MOO

PEN

ANNA DUBROVS

cl

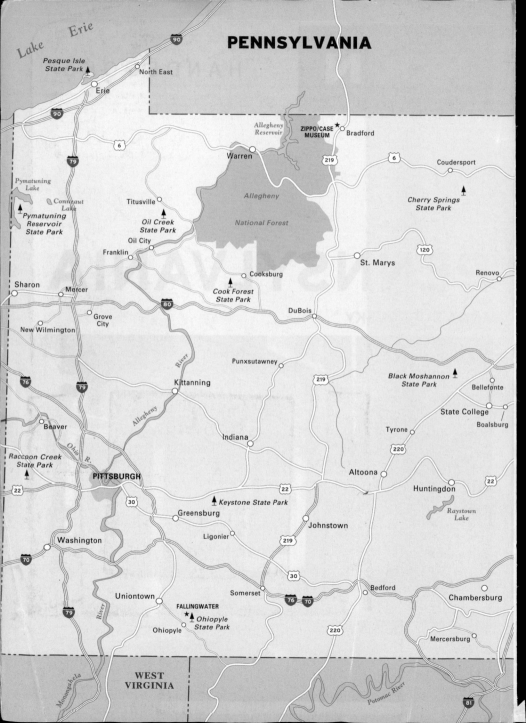

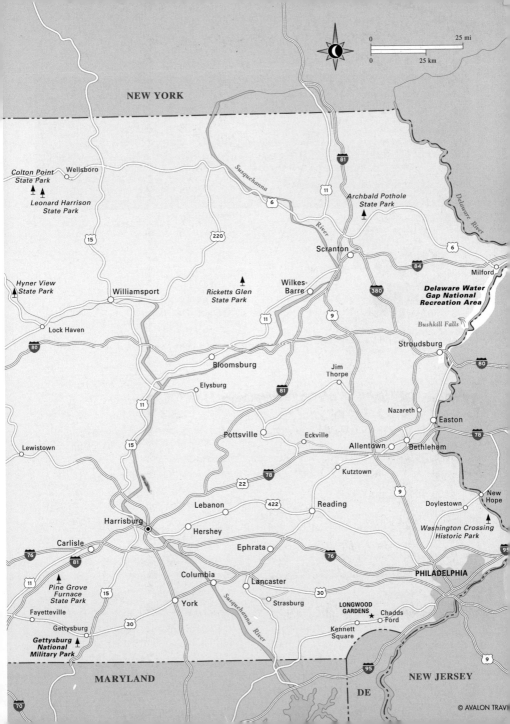

Contents

Discover Pennsylvania

If there's one thing Pennsylvania's founder insisted on, it's that everyone feel welcome. Centuries before New York's Greenwich Village and San Francisco's Haight-Ashbury district gained fame as centers of countercul-ture, William Penn's colony was the place where people could let their freak flags fly. It's thanks to Billy that Pennsylvania is home to the oldest Amish community in the world. It's thanks to him that today's visitor can, in less than 90 minutes, go from one of the largest cities in the country to a place where horse-drawn buggies share the road. "Something for everyone" may be the most tired phrase in destination marketing, but Pennsylvania really means it.

The state that goes by "PA" is a magnet for history buffs, art en-thusiasts, and nature lovers. It's where the nation's founders came up with "life, liberty, and the pursuit of happiness." It's where four score and seven years later, President Abraham Lincoln delivered the timeless speech that began: "Four score and seven years ago our fathers brought forth on this continent a new nation." Pennsylvania is where Andy War-hol first touched a drawing pencil and where Andrew Wyeth painted his whole life. It's where you'll find the only U.S. museum dedicated to hiking and the largest herd of free-roaming elk east of the Rockies.

Pennsylvania is a wide expanse of mostly wilderness and farmlands

flanked by two cosmopolitan cities. In the southeast corner: Philadelphia, the nation's birthplace. In the southwest corner: Pittsburgh, the manufacturing powerhouse turned cultural hub. The towns in between jockey for distinction: "The Sweetest Place on Earth" (Hershey), the "Factory Tour Capital of the World" (York), "Antiques Capital USA" (Adamstown), and a borough made famous by a groundhog (Punxsutawney), to name a few.

The Commonwealth is a study in the art of the comeback. Pittsburgh, described by one 19th-century writer as "hell with the lid off," topped Forbes.com's list of "America's most livable cities" in 2010. In the Lehigh Valley, a shuttered steel works has been reincarnated as a casino. Forests depleted by logging have risen again. Abandoned railroad lines have morphed into multiuse trails. For visitors, too, Pennsylvania is a place of renewal.

It's safe to say that William Penn would be pleased at the shape his land has taken. Welcome.

Planning Your Trip

▶ WHERE TO GO

Philadelphia

The state's largest city is rich in historic and cultural attractions. A thorough exploration of Independence National Historical Park is a better primer on the founding of this nation than any textbook, and the city's art museums are too numerous to see in a day. Known for cheesesteaks and rabid sports fans, the City of Brotherly Love has reached new heights of hipness in recent years, with galleries and eateries sprouting in the unlikeliest places. Idyllic towns such as Kennett Square and New Hope lure Philadelphians past the city limits.

Pennsylvania Dutch Country

With its Germanic heritage, fabled cuisine (pass the shoofly pie), and unmatched concentration of Amish, this region ranks as Pennsylvania's most unique. Gettysburg, site of the Civil War's bloodiest battle, reels in school groups and history buffs, while Hershey defends its title as "The Sweetest Place on Earth."

Pocono Mountains

Pennsylvania's winter sports capital holds as much, if not more, appeal during the warmer

Philadelphia's Swann Memorial Fountain, by sculptor Alexander Stirling Calder and architect Wilson Eyre

Amish buggy

months, thanks to its rivers, lakes, waterfalls, and trails. Let's not forget its many resorts, where there's never a dull moment. Though most are geared toward families, the champagne glass whirlpool is alive and well in the Poconos.

Pittsburgh

Once known as the Smoky City, the Burgh has risen from the ashes to become a cultural hotbed. It boasts the world's largest single-artist museum and the state's largest

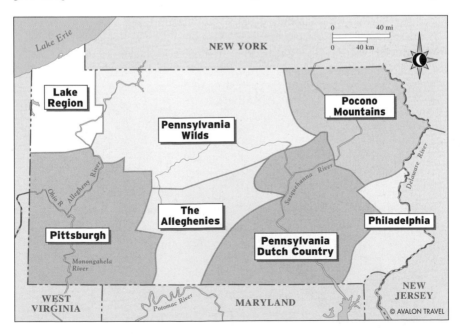

IF YOU HAVE . .

- **A WEEKEND:** Get to know the City of Brotherly Love.
- **A LONG WEEKEND:** Add a day trip to the Brandywine Valley.
- **5 DAYS:** Unwind in Amish country, where time seems to slow down.
- **10 DAYS:** Continue in a clockwise loop through the Commonwealth, taking in Gettysburg, Pittsburgh, Presque Isle, and the Wilds.

Philadelphia

Amish country

Gettysburg

history museum, not to mention the NFL's winningest football team. Fallingwater, the world-renowned work of architecture, is one of many reasons to explore its surrounds.

The Alleghenies

Rail fans flock to this mountainous region to drink in the famous Horseshoe Curve, walk through the nation's first railroad

"Dippy," a fiberglass model of a *Diplodocus* dinosaur, outside the Carnegie Museum of Natural History in Pittsburgh

Nittany Lion shrine

Punxsutawney Phil

tunnel, and ride a steam locomotive on the only original narrow-gauge railroad east of the Rockies. Motorcyclists flood the so-called Flood City in June, and football fever strikes State College in the fall.

Lake Region

Pennsylvania's northwest corner shines in the summer months, when Erie's natural harbor teems with pleasure boats and the sandy beaches of Presque Isle are open for business. Families pack swim gear and stale bread for pilgrimages to manmade Pymatuning Lake, where fish and waterfowl compete for crumbs. As the birthplace of the modern oil industry, this region also attracts history buffs.

Pennsylvania Wilds

Home to the largest herd of free-roaming elk east of the Rockies, a national forest, and the so-called Grand Canyon of Pennsylvania, this lightly populated region is a nature lover's wonderland. It's also home to a major celebrity: Punxsutawney Phil.

▶ WHEN TO GO

Like the rest of the northeastern United States, Pennsylvania experiences all four seasons. There's no best or worst time to visit because the state has plenty to offer year-round, but some areas are better at certain times than others.

Summer is the season to take advantage of Pennsylvania's lakes: loll on the beaches of Presque Isle, feed the ducks at Pymatuning, sail Lake Arthur in Moraine State Park, pilot a houseboat around Raystown Lake, or zoom around Lake Wallenpaupack. It's also a great time to visit Hershey, where a chocolate empire

snow-covered barn in the Pennsylvania Wilds

has given rise to an amusement park and zoo, among other family-friendly attractions.

It's not called Pennsylvania, as in "Penn's Woods," for nothing. This is a tree-blanketed state, which makes fall a fabulous time to visit. Head to the northern half of the state — Allegheny National Forest, Pine Creek Gorge, or the Poconos — for landscapes ablaze in color. While you're there, be sure to visit Benezette, the epicenter of Pennsylvania elk country. September and October are when the elk get it on, and they're apt to do it in the open.

Speaking of wildlife, fall is the best time to visit Hawk Mountain Sanctuary, which lies in the flight path of thousands of migrating raptors. 'Tis also the season to cruise the farmlands of Pennsylvania, stopping to pick apples, stomp grapes, and take a hayride. Agriculture is the state's number one industry, so you never have to go far to find farmlands.

If possible, head to Lancaster County, where Amish farmers rely on horsepower of the four-legged variety to work their fields.

Ah, winter. Love it or hate it, the season of snow and ice brings unique opportunities. Pennsylvania's top snow sports destinations are in opposite corners of the state: the Laurel Highlands in the southwest and the Pocono Mountains in the northeast. In early February, head to Punxsutawney to join the Groundhog Day hubbub.

Rainfall and melting snow and ice make springtime ideal for hitting the rivers. The Youghiogheny, which runs through Ohiopyle State Park in the Laurel Highlands, and the Lehigh Gorge in the Poconos region are popular for white-water rafting and kayaking. Spring is also a swell time to tour the state's largest cities, Philadelphia and Pittsburgh, before they're beset with the humidity and crowds of summer.

Explore Pennsylvania

▶ THE BEST OF PENNSYLVANIA

Pennsylvania is a large state, and few visitors set out to see east, west, north, and south in one go. To pull it off, you'll need 10 days, a car, and a copy of *Moon Pennsylvania* (but of course). The following itinerary assumes travel during the warmer months, when the bulk of attractions are open and the roads more inviting.

Day 1

It only makes sense to begin in the nation's birthplace: Philadelphia. Pick up a timed ticket to Independence Hall at the Independence Visitor Center, loading up on maps and brochures while you're at it. Make your way to the Liberty Bell, and if there's still time before your Independence Hall tour, take

a constitutional through the Rose Garden and Magnolia Garden or leafy Washington Square. After your tour, try a Supreme Court robe on for size at the National Constitution Center. Come sundown, head to the neon-lit, Cheese Whiz–stained intersection of 9th Street and Passyunk Avenue in South Philly, home to rival cheesesteakeries Pat's King of Steaks and Geno's Steaks.

Day 2

Do some time at Eastern State Penitentiary before sprinting up the so-called Rocky steps and getting lost in the period rooms of the Philadelphia Museum of Art. Then take a stroll along the picturesque Benjamin Franklin Parkway and your pick of museums:

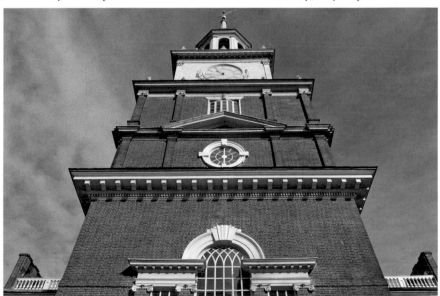

clock tower of Independence Hall

facade of the Philadelphia Museum of Art

the Rodin Museum, The Franklin Institute science museum, or The Academy of Natural Sciences. Finally, treat your culturally enriched self to a show on the Avenue of the Arts and a cocktail at The Ritz-Carlton.

Day 3

Head south on U.S. 1 to the Brandywine River Museum, home to works by three generations of Wyeths. Down the road you'll find Chaddsford Winery, Pennsylvania's largest maker of grown-up grape juice, and then stunning Longwood Gardens. In the evening, kill two birds (shopping and dining) with one stone: Simon Pearce on the Brandywine.

Day 4

It's time for Intercourse (go ahead, snigger away), one of several Lancaster County burgs with an eyebrow-raising name. Taste your way through Kitchen Kettle Village, then drive west on Route 340 to Plain & Fancy Farm, where you can learn all about Amish life and

eat your weight in Pennsylvania Dutch–style foods. After a buggy ride through the Amish countryside, shop your heart out at the Rockvale and Tanger outlet malls.

Jack Meyer, owner of Aaron and Jessica's Buggy Rides

A WEEKEND WITH THE KIDS

These weekend excursions are designed for summertime, when kids are out of school and amusement parks are open.

HERSHEY

The so-called Sweetest Place on Earth is packed with attractions, so go easy on day one to avoid burnout by day two. Start at **The Hershey Story,** which tells the story of Milton Hershey and his eponymous chocolate company and town. Children as young as 4 can experiment in the museum's Chocolate Lab. Then hop a shuttle to **Hershey's Chocolate World,** where singing cows (of the animatronic breed) lend insights into the field-to-factory process of making chocolate. Treat yourself – and the kids, of course – to a chocolate milkshake before you leave. In the late afternoon, stroll through the **Hershey Gardens,** which has a popular butterfly exhibit, and **The Hotel Hershey,** home to a sweets shop where you can decorate your own cupcakes. Spend the night at the more affordable **Hershey Lodge,** which offers such activities as drive-in movies and family bingo. You'll need lots of energy for the next day's romp through **Hersheypark** and **ZooAmerica.**

LANCASTER COUNTY

Spend day one at **Dutch Wonderland,** being sure to catch a high-dive show. Bed down at the adjacent **Old Mill Stream Campground** or at **Verdant View Farm B&B,** where the kids can give milking a go in the morning. On day two, get lost in the Amazing Maize Maze at **Cherry Crest Adventure Farm** and your fill of whoopie pies at **Hershey Farm Restaurant.**

BUCKS COUNTY AND THE LEHIGH VALLEY

Visit Easton's **Crayola Factory** and **National Canal Museum,** where the kids can make like Picasso and build a bridge, respectively. In the evening, take in a double feature at **Becky's Drive-In,** dining on hot dogs, fresh-cut fries, and funnel cake. Spend the night in Easton or Bethlehem and wake up ready to tackle **Sesame Place** or **Dorney Park & Wildwater Kingdom,** the former being best suited to kids still young enough to idolize Big Bird and Snuffleupagus.

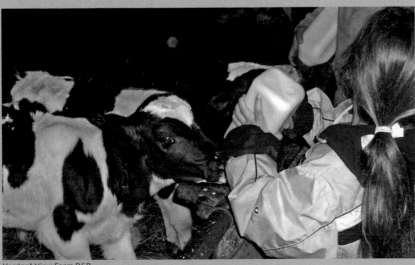

Verdant View Farm B&B

Day 5

Head west on U.S. 30 to Gettysburg, site of the Civil War's bloodiest battle. Take your pick of battlefield tours — horseback and Segway are two ways to go — and don't leave Gettysburg National Military Park without seeing the cyclorama in the visitors center. For dinner, indulge in colonial-style chow at the Dobbin House Tavern. Bed down among (friendly) ghosts at the Best Western Gettysburg Hotel or drive about 80 miles west to the Omni Bedford Springs Resort, cutting the next day's travel time by more than half.

Day 6

Get an early start. Today's destination is the Laurel Highlands, home to Frank Lloyd Wright's Fallingwater. On your way to the

RIDE THE RAILS

Pennsylvania is a rail fan mecca, with about 10 museums dedicated to trains and trolleys, motels made of railroad cars, B&Bs boasting prime views of active tracks, and tourist railroads in every region. Here are a dozen places where you can ride the rails.

PHILADELPHIA

New Hope & Ivyland Railroad: Soak in beautiful Bucks County from the comfort of a 1920s passenger coach or antique bar car.

DUTCH COUNTRY

Strasburg Rail Road: Based across from the Railroad Museum of Pennsylvania, America's oldest operating short-line railroad chugs through Amish farmlands.

Hawk Mountain Line: Proximity to the famous Hawk Mountain Sanctuary gives this tourist railroad its name.

POCONO MOUNTAINS

Lehigh Gorge Scenic Railway: The open-air car is *the* place to be on the journey from Jim Thorpe.

Stourbridge Line Rail Excursions: Kids just love it when gunmen on galloping horses ambush the train.

Steamtown National Historic Site: Take advantage of the rare opportunity to ride in the cab of an operating steam engine. Located on the grounds of Steamtown, the **Electric City Trolley Museum** offers excursions to PNC Field, home of the Scranton/Wilkes-Barre Yankees.

at Steamtown National Historic Site

architectural masterpiece, pay your respects to victims of the 9/11 attacks at the Flight 93 National Memorial.

Day 7

Start your day in Pittsburgh with a visit to the Andy Warhol Museum, then head to the Mattress Factory for more jaw-dropping art or the National Aviary for something to tweet

about. Make your way to Station Square and dine at the Grand Concourse before ascending Mount Washington via the Monongahela Incline. When you're done oohing and aahing over the view, report to party central: the South Side's East Carson Street.

Day 8

Set out on I-79 north for Erie. Stop at the

at Strasburg Rail Road

PITTSBURGH

Duquesne and Monongahela Inclines: Views of Pittsburgh's spectacular skyline await at the top of these 19th-century funiculars.

Pennsylvania Trolley Museum: Admission to this Washington County museum includes unlimited trolley rides.

THE ALLEGHENIES

Johnstown Inclined Plane: Built in the aftermath of the Great Johnstown Flood of 1889, the world's steepest vehicular inclined plane carried people to safety during subsequent floods.

East Broad Top Railroad: The only original narrow-gauge railroad east of the Rockies offers excursions on weekends June–October, as does its neighbor, the **Rockhill Trolley Museum.**

LAKE REGION

Oil Creek & Titusville Railroad: You'll learn about Pennsylvania's important place in oil history during your trip through "the valley that changed the world."

THE WILDS

Tioga Central Railroad: Dining aboard the Tioga Central is a trip back in time.

The author views the massive cyclorama at Gettysburg National Military Park.

Tom Ridge Environmental Center as you enter Presque Isle State Park, home to the finest beaches in the Commonwealth. Ride a coaster or two at Waldameer, order an "orange vanilla twist" cone at nearby Sara's, and call it an early night. You'll need plenty of shut-eye for day 9.

Day 9

The bad news: You'll spend about four hours behind the wheel on your eastward journey to the so-called Grand Canyon of Pennsylvania. The good news: U.S. 6 winds through gorgeous country, including Allegheny National Forest. Stretch your legs on the trails of Leonard Harrison State Park before watching the sun set over the "Grand Canyon," i.e., Pine Creek Gorge.

Day 10

Devote the last day to outdoor adventure in the Poconos, where the options are virtually endless.

gazing down at Pine Creek Gorge, Pennsylvania's Grand Canyon

▶ WEEKEND GETAWAYS

You don't have to hit up your boss for vacation time to get to know Pennsylvania. Seeing it bit by bit is a good way to go, and the state has no shortage of juicy bits. Here are some two-day itineraries to get you started.

From Philadelphia

While walking and public transportation are the easiest ways to get around Philly, you'll need a car for the following escapes.

WYETH COUNTRY

Wake up early and drive to Delaware's Nemours Mansion & Gardens, 30 miles southwest of Philly, in time for the first tour of the day. (Reservations are strongly recommended. If you're traveling January–April, when the magnificent French-style estate is closed to the public, head to nearby Winterthur Museum & Country Estate instead.) After your tour, cross back into Pennsylvania and have lunch at Talula's Table in historic Kennett Square, so-called Mushroom Capital of the World. Devote the afternoon to the horticultural wonderland that is Longwood Gardens. The next day, visit the Brandywine River Museum, home to a remarkable collection of works by three generations of Wyeths. If you're there April–November, take advantage of the opportunity to tour Kuerner Farm, the inspiration for nearly 1,000 works by Andrew Wyeth, one of the most celebrated artists of the 20th century. Treat yourself to a tasting at Chaddsford Winery before returning to the big city.

BUCKS COUNTY

Drive to Doylestown, 25 miles north of Philly, to marvel at the Mercer Museum and Fonthill, concrete castles built by one incorrigible collector. Then follow U.S. 202 north

in New Hope

to New Hope (10 miles), stopping to browse the 70 specialty shops of Peddler's Village along the way. After checking into a B&B in the New Hope area, head to Marsha Brown for New Orleans–style fine dining. (It's not a bad idea to book a table in advance.) Devote the next day to exploring the boutiques and galleries of New Hope and its across-the-Delaware neighbor, Lambertville. To return to Philly, take Route 29 south to I-95 south.

AMISH COUNTRY

Drive to the Strasburg Rail Road, about 60 miles west of Philly, to ride a coal-burning steam train through Amish farmlands. Enjoy a light lunch, a decadent dessert, and a view of the horse-and-buggy traffic through Strasburg's main intersection at the Strasburg Country Store & Creamery. Then make your way to Intercourse (9 miles) via Route 896 north and Route 340 east to sample the likes of pepper jam and chow-chow at Kitchen

Kettle Village. Check out The People's Place Quilt Museum before checking into AmishView Inn & Suites, midway between Intercourse and Bird-in-Hand on Route 340. For dinner, pig out at Shady Maple Smorgasbord (11 miles). Devote the next day to the Plain & Fancy Farm complex, learning about the Amish way of life, experiencing a family-style meal at the on-site restaurant, and clip-clopping through the countryside with Aaron and Jessica's Buggy Rides.

From Pittsburgh

Pittsburgh's surroundings are particularly appealing to outdoorsy types, and the following itineraries are weather dependent.

MORAINE AND McCONNELLS MILL

In the heat of summer, pack the makings of a cookout, drive 40 miles north to Moraine State Park, rent a pontoon boat and gas grill, and while away the day on Lake Arthur. After a night under the stars at Bear Run Campground, hit the trails of McConnells Mill State Park (5 miles). Chow down at North Country Brewing Co. before heading back to the Burgh.

WRIGHT AWAY

Drive to fabulous Fallingwater, 60 miles southeast of Pittsburgh, and learn how far over budget architect Frank Lloyd Wright went. In the afternoon, tour Kentuck Knob, one of his lesser-known creations, taking time to explore the sculpture-studded grounds. (Reservations are recommended for both Wright houses.) Rough it at a tent site in Ohiopyle State Park or do the opposite at Nemacolin Woodlands Resort. In the morning, rent a bike in Ohiopyle and pedal part of the Great Allegheny Passage before finding your way to the moving Flight 93 National Memorial (45 miles).

COOK FOREST

Drive to Cook Forest State Park, 90 miles north of Pittsburgh, to size up the towering pines and hemlocks of the "Forest Cathedral." Spend the night at Gateway Lodge and paddle the Clarion River in the morning.

Frank Lloyd Wright's Fallingwater

► THINK YOU'VE SEEN IT ALL?

If you live in Pennsylvania or visit often, you might think you've seen it all. But the Keystone State, as we call it, is always evolving. For instance, 10 casinos have sprouted since state lawmakers legalized slots gambling in 2004. (Table games were green-lighted in 2010.) In 2009 the African American Museum in Philadelphia unveiled a new core exhibition, and the August Wilson Center for African American Culture opened in downtown Pittsburgh. In 2008 a new Major League-affiliated baseball team, the Lehigh Valley IronPigs, began play in Allentown's brand-new ballpark, and in 2010 the state welcomed a Major League Soccer franchise, the Philadelphia Union. Here are some other recent developments.

Philadelphia

Having long outgrown the home built for it in the 1920s, the venerable Philadelphia Museum of Art expanded into an Art Deco landmark across the way in 2007. Known as the Perelman Building, it showcases some of the museum's more cutting-edge collections. The kid-tastic Please Touch Museum relocated to historic Memorial Hall, built for the 1876 Centennial Exposition, in 2008.

The 58-story Comcast Center snagged the title of Pennsylvania's tallest building when it opened in 2008. The colossal LED wall in its main lobby is a must-see if you're in the area. A great time to be in the area: Philly Beer Week. First held in 2008, the 10-day celebration impressed *Maxim* magazine, which crowned the City of Brotherly Love "best beer town" in 2010. Philadelphia's cred as a shopping town got a boost in 2009, when Walnut Street welcomed Pennsylvania's first Barneys CO-OP.

The Northern Liberties neighborhood — "NoLibs" to those in the know — is in the midst of an extreme makeover. Phillies fans gather at the Piazza at Schmidts, an open-air plaza that opened in 2009 as part of an ambitious, expensive development project, to watch games on a large high-definition screen.

Pennsylvania Dutch Country

If you visited Gettysburg as a grade-schooler, you've got quite a few reasons to return. One: the new Museum and Visitor Center at Gettysburg National Military Park. Opened in 2008, it houses the largest painting in America, a spectacular cyclorama that's looking better than ever on the heels of a five-year, $13 million restoration. Two: the David Wills House. The museum celebrated its grand opening on February 12, 2009, Abraham Lincoln's 200th birthday — quite fitting considering that the lanky president slept in the house when in town to deliver the immortal Gettysburg Address.

Lincoln's statue points to the bedroom in the David Wills House where he slept the night before he delivered the Gettysburg Address.

The 2009 opening of The Hershey Story, The Museum on Chocolate Avenue gave families another reason to visit "The Sweetest Place on Earth," as if they needed one. And the 2010 opening of the Appalachian Trail Museum near the midpoint of the famous Georgia-to-Maine footpath gave Pennsylvania bragging rights as the first state with a museum dedicated to hiking.

Pocono Mountains

The 2005 opening of Great Wolf Lodge and its massive indoor water park inspired Split Rock Resort & Golf Club to open its own indoor water park in 2008.

Pittsburgh

In 2007 the Carnegie Museum of Natural History unveiled an amped-up iteration of its already-heralded exhibition on dinosaurs. Two years later the Carnegie Science Center unveiled Roboworld, the largest permanent robotics exhibition in the country. Not to be outdone, the nearby National Aviary gave us Penguin Point, an open-air home for African penguins. Also in 2009, the ToonSeum opened in a downtown storefront. It's one of only a handful of museums dedicated to the cartoon arts.

In the Laurel Highlands region, Nemacolin Woodlands Resort rolled out the red carpet for Fido and Fluffy with the 2009 opening of the Nemacolin Wooflands Pet Resort & Spa. Seven Springs Mountain Resort stepped up its game with a full-service spa and a sporting clays complex.

The Alleghenies

Two decades after the grand but battered Bedford Springs Hotel shut its doors, investors treated it to a $120 million makeover. Now called the Omni Bedford Springs Resort, the hotel once known as President James Buchanan's "summer White House" is still saturated with history.

The 2009 opening of the Allegrippis Trail System turned Raystown Lake into a premier destination for mountain bikers.

Lake Region

You can't beat the views from the observation tower at the Tom Ridge Environmental Center, gateway to Presque Isle State Park since 2006. With binoculars, you can even see the expressions of sheer joy (and occasional terror) on the faces of thrill-seekers at Waldameer and Water World. The amusement park added the wooden Ravine Flyer II to its coaster collection in 2008, snagging a Best New Ride award from *Amusement Today*.

The Wilds

Opened in September 2010, the 8,400-square-foot Elk Country Visitor Center is the best place to learn about the only wild elk herd in the Northeast. There's a good chance you'll spot some of the majestic creatures while on the property, with its food plots and viewing blinds.

elk viewing in The Wilds

riding on the Allegrippis Trail System

In 2003, an F1 tornado took out 11 of the 20 towers supporting the Kinzua Viaduct, once the highest and longest railroad bridge in the world. The era of excursion trains on the "tracks across the sky" was over, but 2011 will bring a new reason to visit the viaduct: the Kinzua Sky Bridge, a glass-floored overlook at the end of the surviving towers.

► READY, AIM, FIRE!

A great deal of blood was shed in Pennsylvania during the 18th and 19th centuries, and war history buffs have been drawn here ever since. The French and Indian War (1754–1763), a power struggle between Great Britain and France that snowballed into the global Seven Years' War, began in present-day Pennsylvania. The Revolutionary War (1775–1783), which ended British rule in America, came to Philadelphia in 1777, forcing the Founding Fathers to flee to a more westerly Pennsylvania town. And the most harrowing battle of the Civil War (1861–1865) was fought on Pennsylvania soil. Books can teach us a lot about military history, but they're no substitute for standing on hallowed ground. Because war-related sites tend to be clustered, you can see a lot in just two days. Wear comfortable shoes that you wouldn't mind getting dirty, as many sites call for walking on natural terrain.

French and Indian War

This war began over control of the "forks of the Ohio River" in present-day Pittsburgh, so it only makes sense to begin your tour there. The Fort Pitt Museum marks the contested spot. Up next: the Senator John Heinz History Center, where the Clash of Empires exhibit tells the story of the protracted war. The following day, drive 60 miles south to Fort Necessity National Battlefield, where a young George Washington fought his first battle — and surrendered for the first and last time. Don't dawdle too long because the museum at Fort Ligonier, about 40 miles away, is a must-see. If possible, time your trip to coincide with October's Fort Ligonier Days, featuring reenactments of a dramatic 1758 battle.

Revolutionary War

Start the morning at Independence National Historical Park in Philadelphia, where on July 4, 1776, representatives of the 13 colonies adopted the Declaration of Independence. Pay your respects to the Revolutionary War's fallen at the Tomb of the Unknown Soldier, pop by the Betsy Ross House, and quaff a beer based on Ben Franklin's fave recipe at City Tavern. Get an early start to day 2 and drive north to Washington Crossing Historic Park, commemorating the site from which General George Washington and his men crossed the Delaware River on Christmas night 1776. Leave plenty of daylight for Valley Forge National Historical Park, where Washington's army suffered through the winter of 1777–1778, about an hour away. If you don't mind the cold, plan your trip around the annual reenactment of the famed Delaware crossing, held on Christmas Day.

Civil War

Devote the first day to Gettysburg National Military Park, site of the bloodiest battle between North and South, and if time permits, visit the Shriver House Museum to learn about the civilian experience. Come evening, tiptoe around town with a lantern-toting guide on a Ghosts of Gettysburg tour. The next day, head north on U.S. 15 to Harrisburg and pay a visit to the singular National Civil War Museum and the John Harris-Simon Cameron Mansion, whose porch served as a reviewing stand for a parade of the Union's African American soldiers. If you don't mind crowds, consider visiting Gettysburg during the annual reenactment of the July 1–3 battle.

detail of Delaware's monument at Gettysburg, by sculptor Ron Tunison

PHILADELPHIA

Pennsylvania's largest city hardly needs introduction. Anyone with a basic knowledge of U.S. history—or a DVD collection that includes the *Rocky* saga, for that matter—knows a thing or two about Philadelphia. It's where the Founding Fathers wrestled with the wording of the Declaration of Independence and the U.S. Constitution. It's where Ben Franklin came up with so many bright ideas. It's where Rocky Balboa trained for his shot at the world heavyweight championship.

Philadelphia was founded by William Penn in 1682, not long after King Charles II of England granted him a colony as payment for a debt owed to his late father. It was the monarch who named the colony Pennsylvania, meaning "Penn's woods," in honor of Penn's papa. But "Philadelphia" was Penn's idea. As a Quaker,

Penn was no stranger to persecution, and he wanted his colony to be a live-and-let-live sort of place. He derived the name for his capital city from the Greek *philos*, or "love," and *adelphos*, or "brother." In part because of Penn's insistence on religious freedom, the City of Brotherly Love grew into the largest city in the colonies and the second largest in the British Empire after London.

Fast forward to 1774. The 13 American colonies aren't so jazzed about British policies. Delegates from 12 meet in Philadelphia, the geographic center of the colonies, and send King George III a message: ease up or else—or something to that effect. The king doesn't pay much heed to the First Continental Congress, and in May 1775, the Second Continental Congress convenes

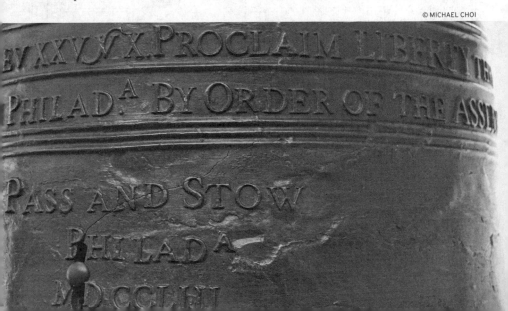

HIGHLIGHTS

(Independence Hall: It's here that the Founding Fathers debated and drafted the Declaration of Independence and later the Constitution. Timed tickets go fast during peak tourist season (page 32).

(National Constitution Center: Learn about the nation's supreme law, pose with life-sized statues of its framers, and slip into a Supreme Court robe at this expansive museum (page 34).

(City Hall: Philadelphia's elaborately adorned seat of government is the largest municipal building in the country, and the view from its observation deck is tops (page 43).

(Masonic Temple: The mothership of Pennsylvania Masonry offers a smorgasbord of architectural styles under one roof (page 45).

(Reading Terminal Market: In business since 1892, this indoor farmers market is a great place to grab lunch and people-watch (page 48).

(Philadelphia Museum of Art: The nation's third-largest art museum is home to more than 225,000 objects, including a bronze statue of fictional boxer Rocky Balboa. Don't forget to sprint up the "Rocky steps" (page 53).

(Eastern State Penitentiary: Opened in 1829, this sprawling prison served as a model for hundreds around the world, horrified Charles Dickens, and hosted Al "Scarface" Capone. It's a tourist attraction now, but it hasn't lost its eerie edge (page 54).

(Longwood Gardens: This Brandywine Valley treasure is quite simply one of the nation's premier horticultural attractions (page 102).

LOOK FOR **(** TO FIND RECOMMENDED SIGHTS, ACTIVITIES, DINING, AND LODGING.

in Philadelphia. By now, the colonies and Great Britain are at war. The delegates get down to business, creating the Continental Army and appointing George Washington as commanding general. On July 4, 1776, they approve the Declaration of Independence, formally cutting ties with the British Empire. The following year, as British troops occupy Philadelphia, the Congress relocates to York, Pennsylvania. But Philadelphia's role in early American history is far from over.

To tell you what happened next would take some of the fun out of exploring Philadelphia and its surrounds. Find out for yourself at Independence Hall, where the Founding Fathers made so many important decisions; at Valley Forge, where Washington and his troops spent the winter of 1777–1778, after

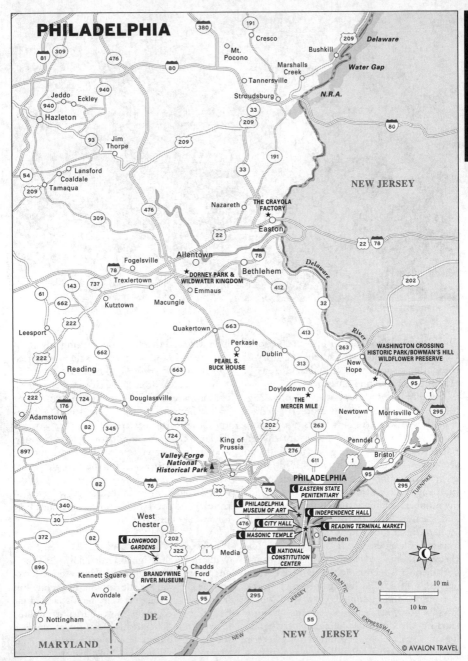

PHILADELPHIA

81 309 476 80

191 Cresco Delaware
380 209

Mt. Pocono Bushkill
Marshalls Creek Water Gap
Tannersville
Stroudsburg N.R.A.
33
209

940 Jeddo Eckley
940
Hazleton
93 Jim Thorpe
209
191
33

54 Lansford Coaldale
209 Tamaqua

NEW JERSEY

309 476 Nazareth THE CRAYOLA FACTORY ★
22 Easton
22 78

Fogelsville Allentown
78 78
143 737 Trexlertown DORNEY PARK & ★ Bethlehem
WILDWATER KINGDOM Delaware
61 662 Emmaus 412
Kutztown Macungie 32
222
662 Quakertown 663
Leesport 222 Perkasie Dublin River
662 PEARL S. ★ 263
BUCK HOUSE 313 WASHINGTON CROSSING
Reading 663 New HISTORIC PARK/BOWMAN'S HILL
Hope WILDFLOWER PRESERVE ★
222 724 Doylestown 95
176 Douglassville THE ★ 1
Adamstown 82 345 MERCER MILE Newtown Morrisville 295
422 202 263 Penndel
897 724 King of 611 Bristol
Prussia 276 1 95
82 Valley Forge 30 76 295
National PHILADELPHIA TURNPIKE
340 76 Historical Park 76 EASTERN STATE (★
30 PENITENTIARY
West PHILADELPHIA (★
372 82 Chester MUSEUM OF ART INDEPENDENCE HALL (★
202 476 (CITY HALL
896 322 (MASONIC TEMPLE (READING TERMINAL MARKET
LONGWOOD 1 Media Camden
GARDENS (NATIONAL
Kennett Square Chadds CONSTITUTION
Avondale BRANDYWINE Ford CENTER
1 RIVER MUSEUM ★ ATLANTIC
Nottingham 82 95 295 CITY EXPRESSWAY

DE 55

MARYLAND NEW JERSEY

0 _____ 10 mi
0 _____ 10 km

© AVALON TRAVEL

PHILADELPHIA

© ROADRUNNER/123RF.COM

Independence Hall

Philadelphia fell to the British; at the National Constitution Center, which tells the story of the nation's supreme law; and at dozens of other historic sites and museums.

If Philly had nothing but its historical significance going for it, it would still attract enough tourists to support fleets of open-top buses, faux trolleys, and horse-drawn carriages. It has much more going for it. It's an arts town—home to the nation's third-largest art museum, more Auguste Rodin sculptures than any place outside of Paris, an astounding number of outdoor murals and sculptures, and theaters both historic and thoroughly modern. It's a sports town, with teams in all four major leagues. And it's a food town. The cheesesteak may be its most famous dish, but Philadelphia is increasingly recognized for its profusion of BYOBs (bring-your-own-bottle restaurants) and gastropubs (bars with superb food). A growing number of celebrity restaurateurs are extending their culinary tentacles into the city. "Philadelphia's evolution from day trip to destination city is such that you can spend a long weekend there without visiting any 18th-century sites, and not even miss them," asserted *The New York Times* in 2009.

Several areas around the city are also worthy of a long weekend. To its west is the Brandywine Valley, home to stunning Longwood Gardens and other former estates of the uber-wealthy du Pont clan. To its north is Bucks County, known for its concrete castles and boutique shopping. Farther north is the Lehigh Valley, where you can catch two movies for $8 at the nation's oldest drive-in theater. New Jersey, to the east and south of Philadelphia, is a subject for another book.

PLANNING YOUR TIME

William Penn designed Philadelphia as a rectangular gridiron sandwiched between two rivers: the Delaware in the east and the Schuylkill in the west. Though the city has expanded far beyond his rectangle, most tourist attractions lie within it. The area is blessedly compact—roughly 25 blocks from river to river—and easy to navigate by foot. Most historic sites are concentrated near the Delaware, and while it would take three or more days of morn-to-eve sightseeing to experience them all, it's possible to hit the highlights in one day. First order of business: Get a timed ticket for Independence Hall at the Independence Visitor Center.

Many of Philadelphia's art and science museums are conveniently clustered around the Benjamin Franklin Parkway, close to the Schuylkill, so visiting two or even three in one day isn't out of the question. After museum hours, soak in the scenery, boathouses, and sculptures along Kelly Drive. If you're traveling with children, set aside a day to explore the Philadelphia Zoo, across the Schuylkill, or Adventure Aquarium, across the Delaware in Camden, New Jersey. If, on the other hand, you're traveling with your better half, book a B&B in the winery-rich Brandywine Valley or Bucks County.

Sights

Philadelphia is rich in historic and cultural attractions, some of which can be enjoyed at little or no cost. Admission to Independence Hall and the Liberty Bell Center, two major tourist draws, doesn't cost a cent. You can stroll down the nation's oldest residential street, Elfreth's Alley, for free and see where Betsy Ross sewed so many flags for just $3. If you're an art lover on a tight budget, you're going to love this city. It's home to more than 2,800 murals and, according to the Smithsonian Institution, more outdoor sculptures than any other U.S. city. And while guided tours of the city can cost a pretty penny, an all-day pass to ride the Phlash—a purple trolley-like vehicle that stops at more than 25 key locations—is just $5.

If you plan on seeing several higher cost attractions, consider investing in a CityPass or Philadelphia Pass. A **CityPass** (888/330-5008, www.citypass.com/philadelphia, $59 per person, children 2–12 $39) is a booklet of tickets good for admission to five attractions—The Franklin Institute, Adventure Aquarium, the Philadelphia Zoo, the Academy of Natural Sciences or the National Constitution Center, and the Please Touch Museum or Eastern State Penitentiary—plus 24 hours of hop-on, hop-off privileges with Philadelphia Trolley Works and The Big Bus Company. It's valid for nine days and cuts the cost of all that sightseeing by almost half. A **Philadelphia Pass** (888/567-7277, www.philadelphiapass.com, $49–115 per person, children 2–12 $39–95) is a smart card good for admission to about 35 attractions in and around the city. The cost of the pass depends on how long it's valid. One-day, two-day, three-day, and five-day passes are available, and the more attractions you hit, the more you save. One of the best things about both passes is that you don't have to wait in line at some attractions. They're to Philadelphia sightseeing what first-class tickets are to air travel.

HISTORIC DISTRICT
The section of Philadelphia now known as the Historic District was, for a while there, the center of America. It's here that delegates from the American colonies debated and adopted the U.S. Declaration of Independence, a silver-tongued "buh-bye" to Great Britain, in 1776. It's here that another enduring document, the United States Constitution, was approved in 1787. The young nation's leaders met here from 1790 to 1800, while Washington, D.C., was taking shape. Quite a few of the buildings where the Founding Fathers conducted their business, clinked glasses, or crawled into bed are still standing, which is why the area is often called "America's most historic square mile." Millions of people visit each year to walk in their footsteps.

Walking is, in fact, the best way to experience the Historic District, which is compact and dense with museums and monuments. It comprises two neighborhoods adjacent to the Delaware River: Old City and Society Hill to

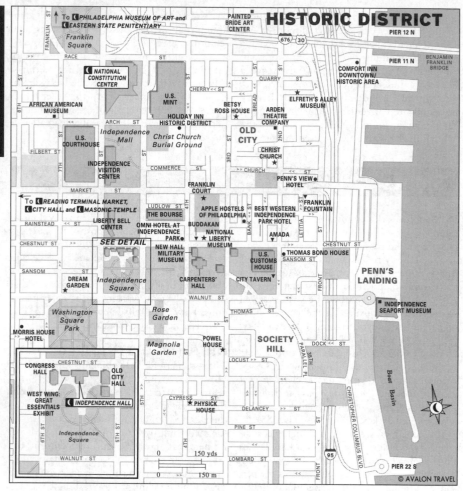

its south. Contrary to its name, Old City is a magnet for the young and hip of Philadelphia. Once teeming with industry, it's now peppered with galleries and boutiques. There's no better time to visit than the first Friday of the month, when many stay open as late as 9 P.M. as part of **First Fridays in Old City** (215/625-9200, www.oldcityarts.org). Society Hill was home to many politicians and power brokers during Philadelphia's tenure as the nation's capital but eventually went to pot. In the 1950s the city undertook a revitalization of the crime-ridden slum, acquiring colonial houses and selling them to people on the condition that they be restored. Today it's one of the poshest neighborhoods in Philly.

Its upscale shopping and dining attract the moneyed, but the Historic District is also a magnet for travelers on a tight budget. It's home to one of only a handful of hostels in Pennsylvania. Many of its major attractions are part of **Independence National Historical**

Park (www.nps.gov/inde), and admission to all but one park site is free. Guided tours are a great way to experience historic Philadelphia, but if you're there on a summer day and short on cash, look for teak benches marked "Once Upon a Nation." They're staffed by "storytellers" who dispense information about the area and America's birth—for free.

It's best to start your visit at the **Independence Visitor Center** (6th and Market Streets, 215/965-7676, www.independence visitorcenter.com, opens at 8:30 A.M. daily, closes at 7 P.M. Memorial Day–Labor Day, 5 P.M. in winter, and 6 P.M. during remainder of year), a large modern building sandwiched between the Liberty Bell Center and the National Constitution Center, two can't-miss sights. As the official visitors center for Philadelphia and its environs, it's stocked with maps and brochures and staffed by helpful sorts—some of them conspicuous in 18th- or 19th-century attire. Exhibits and free films help the orientation process. Tickets for a variety of tours and area attractions are sold here. If you're visiting March through December and plan to tour Independence Hall—and you should—you'll need a free timed-entrance ticket. Day-of tickets are distributed at the Visitor Center. Early birds get the greatest choice of times; during peak season it's not unusual for tickets to be gone by 1 P.M. To ensure that tickets will be waiting for you, reserve them by phone or online (877/444-6777, www.recreation.gov, $1.50 per ticket surcharge). Tickets aren't required to tour Independence Hall in January or February.

Liberty Bell Center

Like New York's Statue of Liberty, the much-photographed Liberty Bell is an international icon of escape from oppression. How it came to symbolize freedom, justice, and all that good stuff is the subject of exhibits in its home since 2003, the Liberty Bell Center (6th and Market Streets, 215/965-7676, www.nps.gov/inde, hours vary by season but generally open 9 A.M.–5 P.M. daily, free admission). The fact that it's been mute for more than 150 years and still speaks to so many people is curious indeed.

Its history begins in 1751, when the Pennsylvania Assembly ordered a new bell for the State House (now Independence Hall) from a London foundry. The splurge was occasioned by the 50th anniversary of the Pennsylvania Charter of Privileges, which codified William Penn's ideals of religious toleration and political rights. The speaker of the Assembly chose an apt Bible quotation to be inscribed on the bell: "Proclaim liberty throughout all the land unto all the inhabitants thereof." No sooner was it hung than the bell cracked. Two local craftsmen, John Pass and John Stow, were tasked with melting and recasting it. They took the liberty of putting their surnames on the bell—and a lot of flak for its tone.

Anyone agitated by its E-flat strike note would have been frequently agitated. The bell was rung to call lawmakers together, to summon the citizenry for announcements, and to mark important occasions. It's often said that the bell tolled for the first public reading of the Declaration of Independence in 1776, but historians pooh-pooh that because the State

The Liberty Bell's glass-enclosed home allows a view of Independence Hall.

House steeple was in shabby condition at that time.

Eventually the bell suffered a thin crack, which was purposely widened to keep the edges from vibrating against each other. When the bell tolled in celebration of the late George Washington's birthday in February 1846, the crack expanded something awful. "It received a sort of compound fracture in a zig-zag direction through one of its sides which put it completely out of tune and left it a mere wreck of what it was," reported the *Public Ledger,* a daily newspaper of the time.

By then the bell had achieved iconic status, thanks to abolitionists who had adopted it as a symbol of their cause. After the Civil War, the fatally cracked bell traveled the country, serving as a reminder of days when Americans were united in their quest for independence. Pass and Stow's 2,080-pound bell came home to Philadelphia in 1915, but a replica forged that year was used to promote women's suffrage. It appeared in different cities with its clapper chained to its side, a metaphor for the silencing of women, and was finally rung when they won the right to vote in 1920. To this day, oppressed groups evoke the image of the Liberty Bell. That its evocative power transcends nationality is evidenced by the variety of languages that mingle in the glass-walled Liberty Bell Center. The bell itself is cleverly displayed at the southern end of the building, where Independence Hall serves as backdrop.

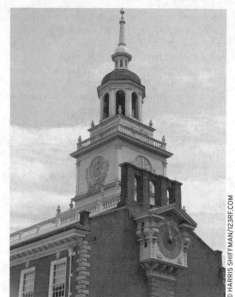

© HARRIS SHIFFMAN/123RF.COM

historic Independence Hall

(Independence Hall

If Philadelphia is the nation's birthplace, then Independence Hall (Chestnut St. between 5th and 6th Streets, 215/965-7676, www.nps.gov/inde, hours vary by season but generally open 9 A.M.–5 P.M. daily, free tours, timed ticket required Mar.–Dec.) can well be thought of as the womb. Within its walls, the Founding Fathers debated and drafted the Declaration of Independence and later the Constitution. George Washington himself presided over the Constitutional Convention, and the mahogany armchair in which he sat is among the furnishings visitors see today.

The Georgian-style brick structure was built as the State House while Pennsylvania was still a British colony. Construction began in 1732 and continued for two decades. The legislature began meeting in the Assembly Room long before the ambitious building project was completed. (Even unfinished, the State House was a more dignified meeting place than private homes and taverns.) When tensions between American colonists and Great Britain erupted into war in 1775, the Second Continental Congress began meeting in the Assembly Room. Composed of delegates from the 13 colonies, including Benjamin Franklin and Thomas Jefferson, the Congress made one history-making decision after another in that room. It appointed Washington as commander in chief of the Continental Army (1775), adopted the Declaration of Independence (July 4, 1776), and settled on the design of the American flag (1777).

In September 1777 the Congress fled to York, Pennsylvania, as British forces occupied Philadelphia. During the occupation, which lasted until the following summer, the State House served as a hospital, prison, and barracks. There was much remodeling after Washington's troops regained control of the city and the Congress returned. In 1783, as the Revolutionary War drew to a close, the nation's governing body relocated from Philly. Pennsylvania's legislature reoccupied its chamber, only to surrender it to the framers of the Constitution in May 1787. The nation's supreme law was signed on September 17, and the State House reverted to its intended use until 1799, when the Pennsylvania capital was moved to Lancaster.

The building saw many alterations and uses in the 19th century. At one point it housed a museum of natural history. At another, its basement served as the city's dog pound. Since the creation of Independence National Historical Park in 1948, it has been returned to its late-18-th-century appearance. Tours start in the East Wing, attached to the main building by a colonnade. Be sure to visit the West Wing, which is not part of the tour. It's home to the **Great Essentials Exhibit** (9 A.M.–5 P.M. daily, free admission), which displays surviving copies of the Declaration of Independence, Articles of Confederation (the nation's first constitution), and the Constitution. There's also a silver inkstand said to have been used during the signing of the Declaration and Constitution.

Flanking Independence Hall are two park sites worth a quick peek. Constructed in the 1780s as the county courthouse, **Congress Hall** (Chestnut and 6th Streets, 9 A.M.–5 P.M. daily, free admission) is so named because the newly formed U.S. Congress met there during Philadelphia's 1790–1800 tenure as the nation's capital. Almost all the chairs on the second floor, which was occupied by the Senate, are authentic. Note the "spitting boxes" near the fireplaces. (Chewing tobacco didn't

ROSE GARDEN, MAGNOLIA GARDEN, AND *DREAM GARDEN*

There are plenty of ways to kill time while waiting for a tour of Independence Hall. The Historic District is packed with museums and other attractions. Some, of course, can take hours to explore. If half an hour is all you've got and it's a beautiful warm day, head to the **Rose Garden,** centerpiece of a landscaped area between Locust and Walnut Streets and 4th and 5th Streets. Planted by the Daughters of the American Revolution in honor of the men who penned the Declaration of Independence, the garden features antique roses. Among the 90-some varieties are "Old Blush" and the unusual green rose. Most flower only once a year, peaking in June. The cobblestone-paved entrance to the garden was once the courtyard of a stable. If you still have time, cross Locust Street to admire the smaller **Magnolia Garden,** a tribute to the Founding Fathers by the Garden Club of America. The 13 hybrid magnolias around its walled perimeter represent the original colonies. They bloom in early spring.

In the colder months, you can pass the time gazing at the *Dream Garden* (Curtis Center, 6th and Walnut Streets, 215/238-6450, 8 A.M.-6 P.M. Mon.-Fri., 10 A.M.-1 P.M. Sat.), a dazzling glass mosaic in the lobby of a somber 19th-century office building. Measuring 15 feet high and 49 feet wide, the leafy landscape was designed by Philadelphia-born artist Maxfield Parrish and executed by stained-glass guru Louis Comfort Tiffany in 1916. It comprises more than 100,000 pieces of Favrile glass in 260 colors. The masterpiece was commissioned by Curtis Publishing Company, which published such magazines as *The Saturday Evening Post* and *Ladies' Home Journal,* for its Philadelphia headquarters. In 1998 it was purchased by casino developer Steve Wynn, who planned to move it from the City of Brotherly Love to Sin City. Philadelphia's intelligentsia rose up in protest, and the Pew Charitable Trusts forked out $3.5 million to keep *Dream Garden* in its original home.

carry warning labels back then.) **Old City Hall** (Chestnut and 5th Streets, hours vary by season, free admission) is so named because it was built as Philadelphia's second city hall. It was home to the U.S. Supreme Court from its completion in 1791 to 1800, when the federal government moved to Washington, D.C.

◖ National Constitution Center

The first museum dedicated to the U.S. Constitution (525 Arch St., 215/409-6600, www.constitutioncenter.org, 9:30 A.M.–5 P.M. Mon.–Fri., 9:30 A.M.–6 P.M. Sat., noon–5 P.M. Sun., admission $12, seniors $11, children 4–12 $8, additional charges for traveling exhibitions apply) opened on July 4, 2003, a day that marked the adoption of another formulated-in-Philly document, the Declaration of Independence. It's one of the flashier sights in town—not surprising given its $185 million price tag. The visitor experience begins with *Freedom Rising*, a multimedia presentation in a star-shaped theater with a 360-degree screen. It's a stirring introduction to the Constitution's main themes.

Anyone interested in the nitty-gritty can spend the better part of a day at the museum, which presents the story of the nation's supreme law through more than 100 exhibits. But an hour or two is enough to hit the highlights, including Signers' Hall, featuring life-sized bronze statues of the 39 men who signed the Constitution and three dissenters. Feel free to give the Founders congratulatory pats on the back or even grateful hugs; this is a museum that encourages interaction. Visitors can take the presidential oath of office, try a Supreme Court robe on for size, email elected officials, and make paper using 18th-century methods.

Be sure to check the calendar of events, available on the museum's website. The Constitution Center serves as a sort of town hall, regularly hosting prominent lawmakers, scholars, authors, and other expert sorts. In March 2008 then-Senator Barack Obama delivered his seminal speech on race ("I am the son of a black man from Kenya and a white woman from Kansas . . .") there. The following month the museum hosted the final debate

the National Constitution Center

© KARRIE GAVIN

between the presidential hopeful and his Democratic primary rival, Hillary Clinton.

The Constitution Center's glass-enclosed Delegates' Café is a good place to fuel up for more sightseeing.

Franklin Square

Visitors to the Historic District run a real risk of information overload. To the rescue: Franklin Square (6th and Race Streets, 215/629-4026, www.historicphiladelphia.org), a lovely park within skipping distance of the Constitution Center. It's arguably the most kid-friendly spot in the area, with a distinctive playground, old-fashioned carousel ($3, children 3–12 $2), and Philadelphia-themed mini golf course ($8, children 3–12 $6). On the 18th hole, players putt through the crack in the Liberty Bell.

It's not a bad idea to come hungry. In 2009 the city's most prolific restaurateur, Stephen Starr, opened **SquareBurger** on the 7.5-acre green. It offers burgers (including a veggie version), hot dogs, root beer floats, shakes, and sundaes—all for under $6. SquareBurger's "cake shake," made with vanilla ice cream and Tastykake snacks, is an utterly unique indulgence.

Franklin Square is one of five squares included in William Penn's original plan for the city. Initially known as Northeast Square, it served as a cattle pasture, burial ground, and military drill site before the city reclaimed it as a park in 1837, erecting an elegant marble fountain. By the turn of this century, the park was in sorry shape. A 2006 facelift transformed the desolate square block into a swell family destination. The original fountain remains its centerpiece.

African American Museum in Philadelphia

Founded in 1976, less than a decade after the assassination of Martin Luther King Jr. and the ensuing riots, the African American Museum (701 Arch St., 215/574-0380, www.aampmuseum.org, 10 A.M.–5 P.M. Tues.–Sat., noon–5 P.M. Sun., admission $10, seniors $8, students and children 4–12 $8) was the first

institution of its kind to be funded by a major city. Its large collection of art and artifacts documents the history and culture of the African diaspora. In 2009 the Smithsonian affiliate unveiled a new core exhibition with a high-tech twist. Audacious Freedom: African Americans in Philadelphia 1776–1876 brings unsung heroes to life by way of video projections. When approached by a visitor, each trailblazer sounds off about life during the time period. Think of it as a cross-era cocktail party.

Carpenters' Hall

Most visitors to historic Philadelphia quickly learn that Independence Hall was the meeting place of the Second Continental Congress, the esteemed assemblage responsible for the Declaration of Independence. Fewer come to appreciate that nearby Carpenters' Hall (Chestnut St. between 3rd and 4th Streets, 215/925-0167, www.carpentershall.org, 10 A.M.–4 P.M. Tues.–Sun. Mar.–Dec. and Wed.–Sun. Jan.–Feb., free admission) hosted the First Continental Congress, which convened in the fall of 1774 to coordinate resistance to a series of heavy-handed laws imposed by Britain. Composed of delegates from 12 of the 13 colonies, the Congress organized a boycott of British goods, petitioned King George III to redress colonists' grievances, and resolved that a second Congress would meet if the monarch turned a deaf ear. The monarch turned a deaf ear.

Among the exhibits in Carpenters' Hall is a room furnished as it might have been in 1774. You'll also find a parade float built to celebrate ratification of the Constitution, a banner carried in the parade, a remarkably detailed model illustrating the hall's construction, and early carpentry tools.

The Georgian-style gem was constructed from 1770 to 1774 as a meeting hall for the Carpenters' Company, a trade guild whose members built much of colonial Philadelphia. Practical men, they immediately began renting out space in their new headquarters. The list of tenants is long and includes the nation's first lending library and the American Philosophical Society, both founded by Benjamin Franklin.

In 1798 the hall was leased to the Bank of Pennsylvania and later that year became the target of America's first bank robbery. (The inside job netted $162,821, which was returned in exchange for a pardon.) The Carpenters' Company, founded in 1724, still holds regular meetings, making it the oldest trade guild in the country.

Next door to Carpenters' Hall is the **New Hall Military Museum** (215/965-7676, www .nps.gov/inde, hours vary by season, free admission), a reconstruction of a building the Carpenters' Company erected in 1790. The original was promptly occupied by the nation's first secretary of war and his staff. Appropriately enough, the museum is devoted

SIGHTSEEING TOURS

Taking a guided tour can be a fun and educational way to start your visit to Philadelphia. Options range from your basic history tour to a bar crawl led by a guide in colonial garb. Old City is usually best explored on foot, with lots of sights within close proximity of one another, but to cover larger areas – or when hot temperatures make it unpleasant to do much walking at all – there are also bus, trolley, carriage, Segway, and bike tours to choose from.

ON FOOT

The 75-minute **Constitutional Walking Tour** (Independence Visitor Center, 6th and Market Streets, 215/525-1776, www.theconstitutional. com, daily Apr.-Nov., $17.50 per person, children 3-12 $12.50, family of four $55) covers about 20 Historic District sites, including the Betsy Ross House, Christ Church, and the National Constitution Center. (Note that the price of the tour does not include admission tickets.) For $15 you can download the tour to your portable media player and go at your own pace.

On a 90-minute **Candlelight Ghost Tour** (Signers Garden, 5th and Chestnut Streets, 215/413-1997, www.ghosttour.com, evenings Apr.-Nov., $17 per person, children 4-12 $8, reservations required), you'll hear tales of the spirits believed to roam "America's most historic and most haunted city." The **Haunted Trolley Tour** (outside the Bourse, 11 S. 5th St., $30 per person, children 4-12 $20), also 90 minutes long, covers more ground but spends less time at each site. Tickets for both tours are available at the Independence Visitor Center, but you'll save $2 per adult ticket if you purchase in advance by phone or online.

Historic Philadelphia Inc. (Historic Philadelphia Center, 6th and Chestnut Streets, 215/629-4026, www.historicphiladelphia.org), the organization responsible for the "storytellers" stationed at benches throughout the Historic District, offers a variety of unique tours April–October. Costumed actors debate going to war with England during the **Turmoil & Treason: The Path to Independence** tour ($20 per person, seniors and students $18, children 12 and under $15). On the **Colonial Kids Quest** ($17 per person, children 2 and under free), kids play detective and look for a missing copy of the Declaration of Independence, while on the **Tippler's Tour** ($35 per person, seniors and students $30), adults enjoy drinks, snacks, and song at four watering holes. **Independence After Hours** ($75 per person, seniors and students $70, children 12 and under $50) features a three-course dinner at historic City Tavern and an exclusive opportunity to visit Independence Hall after it's closed to the public. Historic Philadelphia Inc.'s already impressive **Lights of Liberty Show,** which tells the story of the American Revolution through audio and giant laser-light images projected onto the buildings of Independence Hall, recently underwent a $10 million makeover. The new and improved show, featuring 3D technology, was scheduled to debut in spring 2011.

The nonprofit **Friends of Independence National Historical Park** (215/861-4971, www. friendsofindependence.org) offers free **Twilight Tours** (Signers Garden, 5th and Chestnut Streets, 6 P.M. daily July 5–Labor Day) of the park. Check the Independence National Historical Park (215/965-2305, www.nps.gov/ inde/) website for information on free ranger-guided tours.

to the early history of the U.S. Army, Navy, and Marine Corps.

Franklin Court

Benjamin Franklin (1706–1790), signer of the Declaration of Independence and the Constitution, spent the last five years of his life in a house across Chestnut Street from Carpenters' Hall. The site of his home is now known as Franklin Court (between Market and Chestnut Streets and 3rd and 4th Streets, 215/965-7676, www.nps.gov/inde, call or check website for hours) and serves as a tribute to the preternatural polymath. Author and printer, politician and diplomat, scientist and inventor, Franklin gets a lot of props in his adopted

---

ON WHEELS

Philadelphia Trolley Works and **The Big Bus Company** tours (215/389-8687, www.phillytour.com, 9:30 A.M.-6 P.M. daily Apr.-Nov. and 10 A.M.-4 P.M. daily Dec.-Mar., 24-hour pass $27 per person, seniors $25, children 4-12 $10, 48-hour pass $43 per person, seniors $40, children 18) depart from the northeast corner of 5th and Market Streets and allow you to hop off and on at about 20 stops around the city, including Chinatown, City Hall, Eastern State Penitentiary, the Philadelphia Museum of Art, the Philadelphia Zoo, and Penn's Landing. The road trolleys and double-decker London-style buses are operated by the same company, and passes are good for both vehicle types. The related **76 Carriage Company** (215/923-8516, www.phillytour.com, daily year-round) offers horse-drawn carriage rides departing from 5th and Chestnut Streets. They range from 15 minutes to an hour and cost $30-80 for up to four people. Avoid taking a carriage ride on the hottest summer days – the horse will be even hotter than you are.

I Glide Tours (215/735-1700, www.iglidetours.com, daily Mar.-Nov., reservations required) offers a chance to see Philly via the Segway PT, a two-wheeled, self-balancing electric vehicle. Daytime tours last 2.5 hours and cost $69 per person. Ninety-minute evening tours are $49. Both begin with an instructional period for novice gliders. Your guide will offer unique facts about Philadelphia as you glide through Fairmount Park, along the Benjamin Franklin Parkway, and elsewhere. Participants must be 13 years old and weigh 100-285 pounds, and minors must be accompanied by a parent or guardian.

Philadelphia Bike Tours (215/514-3124, www.philadelphiabiketour.com) offers three-hour river-to-river bicycle tours ($68 per person), as well as customized tours for groups of four or more. Tours are generally offered on weekends only, but weekday tours can sometimes be arranged. Call 24 hours in advance to book. Valid ID and a credit card are required, and minors must be accompanied by a parent or guardian. If you prefer to pedal at your own pace, you can have a bike, helmet, and lock delivered to your hotel ($57/12 hours).

– Contributed by Karrie Gavin,
author of Moon Philadelphia

© ANNA DUBROVSKY

a carriage ride through Old City

hometown of Philadelphia. A river-spanning bridge, a public square, a science museum, a scenic boulevard, and even an ice cream shop bear the name of the Boston-born brainiac, whose formal schooling ended when he was a preteen. But only at Franklin Court can you peer into his privy pit.

Franklin's home was razed about 20 years after his death, but remains of the toilet and foundation can be seen through viewing portals set into the ground. A steel "ghost structure," erected in 1976 in celebration of the nation's bicentennial, represents the three-story house. Below ground is a museum devoted to Franklin and particularly his inventions. You'll find a reproduction of an "armonica," the musical instrument he created after seeing waterfilled wine glasses being played. Mozart wrote a piece specifically for it.

Five row houses at the Market Street end of Franklin Court also yield insights into his life and legacy. (Add "real estate investor" to his titles: He built three of them in the 1780s as rental properties.) At 314 Market is a postal museum featuring Pony Express packages. Next door is the only active post office in the country that doesn't fly an American flag—because there wasn't one when Franklin became the first Postmaster General of the United States in 1775. Another of the row houses displays 18th-century printing and binding equipment.

The Founding Father's passing at the ripe age of 84 was mourned throughout America and France, its Revolutionary War ally. An estimated 20,000 people gathered for his funeral at **Christ Church Burial Ground** (Arch St. between 4th and 5th Streets, 215/922-1695, www.christchurchphila.org, 10 A.M.–4 P.M. Mon.–Sat. and noon–4 Sun. Mar.–Nov., noon–4 P.M. Sun.–Fri. and 10 A.M.–4 P.M. Sat. in Dec., closed Jan.–Feb., admission $2, students $1), which is a short walk from Franklin Court and worth a visit. Almost 300 years old, the graveyard is peppered with 1,400 markers. Franklin is one of five Declaration of Independence signers interred there, along with a host of other colonial- and Revolutionary-

era bigwigs. Guided tours start on the hour. Some visitors believe that tossing a penny on Franklin's gravestone brings good luck. Keep in mind that the thrifty Renaissance man coined the phrase "A penny saved is a penny earned."

National Liberty Museum

A paean to heroism, the National Liberty Museum (321 Chestnut St., 215/925-2800, www.libertymuseum.org, 10 A.M.–5 P.M. daily Memorial Day–Labor Day and Tues.–Sun. rest of year, admission $7, seniors $6, students $5, children 5–17 $2) tells the stories of courageous people from throughout the ages, including Biblical figures, Anne Frank, Nelson Mandela, and the astronauts of the ill-fated space shuttle *Columbia*. A three-story exhibit through its center pays tribute to the heroes of 9/11. The point of it all is to foster "good character, civic responsibility, and respect for all people." And while some exhibits come off as sensitivity training on steroids—witness the paper shredder that allows visitors to symbolically destroy negative words—others are mesmerizing. Particularly yummy is an installation sculpture featuring two life-sized children made of jellybeans.

The museum at the foot of Franklin Court also houses an impressive collection of contemporary glass art, including Dale Chihuly's 21-foot *Flame of Liberty*. Why glass art? Because, like freedom, it's both beautiful and fragile.

Betsy Ross House

Betsy Ross, one of the most famous figures in American history, is known for one thing: sewing the nation's first flag. Whether she did that one thing has long been a matter of debate. Witness the measured wording on the historic marker near the Betsy Ross House (239 Arch St., 215/686-1252, www.betsyrosshouse.org, 10 A.M.–5 P.M. daily, admission $3, children 12 and under and students $2, admission with audio tour $5), where she supposedly lived when she supposedly stitched the flag in 1776: "Credited with making the first stars and stripes flag, Ross was a successful upholsterer." The dearth of evidence doesn't stop hundreds

© DAVID OAKES/123RF.COM

Betsy Ross House

of thousands of people from visiting the circa 1740 row house every year. After all, the version of events sworn to by Betsy's family hasn't been *discredited*. And there's no debating that she was a gutsy patriot, a working mother who produced flags for the government for half a century.

It doesn't take long to explore the little house, which is furnished with period antiques and some reproductions. Several items that belonged to the thrice-widowed tradeswoman are on display. Visitors can learn about the "life and times of the remarkable woman behind the legend" via a 25-minute audio tour. A longer, livelier version is available for youngsters. The highlight of the museum is its first-floor upholstery shop, where an actress portraying Betsy welcomes visitors as if they were potential customers. She fields questions about everything from making draperies to her acquaintance with George Washington, so ask away.

Elfreth's Alley

Popularly known as the nation's oldest residential street, Elfreth's Alley (off 2nd St., between Arch and Race Streets, www.elfreths alley.org) is a charming swatch of the city. The 30-some houses that line it were built between the 1720s and 1830s and have been so meticulously restored that the block feels like a movie set—or a time warp. Here's a horse post. There's a shoe scrape. Up there: That's a "busybody," a set of mirrors that allow a person on the second floor to see who's knocking on the front door.

Like the cobblestone street, the houses are tiny by today's standards. They weren't built for the city's nabobs. In the 18th and early 19th centuries, Elfreth's Alley was the address of numerous artisans and craftsmen, many of whom conducted business out of their homes. Opportunity-seeking immigrants from Germany, Ireland, and other parts of Europe flooded the neighborhood in the 19th century. By the start of the Great Depression, this had become a blighted block. Its present prettiness—and very existence—owes much to the Elfreth's Alley Association, founded in the 1930s to rescue buildings from the wrecking ball. The organization operates the **Elfreth's Alley Museum** (Houses 124 and 126, 215/574-0560, 10 A.M.–5 P.M. Mon.–Sat. and noon–5 P.M. Sun. Mar.–Oct., 10 A.M.–5 P.M. Thurs.–Sat. and noon–5 P.M. Sun. Nov.–Feb., self-guided tour $3, children 6–12 $1, guided tour $5, children 6–12 $2, family $12), which focuses on the lives of working people. It's located in the only two houses open to the public. The others are private homes. Many residents throw open their doors during two annual fundraisers for preservation programs: **Fete Day,** a celebration of colonial history usually held on the first or second Saturday in June, and **Deck the Alley** in early December.

Physick and Powel Houses

The narrow houses along Elfreth's Alley reflect the lifestyles of early Philadelphia's blue-collar citizens. To see how the other half lived, head south to Society Hill, where two elegant 18th-century townhouses are open for tours

PHILADELPHIA

noon–4 P.M. Thursday–Saturday and 1–4 P.M. Sunday. The Physick and Powel Houses, as they're known, are rented for special events, and tours may be limited on Saturdays. Call ahead to avoid crashing a party.

Built in 1765, the Powel House (244 S. 3rd St., 215/627-0364) was home to Philadelphia's last mayor under British rule and first mayor after the creation of the United States, one of its wealthiest citizens. Samuel Powel wasn't a self-made man. His grandfather, an orphan, had arrived in the colonies in 1685, worked hard, married well, and amassed a fortune, the bulk of which Powel inherited upon turning 18. The scion purchased the Georgian-style brick mansion in 1769. He and his wife entertained frequently, welcoming the likes of George and Martha Washington, John Adams, and Benjamin Franklin. A thank-you note from the nation's first president is on display. The house museum's collection also includes a lock of Washington's hair and wood from his coffin.

In the early 20th century, the now-dilapidated building was slated for demolition. The Philadelphia Society for the Preservation of Landmarks (www.philalandmarks.org), which manages the Physick and Powel Houses, was formed to save it. Today the house looks much as it did during Powel's residency, which is to say absolutely fabulous.

The 1786 Physick House (321 S. 4th St., 215/925-7866) is named for Dr. Philip Syng Physick, often referred to as the "father of American surgery." Physick was one of the few doctors who remained in Philadelphia during the yellow fever epidemic of 1793, which killed several thousand people (including Powel). He moved into the four-story, 32-room townhouse in 1815, while undergoing a messy divorce, and lived there until his death in 1837. It's notable as the only freestanding Federal-style townhouse remaining in Society Hill and for its unusually large city garden, adorned with classical statuary and plants popular in the 19th century. Inside, you'll find excellent examples of neoclassic furnishings in one period room after another. The second floor serves as a museum

devoted to Physick's medical career. The surgeon, who was so grossed out by boiling cadavers that he almost dropped out of med school, invented a number of surgical instruments and techniques. He also created America's first carbonated beverage, which he used to treat patients with gastric disorders.

General admission to each house is $5. Seniors and students pay $4, and families enjoy a discounted rate of $12.

Penn's Landing and Camden Waterfront

The Historic District's Delaware River waterfront has been a hot topic among developers and city planners for decades. In 2008 Philadelphia's mayor griped that the area, known as Penn's Landing, had "been the target of big ideas that went nowhere" for too long and appointed a new board to oversee it. Bottom line: It's an area in flux. But there's plenty to see and do at Penn's Landing and across the river in Camden, New Jersey.

A mecca for maritime history buffs, Penn's Landing is home to the **Independence Seaport Museum** (211 S. Columbus Blvd. and Walnut St., 215/413-8655, www.phillyseaport.org, 10 A.M.–5 P.M. daily, admission $12, seniors $10, children and students $7) and several storied ships. The museum covers everything from the science of buoyancy to the immigrant experience to the history of undersea exploration. A boatload of interactive exhibits make it fun for kids. They can play at unloading cargo using a miniature crane, stretch out on a hard bunk in steerage, and crawl through a full-size replica of a 19th-century boat used to fish for shad. The 22-foot skiff was built in the museum's boatbuilding and restoration shop, Workshop on the Water, which offers occasional classes. Tip for travelers on a tight budget: From 10 A.M. to noon on Sundays, the Seaport Museum has a pay-what-you-wish policy.

Admission includes tours of two former U.S. Navy vessels docked beside the museum. The **Becuna,** a 307-foot submarine launched in 1944, prowled the Pacific Ocean for Japanese ships during World War II, eavesdropped on Soviet submarines in the Atlantic during the Cold War, and served in the Korean and Vietnam Wars before she was decommissioned in 1969. Launched in 1892, the *Olympia* made a name for herself during the Spanish-American War. She's the sole surviving naval ship of that 1898 conflict and the oldest steel warship afloat in the world. (In 2010 the museum announced that it couldn't afford the repairs needed to keep the 344-foot cruiser from sinking, leaving its future uncertain.)

Penn's Landing is also home to a venerable tall ship. The *Gazela,* a wooden barkentine built in Portugal more than a century ago, still sails. When she's not off visiting other ports, you'll find her at the northern end of Penn's Landing, near the Market Street footbridge across I-95. She's lovingly maintained by members of the Philadelphia Ship Preservation Guild (215/238-0280, www.gazela.org), who will show you around if you ask nicely. The nonprofit group doesn't charge for tours of *Gazela* or *Jupiter,* a 1902 iron tugboat under its care, but donations are always welcome.

You can't hitch a ride on the vintage vessels, but pleasure trips from Penn's Landing are available. The three-deck *Spirit of Philadelphia* (401 S. Columbus Blvd., 866/455-3866, www.spiritofphiladelphia.com) cruises the Delaware year-round. With its all-you-can-eat buffets, full-service bars, dance floors, and DJs, the ship offers a taste of the Carnival Cruise life. Fair warning: The waitstaff sometimes break into song. Tickets aren't cheap, ranging from $32 for two-hour "midnight moonlight" cruises to upwards of $100 for a dinner cruise on 4th of July weekend.

Another way to get a boat's-eye view of Philadelphia is to hop aboard the **RiverLink Ferry** (215/925-5465, www.riverlinkferry.org, service daily Memorial Day–Labor Day, weekends in May and Sept., round-trip fare $7, seniors and children 3–12 $6), which shuttles between Penn's Landing and Camden's waterfront. The ferry departs from its terminal near the Seaport Museum every hour on the hour starting at 10 A.M., arriving in New Jersey

12 minutes later. It makes its last run from Camden at 5:30 or 6:30 P.M.

With a population of roughly 80,000, the city of Camden is quite small relative to Philadelphia. But it has something its neighbor doesn't: an aquarium. The RiverLink Ferry pulls right up to **Adventure Aquarium** (1 Riverside Dr., Camden, 856/365-3300, www.adventureaquarium.com, 9:30 A.M.–5 P.M. daily, admission $21.95, children 2–12 $17.95), a watery wonderland complete with 3,000-pound hippos. Its shark-petting pool is a huge hit with kids. Tickets are steep, and there's a lot to see, so come at least three hours before closing. Adjacent to the aquarium is the **Camden Children's Garden** (3 Riverside Dr., Camden, 856/365-8733, www.camdenchildrensgarden.org, 10 A.M.–4 P.M. Fri.–Sun., call for winter schedule, admission $6, children 3–11 $5, admission from aquarium $3.50), a four-acre "horticultural playground" operated by the nonprofit Camden City Garden Club. Its buds and butterflies are no match for the aquarium's razzle-dazzle, but it's far less crowded and more affordable.

A visit to Camden isn't complete without a tour of the **Battleship New Jersey** (100 Clinton St., Camden, 866/877-6262, www.battleshipnewjersey.org, 9:30 A.M.–3 P.M. Sat.–Sun. Feb.–Mar. and daily in Apr., 9:30 A.M.–5 P.M. daily May–Labor Day, 9:30 A.M.–3 P.M. daily Sept.–Dec., self-guided tour $18.50, seniors and children $6–11 $14, guided tour $19.95, seniors and children $15), one of the biggest battleships ever. The 45,000-ton behemoth was built in Philadelphia and launched in 1942, a year to the date after the Japanese attack on Pearl Harbor. *New Jersey* racked up so many service stars over the next five decades that she's considered America's most decorated battleship. Visitors get to peer into her nooks and crannies.

Philadelphia's Magic Gardens

South Street, which forms the border between posh Society Hill and gritty South Philly, is one of those rare roads with an identity all its own. Like L.A.'s Hollywood Boulevard, New

© JEFF FADELLIN / COURTESY MAGIC GARDENS

Explore the uniquely colorful tiled corridors and tunnels of Philadelphia's Magic Gardens.

York's Broadway, and New Orleans's Bourbon Street, South Street is more a destination than a route from here to there. It's Philadelphia's center of counterculture, nightlife capital, and most eclectic shopping district. It's also Isaiah Zagar's canvas. Since the late 1960s, the artist has been plastering the South Street area with mosaic murals that make you stop in your tracks. They're shimmering collages of mirrors, tiles, colored glass, and found objects. In a city awash with public art, Zagar's 100-plus creations are unmistakable. Philadelphia's Magic Gardens (1020 South St., 215/733-0390, www .philadelphiasmagicgardens.org, 11 A.M.–6 P.M. Sun.–Thurs., 11 A.M.–8 P.M. Fri.–Sat., closes an hour earlier Sun.–Thurs. Nov.–Mar., admission $4, children 6–12 $2) is his most ambitious creation—his "opus," as he calls it. As colorful and textured as a coral reef, it consists of a fully mosaiced gallery and a mazelike outdoor installation covering half a block. Disfigured bicycle wheels, bottles, Christmas ornaments, folk art from far-flung places, pottery shards, and perseverance went into its

making. When Zagar began the project in 1994, his canvas was a vacant lot. Eight years later, his work still in progress and South Street property values on the rise, the owner of the lot decided to sell. Monies were raised and a nonprofit formed to save the Magic Gardens from the bulldozer.

Like most gardens, this one is best visited in the warmer months. On weekends from April through October, trained interpreters lead hour-long walks through the neighborhood, explaining Zagar's approach and the personal and community stories depicted in his murals. If you don't catch a walking tour ($10 for adults, $6 for children), be sure to pick up a brochure that lists the addresses of more than 60 murals. During the colder months, you can get a guided tour of the Magic Gardens and a nearby Zagar-zapped building that isn't normally open to the public ($7 for adults, $5 for children). Two-day mosaic workshops with Zagar himself ($300 for new students, $50 for alumni) are offered monthly from March through October. The gray-haired artist, whose studio overlooks his opus, teaches the fundamentals of breaking tile, cutting mirror, gluing, and grouting—then gives participants a go at a mural.

CENTER CITY

Center City is to Philadelphia what "downtown" is to most American cities: its commercial heart. It's a place of skyscrapers, men in suits, upscale restaurants, and brand-name hotels. At the center of it all is City Hall, a dramatic building made more dramatic by elaborate nighttime lighting. If you're adrift in Center City, the seat of government is a handy navigation tool. Addresses with an "S" prefix, as in 99 S. 17th Street, are south of Market Street, the east–west thoroughfare interrupted by City Hall, and addresses with an "N" prefix are north of it. The higher the house number, the farther it is from Market. (You won't find "E" and "W" prefixes in Center City addresses because the house number and street name tell you everything you need to know; e.g., 1610 Walnut Street is on Walnut Street between 16th and 17th Streets).

In addition to being the commercial and governmental center of Philadelphia, Center City is a cultural mecca. A portion of Broad Street, the north–south thoroughfare interrupted by City Hall, has been dubbed Avenue of the Arts for its concentration of concert halls and theaters.

◖ City Hall

City Hall (Broad and Market Streets, tour office room 121, 215/686-2840, www.philadelphiacityhall.org, observation deck access 9:30 A.M.–4:15 P.M. Mon.–Fri., guided tour 12:30 P.M. Mon.–Fri.) is a building of many distinctions. When construction began in 1871, it was to be the tallest building in the world. The project dragged on for so long that by the time of its completion in 1901, the Washington Monument and Eiffel Tower stood higher. Still, City Hall had bragging rights as the tallest *habitable* building in the world—for a few years anyway. At 37 feet, the bronze statue of city founder William Penn that crowns its central tower is the tallest statue atop any building. Long after skyscrapers twice

view of Center City from the steps of the Philadelphia Museum of Art

© ANNA DUBROVSKY

the ornate four-faced clock on the tower of Philadelphia's City Hall

© NATALIA BRATSLAVSKY/123RF.COM

© ANNA DUBROVSKY

Philadelphia City Hall

its height dotted the globe, City Hall remained Philadelphia's tallest thanks to a gentleman's agreement that no building would tower over Billy Penn's head. The agreement was broken in the mid-1980s, when One Liberty Place went up, and today City Hall barely makes the top 10. But it hangs on to several distinctions: world's tallest occupied masonry structure, America's largest (and most expensive) municipal building, and one of the continent's finest examples of Second Empire architecture. It's such a fine example, in fact, that a tourist could snap some pics and convince folks back home that he'd been to Paris.

There's plenty to see without stepping foot inside the building, including some 250 sculptures and motifs by Alexander Milne Calder, the Scottish-born son of a tombstone carver and grandfather of the Calder renowned for his sculptural mobiles. He devoted two decades to City Hall's ornamentation. In addition to the colossal Penn statue, Calder's crowning work (literally and figuratively), the central tower is adorned with bronze statues depicting Native American and Swedish settlers. An eagle with a wingspan of 15 feet is perched above each face of the tower's four-faced clock. The many sculptures closer to eye level include representations of continents, various arts and sciences, commerce, agriculture, and justice. Be sure to check out the courtyard's western entrance, though it's the smallest and least ornate of the four. With its carvings of thorns, thistles, and menacing serpents, it's hardly inviting. But Calder knew what he was doing: The portal was used by horse-drawn vans carrying accused criminals.

City Hall isn't nearly as ornate inside as it is outside. Its more lavish spaces are the focus of 90-minute tours ($10 per person, seniors and children 3–18 $8) that depart from room 121 at 12:30 P.M. weekdays. The tours conclude with an elevator ride to an observation deck below the Penn statue. You don't have to take the tour to enjoy the panoramic view. The elevator ferries visitors to the observation deck from 9:30 A.M. to 4:15 P.M. weekdays. It only fits four, and the view is fantastic, so it's not unusual for timed tickets ($5 per person, seniors $3, children 3–18 $4) to sell out by noon.

◖ Masonic Temple

Philadelphia's Masonic Temple (1 N. Broad St., 215/988-1917, www.pagrandlodge.org, tours Tues.–Sat., admission $8, students $6, seniors and children 12 and under $5, family $20), just across the street from City Hall, is easily mistaken for a church. It's imposing, topped with turrets and spires, and clearly not of this

---

SCULPTURE AND SYMBOLISM NEAR CITY HALL

More than 250 sculptures designed by Alexander Milne Calder adorn the magnificent City Hall. While you're in the area, be sure to check out these other unique sculptures.

CLOTHESPIN

Across 15th Street from City Hall stands Claes Oldenburg's 45-foot steel *Clothespin*. Sleek and modern, it offers a stark contrast to City Hall's ornate design. Oldenburg has compared his clothespin to Constantin Brancusi's *The Kiss,* and many agree that the shape is reminiscent of lovers holding one another. The *Clothespin* has also been viewed as a symbol of holding, or clipping, the old with the new in Philadelphia.

LOVE

At the intersection of 15th Street and John F. Kennedy Boulevard is John F. Kennedy Plaza, known to locals as Love Park because of the sculpture by Robert Indiana that stands proudly at its center. It is said that the crooked "O" in the bright-red letters that spell "love" is there to remind us that nothing – including love – is perfect. Positioned at an angle so the Benjamin Franklin Parkway spreads out behind it with the Philadelphia Museum of Art in the distance, the sculpture was installed for the city's bicentennial in 1976 and quickly became an iconic image of the City of Brotherly Love.

GOVERNMENT OF THE PEOPLE

Just north of City Hall across John F. Kennedy Boulevard, you can't miss Jacques Lipchitz's large *Government of the People,* one of several art installations in the plaza of the Municipal Services Building. The abstract bronze sculpture of hands and limbs gripping each other was built in the 1970s during the era of the polarizing mayor Frank Rizzo. Nearby stands a large replica of Rizzo himself, who fittingly has his back to Lipchitz's statue. He purportedly cut off city funding for the statue that he hated and was quoted as saying "It looks like some plasterer dropped a load of plaster." Ah, the history of Philadelphia municipal politics.

– Contributed by Karrie Gavin,
author of Moon Philadelphia

© BEN SUTHERLAND

© RITU JETHANI/123RF.COM

Masonic Temple

century or the last. Divine: yes. Ecclesiastical: no. Dedicated in 1873, the temple is the mothership of Pennsylvania Masonry. Though its origins are obscure, Masonry is considered the world's oldest fraternal organization. Some of the fraternity's practices are as shrouded in secrecy as an Apple product launch, but you don't have to whisper a password to pass through the temple's grand entrance gate. Guided tours are offered at 10 A.M., 11 A.M., 1 P.M., 2 P.M., and 3 P.M. Tuesday–Friday and 10 A.M., 11 A.M., and noon Saturday.

The place is an architectural wonderland, with each of seven resplendent meeting halls paying tribute to a different style. The Grecian-themed Corinthian Hall shares the second floor with Egyptian Hall, Ionic Hall, and rooms decorated in the Italian Renaissance and Rhenish Romanesque styles. Groin vaults, pointed arches, and pinnacles abound in the third-floor Gothic Hall, with its hand-carved furniture. Oriental Hall, located on the first floor, is not

what its name suggests. It's patterned after the Alhambra, the exquisite Moorish-style palace complex in Granada, Spain. Be sure to check out its ceiling, which is divided into thousands of panels of various shapes.

You don't have to tour the building to visit the **Masonic Library and Museum** (9 A.M.–5 P.M. Tues.–Fri., 9 A.M.–noon Sat., admission $3), which displays the Masonic apron presented to George Washington by the Marquis de Lafayette, the French aristocrat who served in Washington's Continental Army during the Revolutionary War. Washington is one of more than a dozen U.S. presidents on the Masonry's long list of "brothers." Other notable pieces in the collection include a reverse glass painting of Washington being lifted into the heavens, Benjamin Franklin's circa 1779 Masonic sash, and the Masonic apron of General Tom Thumb, the dwarf whose circus performances made him an international celebrity in the mid-1800s.

Comcast Center

At 975 feet, the Comcast Center (17th and Arch Streets) is Pennsylvania's tallest building. Its opening in 2008 bumped One Liberty Place, the skyscraper that ended City Hall's reign as the tallest building in town, out of the top slot. Most office buildings don't hold much interest for anyone who doesn't work in them, but the 58-story Comcast Center, headquarters to the largest U.S. cable company, is something of a tourist attraction. That's because of the colossal LED wall in its main lobby. **The Comcast Experience,** as it's called, is 83.3 feet wide, 25.4 feet high, and packed with 10 million pixels for phenomenal picture quality. You can think of it as a high-definition TV on steroids. Or you can think of it as installation art.

From 6 A.M. to midnight, the video wall pulses with ever-changing images of everything from Philly's historic sites to outer space.

Nature footage might follow an artsy dance sequence. At times the visual mimics the lobby's wood paneling, blending in like a bullfrog on a pebbled shore. You never know what you'll see because a virtual "video jockey" selects from thousands of hours of content. One thing's for sure: A workplace can be a fun place.

Pennsylvania Academy of the Fine Arts

In a lesser city, a museum as impressive as the Pennsylvania Academy of the Fine Arts (118 and 128 N. Broad St., 215/972-7600, www.pafa.org, 10 A.M.–5 P.M. Tues.–Sat., 11 A.M.–5 P.M. Sun., admission to permanent collection $10, seniors, students, and children 13–18 $8, admission to permanent collections and special exhibitions $15, seniors, students, and children 13–18 $12) could well top the list of cultural attractions. But Philadelphia

THE CURSE OF BILLY PENN

If you believe a broken mirror brings seven years' bad luck, rub a rabbit's foot with regularity, or stay in bed on Friday the 13th, you'll probably believe in the Curse of Billy Penn. Billy Penn – that's Philadelphia founder William Penn if you're not from these parts – has neither confirmed nor denied the existence of said curse, which may have something to do with the fact that he's been dead for almost 200 years. Anyhow, we digress. The story of the curse goes something like this.

For more than 80 years after its completion in 1901, City Hall stood taller than any other building in Philadelphia. It's not that developers couldn't build taller. By 1980, buildings two times and even three times its height had risen in New York and Chicago. The technology was there. In Philadelphia, however, a gentleman's agreement dictated that the statue of Billy Penn at the tippy-top of City Hall remain the highest point in the city. The agreement was finally cast aside in the mid-1980s, and a 61-floor skyscraper sprouted two blocks from City Hall. Soon it was joined by other soaring towers.

As the city's skyline changed, so did the luck of its sports teams. Between the mid-1970s and early '80s, the Philadelphia Flyers had won two Stanley Cups (1974 and 1975), the Phillies had won a World Series (1980), the 76ers had won an NBA championship (1983), and the Eagles had reached the Super Bowl (1981). But the two decades starting in the mid-'80s were trying times for Philly sports fans. The four major sports teams had close-but-no-cigar seasons. It didn't escape notice that the streak of championships ended around the time that the gentleman's agreement was breached.

Had the breach unleashed a curse? Lots of people talked about it. Few would admit to believing it. But when the Comcast Center marked its near-completion with a "topping out" ceremony in 2007, a statue of William Penn sat on the beam hoisted to the highest point of Philadelphia's newest tallest skyscraper. Just to be safe.

The following year, the Philadelphia Phillies defeated the Tampa Bay Rays for their second World Series title. The curse – if there was one – was broken.

offers art lovers a veritable buffet, and PAFA is often passed up for meatier fare like the Philadelphia Museum of Art and the Barnes Foundation. It's a shame, because its collection of 19th- and 20th-century American art is really quite something. Among the artists represented are Winslow Homer, John Singer Sargent, and Edward Hopper. PAFA is an art school as well as a museum—the oldest in the nation in both respects—and its collection abounds with works by its founders, faculty, and alumni, including Charles Willson Peale, William Rush, Thomas Eakins, Mary Cassatt, and Violet Oakley. The museum doesn't shun modern and contemporary American artists. You can expect to see a fairly even mix of historical and contemporary art if you take in all of its permanent and special exhibitions.

Two strikingly different buildings make up the PAFA campus, and you'll find galleries in both. The older of the two is known as the Historic Landmark Building and dates to 1876. It's considered one of the premier examples of Victorian Gothic architecture in the country. PAFA opened the adjacent

Samuel M. V. Hamilton Building in 2005 as part of its 200th anniversary celebration. Built as an automobile showroom and storage facility in the early 1900s, the ingeniously repurposed building is used for most traveling exhibitions.

Docent-led tours of the galleries are generally offered at 11:30 A.M. and 12:30 P.M. on Tuesdays, Thursdays, and Fridays and 1 and 2 P.M. on Wednesdays, Saturdays, and Sundays. They're included in the price of admission. Admission to the Morris Gallery in the Historic Landmark Building is free.

(Reading Terminal Market

The Reading Railroad was forced into bankruptcy several decades ago, but the indoor farmers market that bears its name pulses with activity seven days a week. Reading Terminal Market (12th and Arch Streets, 215/922-2317, www.readingterminalmarket .org, 8 A.M.–6 P.M. Mon.–Sat., 9 A.M.–5 P.M. Sun.) is a regular stop for local chefs and other gastronomes foraging for fresh produce, eggs, dairy products, meats, seafood, and specialty

The Reading Terminal Market is a gastronome's delight.

foods. More than a third of its 80-some stands are eateries, making the market an extremely popular lunchtime destination. The dizzying array of options—from spicy Cajun fare to savory crepes to caviar—can breed indecision. You can't go wrong with the mac and cheese from **Delilah's,** which has won raves from Oprah. If you're a fan of Pennsylvania Dutch cuisine, come Wednesday–Saturday, when Amish and Mennonite vendors fill out the northwest corner of the market house. Top off a meal at the excellent **Dutch Eating Place** with hand-dipped ice cream straight from Lancaster County at **Miller's Twist.** Handcrafted jewelry, new and used books, housewares, bath products, and other non-edibles are also on offer.

The market opened its doors in 1892 as part of the Reading Railroad's new train depot and company headquarters. In an age before refrigerated trucks, its location couldn't have been more ideal for shipping and receiving goods. At one point, a free service made it possible for a suburban housewife to "shop" at the market without venturing into the city. Her grocery order would be placed on a train bound for her town and held at the station until she came for it. The market's continued existence was threatened by the demise of the Reading Railroad in the 1970s and the subsequent decision to incorporate the terminal into the design of a new convention center. Philadelphians demanded that the venerable market be preserved, and preserved it was. Meeting facilities replaced train tracks and platforms above the street-level market.

The area is well served by public transportation, but if you must drive, park in the garage at 12th and Filbert and bring your ticket. Any merchant will validate the ticket with a purchase of $10 or more, entitling you to two hours of parking for a flat rate of $4. Regular garage rates apply after two hours.

Chinatown

Philadelphia's Chinatown (9th St. to 11th St. between Arch and Vine Streets) doesn't approach New York's or San Francisco's in scale or sales of knockoff handbags and Rolexes. But if you're in the market for canned shark fin soup, roasted eel, dried squid, or porcelain dragons, the compact enclave just east of the Pennsylvania Convention Center won't disappoint. It's packed with restaurants and stores of the Asian variety. (Vietnamese, Burmese, Malaysian, Thai, and Japanese eateries have sprung up among the Chinese businesses, but "Asiatown" doesn't have the same ring as "Chinatown," does it?) A plaque marks the Race Street site of the district's first Chinese restaurant, which opened in 1870.

The landmark most associated with Chinatown is of fairly recent vintage. **Chinatown Friendship Gate** (10th St. near Arch St.), a symbol of friendship between Philadelphia and its sister city of Tianjin, China, was dedicated in 1984 by officials from both cities. Artisans from China had a hand in the creation of the colorful portal, which stands 40 feet tall and proclaims "Philadelphia Chinatown" in large Chinese characters. The temptation to stand beneath it for a photo op is strong but, given the nature of Center City traffic, best resisted.

If you're curious about Chinatown's history and food, hook up with local chef and media darling Joseph Poon. His **Wok 'N Walk Tour** (Chef Kitchen, 1010 Cherry St., 2nd floor, 215/928-9333, www.josephpoon.com, $60) includes a Tai Chi demonstration, visits to a fortune cookie factory and a Chinese herbal medicine shop, and a four-course lunch or dinner.

Mütter Museum

Best visited on an empty stomach, the Mütter (19 S. 22nd St., 215/563-3737, www.collphyphil .org, 10 A.M.–5 P.M. Mon.–Fri., 10 A.M.–5 P.M. Sat.–Sun., admission $14, seniors, students, and children 6–17 $10) houses an unforgettable collection of what physicians of yore called "nature's books." We call them body parts. Its treasures are truly one of a kind. They include bladder stones removed from U.S. Chief Justice John Marshall, tissue from the thorax of President Abraham Lincoln's assassin, and a tumor taken

© ANNA DUBROVSKY

Mütter Museum

from President Grover Cleveland's jaw during a secret surgery aboard a private yacht. The museum is home to the tallest skeleton on display in North America and a wax model of a human head that sprouted a horn. Perhaps most disturbing is the preserved colon of a man so constipated that he was carrying some 40 pounds of feces when he died at the age of 29. Giant doesn't begin to describe the swollen organ.

The Mütter is part of the College of Physicians of Philadelphia, a professional medical organization founded in 1787. Members started the museum in the mid-1800s to help educate future doctors about the human body and its myriad afflictions. Like library books, its specimens were borrowed and studied. The 1874 autopsy of conjoined twins Chang and Eng—the original "Siamese twins"— was performed in the museum. Their bodies were returned to their adopted home of North Carolina, where they'd married sisters and fathered 21 children, but the Mütter was allowed to keep their fused livers. They're on display beneath a plaster cast of the twins' torsos, which were connected by a band of skin and cartilage.

The small gift shop is guaranteed to turn exhibit-induced grimaces into smiles. Its inventory includes plush toys of deadly microbes, syringe-shaped pens, skull-shaped beads, gummy maggots, and, of course, the game Operation. Still queasy? Get some air in the college's lovely garden, which is planted with more than 50 medicinal herbs and dotted with benches.

BENJAMIN FRANKLIN PARKWAY AND FAIRMOUNT PARK

Examine a Philadelphia map and you can't help but think: *One of these things is not like the others.* Per William Penn's 17th-century plan, Philly is a city of parallel lines and right angles. Bucking the trend—daring to be diagonal—is the Benjamin Franklin Parkway. Penn was long dead by the time construction of the mile-long parkway began in 1917. Designed by landscape architect Jacques Gréber and inspired by the Champs-Élysées in his hometown of Paris, the road starts near City Hall, carves a circle through Logan Square, and terminates at the magnificent Philadelphia Museum of Art, known simply as the Art Museum. Trees, sculptures, and flags representing some 90

CITY OF MURALS

With more than 3,000 murals, Philadelphia has been called the world's largest outdoor art gallery. The colorful, larger-than-life artworks brighten schools, community centers, businesses, and homes from Center City to outlying neighborhoods that most tourists never see. In parts of the city where urban blight is at its worst, they bring beauty and a sense of community pride, while mural tours give visitors an interesting and safe way to explore these areas.

Philadelphia's **Mural Arts Program** (877/887-8225, www.muralarts.org) traces its roots to the mid-1980s, when the city was plastered with graffiti. Muralist and community activist Jane Golden was hired to redirect the energies of graffitists into mural painting. She still runs the program, which has not only alleviated much of the graffiti problem but also empowered young artists and contributed to neighborhood revitalization in many parts of the city. Professional artists are hired to work closely with residents to create murals that tell the stories of the spaces they inhabit.

While the magnificent works of art speak for themselves, a guided tour is the best way to experience them. The Mural Arts Program offers **trolley tours** ($25 per person, seniors $23, children 12 and under $15) of various sections of the city on Saturdays and Sundays April–November and Wednesdays May–November. They begin at 10 A.M. and last an hour and a half to two hours. The **Mural Mile Walk** ($17 per person), offered at 11:30 A.M. daily May–October, covers 2.5 miles and 17 murals in Center City. If the guided tour is sold out, you can rent an MP3 player and headphones for a **self-guided version** ($10). Trolley and walking tours depart from the Independence Visitor Center at 6th and Market Streets, rain or shine. Reservations are strongly recommended. **Bike tours** ($17 per person) are offered on occasion. One of the newest and most unusual tour options is known as **Love Letter** ($17 per person) and features 50 rooftop murals in West Philly. Participants take in the artworks from SEPTA's elevated train and several platforms. The tour departs from the Love Park Welcome Center at 1600 JFK Boulevard at 10 A.M. Saturday year-round.

Be sure to check the website for a full schedule of tours and special events, as the Mural Arts Program is always expanding to offer more murals and more ways to experience them.

– Contributed by Karrie Gavin, author of Moon Philadelphia

Philadelphia Muses by Meg Saligman, 13th & Locust Streets, Center City

nations line the grand boulevard. (Looking for a particular flag? With a few exceptions, they're hung alphabetically.) Like Center City's Avenue of the Arts, the parkway is a cultural mecca. In addition to the Art Museum, it's home to the nation's oldest natural history museum and a splendid science museum. It's also home to the largest collection of Auguste Rodin sculptures outside Paris. Soon it will be home to the **Barnes Foundation** (www .barnesfoundation.org), renowned for its extensive holdings of works by the likes of Picasso, Matisse, Cezanne, and Renoir. Based in the burbs since its founding in the 1920s, the foundation broke ground for a new building on the parkway in late 2009. Plans call for a 2011 completion.

"Fairmount Park" refers to both Philadelphia's park system and its largest green space. At roughly 4,200 acres, the latter is one of the largest municipal parks in the country. (For comparison's sake, New York's Central Park covers an area of 843 acres.) It stretches north from the Philadelphia Museum of Art, hugging both sides of the Schuylkill River. The portion east of the river is sometimes called East Fairmount Park and the portion west of it—you guessed it—West Fairmount Park. Winding through East Park is the spectacularly scenic Kelly Drive, named for a former city councilman, Olympic rower, and brother of actress-turned-princess Grace Kelly. There are so many statues along Kelly Drive that it's better experienced by foot or bicycle than by car. West Park is home to the nation's oldest zoo, the city's children's museum, and its premier outdoor concert venue, the Mann Center for the Performing Arts.

The Academy of Natural Sciences

Due to celebrate its 200th birthday in 2012, the Academy of Natural Sciences (19th St. and Benjamin Franklin Parkway, 215/299-1000, www.ansp.org, 10 A.M.–4:30 P.M. Mon.–Fri., 10 A.M.–5 P.M. Sat.–Sun., admission $12, seniors, students, and children 3–12 $10, additional fee of $2 for live butterfly exhibit) is the oldest natural history museum in the western hemisphere. As in most natural history

museums, visitors spend a good deal of time looking at dead things. Critters from around the world strike permanent poses in 37 dioramas, most of which were created in the 1920s and '30s, before television brought the animal kingdom into people's living rooms. The skeletal remains of prehistoric beasts fill Dinosaur Hall. But living, breathing beings also have a place in this museum. Its Live Animal Center is home to more than 100 birds, reptiles, amphibians, and other animals, all of which are injured or were born in captivity and wouldn't make it in the wild. They take turns starring in daily naturalist shows and delighting children in the museum's hands-on discovery center. The academy also boasts a live butterfly exhibit.

The Franklin Institute

It's no surprise that Philadelphia's science museum is named for favorite son Ben Franklin, whose 18th-century discoveries are still remembered. Founded in 1824, The Franklin Institute (20th St. and Benjamin Franklin Parkway, 215/448-1200, www.fi.edu, 9:30 A.M.–5 P.M. daily, admission $15.50, seniors $14.50, children 4–11 $12, additional charges for IMAX and Franklin theaters) became a venue for showcasing new technologies. In 1893 Nikola Tesla demonstrated the principle of wireless telegraphy at the institute. The first public demonstration of an all-electronic television system took place there in 1934, the same year the museum moved to its current home and opened to the public. A 20-foot-high marble statue of a seated Ben Franklin dominates its dramatic rotunda, which was modeled after Rome's Pantheon. The Founding Father's presence is also felt in an exhibit devoted to electricity, which features an electronic version of his book *Experiments and Observations in Electricity,* along with a dance floor that generates power as visitors bust a move. The institute's bioscience exhibit, with its giant walk-through model of a human heart, is a perennial favorite. (Cool factoid: The two-story heart would fit nicely inside a 220-foot-tall person.) If you're the queasy sort, steer clear of the exhibit's full-size re-creation of a surgery room, where the "patient" is forever undergoing open-heart surgery. The aviation exhibit offers would-be pilots a chance to climb into a flight simulator ($5) and pull maneuvers including a 360-degree roll. One of the newest exhibits, Amazing Machine, pays tribute to vacuum cleaners, power drills, and other technologies we take for granted.

The institute has three state-of-the-art theaters: a digital projection planetarium, an IMAX theater, and the Franklin Theater, which specializes in 3D films. Museum tickets include admission to one planetarium show. Tickets to shows in the IMAX theater can be purchased individually or as part of a package that includes museum admission. Franklin Theater tickets can only be purchased as part of a package.

Rodin Museum

The Rodin Museum (22nd St. and Benjamin Franklin Parkway, 215/568-6026, www.rodin museum.org, 10 A.M.–5 P.M. Tues.–Sun., suggested donation $5) is home to more than 120 works by its namesake sculptor, including a bronze cast of *The Thinker,* perhaps the most famous sculpture in the world. You'd have to go to Paris to find a larger collection of the Frenchman's masterpieces. The museum, which opened its Paris-made gates in 1929, was a gift to the city from movie theater magnate Jules Mastbaum. He began collecting all things Auguste Rodin in 1923 and died three years later, just as his museum project was getting underway.

It's best to visit on a temperate, rainless day, as some sculptures are displayed in the museum's formal gardens and other outdoor spaces. Among them is a bronze cast of the unfinished but incredible *Gates of Hell,* which the artist worked on from 1880 until his death in 1917. Guided tours of the museum are offered at 1:30 P.M. Tuesdays, Thursdays, and Sundays, plus the first and third Saturdays of the month.

Philadelphia Museum of Art

Little needs to be said about the Art Museum (26th St. and Benjamin Franklin Parkway, 215/763-8100, www.philamuseum.org, 10 A.M.–5 P.M. Tues.–Sun., open until 8:45 P.M. Fri., admission $16, seniors $14, students and children 13–18 $12), which is quite simply one of the preeminent cultural institutions in the country. Since its founding in 1876, the museum has amassed more than 225,000 objects representing 2,000 years of creative expression.

© ANNA DUBROVSKY

the Philadelphia Museum of Art and its famous "Rocky" steps

It's worth a visit whether your passion is medieval armor, modern sculpture, or the movie character Rocky Balboa (more on that later). Architecture and decorative arts buffs are particularly well served. The museum, which is in itself an architectural gem, contains about 80 period rooms, including entire furnished rooms from historic houses. One can meander through a French cloister, a Chinese palace hall, a Japanese teahouse, and a stone temple straight from India in the space of 10 minutes. The nation's third-largest art museum has more than 200 galleries, so if you're dead set on seeing the whole thing, arrive while the neoclassical temple of art is still bathed in morning light. Better yet, come on a Friday, when select galleries stay open into the evening as part of **Art After 5,** a sort of cocktail party complete with live music. If money is tight, visit on the first Sunday of the month, when the price of admission is up to you.

photo op with the statue of Rocky Balboa outside of the Philadelphia Museum of Art

Having long outgrown the home built for it in the 1920s, the museum expanded into an Art Deco landmark across the way in 2007. Tickets to the main building include admission to the **Perelman Building** (Fairmount and Pennsylvania Avenues, 10 A.M.–5 P.M. Tues.–Sun., admission $8, seniors $7, students and children 13–18 $6), which showcases some of the museum's more cutting-edge collections. A shuttle between the two buildings operates every 10–15 minutes.

It's not unusual for people to visit the main building without stepping foot inside. It sits on a granite hill, and the view from its east entranceway is one of the best in the city. Dead ahead is the plaza known as **Eakins Oval,** featuring a statue of a uniformed George Washington astride a horse, and beyond it, City Hall. The broad steps leading to the entrance are as much a tourist attraction as any in town, having appeared in an iconic scene in *Rocky,* the 1976 sleeper hit starring Sylvester Stallone as a fictional Philly boxer who takes on a heavyweight champ. Not everyone has the stamina to sprint up the steps à la Rocky, but almost every first-time visitor has an "Italian Stallion" moment at the top, posing with arms outstretched for a camera-wielding friend. A bronze statue of the movie character, commissioned by Stallone for a scene in *Rocky III,* can be found near the base of the so-called **Rocky steps.**

❰ Eastern State Penitentiary

When Eastern State Penitentiary (22nd St. and Fairmount Ave., 215/236-3300, www.eastern state.org, 10 A.M.–5 P.M. daily, open until 8 P.M. Wed. June–Aug., admission $12, seniors $10, students and children 7–12 $8) opened in 1829, it was unlike any other prison in the world. For one thing, it was architecturally ingenious, with long cell blocks radiating from a surveillance hub like the spokes of a wheel. In an era when the White House had coal-burning stoves for heat and no running water, Philadelphia's pricey new prison had central heat and flush toilets. Its treatment of inmates was also a radical departure from the norm. Rather than pen them up like cattle, Eastern State assigned each prisoner a private cell complete with skylight. It eschewed corporal punishment, adhering to a Quaker-influenced formula for reforming criminals: strict isolation plus labor. The prison was so serious about curbing interaction that inmates were hooded when it was necessary to move them. Left alone with their thoughts and a Bible, criminals would come to realize the error of their ways and become genuinely penitent—or so thought proponents of the "penitentiary."

Charles Dickens thought otherwise. "I hold this slow and daily tampering with the mysteries of the brain to be immeasurably worse than any torture of the body," he wrote after an 1842 visit. Some 300 prisons around the world emulated Eastern State's design and system of solitary confinement, but detractors like Dickens eventually prevailed. By the time Al "Scarface" Capone was booked into the prison in 1929, inmates lived two or three to a cell, worked alongside each other in the weaving shops and kitchens, exercised together, and ate together.

After 142 years of use, the prison closed in 1971. In 1994 the National Historic Landmark opened its doors to the public. The *Voices of Eastern State* audio tour, available April–November, covers everything from intake procedures to escape attempts. It's narrated by

© KARRIE GAVIN

Eastern State Penitentiary

actor Steve Buscemi and punctuated with first-hand accounts from former wardens, guards, and inmates.

On select evenings from mid-September to early November, the already eerie site moonlights as a massive haunted house. **Terror Behind the Walls** is too terror-ific for kids under the age of 7 (and even some grown-ups).

Philadelphia Zoo

America's oldest zoo (3400 W. Girard Ave., 215/243-1100, www.philadelphiazoo .org, 9:30 A.M.–5 P.M. daily Mar.–Oct., 9:30 A.M.–4 P.M. daily Nov.–Feb., in-season admission $18, children 2–11 $15, reduced admission Nov.–Feb.) packs a lot into its 42 manicured acres. It's home to more than 1,300 animals representing some 300 species and subspecies: lions, tigers, and bears, of course, but also a host of critters that only an *Animal Planet* addict would recognize. You won't soon forget the wrinkled mug of naked mole-rats in the Rare Animal Conservation Center, the wide-eyed Coquerel's sifakas in the PECO Primate Reserve, or the aquatic acrobatics of the giant river otters in Carnivore Kingdom. Also unforgettable: hovering high above the treetops in the **Channel 6 Zooballoon** (Apr.–Oct. weather permitting, $15 per person, $50 per family of four), the region's only passenger-carrying helium balloon. Not surprisingly, there's more to see and do during the warmer months. From April through October, visitors can hand-feed nectar to colorful lorikeets, take in the scenery from the back of a camel ($6 per person), and cruise Bird Lake in a swan-shaped paddleboat ($6 per person).

The Philadelphia Zoo received its charter in 1859 but didn't open its gates until 1874, after the Civil War. The oldest building on the grounds, **The Solitude,** predates the zoo. Built in 1784 by John Penn, grandson of Pennsylvania founder William Penn, it's the only surviving American residence once owned by a Penn family member. Penn named his elegant manor house after the Duke of Württemberg's La Solitude in Stuttgart's sylvan environs.

Fair warning: Unless you're a zoo member, parking will set you back $12. It is possible to get there via SEPTA, Philly's public transit system, but an easier way to travel between Center City and the zoo is by Phlash trolley (800/537-7676, www.phillyphlash.com, $2 per trip or $5 per day, all-day family pass $10), operating May–October. Phlash trolleys (actually buses in disguise) also stop at the nearby Please Touch Museum, where parking for nonmembers is $8.

Please Touch Museum

The Please Touch Museum (Memorial Hall, 4231 Ave. of the Republic, 215/581-3181, www.pleasetouchmuseum.org, 9 A.M.–5 P.M. Mon.–Sat., 11 A.M.–5 P.M. Sun., admission $15) answers a question for the ages: where to take the kids on a rainy day? Designed for the 7 and under set, it offers several hours' worth of learning experiences disguised as fun. Kids can push a cart through a supermarket, fill up a tank at a gas station, race sailboats, take a spin on a hamster wheel, and enter the magical world of *Alice in Wonderland*. On most days, they can also catch an original theater performance by a cast that includes puppets.

The museum has moved several times since opening in 1976. It settled into its current home, West Fairmount Park's historic Memorial Hall, in 2008. Memorial Hall was one of about 200 buildings erected for the 1876 Centennial Exposition, the first World's Fair held in America, and it's the only major one still standing. The beaux-arts-style building served as the city's art museum until the Philadelphia Museum of Art opened in 1928. Please Touch Museum's Centennial Exploration exhibit gives kids a taste of the atmosphere at the World's Fair, where inventions including the telephone, the typewriter, and root beer were revealed. Its centerpiece, a 20-by-30-foot scale model of the fairgrounds, was first unveiled in 1889.

GREATER PHILADELPHIA
Valley Forge National Historical Park

On September 26, 1777, British troops marched into Philadelphia. If Britain thought that capturing the capital of its rebellious colonies would put an end to the Revolutionary War, Britain thought wrong. That winter, George Washington and his battle-weary army set up camp in the small community of Valley Forge, 20 miles northwest of Philadelphia. The soldiers built a city of 2,000-some huts, miles of trenches, and five earthen forts. In February, a former Prussian army officer with an epic name arrived in camp. The charismatic Baron Friedrich Wilhelm Augustus von Steuben whipped the Continental Army into a finely tuned marching machine. The war for independence would continue for several years, but the six-month encampment at Valley Forge would be remembered as a turning point. In came ready-to-quit rebels. Out went warriors.

The visitors center at Valley Forge National Historical Park (Rte. 23 and N. Gulph Rd., Valley Forge, 610/783-1077, www.nps.gov/vafo, grounds open 6 A.M.–10 P.M. daily, visitors center open 9 A.M.–5 P.M. daily, free admission) offers a good introduction to this chapter of history. The 18-minute film *Valley Forge: A Winter Encampment* plays every half hour 9:30 A.M.–4:30 P.M., and exhibits round out the picture. A map with a suggested auto tour of historic sites is available in several languages. Among the historic sites is **Washington's Headquarters** (9 A.M.–5 P.M. daily), the small building that General George Washington and his military staff called home during the encampment. The soldiers' huts often seen in photos of the national park are reproductions; the hastily built originals are long gone. During the warmer months, the visitors center is the starting point for 40-minute ranger-led tours and 90-minute trolley tours. Rental bikes are available June–Labor Day.

As one of the largest open spaces in southeastern Pennsylvania, the park is as much a destination for outdoor recreation as historical edification. Almost 30 miles of hiking, biking, and horseback riding trails carve through its 3,500 acres. The Horseshoe Trail, which begins near Washington's Headquarters, connects to the legendary Appalachian Trail.

Entertainment and Events

BARS AND LOUNGES
Historic District

Before the construction of Independence Hall, it wasn't unusual for men of state to hold meetings in Philadelphia's taverns. Watering holes served as unofficial places of business even after buildings of government and commerce rose in the burgeoning city. So it's only fitting that the Historic District has a good number of bars. For an 18th-century-style libation, head to **City Tavern** (138 S. 2nd St., 215/413-1443, www.citytavern.com, lunch from 11:30 A.M. daily, dinner from 4 P.M. Mon.–Sat. and 3 P.M. Sun., lunch $10–20, dinner $18–33), a replica of a favorite haunt of the Founding Fathers. There's a small bar area and a cozy sitting room on the first floor of the restaurant, which teamed with locally based Yards Brewing Company to create a line of beers based on recipes endorsed by George Washington, Thomas Jefferson, and Ben Franklin. Try the Tavern Porter, a rich molasses-based brew like the kind General Washington served to his thirsty field officers.

Thirsting for Belgian-style suds? Old City has just the place. **Eulogy Belgian Tavern** (136 Chestnut St., 215/413-1918, www.eulogy bar.com, 5 P.M.–2 A.M. Mon.–Wed., 11 A.M.–2 A.M. Thurs.–Sun., kitchen closes at 10:30 P.M. Mon.–Wed. and 1:30 A.M. Thurs.–Sun., food $8–22) offers more than 300 craft brews, including Eulogy's Busty Blonde, brewed in Belgium exclusively for its Philly namesake. Housed in a 19th-century row house, the Belgian-owned pub is known for its plump mussels, juicy burgers, twice-fried *frietjes*, and second-floor "coffin room," where caskets serve as tables. Be aware that smoking is always permitted on the ground floor and after 10 P.M. on the second floor.

One of Philly's most popular Irish-style joints is **The Plough and the Stars** (2nd St. between Market and Chestnut Streets, 215/733-0300, www.ploughstars.com, 11:30 A.M.–2 A.M. Mon–Fri., 10:30 A.M.–2 A.M. Sat.–Sun.,

kitchen closes at 10 P.M. Mon.–Sat. and 9 P.M. Sun., food $7–24). With its soaring ceilings, Corinthian columns, and 16-foot windows, the Plough is a far cry from the typical breed of Irish pub. And its menu has just a smattering of Irish specialties. But Guinness drinkers claim it pours the perfect pint, and the level of joviality reaches St. Patty's Day proportions on a fairly regular basis. Weekend brunches are a big draw, and Sunday evenings feature a traditional Irish music session.

A do-it-yourself bloody Mary bar is a hallmark of weekend brunches at **National Mechanics** (22 S. 3rd St., 215/701-4883, www.nationalmechanics.com, 5 P.M.–2 A.M. Mon., 11 A.M.–2 A.M. Tues.–Sun., food $6–18). The bar occupies an imposing Greek Revival structure built in the 1830s as a bank for the hardworking mechanics of the Industrial Revolution and pays tribute to the original occupant with its name and decor. Mechanical doodads, homemade lighting fixtures, and stained glass windows embellish a space far cozier than the facade suggests. The menu is succinct but varied, swinging from corn dogs to a flank steak. Servers speak of the veggie burger with a reverential tone usually reserved for meaty fare. Local bands, DJs, poets, performance artists, and other creative types turn out for the vaudevillian Monday Night Club. Come on a Tuesday night for karaoke or a Wednesday night to test your trivia IQ.

For a theatrics-free drinking experience, settle into **The Hill** (301 Chestnut St., 215/923-3711, noon–2 A.M. Mon.–Sat., 11:30 A.M.–2 A.M. Sun., kitchen closes at 1 A.M., food $8–20). Located inside the teensy Society Hill Hotel, a haven for weary travelers for well over a century, the pub takes special pride in its French dip sandwich and "Scully fries," an irresistible nest of yams, russet potatoes, and leeks served with an ancho chile dipping sauce.

Old City doesn't neglect those whose tastes tend toward champagne and swishy cocktails. The drinks menu at **Gigi** (319 Market St., 215/574-8880, www.gigiphilly .com, 11 A.M.–2 A.M. daily, lunch $8–12, dinner $15–34) includes mojitos in a dozen flavors, house-made sangria, and champagnes priced at anywhere from $30 to $275 per bottle. Ample outdoor seating and tasty tapas make it an ideal spot for meeting friends on a warm evening. Get there before 7 P.M. on weeknights for half-price signature cocktails, $4 imported drafts, and other steals. The needle on the neighborhood's swank meter swings to the right on Thursday, Friday, and Saturday nights, when **32° Luxe Lounge** (16 S. 2nd St., 215/627-3132, www.32lounge.com, 10 P.M.–2 A.M. Thurs., 9 P.M.–2 A.M. Fri.–Sat.) opens its doors. A self-described "playground for the active sophisticate," 32° lures celebs and people who spend like them with a VIP section, bottle service, vintage champagnes, and rare cognacs. Not too cool to namedrop, it shares a log of famous guests on its website. Regular guests can rent private liquor lockers for any unfinished bottles.

South Philadelphia

The neighborhoods below South Street are unpretentious and largely tourist-free and, for the most part, so are the bars. On the divey end of the spectrum are **Bob & Barbara's** (1509 South St., 215/545-4511, 3 P.M.–2 A.M. Mon.–Sat., noon–2 A.M. Sun.) and **Tattooed Mom** (530 South St., 215/238-9880, noon–2 A.M. daily, food under $10). Getting sloppy drunk at the hipster havens is cheaper than going to the movies. The throngs chug cans of Pabst Blue Ribbon as if it were holy water. Indeed, B&B's is something of a shrine to the historic brew, plastered as it is with Pabst memorabilia. At Tattooed Mom, where $1 buys a can of PBR 7–11 P.M. Friday–Sunday, the walls are awash in graffiti. Gang turf? Yeah, it's a great place to bring the whole gang, sink into a ratty couch, and have a Scrabble throw-down. Tattooed Mom serves $1.50 tacos (beef and vegetarian versions) on Tuesdays and $0.50 pierogies on Wednesdays. If you enjoy a good drag show, B&B's is the place to be on Thursdays.

Red-walled and dimly lit, the **Royal Tavern**

© ANNA DUBROVSKY

PBR (Pabst Blue Ribbon) is the drink of choice at Bob & Barbara's.

(937 E. Passyunk Ave., 215/389-6694, www .royaltavern.com, 11:30 A.M.–2 A.M. Mon.– Fri., 10 A.M.–2 A.M. Sat.–Sun., food $6–16) is a couple of notches above "dive" and firmly entrenched in the "gastropub" category. Most people come here with food on their minds. The Royal's specialty: gussied up comfort food. Its grilled cheese sandwich is a gooey marriage of smoked gouda, sharp provolone, goat cheese, and rustic French bread. The much-trumpeted burger comes topped with bacon, caramelized onions, smoked gouda, and pickled long hots. And the popcorn—oh, the popcorn—is freshly popped and drizzled with truffle butter. The Royal does right by vegans with a meat-free sloppy joe and grilled tempeh sandwich complete with vegan bacon. In spite of all the chewing, the long, narrow space tends to get loud.

Deciding whether to put **Southwark** (701 S. 4th St., 215/238-1888, www.south warkrestaurant.com, 5 P.M.–2 A.M. Tues.– Sat., 11 A.M.–5 P.M. Sun., kitchen closes at 10:30 P.M. Tues.–Thurs. and 11:30 P.M. Fri.– Sat., dinner $20–25, Sunday brunch $8–15) in the restaurant or bar section of this book was a tough call. It excels as a farm-to-table eatery, even breaking into *Philadelphia* magazine's list of top 50 restaurants in 2009. But locavores wouldn't go hungry if it closed its doors tomorrow; the Slow Food movement is sweeping this city. If Southwark shut down, its cocktails would be missed most of all. Since opening in 2004, the gentlemanly Queen Village joint has carved out a niche by eschewing newfangled libations and nailing classics like the Sazerac, sidecar, and Tom Collins. Its Manhattan is said to be the best in the city, and few U.S. bars can match its gin and rye collection. To boot, its beer selection outshines that of many beer-centric establishments.

Northern Liberties

NoLibs, as the neighborhood north of Old City is known, has starred in something of a Cinderella story in recent years. Publicans, restaurateurs, and developers have played the fairy godmother, transforming a bedraggled and unappreciated area into the belle of the

ball. **Standard Tap** (901 N. 2nd St., 215/238-0630, www.standardtap.com, 4 P.M.–2 A.M. daily, dinner 5 P.M.–1 A.M. daily, brunch 11 A.M.–3:30 P.M. Sat.–Sun., food $9–25) led the charge, setting a high bar when it opened in 1999. Widely regarded as Philadelphia's original gastropub, the Tap looks no further than Pennsylvania and neighboring states for its draft-only beer selection. Asking for a Heineken brands you an outsider. So does asking for a food menu. Chef Carolynn Angle switches things up so frequently that chalkboards have a clear advantage over ink and paper. Servers make no excuses when listed dishes are sold out; that's the way the cookie crumbles when a buy-fresh ethos prevails. Mussels and sausage, duck confit salad, and crispy smelts consistently find their way onto the chalkboards. The first-floor jukebox contains a preponderance of punk and indie rock. Seat yourself upstairs for a quieter good time.

North Third (801 N. 3rd St., 215/413-3666, www.norththird.com, 4 P.M.–2 A.M. daily, dinner 5 P.M.–midnight Sun.–Tues. and 5 P.M.–1 A.M. Wed.–Sat., brunch 10 A.M.–3:30 P.M. Sat.–Sun., food $7–19) is also known for top-notch food, especially its customizable burger. The selection of draft beers is small but well edited. Signature cocktails like the mojito martini and Stoli Doli taste best at a sidewalk table, but be sure to have a look around inside, where it's wall-to-wall artwork and tchotchkes. It's a particularly artsy scene on Tuesday nights, when aspiring filmmakers share their short masterpieces with a sauced-up audience.

Nobody has done more to reshape Northern Liberties than developer Bart Blatstein, who gathered up 28 (largely derelict) acres at the start of the new millennium and plans to spend roughly half a billion dollars by the time he's done with them. As of 2010 he'd completed Liberties Walk, a four-block pedestrian strip framed by new row houses with boutiques and eateries at street level and high-end apartments above, and the Piazza at Schmidts, an enormous open-air plaza surrounded by large mixed-use buildings. Forming the eastern gateway to Liberties Walk are **Bar Ferdinand**

(1030 N. 2nd St., 215/923-1313, www.bar ferdinand.com, 4:30 P.M.–midnight Sun.–Thurs., 4:30 P.M.–1:30 A.M. Fri.–Sat., dinner 5–10 P.M. Sun.–Thurs. and 5 P.M.–midnight Fri.–Sat., brunch 11 A.M.–3 P.M. Sun., tapas $4–13) and **El Camino Real** (1040 N. 2nd St., 215/925-1110, www.bbqburritobar.com, 11 A.M.–2 A.M. Mon.–Fri., 10 A.M.–2 A.M. Sat.–Sun., kitchen closes at 1 A.M., food $8–20). The former is a stylish tapas bar with an exceptional selection of Spanish wines, a beer list that's 10 drafts strong, and a way with fruity drinks. Try the clericot, a refreshing *bebida* of white wine, melons, berries, and citrus fruit, if you're seated outside on a summer day, or the Sol de Cádiz, a pilsner and OJ combo, if you're there for brunch. Dried roses dangle over the wraparound bar, which is plenty wide for an assortment of small plates. Noshes include squid stuffed with shrimp and leeks, seared duck hearts, fried dates, ceviche, and savory filled pastries. Amble over to El Camino Real for a Texas-sized tequila list. The bar at the faux rustic Tex-Mex joint also stocks dozens of whiskeys, daring beers like Rogue's chipotle-infused ale as well as Corona, Tecate, and other south-of-the-border staples, and everything it takes to make a jalapeno margarita.

The Piazza at Schmidts is home to the **Swift Half** (1001 N. 2nd St., 215/923-1600, www .swifthalfpub.com, 11:30 A.M.–2 A.M. daily, kitchen closes at 1 A.M., food $8–24), owned by the husband-and-wife team behind Good Dog, a hallowed Center City watering hole. Those enamored of Good Dog's grittiness and blue-cheese-stuffed burger may be disappointed by its sibling pub. Like all things at the Piazza, which opened in 2009, Swift Half is spick-and-span and modern. Its burger doesn't spew molten cheese. But walk in with an open mind, and you'll leave with a satisfied grin. Its 10 draft brews are predominantly of the craft variety, and 10-ounce pours—normally $3 and just $2 on Mondays—are great for adventurous (and indecisive) drinkers. Small eats like house-made charcuterie and cucumber sandwiches share the menu with comfort fare: truffled mac and cheese, a Reuben with beer-infused

thousand island, house-made pierogies smothered with smoked bacon and caramelized onions, vegetarian shepherd's pie, and the like. Also making the Piazza scene: **P.Y.T.** (1050 N. Hancock St., 215/964-9009, www.pyt philly.com, noon–2 A.M. daily, kitchen open until 1 A.M., food $6–15), a much-hyped bar specializing in burgers and booze-infused ice cream shakes. Yeah, you read that right. The $10 "adultshakes" taste great with P.Y.T.'s sensational onion rings. Burger options include the three-patty Bic Mic and the veggie Shroom Burger, made with two batter-fried portobello caps.

Center City East

The half of Center City east of Broad Street is home to drinking establishments of every stripe, including most of Philadelphia's queer bars. For the laid-back beer drinker, there's **Fergie's Pub** (1214 Sansom St., 215/928-8118, www.fergies.com, 11 A.M.–2 A.M. Mon.–Sat., 5 P.M.–2 A.M. Sun., food $6–13). Irish-born owner Fergus Carey is Philly's favorite publican, a former bartender whose beer-soaked ventures include Monk's Café and Nodding Head in Center City West and Grace Tavern just off South Street. His namesake bar has his conviviality and good taste in beer and offers some form of entertainment most every night. Its Tuesday and Thursday Quizzo games vie for liveliest in the city. Monday night's open mic draws a talented crowd, and traditional Irish music is a Saturday afternoon staple.

Vintage (129 S. 13th St., 215/922-3095, www.vintage-philadelphia.com, 4 P.M.–2 A.M. Mon.–Thurs., noon–2 A.M. Fri.–Sat., kitchen closes at midnight, food $6–18) is a mellow little wine bar invitingly outfitted in exposed brick, artfully arranged wine corks, a chandelier crafted of iron and wine bottles, and flickering votives. It offers 60 wines by the glass and more than 100 by the bottle. Be sure to consult the chalkboards for specials. A nearby sister establishment, **Time** (1315 Sansom St., 215/985-4800, www.timerestaurant.net, 5 P.M.–2 A.M. Mon.–Sat., noon–2 A.M. Sun., kitchen closes at 1 A.M., bar menu $5–16, dinner $16–27) boasts one of the most unusual concepts in Philly. Its second-floor lounge specializes in absinthe, the storied herbal liquor that was banned in the United States until 2007. Guests top off their own "green goddess" with water from glass fountains, and DJs spin house and pop tunes Thursday through Saturday. Whiskey lovers rarely make it upstairs. Time's ground-floor bar is stocked with more than 100 whiskeys, along with 20 draft beers.

The swatch of Center City approximately bounded by Walnut, Pine, 11th and Broad Streets is known as the "Gayborhood." Gone are the gay bathhouses and other red-light establishments that characterized the area in the 1970s. But a good time can still be had here. The up-and-coming nabe with the rainbow-emblazoned street signs is dotted with gay bars and clubs. Named one of the 50 greatest gay bars in the world by *Out* magazine, **Woody's** (202 S. 13th St., 215/545-1893, www.woodys bar.com, 11 A.M.–2 A.M. daily, kitchen closes at 9 P.M., food $5–17) is the unofficial capital of the Gayborhood. It's huge—big enough to call itself a "nightlife complex"—with several bars, a dance floor, and a restaurant. Competitive karaoke is a Monday night tradition, Wednesday college nights attract posses of out-and-proud Penn, Drexel, and Temple students, and the gay '80s are revisited every Sunday.

Q (1234 Locust St., 215/732-1800, www.qphilly.com, 5 P.M.–midnight Mon., 5 P.M.–2 A.M. Tues.–Sat., 11 A.M.–9 P.M. Sun., food $10–22) is a sleeker, trendier option that attracts a sleeker, trendier crowd. Formerly known as Bump, the chic lounge specializes in the sort of frilly cocktails that contain no fewer than four ingredients. The popular Madame Q, a marriage of pear-flavored Grey Goose vodka, elderflower liqueur, Lillet, and champagne, is one of about 10 such cocktails priced at $4–5 5–7 P.M. weekdays *and* Saturday. Wednesday night's drag show and Sunday brunch are big draws, and outdoor seating makes Q a particularly popular hangout in the warmer months.

"Hanging out" takes on a whole new meaning on jockstrap Mondays and underwear Wednesdays at **The Bike Stop** (206 S. Quince St., 215/627-1662, www.thebikestop.com, 4 P.M.–2 A.M. Mon.–Fri., 2 P.M.–2 A.M. Sat.–Sun.), a longtime gathering spot for Philly's leather-loving gays and lesbians. As the only lesbian-centric nightclub in the Gayborhood, **Sisters** (1320 Chancellor St., 215/735-0735, www.sistersnightclub.com, 8 P.M.–2 A.M. Mon., 5 P.M.–2 A.M. Tues.–Sat., noon–2 A.M. Sun., kitchen open 5 P.M.–midnight Wed.–Sat. and noon–2:30 P.M. Sun., food $5–12) has the unenviable task of being all things to all women—and often falls short. But all is forgiven on Twisted Thursdays, when $10 buys eight drink tickets.

Center City West

It's easy as pie to find a watering hole west of Broad Street, especially in the area around Rittenhouse Square. Among the standouts is **Tria** (123 S. 18th St., 215/972-8742, www.tria cafe.com, noon–late night daily, food under $10), which pays homage to the "tasty three-some of fermentation": wine, beer, and cheese. If you have a taste for wine and a date who prefers microbrews, it's the place to go. It's also the place to go if you don't know Chardonnay from Shiraz or cheddar from chèvre but want to learn. Servers are knowledgeable and anything but snooty, and the menus helpfully group each day's offerings under layman's descriptors like "approachable," "stinky," and "extreme." Toothsome small bites, salads, and sandwiches round out the experience for those who come hungry. The concept proved so popular in the Rittenhouse neighborhood that **Tria Washington Square West** (1137 Spruce St., 215/629-9200, 4 P.M.–late night Mon.–Fri., noon–late night Sat.–Sun.) opened in 2007. Both locations slash the price of one unique wine, beer, and cheese every Sunday.

Center City West has perhaps the highest concentration of gastropubs—bars even a teetotaler can love—in the Philadelphia region. A mecca for beer aficionados from well outside the region, **Monk's Cafe** (264 S. 16th St., 215/545-7005, www.monkscafe.com, 11:30 A.M.–2 A.M. daily, kitchen closes at 1 A.M., food $8–32) could do a brisk business even if its food menu

Monk's Cafe has a renowned beer selection.

consisted of peanuts and Fritos. The beer emporium has one of the most impressive bottle selections on the East Coast and a much-ballyhooed array of Belgians on draft. It was the only U.S. bar in the top 10 on *All About Beer Magazine*'s list of "125 Places to Have a Beer Before You Die." But Monk's doesn't rest on its sudsy laurels. Its far-from-standard menu includes meaty frog legs, lightly smoked trout, an ever-popular duck salad, mussels, mussels, and more mussels. Beer plays a supporting role in most dishes.

If you're craving mussels and pommes frites but can't stomach the wait at Monk's, foot it to **Nodding Head Brewery & Restaurant** (1516 Sansom St., 2nd floor, 215/569-9525, www .noddinghead.com, 11:30 A.M.–2 A.M. Mon.–Sat., 11 A.M.–2 A.M. Sun., kitchen closes at midnight Mon.–Sat. and 11 P.M. Sun., food $10–17), a sibling establishment. Not long after it opened its doors in 2000, a customer returned from vacation bearing a small animal figurine with a bobbing head. The brewpub's staff put it on display—and opened the floodgates. Patrons have donated enough

bobbleheads to fill a large display case, decorate the back bar, and relegate hundreds more to storage. Like the doll collection, which includes Ozzy Osbourne, Hello Kitty, and disgraced state senator Vincent Fumo, the brews are wide-ranging. Sample as many as you like before committing to a pint, or order a flight and savor them all. Nodding Head offers seven or eight of its creations daily. The Barbardian chef knows his way around a meat smoker. Nod your head yes to anything spicy, jerked, or pulled.

Patrons of **Good Dog** (224 S. 15th St., 215/985-9600, www.gooddogbar.com, 11:30 A.M.–2 A.M. daily, kitchen closes at 1 A.M., food $9–16) also had a hand in its decor. Framed black-and-white photos of their pooches adorn the walls of the three-level bar and restaurant, which bills itself as "a cozy alternative to the ultra-trendy, exclusive" newcomers to the Philly drinking scene. Good Dog's signature burger is something to bark about: Molten Roquefort cheese erupts from the meat upon first bite. Head to the third floor for pool, darts, and retro arcade games. **Pub &**

PHILADELPHIA

© ANNA DUBROVSKY

Nodding Head Brewery & Restaurant is the sister establishment to Monk's Cafe.

Kitchen (1946 Lombard St., 215/545-0350, www.thepubandkitchen.com, 4 P.M.–2 A.M. Mon.–Fri., 11 A.M.–2 A.M. Sat.–Sun., kitchen closes at 1 A.M., food $15–20), one of the area's newest food-centric bars, is giving Good Dog's burger a run for its money. Its Windsor burger is made with all-natural beef and trimmed with house-cured bacon. The beer-battered onion rings are also a wonder.

Center City has no shortage of Irish pubs, but few have as faithful a following as **The Bards** (2013 Walnut St., 215/569-9585, www.bardsirishbar.com, 11 A.M.–2 A.M. daily, kitchen closes at 10 P.M., food $6–11). It pulls off an Irish literary theme without straying into theme-y territory and pours a good Guinness. The kitchen serves up a handful of Irish classics along with standard bar fare, and the best dessert is the only dessert: Guinness bread pudding.

NIGHTCLUBS

Silk City (435 Spring Garden St., 215/592-8838, www.silkcityphilly.com, bar open 4 P.M.–2 A.M. daily, dinner 5 P.M.–1 A.M. daily, brunch 10 A.M.–4 P.M. Sat.–Sun, food $8–17) is a strange and wonderful beast: a classic diner car that opens to a nightclub complete with disco ball chandeliers. Once frequented by truckers, the neon-lit diner now fills with 20- and 30-somethings hungry for a good time—or just plain hungry. Like owner Mark Bee's other Northern Liberties haunt, North Third, Silk City is known for satisfying eats. The kitchen injects pizzazz into diner standards like meatloaf, fried chicken, and mac and cheese, and the fact that you can wash them down with a Hoegaarden or strawberry martini is icing on the cake. The club side hosts a DJ-driven dance party most nights of the week.

South Philly's **Fluid** (613 S. 4th St., 215/629-3686, www.fluidnightclub.com, open nightly except Tues.) has welcomed a host of superstar DJs since it opened in 1997 and counts Roots drummer Questlove among its resident spinners. Depending on when you come, you could find yourself hitting the dance floor to electronica, funk, house, soul, trip-hop, trance, progressive, drum and bass, jungle, breakbeat, hip hop, rock, or punk. What you won't find is: '80s night.

A little '80s action isn't out of the question at nearby **L'Etage** (624 S. 6th St., 215/592-0656, www.creperie-beaumonde.com, 7:30 P.M.–2 A.M. Fri.–Sat., 7:30 P.M.–1 A.M. Sun. and Tues.–Thurs.), which fancies itself a French cabaret. The club upstairs from the lovely crepe café Beau Monde books DJs on Fridays and Saturdays. Live music, film screenings, burlesque, and other diversions round out the calendar.

LIVE MUSIC
Rock

The **Wells Fargo Center** (3601 S. Broad St., event hotline 215/336-3600, box office 800/298-4200, www.wellsfargocenterphilly.com) may be one of the hardest working arenas in the country. Home to Philadelphia's professional basketball, hockey, and lacrosse teams, it's also the largest concert venue in the region. Acts as varied as Hannah Montana, Metallica, and Barbra Streisand have brought down the house since it opened in 1996. Billy Joel and Bruce Springsteen have sold out so many concerts in the 20,000-seat arena and its predecessor that banners honoring them hang from the rafters.

Venues offering a more intimate live music experience are scattered around town. Best of the bunch is **World Cafe Live** (3025 Walnut St., 215/222-1400, www.worldcafelive.com) in the University City neighborhood, home to the University of Pennsylvania and Drexel University. One expects certain things from a music venue in a collegiate setting: frat boys on the prowl, shooter specials, and sticky floors, for starters. World Cafe Live is not what one expects. It's a grown-up sort of place with two performance spaces. Designed for major acts, Downstairs Live is a three-tiered music hall that's usually furnished with tables and chairs for 300 but can hold as many as 650 for standing-room-only events. (Be aware that a food and beverage minimum applies during seated shows. Fortunately, the grub is quite good.) Upstairs Live is a full-service restaurant open for lunch and dinner on weekdays and dinner on weekends. It lures 9-to-5ers with

happy-hour specials and serves up live music most evenings. World Cafe Live shares a converted factory building with public radio station WXPN, which produces the nationally syndicated *World Cafe* with David Dye.

Several of Philadelphia's best-known music venues can be found in the neighborhoods north of Old City. The largest, **Electric Factory** (421 N. 7th St., 215/627-1332, www.electricfactory.info), can pack in about 3,000 people and caters to all musical tastes. Hard-rocker Ted Nugent, '80s chart-topper Phil Collins, and Courtney Love's Hole took the stage in one recent month. Except for some seats near its two bars, Electric Factory is a standing-room-only venue. Shows are open to all ages unless otherwise specified. Expect to be patted down before entering.

Fishtown institution **Johnny Brenda's** (1201 N. Frankford Ave., 215/739-9684, www.johnnybrendas.com, kitchen open 11 A.M.–1 A.M. daily) is a triple threat: bar, restaurant, and music venue. Its owners also own Standard Tap, a locally legendary gastropub, and they're so serious about serving foods made with fresh, seasonal ingredients that they don't bother printing menus. Look for strategically hung chalkboards if you want to know what's cooking. The beer list consists entirely of locally brewed drafts. "Local" doesn't rule the day in the upstairs performance space, one of several venues favored by homegrown concert promotion company R5 Productions. It's strictly off limits to the underage.

The M-Room (15 W. Girard Ave., 215/739-5577, www.themanhattanroom.com, 4 P.M.–2 A.M. Mon.–Fri., 11 A.M.–2 A.M. Sat.–Sun.) reinvented itself as a bar-cum-music-venue in 2005 after more than three decades as a diner. In 2008 the nabe welcomed yet another watering hole with a soft spot for indie bands. The curiously named **Kung Fu Necktie** (1250 N. Front St., 215/291-4919, www.kungfunecktie.com, 5 P.M.–2 A.M. daily) boasts tables crafted from bowling lanes and bathrooms marked "balls" and "boobs."

Best known for its historic sites, Old City has some serious indie-rock cred thanks to this place: **The Khyber** (56 S. 2nd St., 215/238-5888, www.thekhyber.com). It's unapologetically grungy and all about the music. Want a decent meal before you catch the show? The barkeeps will point you to the door. Mondays are usually reserved for karaoke, but bands take the small first-floor stage almost every other night. The upstairs features a dance floor and $1 PBR (that's scenester-speak for Pabst Blue Ribbon beer) seven nights a week.

A longtime presence on a street synonymous with nightlife, **Theatre of the Living Arts** (334 South St., 215/922-1011, www.livenation.com) is one of the city's larger music venues, holding some 800 on-their-feet fans. Known locally as the TLA, the onetime movie theater has hosted heavyweights such as the Red Hot Chili Peppers, Dave Matthews Band, Bob Dylan, Paul Simon, Jane's Addiction, Radiohead, Nickelback, Norah Jones, John Mayer, and Patti Smith. Vintage concert posters and newspaper clippings serve as decor.

Center City's preeminent rock venue, the **Trocadero Theatre** (1003 Arch St., 215/922-6888, www.thetroc.com), was also a cinema at one point. At other points in its long life—it first opened in 1870 as the Arch Street Opera House—the Victorian theater hosted traveling minstrel shows, vaudeville, and burlesque. It did time as a dance club in the 1980s. The Troc, as the concert hall in the heart of Chinatown is known, can accommodate 1,200 people for shows on its main stage. The Balcony, an intimate venue within the venue, has a capacity of 250. It's used for screenings of recently released films and classics like *Ghostbusters* on "Movie Monday," a regular event for the 21-plus set. Most concerts are all-ages.

Center City's most unusual temple of music is an active church. Built by a large and prosperous congregation in the 1880s, the **First Unitarian Church of Philadelphia** (2125 Chestnut St.) responded to a shrinking urban population a century later not by closing its doors, as many churches did, but by opening them for non-church events. R5 Productions has been staging rock shows in the historic house of worship since the mid-1990s.

Visit www.r5productions.com for a concert calendar.

About half a mile north of the Art Museum in the Fairmount neighborhood, **North Star Bar** (2639 Poplar St., 215/787-0488, www.northstarbar.com, 5 P.M.–2 A.M. daily, kitchen closes at 11 P.M. Sun.–Thurs. and 1 A.M. Fri.–Sat.) compensates for its off-the-beaten-path location by putting bands on its stage almost nightly. Ticket prices rarely top $15, and North Star resists the temptation to overcharge for food. Everything on its sandwich-heavy menu, including a generously sized burger, is under $10.

Jazz

Philly certainly has a place in the annals of jazz. Legendary saxophonist Stan Getz was born in this city. John Coltrane, another tenor master, lived and played here. So did trumpeter John Birks Gillespie, who picked up the nickname "Dizzy" while in town. But Philly has few jazz clubs today. Zanzibar Blue, whose stage was graced by the likes of Maynard Ferguson, Arturo Sandoval, Harry Connick Jr., and Diana Krall, closed in 2007. Ortlieb's Jazzhaus, named one of the top 10 jazz clubs in the country by *Playboy* magazine, closed in 2010 after more than 20 years of showcasing local and visiting talent. Philly's jazz enthusiasts are—how to put it—kind of blue. But they're not high and dry. There's still **Chris' Jazz Cafe** (1421 Sansom St., 215/568-3131, www.chrisjazzcafe.com), which serves up live music every day but Sunday. And then there's the **Philadelphia Clef Club** (738 S. Broad St., 215/893-9912, www.clefclub.org). Founded in 1966 as a social club for members of a black musicians union, it counted Coltrane, Gillespie, Nina Simone, and Grover Washington Jr. among its members. Today it's a nonprofit institution dedicated to the promotion and preservation of jazz music. Its concert calendar is regrettably sparse but worth keeping an eye on. Also worth a gander: www.phillyjazz.org. Maintained by jazz enthusiast and middling saxophonist Jan Klincewicz, the website features a calendar of live jazz events.

PHILADELPHIA

CASINOS

Philadelphia's first casino opened in September 2010, six years after Pennsylvania legalized gambling. **SugarHouse Casino** (1001 N. Delaware Ave., 877/477-3715, www.sugar housecasino.com, open 24 hours) sits along the Delaware River in the Fishtown neighborhood, some of whose residents fought tooth and nail to block the project.

PERFORMING ARTS
Avenue of the Arts

South Broad Street is so crowded with performing arts venues that it's rightly known as the Avenue of the Arts. The venues are a mix of old and new. The most striking is the **Kimmel Center for the Performing Arts** (Broad and Spruce Streets, 215/893-1999, www.kimmel center.org), which opened in December 2001. Described by architect Rafael Viñoly as "two jewels inside a glass box," it consists of two freestanding performance halls between a vaulted glass ceiling. The larger Verizon Hall, which seats 2,500, features acoustics designed specifically for the illustrious **Philadelphia Orchestra** (www.philorch.org). The Perelman Theater has 650 seats and a rotating stage. In addition to the orchestra, the Kimmel Center's resident companies include the **Philly Pops** (www.phillypops.com), helmed by two-time Grammy-winning pianist and conductor Peter Nero, and the Philadelphia Dance Company, better known as **PHILADANCO** (www.phila danco.org). The performing arts complex is open 10 A.M. to 6 P.M. daily, so take a look around if you're passing by. You might catch a free performance on its lobby stage, and you won't believe the views from its glass-enclosed rooftop garden.

One block closer to City Hall is the historic **Academy of Music** (Broad and Locust Streets, 215/893-1999, www.academyof music.org), the oldest grand opera house in the country still used for its original purpose. The long list of renowned artists who have performed at the academy since its opening in 1857 includes Pyotr Ilyich Tchaikovsky, Sergei Rachmaninoff, Anna Pavlova, Maria Callas,

and Luciano Pavarotti. U.S. President Ulysses S. Grant was nominated for his second term here in 1872. The National Historic Landmark rarely gets a rest. It hosts the **Opera Company of Philadelphia** (www.operaphila.org) and the **Pennsylvania Ballet** (www.paballet.org), plus Broadway shows and other touring productions. The ballet company also performs at the adjacent **Merriam Theater** (Broad and Spruce Streets, 215/336-1234, www.uarts.edu), which dates to 1918. The 1,800-seat theater is now part of the University of the Arts, whose students have the privilege of performing on a stage graced by John Barrymore, Katharine Hepburn, Sir Laurence Olivier, and Sammy Davis Jr. The university has a number of other performance spaces, including the **Arts Bank** at Broad and South Streets. Once a bank, the building now houses a 230-seat main stage and a cabaret theater.

Across from the Merriam is the **Wilma Theater** (Broad and Spruce Streets, 215/546-7824, www.wilmatheater.org), which has racked up dozens of Barrymore Awards—the local equivalent of Tony Awards—for its superbly crafted plays. "Dedicated to presenting theater as an art form," the Wilma moved into its 296-seat Avenue of the Arts digs in 1996, after packing smaller houses for 20-some seasons. Serious theater lovers seriously love the theater's tradition of post-show discussions with members of the artistic team and symposiums on topics related to each play. In 2007 the Avenue became home to **Philadelphia Theater Company** (Suzanne Roberts Theatre, Broad and Lombard Streets, 215/985-0420, www.philadelphia theatrecompany.org), a highly respected cradle of contemporary works. Founded in 1974, PTC has about 40 world premieres to its credit, including Terrence McNally's Tony Award–winning *Master Class*. It produced half a dozen world premieres and as many Philadelphia premieres during its first three seasons in its new 365-seat theater, named for actress/benefactor Suzanne Roberts.

Other Center City Theaters

Philadelphia is home to America's oldest art

museum, oldest natural history museum, oldest zoo, and oldest residential street. Perhaps not surprisingly, it's also home to America's oldest theater. The **Walnut Street Theatre** (825 Walnut St., 215/574-3550, www.walnut streettheatre.org) opened in 1809 as an equestrian circus, of all things. By 1812, the horses had been canned and the building converted to a bona fide theater. President Thomas Jefferson was in attendance at the first theatrical production. In 1863 the Walnut was purchased by Edwin Booth, a member of a prominent theatrical family. His actor brother would soon tarnish the family name—and etch his in the history books—by assassinating President Abe Lincoln. The Shubert Organization snapped up the theater in the 1940s and used it as a pre-Broadway testing ground for productions including *A Streetcar Named Desire* starring Marlon Brando and *A Raisin in the Sun* featuring Sidney Poitier. In 1976 the already storied theater hosted the first televised Carter-Ford presidential debate. These days the Walnut is a nonprofit regional theater company that generally serves up light fare: *Dirty Rotten Scoundrels, Hairspray,* Neil Simon's *The Odd Couple,* and the like. It also offers an annual series designed for kids in grades K–6. Deal alert: 22 $10 tickets are available for every Mainstage series performance.

Unlike the Walnut, the **Forrest Theatre** (1114 Walnut St., 800/432-7250, www.forrest-theatre.com) doesn't produce shows. It's what folks in the biz call a road house—a venue for touring companies. Owned by the Shubert Organization, Broadway's biggest bigwig, since it was built in the 1920s, the Forrest gets little use these days. The Academy of Music is the Philly venue of choice for most traveling Broadway productions.

The **Adrienne Theatre** (2030 Sansom St., 215/568-8079, www.adriennelive.org) is the venue of choice for many of Philadelphia's small theater companies. Home to the Wilma Theatre before its 1996 move to the Avenue of the Arts, it has three performance spaces that seat between 55 and 120 people. Its most established resident, **InterAct Theatre Company**

(www.interacttheatre.org), wouldn't touch a zany caper with a 10-foot pole. Founded in 1988, InterAct has a stated mission of stirring things up and a fondness for never-before-seen plays. It commissioned seven in 2008 alone. **Amaryllis** (www.amaryllistheatre .org), another resident theater company, is known for its American Sign Language productions. A few doors down from the Adrienne is the **Philadelphia Shakespeare Theatre** (2111 Sansom St., 215/496-8001, www.philly shakespeare.org), devoted to the prolific playwright's works since 1996.

Thanks to the **Curtis Institute of Music** (1726 Locust St., 215/893-7902, www.curtis .edu) and its "learn by doing" philosophy, Philly's classical music lovers can get a free fix almost every week of the year. Students of the prestigious conservatory perform solo and chamber works most Monday, Wednesday, and Friday evenings throughout the school year, getting even busier in the spring. Recitals take place in Field Concert Hall, a 240-seat auditorium in the institute's main building on Rittenhouse Square. No tickets are required, and seating is on a first-come, first-served basis. Call the student recital hotline at 215/893-5261 for the lowdown on each week's programs. Curtis has about 165 students, all of whom show such artistic promise that they get a full ride. (Leonard Bernstein is an alumnus.) Its symphony orchestra makes appearances in New York's Carnegie Hall as well as Philadelphia's Kimmel Center. Curtis Opera Theatre, composed of vocal and opera students, takes the stage at various local venues.

Historic District

Old City's transformation from abandoned industrial area to hip nabe was helped by the arrival of two arts organizations in the 1980s and '90s. Founded in 1969 as a cooperative art gallery on South Street, the **Painted Bride Art Center** (230 Vine St., 215/925-9914, www.paintedbride.org) relocated to Old City in 1982 and is now better known as a performance space. The Bride, as locals call the mosaic-wrapped building, showcases world and jazz music, dance, theater, and poetry. Its commitment to nurturing emerging artists is unquestioned, but it certainly doesn't discriminate against established ones. The long list of past performers includes rocker Carlos Santana, magicians Penn and Teller, and storyteller Spalding Gray.

"Dedicated to bringing to life the greatest stories by the greatest storytellers of all time," **Arden Theatre Company** (40 N. 2nd St., 215/922-1122, www.ardentheatre.org) serves up a mix of popular plays and musicals, new works, and new spins on popular works. The professional company's 2008 interpretation of Thornton Wilder's *Our Town* found the audience walking to historic Christ Church for the second act. Founded in 1988, the Arden snapped up its 50,000-square-foot Old City home in 1995. The space includes a 360-seat main stage and the 175-seat Arcadia Stage.

Fairmount Park

With covered seating for about 5,000, outdoor seating for 4,500 more, and a 4,000-person lawn, the **Mann Center for the Performing Arts** (52nd St. and Parkside Ave., 215/893-1999, www.manncenter.org) is one of the nation's largest outdoor amphitheaters. Named for a local businessman who championed its construction in the 1970s, the Mann is best known as the summer home of the fabulous Philadelphia Orchestra. In 2010 the orchestra's six-week series included a performance featuring Aretha Franklin on vocals and former Secretary of State Condoleezza Rice on piano. The amphitheater in West Fairmount Park also hosts an incredible variety of traveling acts. Cellist Yo-Yo Ma, crooners Tony Bennett and Julio Iglesias, rockers Cheap Trick and Faith No More, singer-songwriter Rufus Wainwright, and the New York Pops all took the stage in 2010 alone. Picnicking on the lawn is a Philly tradition.

FESTIVALS AND EVENTS
Summer

Philadelphians are treated to a host of free concerts and festivals in the summer months. They take place throughout the city, but **Penn's Landing** in particular is a hive of activity. The nonprofit Delaware River Waterfront Corporation (DRWC), which oversees development of the riverfront, brings all sorts of free entertainment to the Great Plaza at Penn's Landing (Columbus Blvd. at Chestnut St.) from May through September. Movies are screened Thursday evenings in July and August. Friday evenings in August are set aside for smooth jazz. Festivals celebrating the diverse cultures that converge in Philly take place on weekends throughout the summer. A complete schedule of DRWC-produced events is available at www.delawareriverevents.com or by calling 215/922-2386.

Center City's Rittenhouse Square is always a social hub but especially so on Wednesday evenings in August, when it hosts *Philadelphia Weekly*'s **Concerts in the Park** (www.philadelphiaweekly.com/event-series). The free concerts start at 7 P.M.; arrive early to claim a prime picnicking spot. Penn Treaty Park (www.penntreatymusic.com) in the Fishtown neighborhood and Pennypack Park (215/281-7664, www.pennypackpark.com) in Northeast Philadelphia also offer free concerts on Wednesday evenings.

Beer festivals are a summertime tradition in towns across the country, typically involving a couple of party tents, a cadre of craft brewers, and a day or two of mingling and tasting. **Philly Beer Week** (215/985-2106, www.phillybeerweek.org, June, free and paid events) puts them to shame. Inaugurated in 2008, the 10-day celebration features several hundred beer-soaked events at more than 100 venues throughout the city and its suburbs. It's one of the reasons *Maxim* magazine handed the City of Brotherly Love the "crown of Best Beer Town" in 2010. Philadelphia has been a beer-loving town for more than 300 years—let's not forget that the nation's forefathers did a lot of their best work in its taverns—and its craft brewers are heralded at the national and international level. With its list of venues, the Beer Week website is a great resource for beer lovers visiting the city at any time.

Pro cyclists from around the world pour into Philadelphia every June for one of America's premier road races. The single-day **Philadelphia International Championship** (610/676-0390, www.procyclingtour.com/phila-home.htm) was started in 1985 and served as the nation's championship race for its first 20 years. Racers log 156 miles on a circuit linking the Benjamin Franklin Parkway with the hillside neighborhood of Manayunk, and hundreds of thousands of people turn out to watch. Popular race-watching areas include the parkway, the steps of the Philadelphia Museum of Art, Kelly Drive in Fairmount Park, and the most famous and arduous section of the course: a 17 percent grade hill dubbed the Manayunk Wall. Professional female cyclists take to the course the same day for the 57.6-mile Liberty Classic.

A Philly tradition since 1975, the **Odunde Festival** (23rd and South Streets and surrounding area, 215/732-8510, www.odundeinc.org, second Sun. of June, free) is one of the largest African American street festivals in the country. Named for a Nigerian expression for "happy new year," it kicks off with a colorful procession to the Schuylkill River and an offering of fruits, flowers, and prayers. Back at Odunde central, musicians and dancers entertain on two stages while tens of thousands of festival-goers browse a marketplace featuring vendors from various African nations, the Caribbean, and Brazil. Later in June, Northwest Philadelphia's West Oak Lane neighborhood throws a New Orleans–style party. The three-day **West Oak Lane Jazz and Arts Festival** (7100–7400 blocks of Ogontz Ave., 877/965-5299, www.westoaklanefestival.com, free except for cover charges at some venues) attracts some of the biggest names in jazz and about half a million fans. Past headliners have included multi-Grammy-winning singer Al Jarreau, saxophonist Dave Sanborn, and the New Orleans–born Preservation Hall Jazz Band and Dirty Dozen Brass Band. Handcrafted goods and all sorts of edible goodies are on offer. The festival's popularity makes parking in the area a nightmare.

Fortunately, free shuttles operate between the festival and multiple locations in Philadelphia, including the Independence Visitor Center at 6th and Market Streets.

In the city where the Declaration of Independence was signed, Independence Day warrants more than a week's worth of festivities. Named for a convenience store chain that forks over big bucks for the big production, **Wawa Welcome America** (various locations, 215/683-2200, www.welcomeamerica.com, free) kicks off in late June and culminates the evening of July 4 in what's billed as the largest free concert in America. Hall & Oates, Elton John, and the Goo Goo Dolls have headlined the concert on the closed-to-traffic Ben Franklin Parkway in recent years. Welcome America traditions include an all-you-can-eat ice cream festival and **Taste of Philadelphia,** a music-filled showcase of culinary talent. The title sponsor may have started a new tradition in 2010 by serving a mile-long hoagie before a *Rocky* screening at the Philadelphia Museum of Art's "Rocky steps."

Fall

The end of summer is a period of transition in Pennsylvania's largest city. Tourism tapers off, and the city's resident population rebounds with the return of the Jersey Shore set. Just as the weather is starting to cool, two concurrent festivals, the **Philadelphia Live Arts Festival** and **Philly Fringe** (various locations, 215/413-1318, www.livearts-fringe.com, Sept., free and paid events), cause a 16-day spike in the city's cultural temperature. The Live Arts Festival consists of more than a dozen shows by a handpicked collection of cutting-edge performing artists. There's no handpicking when it comes to Philly Fringe, an open invitation to all local performers. Hundreds answer the call. Traditional venues can't contain the smorgasbord of artistic expression, which spills into galleries, restaurants, churches, and even a cemetery. For some Fringe participants, a sidewalk is as good a stage as any.

Designers get a chance to show off their

NOTHING QUITE LIKE A PHILLY NEW YEAR'S

Few cities welcome the new year with as much pomp as Philadelphia. On New Year's Eve, revelers gather at Penn's Landing for a fireworks spectacular. The following day brings an even bigger show: the **Mummers Parade,** a ritual so unique that it landed a *National Geographic* spread in 2001. More razzle-dazzle than many people see in a lifetime, the parade is the culmination of a year's worth of planning by 40-odd clubs whose express purpose is to make the first of the year a magical day. To that end, they create costumes so fantastical that club members – mummers, as they're called – resemble cartoon characters more than humans as they strut and twirl up Broad Street. Such a volume of glitter, sequins, and feathers is rarely seen outside Vegas. It's worth noting that Philadelphia's mummers are not, for the most part, performers by trade. They're notaries and nurses, postal workers and plumbers, realtors and retirees. On the first day of the current millennium, then-mayor Ed Rendell gave mummery a go, donning a dress, a wig, and golden slippers. (Wearing drag didn't hurt the political career of the outgoing mayor, who became Pennsylvania governor three years later.)

The origins of mummery are rather obscure. Some trace its roots to ancient Rome, where laborers ushered in the festival of Saturnalia by donning masks, swapping gifts, and satirizing current affairs. Some credit Swedes who settled in the area in the 1600s. We do know that Philadelphia's first official Mummers Parade was held on January 1, 1901. Like cheesesteaks, the parade has become synonymous with the City of Brotherly Love.

Dress warmly if you're parking yourself on the parade route. The pageantry lasts hours and hours. **MummersFest** (www.fancy brigade.com, admission charged), usually held at the Pennsylvania Convention Center in the days leading up to the parade, offers a temperature-controlled taste of what's in store. The Fancy Brigades, one of several categories of mummers, stage two indoor shows on New Year's Day. Tickets to the **Fancy Brigade Finales** can be purchased online at www.ticket-philadelphia.org or by calling 215/893-1999.

Costumes of Mummers Parades past can be seen any time of year at the **Mummers Museum** (1100 S. 2nd St., 215/336-3050, www. mummersmuseum.com, 9:30 A.M.-4:30 P.M. Wed., Fri., and Sat. and 9:30 A.M.-9:30 P.M. Thurs. May-Sept., 9:30 A.M.-4:30 P.M. Wed.-Sat. Oct.-Apr., admission $3.50, seniors, students, and children under 12 $2.50), located in the South Philly neighborhood that many mummers clubs call home. It's best to visit on a Thursday evening May-September, when a mummers string band provides free entertainment.

Mummers Parade

talents the following month. Billed as the largest U.S. event of its kind, **DesignPhiladelphia** (various locations, www.designphiladelphia.org, Oct., free and paid events) spotlights the work of hundreds of creative folks in disciplines as varied as fashion design and automotive design.

Winter

Thanksgiving morning is turkey-prepping time in millions of households across the country. In Philadelphia, it's parade time. A tradition since 1920, the float-choked **Thanksgiving Day Parade** wraps up around noon, leaving plenty of time to get the gobbler ready for gobbling. While we're on the subject of gobbling, let's talk about the **Wing Bowl** (Wells Fargo Center, 800/298-4200, www.610wip.com, admission charged). Cooked up by a local sports radio station in 1993, the annual wing-eating showdown packs Philadelphia's 20,000-seat indoor arena. Soused spectators and scantily clad "Wingettes" cheer on contestants vying for the title of wing king (or queen). The bacchanalia is usually held on the Friday before the Super Bowl.

Spring

Spring is a fertile time for festivals. Among the standouts is the **Cherry Blossom Festival** (various locations, 215/790-3810, www.jasgp.org/cherryblossomfestival, Mar.–Apr., free and paid events). The celebration of Japanese culture lasts for several weeks—sometimes outlasting the cherry blossoms, or *sakura,* themselves. Sponsored by the Japan America Society of Greater Philadelphia, the festival features drumming and dance performances, traditional tea ceremonies, Japanese movie screenings, and demonstrations of everything from martial arts and swordsmanship to flower arranging and origami. Japan's government presented Philadelphia with a gift of cherry trees on America's 150th birthday in 1926. The ephemeral blossoms can be seen along East Fairmount Park's Kelly Drive and

near **Shofuso** (Lansdowne and Horticultural Drives, 215/878-5097, www.shofuso.com, open weekends in April, Wed.–Sun. May–Sept., Thurs.–Sun. in Oct., call for hours, admission $6, seniors, students, and children 3–17 $3), a 17th-century-style Japanese house and garden in West Fairmount Park.

Formerly known as PrideFest, **Equality Forum** (various locations, 215/732-3378, www.equalityforum.com, late Apr.–early May, free and paid events) is a full week of panel discussions, parties, film screenings, and other events geared toward the gay, lesbian, bisexual, and transgender community. Its social highlight is **SundayOUT!**, a street festival complete with a same-sex commitment ceremony. Philly's LGBT citizenry also looks forward to the **PrideDay** parade each June and the **OutFest** block party each October, both organized by the volunteer organization Philly Pride Presents (215/875-9288, www.phillypride.org).

The tony Rittenhouse Square neighborhood welcomes spring with an uncommonly chic street festival. The **Rittenhouse Row Spring Festival** (Walnut St. between Broad and 19th Streets, www.rittenhouserow.org, first Sat. of May, free) features gourmet food booths and wine and cocktail tastings. Models walk a runway in looks available in local shops.

Collegiate rowing teams from across North America converge on Philadelphia for the **Dad Vail Regatta** (215/542-1443, www.dadvail.org, early May), two days of racing on the Schuylkill River. Named for Harry Emerson "Dad" Vail, who coached University of Wisconsin rowers in the early 1900s, the nation's largest collegiate regatta is a beautiful sight. Grandstands in East Fairmount Park afford the best views of the finish line. Kelly Drive is closed to regular traffic during the regatta, but the grandstands can be reached by shuttle bus from the Art Museum and Boathouse Row, a set of Victorian boathouses along the southern end of Kelly Drive.

Shopping

HISTORIC DISTRICT

If you're looking for mainstream retailers—J. Crew, H&M, Ann Taylor, and the like—head to the Rittenhouse Square area. If you're looking to adorn your person or your abode with rare finds, Old City has you covered. Philadelphia's most historic neighborhood is peppered with chic boutiques and art galleries beloved by young, hip (and relatively well-off) shoppers. Wandering aimlessly is as good a strategy as any for exploring the neighborhood's retail offerings. If time is of the essence, concentrate on the square blocks bounded by Front and 3rd Streets and Market and Race Streets. The first Friday of every month is a particularly good day for an Old City excursion because dozens of shops and galleries stay open as late as 9 P.M.

Among the area's gems are **Vagabond Boutique** (37 N. 3rd St., 267/671-0737, www.vagabondboutique.com, open daily) and **J. Karma Boutique** (62 N. 3rd St., 215/627-9625, www.jkarmaboutique.com, open daily), just steps apart on the block of North 3rd between Market and Arch Streets. Vagabond owners Mary Clark and Megan Murphy deal in hand-knit sweaters by Mary, hand-sewn pieces by Megan, and threads by other creative sorts, some of them local. Head to the back room for yarn, children's clothing, accessories, housewares, and monthly art exhibitions. Named for owner Jeanne O'Karma, J. Karma is a trove of women's accessories. Jewelry by local designers sparkles alongside imported sterling silver pieces. Shoe and handbag addicts can get their fix and then some.

Sugarcube (124 N. 3rd St., 215/238-0825, www.sugarcube.us, open daily) makes life a little sweeter with its carefully curated collection of men's and women's fashions by indie designers. Bicycles and canine friends are welcome inside. If you haven't maxed out the plastic, try **Third Street Habit** (153 N. 3rd St., 215/925-5455, www.thirdstreethabit.com, open daily), named best women's boutique by *Philadelphia*

magazine soon after its 2004 opening. If of-the-moment labels like Earnest Sewn, Ella Moss, Graham & Spencer, and Rag & Bone make your heart pitter-patter, then shopping here could easily become a habit. Vagabond, Sugarcube, and Third Street Habit all carry select vintage duds.

Old City has no shortage of stores devoted to beautifying the home. Housed in a converted police station, **Bruges Home** (323A Race St., 215/922-6041, www.brugeshome .com, open daily) abounds with arresting pieces from around the globe. Owner Ed Gray is inspired by the Belgian proclivity for combining natural elements with streamlined design. It's a pricey aesthetic. A set of three petrified logs on metal stands sells for close to $1,000. A chandelier crafted of found driftwood commands three times that. A museum devoted to contemporary wood art, particularly lathe-turned pieces, makes a trip to Old City's northern fringe more than worthwhile. The **Wood Turning Center** (501 Vine St., 215/923-8000, www.woodturningcenter.org, open Tues.–Sat.) doesn't charge an admission fee, but it's easy to drop a week's salary in its spacious store.

SOUTH PHILADELPHIA

South Philly's northern boundary, **South Street,** is a retail melting pot. Sex shops share the corridor with Starbucks. Tattoo parlors co-exist with darling boutiques. Foot Locker is just steps from a store specializing in pimp-worthy shoes made of exotic skins (alligator, stingray, lizard, and the like). The street stretches from the Delaware River in the east to the Schuylkill River in the west, but most of the action is concentrated between Front and 10th Streets. The action spills over to some surrounding blocks. South 4th Street, also known as Fabric Row, is especially colorful—the place to go for a body piercing or a bolt of fabric.

East Passyunk Avenue, which runs diagonally across South Philly, is coming into its own as a shopping destination. The stretch between 11th and 13th Streets is home to **Metro Mens Clothing** (1615 E. Passyunk Ave., 267/324-5172, metromensclothing.com, open daily), which sells exactly what its name suggests; **Green Aisle Grocery** (1618 E. Passyunk Ave., 215/465-1411, www.greenaislegrocery .com, open daily), a self-described "boutique" market co-owned by *Philadelphia Weekly* food critic Adam Erace; and **JimmyStyle** (1820 E. Passyunk Ave., 267/239-0598, shopjimmystyle. com, open Tues.–Sun.), stocked with funky home accessories. All three opened in 2009.

Fabric Row

To the Yiddish-speaking Jews who populated Philadelphia's southern outskirts a century ago, what's now called Fabric Row (S. 4th St. between South and Catharine Streets, www.fabric row.com) was known as "Der Ferder" (The Fourth). In the early 1900s it was chockablock with pushcarts and stands loaded with fabrics, produce, and other goods. The city outlawed pushcarts in the 1950s, but by then, many of the fabric merchants had acquired storefronts and a reputation that attracted tailors and

dressmakers from all over Philadelphia. It's still home to more than a dozen fabric-related businesses.

Marmelstein's (760 S. 4th St., 215/925-9862, open Mon.–Sat.), whose founders sold thread, needles, thimbles, and such from a stand, specializes in fabrics and trims for window treatments and upholstery. For cut-to-size foam cushions, come into **Adler's Fabrics** (742 S. 4th St., 215/925-8984, www .adlersfabricsonline.com, open Mon.–Sat.), which also custom-makes bedspreads, duvets, shams, and bedskirts. **Albert Zoll Inc.** (744 S. 4th St., 215/922-0589, www.albertzoll.com, open Mon.–Sat.) is heaven for the home sewer. Family owned and operated for three generations, it carries everything from scissors and chalk to Swarovski crystals and exotic buttons. Brides-to-be flock there for custom veils.

Sprinkled among the fabric establishments are bars and eateries and an eclectic mix of shops, including **Bus Stop** (750 S. 4th St., 215/627-2357, www.busstopboutique.com, open daily except Tues.), a must-stop for ladies who love unique designer shoes, and

© JEDEDIAH DROLET

Fabric Row used to be known as "Der Ferder" (The Fourth).

South Philly's Italian Market

© AMY GIZIENSKI

Bicycle Revolutions (711 and 712 S. 4th St., 215/629-2453, www.bicyclerevolutions.com, open Mon.–Sat.), a surprising hybrid of bike shop and art gallery.

Italian Market

Age hasn't slowed down South Philly's Italian Market (S. 9th St. between Wharton and Fitzwater Streets, www.italianmarketphilly .org), which throbs with activity seven days a week year-round. The outdoor market, said to be the oldest in the country, traces its history to the 1880s, when an Italian immigrant opened a boarding house for his countrymen. Food stalls sprang up to serve the influx of immigrants, and then came butcher shops, cheese shops, bakeries, and restaurants. Some never left. Produce purveyor **P&F Giordano** and meat-centric **Cannuli's,** where you can pick up a whole roasted pig, date to the 1920s. You'll find both along 9th Street between Washington Avenue and Christian Street, the busiest stretch of the market. Across the street from Cannuli's is the gourmet grocery **Di Bruno Bros.,** which

opened in 1939. In recent years Di Bruno has set up shop in the ritzy Rittenhouse Square area and in the Comcast Center, Philly's tallest skyscraper, but the unpolished original has an inimitable old-world charm. The Italian Market has of late made room for merchants of other ethnic backgrounds. Mexican eateries and bodegas are prevalent. Korean barbecue and Vietnamese *pho* (noodle soup) are as easy to come by as a slice of pizza.

Be aware that some street vendors and shop owners take Mondays off. If you're averse to crowds, it's a great day to come. Steel yourself for thick crowds and impossibly tempting foods if you come during the **Italian Market Festival** (www.italianmarketfestival.com) in mid-May.

CENTER CITY
Macy's

The venerable department store chain's Center City emporium (1300 Market St., 215/241-9000, www.macys.com, 10 A.M.–8 P.M. Mon.–Sat., 11 A.M.–7 P.M. Sun.) holds as much appeal for architecture and history buffs as it does for fashionistas. It occupies a stately tower built a century ago as the flagship of Philadelphia native John Wanamaker's retailing empire. No less a dignitary than U.S. President William Howard Taft dedicated the department store, which bore the Wanamaker name until a buyout in the 1990s, then went by several others before opening as a Macy's in 2006. Hour-long tours (215/241-9000 ext. 2408, $10 per person) of the National Historic Landmark leave from the first-floor visitors center at 3:30 p.m. on weekdays and most Saturdays. The building's soaring atrium features a pipe organ that Wanamaker purchased in 1909 and enlarged to its current glory. With nearly 28,500 pipes and the prowess of three symphony orchestras, it's said to be the largest playable instrument in the world. Macy's shoppers are treated to concerts twice daily Monday through Saturday. The marble-clad atrium is especially magical in March and April, when it's filled with flowers and topiaries from around the world, and during the holiday season, when a Christmas-themed light show runs every hour on the hour. The store offers more than 150,000 square feet of fashion and home decor—enough to overwhelm an unseasoned shopper. Fortunately, an appointment with a Macy's personal shopper (800/343-0120) costs nothing at all.

Antique Row

The stretch of Pine Street between Broad and 9th Streets is peppered with one-of-a-kind shops, about a dozen of which specialize in antique and vintage treasures. **M. Finkel & Daughter** (936 Pine St., 215/627-8199, www.samplings.com, open Tues.–Sun.) boasts two floors of 18th- and 19th-century furniture, but that's not the half of it. It's acclaimed for its selection of antique samplers, or pieces of embroidery. Stained-glass windows and paintings are specialties at **Kohn & Kohn Antiques** (1112 Pine St., 215/317-5300, www.kohnandkohn antiques.com, open by chance or appointment). Steps away is the lovely **Crystal Cage** (1116 Pine St., 215/238-1323, www.thecrystal cage.com, open Wed.–Sun.), whose owner

travels the world in search of artisan-designed jewelry, handbags, hats, and home accents for the boutique.

At 12th and Pine Streets is one of the nation's oldest gay and lesbian bookstores. **Giovanni's Room** (345 S. 12th St., 215/923-2960, www .giovannisroom.com, open daily) has expanded three times since opening on South Street in 1973 and now carries more than 25,000 titles. Maps and advice are generously shared with anyone new to Philly's "Gayborhood."

Midtown Village

Ask a Philly native to point you to Midtown Village, and you're liable to get a "What's dat?" There was no "Midtown Village" in William Penn's 17th-century plan for the city or, for that matter, a decade ago. It's what merchants and restaurateurs in an up-and-coming area better known as the Gayborhood have taken to calling their pocket of Center City. And why shouldn't they get to call it what they please? Where most saw shuttered storefronts and transvestite prostitutes, they saw potential. The heart of the newly hip area is the stretch of South 13th Street between Chestnut and Walnut Streets. Here you'll find **Open House** (107 S. 13th St., 215/922-1415, www.openhouseliving.com, open daily) with its ever-changing collection of modern housewares. The lesbian partners who opened it in 2002 went on to open five other businesses on the same block: restaurants Bindi, Lolita, and Barbuzzo; a gourmet market named Grocery; and **Verde** (108 S. 13th St., 215/546-8700, www.verdephiladelphia.com, open daily), featuring fresh flowers and artisanal chocolates. The entrepreneurial pair hasn't bought up the whole block—yet.

Named for owner Michele Giunta Cimillo's daughter, **Scarlet Fiorella** (113 S. 13th St., 215/922-1955, www.scarletfiorella.com, open daily) is a teeny boutique packed with beautifully restored vintage furniture, eclectic home accents, and some of the hippest children's threads in town. Its sass-emblazoned onesies ("Be good to me and I'll visit you in the nursing home") are hugely popular. **Duross & Langel** (117 S. 13th St., 215/592-7627, www.durossandlangel.com, open daily) is an olfactory delight. It's stocked with its own brand of face, body, and hair care products and offers custom-blended balms for whatever ails you. Cross Sansom Street for clothing and accessories inspired by the late, great tattoo artist Norman "Sailor Jerry" Collins. Not your style? Pop into **Sailor Jerry** (116–118 S. 13th St., 215/531-6380, www.sailorjerry.com, open daily) anyway for a peek at the squid chandeliers.

Jewelers' Row

Philadelphia's diamond district is the oldest in America and second in magnitude only to New York's. Dozens of jewelry stores compete for business along the brick-paved stretch of Sansom Street between 7th and 8th Streets as well as 8th Street between Chestnut and Walnut Streets. Located a (precious) stone's throw from Independence National Historical Park, the area has been bling central since the second half of the 19th century.

Robbins Diamonds (801 Walnut St., 215/925-1877, www.robbinsdiamonds.com, open daily) is a favorite of men ready to pop the question. With goldsmiths and diamond setters on premises, **Campbell & Company** (702 Sansom St., 215/627-4996, www.campbell jewelers.com, open Mon.–Sat.) is a must-stop for anyone interested in a custom-made sparkler. **Unclaimed Diamonds** (113 S. 8th St., 215/923-3210, www.unclaimeddiamonds.com, open daily) offers deals on engagement rings, wedding bands, watches, and other valuables that people put on layaway and never claimed. A handy map of Jewelers' Row businesses is available at www.philadelphiajewelersrow.com.

Rittenhouse Row

The area around leafy Rittenhouse Square is a fashion plate's Eden, a destination for everything from mass-produced tees to haute couture frocks. Walnut and Chestnut Streets are especially crowded with stores. The former is home to Gap, Juicy Couture, Kiehl's, Ann Taylor, American Apparel, Aerosoles, Zara, Armani Exchange, Brooks Brothers, Banana Republic, Club Monaco, Cole Haan, Esprit, Guess, Kenneth Cole, Lucky Brand, Talbots, and more.

At the corner of Broad and Walnut Streets stands **The Bellevue** (215/875-8350, www.bel levuephiladelphia.com, 10 A.M.–6 P.M. Mon.–Sat. and until 8 P.M. P.M. Wed.), a 1904 Beaux Arts building that houses a luxury hotel and stores to match, including Tiffany & Co., Polo Ralph Lauren, and Williams-Sonoma. In 2009 Walnut Street welcomed Pennsylvania's first **Barneys CO-OP** (1811 Walnut St., 215/563-5333, www.barneys.com, open daily), much to the delight of Philly's Carrie Bradshaw wannabes.

Chestnut Street boasts a Sephora and **The Shops at Liberty Place** (1625 Chestnut St., 215/851-9055, www.shopsatliberty.com, 9:30 A.M.–7 P.M. Mon.–Sat., noon–6 P.M. Sun.), an indoor mall with about 30 stores and a food court featuring the excellent Jake's Philadelphia Cheesesteaks. H&M has a presence on Chestnut *and* Walnut.

It's not all chains in this pocket of Center City, dubbed "Rittenhouse Row." Tucked among the nationally recognized stores are gems found nowhere else. **Boyds** (1818 Chestnut St., 215/564-9000, www.boydsphila .com, open Mon.–Sat.), family owned since its founding in 1938, stocks luxury fashions by the likes of Armani, Escada, Gucci, and Dolce & Gabbana, employs an army of tailors, and offers free valet parking. **Petulia's Folly** (1710 Sansom St., 215/569-1344, www.petuliasfolly .com, open daily), a boutique as whimsical as its name, carries hip, upscale home furnishings, women's clothing and accessories, and children's products. Jewelry mavens flock to **Tselaine** (1927 Walnut St., 215/301-4752, open daily) for the sort of baubles seen on starlets and in the pages of *Elle*.

GREATER PHILADELPHIA
King of Prussia Mall

With 400 stores and eateries, including seven department stores, King of Prussia (160 N. Gulph Rd., King of Prussia, 610/265-5727, www.kingofprussiamall.com, 10 A.M.–9 P.M.

Mon.–Sat., 11 A.M.–6 P.M. Sun.) is the East Coast's largest shopping mall. According to mall management, its footprint could accommodate five Great Pyramids or two Louisiana Superdomes. In other words, you'd be wise to wear your comfiest shoes. If money isn't an object, toss your keys to the valets at Neiman Marcus and save your tootsies the trouble of walking from one of 13,000 parking spaces. What's notable about the shopping complex—besides its size—is that it's home to both garden-variety chains (Gap, Old Navy, Express, Victoria's Secret, Forever 21, RadioShack, Foot Locker) and luxury retailers (Thomas Pink, Ralph Lauren, Betsey Johnson, Lilly Pulitzer, Cole Haan, Lacoste, Hermes). Five of its department store anchors—Nordstrom, Neiman Marcus, Lord & Taylor, Sears, and JCPenney—frame a building known as The Plaza. Macy's and Bloomingdales occupy the neighboring Court building. In November and December a courtesy shuttle circles both buildings, making holiday shopping a wee bit less onerous. Like the stores, dining options run the gamut. Shoppers can grab a bite from the likes of Subway and Taco Bell or sit down to a meal at The Cheesecake Factory, Morton's steakhouse, or more than a dozen other restaurants. If you're new to the behemoth mall, stop at a guest services desk and pick up a map. There's one by Rite Aid and another near Lord & Taylor in The Plaza and a third near Bloomingdale's in The Court. If you've traveled far to get your shop on, consider budgeting time for a visit to Valley Forge National Historical Park, just a few minutes away.

Outlet Malls

Cost-conscious clotheshorses have their pick of outlet malls in the Philadelphia area. Located 15 miles northeast of Center City, **Franklin Mills** (1455 Franklin Mills Circle, Philadelphia, 215/632-1500, www.simon.com, 10 A.M.–9:30 P.M. Mon.–Sat., 11 A.M.–7 P.M. Sun.) is a sprawling enclosed mall with about 150 stores and eateries, plus a 14-screen movie theater and a skatepark. A few upscale brands are represented, including Tommy Hilfiger, Brooks Brothers, Saks Fifth Avenue Off 5th, and Neiman Marcus's Last Call. There's a Dave & Buster's on-site for some mid-shopping-spree skee ball. **Philadelphia Premium Outlets** (18 W. Lightcap Rd., Limerick, 610/495-9000, www.premiumoutlets.com, 10 A.M.–9 P.M. Mon.–Sat., 10 A.M.–7 P.M. Sun.) also has about 150 tenants, but its collection of clothing stores is significantly larger. Among them are Sean John, Juicy Couture, Calvin Klein, DKNY, and Elie Tahari. The mall, which opened in 2007, is 35 miles northwest of Center City. The mammoth King of Prussia Mall is on the way.

Sports and Recreation

Philadelphia sports fans have it good: The city has a bushel of professional teams. The Phillies brought home a World Series championship as recently as 2008. But packing stadiums and tailgating aren't the only forms of recreation in Rocky Balboa's hometown. There are parks to explore, rivers to row, and trails to hike and bike, not to mention museum steps to conquer.

PARKS

Philadelphia's park system boasts 63 green spaces spanning more than 9,200 acres, or 10 percent of the land in Philadelphia. Collectively known as **Fairmount Park** (www.fairmountpark.org), they include small urban oases like Rittenhouse Square and unmanicured areas large enough to get lost in, e.g. Wissahickon Valley Park. Most Philadelphians think of Fairmount Park as the lands straddling the Schuylkill River north of the Art Museum, properly known as East and West Fairmount Parks. If you have time for just one outdoorsy activity while in town, go for a bike ride on the Schuylkill River Trail, which runs through East Fairmount Park.

Rittenhouse Square

One of five public squares included in William Penn's 1680s plan for Philadelphia, Rittenhouse Square (between 18th and 19th Streets and Walnut and Locust Streets) has been called the heart of the city. When the weather is nice, you'll find children at play, senior citizens warming the benches, office workers enjoying their lunches, and fat squirrels soliciting handouts. An address near the tree-lined park is a mark of status. Rittenhouse was known as Southwest Square until 1825, when it was renamed for 18th-century astronomer and clockmaker David Rittenhouse. The present layout, with its diagonal walkways and reflecting pool, dates to 1913, when architect Paul Philippe Cret was recruited to spruce it up. Cret would go on to design the Benjamin Franklin Bridge connecting Philadelphia and Camden, New Jersey, and the Rodin Museum, among other memorable structures.

Washington Square

Originally called Southeast Square, Washington Square (Walnut St. between 6th and 7th Streets) is another of Philadelphia's five original squares. It's less trafficked than Rittenhouse despite its proximity to the major historic attractions. Used as a mass graveyard for casualties of the Revolutionary War and for victims of the yellow fever epidemics of the 1790s, it was renamed for the nation's first commander-in-chief and president in 1825. The **Tomb of the Unknown Soldier,** featuring a bronze sculpture of George Washington and an eternal flame, was erected in the 1950s.

Wissahickon Valley Park

Less than 30 minutes north of Center City but a world apart, Wissahickon Valley Park offers 57 miles of trails, a stocked trout stream, and some of the best leaf-peeping in the region. Stretching seven miles from the Chestnut Hill neighborhood in the north to Manayunk in the southwest, it's one of the largest parks in the Fairmount Park system. Wissahickon Creek, which runs through its length, was once lined with water-powered mills and taverns. The only remaining example is the **Valley Green Inn** (Valley Green Rd. at Wissahickon, 215/247-1730, www.valleygreeninn.com, lunch noon–4 P.M. Mon.–Fri. and 11 A.M.–4 P.M.

Wissahickon Valley Park

Sat., Sun. brunch 10 A.M.–3 P.M., dinner 5–9 P.M. Sun.–Thurs. and 5–10 P.M. Fri.–Sat., lunch $6–15, brunch $19–23, dinner $17–29), built in 1850. Originally known as Edward Rinker's Temperance Tavern, it now serves new American cuisine in a cozy and romantic setting. Hitching posts are still found out front.

There are multiple entry points to the 1,800-acre park, but if you're unfamiliar with the area, you're best off parking near the restaurant. Use the public restrooms, then set out on Forbidden Drive, the wide and flat gravel road that parallels the creek. You'll find plenty of opportunities to veer off onto more rugged trails. A very basic map of the park is available on the website of the nonprofit **Friends of the Wissahickon** (8708 Germantown Ave., 215/247-0417, www.fow.org). You can purchase a detailed fold-out map through the website and at locations including the group's headquarters in Chestnut Hill and the Valley Green Inn.

SCHUYLKILL RIVER TRAIL

The Philadelphia region boasts hundreds of miles of trails that range from paved to rocky, flat to steep, and crowded to rarely trodden.

None are so popular as the multi-use Schuylkill River Trail (484/945-0200, www.schuylkill rivertrail.com), a work in progress expected to cover 130 miles when completed. It's already possible to travel from Center City to Valley Forge National Historical Park, a distance of about 20 miles, via the riverside trail. The Philadelphia section, which hugs the Schuylkill River's east bank, stretches north from Locust Street, passes the Philadelphia Museum of Art and Boathouse Row, and continues through the charming Manayunk neighborhood. It's accessible via ramps from Market and Chestnut Streets, stairs from Walnut Street, and street-level crossings at Locust and Race Streets, among other places.

The trailhead near **Lloyd Hall** (1 Boathouse Row on Kelly Dr., 215/685-3936), a community rec center just north of the Art Museum, is particularly popular because of the availability of parking, restrooms, drinking water, and **bicycle and inline skate rentals** (10 A.M.–6 P.M. Sat. and 10 A.M.–4 P.M. Sun. Apr.–Oct., 215/568-6002, www.breakaway bikes.com, $10 per hour or $50 per day, overnight rentals available). You can also rent a

© KARRIE GAVIN

Boathouse Row is home to Lloyd Hall, a community recreation center.

bike at Manayunk's **Human Zoom** (4159 Main St., 215/487-7433, www.humanzoom .com, 10 A.M.–7 P.M. Mon.–Fri., 9 A.M.–6 P.M. Sat., 10 A.M.–4 P.M. Sun.).

WATER ACTIVITIES

Philadelphia is known as a center for rowing, and the set of boathouses sandwiched between Kelly Drive and the Schuylkill River just north of the Art Museum is one of the most recognizable sights in the city. But unless you belong to a local rowing club, boating opportunities are quite limited. Your best bet is to consult the website of the **Schuylkill River Development Corporation** (215/222-6030, ext. 103, www .schuylkillbanks.org), which organizes kayak and riverboat tours from a dock under the Walnut Street Bridge on the east bank of the Schuylkill. Guided kayak tours, offered on select Saturdays and Sundays from mid-June through early October, range $40–80 per person and include a how-to lesson and all equipment. Tours on the RiverLoop (888/748-7445), generally offered Thursday evenings and Saturday and Sunday afternoons, are $20–25 per adult and $15–20 for students and children 12 and under. The boat has indoor and outdoor seating and a cash bar.

If you've always wanted to give rowing a go, register for a **PA Rowing Camps** (267/971-9073, www.parowing.com) course, open to anyone age 13 and older. You don't need to have any knowledge of the sport or any equipment, but you do need to know how to swim.

SPECTATOR SPORTS

Philadelphia is one of about a dozen U.S. cities with teams in all four major sports leagues: Major League Baseball, the National Hockey League, the National Football League, and the National Basketball Association. In 2010 the Philly area welcomed a Major League Soccer franchise. Sports addicts can also get their fix from minor league baseball, arena football, professional indoor soccer or lacrosse, or professional team tennis. A discussion of the sports scene isn't complete without mention of the fierce hoops rivalries between local colleges.

Baseball

In 2007 the **Philadelphia Phillies** (Citizens Bank Park, 1 Citizens Bank Way, 215/463-1000, www.phillies.com) became the first American professional sports franchise to lose 10,000 games. So you can imagine the city's elation when the team beat the Tampa Bay Rays in the 2008 World Series. Founded in 1883, the franchise had captured baseball's highest prize only once before, in 1980. The Phillies made it back to the World Series in 2009 but fell to the New York Yankees four games to two.

Their current home, the 43,651-seat Citizens Bank Park, opened in 2004. While some die-hard fans decried the move from Veterans Stadium, demolished that same year, "The Bank" has proved a hit. The open outfield affords a scenic view of the Center City skyline, and the food is said to be the best in baseball. People for the Ethical Treatment of Animals, or PETA, has crowned it the most vegetarian-conscious ballpark.

For minor league baseball and the joy it brings, cross the Delaware River into New Jersey. The **Camden Riversharks** (Campbell's Field, 401 N. Delaware Ave., Camden, NJ, 866/742-7579, www.river sharks.com) play in the Atlantic League of Professional Baseball, which isn't affiliated with MLB. The view of the Benjamin Franklin Bridge and Philadelphia from their riverfront ballpark is worth the ticket price alone. Built in time for the franchise's first season in 2001, Campbell's Field seats 6,400 and features family-friendly amenities such as a rock-climbing wall and a carousel.

Basketball

The **Philadelphia 76ers** (Wells Fargo Center, 3601 S. Broad St., 800/298-4200, www.nba .com/sixers) have been very good and very bad. Since moving to the city in 1963, the pro basketball franchise has won two NBA championships—one in 1967 and the other in 1983. In between, it set a league record for fewest wins in a season, finishing the 1972–73 season with a 9–73 record. What the Sixers lack in consistency they make up for in star power. The roster has included some of the greatest players in basketball history: Wilt Chamberlain, Julius "Dr. J" Erving, Moses Malone, Charles Barkley, and Allen Iverson. Sixers management has riled fans by letting superstars slip through its fingers. Chamberlain was traded to Los Angeles, Malone to Washington, and Barkley to Phoenix. Iverson, who was sent to Denver in 2006 after 10 successful years with the Sixers, returned in 2009, giving fans hope that disadvantageous trades were a thing of the past. The home arena, known by several names since its 1996 opening, was rechristened the Wells Fargo Center in 2010.

Local basketball fans also relish the intense rivalries between five area universities—the University of Pennsylvania, La Salle, Saint Joseph's, Temple, and Villanova—known as the **Big 5** (www.philadelphiabig5.org).

Football

In a passionate sports town, no team inspires more passion than the **Philadelphia Eagles** (Lincoln Financial Field, 1 Lincoln Financial Field Way, 215/336-2000, www.philadelphia eagles.com). The club's popularity—and the scarcity of tickets—can't be explained by Super Bowl trophies. Established in 1933, the Eagles have not a one. (To be fair, they did win three NFL championships before the Super Bowl was first played in 1967.) "Da Iggles" have been perennial contenders since Andy Reid became head coach in 1999, playing in five conference championship games and advancing to the Super Bowl once. Despite exciting games and a roster stocked with high-profile players, the team's failure to bring home the ultimate prize looms large over the city. Fans grow crankier with each passing year, turning Lincoln Financial Field into a cauldron of noise, heightened emotions, and the occasional drunken brawl. Be warned: If you show up at the stadium (or a sports bar) wearing the opposing team's jersey, you *will* catch heat—or worse.

The waiting list for season tickets is famously long, and single-game tickets generally sell out within minutes of going on sale. Information on buying individual tickets from season ticket holders is available on the team's website. Other options for snagging tickets: eBay, Craigslist, and scalpers. They won't come cheap, and you'll risk arrest if you go the scalper route.

If you need a football fix and Eagles tickets are out of reach, you're not out of luck. Founded in 2004, Philadelphia's Arena Football League franchise won its first ArenaBowl in 2008, just months before league owners canceled the 2009 season in the face of financial woes. The **Philadelphia Soul** (Wells Fargo Center, 3601 S. Broad St., 800/298-4200, www.philadelphiasoul.com) were poised to return to competition in a reorganized AFL in spring 2011. Named for a style of soul music associated with Philadelphia, the team was originally co-owned by New Jersey–born rocker Jon Bon Jovi.

Hockey

The "Broad Street Bullies," as the **Philadelphia Flyers** (Wells Fargo Center, 3601 S. Broad St., 800/298-4200, http://flyers.nhl.com) are known, are arguably the most successful of the city's pro franchises. Added to the NHL in 1967, the Flyers won back-to-back Stanley Cups in 1973–1974 and 1974–1975, earning their nickname along the way. They have appeared in the playoffs more times than any other expansion team, and their 2009–2010 Eastern Conference championship brought their all-time winning percentage to 0.576, the second highest in the NHL. Do home games sell out? You bet.

The bruising style that worked for them in the 1970s made the Flyers local heroes and one of the most reviled teams in the league. Fans still eat up the rough-and-tumble approach. A crunching check or violent confrontation between two enforcers can get the Philly crowd more juiced than a wicked pass or sweet goal. Hockey tends to takes a back seat to the other three major sports in terms of overall effect on the city, but when the

Flyers are doing well, fair-weather fans come out in droves.

Soccer

In 2010 Major League Soccer awarded Philadelphia an expansion team. An 18,500-seat soccer stadium rose in the satellite city of Chester, and the **Philadelphia Union** (PPL Park, One Stadium Dr., Chester, 877/218-6466, www.philadelphiaunion.com) began play in March 2010. By the time their riverfront stadium celebrated its grand opening that June, season tickets had sold out. The team's name alludes to the union of the 13 American colonies in the Revolutionary period, when Philadelphia was the de facto capital. Players wear navy blue and gold—just like soldiers in George Washington's Continental Army.

Philadelphia has been home to a professional indoor soccer team since the mid-1990s. The **Philadelphia KiXX** (The Liacouras Center, 1776 N. Broad St., 800/298-4200, www .kixxonline.com) have won two Major Indoor Soccer League championships since the turn of the century but have failed to qualify for the playoffs in recent years. The regular season begins in November and ends in late March.

Other Spectator Sports

The **Legendary Blue Horizon** (1314 N. Broad St., 215/763-0500, www.legendaryblue horizon.com) in North Philly is one of the nation's iconic boxing institutions. It has reared dozens of future world champions since its first fight in 1961.

The National Lacrosse League's **Philadelphia Wings** (Wells Fargo Center, 3601 S. Broad St., 800/298-4200, www.wingslax.com) are famous for their rabid fans, who have turned heckling of opposing players into an art form. If you leave a game without a hoarse throat, you've missed half the fun.

Heckling during a **Philadelphia Freedoms** (the Pavilion at Villanova University, Villanova, 610/896-2890, www.philadelphia freedoms.com) game will get you the boot. One of 10 teams in the World TeamTennis Pro League, the Freedoms counted Andy Roddick among their ranks in 2010. Cofounded in the 1970s by tennis great Billie Jean King and then-husband Larry King, World TeamTennis is a coed sport. Each match consists of five sets: men's and women's singles, men's and women's doubles, and mixed doubles.

Accommodations

HISTORIC DISTRICT
Under $100

A short walk from the Liberty Bell Center, Independence Hall, and other marquee attractions, **Apple Hostels of Philadelphia** (32 S. Bank St., 215/922-0222, www.applehostels .com, $30–91) is as cheap as it gets in Old City. It's not for everyone: Guests must provide a foreign passport, Canadian driver's license, or out-of-state college ID upon check-in. The neighborhood's only hostel offers female-only, male-only, and couples-only dorms, plus private and semi-private rooms. Rates include bed linens, wireless Internet, weekly pub crawls, laundry detergent, and all the coffee and tea you can drink.

$100-250

Don't let "Best Western" fool you. With its grand staircase, high ceilings, and period-style furnishings, the **Best Western Independence Park Hotel** (235 Chestnut St., 215/922-4443, www.independenceparkhotel.com, $119–299) is no cookie-cutter chain hotel. More than 150 years old, the five-floor Italianate building was designed by an architect better known for churches and served as both a brewery and dry goods store before opening as a hotel in the 1980s. Book well in advance: the National Register of Historic Places property has just 36 guest rooms and a prime location.

You can't throw a rock from the roof of the seven-floor, 364-room **Holiday Inn Historic**

District (400 Arch St., 215/923-8660, www .holidayinn.com, $160–400) without hitting a historic something or other. It's that centrally located. The roof, incidentally, features a nice little swimming pool. You couldn't ask for a better amenity on a hot summer day, especially if you're traveling with kids. Parking is $22 per night.

The 350-room **Hyatt Regency Philadelphia at Penn's Landing** (201 S. Columbus Blvd., 215/928-1234, www.pennslanding.hyatt.com, $133–340) also boasts a pool with a view. It's indoors but bathed in natural light thanks to three walls of windows and a skylight. In the warmer months you can sip a cocktail and catch some rays on the adjoining sundeck. Request a room on the upper floors, and specify city or river view. Fresh off a 2008 renovation, rooms feature the signature Hyatt Grand Bed, dark wood furnishings, leather lounge chairs, and 32-inch LCD televisions. The **Sheraton Society Hill Hotel** (2nd and Walnut Streets, 215/238-6000, www.sheratonsocietyhill hotel.com, $129–329), with 365 recently updated guest rooms, is another recommendable option in the Penn's Landing area.

Be sure to ask for a room with a river view at the **Comfort Inn Downtown/Historic Area** (100 N. Christopher Columbus Blvd., 215/627-7900, www.comfortinn.com, $140–250), a stone's throw from the Ben Franklin Bridge. I-95 stands between the 185-room hotel and Old City's historic attractions, but guests needn't worry about navigating. Transportation to sights such as the Betsy Ross House, Reading Terminal Market, City Hall, and the Rodin Museum is on the house, as is breakfast and high-speed Internet access. Parking will set you back $23 per night.

It's not all chains in the Historic District. Take the **Thomas Bond House** (129 S. 2nd St., 215/923-8523, www.thomasbondhousebandb .com, $115–190), a charming B&B across from City Tavern. Built in 1769, the townhouse is named for its first tenant, an acclaimed surgeon and friend of Ben Franklin, with whom he founded the nation's first public hospital. Its 12 guest rooms feature period furnishings and private baths, some with whirlpool tubs. Bear in mind that the four-story house doesn't have an elevator. Rates include wireless Internet access, local phone calls, a continental breakfast on weekdays, a full breakfast on weekends, and wine and cheese every evening. Parking is available next door at a daily rate of $18.

A National Historic Landmark, the **❗ Morris House Hotel** (225 S. 8th St., 215/922-2446, www.morrishousehotel.com, $179–349) was built in 1787 as a home for one of Philadelphia's most prominent families. It boasts an idyllic private garden and 15 rooms decorated in a variety of styles, from Victorian to ultra-modern. All welcome guests with Godiva chocolates, fresh flowers, and 600-count sheets. Rates include a continental breakfast and afternoon tea complete with house-made cookies. Drop by the onsite **M Restaurant** (215/625-6666, 5–10 P.M. Tues.–Sat., $18–28) 5–7 P.M. any weekday but Monday for $6 martinis.

Over $250

Smack dab in the heart of the historic district, the **Omni Hotel at Independence Park** (401 Chestnut St., 215/925-0000, www.omni hotels.com, $189–459) is what you'd expect from the brand: luxurious. Readers of *Travel + Leisure* ranked it among the 500 best hotels in the world in 2010. The smallest of its 150 guest rooms and suites is a spacious 375 square feet. Treat yourself to a bamboo massage or pilates session at the on-site **Lux Spa & Fitness** (215/931-4248, www.luxspaandfitness.com, 6 A.M.–8 P.M. Mon.–Fri., 8 A.M.–8 P.M. Sat., 8 A.M.–1 P.M. Sun.), and don't forget to pack a swimsuit. Parking at the nearby Bourse Garage is $25 per 24-hour period, with no in-and-out privileges. If you plan on getting around by car, valet parking is a better deal.

Opened in 1990 in what used to be a shipping warehouse, the **Penn's View Hotel** (Front and Market Streets, 215/922-7600, www.pennsviewhotel.com, $189–299) has since expanded into two adjacent buildings on North Front Street. Its success is no surprise. The hotel is owned and operated by the Sena family, who honed their hospitality skills at nearby La Famiglia Ristorante, a local favorite since 1976. Some rooms feature balconies and others Jacuzzi tubs. The on-site **Ristorante Panorama** (215/922-7800, noon–10 P.M. Mon.–Thurs., noon–11 P.M. Fri., 5:30–11 P.M. Sat., 5–9 P.M. Sun., $13–29) is famous for its extensive selection of wines by the glass, made possible by a custom-built wine preservation and dispensing system. Five-wine flights and 3-ounce pours give you the chance to taste very expensive vintages without shelling out for a glass or bottle.

CENTER CITY
$100-250

With 1,332 rooms on 23 floors, the **Philadelphia Marriott Downtown** (1201 Market St., 215/625-2900, www.marriott .com, $169–269) isn't just the largest hotel in town. It's the largest in the state. Attached to the Pennsylvania Convention Center via skybridge, the colossus is one of three Marriotts in the immediate area. Just across 13th Street is the 498-room **Courtyard Philadelphia Downtown** (21 N. Juniper St., 215/496-3200, www.marriott.com, $169–279), which opened in 1999 in what had been the City Hall Annex. Built in 1926, the 16-story tower is resplendent with bronze-framed windows, coffered plaster ceilings, marble finishes, and ornate chandeliers. Guest rooms boast 11-foot ceilings and 42-inch LCD TVs. Request a room with a view of City Hall, which looks especially enchanting after sundown. Rounding out the Marriott triumvirate is the **Residence Inn Philadelphia Center City** (1 E. Penn Square, 215/557-0005, www.mar riott.com, $169–369), designed for extended stays. Its 269 suites have fully equipped kitchens, and guests can leave the grocery shopping to staff.

If cost is a concern, you'd be wise to investigate the area's independent hotels and B&Bs. The **Latham Hotel** (135 S. 17th St., 215/563-7474, www.lathamhotel.com, $119–169) is a good choice. Convenient to upscale shopping and the Avenue of the Arts, it offers 139

Victorian-ish rooms in a century-old building. For contemporary decor, try the **The Independent** (1234 Locust St., 215/772-1440, www.theindependenthotel.com, $159–269) in Midtown Village, a.k.a. the "Gayborhood." A colorful 30-foot-tall mural of Independence Hall greets guests in the lobby of the boutique hotel, which opened in 2008 in a restored Georgian Revival building. Its 24 guest rooms feature hardwood floors, 32-inch HDTVs, microwaves and refrigerators, and bathrooms with tin ceiling tiles. Some have fireplaces, others exposed brick walls or lofts. Breakfast and wine-and-cheese receptions are on the house. A few doors away, **Uncle's Upstairs Inn** (1220 Locust St., 215/546-6660, $100) offers six bargain-priced rooms above a low-key gay bar. Another Gayborhood option: the 48-room **Alexander Inn** (12th and Spruce Streets, 215/923-3535, www .alexanderinn.com, $119–169), which takes its design cues from Deco-era cruise ships. Rates include a buffet breakfast and access to an always-stocked snack bar. The hotel is popular among return visitors, so booking well in advance is advised.

Located on a quiet, tree-lined street a stone's throw from Antique Row, **Clinton Street Bed & Breakfast** (1024 Clinton St., 215/802-1334, www.1024clintonstreetbb.com, $149–199) has seven spacious suites with private bathrooms and galley or full kitchens, which innkeeper Kathleen Rabun is happy to stock with the makings of a continental breakfast. The 1836 townhouse is equipped with satellite TV and wireless Internet.

◖ **La Reserve** (1804–1806 Pine St., 215/735-1137, www.lareservebandb.com, $80–160) is another great deal in a great location. Three blocks south of Rittenhouse Square, the B&B consists of two 1850s townhouses with a combined 12 guest rooms and suites. The executive suites, with their kitchenettes and separate living rooms, were designed with extended stays in mind, for which discounts are available. Guests are welcome to tickle the ivories of the vintage Steinway in the sunny parlor, and breakfast is made to order. Even closer

La Reserve is three blocks south of Rittenhouse Square.

to Rittenhouse and costlier for it, **Lippincott House** (2023–2025 Locust St., 215/523-9251, www.lippincotthouse.com, $199–249) offers four beautifully decorated rooms, a game room complete with antique pool table, and a media room with theater-style seating. Built in 1897, the exquisite manse was opened as a B&B in 2008. Owners Jack Eldridge and Mary Beth Hallman are hosts extraordinaire, adept at everything from recommending restaurants to orchestrating picture-perfect marriage proposals.

Over $250
The domed lobby of 🄲 **The Ritz-Carlton, Philadelphia** (10 Avenue of the Arts, 215/523-8000, www.ritzcarlton.com $359–509) is worth a visit even if a room there is entirely out of your price range. Modeled on Rome's Pantheon, it's one of the grandest spaces in Center City and home to **10 Arts Bistro & Lounge** (215/523-8273, www.10arts.com, breakfast 6:30–11 A.M. Mon.–Fri. and 7 A.M.–noon Sat.–Sun., lunch 11:30 A.M.–2 P.M.

Mon.–Fri., dinner 5:30–10 P.M. Tues.–Sat., lounge open 11 A.M.–11 P.M. Sun.–Thurs. and 11 A.M.–12:30 A.M. Fri.–Sat., breakfast $13–20, lunch $15–28, dinner $26–59), a creation of French-born uber-chef Eric Ripert. Chef de cuisine is Jennifer Carroll, a hometown girl who served as sous chef at Ripert's revered Le Bernardin in New York City and was the last contestant given the boot before the finale of Bravo's *Top Chef* season 6. The restaurant, which opened in 2008, is a AAA Four Diamond winner. You don't have to spend a lot to soak up its sophisticated ambience. Lilliputian lobster rolls and burgers sell for $5 in the lounge. The landmark hotel, a bank in a previous incarnation, also boasts an award-winning spa. It has 300 guest rooms and suites ranging 280–1,900 square feet. Housekeeping visits twice daily, and room service is available around the clock. Fancy a bath strewn with rose petals? A butler will be happy to oblige.

Count on the **Loews Philadelphia Hotel** (1200 Market St., 215/627-1200, www.loews hotels.com, $169–329) for sleek, modern digs. Built in 1932 as the headquarters for the Philadelphia Savings Fund Society, Philly's first modern skyscraper has 581 guest rooms and suites and a 15,000-square-foot wellness center complete with lap pool. A 27-foot high "PSFS" sign still graces its roof. Another deluxe option in the center of town: the 294-room **Westin Philadelphia** (99 S. 17th St., 215/563-1600, www.westinphiladelphia hotel.com, $179–529). Guests are invited to gather in the understated lobby at the start of each evening for food, drink, and tête-à-tête. Call ahead if you're bringing a canine friend. The hotel will prepare a dog-friendly version of its signature Heavenly Bed.

For digs near Philadephia's favorite public square, you can't beat **The Rittenhouse** (210 W. Rittenhouse Square, 215/790-2523, www.ritten househotel.com, from $270), which may well be Philadelphia's most lauded hotel. A AAA Five Diamond winner since 1991, it's been rated the number one hotel in Pennsylvania and among the 100 best in the world. It was good enough for Denzel Washington and Tom Hanks during filming of *Philadelphia*. And the on-site **Lacroix** (215/546-9000, www.lacroixrestaurant.com, breakfast 6:30–11 A.M. daily, lunch 11 A.M.–2:30 P.M. Mon.–Sat., Sun. brunch 11 A.M.–2:30 P.M., dinner 5:30–10 P.M. Sun.–Thurs. and 5:30–10:30 P.M. Fri.–Sat., breakfast $7–22, lunch $14–26, dinner $34–95) was hailed as the nation's best new restaurant when it opened in 2003. Sunday brunch is a $59 extravagance with live music, chocolate fountains, and a liquid nitrogen station. The Rittenhouse has 98 oversized guest rooms and suites, some commanding upwards of $3,000 per night. Marble bathrooms boast mini TVs. Bring your swim duds for the indoor pool and outdoor sundeck.

Just off Rittenhouse Square is a more intimate alternative: the 24-room **Rittenhouse 1715** (1715 Rittenhouse Square St., 215/546-6500, www.rittenhouse1715.com, from $249).

BENJAMIN FRANKLIN PARKWAY
$100-250
The **Best Western Center City** (501 N. 22nd St., 215/568-8300, www.bestwesternpa.com, $89–149) is a rare breed of Philadelphia hotel: It doesn't charge a cent for parking. Add to that its reasonable room rates, and you're looking at one of the best lodging deals in town. The 183-room hotel is otherwise unremarkable. Amenities include a fitness center, outdoor swimming pool, and sports bar. Did we mention the free parking?

The **Windsor Suites** (1700 Benjamin Franklin Parkway, 215/981-5678, www.windsor hotel.com, $109–299) is right on the tree-lined parkway and endowed with a rooftop pool. Its apartment-style accommodations add up to big savings for travelers who do their own cooking. Request an upper-floor room for the best views.

Over $250
Popular among visiting b-ballers for its extra-long beds, the **Four Seasons** (1 Logan Square, 215/963-1500, www.fourseasons .com/philadelphia, from $395) is as swanky—and spendy—as it gets in the City of Brotherly Love. A so-called moderate room measures 500 square feet. Appropriately enough, the Philadelphia branch of the luxury chain pays tribute to the Federal period, when America was in its infancy, in its design aesthetic. The 364-room hotel is home to the French-influenced **Fountain Restaurant** (breakfast 6:30–11 A.M. Mon.–Fri., 7–11 A.M. Sat., 7 A.M.–noon Sun., lunch 11:30 A.M.–2:30 P.M. Mon.–Sat., dinner 5:45–10 P.M. Tues.–Sun.), regularly ranked among the nation's best, and a spa with a palm-flanked lap pool. It's the Four Seasons. Enough said.

FAIRMOUNT PARK
Under $100
Philadelphia isn't off limits to penny-pinching globetrotters thanks to **Chamounix Mansion** (3250 Chamounix Dr., 215/878-3676, www .philahostel.org, $20–23 per person, children 16 and under $8), which isn't nearly as opulent as its name suggests. Built in 1802 as a country retreat for a wealthy Philadelphia merchant, it was saved from demolition in

the mid-1900s by community members who agitated for its conversion to a youth hostel. There are 80 beds between the mansion and carriage house, most in dorm-style rooms. The awesomely low rates include linens, as sleeping bags are prohibited. Billed as the nation's first urban youth hostel, Chamounix is actually in West Fairmount Park, across the Schuylkill and well north of Center City. But with free bikes at their disposal and public transportation nearby, guests have no excuse for staying in. In fact, they must leave the hostel by 11 A.M. each day and return no earlier than 4:30 P.M., heeding a midnight curfew.

Food

Philadelphia's food scene has matured into one of the best, most talked-about in the country, with new eateries popping up every year. Decades-old mom-and-pops share the streets with stylish destination restaurants helmed by renowned chefs. Cozy neighborhood BYOBs boast loyal followings. And gastropub dining is more appealing than ever thanks to a smoking ban passed in 2007.

It goes without saying that Philadelphia's food scene extends far beyond cheesesteaks. That said, unless you're a vegetarian, there is no excuse for not sampling one of the greasy delights while in town. They're just not the same anywhere else. Philly's other culinary trademarks include soft pretzels, hoagies (elsewhere known as sub sandwiches), and water ice (the frozen dessert most Americans know as Italian ice). And no visit to Philadelphia is complete without a stop at Reading Terminal Market or the Italian Market, both of which offer a wide selection of delectable eats and a unique atmosphere.

The availability of healthy options has also improved in recent years, with many restaurants focusing on fresh, locally grown ingredients—which isn't hard considering the wealth of farms around the city.

HISTORIC DISTRICT
Asian
Few people have played a bigger role in Philadelphia's culinary renaissance than Stephen Starr, who has opened more than a dozen restaurants since the mid-'90s. Perhaps the most famous is **Buddakan** (325 Chestnut St., 215/574-9440, www.buddakan.com, 11:30 A.M.–2:30 P.M. and 5–11 P.M. Mon.–Thurs., 11:30 A.M.–2:30 P.M. and 5 P.M.–midnight Fri., 5 P.M.–midnight Sat., 4–10 P.M. Sun., $14–40), offering "modern Asian cuisine" in a low-lit space presided over by a massive Buddha statue. The decor is over the top (if not cheesy), and there are certainly more authentically Asian restaurants in town. But Buddakan can be counted on for a night-on-the-town vibe, delicious drinks, and undeniably tasty, creative dishes. Starr joined forces with Masaharu Morimoto of *Iron Chef* fame to open **Morimoto** (723 Chestnut St., 215/413-9070, www.morimotorestaurant.com, 11:30 A.M.–2 P.M. and 5–10 P.M. Mon.–Wed., 11:30 A.M.–2 P.M. and 5–11 P.M. Thurs., 11:30 A.M.–2 P.M. and 5 P.M.–midnight Fri., 5 P.M.–midnight Sat., 5–10 P.M. Sun., sushi rolls $8–12, lunch sets $16–38, dinner entrees $23–42) in 2001. Though the Japanese-born chef now spends most of his time in New York, his first American restaurant is still a jewel. Guests are treated to something of a light show in the ultramodern dining room. But the real treat is the food: exquisitely prepared sushi, entrees like "Morimoto surf and turf" (kobe filet and hamachi ribbons), and several eat-till-you-die *omakase* (chef's choice) options.

Colonial American
City Tavern (138 S. 2nd St., 215/413-1443, www.citytavern.com, 11:30 A.M.–9 P.M. Mon.–Thurs., 11:30 A.M.–10 P.M. Fri.–Sun., lunch $10–20, dinner $18–33) looks older than its

years, which is exactly what its builders had in mind. Completed in time for the U.S. bicentennial in 1976, the restaurant is a historically accurate reconstruction of the original City Tavern, built in 1773 and frequented by the likes of George Washington, Benjamin Franklin, John Adams, and Thomas Jefferson. Chef-proprietor Walter Staib also strives for historical accuracy. Waiters in 18th century garb serve up braised rabbit legs, medallions of venison, Martha Washington-style turkey pot pie, and other foods inspired by olden days. The commendable children's menu includes "meat and cheese pie," billed as a colonial version of lasagna. Don't miss the sweet potato and pecan biscuits, said to have been a favorite of Thomas Jefferson.

Italian

Designed to evoke the feel of a seaside holiday in Italy, **Positano Coast by Aldo Lamberti** (212 Walnut St., 215/238-0499, www.positano coast.net, 11:30 A.M.–10:30 P.M. Mon.–Thurs., 11:30 A.M.–11 P.M. Fri., noon–11 P.M. Sat., 12:30–10:30 P.M. Sun., lunch $7–16, dinner $12–40) is awash in whites and blues. Request outdoor seating for the full away-from-it-all effect. Appropriately enough, the restaurant specializes in fish and seafood, including *crudo*, or Italian-style sashimi. Choose from an extensive selection of wines and organic cocktails. Positano Coast is known for its happy hour (4:30–7:30 P.M. Mon.–Fri. and all day Sun.), featuring $3 beers and $5 wines and cocktails.

Mexican

Xochitl (408 S. 2nd St., 215/238-7280, www .xochitlphilly.com, 5 P.M.–midnight Sun.– Wed., 5 P.M.–1 A.M. Thurs.–Sat., bar open until 2 A.M. daily, $15–22) offers upscale, creative twists on Mexican fare in a cozy setting. Start with the delicious guacamole, prepared tableside and served with house-made tortilla chips, *sopa Azteca*, or ceviche tostada. Finish with the apple cider churros, which are out

Positano Coast by Aldo Lamberti

© ANNA DUBROVSKY

of this world. Xochitl (pronounced so-cheet) boasts an extensive list of tequilas, available by the shot or flight.

New American

Farmicia (15 S. 3rd St., 215/627-6274, www.farmiciarestaurant.com, 11:30 A.M.–3 P.M. and 5:30–10 P.M. Tues.–Thurs., 11:30 A.M.–3 P.M. and 5:30–11 P.M. Fri., 8:30 A.M.–3 P.M. and 5:30–11 P.M. Sat., 8:30 A.M.–3 P.M. and 5–9 P.M. Sun., breakfast under $10, lunch/brunch under $13, dinner $15–28) is fairly atypical as Old City spots go. Its farm-fresh cuisine and friendly, relaxed atmosphere are a refreshing departure from the look-at-me approach taken by some of its neighbors. The menu emphasizes local, seasonal ingredients and always includes several vegetarian options. Farmicia boasts a full bar, but you can bring your own wine at no charge.

Part of Stephen Starr's ever-expanding gastronomic empire, **Jones** (700 Chestnut St., 215/223-5663, www.jones-restaurant.com, 11:30 A.M.–midnight Mon.–Thurs., 11:30 A.M.–1 A.M. Fri., 10 A.M.–3 P.M. and 5 P.M.–1 A.M. Sat., 10 A.M.–3 P.M. and 4–11 P.M. Sun., $10–22) takes its design cues from the Brady Bunch era. But don't let the shag carpeting fool you; it wouldn't be a Starr restaurant without some contemporary twists. The focus here is comfort foods: fried chicken and waffles, grilled cheese, meat loaf with whipped potatoes, beef brisket, and even matzo ball soup. But you'll also find sesame-seared tuna, a vegetarian soy burger, and pasta with crabmeat. Like most Starr establishments, Jones offers a great selection of tasty if overpriced drinks.

Spanish

Chef Jose Garces is threatening to overtake Stephen Starr as Philly's most prolific restaurateur. The "Latin Emeril," as he's known, has opened half a dozen restaurants in the City of Brotherly Love since 2005 and shows no signs of slowing down. **(Amada** (217–219 Chestnut St., 215/625-2450, www.amadarestaurant.com, 11:30 A.M.–2:30 P.M. and 5–10 P.M. Mon.–Thurs., 11:30 A.M.–2:30 P.M. and 5 P.M.–midnight Fri.–Sat., 4–10 P.M. Sun., tapas $5–19) was the very first and an immediate hit. It specializes in authentic Spanish tapas—from artisanal olives and aged Manchego to lamb meatballs and grilled baby squid. The vibe is always stylish, fun, and energetic, but especially so on Wednesdays and Fridays with flamenco dancing.

Coffee and Sweets

Opened in 2004 by brothers with a passion for history and an eye for antiques, **The Franklin Fountain** (116 Market St., 215/627-1899, www.franklinfountain.com, noon–midnight daily) is part ice cream parlor, part time machine. Don't be surprised if "Gee whiz!" rolls off your tongue when you step inside; the place is a dead ringer for a turn-of-the-century soda fountain, complete with soda jerks in period attire. Order a soda or phosphate and they'll reach for the silver-plated spigots of a 1905 draft tower, believed to be the oldest operating soda fountain in the country. Don't be shy about asking for samples of the handmade ice cream, and do try the teaberry, a tribute to Clark's Teaberry chewing gum. Hardly old-timey, prices for signature sundaes like the Stock Market Crunch (rocky road ice cream with peanut butter sauce and crumbled pretzels) range from $8–15. Not a bad deal for time travel.

SOUTH PHILADELPHIA
Brunch

Thoughts of **(Sabrina's Café** (910 Christian St., 215/574-1599, www.sabrinascafe.com, 8 A.M.–10 P.M. Tue.–Sat., 8 A.M.–4 P.M. Sun.–Mon., $6–20) propel many a hungover local out of bed. Quite simply the best brunch spot in Philadelphia, Sabrina's offers standard breakfast fare along with showstoppers like challah French toast stuffed with cream cheese and bananas. Expect a long wait on weekends. That's worth saying again: Expect

Brunch at Sabrina's Cafe is worth the wait.

a long wait. The cozy eatery doesn't accept reservations, but you can ring before you arrive to put your name on the waiting list. Its owners opened a second location, **Sabrina's Cafe and Spencer's Too** (1804 Callowhill St., 215/636-9061, hours and prices same as above) not far from the Philadelphia Museum of Art.

If the line at Sabrina's is simply unbearable, mosey over to **Sam's Morning Glory Diner** (10th and Fitzwater Streets, 215/413-3999, www.themorninggdiner.com, 7 A.M.–4 P.M. Mon.–Fri., 8 A.M.–3 P.M. Sat.–Sun., under $10), where the wait might be marginally shorter. Check your diet at the door of the hipster-filled joint, and tuck into a frittata or the French toast stuffed with caramelized bananas and mangos. House-made ketchup adds an unusual zing to things.

Moroccan

Tucked away in an alley off South Street, **Marrakesh** (517 S. Leithgow St., 215/925-5929, www.marrakesheastcoast.com, 5:30–11 P.M. Sun.–Thurs., 5:30 P.M.–midnight Fri.–Sat.) is

worth searching out. Its mazelike interior is dimly lit and eminently romantic. Waiters in traditional Moroccan garb serve a lovely multi-course meal (about $30 per person) that you eat with your hands. Go hungry, allow at least two hours, and pace yourself. Each course is more delicious than the last. Marrakesh has a short wine list, but you're welcome to bring your own.

Seafood

It can take upwards of an hour to get a table at **Dmitri's** (795 S. 3rd St., 215/625-0556, www.dmitrisrestaurant.com, 5:30–10 P.M. Mon.–Thurs., 5:30–11 P.M. Fri.–Sat., 5–10 P.M. Sun., $10–18), a tiny corner BYOB that doesn't accept reservations. But the Mediterranean-inspired seafood will turn your wait-induced frown upside down. Don't pass up the perfect hummus in your rush toward the clams, mussels, smelts, and squid. Dmitri's also has locations in **Center City** (2227 Pine St., 215/985-3680) and **Northern Liberties** (944 N. 2nd St., 215/592-4550).

Vegan

Owned and operated by the husband-and-wife team of Rich Landau (executive chef) and Kate Jacoby (pastry chef), **Horizons** (611 S. 7th St., 215/923-6117, www.horizonsphiladelphia.com, 6–10 P.M. Tues.–Thurs., 6–11 P.M. Fri.–Sat., $19–21) is proof that veganism and fine cuisine aren't mutually exclusive. In 2009 the couple made culinary history by cooking the first vegan dinner at the James Beard House in New York City. Landau and team turn seitan, tofu, tempeh, and every vegetable under the sun into dishes both colorful and flavorful. The menu changes seasonally, with Jamaican bbq seitan, red curry tofu banh mi, and cauliflower risotto all making appearances. On Tuesdays through Thursdays you can enjoy a six-course tasting menu for $55. Great wines, beers, and specialty drinks are available.

NORTHERN LIBERTIES
Brunch

Honey's Sit 'n Eat (800 N. 4th St.,

215/925-1150, www.honeys-restaurant.com, 8 A.M.–10 P.M. Mon.–Fri., 8 A.M.–9:30 P.M. Sat., 8 A.M.–4:30 P.M. Sun., $5–12) is a strange and wonderful beast. Popular with hipsters, it pays tribute to Jewish and Southern cuisines in equal measure. That's right: nova lox on the same menu as biscuits and sausage gravy. The breakfast menu, available all day long, also includes ethnically ambiguous fare like giant buttermilk pancakes. The lunch options are also superb. Don't overlook the long list of specials, which may include such must-haves as fried green tomatoes and lobster macaroni and cheese.

CENTER CITY EAST

The half of Center City east of Broad Street is packed with restaurants, with the greatest concentrations in Chinatown, along the Avenue of the Arts, and in the area known as Midtown Village, or the Gayborhood.

Asian

1225 Raw Sushi and Sake Lounge (1225 Sansom St., 215/238-1903, www.rawlounge .net, 11:30 A.M.–2:30 P.M. and 5–9:45 P.M. Mon.–Wed., 11:30 A.M.–2:30 P.M. and 5–10:45 P.M. Thurs., 11:30 A.M.–2:30 P.M. and 5 P.M.–11:30 P.M. Fri., noon–3 P.M. and 5–11:30 P.M. Sat., noon–3 P.M. and 5–9:45 P.M. Sun., $10–19) offers a lounge-like atmosphere with its red walls, bamboo ceiling, and high-backed booths, plus a courtyard for al fresco dining. Its salads, small plates, and traditional dishes don't disappoint, but it does sushi better than anything else. As its name suggests, 1225 is known for its sake selection. You can try four for $18.

Italian

Mercato (1216 Spruce St., 215/985-2962, www.mercatobyob.com, 5–10:30 P.M. Mon.–Thurs., 5–11 P.M. Fri.–Sat., 5–10 P.M. Sun., $16–29), a tiny, cash-only BYOB, is always noisy and crowded. The culprits: close tables, an open kitchen, and the restaurant's immense popularity. Start with bread, artisan cheeses, and an olive oil tasting. You can't go wrong

with anything on the menu, but standouts include the whole grilled artichoke appetizer and pan-seared diver scallops over risotto. The desserts are also excellent. Mercato doesn't take reservations, so you can expect a wait, especially on weekends.

Mexican

The fetching **Lolita** (106 S. 13th St., 215/546-7100, www.lolitabyob.com, 5–10 P.M. Sun.–Tues., 5–10:30 P.M. Wed.–Thurs., 5–11 P.M. Fri.–Sat., $18–25), with its exposed brick walls, open kitchen, and just-right lighting, is one of three restaurants chef Marcie Turney and partner Valerie Safran have opened since 2002. (The other two, the "modern Indian" BYOB **Bindi** and the Mediterranean restaurant and bar **Barbuzzo**, are just a few doors away.) Lolita is out to prove that "Mexican cuisine can be as sophisticated and divine as any other type of food," which can be translated as: This ain't Qdoba, people. You'll find dishes such as hazelnut-crusted duck breast and spice-rubbed pork chop but nary a burrito. Bring your own wine or, better yet, tequila. Lolita always has fresh-squeezed margarita mix on hand. There's a liquor store around the corner at 12th and Chestnut Streets.

Vietnamese

Located in the heart of Chinatown, the warm and inviting **Vietnam Restaurant** (221 N. 11th St., 215/592-1163, www.eatatvietnam .com, 11 A.M.–9:30 P.M. Sun.–Thurs., 11 A.M.–10:30 P.M. Fri.–Sat., $10–15) is one of Philly's most popular ethnic eateries. You won't go wrong with anything on the reasonably priced menu. The crispy spring rolls and delicate rice-paper rolls are top-notch. If you're unfamiliar with Vietnamese cuisine, take your pick of the clay-pot dishes or vermicelli noodle bowls. You may have to wait for a table on weekends; the bar's strong specialty drinks help pass the time. If the wait is too long for your tastes, defect to Vietnam's main competitor, **Vietnam Palace** (222 N. 11th St., 215/592-9596, www .vietnampalacephilly.com, 11 A.M.–9:30 P.M. Sun.–Thurs., 11 A.M.–10 P.M. Fri.–Sat., $8–15),

CHEESESTEAKS 101

As much as I'd love to give you a definitive answer to the question of where to get the best cheesesteak in Philly, there just isn't one. The argument will never be settled because it's truly a matter of personal preference. Some like the roll toasted and crispy, while others prefer it soft and chewy. Some like a cheesesteak dripping with grease, while others complain that too much grease makes the roll soggy. Some like the meat diced as thinly as possible, while others prefer slightly larger slices or even small chunks. Some love yellow Cheez Whiz, but most opt for American or provolone cheese. The one indisputable fact is that cheesesteaks are just not the same anywhere else. The closest I've come to a perfect cheesesteak outside of Philly is at the New Jersey shore, and not surprisingly, it turned out the chef hailed from Philly. While it's a fact that locals eat cheesesteaks regularly, we try to keep our consumption in check. Let's be honest, they're not exactly health food.

WHAT MAKES A GREAT CHEESESTEAK

All good cheesesteaks start with a roll that is chewy – not airy or tough – and many of the best spots in town use Amoroso's brand, a local company that's been around since 1904. The meat should generously fill the roll – leaving an inch of meatless roll is a definite no-no. Fried onions and either hot or sweet peppers are common additions, but beyond that, you're getting into fancy-schmancy territory. Some like to add pizza sauce, making it a pizza steak, or tomato, lettuce, onion, and mayo, making

it a cheesesteak hoagie. Others opt for the only slightly healthier chicken cheesesteak, in which chicken is substituted for the beef. (It's technically a misnomer to call it a chicken cheesesteak since there is no steak involved, but cheesechicken just doesn't have the same ring to it.) While each of these varieties is delicious in its own right, cheesesteak virgins are advised to keep it simple and stick with the classic beef cheesesteak (with fried onions and hot or sweet peppers if you like) and American cheese.

HOW TO ORDER

While not everyone is hardcore about ordering correctly, in South Philly or anywhere there is a long line, it's best to know what you're doing. First, don't *ever* order a "Philly cheesesteak." You're in Philly, so that part goes without saying. The basic rule of thumb is to minimize the words you need to convey what you want, so don't bother saying the word "cheesesteak" if that is the main thing the establishment serves. Cheesesteak is implied, so you can just give the specs: "Whiz wit" means Cheez Whiz with fried onions, and "prov without" means – yes, you guessed it – provolone cheese without fried onions.

These rules are most strictly observed at **Pat's King of Steaks** (215/468-1546, www .patskingofsteaks.com) and **Geno's Steaks** (215/389-0659, www.genosteaks.com), the famous dueling spots at the intersection of 9th Street and Passyunk Avenue in South Philly. Of the two, I prefer Pat's to the neon-bedazzled Geno's, in part because the meat at Pat's is

just across the street. And if you happen to be in University City when a Vietnamese food craving hits, head to Vietnam's stylish sister, **Vietnam Café** (816 S. 47th St., 215/729-0260, www.eatatvietnam.com/vietnam_cafe.php, $10– 15), which opened in 2009.

Coffee and Sweets

Capogiro Gelato Artisans (119 S. 13th St.,

215/351-0900, www.capogirogelato.com, 7:30 A.M.–10 P.M. Mon.–Thurs., 7:30 A.M.– midnight Fri., 9 A.M.–midnight Sat., 10 A.M.–10 P.M. Sun.) serves deliciously dense Italian-style ice cream in countless flavors that change with the seasons. In addition to traditional flavors like chocolate and hazelnut, you'll find creations like pear with Wild Turkey bourbon, pineapple with mint, and lemon and

chopped more finely and in part because of the questionable sign at Geno's that reads: "This is America, when ordering please speak English." While there are certainly better cheesesteaks out there, this corner offers a worthwhile cultural experience. Perhaps best of all, it is the only place where you can find cheesesteaks (and cheese fries if you really want to go all out) 24 hours a day. While you wait in line, be sure to check out the autographed photos of celebs on the walls of both – everyone from Justin Timberlake to Oprah has been here.

WHERE TO GET THE BEST
You're never far from a great cheesesteak in Philly. They're served in every neighborhood, at diners and in bars, out of food trucks and storefront windows, and even in restaurants serving upscale twists on the classic sandwich. Here are a few of my faves, but if you find yourself wanting a cheesesteak and not in close range of any of these spots, just ask a local to point you In the right direction. Almost as famous as Pat's and Geno's, and far superior, is **Jim's Steaks** (400 South St., 215/928-1911, www.jimssteaks.com, 10 A.M.-1 A.M. Mon.-Thurs., 10 A.M.-3 A.M. Fri.-Sat., 11 A.M.-10 P.M. Sun.), which has locations in West and Northeast Philly as well as on South Street.

Other great spots to try are: **Sonny's Famous Steaks** (228 Market St., 215/629-5760, 11 A.M.-10 P.M. Sun.-Thurs., 11 A.M.-3 A.M. Fri.-Sat.) in Old City; **Tony Jr's** (118 S. 18th St., 215/568-4630, 10 A.M.-9 P.M. Mon.-Fri., 11 A.M.-9 P.M. Sat., 11 A.M.-7 P.M. Sun.) near Rittenhouse Square; **Tony Luke's** (39 E. Oregon Ave., 215/551-5725,

© ANNA DUBROVSKY

www.tonylukes.com, 6 A.M.-midnight Mon.-Thurs., 6 A.M.-2 A.M. Fri.-Sat.) and **John's Roast Pork** (14 E. Snyder Ave., 215/463-1951, www.johnsroastpork.com, 6:45 A.M.-3 P.M. Mon.-Fri.) in South Philly; **Chubby's** (5826 Henry Ave., 215/487-2575, 11 A.M.-midnight Mon.-Thurs., 11 A.M.-2 A.M. Fri.-Sat., 11 A.M.-11 P.M. Sun.) in Roxborough; and **McNally's** (8634 Germantown Ave., 215/247-9736, www.mcnallystavern.com, 11 A.M.-11 P.M. Mon.-Sat., noon-8 P.M. Sun.) in Chestnut Hill.

*– Contributed by Karrie Gavin,
author of Moon Philadelphia*

---

ginger with Sailor Jerry rum. Ideal for a sweet ending to a date or a break in a day of shopping, Capogiro now has four Philadelphia locations (the others are at 117 S. 20th St., 3925 Walnut St., and 1625 E. Passyunk Ave.). A small cone will set you back almost $5, but it's worth every cent.

Naked Chocolate Café (1317 Walnut St., 215/735-7310, www.nakedchocolatecafe

.com, 10 A.M.–11 P.M. Mon.–Thurs., 10 A.M.–11:30 P.M. Fri.–Sat., 11 A.M.–9 P.M. Sun.) has been expanding waistlines and lightening wallets since 2006. It offers frozen and hot chocolate drinks, fine chocolates made in-house, and decadent baked goods. The father-and-daughter venture attracts well-coiffed locals, who come for the people-watching as much as the sugar fix.

CENTER CITY WEST

The western half of Center City is home to many of Philly's most elegant restaurants, but you can find a meal in any price range. The section of Walnut Street between Broad and 18th Streets is lined with restaurants, with additional options on side streets.

Markets

Di Bruno Bros. (1730 Chestnut St., 215/665-9220, www.dibruno.com, 9 A.M.–9 P.M. Mon.–Fri., 9 A.M.–7 P.M. Sat., 9 A.M.–6 P.M. Sun., espresso bar opens at 7 A.M. daily), Philadelphia's answer to Dean & DeLuca, began in 1939 as a small grocery store in the Italian Market. The original store (930 S. 9th St., 215/922-2876, 8 A.M.–6 P.M. Tues.–Sat., 8 A.M.–4 P.M. Sun.) still does a brisk business, but its selection of gourmet foods pales in comparison to that of the two-level Chestnut Street location. The latter is a popular lunch spot. Its upstairs café (11:30 A.M.–3 P.M. Mon.–Fri., 11:30 A.M.–4 P.M. Sat., 10:30 A.M.–3 P.M. Sun.) offers salads, sushi, deli sandwiches, and hot entrées. Both stores set out so many samples that it's possible to sate your hunger without spending a cent.

Mexican

Tequilas (1602 Locust St., 215/546-0181, www.tequilasphilly.com, 11:30 A.M.–2 P.M. and 5–10 P.M. Mon.–Thurs., 11:30 A.M.–2 P.M. and 5–11 P.M. Fri., 5–11 P.M. Sat., 5–10 P.M. Sun., $10–24) offers authentic Mexican fare in the elegant setting of a converted brownstone. You'll find high ceilings, dim lighting, and a grand bar stocked with more than 90 varieties of tequila. Start with the limey ceviche or divine guacamole and proceed to the finely tuned meat and seafood entrées (some of which are available in vegetarian versions). Wash it all down with a rose-infused margarita. And be sure to let the staff know if you're celebrating a birthday; they'll serenade you in Spanish and treat you to a shot of sweet tequila.

New American

Opened in 1996, **Audrey Claire** (276 S. 20th St., 215/731-1222, www.audreyclaire .com, 5–10 P.M. Sun.–Thurs., 5–10:30 P.M. Fri.–Sat., $16–24) remains immensely popular. The cash-only BYOB near Rittenhouse Square—a spec of a space—serves up Mediterranean-inspired dishes. The seared brussels sprouts with parmesan are unlike anything your mother tried to feed you. Owner Audrey Claire Taichman is also responsible for **Twenty Manning Grill** (261 S. 20th St., 215/731-0900, www.twentymanning.com, open for dinner daily, $11–24) across the street. Completely revamped in 2010, it has made a host of new fans with its lobster shepherd's pie, short ribs, signature burger, and other upscale comfort foods. Unlike its older sister restaurant, Twenty Manning sells alcoholic drinks. Both boast sidewalk seating.

One of the few restaurants directly on Rittenhouse Square, **Rouge** (205 S. 18th St., 215/732-6622, www.rouge98 .com, 11:30 A.M.–10 P.M. Mon.–Tues., 11:30 A.M.–11 P.M. Weds.–Thurs., 11:30 A.M.–midnight Fri., 10 A.M.–10 P.M. Sat.–Sun., bar open as late as 2 A.M., lunch/brunch $9–23, dinner $16–35) is always packed—usually with yuppies letting their highlighted hair down. Snagging a table from happy hour onwards can be difficult, especially when the weather allows for sidewalk seating, but you can enjoy a drink at the elegant bar while you wait. It affords an excellent view of the square. Prices reflect the prime location. Fortunately the food—American with a French flair—is quite good.

Coffee and Sweets

Local roaster **La Colombe Torrefaction** (130 S. 19th St., 215/563-0860, www.la colombe.com, 7:30 A.M.–6:30 P.M. Mon.–Fri., 8:30 A.M.–6:30 P.M. Sat.–Sun.) supplies beans to some of the chicest restaurants and hotels on the East Coast, including the eponymous eateries of celebrity chefs Daniel Boulud and Jean-Georges Vongerichten in New York City. Its flagship café is just off Rittenhouse Square. Don't be daunted by the line to the register, which has a tendency to stretch out the door. There's no menu overhead, coffee and espresso

© METROPOLITAN BAKERY

Metropolitan Bakery, Rittenhouse Square

drinks come in one size only, and pastry offerings are few, all of which makes for speedy service. For a wide selection of sweets, stroll to **Metropolitan Bakery** (262 S. 19th St., 215/545-6655, www.metropolitanbakery.com, 7:30 A.M.–7 P.M. Mon.–Fri., 8 A.M.–6 P.M. Sat.–Sun.) on the opposite side of the square. It's a wee wonderland of artisanal breads, handsome desserts, and treats that straddle the line, like a chewy loaf made with sour cherries and bittersweet chocolate. The millet muffins and French berry rolls are particularly beloved. Founded in 1993 by two alumni of the celebrated White Dog Café, Metropolitan now boasts five locations.

BENJAMIN FRANKLIN PARKWAY

There aren't many restaurants directly on the Parkway but plenty within a short walk. In 2010 the Philadelphia Museum of Art hired Stephen Starr, the locally famous restaurateur, to reinvent its eateries. You don't need a museum ticket to patronize them.

American

Located a short walk from the Art Museum in the Fairmount section of Philly, **Bridgid's** (726 N. 24th St., 215/232-3232, www.bridgids.com, 4:30–11 P.M. Mon., 11:30 A.M.–3 P.M. and 4:30–11 P.M. Tue.–Fri., 4:30–11 P.M. Sat., 11 A.M.–2 P.M. and 4–9 P.M. Sun., dinner $14–19) has all the right ingredients: affordable, delicious food, an impressive beer list, and a cozy atmosphere complete with fireplace. It's no wonder it's so popular with locals. The menu changes daily, but you can expect to find fresh salmon or tuna, prepared a little differently each day, along with comfort foods like honey-fried chicken. The fantastic Sunday brunch (11 A.M.–2 P.M.) features such dishes as cornflake-crusted French toast, spiced shrimp over buttered grits, and fried chicken on a waffle.

WEST PHILADELPHIA

It's a shame that so many visitors to the city never cross the Schuylkill River. West Philly, especially the section known as University

City, has a wide variety of restaurants, many of which can be enjoyed on a student's budget.

New American

The oldest continually operating BYOB in the city, **Marigold Kitchen** (501 S. 45th St., 215/222-3699, www.marigoldkitchenbyob.com, 5:30–9:30 P.M. Wed.–Thurs., 5:30–10:30 P.M. Fri.–Sat., 10:30 A.M.–2:30 P.M. and 5:30–9:30 P.M. Sun., dinner $20–31, Sun. brunch $7–14) has seen chefs come and go and reinvented itself again and again. The cozy atmosphere in the converted row home remains a constant. Marigold's latest incarnation as a new American restaurant has been well received. The menu changes on an almost daily base; don't hesitate to call and ask what's cooking. The Sunday brunch is not to be missed.

The one-of-a-kind (**White Dog Café** (3420 Sansom St., 215/386-9224, www.whitedog.com, 11:30 A.M.–10 P.M. Mon., 11:30 A.M.–midnight Tue.–Thurs., 10:30 A.M.–midnight Sat., 10:30 A.M.–10 P.M. Sun., lunch $12–16, dinner $20–36, bar menu $6–14) owes its success to longtime community activist Judy Wicks, who opened it in 1983 and went on to prove that progressive and socially conscious business models can work. Local farmers deliver organic produce and humanely raised meats to the restaurant, which composts in its backyard to reduce waste. Wicks sold her baby in 2009 but remains involved in its management. Housed in three adjacent Victorian brownstones, the restaurant can still be counted on for inspired contemporary American cuisine. If you're on a budget, have a seat in the bar and order a Leg Lifter Lager (the White Dog's private label beer) and a hot dog (all-natural, of course).

Information and Services

Located in the heart of the Historic District, the airy **Independence Visitor Center** (6th and Market Streets, Philadelphia, 215/965-7676, www.independencevisitorcenter.com, opens at 8:30 A.M. daily, closes at 7 P.M. Memorial Day–Labor Day, 5 P.M. in winter, and 6 P.M. during remainder of year) is a gold mine of information about what to do in Philadelphia and its environs. It also boasts one of the largest gift shops in the region. If you're driving to Philadelphia via I-95 North, you can load up on brochures at the state-run welcome center a half mile north of the Pennsylvania-Delaware line. Personalized travel counseling is available 7 A.M.–7 P.M. daily; the restrooms are always open. If you're the sort of traveler who likes to get the scoop before leaving home, you'll like the website of the Greater Philadelphia Tourism Marketing Corporation, **visitphilly.com,** and its companion blog, uwishunu.com.

Philadelphia has two major dailies: *The Philadelphia Inquirer* and the *Philadelphia Daily News,* which have been owned by the same company since 2006 and share the website philly.com. Both are morning papers, and that's about where the similarities end. The Inky, as *The Inquirer* is known, is one of the oldest and most venerable newspapers in the country. It's a broadsheet as opposed to the *Daily News,* a tabloid known for its sports coverage and quick-read stories. The Inky's circulation and Pulitzer Prize count trounce the tab's by about 3 to 1. But the *Daily News* isn't to be taken too lightly. In 2010 it snagged a Pulitzer for investigative reporting for a series that exposed a rogue police narcotics squad. Some public transit commuters get their news from *Metro* (www.metro.us), a free daily newspaper designed to be digested in 20 minutes. It's available at transportation hubs. When it comes to planning their leisure time, many young Philadelphians reach for the free weeklies *PW* (www.philadelphiaweekly.com) and *City Paper* (www.citypaper.net). The former is distributed on Wednesdays and the latter on Thursdays. Both keep a trained eye on the city's food, arts, and entertainment landscape. *Philadelphia* (www.phillymag.com), a monthly lifestyle magazine, has an affluent, older readership.

© KARRIE GAVIN

The Independence Visitor Center has a plethora of information on Philadelphia.

Getting There

Philadelphia can be reached by plane, train, automobile, bus, and even boat.

BY LAND

Philadelphia is an easy drive from several major cities: about two hours from New York and Baltimore and three hours from Washington, D.C. All told, about a quarter of the U.S. population lives within a half-day's drive of the City of Brotherly Love. While road trips can be fun, parking in Philly isn't. So even if you live within driving distance, consider taking public transportation. Options abound. **30th Street Station** (2955 Market St.), located just across the Schuylkill River from Center City, is one of the nation's busiest intercity passenger rail stations. It's a stop along several **Amtrak** (800/872-7245, www.amtrak.com) routes, including the Northeast Regional, which connects Boston, New York, Baltimore, and Washington, D.C., among other cities; the Pennsylvanian, which runs between New York and Pittsburgh; and the Cardinal, running between New York and Chicago. Amtrak's high-speed (and high-priced) Acela Express service cuts the New York–Philadelphia trip to an hour and 10 minutes. **NJ Transit** (973/275-5555, www.njtransit.com) provides rail service between 30th Street Station and Atlantic City, New Jersey. The Port Authority Transit Corporation, or **PATCO** (215/922-4600, www.ridepatco.org), provides rapid transit between Center City and points in Camden County, New Jersey.

The Southeastern Pennsylvania Transportation Authority, or **SEPTA** (215/580-7800, www.septa.org), is an uncommonly versatile public transit agency, operating buses, subway trains, trolleys, trackless trolleys, and commuter and high-speed rail trains. It

a train crosses the Schuylkill River

provides service to Philadelphia from innumerable suburbs as well as a handful of points in New Jersey and Delaware. In the New Jersey capital of Trenton, SEPTA's R7 line connects to NJ Transit's Northeast Corridor rail line, which continues all the way to New York City.

Thanks to competition among intercity bus companies, traveling to Philly can be dirt cheap. **Greyhound** buses (local 215/931-4075, general 800/231-2222, www.greyhound.com) collect Philly-bound travelers from all over the country and deposit them at 10th and Filbert Streets in Center City. **Megabus** (877/462-6342, http://us.megabus.com) offers daily service between Philadelphia and 10 cities including Pittsburgh, Baltimore, Boston, Washington, D.C., and Toronto. Its double-decker buses, complete with free Wi-Fi and power outlets, arrive at and depart from JFK Boulevard near the west entrance to 30th Street Station. **New Century Travel Bus** (215/627-2666, www.ntbus.com) provides daily service between Philadelphia, New York City, Baltimore, Washington, D.C., and Richmond, Virginia. Its Philly pick-up and drop-off point is near the intersection of North 11th and Arch Streets in Center City, spitting distance from Reading Terminal Market. Travel website www.GotoBus.com sells tickets for New Century and other "Chinatown bus" lines—so called because many trips originate in Asian enclaves.

NJ Transit buses travel between Philly and points in Jersey, including the popular Cherry Hill Mall, the beach communities of Cape May and Wildwood, and Six Flags Great Adventure in the town of Jackson.

BY AIR

Philadelphia International Airport (215/937-6937, www.phl.org), or PHL, boasts seven terminals, four runways, and about 600 daily departures to 120 cities. It's served by 20-plus airlines, including budget carriers Southwest Airlines, AirTran Airways, and siblings Frontier Airlines and Midwest Airlines. Among its amenities: children's play areas near gates A1 and D10, a full-service postal facility, Travelex currency exchange booths, and more than 150 stores and eateries, including duty-free shops for international passengers. Wireless Internet access is free on weekends, but a fee applies on weekdays. College students can dodge the fee by presenting a student ID at an airport information counter, found in each terminal.

Located seven miles southwest of Center City, the airport offers the usual array of ground transportation options, including rental cars, taxis, and shared-ride vans. Taxis charge a flat rate of $28.50 per trip between the airport and the "Center City zone," defined as the area bounded by Fairmount Avenue in the north, South Street in the south, the Delaware River in the east, and the Schuylkill River in the west, plus a portion of West Philly between the Schuylkill River and 38th Street. On trips from the airport, there's a surcharge of $1 for every passenger over age 12 after the first passenger. If you've flown in alone, it could pay to make a friend or two while queuing for a taxi. The flat rate and passenger surcharges are collected when the first passenger is dropped off, and the driver resets the meter before heading to the next destination. For travel from the airport to anywhere but Center City, metered rates apply: $2.70 when your tush hits the seat and $0.23 for each 0.10 mile, plus change for wait time in traffic. Trips from the airport are subject to an $11 minimum. A tip of 15–20 percent is customary. Drivers accept credit cards.

SEPTA offers rail service from the airport. A one-way trip to West Philly or Center City on its Airport Line (R1) is $7. Stops include 30th Street Station and Suburban Station at 16th Street and JFK Boulevard, both of which are major transit hubs. Trains pick up airport passengers every half hour from shortly after 5 A.M. to shortly after midnight.

The airport website has a directory of ground transportation providers. Call 215/937-6958 to chat with a ground transportation specialist.

BY SEA

OK, so "by sea" is a bit of hyperbole. Philadelphia, as we all know, isn't a coastal city. But it is a port city, and arriving by boat is possible in the warmer months. The **RiverLink Ferry** (215/925-5465, www.riverlinkferry.org, service daily Memorial Day–Labor Day, weekends in May and Sept., round-trip fare $7, seniors and children 3–12 $6) shuttles between Philly and its New Jersey neighbor, Camden. Sadly, the scenic trip across the Delaware River lasts less than 15 minutes.

Getting Around

A car is entirely unnecessary for getting around Center City. In fact, having one can be a downright pain. Street parking is a competitive sport, and parking garages are pricey. If you're able-bodied and not in a hurry, walking is the best way to explore the heart of Philly. You can flag a cab when your tootsies get tired. The extensive public transportation network can be intimidating, but studying it is worthwhile if you're in town for more than a couple of days.

A car is advisable if you plan to spend much time outside of Center City. Good luck getting to gorgeous Wissahickon Valley Park without one.

BY FOOT

Center City is eminently walkable. For one thing, it's compact. Just 25 blocks separate

the rivers that serve as its eastern and western boundaries. For another, it's easy to navigate. Founder William Penn is largely to thank for that, having called for a grid street plan. Most north–south streets are numbered. If the numbers are getting lower, you're heading east, toward the Delaware River. If they're getting higher, you're on your way to the Schuylkill. (It's worth noting that there's no 1st Street or 14th Street. What would be 1st is named Front Street, and what would be 14th is Broad Street, a.k.a. Avenue of the Arts.) A preponderance of east–west streets have tree names, as in Chestnut, Walnut, Spruce, and Pine. East–west Market Street separates Center City roughly in half. Addresses with an "S" prefix, as in 99 S. 17th Street, are south of

Market, and addresses with an "N" prefix are north of it.

A number of Philly outfits offer suggested walking tours. **The Constitutional Walking Tour of Philadelphia** (215/525-1776, www.the constitutional.com), which provides guided tours of the Historic District April–November, distributes a self-guided tour brochure with information on 30-plus sites. You'll find it at the Independence Visitor Center and attractions and hotels in the surrounding area. Interactive and printable versions are available on The Constitutional's website. The nonprofit **Preservation Alliance** (215/546-1146, www .preservationalliance.com), whose volunteers lead architecture walking tours of neighborhoods throughout the city May–October, offers several self-guided tours on its website.

BY TAXI

Taxis prowl the streets of Center City at all hours. In less trafficked parts of town, you can call for a cab. Taxi companies include PHL Taxi (215/232-2000, www.phltaxi.net), Yellow Cab (267/672-7391, www.ridewith pride.com), and Olde City Taxi (215/708-8888, www.215airport.com). All rides are metered with the exception of those between Center City and the airport, when a flat rate of $28.50 applies. The meter reads $2.70 to start, and the fare climbs by $0.23 with each tenth of a mile traversed. Any time spent in traffic also factors into the cost. Rates are regulated by the Philadelphia Parking Authority and must be posted in all cabs. It's customary to tip drivers $1 or $2 for rides within Center City and 15–20 percent of the fare for longer trips. Need a spiffier ride? Call Friendly Express Limousine (215/604-0861, www.felimo.com) for a luxury sedan or stretch limo.

BY PUBLIC TRANSPORTATION

Mastering Philadelphia's public transit system, commonly known as **SEPTA** (215/580-7800, www.septa.org), is no small thing. The multimodal system, which serves a five-county, 2,202-square-mile area, consists of almost

GETTING THERE IN A PHLASH

One of the cheapest and easiest ways to travel between Philadelphia's major attractions is aboard a **Phlash bus** (800/537-7676, www.phillyphlash.com). Operating daily May through October, the buses are easily recognized by their trolley-like exterior and purple paint jobs. The Phlash route stretches from Penn's Landing in the east to the Philadelphia Zoo and Please Touch Museum in the west, with stops at more than 20 attractions in between. You can pay $2 each time you board or purchase an all-day pass for just $5. An all-day family pass, good for two adults and two children ages 6-17, is a steal at $10. Younger children and seniors ride for free. Service begins at 10 A.M., and the last pickup time from most stops is between 6 and 7 P.M. The wait for a purple ride is rarely longer than 12 minutes. Stops include:

6th and Market Streets
Independence Visitor Center, Liberty Bell Center, Independence Hall

7th and Arch Streets
African American Museum

6th and Race Streets
National Constitution Center, Franklin Square

12th and Market Streets
Pennsylvania Convention Center, Market East Station, Reading Terminal Market, bus terminal, Chinatown

Juniper and Market Streets
City Hall, Masonic Temple, Pennsylvania Academy of the Fine Arts (two blocks north)

22nd Street and the Benjamin Franklin Parkway
Rodin Museum, Eastern State Penitentiary (six blocks north)

26th Street and the Benjamin Franklin Parkway
Philadelphia Museum of Art, Fairmount Water Works, Boathouse Row, Fairmount Park

150 fixed routes. More than 100 of those are bus routes. SEPTA also operates trolley lines, a high-speed rail line, commuter rail lines (known locally as Regional Rail), and two subway/elevated lines.

Trip planning is a cinch if you have access to the Web. Simply enter your starting location and destination in the Trip Planner feature on SEPTA's website, then click Plan My Trip. The resulting itinerary includes information on how long the trip should take and how much it will cost you. The base cash fare for bus, subway, and trolley service is $2. Exact fare must be used. Regular riders save time and money by purchasing tokens, which cost $1.55 apiece, or weekly or monthly passes. If your trip calls for switching buses or modes of transport and you're not a pass holder, be sure to buy a transfer or two at the start of your trip. They're $1 apiece. Transfers aren't required when switching between subway and trolley lines at the 15th Street/City Hall, 13th Street/Juniper, and 30th Street Stations. Regional Rail fares are a different animal. A one-way ticket can cost anywhere from $3.50 to $10 depending on where you're going, when you're traveling, and whether you pay in advance or on the train. Senior citizens don't pay a cent to ride buses, subways, or trolleys and get discounts on Regional Rail travel. Up to two children age four and under can ride for free with a fare-paying adult. Discounts are available for riders with disabilities.

SEPTA offers two one-day passes custom-made for tourists. Priced at $7, the **Convenience Pass** is good for eight rides on any bus, subway, or trolley route. The **Independence Pass,** valid for unlimited travel on all SEPTA lines and Phlash, is $11 per person or $28 for a family of up to five. The passes can be purchased at SEPTA sales offices, on Phlash buses, and online at shop.septa.org.

Brandywine Valley

As it winds its way from southeastern Pennsylvania to the northern Delaware city of Wilmington, Brandywine Creek crosses what geologists refer to as a fall line. In laymen's terms, it takes a nosedive. That nosedive made the Brandywine Valley attractive to water-powered industries—flour mills, cotton mills, and the like—in days of yore. In 1802 a French immigrant by the name of Eleuthère Irénée (E. I.) du Pont began construction of a gunpowder works along the creek, often referred to as the Brandywine River. It wasn't long before his company was the nation's largest gunpowder producer, and the du Ponts grew wildly wealthy. The Brandywine Valley's present popularity as a tourist destination has much to do with their wealth. It was a du Pont who created Longwood Gardens, one of the nation's premier horticultural attractions. It was a du Pont who built the magnificent Nemours Mansion and its garden, one of the finest examples of a formal French garden outside of France. And it was a du Pont who turned Winterthur, another family estate, into a showplace for American decorative arts. You'll hear a lot about the du Ponts if you pay the region a visit.

You'll also hear a lot about the Wyeths, often called America's first family of art. Three generations of Wyeth artists have lived and painted in the Brandywine region, capturing its people and landscapes on canvas. The Brandywine River Museum boasts a renowned collection of works by members of the uber-talented clan, including Andrew Wyeth, one of the most celebrated and influential artists of the 20th century.

The region boasts some cute-as-a-button towns, including West Chester, which brazenly bills itself as "the perfect town," and Kennett Square, the so-called Mushroom Capital of the World. More than 60 percent of the mushrooms consumed in the United States are grown in the Kennett Square area, and every restaurant worth its salt features a mushroom

BRANDYWINE VALLEY

soup. The annual Mushroom Festival, held the weekend after Labor Day, showcases mushrooms in every imaginable form, including ice cream. In recent years the Brandywine Valley has become associated with another crop: wine grapes. It's home to more than a dozen wineries, including Pennsylvania's largest.

SIGHTS
◖ Longwood Gardens

Longwood Gardens (1001 Longwood Rd., Kennett Square, 610/388-1000, www.longwood gardens.org, opens at 9 A.M. daily, closing time varies, admission $16, seniors $14, children 5–18 and students $6) is one of Pennsylvania's most exquisite spots, the sort of place people come back to again and again. It's unusual among horticultural showplaces in the Northeast in that it's open 365 days a year. In fact, Longwood is busiest not in spring or summer but from Thanksgiving through early January, when fountains dance to holiday music and ice dancers perform under the stars. Its 1,050 acres of gardens, woodlands,

© ANNA DUBROVSKY

Longwood Gardens

and meadows were shaped by many hands, but the greatest credit is due to Pierre S. du Pont (1870–1954), whose French-born great-grandfather founded the DuPont chemical company.

In 1906, Pierre purchased a property of about 200 acres from a Quaker family by the name of Peirce. The Peirces' 1730 farmhouse became his weekend residence, and the creation of Longwood Gardens began. Pierre drew inspiration from Italian villas and French chateaux but had a tendency to supersize. Longwood's Italian Water Garden, for example, was inspired by a garden near Florence. But where the original had only a few fountains, the Longwood version boasts 18 pools and 600 jets.

Budget at least an hour to take in the 20 outdoor gardens, including the otherworldly Topiary Garden, the Bee-aMazed Children's Garden, and the 600-foot-long Flower Garden Walk, whose beds are replanted with more than 120,000 spring bulbs every October. You'll need at least two hours for the Longwood

Conservatory, which houses everything from cacti to a colossal pipe organ.

Longwood's **Terrace Restaurant,** famous for its mushroom soup, offers both cafeteria-style and fine dining. The cafeteria is open 10 A.M.–4 P.M. Reservations are strongly recommended for the fine dining room, named 1906 after the year Pierre purchased the grounds; 1906 is open for lunch ($12–30) daily and dinner ($18–55) seasonally. Alternatively, bring a cooler of food and a bottle of wine. Longwood's picnic area, open mid-April through Christmas, has tables, grills, and restroom facilities. It's a short drive from the main parking lot.

Delaware's du Pont Sights

Longwood's creator wasn't the only du Pont with lavish tastes. The Wilmington, Delaware, area boasts three du Pont estates-turned-museums, each good for several hours of oohs and aahs. Just six miles south of Longwood on Route 52 is **Winterthur Museum & Country Estate** (5105 Kennett Pike, Winterthur, DE, 302/888-4600, www.winterthur.org,

10 A.M.–5 P.M. Tues.–Sun. early Mar.–mid-Nov. and daily during holiday season, general admission $18, seniors and students $16, children 2–11 $5), home to a vast collection of Americana and a splendid naturalistic garden. E. I. du Pont, who founded the company that made his family one of the wealthiest in America, purchased the land that would become Winterthur in the 1810s. But it wasn't until his great-grandson Henry Francis du Pont (1880–1969) got his hands on the property a century later that it evolved into the extraordinary estate it is today.

Henry doubled the size of the existing mansion, installing historical architectural interiors and filling the rooms with his burgeoning collection of American decorative arts. By the time the mansion opened as a museum in 1951, he had created 175 period rooms. First Lady Jacqueline Kennedy was so wowed during a 1961 visit that she invited Henry to head the committee overseeing the restoration of the White House. General admission includes an introductory tour of the mansion, admittance to galleries displaying highlights from Winterthur's collection of more than 85,000 objects made or used in America from 1640 to 1860, and free rein of the Winterthur Garden. A tram tour of the 60-acre garden is offered when weather permits. The last house tour begins at 3:30 P.M. Winterthur (pronounced "winter-tour") also offers one- and two-hour in-depth tours that cost an additional $12 and $22, respectively. Reservations are strongly recommended for in-depth tours.

While Henry amassed all things American, another great-grandson of E. I. du Pont lived in French-style splendor a few miles away. Alfred I. du Pont (1864–1935) built **Nemours Mansion & Gardens** (Rte. 141 and Alapocas Rd., Wilmington, DE, 302/651-6912, www.nemoursmansion.org, open Tues.–Sun. May–Dec., admission $15) to please his second wife, a Francophile who also happened to be his cousin. The spectacular Louis XVI–style mansion and formal French gardens, modeled after those at Versailles's Petit Trianon, reopened in 2008 after a three-year renovation to the

tune of $39 million. Tours depart three times a day Tuesday through Saturday and twice on Sundays, lasting 2.5–3 hours. Reservations are strongly recommended. Nemours is closed January through April.

Wondering how the du Ponts earned all that dough? Head to **Hagley Museum and Library** (200 Hagley Rd., Wilmington, DE, 302/658-2400, www.hagley.org, museum open 9:30 A.M.–4:30 P.M. daily, admission $11, seniors and students $9, children 6–14 $4), located on the site of the gunpowder works E. I. du Pont established in 1802, three years after fleeing France amid the turmoil and bloodshed of the French Revolution. In time the company established a virtual monopoly on the U.S. gunpowder industry, raking in more than $1 billion during World War I. Spanning 235 acres along the Brandywine River, Hagley features restored gunpowder mills, the remains of a workers' community, and the first du Pont home in America. Exhibits in the visitors center tell the story of the DuPont company, which evolved from America's largest explosives manufacturer into its largest chemical company. Shuttle buses bound for Eleutherian Mills, the du Pont home, depart from the visitors center every half hour 10 A.M.–3:30 P.M. (except from early Jan. to mid-Mar., when departures are limited to 10:30 A.M. and 1:30 P.M.).

Brandywine River Museum

Museums with an emphasis on regional art rarely enjoy international renown. The Brandywine River Museum (1 Hoffman's Mill Rd., Chadds Ford, 610/388-2700, www .brandywinemuseum.org, 9:30 A.M.–4:30 P.M. daily, extended hours for several days after Christmas, admission $10, seniors/students/ children 6–12 $6) is an exception, thanks in large part to one family with a surfeit of talent. Opened in 1971 in a converted Civil War–era gristmill, the museum on the banks of the Brandywine is home to an unparalleled collection of works by three generations of Wyeths. Patriarch N. C. Wyeth (1882–1945) moved to the Brandywine region in 1902 to study with famed illustrator Howard Pyle. He married and

Brandywine River Museum

settled in the village of Chadds Ford, present-day home of the Brandywine River Museum. Pyle's star pupil became one of America's foremost commercial artists, painting advertisements for the likes of Coca-Cola and Cream of Wheat and illustrating such literary classics as *Treasure Island, Robin Hood, The Last of the Mohicans,* and *Robinson Crusoe.*

Three of his five children also became artists, including daughters Henriette and Carolyn, who are well represented in the museum's collection. But it was his youngest child who made the greatest mark. Realist painter Andrew Wyeth (1917–2009) was the first artist awarded the Presidential Medal of Freedom, the nation's highest civilian honor; the first living artist to have an exhibition at the White House; and the first living American artist to have an exhibition at London's Royal Academy of Arts. His 1948 painting *Christina's World,* part of the permanent collection of the Museum of Modern Art in New York, is one of the best-known images of the 20th century. Born in 1946, son Jamie Wyeth was only 20

when his first one-man show opened in New York and less than 30 at his first retrospective. He's known for portraits of larger-than-life figures such as John F. Kennedy, Rudolf Nureyev, and Andy Warhol, as well as large-scale animal portraits. Hundreds of other artists, including Pyle and many of his students, are represented in the museum's collection of more than 3,000 works.

Audio tours are available for $3, but the best way to experience the museum is at the side of Victoria Wyeth, Andrew Wyeth's only grandchild. Daughter of his elder son, an art dealer, Victoria leads tours at 2 and 3 P.M. most Mondays through Thursdays and 1, 2, and 3 P.M. most Fridays. Some tours focus on her grandfather and others on her uncle. Tickets are free with museum admission and are issued on a first-come, first-served basis. Call 610/388-8326 to confirm her availability on a particular day. Private tours can be arranged for a fee.

For even more insight into America's first family of art, tour the **N.C. Wyeth House and**

Studio and the **Kuerner Farm.** In 1911, N. C. used the proceeds from his *Treasure Island* illustrations to buy 18 acres of hillside land in Chadds Ford. He built a house and studio and raised his uber-talented brood there. His daughter Carolyn, who studied with him for nearly 20 years, lived in the house and painted in the studio until her death in 1994. In 1932, when Andrew was 15, he came upon the farm of German immigrants Karl and Anna Kuerner, about a mile from his family's home. Over the next seven decades, nearly 1,000 works of art emerged from his fascination with the Kuerners and their farm. Both properties are now owned by the museum and open for tours from April through mid-November. Tours of the Wyeth clan's former home are offered daily except Monday, while tours of the farm are offered Thursday–Sunday. Tickets are $5 in addition to regular museum admission and must be purchased in person at the museum. Both sites are reached by shuttle bus from the museum.

Brandywine Valley Wine Trail

The Brandywine region boasts nearly a dozen wineries, including Pennsylvania's largest. Most band together under the Brandywine Valley Wine Trail (610/444-3842, www.bvwinetrail.com) banner, and the website is a good first stop on your wine-tasting journey. You'll find directions to participating wineries, their hours, and information on concerts, picnics, sales, and other winery happenings. **Chaddsford Winery** (632 Baltimore Pike, Chadds Ford, 610/388-6221, www.chaddsford.com, noon–6 P.M. daily, tasting $8) is a good second stop. Though it's the largest of Pennsylvania's 100-plus wineries, Chaddsford is hardly the large and impersonal operation that the distinction implies. Founded in 1982 by husband and wife Eric and Lee Miller, the winery occupies a renovated barn along U.S. 1, midway between Longwood Gardens and the Brandywine River Museum. Eric, who regularly leads tours of the winemaking and barrel-aging cellars, had already helped his father build a winery in New York's Hudson Valley. But he wanted to make world-class European-style wines, and to do that he needed superlative grape-growing conditions. The couple searched up and down the East Coast before settling in the Brandywine region. Their 30-acre vineyard is about half an hour north of the winery. Chaddsford, which produces roughly 25,000 cases a year, specializes in dry reds but also turns out award-winning whites and a different sweet wine each season. Fall's Spiced Apple, which can be served cold or hot, is a big seller. About five miles away is the vineyard and tasting room of **Penns Woods Winery** (124 Beaver Valley Rd., Chadds Ford, 610/459-0808, www.pennswoodswinery.com, by appointment Mon.–Thurs., 11 A.M.–6 P.M. Fri.–Sun., tasting $7), known for its Traminette, a hybrid white wine, and Ameritage Reserve, a blend of many grapes. The tasting room is an intimate space, so parties of six or more are encouraged to make appointments. The off-site winery can be visited by appointment.

Paradocx Vineyard (1833 Flint Hill Rd., Landenberg, 610/255-5684, www.paradocx.com, noon–5 P.M. Sat.–Sun., tasting $7) grows grapes and produces wines on one picturesque property. The 5,000-case winery is owned by two couples, all practicing physicians. (Hence its name, a play on "pair of docs.") The tasting room at the vineyard and winery is open only on weekends, but you can sample the full line of Paradocx wines any day in Kennett Square (The Shoppes at Longwood Village, 879 E. Baltimore Pike #B, Kennett Square, 11 A.M.–7 P.M. Sun.–Thurs., 11 A.M.–8 P.M. Fri.–Sat., tasting $7).

Kreutz Creek Vineyards (553 S. Guernsey Rd., West Grove, 610/869-4412, www.kreutzcreekvineyards.com, 11 A.M.–6 P.M. Sat.–Sun., tasting $7), which serves wine slushies at its summer concerts, is just four miles from Paradocx's Flint Hill location.

Bubbly buffs should head to **Stargazers Vineyard** (1024 Wheatland Dr., Coatesville, 610/486-0422, www.stargazersvineyard.com, noon–5 P.M. Sat.–Sun. or by appointment, tasting $5), first planted in 1979. The on-site winery, established in 1996, is the only one in the region to produce sparkling wines. Stargazers

PHILADELPHIA

is about 10 miles west of West Chester and 10 miles north of Longwood Gardens and Kennett Square.

Members of the Brandywine Valley Wine Trail collaborate on two "passport" events: the **Harvest Festival** (late Sept./early Oct.), a grape-stomping good time, and **Barrels on the Brandywine** (weekends in Mar.), a celebration of the newest vintages. Passports, which can be purchased online or at the wineries, entitle holders to tastings at all member wineries.

No longer a wine trail member but an absolute must for oenophiles: **Va La Vineyards** (8820 Gap Newport Pike, Avondale, 610/268-2702, www.valavineyards.com, noon–5:30 P.M. Thurs.–Fri., noon–6 P.M. Sat.–Sun., call ahead to verify hours, tasting $10–20), which produces small batches of unique wines, relying almost exclusively on its 6.73 acres of grapes.

QVC Studio Tour

A tour of QVC's world headquarters (1200 Wilson Dr., West Chester, 800/600-9900, www.qvctours.com, tours at 10:30 A.M., noon, 1 P.M., 2:30 P.M., and 4 P.M. daily, admission $7.50, children 6–12 $5) is to fans of home shopping what Universal Studios Hollywood is to movie buffs: a peek behind the curtain. Guided walking tours begin with a short video introduction to the TV retailer, founded in 1986 with the goal of providing "Quality, Value, and Convenience," and culminate in a bird's-eye view of the sprawling studio from a perch within earshot of the producer's booth. QVC broadcasts live 24 hours a day, 364 days a year in the United States, so the odds of seeing a program in progress are overwhelming. In addition to the regular tour, which lasts 60–75 minutes, QVC offers a three-hour "all access tour" once or twice a week. The $75-per-person tour includes lunch in the corporate cafeteria. Reservations are required and can only be made online. Don't underestimate QVC's popularity: It's not unusual for the pricey tour to sell out. The QVC Studio Store, open 10 A.M.–5:30 P.M. daily, offers an ever-changing selection of beauty products, jewelry, kitchenware, home decor, and other products.

American Helicopter Museum & Education Center

A stone's throw from QVC is the only U.S. museum devoted exclusively to rotary-wing aviation. Opened in 1996, the American Helicopter Museum (1220 American Blvd., West Chester, 610/436-9600, www.helicoptermuseum.org, 10 A.M.–5 P.M. Wed.–Sat., noon–5 P.M. Sun., last admission 4 P.M., admission $10, seniors $8, children over 2 and students $7) is home to more than 30 civilian and military helicopters, autogiros, and convertiplanes. Its collection includes the oldest existing U.S.-built rotorcraft, an experimental "flying jeep," and a prototype V-22 Osprey, which boasts the vertical lift capabilities of a helicopter and the speed of a turboprop plane. Most are displayed indoors, and some can be explored inside and out. Videos and exhibits chronicle the evolution of rotary aircraft. Call ahead if you're keen on taking to the skies. Helicopter rides are just $40 per person during **RotorFest** (Sept./Oct., admission charged), billed as the world's largest all-helicopter air show.

Newlin Grist Mill

Set within a 150-acre park, the Newlin Grist Mill (219 Cheyney Rd., Glen Mills, 610/459-2359, www.newlingristmill.org, visitors center open 9 A.M.–4 P.M. daily, park open 8 A.M.–dusk daily) is the only working 18th-century gristmill in Pennsylvania. The water-powered mill was built in 1704 and operated commercially until 1941, grinding wheat, corn, oats, buckwheat, and rye. Today it grinds corn into cornmeal that can be purchased in the visitors center, a former railroad station and post office. Adjacent to the mill is a two-story stone house built in 1739 for the miller. Admission to the park is free, but tours of the mill and miller's house are $5 per person. They're offered at 11 A.M. and 2 P.M. daily and last 45 minutes to an hour. On weekends tours are also offered at 10 A.M. and 1 P.M. There's no charge for tours during the **Fall Harvest Festival** (first Sat. in Oct., free), featuring demonstrations of period crafts, pumpkin decorating, hayrides, and other family-friendly fun.

The park attracts nature lovers as well as history buffs. Eight miles of hiking trails and the West Branch of Chester Creek, a popular trout stream, run through it. Stream fishing is reserved for fly fishers with a seasonal park pass. Pond fishing (9 A.M.–4 P.M. weekends Apr.–Oct., $5 per person plus $4 per fish caught) is open to all visitors.

ENTERTAINMENT AND EVENTS
Festivals and Events

The Brandywine Valley is horse country, and many of its main spring and summer events fall in the equestrian category. The equestrian season opens with **Point-to-Point** (302/888-4600, www.winterthur.org, early May, admission charged), a day of steeplechase racing and tailgate picnicking amid the splendor of Henry Francis du Pont's Winterthur estate in Delaware. Almost as impressive as the racehorses are the antique Rolls-Royces, Bentleys, steam autos, and horse-drawn carriages rolled out for the occasion.

The 80th running of the **Radnor Hunt Races** (Malvern, 610/647-4233, www.radnorraces.org, third Sat. in May, admission charged) took place in 2010. Proceeds from the steeplechase event benefit the land-preservation programs of the Brandywine Conservancy, the Chadds Ford–based nonprofit that operates the Brandywine River Museum. Admission passes must be purchased in advance.

Started in 1896, when horses were still a primary mode of transportation, the **Devon Horse Show and Country Fair** (Devon, 610/688-2554, www.thedevonhorseshow.org, late May/early June, admission charged) is the oldest and largest outdoor multi-breed horse competition in the country. The event, which has grown from one day to 11, has raised more than $14 million for Bryn Mawr Hospital in suburban Philadelphia.

Other equine-centric traditions include the **Ludwig's Corner Horse Show and Country Fair** (Glenmoore, 610/458-3344, www.ludwigshorseshow.org, Labor Day weekend, admission charged) and the three-day **Laurels at**

Landhope Combined Driving Event (West Grove, 610/486-6484, www.laurelscde.org, early Sept., admission charged), featuring the best carriage drivers in the country, an art show, and terrier races. Prefer polo? Sunday afternoon matches at the **Brandywine Polo Club** (232 Polo Rd., Toughkenamon, 610/268-8692, www.brandywinepolo.com, admission charged) are open to the public.

Festivities focused on wine and song abound in the warmer months. More than 20 wineries are represented at the **Wine and Jazz Festival** (610/388-5200, www.longwoodgardens.org, early May, admission charged) at Longwood Gardens. Chaddsford Winery (610/388-6221, www.chaddsford.com) hosts the **Brandywine River Blues Festival** over Memorial Day weekend, the **Labor Day Weekend Jazz Festival,** and outdoor concerts of various genres on Friday nights in between. Reservations are recommended for the concerts, which often sell out. Several other area wineries host summer concerts series. Visit the website of the Brandywine Valley Wine Trail (610/444-3842, www.bvwinetrail.com) for the rundown.

The two-day **Chester County Balloon Festival** (700 Ryan Blvd., Coatesville, 610/873-4002, www.ccballoonfest.com, June, free admission, $5 parking donation requested) is a chance to take flight or simply delight in the sight of mass balloon ascensions and fireworks. Can't stomach the $225-per-person price of a balloon trip? Tethered balloon rides are just $20.

It's not unusual for hundreds of people to run out of Phoenixville's Colonial Theatre screaming at the top of their lungs. It's tradition. Built in 1903, the theater provided the setting for a memorable scene in 1958's *The Blob,* and reenacting it is part of the town's annual homage to the sci-fi flick starring Steve McQueen. Started in 2000, **BlobFest** (227 Bridge St., Phoenixville, 610/917-1228, www.thecolonialtheatre.com, July, free and ticketed events) also features screenings of horror classics, costume and film competitions, and a street fair.

© ANNA DUBROVSKY

PHILADELPHIA

Kennett Square is known as the Mushroom Capital of the World.

Nearly 200 vendors hawk everything from mushroom-shaped jewelry to mushroom ice cream during the **Mushroom Festival** (610/925-3373, www.mushroomfestival.org, weekend after Labor Day, admission $2, free for children under 12), Kennett Square's annual celebration of its number one cash crop. The fungi-themed fête features mushroom soup cook-offs, mushroom growing and cooking demos, an antique and classic car show, and a community parade. Buses whisk festival-goers to local mushroom farms for behind-the-scenes tours ($5 per person).

ACCOMMODATIONS

As befitting a region known for mansions and gardens, wineries and horse farms, the Brandywine Valley has a healthy stock of elegant B&Bs. Fairest of them all is the (**Fairville Inn** (506 Kennett Pike, Chadds Ford, 610/388-5900, www.fairvilleinn.com, $170–265), with 15 rooms and suites spread between three buildings on five bucolic acres. It's conveniently located between Longwood

Gardens and Winterthur on Route 52, but guests have been known to forgo sightseeing in favor of an afternoon on their private deck, by their in-room fire, or in their canopied bed. Breakfast features a buffet of fresh fruit, yogurt, cereal, and house-baked breads and muffins, plus your choice of three hot entrées.

Set on 50 acres, **Sweetwater Farm Bed & Breakfast** (50 Sweetwater Rd., Glen Mills, 610/459-4711, www.sweetwaterfarmbb.com, $150–370) offers the ultimate country retreat. Choose from seven rooms in the manor house, with one wing dating to 1734 and the other to 1815, and seven guest cottages. The Greenhouse Cottage, featuring two bedrooms, a living room with a fireplace and panoramic pasture views, and a full kitchen, can easily accommodate two couples or a family. Five of the cottages are pet-friendly. Amenities include an outdoor pool, a golf green, a fitness center, and a massage room. Owned by Grace Kelly's nephew, Chris Le Vine, and his wife, painter Vicky Le Vine, Sweetwater Farm also boasts a recently planted vineyard.

PHILADELPHIA

© ANNA DUBROVSKY

Faunbrook Bed & Breakfast is less than two miles from West Chester.

For closer-to-town digs, **Faunbrook Bed & Breakfast** (699 W. Rosedale Ave., West Chester, 610/436-5788, www.faunbrook.com, $135–209) is an excellent choice. Less than two miles from the heart of West Chester, the 1860 manse has six antique-filled guest rooms and grand common areas. Once home to a U.S. congressman, it still has a dignified air about it. Breakfast is served by candlelight. The Arts and Crafts–style **Kennett House Bed & Breakfast** (503 W. State St., Kennett Square, 610/444-9592, www.kennetthouse .com, $135–195) is a short stroll from the heart of Kennett Square and a few minutes' drive from Longwood Gardens. With just four guest rooms and suites, it's small enough that inn-keeper Gilja Kusano has no trouble keeping everyone supremely satisfied.

Bed-and-breakfasts aren't for everyone, and the Brandywine Valley is not without recommendable hotels. The 70-room **Inn at Mendenhall** (323 Kennett Pike, Mendenhall, 610/388-1181, www.mendenhallinn.com, $145–229), not far from the Fairville Inn on Route 52,

has an old-world charm despite the fact that it opened in 1990. Each spacious room and suite is equipped with a microwave, refrigerator, coffee-maker, safe, and flat-screen TV. The hotel's sundry shop, fitness center, and business center are accessible 24/7. Rates include wireless Internet access and a breakfast buffet complete with omelet station. Fine dining is available in the on-site **Mendenhall Inn** (lunch 11 A.M.–3 P.M. Sat. Jan.–Nov., 11:30 A.M.–3 P.M. Mon.–Sat. in Dec., Sun. brunch 10 A.M.–2 P.M., dinner 5–9:30 P.M. Mon.–Sat. and 4–8 P.M. Sun., lunch $9–16, dinner $16–30), known for flambéed desserts and an over-the-top Sunday brunch ($26.99 per person, children 12 and under $12.95).

The European-style **Brandywine River Hotel** (1609 Baltimore Pike, Chadds Ford, 610/388-1200, www.brandywineriverhotel .com, $125–209) boasts room service by the excellent Brandywine Prime restaurant, one of its neighbors at the intersection of U.S. 1 and Creek Road. The Brandywine River Museum, a.k.a. the "Wyeth museum," is also a stone's throw from the 40-room hotel.

FOOD
Chadds Ford

Three noteworthy restaurants can be found near the intersection of U.S. 1 (Baltimore Pike) and Creek Road, a stone's throw from the Brandywine River Museum. A humble establishment, **Hank's Place** (1410 Baltimore Pike, 610/388-7061, www.hanks-place.net, 6 A.M.–4 P.M. Mon., 6 A.M.–7 P.M. Tues.–Sat., 7 A.M.–3 P.M. Sun., $2–16) is known for better-than-average diner food, including Greek specialties like gyros and spanakopita. Renowned painter Andrew Wyeth, who died in 2009, was a regular.

Chadds Ford's favorite son was also spotted at the upscale **Brandywine Prime** (1617 Baltimore Pike, 610/388-8088, www.brandy wineprime.com, dinner from 5 P.M. Mon.–Sat. and 4 P.M. Sun., Sun. brunch buffet 10 A.M.–2 P.M., $18–38, brunch $19.95 per person, children 4–12 $10.95), a seafood and steak restaurant with a superb Sunday brunch. Can't afford a meal of butter-poached lobster tail or grass-fed New York strip steak? You're not out of luck. A bar menu with burgers, sandwiches, and pizzas in the $9–14 range is available from 4 P.M. daily. Come on Friday for half-price burgers. Brandywine Prime's neighbor and sister restaurant, **Bistro on the Brandywine** (1623 Baltimore Pike, 610/388-8090, www.bistroonthebrandywine.com, lunch from 11:30 A.M. Mon.–Sat. and noon Sun., dinner from 4 P.M. daily, $8–22) serves French-inspired fare: artisan cheeses, fantastic salads, hearth-baked pizzas, hot sandwiches, and entrées such as steak frites and coq au vin. It offers a modest selection of craft beers and French and American wines; the corkage fee is a reasonable $5. (Chaddsford Winery, open noon–6 P.M. daily, is just a couple of miles away.)

Kennett Square

You need a reservation to eat dinner at ◖ **Talula's Table** (102 W. State St., 610/444-8255, www.talulastable.com, market 7 A.M.–7 P.M. daily, dinner 7–11 P.M. daily), and that's no small matter. The foodie heaven in the heart of Kennett Square accepts just one reservation a day—for that date *the following year*. Chef-owner Bryan Sikora treats one party per night to an eight-course tasting menu that's worth the wait (and the tab, which comes to roughly $125 a head). Fortunately, you don't need foresight to enjoy breakfast or lunch at Talula's, a gourmet market by day. Burgundy snails, artisanal preserves from Armenia, and other delicacies from afar compete for attention with house-made foods, which run the gamut from breads and pastries to barbecue sauce and spiced salts. Talula's even makes its own sausages, bacon, and other charcuterie with locally raised meat. Seating is sparse, so you may want to avoid the lunch rush.

The **Half Moon Restaurant & Saloon** (108 W. State St., 610/444-7323, www.halfmoon restaurant.com, 11:30 A.M.–10 P.M. Mon.–Thurs., 11:30 A.M.–11 P.M. Fri., noon–11 P.M. Sat., $8–32) specializes in wild game and Belgian beers. Its rooftop atrium is one of the most delightful dining spots in the region.

If you're visiting in the warmer months, save room for dessert at **La Michoacana Ice Cream** (231 E. State St., 610/444-2996, www.lamichoa canaicecream.com, noon–9 P.M. Mar.–Oct.), which makes its own ice cream, water ice, and popsicles. The Mexican-owned shop is known for exotic flavors such as avocado, rice pudding, guava, and sweet corn (sprinkled with your choice of cinnamon or hot chili powder).

West Chester

The county seat of Chester County has become something of a dining destination in recent years. More than 50 eateries representing a wide variety of cuisines can be found within its 1.8 square miles. Gay Street is particularly crowded with options, including **Gilmore's** (133 E. Gay St., 610/431-2800, www.gilmores restaurant.com, seatings every 30 min. from 5:30–8:30 P.M. Tues.–Sat., $24–29), an outstanding French restaurant. Chef-owner Peter Gilmore opened the intimate BYOB in 2001 after 22 years as chef de cuisine at Philadelphia's esteemed Le Bec Fin.

West Chester's main intersection of Gay and High Streets is home to an **Iron Hill Brewery**

& Restaurant (3 W. Gay St., 610/738-9600, www.ironhillbrewery.com/westchester, 11 A.M.–11 P.M. Sun.–Mon., 11 A.M.–midnight Tues.–Thurs., 11 A.M.–1 A.M. Fri.–Sat., kitchen closes at 10 P.M. Sun.–Wed., midnight Thurs.–Sat., 9 P.M. Sun., $9–25), one of more than half a dozen that have opened in Pennsylvania and neighboring Delaware since 1996. Even people who detest beer dine here. The food is that good.

Foodies have good reason to venture off Gay Street. Chief among them is **Carlino's** (128 W. Market St., 610/696-3788, www.carlinosmarket.com, 9 A.M.–7 P.M. Mon.–Sat., 9 A.M.–4 P.M. Sun.), a gourmet market with a mind-blowing selection of cheeses. Belly up to the Brie Bar for a custom-made hunk. There's much more to Carlino's than cheese, of course. Load up on cured delicacies at the olive bar and fresh greens at the salad bar, order a deli sandwich or something hot—a pasta dish or hearth-fired pizza, perhaps—and take your bounty to the **Kreutz Creek Vineyards tasting room** (44 E. Gay St., 610/436-5006, www.kreutzcreekvineyards.com, 11 A.M.–8 P.M. Tues.–Thurs., 11 A.M.–9 P.M. Fri.–Sat., tasting $7), a BYOF (bring your own food) establishment that serves up live music on Friday and Saturday evenings. For a truly decadent dining experience, drop by **Éclat Chocolate** (24 S. High St., 610/692-5206, www.eclatchocolate.com, 10 A.M.–6 P.M. Mon.–Fri., 10 A.M.–4 P.M. Sat.) en route and pick up some single-origin mendiants (melt-in-your-mouth chocolate disks) or rose-infused caramels. Owner and master chocolatier Christopher Curtin was the first American to be awarded the honor of German Master Pastry Chef and Chocolatier after nailing a five-day exam in Cologne, Germany.

For great Italian, great wine, and great desserts all under one roof, head to **Limoncello Ristorante** (9 N. Walnut St., 610/436-6230, www.limoncellowc.com, 11 A.M.–10 P.M. Mon.–Fri., noon–11 P.M. Sat., 4–9 P.M. Sun., bar open as late as 2 A.M., $10–35). Opened in 2006, the casually sophisticated restaurant specializes in southern

Carlino's Market in West Chester

Italian cuisine. Its weekday lunch buffet, featuring pizzas, strombolis, pastas, grilled vegetables, and more, is a steal at $9.95. Finish with the signature dessert: a flute of lemon gelato swirled with limoncello, a lemon liqueur.

Incidentally, parking in downtown West Chester is free after 5 P.M. and all day Saturday and Sunday.

A few miles south of downtown is the incomparable **(Dilworthtown Inn** (1390 Old Wilmington Pike, 610/399-1390, www.dilworthtown.com, 5:30–9:30 P.M. Mon.–Fri., 5–9:30 P.M. Sat., 3–8:30 P.M. Sun., $24–48), offering inspired American cuisine and a stellar wine list in a colonial setting. The original section of the three-floor restaurant, which boasts 15 dining rooms and walk-in fireplaces, dates to 1754. The ruins of an old stone stable provide the setting for outdoor dining when weather permits. Candlelight and dishes like wild Burgundy escargot and chateaubriand for two—carved tableside—make the Dilworthtown a romantic choice. Its wine cellar is one of Pennsylvania's largest

and a perennial winner of *Wine Spectator*'s Award of Excellence. Looking to improve your wine IQ? There's a class for you at **The Inn Keeper's Kitchen,** a state-of-the-art demonstration kitchen across from the inn. A course calendar is available on the restaurant's website. The Dilworthtown's neighboring sister restaurant, a stylish bistro in the body of an 18th-century general store, offers a more casual dining experience. "Hip-storic" is how the **Blue Pear Bistro** (275 Brintons Bridge Rd., 610/399-9812, www.bluepearbistro.com, 4 P.M.–midnight Mon.–Sat., $10–25) describes itself. The menu of small plates (oysters, prime filet carpaccio) and medium plates (seared rock bass, steak frites) lends itself to sharing. Head upstairs to sink into a leather settee.

Located midway between West Chester and Chadds Ford on Route 52, **(Simon Pearce on the Brandywine** (1333 Lenape Rd., 610/793-0949, www.simonpearce.com, restaurant open 11 A.M.–3 P.M. and 5–9 P.M. daily, store open 10 A.M.–9 P.M. Mon.–Sat. and 11 A.M.–9 P.M. Sun., lunch and Sun. brunch

Simon Pearce store

$10–16, dinner $19–32) is part glassblowing workshop, part shopping destination, and part fine dining restaurant. Were it not for its sister facility in Quechee, Vermont, you could call it one of a kind. Simon Pearce, a company named for its London-born, Ireland-raised, Vermont-based founder, is best known as a manufacturer of artisan glass and pottery, and the expansive store on the banks of the Brandywine carries a wide selection, including discounted seconds. You'll find Simon Pearce light fixtures, glassware, and tableware in the restaurant, where massive windows and two levels of seating afford every table a creek view. Canoes and tubes float by in the warmer months. The contemporary American fare outshines the ambience, which is no small compliment. Odds are good you'll catch glassblowers at work if you come Wednesday–Sunday.

Coatesville

The Whip Tavern (1383 N. Chatham Rd., 610/383-0600, www.thewhiptavern.com, 11 A.M.–midnight daily except Tues., $8–35) is an out-of-the-way place you won't mind going out of your way for. Opened by a native of Buffalo, New York, the English-style pub in the heart of Brandywine horse country is authentic enough to attract homesick Brits. Bangers and mash, fish and chips, Scotch egg, Welsh rarebit (melted cheeses swirled with beer and served with crostini for dipping), and other dishes popular across the pond share the menu with American favorites. A bias toward locally raised meats runs throughout. The Whip serves more than 50 domestic and imported beers and ciders, some of which you'd be hard-pressed to find elsewhere in the region. Prefer wine or hard liquor? Bring your own. The corkage fee is a kindly $2.50. Be prepared for a wait on Friday and Saturday evenings; reservations aren't accepted.

INFORMATION AND SERVICES

The Brandywine Valley is blessed with several tourism promotion agencies, each of which can provide a wealth of information about the region. Chester County, home to Longwood

Gardens and media giant QVC, is represented by the **Chester County Conference and Visitors Bureau** (610/719-1730, www .brandywinevalley.com). You'll find hundreds of free brochures at the Chester County Visitors Center (300 Greenwood Rd., Kennett Square, 800/228-9933, 11 A.M.–5 P.M. Mon.–Sat., noon–5 P.M. Sun.), built circa 1865 as a Quaker meetinghouse. You'll also find a free exhibit on the building's role in the Underground Railroad. The visitors center is adjacent to Longwood Gardens' main entrance. The **Brandywine Conference and Visitors Bureau** (1 Beaver Valley Rd., Chadds Ford, 610/565-3679, www.brandywinecvb .org, 9 A.M.–4 P.M. Mon.–Fri.) represents Pennsylvania's Delaware County, home to the Brandywine River Museum, and the **Greater Wilmington Convention & Visitors Bureau** (100 W. 10th St., Ste. 20, Wilmington, DE, www.visitwilmingtonde.com, 9 A.M.–5 P.M. Mon.–Fri.) represents Delaware's largest city and its surrounds, where the Nemours Mansion and Winterthur Museum are found.

GETTING THERE AND AROUND

Longwood Gardens, the Brandywine River Museum, and Chaddsford Winery, located within a few miles of each other along U.S. 1, are about 30 miles from the heart of Philadelphia. They're even closer to **Philadelphia International Airport** (PHL, 215/937-6937, www.phl.org), which is about seven miles southwest of Center City. Although the Southeastern Pennsylvania Transportation Authority, or **SEPTA** (215/580-7800, www .septa.org), connects Philadelphia to West Chester, Phoenixville, and other Brandywine towns, exploring the region without a vehicle of your own is tough. If you're dead set against driving, familiarize yourself with the services of the **Transportation Management Association of Chester County** (TMACC, 610/993-0911, www.tmacc.org) and **DART First State** (302/652-3278, www.dartfirst state.com), Delaware's public transportation system.

Bucks County

Like the Brandywine Valley, Bucks County offers a unique blend of bucolic beauty and a bustling arts and culture scene. Popular destinations include Peddler's Village, an old-timey shopping, dining, and entertainment complex, and the lovely towns of New Hope and Doylestown. All three lie along a 10-mile stretch of U.S. 202, about an hour's drive from Center City Philadelphia.

SIGHTS
New Hope
The village of New Hope boasts nearly 200 independently owned shops and galleries, a relatively vibrant nightlife, and a thriving gay culture. It's the sort of place that attracts art-collecting socialites and leather-clad bikers alike. Just across the Delaware River, the New Jersey town of Lambertville tries hard to keep up with its hip neighbor, so be sure to cross the auto/pedestrian bridge that connects them. There's no need to move your car to and fro: The toll-free bridge is less than a quarter-mile long, and the best parts of both burgs are within strolling distance of the river.

If you're a first-time visitor, get your bearings at the **New Hope Visitors Center** (Main and Mechanic Streets, 215/862-5030, www

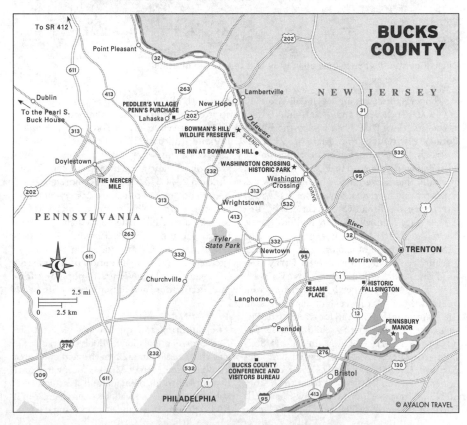

© SIMON HALLETT

Bucks County Playhouse opened in 1939 in a renovated gristmlll.

.newhopevisitorscenter.org, open daily from 10 or 11 A.M. to between 4 and 7 P.M.), built in 1839 as the first town hall. Then pop by the **Bucks County Playhouse** (70 S. Main St., 215/862-2041, www.buckscountyplayhouse.com) to see what's showing. Opened in 1939 in a renovated gristmill, the theater quickly became known as a place to catch premieres of shows that would later open on Broadway. Grace Kelly, Bea Arthur, Liza Minnelli, Robert Redford, Leslie Nielsen, and Merv Griffin have graced its stage.

Should you tire of exploring on foot, take a scenic cruise aboard the **Wells Ferry** (behind The Landing Restaurant, 22 N. Main St., 215/205-1140, www.newhopeboatrides.com, operates May–Oct., weekend departures on the hour noon–7 P.M., call for weekday departures, fare $10, seniors $9, children 2–12 $6) or **Coryell's Ferry** (22 S. Main St., 215/862-2050, operates May–Sept., regular daily departures, fare $10, children 2–12 $5, children under 2 $2). You'll learn a bit about the history of New Hope—which was known as Wells Ferry in the early 1700s and Coryell's Ferry

during the Revolutionary period—during the approximately 40-minute pontoon ride.

Alternatively, take a ride on the **New Hope & Ivyland Railroad** (32 W. Bridge St., 215/862-2332, www.newhoperailroad.com, operates year-round, hourly excursions $16.50–21.50, children 2–11 $13.50–18.50, children under 2 $3, call or check website for special event fares), stretching from New Hope to Lahaska. The tourist railroad has an authentic steam locomotive as well as historic diesel engines, 1920s passenger coaches, and an antique bar car. Hourly excursions give you the option of disembarking near Peddler's Village, a popular shopping destination, and taking a later train back.

The Mercer Mile

The quantity and quality of museums in Doylestown, population 8,200, is remarkable for a town its size. Four are concentrated in an area known as the Mercer Mile. Get an early start if you plan to hit them all, and wear comfortable shoes so you can walk between them. You'll find charming shops and eateries along the way.

Three of the museums owe their existence to one local genius: Henry Chapman Mercer (1856–1930), a lawyer by schooling, an archaeologist and maker of architectural tiles by profession, and an artifact hoarder by passion. In his 50s, Mercer poured his talents into constructing three edifices entirely of reinforced concrete. The first was his dream home, a 44-room castle with 10 bathrooms, 18 fireplaces, 32 stairwells, and more than 200 windows of various shape and size. He named it **Fonthill** (E. Court St. and Rte. 313, 215/348-9461, www.fonthillmuseum.org, 10 A.M.–5 P.M. Mon.–Sat., noon–5 P.M. Sun., last tour at 4 P.M., admission $10, seniors $9, children 5–17 $4). The National Historic Landmark is elaborately adorned with Mercer's own tiles as well as the Persian, Chinese, Spanish, and Dutch tiles he collected. Mercer also collected 7,000 prints from around the world, more than 900 of which are displayed at Fonthill. Access is by guided tour only, and reservations are strongly advised.

Next to his home he built a tile factory. A leading figure in the Arts and Crafts movement,

Mercer produced handmade tiles for thousands of private and public buildings, including the state capitol in Harrisburg and Grauman's Chinese Theatre in Hollywood. Reminiscent of a Spanish mission, his **Moravian Pottery & Tile Works** (130 Swamp Rd., 215/345-6722, www.buckscounty.org/government/departments/tileworks, 10 A.M.–4:45 P.M. daily, last tour at 4 P.M., admission $4.50, seniors $3.50, children 7–17 $2.50) is now maintained as a "working history" museum by the Bucks County Department of Parks and Recreation. Tours, offered every half hour, consist of a 17-minute video and a self-guided walk through the facility, where ceramicists press and glaze tiles in a manner similar to Mercer's. The fabulous gift shop carries reissues of tiles and mosaics in the Arts and Crafts tradition.

The polymath built his final concrete masterpiece, the **Mercer Museum** (84 S. Pine St., 215/345-0210, www.mercermuseum.org, 10 A.M.–5 P.M. Mon.–Sat., noon–5 P.M. Sun., $8 adult, $7 senior, $4 child), to showcase his enormous collection of early American artifacts. Determined to preserve the handmade

The James A. Michener Art Museum, along the Mercer Mile

goods being discarded in favor of machine-made versions, Mercer amassed more than 30,000 objects, from Native American implements dating to 8,000 B.C. and tiny clock-making tools to horse-drawn vehicles and a whaleboat. The collection, which has grown considerably since his death, is regarded as the most complete of its kind. Heads up: The museum isn't heated or cooled, so dress accordingly. Fonthill and the Mercer Museum are administered by the Bucks County Historical Society, which offers a reduced rate ($15, children 5–17 $8) for admission to both.

A stone's throw from the Mercer Museum is the **James A. Michener Art Museum** (138 S. Pine St., 215/340-9800, www.michener museum.org, 10 A.M.–4:30 P.M. Tues.–Fri., 10 A.M.–5 P.M. Sat., noon–5 P.M. Sun., admission $10, seniors $9, college students $7.50, children 6–18 $5), known for its extensive collection of Pennsylvania Impressionist paintings. It also hosts nationally touring exhibits and showcases important regional artists. A permanent exhibit celebrates the career of its namesake, a Doylestown native who rose to fame as an author, snagging a Pulitzer Prize for 1947's *Tales of the South Pacific* and a Presidential Medal of Freedom in 1977. The museum opened in 1988, about a decade before Michener's death, in a building that served as the county jail for more than a century.

Pearl S. Buck House

James Michener wasn't the only prolific, Pulitzer Prize–winning author who called the region home. Raised in China by missionary parents, Pearl S. Buck (1892–1973) settled on a Bucks County farm several years after winning the esteemed award for 1931's *The Good Earth*. There she raised seven adopted children and several foster children and started an international adoption agency that continues today. Now open to the public, the 68-acre estate (520 Dublin Rd., Perkasie, 215/249-0100, www.psbi.org, 11 A.M.–4 P.M. Tues.–Sat. with guided tours at 11 A.M., 1 P.M., and 2 P.M., 1–4 P.M. Sun. with guided tours at 1 and

2 P.M., admission $8, seniors and students $7, children under 6 free) features an 1835 stone farmhouse filled with Buck's belongings, including the Pulitzer, a subsequent Nobel Prize in Literature, and a silk wall hanging from the Dalai Lama. It's surrounded by gardens, greenhouses, and outbuildings including an 1827 barn. You'll find Asian giftware and some of Buck's 50-plus books in the gift shop.

Washington Crossing Historic Park

On December 25, 1776, General George Washington and his ragged troops crossed the ice-choked Delaware River from Pennsylvania to New Jersey. The following morning they marched into Trenton and surprised the heck out of Britain's Hessian mercenaries. Their victory at the Battle of Trenton provided a much-needed lift to morale and prompted new enlistments, paving the way for the successful outcome of the American Revolution. Washington Crossing Historic Park (Rte. 32, between Rte. 532 and Aquetong Rd., 215/493-4076, www.ushistory.org/washingtoncrossing, 9 A.M.–5 P.M. Tues.–Sat., noon–5 P.M. Sun.), which preserves their put-in site, consists of two sections several miles apart. The McConkey's Ferry section, near the intersection of Routes 32 and 532, features a visitors center, an 18th-century inn that served as a guard post during the encampment preceding the river crossing, several early-19th-century structures, and a 20th-century boathouse with replicas of the type of craft used by Washington and his men. The boats are used every Christmas Day in a reenactment of the crossing that changed the course of history. At the other section of the park you'll find more historic structures, the graves of soldiers who died during the winter encampment, and a 125-foot tower completed in 1931 to commemorate the Revolution. Open 10 A.M.–4 P.M. from early April through late November, the tower offers a swell view of the river and surrounding countryside. A towpath connects the two sections, so consider bringing a bike.

Pennsbury Manor

Nestled along the Delaware River, Pennsbury Manor (400 Pennsbury Memorial Rd., Morrisville, 215/946-0400, www.pennsbury manor.org, 9 A.M.–5 P.M. Tues.–Sat., noon–5 P.M. Sun., admission $7, seniors $6, children 3–11 $4, grounds pass $3) is the recreated estate of Pennsylvania founder William Penn (1644–1718). The devout Quaker preferred country living to the hustle and bustle of cities like Philadelphia, which he founded and planned (and retired to in winter, when the Delaware iced over). Pennsbury fell into ruin after his death, and by the 1930s, when the state undertook its reconstruction, no above-ground traces remained. Penn's original instructions and archaeological evidence were used to rebuild the manor house and various outbuildings, including a brewery, an icehouse, a smokehouse, a stable, and a blacksmith's shop. You'll also find a reproduction of the barge Penn used to travel between his country estate and Philadelphia. Ninety-minute tours are offered several times a day April–November and once or twice daily in the off-season. Call or check the website for tour times.

Historic Fallsington

Billed as "the village that time forgot," Historic Fallsington (4 Yardley Ave., Fallsington, 215/295-6567, www.historicfallsington.org, 10:30 A.M.–3:30 P.M. Tues.–Sat. mid-May–mid-Oct., by appt. Tues.–Fri. mid-Oct.–mid-May, admission $6, seniors $5, children $3) consists of more than 90 buildings dating from the 1600s to early 1900s. The village formed around a Quaker meetinghouse built in 1690. Pennsylvania founder William Penn worshiped and preached there while living at Pennsbury Manor, several miles to the south. Guided walking tours, offered every half hour during the regular season, visit three preserved buildings, including a 1760s log house. You're welcome to stroll through the historic district on your own (be sure to grab a pamphlet describing about 20 structures), but don't go turning any doorknobs. Most of the buildings are privately owned.

Sesame Place

Sesame Place (100 Sesame Rd., Langhorne, 215/752-7070, www.sesameplace.com, regular season May–Oct., open daily late May–early Sept., admission $53, seniors $48, children 23 months and younger free) is the nation's only theme park based entirely on the enduring children's television show starring Big Bird, Elmo, and Cookie Monster. Kids can hobnob with all their favorite *Sesame Street* characters in the 14-acre park, designed with the show's demographic in mind. Attractions include Cookie Mountain, a vinyl cone for pint-sized mountaineers, and Ernie's Bed Bounce, a giant air mattress for aspiring moonwalkers. Bring swimwear and a towel for wet attractions such as The Count's Splash Castle, a multi-level play area featuring a 1,000-gallon tipping bucket, and the adult-friendly Big Bird's Rambling River. Admission is pricey (and parking will set you back another $15–25), but tickets are good for a second visit in the same season. The park opens at 10 A.M. and closes between 6 and 9 P.M.

SHOPPING

Boutique shopping is one of Bucks County's biggest draws. New Hope, Doylestown, and Newtown are great places to stroll and spend disposable income. New Hope has a particularly eclectic mix of stores. You'll find everything from antiques to motorcycle leathers to Wiccan supplies along its Main Street. About four miles west of New Hope is the ever-popular **Peddler's Village** (Routes 202 and 263, Lahaska, 215/794-4000, www.peddlers village.com, open daily, hours vary), a 42-acre complex with about 70 specialty shops, six restaurants, a 70-room inn, and a family entertainment area featuring an antique carousel. Designed to evoke colonial America, the "village" hosts Bucks County's biggest annual event: the **Apple Festival** (first weekend in Nov., free). Other Peddler's Village traditions include a gingerbread house display throughout the holiday season, a Christmas parade, and the **Strawberry Festival** in spring.

Adjacent to Peddler's Village is an outlet center, **Penn's Purchase** (U.S. 202, Lahaska,

215/794-0300, www.pennspurchase.com, 10 A.M.–8 P.M. Mon.–Thurs., 10 A.M.–9 P.M. Fri.–Sat., 11 A.M.–6 P.M. Sun.), with about 35 stores, including Coach, Izod, Orvis, and Jones New York.

Flea market enthusiasts can also find their bliss in the region. **Rice's Sale & Country Market** (6326 Greenhill Rd., New Hope, 215/297-5993, www.ricesmarket.com, 7 A.M.–1 P.M. Tues. year-round and Sat. Mar.–Dec.), a 30-acre open-air market, hosts as many as 700 vendors on a typical day. The indoor/outdoor **Golden Nugget Antique Flea Market** (1850 River Rd., Lambertville, 609/397-0811, www.gnmarket.com, 6 A.M.–4 P.M. Wed. and Sat.–Sun.), across the Delaware River in New Jersey, is another gem.

ACCOMMODATIONS

You'll have no trouble finding distinctive accommodations in Bucks County, especially in and around New Hope. At the top of the heap: **The Inn at Bowman's Hill** (518 Lurgan Rd., New Hope, 215/862-8090, www.theinnatbowmanshill.com, $285–535), set on five idyllic acres on New Hope's outskirts. The romantic B&B was named best "weekend hideaway" in *Philadelphia* magazine's 2010 Best of Philly issue, and it's the only AAA Four Diamond lodging in the county. Its six guest rooms and suites feature king-sized featherbeds, fireplaces, and bathrooms with all the bells and whistles. Want a massage in the privacy of your room? No problem. Want breakfast in bed? No problem. Want to collect your own organic eggs from the resident hens? Feel free. The 134-acre **Bowman's Hill Wildflower Preserve** (1635 River Rd., New Hope, 215/862-2924, www.bhwp.org, grounds open 8:30 A.M.–sunset daily, visitors center open 9 A.M.–5 P.M. daily, admission $5, seniors and students $3, children 4–14 $2), home to 800 species of plants native to Pennsylvania, is a stone's throw away.

The **Logan Inn** (10 W. Ferry St., New Hope, 215/862-2300, www.loganinn.com, $120–195) is another excellent choice. Opened as the Ferry Tavern in 1727, it's the oldest continuously run inn in Bucks County and one of the oldest in

the U.S. It's no coincidence that lantern-lit **Ghost Tours of New Hope** (215/343-5564, www.ghosttoursofnewhope.com, 8 P.M. Sat. June–late Nov. and Fridays throughout Oct., $10 per person) begin outside its doors: The 16-room inn is said to be extremely haunted. Good luck booking the legendary Room 6 in October, when paranormal investigators flock to town. The Logan Inn is also known for fine food. Its restaurant (lunch 11 A.M.–4 P.M. daily, brunch 9 A.M.–1 P.M. Sat.–Sun., dinner from 5 P.M. daily, lunch $10–24, brunch $13–27, dinner $10–49, tavern menu $10–19) features steaks and seafood, and the patio is one of the best people-watching spots in town.

Just across the Delaware, **The Lambertville House** (32 Bridge St., Lambertville, NJ, 609/397-0200, www.lambertvillehouse.com, $200–385) also offers excellent people-watching. Have a seat on the porch of the hotel bar (Left Bank Libations), order a martini or single-malt scotch, and enjoy the parade of people crossing between Lambertville and New Hope. The boutique hotel, which dates to 1812, is a perennial winner of the AAA Four Diamond award and a Select Registry member. All 26 of its guest rooms boast jetted tubs, and all but three have gas fireplaces. Some even have a second fireplace near the whirlpool.

Wedgwood Inn (111 W. Bridge St., New Hope, 215/862-2570, www.wedgwoodinn.com, $95–295) owners Nadine and Carl Glassman are so good at what they do that they run training programs for aspiring innkeepers. The couple offers 18 rooms and suites spread between three 19th-century houses a short walk from the heart of New Hope and the bridge to Lambertville. Guests enjoy a continental-plus breakfast, discounts on tickets to the Bucks County Playhouse, and a tot of house-made almond liqueur when it's time to turn in.

Built in the 1740s, the **Black Bass Hotel** (3774 River Rd., Lumberville, 215/297-9260, www.blackbasshotel.com, $195–395) reopened in 2009 after years of neglect followed by a 14-month, multimillion-dollar renovation. The boutique hotel, situated along the Delaware about six miles north of New Hope, has eight luxuriously appointed suites, most with river views. Its riverside restaurant (breakfast 7:30–9:30 A.M. daily, lunch 11:30 A.M.–3 P.M. Mon.–Sat., Sun. brunch 11 A.M.–2:30 P.M., dinner 5:30–9:30 P.M. Mon.–Thurs., 5:30–10 P.M. Fri.–Sat., 4:30–8:30 P.M. Sun., tavern menu 3 P.M.–close Mon.–Fri., breakfast $24.95 per person, lunch $8–17, dinner $21–38, tavern menu $9–16) is renowned for its view, signature crab dish, and exquisite Sunday brunch ($32.50 per person, children 4–12 $18).

A few miles west of New Hope and only a minute from Peddler's Village, **Ash Mill Farm Bed & Breakfast** (5358 York Rd., Holicong, 215/794-5373, www.ashmillfarm.com, $130–295) offers spacious accommodations on a working sheep farm. Feeding the sheep and pygmy goats is permitted, but unlike some farm B&Bs, Ash Mill doesn't market itself to families with young kids (children 13 and older are welcome). So count on peace and quiet as you enjoy a massage in the cleverly named spa barn, The New Ewe. Children of all ages are welcome at the **Golden Plough Inn** (U.S. 202 and Street Rd., Lahaska, 215/794-4004, www.golden ploughinn.com, $129–359), with 71 rooms and suites situated throughout Peddler's Village. Many feature gas fireplaces and two-person whirlpools. Rates include a voucher toward breakfast in a Peddler's Village restaurant.

Convenient to the Mercer and Michener museums, the **Doylestown Inn** (18 W. State St., Doylestown, 215/345-6610, www.doyles towninn.com, $155–230) features 11 elegantly furnished rooms with mini bars and jetted tubs. Parking, wireless Internet, and a continental breakfast are on the house. An off-the-beaten path alternative: **Highland Farm Bed & Breakfast** (70 East Rd., Doylestown, 215/345-6767, www.highlandfarmbb.com, $160–300). Just minutes from the heart of town, the three-story manse was once home to Oscar Hammerstein II—as in half of the famous Rodgers and Hammerstein songwriting duo. Hammerstein (1895–1960) worked on the lyrics to *Oklahoma* on its wraparound porch and entertained such guests as Stephen Sondheim in its grand living room. Today the living room is the setting for wine and cheese receptions for guests of the four-room B&B.

Visit the website of the **Bucks County Bed and Breakfast Association** (www.visitbucks .com) for more options.

FOOD

New Hope and its across-the-Delaware neighbor, Lambertville, have several top-notch restaurants. A true original, ◖ **Marsha Brown** (15 S. Main St., New Hope, 215/862-7044, www.marshabrownrestaurant.com, lunch 11:30 A.M.–4 P.M. daily, dinner 5–10 P.M. Mon.–Thurs., 5–11 P.M. Fri., 4:30–11 P.M. Sat., 4:30–9:30 P.M. Sun., lunch $9–15, dinner $18–42) offers New Orleans–style cuisine and Southern hospitality in a former church complete with stained-glass windows. The dinner menu features upscale versions of Creole classics like gumbo ya ya and jambalaya, a raw bar, Maine lobster, and steak dishes. Come for lunch to soak in the stylish atmosphere (and sink your teeth into a Black Angus burger or po' boy sandwich) at half the cost.

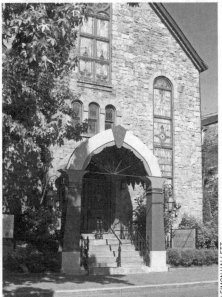

© SIMON HALLETT

Marsha Brown, housed in a former church

Housed in a restored 19th-century train station on the banks of the Delaware, **Lambertville Station** (11 Bridge St., Lambertville, 609/397-8300, www.lambert villestation.com, 11:30 A.M.–9:30 P.M. Mon.–Thurs., 11:30 A.M.–11 P.M. Fri.–Sat., 10:30 A.M.–9:30 P.M. Sun., lunch $9–16, dinner $17–30) is a superb choice any time of year but especially in the warmer months, when its outdoor dining area is open and the on-site herb garden is in full bloom. Specialties include Chesapeake Bay crab cakes and roasted rack of lamb. The Sunday brunch buffet (10 A.M.–3 P.M., $28.95 per person, children 3–10 $16.95), served in the ballroom of the 45-room **Inn at Lambertville Station** (609/397-4400, $125–305), is a worthy splurge. An à la carte brunch menu ($9–19) is available.

Peddler's Village (Routes 202 and 263, Lahaska, 215/794-4000, www.peddlers village.com), the popular shopping destination between New Hope and Doylestown, is home to half a dozen eateries. They include the **Cock 'n Bull** (lunch 11 A.M.–3 P.M. Mon.–Sat., Sun. brunch 9:30 A.M.–2 P.M., dinner 4:30–8 P.M. Mon.–Thurs., 4:30–9 P.M. Fri., 4–9 P.M. Sat., 3–8 P.M. Sun., lunch $8–15, dinner $14–36), which has been serving American classics in a colonial-style setting since the 1960s. All-you-can-eat enthusiasts flock to the Sunday brunch buffet ($21.95 per person, children $10.95) and King Henry's Feast 4:30–9 P.M. Thurs., $36.95 per person, children $18.95), featuring a raw bar, a hot buffet stocked with lobster and crab legs, and a carving station. In 2010 Peddler's Village unveiled a new restaurant, **Earl's Bucks County** (11:30 A.M.–10 P.M. Tues.–Sat., 11 A.M.–8 P.M. Sun., $8–36), with a frequently changing menu that showcases local foods. Both the Cock 'n Bull and Earl's Bucks County offer children's menus.

In Doylestown, try the **Pennsylvania Soup & Seafood House** (22 S. Main St., Doylestown, 215/230-9490, www.pasoupandseafood.com, 11 A.M.–3 P.M. Mon., 11 A.M.–7 P.M. Tues., 11 A.M.–8 P.M. Wed.–Thurs., 11 A.M.–9 P.M. Fri.–Sat., lunch under $15, dinner $9–25), which is known for exactly what its name suggests. Head chef Keith Blalock is known around town as "the soup guy." His lobster bisque, Tuscan onion, and mulligatawny make it easy to stick to a liquid diet.

INFORMATION AND SERVICES

You'll find a wealth of information about the region, including itineraries focused on wineries and covered bridges, on the website of the **Bucks County Conference and Visitors Bureau** (www.buckscountycvb.org). Its main visitors center (3207 Street Rd., Bensalem, 215/639-0300, 9 A.M.–5 P.M. daily) features an orientation theater, a large gift shop, and an interactive exhibit on the region's arts heritage. The CVB also has visitors centers in New Hope (Main and Mechanic Streets, 215/862-5030, www.newhopevisitorscenter.org, open daily from 10 or 11 A.M. to between 4 and 7 P.M.), at Peddler's Village (Routes 202 and 263, Lahaska, 215/794-3130, open daily from 10 or 11 A.M. to between 5 and 9 P.M.), and in Quakertown (2170 Portzer Rd., 8:30 A.M.–4:30 P.M. Mon.–Thurs., 8:30 A.M.–4 P.M. Fri.).

GETTING THERE AND AROUND

Central Bucks County, where New Hope, Doylestown, and Peddler's Village are found, is about 30 miles north of Philadelphia and 75 miles southwest of New York City. The nearest major airports are **Philadelphia International Airport** (215/937-6937, www.phl.org) and **Lehigh Valley International Airport** (800/359-5842, www.lvia.org), whose booking codes are PHL and ABE, respectively. Newark Liberty International Airport (973/961-6000, www.panynj.gov), or EWR, isn't much farther away. **Amtrak** (800/872-7245, www.amtrak .com) can get you to Trenton, New Jersey, 17 miles southeast of New Hope. The Southeastern Pennsylvania Transportation Authority, or **SEPTA** (215/580-7800, www.septa.org), provides regional rail service between Philadelphia and Doylestown, and **Trans-Bridge Lines** (610/868-6001, www.transbridgelines.com) offers bus service between New York City and New Hope, Doylestown, and Peddler's Village.

While you can certainly make do without a car in these popular destinations, you'll want one for traveling between them and exploring the surrounding countryside. If you're fit, of course, a bicycle will do. **New Hope Cyclery** (404 York Rd., New Hope, 215/862-6888, www.newhopecyclery.com, 10 A.M.–6 P.M. Mon.–Wed., 10 A.M.–8 P.M. Thurs.–Fri., 10 A.M.–6 P.M. Sat., 10 A.M.–4 P.M. Sun.), which rents mountain bikes, tandems, and child trailers, is a stone's throw from Trans-Bridge's New Hope stop.

Lehigh Valley

About an hour north of Philadelphia, the Lehigh Valley is better known for what it was than what it is. Home to the cities of Allentown, Bethlehem, and Easton, the region used to be a cradle of industry. Most anyone who owned a radio in the early 1980s knows about the erosion of its manufacturing base, memorialized in Billy Joel's "Allentown" *(Well we're living here in Allentown / And they're closing all the factories down / Out in Bethlehem they're killing time / Filling out forms / Standing in line)*. When Bethlehem Steel, once the second-largest steel producer in the United States after Pittsburgh-based U.S. Steel, made its last cast in November 1995, the hard job of redefining the valley began.

Today a casino stands on the site of the shuttered steel works. That's part of the "new" Lehigh Valley. But much of what's attractive about the region is really quite old. Bethlehem, founded in 1741 by Moravian missionaries, boasts more 18th-century buildings than West Virginia's Colonial Williamsburg. It's home to the oldest continually operated bookstore in the world, the Moravian Book Shop, and the oldest Bach choir in the country. Martin guitars, beloved by musicians from Johnny Cash to John Mayer, have been made in nearby Nazareth since the 1830s. The Martin Guitar Museum is a must-see for music lovers. (Alas, it's not open on weekends, so plan accordingly.) Crayola has been making crayons in Easton since the early 1900s. Its visitors center, The Crayola Factory, is a must-stop for pint-sized Picassos. Allentown, Pennsylvania's third-largest city, boasts one of the oldest fairs in the United States. The country's oldest drive-in theater is a 15-minute drive from town.

SIGHTS
Dorney Park & Wildwater Kingdom
One of the most popular amusement parks on the East Coast, Dorney Park (3830 Dorney Park Rd., Allentown, 610/395-3724, www.dorneypark.com) boasts 50-odd rides, games galore, and a 600-seat theater used for ice shows as well as song and dance revues. Among its rides is the Talon, tallest and longest inverted roller coaster in the Northeast. Its newest coaster, Possessed, features a 90-degree ascent and speeds of up to 70 miles per hour. Prefer tamer attractions? Dorney Park has plenty. Camp Snoopy, a two-acre play area themed around the Peanuts comic strip, is home to about a dozen tyke-friendly rides, some of which are scaled-down versions of park favorites. Dorney Park traces its history to 1860, when Solomon Dorney opened a fish hatchery and several picnic groves along Cedar Creek. By the end of the 19th century, Dorney's Trout Ponds and Summer Resort had grown to include a hotel and restaurant, a Ferris wheel and other mechanical rides, a bowling alley, and a swimming pool. The Whip, a mild ride added in 1920, and a wooden coaster built in 1923 remain in service today. Wildwater Kingdom, which opened in 1985, has two wave pools, two winding rivers, and about 10 major water-slide rides. Access to the water park is included in regular admission.

Dorney Park and Wildwater Kingdom are open daily from Memorial Day weekend through Labor Day. Dorney Park is also open several weekends outside of the summer season. The amusement park generally opens at

© STEVE WINTON

the Woodstock Express in Dorney Park

10 A.M.; Wildwater Kingdom opens at the same time or an hour later. Regular admission during the summer season is $43.99. Seniors (62 and older) and juniors (guests under 48 inches tall) pay $22.99. There's no charge for children 2 and younger. Two-day and "starlight" tickets are also available. Unless you have a season pass, expect to spend $10–12 on parking.

Dorney Park puts on a spooky face for six weekends leading up to Halloween. Its daytime look, **Boo! Blast,** is appropriate for all ages. **Halloween Haunt** (http://haunt.dorneypark .com), its evening look, isn't recommended for children under 13.

Drive-In Theaters

Opened in 1934, **Shankweiler's** (4540 Shankweiler Rd., Orefield, 610/481-0800, www.shankweilers.com) is the oldest drive-in movie theater in America. Prices hark back to the good old days: $8 per adult and $4 per child 3–12 for a double feature. And they don't sock it to you at the snack bar. A cheeseburger and funnel cake will set you back less than $5. About 15 minutes northwest of Allentown, the theater is generally open weekends in April and May and daily June through Labor Day. Weekends in September aren't out of the question.

About 10 miles farther north is **Becky's Drive-In** (4548 Lehigh Dr., Walnutport, 610/767-2249, www.beckysdi.com), which makes a point of showing child-appropriate movies on Fridays and Saturdays and offers pony rides to boot. In continuous operation since 1946, the theater boasts two movie screens and double features for $10 per adult, $5 per child 3–12.

Sands Casino Resort Bethlehem

In 2009 Bethlehem joined the growing list of Pennsylvania casino towns. The Sands Casino Resort Bethlehem (77 Sands Blvd., Bethlehem, 877/726-3777, www.pasands.com, open 24 hours) represents one of the most ambitious brownfield redevelopment projects in the United States. Built on the site of the shuttered Bethlehem Steel mill, it pays tribute to the one-time industrial giant with design elements such as brick walls and exposed steel beams. Orange tube lights meant to evoke glowing hot steel dangle over the gambling floor. Crystal chandeliers hang from large "gears" in a swanky lounge named Molten. Owned by Las Vegas Sands, whose portfolio includes The Venetian and The Palazzo on the Las Vegas Strip, the casino opened with 3,000 slot machines and plans to add as many as 2,000 more. Table games debuted in July 2010, three months after the state Gaming Control Board gave its blessing.

The casino is home to **Emeril's Chop House** (5–10 P.M. Sun.–Thurs., 5–11 P.M. Fri.–Sat., bar opens at 3 P.M., $22–40), celebrity chef Emeril Lagasse's first restaurant in the northeastern U.S., as well as **Burgers and More by Emeril** (11 A.M.–10 P.M. Sun.–Mon. and Wed.–Thurs., 11 A.M.–11 P.M. Fri.–Sat., $7–14), his first-ever burger joint. Other dining options include an Irish pub and an outpost of New York's famous Carnegie Deli. Initial plans called for a hotel and shopping mall to open at the same time as the casino, but economic conditions forced Sands to tackle the project in phases. The hotel, which will have 300 rooms and 22 executive suites, is expected to open in spring 2011.

Lost River Caverns

Lost River Caverns (726 Durham St., Hellertown, 610/838-8767, www.lostcave.com, 9 A.M.–6 P.M. daily Memorial Day weekend–Labor Day, 9 A.M.–5 P.M. daily rest of year, admission $10.50, children 3–12 $6.50), a panoply of stalactites, stalagmites, helictites, and other crystal formations, is just off Route 412 about five miles south of Bethlehem. Thirty-minute tours of the limestone cavern, discovered in 1883 during a quarrying operation, are offered at frequent intervals. One of its five chambers was dedicated as a nonsectarian chapel in 1949, and more than 80 couples have said "I do" there. It's a constant 52 degrees underground, so dress accordingly. The on-site Gilman Museum houses fossils, minerals, gems, and a collection of antique weapons. There's no charge for trailer camping or picnicking on the grounds.

The Crayola Factory

Despite its name, The Crayola Factory (30 Centre Square, Easton, 610/515-8000, www.crayolafactory.com, Memorial Day–Labor Day 9:30 A.M.–5 P.M. Mon.–Sat., 11 A.M.–5 P.M. Sun., fall/winter/spring 9:30 A.M.–3 P.M. Tues.–Fri., 9:30 A.M.–5 P.M. Sat., noon–5 P.M. Sun., admission $9.75, seniors $9.25, children 2 and under free) is not where the world's most famous crayons are manufactured. It's a kid-centric museum of sorts. Visitors can learn about the history of Crayola, which has called Easton home since the early 1900s, see how Crayola crayons and markers are made, and channel their inner Picasso using the company's latest products. (Don't miss the chance to paint with melted crayon wax.) Just outside is The Crayola Store, featuring the world's largest crayon. Measuring 15 feet long and weighing 1,500 pounds, the colossal blue crayon was made with crayon nubs sent by children from around the country.

It's a good idea to purchase tickets in advance if you're visiting during the busiest times of year: July and August, Thanksgiving weekend, winter break, and spring break. Tickets can be purchased online or by phone 8:30 A.M.–4:30 P.M. Monday–Saturday. The Crayola Factory shares a building with the National Canal Museum. Admission includes both attractions.

National Canal Museum

Easton is home to the only museum dedicated to America's towpath canals, the highways of yesterday. Created with kids in mind, the National Canal Museum (30 Centre Square, Easton, 610/515-8000, www.canals.org, Memorial Day–Labor Day 9:30 A.M.–5 P.M. Mon.–Sat., 11 A.M.–5 P.M. Sun., fall/winter/spring 9:30 A.M.–3 P.M. Tues.–Fri., 9:30 A.M.–5 P.M. Sat., noon–5 P.M. Sun., admission $9.75, seniors $9.25, children 2 and under free) is packed with interactive exhibits. Visitors can float a boat down a 90-foot-long model canal complete with locks and incline planes, learn how to harness a mule, and build a bridge. The museum also features an interactive exhibit on the Lehigh Valley's railroading heritage. Tickets are good for admission to The Crayola Factory, located in the same building.

If you're visiting in the summer months,

you can get a taste of canal travel aboard the *Josiah White II*. The mule-drawn boat plies a restored section of the Lehigh Canal in Easton's Hugh Moore Park (2750 Hugh Moore Park Rd.). Tickets ($9.25 per person, seniors $8.75, children 3–15 $6.50) can be purchased at the park. Combo tickets ($16.50 per person, seniors $15.50, children 3–15 $14.50) good for a boat ride and admission to the canal museum and The Crayola Factory are available.

Martin Guitar Museum and Factory Tour

The Martin Guitar Company is as rare as an original Martin D-45, which sells for as much as $1 million on eBay. For one thing, it's more than 175 years old. The company properly known as C. F. Martin & Co. traces its history to 1833, when Christian Frederick Martin emigrated from his native Germany, opened a music shop in lower Manhattan, and began making guitars in the back room. Five years later he relocated to the tiny Pennsylvania town of Nazareth, where Martin guitars have been made ever since. The fact that most Martins are still built in the United States distinguishes the company from so many manufacturers. Dynastic leadership also sets it apart. Current CEO Chris Martin IV is the great-great-great grandson of its founder. The Martin Guitar Museum (510 Sycamore St., Nazareth, 610/759-2837, www.mguitar.com, 8 A.M.–5 P.M. Mon.– Fri., free admission), located at the company's main facility, tells its unique story. Home to more than 170 rare guitars, including a D-45 built for Country Music Hall of Famer Gene Autry in 1933, also offers snapshots of music history. The list of seminal musicians who have played a Martin includes Elvis and Eric Clapton, Jimmy Buffet and Johnny Cash, Paul Simon and Sting, Buddy Guy and Beck. Visitors can get their hands on high-end and limited-edition models in the Pickin' Parlor or test out Martin's top-selling guitars and new offerings in the 1833 Shop, which also carries branded apparel, souvenirs, and collectibles.

Factory tours are offered at regular intervals 11 A.M.–2:30 P.M. weekdays. Guides give an overview of the 300-plus steps required to turn rough lumber into a Martin. The free tours,

Johnny Cash played a Martin guitar.

© ALEX HARDEN (ALEXHARDEN.ORG)

available on a first-come, first-served basis, last about an hour. Anyone with more than an idle curiosity in the art of guitar-making should pay a visit to the **Guitarmaker's Connection** (10 W. North St., Nazareth, 9 A.M.–4 P.M. Mon.–Fri.), located in the original Martin factory. The store offers a unique collection of luthier tools, guitar parts, and kits.

ENTERTAINMENT AND EVENTS
Festivals and Events

The **Pennsylvania Shakespeare Festival** (2755 Station Ave., Center Valley, 610/282-9455, www.pashakespeare.org), a professional theater company in residence at DeSales University, offers more than 200 performances of works by its namesake and other master dramatists from late May through early August. Founded in 1992, the company performs in two theaters in the university's Labuda Center for the Performing Arts. Bring a picnic dinner and a bottle of wine for the Renaissance-themed "Green Show," a free program held on the lawn prior to evening performances.

More than a million people pour into downtown Bethlehem over 10 days starting the first Friday in August. The draw: **Musikfest** (610/332-1300, www.musikfest.org). First held in 1984, the (mostly) outdoor festival features more than 300 (mostly) free performances on upwards of a dozen stages, dubbed "platzes" in honor of the city's Germanic heritage. Just about every music genre is represented, from Afrobeat to jazz to pop to zydeco. Musikfest is perhaps as famous for its official beer mugs as its music lineup. Mug holders enjoy cheap refills at beer tents and bars.

A tradition dating to 1852, **The Great Allentown Fair** (Allentown Fairgrounds, 302 N. 17th St., Allentown, 610/433-7541, www.allentownfairpa.org, week ending on Labor Day, admission charged) is unique among agricultural showcases in its track record of lassoing big-name entertainers. In 2010 the weeklong extravaganza featured pop sensation Justin Bieber, country superstar Keith Urban, prolific alt-rock band Weezer, and the legendary Rush, among others.

Inspired by the open-air markets held throughout Germany during the Christmas season, **Christkindlmarkt Bethlehem** (downtown Bethlehem, 610/332-1300, www.christmascity.org, Nov./Dec., admission charged) is a chance to stock up on holiday ornaments and handcrafted gifts, listen to live Christmas music, sample German fare, and watch ice carvers and other artisans at work. *Travel + Leisure* magazine named it one of the top holiday markets in the world.

SPORTS AND RECREATION
Bear Creek Mountain Resort & Conference Center

About 15 miles southwest of Allentown, Bear Creek Mountain Resort (101 Doe Mountain Ln., Macungie, 610/682-7100, www.bcmountainresort.com) offers snow sports in the winter and diversions such as mountain biking in the off-season. Opened in 1968 as Doe Mountain, the ski area has expanded to include 21 trails, four chair lifts, and three terrain parks. An adult all-day lift ticket is $46 on weekdays, $61 on weekends and holidays. Skiers and snowboarders 6–21 and 62–69 pay $40 on weekdays, $49 on weekends. Anyone 5 and under or 70 and over can hit the slopes for free. Four-hour tickets and evening tickets are also available. Snow tubing is an option on weekday evenings and all day on weekends.

Skiers staying at the rustic-chic **Inn at Bear Creek** (610/641-7101, $151–310) can defrost in indoor or outdoor hot tubs. Steps from the chairlifts, the hotel features 118 rooms and suites, indoor and outdoor pools, and a fitness center. Warm-weather amenities include a pair of lighted tennis courts and a five-acre pond stocked with bass. A handful of kayaks are available to guests. Nonguests can get in on the fishing for $15. The resort's hiking and biking trails are open to the public free of charge. Don't come expecting lift service. The ski slopes are off-limits in the off-season. **The Spa at Bear Creek** (610/641-7174) and **The Grille at Bear Creek** (610/641-7149, $8–29) are open year-round to guests and nonguests alike.

Dutch Springs

As scuba destinations go, Pennsylvania is no Cozumel. But it is lucky enough to have Dutch Springs (4733 Hanoverville Rd., Bethlehem, 610/759-2270, www.dutchsprings.com, general admission $10–24, children 5–9 $8–15, scuba diving $35 per day), one of the largest freshwater scuba diving facilities in the country. The 50-acre lake, a flooded former quarry, is as deep as 100 feet in some areas and boasts 20- to 30-foot visibility. It's filled with sunken treasures: boats, trucks, a school bus, a Cessna plane, a Sikorsky H-37 helicopter, and more. Divers and snorkelers also encounter a variety of aquatic life, including koi, largemouth bass, bluegills, and zebra mussels. The diving season begins in April and stretches into November. Dutch Springs offers air and nitrox fills and rents tanks and weights. (Call ahead to reserve rental equipment.) Divers must bring all other necessary equipment. A wetsuit no thinner than 7 millimeters, a hood, and gloves are advisable even in the summer, as temperatures at the bottom of the lake hover in the 40s year-round.

Non-divers can have a good time, too. Dutch Springs rents ocean kayaks (one-person $6 per hour, two-person $7 per hour) and paddleboats ($7 per hour). The Aqua Park at Dutch Springs, a cordoned section of the lake, features a water trampoline and inflatable water slides. For landlubbers, there's Sky Challenge, a combination rock-climbing wall and ropes course. General admission includes access to the Aqua Park and Sky Challenge, open 10 A.M.–5 P.M. daily Memorial Day weekend through Labor Day.

Tent and RV camping are permitted on Friday and Saturday nights (and holiday Sundays) May through October. Campers can avail themselves of two bathhouses with heated showers and toilets. Utility hookups aren't available, and alcohol and open fires are prohibited. The camping fee is $10 per person per night, or $5 for children 5–9, plus the next day's admission. No reservations needed.

Spectator Sports

In 2008 the Lehigh Valley welcomed its first Major League-affiliated baseball team since the Allentown Red Sox relocated to western Pennsylvania nearly 50 years earlier. The **Lehigh Valley IronPigs** (Coca-Cola Park, 1050 IronPigs Way, Allentown, 610/841-7447, www.ironpigsbaseball.com) have gotten off to a shaky start stats-wise, but that hasn't stopped fans from packing Allentown's new ballpark, featuring a 360-degree concourse. The team is the AAA affiliate of the Philadelphia Phillies, which made the World Series in 2008 and 2009, winning the first year and losing the second. Its name, an homage to the region's steel-making heritage, was derived from the term pig iron, which refers to ingots of crude iron that can be used to produce steel. Mascot Ferrous and his female sidekick, FeFe, owe their monikers to the chemical name for iron.

The **Valley Preferred Cycling Center** (1151 Mosser Rd., Breinigsville, 610/395-7000, www.thevelodrome.com) has been bringing the world's best track cyclists to rural Lehigh County since the mid-1970s. The velodrome hosts races most Tuesdays, Fridays, and Saturdays during the summer. Racing legends including Greg LeMond and Bobby Julich have been known to show up at its cycling-specific flea markets, held each spring and fall.

ACCOMMODATIONS

The Lehigh Valley's hotels and motels are mostly of the chain variety, but unique accommodations aren't impossible to find. The **Ⓒ Historic Hotel Bethlehem** (437 Main St., Bethlehem, 800/607-2384, www.hotel bethlehem.com, $149–299) fits the bill. Built in the Roaring Twenties to cater to clients of the mammoth Bethlehem Steel Corporation, the 128-room hotel features old-school grandeur, modern amenities, and a few friendly ghosts—or so it's said. It sits on the site of the first house built by Bethlehem's Moravian settlers, where on Christmas Eve of 1741 the missionaries named their community after the birthplace of Jesus Christ. The hotel's fine dining restaurant, **1741 on the Terrace** (www.1741ontheterrace.com, 5–9 P.M. Sun.–Thurs., 5–10 P.M. Fri.–Sat., $17–45), boasts views of surviving mid-1700s buildings and some of the best food in the Lehigh Valley. The more casual **Tap Room** (6:30 A.M.–11 P.M. daily, $7–30) specializes in comfort dishes. Its wild mushroom meatloaf is a top seller. If you're not staying or dining at the Hotel Bethlehem, at least stop in to see the set of murals commissioned from artist George Gray in the 1930s. Hung in the aptly named Mural Ballroom, they chronicle Bethlehem's evolution from religious settlement to industrial center.

The **Grand Eastonian Suites Hotel** (140 Northampton St., Easton, 610/258-6350, www.grandeastoniansuiteshotel.com, $139–159, weekly and monthly rates available), overlooking the Delaware and Lehigh Rivers, has a similarly long and rich history. Opened in 1927 as The Hotel Easton, it hosted the likes of Eleanor Roosevelt, heavyweight champion Jack Dempsey, musician Tiny Tim, and John F. Kennedy before running into hard times in the 1980s and closing its doors. When a New York–based nonprofit dedicated to sustainable development purchased it in 2000, there were still unfinished drinks on the bar and unmade beds in the rooms. In the ensuing renovation, which preserved the brick and limestone facade and the original entrance, 140 guest rooms were transformed into 30 condos—just in time for a major downturn in real estate. With more than two-thirds of the units still unsold in 2008, the building returned to its roots as a hotel. Its suites boast handsome wood floors, kitchens with slate countertops and stainless steel appliances, spa tubs, fireplaces, flat-screen TVs, and free high-speed Internet. An indoor pool, a fitness center, and free parking round out the amenities.

The **Sayre Mansion Inn** (250 Wyandotte St., Bethlehem, 610/882-2100, www.sayremansion.com, $160–325) is another excellent choice in town. Built in the 1850s for the chief engineer of the Lehigh Valley Railroad, the Gothic Revival–style mansion has nearly 20 guest rooms and suites, including a unique glass-topped room known as the Conservatory. The recently refurbished carriage house, built at the same time as the main house, boasts three spacious suites with original hardwood floors. Breakfast is an elegant affair.

For a romantic getaway, the **Glasbern Country Inn** (2141 Pack House Rd., Fogelsville, 610/285-4723, www.glasbern.com, $150–475) is unrivaled in the region. Located on a 100-acre working farm just west of Allentown, it features 38 rooms and suites in seven renovated farm buildings. The former stables house loft suites with cathedral ceilings and spiral staircases leading to a large whirlpool. Rates include a hearty breakfast complete with house-made granola and bread. By evening the dining room transforms into a fine dining restaurant (seatings 5:30–8:30 P.M., reservations required) serving contemporary American cuisine. The farm's pasture-raised meat plays a prominent role in the seasonal menus. The restaurant offers an à la carte menu ($18–38) Sunday through Friday and a prix fixe ($55 per person) on Saturdays. An adjacent pub offers a more casual dining option.

FOOD

The sting of Bethlehem Steel's demise was still fresh when the **Bethlehem Brew Works** (569 Main St., Bethlehem, 610/882-1300, www.thebrewworks.com, 11 A.M.–11 P.M. Sun.–Wed., 11 A.M.–midnight Thurs.–Sat., bar open until 2 A.M. daily, $8–29) opened in 1998. So it was only fitting that the brewpub pay tribute to the region's steelmaking heritage. Brick walls, exposed ducts, and furnishings accented with textured sheet metal contribute to an industrial vibe. A mural of Bethlehem Steel's once-mighty blast furnaces flanks gleaming beer tanks, where brews such as Steelworker's Oatmeal Stout and Blastberry Wheat mature. The food is respectable. Specialties include the Foundry Bratwurst, a locally made sausage topped with sauerkraut soaked in the Brew Works' own Valley Golden Ale, and a pulled-pork sandwich with beer-infused barbecue sauce. Picky eaters will appreciate the option to "forge" their own beef, turkey, chicken, or veggie burger. The Brew Works isn't afraid to showcase beverages besides its own. It prides itself on its selection of single malt scotches and small-batch bourbons. Head to the Steelgaarden lounge downstairs from the restaurant for a menu of more than 100 bottled Belgian beers.

In 2007 an abandoned furniture store building in downtown Allentown was reborn as the **Allentown Brew Works** (812 W. Hamilton St., Allentown, 610/433-7777, 11 A.M.–11 P.M. Sun.–Thurs., 11 A.M.–midnight Fri.–Sat., bar open until midnight Sun.–Thurs. and 2 A.M. Fri.–Sat.). The steel theme of the Bethlehem original wasn't carried over, but the menu is largely the same. The place is massive. Mingle with mostly professional 20- to 50-somethings on the ground floor or enjoy a bird's-eye view from a table on the mezzanine. Popular on weekends, the second-floor High Gravity lounge specializes in high-alcohol beers like Weyerbacher Blasphemy (11.8 percent) and Samichlaus (14 percent), brewed in Austria once a year. The lower-level Silk has the hallmarks of an ultra lounge, including a VIP area and bottle service. A patio area dubbed Der Biergarten rounds out the array of atmospheres. In 2009 a third Brew Works opened at the Allentown Municipal Golf Course. **Brew Works on the Green** (3400 W. Tilghman St., Allentown, 484/223-2020) serves breakfast, lunch, and dinner seven days a week.

For contemporary Italian cuisine and a little shopping on the side, head to **Melt** (2805 Center Valley Parkway, Center Valley, 610/798-9000, www.meltgrill.com, 11 A.M.–11 P.M. Mon.–Thurs., 11 A.M.–midnight Fri.–Sat., 11 A.M.–10 P.M. Sun., lunch $9–35, dinner $13–39). Located at The Promenade Shops at Saucon Valley, an upscale "lifestyle center" between Allentown and Bethlehem, the 350-seat restaurant offers the likes of bresaola (air-cured beef), osso bucco, and *spiedini* (skewers of mixed seafood). With its floor-to-ceiling wine wall, curved banquettes, and cylindrical chandeliers, it wouldn't be out of place in L.A. or Las Vegas. Its rooftop lounge, Level3 (www.level3lounge.com, 5 P.M.–2 A.M. Thurs.–Sat. in summer), is as swanky as it gets in the Lehigh Valley. Melt is not to be confused with Bethlehem's **Melting Pot** (1 E. Broad St., Bethlehem, 484/241-4939, www.melting pot.com, 5–10 P.M. Mon.–Thurs., 5–11 P.M.

Fri., 4–11 P.M. Sat., 4–9 P.M. Sun., $16–28) franchise, which specializes in fondue.

For Italian in an intimate setting, it doesn't get better than **Sette Luna** (219 Ferry St., Easton, 610/253-8888, www.setteluna.com, 11:30 A.M.–9:30 P.M. Mon.–Thurs., 11:30 A.M.–10:30 P.M. Fri., noon–10:30 P.M. Sat., 10:30 A.M.–9 P.M. Sun., lunch $7–20, dinner $11–24, Sunday brunch $9–15). The trattoria in Easton's historic district is known for its crispy pizzas, house-made desserts, and Sunday jazz brunch.

INFORMATION AND SERVICES

Discover Lehigh Valley (610/882-9200, www.discoverlehighvalley.com), the region's official tourism promotion agency, is a great source of information. Visit the website to request free brochures or page through a digital version of the *Lehigh Valley Map & Guide*. If you're already in the area, you can load up on brochures at visitors centers in Allentown (840 Hamilton St., 610/973-2140, 10 A.M.–4 P.M. Mon.–Fri.), Bethlehem (505 Main St., 610/691-6055, 10 A.M.–5 P.M. Tues.–Sat., noon–5 P.M. Sun.), and Easton (National Canal Museum, 30 Center Square, 484/546-0594, 9:30 A.M.–5 P.M. Mon.–Sat., 11 A.M.–5 P.M. Sun.).

GETTING THERE AND AROUND

Allentown, the largest city in the Lehigh Valley, is about 60 miles north of Philadelphia and 90 miles east of New York City. It's accessible via I-78 and I-476. **Lehigh Valley International Airport** (800/359-5842, www.lvia.org), with a booking code of ABE, is less than 10 miles from downtown Allentown and Bethlehem. It's served by airlines including US Airways, United, Delta, and low-cost AirTran. Intercity bus service to the area is available through **Greyhound** (800/231-2222, www.greyhound.com) and its interline partners. Local bus service is provided by the **Lehigh and Northampton Transportation Authority** (610/776-7433, www.lantabus.com), or LANTA.

PENNSYLVANIA DUTCH COUNTRY

The portion of the state referred to as Pennsylvania Dutch Country has no blockbuster cities. Its largest, Reading, has a mere 80,000 residents. And yet it receives more visitors than Philadelphia, more visitors than Pittsburgh—more visitors than any other region in the state. Part of the reason is the public's fascination with the Amish, whose way of life is in sharp contrast to the average American's. Lancaster County, the most popular destination in Dutch Country, boasts the largest concentration of Amish in the world. Their use of horse-drawn buggies, adherence to strict dress codes, and rejection of technologies including television and computers makes them exotic. A casual drive through Lancaster County's fertile farmlands has a safari-esque quality. ("Look, honey, buggy at 3 o'clock!") Unlike giraffes and elephants, the Amish take offense to being photographed, so resist the temptation to aim your camera at the farmer working his fields with mule-drawn equipment, the children driving a pony cart, or the women selling their pies and preserves at a market stand.

There's more to the region's allure than the Amish experience. Less than 40 miles from the heart of Amish country is the town of Hershey, the product of one chocolatier's expansive vision. Few places offer as high a concentration of family-friendly attractions as the "Sweetest Place on Earth." In the southern part of Pennsylvania Dutch Country is the town of Gettysburg, site of the Civil War's bloodiest battle and President Abraham Lincoln's most memorable speech. The place throbs with history—and not just on days when it's awash

DUTCH COUNTRY

HIGHLIGHTS

◖ **Amish Attractions:** If you learned everything you know about the Amish from the movie *Witness*, you've got a lot to learn. Get schooled at Plain & Fancy Farm, the Amish Farm and House, or the Mennonite Information Center (page 136).

◖ **Strasburg Rail Road** and the **Railroad Museum of Pennsylvania:** The nation's oldest operating short-line railroad and the state's official train museum are across-the-street neighbors in "Train Town USA" (page 146).

◖ **Air Museums:** With two aviation museums within 20 miles of each other, greater Reading could well be called "Plane Town USA." Take to the skies in an antique plane, or take a trip back in time during the Mid-Atlantic Air Museum's World War II Weekend (page 181).

◖ **Hawk Mountain Sanctuary:** Some 20,000 hawks, eagles, and falcons soar past this raptor sanctuary on their southward journeys. The sight is awe-inspiring and the hiking terrific (page 183).

◖ **The Hershey Story:** One of Pennsylvania's newest museums, The Hershey Story offers hands-on experience in chocolate-making (page 194).

◖ **Hersheypark:** Hershey's century-old amusement park has been adding coasters like they're going out of style (page 195).

◖ **Gettysburg National Military Park:** Site of the Civil War's most hellish battle, this national park is heaven for history buffs (page 234).

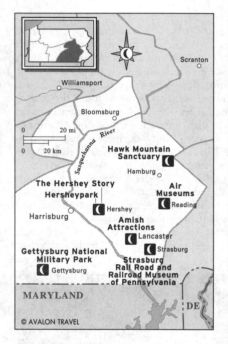

LOOK FOR ◖ TO FIND RECOMMENDED SIGHTS, ACTIVITIES, DINING, AND LODGING.

with musket-toting reenactors. The region is also home to the state capital, Harrisburg, and York County, the self-proclaimed "Factory Tour Capital of the World."

Travelers unfamiliar with the term Pennsylvania Dutch may wonder what south-central Pennsylvania has to do with the Netherlands. The answer is: nada. "Dutch," in this case, is generally regarded as a corruption of the word *Deutsch,* the German word for "German." Tens of thousands of

German-speaking Europeans immigrated to Pennsylvania in the 18th century (before Germany as we know it existed). They, their descendants, and their English-influenced dialect came to be called Pennsylvania German, or Pennsylvania Dutch. A common misconception is that "Pennsylvania Dutch" is synonymous with "Amish." In fact, the Amish made up a very small percentage of the Germanic settlers. The overwhelming majority were affiliated with Lutheran or Reformed churches. But the Amish

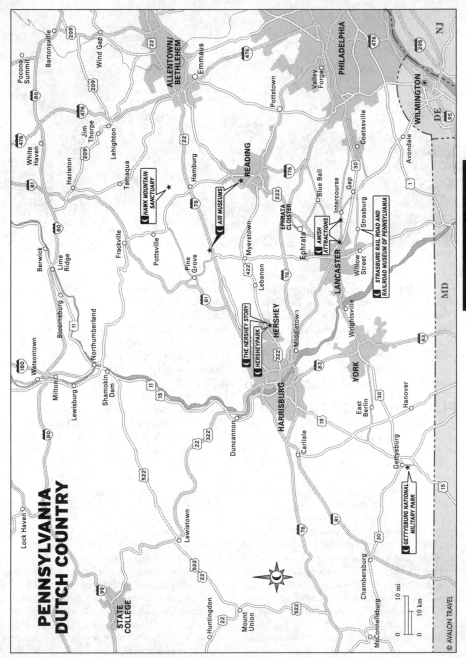

PENNSYLVANIA
DUTCH COUNTRY

© AVALON TRAVEL

laundry day in Lancaster County

and a handful of related "plain" groups have emerged as the guardians of the Pennsylvania Dutch dialect. They speak it at home and among friends. Amish children learn English as part of their formal education, which typically takes place in a one-room schoolhouse (think *Little House on the Prairie*) and ends after the eighth grade. *Wilkom* to Pennsylvania Dutch Country.

PLANNING YOUR TIME

You could spend weeks exploring the small, smaller, and smallest towns of Pennsylvania Dutch Country, but three or four days is sufficient time to hit the highlights. Plan to spend at least a day tootling around Lancaster County's Amish countryside, sharing the roads with horse-drawn buggies and buying direct from farmers and bakers, quilters and furniture makers. Keep in mind that the Amish and their "plain" cousins don't do business on Sundays. See to it that you eat at a restaurant serving Pennsylvania Dutch fare, preferably one that offers family-style dining. If your agenda also includes outlet shopping, save it for the evening. The Rockvale and Tanger outlets, just minutes apart along Lancaster County's main east–west thoroughfare, are open until 9 P.M. every day but Sunday,

when they close a few hours earlier. Anyone into antiques should plan to spend Sunday in Adamstown, a.k.a. "Antiques Capital USA," about 20 miles northeast of Lancaster city.

The Lancaster area is a good base of operations for exploring other parts of Pennsylvania Dutch Country. Reading is about 30 miles to Lancaster's northeast, Hershey and Harrisburg are 30–40 miles to its northwest, and Gettysburg is 55 miles to its southwest. There was a time when demand for rooms in Lancaster County far exceeded supply. Some visitors slept in their cars; others settled for hotels and motels as far as an hour away. The local chamber of commerce beseeched residents with spare rooms to open their doors to Amish-obsessed tourists, and many answered the call. Today the county boasts more than 150 B&Bs. Book a stay at a farm B&B to learn about Lancaster County's leading industry. (Tourism is a close second to agriculture.)

If you have kids, a visit to Hershey is nonnegotiable. You'll run yourself ragged trying to hit all the attractions in one day, so set aside two. A day is generally enough for Gettysburg, but ardent history buffs and ghost hunters can keep busy for several. York County's wineries and the Reading area's air museums are also worth a day trip.

Lancaster County

In January 1955, *Plain and Fancy* opened on Broadway. The musical comedy is the story of two New Yorkers who travel to Bird-in-Hand, Pennsylvania—a real-life village amid Lancaster County's Amish farmlands—to sell a piece of property they've inherited. There, just a few hours from home, they encounter a way of life completely foreign to them. The Amish, or "plain," lifestyle was completely foreign to most play-goers, too. A modest success on Broadway, the show sparked enormous interest in its setting. Before *Plain and Fancy,* Lancaster County was lucky to get 25,000 visitors a year. After, the number rocketed to more than two million. Tourists traipsed through farm fields, knocked on doors, and peered through windows in their quest for a close encounter of the Amish kind. Today there's no need to trespass. Lancaster County, which now welcomes upwards of 10 million visitors annually, is flush with information centers, attractions, and tour operators offering an Amish 101 curriculum.

About 250,000 Amish live in North America, according to the Young Center for Anabaptist and Pietist Studies at Lancaster County's Elizabethtown College. Though the church originated in Europe, it's extinct there. Lancaster County is home to about 30,000 Amish—roughly half of Pennsylvania's Amish—and is neck and neck with Ohio's Holmes County for the distinction of having the world's largest Amish settlement. It also holds the distinction of having the oldest surviving Amish settlement in the world. The first ship carrying a significant group of Amish from their homelands in central Europe to the New World docked in Philadelphia in 1737. Some of the Amish passengers made their home in Lancaster County; a larger number settled 20-odd miles away in present-day Berks County. While the Amish all but disappeared from Berks County by the early 1800s, Lancaster County had six congregations (known as church districts) at the close of

DUTCH COUNTRY

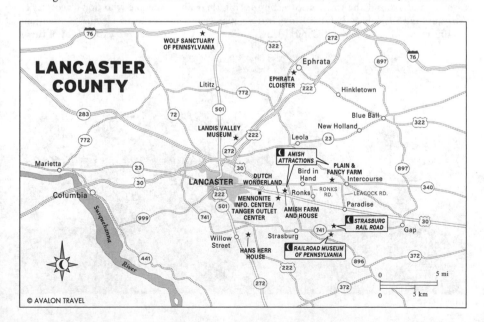

© AVALON TRAVEL

the century. Their numbers have soared since then, more than doubling between 1980 and 2000 and climbing more than 30 percent in the first decade of this century. Large families have a lot to do with the vigorous growth: Most Amish couples have five or more children. And while Amish teens are allowed a period of *rumspringa*, or "running around," during which they decide whether to join the church, very few leave the fold. Given the chance to drive cars and dress how they please, more than 85 percent ultimately choose the horse and buggy as their mode of transport and the distinctive garb that sets them apart from the "English;" i.e., everyone else.

As you explore the region, keep in mind that that not all traditionally dressed people are Amish. Some conservative Mennonite and Brethren groups also practice "plain" dress. You may not be able to tell them apart, but each has distinguishing characteristics.

There's more to Lancaster County than its Amish population. The county seat, Lancaster city, boasts a thriving arts scene. Rail fans will find an abundance of train-related attractions in and around the town of Strasburg. Antiques enthusiasts will fall in love with Adamstown, a.k.a. "Antiques Capital USA."

Bargain hunters can get their fix at a pair of outlet malls along U.S. 30. Anyone fascinated by the Amish and their strict codes of conduct will likely be fascinated by the towns of Lititz and Ephrata. The former began as an experiment in utopia by members of a Protestant denomination that prohibited everything from dancing to changing professions without approval from church elders. The latter was home to a religious group so disdainful of worldly pleasures that its members slept on wooden pillows. Other Lancaster County communities are remarkable for their names: Intercourse, Paradise, Blue Ball, Fertility, and, of course, Bird-in-Hand.

◖ AMISH ATTRACTIONS

If you're visiting Lancaster County for the number one reason people visit Lancaster County—to see the Amish—you may be at a loss as to where to start. Unlike malls and museums, amusement parks and ski resorts, the Amish are an attraction without an address. You can't punch "Amish" into your GPS and get turn-by-turn directions. They're people living their lives—people who don't necessarily appreciate being the focus of tourists' attention. And while it's not hard to catch sight of them

buggy ride

© ANNA DUBROVSKY

living their lives, you'll shortchange yourself if you don't garner some understanding of why they live the way they do.

Plain & Fancy Farm, the Amish Farm and House, and the Mennonite Information Center are great places to acquaint yourself with the ways of the Amish. Visiting one is quite enough. Each offers a hearty menu of get-to-know-the-Amish options. Choosing between the attractions is a matter of taste. Plain & Fancy is smack dab in the heart of Amish country, while the other two are located along U.S. 30, a major east–west thoroughfare. It's the only one that offers buggy rides through the countryside and the opportunity to visit an Amish family in their home. But it's also the priciest of the three. The Amish Farm and House is your best bet if you're traveling with kids. It's crawling with animals and offers a variety of children's activities, including pony rides, a corn maze, and "Buttercup," a life-sized fiberglass cow always ready to be milked. While all three offer driving tours of Amish farmlands, the Mennonite Information Center is unique in that it doesn't operate tour vans or buses. Instead, a guide will climb into your car and lead you on a personal tour. It's the way to go if you tend to ask a lot of questions. It's also a great value: just $44 for a vehicle carrying as many as seven people. On the downside, the Mennonite Information Center is closed on Sundays.

Plain & Fancy Farm

In 1958, a few years after *Plain and Fancy* hit the Broadway stage, a man named Walter Smith built an Amish-style house and barn along Route 340, midway between the villages of Bird-in-Hand and Intercourse, with the intent of giving house tours and holding barn dances. Shrewdly, he named the property after the Broadway musical that ignited so much interest in Amish country. Half a century later, Plain & Fancy Farm (3121 Old Philadelphia Pike, Bird-in-Hand, www.plain andfancyfarm.com) offers everything a tourist could ask for: food, lodging, souvenirs, and an excellent orientation to the Amish way of life.

(Alas, it doesn't offer dances. The barn Mr. Smith built opened as Lancaster County's first family-style restaurant in 1959.)

Begin your orientation to the Amish way of life at the **Amish Experience Theater** (717/768-3600, ext. 210, www.amish experience.com, show begins on the hour 9 A.M.–5 P.M. Mon.–Sat. and 11 A.M.–5 P.M. Sun. Apr.–Oct., 10 A.M.–5 P.M. Mon.–Sat. and 11 A.M.–5 P.M. Sun. Nov.–Dec., call or check website for winter hours, admission $9.95, children 4–12 $6.95). This is not your garden-variety movie theater. Designed to look like a barn, it features five screens, a fog machine, and other bells and whistles that produce three-dimensional effects. *Jacob's Choice*, the film for which the theater was built, packs some 400 years of history into 40 minutes. It's the contemporary story of an Old Order Amish family and the teenage son torn between joining the church and leaving the fold for a modern life. As the title character learns about the persecution Anabaptists faced in Europe and their journey to the New World, so does the audience. Consider yourself warned: The early history of Anabaptism is rated R for violence. Filmed locally in 1995, *Jacob's Choice* doesn't dwell on the blood and gore, but a burning-at-the-stake scene could rattle children.

Tickets for tours of the house Mr. Smith built back in 1958 are sold in the theater lobby. Now known as the **Amish Country Homestead** (717/768-3600, ext. 210, www .amishexperience.com, admission $9.95, children 4–12 $6.95), the nine-room house is continually updated to reflect changes in the Amish lifestyle. (Contrary to popular belief, the Amish don't live just as they did centuries ago. For one thing, they have refrigerators.) The schedule varies throughout the year, but during peak season—April through October—tours begin at 15 minutes before the hour 9:45 A.M.–3:45 P.M. Monday–Saturday and 10:45 A.M.–3:45 P.M. Sunday, with an additional tour at 4:15 P.M. daily. Guides explain such head-scratchers as why the Amish eschew electricity but use refrigerators and other appliances powered by propane gas. The tour takes about 40 minutes. A package rate for admission to *Jacob's Choice* and the house is available.

Driving tours of the farmlands that surround Plain & Fancy depart from the theater lobby. The two-hour **Amish Farmlands Tour** (717/768-3600, ext. 210, www.amish experience.com, $29.95 per person, children 4–12 $14.95) is offered Saturdays in March, daily from late March through November, and weekends in December. Stops may include roadside produce stands, bakeries, a wine shop, and a working farm. Ask about the SuperSaver Package if you're interested in *Jacob's Choice*, the house tour, and the Farmlands Tour. Offered weekday evenings from mid-June through October, the **V.I.P. Tour** ($45.95 per person) is a pricey but priceless experience. You don't have to be a "very important person" to sign up for the three-hour excursion. V.I.P., in this case, stands for "Visit in Person." The tour visits an Amish dairy farm during milking time, proceeds to a meeting with an Amish quilter, furniture maker, basket weaver, or other craftsperson, and culminates in a sit-down chat with an Amish family in their home. V.I.P. Tours are limited to 14 people and normally sell out, so you'll want to purchase tickets in advance.

No reservation needed to hit the back roads in a horse-drawn buggy or wagon. **Aaron and Jessica's Buggy Rides** (9 A.M.–dusk Mon.–Sat. and 10 A.M.–5 P.M. Sun. Apr.–Nov., 9 A.M.–4:30 P.M. Mon.–Sat. Dec.–Mar., 717/768-8828, www.amishbuggyrides .com) depart from Plain & Fancy Farm every 10 minutes or so. Trips range from 20 minutes to over an hour, with prices starting at $10 for adults and $6 for children 3–12. Children 2 and under ride for free. Aaron and Jessica's—named for owner Jack Meyer's oldest daughter and her first horse—bills itself as the county's only buggy tour operator staffed entirely by "plain" people (except on Sundays, which they set aside for worship).

Spending the night at Plain & Fancy Farm is as easy as booking a stay at the amenity-rich **AmishView Inn & Suites** (866/735-1600, www.amishviewinn.com, room $114–214,

Jack Meyer, owner of Aaron and Jessica's Buggy Rides

© ANNA DUBROVSKY

suite $174–424). Ask for a room on the backside of the hotel, where you'll enjoy gorgeous vistas of Amish farms.

The Amish Farm and House

The easiest way to find the Amish Farm and House (2395 Lincoln Hwy. East, Lancaster, 717/394-6185, www.amishfarmandhouse.com, 10 A.M.–4 P.M. daily Jan.–Mar., 9 A.M.–5 P.M. Apr.–May, 8:30 A.M.–6 P.M. June–Aug., 9 A.M.–5 P.M. Sept.–Oct., 9 A.M.–4 P.M. Nov.–Dec., general admission $8.25, seniors $7.50, children 5–11 $5.25) is to look for its neighbor, a Target. The bullseye logo of the discount store, which opened in 2005 on property carved from the hundreds-year-old farm, is far easier to spot than the 70-foot windmill or barn and silo that once dominated the skyline. Their juxtaposition is emblematic of the Amish community's insoluble dilemma: modernity.

Opened to the public in July 1955, the Amish Farm and House bills itself as the first tourist attraction in Lancaster County and the first Amish attraction in the United States. The operating farm has since shrunk from 25 acres to 15 (making room for Target, PetSmart, Panera, etc.), but there's more to see than ever. Start with a guided tour of the farmhouse, included in general admission. Built in 1805 of limestone quarried on the property, the house has counted Quakers, Mennonites, and Amish as residents. Today it's furnished in the manner of a typical Amish home. The front room features wooden benches arranged in preparation for a church service, opening the door for a discussion of why the Amish worship in their homes and other aspects of their religion. Their manner of dress is explained in the bedrooms. After the 45-minute tour, explore the farm at your own pace. Children love the chicken house, the 1803 stone bank barn with its cows, horses, and pigs, and the outdoor animal pens. A goat playground makes for a great photo op with the frisky ruminants. Kids (we're talking humans now, not goats) also enjoy the corn maze, up and running mid-July through October, and tootling around on Amish scooters when weather permits. Other farm features

amid malls, the Amish Farm and House

© ANNA DUBROVSKY

the goat playground at the Amish Farm and House

include an original tobacco shed, one of the few remaining lime kilns in Lancaster County, a working waterwheel, a circa 1855 covered bridge, and a one-room Amish schoolhouse built specifically for tourists in 2006. A quilter and woodcarver are on-site April through October, demonstrating their skills and selling their works. You'll catch a blacksmith pounding away in the Civil War–era blacksmith shop during special events such as **Sheep Shearing Days** (late Apr./early May). Short **buggy rides** ($5 per person) around the property are offered in June, July, and August.

A 90-minute **bus tour of the countryside** (adults $18.95, children 5–11 $12.95, children 4 and under $4.95) leaves from the Amish Farm and House multiple times a day year-round. Call or check the website for a schedule of tour times. It's a good idea to make a reservation, especially if visiting April through October. The tour includes a stop at at least one Amish business (except on Sundays, when the Amish don't conduct business). The package rate for touring the house, farm, and countryside is $25.95

for adults, $15.95 for children 5–11, and $4.95 for children 4 and under. The Amish Farm and House also offers bus tours of downtown Lancaster (April–Oct.) and the region's covered bridges (mid-June–Oct.).

Mennonite Information Center

Don't be put off by its name. You *will* learn about the Amish at the Mennonite Information Center (2209 Millstream Rd., Lancaster, 717/299-0954, www.mennoniteinfoctr.com, 8 A.M.–5 P.M. Mon.–Sat. Apr.–Oct., 8:30 A.M.–4:30 P.M. Mon.–Sat. Nov.–March), located next to Tanger Outlet Center. Start by watching the three-screen feature *"Who Are the Amish?"* (on the hour 9 A.M.–4 P.M., admission $5, seniors $4.50, children 7–12 $3). It answers such questions as: How many are there? Why do they dress that way? Why do they drive buggies? And what do they have against electricity? The images are beautiful and the narration intelligent, but at 30 minutes long, the movie won't necessarily hold the attention of young children. Also showing: the 17-minute *Postcards from a Heritage of Faith,* which elucidates the similarities and differences between the Amish and Mennonites, both of which trace their roots to the Anabaptist movement in 16th-century Europe. There's no charge to see the shorter film, shown on the half hour from 8:30 A.M. to 4:30 P.M. except from November through March, when the last showing is at 3:30 P.M. Admission to the information center's exhibits on Anabaptist life is also free.

Movies and exhibits are nice, but what sets the Mennonite Information Center apart are its **personal tours of Amish country.** For less than the cost of two seats on many bus tours, a guide will hop in your vehicle and point the way to Amish farms, one-room schoolhouses, quilt shops, covered bridges, etc. All guides have a Mennonite or Amish heritage and have lived in Lancaster County for most, if not all, of their lives. A two-hour tour for a carful of up to seven people is $44. Each additional hour is $14. Call ahead to arrange for a guide to meet you at a specified time or just show up and request a tour. The wait for a guide is rarely longer than 30 minutes. Another great service from the Mennonite Information Center is its list of **Mennonite guest homes,** available on its website or in pamphlet form at the info center.

The information center is home to a life-sized reproduction of the portable place of worship described in the Biblical account of the Israelites' exodus from ancient Egypt. A wax figure of the high priest sports a breastplate of gold and precious stones. The **Biblical Tabernacle Reproduction** (admission $7, seniors $6, children 7–12 $4) can only be seen by guided tour. Tours begin on the hour 9 A.M.–4 P.M. from April through October and 10 A.M.–3 P.M. in March and November. From December through February they're offered at 10 A.M., noon, and 2 P.M. A package rate for admission to *"Who Are the Amish?"* and the tabernacle reproduction is available. The reproduction has no real connection to Lancaster County's Anabaptist communities. It was constructed in the 1940s by a Baptist minister in St. Petersburg, Florida, purchased by Mennonites in the 1950s, and installed in

its current home in the 1970s. The information center sells a variety of tabernacle model kits, fair-trade handicrafts from around the world, and a wide selection of books about Anabaptist history and faith.

Next door to the info center is the headquarters of the **Lancaster Mennonite Historical Society** (2215 Millstream Rd., 717/393-9745, www.lmhs.org, 8:30 A.M.–4:30 P.M. Tues.–Sat.), which also boasts a fantastic bookstore. It's home to a museum (admission $5, seniors $4.50, children 7–12 $3) showcasing Pennsylvania German artifacts, a 30,000-book library, and the largest Mennonite archives in the eastern United States and Canada.

DOWNTOWN LANCASTER

It's not unusual for tourists to come and go from Lancaster County without so much as stepping foot in downtown Lancaster. Many are entirely unaware that the county has an urban center. It's hard to blame them. Lancaster County's countryside and quaint towns have gotten all the press for decades. It doesn't help that its major east-west thoroughfare, U.S. 30, bypasses downtown Lancaster altogether. Well, downtown's museums and merchants have had just about enough of being ignored. Revitalization efforts in recent years have given downtown a fresh look and its boosters more cred. Now, in addition to boasting the oldest continuously operated farmers market, theater, and tobacco shop in the U.S., downtown boasts a new convention center and adjoining 19-floor hotel. New restaurants, stores, and galleries add to its promotional arsenal. Plan on devoting a day to downtown. Make it a Tuesday, Friday, or Saturday, when the farmers market is open. Ideally, make it the first Friday of any month, when museums, galleries, and shops stay open as late as 9 P.M. **First Fridays** (717/509-2787, www.lancasterarts .com) feature special exhibitions, artists receptions, and live entertainment.

Guided Tours
The city of Lancaster is so steeped in history—it was capital of the 13 colonies for one day during the American Revolution and capital

of Pennsylvania for 13 years—that a guided tour is a good idea. You can choose your mode: walking, gliding, or riding.

Led by a volunteer guide in 18th- or 19th-century garb, the **Historic Lancaster Walking Tour** (Lancaster Visitors Center, 5 W. King St., 717/392-1776, www.historiclancaster walkingtour.com, $7 per person, seniors $6, children $1) visits more than 50 sites. Allow about 90 minutes for the tour, which begins with a DVD presentation. It's offered daily April–October. On Tuesdays, Fridays, and Saturdays, when nearby Central Market is open, tours depart at 10 A.M. and 1 P.M. Only a 1 P.M. tour is offered on other days.

If you prefer gliding to walking, head over to **Red Rose Seg Tours** (305 N. Queen St., 717/393-4526, www.redrosesegtours.com, guided tour $55–65 per person, mini-glide $25). Opened in 2009 by a local couple that became enamored of Segway tours during their travels, Red Rose offers general tours of downtown as well as arts- and ghost-themed tours. You don't need gliding experience, but you do need a valid driver's license. Each hour-long tour is preceded by 20–30 minutes of training and practice. The tours are offered Wednesday–Sunday from March through December. Call or visit the website for departure times. Tours are available by appointment in January and February. Want the Segway experience but not the tour? Schedule a "mini-glide."

The **Amish Farm and House** (2395 Lincoln Hwy. East, 717/394-6185, www.amishfarm andhouse.com), located on U.S. 30 several miles east of downtown Lancaster, offers a two-hour bus tour of the city. Departing at 10 A.M. on Tuesdays, Fridays, and Saturdays from April through October, the tour is $29.95 for adults, $19.95 for children 5–11, and $4.95 for younger children.

Central Market

Central Market (23 N. Market St., 717/735-6890, www.centralmarketlancaster.com, 6 A.M.–4 P.M. Tues. and Fri., 6 A.M.–2 P.M. Sat.) is the pulsing heart of the city. Granted, the indoor farmers market pulses just three days

Central Market in downtown Lancaster

© ANNA DUBROVSKY

a week, but given its advanced age, it's incredible that it pulses at all. Central Market is the oldest continually operated farmers market in the country. When Lancaster was laid out in the 1730s, a lot adjacent to the town square was designated as a public marketplace in perpetuity. In its early years, the market was simply an open space where farmers and others could sell their wares. The current market house, an eye-catching Romanesque Revival structure with two towers and ornate brick and stone work, was built in 1889. Many of the 60-some market stands have been operated by multiple generations of the same family. The Stoner's vegetable stand, famous for its arugula, has been around for more than a century. Fresh produce isn't the half of it. Central Market is one-stop shopping for everything from hand-stitched Amish quilts to foie gras. There's beef, poultry, and fish; milk and cheeses; breads and pastries; coffees and teas; candies and candles; preserves and prepared foods. There's even a stand specializing in horseradish products. Beware the fan that circulates the scent of fresh grated horseradish. Come on the early side for the best selection. On Tuesdays and Fridays, many of the vendors call it quits at 3 P.M., an hour before the market closes.

Heritage Center Museum

A stone's throw from Central Market is a building that once served as Lancaster's city hall and even as Pennsylvania's capitol. (Lancaster had a 13-year run as the state capital, ceding the role to Harrisburg in 1812.) Today it's one of two 1790s buildings constituting the Heritage Center Museum (5 W. King St., 717/299-6440, www.lancasterheritage.com, 9 A.M.–5 P.M. Mon.–Sat., 10 A.M.–3 P.M. Sun., open until 9 P.M. First Fridays, free admission), which houses an extensive collection of 18th- to 20th-century decorative arts indigenous to south-central Pennsylvania. The stories of groups who settled in the region, including the Amish, Mennonites, Quakers, and Moravians, are told through their furniture, folk art, and other works. The exhibits are worth a look, especially because admission is free, but the museum's best feature is its store. It's chock-full

of jewelry, pottery, carvings, clocks, glassware, and other creations by area artisans. If the size doesn't fit or the color doesn't suit, don't lose heart. Many of the artisans are happy to customize pieces.

Lancaster Quilt & Textile Museum

The Heritage Center's sister museum, the Lancaster Quilt & Textile Museum (37 Market St., 717/397-2970, www.quiltandtextile museum.com, 10 A.M.–5 P.M. Mon. and Wed.–Thurs., 9 A.M.–5 P.M. Tues. and Fri.–Sat., open until 9 P.M. First Fridays, admission $6, students $4, children 17 and under free, no charge after 5 P.M. on First Fridays), is also a few paces from Central Market. The museum was conceived in 2002, when the Heritage Center got its hands on a blockbuster collection of 19th- and 20th-century Amish quilts known as the Esprit Collection. Started by Esprit Corp. founder Doug Tompkins, it's regarded by many scholars as the finest collection of its kind. The Heritage Center, which had its own hoard of quilts and textiles made in

If you catch the quilting bug at the Lancaster Quilt & Textile Museum, pick up a quilt kit at the museum store.

© WWW.DISCOVERLANCASTERPA.COM

The Lancaster Quilt & Textile Museum is home to the famed Esprit Collection.

south-central Pennsylvania, then got its hands on a grand Beaux Arts building. Originally owned by a community bank that didn't survive the Great Depression, the 1912 building had stood empty for much of its life. It opened as the Quilt & Textile Museum in 2004. The marriage of cosmopolitan architecture and folk art works. If you catch the quilting bug, pop into the museum store for a do-it-yourself kit. The store also sells Amish-made quilts, including Esprit Collection reproductions, and unique items such as framed miniature quilts.

Art Museums and Galleries

Art lovers can fill a day exploring Lancaster's museums and galleries. There are more than a dozen within a few blocks of Penn Square (intersection of King and Queen Streets). The section of Prince Street between King Street and Walnut Street to its north is especially crowded with galleries. Very definitely worth a stop: the **Red Raven Art Company** (138 N. Prince St., 717/299-4400, www.redravenartcompany.com, 10 A.M.–5 P.M. Tues. and Thurs.–Sat., open

until 8:30 P.M. First Fridays), which showcases the works of a band of fine artists from the area. Red Raven sets aside space for fledgling artists— art students even—and doesn't take a commission on their sales. If you lean more toward folk art than fine art, you'll love **CityFolk** (146 N. Prince St., 717/393-8807, www.lancasterarts .com, 10 A.M.–5 P.M. Mon.–Sat., winter hours 10 A.M.–4 P.M. Tues.–Sat., open until 9 P.M. First Fridays) with its ever-changing galleries of furniture, paintings, carvings, pottery, and other works by artists and craftspeople from around the country. CityFolk also offers antiques and garden art. A handy map of the city's arts and cultural venues is available on the website of the nonprofit LancasterARTS (717/509-2787, www .lancasterarts.com), their tireless promoter.

A short walk east of Penn Square is the one-time home of Lancaster's most acclaimed artist, the modernist painter Charles Demuth. It's now open to the public as the **Demuth Museum** (120 E. King St., 717/299-9940, www.demuth.org, 10 A.M.–4 P.M. Tues.–Sat., 1–4 P.M. Sun., closed Jan., free admission).

Demuth was born in Lancaster in 1883 and died there in 1935 but moved in avant-garde circles in places as far-flung as Paris, New York, and Bermuda. He was very much appreciated during his lifetime, earning a place in the permanent collection of New York's Metropolitan Museum of Art by his 40s. Among his best-known works is the Precisionist masterpiece *My Egypt,* inspired by grain elevators in Lancaster and snapped up by the Whitney Museum in New York. Demuth's eponymous museum boasts 40 works from throughout his career, plus an extensive archive and library. One of its main galleries is the artist's former studio, a second-floor room overlooking a garden that was tended by his mother. A fertile source of inspiration for his floral watercolors, the garden is open to museum visitors. Rotating exhibits showcase works by Demuth's contemporaries or artists with a thematic or stylistic connection to him. Next door to the museum is the **Demuth Tobacco Shop** (114 E. King St., 717/397-6613, www.demuthtobaccoshop .com, 9 A.M.–5 P.M. Mon.–Fri., 9 A.M.–3 P.M. Sat.), which was owned by the Demuth family for more than two centuries. Established in 1770, it's said to be the oldest tobacco shop in the country.

Not to be forgotten is the **Lancaster Museum of Art** (135 N. Lime St., 717/394-3497, www.lmapa.org, 10 A.M.–4 P.M. Tues.–Sat., noon–4 P.M. Sun., open until 8 P.M. First Fridays, free admission), home to an extensive collection of works by contemporary regional artists. Perhaps more striking than any piece in the collection is the museum's home: a remarkably intact example of Greek Revival–style domestic architecture. The Grubb Mansion, as it's called, was built in the 1840s for an iron master with an eye for art.

Lancaster Science Factory

Geared for children 7–13, the Science Factory (454 New Holland Ave., 717/509-6363, www .lancastersciencefactory.org, 10 A.M.–5 P.M. Mon.–Sat. and noon–5 P.M. Sun., closed Mon. Sept.–May, admission $7.50, seniors $6.50, children 3–15 $6) features dozens of interactive exhibits that help visitors—even those well over 13—understand such things as electricity, magnetism, acoustics, and fluid dynamics. If your kids like blowing bubbles, they'll love the "minimal surfaces" exhibit. Budding Beethovens can experiment with the "bongophone," a bongo/xylophone. The Fac, which opened in 2008 after five years in the making, isn't the only science museum in Lancaster. Less than two miles away is the **North Museum of Natural History & Science** (400 College Ave., 717/291-3941, www.northmuseum.org, 10 A.M.–5 P.M. Tues.–Sat., noon–5 P.M. Sun., museum admission $7, seniors and children 3–17 $6, museum and planetarium admission $8.50, seniors and children $7.50), which boasts a dinosaur gallery, a live animal room, and a planetarium. Located on the campus of Franklin & Marshall College since the 1950s, the museum plans to build a new facility nearby.

"TRAIN TOWN USA"

The town of **Strasburg,** some nine miles southwest of downtown Lancaster, bills itself as "the real Lancaster County." Which is to

Strasburg Rail Road

say that it has changed little in the last couple of centuries. Buggies clip-clop through the town square at the intersection of Routes 741 and 896. Families stream in and out of the old-timey **Strasburg Country Store & Creamery** (1 W. Main St., Strasburg, 717/687-0766, www.strasburg.com, 11 A.M.–10 P.M. Mon.–Sat., noon–10 P.M. Sun.), where scoops of homemade ice cream are pressed into just-made waffle cones. Much of *Witness,* the 1985 romantic thriller that did more for tourism to Amish country than any marketing campaign, was filmed on a farm nearby.

But what brings tourists here by the busload is train mania. There are half a dozen train-related attractions within two miles of the square, including the **Red Caboose Motel & Restaurant** (312 Paradise Ln., Ronks, 717/687-5000, www.redcaboosemotel.com, lodging $69–159, dining $4–17), where rail fans bed down and chow down in refurbished train cars. The Strasburg area is such a magnet for "foamers," as the most zealous of rail fans are known, that it's sometimes called "Train Town USA" (not to be confused with "Railroad

City," a.k.a. Altoona, three hours away). The oldest of the attractions and a good place to start is the Strasburg Rail Road. Don't leave town without a visit to the Choo Choo Barn, where you can see the historic railroad and much more in miniature.

From the town square, head east on Route 741 (Main Street). You'll see the Choo Choo Barn and Strasburg Train Shop on your right after half a mile. Half a mile later, you'll arrive at the Strasburg Rail Road and Railroad Museum of Pennsylvania, located on opposite sides of Route 741. Continue to the next intersection and turn left onto Paradise Lane to check into the Red Caboose or check out the National Toy Train Museum.

◖ Strasburg Rail Road and the Railroad Museum of Pennsylvania

Incorporated in 1832, the Strasburg Rail Road (300 Gap Rd., Ronks, 717/687-7522, www.strasburgrailroad.com, regular train ticket $14–25, children 3–11 $7–25, toddlers free–$25) is America's oldest operating short-line

Railroad Museum of Pennsylvania

© ANNA DUBROVSKY

railroad. It was almost abandoned in the late 1950s, after an upsurge in the use of highways for freight transportation and a series of storms that destroyed parts of its 4.5-mile track. But rail fans came to its rescue, turning it into a tourist attraction and a time capsule of early-20th-century railroading. The railroad offers trips to Paradise and back—as in Paradise, PA—every month but January. As its painstakingly restored trains steam past fields still plowed by horses and mules, conductors share tidbits about the railroad's history and the Amish lifestyle. Horse-drawn buggies wait at railroad crossings. In the hopes that future generations of riders are treated to the same tranquil scenery, a nickel of every ticket sold goes toward farmland preservation. Ticket prices vary widely depending on the type of passenger car. A ride in an open-air car, for example, is $16 for adults, $9 for children 3–11, and $2 for tots, while seats in the plush President's Car, once used by the top brass of the Reading Railroad, are $25 regardless of age. Combo tickets good for a train ride and admission to the nearby Railroad Museum of Pennsylvania are available. In addition to regular rides, which depart as frequently as every half hour on operating days, the Strasburg Rail Road offers a variety of themed excursions. It's a good idea to purchase tickets in advance for the Wine & Cheese Train ($35), murder mystery dinners ($59.95, children 5–11 $39.95), Santa's Paradise Express ($17–25, children 3–11 $10–25, toddlers $3–25), and other special trips. For several days each June, September, and November, fans of Thomas the Tank Engine can ride behind a full-sized steam locomotive based on the storybook character. **Day Out With Thomas** tickets are $18 for passengers 2 and older.

The nine-mile round-trip takes just 45 minutes, but if you're into trains or traveling with kids, plan to spend a couple of hours or longer at the home station. A guided tour of the railroad's mechanical shop ($16 with train ticket stub, $25 without) is offered at noon on most operating days. The 50-minute tour is limited to 25 people and often sells out. Rail fans will also want to visit an 1885 switch tower

© WWW.DISCOVERLANCASTERPA.COM

The Thomas the Tank Engine chugs into Strasburg Rail Road each June, September, and November.

(suggested donation $2) that affords a bird's-eye view of approaching trains. Kids can operate a vintage pump car or take a ride in a circa 1920 miniature steam train. Wee ones can pilot hand-propelled "cranky cars" dating to the 1930s. The station also features several stores geared toward train lovers, a café, and a sweets shop. Consider packing a picnic basket or buying a boxed lunch at the station and disembarking the train at Groff's Grove, a picnic area near Cherry Crest Adventure Farm and its Amazing Maize Maze. (The Strasburg Rail Road sells discounted Cherry Crest tickets.) Just don't miss the last train back.

Directly across the street from the Strasburg Rail Road, the Railroad Museum of Pennsylvania (300 Gap Rd., Ronks, 717/687-8628, www.rrmuseumpa.org, 9 A.M.–5 P.M. Mon.–Sat. and noon–5 P.M. Sun., closed Mon. Nov.–Mar., admission $10, seniors $9, children 3–11 $8) boasts a world-class collection of railroad artifacts, including many last-of-their-kind locomotives. More than 50

DUTCH COUNTRY

locomotives and railroad cars are housed in its 100,000-square-foot exhibit hall. Dozens of others reside in the restoration yard, which is open to visitors when weather and staffing permit. Behind-the-scenes tours of the restoration shop, normally closed to the public for safety reasons, are offered at noon and 4 P.M. most days. The fee is $10 per person and directly benefits the restoration program.

Rail fans hoping to find a rare "Big Boy" steam locomotive will be disappointed. The museum, which opened in 1975, is owned and operated by the Pennsylvania Historical and Museum Commission and endeavors to preserve objects relating to the history of railroading in Pennsylvania. The legendary Big Boys didn't ply Pennsylvania's rails. With its 195-ton engine, Pennsylvania Railroad "Mountain" No. 6755 is the largest and heaviest steam locomotive in the museum's collection. Another highlight of the collection: Pennsylvania Railroad E6 No. 460, a steam locomotive dubbed the "Lindbergh Engine." After Charles Lindbergh completed the first nonstop solo flight across the Atlantic in 1927, the aviator was summoned to Washington, D.C., for a fete in his honor. Fiercely competitive news organizations hired airplanes to fly films of the event to New York; one engaged the Pennsylvania Railroad. No. 460 made the run in record time, and the film it carried was the first to arrive in theaters. Word spread that the locomotive had outraced airplanes. (In reality, credit goes to the maverick news organization, which managed to process, edit, and copy its film en route. But it certainly helped that No. 460 traveled at speeds of up to 115 miles per hour.)

National Toy Train Museum

Real trains are well and good, but there's something enchanting about their much-shrunken kin. Which makes the National Toy Train Museum (300 Paradise Ln., Strasburg, 717/687-8976, www.nttmuseum.org, 10 A.M.–5 P.M. Fri.–Mon. May–Oct., 10 A.M.–5 P.M. Sat.–Sun. in Apr. and Nov.–Dec., admission $6, seniors $5, children 6–12 $3, family $15) an exceptionally enchanting place. It houses one of the most extensive collections of toy trains in the world. More than 100 different manufacturers are represented in the museum's collection, which includes some of the earliest and rarest toy trains. It also includes some model trains. (What's the difference? Toy trains are generally marketed to youngsters and not necessarily based on real trains. Model trains aspire to look

the National Toy Train Museum

every bit like real trains.) The museum, which aspires to look like a Victorian-era station, has five large train layouts. Each has trains of a different scale and represents a different period of the 20th century. Visitors have the opportunity to operate many choo-choos themselves.

The museum is operated by the Train Collectors Association, which has its national headquarters there. Those new to "the world's greatest hobby," as the TCA calls it, can learn the ropes via video presentations in the museum. Seasoned collectors can bury their noses in repair guides, trade catalogs, and other materials in the reference library. While the museum is closed January–March, the library is open five days a week year-round. Call for hours.

Choo Choo Barn

Model train enthusiasts can also find nirvana at the Choo Choo Barn (226 Gap Rd., Strasburg, 717/687-7911, www.choochoobarn.com, 10 A.M.–5 P.M. daily mid-Mar.–Dec., admission $6, children 4–12 $3.25), which predates the National Toy Train Museum. The family-owned attraction has just one layout: a massive, marvelous display featuring 22 trains and more than 150 animated figures and vehicles. Local landmarks including the Strasburg Rail Road and Dutch Wonderland amusement park are represented. There's an Amish barn-raising and an operating quarry, a zoo and a three-ring circus, a baseball game and a ski slope. There's even a fire scene, complete with flames.

The Choo Choo Barn traces its history to 1945, when Strasburg native George Groff, recently returned from war, gave his toddler son a Lionel train set for Christmas. With each year, the train display in their basement grew bigger and more elaborate. They began opening it to townspeople and local school groups at Christmastime. In 1961 the Groffs moved their now 600-square-foot layout to a barn-like building just west of the recently reopened Strasburg Rail Road. The Choo Choo Barn proved a hit, and the display has since grown to more than 1,700 square feet. The family

business has grown to include several specialty shops next to the Barn. The **Strasburg Train Shop** (717/687-0464, www.etrainshop.com), which caters to the layout builder, is known as the place to go for uncommon things such as garbage cans. **Thomas' Trackside Station** (717/687-7911, www.ttstation.com) carries more than 1,200 items related to the *Thomas and Friends* children's television series and the distinction of being the only all-Thomas store in the country. The Groffs also opened a shop specializing in railroading books and videos. The shops are open 10 A.M.–5 P.M. daily.

OTHER SIGHTS
President James Buchanan's Wheatland

The only U.S. president from Pennsylvania lived—and died—on a handsome estate west of downtown Lancaster. James Buchanan, also remembered as the only bachelor to lead the nation, was secretary of state when he moved to Wheatland (230 N. President Ave., Lancaster, 717/392-4633, www.lancasterhistory.org, tours on the hour 10 A.M.–3 P.M. Tues.–Sat. Apr.–Oct., 10 A.M.–3 P.M. Fri.–Sat. Nov.–Dec., weekdays by appointment Jan.–Mar., call or check website for special Christmas week hours, admission $8, seniors $7, students 12 and older $6, children 6–11 $3) in 1848. He announced his 1856 presidential campaign on the front porch of the Federal-style mansion. Reviled for his wishy-washiness on the subject of slavery and his handling of the secession crisis, the 15th president penned a defensive memoir after retiring to Wheatland in 1861. His writing desk is among the many artifacts displayed throughout the manse today. The collection includes everything from his White House china to his bathing tub and even a bottle of 1827 Madeira, now half evaporated, from his wine cellar. Tours leave from the visitors center behind the mansion, where exhibits and a short film introduce the man who reportedly had these words for his successor, Abraham Lincoln, on inauguration day in 1861: "If you are as happy in entering the White House as I shall feel on returning to Wheatland, you are

© ANNA DUBROVSKY

President James Buchanan's Wheatland

a happy man indeed." Buchanan died at his beloved Wheatland in 1868 and is buried at Woodward Hill Cemetery in Lancaster.

Wheatland shares its grounds and parking lot with **Lancaster County's Historical Society** (9:30 A.M.–9:30 P.M. Tues. and Thurs., 9:30 A.M.–4:30 P.M. Wed. and Fri.–Sat.), offering free changing exhibitions on local history.

Dutch Wonderland

Dutch Wonderland (2249 Lincoln Hwy. E., Lancaster, 717/291-1888, www.dutchwonderland.com) doesn't boast of adrenaline-pumping rides like many amusement parks. Its coaster count has stood at two for more than a decade, and you wouldn't call them hair-raising. "Kid-friendly" is what the park calls them. Founded in 1963 by a potato farmer with no experience in the amusement park industry, Dutch Wonderland is kid-friendly through and through. The 48-acre park, fronted by a castle facade visible from U.S. 30, bills itself as "A Kingdom for Kids." In addition to 30-some rides, none of which have a minimum height

requirement of more than 42 inches, Dutch Wonderland offers a variety of live shows daily. They're all quite delightful but none so much as the high-dive shows at Herr's Aqua Stadium. Performers twist, somersault, and splash their way through Disneyesque storylines. Duke's Dance Party, an interactive show hosted by a purple dragon with more than a passing resemblance to Barney, is also worth attending. Bring swimsuits for Duke's Lagoon, the park's water play area.

Dutch Wonderland is open weekends in May, daily from late May through Labor Day, and a few weekends after Labor Day. Gates open at 10 A.M. and close between 6 P.M. and 8:30 P.M. A variety of admission plans are available. One-day admission is $31.95 for guests ages 3–59, $26.95 for adults 60–69, $19.95 for those 70 and older. Hang on to your ticket stub in case you decide to come back the next day; consecutive-day admission is $25.95. Arrive within three hours of closing for twilight rates: $23.95 for guests ages 3–59, $22.95 for those 60 and older. A two-day flex pass, good for visits on any two days during the season, is $46.95 for anyone 3 or older. If your summer plans also include a visit to Hersheypark in nearby Hershey, ask about combo tickets. Hershey Entertainment & Resorts acquired Dutch Wonderland in 2001.

The park reopens in October for several weekends' worth of Halloween-themed fun and again during the holiday season, when it's draped in twinkling lights and visited by Santa.

Cherry Crest Adventure Farm

Dutch Wonderland isn't the only must-stop attraction for pint-sized visitors to Lancaster County. There's also Cherry Crest Adventure Farm (150 Cherry Hill Rd., Ronks, 717/687-6843 www.cherrycrestfarm.com), where every summer a five-acre cornfield is transformed into the Amazing Maize Maze. This maze is no cakewalk. It takes most visitors about an hour to find the exit. But there's no danger of getting hopelessly lost—or bored for that matter. Helpful "Maze Masters" are always on hand, and the paths are peppered with clues and diversions. There's even a Corn Café for mid-adventure refreshment. The maze, open from July 4 though early November, isn't the only attraction on the working farm. You can crawl through a hay tunnel, slide down a hay chute on a burlap sack, or hurl pumpkins with huge slingshots. You can ride pedal karts or a tractor-pulled wagon. You can even watch chicks hatch and hold the little fuzzballs. Now that's agritainment.

Cherry Crest is open Tuesday–Saturday from July 4 to Labor Day; Friday–Saturday and select other dates in September; and Thursday–Saturday from October until it closes in November. Hours vary. Admission to the maze and more than 30 other attractions is $14.95 for visitors 12 and older, $12.95 for kids 3–11. If you want to pass on the maze, admission is $11.95. Cherry Crest is also open on Saturdays and select other dates from Memorial Day weekend through June, offering a limited number of attractions for $8.95. There's an additional fee for the Make-a-Friend Workshop

(717/768-0152, www.makeafriendwork shop.com), available May–November. Kids can create a doll dressed in Amish-style garb or build a wooden barn, steam train, or tractor and wagon. The doll clothes and wooden pieces are Amish-made. Cherry Crest, which is not an Amish farm, is just east of Strasburg, less than three miles from the Strasburg Rail Road. In fact, the railroad's excursion trains run right through it. A "Railroad Farm Fun Pass," good for same-day adventuring at both attractions, is available.

Kitchen Kettle Village

Pat Burnley had two kids under 5 and was in the hospital about to give birth to a third when her husband, Bob, arrived with unexpected news: "We bought a business!" he told her. The business assets consisted of gas burners, a stack of two-gallon kettles, and a few jelly recipes. They set up shop in their garage. As word spread of the jelly "kitchen" in the Lancaster County town of Intercourse, more

Kitchen Kettle Village

© ANNA DUBROVSKY

DUTCH COUNTRY

© ANNA DUBROVSKY

the Jam & Relish Kitchen at Kitchen Kettle Village

and more people stopped to watch the process and have a taste. The business has come a long way from its humble beginnings in 1954. What used to be the family homestead is now Kitchen Kettle Village (3529 Old Philadelphia Pike, Intercourse, 717/768-8261, www.kitchen kettle.com, 9 A.M.–6 P.M. Mon.–Sat. May–Oct., 9 A.M.–5 P.M. Nov.–Apr.), home to about 40 specialty shops, a pair of restaurants, and a handful of kid-centric attractions. To call it a mall would fail to convey its quaintness. Think of it as a mall in a fairy tale—the sort of place where Snow White would buy ribbons for her hair. The canning kitchen is still the heart of it all. Its repertoire has grown to include not just jellies, jams, and preserves but also relishes, pickles, mustards, salad dressings, grilling sauces, and salsas—more than 80 products in all. The operation long outgrew the garage, but some things haven't changed: All products are made by hand in small batches, and visitors get a front-seat view. (Because the kitchen is staffed by Amish women, photos aren't permitted.) Plenty of visitors have discovered a taste

for pickled beets or pepper jam in the store section of the **Jam & Relish Kitchen,** which abounds with samples. An attached bakery fills the air with the smells of shoofly pie, whoopie pies, molasses snaps, snickerdoodle cookies, and other local favorites.

Many of the village's shops feature locally made foods or goods, including ice cream from a dairy farm just a few miles away, fudge and kettle corn made on-site, hand-loomed clothing, fabric bags, quilts, and pottery. The house Pat Burnley (née Kling) grew up in is now the **Kling House Restaurant** (8 A.M.–3 P.M. Mon.–Thurs., 8 A.M.–4 P.M. Fri.–Sat., breakfast $4–9, lunch $8–15), which serves the likes of cinnamon-raisin French toast and baked oatmeal for breakfast, a variety of sandwiches, flatbread pizzas, and entrées for lunch, and a killer coconut cream pie. Pat herself can sometimes be found bussing tables. There's also a cafeteria-style restaurant.

Kitchen Kettle Village is home base to **AAA Buggy Rides** (717/989-2829, www.aaabuggy rides.com, 9 A.M.–6 P.M. Mon.–Sat. weather permitting), which offers a 55-minute excursion ($16, children 3–12 $8) that goes through a covered bridge as well as a 35-minute trip ($12, children $6). Reservations aren't required. The village also features pony rides, a petting zoo, and a playground. Want to stick around after it closes to the public? **The Inn at Kitchen Kettle Village** ($89–199) offers a variety of lodging options, including standard rooms in small cottages with yards and porches and suites that sleep up to six. Rates include breakfast at the Kling House every day except Sunday. Book well in advance if you're coming for the **Rhubarb Festival** (third weekend in May), the **Berry Jam Festival** (third weekend in June), or another of the village's annual events.

Landis Valley Museum

Born two years apart in the 1860s, brothers Henry and George Landis had a lot in common. Both became engineers. Neither married. They were the kind of people who never threw anything away—the kind who collected things other people regarded as valueless. By 1925 the brothers had amassed so many objects

reflective of Pennsylvania German rural life that they opened a small museum on their homestead a few miles north of downtown Lancaster, charging visitors 25 cents apiece. They died a year apart in the 1950s, but the museum (2451 Kissel Hill Rd., Lancaster, 717/569-0401, www.landisvalleymuseum.org, 9 A.M.–5 P.M. Mon.–Sat., noon–5 P.M. Sun., admission $12, seniors $10, children 3–11 $8) lives on. Owned by the state since 1953, it has grown into an assemblage of 30-plus historic and recreated buildings housing a collection of more than 100,000 farm, trade, and household artifacts. While some historic buildings are original to the site, including the Landis brothers' 1870s house, many were relocated here over the years. They include a blacksmith shop, a circa 1800 log building that houses exhibits on early printing and leatherworking, and a late 1800s schoolhouse complete with authentic furnishings. Rather than a time capsule of a particular era, Landis Valley is a repository for all things illustrative of PA Dutch village and farm life from the mid-1700s to mid-1900s. Costumed interpreters are often on

the Landis Valley Museum

hand to demonstrate skills such as open-hearth cooking, horse-drawn plowing, tinsmithing, woodcarving, and weaving. Heirloom gardens and heritage breed farm animals help bring the past to life. Be sure to stop by the museum store, which features traditional handicrafts.

Landis Valley Museum shares a parking lot with **Hands-on House** (721 Landis Valley Rd., Lancaster, 717/569-5437, www.handsonhouse.org, 10 A.M.–5 P.M. Mon.–Thurs. and Sat., 10 A.M.–8 P.M. Fri., noon–5 P.M. Sun. Memorial Day–Labor Day, 11 A.M.–4 P.M. Tues.–Thurs., 11 A.M.–8 P.M. Fri., 10 A.M.–5 P.M. Sat., noon–5 P.M. Sun. Labor Day–Memorial Day, admission $7), a museum designed for children 2–10.

Hans Herr House

Built in 1719, the Hans Herr House (1849 Hans Herr Dr., Willow St., 717/464-4438, www.hansherr.org, 9 A.M.–4 P.M. Mon.–Sat. Apr.–Nov., tour $5, children 7–12 $2) is the oldest structure in Lancaster County and the oldest Mennonite meetinghouse in the western hemisphere. Though named for the Mennonite bishop whose flock established the first permanent European settlement in present-day Lancaster County, the stone house was actually built by his son Christian. The younger Herr was also a bishop, and worship services were held in his Germanic abode. It was home to several generations of the family until the 1860s, after which it was used as a barn and storage shed. Today it's the centerpiece of a museum complex that also includes two 19th-century Pennsylvania German farmhouses, several barns and other outbuildings, and a collection of farm equipment spanning three centuries. You can explore the grounds at your own pace—for free—but must be accompanied by a guide inside the Hans Herr House, restored and furnished to reflect the period 1719–1750. The last house tour begins at 3:15 P.M. Aficionados of 20th-century American art may recognize its exterior. The great Andrew Wyeth, a descendant of Hans Herr, captured the house on canvas before its restoration.

National Watch & Clock Museum

The largest and most comprehensive horological collection in North America can be found in the river town of Columbia, about 10 miles west of Lancaster. I know what you're thinking: "horo-huh?" Horology is the science of measuring time. Sounds like staid stuff, but a visit to the National Watch & Clock Museum (514 Poplar St., Columbia, 717/684-8261, www.nawcc.org, 10 A.M.–4 P.M. Tues.–Sat. Dec.–Mar., 10 A.M.–5 P.M. Tues.–Sat. and noon–4 P.M. Sun. Apr.–Nov., also open Mondays Memorial Day–Labor Day, admission $8, seniors $7, children 5–16 $4, family $20) will convince you otherwise. Located in the world headquarters of the National Association of Watch and Clock Collectors, the museum traces the history of timekeeping from ancient times to present day. Sundials, it turns out, weren't the only timepieces in the days before mechanical clocks. Learn how bowls of water, candles, oil lamps, and incense were used to measure the passage of time. The museum's tick-tocking treasures include early English tall-case clocks, enchanting German musical clocks, vintage and modern wristwatches, and pocket watches spanning three centuries, including one carried by Caroline Bonaparte, youngest sister of Napoleon I. Its collection, which has grown to more than 12,000 items, is strongest in 19th-century American clocks and watches. The doozy: a so-called monumental clock made in Hazleton, Pennsylvania, by one Stephen Engle. Designed to awe and amuse audiences, monumental clocks had their heyday in the late 19th century, touring the United States and Europe like so many modern rock stars. Engle spent more than 20 years crafting his 11-foot-tall clock, which has 48 moving figurines and can display such information as month, day of the week, and moon phase along with time. Finishing it around 1878, he entrusted it to promoters who touted it as "The Eighth Wonder of the World" as they hauled it around the eastern U.S., charging adults a quarter and children 15 cents to see it. In 1951, after an appearance at the Ohio State Fair, the clock vanished. Members of

© ANNA DUBROVSKY

the National Watch & Clock Museum

the National Association of Watch and Clock Collectors spent years hunting for it, finally discovering it in a barn in 1988. Museum staff animate the clock at the top of each hour. The eclectic cast of characters that emerge from its three towers includes Jesus and Satan, three Marys and the 12 apostles, Revolutionary War soldiers and paragon of bravery Molly Pitcher, and Engle himself.

Lititz

In a county studded with lovely little towns, Lititz is generally regarded as the loveliest one of all. The clip-clop of Amish buggies that contributes so much to the appeal of Bird-in-Hand, Intercourse, Strasburg, and other communities west of Lancaster is rarely heard in Lititz. What draws visitors to the borough nine miles north of downtown Lancaster is a combination of historical ambience, boutique shopping, and a busy calendar of events. It doesn't hurt that the smell of chocolate wafts through the streets.

Most of the shops, galleries, eateries, and landmarks lie along East Main Street (Route 772) or Broad Street (Route 501), which meet in the center of town. Be aware that many are closed on Sundays. The second Friday of the month is a great day to visit because merchants pull out all the stops for **Lovin' Lititz Every 2nd** (717/626-6332, www.lititzpa.com, 5–9 P.M.), featuring free entertainment and free parking throughout town. Lititz is also a great place to be on Independence Day. First held in 1818, the **Fourth of July Celebration** (717/626-8981, www.lititzspringspark.org, admission charged) in Lititz Springs Park is the oldest continuous observance of the national holiday. The daylong festivities conclude with the lighting of 7,000 candles and a fireworks show.

Lititz boasts a unique history. It was founded in 1756 by members of the Moravian Church, an evangelical Protestant denomination that originated in the modern-day Czech Republic. For almost 100 years, only Moravians were permitted to live in the village. A group of strict church elders oversaw all aspects of day-to-day

© ANNA DUBROVSKY

historic Lititz

life, calling the shots in economic as well as religious matters. After opening its doors to outsiders in the 1850s, Lititz became a stop on the Reading and Columbia Railroad and a summer resort area. Lititz Springs Park and the limestone springs that give it its name were the main attraction. A replica of the passenger depot that stood at the entrance to the park from 1884 to 1957 houses the **Lititz Welcome Center** (18 N. Broad St., 717/626-8981, www .lititzspringspark.org, 10 A.M.–4 P.M. Mon.– Sat. and until 8 P.M. on the second Fri. of the month). On the opposite side of the train tracks, which are still used for moving freight, is the **Wilbur Chocolate Company** (48 N. Broad St., 717/626-3249, www.wilburbuds .com, store and museum open 10 A.M.–5 P.M. Mon.–Sat., free admission). Founded in 1884 in Philadelphia, based in Lititz since the 1930s, and owned by agribusiness conglomerate Cargill since 1992, Wilbur manufactures chocolate and other ingredients for the baking, candy, and dairy industries. It's best known to consumers for chocolates that resemble a

flower bud. (Wilbur Buds also bear a striking resemblance to Hershey's Kisses, which at more than 100 years old aren't quite as old as the squatter Buds.) The factory store offers free samples of the signature confection and a wide selection of other goodies, including fudge, marshmallows, almond bark, and peanut butter meltaways made on the spot. The attached Candy Americana Museum showcases antique candy machinery, cocoa tins, chocolate molds and boxes, marble slabs and rolling pins, and more than 150 porcelain chocolate pots from around the world.

As if sweet tooths needed another reason to visit Lititz, a chocolate-centric eatery opened in 2005. **Café Chocolate of Lititz** (40 E. Main St., 717/626-0123, www.chocolatelititz.com, 10 A.M.–5 P.M. Sun.–Thurs., 9 A.M.–9 P.M. Fri.–Sat., $6–10) is all about dark chocolate, eschewing varieties with less than 50 percent cocoa solids. Owner Selina Man also eschews foods with preservatives, buying organic whenever possible. The menu is short but varied, representing several cuisines. That makes choosing a wine or beer to bring to the BYOB a bit tricky: What pairs well with chocolate-drizzled crepes, mulligatawny soup, *and* "chili con chocolate" with smoked turkey or vegan sausage? A chocolate fountain in the front window reminds passersby of the house specialty: a $20 chocolate fondue for two (or even four).

The food lover's tour of Lititz doesn't end there. Just a couple of blocks from Café Chocolate is the **Julius Sturgis Pretzel Bakery** (219 E. Main St., 717/626-4354, www.juliussturgis.com, store 10 A.M.–4 P.M. Mon.–Fri. and 9 A.M.–5 P.M. Sat. Jan.–mid-Mar., 9 A.M.–5 P.M. Mon.–Sat. mid-Mar.–Dec., tour $3, children $2). Established in 1861, it's regarded as America's first pretzel bakery. Tours are offered from a half hour before the bakery store opens to a half hour before it closes and include a hands-on lesson in pretzel twisting. The bakery, with its original brick ovens, doesn't do a whole lot of baking these days. Soft pretzels are made in-house, but the many varieties of hard pretzels available in the store come from Tom Sturgis Pretzels, a Reading-area bakery founded by Julius's grandson.

The sturdy stone house that Julius turned into a pretzel bakery was built in 1784. It's one of more than a dozen 18th-century buildings still in use on East Main Street. Another houses the **Lititz Museum** (145 E. Main St., 717/627-4636, www.lititzhistoricalfoundation.com, 10 A.M.–4 P.M. Mon.–Sat. Memorial Day–last Sat. in Oct. and Fri.–Sat. Nov.–Sat. before Christmas, free admission), the place to go for a primer on the town's history. The Lititz Historical Foundation, which operates the museum, offers tours of the neighboring **Johannes Mueller House** (admission $5, seniors $4, high school students $3) from Memorial Day through the last Saturday in October. Built in 1792, the stone house remains practically unchanged and is furnished with hundreds of artifacts from the late 1700s and early 1800s. Tours are led by costumed guides and take approximately 45 minutes.

Wolf Sanctuary of Pennsylvania

Despite its official-sounding name, the Wolf Sanctuary (465 Speedwell Forge Rd., Lititz, 717/626-4617, www.wolfsancpa.com) is not a state facility. It's the pet project of one Lancaster County family, the Darlingtons, with a lot of land and a love for the animal portrayed so harshly in fairy tales. The Darlingtons began taking in wolves and wolf hybrids in the 1980s, after the state forbade keeping them as house pets. Today about 40 onetime pets—who can't be released into the wild because they rely on humans for food—roam 20-odd acres of the family's property. Public tours of the fenced refuge are offered Tuesdays, Thursdays, Saturdays, and Sundays. Reservations are required for the weekday tours, which start at 10 A.M. and cost $15 per adult, $14 per senior, and $13 per child 12 and under. You can just show up for weekend tours, offered at 10 A.M. June–September and noon October–May. They're $12 per adult, $11 per seniors, and $10 per child. Once a month, on the Saturday closest to the full moon, the sanctuary is open to the public in the evening. By the Light of the Moon tours (7:30–10 P.M., $20 per person, reservations requested), closed to children under 16, feature a campfire and live acoustical music. Private tours are available by appointment and cost $25 per person. The tours are a bit of a hike, so dress accordingly. It's best to visit during cold weather, which wolves prefer. On hot days Blazer, Frodo, Kojac, and other sanctuary residents are loath to emerge from holes they dig beneath their shelters.

If you're interested in spending hours or even days with the wolves, you're in luck. In 2005 the Darlingtons opened a B&B on their 100-plus acre property, which was the site of an iron forge from the 1760s to 1850s. **Speedwell Forge B&B** (717/626-1760 www.speedwellforge.com, $125–250) offers three guest rooms in what used to be the ironmaster's mansion and two private cottages. Grandest of them all is the Paymaster's Office cottage, so named because it's where forge employees were paid. The honeymoon-worthy retreat boasts a vaulted ceiling, massive brick fireplace, king-sized bed, and in-room whirlpool bath. The former paymaster's window separates the main room from a kitchenette. A less expensive alternative for romantics is the mansion's master bedroom, featuring a canopy bed and claw-foot whirlpool bath for two.

Ephrata Cloister

The town of Ephrata, about 15 miles north of downtown Lancaster, is best known as the onetime home of a religious community whose faithful ate meager rations and slept on wooden benches with blocks of wood for pillows. The Ephrata Cloister (632 W. Main St., Ephrata, 717/733-6600, 9 A.M.–5 P.M. Mon.–Sat., noon–5 P.M. Sun., closed Mon. and Tues. Jan.–Feb., admission $9, seniors $8, children 3–11 $6) was the hub of their community and home to members who chose a celibate life. The buildings where white-robed Brothers and Sisters lived, worked, and prayed in the 1700s are now open to the public.

Their leader, Conrad Beissel, was born in Germany in 1691. As a young man he was drawn to Pietism, a movement by religious purists to reform the state-supported Protestant churches. Banished from his homeland, he immigrated to Pennsylvania like so many German pietists drawn by William Penn's promise of religious freedom. In 1724 he was tapped to lead a newly formed German Baptist Brethren congregation, where his promotion of celibacy and other radical ideas caused a fissure. He left the church and in 1732 settled along the banks of the Cocalico Creek in northern Lancaster County to lead a hermit's life. Hermit-hood was not to be. The charismatic theologian was soon joined by followers, and their settlement became known as Ephrata, a biblical reference. At its zenith in the mid-1800s, the community consisted of about 80 celibate members and 200 "householders" who lived on farms around the Cloister. The community became known for its Germanic calligraphy, publishing center, and original a cappella music. Beissel prescribed a special diet for members of the choir, who sang at an otherworldly high pitch. Today the music composed by Beissel and crew is performed by the Ephrata Cloister Chorus at occasional concerts.

Beissel died in 1768 and was buried in a graveyard on the cloister grounds. His successor wasn't married to the idea of monastic life. After the death of the last celibate member in 1813, householders formed the German Seventh Day Baptist Church. The congregation disbanded in 1934, and several years later the state purchased the Cloister property, now a National Historic Landmark. Some of the original buildings, including a worship hall known as the saal, can only be viewed during guided tours, which are offered daily. You can explore other structures on your own.

ENTERTAINMENT AND EVENTS
Concert Venues
American Music Theatre (2425 Lincoln Highway East, Lancaster, 717/397-7700, www.amtshows.com) has presented concerts by Joe Cocker, Vince Gill, The Beach Boys, The B-52s, Huey Lewis and the News, Melissa Etheridge, Clay Aiken, and a host of other big-name entertainers since opening in 1997. It produces a handful of original shows each year, including a glitzy Christmas revue. The 1,600-seat theater is across U.S. 30 from the Rockvale Outlets.

Performing Arts
Downtown Lancaster is home to one of the oldest theaters in the country. Built in 1852 on the foundation of a pre-Revolutionary prison, the **Fulton Theatre** (12 N. Prince St., Lancaster, 717/397-7425, www.thefulton.org) hosted lectures by Mark Twain and Horace Greeley, performances by Sarah Bernhardt and W. C. Fields, a production of *Ben-Hur* featuring live horses in a spectacular chariot-racing scene (fistfights broke out at the box office when tickets went on sale), and burlesque in its first 100 years. In the 1950s and '60s it served primarily as a movie house. Since then the Fulton has reinvented itself as a producer of professional theater. Productions range from small-cast plays such as *Doubt* to beloved musicals such as *Les Misérables* and *Hello, Dolly!* Each season features a handful

© CICERO DONNELLY

Fulton Theatre in downtown Lancaster

of shows designed for pint-sized theater-goers. The auditorium, which seats about 700, was restored to its original Victorian splendor in 1995. It's one of a dwindling number still using sandbags and hemp ropes to move scenery. A 100-seat studio theater added during the $9.5 million renovation and expansion is used for an annual cabaret series. Named for a Lancaster County native credited with developing the first commercially successful steamboat, the Fulton is the primary venue of the professional **Lancaster Symphony Orchestra** (www.lancastersymphony.org).

Lancaster County has not one but two dinner theaters. In business since 1984, **Rainbow Dinner Theatre** (3065 Lincoln Highway East, Paradise, 800/292-4301, www.rainbow dinnertheatre.com) bills itself as America's only all-comedy dinner theater. It produces four knee-slappers per year, including a Christmas-themed show. The **Dutch Apple Dinner Theatre** (510 Centerville Rd., Lancaster, 717/898-1900, www.dutchapple.com) serves up more shows, and its menu includes dramatic fare such as *Rent*. Both offer buffet-style dining. The theaters are set back from the road and easily missed. Rainbow is behind the Best Western Revere Inn & Suites on U.S. 30, about three miles east of the Rockvale Outlets. The Dutch Apple shares a driveway with the Heritage Hotel—Lancaster, just off the Centerville exit of U.S. 30.

Sight & Sound Theatres

With two theaters in Lancaster County and a third in Branson, Missouri, Sight & Sound (800/377-1277, www.sight-sound.com) is the nation's largest Christian theatrical company. Founded in the 1970s by a Lancaster County native, it pulls out all the stops to dramatize biblical stories such as Noah's wet and wild journey, Joseph's journey from slavery to

© SIGHT & SOUND THEATRES

a scene from *Joseph,* at the Sight & Sound's Millennium Theatre

power, and the birth of Jesus. Think elaborate sets and special effects, professional actors and live animals. The Lancaster County theaters are a half mile apart along Route 896, between U.S. 30 and the town of Strasburg. Larger of the two, the **Millennium Theatre** (300 Hartman Bridge Rd., Ronks) is a vision inside and out. The sprawling, pastel-hued palace features three exterior domes (representing the Trinity), a wraparound stage double the size of Radio City Music Hall's, and the largest moving light system on the East Coast. Four-legged cast members amble to their spots—and "dressing rooms"—via specially designed passageways under the theater floor. Behind-the-scenes tours, offered March through October, are nearly as fascinating as the productions. The 643-seat **Living Waters Theatre** (202 Hartman Bridge Rd., Ronks) is Sight & Sound's original home.

Festivals and Events

What started in 1980 as a jousting demo to draw attention to a new winery has grown into one of Pennsylvania Dutch Country's marquee attractions. Jousting is just the tip of the lance at the **Pennsylvania Renaissance Faire** (2775 Lebanon Rd., Manheim, 717/665-7021, www.parenfaire.com, admission charged), which brings some 250,000 people to Mount Hope Estate & Winery over the course of 12 weekends from early August to late October. Transported to Elizabethan England, Fairegoers party like it's 1589 alongside sword swallowers and fire breathers, magicians and musicians, jugglers and jesters. The Ren Faire features more than 70 shows per day, including performances of Shakespeare's plays in a three-story replica of London's Globe Theatre. Human pawns, knights, and bishops battle it out on a 40-foot-by-40-foot chessboard. Merchants in period costumes demonstrate glassblowing, pottery throwing, leather working, bow and arrow making, and more. Even the food vendors wear the clothes and talk the talk of Shakespeare's day as they serve up everything from gelato to giant turkey legs. "Drynke" options include wine, mead, beer, and soft drinks made on-site. Admission is $29.95 for adults, $9.95 for children 5–11. Buy tickets online for savings of $5 per adult ticket. Though best known for the Ren Faire, Mount Hope Estate hosts a variety of entertainment throughout the year, including improv comedy, murder mystery dinners, and a Celtic festival. Located 15 miles north of Lancaster, the National Register–listed property was home to a prominent iron-making family in the 19th century.

Lancaster's Long's Park (1441 Harrisburg Pike, Lancaster, 717/735-8883, www.longs park.org) is another site of much merrymaking. The city park just off U.S. 30 is a poultry-lover's paradise on the third Saturday of May, when the Sertoma Club of Lancaster holds its annual fund-raiser for the park. Members of the civic organization serve more than 30,000 chicken dinners over the course of eight hours. The **Sertoma Chicken BBQ** (717/354-7259, www.lancastersertomabbq.com, tickets $8 in advance, $9 at the park), a tradition since 1953, held the Guinness World Record for most meat consumed at an outdoor event for more than a decade, losing it to a Paraguayan shindig in 2008. June marks the start of the **Long's Park Summer Music Series** (7:30 P.M. Sun. June–Aug.), another decades-old tradition. Bring blankets, lawn chairs, and nibbles for the free concerts. Alcohol isn't permitted in the 80-acre park. The music series is funded in part by proceeds from the **Long's Park Art & Craft Festival** (one-day tickets $8 in advance, $10 at the park), held over Labor Day weekend. The four-day festival showcases the work of 200 artists and craftspeople from across the country.

SHOPPING
Outlet Malls
Lancaster County's two outlet malls are just a couple of minutes apart on U.S. 30. **Rockvale Outlets** (35 S. Willowdale Dr., Lancaster, 717/293-9595, www.rockvalesquare outlets.com, 9:30 A.M.–9 P.M. Mon.–Sat., 11 A.M.–5 P.M. Sun.) features about 100 stores, including Lane Bryant, Jones New York,

Pendleton, Casual Male XL, Izod, Gymboree, and Disney Store. It's a great place to shop for the home, counting Pottery Barn, Restoration Hardware, Lenox, and Corningware Corelle Revere among its tenants.

Tanger Outlet Center (311 Stanley K. Tanger Blvd., Lancaster, 717/392-7260, www .tangeroutlet.com, 9 A.M.–9 P.M. Mon.–Sat., 10 A.M.–6 P.M. Sun.), located across U.S. 30 from Dutch Wonderland amusement park, is smaller but chicer, offering designer brands such as Polo Ralph Lauren, Kenneth Cole, Calvin Klein, Brooks Brothers, Coach, and Movado.

"Antiques Capital USA"
Located just off exit 286 of the Pennsylvania Turnpike, the little burg of Adamstown has made a big name for itself in antiquing circles. The self-proclaimed antiques capital of the United States is crowded with antiques shops, malls, and markets, most of which can be found along North Reading Road (Route 272). Sundays are a big day in "Antiques Capital USA" (www.antiquescapital.com). That's when **Renninger's Antiques Market** and the **Black Angus Antiques Mall** are open. The former (2500 N. Reading Rd., 717/336-2177, www.renningers.com, indoor market 7:30 A.M.–4 P.M. Sun., outdoor market opens at 5 A.M.) features upwards of 300 booths indoors and, weather permitting, hundreds more outdoors. Bring a flashlight to get in on the early morning action. The 70,000-square-foot Black Angus Antiques Mall (2800 N. Reading Rd., 717/484-4386, www.stoudts.com, mall 7:30 A.M.–4 P.M. Sun., outdoor pavilions 5 A.M.–noon) is part of a sprawling complex of businesses operated by husband and wife Ed and Carol Stoudt. More than 300 dealers set up shop in the mall, selling everything from fine art and early American furniture to tools and small collectibles. Outdoor pavilions accommodate about 100 more.

At 1 P.M., take a break from shopping for a free tour of **Stoudt's Brewing Company.** Frequent visitors to Europe, the Stoudts established the microbrewery in 1987 with the goal of making an authentic German-style beer. And they succeeded: Gold Lager and Pils, the brewery's German-style flagship beers, have racked up awards and accolades. Its top seller, however, is an American pale ale sold in bottles emblazoned with the stars and stripes. Brewery tours, also offered at 3 P.M. Saturdays, meet in the lobby of the adjacent **Black Angus Restaurant & Pub** (4:30–10 P.M. Mon.–Thurs., noon–10 P.M. Fri.–Sat., 11:30 A.M.–8 P.M. Sun., dining room menu $18–39, pub menu $9–19), a.k.a. "the house that beef built." The antiques-filled eatery has specialized in steaks since Ed Stoudt opened it in 1962. All dinners are served with bread made in the **Wonderful Good Market** (9 A.M.–5 P.M. Fri.–Sat., 7:30 A.M.–3 P.M. Sun.), the Stoudts' bakery, creamery, and specialty foods store.

Adamstown offers plenty of antiquing on days other than Sunday. **Heritage Antique Center** (2750 N. Reading Rd., 717/484-4646, www.heritageantiquecenter.com), one of the area's oldest antiques stores, and the **Antiques Showcase & German Trading Post** (2152 N.

Reading Rd., 717/336-8847, www.blackhorse lodge.com), with nearly 300 showcases full of fine antiques and investment-grade collectibles, are open 10 A.M.–5 P.M. seven days a week. Not to be missed if you visit on a weekend: **The Country French Collection** (2887 N. Reading Rd., 717/484-0200, www.countryfrench antiques.com, noon–4 P.M. Fri.–Sun. and by appointment), which imports 18th- and 19th-century antiques from France and England and restores them to pristine condition.

For several days every April, June, and September, Adamstown's antiquing scene goes into overdrive. Outside markets mushroom and inside markets keep longer hours during the **Antiques Extravaganzas,** which attract dealers from across the country.

Mud Sales

Held at fire companies throughout Lancaster County, "mud sales" are a chance to get dirt-cheap prices on everything from antiques to aluminum siding, lawn equipment to livestock, homemade food to horse carriages. Teeming as they are with Amish and Mennonite buyers

© WWW.DISCOVERLANCASTERPA.COM

Mud sales, named for the condition of the thawing spring ground, are held annually throughout Lancaster County to benefit local fire companies.

and sellers, these fund-raising sales/auctions are also a cultural immersion experience. Why are they called mud sales? Because most take place between mid-February and mid-April, when the ground is thawing—though it's not unheard of for fire companies to hold mud sales in the middle of summer. Visit www.padutch country.com or call 717/299-8901 for a schedule of sales, which begin bright and early.

Quilts and Fabrics

Mud sales are great places to buy locally crafted quilts, but if your visit to Lancaster County doesn't coincide with one, you're not out of luck. Quilt shops are more common than stoplights in the Amish countryside. Most sell a variety of handicrafts. (This author's fave: the ingenious pillow-blanket hybrid known as the "quillow.") Many are home-based businesses, allowing shoppers a glimpse into the everyday lives of locals. Just about all quilt shops are closed on Sundays. The **Quilt Shop at Miller's** (2811 Lincoln Highway East, Ronks, 717/687-8439, www.quiltshopatmillers.com, 10 A.M.–8 P.M. daily June–Aug., 10 A.M.–7 P.M. Mon.–Sat. and 10 A.M.–6 P.M. Sun. Sept.–Dec. and Apr.–May, 10 A.M.–5 P.M. Wed.–Sun. Jan.–Feb.) is an exception. It's right next to the popular Miller's Smorgasbord on U.S. 30, about a mile and a half east of Route 896.

Intercourse is a good place to start a quilt-shopping spree. The village along Route 340 (Old Philadelphia Pike) is home to **The People's Place Quilt Museum** (3510 Old Philadelphia Pike, Intercourse, 800/828-8218, www.ppquiltmuseum.com, 9 A.M.–5 P.M. Mon.–Sat., free admission), which is best known for showcasing antique Amish and Mennonite quilts but has also mounted exhibitions of contemporary quilts, African American quilts, and antebellum album quilts since its 1988 opening. The museum store is a trove of folk art from around the country. You'll find miniature quilts created with antique fabrics, loom-woven wool table runners, dolls with patchwork skirts and tiny accessories, Shaker boxes, wire-wrap jewelry, and more. The museum occupies the second floor of **The Old**

Country Store (800/828-8218, www.theold countrystore.com, 9 A.M.–6:30 P.M. Mon.–Sat. June–Aug., 9 A.M.–5 P.M. Mon.–Sat. Sept.–May), stocked with thousands of items made by local craftspeople, most of them Amish or Mennonite. In addition to hundreds of quilts, it carries potholders and pottery, Christmas ornaments and cornhusk bunnies, faceless Amish dolls and darling stuffed bears, pillows of various sizes and paper cuttings known as *scheren-schnitte*. With its selection of more than 6,000 bolts of fabric, the store is as much a starting point for needlecraft projects as a showplace for finished products. Quilt books, color-coordinated fabric packs, and pattern kits are also on offer.

In the complex of shops known as Kitchen Kettle Village is the airy **Village Quilts** (3529 Old Philadelphia Pike, Intercourse, 717/768-2787, www.kitchenkettle.com/quilts, 9 A.M.–5 P.M. Mon.–Sat.), which commissions works from a select group of home quilters. Each masterpiece is signed and dated and comes with a certificate for insurance purposes. The shop offers one-on-one quilting instruction ($80 for 90 minutes) by appointment. It can also arrange for a professional quilter to hop in your car and accompany you to other area shops. Call at least two weeks in advance to book a **Quilt Shop Hop** (10 A.M. Mon.–Fri., $150 for 2 people, $25 per additional person), which includes a stop for lunch.

A few minutes east of Intercourse along Route 340 is **Esh's Handmade Quilts** (3829 Old Philadelphia Pike, Gordonville, 717/768-8435, 9 A.M.–6 P.M. Mon.–Sat.), a small shop on a family dairy farm. And a few minutes west of Intercourse is **The Quilt & Fabric Shack** (3137 Old Philadelphia Pike, Bird-In-Hand, 717/768-0338, www.thequiltandfabricshack .com, 9 A.M.–5 P.M. Mon.–Sat.), boasting a large selection of quilts made by local Amish and Mennonites and four rooms of all-cotton fabrics. Its bargain room features some 700 bolts priced at $3 per yard. Just northwest of Intercourse along Route 772, **Family Farm Quilts** (3511 W. Newport Rd., 717/768-8375, www.familyfarmquilts.com, 9 A.M.–5 P.M.

Mon.–Sat.) counts more than 200 local women among its quilt suppliers. Its selection of handicrafts includes purses made of antique quilts, placemats, chair pads, children's toys, and baskets.

Witmer Quilt Shop (1070-76 W. Main St., New Holland, 717/656-9526, 8 A.M.–8 P.M. Mon. and Fri., 8 A.M.–6 P.M. Tues.–Thurs. and Sat.), located five miles north of Intercourse along Route 23, is remarkable for its selection of lovingly restored antique quilts. Emma Witmer's shop/home is also stocked with more than 100 new quilts, many in patterns she herself designed. Give her a few months and she'll give you a custom quilt. Drive less than half a mile west on Route 23 and turn right onto North Groffdale Road to reach the Amish dairy farm that's home to **Smuckers Quilts** (117 N. Groffdale Rd., New Holland, 717/656-8730, 8 A.M.–8 P.M. Mon.–Sat.), specializing in traditional patterns. A left onto South Groffdale will bring you to the Amish poultry farm that's home to **Country Lane Quilts** (221 S. Groffdale Rd., Leola, 717/656-8476, 8:30 A.M.–5 P.M. Mon.–Sat.). If you continue past Groffdale, make a left at Hess Road and a right at East Eby Road, you'll arrive at yet another Amish dairy farm with a handicrafts biz: **Riehl's Quilts and Crafts** (247 E. Eby Rd., Leola, 800/957-7105, www.riehlsamishquilts.com, 8 A.M.–5 P.M. Mon.–Sat.).

As you make your way between the shops, each carrying quilts by dozens if not hundreds of local women, keep your eyes peeled for handmade "quilts sold here" signs inviting you to pull into a drive and knock on the door.

Susquehanna Glass Factory Outlet and Tour

Founded in 1910, Susquehanna Glass (731 Ave. H, Columbia, 717/684-2155, www.susquehannaglass.com, store open 9 A.M.–5 P.M. Tues.–Sat., tours 10:30 A.M. and 1 P.M. Tues. and Thurs., reservations required) counts retailers Williams-Sonoma, Restoration Hardware, and David's Bridal among its customers. The glass decorator best known for personalized products offers everything from storage jars to lead crystal bowls at its factory store, located half a mile from the National Watch & Clock Museum in the Susquehanna River town of Columbia. Tours of the factory, where glass is still cut by hand, are offered year-round except when temps creep into the 90s. The tours are free and last 30–45 minutes.

SPORTS AND RECREATION
Spectator Sports

Professional baseball returned to Lancaster in 2005, 44 years after the Lancaster Red Roses folded. Named the **Lancaster Barnstormers** (Clipper Magazine Stadium, 650 N. Prince St., Lancaster, 717/509-3633, www.lancasterbarnstormers.com) by popular vote, the team swept its way to an Atlantic League championship in only its second season. Nearby York was added to the league the following year, and the two cities rekindled their historical "War of the Roses" rivalry. (Back when Lancaster had the Red Roses, York had the White Roses. York's modern-day club is called the Revolution.) Their mayors agreed that the loser of the season-long war would plant a rose garden at the victor's stadium. Clipper Magazine Stadium, built for the Barnstormers, is the first ballpark to boast a bumper boat pond.

Monster truck showdowns, demolition derbies, and other high-octane spectacles bring families to **Buck Motorsports Park** (900 Lancaster Pike, Quarryville, 800/344-7855, www.buckmotorsports.com) on Saturday evenings from May to early October. "The Buck" is 10 miles south of Lancaster on Route 272.

ACCOMMODATIONS

Lancaster County has lodging options aplenty. Its hotels and motels run the gamut from major brands such as Holiday Inn, Comfort Inn, and Travelodge to unique independents such as the **Red Caboose** (312 Paradise Ln., Ronks, 717/687-5000, www.redcaboosemotel.com, $69–159), a motel made of restored railroad cars, and the 97-room **Fulton Steamboat Inn** (Routes 30 and 896, Lancaster, 717/299-9999, www.fultonsteamboatinn.com, $80–180), built to resemble a steamboat and named

Sleep in a restored railroad car at the Red Caboose.

for a Lancaster County native who pioneered steam-powered shipping. Travelers who prefer bed-and-breakfasts can take their pick of more than 150. Indeed, Lancaster County has more B&Bs than any place on the Eastern Seaboard except Cape Cod. They're a diverse bunch: Bed down in an 18th-century stone house, an elegant Victorian manse, or on a working farm. If you travel with young children, you probably eschew B&Bs, but a farm stay is a different animal (hardy har har). It's lodging, education, and entertainment rolled into one—assuming your kids find gathering eggs and bottle-feeding calves entertaining. A list of Lancaster County farms that offer overnight accommodations is available at www.afarmstay.com.

The **Pennsylvania Dutch Convention & Visitors Bureau** (717/299-8901, www .padutchcountry.com) is a great source of information about lodging options. Its website allows for searches by price range and lodging type. The **Mennonite Information Center** (2209 Millstream Rd., Lancaster, 717/299-0954, www.mennoniteinfoctr.com),

best known for its personal tours of the Amish countryside, maintains a list of Mennonite-owned guesthouses, available at the center and on its website.

Under $100

Families can spend the night at **Old Mill Stream Campground** (2249 Lincoln Hwy. E., Lancaster, 717/299-2314, www.oldmill streamcampground.com, $33–43) for a fraction of what it costs to spend the day at the adjacent Dutch Wonderland amusement park. The 15-acre campground, which Hershey Entertainment & Resorts purchased along with Dutch Wonderland in 2001, has more than 160 tent and RV sites open year-round. Amenities include a 24-hour game room, a country store, laundry rooms, and free wireless Internet access.

The **Carriage House Motor Inn** (144 E. Main St., Strasburg, 717/687-7651, www .amishcountryinns.com/motor, $59–109) is a good non-camping option in this price range. Walking distance from the Railroad Museum of

Pennsylvania and the Strasburg Rail Road, it's ideal for rail fans. Dogs are welcome, provided they don't weigh in at more than 75 pounds. Rooms have cable TV and refrigerators, and rates include a continental breakfast. For about the same price, you can spend the night at nearby **Rayba Acres Farm** (183 Black Horse Rd., Paradise, 717/687-6729, www.raybaacres .com, $83–90) or **Neffdale Farm** (604 Strasburg Rd., Paradise, 717/687-7837, www.neffdalefarm .com, $80), both Mennonite-owned.

$100-150

Located just off U.S. 30 west of Lancaster city, the **Heritage Hotel–Lancaster** (500 Centerville Rd., Lancaster, 800/223-8963, www.heritagelancaster.com, $94–124) is a great choice for nightlife-loving travelers. Its restaurant and bar, **Loxley's** (6:30 A.M.–midnight Sun.–Thurs., 6:30 A.M.–2 A.M. Fri.–Sat., breakfast $3–10, lunch and dinner $9–29) attracts locals and hotel guests alike. Named for Robin of Loxley, the archer and outlaw better known as Robin Hood, it boasts a two-level deck that looks like a giant tree house. In keeping with the legend that inspired it, Loxley's donates 5 percent of food purchases to the needy. The hotel has 166 standard-looking guest rooms, a business center, a fitness room, and an outdoor pool. The Dutch Apple Dinner Theatre is right next door.

Sleep under handmade quilts and awake to the clip-clop of Amish buggies at **The Inn at Kitchen Kettle Village** (3529 Old Philadelphia Pike, Intercourse, 717/768-8261, www.kitchenkettle.com, $89–199). Scattered throughout the uber-quaint village, accommodations range from standard rooms in small cottages with yards and porches to suites that sleep up to six. Breakfast at the on-site Kling House Restaurant is free to inn guests Monday–Saturday.

The Strasburg area, known for its train-related attractions, is also heavily trafficked by Amish buggies. Located in the very center of town, the **Strasburg Village Inn** (1 W. Main St., Strasburg, 717/687-0900, www.strasburg .com, mid-June–Oct. $119–149, Nov.–Mar.

$79–99, Apr.–mid-June $99–119) has 10 classically appointed guest rooms and suites with private baths. The circa 1788 house is outfitted with wireless Internet and flat-screen TVs. Also built in the 1780s, the nearby **Limestone Inn B&B** (33 E. Main St., Strasburg, 717/687-8392, www.thelimestoneinn.com, $99–139) has six guest rooms and traces of a previous life: Wood moldings and doors on the third floor, where ceilings are too low for guests taller than 6 feet, bear the initials of boys who boarded there in the mid-1800s while studying at the then-famous Strasburg Academy. (Ceilings in the spacious second floor rooms are plenty high for everyone.) Innkeepers Richard and Denise Waller also own The Iron Horse Inn, an excellent restaurant down the street, so you can safely count on a superb breakfast.

Breakfast at (**Verdant View Farm B&B** (429 Strasburg Rd., Paradise, 717/687-7353, www.verdantview.com, $71–114), one mile east of Strasburg on Route 741, begins with a joining of hands and a rendition of the Johnny Appleseed song (*Oh, the Lord's been good to me . . .*). It's not unusual for two, three, or even four generations of the Ranck family,

Verdant View Farm owner Don Ranck introduces the guests of his B&B to a baby goat.

© ANNA DUBROVSKY

DUTCH COUNTRY

© ANNA DUBROVSKY

General Sutter Inn

which has operated the 118-acre dairy and crop farm for almost a century, to join guests around the table, set with pitchers of raw milk, platters of farm-fresh meat, eggs, and potatoes, and homemade pies. Breakfast isn't the first thing on the menu at Verdant View. Guests can begin the day with a farm tour, complete with opportunities to milk a cow, frolic with kittens, and feed calves, goats, bunnies, and other animals. Overslept? Don't despair. The tour is offered throughout the day, as are tractor-pulled wagon rides and "farmer's apprentice" programs in topics as diverse as making cheese and artificially inseminating cows. (Breakfast and farm experiences aren't offered on Sundays, when the Rancks attend their Mennonite church.) The nine guest rooms, spread between an 1896 farmhouse and the "little white house" down the lane, are nothing fancy. But what it lacks in frills the B&B more than makes up for in hospitality.

The charming town of Lititz has several recommendable accommodations in this price range. Chief among them is the **General Sutter Inn** (14 E. Main St., Lititz, 717/626-2115, www.generalsutterinn.com, $70–189),

offering 16 antique-filled guest rooms and suites. More than 200 years old, the inn took its present name in the 1930s to honor John Augustus Sutter, who established a settlement in California in the 1840s, saw it overrun by gold-seekers, and lived his final years in Lititz. No two rooms are the same, but all feature pillow-top mattresses, down comforters, flat-panel TVs, and wireless Internet. Guests enjoy a complimentary continental breakfast Monday–Friday and $5 off a full breakfast Saturday–Sunday. The **Alden House Bed & Breakfast** (62 E. Main St., Lititz, 717/627-3363, www.aldenhouse.com, $99–149), with seven guest rooms and suites, is another fine choice in the center of town. Breakfast is a multi-course affair.

Over $150

Visitors to downtown Lancaster may find it hard to believe that the **Lancaster Marriott at Penn Square** (25 S. Queen St., Lancaster, 717/239-1600, www.lancastermarriott.com, $139–289) and adjoining Lancaster County Convention Center opened in 2009. The 299-room hotel smack dab in the center of town

© ANNA DUBROVSKY

Lancaster Marriott at Penn Square

looks mighty historical. That's because developers incorporated the Beaux Arts facade of a shuttered century-old department store into its design. A contemporary aesthetic takes over in the soaring lobby and spacious rooms. The hotel boasts an indoor pool and serenity-peddling spa (717/207-4076, www.mandarinrosespa.com, 10 A.M.–6 P.M. Mon.–Sat.). The on-site **Penn Square Grille and Rendezvous Lounge** (717/207-4033, www.pennsquaregrille.com, breakfast 6:30–11 A.M. Mon.–Fri. and 7–11 A.M. Sat.–Sun., lunch 11 A.M.–2 P.M. daily, dinner 5–10 P.M. Sun.–Thurs. and 5–11 P.M. Fri.–Sat., lounge open 11 A.M.–1 A.M. daily, lunch $9–15, dinner $18–36, lounge menu $8–34) offer contemporary American cuisine and 30 wines by the glass. Central Market, the Fulton Theatre, the Demuth Museum, and other downtown attractions are just a hop, skip, and a jump away. On the downside: Hotel parking is $14 per day ($24 if you go the valet route), and surfing the Web will set you back $12.95 daily.

With its brick walls and wood beams, locally crafted furnishings and flat-screen TVs, art gallery and organic restaurant, the (**Lancaster Arts Hotel** (300 Harrisburg Ave., 717/299-3000, www.lancasterartshotel.com, rooms $149–219, suites $269–359) is the city's hippest lodging property by a mile. "Hip" implies new, but the building itself dates to the late 1800s. Built as a tobacco warehouse, it found a new life as a boutique hotel in 2006. Original works by area artists adorn each of 63 guest rooms and suites, some of which boast in-room whirlpools. Amenities include 24-hour business and fitness centers, bicycle rentals, free parking, and free shuttle service within a five-mile radius of the hotel. Internet access and a continental breakfast are also on the house. **John J. Jeffries** (717/431-3307, www.johnjjeffries.com, restaurant 5:30–10 P.M. Mon.–Sat. and 5:30–9 P.M. Sun., bar 4 P.M.–midnight Mon.–Sat. and 4–11 P.M. Sun., $11–29), the on-site restaurant and lounge, bills itself as the leading consumer of local organic meats and vegetables in central PA. Happy hour is 4–6 P.M. daily.

Located midway between the villages of Intercourse and Bird-in-Hand on Route 340, (**AmishView Inn & Suites** (3125 Old Philadelphia Pike, Bird-in-Hand, 866/735-1600, www.amishviewinn.com, room $114–214, suite $174–424) is right in the heart of Amish country. Rooms on the backside of the hotel boast farmland views, and the sight of Amish children heading to school or a farmer working his fields with horse-drawn equipment isn't unusual. That's not the only thing it has going for it. AmishView has an indoor pool and whirlpool, fitness and arcade rooms open 24/7, and a guest laundry. Its 50 guest rooms and suites feature kitchenettes, mahogany furniture, 27-inch TVs with cable channels, CD and DVD players, and free high-speed Internet access. Suites have fireplaces and/or whirlpools. A complimentary country breakfast complete with·made-to-order omelets and waffles is served every morning. Plain & Fancy Farm Restaurant, one of the region's most popular PA Dutch eateries, is just outside the doors. **The Inn & Spa at Intercourse Village** (3542 Old Philadelphia Pike, Intercourse, 717/768-2626, www.amishcountryinns.com/inn,

$159–399), with nine guest rooms and suites, is another upscale option in Amish country. Made for romance, its three "grand suites" feature gas fireplaces, Jacuzzi tubs for two, king-sized beds, and all-cotton bathrobes. Request the Summer House Suite if you're keen on a heart-shaped tub. A five-course breakfast is served by candlelight. Open to the public, the spa (717/768-0555, 9 A.M.–4 P.M. Mon.–Tues., Thurs., and Sat., 9 A.M.–8 P.M. Wed. and Fri.) offers massages, manicures, and other services in a French country setting.

FOOD

Leave your diet at the Lancaster County line. Visiting this corner of the globe without indulging in a Pennsylvania Dutch–style meal is like visiting Disney World and not riding the rides. The cuisine is anything but light, and unless you seek out a restaurant with an à la carte menu (wussy), you're looking at an all-you-can-eat experience. Approach it with the abandon you bring to Thanksgiving dinner. If you're not stuffed to the gills when you leave, you're sort of missing the point. This is the food of hardworking farm families. This is no time to turn down seconds.

It would be unwise to fill up on PA Dutch foods meal after meal, not only because of the effect on your waistline but because Lancaster County has some excellent non-Deutsch eateries. You can find everything from California-style burritos to authentic Cajun cuisine within its borders. The city of Lancaster has experienced a restaurant renaissance over the past decade, and the 2009 completion of a convention center in the heart of downtown augured well for the dining scene.

Pennsylvania Dutch Fare

If you're new to PA Dutch cuisine, you should know a few things. Around here, **chicken pot pie** isn't a pie at all. It's a stew with square-cut egg noodles. A **whoopie pie** isn't a pie either. Think of it as a dessert burger: creamy icing pressed between two bun-shaped cakes. Chocolate cake with white icing is most common, but you'll also encounter variations such

as pumpkin cake with cream cheese icing. The annual **Whoopie Pie Festival** (Hershey Farm Restaurant & Inn, Rte. 896, Strasburg, 717/687-8635, www.whoopiepiefestival.com, third Sat. in Sept., free) features more than 100 varieties. Pennsylvania Dutch Country's most iconic dessert, the **shoofly pie**, is, in fact, a pie with a crumb crust. But it's nothing like the fruit or cream pies served at diners throughout the country. Packed with molasses and brown sugar, the joltingly sweet treat comes in "wet bottom" and "dry bottom" varieties. A wet-bottomed shoofly pie is more gooey and molasses-y than its dry-bottomed cousin. Other regional specialties include egg noodles with browned butter, **chow-chow** (a pickled vegetable relish), **scrapple** (a breakfast food made with pork scraps), and **schnitz un knepp** (a dish consisting of dried apples, dumplings, and ham).

Lancaster County's most popular PA Dutch restaurants generally fall into one of two categories: smorgasbord and family-style. With seating for 1,200 and a seemingly endless array of dishes, ◖ **Shady Maple Smorgasbord** (129 Toddy Dr., East Earl, 717/354-8222, www.shady-maple.com/smorgasbord, breakfast 5–10 A.M. Mon.–Sat., lunch 10:45 A.M.–3:15 P.M. Mon.–Fri., dinner 4–8 P.M. Mon.–Fri. and 10:45 A.M.–8 P.M. Sat.) is the behemoth of the bunch. Don't be surprised to find a waiting line. On Saturday evenings it can take upwards of an hour to get seated. You really need to see this place to appreciate its enormity. Along with Pennsylvania Dutch specialties, lunch and dinner buffets feature everything from pizzas to fajitas to cheesesteaks. Save room for 30-odd dessert options. Lunch costs about $12 and dinner $16–22, depending on the day's specials. Seniors enjoy a 10 percent discount, and children 4–10 eat for half price. (Anyone who has recently undergone a gastric bypass operation also gets a discount.) Shady Maple's breakfast buffet ($9–11 per adult) gets high marks from scrapple fans. A breakfast menu ($3–6) is available on weekdays.

Bird-in-Hand Family Restaurant & Smorgasbord (2760 Old Philadelphia Pike, Bird-in-Hand, 717/768-1550, www.bird-in-hand.com, 6 A.M.–8 P.M. Mon.–Sat., breakfast buffet $9, lunch buffet $10–14, dinner buffet $15–17, age-based pricing for children 4–12) offers both menu and smorgasbord dining for breakfast, lunch, and dinner. Its kids' buffet is designed to look like Noah's Ark, complete with stuffed animals peering through the portholes.

Hershey Farm Restaurant (240 Hartman Bridge Rd., Ronks, 717/687-8635, www .hersheyfarm.com, 8 A.M.–8 P.M. Mon.–Fri. and 7 A.M.–8 P.M. Sat.–Sun., closed Sunday evenings and Mondays Nov.–Apr.) also offers a choice of menu or smorgasbord dining. The on-site bakery is famous for its whoopie pies (Hershey Farm hosts the Whoopie Pie Festival) and triple-layer chocolate cake. A chocolate dipping fountain graces the dessert bar on evenings and weekends. **Miller's Smorgasbord** (2811 Lincoln Hwy. East, Ronks, 717/687-6621, www.millerssmorgasbord.com, breakfast from 7:30 A.M. and lunch/dinner from 11:30 A.M. daily Mar.–Dec., call for Jan.–Feb. hours) is unique in that it accepts reservations and serves alcohol. At $7.95, its weekday breakfast buffet is a steal.

[Plain & Fancy Farm Restaurant (3121 Old Philadelphia Pike, Bird-in-Hand, 717/768-4400, www.plainandfancyfarm.com, lunch/ dinner from 11:30 A.M. daily Mar.–Dec., closed Jan.–Feb.) is Lancaster County's oldest and arguably best destination for family-style dining. Most family-style restaurants in Pennsylvania Dutch Country follow a similar recipe: Guests are seated—often at tables with other parties—and brought platters of food, which are replenished until everyone is sated. Plain & Fancy's "Amish farm feast" ($19 per person, children 4–12 $10) features made-from-scratch fried chicken, baked sausage, chicken pot pie with homemade noodles, real mashed potatoes, and more. The restaurant, which opened in 1959, also offers an à la carte menu (from $8). Its signature dessert, sour cream apple crumb pie, is out of this world. Though it seats 700, you'd be wise to make a reservation.

Good 'N Plenty Restaurant (150 E. Brook Rd., Smoketown, 717/394-7111, www.goodn plenty.com, 11:30 A.M.–8 P.M. Mon.–Sat.) can accommodate more than 600 guests. Choose from a family-style meal ($20 per person,

Good 'N Plenty Restaurant is a great place to have a family-style meal.

© ANNA DUBROVSKY

children 4–12 $10) at a communal table or a "harvest platter" ($11 per person, children 4–12 $7) with a meat dish, two sides, and dessert, served at a private table. Just south of Bird-in-Hand on Route 896, Good 'N Plenty boasts an on-site bakery and a large gift shop. **Stoltzfus Farm Restaurant** (3716 East Newport Rd., Gordonville, 717/768-8156, www.stoltzfusfarmrestaurant.com, 11:30 A.M.–8 P.M. Mon.–Sat. Apr.–Oct. and Fri.–Sat. in Nov., closed Dec.–Mar.), one block east of Intercourse on Route 772, offers family-style dining in a more intimate setting. Amos Stoltzfus and his wife, Mary, began serving meals in their farmhouse in 1968. Their children took over in 1989 and continue to run the show today. The family-style menu ($17 per person, children 4–12 $8) includes sausage made in the on-site butcher shop and homemade ham loaf. An à la carte menu ($5–9) is available 11:30 A.M.–3 P.M.

Lancaster

With close to a dozen cuisines represented under one roof, **Central Market** (23 N. Market St., 717/735-6890, www.centralmar ketlancaster.com, 6 A.M.–4 P.M. Tues. and Fri., 6 A.M.–2 P.M. Sat.) is one of downtown Lancaster's most popular lunch spots. You'll find vendors selling everything from made-to-order salads to homemade rice pudding. Ethnic options include Narai Exotic Thai Cuisine (get there early for the hot-selling fresh spring rolls), Señorita Burrita with its own-made salsas and vegetarian chili, and Saife's Middle Eastern Food. The downsides: Central Market is open just three days a week, and seating is limited. Fortunately, some market vendors have other locations. The original **Señorita Burrita** (227 N. Prince St., 717/283-0940, www .senoritaburrita.net, café opens at 7:30 A.M. Mon.–Fri. and noon Sat., full menu available 11 A.M.–9 P.M. Mon.–Thurs., 11 A.M.–11 P.M. Fri., noon–11 P.M. Sat., $5–9) is just a couple of blocks away. California transplant Jennifer Foster opened the restaurant in 2003 (and the market stand in 2006) to sate her cravings for Mission-style burritos. Choose from specialty burritos such as the Mama Foster (rosemary olive oil tortilla, southwestern chicken, tomato basil rice, black beans, feta cheese, and more) or build your own with ingredients ranging from roasted red pepper hummus to vegan ground "beef" to grilled steak. The hip hangout also offers soups, salads, tacos, nachos, and more than half a dozen variations of rice and beans. Foster and staff grow many of the vegetables they use, buying the rest from local farms or Central Market's produce stands. The java comes from local roaster **Square One Coffee** (145 N. Duke St., 717/392-3354, www .squareonecoffee.com, 7 A.M.–11 P.M. Mon.–Fri., 9 A.M.–11 P.M. Sat.–Sun.), which deals exclusively in Fair Trade Certified and organically grown beans.

The Lancaster Dispensing Co. (33–35 N. Market St., 717/299-4602, www.dispensing co.com, kitchen 11 A.M.–midnight Mon.–Sat. and noon–9 P.M. Sun., bar open until 2 A.M. Mon.–Sat. and 10 P.M. Sun., $4–15) opened next to Central Market in 1978, before Lancaster had a restaurant scene to speak of. Designed with a Victorian pub in mind, DipCo offers a variety of salads, some south-of-the-border specialties, and hearty dinner entrées, but it's the overstuffed sandwiches that keep locals coming back. (The reasonable beer prices don't hurt.) Count on live music most Friday and Saturday nights.

Pick up a bottle of wine on your way to **Rachel's Cafe & Creperie** (309 N. Queen St., 717/399-3515, www.rachelscreperie.com, 7 A.M.–8 P.M. Tues.–Fri., 9 A.M.–8 P.M. Sat., 9 A.M.–3 P.M. Sun., $3–7), where the crepes are piping hot and the fillings inventive. The BYOB pays tribute to France with smoothie names like The Louvre, Monet's Garden, and Napoleon's Weakness but takes an international approach to crepe design. There's the pizza crepe and the Greek crepe, the veggie burrito crepe and the Thai chicken crepe, the smoked salmon crepe and the cheeseburger crepe. There's even a Philly cheese crepe (steak, American cheese, mushroom, scallions, and red onions). Building your own is always an option.

More upscale dining options abound. Lancaster County native Tim Carr lent his

DUTCH COUNTRY

culinary talents to area country clubs before putting his name to a restaurant. Spitting distance from Central Market, **Carr's Restaurant** (50 W. Grant St., 717/299-7090, www.carrsrestaurant.com, brunch 11:30 A.M.–2:30 P.M. Sun., lunch 11:30 A.M.–2:30 P.M. Tues.–Sat., dinner 5:30–9:30 P.M. Tues.–Thurs. and 5:30–10 P.M. Fri.–Sat., brunch $8–20, lunch $7–15, dinner $9–30) puts a sophisticated spin on comfort foods. There's no StarKist in the tuna noodle casserole, an artful presentation of thinly sliced rare tuna and wide noodles tossed with a rich butter sauce and wild mushrooms. The mac and cheese is loaded with Maine lobster chunks. Request a table near the back of the basement-level restaurant, where a glass wall affords a view of the wine cellar. You're welcome to bring your own bottle (a $15 corkage fee applies), but the Carr's selection is one of the best in town. In 2009 Carr opened **Crush Wine Bar** (4:30–9:30 P.M. Tues.–Thurs., 4:30–10 P.M. Fri., noon–10 P.M. Sat.) above his restaurant. On offer: 20-odd wines by the glass and half glass, a carefully curated assortment of beers, several kinds of absinthe, and creative tapas ($6–11). Stop in if only to see what he means by Pennsylvania Dutch "sushi."

A short stroll away, German-born chef Gunter Backhaus presides over **The Loft** (201 W. Orange St., 717/299-0661, www.theloftlancaster.com, lunch 11:30 A.M.–2 P.M. Mon.–Fri., dinner 5:30–9 P.M. Mon.–Sat., lunch $9–14, dinner $16–34), locally famous for its jumbo shrimp cocktail. Backhaus doesn't shy away from the likes of frog legs, snails, and alligator tails—wait'll you see what the man can do with oysters—but timid palates needn't fear. The menu also features rosemary roasted free-range chicken, filet mignon, and lobster tails. Cozy and unpretentious, the restaurant gets its name from the open-beam ceiling in one of two dining rooms. The stems of potted plants cascade over the beams.

With a max capacity of 30 and a no-reservations policy, **Effie Ophelia** (230 N. Prince St., 717/397-6863, www.effieophelia.com, 5–10 P.M. Tues.–Sat., $22–30) might test your patience. But the wait is generally regarded as

worth it, thanks to chef-owner Eric Howton's culinary artistry. An open kitchen allows patrons insight into the creative process. The curiously named BYOB doesn't accommodate parties larger than six.

It's not just dieters who sup on salad at the **Belvedere Inn** (402 N. Queen St., 717/394-2422, www.belvedereinn.biz, lunch 11 A.M.–2 P.M. Mon.–Fri., dinner 5–11 P.M. Sun.–Thurs. and 5 P.M.–midnight Fri.–Sat., bar open 11 A.M.–2 A.M. Mon.–Fri. and 5 P.M.–2 A.M. Sat.–Sun., lunch $7–14, dinner $12–32). The grilled Caesar salad at this elegant restaurant and bar is a thing of legend. Have it plain or choose from toppings including tenderloin tips, sautéed scallops, and grilled salmon. A petite version is available during the dinner hours, when entrées such as wild boar Bolognese and gnocchi with Maine lobster vie for attention. **Crazy Shirley's** (7 P.M.–2 A.M. Wed.–Thurs., 5 P.M.–2 A.M. Fri.–Sat.), a piano bar and lounge on the second floor of the Belvedere, hosts karaoke on Wednesdays, a DJ on Thursdays, and live jazz or blues on Fridays and Saturdays.

You might break into a song after a few sips of the Supercalifragilisticexpialidocious, a signature cocktail at **Checkers Bistro** (300 W. James St., 717/509-1069, www.checkersbistro.com, 11:30 A.M.–10 P.M. Tues.–Sat., bar open until 11 P.M., $8–32). It's a potent mix of vodka, gin, rum, triple sec, and banana liqueur, among other things. Supercalifragilisticexpialidocious is also an apt description for the contemporary restaurant near Lancaster's ballpark. Its small plates menu is particularly appealing, with options both common (chicken wings) and singular (Peking duck tacos). A breakfast menu available 11 A.M.–3 P.M. Saturdays is heavier on drinks than dishes. Wash down the brioche French toast with a Moon River White Sangria, a sparkling concoction of white wine, flavored brandy, and fresh fruit juices.

Like Checkers, **⟨ FENZ Restaurant & Latenight** (398 Harrisburg Ave., Ste. 100, 717/735-6999, www.fenzrestaurant.com, dinner from 5 P.M. Mon.–Sat., lounge opens at 4 P.M., $14–28) excels in cocktails and small plates. Give the pickle fries a chance: the

© ANNA DUBROVSKY

Lancaster's FENZ Restaurant

tempura-battered kosher dill spears are positively addictive. Stylishly appointed with a clientele to match, FENZ has two levels with a bar on each. Have a look at both before settling in; the upstairs generally has a livelier, more youthful vibe. Take a seat at the downstairs bar to watch chef Daniella Ward at work. She's a whiz at vegetarian and vegan entrées. (The restaurant shares a 19th-century foundry building with a yoga studio, so she gets lots of practice.) Don't waste time searching for street parking. There's a lot behind the building, accessible from Charlotte Street.

A discussion of Lancaster's fine dining scene wouldn't be complete without words of praise for **Gibraltar** (931 Harrisburg Ave., 717/397-2790, www.kearesrestaurants.com/gibraltar, lunch 11:30 A.M.–2:30 P.M. Mon.–Fri., dinner 5–10 P.M. Mon.–Thurs., 5–10:30 P.M. Fri.–Sat., 4:30–9:30 P.M. Sun., bar open as late as 2 A.M., lunch $8–19, dinner $19–34), with its Mediterranean-influenced cuisine, *Wine Spectator*-lauded wine list, and gracious service. The seafood is simply phenomenal.

Start off with selections from the raw bar or an order of crab spring rolls and proceed to entrées like whole Adriatic Sea branzino (European seabass), rainbow trout stuffed with crab, and Moroccan spiced colossal shrimp. A tapas menu ($5–17) is available for those in the sharing spirit. Save room for one of pastry chef Anthony Valerio's confections.

Strasburg

Strasburg, with its train-related attractions and proximity to the Sight & Sound Theatres, sees large numbers of tourists. But its restaurants feel refreshingly un-touristy. Smack dab in the center of town, the **Strasburg Country Store & Creamery** (1 W. Main St., 717/687-0766, www.strasburg.com, 11 A.M.–10 P.M. Mon.–Sat., noon–10 P.M. Sun.) is best known as a destination for dessert and a dose of nostalgia. But it also offers soups, salads, sandwiches, and "Strasburgers" served with locally made potato chips. The house specialty is a bread bowl filled with PA Dutch–style chicken corn soup. As for dessert, choose from 20-plus flavors of ice

© ANNA DUBROVSKY

Strasburg Country Store & Creamery

cream and mix-ins such as M&Ms, raisins, and granola. Like the ice cream, the waffle cones are house-made, and the sweet aroma of sizzling batter hangs in the air. For a real indulgence, skip the cone and order an apple dumpling sundae. Ice cream isn't the only dessert option. A wide variety of chocolate-covered goodies vie for attention with fudge and peanut brittle, candy apples and caramel corn. Have a seat inside to soak in the old-timey touches, from vintage Cream of Wheat posters to a 19th-century marble soda fountain. Have a seat outside to watch horse-drawn buggies negotiating the intersection of Routes 741 and 896.

Purchased in 2003 by a husband and wife team with no experience in food service, **(The Iron Horse Inn** (135 E. Main St., 717/687-6362, www.ironhorsepa.com, noon–9 P.M. Mon. and Wed.–Thurs., noon–10 P.M. Fri.–Sat., noon–7 P.M. Sun., lunch $7–10, dinner $9–42) has emerged as one of those rare restaurants that pair fine food with a casual ambience. Denise Waller, one-half of the ownership

team and a nurse by training, buys broccoli, squash, potatoes, and other produce directly from local Amish farmers, shrinking the field-to-table timeline to a few hours in some cases. Lunch at the Iron Horse (a native American term for trains) can be as simple as a grilled ham and cheddar sandwich or as sophisticated as crepes stuffed with lump crabmeat. The asparagus fries—that's right: deep-fried spears of asparagus—go well with any dish. Dinner options range from an Angus beef burger to German/Austrian specialties to the triple steak, a marriage of portobello mushroom, Atlantic salmon, and succulent filet mignon. Chicken and waffles, served here more than a century ago when the building was known as The Hotel Strasburg, is available Sunday through Thursday. The lineup of draft beers features local brews along with German imports, and the wine list includes selections from Twin Brook Winery, about 10 miles east of Strasburg.

Just east of town on Route 741 is an outpost of regional chain **Isaac's Restaurant**

& Deli (226 Gap Rd., 717/687-7699, www .isaacsdeli.com, 10 A.M.–9 P.M. Mon.–Thurs., 10 A.M.–10 P.M. Fri.–Sat., 11 A.M.–9 P.M. Sun., call for winter hours, $6–12). The year was 1983 when two college buddies opened the first Isaac's in downtown Lancaster, and *Miami Vice* was soon to become a TV sensation. Hence the preponderance of pink flamingos in the bird-themed eateries scattered throughout south-central Pennsylvania. The Strasburg location, which shares an address with the Choo Choo Barn, a model railroader's mecca, boasts a dining area decked out like a train car. Its repertoire of made-from-scratch soups is 200 strong, but only the delicious creamy pepperjack tomato is available every day. The long list of sandwiches includes half a dozen veggie options. Pretzel sandwiches like the Salty Eagle (grilled ham, Swiss cheese, mustard) and Mallard (roast beef, bacon, mushrooms, melted cheddar, mild horseradish sauce) are particularly popular. Watching your carbs? Ask for a nest of romaine, mixed greens, or spinach in lieu of bread. You'll also find Isaac's in downtown Lancaster (25 N. Queen St., 717/394-5544), Lititz (4 Crosswinds Rd., 717/625-1181), and Ephrata (120 N. Reading Rd., 717/733-7777), among other places.

Lititz

The historic General Sutter Inn (14 E. Main St., 717/626-2115, www.generalsutterinn.com), located at the junction of Route 501 and East Main Street in the heart of Lititz, offers two restaurants along with 16 antique-filled guest rooms. The elegant **1764 Restaurant** (brunch 11 A.M.–3 P.M. Sun., lunch 11 A.M.–2:30 P.M. Mon.–Fri., 11 A.M.–3 P.M. Sat., dinner 5–9 P.M. Tues.–Thurs., 5–9:30 P.M. Fri.–Sat., 3–8 P.M. Sun., $7–30) isn't as pricey as its white tablecloths suggest. Its menu includes flatbread pizzas, burgers, and sandwiches for under $12 as well as loftier fare such as lobster and truffle mac and cheese and house-made basil gnocchi. The crab cakes sell like hotcakes. Alfresco dining is available Tuesdays through Sundays during the warmer months. The restaurant's name references the year the original inn was built.

(The current structure was built on the foundations of the original in the early 1800s.) In 2010 the inn unveiled a British-style pub, **Bulls Head Public House** (11:30 A.M.–4 P.M. Mon., 11:30 A.M.–10 P.M. Tues.–Thurs., 11:30 A.M.–10:30 P.M. Fri.–Sat., 11:30 A.M.–8 P.M. Sun., bar open until 11 P.M. Tues.–Thurs. and midnight Fri.–Sat., $5–15). Beer lovers are bonkers for the place, which boasts 14 rotating drafts and 80-plus bottles. The menu varies from day to day (check the chalkboard), but typical options include fish and chips, lamb shepherd's pie, chicken and leek pie, Scotch eggs, and mussels with blue cheese and bacon.

Columbia

Order the whoopee pie at **◖ Prudhomme's Lost Cajun Kitchen** (50 Lancaster Ave., 717/684-1706, www.lostcajunkitchen.com, 4:30–11 P.M. Mon., 11 A.M.–11 P.M. Tues.–Thurs., 11 A.M.–midnight Fri.–Sat., 11 A.M.–8 P.M. Sun., $4–22) and what you'll get is a far cry from the classic Pennsylvania Dutch dessert. In place of the mound-shaped cakes: homemade cornbread. In place of the icing center: tender crabmeat. Served with a side of creamy mushroom sauce, the appetizer is a Lost Cajun original. Owners David and Sharon Prudhomme—he of Louisiana, she of New Jersey—brought their brand of Cajun cooking to Pennsylvania Dutch Country in 1992. The name Prudhomme should not be unfamiliar to foodies. David's uncle, Paul Prudhomme, owner of K-Paul's Louisiana Kitchen in New Orleans, is widely credited with popularizing Cajun cuisine. David learned the ropes in the restaurant his uncle opened in 1979. He makes just about everything from scratch—from salad dressings to the turkey andouille sausage that flavors his jambalaya—and still finds time to work the front of the house, where Sharon presides. Adventurous eaters delight in the menu, which includes turtle soup, alligator tail, and deep-fried bison testicles. But what Lost Cajun does best is blackened catfish. Try the melt-in-your-mouth catfish nuggets or the Cajun-meets-Mexican catfish fajita. The casual, playfully decorated restaurant and bar is also famous for its oversized onion rings. You'll need a knife and fork to attack these bad boys.

Mount Joy

Bube's Brewery (102 N. Market St., 717/653-2056, www.bubesbrewery.com) is reason enough to visit the town of Mount Joy, which at 14 miles northwest of Lancaster isn't particularly close to major tourist attractions. The one-of-a-kind Bube's is many things. For starters, it's a trip back in time. Listed in the National Register of Historic Places, the large brewery/restaurant complex looks much as it did in the late 1800s, when German immigrant Alois Bube produced lager beers there. Bube died in 1908, and the buildings were largely untouched until 1968, when restoration work began. Today they house a microbrewery, three restaurants, a store, and an art gallery. Occupying the original bottling plant is the **Bottling Works** (lunch served from 11 A.M. Mon.–Sat. and noon Sun., dinner served from 5 P.M. daily, $6–29), most casual of the restaurants. Its menu is typical of brewpubs: plenty of deep-fried munchies, soups and salads, burgers and sandwiches, and a selection of hearty entrées. Open-air dining is available in the adjacent **Biergarten,** where you'll find the huge boiler that created steam to power Mr. Bube's brewery. Reservations aren't required but are appreciated for groups of six or more.

It's best to make a reservation if you're keen on dining more than 40 feet below ground in the **Catacombs** (dinner served from 5:30 P.M. weekdays and 5 P.M. weekends, $24–39). The fine dining restaurant in the original brewery's stone-walled cellars offers the likes of roast duckling, crabmeat-stuffed lobster tail, and filet mignon amid candlelight. On most Sundays it serves a themed feast with a heaping side of theatrics. Bawdy medieval-themed feasts are most common, but its repertoire also includes Roman-, pirate-, and fairy-themed feasts, Halloween-themed feasts in October, and Christmas-themed feasts in December. Feast tickets must be purchased in advance.

Alois, the third restaurant, occupies the bar and dining rooms of the Victorian hotel Mr. Bube built onto his brewery. It hosts murder mystery dinners on Saturday nights throughout the year and several times a week around Halloween and Christmas. Tickets are $38 and should be purchased in advance.

Bube's Brewery merchandise is available in the **Cooper's Shed**, so called because it served as the original brewery's barrel-working shop. The store is open the same hours as the Catacombs. The **Brewery Gallery** (noon–9 P.M. daily and until 11 P.M. Fri.–Sun., free admission) changes exhibits monthly. The **Inn at Bube's Brewery** opened in 2010, offering rooms in the historic hotel at $100 per night.

INFORMATION

The **Pennsylvania Dutch Convention & Visitors Bureau** (717/299-8901, www.padutchcountry.com) is an excellent source of information about Lancaster County. Visit the website to request its free "getaway guide" or flip through a digital version. At the CVB's main visitors center (501 Greenfield Rd., Lancaster, 9 A.M.–6 P.M. Mon.–Sat. and 9 A.M.–4 P.M. Sun. Memorial Day weekend–Oct., 10 A.M.–4 P.M. daily Nov.–Memorial Day weekend), located just off U.S. 30 at the Greenfield Road exit, you can watch a brief film, load up on maps and brochures, and chat with travel consultants. One-hour tours of the Amish countryside ($20.95 per person, children 12 and under $10.95) depart from the visitors center at 10:30 A.M., noon, 1:30 P.M., and 3 P.M. daily from late May through October and select weekends in early May and November. The CVB also operates a visitors center in downtown Lancaster (1–3 W. King St., Lancaster, 717/299-6440, www.lancasterheritage.com, 9:30 A.M.–5 P.M. Mon.–Sat. and 10 A.M.–3 P.M. Sun. Memorial Day weekend–Oct., 10 A.M.–3 P.M. daily Nov.–Memorial Day weekend) in downtown Lancaster. For information about Pennsylvania Dutch Country as a whole, visit www.dutchcountryroads.com.

GETTING THERE AND AROUND

Lancaster County is about 90 minutes by car from Philadelphia and Baltimore. I-76 (Pennsylvania Turnpike) passes through the northern part of the county, but many of the main attractions lie along or near U.S. 30, which traverses the central part. Cape Air provides regularly scheduled flights between Baltimore/Washington International Thurgood Marshall Airport (BWI) and **Lancaster Airport** (717/569-1221, www.lancasterairport .com), six miles north of the city of Lancaster at the intersection of Route 501 (Lititz Pike) and Airport Road. Lancaster Airport's booking code is LNS. Rental cars are available at the airport. The larger Harrisburg International Airport (HIA) is about 30 miles from Lancaster.

Amtrak (800/872-7245, www.amtrak .com) provides rail service to the city. Bus service is available through **Greyhound** (800/231-2222, www.greyhound.com) and its interline partners. Trains and intercity buses pull into Lancaster Station (53 E. McGovern Ave.), built in 1929 by the Pennsylvania Railroad and now owned by Amtrak. It's about a mile north of downtown.

For getting around Lancaster County, it's best to have your own wheels, but public transportation is available. **Red Rose Transit Authority** (717/397-4246, www.red rosetransit.com) operates 17 bus routes, 11 of which serve Queen Street Station (225 N. Queen St., 717/393-3315, information center open 8 A.M.–5:30 P.M. Mon.–Fri. and 8 A.M.–4:30 P.M. Sat.–Sun.) in downtown Lancaster. The transit authority also operates the **Historic Downtown Trolley** on weekdays. (The trolley itself isn't historic. It's a thoroughly modern vehicle made to look like an old-time trolley.) Stops include Lancaster Station, a park-and-ride lot at Clipper Magazine Stadium, and Queen Street Station. One trolley trip is $1.50. An all-day pass costs $3.25.

Reading and Vicinity

With a population of roughly 80,000, Reading is the largest city in Pennsylvania Dutch Country. It was laid out in 1748 by sons of Pennsylvania founder William Penn and named the seat of Berks County several years later. By then the area was already home to an Amish community, one of the first in the country. Most Amish left Berks County in the latter part of the 1700s and early 1800s for reasons that may have included their pacifism. Reading was a military base during the French and Indian War, and its ironworks helped supply George Washington's troops with ammunition during the Revolutionary War. After Washington famously crossed the icy Delaware River in December 1776 and captured hundreds of Hessian soldiers garrisoned in Trenton, New Jersey, Reading hosted a prisoner-of-war camp.

The construction of the Reading Railroad in the 19th century ushered in the region's economic heyday. Built in the 1830s and '40s, the original mainline stretched south from the coal-mining town of Pottsville to Reading and then on to Philadelphia, a journey of less than 100 miles. Over the next century, the Reading grew into a many-tentacled transportation system with more than 1,000 miles of track. Heavily invested in Pennsylvania's anthracite coal industry, it reigned as one of the world's most prosperous corporations at the turn of the 20th century. Within a few decades, anthracite coal and rail transportation had both fallen out of favor. The railroad filed for bankruptcy and was absorbed by Conrail in the 1970s. But it lives on in the form of a property in the standard version of the board game Monopoly. One of Berks County's 30-plus historical museums and sites is dedicated to the railroad.

Historical attractions notwithstanding, the

DUTCH COUNTRY

© GREATER READING CONVENTION & VISITORS BUREAU

the Reading Pagoda

county is best known as a shopping destination. It's home to an outlet mall and the only Cabela's outdoor megastore in Pennsylvania. It also has much to offer antiques lovers.

By the way, it's pronounced "RED-ing," not "REED-ing."

SIGHTS
The Pagoda

Reading's most prominent landmark is a building of the sort rarely seen outside the Far East. Perched atop Mount Penn, 886 feet above downtown, the Pagoda (Duryea Dr., 610/655-6271, www.readingpagoda.com, noon–5 P.M. Fri.–Sun. mid-June–Labor Day, noon–4 P.M. Sat.–Sun. rest of year, suggested donation $1) has become a symbol of the city. You'll see it in the logos of businesses and civic organizations and on a shoulder patch worn by the men and women of the Reading Police Department. More than a century old, it's believed to be one of only three pagodas of its scale in the country and the only one in the world with a fireplace and chimney. The story of how the multi-tiered tower came to be is as interesting as the structure

itself. "Reading to Have Japanese Pagoda," read a headline in the August 10, 1906, issue of the *Reading Eagle*. The man behind the plan was local businessman William Abbott Witman, who had made himself very unpopular by starting a stone quarrying operation on the western slope of Mount Penn. The Pagoda would cover the mess he'd left on the mountainside. Moreover, it would serve as a luxury resort.

The exotic building was completed in 1908, but Witman's plan to operate it as a mountain retreat was dealt a fatal blow: His application for a liquor license was denied. By 1910, the property was in foreclosure. To save the bank from a loss, local merchant and bank director Jonathan Mould purchased the Pagoda and presented it to the city as a gift. Before radios came into common use, the seven-story structure served as a sort of public announcement system. Lights installed on its roof flashed Morse code to direct firemen and relay baseball scores, political outcomes, and other information. Today the temple of stone and terracotta tiles is a popular tourist stop. Visitors can climb 87 solid oak steps to a lookout offering a view for 30-plus miles. There's a small café and gift shop on the first floor. The Pagoda is quite a sight at night, when it's aglow with red LED lights.

Reading Railroad Heritage Museum

Opened in 2008 in a former Pennsylvania Steel foundry complex, the Reading Railroad Heritage Museum (500 S. 3rd St., Hamburg, 610/562-5513, www.readingrailroad.org, 10 A.M.–4 P.M. Sat., noon–4 P.M. Sun., admission $5, seniors $4, children 5–12 $3) tells the story of the profound impact the railroad had on the communities it served. It's operated by the Reading Company Technical & Historical Society, which began rounding up locomotives and freight and passenger cars several years after the railroad's 1971 bankruptcy filing. The all-volunteer nonprofit is now the proud owner of the nation's largest collection of rolling stock dedicated to a single railroad. Tours of the outdoor display yard begin at 15 minutes past the hour, with the last scheduled at 2:15 P.M.

Reading Public Museum

The Reading Public Museum (500 Museum Rd., Reading, 610/371-5850, www.reading publicmuseum.org, 11 A.M.–5 P.M. Tues.–Thurs. and Sat., 11 A.M.–8 P.M. Fri., noon–5 P.M. Sun., admission $8, seniors, students, and children 4–17 $6) is part art museum, part natural history museum, and part anthropological museum. Founded in 1904 by a local teacher, the museum even has a gallery devoted to its own history. Its fine art collection is particularly strong in oil paintings and includes works by John Singer Sargent, Edgar Degas, Winslow Homer, N. C. Wyeth, George Bellows, Milton Avery, and Berks County native Keith Haring. Among the highlights of its natural history collection are the fossilized footprints of reptiles that roamed the immediate area some 200 million years ago. They were found just a few miles away. The anthropological and historical collections include everything from an Egyptian mummy to 16th-century samurai armor to Pennsylvania German folk art. As if that weren't enough, the museum boasts a 25-acre arboretum and a full-dome planetarium. Admission to star shows, offered most Sunday afternoons, is $7 for adults and $5 for seniors, students, and children 4–17.

GoggleWorks Center for the Arts

Like other cities wrestling with the erosion of their industrial base, Reading has rolled out the red carpet for artists and cultural organizations. In 2005 an abandoned factory in Reading's urban core was transformed into the GoggleWorks Center for the Arts (201 Washington St., Reading, 610/374-4600, www.goggleworks.org, 9 A.M.–9 P.M. Mon.–Sat., 11 A.M.–7 P.M. Sun., free admission). So named because the factory manufactured safety goggles, the arts center boasts several galleries, a film theater, a café, dozens of artist studios, a wood shop, a ceramics studio, a jewelry studio, a glass-blowing facility, dance and music studios, and more. The GoggleWorks Store (10 A.M.–7 P.M. Mon.–Fri., 10 A.M.–6 P.M. Sat., 11 A.M.–5 P.M. Sun.) offers unique handcrafted items.

glassblowing class at the GoggleWorks Center for the Arts

The best time to explore the six-building campus is during a **Second Sunday** open house, when most of the artists are in their studios. Held from 11 A.M.–4 P.M., the event features live music and walk-in workshops. The GoggleWorks and other venues in Reading's emerging arts district are also hopping on the **First Thursday** (www.penncorridor.com) evening of every month. The arts center is a good first stop on a visit to the area because it houses the Greater Reading Visitors Center, stocked with hundreds of brochures.

In 2008 **R/C Reading Movies 11** (30 N. 2nd St., 610/374-2828, www.rctheatres.com) opened a stone's throw from the GoggleWorks. The multiplex boasts Reading's first IMAX auditorium, stadium seating with high-back chairs, and a game room.

Boyertown Museum of Historic Vehicles

The Reading area is so associated with rail transportation that visitors are often surprised to learn of its role in automobile history.

Reading's Duryea Drive is named for Charles Duryea, who in the 1890s founded the first American company to manufacture and sell gasoline-powered vehicles. In 1900 the famous automaker moved from Massachusetts to Reading, in part because the railroad center had iron and steel foundries, machine shops, and skilled workers—everything needed for automobile manufacture. He stayed for 14 years, testing new vehicles on the steep, winding road that would bear his name. Duryea wasn't the only automaker to set up shop in Reading. Eleven companies manufactured automobiles in the city between 1900 and 1934. Most of the 50-odd cars, trucks, and motorcycles displayed at the Boyertown Museum (85 S. Walnut St., Boyertown, 610/367-2090, www.boyertownmuseum.org, 9:30 A.M.–4 P.M. Tues.–Sun., admission $6, seniors $5, students $4) were built in southeastern Pennsylvania. The collection also boasts rare examples of the horse-drawn vehicles that preceded them. It includes an 1875 fire cart hose made in a factory that operated on the site of the museum

© BOYERTOWN MUSEUM OF HISTORIC VEHICLES

Boyertown Museum

from 1872 to 1926 and trucks developed by the Boyertown Auto Body Works, which succeeded the carriage factory and remained in business until 1990. Located about 15 miles east of Reading, the museum hosts an annual antique and classic car show called **Duryea Day.** It's held on the Saturday of Labor Day weekend in Boyertown Community Park.

Before we leave the subject of cars, it should be mentioned that Duryea Drive, where so many early automobiles were tested, is the site of two annual races sponsored by the Pennsylvania Hillclimb Association (www.pahillclimb.org): the **Pagoda Hillclimb** in June and the longer **Duryea Hillclimb** in August.

◖ Air Museums

Berks County is home to not one but two museums dedicated to the history of aviation. Both offer thrill-of-a-lifetime rides in antique planes. Larger and older, the **Mid-Atlantic Air Museum (MAAM)** (11 Museum Dr., Reading, 610/372-7333, www.maam.org, 9:30 A.M.–4 P.M. daily, admission $6, children

6–12 $3) at Reading Regional Airport is home to more than 60 aircraft built from 1928 to the early 1980s. Among them is a Northrop P-61 Black Widow—one of only four in existence. In January 1945, the night fighter crashed into a mountainside on the South Pacific Island of New Guinea. World War II veteran Eugene "Pappy" Strine and his son established the air museum in 1980 for the purpose of recovering the rare aircraft, which had logged only 10 flight hours before stalling and crashing during a proficiency check. Green-lighted by the Indonesian government in 1984, the recovery project took seven years. The effort to restore it to flying condition was nearing completion in 2010. Other highlights of the collection include a North American B-25 Mitchell, a World War II bomber that appeared in half a dozen movies before she was donated to the museum in 1981, and a Douglas R4D-6 Skytrain, which delivered supplies and specialist personnel to combat zones during the war. MAAM's impressive holding of vintage military aircraft and annual **World War II Weekend** have given it a

DUTCH COUNTRY

© PABLO SANCHEZ

Vintage warbirds take to the skies during World War II Weekend at the Mid-Atlantic Air Museum.

reputation as a "warbird" museum, but in fact, about two-thirds of its flying machines were built for civilians.

Reading's airport was used as a military training airfield during World War II, and for three days each summer, it takes on the look and feel of that era. Held the first full weekend in June, WWII Weekend features air and military vehicle shows, battle re-creations, troop encampments, a militaria flea market, and 1940s entertainment, including big band dances. Single-day tickets are $20 in advance or $22 at the gate for adults, $9 in advance or $10 at the gate for children 6–12.

The **Golden Age Air Museum** (Grimes Airfield, 371 Airport Rd., Bethel, 717/933-9566, www.goldenageair.org, 10 A.M.–4 P.M. Sat. and 11 A.M.–4 P.M. Sun. May–Oct., year-round by appointment, admission $5, children 6–12 $3), about 20 miles away, was established in 1997. True to its name, it concentrates on the so-called golden age of aviation: the years between the two World Wars. More than 20 of its 30-some aircraft were built in the late 1910s, '20s, and '30s. The museum is also home to a handful of antique automobiles, including a

1930 Ford Model A roadster. Its **Flying Circus Air Shows,** held in June and August, pay tribute to barnstorming, a popular form of entertainment in the 1920s.

MAAM offers rides in a pair of 1940s aircraft, including an open-cockpit biplane trainer, on the second weekend of May and July–October, as well as during the WWII extravaganza. The cost of the flight, which lasts about 20 to 25 minutes, is $225. Reservations are required. Golden Age Air Museum offers rides in an open-cockpit 1929 biplane year-round by appointment. A 15-minute flight costs $99 for one person, $119 for two. One or two people can fly for 30 minutes for $199 or 60 minutes for $379.

Hopewell Furnace National Historic Site

If you ask a Pennsylvanian about the state's iron and steel heritage, he'll probably tell you about the fire-breathing plants that brought renown to cities such as Pittsburgh, Johnstown, and Bethlehem. Most people don't associate the industry with rural Pennsylvania. They haven't been to Hopewell Furnace National Historic

Hopewell Furnace National Historic Site

Site (2 Mark Bird Ln., Elverson, 610/582-8773, www.nps.gov/hofu, 9 A.M.–5 P.M. Wed.–Sun. and holidays including Memorial Day and Labor Day, restrooms and hiking trails open daily, free admission), which features the restored remains of an iron furnace and the village that grew around it. Established in 1771, Hopewell Furnace was one of dozens of "iron plantations" operating in southeastern Pennsylvania by the time the American colonies declared their independence from Great Britain. It supplied cannons, shot, and shells for patriot troops during the Revolutionary War. During the first half of the 19th century, the charcoal-fired furnace produced a wide variety of iron products, including pots, kettles, flatirons, and hammers, gaining fame for its stoves. Even Joseph Bonaparte, elder brother of Napoleon, ordered a Hopewell stove in 1822. After 112 years of operation, the outdated furnace closed in 1883. The workers and their families packed up and left.

Purchased by the federal government in 1935, the Hopewell Furnace property has been restored to the way it looked during its heyday in the 1830s and '40s. Visitors still have to use their imaginations: The National Park Service lacks the wizardry to recreate the billows of charcoal dust, noises, and stench that emanated from the active furnace. Exhibits in the visitors center and occasional living history programs help the imagination. The core of the Hopewell Furnace experience is strolling through the frozen-in-time village, popping into open buildings, so it's best to visit when the weather is nice. Early September through October is a particularly good time because the park's apple orchard, which includes historic varieties you won't find in the supermarket, is open for picking. The apples are sold by the pound. Hiking enthusiasts should plan to stay a while. More than 40 miles of trails traverse the 848-acre historic site and neighboring **French Creek State Park** (843 Park Rd., Elverson, 610/582-9680, www.dcnr.state.pa.us/stateparks/parks/frenchcreek.aspx).

(Hawk Mountain Sanctuary

Located 25 miles north of Reading, Hawk Mountain Sanctuary (1700 Hawk Mountain Rd., Kempton, 610/756-6000, www.hawk mountain.org, trails open dawn to dusk daily,

DUTCH COUNTRY

© HAWK MOUNTAIN SANCTUARY

one of several Hawk Mountain lookouts

HAVE A LAGER

If Pennsylvania had an official state beer, it would have to be **Yuengling Traditional Lager.** It's so ubiquitous and popular that asking for it by name is oftentimes unnecessary. Most bartenders translate "I'll have a lager" as "Pour me a Yuengling." Pronounced properly (YING-ling), the brand sounds like an import from the Far East. But the brewing company more properly known as D.G. Yuengling & Son has been based in Pottsville, Pennsylvania, since its 1829 founding. Yeah, about its age: Yuengling is America's oldest brewery, a fact

© VINCEGIANTESANO

The Yuengling wagon delivers lager in the Memorial Day Parade in Summit Hill.

---

visitor center open 8 A.M.–5 P.M. daily Sept.–Nov., 9 A.M.–5 P.M. Dec.–Aug.) is one of the best places in the country to watch migrating hawks, eagles, falcons, and other winged predators. During the fall migration, counters may record upwards of 1,000 birds in one day. That's because of the sanctuary's location on the Blue Mountain (a.k.a. Kittatinny) ridge, part of the Appalachian range. In the fall, the topography and prevailing northwesterly winds conspire to create updrafts that allow raptors to glide, soar, and save energy on their southward journeys. Lookouts at Hawk Mountain allow for eye-level views of the majestic birds. Some fly so close that you can't help but duck. The migration begins in mid-August and continues into December, peaking September through November. The very best time to visit is two or three days after a cold front passes. Sightings are considerably less frequent during the northbound migration, when prevailing easterlies push raptors west of the sanctuary. Still, it's possible to spot as many as 300 on a day in April or early May.

Founded in 1934 to stop hunters from shooting the migrants, Hawk Mountain is the world's oldest refuge for birds of prey. The nonprofit charges a fee for use of its eight-mile trail system, which connects to the epic Appalachian Trail. The fee is $5 for adults, $4 for seniors, and $3 for children 6–12 except on national holidays and weekends in September

stamped on every bottle. It survived Prohibition by producing "near beers" – now known as non-alcoholic beers – and celebrated the 1933 repeal of the 18th Amendment by shipping a truckload of real beer to the White House. We don't know how then-president Franklin Roosevelt felt about the suds, but Barack Obama is a fan. When he lost a friendly wager on the outcome of the U.S.-Canada battle for ice hockey gold at the 2010 Winter Olympics, he sent a case of "lager" (as in Yuengling) to the Canadian prime minister.

About 35 miles north of Reading, Pottsville lies in Pennsylvania's coal region, home to the largest fields of anthracite in the country. The city is still recovering from the demise of the anthracite industry after World War II. Yuengling also had it rough in the post-war decades, as the full-flavored products of regional breweries lost favor to lighter national brands. But the company has more than recovered since Richard L. Yuengling Jr. became its fifth-generation owner in 1985. In 1999 it purchased a former Stroh brewery in Tampa, Florida, to keep up with demand. Two years later it opened a third brewery in Port Carbon, just a few minutes from Pottsville. By 2010 demand was again outstripping supply, necessitating an expansion of the newest plant. According to

a 2010 report by the Boulder, Colorado-based Brewers Association, Yuengling is the fourth largest brewing company in the country. Only Anheuser-Busch, MillerCoors, and Pabst sell more suds. Its rapid growth has much to do with the popularity of "lager," introduced in 1987. Yuengling produces half a dozen other beers but sells more lager than all the rest combined.

Free tours of the Pottsville brewery (5th and Mahantongo Streets, 570/628-4890, www.yuengling.com, gift shop open 9 A.M.-4 P.M. Mon.-Fri. year-round and 10 A.M.-3 P.M. Sat. Apr.-Dec.) are offered at 10 A.M. and 1:30 P.M. weekdays year-round and 11 A.M., noon, and 1 P.M. on Saturdays April through December. They include a visit to the "caves" where beer was fermented in years past, ending with free samples. You don't have to be of drinking age to take a tour, but you do have to wear closed shoes. Built in 1831, the facility isn't handicapped accessible.

While in Pottsville, you may want to pay a visit to **Jerry's Classic Cars and Collectibles Museum** (394 S. Center St., 570/628-2266, www.jerrysmuseum.com, noon-5 P.M. Fri.-Sun. May-Oct., admission $8), a tribute to the 1950s and '60s.

and November, when adults and seniors pay $7. The most popular path winds past a series of lookouts and is known, appropriately enough, as the Lookout Trail. The first lookout is only a couple hundred yards from the trailhead and is accessible by all-terrain wheelchair, available at the visitor center. The trail becomes rocky and uneven after the first few overlooks, but soldier on and you'll reap just rewards. At the end of the mile-long trail is the famed **North Lookout,** site of the sanctuary's official hawk count. It's hard to tear yourself away from the panoramic view from 1,490 feet above sea level, so consider bringing a cushion and something to eat or drink. Definitely pack food and water if you plan to tackle longer trails like the four-

mile River of Rocks loop, which drops into a valley and skirts an ice age boulder field. Trail maps are available on the sanctuary's website and in the visitor center.

If you're new to bird-watching, browse the visitor center's educational displays before starting your hike. A bit of time in the Wings of Wonder Gallery, featuring life-sized woodcarvings of each migrating raptor, will do wonders for your ability to identify the real deal. A pocket-sized guide to the various species that pass the sanctuary is available for purchase. You'll more than likely meet longtime visitors as you explore the sanctuary, many of whom can chirp up a storm about spotting and identifying birds. Educators are stationed at some lookouts during busy periods.

Hawk Mountain Line

Known as the Hawk Mountain Line because of its proximity to the bird sanctuary, the Wanamaker, Kempton & Southern (home station 42 Community Center Dr., Kempton, 610/756-6469, www.kemptontrain.com, regular ticket $8, children 3–11 $4) is a tourist railroad consisting of several miles of track purchased from the Reading Railroad in the 1960s and a collection of rolling stock that includes both steam and diesel-electric locomotives. The Reading began pulling up tracks in the 1970s, leaving the WK&S with two dead ends. Regular and themed train rides are offered on weekends April–December. Tickets for regular rides, which last about 40 minutes, can be purchased at the home station up to 10 minutes before departure. Reservations are required for murder mystery events, fall's "harvest moon" and haunted train rides, and December's Christmas-themed trips. The home station is off Route 737 in Kempton, an itty-bitty community about 30 miles north of Reading. From I-78, take exit 35 for Route 143 north or exit 40 for Route 737 north and continue about five miles to Kempton, where signs point the way to the station. Originally part of the vast Reading Railroad network, the station was moved from the southern tip of Berks County to its present location at the northern tip in 1963.

Crystal Cave Park

Discovered in 1871, Crystal Cave (963 Crystal Cave Rd., Kutztown, 610/683-6765, www.crystalcavepa.com, opens at 9 A.M. daily Mar.–Nov., closes between 5 and 7 P.M., admission $11.50, children 4–11 $7.50) is the oldest operating show cave in Pennsylvania. Guides who know their stalagmites from their stalactites lead visitors along concrete pathways, pointing out the "prairie dogs," the "totem pole," the "ear of corn," and other exquisite formations. Tours last 40 to 50 minutes and include a short video presentation on cave geology. It's a constant 54 degrees inside, so dress accordingly.

There's quite a bit to keep visitors entertained outside the cave, including an 18-hole miniature golf course ($4), a panning-for-gemstones attraction ($4.50 per gemstone bag), and an ice cream parlor and restaurant open daily in July and August and weekends in June and September. Amish buggy rides and use of the picnic facilities are included in the price of admission.

ENTERTAINMENT AND EVENTS

Concert Venues

Home to Reading's professional ice hockey and indoor football teams, the **Sovereign Center** (700 Penn St., Reading, 610/898-7469, tickets 800/745-3000, www.sovereigncenter.com, box office 10 A.M.–5 P.M. Mon.–Fri. year-round and 10 A.M.–2 P.M. Sat. Labor Day–Memorial Day) also hosts concerts, professional wrestling, conventions, and other events. Previous performers include Neil Diamond, Lynyrd Skynyrd, Kenny Chesney, Matchbox Twenty, Cher, Elton John, and Sting. Opened in 2001, the arena seats 7,000 for hockey matches and 8,900 for concerts. It's sometimes converted into a smaller, more intimate venue known as the **Reading Eagle Theater.**

Performing Arts

In 2000 the Berks County Convention Center Authority purchased Reading's only surviving movie palace, sank $7 million into renovations, and reopened it as the **Sovereign Performing Arts Center** (136 N. 6th St., Reading, 610/898-7469, tickets 800/745-3000, www.sovereigncenter.com, box office opens at noon on event days). The 1,700-seat theater is home to the **Reading Symphony Orchestra** (www.readingsymphony.org), founded in 1913, and **Reading Civic Theatre** (www.readingcivic.org), which began staging musicals one year later. It also hosts touring Broadway productions, popular music concerts, and other events.

The **Miller Center for the Arts** (4 N. 2nd St., Reading, 610/372-4721 ext. 5500, www.racc.edu/MillerCenter) also welcomes a wide array of touring acts—from modern dance to classical marionette theater. The glass-walled theater on the campus of Reading Area Community College opened in 2007. It seats about 500.

Festivals and Events

First held in 1991, **Berks Jazz Fest** (various venues, tickets 800/745-3000, www.berksjazzfest.com, Mar.) has grown bigger and bigger over the years. Famed trumpeter Wynton Marsalis, who played at the inaugural fest, returned in 2010 with his Jazz at Lincoln Center Orchestra. Other past performers include Eliane Elias, the Dirty Dozen Brass Band, John Tesh, Béla Fleck and the Flecktones, David Sanborn, the Count Basie Orchestra, Buddy Guy, Susan Tedeschi, and Kurt Elling. The 10-day festival is presented by the Berks Arts Council, which is also to thank for a series of free concerts held on Friday evenings in the summer. The **Bandshell Concerts** (City Park, 1261 Hill Rd., Reading, 610/898-1930, www.berksarts.org) showcase various musical genres, including blues, doo-wop, and bluegrass.

Berks County's premier event is the **Kutztown Folk Festival** (Kutztown Fairgrounds, 225 N. White Oak St., Kutztown, 888/674-6136, www.kutztownfestival.com, late June/early July, admission charged, free for children 12 and under), a nine-day celebration of Pennsylvania Dutch culture. Founded in 1950, it's said to be the oldest continuously operated folklife festival in the country. To call it a unique event is an understatement. Where else can you see a reenactment of a 19th-century hanging, watch a Mennonite wedding, take a seminar on the PA Dutch dialect, *and* buy bread baked in an early 1800s oven? The festival also features one of the largest quilt sales in the country. More than 2,500 locally handmade quilts are available for purchase; collectors from around the world attend an auction of the prize-winners. Demonstrations of quilting and other traditional crafts are a hallmark of the event. The words "Pennsylvania Dutch" are practically synonymous with "pig-out," and the Kutztown extravaganza does nothing to dispel that association. All-you-can-eat ham and chicken dinners are a festival tradition, as is roasting a 1,200-pound ox over a bed of coals. The borough of Kutztown is about 20 miles northeast of Reading.

Folks who like it hot descend on an itty-bitty community four miles south of Kutztown for the **Chili Pepper Food Festival** (William Delong Park, 233 Bowers Rd., Bowers, www.pepperfestival.com, Sept., admission by donation). The two-day event features a jalapeno-eating contest, a salsa contest, and even a chili pepper song contest. Excursions to a local chili pepper field are offered both days.

Winter's main event is a Christmas display on steroids. **Koziar's Christmas Village** (782 Christmas Village Rd., Bernville, 610/488-1110, www.koziarschristmasvillage.com, first weekend of Nov. to first weekend of Jan., admission charged) traces its history to 1948, when William M. Koziar strung lights around his house and barn in rural Berks County to the delight of his wife and four children. Each year, he stepped up his game, decorating more and more of his property. The increasingly elaborate display began attracting people from nearby and then people from not-so-nearby. These days more than half a million Christmas lights go into the creation of the winter wonderland. A reflective lake doubles the wow factor. There's more to Koziar's than twinkling lights. It also offers large dioramas of scenes such as "Christmas Beneath the Sea" and "Santa's Post Office," extensive model train layouts, and shops selling ornaments, souvenirs, toys, and other gifts. Santa's on site, of course.

SHOPPING
VF Outlet Center

One of greater Reading's most popular tourist destinations, the VF Outlet Center (801 Hill Ave., Wyomissing, 610/378-0408, www.vfoutletcenter.com, 9:30 A.M.–7 P.M. Mon.–Thurs., 9:30 A.M.–9 P.M. Fri.–Sat., 10 A.M.–5 P.M. Sun. Jan.–Feb., 9:30 A.M.–9 P.M. Mon.–Sat., 10 A.M.–6 P.M. Sun. Mar.–Dec.) has about 50 stores and a rich history. For most of the 20th century, its buildings comprised the Berkshire Knitting Mills. The Berkie, as locals called it, was the world's largest manufacturer of hosiery in the early decades of the century, before seamless nylons became all the rage. In 1969 it was purchased by VF Corporation, which opened a factory store in one end of a manufacturing building. A drop cloth separated the retail and manufacturing areas. The mill ceased operations several years later, but the store remained. Today the VF Outlet store is stocked with brands including Wrangler, Lee, JanSport, and Nautica. Other stores in the mill-turned-mall include Tommy Hilfiger, Liz Claiborne, Timberland, Reebok, OshKosh B'gosh, Black & Decker, and Dooney & Bourke.

Cabela's

The 2003 opening of a Cabela's store less than 20 miles north of Reading warranted a story in *The New York Times* travel section. After all, it was the first Cabela's outpost on the East Coast. The revered retailer of outdoor gear has since expanded into Connecticut and Maine, but the Pennsylvania store (100 Cabela Dr., Hamburg, 610/929-7000, www.cabelas.com, 8 A.M.–9 P.M. Mon.–Sat., 9 A.M.–8 P.M. Sun., call for winter hours) still reels in millions of hunting and fishing enthusiasts a year. The 250,000-square-foot showplace just off I-78 features shooting and archery ranges, massive aquariums, life-sized wildlife dioramas that put many natural history museums to shame, and a restaurant offering sandwiches stuffed with your choice of meats—the choices including elk, wild boar, bison, and ostrich. And then there's the merchandise. The dizzying selection includes everything from guns to outdoor-inspired home decor. Live bait is available for anglers heading to nearby waters. Also available: kennels for shoppers who bring their canine friends, a corral for those who bring their equine friends, and a dump station for those arriving by RV.

Antiques

Antiques lovers can find plenty of what they're looking for in the Reading area. Just 10 miles southwest of Reading, straddling Berks and Lancaster Counties, is the borough of Adamstown, also known as "Antiques Capital USA." See the *Lancaster County* section for the lowdown on Adamstown. Twenty miles northeast of Reading is another antiquing destination: Kutztown's **Renninger's Antiques Market** (740 Noble St., Kutztown, 570/385-0104 Mon.–Thurs., 610/683-6848 Fri.–Sat., www.renningers.com, indoor antiques market 8 A.M.–4 P.M. Sat.). With locations in Adamstown and Florida as well as Kutztown, Renninger's is a big name in antiquing circles. The Kutztown market is open Saturdays and the Adamstown market Sundays, so it's not unusual for treasure hunters to hit both in one weekend. Kutztown's Renninger's began as a farmers market in 1955. Antiques dealers have been setting up shop since 1974. These days you'll find 200 booths in the indoor antiques market and as many as 100 more in the flea market outside. The flea market opens at 7 A.M., an hour before the indoor market. Thanks to large pavilions, it operates even during the winter months. What's for sale? Everything from Indian artifacts and early farm tools to neon beer signs and Pez dispensers.

Three times a year, hundreds of dealers from around the country descend on the grounds for an **Antiques & Collectors Extravaganza** (last full Thurs.–Sat. of Apr., June, and Sept., admission charged). Renninger's Kutztown also hosts a biannual antique radio show. It hasn't forgotten its roots as a farmers market. Open 10 A.M.–7 P.M. Fridays and 8 A.M.–4 P.M. Saturdays year-round, the indoor **Renninger's Farmers Market** has a strong Pennsylvania Dutch flavor. You'll find produce, fresh and smoked meats, baked goods, handmade candies, gourmet coffees and teas, and french fries to die for.

SPORTS AND RECREATION
Spectator Sports

The Reading area boasts minor league baseball, hockey, and soccer franchises, a professional indoor football team, and a drag racing track good for adrenaline-pumping entertainment eight months of the year. The **Reading Phillies** (FirstEnergy Stadium, 1900 Centre Ave., Reading, 610/370-2255, www.reading phillies.com) have been the AA affiliate of the Philadelphia Phillies since 1967. Only one

Minor League Baseball team has had a longer relationship with its parent club. The R-Phils, as they're known, have a devoted following, attracting more fans than any other team in the Eastern League year after year. It doesn't hurt that FirstEnergy Stadium is a classic beauty. Completed in 1951, the ballpark has undergone a series of renovations and additions since the late 1980s. The most ambitious was the construction of a 1,000-square-foot pool behind the right field fence. Game day tickets to the pool pavilion, which boasts a picnic area with TVs on each table, are $23–27 and include an all-you-can-eat buffet complete with barbecued ribs and corn on the cob.

Founded in 2001, Reading's ECHL ice hockey team has yet to bring home a championship. But the **Reading Royals** (Sovereign Center, 7th and Penn Streets, Reading, 610/898-7825, www.royalshockey.com) have produced more than a dozen National Hockey League players, including Los Angeles Kings goaltender Jon Quick, who earned a spot on the U.S. team for the 2010 Olympics. The Royals are affiliated with the NHL's Toronto Maple Leafs and Boston Bruins and the American Hockey League's Toronto Marlies. They share an arena with the **Reading Express** (800/745-3000, www.expressindoorfootball.com), a professional indoor football team that began play in 2006.

On the eve of its 2010 inaugural season, Major League Soccer's Philadelphia Union announced an affiliation with Reading's minor league franchise. Formed 15 years earlier as the alliteratively pleasing Reading Rage, the team was rebranded as **Reading United A.C.** (Exeter Township Senior High School, 201 E. 37th St., Reading, 610/927-4474, www.readingunitedac.com). It competes in the United Soccer Leagues' Premier Development League, considered the fourth tier of competition in North America.

Older than any of the minor league teams, **Maple Grove Raceway** (30 Stauffer Park Ln., Mohnton, 610/856-9200, www.maplegroveraceway.com) has been the site of many firsts in drag racing history. Best known as home

of the annual NHRA (National Hot Rod Association) Toyo Tires Nationals, the quarter-mile strip about 10 miles south of Reading hosts a wide variety of auto-centric events on weekends from March to November. It's best not to blink when jet-powered vehicles take to the track. Opened in 1962, Maple Grove also hosts a spring, summer, and fall flea market.

ACCOMMODATIONS
Reading
Though it's the cultural, governmental, and business capital of Berks County, downtown Reading has few lodging options. Its only hotel is the historic **(Abraham Lincoln** (100 N. 5th St., 610/372-3700, www.wyndhamreadinghotel.com, $99–159), a Wyndham property since 2005. Conveniently located within three blocks of the GoggleWorks Center for the Arts, the Sovereign Center, and the Sovereign Performing Arts Center, the hotel offers 104 rooms and 32 suites, two restaurants, a 24-hour gift shop, and free shuttle service to area businesses and attractions. Abraham Lincoln never slept here. The hotel, which opened in 1930, is named for the nation's 16th president because his great-grandfather lived nearby. Music fans and Marines will be interested to know that John Philip Sousa, the famed composer of military marches, suffered a heart attack while rehearsing in the area in 1932 and died in his 14th floor room at the Abraham Lincoln. With its original chandeliers, stately pillars, and brass and wrought iron railings, the hotel lobby is worth a peek even if you're just passing by.

The great stone mansion now known as the **Stirling Guest Hotel** (1120 Centre Ave., 610/373-1522, www.stirlingguesthotel.net, $150–300) was built in the early 1890s in what was then considered a far suburb of Reading. It's a mere mile north of the city center. Designed in the Châteauesque style for a local iron and steel magnate and named for a castle in Scotland, the mansion has nine sumptuously decorated guest suites. A large Tudor-style carriage house offers six more.

Less than a mile north of the VF Outlet

Center, **The Inn at Reading** (1040 N. Park Rd., Wyomissing, 610/372-7811, www.innatreading.com, $95–149) has 170 traditionally furnished rooms and suites. Amenities include a large outdoor pool open May through September, a half-court basketball court, an exercise facility, and a restaurant modeled on a traditional English pub. Breakfast is on the house Monday–Friday.

Northern Berks County

Pheasants, quail, and chukar, oh my! **Wing Pointe** (1414 Moselem Springs Rd., Hamburg, 610/562-6962, www.wingpt.com) is a resort custom-made for sport-shooting enthusiasts. From September through March, shotgun-toting guests hunt game birds released onto the grounds. Rental dogs and guides are available. The resort 15 minutes from outdoor megastore Cabela's also offers skeet and sporting clays shooting. Its main lodge features four guest suites ($145–191), a common room with a fireplace and large-screen TV, and an outdoor pool and whirlpool. Parties of up to nine people can rent a five-bedroom retreat ($550 for four guests, $83 per additional guest) with plush furnishings, a large modern kitchen, a formal dining room, and its own pool and whirlpool.

For those who venture to these parts to aim binoculars rather than shotguns at birds, there's **(Pamela's Forget Me Not B&B** (33 Hawk Mountain Rd., Kempton, 610/756-3398, www.pamelasforgetmenot.com, $99–159). A short drive from the famed Hawk Mountain Sanctuary and the Appalachian Trail, the B&B is as charming as its name. It offers three suites complete with Jacuzzis and one room with a shared bath. Made for romance, the Cottage Suite features a hand-crafted four-poster bed, gas fireplace, and private deck. (The couple that purchased the B&B in 2006 stayed here as guests on the night of their 1999 engagement.) The comfy Carriage House Suite, which sleeps up to six people, is perfect for families. The remaining suite and guest room are in the main house, dating to 1879 and Victorian in decor.

FOOD

Reading

Most of Reading's recommendable restaurants are concentrated in the gritty downtown area. The most famous, thanks to its longevity and a 2008 visit from the Travel Channel, is **Jimmie Kramer's Peanut Bar** (332 Penn St., 610/376-8500, www.peanutbar.com, 11 A.M.–11 P.M. Mon.–Thurs., 11 A.M.–midnight Fri., noon–midnight Sat., $7–25). At the "bar food paradise," as the Travel Channel dubbed it, patrons are welcomed with a bowl of peanuts and encouraged to toss the shells on the floor. The casual joint is also known for its hot wings, seafood, house-made desserts, and draft beer blends. Opened in 1933 as Jimmie Kramer's Olde Central Cafe, the bar and restaurant originally plied patrons with pretzels. When the pretzels ran out one day in 1935, Jimmie sent someone to a peanut roaster across the street, and the shell-tossing tradition was born. Renamed for the humble legume in 1958, the restaurant is now run by Jimmie's grandson.

One block south of the Peanut Bar is a cluster of three restaurants owned by local chef Judy Henry. **Judy's on Cherry** (332 Cherry St., 610/374-8511, www.judysoncherry.com, open for lunch Tues.–Fri. and dinner Tues.–Sat., lunch $8–14, dinner $9–30), a self-described "hearth-fired Euro café," offers Mediterranean-style fare. The lunch menu features salads, sandwiches, and pasta dishes. Dinnertime selections include the likes of pan-seared golden sea bass and half rack of lamb. Elegant small plates and crispy thin-crusted pizzas are always on offer, and warm focaccia sprinkled with sea salt is free with every meal. The adjoining **Speckled Hen Cottage Pub & Alehouse** (30 S. 4th St., 610/685-8511, www.speckledhenpub.com, 4:30 P.M.–midnight Wed.–Thurs. and 4:30 P.M.–1 A.M. Fri.–Sat. Oct.–Apr., $8–19) offers an altogether different dining experience. Henry transformed downtown Reading's oldest building—a log house built in the 1780s—into the sort of pub you'd find in the countryside of England or Ireland. With its working fireplaces and comfort cuisine (shepherd's pie, bangers and mashed potatoes, meatloaf, beef pot roast, baked mac and cheese, and such), the Speckled Hen hits the spot on a wintry day. Come spring, Henry closes it and opens **Plein Air** (lunch 11:30 A.M.–2 P.M. Wed.–Fri., dinner 5–10 P.M. Wed.–Sat., open mid-May–Sept., $8–18), an outdoor café accessible from either Judy's or the Speckled Hen. The fare is light and summery and the featured cocktail a tangerine mojito with fresh mint.

For margaritas in more than half a dozen flavors, head to **Mezcal's** (150 N. 6th St., 610/685-5272, www.dineindie.com/mezcals, 11 A.M.–3 P.M. Mon., 11 A.M.–8 P.M. Tues.–Thurs., 11 A.M.–9 P.M. Fri.–Sat., noon–8 P.M. Sun., lunch under $10, dinner $7–17). Set in a typical Reading row house, the colorful Mexican eatery offers a lengthy menu and a laid-back vibe.

Downtown's chicest dining establishment is also tucked inside a row house. **Dans Restaurant** (1049 Penn St., 610/373-2075, 5–9:30 P.M. Wed.–Sat., noon–7 P.M. Sun., dinner $19–36, Sun. brunch $7–29) is no longer owned by the two Dans who opened it in 1989 but carries on their mission of providing "a contemporary alternative to the traditional Berks County dining scene." Its French-influenced dinner menu changes weekly. The Sunday brunch, served noon–3 P.M., is the best in town. Choose from such dishes as fried duck eggs, griddle cakes with Ghirardelli white chocolate, and brie and tomato fondue omelet, or splurge on the five-course tasting menu ($29). Dans is quite small, and reservations are very much recommended.

Just outside the downtown area is the lovely **Abigail's Tea Room** (1441 Perkiomen Ave., 610/376-6050, www.abigailstearoom.com, seating 11 A.M.–3 P.M. Wed.–Sat.), which offers a simple lunch menu ($6–9) as well as afternoon tea experiences ($17–20). For the latter, be sure to make a reservation at least a day in advance. Abigail's is Victorian through and through, from its setting—an 1883 manse outfitted with period furnishings and crystal chandeliers—to its delicate floral china. You wouldn't look a bit out of place in a wide-brimmed, feather-trimmed hat. There's a tea-centric gift shop on site, and guess what: Lady Gaga has been photographed with exquisite teacups purchased from the owner's website.

Northern Berks County

With a name like **Deitsch Eck** (87 Penn St., Lenhartsville, 610/562-8520, www.deitscheck.com, 4–8 P.M. Wed.–Thurs., 4–9 P.M. Fri.–Sat., 11:30 A.M.–7 P.M. Sun., $4–15), it has to be Pennsylvania Dutch. Chef-owner Steve Stetzler began working in the corner restaurant (Deitsch Eck means "Dutch Corner") when he was 15 and bought it nine years later in 1997. His mother and sister are among the staff. In addition to heaping portions of PA Dutch cooking, they serve a wide variety of burgers and sandwiches and Italian favorites like veal parmigiana. A meat market in their quaint country town provides the ground beef, hams, pork chops, and sausages.

INFORMATION AND SERVICES

The **Greater Reading Convention & Visitors Bureau** (610/375-4085, www.readingberkspa.com) is a good source of information about the area. Visit the website to request a free copy of its official visitors guide or peruse a digital version. The guide and some 300 brochures are available at the CVB's visitors center in the **GoggleWorks Center for the Arts** (201 Washington St., Reading, 9 A.M.–9 P.M. Mon.–Sat., 11 A.M.–7 P.M. Sun.). For information about Pennsylvania Dutch Country as a whole, visit www.dutchcountryroads.com.

GETTING THERE AND AROUND

Located about 60 miles northeast of Philadelphia and 30 miles northwest of Lancaster, Reading is primarily a drive-to destination. It's accessible by I-78, I-76 (Pennsylvania Turnpike), U.S. 222, and U.S. 422. There hasn't been scheduled service to Reading Regional Airport, home to the Mid-Atlantic Air Museum, for several years. Lehigh Valley International Airport (ABE), served by airlines including Delta, United, and AirTran, is 40 miles from Reading. Harrisburg

DUTCH COUNTRY

International Airport (HIA) and Philadelphia International Airport (PHL) are about 60 miles away. **Schuylkill Valley Airport Shuttle** (610/929-1775, www.svairportshuttle.com) provides van service between Reading Regional and Philadelphia International. The one-way fare is $50 for one adult, $80 for two, and $100 for three. Reservations are required.

Intercity bus service to Reading is available through **Greyhound** (800/231-2222, www.greyhound.com) and its interline partners. Local bus service is provided by the Berks Area Reading Transportation Authority, or **BARTA** (610/921-0601, www.bartabus.com). Call **Reading Metro Taxi** (610/374-5111) if you need a lift.

Hershey and Vicinity

Hershey is a town built on chocolate as surely as if cocoa were used in place of concrete. It owes its name and existence to Milton S. Hershey, founder of the largest chocolate company in North America. Milton Hershey was born in 1857 in a small central Pennsylvania community. His family moved frequently while his father pursued a series of get-rich schemes, and as a consequence, he never advanced past the fourth grade. At 14, he began a four-year apprenticeship with a Lancaster confectioner—and found his calling. But the young candy maker wasn't immediately successful. His first

candy business, in Philadelphia, collapsed after six years. In 1883 he opened a candy shop in New York. Again, his venture failed. Penniless, he returned to Lancaster and gave it a third try, making caramels by day and selling them from a pushcart in the evenings. A large order from a British candy importer and a loan from a local bank marked a turning point for the persistent entrepreneur. His Lancaster Caramel Company soon became one of the leading caramel manufacturers in the country, and he became a very rich man.

At the Chicago World's Fair in 1893,

© RICHARD BITTING

Hershey is called "The Sweetest Place on Earth."

Hershey was transfixed by an exhibit of German chocolate-making equipment. He purchased the machinery and had it installed in the east wing of his caramel factory. The Hershey Chocolate Company was born.

Back then, milk chocolate was a Swiss luxury product. Hershey was determined to develop a formula for affordable milk chocolate, and by the dawn of the new century, he had succeeded. He sold the Lancaster Caramel Company for $1 million, retaining his chocolate-making machinery, and in 1903 broke ground on a new, larger factory. The site: a cornfield in Derry Township, Pennsylvania, about a mile from his birthplace. It wasn't simply nostalgia that brought him back. Hershey needed fresh milk for his milk chocolate, and the area was rich in dairy farms. There was a railroad line and turnpike nearby. The absence of housing and other infrastructure for future employees didn't faze Hershey. He was bent on building not only a manufacturing plant but also a model town.

The intersection of two dirt roads a short distance from the factory became the center of his town. He named one Chocolate Avenue and the other Cocoa Avenue. A trolley system was up and running even before the factory was completed. As Americans fell in love with Hershey's chocolate, homes for workers and executives were built on streets named after cocoa-growing regions: Trinidad, Java, Ceylon, and such. Hershey saw to it that builders used a variety of designs so that the community wouldn't look like a company town. It wasn't long before his eponymous town had a fire company, barber shop, blacksmith shop, gas station, service garage, and weekly newspaper. He had set aside land for a park, and by 1910 it boasted a band shell, swimming pool, zoo, and bowling alley. Today Hersheypark boasts 11 roller coasters and dozens of other rides. Sales of Hershey's chocolates grew even during the Great Depression, and so did the town. Taking advantage of low-cost materials, the chocolate magnate launched a massive building campaign that employed hundreds of people. Among the town's Depression-era landmarks are the

© KATE HOPKINS

DUTCH COUNTRY

The street lights in Hershey are shaped like Hershey's Kisses.

grand Hotel Hershey and Hersheypark Arena, home to the Hershey Bears hockey team (originally named the Hershey B'ars) until 2002 and site of a massive surprise party on Milton Hershey's 80th birthday. He died in 1945 at the age of 88.

The Hershey Company, as it's now named, does business all over the world. It has plants in places as far-flung as Brazil and Mexico. But the company founded by Milton Hershey is still based in the town built by Milton Hershey—a town with streetlights shaped like Hershey's Kisses. It still makes chocolate there. You can smell it in the air. "The Sweetest Place on Earth," as Hershey is called, attracts several million visitors a year. Factory tours are no longer given, but it's still possible to learn a world about chocolate and the man who brought it to the masses. Start at the town's newest attraction, The Hershey Story, The Museum on Chocolate Avenue, for an excellent overview. Of course, if you have kids in tow, as a great deal of visitors do, they'll probably insist on starting at Hersheypark. Wherever you start, pace yourself. This place is right up there with Disney World in its concentration of attractions.

SIGHTS
(The Hershey Story

The Hershey Story (63 W. Chocolate Ave., Hershey, 717/534-3439, www.hersheystory .org, opens at 9 A.M. daily, closing time varies) opened in 2009, the first new landmark building on Chocolate Avenue in 75 years. It delivers exactly what its name promises: the story of the man, the company, and the town named Hershey. The story unfolds on the museum's second floor, where visitors learn about Milton Hershey's childhood and rocky road to success, his chocolate-making innovations and creative promotion strategies, his model town, and his philanthropies. Among the artifacts displayed are a chocolate-mixing machine from the 1920s and a Hershey's Kisses–wrapping machine, both in working order. Admission to the exhibit area is $10 for adults, $9 for seniors, $7.50 for children 3–12.

The main floor features the Chocolate Lab, where kids and adults can get hands-on experience in chocolate-making. Arrive early if you're interested. Classes can only be booked on the day of, and they fill quickly. They're $10 for adults, $9 for seniors, $7.50 for children 4–12. Children under 4 aren't permitted in the lab. Combo tickets are available for visitors who want to take in the exhibits and take part in a class: $17.50 for adults, $16.50 for seniors, $14 for children.

Also on the main floor is Café Zooka, named after one of Milton Hershey's early chocolate novelties. You won't find his Chocolate Zooka Sticks on the menu (they were discontinued in 1904), but you will find a variety of sandwiches, salads, pizzas, and desserts. Leave room for the Countries of Origin Chocolate Tasting, located within the café. You can sample six warm drinking chocolates, each representing a different chocolate-growing region, for $9.95.

Even before his chocolate factory was built, Milton Hershey had laid out the plans for a town. He'd set aside 150 acres along Spring

© THE HERSHEY STORY

The Hershey Story describes the history of the Hershey legacy.

© HERSHEY ENTERTAINMENT & RESORTS

Hersheypark

Creek for a park where his employees could picnic and paddle the day away. The park opened in the spring of 1907 and soon became a tourist attraction, with excursion trains and trolleys delivering fun-seekers from surrounding communities.

◖ Hersheypark

Today Hersheypark (100 W. Hersheypark Dr., Hershey, 717/534-3900, www.hersheypark .com) lures people from across the state and beyond with more than 60 rides and attractions, including 11 roller coasters. The historic park spends generously to stay current. Four of the coasters were installed in the 21st century, including Lightning Racer, the first wooden dueling coaster in the U.S. The newest coaster, Fahrenheit, features trains with stadium-style seating and a 97-degree drop. Bring bathing suits to enjoy Hersheypark's water attractions, which include Tidal Force, one of the tallest splash-down rides in the world; Roller Soaker, an aerial ride that pits riders against spectators armed with water sprayers; and a series of tubing rides. A huge wave pool and 1,300-foot lazy river were added in 2009. For those who prefer to stay firmly planted on the earth, Hersheypark offers shopping and a busy schedule of live entertainment.

The park is open weekends in May, daily from late May through Labor Day, and a few weekends after Labor Day. Gates open at 10 A.M. and close between 6 P.M. and 11 P.M. A variety of admission plans are available. One-day admission is $52.95 for guests ages 9–54, $31.95 for children 3–8 and adults 55–69, $20.95 for those 70 and older. Hang on to your ticket stub in case you decide to come back the next day; consecutive-day admission is $31.95. Arrive within a few hours of closing for special "sunset" rates. Flex passes, good for admission to the park on any two or three days of the season, are available. If your summer plans also include a visit to Dutch Wonderland in Lancaster, part of the Hershey family of attractions, ask about combo tickets. Hersheypark tickets are good for same-day admission to ZooAmerica.

The park opens on select weekends outside of its regular season. **Springtime in the Park** (www.springtimeinhershey.com) is a chance to preview what's in store for summer over several days in April. **Hersheypark in the Dark** (www.halloweeninhershey.com) is several weekends' worth of Halloween-themed fun. The park is also open in late November and throughout December for **Christmas in Hershey** (www.christmasinhershey.com). Meet Santa's

> ## MILTON HERSHEY'S ORPHAN HEIRS
>
> Married for 10 years and unable to have children, Milton Hershey and his wife, Catherine, established a boarding school for orphaned boys in 1909. The Hershey Industrial School, as it was called at the time, had an initial enrollment of 10. Catherine Hershey – "Kitty" to her adoring husband – wouldn't live to see its dramatic expansion. After a long and debilitating muscular illness, she died in 1915. Three years later, Milton Hershey transferred the bulk of his fortune, including his stock in the Hershey Chocolate Company, to the trust created to fund the school. Upon his death in 1945, townspeople streamed into the school's foyer, where his body lay in state. The funeral service was held in the auditorium, with eight boys from the senior class serving as pallbearers.
>
> Renamed the Milton Hershey School (www.mhs-pa.org) in 1951, it began enrolling girls in the 1970s. Today more than 1,200 underprivileged children from pre-kindergarten through 12th grade live and learn on the 9,000-acre campus – at no cost to their families. Milton Hershey's endowment has grown in value to more than $6 billion. The school trust's assets include a 30 percent stake in the Hershey Company and full ownership of Hershey Entertainment & Resorts, the company that runs Hersheypark, ZooAmerica, The Hotel Hershey, the Giant Center, the Hershey Theatre, and other products of Milton Hershey's vision of a town rich in recreational and cultural resources.

reindeer and take in a light show set to holiday tunes at Hersheypark. Then hop in the car and crank up the heater for Hershey Sweet Lights, a drive-thru spectacular located a few minutes from the amusement park.

ZooAmerica

In 1905, a couple from Lebanon, Pennsylvania, approached Milton Hershey with an idea. Several years earlier they'd immigrated from Germany, where they'd owned 12 prairie dogs and a bear cub. Alas, their yard in Lebanon couldn't accommodate their brood. They figured Hershey's proposed park could. ZooAmerica (30 Park Ave., Hershey, 717/534-3900, www.zooamerica.com, open year-round, hours vary, admission $9.50, children 3–8 and seniors $8, free admission with Hersheypark ticket) traces its history to their meeting with the chocolate magnate. The 11-acre zoo is home to more than 200 animals from five regions of North America. Visitors are never terribly far from the critters but have a rare opportunity to get even closer on Wednesday and Saturday evenings. The zoo's After-Hours Tour is a chance to peek behind the curtain, feed the otters, touch a reptile, and more. The two-hour tour, which begins at 8 P.M. April–September and 6 P.M. October–March, costs $35 per person. Participants must pre-register 72 hours in advance. ZooAmerica is connected to Hersheypark by a walking bridge. It also has a year-round, dedicated entrance on Park Avenue (Route 743).

Hershey's Chocolate World

When The Hershey Company ceased stopped factory tours in the 1970s, it gave the public Hershey's Chocolate World (251 Park Blvd., Hershey, 717/534-4900, www.hersheys.com/chocolateworld, open year-round, hours vary). Adjacent to Hersheypark, Chocolate World is part mall, part interactive museum. Its shops sell anything and everything Hershey's, including pillows shaped like packets of Reese's Peanut Butter Cups, Twizzlers-shaped pens, and personalized chocolate bars. A primer on the chocolate-making process is available in the form of a slow-moving amusement ride. Passengers are transported from a tropical rainforest where cocoa beans flourish to a chocolate factory, encountering some singing cows along the way. The ride is free, as is a sample of a Hershey's confection at its conclusion. Other Chocolate World attractions have an admission fee. The Hershey's Really Big 3-D Show, an animated musical complete with rumbling seats and smoke plumes, is $5.95 for adults, $5.45 for seniors, $4.95 for children 3–12. The Chocolate Tasting Adventure, a chance to compare various chocolates under the tutelage of an expert, is $9.95 for adults, $9.45 for seniors, $6.95 for children. Call for tasting times.

To fill up on something other than candy, head to the food court or the Kit Kat "Gimme a Break" Café, which serves hot dogs, sandwiches, nachos, and the like. If you buy nothing else during your visit to Chocolate World, buy a chocolate milkshake. Worth every calorie.

Complimentary shuttle service is available from Chocolate World to The Hershey Story and ZooAmerica. You can also hop aboard an old-fashioned trolley car for a fascinating tour of the town with a ham of a conductor. **Hershey Trolley Works** (717/533-3000, www.hersheytrolleyworks.com, fare $12.95, seniors $11.95, children 3–12 $5.95) tours depart Chocolate World daily rain or shine.

Hershey Gardens

When chocolate magnate and philanthropist Milton Hershey was asked to sponsor a national rosarium in Washington D.C., he decided to create one in his eponymous town instead. "A nice garden of roses," as he called it, opened to the public in 1937 and within five years had blossomed into a 23-acre horticultural haven. Roses are still the specialty at Hershey Gardens (170 Hotel Rd., Hershey, 717/534-3492, www.hersheygardens.org, open daily late Mar.–Oct. and Fri.–Sun. Nov.–Dec., hours vary, admission $10, seniors $9, children 3–12 $6), located across from The Hotel Hershey. More than 7,000 roses of 275 varieties bloom during the summer months. Springtime is pretty special too. That's when 30,000 tulips of 100

varieties blanket the Seasonal Display Garden and daffodils light up the Perennial Garden. Bold-colored chrysanthemums steal the show in fall. But what most visitors go ga-ga over isn't roses or tulips or any flower for that matter. It's the Butterfly House, open from late May through late September. Visitors can observe the entire lifecycle of the ethereal insects. Also popular is the Children's Garden, filled with not only flora but also fun activities.

The Hotel Hershey

The Hotel Hershey (100 Hotel Rd., Hershey, 717/533-2171, www.thehotelhershey.com), a Mediterranean-style product of Milton Hershey's Depression-era building campaign, deserves a spot on your itinerary even if you're not staying there. Grand to begin with, the hotel is grander than ever on the heels of a $67 million renovation and expansion. Some amenities, like the year-round ice-skating rink unveiled in 2009, are exclusively for guests. But nonguests can still have a field day. For starters, they can sink into a chocolate milk bath at The Spa at The Hotel Hershey (717/520-5888,

The Hotel Hershey

© HERSHEY ENTERTAINMENT & RESORTS

a king room at The Hotel Hershey

www.chocolatespa.com), better known by its nickname, the **Chocolate Spa.** Other chocolate-inspired services include a Swedish massage with chocolate-scented oil and an exfoliating treatment with cocoa bean husks. The spa menu also pays homage to Cuba, where Milton Hershey spent much of his time after his wife's death in 1915, buying and building sugar mills. The Noche Azul Soak, for example, is a 15-minute dip in waters infused with Cuba's national flower. The three-story spa overlooks the hotel's formal gardens and reflecting pools.

The hotel's boutiques welcome the general public. Among them is a swimwear store with a particularly large selection of chocolate-brown pieces and a sweets shop where customers can decorate their own cupcakes. One of the oldest and most distinguished restaurants in central Pennsylvania calls the hotel home. The **Circular Dining Room** (breakfast 7–10:30 A.M. daily, brunch noon–2:30 P.M. Sun., dinner 5:30–9 P.M. Mon.–Sat. and 6–9 P.M. Sun., call for lunch hours, dinner $28–39) owes its shape to Milton Hershey, who noticed during his world travels

that guests who tipped poorly were often seated in the corners of restaurants. "I don't want any corners," he reportedly said. He also saw to it that the restaurant had no pillars, having noticed that single diners were often seated at tables with obstructed views. A recent addition to the hotel's dining portfolio, **Harvest** (717/534-8800, 11:30 A.M.–10 P.M. daily, $9–28) offers regional American cuisine made with ingredients found within a 100-mile radius of the hotel. Not interested in spa treatments, shopping, or excellent food? Come to The Hotel Hershey for the view. Situated on a hilltop, it overlooks "The Sweetest Place on Earth."

Antique Auto Museum at Hershey

Home to the Lakeland bus used in the movie *Forrest Gump* and a green Cadillac Seville once owned by actress Betty White, the Antique Auto Museum at Hershey (161 Museum Dr., Hershey, 717/566-7100, www.aacamuseum .org, 9 A.M.–5 P.M. daily, admission $10, seniors $9, children 4–12 $7) is one of the few

DUTCH COUNTRY

Antique Auto Museum at Hershey

attractions in town that have nothing to do with chocolate. An affiliate of the Smithsonian Institution, the museum displays more than 150 cars, motorcycles, and buses—many in elaborate dioramas depicting scenes such as a turn-of-the-20th-century machine shop, a 1940s gas station, and a 1950s drive-in. A highlight of the cruise through time is a restored 1941 Valentine Diner relocated from Wichita, Kansas. The museum frequently stages special exhibitions of loaned vehicles. Among its recent borrowings: turbine-powered, aeronautically inspired concept cars from the General Motors Heritage Center, a pair of stainless steel cars created in the 1960s, and a 1953 Cadillac LeMans, one of only four built and two known to exist. On the first Saturday of each month and throughout the holiday season, visitors can check out the museum's model train display, a miniaturization of small-town America in the 1950s.

Indian Echo Caverns

Geological forces make for family entertainment at Indian Echo Caverns (368 Middletown Rd., Hummelstown, 717/566-8131, www.indian echocaverns.com, 9 A.M.–6 P.M. daily Memorial Day–Labor Day, 10 A.M.–4 P.M. rest of year, admission $13, seniors $11, children 3–11 $7), located four miles west of Hershey off U.S. 322. The first visitors to the limestone caverns were likely Susquehannock Indians seeking shelter from inclement weather. The caverns still do a brisk business on rainy days, when Hersheypark holds less than its usual appeal. Guides point out spectacular formations and share cavern lore during 45-minute walking tours. It's always a cool 52 degrees inside, so dress accordingly. In summer, allot an extra hour if you're bringing kids. The grounds include a playground, a petting zoo, and Gem Mill Junction, where budding prospectors can search for amethyst, jasper, agate, and other treasures.

Hollywood Casino at Penn National Race Course

Not every attraction in the Hershey area was built with kids in mind. Nine miles north of chocolate central, grownups gamble on slots and horses at Hollywood Casino at Penn National Race Course (77 Hollywood Blvd., Grantville, 717/469-2211, www.hcpn.com, open 24 hours). Live thoroughbred races, a tradition since 1972, are held Wednesday–Saturday evenings throughout the year as well as most Tuesdays May–July. The casino, which opened in 2008, is ding-ding-ding 24/7 with the occasional ka-ching! Its 2,300-plus slot machines range from penny slots to $100 slots. Dining options include the upscale **Final Cut Steakhouse** (717/469-3090, 5:30–10 P.M. Wed.–Sat., 4–9 P.M. Sun., $25–42), with a menu biased toward Hereford beef but not averse to lobster tails, grass-fed lamb, and Cornish game hen. There's a buffet restaurant, of course. Lunch is $12.99, dinner $19.99.

Cornwall Iron Furnace

Cornwall Iron Furnace (94 Rexmont Rd., Cornwall, 717/272-9711, www.cornwall ironfurnace.org, 9 A.M.–5 P.M. Thurs.–Sat., noon–5 P.M. Sun., admission $6, seniors $5.50, children 3–11 $4) was retired from service more than a century ago, but it still has a job to do: teaching visitors about the fiery infancy of America's metals industry. Charcoal-fueled furnaces dotted the Pennsylvania countryside in the 18th and 19th centuries, but this one is unique in its intactness. Indeed, the blast furnace and related buildings are regarded as one of the best-preserved 19th-century ironmaking complexes in the world.

Stonemason Peter Grubb established the furnace in 1742, naming the area Cornwall after a region of England. For more than a century and a half, the furnace consumed copious amounts of charcoal, iron ore, and limestone, producing molten iron that was cast into cannons, stoves, and other products. It was abandoned in 1883, rendered obsolete by coal-fueled ironmaking operations. Today the furnace looks much as it did following extensive renovations in the mid-1800s. What used to be the charcoal barn is now a visitors center with interpretive exhibits on mining, charcoal-making, and ironmaking. Other surviving structures include a blacksmith shop, a building where wagons were built

and repaired, and a darling Gothic Revival building that served as a butcher shop for the ironmaster's estate. The iron ore mine, which continued to operate until 1973, is just south of the furnace site and visible from Boyd Street. The open pit mine was sensationally prolific, yielding more than 100 million tons before beginning to flood. Today it's filled with water. Houses built in the 19th century for miners and furnace workers still line Boyd Street.

ENTERTAINMENT AND EVENTS

Performance Venues

Best known as the home arena of the Hershey Bears hockey team, **Giant Center** (550 W. Hersheypark Dr., Hershey, 717/534-3911, www.giantcenter.com) hosts some of the flashiest performers to pass through Hershey. It opened in 2002 with a Cher concert. More recent guests have included 50 Cent, Kelly Clarkson, the Harlem Globetrotters, the Ringling Bros. and Barnum & Bailey circus, and Republican running mates John McCain and Sarah Palin, who held a rally there during the 2008 presidential race. Less-than-famous folks can hit the ice during occasional public skating sessions. The arena seats 10,000–12,500 depending on the nature of the event.

Hersheypark Stadium (100 W. Hersheypark Dr., Hershey, 717/534-3911) can accommodate 30,000 fans for concerts. The outdoor stadium has hosted the likes of The Who, James Taylor, Alabama, U2, Dave Matthews Band, and an 'N Sync 'n' Pink doubleheader. It's also the venue for sporting events such as the Big 33 Football Classic, an annual all-star game between high school players from Pennsylvania and Ohio. Built as part of Milton Hershey's Depression-era building campaign, the stadium at one point served as the summer home of the Philadelphia Eagles. **The Star Pavilion** opened at Hersheypark Stadium in 1996. It's a more intimate open-air venue with reserved and lawn seating for 8,000.

The spectacular **Hershey Theatre** (15 E. Caracas Ave., Hershey, 717/534-3405, www .hersheytheatre.com) also went up during

Mr. Hershey's "Great Building Campaign," which created jobs for an estimated 600 skilled workers. And skilled they were. The lobby boasts a floor laid with polished Italian lava rock, soaring marble arches, and a ceiling adorned with bas-relief images of swans, war chariots, and more. The foyer and auditorium reveal the architect's fondness for Venice, Italy. A winged lion, the symbol of Venice, is mounted above the stage, and the proscenium arch calls to mind an ancient canal bridge. An intricate lighting system creates the illusion of twinkling stars and floating clouds overhead. The 1,904-seat theater hosts touring Broadway shows, concerts, dance performances, and classic films.

If you catch a concert at Giant Center, Hersheypark Stadium, The Star Pavilion, or the Hershey Theatre during Hersheypark's May–September season, you can present your ticket or ticket stub at the amusement park's front gate for a discounted admission price of $33.95. The discount applies the day before, day of, and day after the concert.

Festivals and Events

With Hersheypark closed and temps that dip below freezing, February wouldn't seem like a good time to visit Hershey. If you're a bargain-hunting chocolate lover, it's an ideal time. Each day of **Chocolate-Covered February** (800/437-7439, www.chocolatecoveredfebruary.com) brings a host of chocolate-themed activities along with discounts on everything from museum tickets to spa treatments. The month-long celebration of Hershey's signature foodstuff features chocolate-inspired meals, chef demonstrations, and classes in topics such as truffle-making, chocolate martini mixology, and wine and chocolate pairing.

There's no shortage of entertainment in Hershey during the summer months, but fans of classical and jazz music may wish to head east, to Mount Gretna. The resort community about 12 miles from Hershey has long been known as a cultural mecca. It's home to the **Pennsylvania Chautauqua** (general information 717/964-3270, summer programs

717/964-1830, www.pachautauqua.org), which sponsors Thursday evening organ recitals, Sunday evening "mini concerts," and a host of other cultural and educational programs throughout the summer. **Music at Gretna** (717/361-1508, www.gretnamusic.org), a classical chamber music and jazz festival spanning several weeks, has welcomed the likes of jazz pianist Dave Brubeck and singer/guitarist John Pizzarelli.

Hershey welcomes thousands of antique automobile enthusiasts during the first full week of October. The **Antique Automobile Club of America's Eastern Division National Fall Meet** (717/566-7720, www.hersheyaaca.org), held in Hershey since 1955, is one of the largest antique automobile shows and flea markets in the country.

SHOPPING

The **Outlets at Hershey** (46 Outlet Square, Hershey, 717/520-1236, www.theoutletsat hershey.com, 9:30 A.M.–6 P.M. Mon.–Thurs., 9:30 A.M.–9 P.M. Fri.–Sat., 11 A.M.–5 P.M. Sun.) are just off Hershey Park Drive, within minutes of Hersheypark and other main attractions. The outlet center's 60-some stores include Brooks Brothers, J. Crew, Liz Claiborne, Calvin Klein, Tommy Hilfiger, and Polo Ralph Lauren.

SPORTS AND RECREATION
Spectator Sports

The **Hershey Bears** (Giant Center, 550 W. Hersheypark Dr., Hershey, 717/534-3380, www.hersheybears.com) have competed in the professional American Hockey League without interruption since 1938. Amateur hockey came to Hershey even earlier, in 1931. The popularity of matches between college teams convinced chocolate czar Milton S. Hershey and his longtime chief of entertainment and amusements, John B. Sollenberger, to sponsor a permanent team the following year. They called it the Hershey B'ars and dressed the players in maroon and silver—just like the Hershey Bar. Renamed the Hershey Bears in 1936, the team has brought home at least one Calder

DUTCH COUNTRY

Cup, the AHL's ultimate prize, every decade since the 1940s. The Bears "draw more fans and inspire more passion than just about any team in minor league hockey," *The Washington Post* wrote of the Washington Capitals' affiliate in 2009. Later that year, the Bears became the first team in league history to win 10 championships.

Top high school athletes and their families frequently descend on Hershey. The town hosts the **Big 33 Football Classic** (717/774-3303, www.big33.org), an all-star game that pits Pennsylvania's best against Ohio's, as well as various Pennsylvania Interscholastic Athletic Association (717/697-0374, www.piaa.org) championships.

ACCOMMODATIONS

Hershey Entertainment & Resorts (800/437-7439, www.hersheypa.com), the company founded when Milton Hershey decided to separate his non-chocolate ventures from the business that made them all possible, controls not only most of the tourist attractions in town but also three lodging properties: the upscale Hotel Hershey, the more affordable Hershey Lodge, and the Hershey Highmeadow Campground. There are plenty of other places to bed down, but staying at a Hershey Resorts property has its privileges. Guests of the Hotel Hershey and Hershey Lodge get free admission to the Hershey Gardens and The Hershey Story, while campground guests get discounted admission. Other perks include free seasonal shuttle service to Hersheypark and access to some rides before the gates officially open. Hershey Resorts guests also have the exclusive opportunity to purchase a Hersheypark Sweet Access Pass, bearers of which can cut to the front of most lines and otherwise behave like VIPs.

For obvious reasons, most Hershey hotels charge a heckuva lot more in summer than the rest of the year.

Under $100

Open year-round, **Hershey Highmeadow Campground** (1200 Matlack Rd., Hummelstown, 717/534-8999, www.hershey camping.com, campsites $30–51, cabins $68–135) offers more than 300 tent and RV sites and cabins ranging from rustic to deluxe. The 55-acre campground is minutes from Hersheypark. Amenities include two swimming pools, a game room, basketball and volleyball courts, horseshoe pits, and a country store. Organized activities add to the fun in summer. The campground has 22 cabins without indoor plumbing, plus two deluxe cabins complete with kitchen and bathroom. Cabins sleep anywhere from four to eight people. Campsite and cabin rates are based on occupancy of up to four. There's a $5 per night fee for each additional person. Another good budget option: the family-run **Chocolatetown Motel** (1806 E. Chocolate Ave., Hershey, 717/533-2330, www.chocolatetownmotel.com, $54–140). Even during the busiest weeks of the busy season, rates start at just $89. An outdoor pool adds to its appeal.

$100-300

With 665 guest rooms and suites and 100,000 square feet of function space, **☐ Hershey Lodge** (325 University Dr., Hershey, 717/533-3311, www.hersheylodge.com, summer $290–310, off-season $170–270) is Pennsylvania's largest convention resort. Not surprisingly, it's quite often crawling with convention-goers. But it's also wildly popular with families, won over by amenities including an 18-hole miniature golf course, activities such as poolside movies and family bingo, and appearances by Hershey's product characters. (Who can resist a huggable Hershey's Kiss?) The chocolate theme extends to the decor of the guest rooms, which feature complimentary wireless internet access, refrigerators, and flat-screen TVs. Guests can catch A&E Biography's *Milton Hershey: The Chocolate King* any time of day.

Hershey has several chain hotels in this price range. Closest to the action: **Days Inn Hershey** (350 W. Chocolate Ave., Hershey, 717/534-2162, www.daysinnhershey.com, summer $200–270, off-season $110–160). Owned and operated by a lifelong Hershey resident, the hotel has more to recommend it than convenience. The rooms are spacious and the staff gracious. On-site massages are available. Guests get all sorts of freebies: hotel-wide wireless Internet access, continental breakfast, shuttle service to Hersheypark, 24-hour coffee service, and use of the Gold's Gym less than two miles away. Plus, they get to bring their pets.

Another fine choice is **SpringHill Suites Hershey** (115 Museum Dr., Hershey, 717/583-2222, www.springhillsuiteshershey.com, summer $250–260, off-season $125–160), where Internet access and breakfast are likewise free. It's next door to the Antique Auto Museum and fairly new, having opened in 2000. All guest rooms are studio-suites with a pull-out sofa in addition to one or two beds. Both the Days Inn and SpringHill Suites have an indoor pool and whirlpool, a fitness center, and guest laundry facilities.

For homier digs, head to the **1825 Inn Bed & Breakfast** (409 S. Lingle Ave., Palmyra, 717/838-8282, www.1825inn.com, $114–239). The main house has six country-style guest rooms with private baths. A pair of cottages with a more contemporary aesthetic, king-sized beds, two-person Jacuzzis, and private decks seem to have been designed with honeymooners in mind.

Some of the area's most elegant accommodations can be found on a picturesque horse farm. ☖ **The Inn at Westwynd Farm** (1620 Sand Beach Rd., Hummelstown, 717/533-6764, www.westwyndfarminn.com, $109–259) is just 10 minutes north of Hershey but, as owners Carolyn and Frank Troxell are fond of saying, "a world apart." Their goal is simple: to pamper the heck out of guests. That means refreshments upon arrival, a bottomless cookie jar, and gourmet breakfasts that reflect the season, often flavored with herbs from their own garden. The Troxells are happy to point guests to good restaurants and even arrange for a dinner at the home of an Amish family. Bringing your family? Ask for the carriage house with its full bath, living room, and space enough for six. The main house has nine en suite guest rooms, eight of which have fireplaces, five of which have Jacuzzis, and all of which have charm in spades.

Over $300

Milton Hershey's plan to build a luxury hotel in the midst of the Great Depression met with ridicule. He poured $2 million into the project anyway. When he addressed the first guests of **The Hotel Hershey** (100 Hotel Rd., Hershey, 717/533-2171, www.thehotelhershey .com, summer traditional room $370–430, cottage room $500–535, off-season traditional room $250–390, cottage room $400–495) on May 26, 1933, he also addressed his critics. "When we farmers go to the city, we are impressed by the fine hotels we see there," he said. "So I thought I'd impress the city folks by building a fine hotel on one of our farms. I am of the opinion that there will be a need for this hotel someday, although the prospects do not look very encouraging at the present time." Mr. Hershey's 170-room hotel impressed folks, indeed. Renowned newsman Lowell Thomas, who visited the hotel in its first year, described it as "a palace that out-palaces the palaces of the Maharajahs of India." The Hotel Hershey is even more palatial now, having treated itself to a $67 million facelift and expansion on the occasion of its 75th anniversary. Among the new facilities is an outdoor swimming complex with an infinity-edge pool for grown-ups, a family pool with two large slides, a whirlpool, and an eatery. The pool complex also has 14 swanky cabanas complete with flat-screen TVs, ceiling fans, and refrigerators, available to guests for $200 a day. (The hotel has an indoor pool, so guests can still get their swim on during the colder months.) Also added as part of the expansion: an all-weather ice-skating rink, seven boutique shops, and 10 luxury guest cottages. Bordering dense woods, the four- and six-bedroom cottages are the hotel's poshest accommodations. Guests can reserve individual bedrooms or an entire cottage. The latter affords them access to a great room with a fireplace, French doors opening to a porch, and

pool complex at The Hotel Hershey

© HERSHEY ENTERTAINMENT & RESORTS

other comforts. The hotel's main building has 230 guest rooms and suites, including the especially elegant Milton Hershey Suite with its veranda overlooking the town of Hershey.

FOOD

Two of Hershey's best restaurants are within The Hotel Hershey (100 Hotel Rd., Hershey, restaurant reservations 717/534-8800, www.thehotelhershey.com). Fancier of the two is the ◖ **Circular Dining Room** (breakfast 7–10:30 A.M. daily, brunch noon–2:30 P.M. Sun., dinner 5:30–9 P.M. Mon.–Sat. and 6–9 P.M. Sun., call for lunch hours, dinner $28–39), which dates to the 1930s. Built without corners or pillars as per Milton Hershey's instructions, the restaurant recently underwent a $1 million renovation that included the addition of a 1,200-bottle wine cellar. Its wine list now offers some 350 labels. The dinner menu changes with the seasons and, not surprisingly, makes liberal use of chocolate and cocoa. What may surprise first-time

guests is their use in dishes savory as well as sweet—dishes such as cocoa-seared jumbo scallops and venison chop with cocoa nib jus. On Friday evenings the restaurant offers a six-course chef's tasting menu for $75. The Circular Dining Room's greatest claim to fame is its Sunday brunch. At $39.95 per person (kids 3–8 can dive in for $19.50), the gourmet smorgasbord isn't cheap. But it's possible to eat your money's worth with a couple of trips to the fresh seafood bar. Reservations are required for the Sunday brunch, lunch buffet ($23 per person, children 3–8 $11.50), and dinner. Gentlemen need a jacket and ladies a dress or dress pants for Sunday brunch and dinner. "Resort casual" rules the day at **Harvest** (11:30 A.M.–10 P.M. daily, $9–28), which joined The Hotel Hershey's menu of eateries in 2009. The folks at Harvest are fiercely loyal to local growers and producers, so much so that even the pretzels crushed to coat its chicken tenders hail from within a 100-mile radius of the hotel. Both lunch and dinner menus offer a variety of salads, sandwiches, burgers, and entrées. **Fenicci's of Hershey** (102 W. Chocolate Ave., Hershey, 717/533-7159, www.feniccis.com, 11 A.M.–midnight Mon.–Thurs., 11 A.M.–1 A.M. Fri.–Sat., noon–11 P.M. Sun., $9–28) is spitting distance from Hersheypark, The Hershey Story, and other main attractions, but don't mistake it for a tourist trap. The casual Italian eatery, which dates to 1935, is beloved by generations of locals. It's famous for its upside-down pizza—cheese on bottom, sauce on top—and its homemade meat, marinara, and mushroom sauces. The Italian wedding soup, made daily, is also a hit. The menu is extensive, with five risottos, six parms, and scores of variations on pasta. There's a kids' menu too. Grown-ups have the benefit of a full bar and live music on Friday and Saturday nights.

Also popular with locals, **Fire Alley** (1144 Cocoa Ave., Hershey, 717/533-3200, www.firealley.net, 4–10 P.M. Sun. Thurs., 4–11 P.M. Fri.–Sat., bar closes later, $7–28) is an offshoot of Harrisburg's Fire House, which occupies a restored 19th-century firehouse. What Fire Alley lacks in historical value it makes up for in style. Inside the suburban eatery, murals, awnings, window boxes, and streetlights create the impression of an urban streetscape, complete with graffiti. Fire Alley's cleverest design element is banquette-styling seating at the bar: all the comfort of a booth with readier access to the bartender. It's the food, of course, that accounts for the large roster of regulars. The kitchen does wings, burgers, veal parmesan— stuff you'd expect from a casual eatery—but also mussels steamed in Guinness, seared tuna on seaweed salad, and slow-roasted prime rib. The meatloaf is swaddled in bacon, and the nachos fall in the seafood category. Drop by on a Thursday for $4 margaritas.

The curiously named **What If . . .** (845 E. Chocolate Ave., Hershey, 717/533-5858, www.whatifdining.com, 11 A.M.–10 P.M. Mon.– Thurs., 11 A.M.–11 P.M. Fri.–Sat., 4–10 P.M. Sun., bar menu available for an additional hour Memorial Day–Labor Day $7–32) is in an off-putting location: below street level in the Howard Johnson Inn Hershey. But if you can overlook the lack of natural light, you'll be glad you came. Start with the crab martini and end with the profiterole du jour, made in-house along with every other dessert. In between, tuck into an entrée from the menu of continental cuisine. The extensive wine list is partial to California and the Pacific Northwest.

INFORMATION

The **Hershey Harrisburg Regional Visitors Bureau** (17 S. 2nd St., Harrisburg, 717/231-7788, www.hersheyharrisburg.org, 9 A.M.–5 P.M. Mon.–Fri. and 10 A.M.–3 P.M. Sat., also open 10 A.M.–2 P.M. Sun. in summer) has loads of information about attractions, lodging, and dining in and around Hershey. Visit the bureau's website to request a copy of its current visitors guide or peruse a digital version. For information about Pennsylvania Dutch Country as a whole, visit www.dutchcountryroads.com.

GETTING THERE AND AROUND

Hershey is about 30 miles northwest of Lancaster and 15 miles east of Harrisburg, the state capital. **Harrisburg International Airport** (888/235-9442, www.flyhia.com), about a 20-minute drive from Hershey, is served by Air Canada, AirTran Airways, Continental Airlines, Delta Air Lines, United Airlines, and US Airways. They offer daily nonstop service to about a dozen destinations. Note that while locals refer to the airport as HIA, its Federal Aviation Administration booking code is MDT. That's because of its physical location in the borough of Middletown, about eight miles south of Harrisburg.

Harrisburg is served by **Amtrak** (800/872-7245, www.amtrak.com) and intercity bus companies. Once there, rent a car or hop in a cab to get to Hershey. You can also travel to Hershey from Harrisburg by **Capital Area Transit** (717/238-8304, www.cattransit.com) bus.

Harrisburg and Vicinity

Like many state capitals, Harrisburg isn't much of a vacation destination. It's awfully close to one; Hershey, a.k.a. Chocolate Town, USA, is just 15 miles to its east. Most people come to Harrisburg because they have business there, and more often than not, it's government business. That's not to say there's nothing to see or do in the city, which lies on the east bank of the Susquehanna River. Harrisburg has some excellent museums, including the State Museum of Pennsylvania and the National Civil War Museum. It has a charming park along the river and another *on* the river. It has more minor league teams than you can imagine. In recent years the dining and nightlife scenes have improved to such a degree that it's not unusual for innkeepers in the Hershey area to point guests toward Harrisburg for dinner.

The city owes its name to John Harris, who emigrated from England in the late 17th century, built a home on the river near the present juncture of Paxton and Front Streets, and eventually established the first ferry across the Susquehanna. The ferry played an important role in the westward migration of other pioneers and later in the Revolutionary War, carrying supplies to the Continental army west of the Susquehanna. After the war, John Harris Jr. made plans for a town on his father's land, which had come to be known as Harris's Ferry. Freshly named, Harrisburg was incorporated in 1791. In 1812, it replaced Lancaster as the state capital.

Over the next several decades, Harrisburg emerged as a transportation center, first as a linchpin of Pennsylvania's canal system and then as a railroad hub. During the Civil War, the rail yards teemed with Union soldiers. Hundreds of thousands of men received their instructions at Harrisburg's Camp Curtin. With its transportation arteries and trove of supplies, Harrisburg was a target for Confederate General Robert E. Lee. His troops might have captured the vulnerable capital

Harrisburg skyline

in 1863—they made it as far as Camp Hill, just across the river—had they not received an urgent order to turn south. The Battle of Gettysburg was at hand.

More than a century later, the citizens of Harrisburg would feel threatened once again. In March 1979, the Three Mile Island nuclear power plant, about 15 miles south of the capital, suffered a partial meltdown. Tens of thousands of people fled their homes. The sight of the plant's cooling towers is still somewhat chilling. Current owner Exelon Corp. occasionally invites the public to visit and see that everything is hunky-dory.

It's best to visit Harrisburg during the warmer months, when the Susquehanna calls to boaters and anglers and the riverfront hosts one festival after another. Be sure to venture outside the city. Take a trip on the only remaining ferry across the Susquehanna. Take a hike on the Appalachian Trail. If nothing else, take a look at the city from across the river. Not bad for a place that's rarely seen on postcards.

SIGHTS
Whitaker Center for Science and the Arts

Part science museum, part performing arts center, and part movie theater, the Whitaker Center (222 Market St., Harrisburg, 717/214-2787, www.whitakercenter.org, 9:30 A.M.–5 P.M. Tues.–Sat., 11:30 A.M.–5 P.M. Sun., admission Science Center only $13.75, seniors, students, and children 3–12 $11.75) is downtown Harrisburg's cultural hub. The $53 million center, which opened in 1999, houses the Sunoco Performance Theater and an IMAX theater with an 80-foot-wide screen—the largest in central Pennsylvania. It's also home to the Harsco Science Center, three floors of exhibits about everything from weather systems to the physics of dance. Visitors can venture a hand into a writhing eight-foot-tall tornado, test their physical and mental fitness, assemble telescopes and microscopes, discover how dancers manipulate their center of gravity to appear to be floating during leaps, and more. KidsPlace, a gallery for children 5 and under,

opened in 2008 and features a miniature version of Harrisburg's Broad Street Market, the oldest continuously operated market house in the United States. Other exhibits with a local twist include a model of the Susquehanna River, which passes within a few blocks of the Whitaker Center. Combo tickets for Science Center visitors who want to catch an IMAX documentary are $17.75 for adults and $15.75 for seniors, students with ID, and children 3–12. Hollywood movies shown on the giant screen are $13.75 for adults and $11.75 for seniors, students, and children.

State Museum of Pennsylvania

Free for more than a century, the State Museum of Pennsylvania (300 North St., Harrisburg, 717/787-4980, www.statemuseumpa.org, 9 A.M.–5 P.M. Thurs.–Sat., noon–5 P.M. Sun., admission $5, seniors and children 1–12 $4) implemented an admission fee in mid-2009, citing "budget considerations." But it's still a bargain (and still free on the third Saturday of every month). The four-story circular museum next to the State Capitol offers a well-rounded perspective on Pennsylvania's story. The Hall of Paleontology and Geology introduces visitors to earlier life forms, including a massive armored fish that prowled the seas of Pennsylvania and Ohio some 367 million years ago and the Marshalls Creek Mastodon, a prehistoric elephant whose remains were discovered in the small eastern Pennsylvania community after which it's named. Also popular is the Hall of Mammals, a set of 13 life-sized dioramas of native animals in their natural environments. The Civil War gallery features Peter Rothermel's famous painting of Pickett's Charge at the Battle of Gettysburg. Unveiled in 1870, the plus-sized masterpiece (32 feet long and almost 17 feet high) toured the country, appearing at the World's Fair in Philadelphia in 1876. Though it garnered much praise, it also came under fire. Critics complained that the dying Union soldiers had angelic countenances while the rebels appeared wracked with guilt.

Access to Curiosity Connection, a play area designed for children ages 1–5, is included in

DUTCH COUNTRY

© HERSHEYHARRISBURG.ORG

the State Museum of Pennsylvania in Harrisburg

general admission. The State Museum also houses a planetarium. Planetarium tickets, which include museum admission, are $7 for adults and $6 for seniors and children 12 and under. Additional planetarium shows are $2.

Susquehanna Art Museum

Dismayed that the state capital had no art museum, four art educators set about making one in 1989. Today the Susquehanna Art Museum (301 Market St., Harrisburg, 717/233-8668, www.sqart.org, 10 A.M.–4 P.M. Tues.–Wed. and Fri.–Sat., 4–8 P.M. Thurs., 1–4 P.M. Sun., admission $5, seniors and students $3, children 12 and under free) occupies the first three floors of the Kunkel Building, kitty-corner from the Whitaker Center. Each year, the museum stages four exhibits of museum-quality pieces by internationally recognized artists. Its Doshi Gallery for Contemporary Art, located on the second floor, showcases the works of regional artists.

Civil War Sights

Though enemy forces failed to reach it, Harrisburg was not untouched by the Civil War.

Far from it. The city was a major transportation hub for the North's war effort. Only Baltimore and Washington had more soldiers pass through their railroad stations. It was also a strategic center. More than 300,000 men were processed through **Camp Curtin,** which opened in April 1861 on what was then the northern outskirts of Harrisburg. The Union's first and largest training facility, named for Pennsylvania's governor at the time, closed in November 1865, seven months after the Confederacy surrendered. Today a statue of Governor Andrew G. Curtin stands in a small park one block north of the intersection of Maclay and North Sixth Streets, where soldiers entered the camp. Local citizens donated food and other supplies for the soldiers streaming through Harrisburg. The Ladies Union Relief Association raised funds, knitted socks, and tended the wounded. Fallen Union soldiers were buried at the **Harrisburg Cemetery** at Liberty and North 13th Streets on the eastern end of the city. Established in 1845, the 350-acre cemetery is also the final resting place of some Revolutionary War soldiers and Pennsylvania governors.

At the end of the war, tens of thousands of Union soldiers paraded through the streets of Washington, D.C., past joyous crowds toward a reviewing stand in front of the White House. Excluded from the Grand Review of the Armies were the regiments of the U.S. Colored Troops, including 11 from Pennsylvania. In November 1865, a parade honoring them was held in Harrisburg. African American veterans marched from State and Filbert Streets on the east side of the Capitol to the Front Street home of Simon Cameron, a longtime abolitionist who'd served in the U.S. Senate and, for a spell, as President Abraham Lincoln's secretary of war. He reviewed them from his front porch and delivered a speech in which he promised: "If you continue to conduct yourselves hereafter as you have in this struggle, you will have all the rights you ask for, all the rights that belong to human beings." No other state held such an event. Cameron's residence was donated to the Historical Society of Dauphin County in 1941 and is now known as the **John Harris-Simon Cameron Mansion** (219 S. Front St., Harrisburg, 717/233-3462, www

.dauphincountyhistory.org, 1–4 P.M. Tues.–Fri. and second Sat. of the month Apr.–mid-Dec., admission $8, seniors $7, children 6–16 $6). The house has undergone many additions and renovations since it was built in the mid-1700s for John Harris Jr., who founded Harrisburg on land his father had settled. Cameron was responsible for its makeover into an Italianate-style Victorian, adding a grand staircase and solarium and lowering the floor in the front section of the house by 3 feet to accommodate a pair of 14-foot-tall pier mirrors he'd found in France. Guided tours reveal what else he snapped up on his way to Russia, where he was sent as U.S. ambassador after his scandal-marred stint as war secretary.

Harrisburg's premier Civil War attraction opened in 2001. The **National Civil War Museum** (1 Lincoln Circle at Reservoir Park, Harrisburg, 717/260-1861, www.national civilwarmuseum.org, 10 A.M.–5 P.M. Mon.–Tues. and Thurs.–Sat., 10 A.M.–8 P.M. Wed., noon–5 P.M. Sun., admission $9, seniors $8, students $7, family pass $35) bills itself as a bias-free presentation of the Union and

DUTCH COUNTRY

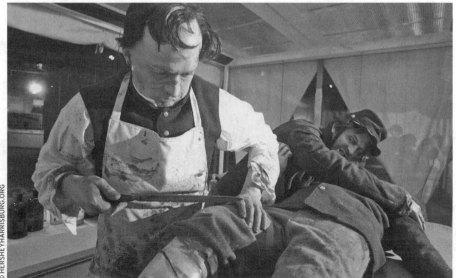

© HERSHEYHARRISBURG.ORG

Realistic mannequins graphically depict Civil War-era life at the National Civil War Museum.

Confederate causes, "the only museum in the United States that portrays the entire story of the American Civil War." Its focus isn't on the famous—President Lincoln, General Robert E. Lee, and such—but on the common soldier and the men and women on the home front. Particular attention is paid to the African American experience. Lifelike mannequins star in depictions of a slave auction, soldier life at Camp Curtin, the amputation of a soldier's leg, and other facts of 19th-century life.

If you just can't get enough of Civil War history, visit www.dutchcountryroads.com and download the *Pennsylvania Civil War Trails* brochure or request that one be sent to you. The brochure will direct you to places of significance along two routes, one starting in Harrisburg and the other in Gettysburg.

Pennsylvania State Capitol

Completed in 1906, the current Capitol (N. 3rd St., between North and Walnut Streets, 800/868-7672, www.pacapitol.com) was the tallest structure between Philadelphia and Pittsburgh for 80 years. It's still among the most ornate. The seat of state power features a spectacular vaulted dome inspired by Michelangelo's design for St. Peter's Basilica in Rome. Architect Joseph Huston incorporated elements of Greek, Roman, Renaissance, and Victorian design into the building, envisioning a "palace of arts." His vision cost a pretty penny, and Huston was sentenced to prison for overcharging the state. There's no charge for guided tours of the Capitol, part of a large complex of government buildings. They're offered every half hour 8:30 A.M.–4 P.M. Monday–Friday and at 9 A.M., 11 A.M., 1 P.M., and 3 P.M. on Saturday, Sunday, and most holidays. Reservations are required for groups of 10 or more and recommended for smaller parties. A welcome center in the East Wing is open 8:30 A.M.–4:30 P.M. Monday–Friday. Its interactive exhibits explain how laws are made. Visitors who call Pennsylvania home can learn about their local legislators and even leave them messages.

Other Harrisburg Sights

The **Broad Street Market** (1233 N. 3rd St., Harrisburg, 717/236-7923, www.broadstreetmarket.org, 7 A.M.–2 P.M. Wed. with limited

the Pennsylvania State Capitol

vendors, 7 A.M.–5 P.M. Thurs.–Fri., 7 A.M.–4 P.M. Sat.) is said to be the oldest continuously operating farmers market in the country. Founded in 1860, it's the sole survivor of six markets that once operated in the city. At its peak in the 1920s, the market just a few blocks north of the State Capitol had more than 725 vendors, many of whom leased space outside and waited years for an indoor stall. Today it has about 40 vendors. They hawk everything from hand-rolled soft pretzels to home decor.

One mile north of the Capitol, the **Pennsylvania National Fire Museum** (1820 N. 4th St., Harrisburg, 717/232-8915, www .pnfm.org, 10 A.M.–4 P.M. Tues.–Sat., 1–4 P.M. Sun., admission $6, seniors $5, students $4, family $20) has fascinating answers to questions you may not have thought to ask. Why were firehouses built with spiral staircases? To keep the horses from climbing them. Why the poles? Because spiral staircases slowed down the firemen. Housed in an 1899 Victorian firehouse, the museum traces the history of firefighting from the days of hand-drawn equipment to modern times.

A mile south of the Capitol is **Tröegs**

Brewing Company (800 Paxton St., Harrisburg, 717/232-1297, www.troegs.com, tasting room and gift shop 10 A.M.–5 P.M. Mon.–Fri., noon–4 P.M. Sat.), established in 1997 by brothers Chris and John Trogner. The natives of nearby Mechanicsburg now distribute their beers not only in Pennsylvania but also in half a dozen other states and Washington, D.C. Tours of the brewery behind such frothy delights as HopBack Amber Ale, Troegenator Double Bock, and the seasonal Mad Elf Ale are offered at 1:30, 2, and 2:30 P.M. on Saturdays and usually last 30–40 minutes. Call to reserve spaces. You can samples the goods any day but Sunday. The tasting room is the only place to get your hands on so-called scratch beers, brewed in very small batches using nontraditional ingredients and techniques.

Lake Tobias Wildlife Park

A little drool never hurt anyone. Bear that in mind as elk, oxen, llamas, and other beasts approach you for a snack at Lake Tobias Wildlife Park (760 Tobias Dr., Halifax, 717/362-9126, www.laketobias.com, 10 A.M.–7 P.M. Sat.–Sun. May–Sept., 10 A.M.–6 P.M. Mon.–Fri. and

© HERSHEYHARRISBURG.ORG

Lake Tobias Wildlife Park

DUTCH COUNTRY

10 A.M.–7 P.M. Sat.–Sun. Memorial Day–Labor Day, 10 A.M.–6 P.M. Sat.–Sun. Oct., zoo admission $4, safari tour $5, children under 3 free), about 20 miles north of Harrisburg off Route 225. Africa it's not, but the family-owned animal park offers a safari experience that visitors aren't soon to forget. Specially designed safari cruisers—think school buses with their top halves hacked off—ply 150 rolling acres home to some 500 animals. Among them are species rarely seen in these parts, including water buffalo, the ostrich-like rhea, and the zonkey, a zebra-donkey hybrid. The last safari tour departs one hour before closing. Come too late and you can still have a close encounter with residents of the petting zoo, which include African pygmy goats, Patagonian cavies, armadillos, green monkeys, lemurs, and spotted sheep. Not-so-petable creatures such as lions, tigers, and bears are exhibited in a zoo-like setting. Anacondas, pythons, snapping turtles, and other reptiles entertain company from Memorial Day weekend through Labor Day. Admission to the reptile building is an extra $1.

Millersburg Ferry and Ned Smith Center

Before bridges spanned the Susquehanna River, people and goods crossed it by ferry. John Harris, the first European to permanently settle in the wilderness that would later become Harrisburg, established the first ferry across the river. It became so popular that settlers began referring to the area not by its Indian name but as Harris's Ferry. Today more than 200 bridges stretch across the Susquehanna, which winds its way south from New York to the Chesapeake Bay, and ferry operations are all but extinct. One survives. Now a nostalgic tourist attraction more than anything else, the Millersburg Ferry (717/692-2442, www.millersburg.com, May–Oct. as water conditions allow, one-way walk-on fare $2, autos $6) began shuttling people, produce, livestock, building materials, and more across a mile-wide section of the Susquehanna in the early 1800s. Traffic was heavy enough to keep four boats busy in the early decades of the 20th century. Today the fleet consists of two

wooden paddleboats that can accommodate four vehicles and 50 passengers. The ferry connects the quaint town of Millersburg, about 25 miles north of Harrisburg, to a modern campground (32 Ferry Ln., Liverpool, 717/444-3200, www.ferryboatcampsites.com, campsites $22–43, cabins and cottages $45–95) on the west bank of the river. It operates 9 A.M.–dusk on weekends from May through October, plus 11 A.M.–5 P.M. on weekdays from June through Labor Day. To reach the Millersburg landing from Harrisburg, take U.S. 22/322 west to Route 147 north. Follow 147 into Millersburg and turn left onto North Street.

Just outside Millersburg is the **Ned Smith Center for Nature and Art** (176 Water Company Rd., Millersburg, 717/692-3699, www.nedsmithcenter.org, gallery and gift shop 10 A.M.–4 P.M. Tues.–Sat. year-round and noon–4 P.M. Sun. Memorial Day–Labor Day, gallery admission $5, seniors and children 12–18 $2), which celebrates the life and works of a local boy turned nationally recognized wildlife artist. Ned Smith (1919–1985) painted almost 120 covers for the Pennsylvania Game Commission's magazine, created the state's first duck stamp, and illustrated 14 books. Original paintings now command upwards of $60,000. Home to a $1.5 million collection of paintings, drawings, field sketches, journal notes, and manuscripts donated by Smith's widow, the center sits on 500 rustic acres crisscrossed by more than 12 miles of trails. Its gallery showcases the work of contemporary artists and photographers, along with selections from the collection. An outdoor amphitheater is in the works.

ENTERTAINMENT AND EVENTS

Performing Arts

The 600-plus seat **Sunoco Performance Theater** within the Whitaker Center for Science and the Arts (222 Market St., Harrisburg, 717/214-2787, www.whitakercenter.org) hosts live theater, music, and dance by touring and local performers. Resident companies include **Theatre Harrisburg** (717/232-5501, www.theatreharrisburg.com), a community theater

CARLISLE: CAR SHOW CAPITAL

If you love cars, you'll love Carlisle. The Cumberland County seat, about 20 miles southwest of Harrisburg, is named for a town in England, and locals usually emphasize its second syllable. But auto aficionados can't be blamed for thinking the "car" in "Carlisle" has something to do with engines and chrome. The town is the site of collector car, truck, and motorcycle events every season but winter.

Carlisle Events (1000 Bryn Mawr Rd., Carlisle, 717/243-7855, www.carlisleevents.com) rented the Carlisle Fairgrounds when it began producing car shows in the mid-1970s. By 1981 the gatherings had grown so popular that the company purchased the property. Today it hosts 10 annual events. Held in April, **Spring Carlisle** is the kickoff to the season and one of the largest automotive swap meets in the world. **Fall Carlisle,** which caps the season, is another opportunity to buy, sell, and celebrate all things automotive. A car auction is held in conjunction with both events. Between them are specialty shows for Corvettes, Fords, GMs, Chryslers, trucks, motorcycles, imports, and tricked-out "performance and style" vehicles. Visit the Carlisle Events website for a complete schedule, admission fees, and more information.

Car enthusiasts have even more reasons to love Cumberland County. Mechanicsburg, 10 miles east of Carlisle, is home to the **Rolls-Royce Foundation** (189 Hempt Rd., Mechanicsburg, 717/795-9400, www.rollsroycefoundation.com), which operates a research library and museum dedicated to Rolls-Royces and Bentleys. It's open to the public 10 A.M.-2 P.M. Tuesday, Wednesday, and Thursday. Mechanicsburg — named for the mechanics of an earlier vehicle make, the Conestoga wagon — also has an automobile racetrack that dates to 1939. Motorsports legends including Ted Horn, A. J. Foyt, and Mario Andretti have raced at the **Williams Grove Speedway** (1 Speedway Dr., Mechanicsburg, 717/697-5000, www.williamsgrove.com). The half-mile speedway hosts weekly sprint car races from February or March through October. Two other racetracks are within a half-hour drive: the **Quarter Aces Drag-O-Way** (1107 Petersburg Rd., Boiling Springs, 717/258-6287, www.quarteracesdragway.com) and the **Shippensburg Speedway** (178 Walnut Bottom Rd., Shippensburg, 717/532-8581, www.shippensburgspeedway.com).

© JOHN LLOYD

A 1958 Rambler is displayed at the 2010 Fall Carlisle.

DUTCH COUNTRY

that dates to 1926, and the **Harrisburg Choral Society** (877/663-4279, www.harrisburg choralsociety.org), which is even older.

Part of the Capitol Complex, **The Forum** (N. 5th and Walnut Streets, Harrisburg, 717/783-9100) is a 1,763-seat concert hall where "star-studded" refers to the architecture as well as some performances. Its ceiling is studded with hundreds of lights of varying levels of brilliance, arranged to depict constellations. Dedicated in 1931, The Forum is home to the **Harrisburg Symphony Orchestra** (717/545-5527, www.harrisburgsymphony.org).

A storm blew the roof off the **Allenberry Playhouse** (1559 Boiling Springs Rd., Boiling Springs, 717/258-3211, www.allenberry.com) during its dedication in 1949. Adhering to the adage that "the show must go on," the theater didn't let a soaked stage get in the way of its 10-week opening season. Today the season lasts more than 40 weeks, starting in March and running through December. The playhouse on the grounds of Allenberry Resort, about 20 miles southwest of Harrisburg, stages musicals, comedies, and dramas with professional actors. Alumni include John Travolta, who sang and danced on the Allenberry stage in 1971, and Norman Fell, best known for his role as Mr. Roper on *Three's Company.* Allenberry guests are part of the cast during "murder mystery weekends," held October–April.

Festivals and Events

Harrisburg kicks off each year with the largest indoor agricultural event in the nation, the **Pennsylvania Farm Show** (717/787-2905 during show, www.farmshow.state.pa.us, Jan., free). Some 6,000 animals and hundreds of thousands of people pass through the Pennsylvania Farm Show Complex & Expo Center (N. Cameron and Maclay Streets, Harrisburg, 717/787-5373, www.pa-farmshowcomplex.com) during the weeklong event. Farmers from across the state show off the fruits of their labors—everything from pecans to powerful Percherons—in the hopes of taking home prize money and bragging rights. Come for an education in the state's number

one industry, and come on an empty stomach. The Farm Show's best feature could very well be its food court, where a baked potato isn't a humdrum side but a tour de force. Food purchases feed the coffers of nonprofit commodity organizations like Pennsylvania Co-Operative Potato Growers Inc. and the Pennsylvania Maple Syrup Producers Council. Celebrity chefs and culinary students conduct cooking demonstrations using Pennsylvania-grown products. Though admission to the Farm Show is free, parking isn't.

Come February, hunting and fishing enthusiasts pack the Farm Show Complex. The **Eastern Sports & Outdoor Show** (800/467-5656, www .easternsportshow.com, admission charged) is a chance for them to check out the newest gear, chat up professional outdoorsmen, book excursions with top guides, and shop for boats, RVs, ATVs, and other cool rides. It's the largest consumer event of its kind in North America.

Harrisburg's largest arts event is the **Patriot-News Artsfest** (717/238-5180, www.harris burgarts.org, Memorial Day weekend). Named one of the top 100 arts events in the country by *Sunshine Artist* magazine, Artsfest brings some 275 artists and craftspeople from around the country to Riverfront Park. Music lovers have as much reason to turn out as art lovers: Free concerts are a festival staple. The Whitaker Center for Science and the Arts hosts an independent film festival in conjunction with Artsfest.

Live music—sans cover charge—is a hallmark of summers in Harrisburg. The city's Department of Parks & Recreation sponsors two outdoor entertainment series. On Saturdays young and old congregate around Reservoir Park's restored 1940s-era bandshell for the latest installment of the **Levitt Live!** (717/255-3020, www.levittlive.com, June–Aug.) series. The genre? Might be classical. Might be reggae. Might be Shakespeare or spoken word. Check the website for the lineup. Reservoir Park, the city's largest park and the site of the National Civil War Museum, is on the eastern end of the city, reachable from downtown by both State and Market Streets. The bandshell is near the entrance at State and 20th Streets.

On Sunday evenings the action shifts to Italian Lake, a diminutive park at Third and Division Streets in the neighborhood known as Uptown. The **Italian Lake Concert Series** (717/255-3020, www.harrisburgevents.com, July–Aug.) brings folk, classical, jazz, and world music to the masses. The masses bring lawn chairs, blankets, and refreshments.

The city marks Independence Day and Labor Day with free festivals in Riverfront Park. Held over July 4 weekend, the **Harrisburg Jazz and Multi-Cultural Festival** attracts gobs of local, regional, and national musicians. There's plenty to keep kids occupied, including amusement rides and video karaoke. A spectacular fireworks display caps three days of virtually uninterrupted music. **Kipona,** held over Labor Day weekend, is Harrisburg's annual homage to the Susquehanna River. (Kipona means "bright, sparkling water" in the Delaware Indian tongue.) It's a blockbuster of a festival. You've got all the fixings of the Jazz and Multi-Cultural Festival: live entertainment on multiple stages, children's activities, fireworks, food, and more food. You've also got a chili cook-off—not just any chili cook-off but the Pennsylvania State Chili Cook-Off (www.chiefchili.com), a qualifying event for the International Chili Society's world championship. The competition is, um, hot. Adding hilarity to the so-called Chili Bowl are eating contests open to the public. Cash, hot sauces, and sympathy go to the man or woman who eats the most jalapenos in 60 seconds. The perennial festival is also the occasion for a Native American encampment on City Island. The powwow, as it's called, features demonstrations of traditional dance, drumming, and arts and crafts. Elk jerky and sassafras tea are on offer. Some 150 artists and craftspeople from around the country sell their works at the southern end of Riverfront Park. There's a fee for admission to the arts area. Other Kipona traditions include canoe races, a bass fishing tournament, a youth street soccer competition, and a karate tournament. Visit the website of the Department of Parks & Recreation, www.harrisburgevents.com, or call 717/255-3020

for more information about Kipona or the Jazz and Multi-Cultural Festival.

SPORTS AND RECREATION
City Island

Harrisburg's recreational hub is a 63-acre city park surrounded by water. The mid-river City Island (717/255-3020, www.harrisburgevents.com) boasts a beach, sand volleyball courts, a multipurpose field, a playground, picnic pavilions, and three marinas. If you don't have a boat of your own, board the *Pride of the Susquehanna* (717/234-6500, www.harrisburgriverboat.com), an old-fashioned paddlewheeler that plies the river May–October. Alternatively, set off in a kayak or canoe from **Susquehanna Outfitters** (717/503-0066, www.susquehannaoutfitters.com, 10 A.M.–6 P.M. Sat.–Sun., weekdays by reservation), which also rents bicycles. Work on your swing on an elaborate 18-hole miniature golf course (717/232-8533) or in the batting cages. Catch pros in action at Metro Bank Park, home to Harrisburg's minor league baseball team (717/231-4444, www.senatorsbaseball.com). Other City Island attractions include an antique carousel and scaled-down versions of a Civil War–era steam train and San Francisco–style trolley.

You can walk or bike to the island from downtown Harrisburg via the Walnut Street Bridge, which was closed to cars after Hurricane Agnes in 1972 and lost some of its western spans in 1996 flooding. Cars access the island via the Market Street Bridge, a stone arch bridge spanning the Susquehanna.

Riverfront Park and Capital Area Greenbelt

After-church strolls through Riverfront Park were de rigueur for Harrisburg's middle and upper classes in the early 1900s. No need to wear your Sunday best for a visit to the 4.5-mile ribbon of lawns and gardens along the Susquehanna, often co-opted for festivals, runs and walks, weddings, and other special events. Stretching from Vine Street up to Vaughn Street, the lush park is punctuated by public art, picnic

DUTCH COUNTRY

tables, benches, and plazas. Paved paths make it ideal not just for strolling but also for inline skating and biking. Riverfront Park is part of the 20-mile Capital Area Greenbelt (717/921-4733, www.caga.org), a mostly paved, mostly car-free recreational route. Rental bikes of all sizes are available at City Island's **Susquehanna Outfitters** (717/503-0066, www.susquehanna outfitters.com, 10 A.M.–6 P.M. Sat.–Sun., weekdays by reservation).

Appalachian Trail

The **Appalachian Trail Conservancy** (304/535-6331, www.appalachiantrail.org), the volunteer-based organization charged with managing and protecting the famous footpath, has an information center about 15 miles southwest of Harrisburg. The center (4 E. 1st St., Boiling Springs, 717/258-5771) is staffed 8 A.M.–3:30 P.M. weekdays year-round. You can get answers to questions about short jaunts, thru-hikes, and everything in between, plus guidebooks, maps, postcards, and A.T. merchandise. It's not unusual to find volunteers doling out information on the front porch on summer weekends.

The A.T. crosses the Susquehanna River at Duncannon, about 15 miles north of the

A MYRIAD OF MINOR LEAGUE TEAMS

Harrisburg doesn't have a single major league franchise, but its sports fans have plenty to cheer about. The Hershey-Harrisburg region has so many professional and semi-pro teams that Street & Smith's *SportsBusiness Journal* named it the nation's top minor league market in 2009. Best known of Harrisburg's franchises is the **Harrisburg Senators** (Metro Bank Park, City Island, Harrisburg, 717/231-4444, www.senatorsbaseball.com), the Class AA affiliate of the Washington Nationals. Formed in 1987, the baseball team won the Eastern League championship in its first season. It won four consecutive championships from 1996 to 1999, becoming the first team in league history to do so. More than 200 of its players have been called up to the majors.

Football fans have a host of teams to watch, including the **Harrisburg Stampede** (717/889-0344, www.harrisburgstampede.com), a 2009 expansion team in the American Indoor Football Association. Home games are held at the Pennsylvania Farm Show Complex & Expo Center (N. Cameron and Maclay Streets, Harrisburg, 717/787-5373, www.pafarmshowcomplex.com), which also hosts the state's annual livestock show – hence the team's name. The season runs from March through June. Harrisburg is also home to two members of the North American Football League: the **Central Penn Piranha** (www.eteamz.com/piranhafootball), which bills

itself as the "winningest team in minor league football history," and the **South Central Yard Dawgs** (www.htosports.com/?djohnson). Their regular season begins in July. Then there's women's full-contact football. The **Central PA Vipers** (www.centralpavipers.com) of the Independent Women's Football League compete for talent with Harrisburg's other women's team, the **Keystone Assault** (717/222-8570, www.keystoneassault.com) of the Women's Football Alliance. Both leagues have 10-week seasons beginning in April.

Harrisburg has something for basketball and soccer fans, too. The **Harrisburg Horizon** (717/986-0499, www.harrisburghorizon.com) won seven consecutive Eastern Basketball Alliance championships from 2002 to 2008. The league's season begins in December and ends in March. The **City Islanders** (717/441-4625, www.cityislanders.com), members of the United Soccer Leagues Second Division, play home games at Skyline Sports Complex, next to Metro Bank Park on City Island. Their season kicks off in April.

The city's hockey fans needn't go far to catch action on ice. In 2009 the **Hershey Bears** (Giant Center, 550 W. Hersheypark Dr., Hershey, 717/508-2327, www.hersheybears.com) became the first team in American Hockey League history to clinch 10 championships.

state capital. Duncannon's **Doyle Hotel** (7 N. Market St., 717/834-6789, www.doylehotel .com) is a legendary stop along the Georgia-to-Maine trail. It's a bit of a dive, but that's part of its charm. The hotel serves food and drink, accepts mail drops, and plasters its walls with photos of thru-hikers. Rooms are $25 per night, and Internet service is free to hikers.

Water Activities

Almost a mile wide at Harrisburg, the Susquehanna River tempts outdoor lovers to float or fish the day away. Among the enablers: **Susquehanna Outfitters** (main parking lot of City Island, 717/503-0066, www.susque hannaoutfitters.com, 10 A.M.–6 P.M. Sat.–Sun., weekdays by reservation, half-day boat rental $39–49, full-day boat rental $52–62, 2-hour bicycle rental $10) with its rental fleet of river canoes and sit-on-top kayaks. Paddlers are shuttled to one of two put-ins upstream, from which they make their back to the outfitter's base on City Island. Paddling is hardly necessary. If you're feeling lazy, the south-flowing Susquehanna will do most of the work for you. Boat rental rates include basic instruction, life jackets, and the shuttle, which departs every two hours 10 A.M.–4 P.M. on weekends and by reservation on weekdays, weather permitting. Paddlers with boats of their own can hitch a ride for $7–10. Susquehanna Outfitters is owned by a local husband and wife who are happy to point you to prime swimming, fishing, and picnicking spots on the island-studded river. They also offer guided tours.

If you want to paddle for days, fishing in secluded coves and sleeping in riverfront campgrounds or primitive island campsites, you want to call **Blue Mountain Outfitters** (U.S. 11/15, 2 miles north of I-81 interchange, Marysville, 717/957-2413, www.bluemountainoutfitters .net, 10 A.M.–8 P.M. Tues., 10 A.M.–6 P.M. Wed.–Sat., open Sun. in warmer months, 1-day boat rental $45–65, each additional day $35–55, reservations recommended). Located several miles north of Harrisburg on the west side of the Susquehanna, Blue Mountain is a full-service paddle sports store with a wide

selection of canoes, kayaks, and accessories. It also sells some camping gear. During the warmer months, it rents canoes, one- and two-person recreational kayaks, and one-person touring kayaks. Paddlers can start at Blue Mountain and float downstream or hop on a shuttle to explore the river's more northerly stretches. The outfitter, housed in an erstwhile train station, offers lifts to put-ins upwards of 40 miles away for multi-day trips. It also facilitates trips on the Juniata River, Sherman Creek, and other nearby waterways when water levels permit. Rental rates don't include shuttle services, which are also available for privately owned boats. Novice paddlers and shutterbugs can leave the piloting to Blue Mountain's pros by booking a trip on the "war canoe"—a 22-foot vessel that can accommodate eight people. The ride is especially thrilling during high water.

The Harrisburg-area section of the Susquehanna is a top-notch smallmouth bass fishery. Anglers can also get bites from catfish, carp, panfish, and other swimmers. Short on poppers, plastic crayfish, or rubber worms? No worries. Harrisburg Mall is home to Pennsylvania's only **Bass Pro Shops** (3501 Paxton St., Harrisburg, 717/565-5200, www.basspro.com, 9 A.M.–9 P.M. Mon.–Sat., 10 A.M.–6 P.M. Sun.). The mammoth store is as much a spiritual experience as shopping experience for fishing and hunting fanatics. With its 60,000-gallon aquarium and wildlife dioramas, it's also a family attraction. The store boasts a rock-climbing wall, a NASCAR simulator, an archery range, and a boat showroom.

Yellow Breeches Creek, which flows through communities to Harrisburg's southwest and dumps into the Susquehanna three miles south of City Island, is among the most popular trout streams in the state. Anglers interested in the stocking program can visit the **Huntsdale State Fish Hatchery** (195 Lebo Rd. in the village of Huntsdale, 12 miles southwest of Carlisle, 717/486-3419, www.fish.state .pa.us, visitor center 8 A.M.–3:30 P.M. daily), which produces brook trout, brown trout, rainbow trout, and golden rainbow trout, along with striped bass, channel catfish, and tiger muskellunge. Fly fishers flock to a mile-long catch-and-release section in the town of Boiling Springs, which has an excellent fly shop, **Yellow Breeches Outfitters** (2 First St., Boiling Springs, 717/258-6752, www.yellow breeches.com, regular season 9 A.M.–5 P.M. Tues.–Thurs., 9 A.M.–6 P.M. Fri., 9 A.M.–5 P.M. Sat., 9 A.M.–4 P.M. Sun., open only Fri.–Sun. in winter). The shop sells a wide variety of rods, reels, waders, and other gear from England-based Hardy & Greys. Other products include Echo rods, Beulah rods, and Patagonia clothing and gear. It offers fly-fishing instruction and guided fishing on the Yellow Breeches, Letort Spring Run, and other fabled streams in the area. Smallmouth guiding on the Susquehanna is also available. A full day with an experienced guide is $250 for one angler, $375 for two. **Allenberry Resort Inn and Playhouse** (1559 Boiling Springs Rd., Boiling Springs, 717/258-3211, www.allenberry.com), at the downstream end of the no-kill area, offers fly-fishing courses on select weekends.

ACCOMMODATIONS

If you're looking for a central location, look no further than the **(Hilton Harrisburg** (1 N. 2nd St., Harrisburg, 717/233-6000, www .hilton.com, $112–239). Just three blocks from the State Capitol Complex and the bridges to City Island, the hotel is connected via an enclosed walkway to the Whitaker Center for Science and the Arts and a shopping center called Strawberry Square. Its 300-plus guest rooms and suites are outfitted with flat-panel TVs, refrigerators, coffee makers, and Hilton's trademark Serenity beds. Guests of Executive Level rooms have access to a private lounge where a complimentary continental breakfast and evening hors d'oeuvres are served. All guests get free wireless Internet access and weekday *USA Today* newspapers. The hotel is at the end of Harrisburg's Restaurant Row, but finding an excellent meal is easier than stepping outside. The Hilton is home the **The Golden Sheaf** (717/237-6400, lunch for hotel guests 11 A.M.–2 P.M. Mon.–Fri., dinner 5:30–10 P.M.

Mon.–Sat., lunch $10–17, dinner $28–48), the city's only AAA Four Diamond restaurant. Its casual restaurant, **Raspberries** (717/237-6419, breakfast 6:30–11 A.M. Mon.–Fri., 7 A.M.–1 P.M. Sat., and 7–11 A.M. Sun., brunch 11 A.M.–2 P.M. Sun., lunch 11:30 A.M.–2 P.M. Mon.–Fri., dinner 5–10 P.M. daily, $10–24), is best known for its outstanding Sunday brunch, set to live music.

Nestled on the west shore of the Susquehanna River, **Bridgeview Bed & Breakfast** (810 S. Main St., Marysville, 717/957-2438, www .bridgeviewbnb.com, single occupancy $100–110, double occupancy $120–130, triple occupancy $160, weeknights $80–120) doesn't have antique furnishings, luxury linens, heaven-scented bath products, or even in-room televisions. Breakfast isn't what you'd call gourmet. It does have killer views of the river and the Rockville Bridge, famous for being the world's longest stone masonry arch railroad bridge. Built in the opening years of the 20th century by the Pennsylvania Railroad, the bridge still sees a good deal of train traffic—which makes the Bridgeview a magnet for train buffs. The B&B, formerly a sporting goods and tackle shop, has 10 en suite guest rooms, three of which have private entrances from outside. The rooms are named for Pennsylvania's great rivers. Fittingly enough, the Susquehanna Room is the largest and most expensive.

FOOD

Pennsylvania's politicos don't have to venture far from the Capitol Complex to strategize or negotiate over a meal that receives bipartisan approval. The strip known as Restaurant Row is a stone's throw away. Roughly defined as the section of 2nd Street between Market and State Streets, Restaurant Row has eateries both casual and upscale, American and ethnic. Consider walking its length before settling on a choice. One you won't regret: **(Café Fresco** (215 N. 2nd St., Harrisburg, 717/236-2599, www.cafefresco.com, 7 A.M.–11 P.M. Mon.–Wed., 7 A.M.–1 A.M. Thurs.–Sat., $4–41). By day, it's a chic but casual spot, offering breakfast items for under $5, sandwiches on rolls or homemade flat bread, wraps, burgers, salads, and pizzas. It glams up in the evening, becoming a destination for swishy cocktails and high-end, Asian-influenced cuisine, though casual fare such as pizzas and a Kobe burger are still on offer. After dinner, you can sashay upstairs to get your groove on. At **Level 2** (717/236-6600, www.level2.us, 8 P.M.–2 A.M. Thurs.–Sat.), one of a handful of nightlife spots in the state capital, the dress code is "fashionable and fierce," and the DJs are tireless. Bottle service is available. For those who come hungry, there's a menu of small plates courtesy of Café Fresco's chef.

If it's Motown or jazz that brings you to the dance floor, show up at **Stock's on 2nd** (211 N. 2nd St., Harrisburg, 717/233-6699, www.stocksonsecond.com, lunch from 11:30 A.M. Mon.–Fri., dinner from 5 P.M. daily, $9–30) on a Saturday night. The music begins at 9:30 P.M., and there's never a cover charge. Another excellent time to visit Stock's: 5–7 P.M. on a weekday. That's when select draft beers are $1, single-liquor well drinks are $2, and everything on the bar and lounge menu is half price. (Don't think typical bar fare. Think lamb sliders, roasted tomato and basil bisque, and chips made from beets as well as tubers.) The restaurant's lunch and dinner menus are also mouthwatering, with crab cakes and Delmonico steak among the specialties. An exhibition kitchen and oversized Leroy Neiman artwork lend to the lighthearted atmosphere. So do the generous martinis.

Ethnic options on Restaurant Row include **Miyako Sushi on Second** (227 N. 2nd St., Harrisburg, 717/234-3250, 11 A.M.–10 P.M. Mon.–Thurs., 11 A.M.–11 P.M. Fri., noon–11 P.M. Sat., $5–19), which offers Japanese-style omelets and casseroles, a variety of teriyaki platters, and udon and soba noodle dishes as well as sushi.

Third Street is home to the *muy excelente* **El Sol Mexican Restaurant** (18 S. 3rd St., Harrisburg, 717/901-5050, www.elsolmexicanrestaurant.net, 11 A.M.–10 P.M. Mon.–Thurs., 11 A.M.–11 P.M. Fri., 4–11 P.M. Sat., $7–24). Owners Juan and Lisa Garcia—he

of the Guadalajara region of Mexico, she of Harrisburg—specialize in dishes from his home state, but they pull off burritos, fajitas, and other familiar fare with equal aplomb. The ceviche, made with tilapia, is an excellent appetizer. Popular entrées include *camarones a la diabla* (shrimp and mushrooms sautéed in a spicy sauce) and *bistek Guadalajara* (steak topped with sautéed vegetables and cheese). Also outstanding are the *molcajetes*—medleys of meat and/or seafood served in the Mexican version of a mortar. All sauces are made from scratch, and customers can dictate the level of spiciness. El Sol also makes its own Mexican beverages, including a sweetened rice drink known as horchata and fresh-squeezed limeade. For those who want something harder, there's beer and a tequila selection unmatched in Harrisburg. Try a tequila flight if you're new to the Mexican liquor.

Across the street at **Bricco** (31 S. 3rd St., Harrisburg, 717/724-0222, www.bricco pa.com, lunch 11:30 A.M.–2:30 P.M. Mon.–Fri., dinner 5:30–10 P.M. Mon.–Sat. and 4:30–10 P.M. Sun., $8–34), executive chef Jason Viscount creates masterly Mediterranean dishes with the help of students from the Olewine School of Culinary Arts at Harrisburg Area Community College. Though inspired by Tuscan cuisine, Bricco sources Pennsylvania products whenever possible. Particularly popular are its raw-bar offerings and pizzas, baked in a stone oven and topped with delicacies such as fig jam, white truffle oil, and local feta. The restaurant, a collaboration between the Olewine School and the managing general partner of the Hilton Harrisburg, boasts an extensive wine list—about 50 varieties by the glass and well over 200 by the bottle. Wine enthusiasts have the opportunity to sample three for $12–16. Formaggi, or cheeses, have a menu of their own. Fall in love with one and you can buy some to take home at **Olewine's Meat and Cheese House** (306 Chestnut St., Harrisburg, 717/724-0246, 11 A.M.–5 P.M. Tues.–Fri., 10 A.M.–2 P.M. Sat.). Located around the corner from Bricco, the shop also sells a wide variety of hand-cut meats, fresh

DUTCH COUNTRY

seafood, and deli sandwiches. Bricco's bakery, **Ciao!** (304 Chestnut St., Harrisburg, 717/724-0236, 6:30 A.M.–4 P.M. Mon.–Fri.) carries artisan breads, breakfast pastries, and desserts.

Housed in a restored 1871 firehouse, **Fire House** (606 N. 2nd St., Harrisburg, 717/234-6064, www.thefirehouserestaurant.com, 11:30 A.M.–10 P.M. Mon.–Thurs., 11:30 A.M.–11 P.M. Fri.–Sat., 4–9 P.M. Sun., $6–35) is worth a visit if only to watch beer pour from a fire hydrant. Food's good, too. Highly regarded for its prime rib, slow-roasted every evening, and baby-back ribs, the casual American eatery also finds a place for pork on its appetizer list. "Pork wings," we're told, are twice the size of hot wings and healthier to boot. The multi-level restaurant's Maryland-style crab cakes are phenomenal, either as an entrée with sweet potato fries or atop a salad.

INFORMATION

The **Hershey Harrisburg Regional Visitors Bureau** (17 S. 2nd St., Harrisburg, 717/231-7788, www.hersheyharrisburg.org, 9 A.M.–5 P.M. Mon.–Fri. and 10 A.M.–3 P.M. Sat., also open 10 A.M.–2 P.M. Sun. in summer) is a good source of information about attractions, lodging, and dining in and around the state capital. Visit the bureau's website to request a copy of its current visitors guide or peruse a digital version.

GETTING THERE AND AROUND

Harrisburg is about 15 miles west of Hershey and 40 miles northwest of Lancaster. **Harrisburg International Airport** (888/235-9442, www.flyhia.com) is served by Air Canada, AirTran Airways, Continental Airlines, Delta Air Lines, United Airlines, and US Airways. They offer daily nonstop service to about a dozen destinations. Note that while locals refer to the airport as HIA, its Federal Aviation Administration booking code is MDT. That's because of its physical location in the borough of Middletown, about eight miles south of Harrisburg.

The Harrisburg Transportation Center, located at 4th and Chestnut Streets, is served by **Amtrak** (800/872-7245, www.amtrak.com), **Greyhound** (800/231-2222, www.greyhound.com), and other intercity bus operators. Local bus services are provided by **Capital Area Transit** (717/238-8304, www.cattransit.com). The base fare is $1.65 for adults, $1.15 for students. Transfers are $0.25. Bus drivers don't make change. Multiple-ride tickets and monthly passes can be purchased at CAT's main office (901 N. Cameron St., Harrisburg, 7:30 A.M.–4:30 P.M. Mon.–Fri., 9 A.M.–1 P.M. last Sat. of every month) and at kiosks in locations including Strawberry Square shopping center (2nd and Market Streets, Harrisburg, 10 A.M.–6 P.M. Mon.–Fri., 10 A.M.–5 P.M. Sat.). They're also available through CAT's website.

York County

Just west of Lancaster County, York County touts itself as the "Factory Tour Capital of the World." Indeed, about a dozen factories open their doors to visitors. Frugal families can live it up here; admission is free in almost every case. So many of the factories are dedicated to guilty pleasures that York County also claims the title of Snack Food Capital of the World. I know what you're thinking: York Peppermint Patties. Alas, the brand born here in 1940 now belongs to Hershey Co., and the minty, chocolatey confections are made elsewhere. But

York County is home to another candy company, potato chip makers Martin's and Utz, and pretzel producer Snyder's of Hanover. The biggest name on the factory circuit has nothing to do with mmmm-mmmm and everything to do with vroom-vroom. Harley-Davidson's York operations attract bikers from across the United States and countries as far-flung as Turkey, China, and Australia.

In recent years, York County has strived to make a name for itself in wine circles. The ranks of the UnCork York Wine Trail swelled

© WWW.YORKPA.ORG

DUTCH COUNTRY

York County is home to the potato chip maker Martin's.

to 13 family-owned wineries in 2009. Napa it's not, but boosters cast that as a virtue. Because the area's wineries are modest operations, visitors can count on face time with people close to the winemaking process—often the owners themselves.

Long before the county became the Factory Tour Capital, its only city, also named York, served as the capital of what would soon be known as the United States of America. The Continental Congress, that body of delegates who spoke for the colonies during the Revolutionary period, met in York for nine months in 1777 and 1778, adopting the Articles of Confederation. The York County Heritage Trust operates several museums and historic sites that offer a window into the past. Murals throughout downtown York also serve as a record of local history.

The county's greatest asset could be its location in the center of Pennsylvania Dutch Country. Gettysburg and its Civil War battlefield are 30 miles west of York. Lancaster's Amish farmlands are about that distance to its

east. The state capital, Harrisburg, is 25 miles north of the city, and Hershey, a.k.a. "The Sweetest Place on Earth," is just 10 miles farther. That makes York County a good base of operations for travelers who want to take in the more touristy areas without paying touristy lodging prices.

FACTORY TOURS

The Factory Tour Capital of the World has more factories than you can visit in a day—or even two—so making your picks is job one. You'll find a complete list of factory tours at www.yorkpa.org, the website of the York County Convention & Visitors Bureau. Not to be missed is **Wolfgang Candy Company** (50 E. 4th Ave., York, 800/248-4273, www.wolfgangcandy.com, walk-in tours on the hour 10 A.M.–2 P.M. Mon.–Thurs. in summer, call or check website for fall–spring schedule, store and museum open 8 A.M.–4:30 P.M. Mon.–Fri. and 10 A.M.–3 P.M. Sat. year-round, free), where you can watch chocolate-covered pretzels, bear-shaped chocolates filled with creamy peanut butter, or other confections take shape. Founded in 1921, the family-owned company still makes chocolate in small batches using vintage equipment. Tours last 45 minutes to an hour and end with free samples. You'll be asked to remove jewelry and don a hairnet (gents with beards or long mustaches get extra nets) before entering production areas. A museum that tells the story of the Wolfgang family's adventure in candy-making and a store, Das Sweeten Haus, are open daily except Sunday. Save room for a milkshake from the old-timey soda fountain.

Less than three miles away is **Harley-Davidson's York Vehicle Operations** (1425 Eden Rd., York, 877/883-1450, www.harley-davidson.com/experience, tours at regular intervals 9 A.M.–2 P.M. Mon.–Fri., tour center and gift shop open 8 A.M.–4 P.M. Mon.–Fri., free). Established in 1973, the motorcycle assembly facility grew into Harley's largest manufacturing site and York County's largest manufacturing employer. But the legendary motorcycle company wasn't immune to the Great Recession of 2009. In mid-year it

announced that the York operations, where Touring and Softail models are assembled, were "not currently competitive or sustainable" and that relocating was under consideration. The community breathed a collective sign of relief at the close of the year, when a combination of union concessions and state incentives convinced the company to stay put and scale back. Tours, which last about an hour, begin with a brief movie, continue through various manufacturing and assembly areas, and conclude at the end of the line, where every motorcycle is roll-tested before being crated and shipped. Children under 12 aren't allowed on the factory floor, but they're welcome in the tour center, which includes exhibits about assembly processes and motorcycles for the straddling.

If you head west on U.S. 30 from Harley, you'll reach **Martin's Potato Chips** (5847 Lincoln Hwy./U.S. 30, Thomasville, 800/272-4477, www.martinschips.com, tours on the hour 9–11 A.M. Tues. by reservation, store open 8:30 A.M.–2:30 P.M. Mon.–Fri., free) in about 15 minutes. But the epicenter of the

© HARLEY-DAVIDSON MOTOR COMPANY

touring Harley-Davidson's York Vehicle Operations

county's snack foods industry is the borough of Hanover, about 20 miles southwest of York. That's where you'll find **Snyder's of Hanover** (1350 York St., Hanover, 800/233-7125 ext. 8592, www.snydersofhanover.com, tours 10 A.M., 11 A.M., and 1 P.M. Tues.–Thurs. by reservation, store open 9 A.M.–6 P.M. Mon.–Sat. and noon–5 P.M. Sun., free), best known for its pretzels. Snyder's snacks are sold on every continent except Africa and Antarctica, so tours of the Hanover facilities are an education in large-scale manufacturing. You'll get to see the raw material warehouse, finished goods warehouse, packing room, and oven room. The one-hour tour includes a primer on potato chip making and finishes in the factory store, where you'll get a free bag of pretzels and bargains on everything from Old Tyme Pretzels, first made in 1909, to the popular flavored pretzel pieces, introduced some 80 years later.

At **Utz Quality Foods** (900 High St., Hanover, 800/367-7629, www.utzsnacks.com, self-guided tours 8 A.M.–4 P.M. Mon.–Thurs., call for Fri. hours, free), you can watch raw spuds become crunchy chips from a glass-lined gallery. Though famous for its chips—Rachael Ray talked up Utz Kettle Classics Potato Chips on her eponymous TV show—the company also makes pretzels, cheese curls, pork rinds, and more. Its outlet store (861 Carlisle St., Hanover, 8 A.M.–7 P.M. Mon.–Sat., 11 A.M.–6 P.M. Sun.) is two blocks from the main plant.

Far smaller than Snyder's or Utz, **Revonah Pretzels** (507 Baltimore St., Hanover, 717/630-2883, www.revonahpretzel.com, tours 9:30 A.M.–noon Tues.–Thurs., reservations recommended, free) takes its name from the town (Revonah is Hanover spelled backwards) and its cues from the past. Pretzels are rolled and twisted by hand, hearth-baked, and slowly hardened in a kiln. Word has it that the Pittsburgh Steelers munch on these when they're on the road. Visitors can sample a "greenie," a pretzel that's crunchy on the outside but still warm and soft on the inside.

If it's a warm, sunny day, be sure to include **Perrydell Farm Dairy** (90 Indian Rock Dam Rd., York, 717/741-3485, www.perrydell farm.com, self-guided tours 7 A.M.–9 P.M.

Pretzels are made by hand at Renovah Pretzels.

Mon.–Sat., noon–6 P.M. Sun., free) on your itinerary. Depending on when you visit the family-owned farm, which eschews artificial growth hormones, you might see cows being milked, calves being fed, or milk being bottled. The oh-so-fresh milk is sold on-site, along with hand-dipped ice cream, locally grown produce, and locally baked goods.

Be sure to wear comfortable, closed-toe shoes when you go factory hopping. Open-toe shoes and heels are prohibited in some areas.

UNCORK YORK WINE TRAIL

Central Pennsylvania's reputation as a wine region is growing, albeit slowly, in part because its wineries are within easy reach of metropolitan areas and in part because of savvy marketing. Even people who don't much care for wine are lured to the wineries by concerts, pig roasts, chances to stomp grapes à la Lucy Ricardo, and other crowd-pleasing programming. One of the happening-est spots in York County is **Moon Dancer Vineyards & Winery** (1282 Klines Run Rd., Wrightsville, 717/252-9463, www .moondancerwinery.com, noon–5 P.M. Wed.– Thurs., noon–9 P.M. Fri., 11 A.M.–6 P.M. Sat.– Sun.). It hosts live music on Fridays, Saturdays, and Sundays year-round and annual jazz, bluegrass, folk, and reggae festivals. In the warmer months, visitors can mingle on the patio or picnic on the grounds of the French chateau–like winery overlooking the Susquehanna River. In the colder ones, they're invited to sip hot mulled wine by a fire.

Of course, winemaking is the primary business of Moon Dancer and other wineries along the Uncork York Wine Trail (www.uncorkyork .com). And they're turning out some high-caliber wines, from sweet wines infused with apples, peaches, and other fruits so plentiful in Pennsylvania to European-style dry wines. Boasts one area winemaker: "California wine tastes like sunshine. Big deal. Mine tastes like earth and the four seasons." The oldest winery in York County, **Naylor Wine Cellars** (4069 Vineyard Rd., Stewartstown, 800/293-3370, www.naylorwine.com, 11 A.M.–6 P.M. Mon.– Sat., noon–5 P.M. Sun.) has collected medals at

Wine that "tastes like earth and the four seasons" can be found along the Uncork York Wine Trail.

© WWW.YORKPA.ORG

statewide and international competitions. Be sure to sample the award-winning Cabernet and the port-style Essence of Chambourcin. Tours of the winery are free and require no advance notice. If you're interested in touring the vineyard with its labrusca, vinifera, and French-American grapes, call ahead to make arrangements. On Saturday evenings in the summer, Naylor hosts dances to big band music. "Wine dinners" draw visitors in the winter.

Allegro Vineyards (3475 Sechrist Rd., Brogue, 717/927-9148, www.allegrowines .com, 1–5 P.M. Wed.–Sun.) grows six varieties of grapes on five acres, including Cabernet Sauvignon and Chardonnay. Founded by musician brothers, Allegro opened to the public in 1981. It's now owned by husband and wife Carl Helrich and Kris Miller, but the wine list is still sprinkled with musical references. There's a dessert wine named Aria, a sparkling wine called Serenade, and the 2005 Cadenza, Allegro's Bordeaux-inspired flagship red. Check the website for a calendar of concerts and other events at the winery and **Allegro Wine Gallery** (2549 S. Queen St., York, 717/741-3072, noon–6 P.M. Sun.–Thurs., noon–8 P.M. Fri., 11 A.M.–7 P.M. Sat.), a shop-cum-gallery in the Olde Tollgate Village shopping center, a few miles south of downtown York.

There's no better time to visit the UnCork York wineries than during **Tour de Tanks**, a celebration of new vintages held weekends in March. A $20 ticket gives you access to the cellars of all participating wineries, where you can taste the season's upcoming wines before they're bottled. Winemakers are on hand to answer questions. Visit the UnCork York website for more information about the event, a complete list of wineries, a downloadable map of the trail, and a list of hotels and B&Bs that offer wine-themed packages.

OTHER SIGHTS
Central Market

York's public market house is a can't-miss if you're in town on a Tuesday, Thursday, or Saturday. Built in 1888, Central Market (34 W. Philadelphia St., York, 717/848-2243, www.centralmarketyork.com, 6 A.M.–2 P.M. Tues., Thurs., and Sat.) is not just a showcase for area farmers but also a hopping lunch spot. In fact, lunch counters outnumber produce stands by more than three to one. You'll find Greek food, Puerto Rican food, and Italian food. You'll find soups and sandwiches at Busy Bee, opened in 2009 by the chef de cuisine of York's exclusive Lafayette Club. Roburrito's, a popular local burrito joint, also joined the vendor ranks in 2009. You can't miss its stand, which resembles a foil-wrapped burrito and serves up venison-stuffed burritos during deer season. Fresh-cut french fries, freshly baked cupcakes, and hot pretzels make it nearly impossible to avoid an indulgence.

York County Heritage Trust

History buffs will be happy to find more than half a dozen museums and historic sites within walking distance of each other in downtown York. Operated by the York County Heritage Trust (250 E. Market St., 717/848-1587, www.yorkheritage.org), they include the **Agricultural and Industrial Museum** (217 W. Princess St., 10 A.M.–4 P.M. Tues.–Sat.), which houses artifacts spanning three centuries. Its collection includes a 72-ton A-frame ammonia compressor, once used to manufacture large blocks of ice; a three-story gristmill; and locally made tractors and farm tools. Exhibits cover topics as diverse as casket manufacturing, piano and organ manufacturing, and York's industrial contribution to World War II. The 12,000-square-foot transportation wing showcases automobiles made in York, a Conestoga wagon, and a 1937 Aeronca K airplane.

Just two blocks away is the **Colonial Complex** (corner of W. Market St. and N. Pershing Ave., 10 A.M.–4 P.M. Tues.–Sat., closed mid-Dec.–late Mar.), four buildings that transport visitors to earlier times. Among them is the **Golden Plough Tavern**, the oldest structure in town. Built in 1741, it served as a hotel and restaurant and today is furnished with Pennsylvania furniture predating 1760. Adjacent to it is the **General Gates House,** built circa 1751 by the tavern's second owner. It's named for General Horatio Gates, the Revolutionary War hero who lived in the house during York's turn as the de facto capital of the American colonies. In 1777, as Philadelphia fell into the hands of the British, the Continental Congress moved west, spending one day in Lancaster before crossing the Susquehanna River and settling in York on September 30. After Gates defeated the British near Saratoga, New York, the Congress invited him to York, where he was feted and named president of the Board of War. Some members of Congress had bigger plans for him. Unimpressed with General George Washington's command of the Continental Army, they plotted to replace him with Gates. The "Conway Cabal," as the intrigue was dubbed, unraveled when France's Marquis de Lafayette proposed a toast to General Washington during a banquet at the Gates House. Eager for France's support in the war against Britain, the conspirators quit their plotting. Today the house reflects the year— 1778—when history was made there.

DUTCH COUNTRY

Across the street from the Gates House and tavern is a reconstruction of the courthouse where Congressional delegates met during their nine-month stay in York. The original courthouse was located two blocks away. Behind the Gates House and tavern is the **Barnett Bobb Log House,** built in the early 1800s and named for its builder, a German immigrant. It's furnished to reflect family life in the 1830s. Tours of the Colonial Complex begin in the yard behind the Gates House. They're usually offered at 10 A.M., 11 A.M., 1 P.M., 2 P.M., and 3 P.M., but check the website or call 717/846-6452 to confirm. Public tours are curtailed when school groups descend on the historic sites.

A few blocks east of the Colonial Complex is a onetime car dealership that now houses the Heritage Trust's main offices, an extensive research library, and the **Historical Society Museum** (250 E. Market St., 10 A.M.–4 P.M. Tues.–Sat.), with more than 10,000 square feet of exhibitions on everything from quilts to tall case clocks. About half a mile east of the Colonial Complex is the **Fire Museum** (757 W. Market St., 10 A.M.–4 P.M. Sat., closed mid-Dec.–late Mar.). Its collection of firefighting artifacts includes horse-drawn fire carriages, vintage fire trucks, and old-fashioned alarm systems.

Tickets good for all Heritage Trust sites are sold at each of the sites. One-day tickets are $10 for adults and $5 for children 8–18. Two-day tickets and family passes are available.

USA Weightlifting Hall of Fame

If you've ever done bicep curls or bench presses, "York" probably rings a bell. The name is emblazoned on barbells, dumbbells, and other weightlifting equipment made by York Barbell, founded in York in 1932. The company is now Canadian-owned, but it still has administrative offices just north of the city. A statue of a weightlifter in a blue singlet, barbell hoisted overhead, still revolves atop the adjacent factory, turning the heads of motorists on nearby I-83. And the Weightlifting Hall of Fame (3300 Board Rd., York, 800/358-9675, www.yorkbarbell.com, 10 A.M.–4:30 P.M. Mon.–Sat.,

free admission) still welcomes fans of strength sports. Located on the first floor of York Barbell's administrative building, the Hall of Fame is part history museum and part homage to company founder and weightlifting legend Bob Hoffman. Raised near Pittsburgh, Hoffman was a sickly, reed-thin kid. In 1919, after serving overseas in World War I, he moved to York and cofounded an oil burner company. Determined to build not just his business but also his body, Hoffman bought a barbell. By the late 1920s, the now-buff businessman was training other lifters and hiring them to work in his factory, which he eventually transformed from York Oil Burner into York Barbell. In 1946, when the United States won its first weightlifting world championship, four of the six teammates worked for York Barbell. Hoffman coached the U.S. Olympic team from 1948 to 1964, and in 1970, the International Weightlifting Federation crowned him the "Father of World Weightlifting." By then, York also had a fanciful title: "Muscletown USA."

A 7.5-foot bronze statue of Hoffman stands outside the entrance to the Weightlifting Hall of Fame. The two-story lobby features a bronze bust of Hoffman, who died in 1985, and dumbbells and barbells from the 19th and early 20th centuries. Exhibits trace the evolution of strength sports, highlighting legendary strongmen such as Joe "The Mighty Atom" Greenstein, whose feats of strength included biting nails in half, and John Grimek, a longtime employee of York Barbell as well as a two-time Mr. America and 1948's Mr. Universe. Highlights of the collection include a seven-foot Travis dumbbell weighing more than 1,600 pounds. Its lifter and namesake, Warren Lincoln Travis, weighed just 180 ponds during his zenith in the early 1900s.

Haines Shoe House

Worth a stop if you're tootling along U.S. 30 or Route 462 (a.k.a. the Lincoln Highway) in western York County is the Haines Shoe House (197 Shoe House Rd., Hellam, 717/840-8339, www.shoehouse.us, 11 A.M.–5 P.M. Wed.–Sun. June–Aug., 11 A.M.–5 P.M. Sat.–Sun.

Sept.–Oct., by appointment Nov.–May, admission $4.50, children 4–12 $3). Built in 1948, the shoe-shaped house was an advertising gimmick by "Shoe Wizard" Mahlon Haines, whose shoe empire grew to more than 40 stores in central Pennsylvania and northern Maryland. At first, the eccentric millionaire invited elderly couples to spend an expense-free weekend in the three-bedroom, two-bath shoe house, where they had a maid, cook, and chauffeur at their disposal. In 1950 he extended the invitation to honeymooning couples from any town with a Haines shoe store. After his death in 1962, the house became an ice cream parlor. Today the roadside oddity is a museum dedicated to Haines, who staged safaris on his nearby "Wizard Ranch" and used to stop smokers on the streets of York, offering them cash if they promised to quit.

The shoe motif is ubiquitous throughout the property. You'll find it on the wooden fence that surrounds the house and in the stained glass windows. There's even a shoe-shaped doghouse. Guided tours reveal other novelties, including a curved eating booth in the kitchen, located in the heel of the shoe house. Ice cream and other snacks are sold on site, along with kitschy gifts like shoe house lamps with lighted windows.

Maize Quest Fun Park

In 1997, Hugh McPherson carved a maze into a cornfield on Maple Lawn Farms in southern York County. It proved such a hit that in 2000, the Penn State graduate added a straw bale maze, a fence maze, and a maze of living bamboo. Year after year, Maize Quest Fun Park (2885 New Park Rd., New Park, 866/935-6738, www.mazefunpark.com) unveiled new attractions. Today it boasts more than 20, including an 80-foot-long tube slide, a maze lined with misters designed for cooling livestock, and a mammoth indoor playground. Most attractions open in early June. The signature cornfield maze, which reflects a different theme each year, is revealed in August. Themes have included "Ice Age Adventure," "Space Explorers," and "The Vikings!" Maize

Quest is open Fridays, Saturdays, and Sundays through mid-November. Admission is $9.50 for adults, $7.50 for children 2–12. The indoor playground, designed for kids ages 2–10, is open Saturdays from early December to early June. Admission for kids is $7.50; there's no charge for adults. Call or check the website for hours.

ENTERTAINMENT AND EVENTS
Performing Arts

Downtown York's **Strand-Capitol Performing Arts Center** (50 N. George St., York, 717/846-1111, www.strandcapitol.org) plays host to touring musicians, dance companies, comedians, and acrobats. The **York Symphony Orchestra** (717/812-0717, www.yorksymphony.org), which has performed without interruption since the Depression, can also be seen there. "There" is actually a five-building complex that includes two historic theaters. What's now known as the Capitol Theatre opened in 1906 as a dance hall and later became a movie house. The larger, grander Strand Theatre opened in 1925 primarily for vaudeville and silent movies. Both closed in the late 1970s as suburbia sucked the life out of downtown. But a movement to reopen them quickly took shape, and the Strand and Capitol reopened their doors in 1980 and 1981, respectively. At 500 seats, the Capitol is less than half the size of the Strand, but it boasts a restored 1927 Mighty Wurlitzer. The organ is put to use before classic film showings, which sometimes involve audience participation (e.g., singing along to *The Sound of Music* or dressing like the title character in *The Big Lebowski*). Contemporary independent and foreign films are also shown at the Capitol.

Festivals and Events

Thousands of gleaming vintage cars of every description roll into York for **Street Rod Nationals East** (901/452-4030, www.nsra-usa.com, early June, admission charged), one of about a dozen annual events hosted by the National Street Rod Association. The street rods—vintage vehicles that have been modernized with features such as air conditioning and cruise control—congregate on the grounds of the York Expo Center (334 Carlisle Ave., York, 717/848-2596, www.yorkexpo.com), where auto enthusiasts can get a close look and chat up the owners. Spectators line the streets of York for a parade of the candy-colored cars.

In September the Expo Center hosts its signature event, the 10-day **York Fair** (717/848-2596, www.yorkfair.org, opens first Friday after Labor Day, admission charged). The fair dates to 1765—11 years before the nation was founded—and bills itself as America's first and oldest. It was interrupted during the Civil War, when the fairgrounds served as a hospital for wounded soldiers, and in 1918 due to a deadly influenza outbreak. But the fair hasn't taken a hiatus since, growing larger and longer with each passing decade. It even remained open in the days following the 9/11 attacks, in celebration of American culture and spirit.

SPORTS AND RECREATION
Heritage Rail Trail

The 21-mile Heritage Rail Trail (717/840-7440, www.yorkcountyparks.org) stretches from York City to the Mason-Dixon line, where it connects to Maryland's 20-mile Northern Central Railroad Trail. Hiking, bicycling, horseback riding, cross-country skiing, and snowshoeing are permitted on the 10-foot-wide path. The parking lot for the York City trailhead is on Pershing Avenue near the Colonial Courthouse. Traversing the trail is part exercise, part history lesson. About six miles south of the reconstructed courthouse is the 370-foot Howard Tunnel, the oldest continuously operational railroad tunnel in the world. The rail line adjacent to the Heritage Rail Trail was a vital link between Washington, D.C., and points north in the 19th century. As such, it was a prime target for Confederate troops during the Civil War. After the Battle of Gettysburg, President Lincoln traveled via these rails to deliver the Gettysburg Address, stretching his legs at York County's Hanover Junction station, located on Route 616 about six miles south of U.S. 30.

Restored to its 1863 appearance, the station at the midpoint of the Heritage Rail Trail is now a Civil War museum. Another historic station at Front and Franklin Streets in New Freedom, 1.5 trail miles north of the state line, is now a railroad museum. Check the York County Parks website for information on when the museums are open.

A good place to start if you're looking to rent a bicycle is Seven Valleys, a small borough just north of Hanover Junction. There you'll find **Serenity Station** (11 Church St./Rte. 214, Seven Valleys, 717/428-9575, www.serenity-station.com, 11 A.M.–8 P.M. Mon.–Thurs., 11 A.M.–9 P.M. Fri., 8 A.M.–9 P.M. Sat., 8 A.M.–8 P.M. Sun., open until 9 P.M. daily June–Aug.), a bike shop, day spa, and restaurant rolled into one. Single, tandem, and recumbent bikes can be rented by the hour or day. Child seats and trailers are available. The Heritage Rail Trail is just behind Serenity Station, which also sells bike parts and offers repair services. Call at least 48 hours in advance if you'd like a hot stone deep tissue massage, a detox wrap, or other spa service. Serenity Station's restaurant ($5–17) offers salads, sandwiches, grilled panini and wraps, and personal pizzas. The dinner menu is a touch fancier, featuring entrées like pepper-encrusted steak tenderloin and seafood tossed with rotini pasta. Breakfast is served on Saturdays and Sundays. Also adjacent to the rail trail is **Four Springs Winery** (50 Main St., Seven Valleys, 717/428-2610, www.fourspringswinerypa.com, 1–6 P.M. Fri. and Sun., 11 A.M.–6 P.M. Sat.), one of about a dozen wineries along the UnCork York Wine Trail. It's not unusual to see spandex-clad cyclists sampling the fruit-driven wines before continuing on their way.

Kayaking

Worth a visit if only to gaze at the scenic Susquehanna River from its front porch, **Shank's Mare** (2092 Long Level Rd., Wrightsville, 717/252-1616, www.shanksmare.com, 10 A.M.–8 P.M. Mon.–Fri., 10 A.M.–5 P.M. Sat., noon–5 P.M. Sun. in summer, call or check website for non-summer hours) rents

© ANNA DUBROVSKY

Shank's Mare outfitters

single, tandem, and triple kayaks. You don't need any experience to take to the water in one of the outfitter's sit-on-top kayaks. Birders come from hundreds of miles away to paddle to the Conejohela Flats, a series of small islands and mud flats that attract scores of migratory shorebirds in spring and fall. On a calm day, it takes about 40 minutes to paddle from Shank's Mare to the Audubon-designated Important Bird Area.

The family-owned outfitter, housed in an 1890s general store, offers guided paddles, kayaking instruction, hiking tours of Moon Dancer Vineyards and other nearby areas, and programs on topics such as local geology and kayak fishing. It also sells kayaks, cross-country skiing gear, local trail maps, and outdoor clothing, including shirts, hats, and other items emblazoned with its motto, "Go Play Outside." The 193-mile **Mason Dixon Trail** (www.masondixontrail.org) passes right by Shank's Mare.

Ski Roundtop

About midway between York and Harrisburg, Ski Roundtop (925 Roundtop Rd., Lewisberry, 717/432-9631, www.skiroundtop.com, 8-hour lift ticket $47–56, children 6–12 $42–49, ski rental $35, snowboard rental $40, snow tubing 1-hour session $14–20) has 16 trails, three terrain parks, and one half-pipe. In addition to all-day and nighttime lift tickets, the resort offers four- and eight-hour "flex" tickets activated at the time of purchase. One- and two-hour tickets are available for snow tubing sessions, which begin at the top of each hour. Kids 2–4 have a tubing hill all to themselves and can ride all day for just $7. Homemade contraptions of cardboard, tape, and glue careen down the tubing runs during Ski Roundtop's annual **Cardboard Derby**, held January 31.

Roundtop Mountain Adventures, the resort's summertime persona, features the Vertical Trek, a descent of more than 600 vertical feet via zip lines, rope bridges, Tarzan swings, and other means. Reservations are highly recommended for the treks, which can take up to four hours. Other summertime activities include tubing on turf-covered runs, bumper boating, and "zorbing"—rolling downhill in a large inflatable orb. The resort's paintball facility is open year-round. Groups can polish their teamwork skills on a pair of ropes courses.

AvalancheXpress

The snow tubing hill at York's Heritage Hills Golf Resort, AvalancheXpress (2700 Mount Rose Ave., York, 877/782-9752, www.avalanchexpress.com, day pass $18–26, children 6 and under $10–14), has multiple runs ranging from a kiddie slope to "Xtreme" lanes with daredevils in mind. Plan to make a day of it; AvalancheXpress doesn't sell passes by the hour. There are fire pits, picnic tables, outdoor concessions, and an indoor bar for relaxing and refueling between runs. You'll find the shortest lines on weekdays and the longest on Saturday afternoons.

Spectator Sports

Almost four decades after the York White Roses hung up their uniforms, professional baseball returned to York. The **York Revolution** (Sovereign Bank Stadium, 5 Brooks Robinson Way, York, 717/801-4487, www.yorkrevolution.com), a member of the Atlantic League of Professional Baseball, played its inaugural season in 2007. The Revs have a friendly rivalry with the Lancaster Barnstormers across the Susquehanna River, with each trying to best the other in a "War of the Roses" series. (The name is a nod to the War of the Roses between the Houses of York and Lancaster in 15th-century England.)

ACCOMMODATIONS

Built during the Roaring Twenties, **[The Yorktowne Hotel** (48 E. Market St., York, 717/848-1111, www.yorktowne.com, $109–300) is resplendent with high ceilings, brass and crystal chandeliers, and wood paneling. Just as impressive is the service; some of the staff have worked at the downtown landmark for upwards of 20 years. The Yorktowne is conveniently located within walking distance of the Colonial Complex, the northern terminus of the Heritage Rail Trail, Central Market, and the Strand-Capitol Performing Arts Center.

And it's home to **The Commonwealth Room** (5:30–9:30 P.M. Tues.–Sat., $26–38), York County's only AAA Four Diamond restaurant, plus a cocktail lounge open nightly until 1:30 A.M. The 121 guest rooms and suites have period furnishings and modern conveniences including complimentary Internet access.

You don't have to be a golfer to appreciate the amenities at **Heritage Hills Golf Resort** (2700 Mount Rose Ave., York, 877/782-9752, www.hhgr.com, $149–179). Just minutes from downtown York, the property boasts a spa open seven days a week, an 18-hole mini golf course, and a busy entertainment calendar. The patio of Knickers Pub, a casual eatery overlooking the golf course, is a locals' favorite in summertime. AvalancheXpress, the resort's snow tubing hill, draws crowds in winter. An indoor water park is in the works. If golf is your thing, be sure to inquire about "stay-and-play" packages. Heritage Hills also offers spa packages, snow tubing packages, romantic packages, and even hot air balloon packages. (Balloons lift off from the golf course at sunrise or before sunset.)

York County has no shortage of excellent B&Bs. Among them: the **Lady Linden Bed and Breakfast** (505 Linden Ave., York, 717/843-2929, www.ladylindenbedandbreakfast.com, $129), a meticulously restored 1887 Queen Anne Victorian with two guest suites. The house is impeccably decorated, the linens are silky soft, and breakfast is a four-course affair. **The Beechmont** (315 Broadway, Hanover, 800/553-7009, $109–169) is an excellent choice in southern York County. Owner Kathryn White received the Pennsylvania Tourism & Lodging Association's Innkeeper of the Year Award in 2009. The Select Registry inn with its seven guest accommodations is convenient to historic Gettysburg. Now an oasis of calm, the house witnessed the Battle of Hanover, which delayed a Confederate cavalry's arrival at the more famous Battle of Gettysburg. White is a font of information about Hanover's role in the Civil War—and a whiz in the kitchen. Exquisite breakfasts are served by candlelight; homemade cookies or other treats are offered in the evenings. A two-night minimum stay applies on weekends April–November.

FOOD

Across the street from York's Central Market, the **White Rose Bar & Grill** (48 N. Beaver St., York, 717/848-5369, www.whiterosebar andgrill.com, kitchen 11 A.M.–10 P.M. Sun.–Thurs. and 11 A.M.–11 P.M. Fri.–Sat., bar open until 2 A.M. Mon.–Sat. and midnight Sun., $5–35) dates to the 1930s. Extensive renovations in recent years have given it a thoroughly modern feel. The appetizer menu includes oysters on the half shell, seared sushi-grade tuna, and plenty of deep-fried goodies, but nothing compares to the soft pretzel sticks topped with crab dip and melted cheese. Meal options range from a simple BLT to Hereford beef filet mignon. Order from the Hot Rock Menu and your seafood or steak will arrive at the table on a hot volcanic rock, where it'll continue to cook while you dig in.

If raw is how you like it, try **Keo Asian Grill and Sushi Restaurant** (15 S. George St., York, 717/848-2510, www.keoasian.com, 11 A.M.–4 P.M. Mon.–Wed., 11 A.M.–9 P.M. Thurs.–Sat., $6–14), a relative newcomer to downtown York's dining scene. The space is small, which can mean a wait during the lunchtime rush, but the sushi is consistently good. Don't eat sushi? Keo has an extensive menu of beef, chicken, seafood, and vegetarian dishes that reflect the cooking traditions of China, Thailand, and other far reaches.

Fresh, seasonal American cuisine is the focus at **Blue Moon** (361 W. Market St., York, 717/854-6664, www.bluemoonfresh.com, lunch 11:30 A.M.–2:30 P.M. Tues.–Fri., dinner 4:30–9:30 P.M. Mon.–Sat., lunch $10–15, dinner $18–36), a lovely bistro with white tablecloths, walls decked with original art, and nary a hint of pretension. The happy hour—Thursdays from 5:30–7:30 P.M.—is among the best around, complete with complimentary hors d'oeuvres. Take your martini to the backyard deck if the weather's nice.

York's most impressive martini list can be found at █ **The Left Bank** (120 N. George St., York, 717/843-8010, www.leftbankyork .com, lunch 11 A.M. Tues.–Fri., dinner 4 P.M. Mon.–Sat., $10–34), a chef-owned fine dining restaurant with a big-city feel. This is where Yorkers come on special occasions. Don't think "Philly cheesesteak" and "fancy" belong in the same sentence? You haven't tried chef David Albright's cheesesteak appetizer, made with beef tenderloin, bruschetta, and basil aioli. The seafood entrées are outstanding, as is the service. Don't hesitate to ask the waitstaff for wine recommendations.

If your visit to York County includes winetasting at Moon Dancer Vineyards or kayaking from Shank's Mare, plan on dining at the **John Wright Restaurant** (N. Front St., Wrightsville, 717/252-0416, www.johnwright restaurant.com, 8 A.M.–3 P.M. Mon.–Wed., 8 A.M.–9 P.M. Thurs.–Sat., 11 A.M.–4 P.M. Sun., $4–20), which occupies a restored warehouse along the Susquehanna River. Heck, plan on dining there if you're anywhere within a 20-mile radius. The casual atmosphere, comfort foods, and killer views make it worth a drive. (You can also kayak to it.) Come for Sunday brunch if you get the chance, when the menu includes French toast with roasted peaches, smoked salmon soufflé, and a 5-ounce burger with your choice of fixings, plus $3 Bloody Marys and mimosas. Also on premises: the John Wright Store (8 A.M.–5 P.M. Mon.–Wed., 8 A.M.–8 P.M. Thurs.–Sat., 11 A.M.–5 P.M. Sun.), which sells cast iron home and garden products made by the locally based company of the same name as well as accessories by the likes of Vera Bradley.

INFORMATION

If you're arriving in York County via I-83 north, look for the state-run welcome center 2.5 miles north of the Pennsylvania-Maryland line. Personalized travel counseling is available 7 A.M.–7 P.M. daily; the restrooms are always open.

Visit the website of the **York County Convention & Visitors Bureau** (717/852-9675, www.yorkpa.org) to request a free

DUTCH COUNTRY

visitors guide or peruse a digital version. The CVB operates a visitors center in downtown York (155 W. Market St., 9:30 A.M.–4 P.M. daily) and another at the Harley-Davidson plant (1425 Eden Rd., York, 9 A.M.–5 P.M. daily). For information about Pennsylvania Dutch Country as a whole, visit www.dutch countryroads.com.

GETTING THERE AND AROUND

York County shares its southern border with Maryland. Its county seat and largest municipality, York, is about 50 miles north of Baltimore and 25 miles south of Harrisburg via I-83. U.S. 30 provides east–west access to the city, which is about 30 miles from Gettysburg to its west and Lancaster to its east.

Harrisburg International Airport (888/235-9442, www.flyhia.com), about half an hour's drive from York, is served by Air Canada, AirTran Airways, Continental Airlines, Delta Air Lines, United Airlines, and US Airways. They offer daily nonstop service to about a dozen destinations. Note that while locals refer to the airport as HIA, its Federal Aviation Administration booking code is MDT. That's because of its physical location in the borough of Middletown, about eight miles south of Harrisburg. **Baltimore/Washington International Thurgood Marshall Airport** (800/435-9294, www.bwiairport.com) is farther—about an hour from York assuming minimal traffic—but considerably larger. It's served by about 25 commercial airlines.

Intercity bus service to York is available through **Greyhound** (800/231-2222, www .greyhound.com) and its interline partners. York County's public bus system is **Rabbittransit** (800/632-9063, www.rabbittransit.org).

Gettysburg and Vicinity

Few places in America have the name recognition of Gettysburg. There's hardly an eighth grader who hasn't heard of the town, which has but 8,000 residents and welcomes some three million visitors a year. It earned its place in the history books in 1863, when it was the setting for the Civil War's bloodiest battle and President Abraham Lincoln's most famous speech. The former took place in July of that year, when more than 165,000 soldiers converged on the crossroads town. Over the first three days of the month, a Union army under the command of General George G. Meade desperately and successfully defended its home territory from General Robert E. Lee's Confederate forces. The war would continue for almost two more years, but the Confederacy's hopes for independence effectively died on the Gettysburg battlefield. The hellish battle's human toll was astronomical: 51,000 soldiers were dead, wounded, or missing. Interestingly, only one of Gettysburg's 2,400 citizens was killed during the biggest battle ever fought on this continent. The casualty was a young woman named Jennie Wade, and the bullet-riddled house in which she died is now a museum named for her.

In the aftermath of the battle, the townspeople dedicated themselves to caring for the wounded and burying the dead. A group of prominent residents convinced the state to help fund the purchase of a portion of the battlefield to serve as a final resting place for the Union's defenders. Gettysburg attorney David Wills was appointed to coordinate the establishment of the Soldiers' National Cemetery, and he invited President Lincoln to deliver "a few appropriate remarks" at the dedication ceremony on November 19. The lanky commander-in-chief arrived by train the previous day and strolled down Carlisle Street to Wills's stately home on the town square. There, in a second-floor bedroom, he polished his talk. The National Park Service acquired the house in 2004 and opened it as a museum in 2009. Lincoln was not the featured speaker at the

The Pennsylvania memorial, Gettysburg's most visited, is a tribute to all the Pennsylvania soldiers who fought there.

These simple stones in Gettysburg National Cemetery mark the graves of unidentified soldiers who were killed in the battles.

dedication of the cemetery. That honor went to politician and orator Edward Everett, who waxed on for two hours. But Lincoln's two-minute Gettysburg Address—so succinct that a photographer on the scene failed to snap a picture—is regarded as the rhetorical zenith of his career and one of the greatest speeches in history.

America's four-year civil war was fought on many battlegrounds, but none is as hallowed as Gettysburg's. Established in 1895, Gettysburg National Military Park was the first historic site owned by the U.S. government. As the only major Civil War battlefield in a northern state and an easy trip from population centers such as Philadelphia and Baltimore, it attracted scores of veterans and other visitors. The battlefield's popularity as a tourist destination bred commercial development in the 20th century. At one point there was even a casino on what is now park property. In recent years, preservationists have gotten the upper hand. Commercial establishments have been given

the boot. Billboards have vanished. In 2000, on the anniversary of the final day of the battle, locals cheered as an observation tower built in the 1970s on private land adjacent to the park was demolished with explosives. The National Park Service is even removing trees from parts of the battlefield, planting them in others, and reconstructing long-gone farm lanes and roads so that the landscape looks more like it did in 1863. Bottom line: There hasn't been a better time to visit Gettysburg in the last century. The picture of what transpired there is getting clearer and clearer.

When to visit? That depends on your interests and tolerance for crowds. The Gettysburg area is busiest in early July, during the annual battle reenactment, which is held not on the battlefield but on private land. The town swarms with tourists and rifle-toting reenactors, and the weather tends toward hot and humid. Visitation tapers off as the summer draws to a close, then picks up in October, when paranormal enthusiasts flock to what they believe is one of the most haunted places in the country. Mid-November brings scores of Lincoln scholars and admirers. They discuss his life and legacy at an annual symposium before joining in a town-wide celebration of his famous address. Winter is the slow season, an ideal time for hushed contemplation of the carnage that took place here and the courage that shaped this country. Some Gettysburg attractions are closed during the coldest months, but the battlefield is open daily year-round. Things pick up in April with the arrival of busload after busload of schoolchildren. By June, tourism is in full swing.

The battlefield is certainly the area's biggest draw, but there are more than a dozen other sights of interest to history buffs. Downtown Gettysburg is itself a historical attraction: About 60 percent of its buildings predate the battle. One of the most popular tourist stops isn't about history at all. It's a museum housing one man's collection of elephants (man-made, not living). Another non-historical attraction, the Land of Little Horses (living, not man-made), scores big with kids.

❰ GETTYSBURG NATIONAL MILITARY PARK

Expect to spend the better part of a day at Gettysburg National Military Park (717/334-1124, ext. 8023, www.nps.gov/gett, 6 A.M.–10 P.M. daily Apr.–Oct., 6 A.M.–7 P.M. daily Nov.–Mar., free admission), site of the Civil War's biggest and bloodiest battle. Run by the National Park Service, the 6,000-acre battlefield is not only one of the nation's most popular historical attractions but also one of the world's most extraordinary sculpture gardens. It's dotted with more than 1,300 monuments, markers, and memorials. The oldest was dedicated on July 1, 1869, the sixth anniversary of the first day of fighting. State after state commissioned monuments in the late 1800s. Visitors encounter equestrian bronzes of the battle's commanders, tributes to common soldiers, a statue of a civilian hero, and another of a priest who gave absolution to Irish soldiers as they prepared for battle.

It's best to begin your visit at the **Museum and Visitor Center** (1195 Baltimore Pike/Rte. 97, Gettysburg, 717/338-1243, reservations

the Louisiana monument, sculpted by Donald De Lue

the North Carolina monument, sculpted by Gutzon Borglum

© CARL SHUMAN

DUTCH COUNTRY

The cyclorama in the Visitor Center is a 360-degree painting of Pickett's Charge.

717/334-2436, www.gettysburgfoundation.org, 8 A.M.–6 P.M. daily Apr.–Oct., 8 A.M.–5 P.M. daily Nov.–Mar., admission to film/cyclorama/museum $10.50, seniors $9.50, children 6–18 $6.50), operated by the nonprofit Gettysburg Foundation. There you can orient yourself to the park and learn about the nightmarish clash of armies. Be sure to ask for a schedule of lectures, guided walks, and other special programs, which are especially frequent from mid-June through mid-August. If you plan on touring the battlefield on your own, pick up an official park map and guide (also available at www.nps.gov/gett). It offers a 24-mile auto tour with 16 stops on the battlefield and a couple more in downtown Gettysburg. Brief descriptions of what transpired at each battlefield stop are included. For detailed descriptions of the three-day battle, you can buy an audio tour CD in the museum bookstore or hire a federally licensed guide, who for $55 will get behind the wheel of your car and take you and as many as five other passengers on a two-hour personalized tour. The highly knowledgeable guides

are available on a first-come, first-served basis as soon as the Visitor Center opens, but reservations are recommended. Bus tours with a licensed guide ($28 per person, children 6–12 $17) are also offered.

The Visitor Center, which opened in 2008, is home to a colossal cyclorama depicting Pickett's Charge, a futile infantry assault ordered by Confederate General Robert E. Lee on the final day of battle. It's said that veterans wept at the sight of artist Paul Philippoteaux's 360-degree painting when it was unveiled in 1884. In the 1960s the Park Service commissioned architect Richard Neutra to create a cylindrical home for the masterpiece. But climate control proved a problem in Neutra's modernistic building, and the cyclorama was rehung in the new Visitor Center after several years of painstaking and costly restoration. The largest painting in the country—42 feet high and slightly longer than a football field—is now displayed with a canopy overhead and a diorama that carries the moving scene into the foreground, features that had been lost for more than a century. A sound and light show amps up the drama. The cyclorama experience is preceded by a 22-minute film, *A New Birth of Freedom,* narrated by Morgan Freeman. Timed tickets are issued for the film and cyclorama. Ticket holders can explore the **Gettysburg Museum of the American Civil War** at their own pace. Its 12 galleries include artifacts, films, and interactive exhibits that place the Battle of Gettysburg in the larger context of the deadliest war in American history.

The **Gettysburg National Cemetery,** where President Lincoln delivered his famous Gettysburg Address, is a short walk from the Visitor Center. It's open from dawn to sunset and closed to vehicular traffic. Walking tour brochures are available at the Visitor Center and can be downloaded from the Park Service's Gettysburg website. Work on the cemetery, located on the battlefield, began soon after the bloodshed ended. Thousands of Union and Confederate dead had been hastily buried on or near the battlefield, many of them in shallow graves. Heavy rains would expose decaying bodies, a grisly sight that helped convince Pennsylvania governor Andrew Curtin to appropriate state funds for the cemetery project. About 3,500 Union soldiers were interred there. The Confederate dead remained in scattered graves until the 1870s, when they were relocated to cemeteries in the south. Today the Soldiers' National Cemetery is the final resting place for veterans from all of America's wars through Vietnam. It's the setting for several annual events, including a Memorial Day service and a commemoration of the Gettysburg Address held each November.

Adjacent to the battlefield is the **Eisenhower National Historic Site** (717/338-9114, ext. 10, www.nps.gov/eise, 9 A.M.–4 P.M. daily, admission $7.50, children 6–12 $5), the one-time home and farm of President Dwight D. Eisenhower. The Texas-born Army general and 34th president first visited Gettysburg as a cadet at the U.S. Military Academy at West Point and returned during World War I to run a training camp. After commanding the Allied forces during the second World War, "Ike"

came to Gettysburg with his wife, Mamie, in search of a retirement home. They bought a 189-acre farm in 1950, but retirement eluded them. General Eisenhower left for Europe to assume command of the North Atlantic Treaty Organization, returning to the United States to run for president in 1952. During his two-term presidency, the Eisenhowers spent weekends and holidays at their Gettysburg home. The president entertained world leaders there, introducing them to his show herd of black Angus cattle and chatting with them on his porch. The Eisenhowers finally retired to their farm in 1961 and donated it to the National Park Service in 1967, two years before the general's death. Mrs. Eisenhower continued to live there until her death in 1979. The house has changed little since then. Furnishings include a coffee table given to the Eisenhowers by the first lady of South Korea, a rug from the shah of Iran, and a desk fashioned from old floorboards removed from the White House during a 1948 renovation. Visitors can also explore the grounds, which include a putting green, a skeet range, rose gardens, and a garage that still houses the Eisenhowers' jeep, golf carts, and station wagon. Some 40 to 50 Angus still graze the pastures. Due to limited on-site parking and space in the home, visitors must arrive by shuttle bus from the Visitor Center at Gettysburg National Military Park.

OTHER SIGHTS
David Wills House
In the aftermath of the Battle of Gettysburg, when dead and wounded soldiers outnumbered civilians 11 to one, the home of local attorney David Wills became a center of recovery efforts. He gathered supplies for the wounded, sought compensation for farmers who'd suffered losses during the battle, and coordinated the establishment of a permanent cemetery for the Union dead. Less than three weeks before the dedication of the cemetery, Wills wrote a letter to President Abraham Lincoln inviting him to deliver "a few appropriate remarks" at the event. He had already booking famed orator Edward Everett as the main speaker. The

President Lincoln points to the bedroom in the David Wills House where he slept the night before he delivered the Gettysburg Address in a statue titled *Return Visit*.

president accepted and arrived in Gettysburg a day ahead of the November 19 dedication. Mrs. Wills had prepared her own bedroom for the president. It was there that he put the finishing touches on his Gettysburg Address. Admirers gathered outside the house could see him pacing back and forth through the second-story windows.

In 2009, on Lincoln's 200th birthday, the National Park Service opened the house as a museum that tells the story of the town's recovery and Lincoln's visit. The David Wills House (8 Lincoln Square, Gettysburg, 866/486-5735, www.davidwillshouse.org, 9 A.M.–6 P.M. daily May–Aug., 9 A.M.–5 P.M. daily except Tues. Mar.–Apr. and Sept.–Nov., 9 A.M.–5 P.M. daily except Tues. and Wed. Dec.–Feb., admission $6.50, seniors $5.50, children 6–18 $4) features the recreated Lincoln bedroom with Mrs. Wills's original bed. The office where David Wills received letters from families looking for sons lost in battle is also restored to its 1863 appearance. Other rooms have exhibits on Gettysburg before and after the battle,

Lincoln's immortal words, and the preservation and restoration of the Wills house. The collection includes Lincoln's saddle cover and a telegram sent to the president at the house.

There's a municipal parking garage a block away on Race Horse Alley. Freedom Transit (717/846-7433, www.ridethetrolley.com) trolleys provide service from the Gettysburg National Military Park Museum and Visitor Center and other locations.

Shriver and Jennie Wade Houses

Just a few blocks from the David Wills House are two house museums that explore the civilian experience during the Civil War. Tours of the **Shriver House Museum** (309 Baltimore St., Gettysburg, 717/337-2800, www.shriverhouse .org, 10 A.M.–5 P.M. Mon.–Sat. and noon–5 P.M. Sun. Apr.–mid-Nov., 10 A.M.–5 P.M. Sat. in Dec., 10 A.M.–5 P.M. Sat. and 10 A.M.–2 P.M. Sun. in Mar., admission $7.50, seniors $6.85, children under 13 $4.85) are conducted by guides in period attire. Candlelight tours are offered on Saturday evenings in December,

GETTYSBURG GUIDES

It's easy to explore Gettysburg on your own and especially so when you have this book in hand. But if you're hazy on Civil War history, a tour can make for a richer experience. Tour operators are a dime a dozen. Which one is right for you depends on your preferred mode of transport and whether you're keen on a live guide or satisfied with recorded commentary.

Many Gettysburg tours are led by members of the **Association of Licensed Battlefield Guides** (717/337-1709, www.gettysburgtourguides.org). These guys have spent years if not decades studying the Battle of Gettysburg. Licensure applicants must first pass a written exam given every other year. The highest scorers must prove themselves further by passing an oral test. If you're the sort who appreciates a lot of detail and asks a lot of questions, hire a licensed guide who will take the wheel of your car and show you around. A standard auto tour of the battlefield is two hours long. Guides are available on a first-come, first-served basis at the Gettysburg National Military Park Museum and Visitor Center (1195 Baltimore Pike/Rte. 97, Gettysburg, 8 A.M.–6 P.M. daily Apr.–Oct., 8 A.M.–5 P.M. daily Nov.–Mar.). You can also reserve a tour in advance by calling 717/334-2436 or visiting www.gettysburgfoundation. org. During busy times of year, it's not unusual for all available guides to be booked up early in the day. Guide fees are $55 for a vehicle of 1-6 people, $70 for a vehicle of 7-15. It's customary to tip your guide if you're satisfied. Bus tours with a licensed guide ($28 per person, children 6-12 $17) also leave from the visitors center. Allow 2.5 hours for the bus tour. If you'd like a specialized tour of the battlefield or town, contact the Association of Licensed Battlefield Guides directly.

Bus tours with a licensed guide also depart from the **Gettysburg Tour Center** (778 Baltimore St., Gettysburg, 717/334-6296, www.gettysburgbattlefieldtours.com), located across from the Soldiers' National Cemetery. But the commercial tour company is best known for its open-air double-decker bus tours, featuring "dramatized audio" complete with booming cannons and cracking rifles. The two-hour tour ($24.95 per person, children 6-12 $14) is offered so long as weather permits. Gettysburg Tour Center operates several area attractions, including the Jennie Wade House and the Hall of Presidents and First Ladies. Combo packages are available.

You can feel like General Lee by touring the battlefield on horseback. **Artillery Ridge Campground** (610 Taneytown Rd., Gettysburg, 717/334-1288, www.artilleryridge.com), just across the street from the battlefield, offers two-hour horseback tours ($72 per person) daily April through October and weekends in November. When a licensed guide can't be along for the tour, riders listen to a recorded narrative. Riding experience isn't necessary; reservations are. Another option: gliding around the battlefield on a Segway. **SegTours** (717/253-7987, www.segtours.com) offers a 2.5-hour tour that takes in the most famous battlefield sites ($65 per person) and a shorter tour to a lesser-known part of the battlefield ($45 per person). Riders listen to a recorded narrative as they're escorted along a prescribed route. For an additional fee, a licensed guide will come along for the ride. Reservations are recommended for audio tours and required if you want a live guide. The SegTours field office is in the rear parking lot of the Reliance Mine Saloon on Taneytown Road (Route 134), about 100 yards north of the entrance to the Soldiers' National Cemetery. Tours depart on a regular schedule March–November.

If you want to burn off some calories while exploring the battlefield, take a bicycle tour. **GettysBike** (241 Steinwehr Ave., Gettysburg, 717/752-7752, www.gettysbike.com) tours generally last three hours and cover nine miles. A licensed guide always comes along. Group tours are $61 per person, $30 for children 13 and under. Bring your own bike for a discount. Families with children under 10

© ANNA DUBROVSKY

Licensed Battlefield Guide Terry Latschar leads a horseback tour of the battlefield.

must reserve a private tour, which costs $102 per person, $52 per child. Reservations are required.

While most tours focus on the battlefield and the clashes of troops that culminated in a Union victory, the nonprofit **Main Street Gettysburg** (717/339-6161, www.mainstreetgettysburg.org) offers guided walking tours of downtown that illumine the civilian experience. One need only to look at a map of Gettysburg National Military Park to realize that the town must have been deeply scarred. The battlefield enfolds the town – the last in America to be occupied by an invading army. When the bullets stopped flying, Gettysburg citizens emerged from hiding places to an Armageddon-like scene. The town became a hospital and morgue and every citizen a first responder. Offered April through October, the 90-minute walking tours ($10 per person, seniors and children 5-12 $8) depart from the historic Gettysburg Hotel at 1 Lincoln Square.

Gettysburg's "nearly departed" are the subject of much interest within the paranormal community. The site of so much Civil War carnage is regarded as one of the most haunted places in the county. If you're not terribly squeamish, an evening ghost-themed tour may be for you. The original and most reputable operator is **Ghosts of Gettysburg** (271 Baltimore St., Gettysburg, 717/337-0445, www.ghostsofgettysburg.com), open every season but winter. Its walking and bus tours, led by guides in period attire with candle lanterns in hand, are based on the books of historian, ghost hunter, and former National Park Service ranger Mark Nesbitt. Walking tours are $9.50-10 per person, free for children 7 and under. Bus tours are $18 per person, $16 for children 5-10, and off-limits to children under 5.

when the house is decorated for Christmas, 1860s style. George Washington Shriver paid $290 in 1860 for what was then considered a double lot on the edge of town. He built a home for his family, opening a saloon in the cellar and a 10-pin bowling alley in an adjacent building. The family was just settling in when the Civil War erupted in 1861 and Shriver answered President Lincoln's call for troops. When the war came to Gettysburg in the summer of 1863, he was still away. While his wife, Hettie, and two young daughters hunkered down at her parents' farm about three miles away, Confederate soldiers occupied their home. Today visitors learn about life during the Civil War as they tour all four floors of the house, including the attic used by Confederate sharpshooters. The bowling alley is no longer standing, but the saloon has been recreated. During the 1996 restoration of the Shriver home, three live Civil War bullets and period medical supplies were discovered under floorboards. They're among the artifacts displayed in the museum shop next door.

The nearby **Jennie Wade House** (548 Baltimore St., Gettysburg, 717/334-4100, www .gettysburgbattlefieldtours.com, 9 A.M.–7 P.M. daily in summer, 9 A.M.–5 P.M. in spring and fall, admission $7.25, children 6–12 $3.50) is a shrine to its namesake, the only civilian casualty of the Battle of Gettysburg. Jennie Wade was baking bread for Union soldiers when bullets ripped through the door of the house, taking her life. She was 20 years old and engaged to a childhood friend who'd been mustered into the service two years earlier. He died just nine days later of wounds sustained in a Virginia battle, never knowing of his sweetheart's fate.

General Lee's Headquarters Museum

On the first day of the Battle of Gettysburg, Confederate General Robert E. Lee established his personal headquarters in a stone house at the center and rear of his battle lines. There, he and his commanders pondered the problems of the great battle, which ended in a victory for the Union. Fifty-nine years after Lee

escaped south, the house was opened to the public as a museum named for him. General Lee's Headquarters Museum (401 Buford Ave., Gettysburg, 717/334-3141, www.civilwarhead quarters.com, 9 A.M.–5 P.M. mid-Mar.–Nov., extended summer hours, admission $3, free for children under 16 and local residents) is one of the oldest museums in Gettysburg and unique in its focus on the Confederate cause. It's also unique in that visitors can spend a night upstairs. Call 717/334-3141 or visit www .thegettysburgaddress.com for more information about the **Quality Inn at General Lee's Headquarters** ($75–240). The historic inn has hosted such bigwigs as General George Patton and President Dwight Eisenhower as well as the last surviving Confederate widow.

Wax Museums

The little town of Gettysburg is home to not one but two wax museums. More than 300 life-sized wax figures depict events of the nation's deadliest war at the **American Civil War Museum** (297 Steinwehr Ave., Gettysburg, 717/334-6245, www.gettysburgmuseum.com, 9 A.M.–5 P.M. daily Mar.–Dec., open weekends and holidays in Jan. and Feb., extended spring and summer hours, admission $5.50, children 6–17 $3). Visitors learn about the economical, social, and political causes of the war, the assassination of President Abraham Lincoln, and everything in between. The sounds of bullets and battle cries echo in the auditorium, where the Battle of Gettysburg is recreated. The onsite **Gettysburg Gift Center,** 3,200 square feet of collectibles, art, books, games, clothing, and home decor, is arguably the best gift shop in town.

A stone's throw from the main entrance to Soldiers' National Cemetery, the **Hall of Presidents and First Ladies** (789 Baltimore St., Gettysburg, 717/334-5717, www.gettys burgbattlefieldtours.com, 9 A.M.–7 P.M. in summer, 9 A.M.–5 P.M. in spring and fall, admission $7.25, children 6–12 $3.50) features wax figures of every American president. Extra attention is paid to 34th President Dwight D. Eisenhower, who bought a home in Gettysburg not long before winning the presidency and lived out his days there. The museum also has a collection of doll-sized first ladies in their inaugural gowns.

Land of Little Horses Farm Park

Admission isn't cheap, but the Land of Little Horses (125 Glenwood Dr., Gettysburg, 717/334-7259, Dec.–Mar. 717/334-5236, www.landoflittlehorses.com, 10 A.M.–5 P.M. Mon.–Sat. early June–late Aug., Sat. and Sun. only through Oct., admission $13.95, children 2–11 $11.95) is a hit with little 'uns. Just a few miles west of downtown Gettysburg, the "performing animal theme park" is home to not only miniature horses but also goats, sheep, donkeys, emus, and other critters happy to eat out of your hand. The performers among them take the stage twice daily Monday through Saturday and once on Sunday. Two dollars buys a wagon or pony ride. (Alas, if you're over 70 pounds, no pony ride for you.) A gift shop, snack bar, and guesthouse are on-site.

Mister Ed's Elephant Museum

Ed Gotwalt's passion for all things pachyderm started on his wedding day more than 40 years ago, when he received an elephant knickknack as a good luck charm. By 1975 his elephant collection had grown so large that his wife made him open a museum to get them out of the house. Miss Ellie Phant, a life-sized talking elephant with animated eyes and ears, greets visitors at Mister Ed's Elephant Museum (6019 Chambersburg Rd., Orrtanna, 717/352-3792, www.mistereds.com, 10 A.M.–5 P.M. daily, free admission), located on U.S. 30 about 12 miles west of Gettysburg. It doesn't cost a cent to see Gotwalt's collection, which ballooned to more than 10,000 elephants after an anonymous donor left him some 4,000 in her will. There are stone elephants, wood elephants, metal elephants, and plush elephants. There's an elephant potty chair and an elephant hair dryer. There are even elephant-embroidered pillowcases that once belonged to Cher. It's safe to say you'll never see any place like it. Elephants aren't the only draw. A onetime peanut dealer,

Gotwalt sells mountains of nuts and candy, including nostalgic varieties like wax bottles and Pez.

Appalachian Trail Museum

After 12 years in the making, the Appalachian Trail Museum (1120 Pine Grove Rd., Gardners, 717/486-8126, www.atmuseum.org, noon–4 P.M. daily Memorial Day–Labor Day and weekends in spring and fall, free admission) opened in 2010 in a former gristmill about 20 miles north of Gettysburg. It pays tribute to pioneer hikers such as Earl Shaffer, the first person to thru-hike the trail, and "Grandma" Gatewood, so nicknamed because she was 67 when she became the first female to complete the journey alone. A pillowcase she used as a pack is among the artifacts displayed in the first museum dedicated to the famed footpath. There's even an exhibit on Ziggy, who in 1990 became the first feline to conquer the Georgia-to-Maine trail. (To be fair, the cat spent most of the journey riding on the backpack of hiker Jim "the Geek" Adams, but he contributed much in the way of mice patrol at trail shelters.) Highlights of the collection include a trail shelter that Shaffer, a native of nearby York County, built about a decade after his 1948 history-making hike. The shelter was painstakingly dismantled at its original site on a mountain north of Harrisburg and reassembled in the museum.

Visitors stand a good chance of rubbing shoulders with modern-day thru-hikers because the museum is just a few hundred yards off the A.T. in **Pine Grove Furnace State Park** (717/486-7174, www.dcnr.state.pa.us/stateparks/parks/PineGroveFurnace.aspx), which marks the midpoint of the 2,179-mile trail. Tradition dictates that thru-hikers stop at the park's general store, across the road from the museum, and face a test of mettle known as the "half-gallon challenge." Those who succeed, i.e., eat a half gallon of ice cream, are rewarded with a commemorative wooden spoon. Word has it that chunky flavors are harder to finish.

The state park is named for an ironworks founded in 1764, and the charcoal iron furnace that operated until 1895 is still standing. A mansion built in 1829 for the ironmaster's family is now a youth hostel (717/486-7575) along the Appalachian Trail. It closed for extensive renovations in 2010 and was expected to reopen in spring 2011. The 696-acre park also features a campground and two small lakes with beaches and a boat rental. Pine Grove allows overnight parking for anyone who wants to hit the A.T., but registration at the park office is required. The office is at the intersection of Route 233 and Pine Grove Road, a few hundred feet from the museum.

National Apple Museum

Adams County, of which Gettysburg is the county seat, is one of the largest apple producers in the country and the heart of Pennsylvania's fruit belt. It's home to grower-owned applesauce maker Musselman's, a Mott's plant, and the National Apple Museum (154 W. Hanover St., Biglerville, 717/677-4556, www.national applemuseum.com, 10 A.M.–4 P.M. Sat. and 1–4 P.M. Sun. May–Oct., admission $2, seniors $1.75, children 6–16 $1). Miles and miles of orchards make for scenic drives, especially when the trees are in bloom. (See www .gettysburgwineandfruittrail.com for suggested routes north and west of Gettysburg.)

ENTERTAINMENT AND EVENTS
Performing Arts

The **Majestic Theater** (35 Carlisle St., Gettysburg, 717/337-8200, www.gettysburg majestic.org) was the largest vaudeville and silent movie theater in south-central Pennsylvania when it opened in 1925. President Dwight D. Eisenhower and First Lady Mamie Eisenhower attended performances in the 1950s, often with world leaders in tow. In 1993 the Majestic hosted the world premiere of *Gettysburg,* one of the longest films ever released by a Hollywood studio at more than four hours. Today it hosts live performances by the likes of the Moscow Circus, the Temptations, and pianist Jim Brickman. Two cinemas with stadium seating and a pair of "cuddle up" seats in every row

were added as part of a $16 million renovation in recent years. Art films are shown nightly.

Festivals and Events

The blooming of Adams County's fragrant blossoms is cause for a celebration: the **Apple Blossom Festival** (717/677-7444, www.uasd .k12.pa.us/upperadams/Fruitgrowers/festival, admission $5, children under 12 free), takes place the first weekend in May. Free orchard tours, pony and wagon rides, apple-bobbing and pie-eating contests, antique cars, arts and crafts, live entertainment, and an apple queen contest are all part of the fun. The fall harvest is occasion for Adams County's biggest to-do, the **National Apple Harvest Festival** (717/677-9413, www.appleharvest.com, first two weekends in Oct., admission $9, seniors $8, children under 12 free). Both festivals are held at the South Mountain Fair Grounds, 10 miles northwest of Gettysburg on Route 234. A different crop gets the limelight in June.

A bin of apples sits ready for cooking at the National Apple Harvest Festival.

The **Pennsylvania Lavender Festival** (145 Tract Rd., Fairfield, 717/642-6387, www.palavenderfestival.com, Father's Day weekend) is held at Willow Pond Farm in Fairfield, about 15 minutes west of Gettysburg. Owners Tom and Madeline Wajda grow more than 100 different lavenders along with other herbs and perennial plants. Festival-goers can tour the lavender field, cut their own lavender, and make lavender wands. Lectures and workshops on growing lavender, herbal medicines, cooking with fresh herbs, edible topiaries, and other topics are offered throughout the three-day festival. The certified organic farm is also open to visitors 9 A.M.–5 P.M. Thursday–Saturday from April to Christmas and noon–5 P.M. on Sundays from April to mid-June and in November and December. Visit the farm's website, www.willowpondherbs.com, for more information on its demonstration gardens and shop, which sells herbal jellies, vinegars, honeys, teas, and more.

A tradition since 1979, the **Gettysburg Bluegrass Festival** (3340 Fairfield Rd., Gettysburg, 717/642-8749, www.gettysburg bluegrass.com) is actually two four-day festivals: one in May and another in August. Both are held at Granite Hill Camping Resort, about five miles west of Gettysburg on Route 116. Top bluegrass and traditional country musicians turn out for the acclaimed festivals. Legendary mandolinist John Duffey played every one from 1979 until his death in 1996, and singer/fiddler Alison Krauss, who first played the festival as a high school senior, continued showing up through the year she was crowned Female Vocalist of the Year by the Country Music Association. Single- and multiday tickets can be purchased at the gate (cash only) or in advance at a discount.

Thousands of reenactors take part in the annual **Gettysburg Civil War Battle Reenactment** (717/338-1525, www.gettys burgreenactment.com, early July), firing period

Union soldiers fire a cannon during the annual Gettysburg Civil War Battle Reenactment.

DUTCH COUNTRY

© GETTYSBURG CONVENTION & VISITORS BUREAU

DUTCH COUNTRY

Confederate soldiers line up in formation before reenacting a battle during the annual event.

weapons and feigning death on farm fields just a few miles from the original battlefield. Half a dozen clashes are staged over several days. Spectators can stroll through the soldiers' camps, listen to live Civil War music and period speakers, watch period demonstrations, and shop for period wares. Admission at the gate is $30 for adults, $15 for children 6–12. You'll save if you order tickets in advance. Arrive early to claim a spot near the front of battle viewing areas. It's a good idea to bring folding chairs, binoculars, and sunscreen. Limited bleacher seating is available for an additional $10 per person per day and usually sells out before the event.

A host of events commemorate President Abraham Lincoln's most famous speech, delivered at the dedication of the Soldiers' National Cemetery less than five months after the Battle of Gettysburg. Held on the anniversary of his Gettysburg Address, **Dedication Day** (717/334-1124, www.nps.gov/gett, Nov. 19) begins with a wreath-laying ceremony at the cemetery. Locally based and nationally renowned Lincoln actor Jim Getty recites the short address after an oration by a person of

note. Past speakers have included actor Richard Dreyfuss, newsman Tom Brokaw, aviator Neil Armstrong, and Chief Justice William Rehnquist. The Saturday closest to November 19 is **Remembrance Day** (717/334-6274, www.gettysburg.travel) in Gettysburg. A parade of reenactors—Union and Confederate troops, drummer boys and generals on horseback, women and children in 1800s attire—winds through town and ends at the national military park. As the day draws to a close, a luminary candle is placed on each Civil War grave in the national cemetery. The cost to sponsor a candle for the **Remembrance Illumination** (717/338-1243, www.gettysburgfoundation.org) is, appropriately enough, $18.63.

SHOPPING
Downtown Gettysburg
You won't find the Gap or a Starbucks in downtown Gettysburg. Its shops are of the independent variety, and many offer things you'd be hard-pressed to find in a big city: Civil War collectibles, military artifacts from the American Revolutionary War and onwards,

and anything a reenactor could want, from candle lanterns to cavalry swords. Dale Gallon and Mort Kunstler, two of the nation's premier historical artists, each have eponymous galleries in town: the **Gallon Historical Art Gallery** (9 Steinwehr Ave., 717/334-8666, www.gallon.com, 10 A.M.–5 P.M. Mon.–Sat. and noon–3 P.M. Sun.) and the **MKunstler Gallery** (10 York St., 717/334-0513, www .mkunstlergallery.com, call for hours).

Greater Gettysburg

Pennsylvania's sales tax exemption on clothing lures many a Marylander to the **Outlet Shoppes at Gettysburg** (1863 Gettysburg Village Dr., Gettysburg, 717/337-9705, www.theoutletshoppesatgettysburg.com, 10 A.M.–9 P.M. Mon.–Sat., 10 A.M.–6 P.M. Sun.) at U.S. 15 and Baltimore Street (Route 97). Retailers include Liz Claiborne, Jones New York, Old Navy, Naturalizer, Nautica, and Izod. There's a 10-screen cinema (717/338-0101) and hotel on-site.

Five miles south of downtown Gettysburg on U.S. Business Route 15 south is the flagship store of The Boyds Collection Ltd., best known for its plush bears and resin figurines. Billing itself as the "World's Most Humongous Teddy Bear Store," **Boyd's Bear Country** (75 Cunningham Rd., Gettysburg, 866/367-8338, www.boydsbearcountry.com, 10 A.M.–6 P.M. daily) carries collectibles available nowhere else, including a top-hatted Abraham Lincoln bear. In addition to Boyds products, the store sells collectibles and home decor from Gund, Yankee Candle, and more than 20 other companies. The four-story red barn is as much a family-fun destination as it is a store. Inside is a free museum that tells the Boyds story, a portrait center, and the Boyds Super Duper Bear Factory, where visitors can make their own bean-filled animal friend. Kids can adopt a plush canine at the Pups 'n Pals Adoption Center or take home a swaddled bear cub from the Boyds Teddy Bear Nursery. There's a deli open daily and a buffet-style eatery open on weekends. There's even a Guest Relations Center with information about area attractions, hotels, and more.

The quiet, tree-lined borough of **New Oxford,** 10 miles east of Gettysburg on U.S. 30, is an antiquing mecca with more than 500 dealers. A partial list of dealers can be found at www.newoxfordantiques.com, website of the New Oxford Antique Dealers Association.

SPORTS AND RECREATION

About 20 minutes from Gettysburg, **Liberty Mountain Resort** (78 Country Club Trail, Carroll Valley, 717/642-8282, www.ski liberty.com, 8-hour lift ticket $47–58, children 6–12 $42–52, ski rental $38, snowboard rental $44, snow tubing 1-hour session $15–20) offers skiing, snowboarding, and snow tubing when weather permits. A sister resort of York County's Ski Roundtop, Liberty Mountain has 16 trails, three terrain parks, and a 500-foot half-pipe. Skiers and snowboarders can choose from all-day, two-day, nighttime, and "flex" lift tickets good for four or eight hours from the time of purchase. Rossignol skis and Burton snowboards are available for rent. **Boulder Ridge Snow Tubing,** on the backside of the mountain, boasts more than a dozen lanes. One- and two-hour tickets are available for tubing sessions, which begin at the top of each hour. Kids 2–4 can tube all day in an area set aside for them for $9. The slopeside Liberty Mountain Hotel has 40 rooms ($125–149) and a suite with a kitchenette and hot tub ($189–209). Guests get free wireless Internet access and breakfast. Child care is available at $14–16 per hour. There's championship golfing next door to Liberty Mountain at **Carroll Valley Resort** (121 Sanders Rd., Fairfield, 717/642-8211, www.carrollvalley.com, accommodations $119–169).

ACCOMMODATIONS

Gettysburg has loads of lodging properties, many of which have a story to tell. There are B&Bs scarred by bullets and rooms once occupied by generals. You can unwind in a place that once crawled with wounded soldiers. If you visit when the town is crawling with tourists, expect two- or three-night minimums at many properties. Rates are at their lowest from December through March.

Under $100

Camping is a popular and inexpensive way to stay near the battlefield during the high season. Gettysburg has half a dozen campgrounds. If your idea of camping is quietly communing with nature with nothing but critters for company, you may be in for a shock. These campgrounds are fairly bustling places. Some have cottages so luxurious they make hotel rooms look rustic, and all offer a host of modern amenities. **Drummer Boy Camping Resort** (1300 Hanover St., Gettysburg, 800/293-2808, www.drummerboycampresort.com, tent sites $32–53 per night or $179–199 weekly, hookup sites $36–69 per night or $224–296 weekly, cabins $55–135 per night or $349–560 weekly, cottages $145–275 per night or $835–1,395 weekly) has, in addition to more than 400 campsites and about 50 cabins and cottages, two heated pools, a 250-foot water slide, a mini golf course, a game room, basketball and volleyball courts, and a pond where campers can fish without a license. Add to that a full schedule of activities and it's a wonder that campers ever leave the 95-acre resort. Drummer Boy is a few minutes east of downtown on Route 116.

A few minutes west of downtown on 116 is the 260-site **Gettysburg Campground** (2030 Fairfield Rd./Rte 116 W., Gettysburg, 717/334-3304, www.gettysburgcampground.com, tent sites $30–38 per night or $180–198 weekly, hookup sites $37–52 per night or $222–276 weekly, cabins $58–75 per night or $348–390 weekly, cottages $120–155 per night or $720–810 weekly). It too has amenities up the wazoo. Try to snag a campsite along Marsh Creek.

$100-200

Gettysburg's most iconic hotel, the **(Best Western Gettysburg Hotel** (1 Lincoln Square, Gettysburg, 717/337-2000, www.hotelgettysburg.com, peak season $138–390, winter $100–250), is said to have a friendly ghost. You may or may not encounter the civil war nurse and wandering soul named Rachel during your stay. You'll definitely encounter friendly staff. The hotel in the center of town, just steps from the house where President Lincoln polished his Gettysburg Address, is steeped in history. Its story begins in 1797, when a tavern opened its doors on the site. It withstood the bloody and pivotal battle of 1863 but was replaced in the 1890s by the current structure, which was christened the Hotel Gettysburg. In 1955 the hotel served as President Eisenhower's national operations center while he recuperated from a heart attack at his Gettysburg home. Eisenhower and his wife were the hotel's last guests before it closed its doors in 1964, rendered unprofitable by changes in travel habits. Ravaged by fire in 1983, the building was painstakingly restored and opened as a Best Western in 1991, grand as it ever was. The hotel has 119 guest accommodations, almost half of which are suites; a rooftop swimming pool; a fine dining restaurant open for breakfast and dinner; and an English-style pub with a mahogany bar shipped from across the pond. Check the website for a list of packages that bundle accommodations with activities such as skiing and theater-going.

Also historic but considerably smaller, the **James Gettys Hotel** (27 Chambersburg St., Gettysburg, 717/337-1334, www.jamesgettyshotel.com, $140–250) is half a block from the town square. Named for the founder of Gettysburg, it dates to 1804 and looks much as it did in the 1920s. Like the Gettysburg Hotel, it closed in the 1960s and reopened as an emulation of its former self in the 1990s. The James Gettys has a dozen suites, each with a bedroom, sitting room, kitchenette, and private bath. A complimentary continental breakfast is delivered to the suites daily. Housekeeping has been known to leave behind dark chocolates in the shape of the hotel.

With more than 300 guest rooms and suites, the **Eisenhower Hotel** (2634 Emmitsburg Rd., Gettysburg, 717/334-8121, www.eisenhower.com, $119–149) is the largest hotel in the area. Amenities include an indoor pool and Jacuzzi, a fitness room, dry saunas, a casual eatery, and a business center. A fun park on the hotel grounds features two go-kart tracks, 36 holes of miniature golf, a 14-acre fishing lake, and batting cages. Downtown Gettysburg is five miles to the north and the battlefield even closer.

B&B options in downtown Gettysburg include the impeccable **((Brickhouse Inn Bed & Breakfast** (452 Baltimore St., Gettysburg, 717/338-9337, www.brickhouseinn.com, $115–184). The older of its two buildings dates to the 1830s and was occupied by Confederate sharpshooters during the Battle of Gettysburg. Its south wall still bears the scars of Union bullets. The main house is an 1898 Victorian with original wood floors and chestnut trim. Between them they have 14 guest rooms and suites, each named for a state represented in the bloody battle. Breakfast always includes a hot entrée and the B&B's signature shoo-fly pie. Proprietors Tessa Bardo and Brian Duncan will give you the shirts off their backs but not the secret family recipe.

The **Brafferton Inn** (44 York St., Gettysburg, 717/337-3423, www.brafferton .com, $129–219) is another excellent choice. It has 18 uniquely decorated guest rooms and suites in four buildings—including the oldest deeded house in Gettysburg. The Brafferton is so centrally located—just half a block from the town square—that it can't offer private parking to all guests. Metered street parking is free 8 P.M.–8 A.M. and all day Sunday. Parking is also available in a municipal garage that charges 50 cents per hour.

The **Gaslight Inn** (33 E. Middle St., Gettysburg, 717/337-9100, www.thegaslight inn.com, $115–170) is yet another "in-town oasis," as innkeepers Mike and Betty Hanson put it. Their 1872 house has nine guest rooms, some of which boast Jacuzzis or steam baths, and a pair of furry residents: a Yorkie and a Pomeranian.

A few miles south of town is a countryside oasis, the **Lightner Farmhouse Bed & Breakfast** (2350 Baltimore Pike, Gettysburg, 717/337-9508, www.lightnerfarmhouse.com, $139–189). Built shortly before the Battle of Gettysburg, the Federal-style farmhouse was used as a hospital for three weeks after the bloodshed. Nothing gory about the place today. Innkeepers Dennis and Eileen Hoover aim to provide "outrageous service," whether preparing breakfast or arranging a crash course

in paranormal investigation. The B&B has five en suite rooms, a suite that sleeps up to four, and a two-floor cottage with a private wraparound deck. Quilt designs inspired their decor. Nature trails wind through the 19-acre property.

Built circa 1797, the **Cashtown Inn** (1325 Old Rte. 30, Cashtown, 717/334-9722, www .cashtowninn.com, $140–185) was the first stagecoach stop west of Gettysburg. It owes its name to its original innkeeper, who accepted only cash, and gave its name to the village it calls home. These days, credit cards are welcome at the inn, which is known as much for its cuisine as its cozy accommodations. Its four rooms and three suites are named for Confederate generals, some of whom made their headquarters there during the summer of 1863. More recent (and welcome) guests have included actor Sam Elliott, who bunked there while filming the 1993 movie *Gettysburg,* and paranormal investigator Jason Hawes, who featured the Cashtown in an episode of his Syfy series, *Ghost Hunters.* Room rates include breakfast.

FOOD

Gettysburg is no dining mecca, but it offers a rare opportunity for culinary time travel. A number of restaurants specialize in period fare. Best of the bunch: the **Dobbin House Tavern** (89 Steinwehr Ave., Gettysburg, 717/334-2100, www.dobbinhouse.com), offering colonial and continental cuisine in Gettysburg's oldest building. The Dobbin House was built in 1776—the same year the American colonies declared their independence from Great Britain—as a home for an Irish-born minister and his large brood. It served as a station on the Underground Railroad in the mid-1800s and as a hospital in the immediate aftermath of the Battle of Gettysburg. Great pains have been taken to restore the house-turned-restaurant to its 18th-century appearance. Many of the antique furnishings match descriptions in the inventory of the minister's estate. The china and flatware match fragments unearthed during an excavation of the cellar. For casual dining, head to the basement Springhouse Tavern (open daily from 11:30 A.M., $8–25). With three natural springs and two fireplaces, it's a cozy and romantic spot (that can be clammy in winter and humid in summer). Specials include spit-roasted chicken, chargrilled strip steak, and barbecued ribs, all served with a hearth-baked roll. Fine dining is available in six candlelit rooms known as the Alexander Dobbin Dining Rooms (open daily from 5 P.M., $19–37). The "bedroom" features a table beneath a lace bed canopy. Servers in period attire help satisfy the craving for history that brings most visitors to Gettysburg. Reservations are accepted for the dining rooms but not the tavern, where you can expect a considerable wait on summer weekends.

The **Farnsworth House Inn** (401 Baltimore St., Gettysburg, 717/334-8838, www.farns worthhouseinn.com, dining rooms 5–9 P.M. daily, call for winter hours, $18–25) is another popular destination for period dining complete with costumed servers. Game pie, the house specialty, is a stew of turkey, pheasant, and duck topped with a golden egg crust. Built in the early 1800s, the house sheltered Confederate sharpshooters during the Battle of Gettysburg. It's believed that one of the Southerners accidentally shot Jennie Wade, the only civilian killed during the three-day struggle. Oil paintings of the commanding officers at Gettysburg and photos by famed Civil War photographer Mathew Brady decorate the bullet-scarred house, which has been restored to its 1863 appearance. Its tavern (11:30 A.M.–10 P.M. daily, call for winter hours, $8–12), popular with reenactors, offers hot and cold sandwiches, pork and sauerkraut, meatloaf, and more. Garden dining is available in the warmer months.

Eight miles west of Gettysburg on Route 116, the **Fairfield Inn** (15 W. Main St., Gettysburg, 717/642-5410, www.thefairfieldinn.com, lunch 11 A.M.–4 P.M. Fri.–Sat., brunch 11 A.M.–3 P.M. Sun., dinner 5–9 P.M. Tues.–Sat. and 3–8 P.M. Sun., lunch $6–12, dinner $17–32) has hosted such VIPs as Thaddeus Stevens and President Dwight D. Eisenhower since opening in 1757. The day after the Battle of Gettysburg, as the weary Confederate army retreated west through Fairfield, the inn hosted their generals. Today's guests can sup on hearty ham and

the Farnsworth House Inn

bean soup and chicken and biscuits, just like General Robert E. Lee, or choose from dishes like Tuscan penne, fried haddock, and roasted half duck with balsamic fig reduction. Sunday brunch ($18 per person, children 5–12 $7) is a three-course affair.

If you're not into period dining, you're not out of luck. The Gettysburg area has some recommendable restaurants that go a different route. **Gettysburg Eddie's** (217 Steinwehr Ave., Gettysburg, 717/334-1100, www.gettys burgeddies.com, 11 A.M.–10 P.M. Sun.–Thurs., 11 A.M.–10:30 P.M. Fri.–Sat., bar open until 11 P.M. Sun.–Thurs. and midnight Fri.–Sat., call for winter hours, $8–27), across the street from Soldiers' National Cemetery, is a casual, welcoming spot with a stamp of approval from the sustainability-promoting Green Restaurant Association. Named for Baseball Hall of Fame pitcher Eddie Plank, born in 1875 on a farm north of Gettysburg, the restaurant has an expansive menu that includes foot-long franks, steaks (cut in house daily), sizzling fajitas, and pasta dishes. The house-made peanut butter pie is a home run. Big LCD TVs and a full-

service bar make Eddie's a popular place to watch college and pro sports.

Herr Tavern & Publick House (900 Chambersburg Rd., Gettysburg, 717/334-4332, www.herrtavern.com, lunch 11 A.M.–3 P.M. Wed.–Fri. and 11:30 A.M.–3 P.M. Sat., dinner 5–9 P.M. daily, lunch $8–13, dinner $24–34) is an excellent choice for fine dining. Servers are happy to talk guests through the creative menu, which changes weekly, and extensive wine list, a winner of *Wine Enthusiast Magazine*'s Unique Distinction Award. Built in 1815, the tavern was turned into a Confederate hospital during the 1863 clash of armies. It's said that amputated limbs were thrown out of a window into a waiting wagon. Given the gruesomeness of what went down, it's no wonder the staff have some ghost stories to share. Herr Tavern is just west of downtown Gettysburg on U.S. 30. A few miles farther west is another historic and reportedly haunted dining destination. The **◖ Cashtown Inn** (1325 Old Rte. 30, Cashtown, 717/334-9722, www .cashtowninn.com, lunch 11:30 A.M.–2 P.M. and dinner 5 P.M. Tues.–Sat., lunch $6–14, dinner

the Cashtown Inn

$19–32) was also overrun by Confederates during the battle. The general who assumed command of the defeated army's retreat made it his headquarters. Its current owners have resisted the temptation to lure history-hungry tourists with period fare, offering New American cuisine instead. They rely on local farmers and producers for everything from eggs and apples to wines and beers.

If you don't mind a bit of a drive, head to the **Altland House** (Center Square, Abbottstown, 717/259-9535, www.altlandhouse.com), a hotel about midway between Gettysburg and York on U.S. 30. Its main restaurant, **Lulu's Grille and Spirits** (11 A.M.–8 P.M. Tues., 11 A.M.–9 P.M. Wed.–Sat., 11 A.M.–8 P.M. Sun., lunch $7–17, dinner $10–28), is a popular spot for celebrating anniversaries and other special occasions. "Trends" (as in the chef's latest creations) share the menu with "traditions" (as in chicken and crab casserole and meatloaf with red-skinned mashed potatoes). The hotel's **Underside Pub and Eatery** (5–11 P.M. Wed.–Sat., $8–28) offers a more casual setting and live entertainment most Friday and Saturday evenings. You can order off the pub menu at Lulu's and vice versa.

INFORMATION

Visit the website of the **Gettysburg Convention & Visitors Bureau** (717/334-6274, www.gettysburg.travel) to request a free copy of its official visitors guide or peruse a digital version. The CVB operates information desks in the Gettysburg National Military Park Museum and Visitor Center and the David Wills House. For information about Pennsylvania Dutch Country as a whole, visit www.dutchcountryroads.com.

GETTING THERE AND AROUND

Gettysburg is in the center of Adams County, which hugs the Pennsylvania-Maryland line just west of York County. The town is about 40 miles southwest of Harrisburg and 60 miles northwest of Baltimore. **Harrisburg International Airport** (888/235-9442, www.flyhia.com) is served by Air Canada, AirTran Airways, Continental Airlines, Delta Air Lines, United Airlines, and US Airways. They offer daily nonstop service to about a dozen destinations. Note that while locals refer to the airport as HIA, its Federal Aviation Administration booking code is MDT. That's because of its physical location in the borough of Middletown, about eight miles south of Harrisburg. The larger **Baltimore/Washington International Thurgood Marshall Airport** (800/435-9294, www.bwiairport.com) is served by about 25 commercial airlines. Private aircraft can fly into **Gettysburg Regional Airport** (www.flyhia.com) just west of town.

There's no passenger train or commercial bus service into Gettysburg. It's very much a driving destination. Public transportation within Gettysburg debuted in 2009. **Freedom Transit** (717/845-7433, www.ridethetrolley.com) operates trolley-like buses on three fixed routes. The tourist-oriented route, named the Lincoln Line, connects downtown Gettysburg and Gettysburg National Military Park. Lincoln Line service is available 8 A.M.–10 P.M. daily April–November and on a more limited basis in the winter. The cash fare is $1, and transfers are free. An all-day pass is $3 and can be purchased on Freedom Transit's website. Ten-ride and monthly passes are also available. Seniors and children 5 and under ride for free.

POCONO MOUNTAINS

Like New York's Catskills and the Berkshires of Massachusetts and Connecticut, Pennsylvania's Poconos are synonymous with R&R. Less than two hours by car from New York City and Philadelphia, the highlands of northeast Pennsylvania have provided respite from the rigors of urban life since the early 1800s, when people arrived by wagon to "take in the air" and scenery. For decades, the big draw was the dramatic Delaware Water Gap, a pass through the mountains carved by the Delaware River. Touted as one of the country's 15 scenic marvels in a 19th-century guidebook, the Gap gave birth to a thriving resort industry. In a 1908 ad in *The New York Times,* one hotel promised "commanding views for 30 miles in every direction of the grandest scenery east of the Rockies" (and, of course, "most modern

sanitary arrangements"). It wasn't unusual for mom and the kids to spend whole summers at the Gap. Dads arrived by the trainful on weekends.

The Gap's popularity as a resort area waned in the years following World War I, in part because cars changed the way people vacationed. But the Poconos region was far from finished as a vacation destination. In the mid-1920s, an energy company dammed a creek near the town of Hawley, 20 miles north of the Gap. The hydroelectric project created a recreational gem: Lake Wallenpaupack. With 52 miles of shoreline, it was the largest man-made lake in Pennsylvania. (It's since slipped to third.) During World War II, many young GIs whisked their girlfriends to the Poconos before shipping overseas or while on leave. When

© INAJEEP

HIGHLIGHTS

◖ Delaware Water Gap National Recreation Area: Canoeists are cuckoo for this park, which features 40 miles of calm river. Invest in a mask and snorkel for a face-down drift down the Delaware (page 255).

◖ Bushkill Falls: This privately owned piece of nature's artwork is hyped as "The Niagara of Pennsylvania." Hyperbole? You decide (page 258).

◖ Lehigh Gorge State Park: Roiling white water and a 25-mile rail-trail make this park a must-visit for active sorts. Feeling lazy? Hop on the train that chugs through the river gorge (page 268).

◖ Hickory Run State Park: The otherworldly boulder field in the northeast corner of this expansive state park is a National Natural Landmark (page 270).

◖ Ski Areas: With nearly a dozen major ski areas, northeast Pennsylvania is the state's sports capital (page 271).

◖ Ricketts Glen State Park: Home to the 94-foot Ganoga Falls – and 21 other named waterfalls – this exceptionally scenic park is hiker heaven (page 296).

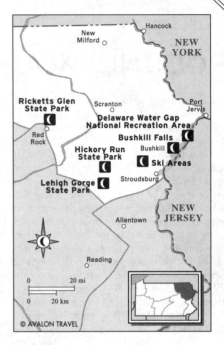

LOOK FOR ◖ TO FIND RECOMMENDED SIGHTS, ACTIVITIES, DINING, AND LODGING.

Johnny came marching home, he was itching to get married. The post-war surge in marriages spawned a proliferation of honeymoon resorts in the Poconos. In 1971 a photo of lovebirds smooching in the heart-shaped hot tub of one such resort appeared in *Life* magazine, sealing the region's reputation as "Honeymoon Capital of the World."

By then, the region was also enjoying a reputation as a ski destination. Pennsylvania's first commercial ski area opened in the Poconos—part of the vast Appalachians—in the 1940s and helped to pioneer snowmaking technology in the 1950s. The industry snowballed in the years that followed. Today there are nearly a dozen major ski areas in northeast

Pennsylvania. Thanks to arsenals of snow guns, they're not completely at the mercy of Mother Nature.

Because of the concentration of ski slopes, some people think of the Poconos as a winter destination first and foremost. That's a mistake. Indeed, winter is the off-season for many hotels and other tourism-reliant businesses in these parts. There's plenty to do in the warmer months, thanks largely to the region's rivers and lakes. The water gap that captivated Victorian-era urbanites is now the centerpiece of a large national park beloved by canoeists for its 40 miles of calm river. To its west is a state park encompassing 30 bumpy miles of the Lehigh River, a tributary of the Delaware.

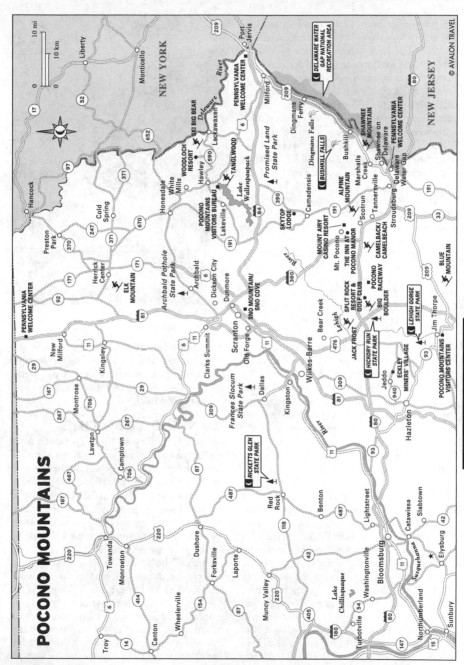

POCONO MOUNTAINS

POCONO MOUNTAINS

© AVALON TRAVEL

NEW YORK

NEW JERSEY

DELAWARE WATER GAP NATIONAL RECREATION AREA

PENNSYLVANIA WELCOME CENTER

Port Jervis

Milford

Dingmans Ferry

Dingmans Falls

BUSHKILL FALLS

Bushkill

SHAWNEE MOUNTAIN

Shawnee on Delaware

PENNSYLVANIA WELCOME CENTER

Delaware Water Gap

Marshalls Creek

Tannersville

Stroudsburg

Scotrun

CAMELBACK/ CAMELBEACH

BLUE MOUNTAIN

ALPINE MOUNTAIN

Camadensis

MOUNT AIRY CASINO RESORT

THE INN AT POCONO MANOR

Mt. Pocono

POCONO RACEWAY

SPLIT ROCK RESORT & GOLF CLUB

BIG BOULDER

LEHIGH GORGE STATE PARK

Jim Thorpe

JACK FROST

HICKORY RUN STATE PARK

POCONO MOUNTAINS VISITORS CENTER

ECKLEY MINERS' VILLAGE

Jeddo

Hazleton

SKYTOP LODGE

SNO MOUNTAIN/ SNO COVE

Bear Creek

Wilkes-Barre

Scranton

Old Forge

Dunmore

Dickson City

Archbald

Archbald Pothole State Park

ELK MOUNTAIN

Herrick Center

PENNSYLVANIA WELCOME CENTER

Clarks Summit

Dallas

Frances Slocum State Park

Kingston

Kingsley

New Milford

Montrose

Lawton

Camptown

PICKETTS GLEN STATE PARK

Red Rock

Benton

Lightstreet

Slabtown

Catawissa

Elysburg

Bloomsburg

Washingtonville

Lake Chilliisquaque

Turbotville

Northumberland

Sunbury

Muncy Valley

Laporte

Forksville

Dushore

Wheelerville

Canton

Troy

Towanda

Monroeton

Liberty

Monticello

Hancock

Preston Park

Cold Spring

Honesdale

White Mills

Hawley

WOODLOCH RESORT

SKI BIG BEAR

TANGLWOOD

Lackawaxen

POCONO MOUNTAINS VISITORS BUREAU

Lakeville

Lake Wallenpaupack

Promised Land State Park

Delaware River

10 mi

10 km

POCONO MOUNTAINS

Lehigh Gorge State Park, as it's called, offers white-water boating in spring, summer, and fall. The Lackawaxen River, which flows through the quaint towns of Honesdale and Hawley on its way to the Delaware, is a magnet for fly fishers. And then there are the lakes—more than 150 in all. Still the largest in northeast Pennsylvania, Lake Wallenpaupack is alive with powerboats, Jet Skis, and sailboats when it's not frozen. (The "Pack" isn't totally useless when it is frozen. The annual Ice Tee Golf Tournament takes place atop it. Great ice fishing, too.)

The region's reputation as a honeymoon destination began to wane in the 1980s, as more and more newlyweds jetted to faraway places like Paris and Hawaii. Out of favor and out of date, several Poconos couples' resorts closed in the 1990s. Three remain, so it's still possible to book a room that would make Austin Powers go "Yeah, baby!" Round beds: check. Champagne glass hot tubs: check. In-room heart-shaped pools: yeah, baby.

PG-rated fun can be had at any number of family resorts. The activities lists at some of these places include everything from arts and crafts to horse-drawn sleigh rides to Wii. Another family-friendly destination: Pocono Raceway. The 2.5-mile super speedway hosts three NASCAR series races each summer. It's the only NASCAR track in Pennsylvania and one of only four in the northeastern United States, which helps explain why its marquee events attract tens of thousands of fans.

Just west of Poconos country are the cities of Scranton and Wilkes-Barre, former nerve centers of the anthracite coal-mining industry. They're hard at work reinventing themselves. With a population of about 72,000, Scranton is the largest city in northeast Pennsylvania and among the 10 largest in the state. It's home to the only "Big Boy" steam locomotive in the East, which puts it on the bucket list of many a rail fan. Wilkes-Barre's Mohegan Sun at Pocono Downs was the first casino to open in Pennsylvania after lawmakers legalized electronic gaming in 2004. It's now one of two in this corner of the state. The other, Mount

© JEFF GREENBERG

jet skiers on Lake Wallenpaupack

Airy Casino Resort, was built on the site of a razed Poconos couples resort. By the look of their parking lots, northeast Pennsylvania may soon be synonymous with R&R&R (rest and recreation and risk).

PLANNING YOUR TIME

How you organize your time depends on what brought you to this corner of Pennsylvania. If it's an outdoor activity such as skiing or snowboarding or white-water rafting, you probably live within a couple of hours' drive, and you're probably looking at a day trip. If it's reconnecting with your honey or your family at an amenity-rich resort, you're probably looking to stay for as long as you can afford.

Railroad buffs should devote half a day to Scranton, home to Steamtown National Historic Site and the Electric City Trolley Museum. Steamtown is one of several places in northeast Pennsylvania where you can hop aboard a vintage railcar. The truest of rail fans will also want to ride the Stourbridge Line through the Lake Region and the Lehigh

© DIANA WILLIAMS MORGAN

Train buffs will enjoy touring Steamtown in Scranton.

Gorge Scenic Railway out of Jim Thorpe. Fans of *The Office* may also wish to devote a few hours to Scranton, the setting for the hit TV sitcom. Northeast Pennsylvania was at one time a world leader in coal production, and some communities have transformed the detritus of that industry into tourist attractions. History buffs can descend into once-active mines in Scranton and Lansford, tour the company town of Eckley, and visit the jail where Irish miners fingered as murderous "Molly Maguires" were hanged.

Pocono Mountains

Geologically speaking, the Poconos aren't actually mountains. They're part of the Allegheny Plateau, which in turn is part of the Appalachian Plateau. Not being a geologist, this writer is ill-equipped to explain the differences between plateaus and mountains. Suffice it to say that the Poconos are no Rockies. "Hilly" is a better descriptor than "mountainous" for the four counties marketed under the Pocono Mountains banner. The county seats—Carbon County's Jim Thorpe, Monroe County's Stroudsburg, Pike County's Milford, and Wayne County's Honesdale—are

charming little towns. But small-town charm isn't what lures the majority of visitors to the Poconos. Most come for the sprawling resorts, snow-covered slopes, or some form of waterlogged adventure.

◖ DELAWARE WATER GAP NATIONAL RECREATION AREA

The Delaware Water Gap, a wide chasm cut through Kittatinny Ridge by the Delaware River, attracted urbanites by the trainful in the latter half of the 1800s. Why? "From the

© POCONO MOUNTAINS VISITORS BUREAU/800POCONOS.COM

Delaware Water Gap beach

mountain peaks on every hand open magnificent vistas, and from the river both below and above the chasm views are of marvelous extent," crowed *The New York Times* in June 1897, ticking off names of prominent New Yorkers recently arrived in the area. "Spurs jutting out from the main range give endless variety to the landscape, while hollows, gaps, and ravines add their countless beauties." As one of the most popular summering spots in the eastern United States, the Gap got a lot of ink in *The Times*. Its popularity persisted into the early 20th century. Theodore Roosevelt paid a visit to the palatial Water Gap House, one of many hotels in the area, in 1910. A young Fred Astaire returned repeatedly with his family.

But the advent of automobiles expanded the realm of possibility for vacationers. In: the weekend road trip. Out: summering at large hotels near rail lines. It didn't help that the Water Gap House and the Kittatinny Hotel, grandest of the Gap's hotels, burned to the ground in 1915 and 1931, respectively. The

Great Depression dealt a fatal blow to most of the remaining hotels and boarding houses.

Today the Gap is enjoying another heyday—not as a resort area but as a recreation area. Its core constituency is outdoorsy people rather than society people. The chasm in Kittatinny Ridge is the centerpiece of Delaware Water Gap National Recreation Area (www .nps.gov/dewa), one of the 10 most visited areas in the National Park System. Established in 1965 under President Lyndon Johnson, the park encompasses 40 miles of the Delaware River, which forms the boundary between Pennsylvania and New Jersey, and 67,000 acres of river valley in both states.

Getting your bearings is job one. The park is about five miles wide and 35 miles long, with the geologic Gap and the village named for it at its south end and the pretty town of Milford at its north end. U.S. 209 is the major north–south artery on the Pennsylvania side. The exceptionally scenic Old Mine Road runs the length of the park on the New Jersey side. There are only three bridges spanning the

Delaware within the park: the I-80 bridge at the south end of the park; the privately owned Dingmans Bridge linking Pennsylvania Route 739 and New Jersey Route 560; and the U.S. 206 bridge near Milford. Maps and brochures are available on the park website, but you can save a lot of printer ink by stopping at one of two seasonal visitors centers staffed by rangers. The **Kittatinny Point Visitor Center** (off I-80 just east of Delaware River bridge, NJ, 908/496-4458) at the south end of the park and the **Dingmans Falls Visitor Center** (Johnny Bee Rd. off U.S. 209, Dingmans Ferry, PA, 570/828-2253) about 26 miles north of I-80 are open daily Memorial Day weekend through Labor Day weekend and weekends in the fall. Weekday visitors can also get information at park headquarters (River Rd. off U.S. 209, Bushkill, PA, 570/426-2452, 8 A.M.–4:30 P.M. Mon.–Fri.), open year-round.

Boating and Swimming

If you've come to float down the river, as many people do, you can get all the information and equipment you need from one of the dozen or so commercial liveries authorized to drop off and pick up paddlers within the recreation area. They generally open sometime in April or May and close at the end of October. More than 400 miles long, the Delaware is the longest undammed river east of the Mississippi. The Middle Delaware River, which flows through the recreation area, is calm enough for even novice paddlers to navigate sans guide. On hot days it's not unusual for people to jump ship and float awhile in their life jackets. Liveries near I-80 and the south end of the park include **Adventure Sports** (U.S. 209, Marshalls Creek, 570/223-0505, www.adventuresport.com) and **Chamberlain Canoes** (River Rd., Shawnee on Delaware, 800/422-6631, www.chamberlain canoes.com). Both rent canoes, kayaks, and rafts for trips ranging from an hour or two to several days. Chamberlain Canoes also offers tubes. Most liveries closer to the north end of the park facilitate trips on the Upper Delaware, with its abundant white water, as well as the placid Middle Delaware. Best of the bunch:

Kittatinny Canoes (800/356-2852, www.kittatinny.com), which has a massive fleet of canoes, rafts, kayaks, and tubes that it dispatches from various locations, plus two riverfront campgrounds and a paintball operation. In business since 1941, it even provides pickup service for customers who arrive in the riverfront city of Port Jervis, New York, by Metro-North train or Short Line bus.

The Middle Delaware is an exceptionally clean river, so don't hesitate to take a dip. Two beaches, both on the Pennsylvania side of the park, are staffed with lifeguards in summer: **Smithfield Beach** (River Rd., 3.2 miles north of the village of Shawnee on Delaware) and **Milford Beach** (off U.S. 209 near Milford). A per-vehicle fee of $7 on weekdays and $10 on weekends and holidays is collected. Beach users who arrive by foot or bicycle pay $1 apiece. Swimming is prohibited in certain areas, including within 50 feet of any boat launch. Invest in a snorkel and mask for a memorable drift down the river. Scuba diving is permitted.

Fishing

Prefer catching fish to swimming with them? Smallmouth bass, muskellunge, walleye, catfish, and panfish are found in the Delaware River. Schools of hard-fighting shad, which live in the ocean but migrate upstream to spawn, reach the park around May. A license from either Pennsylvania or New Jersey will do for fishing on the Delaware or from its banks. To fish in its trout-laden tributaries or in small lakes and ponds, you'll need the appropriate state license.

Hiking

The river may be its main attraction, but DWGNRA (that's Delaware Water Gap National Recreation Area for the texting generation, LOL) has plenty to offer to landlubbers, starting with 100 miles of trails. More than 25 miles of the famed Appalachian Trail are within the recreation area. Thru-hikers cross the geological Gap via a walkway along I-80. Climbing the Gap's gateposts—Mount Tammany in New Jersey

© WALKING GEEK

Lovely trails wind through Delaware Water Gap National Recreation Area.

and Mount Minsi in Pennsylvania—is popular with day hikers. But you don't have to climb more than 1,000 vertical feet for a visual feast. Several short trails on the Pennsylvania side of the park lead to striking waterfalls. Near the village of Dingmans Ferry, a Delaware River tributary named Dingmans Creek dives 130 feet. **Dingmans Falls** was privately owned from 1888 to 1975, when the federal government snapped it up, and tourists used to pay for the privilege of seeing it. The base of the falls is at the end of a flat, wheelchair-accessible boardwalk only a quarter of a mile long. Some 240 steps lead to the top. Signs near milepost 14 of U.S. 209 point the way to the Dingmans Falls trailhead and visitors center. The eponymous falls of Raymondskill Creek, which empties into the Delaware a few miles farther upstream, are only a little harder to get to. A short hike through hemlock forest puts you at the upper falls; steep, uneven stairs descend to the middle falls. Look for Raymondskill Road near milepost 18 of U.S. 209.

Guided hiking tours are available through **Edge of the Woods Outdoor Outfitters** (110 Main St., Delaware Water Gap, 570/421-6681, www.edgeofthewoodsoutfitters.com). The store, which carries an impressive selection of outdoor equipment and apparel, also provides shuttle services for Appalachian Trail hikers ($2 per mile one way) and rents mountain bikes ($20 for one hour, $25 for two hours).

Rock climbing and **horseback riding** are among the other land-based activities enjoyed in the park. In winter it's the nearby ski slopes that draw the crowds, but the swish of cross-country skis and shrills of bald eagles break the silence near the icy Delaware.

VICINITY OF NATIONAL RECREATION AREA
◖ Bushkill Falls

A place that bills itself as "The Niagara of Pennsylvania" had better deliver, and Bushkill Falls (Bushkill Falls Rd., off U.S. 209, Bushkill, 570/588-6682, www.visitbushkillfalls.com, opens at 9 A.M. Apr.–Oct., Nov. weather permitting, admission $10, seniors $9, children 4–10 $6) does. No, you can't don a plastic raincoat

© POCONO MOUNTAINS VISITORS BUREAU/800POCONOS.COM

Bushkill Falls

and ride into a waterfall basin aboard a steamship. But you can get close enough to a towering waterfall for a mist bath. You can marvel at the power and beauty of churning water, fill up on fudge and ice cream, and load up on souvenirs. Unlike Niagara, Bushkill Falls is a privately owned attraction. When Charles E. Peters opened it to the public in 1904, charging 10 cents for admission, a single path and a swinging bridge brought visitors to the head of a 100-foot waterfall now known as the Main Falls. Today a series of mostly easy trails connects eight waterfalls. The original is still the best. A 15-minute walk yields a good view of it. For even better vantage points and access to a second waterfall, follow the popular yellow-marked trail, which takes about 45 minutes and crosses several wooden bridges strung across roaring waters. Avid hikers can take in all eight waterfalls via the two-mile Bridal Veil Falls Trail.

Still owned by the Peters family, Bushkill Falls has added a host of kid-friendly amenities over the years. It's now possible to play a round of miniature golf ($5 including souvenir golf ball), ride a paddleboat ($3 per person), fish the still waters of a pair of lakes (permit $3, gear $6), and mine for gemstones ($6–8) without leaving the grounds. Free exhibits on the Lenni Lenape, who inhabited the area hundreds of years ago, and Pennsylvania wildlife feature a full-sized longhouse and mounted animals, respectively. In addition to fudge and ice cream, food options include burgers, pizza, and funnel cakes. Do-it-yourselfers can prepare a feast at the free picnic area with its charcoal grills. The grounds close between 4 P.M. and 7 P.M. depending on the time of year and day of week. Shops and activity areas close an hour before the grounds.

Grey Towers National Historic Site

The onetime home of Gifford Pinchot, America's first forester and founder of the U.S. Forest Service, is open to the public as Grey Towers National Historic Site (Pine Acres Ln. and Old Owego Turnpike, Milford, 570/296-9630, www.fs.fed.us/na/gt, open Memorial Day weekend–Oct., weekends in Nov., and most days in mid- and late Dec., admission $6, seniors $5, children 12–17 $3). Pinchot was still a kid when his father, having made a fortune in the wallpaper business in New York, retired and moved his family to his hometown of Milford. Fresh out of his teens, Pinchot decided to pursue forestry. But in the 1880s, such a profession didn't yet exist in America. After graduating from Yale University in 1889, he enrolled at L'Ecole Nationale Forestiere in France but dropped out after a year, thirsting for practical experience. His family's wealth and connections helped pave the way for his ascension, in less than a decade, to head of the U.S. Department of Agriculture's small Division of Forestry, which would become the larger Forest Service within a few years. Under his watch, the number of national forests climbed from 32 in 1898 to 149 in 1910. A confidant of President Theodore Roosevelt, Pinchot was fired by his successor, William Taft. But he remained in the public eye, forming and financing the National Conservation Association and serving two terms as Pennsylvania governor.

POCONO MOUNTAINS

© POCONO MOUNTAINS VISITORS BUREAU/800POCONOS.COM

Grey Towers

During World War II he developed a special fishing kit for Navy sailors adrift in lifeboats and was credited with saving countless lives. Pinchot died in 1946 at the age of 81.

His son donated Grey Towers, the family's Milford estate, to the Forest Service in 1964. Visitors must be accompanied by a guide to enter the mansion, which resembles a medieval French castle. Built in the 1880s, the house originally had 43 rooms. Gifford Pinchot's wife, Cornelia, found it rather dreary and had dividing walls knocked down to create larger rooms. "She's revised and edited and altered this house practically beyond recognition," he told the *Saturday Evening Post* in 1922. She also oversaw the construction of a playhouse for their son, a stone archives for her husband's papers, and even a moat. The moat might have been her crowning achievement were it not for the Finger Bowl, a unique outdoor dining table designed to seat up to 18 people. The table consists of a pool of water surrounded by a stone ledge wide enough to accommodate a place setting. Food was floated on the water in wooden bowls.

One-hour tours of the first-floor rooms and several garden areas are offered 11 A.M.–4 P.M. daily from Memorial Day weekend through October. On Saturdays and Sundays, three-floor tours are available at 10 A.M. and 4 P.M. Call or check the website for tour times in November and December.

The Columns

A bloodstained American flag is the artifact extraordinaire at the museum of the Pike County Historical Society, a.k.a. The Columns (608 Broad St., Milford, 570/296-8126, www.pike countyhistoricalsociety.org, 1–4 P.M. Wed.–Sun. July–Aug., 1–4 P.M. Wed. and Sat.–Sun. Sept.–June, admission $5, students $3, children 12 and under free). The large 36-star flag was draped over a balustrade in Ford's Theatre on the night of April 14, 1865, when John Wilkes Booth shot Abraham Lincoln in the back of the head. Thomas Gourlay, a part-time stage manager at the Washington D.C. theater, placed the flag under the mortally wounded president's head. Gourlay kept the flag and gave it to his daughter, who moved to Pennsylvania's Pike County in 1888. Her son donated the flag to the historical society, along with other artifacts from the Civil War era. Stage costumes worn by his famous mother, who had a lead role in the play that was in progress when Lincoln was assassinated, are highlights of the museum's collection of 18th- and 19th-century clothing. The Columns, a 1904 Neoclassical mansion, also houses Native American artifacts, early medical equipment and beauty equipment, antique musical instruments, and a stagecoach built in the mid-1800s. One of the 11 exhibit rooms is dedicated to the brilliant logician and scientist Charles Sanders Pierce, who moved to Milford in the late 1800s. Pierce's ideas influenced the likes of Albert Einstein long after his 1914 death.

LAKE REGION

More than 100 of the approximately 150 lakes in the Poconos are located in what's known, appropriately enough, as the Lake Region. Largest of them is the 5,700-acre Lake Wallenpaupack.

Created in the 1920s by an energy company, the lake provides more than hydroelectric power. It's the place to go for powerboating in the Poconos. It's also a popular destination for sailing, fishing, and camping. The countless residential and vacation homes that ring the lake are testament to its recreational appeal. In 2005 *The New York Times* observed that an increasing number of New Yorkers were weekending in the itty-bitty town of Hawley, just north of Lake Wallenpaupack, drawn by its "old-fashioned charm" and the body of water in its backyard.

The largest town in the Lake Region is Honesdale, about 15 minutes from Hawley. With its Victorian architecture, tall church steeples, and quaint shops, the Wayne County seat is worth a stroll. Honesdale is charming enough to have inspired the lyrics of *Winter Wonderland,* written in 1934 by Honesdale native Dick Smith and recorded by everyone from Perry Como to Ozzy Osbourne.

Flowing through the Lake Region is the Lackawaxen River, a 25-mile tributary of the Delaware that's beloved by fly fishers. Bald eagles seem to love it too, which brings out the birders. In 2010 the state Department of Conservation and Natural Resources named the Lackawaxen "River of the Year," calling it a "recreational treasure."

Lake Wallenpaupack

Lake Wallenpaupack—fun to say, tricky to spell—was the largest man-made lake in the state upon its creation for hydroelectric purposes in the mid-1920s. Since then it's been relegated to number three by Pymatuning Reservoir and Raystown Lake in northwest and central Pennsylvania, respectively. But the "Pack" is plenty big for boating, even of the *vroom-vroom* variety. For no-fee boat launching, head to Mangan Cove, off Route 590 about a mile west of the junction of Route 590 and U.S. 6.

If you don't have your own vessel, you're not out of luck. **Pocono Action Sports** (969 Rte. 507, Greentown, 570/857-0779, www .lighthouseharbor.com, 9 A.M.–5 P.M. daily June–Sept.) rents powerboats along with water

skis, wakeboards, kneeboards, and tubes. Sailboats are also available for those with sailing experience. Boats can be rented for a full day (9 A.M.–5 P.M.) or half a day (8:30 A.M.– 12:30 P.M. or 1–5 P.M.). Full-day rental rates range from $210 for a 19-foot sailboat to $395 for a 22-foot pontoon boat that holds up to 10 people. Water skis and other tow-riffic accessories are $35 per day. Located at Lighthouse Harbor Marina, Pocono Action Sports also offers waterskiing and wakeboarding lessons on weekends by appointment.

If Jet Skiing is more your speed, **Rubber Duckie Boat Rentals** (junction of Routes 507 and 390, Tafton, 570/226-3930, www.rubber duckieboatrentals.com, 9 A.M.–6 P.M. daily May–late Oct.) is the place to go. Three-seater Sea Doo personal watercraft are $70 for half an hour, $110 for an hour. Prices include fuel. Rubber Duckie also rents powerboats, Sunfish sailboats, and canoes by the hour. Sunfish are simple enough for sailing virgins. Waterskis, wakeboards, kneeboards, and tubes are available. Pack a cooler for an island picnic. Lake Wallenpaupack's four islands—Epply, Kipp, Burns, and Cairns—have grills and tables. All but Burns have toilet facilities. Camping, open fires, and alcoholic beverages are prohibited on the islands.

Perfect for anyone who wants to get on the water but leave the navigating to pros, the **Wallenpaupack Scenic Tour Boat** (2487 U.S. 6, Hawley, 570/226-3293, www.wallen paupackboattour.com, ticket $14, seniors $13, children 12 and under $10) is an hour-long cruise aboard a patio boat. (Not to be confused with a party boat. There's no food, booze, or DJ on this ride.) In summer, tours depart every hour on the hour 11 A.M.–6 P.M. daily. Sunset cruises are offered on occasion. The tour boats also ply the lake on weekends in late spring and early fall, pushing off every hour from noon to 4 P.M., weather permitting.

The lake, its islands, and most of its 52-mile shoreline are property of PPL Corp., which gave birth to the lake when it dammed Wallenpaupack Creek. The Allentown-based energy company

© RARE BRICK PHOTOGRAPHY

sunset at Lake Wallenpaupack

maintains four **campgrounds** for the general public. Each has tent and trailer sites, a small general store, picnic grounds, and boat docking and launching facilities. The campgrounds are open from the last Saturday in April to the third Sunday in October; a limited number of seasonal campsites are available. Contact the campgrounds directly for camping and docking/launching rates and to make reservations.

With 29 sites, **Caffrey** (431 Lakeshore Dr., Lakeville, 570/226-4608) is the smallest of the campgrounds. Good prevailing westerlies make it popular with sailboaters. **Ironwood Point** (155 Burns Hill Rd., Greentown, 570/857-0880, www.ironwood point.com) is situated on a wooded hill overlooking the lake. Among its approximately 60 campsites are 13 lakefront sites for walk-in camping. Located at the southern tip of the 13-mile lake, **Ledgedale** (153 Ledgedale Rd., Greentown, 570/689-2181) has 70 campsites. It's adjacent to PPL's **Ledgedale Natural Area** (Kuhn Hill Rd., Greentown, open dawn to dusk), an 80-acre wooded tract with abundant wildlife and two miles of hiking trails. Just off U.S. 6, **Wilsonville** (113 Ammon Dr., Hawley,

570/226-4382, www.wilsonvillecampground .com) is the largest of PPL's campgrounds with 160 sites and closest to the dam. It's adjacent to the only **public beach** (U.S. 6 just west of Rte. 507 junction, behind Lake Wallenpaupack Visitors Center) on Lake Wallenpaupack. Operated by Palmyra Township, the beach is open 9 A.M.–6 P.M. daily from Memorial Day weekend through Labor Day weekend. Admission is $3 for adults, $1 for children under 10. Swimming is prohibited at PPL's recreation areas. So are pets and alcohol.

Hunting isn't permitted on PPL property, but **anglers** are welcome year-round. The "Pack" serves up some big trout and walleye, along with bass, muskellunge, pickerel, and yellow perch. Call **Bill's Guide Service** (570/698-6035 or 570/347-4484, www.billsguideservice.com) or **Ray's Fishing Guide Service** (570/654-5436, www.raysguideservice.webs.com) for a helping hand on the lake. Wallenpaupack Creek and the Lackawaxen River, which the lake drains into, offer mountain stream fishing. Both are stocked by the Pennsylvania Fish & Boat Commission. Anglers on the Lackawaxen should watch for sudden rises in water level, which occur when water is released from PPL's hydroelectric plant. Call 800/807-2474 or visit www.lakelevel ppl.com for information on lake elevation and discharge to the river.

For general information about the lake and the recreational opportunities it affords, go to www.pplpreserves.com. Information about area attractions, lodging properties, and restaurants is available at the Pocono Mountains Visitors Bureau's Lake Wallenpaupack Visitors Center (U.S. 6 just west of Rte. 507 junction, 570/226-2141, 10 A.M.–6 P.M. daily Memorial Day–Labor Day, 9 A.M.–5 P.M. daily rest of year).

Dorflinger Glass Museum

The village of White Mills lies halfway between Hawley and Honesdale on U.S. 6. Blink and you could miss it. There's little to suggest that White Mills was once a bustling industrial center, but that's exactly what it became after Christian Dorflinger came to town in the 1860s. Only in his 30s, the French-born glassmaker had already opened three factories in Brooklyn, New York. Sleepy little White Mills offered an escape from the rigors of city life, but Dorflinger wasn't ready to retire. He built a glass factory in the hamlet, which became home to so many workmen and craftsmen that it could no longer be called a hamlet. The White Mills plant produced some of the most exquisite cut lead crystal in the country. Customers included several U.S. presidents, the Vanderbilts, the Prince of Wales, and Cuban president Mario Menocal, who commissioned a 2,300-piece set of tableware. Dorflinger died in 1915, and his glass empire collapsed several years later, undone by the decline in demand for wine and table services amid World War I and Prohibition.

In 1980 Dorflinger's White Mills estate opened to the public as the **Dorflinger-Suydam Wildlife Sanctuary** (Elizabeth St. and Long Ridge Rd., White Mills, 570/253-1185, www.dorflinger.org, open dawn–dusk daily, free admission). Several miles of trails traverse the 600-acre sanctuary, which is home to the Dorflinger Glass Museum (10 A.M.–4 P.M. Wed.–Sat. and 1–4 P.M. Sun.

May–Oct., Sat.–Sun. only in Nov., admission $3, seniors $2.50, children 6–18 $1.50). Opened in 1989, the museum boasts the largest collection of Dorflinger glass in the country—more than 900 pieces strong. The gift shop demands as much time as the galleries. It's filled with glass treasures, including Christmas ornaments, vases, paperweights, jewelry, and kaleidoscopes.

The wildlife sanctuary hosts the summer-long **Wildflower Music Festival,** which attracts touring performers. Songstress Judy Collins made an appearance in 2009. Dates, times, and ticket prices are available on the sanctuary's website. Bring lawn chairs or a blanket for the natural amphitheater.

Stourbridge Line Rail Excursions

If you've never been on a moving train ambushed by gunmen on galloping horses, you're missing out. Head to Honesdale on a summer Saturday for the "Great Train Robbery," one of a variety of Stourbridge Line Rail Excursions (32 Commercial St., Honesdale, 570/253-1960, www.waynecountycc.com). The 3.5-hour adventure, which includes a one-hour stopover in downtown Hawley for shopping and sightseeing, is $22 for adults, $17 for children 12 and under. Don't tell the kids what's in store, and ready your camera to capture their surprised looks when the marauders materialize.

October's "Fall Foliage" excursions are the Stourbridge Line's most popular. Four and a half hours long, they begin in Honesdale and continue past Hawley to the Victorian village of Lackawaxen, where passengers tour the Zane Grey Museum, located in the house that Western novelist Zane Grey called home in the 1910s. Tickets are $29 for adults, $27 for seniors, $17 for children 12 and under. Other fall excursions include a Halloween-themed trip to a pumpkin patch and, for the 21 and over crowd, "Grape Express," which features wine-tasting at the historic Falls Port Inn and Restaurant in Hawley. Winter brings a chance to share the train with Santa, Rudolph, and friends. The Easter Bunny hops on board for the "Bunny Run" in spring.

© JEFF GREENBERG

Stourbridge Lion replica

Honesdale has a special place in railroading history—so special that the town calls itself the "Birthplace of the American Railroad." On August 8, 1829, a steam locomotive named the Stourbridge Lion left Honesdale and ran about a mile and a half to present-day Seelyville, then returned to its starting point. Built in Stourbridge, England, it was the first locomotive to run on a railway in the United States. Its boiler, virtually all that remains of the history-making locomotive, is now in the possession of the Smithsonian Institution. A full-scale replica of the Lion built from the original plans is the pride and joy of the **Wayne County Historical Society** (810 Main St., Honesdale, 570/253-3240, 10 A.M.–4 P.M. Wed.–Sat. mid-Apr.–Dec. and Sun. when excursion train is running, admission $5, children 7–17 $3).

JIM THORPE AND VICINITY

Tucked into the hills and dotted with striking Victorian buildings, the town of Jim Thorpe was known to 19th-century rail excursionists as the "Switzerland of America." Today it's better known as a gateway to outdoor adventure. Rafters, canoeists, and kayakers come for the Lehigh River, which flows through town. North of town, the Lehigh Gorge offers some of the most exciting white water in the East. South of town, the river snakes languidly toward its confluence with the Delaware. Bikers and hikers come for the river-hugging trail between Jim Thorpe and White Haven to its north. Twenty-five miles long, it attracts cross-country skiers when conditions are right. Blue Mountain Ski Area and Big Boulder are just half an hour from Jim Thorpe, making it a good base of operations for alpine skiing enthusiasts. It's okay if you come unprepared for adventure. Finding an outfitter in Jim Thorpe is easier than finding a Starbucks in Seattle. In 2007 National Geographic *Adventure* magazine named the "unassuming outdoors mecca" one of the nation's best places to live and play.

That's the sentiment local officials were shooting for when they renamed the town for an extraordinarily gifted athlete. Prior to

1954, Jim Thorpe was called Mauch Chunk (pronounced mock-CHUNK). In the 19th century, Mauch Chunk thrived as a transportation hub for the anthracite coal so plentiful in the hills around it. Fortunes were made. Mansions and grand hotels rose. It's said that half of America's millionaires lived in Mauch Chunk at one time. By the 1950s, however, Mauch Chunk was in sorry condition. The decline of the coal and railroad industries and the Great Depression had sapped its wealth. In the hopes that a new name would give it new life as a tourist destination, Mauch Chunk officials struck a deal with the widow of the recently deceased Jim Thorpe, former Olympian and pro football and basketball player. Thorpe had been born in Oklahoma and died in California and had no ties to Mauch Chunk whatsoever. No matter. In exchange for his remains, Mauch Chunk and its neighbor across the Lehigh, East Mauch Chunk, merged under the name Jim Thorpe and erected a 20-ton mausoleum for the Native American sports icon.

The town's turnaround wasn't immediate, but turn around it did. With old mansions and new galleries, ample dining and lodging options, and tourism as its lifeblood, the "Switzerland of America" could easily adopt as its tag line the title of a 1951 biopic starring Burt Lancaster: *Jim Thorpe—All American*.

Mauch Chunk Museum and Old Jail Museum

The local history of the town formerly known as Mauch Chunk is colorful enough to captivate non-locals, particularly anyone interested in the evolution of transportation technologies. The discovery of anthracite coal in the wilderness of northeast Pennsylvania was all well and good, but no one was going to get rich until large quantities could be transported to big city markets. As the saying goes, profit motive is the mother of invention (or something like that). Founded in 1818 as a river landing for a mining company, Mauch Chunk witnessed one engineering breakthrough after another. The Mauch Chunk Museum (41 W. Broadway,

Jim Thorpe, 570/325-9190, www.mauchchunk museum.com, 10 A.M.–4 P.M. Tues.–Sun., admission $5, children under 8 $2) boasts working models of those breakthroughs, including the "bear trap lock" that made it possible for coal-laden arks to travel down the Lehigh River from Mauch Chunk. A 30-foot model illustrates the workings of the famous Switchback Railroad, which relied on gravity to move coal down a mountain and became an enormously popular tourist attraction after its usefulness to the mining industry expired in 1872. Housed in a former church, the museum chronicles not just the town's industrial golden age but also its decline in the early 20th century, its peculiar decision to trade its name for the body and name of a sports icon, and its revitalization as Jim Thorpe.

Just down the street, a jail-turned-museum zeroes in on a grim chapter in local history. In the late 1870s, seven Irish coal miners fingered as murderous "Molly Maguires" were hanged in the jail. The story of the Mollies has been told in so many ways that separating fact from

the Carbon County Jail, where the "Molly Maguires" were executed

JIM THORPE, THE MAN

The Pennsylvania capital of Harrisburg was named for the frontiersman who settled it in the early 1700s. British General John Forbes paid tribute to William Pitt, first Earl of Chatham, when he gave the name Pittsburgh to the settlement at the forks of the Ohio River in 1758. The city of Scranton owes its name to a family of 19th-century captains of industry. Loads of towns in the state named for founder William Penn are eponyms for a long-buried someone or other. The town of Jim Thorpe is uncommon in that it's named for a man who made his mark in the 20th century.

James Francis Thorpe was born in 1887 in a single-room cabin in what is now Oklahoma and was then known as Indian Territory. His Native American name, Wa-Tho-Huk, meant "Bright Path," which was prescient indeed. In 1904 he began attending Carlisle Indian School, a trade school of sorts for Native American youths. It was at the boarding school in Carlisle, Pennsylvania, that Thorpe found his calling: athletics. In addition to playing football under legendary coach Glenn "Pop" Warner, he competed in track and field, baseball, lacrosse, and even ballroom dancing. In 1912 the 24-year-old sailed to Europe for the Stockholm Olympics, training aboard the ship. He won the pentathlon and the decathlon by wide margins, setting records that wouldn't be defeated for decades. "Sir, you are the greatest athlete in the world," gushed Sweden's King Gustav V, who presented Thorpe with his medals. The greatest athlete in the world reportedly replied: "Thanks, King." He was celebrated with a ticker-tape parade in New York.

The following year, things took an ugly turn for "Bright Path." After a newspaper reported that Thorpe had played two seasons of semi-professional baseball in North Carolina, he was stripped of his gold medals. His records were struck from the books. The ordeal didn't sour Thorpe on athletics. The 6-foot-1 phenom played six seasons of professional baseball for teams including the New York Giants (now the San Francisco Giants). Pro football also came calling. He played both sports for several years before retiring from baseball in 1919. His career in pro football continued for another decade and included a stint with the Chicago Cardinals (now the Arizona Cardinals). Thorpe was 41 when he finally hung up his cleats.

Over the next two decades, the father of seven struggled to make a living. He held a string of menial jobs, including as a ditch digger and a bouncer, and succumbed to alcoholism. In 1950 Thorpe was voted greatest athlete of the first half of the century in an Associated Press poll, beating out baseball great Babe Ruth. The following year, when he underwent surgery for a cancerous growth on his lower lip, the Associated Press reported

fiction is Herculean work. By some accounts they were a secret fraternity of Irishmen bent on cold-blooded murder of any mine boss who crossed them. By others, they were principled crusaders for the rights of impoverished workers under the cruel boot of industrialists. There's no disputing that the 1860s and 1870s were bloody times in "black diamond" country. A tour of the Old Jail Museum (128 W. Broadway, Jim Thorpe, 570/325-5259, www .theoldjailmuseum.com, noon–4:30 P.M. daily except Wed. Memorial Day–Labor Day and weekends Sept.–Oct., admission $5, seniors and students $4, children 6–12 $3), a fortress-like structure that served as the county jail from 1871 until 1995, is a walk on the macabre side. "Wander eerie dungeon cells," the ads beckon. "Be locked in a real jail cell." Its most irresistible selling point is a dash of the supernatural. Legend has it that on the day of his execution, one of the condemned coal miners pressed a dirty hand against the wall of his cell and swore that his handprint would remain forever as proof of his innocence. Wardens tried mightily to remove the mark, washing, painting, and even re-plastering the wall. But it always returned, or so it's said. See for yourself in cell 17.

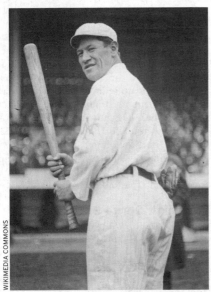

Jim Thorpe in 1913 as a New York Giant

and East Mauch Chunk merged and took the name of the multi-sport star. President Richard Nixon proclaimed April 16, 1973, as "Jim Thorpe Day," noting that "millions of young people who aspire to achievements transcending a disadvantaged background continue to take heart from Jim Thorpe's example." In 1982 his supporters won a hard-fought battle to have his Olympic titles reinstated. Seventy years after demanding the return of its medals, the International Olympic Committee presented replicas to his family.

Visitors to Jim Thorpe, the town, can learn about Jim Thorpe, the man, at the **Jim Thorpe Memorial,** his final resting place. Located along Route 903 on the northeast fringe of town, the memorial features a bronze statue of a football-toting Thorpe and an abstract sculpture, *The Spirit of Thunder and Lightning,* flanked by information panels. Flags representing America, Pennsylvania, and the Olympics stand behind his gravestone, inscribed with the words of King Gustav V. The town pays tribute to its namesake on the third weekend of every May. The **Jim Thorpe Birthday Celebration** (570/325-5810, www.jimthorpe.org, free) kicks off with a Native American ritual at the memorial, but most festivities, including a torch-lighting ceremony and a large Chinese auction, take place at Josiah White Park in the heart of town.

that the patient was "flat broke." He died on March 28, 1953, after suffering a heart attack in his trailer home in Lomita, California.

The posthumous honors were many. In 1954 the Pennsylvania towns of Mauch Chunk

Asa Packer Mansion

Sitting high on a hill overlooking Jim Thorpe is the onetime home of railroad magnate Asa Packer. Born into humble circumstances in Connecticut, Packer was the wealthiest man in Pennsylvania (and one of the wealthiest in the country) by the time he died in 1879. Built in 1861, his mansion (Packer Ave., Jim Thorpe, 570/325-3229, www.asapackermansion.com, 11 A.M.–4:15 P.M. daily Memorial Day–Oct. and weekends Apr.–May and Nov.–mid-Dec., admission $8, seniors $7, children 6–18 $5) is unusual as vestiges of the region's industrial heyday go because it looks essentially as

it did when the Packers called it home. Their personal possessions still fill the 18-room Italianate villa. That's because Asa Packer's daughter Mary Packer Cummings, who died in 1912, willed the mansion and its contents to the town. Then known as Mauch Chunk, the town wasn't certain what to do with the house, and so it stood dormant for 44 years. A local Lions Club opened it to the public in 1956. Among the priceless objects inside is Mary's 1905 orchestrion—basically an orchestra in a box. It's the only working orchestrion of its kind in the country.

The only way to explore the mansion is by

docent-guided tour. Tours are offered every half hour beginning at 11:15 A.M. and can last an hour depending on group size and level of interest. Don't down a Big Gulp before your arrival; there's no public restroom on premises. Docents dole out information about Asa Packer, who arrived in Mauch Chunk in 1832 after hearing that men were needed to captain coal barges. In time he became a contractor for the construction of locks on the Lehigh River. Quite wealthy by the 1850s, he sank his money into a yet-unfinished railroad. The original line of Packer's Lehigh Valley Railroad opened in 1855, stretching from Mauch Chunk to Easton, Pennsylvania. The "Route of the Black Diamond," as the railroad came to be called, proved a gold mine for Packer. Unlike the Lehigh Canal, it could operate even in winter. Packer served two terms in Congress in the 1850s and ran for the Democratic nomination for president and for Pennsylvania's governorship in the 1860s. He also founded Lehigh University in Bethlehem, Pennsylvania.

Next door to the Asa Packer Mansion is another marvelous Victorian. Built in 1874, it was home to Asa Packer's son Harry, a railroad engineer who died just a decade later in his 30s. The mansion may look familiar if you've visited Walt Disney World's Magic Kingdom; it's said to have inspired the Florida theme park's *Haunted Mansion* attraction. Today the **Harry Packer Mansion** (19 Packer Ave., Jim Thorpe, 570/325-8566, www.murdermansion .com, $150–250) is a B&B best known for its murder mystery weekends.

No. 9 Coal Mine & Museum

The coal veins to which Asa Packer owed his mind-blowing wealth were mined by men who lived hand to mouth. Their story takes front and center at No. 9 Coal Mine & Museum (9 Dock St., Lansford, 570/645-7074, www .no9mine.com, museum open Wed.–Sun. year-round, mine tours May–Oct., museum admission $3, with mine tour $7), a 10-mile drive from Jim Thorpe. A train carries visitors into the belly of the anthracite mine, a workplace from 1855 to 1972 and a tourist attraction

since 2002. The guided tour continues on foot to areas including a miner's hospital and a passageway originally used by coal-hauling mules. The museum is located above ground in a former "wash shanty," the coal mine equivalent of a locker room. On display are loads of tools, a tableau of an 1800s miner's kitchen, and life-sized figures of a mine mule and a boy tasked with directing the beast of burden. While the museum is open Wednesday–Sunday year-round, mine tours are limited to May–October. The museum opens at 10 A.M. on tour days and noon on non-tour days, closing at 4. Tours are offered Friday–Sunday in May; Thursday–Sunday from June through August; and Saturday and Sunday only or by appointment after Labor Day.

◖ Lehigh Gorge State Park

Lehigh Gorge (570/443-0400, www.dcnr.state .pa.us/stateparks/Parks/lehighgorge.aspx) is *the* place to go for white-water boating in northeast Pennsylvania. The long, snaking state park contains about 30 miles of the Lehigh River, from the Francis E. Walter Dam in the north to Jim Thorpe in the south. This section of the river offers Class II and III rapids in a season that stretches from March through October and sometimes into November. Left in the hands of Mother Nature, the white-water season would be woefully short. But the U.S. Army Corps of Engineers, which manages the dam, likes to see people have a good time. It releases loads of water on select weekends, providing for rollicking rides even during the hot months of July and August. The white-water release schedule is available at www.nap.usace .army.mil/Projects/FEWalter/index.htm.

Inexperienced boaters should very definitely engage the services of a guide, and there's no shortage of them in or near Jim Thorpe. **Pocono Whitewater** (1519 Rte. 903, 570/325-3655, www.whitewaterrafting.com), **Jim Thorpe River Adventures** (1 Adventure Ln., 570/325-2570, www.jtraft.com), and **Whitewater Rafting Adventures** (U.S. 209 and Hunter St./Rte.93, Nesquehoning, 570/669-9127, www.adventurerafting.com), all

© POCONO MOUNTAINS VISITORS BUREAU/800POCONOS.COM

Lehigh Gorge

within 10 minutes of each other, offer **whitewater rafting** through the park as well as float trips on the milder waters south of Jim Thorpe. There's also a rafting outfitter near the midsection of the park, **Whitewater Challengers** (288 N. Stagecoach Rd., Weatherly, 570/443-9532, www.whitewaterchallengers.com). All four offer kayaking clinics.

It's hard to appreciate the beauty of the deep river gorge with its cascading waterfalls and diverse wildlife when you're paddling furiously. It's easier when you're pedaling. The 25-mile **Lehigh Gorge Trail,** which follows an abandoned railroad corridor along the river, has been called one of "America's sweetest rides" by *Outside* magazine. The **biking** is especially sweet in October, at the peak of fall foliage. Start at the park's northern access area, White Haven, for an all-downhill ride to Jim Thorpe. (It's a very slight downhill grade, so you'll still break a sweat.) All of the above-mentioned outfitters rent bikes. Shuttles to and from the trail are available. In winter the trail is open to **cross-country skiers.** The 15-mile section

from White Haven to Penn Haven Junction is also open to **snowmobilers.** To reach the park's White Haven access area from I-80, take exit 273 and follow Route 940 east to the White Haven Shopping Center. Turn right on Main Street and bear right.

Experienced **hikers** may find the rail-trail a bore. Never boring: the **Glen Onoko Falls Trail,** located on state game lands adjacent to the park. The terrain is steep and sometimes treacherous—"we're always in there rescuing people," confides one park ranger—but the payoff is rich. Come in spring to see the cascading falls at their most ferocious. The trail begins at the park's southern access area, Glen Onoko, reached from Coalport Road in Jim Thorpe.

If you have a mind to raft, bike, and hike all in one day, you may be a little bit crazy, but you're not alone. Pocono Whitewater's "Big Day Out" is a chance to do just that. It starts with a hearty breakfast and ends with dinner around a bonfire. In between, participants bike the rail-trail, hike to the Glen Onoko Falls, and raft the Lehigh. The $89.95 price tag includes all necessary equipment as well as breakfast, a box lunch, and a dinner complete with beer and bonfire. Pocono Whitewater offers the outing at least once a month from April through October and ladies-only versions several times during the season. The outfitter's after-dark rafting trips are also worth checking out.

Lehigh Gorge Scenic Railway

Riding the river is one way to see Lehigh Gorge State Park. Riding the rail-trail alongside the river is another. The deliciously lazy way: riding a train through the river gorge. Lehigh Gorge Scenic Railway (U.S. 209, Jim Thorpe, 570/325-8485, www.lgsry.com, weekends and holidays Memorial Day–Dec.) began offering train excursions in 2006, more than 40 years after railroads in the region put the brakes on passenger service. The one-hour trip begins in Jim Thorpe's historic district at a restored train station that now houses a visitors center. The train follows the curves of the Lehigh River for eight miles before returning the way it came.

If it's a beautiful day, make a beeline for the open-air car or the caboose platform.

〔 Hickory Run State Park

Hickory Run State Park (Rte. 534, 18 miles north of Jim Thorpe, 570/443-0400, www .dcnr.state.pa.us/stateparks/parks/hickoryrun. aspx) is home to one of the most striking geologic features in Pennsylvania: a boulder field born of the last glacial period. The field of loosely packed boulders, a National Natural Landmark, is roughly 400 feet by 1,800 feet and at least 12 feet deep—the largest of its kind in the Appalachian Mountains. Its flatness and barrenness are such a contrast to the ridges and dense woods that surround it that you almost feel transported, *Star Trek*–style, to another planet. Located in the northeast corner of Hickory Run, the boulder field can be reached by car via a park road, by foot, and even by snowmobile.

At nearly 16,000 acres, Hickory Run offers more than boulder hopping. **Hunting** and trapping are permitted in most of the park, which adjoins several state game lands.

Hickory Run State Park

Miles of trout streams make it appealing to **anglers.** The Lehigh River, which flows along the park's western boundary, is home to warmwater game fish and panfish as well as trout. **Hikers** can explore more than 40 miles of trails, which are especially enchanting from mid-June to mid-July, when the mountain laurel and rhododendron are in bloom. In winter, 13 of those miles are open to **cross-country skiers** and 21 to **snowmobilers.** Sand Spring Lake, in the recreational hub of the park, has a sand beach open from late May to mid-September and welcomes ice skaters when conditions permit. Nearby is a disc golf course, a large picnic area, and a modern campground open from the second Friday in April to the third Sunday in October. Rustic **camping** is permitted until mid-December. Reserve campsites online at www.pa.reserveworld.com or by calling 888/727-2757.

█ SKI AREAS

The Pocono Mountains region is the state's number one destination for snow sports, with eight major alpine ski areas offering a total of more than 150 trails. All eight provide for tubing as well as skiing and snowboardin All have ski schools. All but one have what it takes to stay open after night falls. The black-diamond question: How to choose between them?

First off, it's worth noting that these are modest hills relative to those out West. Even **Blue Mountain Ski Area** (1660 Blue Mountain Dr., Palmerton, 610/826-7700, www.skibluemt .com, all-day lift ticket $45–54, children 7–18 $35–38, 10 percent discount off any lift ticket for seniors, all-day equipment rental $33), which boasts the greatest vertical drop in Pennsylvania (1,082 feet), is Smurf-sized compared with Colorado's slopes, where verticals of more than 4,000 feet are not uncommon. So hotshots used to carving turns in places such as Colorado, Montana, and Utah won't have the thrill of their lives in the Poconos. That's not to say that the region's ski areas don't attract plenty of experienced skiers and snowboarders. After all, it's a lot easier and cheaper for Philadelphians with a passion for powder to get to Blue Mountain than to Telluride.

© POCONO MOUNTAINS VISITORS BUREAU/800POCONOS.COM

skiing at Camelback Mountain Resort

POCONO MOUNTAINS

ıt ski areas, Blue Mountain 'hiladelphia and Allentown, first and third most populous ...r that reason, it can get very busy on weekends and holidays. Blue boasts 34 trails on 158 ski-able acres, including three runs more than a mile long. Four terrain parks of varying degrees of trickiness make it popular with the teen set. At the base of the mountain is a huge tubing park with three lifts. Family-sized tubes as well as solo tubes are available. Weekday tubing sessions are six hours long and $23 per person. Weekend tubing sessions are anywhere from 4.5 to 9.5 hours long and range from $27 to $30. Skiers and snowboarders can add tubing to their itinerary for just $10. Babysitting services are available seven days a week for those too wee to hit the slopes. In the warmer months the mountain attracts disc golf and mountain biking enthusiasts.

Camelback Mountain Resort (1 Camelback Rd., Tannersville, 570/629-1661, www.skicamelback.com, all-day lift ticket $43–55, seniors and children 7–18 $31–40, all-day equipment rental $33, snow tubing $25 all day midweek or 3-hour session weekend) has the second greatest vertical drop in the Poconos at 800 feet. Just like Blue, it has 34 trails. Just like Blue, it can get crowded. Camelback's location is a big selling point. It's just over three miles from exit 299 of I-80, a major east–west artery. The Crossings Premium Outlets is also at that exit, which makes Camelback a great choice if part of your party prefers shopping to snow sports.

A great choice if part of your party is pint-sized: **Shawnee Mountain** (Hollow Rd., Shawnee on Delaware, 570/421-7231, www.shawneemt.com, all-day lift ticket $43–50, seniors and college students $33–40, youths 18 and under $32–36, children under 46 inches and seniors 70 and older free, all-day equipment rental $30, snow tubing 2-hour session $20–25). Located east of Camelback and just short of the Pennsylvania–New Jersey line, Shawnee has an excellent reputation for its children's lessons. It even has an intro-to-skiing program for tots three and under. Multi-

day lift tickets can add up to big savings for families. Shawnee offers 700 feet of vertical, 23 trails, two terrain parks, and a seven-chute tubing park. It's unusual in that it rents skiboards (think skis but shorter and wider).

Jack Frost Big Boulder (570/443-8425, www.jfbb.com, all-day lift ticket $42–48, seniors and children 7–18 $32–38, seniors 70 and older free, all-day equipment rental $28–32, snow tubing $25 all day midweek or 3-hour session weekend) offers two ski areas for the price of one. Like Shawnee, they're good training grounds for kids. Dating to the 1940s, Big Boulder (1 S. Lake Dr., Lake Harmony) is the oldest commercial ski area in Pennsylvania. Its builders played a hand in the invention of snowmaking machines. Today it's best known for its terrain parks. Jack Frost (1 Jack Frost Mountain Rd., Blakeslee), which opened in 1972, has 30 trails, twice as many as its older sibling. But it's not equipped for night skiing and closes at 4 P.M. Big Boulder stays open as late as 10 P.M., but on weekdays it doesn't open until 3 P.M. So to get the biggest bang for your buck midweek, hit the Jack Frost slopes in the morning and migrate to Big Boulder in the afternoon. The drive takes about 20 minutes. While a lift ticket purchased at either ski area is valid at both, rental equipment can't be taken from one to the other.

As the region's northernmost ski area, **Ski Big Bear** (Karl Hope Blvd., Lackawaxen, 570/685-1400, www.ski-bigbear.com, all-day lift ticket $41–49, seniors and children 6–12 $34–39, all-day equipment rental $30–32, snow tubing 2-hour session $24) is convenient to New Yorkers. It offers 600 feet of vertical and 18 trails.

With just 500 feet of vertical and three chairlifts, **Alpine Mountain** (Rte. 447, Analomink, 570/595-2150, www.alpinemountain.com, all-day lift ticket $42–49, seniors and children under 17 $32–35, seniors 70 and older $12–18, all-day equipment rental $24–30, snow tubing session $19–23) is on the smaller end of the spectrum. Smallest of them all is **Tanglwood Ski Area** (192 Paper Birch South,

Tafton, 570/226-9780, www.skitanglwood
.com, 9 A.M.–5 P.M., lift ticket $38–46, seniors
and children 6–14 $30–36, seniors 70 and
older free, equipment rental $30, snow tubing
2-hour session $20). It's a two-chairlift opera-
tion with 450 feet of vertical.

A summary of snow conditions at each of the
region's ski areas is available at www.pocono
ski.com or by phone at 570/421-5565.

One of the best tubing parks in the Poconos
isn't affixed to a ski mountain. **Fernwood
Hotel & Resort's Winter Fun Center**
(U.S. 209 and River Rd., Bushkill, 888/337-
6966, www.fernwoodhotel.com, 5–9 P.M.
Mon.–Fri., 10 A.M.–5 P.M. and 6–10 P.M. Sat.
and holidays, 10 A.M.–5 P.M. and 6–9 P.M.
Sun.) has tubes built for one and tubes built
for the whole family. It also has a play area
designed for kids too small to cut it at other
tubing parks. On weekday evenings, all-you-
can-slide passes are $17–25. On weekends and
holidays, daytime passes good for two hours
are $24, and evening passes good from 6 P.M.
to close are $25. Guests of the resort enjoy
discounted rates. Admission to the Tiny Tot
Play Area is $8. Fernwood's horse stables are a
mare's breadth away, making it possible to go
for a giddy-up between tubing runs.

ENTERTAINMENT AND EVENTS
Mount Airy Casino Resort
Most Americans over 30 can hum the once-
ubiquitous jingle for Mount Airy Lodge, which
enjoyed a decades-long reign as America's premier "honeymoon hideaway" before falling
into disrepair. The resort—"Your host with
the most in the Poconos: beautiful Mount Airy
Lodge"—closed its doors in 2001 and was demolished several years later. Built in its place:
Mount Airy Casino Resort (44 Woodland
Rd., Mount Pocono, general information
877/682-4791, hotel and restaurant reservations 877/682-4791, www.mountairycasino
.com, casino open 24 hours), which boasts
more than 2,500 slot machines, about 190
guest rooms and suites, an 18-hole golf course,

a full-service spa, several restaurants, and a
nightclub. Gone are the heart-shaped bathtubs
and floor-to-ceiling mirrors that characterized
its predecessor. The resort's guest accommodations were designed with a four-star rating
in mind, which meant out with the kitsch, in
with the elegant. A waterfall greets guests in
the hotel lobby, masking the noise of the gambling floor above.

Like the old Mount Airy, the new Mount
Airy wants to be known as a destination for
outstanding live entertainment. The 2,000-
seat Crystal Room at Mount Airy Lodge hosted
headliners including Bob Hope, Milton Berle,
Red Buttons, Tony Bennett, and Paul Anka.
Mount Airy Casino's **Gypsies Lounge and
Nightclub** has welcomed *Twist* legend Chubby
Checker, 1960s chart-toppers Herman's
Hermits, and Frank Sinatra Jr., who, inciden-
tally, appeared at the old Mount Airy.

Dining options range from a 24-hour sandwich shop and a 1950s-style diner to the upscale **Red Steakhouse** (dinner Mon.–Tues.
and Fri.–Sun., $29–60, reservations recom-
mended), which specializes in prime aged beef
and seafood. A casino wouldn't be complete
without a buffet. Mount Airy's is best known
for its $24.95 Sunday brunch, which features
a seafood station stocked with oysters, snow
crab, smoked white fish, and more; carving stations; and a Viennese dessert table.

Mount Airy is one of two casinos in northeast Pennsylvania. Mohegan Sun at Pocono
Downs, about an hour away in Wilkes-Barre,
has a harness racing track but no hotel or golf
course.

Pocono Raceway
NASCAR fans flock to Pocono Raceway
(Long Pond Rd. and Andretti Rd., Blakeslee,
800/722-3929, www.poconoraceway.com)
for two 500-mile Sprint Cup Series races: the
Pocono 500 in early June and the Pennsylvania
500 several weeks later. The 2.5-mile track is
triangular in shape with straights of varying
lengths and severe turns, each with a different degree of banking. Nicknamed "The

© POCONO MOUNTAINS VISITORS BUREAU/800POCONOS.COM

Pocono Raceway

Tricky Triangle," it's unlike any other track used for NASCAR's top racing series. In 2010 NASCAR's pickup truck series came to Pocono for the first time. The super speedway's Camping World Truck Series race is known as the Pocono Mountains 125.

Family-owned since its inception in 1968, Pocono prides itself on its fair-like atmosphere. Its motto: "Back to the good old days." (Another point of pride is its titanic toilet facility, 1,000 stalls strong.) Grandstand seating for the Sprint Cup races starts at $45. Ticket holders who want to snag an autograph from their favorite driver or catch a glimpse of teams preparing cars should shell out $50 for the Pre-Race Pit/Paddock Pass, good for all three days of a race weekend. Premium seating options range from an open-air hospitality area ($100 for race day) to air-conditioned skyboxes ($500 for three days). Fans are welcome to pitch a tent or park an RV on the grounds for the duration of a race weekend. Camping options range from $125 for a two-night tent site for two people to $500 per

vehicle plus $50 per person for a three-night trackside RV site.

Wannabe car racers can get their training wheels at Pocono. **StockCar Racing Experience** (570/643-6921, www.877stockcar .com) is a chance to suit up, strap in, and see the track from the inside of a 600-horsepower vehicle. Brave souls can either sit in the passenger seat while an instructor zooms around the track at top speed or take the wheel and follow a leader. A ride-along is $135 for three laps, $269 for six laps. Eight laps in the driver's seat will set you back $499–559, depending on the day. For those who can't get enough, there are 16-, 24-, and 32-lap options, plus opportunities for more advanced training. Drivers must be at least 18 and have experience in operating a manual transmission. Riders can be as young as 14, but both parents must be present for those under 18. StockCar Racing Experience, in business since 1998, also offers a team pro kart racing program. Pocono Raceway is also used by the locally based **Bertil Roos Racing School** (800/722-3669, www.racenow.com), the place to go for seat time in a Formula 2000 race car.

Concert Venues

REO Speedwagon, Air Supply, Alice Cooper, Billy Ray Cyrus, Styx, Loretta Lynn, and Kenny Rogers are among the many and various acts that have played **Penn's Peak** (325 Maury Rd., Jim Thorpe, 866/605-7325, www.penns peak.com), a mountaintop venue with lofty ceilings and a capacity of 1,800. Its luncheon and dinner shows often sell out months in advance. The picturesque views from the Peak's open-air decks and patios are alone worth the price of a ticket.

Ten minutes away is the **Mauch Chunk Opera House** (14 W. Broadway, Jim Thorpe, 570/325-0249, www.mauchchunkoperahouse .com), built in 1881 as a combo farmers market and concert hall. Once a regular stop on the vaudeville circuit, the Opera House became a movie theater in the 1920s and later a warehouse for a pocketbook manufacturer. Today it's once again a venue for live entertainment. Operated by the Mauch Chunk Historical Society, the acoustically superior Opera House seats 350. It's a favorite venue of Canadian folk trio The Wailin' Jennys, who recorded a live album there in 2008. Vaudeville returned to the Opera House in 2010, when it hosted the first annual **Jim Thorpe Burlesque Festival** (www.jimthorpeburlesque.com, March).

The **Sherman Theater** (524 Main St., Stroudsburg, 570/420-2808, www.sher mantheater.com) in downtown Stroudsburg opened on January 7, 1929, with a live performance by Stan Laurel and Oliver Hardy (as in the comedic duo Laurel and Hardy). Today it's best known as a rock venue, hosting both local bands and national acts such as Blues Traveler and Papa Roach, but other music genres, theater, and dance also find their way onto the calendar. Jazz aficionados have been finding their way to the **Deer Head Inn** (5 Main St., Delaware Water Gap, 570/424-2000, www .deerheadinn.com) for more than 50 years. Built as a hotel in the mid-1800s, the four-

story Victorian in the heart of Delaware Water Gap still offers lodging ($90–180 per night), and its proximity to the Appalachian Trail and Delaware Water Gap National Recreation Area makes it a good choice for outdoorsy types. But jazz is its raison d'être. Maestros such as saxophonists Stan Getz and Phil Woods, pianist Keith Jarrett, and guitarist Pat Metheny have played the Deer Head, which offers dinner and live music Thursday through Sunday.

Performing Arts

In 1985 arson claimed a playhouse that had stood since 1904 and earned a spot on the National Registry of Historic Places. Thanks in part to donations from its many fans, the **Shawnee Playhouse** (River Rd., Shawnee on Delaware, 570/421-5093, www.theshaw neeplayhouse.com) rose again. Located on the grounds of The Shawnee Inn and Golf Resort, the playhouse imports non-equity talent from New York City for its main stage season, which runs from May through December and includes both musicals and nonmusicals. The theater's resident Worthington Players perform nonmusicals during the off-season.

Festivals and Events

Unlike many parts of Pennsylvania, the Poconos region really shines in winter. That's due in large part to its abundance of ski areas, but it doesn't hurt that some of its most unique events take place during the frosty months. In 2007 professional ice carver Mark Crouthamel took advantage of a post-New Year's lull in business by creating life-sized sculptures of a log cabin and some critters and inviting the public to come have a look. Thousands turned out for **Crystal Cabin Fever** (Sculpted Ice Works, Rte. 590, Lakeville, 570/226-6246, www.crystalcabinfever.com, Feb., admission $10, children 3–15 $6), now an annual event. Playing on a different theme each year, Crouthamel and team carve an interactive display out of more than 100 tons of ice. A team of sled dogs, a giant polar bear, and caribou greeted visitors during 2009's Alaska-themed event. The bundled-up crowds got a taste of the Caribbean, coral reef and all, the following year. There's always a dual-run ice slide, so wear your waterproof pants. Ice carving competitions are among the highlights of the event, which lasts for two and a half weeks. Another sure-fire cure for cabin fever: the **Ice Tee Golf Tournament** (570/226-3191, www .hawleywallenpaupackcc.com, Feb., registration fee charged), played atop frozen Lake Wallenpaupack. Golfers tee up on two challenging courses complete with water traps.

Summer's can't-miss event is the **Delaware River Sojourn** (609/883-9500, www.delaware riversojourn.org, June, registration fees charged). The weeklong paddling trip is designed to heighten awareness of the ecological and recreational significance of the river, which flows through New York, New Jersey, Pennsylvania, and Delaware. It's open to both novice and experienced kayakers/canoeists, who can sign up for the entire event or a portion of it. Participants catch their winks at campgrounds near the scenic river. Other notable summer happenings include the **Great Tastes of Pennsylvania Wine & Food Festival** (Split Rock Resort, Lake Harmony, 570/722-9111, www.splitrockresort.com, June, admission charged) and the **Poconos' Wurst Festival** (Shawnee Mountain Ski Area, Shawnee on Delaware, 570/421-7231, www.shawneemt .com, July, admission charged). Both are two-day outdoor festivals with a special emphasis on food and drink. The former spotlights wineries from across the state. Authentic German and Polish foods, craft brews, and polka and oompah-pah bands take center stage at the latter. July draws to a close with the three-day **Pocono Blues Festival** (Big Boulder Ski Area, Lake Harmony, 570/443-8425, www.pocono blues.com, admission charged), which attracts world-class musicians.

Jazz fans get their due in September. **Celebration of the Arts** (570/424-2210, weekend after Labor Day, www.cotajazz .org, admission charged), a three-day affair in the town of Delaware Water Gap, showcases musicians with ties to the area—from a jazz orchestra comprising high-school students to maestros such as multi-Grammy winning saxophonist Phil Woods, who cofounded the festival in 1978. Highlights include Jazz Mass, a nondenominational Sunday morning service featuring a big band, a chorus, and vocal soloists. Admission to the mass is free. "The jazz festival," as locals call COTA, also draws attention to area visual artists with a show of musically themed fine art and an array of arts and crafts vendors.

Shawnee Mountain Ski Area hosts three fun-filled fall events, starting with the **Pocono Garlic Festival** (570/369-6814, www.pocono garlic.com, Labor Day weekend, admission charged). Sponsored by the Pocono Garlic Growers Association, it's basically a street fair with a garlicky twist. Expect such unexpected foods as roasted garlic ice cream and garlic funnel cake. A few weeks later, cowboys descend on Shawnee for two days of bronc and bull riding, calf roping, steer wrestling, and other events sanctioned by the Professional Rodeo Cowboys Association. The **PRCA Rodeo & Chili Cook-Off** (570/421-7231, www.shaw neemt.com, late Sept., admission charged) also features barrel-racing cowgirls, live country music, line dancing, and all sorts of barbecue goodness. Lumberjacks show their stuff during the **Autumn Timber Festival** (570/421-7231, www.shawneemt.com, early Oct., admission charged), held during the peak of fall foliage. Festival-goers can board a chairlift or hot air balloon for a bird's-eye view of hills ablaze with color. Tickets to all festivals at Shawnee are cheaper when purchased in advance.

SHOPPING
The Crossings Premium Outlets

With 100 stores, The Crossings Premium Outlets (1000 Rte. 611, Tannersville, 570/629-4650, www.premiumoutlets.com, regular hours 10 A.M.–9 P.M. Mon.–Sat. and 10 A.M.–8 P.M. Sun., winter hours 10 A.M.–6 P.M. Sun.–Thurs. and 10 A.M.–9 P.M. Fri.–Sat.) is good reason for people who aren't fond of outdoor recreation to head to the Poconos. Pennsylvania's sales tax exemption on shoes and apparel lures many New York and New Jersey residents to the outlet mall, located off exit 299 of I-80. In fact, motor coaches originating on Long Island, New York, deposit shoppers there every Monday and Tuesday. Retailers include Jones New York, Nautica, Anne Klein, BCBG Max Azria, Calvin Klein, Kenneth Cole, Juicy Couture, Tommy Hilfiger, Burberry, J. Crew, and Guess. The Pocono Mountains Visitors Bureau has an information center in the food court.

Specialty Shops

Prefer small-town shopping districts to sprawling malls? You'll find what you're looking for in the towns of Jim Thorpe, Stroudsburg, Milford, and, to a lesser degree, Hawley. Not to be missed: **Fretta's Italian Food Specialties** (223 Broad St., Milford, 570/296-7863, www.frettas.com, 8:30 A.M.–6:30 P.M. Tues.–Sat., 9 A.M.–3 P.M. Sun.), which bills itself as the oldest pork store in America. Established in 1906 in New York City's Little Italy neighborhood, the *salumeria* relocated to picturesque Milford in 1998. It carries all sorts of imported goodies, including cheeses, pasta, olive oil, sorbets, and tiramisu. Fourth-generation proprietor Joseph Fretta also prides himself on offering a host of house-made foods: fresh mozzarella, sopressata, capicola, pancetta, pasta sauces, and more. Pop in for a takeout sandwich or pasta dish, and don't leave without a box of Fretta's own cannolis.

Some of the region's most popular specialty shops are quite a ways from Main Street. **Pocono Candle** (1993 Milford Rd./Business U.S. 209, E. Stroudsburg, 570/421-1832, www.poconocandle.com, 9 A.M.–5:30 P.M. Sun.–Thurs., 9 A.M.–7 P.M. Fri.–Sat.) on the outskirts of East Stroudsburg attracts wax-and-wick enthusiasts by the busload. In business for more than 35 years, it sells everything from scented votives to custom-made wedding candles. Kids get a kick out of watching the candle makers at work. Four miles to its north on U.S. 209 is the **Pocono Bazaar** (U.S. 209, Marshalls Creek, 570/223-8640, www.poconobazaar

.com, 9 A.M.–5 P.M. Sat.–Sun. and holidays), a massive year-round flea market. You name it, you'll find it there.

Sweet tooths search out **Callie's Candy Kitchen** (Rte. 390, Mountainhome, 570/595-2280, www.calliescandy.com, 10 A.M.–5 P.M. weekends in Jan. and daily second week of Feb.–Dec.) and **Callie's Pretzel Factory** (Rte. 390/191, Cresco, 570/595-3257, 10 A.M.–5 P.M. weekends second week of Feb.–Apr. and daily May–Dec., closed Jan.) three miles to its south. Owner Harry Callie was 19 when he began selling handmade candy in 1952, and shoppers can still find him hands deep in chocolate. He's known for coating just about anything with the food of the gods, including sunflower seeds, cream cheese, and Twinkies. Chocolate-covered strawberries, made daily, are the biggest sellers. The Candy Kitchen also makes its own lollipops, fudge, brittles, and barks (including *bacon* bark). The Pretzel Factory, which opened in the 1980s in a three-story house, makes hard and soft pretzels as well as flavored popcorn. A window-lined wall gives customers the opportunity to observe the pretzel-making process. Be sure to try the "everything" pretzels, inspired by everything bagels.

SPORTS AND RECREATION

Its ski slopes, hiking trails, rivers, and lakes are enough to keep active sorts busy for weeks on end, but the region's menu of recreational fare doesn't end there.

Dog Sledding

Iditarod dreams? **Arctic Paws Dog Sled Tours** (The Inn at Pocono Manor, Rte. 314, Pocono Manor, 570/839-0123, www.arcticpawsdogsledtours.com) offers a taste of the mushing life. Prior experience driving a team of huskies isn't required. Even young children can give it a go. Mushing, which involves standing at the back of the sled, costs $50 for children and adults alike. The regular rate for simply riding in the sled's basket is also $50; children 5–10 can ride for $25. Be sure to bring cash as credit cards and checks aren't accepted. Reservations are required and should be made through the Arctic

dog sledding at Pocono Manor

Paws website. Dog sledding requires snow, of course, which means the window of opportunity is rather narrow. Typically the Poconos get snow from mid-December to late February. Snowfalls in March aren't out of the question.

Horseback Riding

Horse lovers can have their pick of riding stables in the Poconos. An excellent pick: **Triple W Riding Stables** (291 Beechnut Dr., Honesdale, 570/226-2620, www.triplewstable.com), which offers trail rides of 1–2 hours, hayrides, sleigh rides, and even stage coach rides, all in a secluded mountaintop setting. Packages that combine horseback riding and camping are available. **Mountain Creek Riding Stable** (Rte. 940, Cresco, 570/839-8725, www.mtcreekstable .com), located just minutes from Mount Airy Casino Resort, is another reputable operation.

Paintball

The Poconos region is home to a curiously large number of paintball complexes. The behemoth of the bunch is **Skirmish USA** (211 N. Meckesville Rd., Albrightsville, 800/754-7647, www.skirmish.com), with 50-some playing fields on 700 acres and two castles for the capturing. The three-story Tippmann Castle, larger of the two, has ten towers, spiral staircases, ramparts, and other nifty features that make for epic battles. Another popular field features a replica of a frontier fort. One of the newest fields, "Tippmann City," is a cityscape with more than 25 structures. Skirmish is a sister business of Pocono Whitewater, a Jim Thorpe–based rafting, kayaking, and biking outfitter. A "Battles and Paddles" package is available for those who want to capture the flag one day and conquer the Lehigh River the next. The paintball fields are a half-hour drive from Jim Thorpe. Whitewater Rafting Adventures, another Jim Thorpe-area outfitter, has an on-site paintball operation. With 18 fields, **Pocono Mt. Paintball** (U.S. 209 and Hunter St./Rte.93, Nesquehoning, 570/669-9127, www.adventurerafting.com) doesn't measure up to Skirmish, but its selling points include free hot dogs.

The Paintball Asylum (365 Camelback Rd., Tannersville, 570/629-3852, www.the paintballasylum.com) has lower rates than the previous two. Admission, basic equipment, and 500 paintballs will set you back $34.95, compared to more than $55 at Skirmish and Pocono Mt. Paintball. As one might expect, it has fewer fields: seven on about 30 acres. Coaching clinics are available for beginners or experienced players looking to ratchet up their game. The Paintball Asylum is a good choice if only part of your crew wants to fight it out on the fields. It's on the same property as Angler's Cove, a fish-and-pay facility with four stocked trout ponds, and a stone's throw from Camelback. All three paintball locations are open year-round except in severe weather. Reservations are recommended.

Snowmobiling

So long as Mother Nature provides the snow and you provide a valid driver's license, **Pocono Snowmobile Rentals** (The Inn at Pocono Manor, Rte. 314, Pocono Manor, 570/839-6061, www.poconosnowmobilerentals.com, rate per half hour $35 for single snowmobile, $50 for double) will provide your ride. Reservations are recommended.

Water Parks

Just a couple of months after its ski slopes close, Camelback Mountain Resort opens **Camelbeach** (1 Camelback Rd., Tannersville, 570/629-1661, www.camelbeach.com, general admission $34.99, seniors $23.99, children older than 2 and under 48 inches tall $23.99), a water park with more than two dozen slides. "The Titan," an eight-story tubing slide, is said to be the largest of its kind in the world. Camelbeach also has a lazy river ride, an Olympic-sized swimming pool, a wave pool, and play zones designed for its littlest guests. Park-goers can give boogie boarding or surfing a try at the FlowRider attraction. Boogie board rides are included in the admission price; there's an additional fee during surfing sessions. The water park is open weekends in late May and early June and daily from mid-June through

Labor Day. Park hours are 11 A.M.–6 P.M. or 10 A.M.–7 P.M., depending on the day. Come within three hours of closing for discounted admission of $19.99.

In the Poconos, you don't have to wait for warm weather to enjoy water park action. Just minutes from Camelback ski area, **Great Wolf Lodge** (1 Great Wolf Dr., Scotrun, 800/768-9653, www.greatwolf.com) features a massive indoor water park. The resort, part of a nationwide chain, became the first new Poconos resort in three decades when it opened in 2005. Alas, its water park is reserved for resort guests. Recognizing a good thing, Split Rock Resort & Golf Club opened its own indoor water park in 2008. Its version, **H2Oooohh!** (1 Lake Dr., Lake Harmony, 570/722-9111, www.splitrockresort.com, day pass $34.95–39.95, seniors $15, children older than 2 and under 42 inches tall $29.95–34.95), is open to the general public. It boasts the first indoor FlowRider in Pennsylvania, a handful of slides, a wave pool, play areas for little kids, and hot tubs for big kids. Call or check the website for operating hours. During high season the water park is open as late as 10 P.M. Admission prices dip after 4 P.M.

ACCOMMODATIONS
Family Resorts
FERNWOOD HOTEL & RESORT

Fernwood (U.S. 209 and River Rd., Bushkill, 888/337-6966, www.fernwoodhotel.com, $76–225) is most notable for its location. It's adjacent to Delaware Water Gap National Recreation Area and just minutes from Shawnee Mountain. Unlike some family resorts in the Poconos, Fernwood isn't all-inclusive. (Heck, the place charges guests for wireless Internet access.) So it's an affordable base of operations for vacationers more interested in drifting down the Delaware River, hitting the ski slopes, or exploring the region than reliving sleepaway camp. Guests *can* have an action-packed day without leaving the 440-acre resort. Fernwood boasts an 18-hole par 71 golf course dating to 1969, a snow tubing park, horseback riding stables, and paintball fields, all of which are open to nonguests. Other amenities include indoor and outdoor pools, a fitness center, a mini golf course, a bumper boat pond, and a 10,000-square-foot arcade.

Fernwood offers two types of accommodations: rooms and suites in its aging but tidy hotel and villas that sleep up to six. The latter are a good choice for families who like to do their own cooking. The resort has several restaurants and a food court featuring Pizza Hut. Guests can purchase "EZ Cards," which work like debit cards, for use in the restaurants and other resort facilities.

GREAT WOLF LODGE

A vast indoor water park sets Great Wolf Lodge (1 Great Wolf Dr., Scotrun, 800/768-9653, www.greatwolf.com, $239–510) apart from the pack. With a dozen slides, six pools, two jumbo whirlpools, a lazy river, and a 1,000-gallon soaker bucket, the weatherproof water park is one of the largest in the country. It's always a balmy 84 degrees inside, which makes it a real treat after a day on the slopes of Camelback Mountain Resort, just a

few minutes away. When it's balmy outside, the action spills over to Great Wolf's outdoor water park. (Incidentally, Camelback morphs into an outdoor water park, Camelbeach, when weather permits.) The great thing about Great Wolf's wetlands is that long lines are as rare as lone wolves. That's because access is reserved for guests of the all-suites resort.

Great Wolf, part of a nationwide chain of indoor water park resorts, is one of the newest lodging properties in the Poconos, having opened in 2005. Its 401 suites come in a dozen styles. A real hit with pup-sized guests: themed suites with bunk beds in a walled-off space resembling a cave, tent, or log cabin. PJs are perfectly acceptable attire for nightly story readings in the lobby. Story time immediately follows the 8 P.M. show of Great Wolf's enormous clock tower. Its animatronics inhabitants also come alive at 10 A.M. and 9 P.M. daily. Other resort amenities include Cub Club, an activity and craft center for kids 5–12; Race Zone, where their older siblings can build remote-control vehicles; and an arcade with more than 100 games. Great Wolf has not

Great Wolf Lodge is an amazing indoor water park.

one but two spas (reservations 570/213-6020): the fairly standard Elements Spa and the ice-cream-themed Scoops, designed for kids 12 and under. Mom can enjoy a signature facial while her little princess delights in a brownie-flavored foot soak. On-site eateries include a Starbucks coffee shop and Loose Moose Cottage, which offers breakfast and dinner buffets.

Water park passes are included in standard room rates. The indoor water park is typically open 9 A.M.–9 P.M. Guests are welcome to enjoy the park as early as 1 P.M. on their check-in date and until close on their departure date.

SKYTOP LODGE

If the stately stone manor at the heart of this resort strikes you as an exclusive retreat for the exceptionally wealthy, that's because it used to be. Built in the 1920s, it welcomed the likes of Lucille Ball when Skytop Lodge (1 Skytop, Skytop, 800/345-7759, www.skytop.com) was a private resort. Celebs still check in from time to time, but these days Skytop specializes in giving regular folks the star treatment. At 5,500 acres, the resort is larger than many towns in northeast Pennsylvania. And it offers more recreational opportunities than many towns put together. Among its amenities: a spa, a championship golf course rated 4.5 stars by *Golf Digest,* a private trout stream, a 75-acre lake, 30 miles of hiking trails, paintball fields, a 15-station sporting clays course, an indoor mini golf course, an outdoor ice skating rink, and a 30-foot rock-climbing wall. Skytop even has its own ski hill. (With a vertical drop of 295 feet and four gentle slopes, it won't knock anyone's skis off. But for novices, it's an appealing alternative to crowded public ski areas.) A wintertime visit gives kids the rare opportunity to explore the grounds on snowshoes shaped like dinosaur feet, pilot a sled pulled by Siberian huskies, or zoom down a toboggan run.

In the summer, all-inclusive packages start at $499 per night for two people, not including tax and a 15 percent service charge. Children ages 5–17 can share their parents' room for $45 per night. There's no charge for children 4 and under. The longer the stay, the lower the nightly rate. At other times of year, all-inclusive packages start at $399 per night for two people. Skytop offers room-and-meals rates for guests more interested in long walks or curling up with a book than making use of the recreational facilities.

Guests can choose from a variety of accommodations. Perched on a high plateau, the historic Main Lodge has 125 guest rooms and suites, heavy wooden furniture and plaid accents, and a buttoned-up ambience. In an effort "to maintain an atmosphere of dignity and good taste," Skytop asks that gentlemen wear jackets for dinner in the Main Lodge's Windsor Dining Room. "Appropriate attire" is also expected of ladies and children. Golfers gravitate toward the more intimate Inn at Skytop, located on the course designed more than 80 years ago by the first president of the PGA of America. With its two-story atrium, exposed beams, and cozy cocktail lounge, the 20-room inn recalls a European ski chalet. Its 135-seat restaurant offers floor-to-ceiling windows and a relatively casual dining experience. (Male guests can get away with collared shirts or sweaters. Jeans and T-shirts are still verboten.) Families may prefer to stay in one of Skytop's four-bedroom cottages, which have conveniences such as washers, dryers, and small refrigerators but no common areas. The interconnected bedrooms can be rented individually.

WOODLOCH RESORT

Parents, Better Homes and Gardens, Family Circle, and other national magazines have sung the praises of Woodloch Resort (731 Welcome Lake Rd., Hawley, 570/685-8000, www.woodloch.com), an all-inclusive resort that's all about family. The Lake Region landmark has been owned by the same family—the Kiesendahls—since 1958. Many employees are practically family, having been with the Kiesendahls for decades. And you can guess how guests are treated: like family. Many return year after year in multigenerational posses. Babysitting

snowmobiling at Woodloch Resort

© ANNA DUBROVSKY

is available for an extra charge, but the daily schedule of activities and all facilities are designed with kids in mind. "It's kind of *Dirty Dancing* meets Disney," explains one staffer.

On the Kiesendahls' watch, the resort on Lake Teedyuskung has grown from 12 acres with lodgings for about 40 guests to 1,000-plus acres with lodgings for more than 900. Accommodations range from endearingly outdated rooms with accordion dividers separating living and sleeping areas to modern trilevel houses with five and a half baths, cathedral ceilings, and fireplaces. Rates depend on accommodation type, time of year, and children's ages (the younger, the cheaper). A two-night weekend stay in January or February starts at $1,130 for a family of four with kids ages 7–12. The same family could enjoy a three-night midweek stay for as little as $786. Prices are higher when school's out for summer. A three-night stay in August would cost that family at least $2,104. Rates include three meals a day, almost all activities, and entertainment. Not included: alcohol; snowmobiling; use of the racquetball

courts, rifle range, or batting cages; and golfing at **Woodloch Springs** (1 Woodloch Dr., Hawley, 570/685-8102), an 18-hole par 72 championship course. Vacationers who want to enjoy all the amenities of the family resort but prefer cooking their own meals to dining in the company of hundreds can rent one of the golfing community's privately owned homes.

Lake Teedyuskung is the center of resort activity in summer. Guests can lounge on a sandy beach; fish off the docks for bass, bluegill, and catfish; swim in the shimmering lake or the shamrock-shaped pool along its shore; or take to the water in a canoe, kayak, paddleboat, rowboat, or Sunfish sailboat. Waterskiing is an option for those 13 and older. Winter activities include ice fishing, ice skating, snowshoeing, and snow tubing. Among the year-round options are trapshooting, biking, bumper cars, bingo, and "family Olympics." The resort's social department is never short on ideas.

Woodloch is as famous for its lavish Broadway-style revue as its array of activities. The pyrotechnics-enhanced performance is held Wednesday and Saturday evenings in the resort's capacious nightclub. Entertainment of one sort or another is offered every night of the week. Ray Romano and Darrell Hammond kept Woodloch guests in stitches before starring in *Everybody Loves Raymond* and *Saturday Night Live,* respectively.

Woodloch Resort is not to be confused with The Lodge at Woodloch, an adults-only destination spa more likely to be praised by *Forbes* than *Family Circle.*

Couples Resorts

If you've ever pictured yourself in soft porn, you'll probably enjoy a stay at one of the three remaining couples resorts in the Poconos. The region once known as the "Honeymoon Capital of the World" has lost most of its couples resorts, but the species doesn't appear to be headed toward extinction. Each year, some 65,000 couples vacation at the three resorts, which are jointly owned by **Cove Haven Entertainment Resorts** (800/432 9932, www.covepoconoresorts.com, $340–585), a subsidiary of Starwood Hotels & Resorts Worldwide Inc. They uncork more than 20,000 bottles of champagne and empty twice as many bottles of bubble bath. They splishsplash in hot tubs shaped like hearts and champagne glasses, canoodle in private pools, and "sleep" on round beds under mirrored ceilings. They prove that kitschy and sexy can go hand in hand.

The all-inclusive resorts have much in common. Each offers several suite types, all-you-can-eat breakfast and dinner (and breakfast in bed at no additional charge), a variety of indoor and outdoor activities, and live entertainment nightly. Located on Lake Wallenpaupack, **Cove Haven** (194 Lakeview Dr., Lakeville, 570/226-4506) tends to draw the biggest entertainers. Comedians Howie Mandel and Sinbad, Motown legends The Temptations, and country crooner Billy Ray Cyrus have taken its stage in recent years. **Paradise Stream** (1022-1047 Rte. 940, Mount Pocono, 570/839-8881) has the fewest amenities, but a $20 million renovation in recent years turned it into the hippest

of the three. The poshest digs can be found at **Pocono Palace** (5241 Milford Rd./U.S. 209, East Stroudsburg, 570/588-6692), located just minutes from Delaware Water Gap National Recreation Area. Its multi-level "Roman Tower" suites feature floor-to-ceiling columns, a log-burning fireplace, a heart-shaped pool, a dry sauna, a massage table, and a king-sized round bed. A seven-foot-tall champagne glass whirlpool overlooks the living room. (All three resorts have suites with the enduringly popular champagne whirlpool, created in 1984 by Cove Haven founder Morris B. Wilkins.)

Guests of any of the resorts enjoy unlimited access to amenities at all three. So couples staying at Cove Haven or Paradise Stream, which don't have golf courses, can swing to their heart's content on Pocono Palace's nine-hole regulation golf course. Paradise Stream and Pocono Palace guests can journey to Cove Haven for sailing, snow tubing, or ballroom dancing. All three offer fishing, tennis, indoor and outdoor pools, mini golf, archery, snowmobiling, and ice skating, among other activities.

Other Accommodations
UNDER $100
Campgrounds dot the Poconos region, making it possible to stay very close to major attractions without making a major investment. **Mountain Vista Campground** (50 Taylor Dr., E. Stroudsburg, 570/223-0111, www.mtnvista campground.com, campsite $35–48 per day, $205–325 for 1 week, $370–495 for 2 weeks, rates based on 2 people and 1 camping unit per site) is just minutes from the famed Delaware Water Gap, Bushkill Falls, and Appalachian Trail access points. Open from mid-April through October, the pet-friendly campground has a modest pool and a fishing pond stocked with bass, pickerel, perch, and bluegill. Other amenities include wireless Internet access, a sand volleyball court, tennis and basketball courts, a playground, and the most darling laundry room you ever did see. In addition to wooded campsites for tents and RVs, Mountain Vista offers several types of cabins that sleep

up to four. Cabin rates are $79–124 per day or $459–699 for one week based on double occupancy. Ask about discounted rates for longer stays.

Canoeing, kayaking, rafting, and tubing outfitter Kittatinny Canoes operates two campgrounds along the Delaware River. One, **River Beach** (U.S. 6/209, 3 miles north of Milford, 800/356-2852, www.kittatinny.com, $11–18 per site, $13 per person, $6.95 for children 6–11), is just north of Delaware Water Gap National Recreation Area. The 18-acre campground has about 160 tent and RV sites, a handful of lean-tos, two refreshingly modern bathhouses, a laundry facility, an arcade, and a store that carries new and used canoes and kayaks as well as basic camping gear. Best of all: Campers can begin river trips just steps from their abodes.

In the Lake Region, it doesn't get better than (**Keen Lake Camping & Cottage Resort** (155 Keen Lake Rd., Waymart, 800/443-0412, www.keenlake.com, campsite $31–50 per day, 10 percent discount for stays of 1 week or longer, rates based on 2 people and 1 camping unit per site). Located just off U.S. 6 about seven miles west of Honesdale, the 300-site campground features a privately owned lake teeming with bass, bluegill, calico, perch, pickerel, and catfish. Fishing licenses—and everything from bacon to board games—are available in the camp store. Campers can rent a rowboat, paddleboat, canoe, or kayak for a spin around the 90-acre lake or take a dip in a designated swim area. There's a heated swimming pool for the less adventurous. The well-groomed, pet-friendly campground also has several playgrounds, a game room with pool tables, and a movie lounge with a 60-inch screen. About a dozen cottages and an RV unit are available for rent. Cottage rates are $150–295 per day or $845–1,595 per week. Some are available year-round. The priciest is a rustic three-bedroom cottage on an island accessible only by boat.

If you've come to northeast Pennsylvania to conquer the rapids of Lehigh Gorge State Park, pitch a tent at **Adventure Campground** (288 N. Stagecoach Rd., Weatherly, 570/443-

9532, www.whitewaterchallengers.com, campsite $7.50 per person). Operated by rafting, kayaking, and biking outfitter Whitewater Challengers, the campground is open from early April through October. Bicycles can be rented right at the campground, and the rafting check-in area is just a few minutes away by foot. Campers are invited to start their day with a hot breakfast buffet or adrenaline-pumping zipline ride. Box lunches and dinner buffets are also on offer. Don't have a tent? Reserve a rental tent or one of the campground's rustic bunkhouses ($48 for first night, $45 per additional night, plus per-person site fee). The campground occasionally admits RVs. Call for clearance.

A better choice for RV vacationers is the immaculate **StoneyBrook Campground** (1435 Germans Rd., Lehighton, 570/386-4088, www.stoneybrookestates.com, campsite $35–40 per day for up to 4 people, $225 per week, $450 per month), which opened in 2009. It's about 10 miles south of Jim Thorpe, the southernmost gateway to Lehigh Gorge.

$100-200

Having opened in 2007, **Mount Airy Casino Resort** (44 Woodland Rd., Mount Pocono, 877/682-4791, www.mountairycasino.com, $99–349) offers some of the newest digs in northeast Pennsylvania. Rooms and suites feature modern furnishings, spacious bathrooms, pillow-top beds, LCD TVs, and refrigerators. Guests enjoy free access to high-speed Internet and a 24-hour fitness center. The resort's central location—just minutes from The Crossings Premium Outlets and Camelback Mountain Resort and within half an hour of Delaware Water Gap National Recreation Area and Pocono Raceway—is a major selling point. That being said, it's entirely possible to wile away a day without leaving Mount Airy, even if you're not a gambler. In addition to a 24-hour casino, the resort has an 18-hole golf course, a first-rate spa, and a tradition of booking well-known entertainers. Its restaurants are well above average for the region but on the pricey side. The all-you-can-eat Sunday Signature Brunch, for example, is $24.95 per person.

Start your day with yoga at **Santosha on the Ridge** (Mosiers Knob Rd., Shawnee on Delaware, 570/476-0203, www.santosha ontheridge.com, $145–200), a secluded B&B where worldly comforts aren't sacrificed in the name of inner peace. Innkeeper Leslie Underhill is a yoga teacher and one heckuva cook. Her breakfast specialties include homemade granola with mixed berries from her garden, puff pancake with maple-baked pears, and brie scrambled eggs with sun-dried tomatoes in a puff pastry crust. "Santosha" is Sanskrit for "contentment," and it's not so hard to find when cradled in a hammock on the back deck, where Underhill teaches classes when weather permits. A stone labyrinth helps guests on their inward journey. Another easy walk brings them to the lovely Delaware Water Gap.

The Settlers Inn (4 Main Ave., Hawley, 800/833-8527, www.thesettlersinn.com, $160– 250) is a Lake Region landmark that almost didn't come to be. Construction began in 1927, the year after a hydroelectric dam gave birth to Lake Wallenpaupack and a wave of tourism. When the stock market crashed two years later, work ground to a halt. The lodge remained unfinished through the Great Depression and World War II before finally opening in 1948. Since 1980 it's been in the hands of Jeanne and Grant Genzlinger, whose mastery of the art of hospitality has earned the inn membership in Select Registry and its onsite farm-to-table restaurant a AAA Four Diamond rating. A handsome example of Arts and Crafts style both inside and out, the inn is ideal for travelers who find hotels too impersonal and many B&Bs too frilly. It's also ideal for anglers: The trout-filled Lackawaxen River runs through the property. The inn has 20 guest rooms and a two-bedroom suite perfect for a family. All have private baths, flat-screen TVs, CD players, and wireless Internet access. Many feature fireplaces and hot tubs. Eco-minded types will appreciate room 204 with its bamboo flooring, organic cotton bed covers, and river view. Guests get complimentary access to a state-of-the-art fitness center about 10 minutes away. Standard room rates include breakfast; packages that include dinner are available.

During its heyday in the late 1800s, the

a guest room at The Settlers Inn

town now known as Jim Thorpe was a tourist destination on par with Niagara Falls—so scenic that it earned the epithet "Switzerland of America." More than half a dozen grand hotels catered to the visitors. One of those remains. Built in 1849 and originally called the New American Hotel, it's since been restored and rechristened **The Inn at Jim Thorpe** (24 Broadway, Jim Thorpe, 800/329-2599, www .innjt.com, room $89–172, suite 149–364). The 45-room hotel in the heart of the historic district invites guests to "rediscover a bygone era." Floral carpets, tin ceilings, period furnishings, and a friendly staff aid in that rediscovery. Accommodations range from generously sized standard rooms to suites with whirlpools and gas fireplaces. Rates include a continental breakfast during the week and a hot breakfast buffet on weekends. The hotel has a modest exercise room, a game room with a pool table, and a restaurant and pub. On-site spa services are available. Cast-iron balconies dotted with wicker rockers overlook Broadway's shops, restaurants, and galleries. In the warmer months, The Inn at Jim Thorpe is a popular base camp for adventures in nearby Lehigh Gorge State Park, so book well in advance. No luck? Look for digs in one of its sister properties: **55** (55 Broadway, 800/329-2599, www.innjt.com, $119–275), a recently restored Victorian building across the street from the inn, and **Broadway House** (44–46 W. Broadway, 800/329-2599, www.broadwayguesthouse .com, $99–194), a guesthouse a couple of blocks from the historic downtown.

OVER $200

Its hilltop setting is reason enough to splurge on a stay at **The French Manor** (50 Huntingdon Dr., South Sterling, 570/676-3244, www.the frenchmanor.com, $175–375). Need more reasons? How about its fine dining restaurant, named one of Pennsylvania's best by *Gourmet* magazine? Or its on-site spa, where couples can enjoy side-by-side massages and facials by a crackling fire? **La Spa Forêt,** which opened in 2009, boasts an indoor saltwater pool and hot tub and uses only all-natural products. Ron

and Mary Kay Logan, owners of The French Manor since 1990, are adept at setting the stage for romance. That means no children, breakfast in bed for an additional charge of $10 per person, and picnic baskets on request. A midweek package called "Enchanted Evenings," available year-round, includes chilled champagne upon arrival and candlelit dinners. The Select Registry–endorsed B&B has about 20 rooms and suites in four buildings: a stone chateau built in the 1930s, a remodeled carriage house with country-style furnishings, La Maisonneuve (French for "the new house") with its private balconies and in-room Jacuzzis, and the even newer spa building.

Milford's charming downtown is home to one of only two Relais & Châteaux properties in Pennsylvania: the eminently chic ❰ **Hotel Fauchère** (401 Broad St., Milford, 570/409-1212, www.hotelfauchere.com, regular rates $200–350, winter rates $170–245). When the 19th-century Italianate hotel reopened in 2006 after a three-decade hibernation and five-year restoration, the *New York Post* called it "the smartest hotel to open near the city in a long time." Today's guests walk through the same marble entryway and run their hands along the same mahogany banisters as Henry Ford, Charlie Chaplin, Mae West, Babe Ruth, Franklin D. Roosevelt, and John F. Kennedy. Among the newer features: iPod docking stations, flat-panel TVs, and marble-drenched bathrooms with heated towel racks and floors. The pet-friendly hotel, which has 16 guest rooms, also boasts a fine collection of mid-19th-century landscapes by Hudson River School painters. Its reputation for sumptuous lodging is matched by its culinary cachet. Tables at The Delmonico Room, the Hotel Fauchère's fine dining restaurant, and Bar Louis, its ultramodern bistro, are among the most coveted in northeast Pennsylvania. Overnight guests enjoy priority seating. A continental breakfast is included in room rates.

The reopening of the Hotel Fauchère wasn't the only big story of 2006. That very same year, northeast Pennsylvania sprouted a destination spa: **The Lodge at Woodloch** (109 River Birch

© BRUCE BUCK

guest room at the Hotel Fauchère

Ln., Hawley, 570/685-8500, www.thelodgeat woodloch.com, $249–659 per person not including spa treatments). "Luxury" is a word used liberally in descriptions of the Lake Region resort. It's been named to *National Geographic Traveler*'s "Stay List" and *Condé Nast Traveler*'s "Hot List," voted one of the world's best spas by readers of *Travel + Leisure,* and even been touted as a "top man-cation destination" on ABC News. Built at a cost of $37 million, the adults-only resort on 75 sylvan acres has just 58 guest rooms and suites. Even the smallest of them have private verandas and marble bathrooms with oversized showers. But the resort's showpiece is its spa. Soaking tubs with hydro-massaging waterfalls, an outdoor whirlpool with a radiant-heated deck for year-round enjoyment, and woodland views ensure that guests slip into a blissed-out state even before setting foot in one of the 27 treatment rooms. When they're not luxuriating in the spa, guests can unwind in other ways: kayaking on the private 15-acre lake, for example, or golfing at **Woodloch Springs** (1 Woodloch Dr., Hawley,

570/685-8102, www.woodloch.com/golf), an 18-hole championship course across the street from the resort. Overnight rates include three gourmet meals daily and any nonalcoholic beverages. (Somewhat unorthodoxly, the detox destination offers wine, beer, and cocktails. The spa, however, is a booze-free zone.) The many and various group fitness classes—from inner smile meditation to cardio kickboxing—are also included.

FOOD
Vicinity of Delaware Water Gap National Recreation Area
Located on the grounds of The Shawnee Inn and Golf Resort, **C The Gem and Keystone** (River Rd., Shawnee on Delaware, 570/424-0990, www.gemandkeystone.com, 11:30 A.M.–10 P.M. Sun.–Thurs. with bar open until 11 P.M., 11:30 A.M.–midnight Fri.–Sat., $8–29) is a tree hugger of an eatery with a snappy slogan: "Beer from here. Food from near." It's not a coincidence that the slogan puts suds before eats. Dishes are designed to

pair with all-natural ShawneeCraft ales and lagers, brewed within a short walk of The Gem. (Tours of the brewhouse are available by appointment. Call 570/424-4000, ext. 1295.) Signature entrées include beer barbecued chicken, Bavarian braised pork, and pretzel-crusted salmon. Vegetarians won't go hungry with options such as vegetarian chili, vegetarian pot pie, and a portobello burger. Rest assured that the meats are all-natural, the seafood sustainable, and the doggie bags biodegradable. A kid's meal is free with the purchase of each adult dinner entrée. Other money savers: happy hour specials 8–10 P.M. and the "Perfect Tens Menu" with its selection of $10 dinners. Jazz musicians jam every other Thursday, and bands perform most Fridays and Saturdays.

Fresh food, full-bodied flavors, and fair prices can add up to a line out the door of **Saen Thai Cuisine** (Shawnee Square, Shawnee on Delaware, 570/476 4911, 11:30 A.M.–2 P.M. and 5:30–9 P.M. Tues.–Fri., noon–2 P.M. and 5:30–9 P.M. Sat.–Sun., $8–23), which doesn't take reservations. It's not a bad idea to arrive about 20 minutes before the place opens for dinner on a weekend. Once inside the exotically decorated eatery, you'll be greeted warmly. Owner Boon Pruettipun often weaves between the closely arranged tables to chat up patrons. Everything is superb, from the spring rolls to the curries to the exquisitely presented specials.

Once called "the prettiest county seat in America" by *The Atlantic* magazine, Milford can also brag of several outstanding restaurants. The chic and history-rich **Hotel Fauchère** (401 Broad St., Milford, 570/409-1212, www.hotelfauchere.com) is home to not one, but two. Its reputation as a culinary destination dates to the 1860s, when a Swiss-born chef named Louis Fauchère took over the hotel. An 1888 portrait of Fauchère presides over its fine dining restaurant, **The Delmonico Room** (breakfast 8–11 A.M. Mon.–Sat. and jazz brunch 9 A.M.–2:30 P.M. Sun. year-round, lunch 11:30 A.M.–2 P.M. Thurs.–Sat. in summer, dinner Thurs.–Sun. in summer and Fri.–Sun. in winter, breakfast $7–11, lunch $16–22, dinner $32–42, tasting menus offered), where

modern interpretations of classic cuisine are served on Bernardaud china. The service is superlative and the setting romantic. Though it's decorated with vintage menus from famed European restaurants, The Delmonico Room is actually named for a New York City establishment: Delmonico's. Fauchère served as master chef at the venerable restaurant, best known for creating the Delmonico steak, before moving to Milford. Delmonico steak is on the menu at **Bar Louis** (summer hours 11:30 A.M.–10 P.M. Sun.–Thurs. and 11:30 A.M.–11 P.M. Fri.–Sat., winter hours 11:30 A.M.–3 P.M. and 5–9 P.M. Wed.–Thurs., 11:30 A.M.–3 P.M. and 5–11 P.M. Fri., 11:30 A.M.–11 P.M. Sat., and 11:30 A.M.–9 P.M. Sun., $12–36), named for Fauchère himself. The sleek, sexy bistro on the hotel's ground level is famous for its specialty cocktails and sushi pizza (ahi tuna atop a crust of flash-fried tempura-battered rice). Also notable: the house-cured meats and olives and signature burger with black truffle fries. An enormous framed photo of Andy Warhol planting a smooch on John Lennon's cheek sits behind the minimalist bar. It's all so very SoHo that you're liable to feel disoriented upon emerging onto Milford's sleepy main drag.

Something you'll never see in a New York City eatery: a working 19th-century waterwheel. Milford's **Waterwheel Café, Bakery and Bar** (150 Water St., Milford, 570/296-2383, www.waterwheelcafe.com, café 8 A.M.–3:30 P.M. daily and 5:15–9:30 P.M. Thurs.–Sat., bar 5–10 P.M. Thurs.–Sat., breakfast and lunch $3–12, dinner $16–28) offers diners a view of water rushing over a three-story waterwheel built in the early 1800s to power grain-grinding equipment. Contemplate the power of moving water as you power up for your day with a house-baked scone, whole-wheat pancakes, or a plate of sirloin steak and eggs. The Waterwheel spans the globe for its lunchtime options, which include Vietnamese rice noodle salad, a Mediterranean sampler plate, and a sandwich of duck liver mousse on brick-oven Italian bread. Dinner at the café is a relaxed fine dining affair with a menu heavy on modern Vietnamese cuisine. A bar menu is available

© BRUCE BUCK

Bar Louis at Hotel Fauchère

for lighter appetites. Beer, wine, and cocktails are served any time of day, as are divine pastries, cakes, and pies. The Waterwheel's Thursday night blues jam attracts some of the best musicians in the region, and many a weekend features live music.

Lake Region

For a town of just 4.2 square miles, Honesdale has a surprising assortment of diners and pizzerias. Established in 1930 by a family of Greek immigrants, **The Towne House Diner** (920 Main St., Honesdale, 570/253-1311, www .townehousediner.com, 7 A.M.–8 P.M. Sun.–Thurs., 7 A.M.–9 P.M. Fri., $3–14) has downhome food down pat. Fred Chalmers has owned the place since the 1970s, and his Greek chef, Peter Papoutsakis, has been serving up everything from burgers to sautéed baby beef liver for more than a quarter of a century. Breakfast buffs can order an omelet or a stack of pancakes any time of day. The decor is strictly old-school, plaid curtains and all, but the mini jukeboxes on the tables offer several eras' worth of tunes. (Vanilla Ice sounds even sillier after a

little Bing Crosby.) The Towne House is conveniently located near the departure station for Stourbridge Line train excursions.

The European-style **《 Branko's Patisserie du Jour** (501 Main St., Honesdale, 570/253-0311, www.brankos-patisserie.com, 6:30 A.M.–3 P.M. Tues.–Thurs., 7 A.M.–5 P.M. Fri.–Sat., 8 A.M.–2 P.M. Sun., breakfast $1–8, lunch $5–20) is a departure from the typical. Chef Branko Bozic, a silver-haired gent from Germany, worked in high-end restaurants across Europe and in Las Vegas and served as personal chef to Pennsylvania governor Bob Casey in the early 1990s before opening this café in 2005. The vibe is casual, but the soups, salads, and sandwiches are très sophisticated. Rare-grilled duck breast finds its way onto organic greens. Salami from Barcelona meets French brie on house-baked bread. Bozic is a skilled pastry chef, and his fruit tarts and Parisian chocolate domes are to die for. Once a month from September through May, the patisserie offers a prix fixe dinner ($59.95 per person) in a candlelit setting. Reservations go quickly.

The historic **Hotel Wayne** (1202 Main St.,

Honesdale, 570/253-3290, www.hotelwayne .com, restaurant 11:30 A.M.–9 P.M. daily, bar open as late as 2 A.M., $7–22) is home to the only classy, smoke-free bar in town. Originally built in 1827, the hotel was rebuilt in 1895 and extensively renovated in 2009. Its turn-of-the-20th-century ambience remains intact, owing in part to lofty tin ceilings and oversized windows. The bar boasts the largest selection of microbrews and craft beers in the area. Bistro 1202, the hotel's restaurant, serves middling contemporary American cuisine. Its menu is available in the bar and on the outdoor porch. Order the fresh-cut chips tossed with blue cheese, scallions, and white truffle oil to start. Post-renovation, Hotel Wayne has been an up-and-coming hangout for tourists and locals alike, so a reservation isn't a bad idea.

The itty-bitty borough of Hawley, about 10 miles southeast of Honesdale, offers the sort of fine dining usually associated with metropolises. Farmers and producers within an hour's drive provide a great deal of what's served at **The Settlers Inn** (4 Main Ave., Hawley, 800/833-8527, www.thesettlersinn.com, breakfast 7:30–10 A.M. daily, lunch noon–2:30 P.M.

Fri.–Sat., brunch 11:30 A.M.–2:30 P.M. Sun., dinner 5 P.M.–close daily, breakfast $6–10, lunch $9–12, dinner $26–37), a small hotel and immensely popular restaurant on the banks of the trout-rich Lackawaxen River. Brook trout is a favorite ingredient of innkeeper, longtime fisherman, and self-taught chef Grant Genzlinger. He smokes it in house and serves it with horseradish cream as an appetizer. A trout dish often tops the list of dinner entrées. Pennsylvania's state fish even finds its way onto the breakfast menu in the form of a crepe-accompanying mousse. Portions are on the small side, so don't shy away from the soups and other starters. The baked onion soup with Amish-made Swiss cheese hits the spot in winter. If the dinner menu doesn't fit your budget, consider dining in the inn's cozy tavern. You'll find the same farm-to-table philosophy and no entrée over $15. In the warmer months, snag a table on the river-facing terrace.

A touch more casual, the **Falls Port Inn and Restaurant** (330 Main Ave., Hawley, 570/226-2600, www.thefallsportinnand restaurant.com, regular hours 11:30 A.M.–3 P.M. and 5–10 P.M. Mon.–Sat., 5–9 P.M. Sun., call

© RARE BRICK PHOTOGRAPHY

The Settlers Inn

or see website for winter hours, lunch $8–10, dinner $17–60) is known for its hand-cut steaks, grilled over an open flame. Ask your server about the "heart attack steak toppings." Service can be a bit slow, but the owners are friendly, and the food is generally delicious. Classical music complements the Victorian decor. The tavern adjacent to the dining room gets busy around 9 P.M. as locals and inn guests mingle over top-shelf spirits and fine wines.

Dinner at **Torte Knox** (301 Main Ave., Hawley, 570/226-8200, www.torteknox.com) is more experience than meal and very much a splurge. Owner and chef Sheelah Kaye-Stepkin, a former actress and cooking show hostess, serves up stories from the culinary trenches as she prepares a tasting menu in full view of guests. Hers are dishes you're not likely to try at home: soft-shell crabs with underbellies painted in apricot coulis, for example, or quail stuffed with handmade brioche. Offered most Saturdays, the experience begins at 6:30 P.M. and lasts well into the evening. The $125-per-person price tag doesn't include beverages. If you're interested in wine pairings, mention so when making a reservation. Torte Knox also offers brunch 10 A.M.–2 P.M. on Sundays. Entrées are $8–20 and include Kaye-Stepkin's signature lobster Benedict. Her culinary chops are matched by her talent for remodeling. Torte Knox, a recreational cooking school as well as restaurant, occupies the former First National Bank of Hawley.

Jim Thorpe

Historic Jim Thorpe is home to the artfully modern **Ⓒ Flow** (268 W. Broadway, Jim Thorpe, 570/325-8200, www.flow restaurant.com, 11 A.M.–9 P.M. Wed.–Thurs., 11 A.M.–10 P.M. Fri.–Sat., 11 A.M.–9 P.M. Sun., lunch $5–7, dinner $16–29), named for the underground stream visible through a glass enclosure in the dining room. Flow is extremely rigid in one respect: It serves only chemical-free meats, dairy products, and vegetables. The dinner menu, as spare as the decor, is rewritten almost daily to reflect the latest offerings of area farmers and producers. Popular items include

organic foie gras, homemade gnocchi, and "starving artist" specials such as meatloaf made with grass-fed beef. Seven-dollar sandwiches dominate the lunch menu. Portions are enormous, and the selection of Pennsylvania beers and wines is extensive. Flow, which opened in 2008, occupies a mid-19th-century building that opened as a water-powered wire mill and once served as a warehouse for adult toys. Nationally renowned illustrator Victor Stabin and his wife transformed it into the Carbon County Cultural Project (www.thecccp.org). It's as much an arts destination as a dining destination, housing galleries that display works by Stabin and other select artists.

Moya (24 Race St., Jim Thorpe, 570/325-8530, www.jimthorpemoya.com, 5–9 P.M. Mon.–Tues. and Thurs., 5–10 P.M. Fri.–Sat., 5–8 P.M. Sun., $20–26) also pairs exceptional food with art. Owner and chef Heriberto Yunda got his culinary start cooking for American oil company executives in his native Ecuador and lent his talents to restaurants in New York City and Istanbul before moving to Pennsylvania in 2002. Named for his hometown, Moya is decorated with his wife's abstract paintings: riots of color against butternut squash-hued walls. The menu changes frequently but always offers an eclectic variety of dishes. Polenta with gorgonzola sauce, roasted quail, seafood stew, and braised lamb shank have all made the cut. Moya draws a lot of locals and is always packed on weekends; a reservation will spare you the disappointment of being turned away. The service can be hit or miss, especially when the house is full, but the food is unassailable.

Also chef-owned, **Café Origins** (107 Broadway, Jim Thorpe, 570/325-8776, www.cafeorigins.com, noon–9 P.M. daily except Tues. July–Aug., weekends and holidays only Apr.–June and Sept.–Nov., $10–17) specializes in Eurasian-inspired vegetarian and vegan fare. The hippie haven doesn't discriminate against omnivores: Its lengthy menu includes a smattering of chicken, salmon, and shrimp options. Because everything is made from scratch, the cooks can accommodate gluten-free diets and other culinary sensitivities. Owner Denise

O'Donnell is known around town as "the elephant lady." That's because the Buddhist vegetarian volunteers as a mahout, or elephant keeper, in Thailand on a fairly regular basis. Adorned as it is with Tibetan tankas, statues carved from mango wood, a Buddhist altar complete with incense, and—no lie—paintings created by elephants, Café Origins isn't exactly toddler-proof. Adult beverages are allowed. The restaurant waives its $5 corking fee for wines from the nearby Big Creek Vineyard shop (27 Race St., Jim Thorpe, 1–5 P.M. Sun.–Thurs., 1–7 P.M. Fri.–Sat.). Its own selection of drinks includes delish smoothies made with organic fruit and soy milk.

Just down the street, the **Albright Mansion** (66 Broadway, Jim Thorpe, 570/325-4440, www.albrightmansion.com, 8 A.M.–3 P.M. Sun.–Thurs., 8 A.M.–9 P.M. Fri.–Sat., breakfast and lunch $4–10, dinner $17–26) offers "elegant, inexpensive, fine cuisine" in the onetime home of a Civil War general. It's known for its breakfasts, available 8 A.M.–noon daily. Power up with the full English breakfast, complete with banger and grilled tomato, or the sublime eggs Benedict. The BYOB restaurant serves lunch and a proper tea starting at noon and dinner on Fridays and Saturdays. Entrées are accompanied by a complimentary pour of matching wine.

With its full-service bar and laid-back atmosphere, **Molly Maguires Pub & Steakhouse** (5 Hazard Square, Jim Thorpe, 570/325-4563, www.jimthorpedining.com, kitchen 11 A.M.–10 P.M. Sun.–Thurs., 11 A.M.–11 P.M. Fri.–Sat., last call 1:45 A.M., $6–22) is often the most happenin' spot in Jim Thorpe. Its proprietors hail from Dublin, and the kitchen dishes out some Irish classics along with plenty of American pub grub. Mollies, as locals call the place, showcases live music on weekends. An outdoor deck with space for 125 provides an appealing alternative to the sometimes smoky bar area.

INFORMATION

If you're driving to the Poconos from New Jersey or New York, be sure to stop at a state-run welcome center, where you'll be up to your eyeballs in information. The I-80 welcome center is a half mile west of the Pennsylvania–New Jersey line at exit 310. The I-84 welcome center is a mile west of the Pennsylvania–New York line at exit 53. Look for the I-81 welcome center a half mile south of the Pennsylvania–New York line. Personalized travel counseling is available 7 A.M.–7 P.M. daily; the restrooms are always open.

The **Pocono Mountains Visitors Bureau** (1004 Main St., Stroudsburg, 570/421-5791, www.800poconos.com, 8:30 A.M.–5 P.M. Mon.–Fri.) operates several visitors centers. The northernmost is the Lake Wallenpaupack visitors center (U.S. 6 just west of Rte. 507 junction, 570/226-2141, 10 A.M.–6 P.M. daily Memorial Day–Labor Day, 9 A.M.–5 P.M. daily rest of year), located right on the lake with a public beach behind it. The tourism promotion agency also has a presence in Tannersville (food court of The Crossings Premium Outlets, I-80 exit 299, 570/629-1703, 10 A.M.–6 P.M. daily) and Jim Thorpe (historic train station on U.S. 209, 570/325-3673, 9:30 A.M.–5:30 P.M. daily). Visit its website to request free publications or peruse digital versions of skiing and camping brochures. Another handy feature of the website: a summary of snow conditions at each of the region's ski areas. If you don't have access to the Internet, call the 24-hour ski hotline at 570/421-5565. In the fall, that's the number to dial for foliage info.

GETTING THERE AND AROUND

Though mostly rural, the Poconos region is serviced by several major highways: east–west Interstates 80 and 84, north–south I-81, and the Northeast Extension of the Pennsylvania Turnpike (I-476). It's possible to come and go by bus (just ask the sleepy-eyed Poconos residents who commute to Manhattan on weekday mornings), but it's hard to get by without a car during your stay. There are exceptions to that rule. If your destination is one of the region's full-service resorts, it may provide shuttle service from a bus station or airport. If your goal is to hike the famed Appalachian Trail, you can take a **Greyhound** (800/231-2222, www.greyhound.com) or **Martz Trailways** (570/421-3040, www.martzpoconos.com) bus to the town of Delaware Water Gap and walk to two trailheads. Visit the Delaware Water Gap National Recreation Area website (www.nps.gov/dewa) for walking directions. **Pack Shack Adventures** (88 Broad St., Delaware Water Gap, 570/424-8533, www.packshack.com) is also within walking distance of the bus stop. The livery rents canoes, kayaks, rafts, and tubes and provides shuttles to and from the Delaware River.

Passenger airlines won't get you terribly close to the recreational heart of the Poconos. These major airports are 40–70 miles from the national park: Lehigh Valley International Airport (ABE), Wilkes-Barre/Scranton International Airport (AVP), and Newark Liberty International Airport (EWR).

Scranton and Wilkes-Barre

Northeast Pennsylvania's largest cities are the not-so-large cities of Scranton and Wilkes-Barre. Both are county seats—a virtual guarantee of lofty architecture. Both are nestled in river valleys. Just 20 miles apart, they're often joined by a slash in references to the area. (Think Dallas/Fort Worth on a smaller scale.) They share professional sports teams, a philharmonic orchestra, and an airport. They also share an industrial heritage: Both were once booming centers of the anthracite mining industry.

Anthracite is a word rarely heard these days, but for several decades, it was the most popular heating fuel in the northern United States. Sometimes referred to as hard coal or colloquially as "black diamonds," anthracite is special stuff. It has fewer impurities than any other type of coal. It burns longer. And no place in the western hemisphere has more of it than northeast Pennsylvania. Its discovery in the 18th century transformed the region over the course of the 19th. Immigrants poured in to meet the human capital needs of coal companies. Communities were carved out of wilderness. Canal systems were built, and then railroads. The population of Scranton surged from less than 10,000 in 1860 to about 143,000 in 1930. Wilkes-Barre's population shot from less than 5,000 to about 87,000 in that period.

Today their populations are roughly half of what they were in 1930. Why? Because the lust for black diamonds began to wane after World War I. Oil was in; coal was out. On January 22, 1959, an anthracite mine about midway between Scranton and Wilkes-Barre collapsed under the weight of the ice-laden Susquehanna River. An estimated 10 billion gallons of river water coursed through the cavity, flooding mines throughout the area. The Knox Mine disaster, as it came to be called, killed 12 men and the nation's appetite for deep anthracite mining. To appreciate the enormous impact of the

Coal mining was a major industry in the Scranton/Wilkes-Barre area for decades.

PHOTO BY W.J. HARRIS/FROM THE COLLECTION OF JANET LINDENMUTH

POCONO MOUNTAINS

THE OFFICE FAN'S GUIDE TO SCRANTON

The "Scranton Welcomes You" sign is now inside The Mall at Steamtown.

© PETER DUTTON

Millions of people who've never been to Scranton know just where to get a beer if they're ever out this way. That's because they're fans of the American version of *The Office*, a sitcom that's filmed in sunny California but set at the Scranton branch of a fictional paper company. References to actual places in Scranton and the surrounding area are common, which has made the city a pilgrimage site for super fans of the hit NBC show. In October 2007 they flocked to Scranton for the first-ever **The Office Convention** (www.theofficeconvention. com), which featured appearances by many cast members. It remains to be seen whether the lovefest is repeated.

The first order of business for many visiting fans is snapping a photo of the "Scranton Welcomes You" sign that appears in the opening credits. They can approach the city from every possible direction and still not find it. Until a few years ago, there were two

such signs alongside inbound expressways. The bravest of fans – some might call them knuckleheads – would veer off to the side for a photo op. Now it's possible to get a pic without risking life and limb. After the city removed the signs, one was rescued from storage and placed inside **The Mall at Steamtown** (Lackawanna and Penn Aves., downtown Scranton, 570/343-3400, www.themallatsteamtown. com, 10 A.M.-9 P.M. Mon.-Sat., 11 A.M.-6 P.M. Sun.), which itself has gotten shout-outs on the show. Rainn Wilson, who plays uber-quirky officemate Dwight Schrute, has been named an honorary mall guard.

Fans who wish to visit some of the restaurants and bars referenced on *The Office* first have to parse fact from fiction. Office boss Michael Scott loves Hooters and its buxom waitresses, but there's no Hooters in Scranton. The nearest location of the international chain is 60 miles away in New Jersey. There's no Benihana – or "Asian Hooters," as Michael calls it – anywhere near Scranton either. But the oft-mentioned **Cooper's Seafood House** (701 N. Washington Ave., Scranton, 570/346-6883, www.coopers-seafood.com, 11 A.M.-midnight Mon.-Thurs., 11 A.M.-1 A.M. Fri.-Sat., noon-midnight Sun., $8-30) is, indeed, a Scranton institution. The family-owned restaurant, famous for its beer selection and lobster hats, looks like a pirate ship complete with attacking octopus. Patrons can wait for a table inside a lighthouse-shaped bar. Scranton's most famous watering hole may well be **Poor Richard's Pub** (125 Beech St., Scranton, 570/344-4555, www.poorrichardspub.net, 5 P.M.-2 A.M. Mon.-Fri., 2 P.M.-2 A.M. Sat., noon-2 A.M. Sun., kitchen open 6 P.M.-1 A.M. Mon.-Sat. and 1 P.M.-1 A.M. Sun., $2-10). It's referenced in multiple episodes of *The Office*, and in season three, it's where office cutie Pam tells then-boyfriend Roy about her kiss with coworker Jim. Good thing the scene wasn't filmed in the real Poor Richard's because an enraged Roy proceeds to trash the place. Fans expecting a stand-alone pub will be surprised to find that Poor Richard's is actually inside the 34-lane South Side Bowl. The show has also dished out free advertising for **Alfredo's Pizza Cafe** (1040 S. Washington Ave., Scranton, 570/969-1910, www.alfredoscafe.com, 11 A.M.-11 P.M. Mon.-Thurs., 11 A.M.-midnight Fri.-Sat., 11 A.M.-11 P.M. Sun., $6-20), located just around the corner from Poor Richard's, and **Farley's** (300 Adams Ave., Scranton, 570/346-3000, www.farleysrestaurant.com, 11 A.M.-2 A.M. Mon.-Sat., 4:30 P.M.-2 A.M. Sun., opens 1 P.M. Sat. and 4 P.M. Sun. in summer, $6-36), a downtown steak and seafood house.

Viewers with an eye for detail will spot all sorts of Scrantonalia in the Dunder Mifflin Scranton office, from University of Scranton apparel to bobbleheads of Scranton/

Wilkes-Barre Red Barons players (now the Scranton/Wilkes-Barre Yankees). **Crystal Club** sodas, which seem to be the beverages of choice in the office, weren't concocted by set designers. They're made in Scranton by a private company that's been in business for more than a century.

Viewers who know the area will spot all sorts of improbabilities, like Michael and Dwight's train ride to Philadelphia in one episode. There's no passenger train service between the cities. In the season three episode "Beach Games," Michael takes the gang to **Lake Scranton** for a series of competitions to determine his successor. The real Lake Scranton, located southeast of downtown off Route 307, doesn't have a beach. In season two's "Booze Cruise," Michael surprises his motley crew with a January cruise on **Lake Wallenpaupack.** The real Lake Wallenpaupack, about 30 miles east of Scranton in the Poconos, usually freezes in winter; cruises don't resume until spring.

Improbabilities aside, most Scrantonites are tickled by the attention heaped on their city. In 2009 an enterprising group began offering **The Office Fan Tours** (570/963-6363, www.theofficefantours.com), a guaranteed good time. *That's what she said.*

industry on northeast Pennsylvania, just glance at a map. Place names such as Minersville, Port Carbon, Carbondale, Coaldale, and Carbon County say it all. A deeper appreciation can be gained by visiting one or more of the heritage attractions in the region. There's a slew of them in and around Scranton.

Like many rust belt cities, Scranton and Wilkes-Barre are working to reinvent themselves. They landed a minor league baseball team in 1989 and an American Hockey League franchise a decade later. Wilkes-Barre got a casino in 2006. Scranton has gotten loads of priceless publicity since 2005, when the American version of *The Office* debuted. Set in Scranton, the hilarious TV sitcom has given rise to fan tours of the city.

SIGHTS
◖ Ricketts Glen State Park

Exceptionally scenic **hiking** trails make Ricketts Glen (accessible from Routes 487 and 118, 25 miles west of Wilkes-Barre, 570/477-5675, www.dcnr.state.pa.us/stateparks/parks/RickettsGlen.aspx) one of northeast Pennsylvania's main attractions. *Backpacker* magazine has for years heaped accolades on the 13,050-acre park, which boasts 22 named waterfalls. The highest of them, Ganoga Falls, is 94 feet tall. The waterfalls lie in a section of the park known as the Glens Natural Area, a registered National Natural Landmark that's also blessed with giant pines, hemlocks, and oaks. Many of the trees are more than 500 years old—too wide to wrap your arms around and dizzyingly tall. Twenty-six miles of trails crisscross the park. The most talked-about trek is 7.2 miles long and passes by 21 waterfalls. It's called the Falls Trail, for obvious reasons, and it's accessible from several parking areas. The Lake Rose parking lot, at the end of a dirt road across from the park's campground, provides the closest access but fills up quickly. The less convenient options are the beach parking lots and a lot on Route 118 about 2 miles east of the town of Red Rock. It's a challenging trail: often rocky, sometimes slippery, and damn steep here and there. You can skip the lower section,

Ricketts Glen State Park

© LUZERNE COUNTY CONVENTION AND VISITORS BUREAU

trimming the trek to 3.2 miles, and still see most of the waterfalls. The only one of the 22 waterfalls *not* along the Falls Trail, a 36-footer named Adams, is a cinch to reach. It's a few hundred feet from the Evergreen Trail parking lot on Route 118, a stone's throw from the previously mentioned Route 118 parking lot. The one-mile Evergreen Trail is easy hiking through one of the oldest forest stands in Pennsylvania. See if you can spot the hemlock that stood on this continent before Columbus.

Hiking isn't the only draw. The 245-acre Lake Jean allows for swimming and **boating** (electric motors only) in the warmer months and **fishing** year-round. Its 600-foot beach is open from late May to mid-September. Rowboats, paddleboats, kayaks, and canoes are available for rent from mid-May through mid-October. The boat concession is open 10 A.M.–6 P.M. daily from June through August and on weekends the rest of the season. **Hunting** and trapping are allowed on more than 10,000 acres of the park, which abuts some 83,000 acres of state game lands. That adds up to a helluva lot of deer, beaver, bear, coyote, and other critters. **Horseback riding** is permitted on certain trails and roads within the park, but you have to bring your own mount. **Braces Stables** (62 Jamison City Rd., Benton, 570/925-5253, www.bracesstables.com), just outside the park, offers one- to two-hour trail rides for a reasonable $25–40 per person. In winter Ricketts Glen attracts cross-country skiers, snowshoers, snowmobilers, and ice climbers.

The park has a modern campground with 120 tent and trailer sites, some of which are available year-round. More than half are on a peninsula extending into Lake Jean. Ten modern cabins with two or three bedrooms can be rented year-round. Reserve online at www.pa.reserveworld .com or by calling 888/727-2757.

Steamtown National Historic Site

Rail fans have a lot of love for Scranton. It's home to one of eight surviving "Big Boy" steam locomotives and the only one stored east of Wisconsin. Weighing in at 1.2 million pounds, Union Pacific No. 4012 was one of 25 Big Boys built in the 1940s to pull long freight trains over the mountains of Utah and Wyoming. Though it no longer operates, it's among the standouts in the collection of locomotives, passenger cars, freight cars, and maintenance-of-way equipment at Steamtown (intersection of Lackawanna Ave. and Cliff St., downtown Scranton, 570/340-5200, www.nps .gov/stea, open daily, train rides offered seasonally, regular hours 9 A.M.–5 P.M., winter hours 10 A.M.–4 P.M., admission $6, children 16 and under free).

Located on a working railroad yard that dates to 1851, the national park is dedicated to preserving the history of steam railroading in America. It's home to some 25 steam and diesel-electric locomotives. The oldest of them is a freight engine built in 1903 for the Chicago Union Transfer Railway Company. Several are in working order, and visitors can ride behind them in historic commuter cars. Half-hour train rides are offered most days

© JOHN MORGAN

Union Pacific No. 4012, one of eight surviving "Big Boy" locomotives, at Steamtown National Historic Site

POCONO MOUNTAINS

from mid-April to early December. Tickets are $3 for anyone age 6 or older. On days when a steam locomotive is used, visitors can pay $30 for the privilege of riding in the cab and interacting with the crew. Cab ride tickets are limited to four per day and, like the $3 tickets, are sold on a first-come, first-served basis. Reservations are strongly recommended for longer excursions, which are offered on select weekends and range from about two hours to a full day. Guided walking tours of the locomotive shop, part of which dates to the 1860s, are available year-round. The 45-minute look at what it takes to maintain and repair the fire-breathing machines is included in the price of park admission. Other walking tours are offered seasonally. Call or check the website for a schedule of train excursions and walking tours. Allot at least an hour for exploring Steamtown's two museums. One traces the history of railroading from its earliest days to the 1980s; the other focuses on the technology of steam railroading. The museum complex includes a 250-seat theater that shows *Steel and Steam,* an 18-minute film illustrating the profound changes railroads underwent in the early 20th century, every half hour on most days. Steamtown hosts **Railfest,** a celebration of passenger railroading past and present, in the fall, and a lecture series in winter.

Electric City Trolley Museum

It's not its nightlife that earned Scranton the nickname "Electric City." It's the fact that Scranton had a commercially viable electric streetcar system before any other U.S. city. Scranton was a booming industrial metropolis when the Scranton Suburban Electric Railway commenced operation in November 1886. By the time the railway folded in 1954, Scranton's fortunes and population had begun to diminish, and buses were supplanting streetcars across the country. The history of electric railway transit in eastern Pennsylvania is chronicled at the Electric City Trolley Museum (intersection of Lackawanna Ave. and Cliff St., downtown Scranton, 570/963-6590, www

.ectma.org, 9 A.M.–5 P.M. daily Apr.–Dec., Wed.–Sun. Jan.–Mar., trolley rides offered seasonally, museum admission $6, seniors $5, children 4–17 $4), located on the grounds of Steamtown National Historic Site. About a dozen trolleys are on display, the oldest of which dates to 1907. The museum's collection is particularly strong in trolleys of Philadelphia and its western suburbs. Most of its vehicles were in fact built in Philadelphia by the J.G. Brill Company, the world's largest trolley manufacturer in its day.

Looking at historic trolley cars is nice, but it's best to visit when you can ride one. Trolley excursions are offered Thursday–Sunday from May through October. The trolley passes through one of the longest interurban tunnels ever built as it makes its way to PNC Field, home of the Scranton/Wilkes-Barre Yankees. The fare is $8 for adults, $7.50 for seniors, $6 for children 4–17. A combination ticket good for museum admission and a trolley ride is $10 for adults, $9 for seniors, $8 for children.

Scranton was the first U.S. city to have a commercially viable electric streetcar system.

Everhart Museum and Nay Aug Park

When Scranton's Everhart Museum (1901 Mulberry St., Scranton, 570/346-7186, www.everhart-museum.org, open Feb.–Dec., noon–4 P.M. Mon. and Thurs.–Fri., 10 A.M.–5 P.M. Sat., noon–5 P.M. Sun., admission $5, seniors and students $3, children 6–12 $2) opened in 1908, it housed little more than its benefactor's vast collection of mounted birds. But Dr. Isaiah Fawkes Everhart—local physician and businessman, Civil War veteran, and skilled taxidermist—did more than donate his stuffed specimens. He also created an endowment fund for his museum. Many purchases and donations later, the Everhart is the largest public museum in northeast Pennsylvania, with a focus on the visual arts as well as natural history. Its eclectic collection includes a Victorian-era wreath made with human hair, a cast of a stegosaurus skeleton, ceremonial masks from Africa, and painted coffin posts from Egypt. Among the highlights is a mural of prehistoric northeast Pennsylvania by Brooklyn-born Charles R. Knight, who became a renowned artist despite being legally blind. Painted in 1951, it was the last of his great murals.

The museum is located in Scranton's largest city-run park, Nay Aug (570/348-4186, www.scrantonpa.gov), boasting two playgrounds, a pool and water-slide complex, and a rose garden. But its best feature is the rock-strewn Nay Aug Gorge and its waterfalls, designated a National Natural Landmark. The best *manmade* feature is a spectacularly crafted tree house overlooking the gorge.

Anthracite Heritage Attractions

The story of coal mining in northeast Pennsylvania is not a PG one. It's a story of backbreaking work under deplorable conditions, a story of death and disfiguring injuries. It's rated R for violence. If you have the stomach for it, start with a visit to the **Pennsylvania Anthracite Heritage Museum** (McDade Park, Scranton, 570/963-4804, www.anthracitemuseum.org, 9 A.M.–5 P.M. Mon.–Sat.,

noon–5 P.M. Sun., admission $6, seniors $5.50, children 3–11 $4), which focuses on the immigrant experience. Tens of thousands of immigrants from more than three dozen nations settled in the region in the 19th and early 20th centuries to work in the iron, coal, and textile industries. The museum offers a window into their daily lives. Among its exhibits is a recreated kitchen of a typical mine worker's house, circa 1935. The original altar of a Catholic church founded by Irish immigrants in 1902 is the centerpiece of an exhibit on the role of churches in ethnic communities. (Their role was as much temporal as spiritual. Women whose husbands were maimed or killed in the mines often turned to their church for financial assistance.) But the most telling pieces in the collection are black-and-white photographs of men, women, and children building new lives in a nation built on their backs. The museum is located in McDade Park, a county-run oasis reclaimed from coal-mining terrain. The park is a few miles west of downtown Scranton, accessible from Keyser Avenue.

McDade Park is also home to the **Lackawanna Coal Mine Tour** (Scranton, 570/963-6463, www.lackawannacounty.org, 10 A.M.–3 P.M. daily Apr.–Nov., admission $10, seniors $9.50, children 3–12 $7.50), where you can don a hardhat and descend 300 feet below the earth's surface to explore a once-active mine. Honest-to-goodness miners do the guiding. The descent by mine car takes several minutes; the walking portion of the tour lasts an hour and covers about half a mile. It's always 53 degrees inside the mine, so dress accordingly. Tours are scheduled on demand.

About an hour south of McDade Park is **Eckley Miners' Village** (off Rte. 940, 9 miles east of Hazleton, 570/636-2070, www.eckleyminers.org, 9 A.M.–5 P.M. Mon.–Sat., noon–5 P.M. Sun., admission $6, seniors $5.50, children 3–11 $4), an example of a so-called patch town. Hundreds of "patches"—villages owned entirely by mining companies and populated by miners and their families—mushroomed across the anthracite region in the 19th century. Even the stores were company-owned,

© LUZERNE COUNTY CONVENTION AND VISITORS BUREAU

Eckley Miners' Village

and you can bet there were no bargains to be found. Settled in 1854, Eckley had a population of more than 1,000 by 1870. Today it's property of the state and virtually uninhabited. Visitors can stroll through the village-turned-museum, which consists of 58 buildings. It's best to visit between Memorial Day weekend and Labor Day weekend, when guided tours are available. Admission plus a tour is $7.50 for adults, $7 for seniors, $4 for children 3–11. Tours take about an hour and 15 minutes and go inside several buildings, including miners' dwellings and two churches. The "company store," which houses the museum shop, isn't original. It was built as a prop for the 1970 movie *The Molly Maguires,* based on the murderous doings of militant Irish miners. Much of the movie, starring Sean Connery, was filmed in Eckley, which had changed hardly at all in the century since the bloodshed.

Houdini Tour & Magic Show

The legendary Harry Houdini may be dead, but his legacy is alive and well in Scranton. The city's most unique attraction is a show (1433 N. Main Ave., Scranton, 570/342-5555, www.houdini.org, call for show times and prices) put on by a pair of magicians whose idolatry of the escape artist is infectious. Dorothy Dietrich, a platinum blonde famous for duplicating Houdini's escapes and sawing men in half, and Dick Brooks, a.k.a. "Bravo the Great," have been known to levitate audience members. Each magic show—complete with live animals—is complemented by a tour of their collection of Houdini memorabilia, which includes photos, posters, and props. Among the highlights: a pair of handcuffs that belonged to the escapologist himself.

ENTERTAINMENT AND EVENTS

Mohegan Sun at Pocono Downs

Mohegan Sun at Pocono Downs (1280 Rte. 315, Wilkes-Barre, 570/831-2100, www.poconodowns.com, casino open 24 hours), a casino and harness racing track, is the younger sibling of Connecticut's Mohegan Sun. Both are property of the Mohegan Tribe of Connecticut. If you've been to the mammoth original—one of the largest casinos in the country—you'll find Wilkes-Barre's "racino" quaint by comparison. But it's impressive as Pennsylvania casinos go, boasting 2,500 slots, a dozen eateries and bars, and several shops. Nonsmokers, beware: Smoking is permitted in well over half of the casino. The easiest way to find the nonsmoking section is to scan the signage from the bar in the center of the casino. While the casino is closed to anyone under 21, there's no age requirement to enter the racetrack area. Wagering, however, is limited to those 18 and older. Races are held on the 5/8-mile track several evenings a week for all but the coldest months of the year. In summer the racetrack doubles as a concert venue.

Dining options include a buffet restaurant, a sushi bar, and chains Ruth's Chris Steak House, Wolfgang Puck Express, and Johnny Rockets. The standout: **Rustic Kitchen Bistro & Bar** (570/824-6600, 11:30 A.M.–9 P.M. Sun.–Tues., 11:30 A.M.–11 P.M. Wed.–Sat., bar open until midnight Wed.–Sat., $9–35), a Tuscan villa-themed restaurant with a knack for pizzas, creamy clam chowder, and seafood dishes. Its main feature is a state-of-the-art TV studio kitchen complete with tiered seating for audience members. Call or check the casino website for a schedule of live cooking shows.

Mohegan Sun at Pocono Downs, the state's only casino when it opened in 2006, is now one of two in northeast Pennsylvania. Unlike Mount Airy Casino Resort to its east, it doesn't have a hotel. But there are plenty of lodging options within a few minutes drive. Best of the bunch: The Woodlands Inn (1073 Rte. 315, Wilkes-Barre, 570/824-9831, www.thewoodlandsresort.com, $89–200), known for its giant Jacuzzi and jumpin' nightlife.

Concert Venues

The area's largest concert venue is the **Toyota Pavilion at Montage Mountain** (1000 Montage Mountain Rd., Scranton, 570/961-9000, www.livenation.com), a partially covered amphitheater near Sno Mountain Ski Resort. The summer concert venue, which has reserved and lawn seating for about 18,000, has played host to Dave Matthews Band, James Taylor, Def Leppard, and Kanye West, among many other performers.

The **Mohegan Sun Arena at Casey Plaza** (255 Highland Park Blvd., Wilkes-Barre, 800/745-3000, www.mohegansunarenapa.com) is home to the Wilkes-Barre/Scranton Penguins, the American Hockey League affiliate of the Pittsburgh Penguins. Built in 1999, it's also used for everything from college graduation ceremonies to professional wrestling shows. Elton John, Cher, Neil Diamond, Janet Jackson, The Eagles, AC/DC, and Simon & Garfunkel have played the arena, which has 8,000 permanent seats and a capacity of almost 10,000 for concerts. The arena was named for Wilkes-Barre's casino/racetrack in 2010. Previously it was known as the Wachovia Arena.

Performing Arts

The **Scranton Cultural Center at the Masonic Temple** (420 N. Washington Ave., Scranton, 570/346-7369, www.scrantonculturalcenter.org) is arguably the most architecturally impressive building in Scranton. Inaugurated in 1930 as the Masonic Temple and Scottish Rite Cathedral, the neo-Gothic and Romanesque structure was designed by Raymond M. Hood, also responsible for the *Chicago Tribune* building and New York's Rockefeller Center. It's still the hub of Freemasonry activity in the area, but these days it's also a venue for regional and touring performers, including Broadway companies. The stage has been graced by everyone from Yul Brynner in *The King and I* to Britney Spears. A stone's throw from the Cultural Center is Lackawanna College's **Mellow Theater** (Vine St. and N. Washington Ave., Scranton, www.lackawanna.edu), which dates to 1923. It served as a concert hall in its early years, hosting the likes of Sergei Rachmaninoff and John Philip Sousa. By the early 1990s it was vacant and dilapidated. The college reopened the theater in 1999 after an extensive restoration. Named for alumnus and state senator Robert Mellow, it's used by a variety of local arts organizations. The theater, which has a capacity of 1,043, doesn't maintain a box office. Contact the presenting organization for ticket information.

Wilkes-Barre's premier theater is the **F.M. Kirby Center for the Performing Arts** (71 Public Square, Wilkes-Barre, 570/826-1100, www.kirbycenter.org), which opened in 1938 as a majestic single-screen movie palace. The Art Deco theater is one of the few structures in the public square that predates 1972's Hurricane Agnes, when the Susquehanna River spilled into downtown. Bob Hope, Johnny Cash, Dizzie Gillespie, and Aretha Franklin are among the many entertainers who have played the theater. Like the Scranton Cultural Center, it seats 1,800. The **Northeastern Pennsylvania Philharmonic** (570/341-1568, www.nepaphil .org), the only fully professional symphony in the region, regularly performs at both.

Festivals and Events

Like many cities across the country, Scranton and Wilkes-Barre shine a spotlight on local arts one Friday a month. The **First Friday Scranton** (www.firstfridayscranton.com) art walk features exhibits at some 20 downtown galleries and businesses. Attendees can ride a free trolley between the venues. **Wilkes-Barre's art walk** (www.artsyouniverse.com), a more modest affair, takes place on the third Friday of each month so as not to compete with Scranton's.

The **Clarks Summit Festival of Ice** (570/587-9045, www.theabingtons.org/ CSFestivalOfIce) is the hottest event around in February. Held over several days ending on President's Day, the festival kicks off with a parade through the borough of Clarks Summit, about 15 minutes north of Scranton. Ice chips fly as chainsaw-wielding carvers transform blocks of ice into things of beauty. The festival also features live entertainment, children's activities, and the crowning of an ice prince and princess.

Scranton claims to have one of the largest St. Patrick's Day parades in the country, as measured by participants per population. More than 10,000 marchers and float riders take part in the **Scranton St. Patrick's Parade** (www.stpatparade.com, weekend before St. Patrick's Day), which starts in front of St.

Peter's Cathedral on Wyoming Avenue after a special mass and a two-mile foot race along the parade route. St. Peter's hosts a mass in Italian during the city's other marquee ethnic celebration, **La Festa Italiana** (www.lafestaitaliana .org, Labor Day weekend). The three-day celebration features food, continuous live entertainment, and more food.

SPORTS AND RECREATION
Sno Mountain and Sno Cove

Scranton's ski area is much improved since coming under private ownership in 2006. Previously county-owned and called Montage Mountain, Sno Mountain (1000 Montage Mountain Rd., Scranton, 570/969-7669, www .snomtn.com, 8-hour lift ticket $42–51, seniors, children 6–18, and college students $32–40, 1-day equipment rental $28–33) has cut new trails, beefed up its snow-making arsenal, installed a year-round zipline ride, and built a water park from scratch. The ski area has 26 trails, including an intermediate cruising trail that's more than a mile long, and seven lifts. It offers two terrain parks, a half-pipe, and 10 tubing chutes. Skiers and snowboarders can choose from a variety of lift tickets, including flexible four-hour passes, morning passes, and night passes. The tubing hill, serviced by a magic carpet lift, is open after 3 P.M. weekdays and all day weekends and holidays. Tubing is $22 on weekdays and $24–36 on weekends and holidays. Ski and snowboard lessons for children and adults are available.

In late spring Sno Mountain transforms into Sno Cove (www.snocove.com, open Memorial Day–Labor Day, all-day pass $29.95, children under 48 inches tall and seniors $20.95, children under 2 free), a winter-themed water park. Attractions include a wave pool, a lazy river, a bumper boat pond, a funnel-shaped tube ride called Tundra Tornado, and the eight-lane Iceberg Alley Luge, which pits park-goers against each other in a head-first race toward the finish line. For those not in the mood to get wet, there are batting cages, an 18-hole miniature golf course, a skate park, sand volleyball courts, and arcade games. Sno Cove usually opens at

© ANNA DUBROVSKY

Sno Mountain morphs into a water park in the warmer months.

10 A.M. and closes at 7 P.M. Come after 4 P.M. for night rates: $16.95 for anyone 48 inches or taller, $11.95 for children under 48 inches and seniors, free for children 2 and under.

Elk Mountain

About 30 miles north of Scranton, Elk Mountain (344 Elk Mountain Rd., Union Dale, 570/679-4400, www.elkskier.com, all-day lift ticket $52–63, seniors and children 6–12 $41–47, beginner's lift ticket $29–32, all-day equipment rental $24–37) offers some of the most challenging terrain in Pennsylvania. Its tag line: "It's like skiing in Vermont without the drive." Both Sno Mountain and Elk boast a vertical drop of about 1,000 feet, but a higher percentage of Elk's 27 trails are rated "most difficult." Because of its remoteness, Elk is generally less crowded than Sno and more southerly ski areas such as Blue Mountain and Camelback. Unlike the rest, it doesn't offer tubing.

In addition to all-day tickets good from 8:30 A.M. to 10 P.M., Elk offers a variety of cheaper tickets for narrower time frames.

Skiers and snowboarders who just can't get enough can save with two-day tickets. Check Elk's website for a list of nearby hotels and inns. Best of the bunch: **Fern Hall Inn** (Rte. 247, Clifford, 570/222-3676, www.fernhall inn.com, $125–195), a handsome B&B and restaurant on 117 lakefront acres. Ask the exceedingly gracious staff to arrange for a horse-drawn carriage ride during your stay.

Eagle Rock Resort

With just 14 trails, three chairlifts, and a vertical drop of 550 feet, the ski hill at Eagle Rock Resort (1031 Valley of Lakes, Hazleton, general information 888/384-6660, ski information 570/384-1522, golf information 570/384-6616, www.eaglerockresort.com, all-day lift ticket $42, seniors $15, children 7–15 $28, equipment rental $25–35, snow tubing day rate $22) doesn't measure up to Sno Mountain or Elk Mountain. But short lift lines and uncrowded skiing are virtually guaranteed. Eagle Rock is the only choice for people who want to sleep where they ski. Its accommodations include

14 ski-in/ski-out rooms and suites. The slopes are open Friday–Sunday, on holiday Mondays, and daily from Christmas to shortly after New Year's. Lift ticket holders can hit the tubing hill for just $10.

The sprawling resort is better known for its **golfing** than its skiing. Its 18-hole championship golf course, rated four stars by *Golf Digest*, was codesigned by legendary golfer Arnold Palmer and the resort's Texas-based parent company. Weather permitting, it opens at 7 A.M. on Fridays, Saturdays, and holidays; 8 A.M. on Mondays, Wednesdays, and Thursdays; and noon on Tuesdays, always closing at dusk. The pro shop and practice range open 30 minutes before play starts. Peak season green fees for the general public are $55–75. Other resort amenities include a full-service spa and an equestrian center.

Spectator Sports

In 2006 the New York Yankees ended a 28-year relationship with a minor league baseball team in Ohio, naming the Scranton/Wilkes-Barre Red Barons as their new Triple-A affiliate. Sales of Red Barons tickets shot through the roof. Renamed the **Scranton/Wilkes-Barre Yankees** (PNC Field, 235 Montage Mountain Rd., Moosic, 570/969-2255, www.swbyankees.com), the club hasn't had a losing season since.

The National Hockey League's Pittsburgh Penguins also have an affiliate in the area: the **Wilkes-Barre/Scranton Penguins** (Mohegan Sun Arena at Casey Plaza, 255 Highland Park Blvd., Wilkes-Barre, 570/208-7367, www.wbspenguins.com). The "Baby Penguins," as fans call them, play in the American Hockey League.

ACCOMMODATIONS
Under $100

Wilkes-Barre's 104-room **Econo Lodge Arena** (1075 Wilkes-Barre Twp. Blvd., Rte. 309, Wilkes-Barre, 570/823-0600, www.econolodge.com, $70–110) is a gem as budget hotels go. Its parent company has heaped accolades on the pet-friendly (and very people-

friendly) property just off I-81. Rooms are equipped with coffeemakers, microwaves, and refrigerators. Coffee, breakfast, weekday newspapers, and wireless Internet access are complimentary.

$100-200

Scranton's most opulent hotel was once a passenger train station. Built in 1908, the Neoclassical knockout features a breathtaking lobby with a mosaic tile floor, marble walls and columns, and a barrel-vaulted stained-glass ceiling. Indeed, the **(Radisson Lackawanna Station Hotel** (700 Lackawanna Ave., Scranton, 570/342-8300, www.radisson.com/scrantonpa, $89–250) wouldn't look out of place in a city on the world stage. It's an ideal base for exploring this one. Steamtown National Historic Site is just steps away. The Anthracite Heritage Museum, Lackawanna Coal Mine Tour, and Everhart Museum are among the attractions within a short drive. The six-story hotel, listed on the National Register of Historic Places, has 146 traditionally furnished guest rooms and suites, each featuring Radisson's signature Sleep Number bed. It's home to the acclaimed **Carmen's Restaurant** and the more casual **Trax** (kitchen 11 A.M.–midnight, bar open until 2 A.M.), where diners can catch sight of Steamtown's tourist-loaded locomotives.

The opulent choice in the heart of Wilkes-Barre is **The Frederick Stegmaier Mansion** (304 S. Franklin St., Wilkes-Barre, 570/823-9372, www.stegmaiermansion.com, $135–200), a brewmaster's house turned B&B and house museum. "Stegmaier" is synonymous with suds in this northeast Pennsylvania city. The Stegmaier family produced award-winning brews here for more than a century before selling its eponymous brand to another local brewer in 1974. (Just about anyone in Wilkes-Barre can point you to the stately Stegmaier brewery, which has been converted into an office building.) The lavishly decorated 1870 mansion landed a 15-page spread in *Victorian Homes* magazine in 2010. Its guest rooms and suites have private baths and fully stocked kitchenettes. Extended-stay accommodations are available.

Less than a mile from Mohegan Sun at Pocono Downs, **The Woodlands Inn** (1073 Rte. 315, Wilkes-Barre, 570/824-9831, www.thewoodlandsresort.com, $89–200) is an excellent choice if you're in town to try your luck. Good enough for Barack Obama when his presidential campaign arrived in Wilkes-Barre and Grammy winners LeAnn Rimes and Peter Frampton when they played the "racino," the hotel is family-owned and amenity-rich. Most famous of its amenities: a 17,000-gallon Jacuzzi said to be one of the largest on the East Coast. Business travelers make up the bulk of the guests on weekdays, but it's a different scene on weekends. With its smoky dance club, sexy ultra lounge, and outdoor cigar bar overlooking a babbling stream, the hotel has a well-deserved reputation as party central. Other amenities include indoor and outdoor pools, a sushi restaurant, and **Alexander's In the Woods** (570/208-1478), a salon and spa. In summer Alexander's offers alfresco massages

and pedis. The Woodlands has 150 modernly furnished rooms and suites, plus a handful of cabins for extended stays.

FOOD
Scranton Area

The Electric City's most critically acclaimed eatery is found in the magnificent marble-drenched lobby of the Radisson Lackawanna Station Hotel, built in 1908 as a passenger train station. **◖ Carmen's Restaurant** (700 Lackawanna Ave., Scranton, 570/558-3929, www.carmensradisson.com, breakfast 6:30–11 A.M. Mon.–Sat. and 6:30–9:30 A.M. Sun., brunch 10 A.M.–2 P.M. Sun., lunch 11:30 A.M.–2 P.M. Mon.–Fri., dinner 5–10 P.M. Tues.–Sat., breakfast $7–11, Sun. brunch $25.95 for adults and $19.95 for children, lunch buffet $13, dinner $19–35) offers breakfast, lunch, and Sunday brunch buffets. Dinner is a more formal and gastronomically memorable affair. Several entrées are available in half portions—ideal for anyone with a light appetite and parties that can't get enough of delectable

© ANNA DUBROVSKY

guest room at The Woodlands Inn

POCONO MOUNTAINS

PIZZA CAPITAL OF THE WORLD

Leaving the Scranton/Wilkes-Barre region without sampling **Old Forge pizza** is like leaving Philadelphia without sampling a cheesesteak: just *wrong*. A town of about 9,000, Old Forge is the self-proclaimed "Pizza Capital of the World." That's a tall claim, but anyone who's driven down Main Street, Old Forge, is inclined to buy it. It's pizza joint after pizza joint after pizza joint. There are at least a dozen on Main Street alone and more within a few blocks – so many in such close proximity that even New Yorkers and Chicagoans wouldn't begrudge Old Forge its title.

It's not clear how pizza became the trademark of a town formerly associated with anthracite coal. Quizzing locals about causal factors is about as fruitful as pumping pizzeria owners for their cheese blend. This much we know: The anthracite industry attracted many Italians to this corner of the world. They brought their cuisine. It sells.

Old Forge pizza isn't your average pizza.

Old Forge pizza: rectangular instead of round

© ANNA DUBROVSKY

starters such as hazelnut-crusted scallops, lamb lollipop chops, or classic beef carpaccio. Scranton's only AAA Four Diamond restaurant reels in budget-conscious foodies with its "dining at dusk" menu, available 5–6:30 P.M. Monday–Saturday. The three-course prix fixe is $19.99 per person. The adjacent **Carmen's Wine Bar** (5:30–midnight Tues.–Sat.) serves 18 premium wines by the glass and small plates in a relaxed setting.

Like the Neoclassical landmark that houses Carmen's, **Stirna's Restaurant and Bar** (120 W. Market St., Scranton, 570/961-9681, www .stirnas.com, 4–11 P.M. Tues.–Thurs., 4 P.M.–midnight Fri.–Sat., $12–18) has been around for more than a century. Locals of all ages come here for home-style cooking and friendly service. The "Stirna-burger," a quarter-pound of ground beef cooked to order and topped with bacon, is a real crowd-pleaser, but nothing outsells the signature brownie. Whiskey sours are a house specialty.

The best of Scranton's many Italian restaurants is **La Trattoria** (522 Moosic St.,

For one thing, it's not shaped like your average pizza. Instead of round "pies," pizzerias here specialize in rectangular "trays." Servings are referred to not as "slices" but as "cuts." White pizzas are also a specialty, as are double-crust pizzas. For a new taste experience, order a tray of double-crust white pizza. (Not that the "red" pizzas aren't tasty. Ask your waitress if the sauce is made with fresh tomatoes. There's a good chance her reply will be "Sure is, honey.")

Asking around about the best pizzeria won't get you anywhere. Most locals aren't exclusively loyal to one. They'll tell you it's a matter of taste. They'll tell you they're all good. Even the proprietors of pizza joints are more likely to pat each other on the back than undermine each other. If Old Forge's reputation as Pizza Capital rises, they all rise.

Among the veterans of the bunch is **Ghigiarelli's Restaurant** (511 S. Main St., 570/457-2652, 4-10:30 P.M. Tues.-Thurs. and Sat., 3-10:30 P.M. Fri.). According to local lore, Old Forge-style pizza owes its shape to a certain Mrs. Ghigiarelli, who grabbed a rectangular baking pan and made pizza to feed a bunch of card-playing coal miners many decades ago.

Secretary of State Hillary Clinton tucked into a cut at **Revello's Cafe-Pizza** (502 S. Main St., 570/457-9843, www.revellos. com, takeout 11 A.M.-11 P.M. Mon.-Sat. and noon-10 P.M. Sun., dining 4:30-11 P.M. Mon.-Sat. and noon-10 P.M. Sun.), which dates to 1962.

Just as old, **Arcaro & Genell** (443 S. Main St., 570/457-5555, opens at 11 A.M. Tues.-Fri. for lunch, 3-11 P.M. Mon.-Sat.) serves complimentary Tuscan bean salad and a whole lot more than pizza. Start with the portobello stuffed with crabmeat and finish with an espresso. You can't go wrong with the homemade pasta or the single-crust white pizza topped with tomato slices and onions. The restaurant has a *Cheers*-like atmosphere and a 1983 *USA Today* article on the nation's best pizzas hanging by the door. "Crust eater's heaven," the writer calls Old Forge.

Given the number of pizzerias, you'd think getting a table would be easy. Not always. They tend to be crowded on Thursday, Friday and Saturday evenings. Come on a Friday during Lent and you may have to wait for hours. Here's a strategy endorsed by one local: Send members of your party to different pizzerias. Have your cell phones handy. Whoever gets seated first can phone the others.

Old Forge is about five miles southwest of downtown Scranton. Scranton's Main Avenue eventually becomes Main Street, Old Forge. If traveling south on I-81, take exit 182B and turn right onto Davis Street. If traveling north on 81, take exit 182 and turn left onto Davis. Continue to Main Street in the town of Taylor and turn left. Follow Main Street for about a mile and a half to the Pizza Capital.

POCONO MOUNTAINS

Scranton, 570/961-1504, www.thelatrattoria .com, 10:30 A.M.–9 P.M. Mon.–Thurs., 10:30 A.M.–10 P.M. Fri., 4–10 P.M. Sat., 1–7 P.M. Sun., lunch $6–11, dinner $15–24), which makes its pasta on-site. In fact, the stuff isn't even cut until it's ordered. It gets better: Seconds are free. La Trattoria also makes sauces from scratch and bakes its own breads in a wood-fired oven. It's a casual joint with a friendly ambience, equally suitable for a family gathering or a couple's night out. A small, quaint bar serves beer, cocktails, and wines

including La Trattoria's private-label blueberry Pinot Noir, peach Chardonnay, and pomegranate Shiraz, produced at a local winery.

Beloved by young professionals, **Blu Wasabi** (1008 Scranton Carbondale Hwy., Dickson City, 570/307-3282, www.bluwasabi.net, 4:30–10 P.M. Mon.–Thurs., 4:30–11 P.M. Fri.–Sat., $18–48) offers "fine Japanese cuisine" and a degree of hipness uncommon in coal country. Its artfully prepared specialty rolls taste as good as they look, and its steaks—served with sautéed shiitake and oyster mushrooms

Patsel's serves up "creative American" fare.

or teriyaki sauce—are among the best in the area. Blue Wasabi, located about 10 minutes north of downtown Scranton, is also known for its raw bar. Owner Vinny Lam insists on the highest-grade seafood and meats, signing for deliveries three times a week. Service can be a bit slow when Blu is at its busiest, but the chill-out tunes, soft lighting, and hard alcohol make everything all right. Reservations are advisable, especially for a late-ish dinner.

There are a couple of dining gems a few minutes farther north of Scranton. **Formosa** (727 S. State St., Clarks Summit, 570/585-1902, www.formosa1.com, opens for dinner at 5 P.M. Mon.–Sat., $11–28) offers exquisite French-influenced Thai cuisine. The ingredients are fresh as can be, the curry dishes are mild and richly flavored, the waiters are quirky, and there's rarely a wait. **Patsel's** (U.S. 6 and Route 11, Glenburn, 570/563-2000, www.patsels .com, 11:30 A.M.–2:30 P.M. and 5–8 P.M. Wed.–Fri., 5–9 P.M. Sat., 11 A.M.–2 P.M. Sun., lunch $10–14, dinner $18–35, reservations requested) describes its fare as "creative American" and borrows from Mediterranean, Asian, continental, and Southwestern schools

of cooking. Owners Pat and John Atkins involved several local artists and artisans in the design of the restaurant, which opened in 1999. The result is a multi-sensory dining experience, which starts when patrons arrive at the hot pink entry doors. Inside: a floor-to-ceiling raku mural, original paintings, custom-made furniture, and elaborately trimmed windows. In the warmer months, ask for a seat on the patio overlooking flower, water, and herb gardens. Portions are modest; the popular Sunday brunch ($27.50, children 6–12 $13.75) is an all-you-can-eat affair.

Wilkes-Barre Area

Downtown Wilkes-Barre has several recommendable restaurants. Hippest of the bunch is **Rodano's** (53 Public Square, Wilkes-Barre, 570/829-6444, www.rodanos .com, kitchen 11 A.M.–9 P.M. Mon.–Tues., 11 A.M.–10 P.M. Wed.–Thurs., 11 A.M.–11 P.M. Fri., noon–11 P.M. Sat., noon–9 P.M. Sun., bar open as late as 2 A.M., $5–16), a high-ceilinged space with a menu teetering between casual American and Italian fare. Long bar tables that seat up to 12 lend to the sociable vibe of the place, which attracts families and professionals by day and college kids and other party-ready sorts by night. DJs coax revelers onto the dance floor on weekends. Nearby **Cafe Toscana** (1 Public Square, Wilkes-Barre, 570/208-1252, www.cafetoscanarestaurant .com, lunch 11:30 A.M.–3 P.M. Mon.–Fri., dinner 5–10 P.M. Mon.–Sat., $9–23) offers a more buttoned-down dining experience, white tablecloths and all. True to its name, the restaurant specializes in the light, delicate cuisine of northern Italy. The wine list is heavy on Italian reds. Save room for the ricotta cheesecake, profiteroles, limoncello truffle, or another house-made dessert.

For the best sushi in town—and the best hibachi in northeast Pennsylvania—head to **Katana** (41 S. Main St., Wilkes-Barre, 570/825-9080, www.katanawb.com, lunch 11:30 A.M.–2:30 P.M. Mon.–Fri., dinner 5–9:30 P.M. Mon.–Thurs., 5–10 P.M. Fri.–Sat., 5–9 P.M. Sun., $9–26). The owners and chefs hail from Japan and take pride in delivering an authentic Japanese experience, bento boxes and all. It's a great place for a celebration with family or friends; the hibachi tables seat 12 and

can be pushed together for even larger parties. Watch chefs slice, dice, and sear your hibachi meal to perfection or have a seat at the sushi bar for a different display of culinary artistry. The bar features one of the largest selections of single malts in the region.

Cross the Susquehanna River for home-style Greek cuisine in a whimsical setting. **⟨ Theo's Metro** (596 Mercer Ave., Kingston, 570/283-2050, www.theosmetrorestaurant .com, 11 A.M.–10 P.M. daily, lunch $5–10, dinner $14–28) opened in 2001 in what used to be a popcorn factory, and it's decorated with the detritus of the corn-popping trade. Hand-painted tables, floor-to-ceiling murals, water features, and a mini golf course—yes, inside the restaurant—add to the delightfully off-beat ambience. The menu includes burgers, a chicken cheesesteak, and other American fare, but you'd be a fool to pass up Greek specialties like moussaka, spinach pie, stuffed grape leaves, and *youvetsi* (lamb in a clay pot with orzo pasta, tomato sauce, and parmesan cheese). Add a touch of drama to dinner by starting with the *saganaki* (imported Greek cheese dipped in batter, lightly fried, and

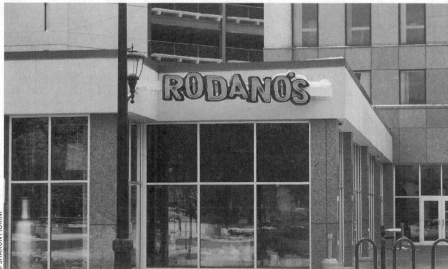

© SHARON FIORINI

Rodano's has DJs and dancing on the weekends.

POCONO MOUNTAINS

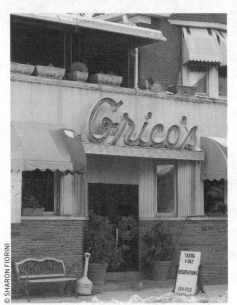

© SHARON FIORINI

Grico's is famous for its very private tables.

flamed tableside with ouzo). The eatery boasts a full bar and a martini list that's as long as the River Styx.

Theo's doesn't have the corner on uncommon decor. **Grico's** (1074 Wyoming Ave., Exeter, 570/654-9120, www.gricosrestaurant .com, opens 5 P.M. Mon.–Sat., last reservation 10 P.M., $12–33), a dinner-only establishment dating to the 1930s, is famous for its curtain-shrouded tables. Rumor has it that mafiosos wined and dined their mistresses in these private "rooms" for two or four. True? Perhaps. This much is certain: They're romantic as all get-out. Grico's, which also has plenty of curtain-free tables, serves the sort of food one associates with mafiosos: fresh clams, pasta dishes, massive steaks, lobster tail, and half a dozen varieties of veal scaloppini, among other things. Plan on being wowed by the dessert tray—and the service.

INFORMATION

Scranton and Wilkes-Barre are the county seats of Lackawanna County and Luzerne County, respectively. The **Lackawanna County Convention & Visitors Bureau** (99 Glenmaura National Blvd., Moosic, 570/496-1701, www.visitnepa.org, 9 A.M.–5 P.M. daily) has a large information center just a couple of minutes from PNC Field and Sno Mountain. The on-site gift shop carries merchandise made locally or related to the area's heritage—everything from locally roasted coffee to coal miners' hats. The **Luzerne County Convention & Visitors Bureau** (56 Public Square, Wilkes-Barre, 888/905-2872, www.tournepa.com, 8:30 A.M.–4:30 P.M. Mon.–Fri.) has its smallish headquarters in the heart of Wilkes-Barre. Visit their websites to request free copies of their respective visitors guides.

GETTING THERE AND AROUND

Scranton and Wilkes-Barre are about two hours from both Philadelphia and New York City. They're accessible via north–south I-81 and the Northeast Extension of the Pennsylvania Turnpike, a.k.a. I-476. Both highways connect to the transcontinental I-80, which is south of the cities.

The **Wilkes-Barre/Scranton International Airport** (570/602-2000, www.flyavp.com), with a booking code of AVP, is served by several major carriers. They offer daily nonstop flights to Chicago, Detroit, Philadelphia, Charlotte, and Newark. Free wireless Internet access is available throughout the terminal building. Rental car counters and a taxi and limo service are located in the baggage claim area. There's no passenger train service to the region. Contact **Greyhound** (800/231-2222, www.greyhound.com) for information on arriving by bus. Scranton's public transportation provider is the **County of Lackawanna Transit System** (570/346-2061, www.colts bus.com). Wilkes-Barre's is the **Luzerne County Transportation Authority** (570/288-9356, www.lctabus.com).

PITTSBURGH

Ask people what they think when they hear "Pittsburgh," and they're liable to answer "steel." What they're picturing is the Pittsburgh of old, a place nicknamed "Smoky City" and described in an 1868 magazine article as "hell with the lid taken off." That image is about as current as petticoats. The city that celebrated its 250th birthday in 2008 is no longer an industrial powerhouse but rather a manicured seat of culture. Its lush parks, rehabilitated rivers, world-class museums, and magical skyline inspire accolades from even the most cosmopolitan of visitors. A writer for *The New Yorker* who visited in 1990 called it one of the three most beautiful cities in the world, along with Paris and St. Petersburg, Russia. "If Pittsburgh were situated somewhere in the heart of Europe," he wrote, "tourists would eagerly journey hundreds of miles out of their way to visit it." Paris has crepes, St. Petersburg has *oladushki,* and Pittsburgh has Pamela's crispy-edged pancakes (more on that later).

Pittsburgh is a work in progress. Something is always being knocked down. Something bigger is always rising. It's as if Pittsburgh never heard of recession. At a time when real estate development was grinding to a halt in cities across the country, officials here were giddily breaking ground and cutting ribbons. That has led to a good amount of grumbling about high taxes and superfluous government spending, but tourism is all the better for it. The past couple of years have seen the addition of a riverfront casino, an African American culture center, and a 23-floor skyscraper, among other big-ticket attractions. A spanking-new hockey arena opened

HIGHLIGHTS

◖ Senator John Heinz History Center: Gain a new appreciation for southwestern Pennsylvania at the state's largest history museum. Betcha didn't know the Big Mac was born here (page 320).

◖ The Andy Warhol Museum: It's perhaps not surprising that a museum dedicated to one of the best-known and most provocative artists of all time could make you say "Wow!" (page 322).

◖ Mount Washington Inclines: You just don't visit Pittsburgh without climbing aboard a cable car at the Monongahela or Duquesne Incline. You just don't (page 329).

◖ Carnegie Museums of Art and Natural History: Born of industrialist Andrew Carnegie's largess, the conjoined museums have grown into international sensations (pages 332 and 333).

◖ Cathedral of Learning: The facade of this architectural paean to higher education is mighty impressive, but what's inside is unique in all the world (page 334).

◖ Phipps Conservatory and Botanical Gardens: Pittsburgh's "crystal palace" is as magical as its nickname suggests (page 337).

◖ Ohiopyle State Park: This gorgeous expanse offers some of the best white-water boating in the eastern United States, plus access to the Great Allegheny Passage rail-trail. To boot, the hiking is outstanding (page 395).

◖ Fallingwater: Sure, it's an hour's drive from the city, but Frank Lloyd Wright's masterpiece is worth crossing an ocean to see. Lots of people do (page 397).

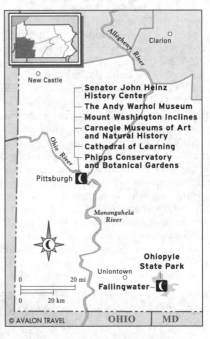

LOOK FOR **◖** TO FIND RECOMMENDED SIGHTS, ACTIVITIES, DINING, AND LODGING.

in time for the 2010–2011 season. Not everything is made from scratch. Shuttered factories, abandoned warehouses, obsolete railyards, and even churches have been repurposed. The Cork Factory doesn't cut corks these days. It's a luxury apartment complex. The opulent Grand Concourse at Station Square isn't a railroad terminal. It's a seafood restaurant. The "Burgh" will make you a believer in reincarnation.

If you're coming from the international airport, your tour begins when you emerge from the tunnels bored through Mount Washington.

The feast laid out before you—rivers, bridges, and uncommonly shaped buildings—has placed Pittsburgh near the top of best-skyline lists. The city is famous for its hills, too. You need only scan the names of its 90-some neighborhoods to understand the topography: Brighton Heights, Highland Park, Southside Slopes, Squirrel Hill. Exploring them is both anthropology and exercise.

Leave time for the countryside. You'll find Amish communities to Pittsburgh's north and a huge concentration of covered bridges to its south. In the Laurel Highlands region southeast of the city, you'll find the state's largest ski resort, highest mountain, largest cave, and most decorated restaurant. You'll also find three houses by Frank Lloyd Wright, America's favorite architect.

Pittsburgh is working overtime to shake its outdated image. It may one day succeed in attracting large numbers of new residents and droves of tourists. In the meantime, be glad it's underrated. You can have your run of the place. You can squeeze into any hot spot save for Heinz Field, where the winningest team in Super Bowl history plays. You can dine without a reservation at just about any restaurant. You can shop without shoving. But hurry. This offer may not last for long.

PLANNING YOUR TIME

The city has enough cultural and historical attractions to keep intensely curious types busy for well over a week, but it's possible to hit the highlights in three days. Oakland, a couple of miles east of Downtown, is a good place to start. Spend a few hours exploring the Carnegie Museums of Art and Natural History before sitting down to lunch at a Craig Street eatery

or, if the weather's nice, in Schenley Plaza. Afterward, take a tour around the world in the magnificent Cathedral of Learning. Its Nationality Rooms are open until 4 P.M. You'll still have time to marvel at the specimens at Phipps Conservatory, the "crystal palace" in Schenley Park. Cross the Hot Metal Bridge for dinner on the South Side and stick around to see why East Carson Street is considered Pittsburgh's nightlife capital.

Devote the following day to the North Side, where the Pittsburgh Steelers and Pirates play. It's home to the National Aviary, the Andy Warhol Museum, and the Mattress Factory, a renowned installation museum. If you're traveling with kids, you'll have to prioritize. The Carnegie Science Center and Children's Museum of Pittsburgh can also be found there. Drive or, better yet, walk across one of the "Three Sisters" bridges into Downtown for dinner. Try to catch a show or concert in the Cultural District. Alternatively, stay on the North Side and try to beat the odds at the Rivers Casino, one of Pittsburgh's newest attractions.

First thing in the morning, find your way to the Strip District, the mile-long neighborhood adjacent to Downtown. Have breakfast at

© ANNA DUBROVSKY

the Phipps Conservatory in Schenley Park

a cable car climbs Mount Washington

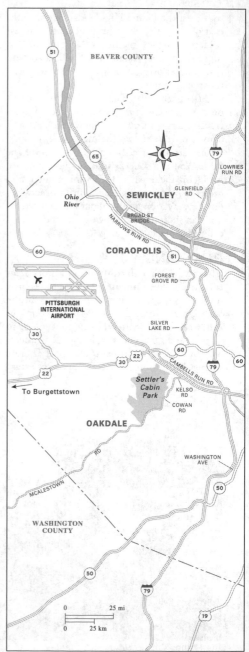

Pamela's, then wander in and out of the specialty foods markets along Penn Avenue. Load up on hard-to-find ingredients and impossible-to-resist delicacies. While you're there, acquire the accoutrements of a Pittsburgh sports fanatic. You can learn what's so special about Pittsburgh at the Heinz History Center, located at the western end of the Strip.

You've saved the best for last. Head toward Station Square on the south shore of the Monongahela River, climb into a cable car at the base of Mount Washington, and ascend to its crest for knock-your-socks-off views of the city. The skyline is particularly dazzling after dark, so have dinner or a cocktail at Station Square or on Mount Washington's Restaurant Row if you arrive earlier.

If you can devote more than three days to the city, get off dry land for a spell. Take a cruise on a Gateway Clipper riverboat or, during the warmer months, set off from Kayak Pittsburgh's base on the North Shore.

Pittsburgh is swell and all, but seriously consider skipping town for a day or two to explore is surrounds. First stop: Frank Lloyd Wright's Fallingwater.

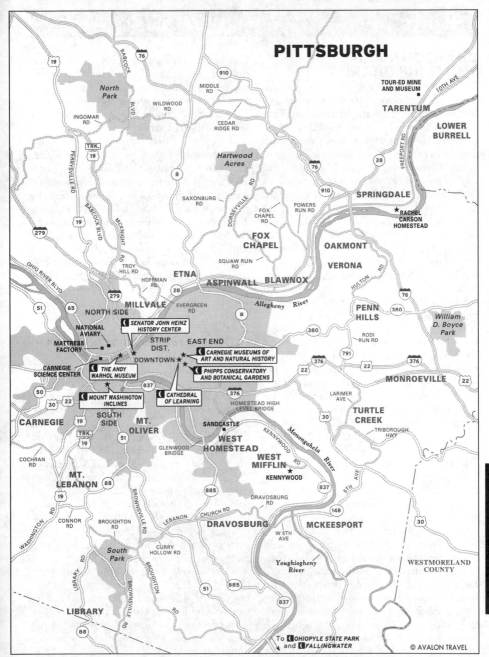

PITTSBURGH

PITTSBURGH

North Park

Hartwood Acres

TOUR-ED MINE AND MUSEUM

TARENTUM

LOWER BURRELL

SPRINGDALE

★ RACHEL CARSON HOMESTEAD

FOX CHAPEL

OAKMONT

VERONA

ETNA

ASPINWALL   BLAWNOX

Allegheny River

PENN HILLS

William D. Boyce Park

MILLVALE

NORTH SIDE

NATIONAL AVIARY

MATTRESS FACTORY

◖ SENATOR JOHN HEINZ HISTORY CENTER

STRIP DIST.

EAST END

◖ CARNEGIE MUSEUMS OF ART AND NATURAL HISTORY

DOWNTOWN

CARNEGIE SCIENCE CENTER

◖ *THE ANDY WARHOL MUSEUM*

◖ PHIPPS CONSERVATORY AND BOTANICAL GARDENS

MONROEVILLE

◖ MOUNT WASHINGTON INCLINES

◖ CATHEDRAL OF LEARNING

HOMESTEAD HIGH LEVEL BRIDGE

TURTLE CREEK

CARNEGIE

SOUTH SIDE

MT. OLIVER

SANDCASTLE

WEST HOMESTEAD

Monongahela River

MT. LEBANON

GLENWOOD BRIDGE

WEST MIFFLIN

KENNYWOOD ★

DRAVOSBURG

MCKEESPORT

WESTMORELAND COUNTY

Youghiogheny River

LIBRARY

To ◖ OHIOPYLE STATE PARK and ◖ FALLINGWATER

© AVALON TRAVEL

Sights

DOWNTOWN AND THE STRIP DISTRICT

Downtown Pittsburgh, a.k.a. the Golden Triangle, sits at the confluence of the Allegheny and Monongahela Rivers, which join to form the Ohio River. The arrowhead-shaped neighborhood has a storied past, which visitors can explore at the Fort Pitt Museum and Senator John Heinz History Center. Today it's the city's financial center, home to corporations including H. J. Heinz Co. and PNC Financial Services. Like many business districts, it's sleepy most weekday nights. But it comes alive on weekends, when Pittsburghers and visitors flock to the 14-square-block Cultural District for live theater, music, and dance.

The Strip District extends from Downtown's northeastern cusp to 33rd Street, hugging the Allegheny River the whole way. Its name implies commerce of the red-light variety, but "the Strip" was and remains a center of sanctioned trade. In the 19th century, mills and factories mushroomed along the river. In the early part of the 20th, the Strip became the hub of Pittsburgh's wholesale produce industry. These days the mile-long neighborhood is famous for its specialty foods markets, which attract gourmets from far outside the city. It's also home to diverse restaurants and bars.

Point State Park

The pretty park at the confluence of Pittsburgh's rivers is ideal for sunbathing in summer. George Washington thought the spot ideal, too. After a stopover in 1753, he advised that the British establish an outpost at the "forks of the Ohio" to gain command of the rivers. Alas, the French also had their eye on the area. In 1754 they chased away a force of Virginians who'd built a weak stockade and proceeded to build a fort they called Duquesne. Britain's attempts to retake control failed until November 1758, when the French burned their fort and fled two days before the arrival of a massive army led by General John Forbes. Upon his arrival, Forbes ordered the construction of a new fort, naming it after British Secretary of State William Pitt. The settlement around Fort Pitt became "Pittsbourgh." (The current spelling appeared in the 1816 city charter.)

A recreated bastion houses the **Fort Pitt Museum** (101 Commonwealth Place, 412/281-9285, www.heinzhistorycenter.org, 10 A.M.–5 P.M. daily, admission $5, seniors $4, students and children 4–17 $3), which tells the story of the French and Indian War. Exhibits also speak to the ensuing hostilities between the British victors and Native Americans. The highlight for anyone under 13 is the trader's cabin with its assortment of animal pelts. A costumed guide explains how Native Americans purchased everything from mirrors to muskets with buckskins and other furry currency. Even adults may be surprised by how many "bucks" equaled a beaver pelt.

The nearby **Fort Pitt Block House** (412/471-1764, 10 A.M.–5 P.M. Wed.–Sun., reduced winter hours, free) is the only original fort structure and the oldest building in Pittsburgh. It was constructed in 1764 to help protect the fort from possible attacks by Native Americans. Eventually the small redoubt was repurposed as a dwelling. Neville Craig, Pittsburgh's first historian, was born there in 1787. In 1894 the property was transferred to the Daughters of the American Revolution, who blocked it from destruction by the Pennsylvania Railroad and preserve it to this day. Its stone foundation, brick walls, ceiling beams, and roof rafters are original, as are the gun loops through which soldiers aimed their muskets. The firing step on the first floor is a recreation.

Most people come to Point State Park (724/865-2131, www.dcnr.state.pa.us/stateParks/parks/point.aspx) not for a history lesson but for a festival, concert, or fireworks display. The fountain at the tip of the park shoots to a height of 150 feet when it's in operation.

CITY OF INDUSTRY

In the winter of 1866, writer James Parton visited a Pittsburgh chockablock with mills, foundries, and factories. He surveyed the city from a hill and marveled at its industrial might. In the story he wrote for *The Atlantic Monthly*, he compared Pittsburgh to another fiery destination:

The entire space lying between the hills was filled with blackest smoke, from out of which the hidden chimneys sent forth tongues of flame, while from the depths of the abyss, came up the noise of hundreds of steam-hammers. There would be moments when no flames were visible; but soon the wind would force the smoky curtains aside, and the whole black expanse would be dimly lighted with dull wreaths of fire . . . if any one would enjoy a spectacle as striking as Niagara, he may do so by simply walking up a long hill to Cliff Street in Pittsburg, and looking over into – hell with the lid taken off.

Mellon Square and Vicinity

Downtown boasts a number of distinctive buildings, ranging from the old and ornate to the modern and sleek. Architecture buffs would be wise to contact the **Pittsburgh History & Landmarks Foundation** (100 W. Station Square Dr., 412/471-5808, www.phlf .org), which organizes free walking tours led by guides who know their Flemish Gothic from their Georgian Classical. One good place to begin a self-guided tour is Mellon Square on Smithfield Street between Oliver and 6th Avenues. When the weather is good, Downtown workers crowd the plaza's terrazzo walks and granite benches. There's no bad seat in the house, but the best face the 1916 **Omni William Penn Hotel** (530 William Penn Place, 412/281-7100, www.omnihotels .com). The oldest hotel in the city underwent a

renovation in 2004 to the tune of $22 million, and many of its original features were restored. Its grand facade whispers of crystal chandeliers and leather armchairs. (You'll find both in the main lobby, along with a grand piano.)

Also flanking Mellon Square is a 31-story skyscraper known as the **Alcoa Building** (425 6th Ave.). Aluminum was used wherever possible when industry giant Alcoa Inc. built the slender tower in 1953. The company relocated to Pittsburgh's North Shore neighborhood in 1998, and today the building is more properly called the Regional Enterprise Tower.

Head west on 6th Avenue for a gander at the **Duquesne Club** (325 6th Ave., 412/391-1500, www.duquesne.org), the Romanesque home of Pittsburgh's oldest private club. Founded in 1873, it welcomed the captains of industry whose names still grace so many Pittsburgh buildings. The current clubhouse, which opened in 1890 and didn't admit women until 1980, was dubbed "the citadel of Pittsburgh tycoonery" by *Time* magazine in 1940.

Across the street are two churches designed in the English Gothic style. **Trinity Cathedral** (328 6th Ave., 412/232-6404, www.trinity cathedralpgh.org) with its striking steeple was dedicated in 1872. It replaced a smaller church that its Episcopalian congregation had outgrown. Its neighbor, the twin-towered **First Presbyterian Church** (320 6th Ave., 412/471-3436, www.fpcp.org), is three decades younger and the third church to be built on this site. All but one of its nave windows were designed and produced by the Tiffany Studios in New York. The graveyard between the churches is older than them both. Native Americans, the French, the British, and American settlers buried their dead here in the 18th century.

Three congregations moved east of Downtown after industrialist Henry Clay Frick purchased their churches and land. In place of one, he built the aforementioned William Penn Hotel. One block south, he replaced a Catholic church with a shopping and office complex designed in the Flemish Gothic style. Completed in 1917, it was known as the Union Arcade. Today it's called the **Union Trust Building**

(435 Grant St.), and the shops are long gone. But do step inside. Four street entrances meet in a rotunda capped by a stained-glass dome—a feature the bishop insisted on when he sold his church to the coke and steel magnate.

Frick's own office was located in the adjacent **Frick Building** (437 Grant St.), which took the place of St. Peter's Episcopal Church. (The church was dismantled and taken in horse-drawn wagons to Oakland, where it was reconstructed—only to be demolished in the 1980s.) The Frick Building had 20 floors when it was completed in 1902. About a decade later, grading of the hill upon which it was built left its basement exposed and its entrance suspended in air. The renovation resulted in a two-story lobby, where you'll find a marble bust of Mr. Frick.

Before the Frick Building went up, the Pittsburgh skyline was dominated by the **Allegheny County Courthouse** (436 Grant St.) across the street. It's still one of the city's most impressive buildings. The courthouse and adjacent jail were designed by Boston architect Henry Hobson Richardson, whose style was so distinctive that it got its own name: Richardsonian Romanesque. He died in 1886, two years before the courthouse was finished, and reportedly had this to say on his deathbed: "If they honor me for the pygmy things I have already done, what will they say when they see Pittsburgh finished?" Quite a lot, in fact. The granite complex with its theatrical towers, turrets, columns, and arches has won more than a few design awards. The jail was closed in 1995, partly on account of a class action brought by a prisoner, and its tenants moved to a boring new building on 2nd Avenue. Several years later, Richardson's jail was converted into a home for the family division of the court. A portion of a cellblock was preserved, and you can learn about prison life with a carefully timed visit. The **Jail Museum** is open 11:30 A.M.–1 P.M. Mondays from February through October. The main entrance to the family court facility and museum is on Ross Street. You can also enter through the courtyard arch on 5th Avenue. The courtyard was used for public hangings until 1911.

PPG Place

The tallest skyscraper in downtown Pittsburgh is the 64-floor U.S. Steel Tower, but the fairest of them all is PPG Place (www.ppgplace.com). Like the aluminum Alcoa Building, both were designed to show off a product: steel in the case of the former and glass in the case of the latter. PPG Industries Inc. entrusted the design of its world headquarters to New York architects Philip Johnson and John Burgee. What they envisioned was no simple skyscraper. PPG Place, finished in 1984 at a cost of $200 million, is a glass-skinned castle complete with neo-Gothic spires—231 of them. Some call it modern; others insist it's postmodern. Regardless, it makes Pittsburgh's skyline instantly recognizable even if you crop out the rivers and bridges.

PPG Place is actually six buildings that occupy several city blocks. The tallest at 40 floors is One PPG Place. Standing between them is

PPG Place towers over the *Gateway Clipper* riverboat.

© GATEWAY CLIPPER, VISITPITTSBURGH

an otherworldly experience. Think Superman's Fortress of Solitude. Images dance across the glass panes, making for a unique photo with every click. Nearly one million square feet of PPG-made reflective glass went into the facades. The purpose of all that glass is not only aesthetic; it helps keep the buildings cool in summer and cozy in winter. You'll also find glass paneling in the lobbies and cracked glass mirrors in the elevators.

From spring through fall, the outdoor plaza features a granite fountain with 140 columns of water. In winter, an ice skating rink takes its place—part of the reason why PPG Place has been likened to New York's Rockefeller Center. The glass-enclosed Wintergarden in One PPG Place hosts exhibits, events, and performances throughout the year, including a gingerbread house competition and train display during the holiday season. It's generally open 6 A.M.–7 P.M. weekdays and 9 A.M.–7 P.M. weekends.

August Wilson Center for African American Culture

Opened in 2009 after more than a decade of planning, the August Wilson Center (980 Liberty Ave., 412/258-2700, www.august wilsoncenter.org, 11 A.M.–6 P.M. Tues.–Sat., free admission) is part museum and part performing arts facility. Its core exhibition, Pittsburgh: Reclaim Renew Remix, features an interactive tool that allows visitors to create video collages celebrating the region's black heritage. Changing exhibits are found throughout the 65,000-square-foot building, an ultramodern composition of metal, stone, and glass on a triangular site. At the center of it all is a 486-seat theater. The August Wilson Center, which functioned as a presenting arts organization for several years before it had a home of its own, has brought the likes of filmmaker Spike Lee, the Alvin Ailey American Dance Theater, and Grammy-winning gospel singer CeCe Winans to Pittsburgh. Its namesake, one of the 20th century's most celebrated playwrights, grew up in the Hill District, just east of Downtown. August Wilson (1945–2005) is best known for a 10-play series often referred to as the Pittsburgh Cycle. Each play depicts African American life in a different decade of the 1900s, and all but one are set in the Hill, once known as a hotbed of jazz. Wilson won Pulitzer Prizes for *Fences* and *The Piano Lesson* and was the first African American to have two plays running on Broadway at the same time.

ToonSeum

One of only a handful of museums dedicated to the cartoon arts, the ToonSeum (945 Liberty Ave., 412/232-0199, www.toon seum.org, 10 A.M.–3 P.M. Wed.–Thurs., 10 A.M.–5 P.M. Fri.–Sat., 10 A.M.–3 P.M. Sun., admission $4, children 12 and under free) relocated from its original home in the Children's Museum of Pittsburgh to a storefront across from the August Wilson Center in 2009. The move opened the door for exhibits of more provocative works. Fear not, Mickey Mouse fans. America's favorite rodent and other beloved characters such as Snoopy, Superman, and SpongeBob SquarePants still have places of honor at the ToonSeum, which changes exhibits every two months. Jean Schulz, widow of Snoopy creator Charles M. Schulz, was one of its earliest supporters. Bit by the cartooning bug? The museum offers cartooning classes for kids and adults.

David L. Lawrence Convention Center

Completed in 2003, the riverfront David L. Lawrence Convention Center (1000 Fort Duquesne Blvd., 412/565-6000, www.pitts burghcc.com) is something of an architectural marvel. Its sloping steel roof and terraces are best viewed from the opposite shore of the Allegheny. The 1.5-million-square-foot building was the first meeting facility in the United States to win LEED (Leadership in Energy and Environmental Design) gold. Daylight satisfies about 75 percent of its lighting needs. All that innovative and earth-friendly design came at a steep price: $375 million. The international design competition alone cost $750,000.

the Senator John Heinz History Center

© ED MASSERY, VISITPITTSBURGH

◖ Senator John Heinz History Center

The Senator John Heinz History Center (1212 Smallman St., 412/454-6000, www.heinzhistorycenter.org, 10 A.M.–5 P.M. daily, Library & Archives 10 A.M.–5 P.M. Tues.–Sat. or by appointment, admission $10, seniors $9, students and children 4–17 $5), located at the Downtown end of the Strip District, is the largest history museum in Pennsylvania. It tackles 250 years of Pittsburgh history, from the pre-Revolutionary period to the present day. The Smithsonian-affiliated museum is anything but stuffy. It's a family-friendly medley of artifacts, artwork, audiovisual programs, and interactive exhibits. Long-term exhibitions include Clash of Empires, which examines the French and Indian War, and Heinz 57, a tribute to the king of condiments. A two-floor exhibition trumpets Pittsburgh's contributions to the world, which include the Ferris wheel and the polio vaccine. And the Special Collections gallery houses ethnic and corporate artifacts of all ilk, including an Oscar de la Renta bikini made with Alcoa-produced aluminum.

Sports junkies can get a fix at the **Western Pennsylvania Sports Museum,** a museum within the museum that celebrates the home runs, touchdowns, goals, and other proud moments of the region's athletes. If "Immaculate Reception" means nothing to you, this is the place to go for a primer in Pittsburgh sports lore.

If the exhibitions leave you with any questions about Pittsburgh, climb to the sixth floor of this former icehouse, where you'll find the Library & Archives. The collection includes 700,000 images, 40,000 books and pamphlets, and the archival collections of some 3,500 families, organizations, and businesses. Professional librarians and archivists are available to assist with genealogical and historical research.

Saints in the Strip

Two Strip District churches warrant a respectful walkabout: **St. Patrick** (1711 Liberty

Ave.) and **St. Stanislaus Kostka** (57 21st St.). The former holds the distinction of being Pittsburgh's first Roman Catholic church, the latter its first ethnic Polish Catholic church. They were merged into one parish (412/471-4767, www.saintsinthestrip.org) in 1993, after decades of population shift to the suburbs.

Western Pennsylvania was almost devoid of Catholics after the British chased away the French in the mid-1700s. In the latter part of the century, the Catholics who called this region home had to make do with occasional and brief visits by priests. About 20 Catholic families lived in Pittsburgh when the first resident pastor arrived in 1808. He laid the cornerstone for a church. St. Patrick was dedicated three years later—without a single pew. Families had their pews built as soon as they could afford a carpenter.

Fire destroyed the church in 1854. Its congregation moved to a new church, only to move again to make way for the Pennsylvania Railroad Company. Version 3.0 was built on the current site at the corner of 17th Street and Liberty Avenue. It survived for 70 years before it, too, succumbed to a fire. The present church was dedicated in 1936. A piece of the Blarney Stone from Blarney Castle in Ireland was placed in the baptistery tower. The lucky charm seems to be working: "Old St. Patrick's," as the church is known, has already outlived its predecessors.

The church courtyard offers calm and solitude of monastic proportions. You'll find a grotto in honor of Our Lady of Lourdes and statues of sundry saints, including the Virgin Mary. The church vestibule features a replica of the Scala Sancta, or "Holy Stairs," in Rome. It's believed that Jesus climbed the 28-step stairway on his way to trial. Only a handful of churches have replicas. At St. Patrick, as in Rome, the steps are ascended on one's knees.

The younger St. Stanislaus Kostka has an older church building. It was consecrated in 1892 and withstood disasters both natural and man-made. During the Great St. Patrick's Day Flood of 1936, water rose as high as the wainscoting, trapping the pastor on the second floor. Later that year, an explosion at the nearby Pittsburgh Banana Company weakened its twin bell towers, and their original bonnets had to be removed. The church's stained glass windows are a must-see. If you're lucky, you'll come on a day when parishioners are selling homemade pierogies to raise dough.

NORTH SIDE

Many of Pittsburgh's main attractions are just north of the Allegheny and Ohio Rivers. The North Side, as the area is called, has undergone a dramatic transformation over the past decade. The Pittsburgh Steelers and Pirates each got a new home there. In 2009, they got a new neighbor: the city's only casino. Two North Side institutions, the Children's Museum of Pittsburgh and National Aviary, undertook major expansions. And the makeover isn't over. Cross one of the bridges that link Downtown and the North Side and it shouldn't be long before you encounter a work crew or detour.

The North Side was once an independent municipality named Allegheny. In 1907, when it was forcibly annexed by Pittsburgh, Allegheny was a sooty city of industry with a charming park, **Allegheny Commons** (412/330-2569, www.alleghenycommons.org), at its center. The residential area east of the park had become known as Deutschtown for its large population of German immigrants. Many well-to-do citizens lived north of the park in the Mexican War Streets section, where streets had been named for the battles (Buena Vista, Monterey, Resaca, Palo Alto) and leaders (Taylor, Sherman, Jackson) of the Mexican-American War. Today, both neighborhoods are national historic districts well worth a stroll on a pleasant day.

The "Three Sisters"

Four vehicular bridges connect Downtown and the North Side, and all of them can be crossed on foot. The busiest is Fort Duquesne Bridge, a double-decker that feeds into an interstate. Its lower-deck walkway makes for a less-than-scenic stroll. For fantastic views sans deafening traffic, try one of the "Three

PITTSBURGH

the Roberto Clemente Bridge, one of the "Three Sisters"

Sisters." There's no Cinderella here; the bridges are all but identical. The yellow triplets were built between 1924 and 1928 on orders of the U.S. War Department, which feared that certain vessels wouldn't be able to pass under the variously designed bridges they replaced. The Sisters were the first self-anchored suspension bridges in the United States and remain the only trio of neighboring, nearly indistinguishable large bridges.

The bridges were originally named for the Downtown streets they adjoin: 6th Street, 7th Street, and 9th Street. Starting in 1999, they were renamed to honor local luminaries. Closest to the tip of Downtown is the **Roberto Clemente Bridge** (6th Street Bridge). Clemente, a National Baseball Hall of Famer, was drafted by the Pittsburgh Pirates in 1954. He remained with the team until 1972, when he died in a plane crash during a relief mission to earthquake-torn Nicaragua. PNC Park, where the Pirates have played since 2001, is a stone's throw from the span's northern end. The bridge is closed to vehicular traffic during

Pirates home games and flooded with fans, vendors, and scalpers.

The Andy Warhol Museum sits near the northern end of the **Andy Warhol Bridge** (7th Street Bridge). The bridge was renamed in 2005 as part of the museum's 10th anniversary celebration. Warhol was a Pittsburgh boy turned pop art sensation. The **Rachel Carson Bridge** (9th Street Bridge) got its new name on Earth Day in 2006. Carson, who ignited the environmental movement with the publication of *Silent Spring*, was born in 1907 in Springdale, about 18 miles north of Pittsburgh along the Allegheny River.

◖ The Andy Warhol Museum

Andy Warhol was born and buried in Pittsburgh, which might have remained a little-known fact were it not for The Andy Warhol Museum (117 Sandusky St., 412/237-8300, www.warhol.org, 10 A.M.–5 P.M. Tues.–Thurs. and Sat.–Sun., 10 A.M.–10 P.M. Fri., admission $15, seniors $9, students and children 3–18 $8). It opened in 1994 to celebrate the

The Andy Warhol Museum is one of the Carnegie Museums in Pittsburgh.

the Carnegie Institute of Technology (now Carnegie Mellon University), Warhol moved to New York and gained recognition as a commercial illustrator. In the early 1960s, he shot to fame as a pop artist with paintings of consumer products such as Campbell's Soup and celebrities including Marilyn Monroe. He also churned out dozens of avant-garde films and survived a murder attempt. The 1970s and '80s were less heady decades, but Warhol remained in the public eye until his death from complications following gallbladder surgery. His body was taken to Pittsburgh and buried at St. John the Baptist Cemetery in the suburb of Bethel Park. Admirers still leave soup cans and other offerings at the gravesite.

Ardent fans and scholars can find art supplies used by Warhol, audiotapes of his conversations with friends, more than 30 of his silver-white wigs, and countless other ephemera at the museum's Archives Study Center, which is open by appointment. The archives include 610 cardboard boxes that Warhol filled—with everything from phone messages to source images for his art—and sent to storage between the early 1960s and late 1980s.

If possible, visit the museum on a Friday evening, when a cash bar and special programs add a twist to the Warhol experience. The museum stays open until 10 P.M., and tickets are half price after 5.

work of the influential artist whose career unfolded in New York City. The Warhol is one of the four Carnegie Museums of Pittsburgh. (As a child, Andy Warhol took free Saturday art classes at the Carnegie in Oakland, a neighborhood east of Downtown.) It's also the largest U.S. museum dedicated to a single artist. The collection includes about 900 paintings and 1,500 drawings, along with sculptures, prints, photographs, films, videos, books, and even wallpaper designed by the artist. The museum was founded in part by the Andy Warhol Foundation for the Visual Arts, created after his 1987 death to manage his estate and provide support to other visual artists. About 500 works from the permanent collection are exhibited at any one time. Exhibitions rotate regularly.

The "pope of pop" was born in 1928 to working-class immigrants from what is now Slovakia. There's another museum devoted to his work in the Slovakian town of Medzilaborce, not far from his parents' birthplace. After graduating with an art degree from

PNC Park

PNC Park (115 Federal St., 412/323-5000, http://pittsburgh.pirates.mlb.com) is the George Clooney of ballparks: handsome, classy, and alone worth your ticket price. Its tenants, Major League Baseball's Pittsburgh Pirates, haven't won a World Series since 1979, so it's a cinch to secure tickets to home games. The 38,000-seat ballpark, named for locally based PNC Financial Services, became the fifth home of the Pirates when it opened in April 2001. It's a nod to early ballparks like Chicago's Wrigley Field and Boston's Fenway Park. Masonry archways, steel truss work, and a natural grass field contribute to the princely feel of the place, but PNC Park's greatest asset is its location on the

EXTREME MAKEOVERS

Demolitions make good spectacles, but many Pittsburgh developers choose instead to adapt old buildings for new purposes. What looks like a church could very well be a brewpub, nightclub, or hookah bar. The building that resembles a warehouse could be gallery space. Extreme makeovers can be found throughout the city. Here's a look at a few:

ANDY WARHOL MUSEUM

The museum, which opened in 1994, occupies a former warehouse built in 1911. It was known as the Frick & Lindsay building when it housed mining supplies and Volkwein Music & Instruments Co. after it became a music store in the 1960s.

CHILDREN'S MUSEUM OF PITTSBURGH

This kid-centric museum occupies the former post office of Allegheny City, the municipality annexed by Pittsburgh in 1907 and now known as the North Side.

CHURCH BREW WORKS

St. John the Baptist Church closed in 1993 due to a decline in parishioners. The brewery and restaurant that took its place fills with revelers on weekends. Brewing kettles occupy the former altar.

PENN BREWERY

This brewery and restaurant opened in the 1980s in the onetime home of the Eberhardt & Ober Brewery, which operated from the 1840s to the early 1900s. A fruits and vegetables wholesaler used the building as a warehouse in the interim.

THE PRIORY HOTEL

A Catholic church called St. Mary's was built on the North Shore in 1852. A priory for the Benedictine priests and brothers who served the parish was added several decades later. Today the priory is a boutique hotel and the church a banquet hall.

SENATOR JOHN HEINZ HISTORY CENTER

The 19th-century building that houses Pennsylvania's largest history museum was once a warehouse for an ice company.

STATION SQUARE

The riverfront shopping, dining, and entertainment complex was once the headquarters of the Pittsburgh & Lake Erie Railroad, which carried materials to and from the steel mills starting in the 1870s.

© VISITPITTSBURGH

Station Square, once a railroad station, is now a shopping and dining complex.

Allegheny River. Many seats offer stellar views of the water, bridges, and Downtown skyline. The home dugout was placed along the third base line instead of the first to give the Pirates a view of Pittsburgh's skyscrapers.

Tours are conducted weekdays from mid-April through late September and one Saturday a month. The walking tours last about 90 minutes and include the Pirates dugout, batting cages, and press box. Tour tickets are available at the main ticket window on the corner of Federal and General Robinson Streets. They're $7 for adults, $5 for seniors, students, and children. Kids five and under can tag along for free.

Heinz Field

Horseshoe-shaped Heinz Field (100 Art Rooney Ave., 412/323-1200, www.steelers.com/heinzfield) sits at the head of the Ohio River. Its open south side features a massive scoreboard and a vista of the Downtown skyline. About 12,000 tons of steel went into the 65,000-seat stadium for the Steelers and their fans, a.k.a. Steeler Nation. Locally based PPG Industries Inc. provided 30,000 gallons of paint and 50,000 square feet of glass. Food manufacturer H. J. Heinz Co., another global company that calls Pittsburgh home, snagged naming rights for $57 million.

Like PNC Park, Heinz Field opened in 2001. (Before that, the Pirates and Steelers shared Three Rivers Stadium, which was imploded when each team got a home of its own.) Unlike the Pirates, the Steelers have a tendency to win games. In 2009, the team became the first in the National Football League to score six Super Bowl titles, and Pittsburgh got a new nickname: "Sixburgh." As a consequence, it's easier to get into heaven than Heinz Field when the Steelers are in the house. The University of Pittsburgh football team also calls the stadium home. Tickets to its games are considerably easier to come by.

Tours are offered weekdays from April through October and one Saturday a month from April through July. Call or check the website for details. The cost is $6.50 for adults, $4 for seniors, students, and children.

Carnegie Science Center

Like the Andy Warhol Museum about a mile away, the Carnegie Science Center (117 1 Allegheny Ave., 412/237-3400, www.carnegiesciencecenter.org, 10 A.M.–5 P.M. Sun.–Fri., 10 A.M.–7 P.M. Sat., admission $17.95, children 3–12 $9.95, admission plus Omnimax film or laser show $22.95, children $14.95) is one of the four Carnegie Museums of Pittsburgh. It's the most kid-friendly and interactive of the four, and its store, XPLOR, is shopping nirvana for the nerdy set. Astronaut food? Check. Submarine models? Check. Permanent exhibitions include Exploration Station—a godsend to parents stumped by their progeny's "why" questions. Aerodynamics, embryology, magnetic forces, and dozens of other concepts and processes are explained. At SciQuest, another permanent exhibition, children can step inside a wind tunnel, experience an earthquake, and learn how bird flight influences airplane designers. The Miniature Railroad & Village offers a bird's-eye view of western Pennsylvania at the turn of the 20th century. Among the 2,000 hand-built replicas of historic structures is Forbes Field, Pittsburgh's beloved, bygone ballpark. Its miniature stands are packed with miniature spectators come to watch the Pirates and Chicago Cubs on opening day 1909. Trains wind around the village, and boats ply its rivers.

The Highmark SportsWorks exhibition, which explores the science of sports and the mechanics of the human body, moved into a brand-new facility in 2009. Also in 2009, the Science Center unveiled Roboworld, the largest permanent robotics exhibition in the country. Pittsburgh is a fitting home for the exhibition. Dubbed "Roboburgh" by *The Wall Street Journal*, the city has one of the leading robotics research centers in the world. Carnegie Mellon University's Robotics Institute, founded in 1979, has spawned dozens of companies. The university's Robot Hall of Fame found a permanent home in Roboworld. Inductees are robots real and fictional, including NASA's Mars Sojourner, Honda's ASIMO humanoid robot, and *Star Wars* heroes R2-D2 and C-3PO.

© CARNEGIE SCIENCE CENTER, VISITPITTSBURGH

Carnegie Science Center

Regular shows at the full-dome digital planetarium and tours of the World War II submarine moored alongside the Science Center are included in the price of admission. There is an additional charge for Omnimax movies (adults $8, children $6) and laser shows in the planetarium (adults and children $8). The Omnimax theater and planetarium stay open late into the evening on Fridays and Saturdays.

Rivers Casino

Luck rules the day at the adjacent Rivers Casino (777 Casino Dr., 412/231-7777, www.therivers casino.com, open 24 hours). Pittsburgh's only casino opened in August 2009 with 3,000 slot machines, adding table games the following year. Luckily for the proletariat, roughly a third of the 3,000 are penny slots. But the Rivers Casino also boasts the state's first $500 slot machine, a posh lounge reserved for the highest rollers, and priceless views of the Ohio River. In short, the casino offers something for everyone. Even non-gamblers should pay a visit, if only to marvel at what $780 million

can build or to quaff a chocolate martini beneath a 70-foot-tall contemporary chandelier in the Drum Bar. (Be aware that you have to play to park for free in the immense garage. A single round with a one-armed bandit will do ya, parking-wise.)

On-site restaurants include the upscale **Andrew's Steak and Seafood** (5–9:30 P.M. Sun.–Thurs., 5–11 P.M. Fri.–Sat., $18–55), notable for its chilled seafood and selection of wines by the glass. It's named for Carnegie, Mellon, and Warhol—three Andrews who made Pittsburgh proud. The casual, self-serve **Cíao** (7 A.M.–11 P.M. Sun.–Thurs., 7 A.M.–1 A.M. Fri.–Sat., $5–8) features pastries, paninis, wraps, and an Italian-made wine-dispensing system. Of course, a casino wouldn't be complete without an all-you-can-eat buffet. Eats at the **Grand View Buffet** (lunch 11 A.M.–3 P.M. Mon.–Sat. and 10 A.M.–3 P.M. Sun., dinner 4–9 P.M. Sun.–Thurs. and 4–11 P.M. Fri.–Sat., lunch $13.95, dinner $24.95) range from Italian staples to Mongolian stir-fry.

Children's Museum of Pittsburgh

Architecture and history buffs have as much reason as kiddies to visit the Children's Museum of Pittsburgh (10 Children's Way, 412/322-5058, www.pittsburghkids.org, 10 A.M.–5 P.M. Mon.–Sat., noon–5 P.M. Sun., admission $11, seniors and children 2–18 $10). It's housed in two historic landmarks. The older of the two, notable for its copper dome, served as the post office for Allegheny City before its annexation by Pittsburgh in 1907. The younger opened in 1939 as a planetarium. They're linked by an eye-catching contemporary structure of polycarbonate and glass.

Inside, it's back-to-back playgrounds. At the Studio, children can try their hand at painting, sculpting, printmaking, papermaking, and other art forms. The exhibition also has something for grown-ups: prints by Andy Warhol, Jasper Johns, and other noteworthy artists. In the Garage and Workshop, young handymen (and -women) can change a tire, crank up a transmission, hammer a nail, or take apart a stereo to see how it works. The Attic includes the Gravity Room, where just about everything is tilted at a 25-degree angle, and the Phosphorescent Room, where kids can capture their shadows with a strobe light. In Pittsburgh, no major children's attraction would be complete without a tribute to the homegrown public television series *Mister Rogers' Neighborhood*. The museum boasts a replica of Mister Rogers' television house and Neighborhood of Make-Believe. Children are welcome to try the cardigans on for size.

National Aviary

Just west of the Children's Museum is one of the largest aviaries in the United States. The National Aviary (700 Arch St., 412/323-7235, www.aviary.org, 10 A.M.–5 P.M. daily, opens 9 A.M. Memorial Day–Labor Day, admission $10, seniors $9, children 2 and older $8.50) is home to more than 600 birds, including many species that are threatened or endangered in the wild. Free-flight rooms and public feedings allow for close encounters of the bird kind. Visitors can toss fish to the pelicans, hand-feed nectar to the rainbow lorikeets, or watch the aviary's "chefs" prepare vittles for condors, macaws, and other residents. In 2009 the aviary unveiled Penguin Point, part of a multimillion-dollar expansion. The open-air exhibit features about a dozen African penguins, also known as jackass penguins because of their donkey-like bray. They include Sidney (as in Pittsburgh Penguins captain Sidney Crosby) and Stanley (as in hockey's holy grail, the Stanley Cup). An acryllic-fronted pool and crawlspaces make it possible to observe their underwater antics.

Mattress Factory

The historic Mexican War Streets are home to a museum of ultra-contemporary art. Billed as a "research and development lab for artists," the Mattress Factory (500 Sampsonia Way, 412/231-3169, www.mattress.org, 10 A.M.–5 P.M. Tues.–Sat., 1–5 P.M. Sun., admission $10, seniors $8, students $7, children under 6 free) exhibits room-sized works created on-site. Its 16 permanent installations include works by James Turrell, Bill Woodrow, and William Anastasi. Each year, 8–10 new works are exhibited for several months at a time. The museum's expansion has made it an engine for community development as well as artistic expression. It has purchased nine properties since 1975, turning them into galleries, artist residences, offices, public spaces, a parking lot, and even an artist-created garden. The first acquisition was a former mattress warehouse built at the turn of the 20th century.

Allegheny Observatory

The heavens seem almost within reach when viewed through the 13-inch Fitz-Clark refractor at the Allegheny Observatory (159 Riverview Ave., 412/321-2400, www.pitt.edu/~aobsvtry, tours April–Oct., free). The observatory in Riverview Park, four miles north of Downtown, is a University of Pittsburgh research laboratory and only occasionally open to the public. Free tours are offered Thursdays May–August and Fridays April–October. All tours begin at 8 P.M. with a short slide or film presentation and end about two hours later at the Fitz-Clark. On the third Friday of every month except December, local astronomers and physicists give public lectures on topics such as *The Mysteries of Quantum Mechanics* and *Measuring the Universe with the Wilkinson Microwave Anisotropy Probe.* An open house is held once a year, usually in the fall. It's the only opportunity you'll get to peer through a telescope that puts the Fitz-Clark to shame. Reservations are required for all tours, lectures, and the open house. Lectures are so popular that reservations are only accepted the Monday following the previous lecture.

SOUTH SIDE AND MOUNT WASHINGTON

It's been said that the South Side has both types of "blue hairs." One type is fond of studded collars and punk rock; the other favors sensible shoes and Dean Martin. That diversity is part of what makes the area so interesting. What's referred to as the South Side is actually several neighborhoods near the southern banks of the Monongahela River. The smallest of these is the South Shore, dominated by a dining and entertainment complex called Station Square. Overlooking it is Mount Washington, once called Coal Hill for its abundant coal seams, which supplied fuel to Pittsburgh's settlers and, later, its riverbank industries. The growth of these industries in the mid-19th century created more and more jobs—and a shortage of housing in the flatlands. So workers built houses on Pittsburgh's hillsides. For a while, they commuted on foot, trudging up steep paths after a hard day's work in the plants. The first people-moving incline opened in 1870. In the 25 years that followed, more than 15 others were built. Two remain, a mile apart on Mount Washington. The hilltop is now accessible by car, but some of its residents still use the inclines to commute to jobs in Downtown or the South Side. They're also popular among tourists (and lovebirds) for the vista from up top.

If Pittsburgh has a main drag, it's East Carson Street in the South Side Flats. The low-lying neighborhood was once crowded with glass-making factories and, later, iron and steel operations. Today it's chockablock with restaurants, bars, and stores. Should gluttony

get the best of you there, press on toward the South Side Slopes. The neighborhood's steep streets rival a treadmill at its highest setting. Sweat isn't the only payoff; a perch in the hills affords views that rival Mount Washington's.

Smithfield Street Bridge

Some years ago, the Pennsylvania Department of Transportation decided to demolish the Smithfield Street Bridge, which connects Downtown and the South Side, and replace it with a modern bridge. Preservationists lobbied to save it and won. Instead of being torn down, the oldest steel bridge in the United States got a new deck, a paint job, and an extra traffic lane (in place of an obsolete streetcar rail line). The bridge is actually the third to be built on the site. The first, built in 1818, was made of wood. It was felled by the Great Fire of 1845, along with more than a thousand buildings. The second was a wire-rope suspension bridge designed by John A. Roebling, the German-born civil engineer also responsible for New York's Brooklyn Bridge. By the 1870s, the heavily trafficked bridge had begun to show signs of strain. The truss bridge that stands there today was constructed in the early 1880s.

The Smithfield Street Bridge is a National Historic Landmark, but what really distinguishes it from so many bridges in Pittsburgh and across the country is the foot traffic. Downtown workers who live south of the Monongahela River stream across the bridge in the morning and again come quitting time. For visitors staying in Downtown hotels, the bridge's pedestrian walkways are a great way to reach the restaurants and nightspots of Station Square and the famous Mount Washington inclines.

Station Square

As a shopping destination, Station Square (intersection of Smithfield Street Bridge and East Carson St., 800/859-8989, www.stationsquare .com) leaves much to be desired. You probably won't recognize the retailers. You probably won't leave with shopping bags slung over your shoulders. But if you're in the market for a Terrible Towel—the local sports fan's favorite accessory—you won't be disappointed. Many of the merchants specialize in Pittsburgh mementos and other knickknacks. What's noteworthy about the Shops at Station Square (10 A.M.–9 P.M. Mon.–Sat. and noon–5 P.M. Sun. Mar.–Dec., 10 A.M.–7 P.M. Mon.–Thurs., 10 A.M.–9 P.M. Fri.–Sat., and noon–5 P.M. Sun. Jan.–Feb.) is that they occupy restored railroad buildings. Once upon a time, these buildings belonged to the Pittsburgh & Lake Erie Railroad, the "Little Giant" that moved so much tonnage between points in Pennsylvania and Ohio when steel was king. When the mills declined, so did the railroad. By the 1970s, the massive Pittsburgh terminal on the south bank of the Monongahela River was in danger of becoming a commercial cemetery. The Pittsburgh History and Landmarks Foundation stepped in to give the property a second life, building a hotel, parking lots, and a dock and converting the railroad terminal to a fine restaurant before selling to a developer in 1994. Today, Station Square is a 52-acre complex with more than a dozen restaurants, a handful of nightclubs, a new amphitheater that seats 4,000, and a 47-slip marina.

All that jazz doesn't obscure its railroad roots. Five freight cars remain in the shopping mall. On weekends, a trackless kiddie train winds around the shops. A ticket to ride the Station Square Express can be purchased for $1. The Grand Concourse seafood restaurant, with its stained-glass cathedral ceiling and brass accents, looks very much as it did when it served as a passenger terminal. The outdoor Bessemer Court is named for a rare artifact displayed there: a 1930s Bessemer converter, which was used to convert molten iron into steel. The 10-ton machine is easy to miss if you arrive when the Fountain at Bessemer Court is in full swing. This ain't no garden-variety gusher; it's the Vegas showgirl of water fountains. Hundreds of rainbow-colored water jets dance to music by the likes of Frank Sinatra, Celine Dion, and Christina Aguilera (who, incidentally, grew up in the suburbs of Pittsburgh). The fountain operates 9 A.M. to midnight from late April through early November. Shows begin every 20 minutes.

Station Square is a hub for tour operators. The busiest of those is the **Gateway Clipper Fleet** (412/355-7980, gatewayclipper.com) of five riverboats that ply the three rivers year-round. If the boats look up in years, it's because they're reproductions of vessels of yore. The largest is the *Gateway Majestic,* which has a capacity of 1,000 passengers. The smallest, the *Gateway Countess,* is the fastest of the fleet and also its only open-air boat. Excursions range from one-hour sightseeing tours to dinner-and-dancing cruises to full-day trips. The fleet also shuttles sports fans to PNC Park and Heinz Field on game days.

Station Square is also home to **Just Ducky Tours** (412/402-3825, www.justduckytours .com, daily Apr.–Oct., weekends in Nov.), Pittsburgh's only land-and-water tours. These vehicles are no reproductions; they're amphibious trucks built by General Motors for use in World War II. The DUKWs, as they're called, cross the Monongahela River for a tour of Downtown. Tours last about an hour and depart every 90 minutes or so.

For the sightseer who prefers dry land, there's **Segway in Paradise** (412/337-3941, www.segwayinparadise.com), which occupies a storefront in the mall. You can hop aboard a two-wheeled personal transporter for a spin around Station Square or a two-hour guided tour of Downtown. During the warmer months, tours depart at 9:30 A.M. and 1 P.M. daily. No experience is necessary. The $59 tour includes a 20-minute training session.

◖ Mount Washington Inclines

Three 19th-century inclines remain in Pennsylvania, and two of those climb Mount Washington. (The third is in Johnstown, about 65 miles east of Pittsburgh.) They've been around for so long that you might think twice about boarding the cable cars. Board. The views more than compensate for the fear factor.

The **Monongahela Incline** (lower station Carson St. near Smithfield Street Bridge, 412/442-2000, www.portauthority.org, 5:30 A.M.–12:45 A.M. Mon.–Sat., 8:45 A.M.–midnight Sun. and holidays, one way $2, round-trip $2.50, children 6–11 $1 one way, $1.25 round-trip) is the oldest and steepest incline in all of America. It's also the oldest cable car operation—three years older than San Francisco's famous cable cars. The incline began operating in 1870. Its cars, which were replaced in the 1980s, ply two parallel tracks at about six miles per hour. The creaks and groans of the machinery recall a wooden roller coaster. Rest easy; there's no plunge after the "Mon Incline" summits. The lower station is a short walk from the Smithfield Street Bridge and across the street from Station Square, where you can park for a modest fee.

The **Duquesne Incline** (lower station 1197 W. Carson St., 412/381-1665, www.incline .pghfree.net, 5:30 A.M.–12:45 A.M. Mon.–Sat., 7 A.M.–12:45 A.M. Sun. and holidays, $2 each way, children 6–11 $1, seniors free), one mile west, opened in 1877. It joined three other Mount Washington inclines but didn't lack for passengers. In 1880, *Scientific American* magazine wrote of the Duquesne Incline: "On Sundays during the summer, 6,000 passengers

are carried during the day and evening, the cars ascending and descending as rapidly as filled and emptied." Ridership shrank after the advent of the automobile, and in 1962, the company that owned the incline decided not to invest in sorely needed repairs. The incline was shut down. A group of Mount Washington residents took up its cause, raising $15,000 in six months through the sale of souvenir tickets, baked goods, and shares in the incline company. Repairs were made, and the incline reopened. Shortly afterward, the Port Authority of Allegheny County purchased the incline and leased it to its rescuers. Inflation hasn't affected the lease fee: $1 per year. (The transportation authority promptly donates the dollar to the Society for the Preservation of The Duquesne Heights Incline, the nonprofit that operates the incline.)

There's free parking across the street from the lower station, between West Carson Street and the Ohio River. Follow the pedestrian bridge that crosses West Carson to reach the station. You'll board one of two original Victorian cable cars and gain 400 feet of elevation in less than

© NATALIA BRATSLAVSKY/123RF.COM

the Duquesne Incline

STEP AEROBICS

The fitness quest can be costly. Gym memberships cost upwards of $50 a month. Personal trainers can charge as much as some lawyers. In the Steel City, however, it's possible to get buns of steel without spending a cent. Pittsburgh has at least 738 outdoor staircases comprising 45,000 steps. No city in the country has more, and no neighborhood in Pittsburgh has more than the South Side Slopes. Rising from the Monongahela River, the nabe rewards those who conquer its steps with knockout views. (Mount Washington with its inclined planes gets a great deal more press, but when you visit the Slopes, you get the satisfaction of *earning* the panorama.) Driving through the Slopes is almost as challenging as hoofing it. The streets are narrow and winding and in some spots so steep that you can't see the road for the car hood. If you're working your way down and see an oncoming car, it's customary to pull to the side so the climber can have the right of way. Complicating driving is the matter of "paper" streets, so called because they exist on paper, but a motorist who attempted one would be screwed. They're actually staircases, and Pittsburgh has 334 of them. Perfect example: Eleanor Street in the Slopes. On a map, the street appears to extend from Josephine Street at the base of the Slopes to way-up-there Arlington Avenue. In actuality, Eleanor morphs into a staircase one block from Josephine and then back into a drivable street two blocks later.

During Pittsburgh's industrial heyday, the staircases linked hilltop communities with the steel mills and other workplaces on the riverbanks. The Slopes were home to Poles, Germans, and other immigrants. Their faith left an indelible mark on the neighborhood. It's dotted with churches and a larger number of former churches, rectories, and convents. Yard Way, the longest of the paper streets, climbs from a street named Pius toward a street named St. Paul, which curves its way to an avenue named Monastery, home to St. Paul of the Cross Monastery. To reach Yard Way from bustling East Carson Street in the South Side Flats neighborhood, head away from the river on South 18th Street. Shortly after crossing railroad tracks, 18th veers to the left and then comes to a fork. Bear right to stay on 18th, then take the first right onto Pius Street. Yard Way is two blocks down.

Good to have if you're interested in exploring more staircases is Bob Regan's *The Steps of Pittsburgh: Portrait of a City* ($21.95, 866/362-0789, www.thelocalhistorycompany.com). Or mark your calendar for the South Side Slopes Neighborhood Association's **StepTrek** (412/488-0486, www.steptrek.org, Oct., registration $15, early bird price $12, children under 12 free). Armed with maps and course descriptions, participants in the noncompetitive event climb about half of the Slopes' 5,447 steps.

three minutes. At the upper station, you'll find a free museum, gift shop, and observation deck with two binocular telescopes. Fifty cents buys you access to a viewing platform where you can watch the hoisting equipment in action.

Grandview Avenue

Both funiculars deposit passengers on Mount Washington's Grandview Avenue, the most stroll-worthy stretch in Pittsburgh. George Washington is said to have spotted the forks of the Ohio River from this bluff. He saw a highly strategic site for a fort. What we see today is an acclaimed cityscape. In 2003, *USA Weekend* magazine named the nighttime view from Mount Washington to its list of 10 most beautiful places in America. The daytime view is pretty righteous too. Pittsburghers rarely fail to bring out-of-town guests here.

The historic inclines aren't the only way to reach Grandview Avenue, which clings to the rim of the hill for about a mile and a half. PJ McArdle Roadway and Sycamore Street also climb to the penthouse of Pittsburgh. Street parking is plentiful unless you arrive on the Fourth of July or another occasion for fireworks. Once on foot, make your way to one of the observation decks that jut over the hillside. You may have to bypass a wedding party or gaggle of prom-goers. This is the mother of Pittsburgh photo ops. The western (Duquesne Incline) end of Grandview is crowded with restaurants of the special occasion variety, many of which are open only for dinner. They could serve gruel and still be packed on Valentine's Day. The views from their dining areas are that romantic.

Community development types try mightily to prove that Mount Washington has more to offer than breathtaking views and "Restaurant Row." At the eastern end of Grandview, near the Monongahela Incline, signs point the way to the homey Shiloh Street business district. You'll find ATMs, several murals, and casual eateries like the aptly named **Packs-N-Dogs** (223 Shiloh St., 412/431-1855), which offers specialty beers and hot dogs (all-beef or veggie).

St. John the Baptist Ukrainian Catholic Church

The eight-domed St. John the Baptist Ukrainian Catholic Church (109 S. 7th St., 412/431-2531, www.stjohnspittsburgh.com) is an eye-catcher. The Byzantine-style church was built in 1895 by Ukrainian immigrants who worked in Pittsburgh's mills, factories, and mines. But there's nothing workaday about it. Its towers, stained-glass windows, and domes topped with Greek crosses set it apart from the slope-roofed houses that surround it and the Victorian storefronts that line East Carson Street. It's not just the architecture that offers a taste of Eastern Europe. Every week, parishioners gather in the basement to make pierogies: dumplings stuffed with potato, cheese, or sauerkraut. Pierogi sales are held Thursdays from 10 A.M. to 3 P.M. A dozen of the potato or kraut varieties costs $6; cheese pierogies are $9 a dozen.

OAKLAND AND POINTS EAST

In the 19th century, pollution and overcrowding drove some Pittsburghers to the city's outskirts. Oakland, about three miles east of

Downtown, started as an elite enclave. By the 1920s, thanks in no small part to its moneyed residents, Oakland had blossomed into an academic and cultural powerhouse with two major universities, a pair of world-class museums, and outstanding hospitals.

First stop for many visitors are three connected buildings that house the Carnegie Museum of Art, the Carnegie Museum of Natural History, Carnegie Music Hall, and the main branch of the Carnegie Library of Pittsburgh. Schenley Park fans out behind them, offering relaxation, recreation, and, frequently, free entertainment. Oakland's most arresting free building, the 42-story Cathedral of Learning, can be seen from points near and far, guiding home coeds who wander too far from the campuses of Carnegie Mellon University or University of Pittsburgh. Central Oakland is awash in the sort of restaurants, bars, and coffee shops favored by students.

East of Oakland are the neighborhoods of Squirrel Hill, Shadyside, and Bloomfield. Squirrel Hill is the center of Jewish culture in the city. Dotted with synagogues, it's the place to go for a breakfast of bagels and lox. When a Dunkin' Donuts opened on one of the neighborhood's main thoroughfares in 2009, it resolved to adhere to Jewish dietary laws. (Vegetarians can rest assured that its breakfast sandwiches are made with meatless versions of sausage and bacon.) Shadyside is among the most affluent neighborhoods in Pittsburgh. Its Walnut Street shopping district is home to the likes of Williams-Sonoma and Pottery Barn. The parallel Ellsworth Avenue is known for its nightlife offerings, including a couple of queer-friendly joints. Bloomfield is Pittsburgh's Little Italy. On Liberty Avenue, its main drag, parking meters are painted the colors of the Italian flag. These and other neighborhoods are collectively known as the East End.

◖ Carnegie Museum of Art

Don't have the budget to visit the Parthenon in Greece? Head to the Carnegie Museum of Art (4400 Forbes Ave., 412/622-3131, www.cmoa .org, 10 A.M.–5 P.M. Tues.–Sat., 10 A.M.–8 P.M.

Thurs., noon–5 P.M. Sun., admission $15, seniors $12, students and children $11, children under 3 free, includes same-day access to Carnegie Museum of Natural History), where you'll find the Hall of Sculpture, a replica of the ancient temple's heavily columned inner sanctuary. It's made of white marble from the same quarries that provided stones for the 5th century B.C.E. Parthenon. Decorative arts objects from more recent centuries are displayed on the balcony of the hall, along with several works from the museum's celebrated architectural cast collection. More than 140 pieces from that collection, the largest in the country, reside in the Hall of Architecture. Plaster casts of architectural and sculptural masterpieces were in hot demand in the 19th century. The industrialist and philanthropist Andrew Carnegie, who founded museum in 1895, saw them as a way to bring the world's masterworks to Pittsburgh. Today, few sizable collections remain. Only the Victoria and Albert Museum in London and Musée National des Monuments Français in Paris have architectural cast collections that rival Pittsburgh's. The Carnegie collection includes not only architectural casts but also casts of famed sculptures such as the *Venus de Milo* and Myron's *Discobolus* (Discus Thrower). Much newer than the halls of Sculpture and Architecture, which opened in 1907, is the Heinz Architectural Center. It opened in 1993 to collect and showcase architectural drawings and models.

The Carnegie, of course, isn't just about architecture. It has a dozen galleries devoted to art from ancient times to the 20th century and several more filled with contemporary works. In fact, the Carnegie has been called the first museum of modern art. Andrew Carnegie wished that it be filled not with the works of the long-dead but rather with the art of "tomorrow's old masters." Early acquisitions included paintings by Winslow Homer, James A. McNeill Whistler, and other artists who were still ticking. About every three years, the museum presents the Carnegie International, an exhibition of contemporary art from around the world. The exhibition draws the art world to Pittsburgh, which is exactly what Andrew Carnegie had in mind when he established the tradition in 1896. Featured artists have included Mary Cassatt, Henri Matisse, Edward Hopper, Andy Warhol, and Willem de Kooning. The 2008 Carnegie International showcased works by about 40 artists whose names generally aren't recognized outside art circles—yet. The museum's permanent collection includes more than 300 works purchased from its Carnegie Internationals.

◖ Carnegie Museum of Natural History

Three years after opening his eponymous museums, Andrew Carnegie set his sights on bagging a dinosaur. In 1899, a bone-digging crew bankrolled by Carnegie discovered the skeleton of an 84-foot sauropod in southeastern Wyoming. A longer dinosaur had never been found. Exhibiting the colossal fossil—named *Diplodocus carnegii* in recognition of its benefactor—required a $5 million museum expansion. "Dippy," as the dinosaur came to be known, wasn't alone for long. In 1909, Carnegie's bone hunters discovered a hoard

© IOANA BARZA

PITTSBURGH

statue of "Dippy" outside of the Carnegie Museum of Natural History

of Jurassic dinosaur fossils near Jensen, Utah. The site produced about 20 mountable skeletons, six of which joined Dippy at the Carnegie Museum of Natural History (4400 Forbes Ave., 412/622-3131, www.carnegiemnh.org, 10 A.M.–5 P.M. Tues.–Sat., 10 A.M.–8 P.M. Thurs., noon–5 P.M. Sun., admission $15, seniors $12, students and children $11, children under 3 free, includes same-day access to Carnegie Museum of Art). The Carnegie boasts the third-largest display of real mounted dinosaurs in the United States, after the National Museum of Natural History in Washington, D.C., and the American Museum of Natural History in New York City.

The museum's interactive fossil dig, Bonehunters Quarry (1–3 P.M. Tues.–Wed. and Fri., 1–7 P.M. Thurs., 10 A.M.–4:30 P.M. Sat., and noon–4:30 P.M. Sun.), gives children 10 and under a chance to play paleontologist. Using a chisel and brush, they can help excavate a dinosaur or other beast of yore. It's also open to the public 10 A.M.–1 P.M. weekdays when not in use by school groups. There's no pretending at PaleoLab, the museum's on-site fossil preparation lab. Visitors can watch real preparators clean and prepare real fossils.

Dinosaurs may be its main draw, but the Carnegie has other distinguished exhibitions. The museum has been building its collection of ancient Egyptian artifacts ever since Andrew Carnegie donated a mummy and its sarcophagus. The collection now includes more than 2,500 artifacts dating back to 3100 B.C.E., about 600 of which are displayed in the Walton Hall of Ancient Egypt.

◖ Cathedral of Learning

If Dippy's head were turned toward Forbes Avenue, he would be gazing at the second-tallest university building in the world. The 42-story Cathedral of Learning (4200 5th Ave., 412/624-4141, www.pitt.edu) was robbed of the number one spot by a Moscow building with fewer stories and an oversized spire. The geographic and symbolic heart of the University of Pittsburgh was designed in the early 1920s by one of the foremost neo-Gothic

the Cathedral of Learning

© ANNA DUBROVSKY

architects of the time and was to be the tallest building in Pittsburgh. By the time the limestone skyscraper was dedicated in 1937, the 44-story Gulf Tower had risen in Downtown. But the Cathedral didn't fail to make its point that scholarliness is next to godliness. Its three-story foyer, known as the Commons Room, is so churchlike that you half expect to find kneeling parishioners beneath the soaring arches. Instead, you find students hunched over books and laptops. Any prayers are silent.

The Cathedral houses classrooms, administrative offices, libraries, and several departments. It attracts non-students because of its dramatic design and the equally dramatic views from its upper levels. But the main attraction is a set of classrooms gifted to the university by the city's ethnic communities. Each of the **Nationality Rooms** (412/624-6000, www .pitt.edu/~natrooms, 9 A.M.–4 P.M. Mon.–Sat., 11 A.M.–4 P.M. Sun., admission $3, children 8–18 $1, booklet with brief descriptions $1.25) depicts a culture in a period prior to the 19th century. The first four rooms were dedicated in 1938 and the 27th in 2008. Several others are in the works. Chancellor John G. Bowman, who dreamed up the Cathedral, invited local immigrants and their descendants to create classrooms that would evoke pride in their heritage. In many cases, their fundraising and designing efforts were aided by their motherlands. The Chinese Classroom, inspired by a palace hall in Beijing's Forbidden City, features a round teakwood table and a slate portrait of Confucius. The Armenian Classroom with its domed ceiling emulates a 10th- to 12th-century monastery, and the Greek Classroom represents 5th-century B.C.E. Athens. Classrooms are off-limits when they're in use, so it's a good idea to visit on a weekend or any day from May through August. Audio tours are available during those times. The last tour is dispatched from the information center near the 5th Avenue entrance at 2:30 P.M. The best time to visit is from mid-November to mid-January, when the classrooms are dressed in holiday finery. For a free tour with a guide who knows every nook and cranny, come the day after Thanksgiving or December 27–31. On those days, the information center opens at 10 A.M., and tours depart about every two hours 10:30 A.M.–2:30 P.M.

Philadelphia-born architect Charles Klauder designed two buildings to accompany his Cathedral. The university's interdenominational **Heinz Chapel** (1212 Cathedral of Learning, 412/624-4157, www.heinzchapel .pitt.edu), on the Bellefield Avenue side of the Cathedral, hosts about 1,500 events a year. A lot of those are weddings, but choral and organ concerts are held occasionally, and many of them are free. *Where's Waldo* whizzes will get a kick out of scanning the stained glass windows for 391 famous figures. At 73 feet, the transept windows are among the tallest in the world.

The **Stephen Foster Memorial** (4301 Forbes Ave., 412/624-4100) is just outside the Forbes Avenue doors of the Cathedral. In addition to two theaters used for productions of the university's Department of Theatre Arts, the Foster Memorial houses a library with one of the nation's top collections of 19th-century American music. A museum (9 A.M.–4 P.M.

Mon.–Fri.) dedicated to the composer and Pittsburgh native for whom the building is named offers guided tours for $1.50 for adults and $1 for senior citizens and children; unguided tours are free. Call in advance to arrange for a guide.

Schenley Plaza

Not so long ago, the verdant public park across from the Cathedral of Learning was a parking lot. Today Schenley Plaza (4100 Forbes Ave., 412/682-7275, www.pittsburghparks.org/ schenleyplaza) is a popular sunbathing and picnicking spot and a frequent venue for free concerts, yoga classes, and other mind-expanding stuff. New Yorkers may experience a touch of déjà vu. The Schenley Plaza design team drew on the Big Apple's Bryant Park for inspiration, borrowing elements such as a carousel, a great lawn, flower gardens, and food kiosks. There's a tented area for the fair-skinned and free wireless Internet access for the plugged-in. A full-service restaurant could be on the horizon. The Victorian-style carousel operates April through October (10 A.M.–8 P.M. Mon.–Fri., 10 A.M.–6 P.M. Sat., and 11 A.M.–6 P.M. Sun.). Ride tokens are $1.25.

Mosey across Schenley Drive for a look at the **Mary Schenley Memorial Fountain.** Dedicated in 1918 and restored in 2008, the sculpture and fountain titled *A Song to Nature* depicts Pan, the goat-legged god of woods, being serenaded by a nymph. Its sculptor, Victor David Brenner, may not be a household name, but just about every American household has a Brenner in its collection. He designed the likeness of President Lincoln on the U.S. penny.

Sitting behind the fountain is the **Frick Fine Arts building,** home of the University of Pittsburgh's History of Art and Architecture Department and Studio Arts Department. The Italian Renaissance edifice also houses one of the country's premier fine arts libraries. What makes it of interest to non-academics is the collection of art copies displayed in the cloister. "Copies" doesn't exactly sell them, but these scale reproductions of 15th-century Italian

© ANNA DUBROVSKY

Schenley Plaza

Renaissance paintings are masterpieces in their own right. They're the work of Russian artist Nicholas Lochoff, commissioned in 1911 by the Moscow Museum of Fine Arts. Stranded in Italy after the Russian Revolution of 1917, Lochoff sold off most of his replicas. Helen Clay Frick, daughter of industrialist Henry Clay Frick, rounded them up after the artist's death in 1948 and donated them to the university. If you can't make it to Italy to see Botticelli's *Birth of Venus,* make it to the Frick Fine Arts building.

For many years, Schenley Plaza had a neighbor nicknamed the House of Thrills. Officially known as Forbes Field, it was the third home of the Pittsburgh Pirates and the first home of the Pittsburgh Steelers. The 1909 stadium where Babe Ruth hit his last three home runs closed in 1970, but its remnants still attract sports fans. Look for the stadium's flagpole and part of the outfield wall to the right of the Frick Fine Arts building. Baseball fans gather here every October 13 to celebrate Bill Mazeroski's ninth-inning home run in the final game of the 1960 World Series, which gave the Pirates a 10-9 win over the New York Yankees. Cross the street and enter Wesley W. Posvar Hall to see the home plate used in the stadium's final game. It's embedded in the ground floor, beneath glass, not far from its original spot. (Baseball fans can forgive the historical inaccuracy. If placed in its original spot, home plate would be displayed in a women's restroom.)

Schenley Park

Beauteous as it is, Schenley Plaza is but a gateway to a much larger oasis, Schenley Park (412/682-7275, www.pittsburghparks.org/schenley). The 456-acre park is home to an ice-skating rink, an outdoor swimming pool, golf and disc golf courses, and a sports complex, among other facilities. A good place to start is the lovely **Schenley Park Café** (Panther Hollow Rd. and Schenley Dr., 412/687-1800, 10 A.M.–4 P.M. daily, closed Mon. in winter), which doubles as a visitors center. You'll find light lunch fare, coffee and espresso drinks, and desserts, along with free wireless Internet access. Trail maps are $2. There are trailheads behind the café. Free concerts are held on the tented patio 12:30–3:30 P.M. on Sundays in summer and fall. Consult the park website for a list of **Sundays in the Park** performers.

Grassy **Flagstaff Hill,** across from Phipps Conservatory and Botanical Gardens, is awash with sunbathers on summer days. On

---

THE INCORRIGIBLE HEIRESS

The woman for whom Schenley Park and Schenley Plaza are named started life as Mary Elizabeth Croghan. She gained the Schenley name – and created an international scandal – at the age of 15, when she eloped with a 43-year-old captain in the British Army. The 1842 elopement made headlines not just because of their age difference but because Mary Croghan Schenley stood to inherit large tracts of land amassed by her maternal grandfather, one of Pittsburgh's earliest captains of industry. Distraught, her widowed father wrangled control of the estate and arranged for it to be placed in trust after his death. For a while, the lovebirds in England barely scraped by. But father and daughter eventually reconciled. Upon his death in 1850, she received her full inheritance.

In 1889, Pittsburgh's director of public works learned that a real estate developer's agent planned to travel to London to persuade Mary to sell a swath of land then known as Mt. Airy Tract. The city official had another idea for the property: a grand park. He dispatched a Pittsburgh lawyer, who beat the agent to England by two days. The quick-footedness paid off. Mary gave the city 300 acres of Mt. Airy Tract, stipulating that the park be named after her and never sold. Over the next few years, the city purchased an additional 120 acres of her property and some adjoining land to complete Schenley Park.

Wednesday and Sunday nights, it's packed with movie buffs and their picnic baskets. Starting at sundown, hits such as *Slumdog Millionaire* and *Iron Man* are projected onto a large screen. (You can be assured of a kid-friendly flick like *WALL-E* on a Sunday.) Flagstaff Hill is one of several Cinema in the Park (www.city .pittsburgh.pa.us/parks, 412/937-3039) sites in the city.

In winter, the action shifts to the **Schenley Park Skating Rink** (Overlook Dr., 412/422-6523, www.city.pittsburgh.pa.us/parks, admission $4, seniors and children 17 and under $3, skate rental $2.50). The outdoor rink generally opens in early November and closes in late March. Public skating times vary from day to day.

The 18-hole **Bob O'Connor Golf Course** (E. Circuit Rd., 412/622-6959, www.thefirst teepittsburgh.org) is open year-round. So is the **Schenley Oval Sportsplex** (Overlook Dr., 412/255-2539, www.city.pittsburgh.pa.us/ parks), which has 13 tennis courts, a 400-meter running track, and a sports turf soccer field.

⊄ Phipps Conservatory and Botanical Gardens

Cacti and bonsai and tree ferns, oh my! The crown jewel of Schenley Park is Phipps Conservatory and Botanical Gardens (1 Schenley Park, GPS: 700 Frank Curto Dr., 412/622-6914, http://phipps.conservatory. org, 9:30 A.M.–5 P.M. daily and until 10 P.M. Fri., admission $10, seniors and students $9, children 2–18 $7). The "crystal palace," as the steel and glass structure has been called, is as wondrous as the botanical treasures inside. It opened in 1893, stocked with tropical plants from that year's Chicago World's Fair. Today the Victorian greenhouse has 19 indoor and outdoor gardens whose oxygen-producing inhabitants range from towering palm trees to rare miniature orchids. A good mix of permanent and changing displays make repeat visits a must for the horticulturally inclined. Come in fall or winter to catch the conservatory's miniature train display. In spring and summer, you can watch butterflies emerge from chrysalises.

© ANNA DUBROVSKY

The Phipps Conservatory in Schenley Park features 19 gardens.

On weekends throughout the year, Phipps offers educational programs on everything from origami to moss gardening. They're free with admission.

You don't need to pay admission to browse the extensive selection of gardening supplies, books, and doodads in the gift shop or eat in the airy cafe, where the forks are compostable and the produce largely local. An otherworldly golden chandelier hovers over the LEED-certified welcome center. It's one of several installations by renowned glass sculptor Dale Chihuly at the conservatory, which was a gift to the city from Henry Phipps, Andrew Carnegie's partner in Carnegie Steel Company.

Soldiers & Sailors Memorial Hall & Museum

"Honor them with your presence" is the battle cry of the Soldiers & Sailors Memorial Hall & Museum (4141 5th Ave., 412/621-4253, www.soldiersandsailorshall.org, museum 10 A.M.–4 P.M. Tues.–Sat., admission by donation). The grand Greco-Roman structure opened in 1910 as a tribute to local Civil War veterans. Since then, Soldiers & Sailors has broadened its scope to include all men and women who have served the United States in its military endeavors. Visitors can hup-two-three-four through four exhibit-filled corridors. Bronze plaques on their outer walls are engraved with the names of 25,000 men from the Pittsburgh area who served in the Union Army during the Civil War. It's interesting to note that three of the corridors are named for cardinal points—West Hall, North Hall, and East Hall—while the fourth is called Front Hall. That's because the Civil War vets who ran the place a century ago refused to see "South" on their building. The "Slave to Soldier" exhibit in the Gettysburg Room explores the experience of African Americans in the military. Scantily clad coeds dot the museum's expansive lawns in summer.

Rodef Shalom Biblical Botanical Garden

You needn't be a believer to appreciate the

© ANNA DUBROVSKY

Soldiers & Sailors Memorial Hall & Museum

Rodef Shalom Biblical Botanical Garden (4905 5th Ave., 412/621-6566, www.biblicalgarden pittsburgh.org, 10 A.M.–2 P.M. Sun.–Thurs., 7–9 P.M. Wed., noon–1 P.M. Sat. early June to mid-Sept., free), a microcosm of Holy Land horticulture. Think olives, dates, pomegranates, and figs. In addition to more than 100 plants grown in ancient Israel, the garden features botanical eponyms of biblical characters, e.g., Moses in the Basket and Joseph's Coat. A stream representing the River Jordan runs through it. Trained docents lead free tours on the first Wednesday of the month at 12:15 P.M. Being Mediterranean or tropical, most of the plants are trucked off to greenhouses before the first frost.

Frick Art & Historical Center
In December 1881, industrialist Henry Clay Frick married Adelaide Howard Childs. After their wedding trip, the couple purchased an Italianate-style house on the corner of Penn and South Homewood Avenues, about two miles east of Oakland. They named it Clayton,

and it served as the family's primary residence until 1905, when they moved to New York. Today Clayton is one of three museums on the grounds of the Frick Art & Historical Center (7227 Reynolds St., 412/371-0600, www .frickart.org, 10 A.M.–5 P.M. Tues.–Sun.) More than 90 percent of the furniture and artifacts in the restored home, which opened to the public in 1990, are original. The only way to see them is via docent-led tour ($12, seniors and students $10, children 16 and under $6). Tour times vary, and reservations are strongly recommended.

There's no charge for admission to the intimate Frick Art Museum, which houses the personal collection of Helen Clay Frick, Henry and Adelaide's younger daughter. Helen, who returned to Pittsburgh in 1981 and lived at Clayton until her death in 1984, was particularly fond of early Renaissance painting and 18th-century French painting and decorative arts. The museum hosts traveling exhibitions, adult workshops, film screenings, and lectures by artists and art educators. Guided tours of the

PITTSBURGH

current exhibition are provided Wednesdays, Saturdays, and Sundays at 2 P.M. They're usually free, but the museum asks for a donation for some exhibitions. Henry Clay Frick's 1914 Rolls Royce Silver Ghost and an 1898 Panhard believed to be the first car in Pittsburgh are among 20-some vintage automobiles on view in the Car and Carriage Museum. Admission is free, as is a cell phone tour.

What used to be the Frick children's playhouse is now a visitors center and museum shop. Check out the remains of their bowling alley in the floor of the shop. No ordinary museum commissary, the **Café at the Frick** (11 A.M.–5 P.M. Tues.–Sun., $11–22, reservations recommended) offers one of the loveliest lunches in Pittsburgh. Seasonal menus feature uncommon soups, salads, and sandwiches, plus several flawless entrées. The vegetables and herbs couldn't be fresher; they're grown in the on-site garden and greenhouse. Tea service is available after 2:30 P.M.

Pittsburgh Zoo & PPG Aquarium

More than a century old but not the least bit timeworn, the 77-acre Pittsburgh Zoo & PPG Aquarium (1 Wild Place, GPS: 7340 Butler St., 412/665-3640, www.pittsburghzoo.org, summer 9 A.M.–6 P.M. daily, gates close at 4:30 P.M., fall and spring 9 A.M.–5 P.M. daily, gates close at 4 P.M., winter 9 A.M.–4 P.M. daily, gates close at 3 P.M., admission $12, seniors $11, children 2–13 $10 Apr.–Nov., discounted rates Dec.–Mar.) is home to thousands of animals representing more than 400 species. Thanks to extensive renovations that began in 1980, they reside in naturalistic habitats, including the five-acre indoor Tropical Forest and the African Savanna. Kids Kingdom, one of the top-ranked children's zoos in the country, features animals native to Pennsylvania along with more exotic creatures such as camels and venomous lizards known as Gila monsters. (No worries—no Gilas in the petting area.) At Water's Edge, visitors can make the acquaintance of polar bears and sea otters. The state-of-the-art PPG Aquarium is home to penguins, sharks, and one very shy giant Pacific octopus. Don't rush past the tank at its entrance, which at first glance appears to hold little more than seaweed. Look closer; it's the domicile of otherworldly, utterly mesmerizing sea dragons.

GREATER PITTSBURGH

Allegheny County has 130 municipalities, more than any other county in the state. None match Pittsburgh, the county seat, in size or sophistication. When Pittsburghers leave the city limits, it's often to shop at sprawling suburban malls. But many also owe fond memories to outskirts attractions, including an amusement park designated a National Historic Landmark.

Kennywood

It didn't make headlines when members of the National Amusement Park Historical Association named Kennywood (4800 Kennywood Blvd., West Mifflin, 412/461-0500, www.kennywood.com, admission $36.99, seniors $17.99, children under 46 inches tall $23.99, children 2 years and under free, reduced rates after 5 P.M.) their favorite traditional park in 2009. The park had captured the top spot every year but once since 1992. About 10 miles southeast of Downtown, Kennywood is virtually synonymous with summer fun for generations of Pittsburghers. Don't let its status as America's favorite traditional park fool you; this ain't no namby-pamby relic of bygone days. Founded in 1898 as a small trolley park, Kennywood has weathered everything from World War II to competition from Disneyland by enhancing its portfolio of rides. Today it's a well-balanced mix of classic and cutting-edge thrills. Its five roller coasters include two wooden beauties erected in the 1920s—Jack Rabbit and Racer—as well as Phantom's Revenge, a 21st-century steel machine with a peak speed of 85 mph. Also on tap: water rides, dark rides, and upside-down action for serious adrenaline junkies. Kiddieland caters to tots with rides such as Lil' Phantom, a pint-sized coaster that maxes out at 15 mph. Famous for its fresh-cut Potato Patch fries, Kennywood is one of the few amusement parks that still permit guests to bring their own grub. Alcohol isn't allowed.

The park is open daily from mid-May to late August and some weekends before and after that period. The shortest lines tend to be on Sundays in May and June, weekdays throughout the summer, Memorial Day, and July 4. The front gates open at 10:30 A.M., and rides begin a half hour later. Quittin' time is based on weather and crowd size but usually around 10 P.M. The park marks the end of each season with two weeks of nightly parades in August. It reopens on weekend evenings in October for ghoul-themed **Phantom Fright Nights** (www.phantomfrightnights.com, admission $25.99), not recommended for children under 13.

Sandcastle

Opened in 1989 on a former railroad yard for a massive steel-producing plant, Sandcastle (1000 Sandcastle Dr., Pittsburgh, 412/462-6666, www.sandcastlewaterpark.com, admission $29.99, seniors and children under 48 inches tall $19.99, reduced rates after 3 P.M.) quickly became Pittsburghers' favorite place to cool off on sweltering days. The water park on the banks of the Monongahela River has 14 waterslides and a 300,000-gallon wave pool. Those who prefer calmer waters can float down the quarter-mile Lazy River, wade in the Sandbar Pool, or soak in the world's biggest hot tub. Tykes get a pool and play area of their own.

Arrive by boat and dock at Sandcastle for free; drive and shell out $6 for parking. The water park is open daily from mid-June to late August and several weekends before and after that period. Gates generally open at 11 A.M. and close at 6 or 7 P.M. The fun continues into the evening on "Jukebox Sunday Nights" (weekly, admission $7.99, reduced rate after 8 P.M.), featuring music and dancing, and "Dive-In Movie Nights" (select Sundays, admission $9.99, free with same-day Sandcastle ticket), when family-friendly flicks are projected onto a poolside screen.

Other Sights

Published in 1962, Rachel Carson's *Silent Spring* drew public attention to the dangers of chemical pesticides and helped kick-start the environmental movement. Her legacy draws nature lovers to the **Rachel Carson Homestead** (613 Marion Ave., Springdale, 724/274-5459, www.rachelcarsonhomestead.org, tour $5, seniors and children over 5 $3) in suburban Springdale, about half an hour from Downtown Pittsburgh. Tours of the clapboard house in which Carson was born and raised are available 10 A.M.–4 P.M. weekdays by appointment. No appointment is necessary to explore the grounds, open year-round. Interpretive signage dots the quarter-mile Wild Creatures Nature Trail. The gift shop, open 9 A.M.–5 P.M. weekdays, sells books by and about the scientist-cum-writer who was awarded the Presidential Medal of Freedom after her death in 1964. Organic free-trade coffee and other eco-friendly products are also on offer.

Eco-friendly it's not, but coal mining is a fascinating process, and it's expertly explained at the **Tour-Ed Mine and Museum** (748 Bull Creek Rd., Tarentum, 724/224-4720, www.tour-edmine.com, 10 A.M.–4 P.M. daily except Tues. Memorial Day–Labor Day, admission $8, children 12 and under $6.50), several miles northeast of the Rachel Carson Homestead. Real miners do the explaining as they lead hard-hatted visitors through a mine 160 feet below the earth's surface. It's chilly down there—52 to 55 degrees even in summer—so dress accordingly. Records of mining activity at the site date to 1850. Visitors learn how mining tools and methods have evolved since then. The museum is packed with thousands of artifacts and features the recreated home of an 1850s miner. Also on-site: a 1785 log house, a strip mine, a sawmill, a railroad caboose, and a mine rescue vehicle. In October, Tour-Ed transforms into the spine-tingling **Haunted Mine** (www.thehauntedmine.com, 7–10 P.M. Thurs., 7–11 P.M. Fri.–Sat., admission $10).

PITTSBURGH

Entertainment and Events

Anybody who complains about the entertainment scene in Pittsburgh either isn't looking or can't afford the ticket prices. Look no further than the event listings in the weekly *Pittsburgh City Paper* (www.pghcitypaper.com) for ways to unwind, whether your tastes lean toward death metal or modern dance. The pickings are particularly plenteous in summer, when many parks double as concert venues and open-air theaters, festivals abound, and the likes of Jimmy Buffett and Phish play the First Niagara Pavilion.

It's worth noting that Pittsburgh's cultural breadth has grown over the past several decades even as the population has shrunk. Galleries, artist studios, and dance companies have sprung up in both chic and rumpled sections of town. Nowhere is the phenomenon more striking than in Downtown, where a 14-square-block Cultural District has risen from the proverbial ashes. Herds of smartly dressed theater-goers roam the streets. The corner of 7th Street and Penn Avenue, once home to Doc Johnson's International House of Love Potions and Marital Aids, is now an outdoor exhibition space for temporary installations. Empty storefronts: gone. Cocktails and ceviche: check.

BARS AND LOUNGES

It shouldn't come as a surprise that a sports-obsessed city with several colleges would support numerous bars. It may come as a surprise that Pittsburgh's watering holes are a diverse bunch, with sticky-floored, student-packed, Bud-and-wings joints only a slim majority. This is a town that's coming around to delicate cocktails and craft beers. Don't believe it? Witness the queue of hipsters, glass jugs in hand, at **East End Brewing Company** (6923 Susquehanna St., 412/537-2337, www.eastendbrewing.com, growler hours 5–7 P.M. Tues.–Thurs., 4–8 P.M. Fri., noon–5 P.M. Sat.), a microbrewery that's decidedly off the beaten path. The **Steel City Big Pour** (www.constructionjunction.org, Sept.), a craft beer festival born in 2007, "sold

out faster than a Hannah Montana concert," as one blogger put it, in its second and third years. Rest assured, whether your tastes run toward gritty or glam, you'll find your *Cheers* here.

Generally speaking, head Downtown for bars filled with smartly dressed professionals and theater-goers and a wide selection of drinks that end in "tini." To barhop with herds of 20-somethings, hightail it to East Carson Street on the South Side. When the Steelers or Pirates are playing, bob in a sea of black and gold on the North Shore.

Downtown and the Strip District

The house drinks at **Seviche** (930 Penn Ave., 412/697-3120, www.seviche.com, 5 P.M.–1 A.M. Mon.–Sat., tapas $8–12) are the caipirinha and pisco sour, but who can resist the mojito list? Classic mojito, pomegranate mojito, key lime mojito—and that's not the half of it. Arrive before 7 P.M. Monday–Thursday to enjoy them at half price. The high-ceilinged, multihued bar, offspring of its French proprietor's love affair with Latin culture, also has a sweet selection of South American and Spanish wines and beers. (Yankee brews such as Blue Moon and Bud Light are available.) Food-wise, Seviche specializes in—what else?—ceviche, offering an assortment of fresh seafood and seven different preparations. Be sure to sample Fire and Ice, traditional ceviche made spicier with habanero peppers and topped with homemade prickly pear granita. On Monday nights, tables are moved aside for salsa dancing.

Brick-lined and romantically lit, **Olive or Twist** (140 6th St., 412/255-0525, www .olive-twist.com, 11:30 A.M.–2 A.M. Mon.–Fri., 5 P.M.–2 A.M. Sat., food $7–26) is a martini bar par excellence. The 'tini options number more than 20 and range from the classic marriage of gin and vermouth to liquid desserts like the Chocolate Covered Cherry. Pennsylvania-made potato vodka gives the Keystone Dirty Martini its name. Above-average appetizers, sandwiches, and entrées make Olive or Twist a fine choice for a meal. The same is true of **Tonic Bar & Grill** (971 Liberty Ave., 412/456-0460, www.tonicpitts burgh.com, 11 A.M.–midnight Mon.–Sat., food $10–22), where freshly squeezed fruit juices give extra goodness to drinks like the Goose & Juice and Lemon Drop Martini. Burgers come in your choice of Angus beef, chicken, turkey, or veggie.

Many of the Strip District's gems are along Penn Avenue. On a nice day, take in the streetscape from the deck of **Roland's Iron Landing**, upstairs neighbor to **Roland's Seafood Grill** (1904 Penn Ave., 412/261-3401, www.rolandsseafoodgrill.com, 11 A.M.–1 A.M. Sun.–Thurs., 11 A.M.–2 A.M. Fri.–Sat., kitchen closes at 10 P.M. Sun.–Thurs. and midnight Fri.–Sat, food $8–38). Downstairs: 30 draft beers, game room, raw bar, and extensive menu. Upstairs: coolers packed with bottled beers and fewer food options. You can order the famous hot lobster roll no matter where you sit. The wood-fired pizzas are delightful and a great deal when shared.

For Irish-style carousing, head to **Mullaney's Harp & Fiddle** (2329 Penn Ave., 412/642-6622, www.harpandfiddle.com, 11:30 A.M.–1 A.M. Tues.–Thurs., 11:30 A.M.–2 A.M. Fri.–Sat., food $8–17). The mostly middle-aged members of the Pittsburgh Ceili Club turn out every Tuesday evening for something akin to square dancing.

DJs lure pretty young things to the dance floor at **Firehouse Lounge** (2216 Penn Ave., 412/434-1230, www.firehouse-lounge .com, 5 P.M.–2 A.M. Mon. and Wed.–Thurs., 4 P.M.–2 A.M. Fri., 7:30 P.M.–2 A.M. Sat., kitchen closes at 11 P.M., small plates $4–9), a stylish cocktail bar with long banquettes, low tables, soaring windows, and—most strikingly—zero televisions. The lounge occupies the second floor of a former fire station. At **Embury,** its first-floor sister establishment, a cocktail savant tends a small bar stocked with absinthe, chartreuse, handcrafted bitters, and other rarely seen liquors.

North Side

You can't swing a bat without hitting a sports bar outside PNC Park, home of the Pittsburgh Pirates. Irish stylings are so prevalent as to warrant comparisons to Chicago's Wrigleyville. In fact, **Mullen's Bar and Grill** (200 Federal St., 412/231-1112, www.mullensbarandgrill .com, 11 A.M.–2 A.M. Tues.–Sat., food $6–10) is a younger sibling of a Wrigleyville watering hole. Neither Mullen's nor **McFadden's** (211 N. Shore Dr., 412/322-3470, www.mc faddenspitt.com, 11 A.M.–2 A.M. Mon.–Fri., 5 P.M.–2 A.M. Sat., kitchen closes at 10 P.M., food $8–25), which has its roots in New York City, offers much in the way of Irish cuisine. If it's corned beef and cabbage you're after, head to **Finnigan's Wake** (20 E. General Robinson St., 412/325-2601, www.finniganspittsburgh .com, 11 A.M.–2 A.M. Mon.–Sat., Sunday hours vary, kitchen closes at 11 P.M. Mon.–Thurs. and midnight Fri.–Sat., food $9–11). All three are packed when the Pirates or Steelers are playing but rather cheerless otherwise.

A touch more upscale, **Atria's Restaurant and Tavern** (103 Federal St., 412/322-1850, www.atrias.com, 11 A.M.–11 P.M. Mon.–Thurs., 11 A.M.–midnight Fri.–Sat., 11 A.M.–9 P.M. Sun., food $9–25) makes a mean sherry crab bisque. The local chain snagged some choice real estate. It's in PNC Park but accessible from the street.

A sports bar named **SoHo** (203 Federal St., 412/321-7646, www.sohopittsburgh.com, 11 A.M.–2 A.M. daily May–Oct., 11 A.M.–1 A.M. daily Nov.–Apr., kitchen closes one hour before bar, food $9–27) makes about as much sense as an art gallery named Sluggers. It makes a little more sense when you consider that SoHo doubles as the on-site restaurant of the North Shore's SpringHill Suites, a hotel "designed for the modern lifestyle." The Terrible Towel crowd will find what it's looking for (13 wide-screen televisions and bottles of Iron City), as will the suit-and-tie crowd (filet mignon and a martini menu). Appetizers include the rather avant-garde buffalo pierogies: handmade potato and cheese pierogies sautéed with onions and butter and tossed in hot sauce. Don't be surprised if a few Pirates belly up to the large central bar after a winning game.

There's good reason to leave the orbit of the stadiums, namely **Max's Allegheny Tavern** (537 Suismon St., Pittsburgh, 412/231-1899, www.maxsalleghenytavern.com, 11 A.M.–10 P.M. Mon.–Thurs., 11 A.M.–11 P.M. Fri.–Sat., 9:30 A.M.–9 P.M. Sun., food $6–18). The bar and restaurant in the heart of Deutschtown dates to the turn of the previous century. Look for the framed opening in the ceiling of one dining room; it's all that remains of a dumbwaiter that used to carry German-style meals from the second-floor kitchen. German dishes remain Max's stock-in-trade. Wash down the *hasenpfeffer* (braised rabbit in spiced red wine sauce) with a Hacker-Pschorr, Spaten, or other German brew. On days when the Steelers play at home, Max's offers complimentary shuttle service to Heinz Field.

South Side

No debate about it: The South Side's East Carson Street is party central. There's a bar—or two or three—on nearly every block in the business and entertainment district, roughly defined as the section between 9th and 28th Streets. It's been called the longest continuous stretch of bars in the country. Shot-n-beer joints predominate, but there's sleek sprinkled into the mix and even the occasional velvet rope. Word of caution: If you're over 25, you might feel downright geriatric as you navigate this swiftly flowing river of youth. Word of caution II: Tattoo parlors are almost as ubiquitous as bars. Just say no to spur-of-the-moment body art.

When it comes to beer selection and bar food, **Fat Head's Saloon** (1805 E. Carson St., 412/431-7433, www.fatheads.com, food $8–20) is head and shoulders above the rest. Its 42 draft beers are mainly of the craft variety and invariably include a hand-pumped "real ale." No need to crane your neck for a gander at the tap handles; a large board over the bar advertises the day's lineup. (The bar's eponymous suds aren't brewed on site but rather imported from a Cleveland suburb, where the first

Fat Head's Saloon on East Carson Street

© ANNA DUBROVSKY

Carson City Saloon is a bank-turned-bar.

Fat Head's franchise opened in 2009.) Munchies include mussels steamed with Sierra Nevada Pale Ale and deep-fried shrimp coated in one of 13 wing sauces. Consider splitting one of the ginormous "headwiches." The Southside Slopes Headwich, an incomparable combo of kielbasa, fried pierogies, American cheese, and grilled onions, weighed in at number five when men's mag *Maxim* scoured the U.S. for the best "meat hog" sandwiches.

Speaking of ginormous, the specialty drinks at **Carson City Saloon** (1401 E. Carson St., 412/481-3203, www.carsoncitysaloon.com, 11:30 A.M.–2 A.M. daily, food $7–11) include the prophetically named Call A Cab, a 64-ounce bowl of Lord-knows-what that's meant to be shared. Some people aren't good at sharing, and those people are more than welcome at Carson City, which prides itself on "a complete lack of social morality." Draft options usually include a few fruity imports, a.k.a. girly beers. Check out the wheelchair-accessible bathroom; it was a vault when the building was a bank.

You'd be hard-pressed to find traces of its past

life as a Greek pastry shop at the posh **Elixir Ultra Lounge** (1500 E. Carson St., 412/481-1811, www.elixirpgh.com, 5 P.M.–2 A.M. Tues.–Sat. 8 P.M.–2 A.M. Sun.). The succinct dress code says it all: "fashionable."

Theme bars are fairly in vogue on the South Side. The volcano-inspired **Lava Lounge** (2204 E. Carson St., 412/431-5282, www.lavaloungepgh.com, 4 P.M.–2 A.M. Mon.–Sat., 8 P.M.–2 A.M. Sun.) attracts an artsier-than-average crowd. Its proprietors also own the Beehive coffee house, an East Carson institution, so perhaps it's not surprising that the drinks menu includes a good number of coffee cocktails and so-called coffee shots. Don't bother asking for a food menu; Lava Lounge offers meatballs on Mondays, tacos on Tuesdays, wings on Wednesdays, and veggie versions of all three. Nightly diversions range from DJ dance parties to spelling bees. It's all very e-c-l-e-c-t-i-c.

Lava Lounge's owners journeyed to Bali for bamboo, beads, masks, and other decorations when they decided to open a retro-style tiki bar a couple of blocks away. Buy a tropical cocktail at **Tiki Lounge** (2003 E. Carson St., 412/381-8454, www.tikilounge.biz, 4 P.M.–2 A.M. Mon.–Sat., 8 P.M.–2 A.M. Sun.) and you can keep the kitschy mug it comes in. DJs spin hits on weekends; a jukebox provides the tunes on school nights.

Bookworms are welcome at **The Library** (2302 E. Carson St., 412/715-9344, www.thelibrary-pgh.com, 4 P.M.–2 A.M. Mon.–Fri., 11 A.M.–2 A.M. Sat. and Sun., kitchen closes at 1 A.M. daily, food $7–28), where the menus are peppered with literary references and pasted into books. Popular starters include Edgar Allen Potatoes: regular or sweet potato fries served with aioli. Animal Farm is another best-seller. The sandwich, made with freshly sliced turkey, peppered bacon, gouda, and a fried egg, is served on a pretzel bun baked a few doors down at The Pretzel Shop. Let's not forget that The Library has a swell selection of craft brews and a charming rooftop patio.

Spandex never goes out of style at **OTB (Over The Bar) Bicycle Café** (2518 E. Carson

PITTSBURGH

St., 412/381-3698, www.otbbicyclecafe.com, 11 A.M.–2 A.M. Mon.–Fri., noon–2 A.M. Sat.– Sun., kitchen closes at 10 P.M. Mon.–Sat. and 8 P.M. Sun., food $6–9). The watering hole is a tribute to two-wheeled travel, with bicycles hanging from the ceiling, gears decorating the walls, and sconces made of spokes. Be sure to check out the toilet paper holders, also made from bike parts. The place attracts bike messengers and other cyclists, natch, but also motoring folk reared on Skippy. (The astonishingly popular and protein-rich Dirt Rag Delight is a burger smothered in peanut butter. That's right, peanut butter.) Vegetarians were very much in mind when the OTB team drafted a menu riddled with cycling references.

So long, Spandex. Hello, tartan. **Piper's Pub** (1828 E. Carson St., 412/381-3977, www .piperspub.com, 11 A.M.–2 A.M. Mon.–Sat., 9 A.M.–2 A.M. Sun., kitchen closes at 11 P.M. Mon.–Sat. and 10 P.M. Sun., food $8–23) promises "a taste of the British Isles," and lad does it deliver. Draft brews include Guinness, Smithwick's, and Old Speckled Hen, but it's the scotch list that really sets Piper's apart. That and vittles rarely seen in these parts, including Scotch eggs (hardboiled eggs wrapped in sausage meat, breaded, and deep-fried). In a city obsessed with Super Bowl wins, Piper's tunes its tellies to football matches of a different sort.

A Bavarian-style *bier* hall is one the newest additions to the South Side suds scene. The humongous **Hofbräuhaus Pittsburgh** (2705 S. Water St., 412/224-2328, www.hofbrauhaus pittsburgh.com, 11 A.M.–midnight Sun.–Wed., 11 A.M.–1 A.M. Thurs., 11 A.M.–2 A.M. Fri.– Sat., food $8–20) couldn't be more cartoonish if Walt Disney himself had risen from the dead to design it. Picture female servers clad in dirndls. Picture men in lederhosen playing oompah music. Picture 300 stein-waving Pittsburghers lending their voices to "Sweet Caroline" or "Brown Eyed Girl." (That's right, 300 Pittsburghers in a bar without televisions.) Picture, in short, a rollicking good time. Modeled after Munich's famous Hofbräuhaus, the Pittsburgh branch employs a

brew master from Germany who supervises the production of four year-round beers and a seasonal unveiled on the first Wednesday of every month. You can order a burger or fettuccine alfredo, but *come on,* this is the Hofbräuhaus. Stick to specialties you can't pronounce, like the Würstlteller, a sampler of three wursts. And do try the soft pretzels, imported from Germany and served with homemade beer-infused cheese. Hofbräuhaus is two blocks north of East Carson in the SouthSide Works development. Revelers spill from the *bier* hall into a riverside *biergarten* in summertime.

Oakland and Points East

Gooski's (3117 Brereton St., 412/681-1658) is the most celebrated of Pittsburgh's neighborhood dives. Regular beer and food prices rival happy hour specials at other bars. (Order the 50-count bucket of wings, and your per-wing cost plummets to something like 35 cents. Better yet, order the pierogies. The neighborhood is named Polish Hill, after all.) The anyone-goes vibe is also appealing. A Klingon could belly up to the bar and drink in peace.

Best beer selection in the Burgh? Easy. The selection at **Sharp Edge** (302 S. Saint Clair St., 412/661-3537, www.sharpedge beer.com, 11 A.M.–midnight Mon.–Thurs., 11 A.M.–1 A.M. Fri.–Sat., 11 A.M.–10 P.M. Sun.) in the Friendship section of town is only rivaled by the selection at its four sister bars. Simply put, the beer list goes on and on. And on. Sharp Edge is nationally recognized for its Belgians but doesn't discriminate against brews of other provenance. Even Sri Lanka and Croatia are represented. Bewildered by the array? You can fall back on the hops-heavy house beer, Over the Edge, or take a chance on the "mystery beer." Sharp Edge sponsors a European beer festival in June and an annual homebrew competition. The latter's winning entry is commercially brewed and added to the draft offerings.

The Art Deco **Kelly's Bar & Lounge** (6012 Penn Circle S., 412/363-6012) evokes an era when dudes called chicks "doll" and *Double Indemnity* was in theaters. Contrived? Hardly.

© ANNA DUBROVSKY

Kelly's Bar & Lounge has a patio in the back.

This place has been around since the 1940s. Order a classic cocktail—a Sidecar, perhaps—for maximum effect. The beer selection is quite good, and the mac and cheese worth every calorie. Wondering why so many 30-something bohos head toward the bathrooms and never return? There's a no-frills patio out back.

Nearby **AVA** (126 S. Highland Ave., 412/363-8277, www.avapgh.net, 8 P.M.–2 A.M. Mon. and Sat., 6 P.M.–2 A.M.Tues.–Fri., open Steelers Sundays) serves up live jazz on Monday evenings. DJs entertain an eclectic crowd most other nights, spinning the sort of tunes that would be at home on a *Buddha Bar* or *Café del Mar* compilation. Come on a Wednesday for taco wings—grilled chicken wings topped with a taco seasoning–based sauce—prepared on a grill just outside AVA's doors. On Sundays when the Steelers are playing, fans are invited to BYOM (bring your own meat) and plunk it on the grill. Games are projected on a wall.

A hallway connects AVA and **Shadow Lounge** (5972 Baum Blvd., 412/363-8277, www.shadowlounge.net), a "performance

lounge" with the look of a *Rent* set and bohemian regulars to match. Poets, emcees, and singers take turns on the stage on Tuesdays; acoustic musicians and rock bands show their stuff on Wednesdays. The third Monday of each month is reserved for aspiring comedians. You don't need experience to join the lineup—just cojones.

NIGHTCLUBS

Nightclubs tend to come and go (or at least change ownership and names) with a rapidity that's maddening to guidebook writers. Just a few years ago, the Strip District was *the* place to shake it. Ask a club-goer about the Strip today, and you'll probably get a roll of the eyes that says *sooo over*. Of this you can be sure: You'll find a dance floor at Station Square (125 W. Station Square Dr.). The riverfront development has enough nightclubs that a closure won't screw up your plans to git down. Among them: **Saddle Ridge** (412/434-8100, www.saddleridgepittsburgh.com, 7 P.M.–2 A.M. Thurs.–Sat.), where hats are more than welcome, particularly those of the cowboy variety. The "rock-n-country saloon" features a mechanical bull, skimpily attired female servers, and free line dancing lessons on Fridays and Saturdays. On balmy nights, trot next door to **Barroom Pittsburgh** (www.barroompgh.com, 8 P.M.–2 A.M. Thurs.–Sat.), a nightclub with a Texas-sized deck. Still searching for nightclub nirvana? Try **Zen Social Club** (412/918-1637, www.zensocialclub.com, call for hours), an Asian-inspired enterprise complete with paper lanterns, a two-story waterfall, and mixed drinks with cutesy names like Zentini and Sake to Me. Reserve a VIP table for bottle service. Zen is operated by the Pittsburgh Generation X Association, dedicated to curbing the migration of young, hip Pittsburghers to cities more tantalizing to young, hip people.

Should you tire of the Station Square scene, head east on Carson Street to **Diesel Club Lounge** (1601 E. Carson St., 412/431-8800, www.liveatdiesel.com, 9 P.M.–2 A.M. Wed.–Sun.). Lighting maestros from Miami had a hand in its design, which helps explain why the slick, multilevel nightclub looks more South Beach than South Side. Lavish VIP lounge with private mini bars: check. Skyboxes: check. Valet service: check (at least on Fridays and Saturdays). The computer-controlled lighting system—1,200 LEDs strong—is occasionally upstaged by national music acts. Blues chanteuse Shemekia Copeland and a retooled version of 1980s icon Berlin visited in 2009.

LIVE MUSIC

The opening of the **Consol Energy Center** (1001 5th Ave., general information 412/642-1800, tickets 800/745-3000, www.consolenergycenter.com) in August 2010 changed the city's concert landscape. The Pittsburgh Penguins' new home is not only bigger than their previous digs, but also better equipped for over-the-top stage shows. Which means that big-name artists no longer have reason to bypass Pittsburgh. Paul McCartney christened the new venue; Lady Gaga had committed to two shows before it even opened. The $321 million arena seats about 14,500 for end-stage concerts and almost 20,000 for center-stage concerts. Other sporting venues that double as concert halls include the University of Pittsburgh's **Petersen Events Center** (3719 Terrace St., general information 412/648-3054, tickets 800/745-3000, www.petersenevents center.com) and Duquesne University's **A.J. Palumbo Center** (600 Forbes Ave., general information 412/396-5140, tickets 800/745-3000, www.duq.edu/palumbo-center).

The region's largest concert venue, **First Niagara Pavilion** (665 Route 18, Burgettstown, 724/947-7400, www.livenation .com), boasts pavilion and lawn seating for more than 20,000. It's about 25 miles west of Downtown, but the acts are generally worth the trek. The more centrally located **Trib Total Media Amphitheatre at Station Square** (1 W. Station Square Dr., 412/642-1100, www .tribtotalmediaamp.com) has hosted acts as wide-ranging as Lil' Kim, Maroon 5, B.B. King, and Ted Nugent in recent years.

This author's vote for most unique venue goes to the **Pepsi-Cola Roadhouse** (565 Route 18, Burgettstown, 724/947-1900, www.pepsi roadhouse.com), located a stone's throw from the First Niagara Pavilion. Audience members sit four to a table, feasting on roasted chicken and barbeque ribs while tapping their toes to the likes of Kenny Rogers, Tim McGraw, and Loretta Lynn. All Roadhouse shows are open to all ages. **Mr. Small's Theatre** (400 Lincoln Ave., Millvale, general information 412/821-4447, tickets 866/468-3401, www.mrsmalls .com) is runner-up in the "most unique" category. Housed in a former Catholic church, the venue boasts 40-foot-ceilings, hardwood floors, and heavenly acoustics. It's generally a standing-room-only venue and has a capacity of 650. The Mr. Small's complex also includes recording studios that count the Black Eyed Peas, 50 Cent, Meatloaf, Live, and Ryan Adams among their clients. What used to be the priest's living quarters is now a "rock hostel" for visiting artists. Believe it or not, Mr. Small's isn't the only church turned church of rock. So is the Strip District's **Altar Bar** (1620 Penn Ave., general information 412/263-2877, tickets 800/745-3000, www.altarbarpittsburgh.com), dedicated to "resurrecting live music in Pittsburgh," and the South Side's dueling piano bar, **Charlie Murdochs** (1005 E. Carson St., 412/431-7464, www.charliemurdochs.com).

The South Side's most revered music venue is **Club Cafe** (56-58 S. 12th St., general information 412/431-4950, tickets 866/468-3401, www.clubcafelive.com), an intimate nightclub that books biggish singer-songwriters, e.g. Jill Sobule and Marshall Crenshaw. Norah Jones made an appearance not long before collecting multiple Grammys for her debut album. Acts filed under "rock" or "blues" also play Club Cafe, which has a capacity of 150. All shows are 21 and over. More than 100 years old, the nearby **Rex Theater** (1602 E. Carson St., 412/381-6811, www.rextheater.com) recently underwent a renovation that included removal of reclining seats dating to its movie house days and installation of top-of-the-line sound and lighting systems. The concert promoter responsible for the overhaul prides himself on reeling in a range of acts—from folk to heavy metal.

The Bloomfield neighborhood also attracts music fans. Artsy types gravitate toward **Brillobox** (4104 Penn Ave., general information 412/621-4900, tickets 866/468-3401, www.brillobox.net, 5 P.M.–2 A.M. Tues.–Fri., noon–2 A.M. Sat.–Sun.), where local and touring indie bands dish up contemplative lyrics. The venue is perhaps better known for DJ dance parties such as "Pandemic," a global music blowout held on the first Friday of each month. Its dinner and weekend brunch menus include vegetarian-friendly fare. More comfortable surrounded by neon beer signs than original art? Try **Howlers Coyote Cafe** (4509 Liberty Ave., 412/682-0320, www.howlerscoyotecafe.com, 3 P.M.–2 A.M. Mon.–Fri., 5 P.M.–2 A.M. Sat.–Sun.), neighborhood bar by day, music venue by night (or at least Wednesday through Sunday nights). Roots, rock, country, jazz, blues, metal—"the Coyote," as locals call it, doesn't discriminate. The nearby **Bloomfield Bridge Tavern** (4412 Liberty Ave., 412/682-8611, www.bloomfield bridgetavern.com, 5 P.M.–2 A.M. Tues.–Sat., kitchen closes at 11 P.M., food $4–10) bills itself as "the Polish party house," but don't expect an earful of polka. Known for its pierogies and other Polish grub, the BBT offers live music on Friday and Saturday nights. The bands are predominately local and play for the door, so don't be surprised if three-quarters of the patrons know the lead singer. The stage is open to all on Tuesdays, DJs do the drum and bass thang on Wednesdays, and dollar bottles bring in frugal folk on Thursdays.

Heart jazz? Head to **Little E's** (949 Liberty Ave., 2nd floor, 412/392-2217, www.littlees jazz.com) in downtown Pittsburgh. Blues fans should find their way to Blawnox, about 10 miles northeast of Downtown. **Moondog's** (378 Freeport Rd., Blawnox, 412/828-2040, www.moondogs.us) has been bringing rock and blues acts to the Allegheny River burgh for nearly two decades.

PERFORMING ARTS
Cultural District
Bordered by the Allegheny River on the north,

10th Street on the east, Stanwix Street on the west, and Liberty Avenue on the south, the Cultural District boasts half a dozen theaters. Think of it as a miniature version of New York's Broadway theater district. Not unlike Times Square, it's the stardust-sprinkled reincarnation of a seedy section of town. The transformation can be traced to the mid-1960s, when H. J. Heinz Company Chairman Jack Heinz resolved to turn a shuttered movie palace into a new home for the Pittsburgh Symphony Orchestra. In 1971, the former Loew's Penn Theater was dedicated as **Heinz Hall** (600 Penn Ave., 412/392-4900, www.pittsburghsymphony.org), a vision in red velvet, Italian marble, crystal, and 24-karat gold leaf. It's enough to give you goosebumps even before the renowned Pittsburgh Symphony starts playing. For extra goosebumps, come on a night when the 115-voice **Mendelssohn Choir of Pittsburgh** (www.themendelssohn .org) is also under the spell of the conductor's baton. In addition to classical music performances, the **Pittsburgh Symphony** offers 45-minute kid-friendly concerts and a pops series. Principal conductor of the latter is none other than Marvin Hamlisch, the much-celebrated composer of more than 40 movie scores and the Broadway musical *A Chorus Line*. Heinz Hall also hosts free concerts by the **Pittsburgh Youth Symphony Orchestra** (412/392-4872, www.pittsburghyouthsymphony.org), touring Broadway shows, and other guest performances. And it's home to the annual **Pittsburgh Speakers Series** (412/392-4900, www.pittsburghspeakersseries.org), seven lectures by seven "heroes and legends," e.g. Madeleine Albright, Salman Rushdie, Walter Cronkite, and Colin Powell.

Jack Heinz's recycling of a 1927 theater scheduled for demolition inspired further development in the "red light" district. In the mid-1980s, the newly formed Pittsburgh Cultural Trust undertook a $43 million restoration of another former movie house a block away. Billed as "Pittsburgh's Palace of Amusement" when it opened in 1928, the resplendent Stanley Theater had fallen into

the Benedum Center

disrepair and into the hands of a rock concert promoter by the late 1970s. (Reggae maestro Bob Marley played his final concert there in 1980.) It reopened in 1987 as the **Benedum Center** (719 Liberty Ave., 412/456-666, www.pgharts.org), a dead ringer for the Stanley on opening night in 1928, right down to the original 4,700-pound chandelier. The Benedum hosts performances by the **Pittsburgh Opera** (412/281-0912, www.pittsburghopera.org) and **Pittsburgh Ballet Theatre** (412/281-0360, www.pbt.org), along with musical theater productions by **Pittsburgh CLO** (412/281-3973, www.pittsburghclo.org). Touring Broadway companies frequently take the stage. Other recent visitors include magician David Copperfield and Christian songster John Tesh. The Benedum is the largest theater in the Cultural District.

The Cultural Trust's next project was the **Byham Theater** (101 6th St., 412/456-6666, www.pgharts.org), which opened in 1904 as

a vaudeville house named the Gayety and became the Fulton movie theater in the 1930s. Look for its original name in the salvaged mosaic tile floor in the entry vestibule. Less ornate than Heinz Hall or the Benedum, the 1,300-seat Byham draws a more casual crowd with dance and theater performances, live music, films, and lectures. The mural on the Fort Duquesne Boulevard facade of the Byham is a tribute to Pittsburgh's steel heritage.

In 1995, the nonprofit Cultural Trust snapped up the 194-seat **Harris Theater** (809 Liberty Ave., 412/682-4111, www.pghfilmmakers.org), formerly known as the Art Cinema. What had started as Pittsburgh's first "art movie" house had morphed into a triple-X theater in the 1960s. Today the Harris is frequented by connoisseurs of classic, independent, and foreign films. It also serves as an intimate setting for live performances.

Next, the Cultural Trust undertook its first from-scratch theater project. Building the **O'Reilly Theater** (621 Penn Ave., 412/316-1600, www.ppt.org) cost less than renovating the Benedum, even with hotshot architect Michael Graves on the job. The 650-seat theater opened in December 1999 with the world premiere of Pittsburgh-bred playwright August Wilson's *King Hedly II*. It's the only Downtown venue with a thrust stage, surrounded by seats on three sides. As the permanent home of the professional **Pittsburgh Public Theater,** good for more than 200 performances a year, the O'Reilly rarely gets a rest.

Graves also signed on to design **Theater Square** (655 Penn Ave.), completed in 2003. The nine-story complex houses a large parking garage and a box office (412/456-6666, www.pgharts.org, 9 A.M.–9 P.M. Mon.–Sat., noon–6 P.M. Sun.) that sells tickets to Cultural District events. It's also home to the area's newest performance venue, the 253-seat **Cabaret at Theater Square** (412/325-6769, www.pgharts.org), where Pittsburgh CLO dishes out toe-tapping, nuance-eschewing shows such as *Forever Plaid* and *Nunsense*. Ticket holders can arrive up to 90 minutes before curtain to have a meal or drinks at the theater. The Cabaret can also be counted on for late-night entertainment most Friday and Saturday evenings.

Carnegie Library Music Hall

Steel magnate Andrew Carnegie envisioned more than a book-lending enterprise when he footed the bill for the Carnegie Library of Homestead (510 E. 10th Ave., Munhall, 412/368-5225, www.librarymusichall.com). Dedicated in 1898, the French Renaissance–style library overlooking his Homestead Steel Works had a 1,000-seat music hall and an athletic wing with an indoor pool. "Recreation of the working man has an important bearing upon his character and development," Carnegie explained. The steel plant is gone, but the library is still in the recreation business. Not to be confused with Carnegie Music Hall in the Oakland section of Pittsburgh, Carnegie Library Music Hall (412/368-5225, www.librarymusichall.com) has in recent years hosted musicians Brian Wilson and Arlo Guthrie, comedians including Paula Poundstone, and the Banff Mountain Film Festival.

Carnegie Music Hall

Come early if you're coming to the 1,928-seat Carnegie Music Hall (4400 Forbes Ave.), part of the complex that includes the Carnegie Museums of Art and Natural History. Its most magnificent feature is its anticipation-heightening foyer, 45 feet high, liberally gilded, and ringed with fat columns of green Tinos marble. The hall itself, humble by comparison, is the setting for concerts presented by the **Pittsburgh Chamber Music Society** (412/624-4129, http://pittsburghchambermusic.org), which imports the world's most celebrated ensembles. It's also one of the stomping grounds of the **River City Brass Band** (412/434-7222, www.rcbb.com), 28 brass players and percussionists with a repertoire that ranges from traditional marches to Hollywood tunes. The **Drue Heinz Lectures** (412/622-8866, www.pittsburghlectures.org) bring literary luminaries to Carnegie Music Hall on select Monday evenings. Speakers have included man-in-white Tom Wolfe, *Eat, Pray,*

Love author Elizabeth Gilbert, and magazine doyenne Tina Brown. Balcony-supporting columns make for some obstructed views; steer clear of them when reserving tickets.

Carnegie Lecture Hall, a smaller venue in the same complex, is home to a lecture series for pint-sized bookworms, **Black, White & Read All Over** (412/622-8866, www.pittsburghlectures.org). Fans of traditional and contemporary roots music fill the 600-seat hall for concerts presented by **Calliope: The Pittsburgh Folk Music Society** (412/361-1915, www.calliopehouse.org).

City Theatre

Not content to recycle tried-and-true theatrical works, City Theatre (1300 Bingham St., 412/431-2489, www.citytheatrecompany.org) embraces the edgy and new. Expect a good number of world premieres in a typical season. The 270-seat main stage and a second smaller theater are a block from the South Side's carousing corridor, East Carson Street. For $5, patrons can park at the theater for a couple of hours before and after performances and hoof it to shops, restaurants, and watering holes.

Hillman Center for Performing Arts

Shady Side Academy's Hillman Center for Performing Arts (423 Fox Chapel Rd., 412/968-3040, www.shadysideacademy.org) is no ordinary high school auditorium. But then, Shady Side Academy is no ordinary high school. The suburban prep school that counts Pulitzer Prize–winning author David McCullough among its alumni unveiled two state-of-the-art theaters in 2004 and plunged into programming two years later. Its professional performance series serves up predominantly lighthearted fare. Cast members of NBC's *Dancing with the Stars* and the celebrated New York comedy show Chicago City Limits have played the Hillman Center in recent years.

Kelly-Strayhorn Theater

The multi-use Kelly-Strayhorn Theater (5941

Penn Ave., 412/363-3000, www.kelly-strayhorn .org) has an ambitious agenda: support the arts *and* revitalize an urban neighborhood considered blighted at worst and transitional at best. The last of nine theaters from East Liberty's golden era, the 350-seat Kelly-Strayhorn is named for Hollywood musicals megastar Gene Kelly and jazz composer Billy "Sweet Pea" Strayhorn, two of Pittsburgh's favorite sons. Not surprisingly, it usually showcases home-grown talent.

New Hazlett Theater

The North Side's New Hazlett Theater (Allegheny Square East, 412/320-4610, www .newhazletttheater.org) has withstood some hard knocks. Dedicated in 1890 as Carnegie Hall (by the sitting U.S. president, no less), it almost met the wrecking ball in the 1960s. Saved by community activism and renamed the Hazlett Theater, the landmark took another blow in 1999, when Pittsburgh Public Theater relocated to the downtown Cultural District after 24 seasons in residence. But things are looking sunnier since a $2 million facelift put the "New" in its name in 2006. The utilitarian performance space with its movable scaffold seating is frequently booked for plays, concerts, and other arts programs. Marquee performers rarely come here, but Pittsburghers with progressive tastes often do.

Pittsburgh Playhouse

Point Park University's Pittsburgh Playhouse (222 Craft Ave., 412/621-4445, www.pitts burghplayhouse.com) is the three-theater home of four companies. The REP, the professional one in the bunch, cherry picks plays with a Pittsburgh connection or themes that resonate here. The rest are student companies: one theater, one children's theater, and one dance. Add 'em up and you get 18 major productions and 235 performances a year.

Purnell Center for the Arts

Carnegie Mellon University's Purnell Center for the Arts (5000 Forbes Ave., 412/268-2407, www.cmu.edu/cfa/drama), unveiled in 2000, was funded almost entirely by alumni of the School of Drama. That should tell you something about the caliber of the oldest degree-granting drama program in the United States—and its productions. The Purnell Center houses a proscenium theater with seating for more than 400 and a smaller black-box theater, plus myriad classrooms, rehearsal and movement studios, production shops, and a large art gallery.

Stephen Foster Memorial

The University of Pittsburgh Department of Theatre Arts has its pick of three performance spaces. Two of those, the 478-seat Charity Randall Theatre and 153-seat Henry Heymann Theatre, are found in the Stephen Foster Memorial (4301 Forbes Ave., 412/624-7529, www.play.pitt.edu) on the Cathedral of Learning green. Pitt's budding thespians often share the stages with professionals. The university is good for a few major productions a year and a larger number of student-directed laboratory productions. The latter are staged at Studio Theatre, a black-box space in the Cathedral.

FESTIVALS AND EVENTS
Year-Round

Missed the Pittsburgh Three Rivers Regatta or Light Up Night? You're out of luck for another year. Missed a **JazzLive** (412/456-6666, www.pgharts.org) performance? Catch next week's. The free showcase of area jazz talent takes place every Tuesday at 5 P.M. in the downtown Cultural District. In summer, bob your head to the beat at Katz Plaza at the corner of 7th Street and Penn Avenue. JazzLive moves into the adjacent Theater Square building (655 Penn Ave.) in September.

Also the work of the Pittsburgh Cultural Trust, **Gallery Crawl in the Cultural District** (412/456-6666, www.pgharts.org, free) is a quarterly roving soiree featuring live music, cheap eats, and lots and lots of art. Galleries keep their doors open until 9 P.M. for the Friday evening crawls.

Local knitters, crocheters, potters,

jewelry-makers, and other glue-gun packers peddle their wares at **I Made It! Market** (www .imadeitpgh.com, free), a nomadic craft fair that occurs six to eight times a year. Pretty good chance you'll find your new favorite fingerless gloves there. Add your email address to the mailing list for updates about the market's whereabouts.

Summer

Pittsburghers elevate picnicking to an art form during **First Fridays at the Frick** concerts (412/371-0600, www.thefrickpittsburgh.org, first Friday June–Sept., $5 suggested donation), which signal the start and end of summer in this city. Think wine and Brie. Think flickering candles. Think you'll find a spot for your blanket just before show time? Think again. Regulars begin laying claim to sections of lawn at the Frick Art & Historical Center an hour and a half before the night's musical guests take the stage. It doesn't seem to matter what kind of music is on tap. African-inspired jazz, reggae, Celtic music—clinking glasses of Chardonnay complement them all.

What started in 1960 as an effort by museum types to bring the arts to non-museum types has blossomed into the something-for-everyone **Three Rivers Arts Festival** (412/456-6666, www.artsfestival.net, June, free). The 10-day festival draws hundreds of thousands of people to Point State Park and other Downtown festival sites. Some come for the original art works and handmade fine crafts of about 260 artists, fewer than half of whom are from Pennsylvania. Some come for corn dogs, chicken on a stick, chocolate-covered strawberries, or other festival foods. The lineup of free performances lures everyone else.

Machines capable of speeds of 130 mph ply local waterways during the **Three Rivers Regatta** (412/875-4841, www.threerivers regatta.net, July 4 weekend, free). But the spectacle-packed weekend isn't just about powerboat racing. Recent regattas have treated the masses to motocross and water-ski stunt shows, competitive-eating and bass-fishing contests, car-rollover simulations courtesy of the

Pennsylvania State Police, fireworks, and even a high-wire trek across the Allegheny River by professional daredevil Nik Wallenda—sans safety net. The likes of Three Dog Night and country crooner Steve Azar lend their musical talents to the show of muscle.

If you find yourself driving alongside a "gullwing" Mercedes-Benz or a 1959 Ferrari, chances are it's **Pittsburgh Vintage Grand Prix** time (412/299-2273, www.pvgp.org, July, free). The 10-day tribute to classic and exotic cars started as a one-day race in 1983 and has grown to include shows, cruises, and races in half a dozen locations. It culminates the third weekend in July with a show of some 2,000 beauts and a series of vintage sports car races at Schenley Park. Nowhere else in the nation can you see such races on city streets.

Unlike the regatta, the Grand Prix races, and many other outdoor events, the **Pittsburgh Blues Festival** (412/460-2583, www.pgh blues.com, July, $22 in advance, $25 at gate, weekend pass $40, family pack $95) isn't free. But $40 isn't a bad deal for a weekend of first-rate blues, especially when you consider that proceeds benefit the Greater Pittsburgh Community Food Bank. (A bag of nonperishable foods will get you past the gate on Friday night.) The festival takes place at Hartwood Acres, an Allegheny County park about 11 miles northeast of downtown Pittsburgh.

Jazz fans can get their fix in two Pittsburgh parks, thanks to the **Stars at Riverview** and **Reservoir of Jazz** series. Area jazz artists perform Saturday evenings throughout the summer in Riverview Park and Sunday evenings in August in Highland Park. The city doesn't neglect its classical music–loving citizens. Sunday mornings find **Bach, Beethoven and Brunch** concerts at Mellon Park. All of the jazz and classical concerts are free and BYOG (bring your own grub). For dates, times, and directions, consult the Citiparks website (www.city .pittsburgh.pa.us/parks) or call 412/255-8975.

The city is especially good to movie buffs, treating them to an alfresco flick every night of the week in summer. **Cinema in the Park** locations vary from night to night, but show time is always dusk. Check the Citiparks website (www .city.pittsburgh.pa.us/parks) or call 412/937-3039 for locations and movie listings.

Fall

The splendid and cleverly titled **A Fair in the Park** (412/370-0695, www.afairinthepark .org, weekend after Labor Day, free) is a great opportunity to get a jump on holiday shopping. Presented by the Craftsmen's Guild of Pittsburgh, the showcase of high-quality crafts takes place at Mellon Park in the city's Shadyside neighborhood.

A jolly good time, the **Pittsburgh Irish Festival** (412/422-1113, www.pghirishfest.org, weekend after Labor Day, admission $3–10) could make you fall in love with the Emerald Isle—maybe even enough to fork over 15 bucks for a bag of soil presumably gathered there. The three-day festival is heavy on music and dance but dutifully showcases other aspects of Celtic culture, including sports, crafts, cuisine, and even native dog breeds. It's set at the appropriately emerald Riverplex, Sandcastle's oversized picnic grounds along the Monongahela River.

No experience necessary to try your hand at one of the earliest forms of boat competition during the **Pittsburgh Dragon Boat Festival** (www.pdbf.org, Sept., free), a daylong celebration of Asian cultures at the South Side's Riverfront Park. If powering a 44-foot-long boat with an intricately carved dragon head at its fore doesn't appeal, you can learn another ancient skill: using chopsticks. (Fear not, forks are on hand for the less nimble-fingered.) The festivities also feature traditional Asian music and dance, arts and crafts for the kiddies, and demonstrations of tai chi and Chinese yo-yo.

Winter

Downtown slips into her holiday threads on **Light Up Night** (412/566-4190, www.down townpittsburgh.com, Nov., free) and, *girrrl*, we're talking serious bling-bling. An estimated 200,000 people turn out to see buildings and trees dripping with the electric equivalent of diamonds. Highlights include the unveiling of holiday window displays at Macy's, the lighting of towering Christmas trees, and, of course, the arrival of Santa. Across the Monongahela, Station Square also gets its twinkle on.

Local charities reap the proceeds of the **Celebration of Lights** (late Nov. to first week of Jan., 6–10 P.M. Sun.–Thurs., 6–11 P.M. Fri.–Sat., suggested donation $12 per car) at Hartwood Acres. Visitors drive through a three-mile wonderland of lights and moving displays.

First of all, **First Night Pittsburgh** (412/456-6666, http://firstnightpgh.com, Dec. 31) takes place on the last night of the year, not the first. Second of all, it's not the bacchanalia you may have come to expect from New Year celebrations. First Night is family-friendly and, like all projects of the Pittsburgh Cultural Trust, arts-focused. You can learn to rumba, pick up puppetry, take in a magic show, sway to gospel, listen to a steel drum band, and catch a performance by Croatian folk dancers—all before counting down to midnight. The grand finale: fireworks, of course. The Cultural Trust squeezes more than a hundred programs into the six-hour party, which spans dozens of Downtown locations. A First Night button is required for indoor events; unless you're part Inuit or otherwise immune to Pittsburgh winters, shell out the $8. Children five and under can tag along for free.

Spring

Pittsburgh's **St. Patrick's Day Parade** (www.pittsburghirish.org/parade, mid-Mar., free) traces its history to 1869. It's so old that some thoroughfares of parades past no longer exist. And while the tribute to Ireland's favorite patron saint was suspended for several decades in the 1900s, it has taken a firm hold on Pittsburghers' affections in recent ones—so much so that the great blizzard of 1993, which closed airports and highways, couldn't stop it. The parade always takes place on a Saturday; if St. Patrick's Day falls on any other day, the floats, marching bands, and nimble-footed dancers snake their way through Downtown on the Saturday preceding it. Expect a fair number of inebriated spectators. Their shenanigans have prompted condemnations from parade organizers and increased police presence in recent years.

Performing arts groups from as far away as Spain and the Republic of Congo entertain at the **Pittsburgh International Children's Festival** (412/456-6666, www.pghkids.org, May). The five-day event in Oakland is one of the nation's only international theater festivals for kids. All featured performances require tickets, which can be purchased in advance or at the on-site box office. Seeing as how kids are the intended audience, free "lap passes" are reserved for those under two.

Shopping

Come Black Friday, you'll find more traffic leaving Pittsburgh than coming into it. The biggest malls, not surprisingly, are outside the city limits. They're in Monroeville, Robinson Township, Ross Township, and other suburbs. But the city isn't without its shopping destinations. It has one of the more pleasant malls in southwestern Pennsylvania—SouthSide Works—and several shopping districts with a good number of independent, one-of-a-kind stores.

DOWNTOWN AND THE STRIP DISTRICT

Pittsburgh's business core doesn't top any lists of shopping meccas, but it is home to a massive **Macy's** (400 5th Ave., 412/232-2000, www.macys.com, 10 A.M.–7 P.M. Mon.–Fri., 10 A.M.–6 P.M. Sat., noon–5 P.M. Sun.). It wasn't so long ago that the grand department store on the corner of 5th Avenue and Smithfield Street was known as Kaufmann's. It was, in fact, the flagship store of the homegrown chain. Locals tsk-tsked Macy's parent Federated Department Store Inc. for erasing the Kaufmann's name, but there's nary a complaint about the store's selection of clothing, jewelry, housewares, and more. Macy's curries favor by continuing a tradition started by Kaufmann's: the Celebrate the Season Holiday Parade, held a couple of days after Thanksgiving. Its holiday window displays also draw crowds.

Downtown's neighbor to the northeast, the Strip District, is hog heaven for foodies. It's home to block after block of specialty foods purveyors, including a store wholly devoted to spices. This is where chefs go to shop. If cooking isn't your thing, go anyway, preferably on a Saturday morning. That's when the crowds are thickest and the air permeated with the smells of street foods. That's when the Strip is more of an experience than a shopping trip.

The narrow strip of a neighborhood is bordered by the Allegheny River on the north, 11th Street on the east, and 33rd Street on the west. Most must-stops are clustered along **◖ Penn Avenue between 17th and 22nd Streets.** At Penn and 21st, there's **Mon Aimee Chocolat** (2101 Penn Ave., 412/395-0022, www.monaimeechocolat.com, 8:30 A.M.–5 P.M. Mon.–Fri., 7:30 A.M.–5 P.M. Sat., 10 A.M.–3:30 P.M. Sun.), an Elysium of specialty and artisanal chocolates. If it's a cold day, treat yourself to a swig of delectable hot chocolate. Sweet tooths had also better visit **Fudgie Wudgie** (1728 Penn Ave., 412/402-0515, www.fudgiewudgie.com, 9 A.M.–5 P.M. Mon.–Fri., 9 A.M.–5:30 P.M. Sat., 10 A.M.–4 P.M. Sun.), where colorful bricks of fudge line a curvaceous counter. Samples are easy to score. Fudge and chocolate-covered goodies don't travel far to get to the store. Six blocks away is Fudgie Wudgie's headquarters and factory, where workers use wooden paddles to stir together locally produced cream, imported Belgian chocolate, and other premium ingredients.

Coffee connoisseurs can get the buzz of their lives in the Strip, where three local roasters peddle their beans within four blocks of each other. Across Penn Avenue from Mon Aimee is **La Prima Espresso Bar** (205 21st St., 412/281-1922, www.laprima.com,

6 A.M.–4 P.M. daily), run by the only certified organic coffee roaster in Pittsburgh. It's a slice of Italy is what is. Take your espresso or cappuccino next door to **Colangelo's** (207 21st St., 412/281-7080, www.colangelosbakery.com, 7 A.M.–3 P.M. Mon.–Sat.), order a slice of thin, from-scratch pizza, and have your snack at one of the bistro's high, chair-less tables. A quarter of a mile away is **Prestogeorge Fine Foods** (1719 Penn Ave., 412/471-0133, 8 A.M.–4 P.M. Mon.–Thurs., 8 A.M.–5 P.M. Fri., 7 A.M.–5 P.M. Sat.) with its 400-plus varieties of coffee and loose leaf tea. You'll be greeted by the aroma of freshly roasted beans and red-aproned specialists who can steer you toward a selection that's just right for your palate.

The legendary selection of cheeses at **Pennsylvania Macaroni Co.** (2010–2012 Penn Ave., 412/471-8330, www.pennmac.com, 6:30 A.M.–4:30 P.M. Mon.–Sat., 9:30 A.M.–2 P.M. Sun.) can be downright overwhelming. Try this: Say "just surprise me" to the deli staff. What you'll taste will likely become a lifelong addiction. Penn Mac, as locals call it, was founded in 1902 by three Sicilian brothers, and the family is still at the wheel. Pasta manufacturing was its first business; today it offers more than 5,000 specialty products, including all things Italian. Pasta remains a strong suit. Try the fresh egg pappardelle—next best thing to having a nanna in your kitchen.

Five Greek brothers who landed in America in 1907 opened **Stamoolis Brothers Co.** (2020 Penn Ave., 412/471-7676, www.stamoolisbros.com, 7 A.M.–4 P.M. Mon.–Fri., 8 A.M.–4 P.M. Sat.). Olives of many shades, sizes, and tastes can be found here, along with stuffed grape leaves, spanakopita, and other Mediterranean specialties. The Strip has Asian and Mexican markets too.

If fresh fish is what you're after, join the sea of customers at **Wholey's** (1711 Penn Ave., 412/391-3737, www.wholey.com, 8 A.M.–5:30 P.M. Mon.–Thurs., 8 A.M.–6 P.M. Fri., 8 A.M.–5 P.M. Sat., 9 A.M.–4 P.M. Sun.). It has whole fish on ice and live ones swimming in

tanks, fresh fillets and steaks, smoked fish, lobster, crab, squid, and more. Wholey's (pronounced "woolies") also sells cleaned rabbit and other meats. If your hunt for the perfect cut whets your appetite, order up a fried fish sandwich or something from the on-site sushi bar, then head upstairs for seating.

Because the littlest ingredients can make the biggest difference, it's prudent to stop by **Penzeys Spices** (1729 Penn Ave., 412/434-0570, www.penzeys.com, 9 A.M.–5 P.M. Mon.–Sat., 9 A.M.–3 P.M. Sun.). Just try to name a spice that's not in stock. Penzeys carries everything from salt and pepper to ajwain seeds from Pakistan and whole Turkish mahlab. It also has a wide array of hand-mixed seasonings that simplify cooking. With locations across the country, Penzeys is one of the few Strip merchants that's not locally based. If you're not locally based, you'll be happy to know that many Strip favorites, including Prestogeorge, Penn Mac, and Wholey's, do a brisk business on the Internet.

Neighbors in the Strip (1212 Smallman St., mezzanine level, 412/201-4774, www.neighborsinthestrip.com, 8:30 A.M.–5 P.M. Mon.–Fri.) distributes free maps that are very handy, though not comprehensive. Pick one up in the Strip or request one online. The website is a good source of information about the neighborhood's history.

SOUTH SIDE

It's easy to while away a day shopping in the **East Carson Street business district**, roughly bounded by 9th and 28th Streets. Figure 20 minutes per block, 20 blocks, and, just like that, seven hours gone. If you're an architecture buff, allow more time to admire the nation's longest Victorian-era business district. What's remarkable is that just a few decades ago, after the city's steel industry ground to a halt, East Carson practically had tumbleweeds blowing through it.

Where once stood a massive steelmaking enterprise, now stands an open-air mall. Actually, "mall" doesn't tell the whole story. **SouthSide**

Works (riverfront between 26th and Hot Metal Streets, 412/481-1750, www.southsideworks .com) is what developers call a lifestyle center. The retail/dining/entertainment/residential/office complex, complete with a tastefully landscaped "town square," officially opened in 2004 and hasn't stopped growing. It's home to a 10-screen movie theater, a yoga studio, and about 30 retailers, including H&M, Urban Outfitters, REI, Sur La Table, and American Eagle Outfitters, whose corporate overseer is also a tenant. Independently owned stores are sprinkled into the mix. Among the dining options are Cheesecake Factory and McCormick & Schmick's Seafood Restaurant. Maps of the property and information about upcoming events are available at a guest services kiosk on the corner of East Carson and 27th Streets.

Heading west on East Carson Street from SouthSide Works, you'll find small, one-of-a-kind stores interspersed with bars and eateries, tattoo parlors and Chinese massage parlors, hookah lounges and live music venues. There's a shop that specializes in designer jeans and a shop that carries *Star Wars* figurines. Funky T-shirts, fishnets in every shade, and toys of the adult variety can be found at "anti-fashion" boutique **Slacker** (1321 E. Carson St., 412/381-3911, www.slackernet.com, noon–9 P.M. Mon.–Sat., noon–8 P.M. Sun.), where the magazine racks carry the latest issue of *Witches & Pagans, Weed World,* and *The Nation.* Unique in a different way is **The E House Company** (1511 E. Carson St., 412/488-7455, www.ehousecompany.com, 11 A.M.–7 P.M. Mon.–Thurs., 11 A.M.–8 P.M. Fri.–Sat., noon–5 P.M. Sun.), a heavenly scented port of call for environmentally conscious consumers. Organic cotton underthings, bamboo fiber towels, and bags made from discarded vinyl billboards are displayed on fixtures fashioned from scrap iron and reclaimed barn wood.

East Carson even has a magic shop, **The Cuckoo's Nest** (1513 E. Carson St., 412/481-4411, www.thecuckoosnest.com, 10:30 A.M.–5 P.M. Mon.–Tues. and Thurs.– Fri., 10:30 A.M.–8 P.M. Wed., 10:30 A.M.– 4:30 P.M. Sat., 11 A.M.–4 P.M. Sun.), where

aspiring illusionists can stock up on top hats, trick coins, and much more. "Please choose carefully," read the signs. "Magic is NOT returnable."

OAKLAND AND POINTS EAST

Leave the heart of Oakland by way of Forbes Avenue and you'll find yourself, two miles later, in the commercial center of Pittsburgh's Squirrel Hill neighborhood. Best known for its large Jewish population, Squirrel Hill is home to **Pinskers Judaica Center** (2028 Murray Ave., 412/421-3033, www.judaism.com, 10 A.M.–6 P.M. Mon.–Thurs., 10 A.M.–2 P.M. Fri., 10 A.M.–5 P.M. Sun.), a source for Jewish books and gifts since 1954. But the shopping on its main thoroughfares, **Forbes and Murray Avenues,** is mostly of the secular variety. Just a block from Pinskers is **Jerry's Records** (2136 Murray Ave., 412/421-4533, www.jerrysrecords.com, 10 A.M.–6 P.M. Mon.–Sat., noon–5 P.M. Sun.), a magnet for vinyl enthusiasts from near and far. Like its albums, which number well over a million, the expansive store is a relic of another era. *Paste Magazine* crowned it the "best place to spot world-renowned crate diggers—and nab a bargain at the same time" in 2008.

With its whimsical sign and obsequious staff, **Littles Shoes** (5850 Forbes Ave., 412/521-3530) is also a throwback to an earlier time. But its footwear is very much in vogue. Customers range from UGG-coveting tweens to aging fashionistas who began shopping there when *they* were in their tweens. The nearby **Pussycat** (5824 Forbes Ave., 412/521-5977, www.anotherpussycat.com, 10 A.M.–6 P.M. Mon., Wed., and Fri.–Sat., 10 A.M.–7:30 P.M. Tues. and Thurs., noon–4:30 P.M. Sun.) recently celebrated its 40th year in the lingerie biz. The boutique's window displays turn the heads of teenage boys. High-end labels such as Cosabella, Simone Perele, and Prima Donna keep women coming back. Owner and bra authority Gail Gross is often on hand for consultations. Fashion-forward gents have a friend in **Charles Spiegel for Men** (5841 Forbes

Ave., 412/421-9311, www.charlesspiegel.com, 10 A.M.–6 P.M. Mon., Wed., and Fri.–Sat., 10 A.M.–9 P.M. Tues. and Thurs., noon–5 P.M. Sun.) across the street.

Just north of Squirrel Hill is one of Pittsburgh's most affluent nabes. Shadyside has a couple of shopping corridors. **Walnut Street** between South Negley and South Aiken Avenues is lined with big-name stores including Williams-Sonoma, Pottery Barn, Sephora, Ann Taylor, Gap, J. Crew, Banana Republic, Victoria's Secret, and Apple. There are independents in their midst and along the side streets. **Schiller's Pharmacy** (811 S. Aiken Ave., 412/621-5900, www.schillersrx .com, 9 A.M.–7 P.M. Mon.–Fri., 9 A.M.–5 P.M. Sat., 10 A.M.–3 P.M. Sun., closes 2 P.M. Sun. in summer) on the corner of Walnut and South Aiken has been a Shadyside institution for more than a century. It sells not just meds but also high-end fragrances, cosmetics, and bath and body products. One of the shopping district's most unusual stores is **Kards Unlimited** (5522 Walnut St., 412/622-0500, www.kards unlimited.blogspot.com, 9:30 A.M.–9 P.M. Mon.–Sat., noon–5 P.M. Sun.). True to its curiously spelled name, it has a vast selection of greeting cards, plus stationery, gift wrap, photo albums, and other stuff you'd expect from a card store. It also has Star Trek lunch boxes, Pittsburgh Steelers checker sets, bendable Simpsons dolls, Jesus and Moses action figures, temporary tattoos for talking hands, and so much more. In short, the family-owned store has a fantastic sense of humor.

Locally owned businesses predominate on Shadyside's **Ellsworth Avenue.** The street runs parallel to Walnut, but its small commercial stretch is on the opposite side of South Negley. Fans of vintage wear are especially well served here.

The riverfront neighborhood of Lawrenceville is a study in arts-driven urban revitalization. It's the larger part of the two-neighborhood 16:62 Design Zone (www.1662designzone.com), an arts and interior design district that extends from the 16th Street Bridge in the Strip District to the 62nd Street Bridge in Lawrenceville. The zone is home to more than 100 shops, artisan studios, galleries, and professional services firms. Many are located along Lawrenceville's **Butler Street.** Shoppers should focus their energies on the stretch between 35th and 47th Streets, where the addictive **Sugar** (3703 Butler St., 412/681-5100, www.sugarboutique-style. blogspot.com, 11 A.M.–6 P.M. Wed. and Sat.– Sun., 11 A.M.–7 P.M. Thurs.–Fri., other hours by appointment) can be found. The boutique features fashions from emerging designers, including some of Pittsburgh's own.

Divertido (3701 Butler St., 412/687-3701, www.divertidoshop.com, 11 A.M.–6 P.M. Tues.–Wed. and Fri.–Sat., 11 A.M.–8 P.M. Thurs., 11 A.M.–3 P.M. Fri.) also taps local talent. Its eclectic offerings include handmade bags and jewelry, original art, and unconventional baby garb. At the other end of the shopping corridor is **Jay Design** (4603 Butler St., 412/683-1184, www.jaydesign .com, 10 A.M.–6 P.M. Mon.–Wed. and Fri., 10 A.M.–9 P.M. Thurs., 10 A.M.–5 P.M. Sat., 11 A.M.–5 P.M. Sun.), a showplace for exquisite, handmade soaps. You'll know it by the bathtub in the window.

GREATER PITTSBURGH

Like SouthSide Works, **The Waterfront** (149 W. Bridge St., Homestead, 412/476-8889, www.waterfrontpgh.com, shopping 10 A.M.–9 P.M. Mon.–Sat., noon–6 P.M. Sun.) is an open-air shopping center on riverfront once occupied by an immense steel producer. A line of towering smokestacks near its 22-screen movie theater pays homage to the Homestead Works, silenced in 1986 after 105 years. Far bigger than SouthSide Works, the Waterfront has room enough for Costco, Lowe's, Target, Best Buy, Petco, Office Depot, and other megastores. Clothiers including Ann Taylor Loft, Victoria's Secret, Wet Seal, and Children's Place can also be found among its 70-plus stores, restaurants, and entertainment venues. The shopping complex is six miles from downtown Pittsburgh on the south bank of the Monongahela River.

Sports and Recreation

Pittsburgh has a well-earned reputation as a sports town. The birthplace of NFL greats Johnny Unitas and Dan Marino became known as the "City of Champions" in the 1970s, when the Pirates won the last two of their five World Series titles and the Steelers claimed Super Bowl title after Super Bowl title after Super Bowl title. The Pittsburgh Penguins captured the world's attention in the early 1990s, bringing home the Stanley Cup twice in two years. If there was any doubt about Pittsburgh's eminence in pro sports, it vanished in 2009. In February, the Steelers defeated the Arizona Cardinals 27–23 in Super Bowl XLIII, becoming the first team to win six NFL championships. Four months later, the Penguins triumphed over the Detroit Red Wings, four games to three, in the Stanley Cup Final. There's only one way to describe the elation that washed over Pittsburgh in both instances: *You had to be there.* An estimated

375,000 people turned out for the Penguins' victory parade in the middle of a Monday. (Let's put that figure in perspective. According to the U.S. Census Bureau, Pittsburgh's population slipped to about 310,000 in 2008.) No one was surprised later that year when *Sporting News* magazine handed Pittsburgh the title of "Best Sports City."

The Steelers and Penguins aren't the only heroes around here. The University of Pittsburgh's Panthers football team, which shares the Steelers' home stadium, has won nine national championships. The men's basketball team advanced to its eighth straight NCAA Tournament in 2009. Two private universities, Robert Morris and Duquesne, also boast strong basketball programs. The Robert Morris Colonials won the 2009 Northeast Conference championship game, reaching the NCAA Tournament for the first time in 17 years.

There are those who argue that the real

© ANNA DUBROVSKY

You had to be there: Steelers fans celebrate the Super Bowl XLIII victory at Jerome Bettis' Grille 36.

PITTSBURGH

heroes of Pittsburgh sports are the fans—"fans like no other," as *Sporting News* put it. "Enthusiastic" doesn't begin to describe them. "Rabid" comes close. A wardrobe without a black and gold sports jersey is something of an anomaly. (Pittsburgh is unique in that all of its major pro sports teams wear the same colors, although the Penguins occasionally don uniforms dominated by powder blue.) The citizenry's favorite accessory: the Terrible Towel, an emblem of devotion to the Steelers. Steeler Nation, as the team's fan base is called, has no geographic boundaries. Its members can be found all across the country, due in part to the team's successes and perhaps in larger part to the collapse of the city's steel industry in the early 1980s, which created a diaspora of Steelers fans.

Of course, cheering on the teams isn't the only pastime in the city of three rivers. As one might expect, boating and fishing are among the ways to unwind. The city and its environs also afford opportunities for hiking, biking, rock-climbing, cross-country skiing, snowshoeing, and more. If you're new to any of these activities or unfamiliar with the area, consider a **Venture Outdoors** (412/255-0564, www.ventureoutdoors.org) outing. The nonprofit recreation company offers a year-round calendar of group activities, from early morning paddles to sunset hikes to overnight bike tours. Instruction and gear are provided. VO folk like noshing almost as much as they like nature; a good number of excursions start or end with food and drink. If you prefer to go it on your own, visit the website of **Walls Are Bad** (www .wallsarebad.com), a campaign to promote outdoor recreation in southwestern Pennsylvania, for a wealth of suggestions.

PARKS
Schenley Park
Schenley Park (412/682-7275, www.pitts burghparks.org/schenley) is a 456-acre park home to an ice-skating rink, an outdoor swimming pool, golf and disc golf courses, and a sports complex, among other facilities.

Grassy **Flagstaff Hill,** across from Phipps Conservatory and Botanical Gardens, is awash with sunbathers on summer days. In winter, the action shifts to the **Schenley Park Skating Rink** (Overlook Dr., 412/422-6523, www.city .pittsburgh.pa.us/parks, admission $4, seniors and children 17 and under $3, skate rental $2.50). The outdoor rink generally opens in early November and closes in late March. Public skating times vary from day to day (4–6:30 P.M. Mon., 7–9 P.M. and 9:30–11:30 P.M. Tues., 1:30–3:30 P.M. Wed., 7–9 P.M. Thurs., 7–9 P.M. and 9:30–11:30 P.M. Fri., and 1:30–3:30 P.M., 4–6:30 P.M., and 7–9 P.M. Sat.–Sun., along with 9:30–11:30 P.M. Sat.); all 9:30 P.M. sessions are open to adults only.

The 18-hole **Bob O'Connor Golf Course** (E. Circuit Rd., 412/622-6959, www.thefirst teepittsburgh.org) is open year-round. So is the **Schenley Oval Sportsplex** (Overlook Dr., 412/255-2539, www.city.pittsburgh.pa.us/ parks), which has 13 tennis courts, a 400-meter running track, and a sports turf soccer field.

Frick Park
Schenley Park may be Pittsburgh's most beloved green expanse, but it's not the largest. That distinction goes to Frick Park (412/682-7275, www.pittsburghparks.org/frick), a 561-acre sanctuary that straddles the neighborhoods of Point Breeze, Squirrel Hill, Regent Square, and Swisshelm Park. It's less manicured than Schenley, more woodsy. Most mountain bikers will tell you Frick has the best trails in the city. It's also popular with hikers, though the sound of vehicles on the nearby Parkway East (I-376) can really break one's reverie. Another recreational option: lawn bowling. The park is home to the only public lawn bowling green in the state. For free instruction in the medieval sport, give the **Frick Park Lawn Bowling Club** (412/782-0848, www.lawnbowling .net) a ring. You'll also find off-leash exercise areas for dogs, off-leash exercise areas for kids (a.k.a. playgrounds), and red clay tennis courts dating to 1930. Frick has a number of entrances, some marked by distinctive stone gatehouses. Families with young children

flock to the playgrounds near the intersection of Forbes and South Braddock Avenues and at Beechwood Boulevard and English Lane. Both are good starting points for a walk in the woods, as is the Frick Environmental Center at 2005 Beechwood Boulevard.

Highland Park

The award for grandest entrance goes to Highland Park (412/682-7275, www.pittsburgh parks.org/highland), located in the East End neighborhood of the same name. Follow North Highland Avenue to its northernmost point and you'll pass between sculptures atop tall pedestals, arriving at a Victorian-style entry garden complete with fountain, reflecting pool, and neatly arranged benches. Steps at the far end of the garden lead to the park's iconic feature: a 19th-century municipal reservoir circled by a three-quarter-mile promenade. You'll find walkers and joggers and, sometimes, waterfowl. Road cyclists adore Highland Park for its half-mile velodrome, formerly a driver's training course. The park is also home to the Pittsburgh Zoo & PPG Aquarium, a summer jazz series, several playgrounds, a pair of sand volleyball courts, and the city's only long-course swimming pool (151 Lake Dr., 412/665-3637, open mid-June through Labor Day, 1–7:45 P.M. Mon.–Fri., 1–5:45 P.M. Sat.–Sun., daily admission $4, children 3–15 $3).

Riverview Park

Though considerably smaller than the one at Highland Park, the pool at Riverview Park (Riverview Ave., 412/682-7275, www.pitts burghparks.org/riverview) is a popular summertime destination. The park on Pittsburgh's North Side also draws crowds on Saturday evenings in the summer, when it hosts a jazz concert followed by an outdoor movie—both free. At the heart of the hilly escape is the University of Pittsburgh's Allegheny Observatory. Kids can unleash their inner astronauts at a space-themed playground nearby.

County Parks

City parks are a puny bunch relative to the county's collection of green spaces. **North Park** (Pearce Mill Rd., Allison Park, 724/935-1766, www.alleghenycounty.us/parks/npfac.aspx), the largest of Allegheny County's nine parks, is five times larger than Frick, the city's titan. Three county parks have wave pools, something no Pittsburgh park can boast of.

City folk rarely venture to the oases on Pittsburgh's outskirts—precisely because they're on the outskirts. The exception is **Hartwood Acres** (200 Hartwood Acres, Pittsburgh, 412/767-9200, www.allegheny county.us/parks/hwfac.aspx), a county park so delightful and so adept at staging large events that never mind the drive. At 629 acres, the park about 11 miles northeast of Downtown is one of the smallest in the county network. Its centerpiece is a stately country estate complete with Tudor mansion, stables, and formal gardens. Billed as a window into "the life of leisure and philanthropy so fashionable in the first part of the 20th century," the 1929 mansion is filled with antiques, photographs, and personal items of the family that once called it home. Reservations are recommended for mansion tours (10 A.M.–3 P.M. Mon.–Sat., noon–4 P.M. Sun., admission $6, seniors and children 13–17 $4, children 6–12 $2, children 5 and under $1). Stable tours are $3 and offered only occasionally. For a real taste of life in the Hartwood Mansion, come for afternoon tea. Reservations are required for the intermittent tea parties, which sell out more often than not.

The park's summer concert series is hugely popular. Pittsburghers who never step foot into Downtown's Heinz Hall or Benedum Center turn out to listen to the Pittsburgh Symphony Orchestra or Pittsburgh Opera under the stars. The Hartwood Amphitheatre also welcomes reggae, blues, jazz, and country acts, popular bands such as Sun Volt and the Old 97's, and dance companies including the Pittsburgh Ballet and Duquesne Tamburitzans. In July the park hosts the **Pittsburgh Blues Festival** (412/460-2583, www.pghblues.com, $22 in advance, $25 at gate, weekend pass $40, family pack $95), a weekend of first-rate music and a fund-raiser for the Greater Pittsburgh

PITTSBURGH

Community Food Bank. Local charities also reap the proceeds of Hartwood's **Celebration of Lights** (late Nov. to first week of Jan., 6–10 P.M. Sun.–Thurs., 6–11 P.M. Fri.–Sat., suggested donation $12 per car). Visitors drive through a three-mile wonderland of lights and moving displays. Candlelight tours of the Hartwood Mansion in all its holiday finery are available by reservation. Other annual events at the park include British Car Day and a polo match to benefit the nonprofit Family House, both held in September.

BICYCLING

Pittsburgh's steep hills and tangled streets can be intimidating to novice and new-in-town cyclists. Here to help: **Bike Pittsburgh** (33 Terminal Way, 412/325-4334, http://bike-pgh.org). The advocacy group publishes the free *Pittsburgh Bike Map,* available at its office on the South Side and at like-minded businesses. The map identifies car-free trails, on-street bike routes, steep hills, and *very* steep hills. An online version allows cyclists to explore routes in terrain and satellite modes. The map includes tips for biking across major bridges, like these words of wisdom about Fort Pitt Bridge: "Don't even try to ride in the auto travel lane on this bridge. But there is a little known sidewalk on the downriver side that goes from western Station Square to Point State Park." Handy, huh?

Bike Pittsburgh, founded in 2002, presses for bike lanes and racks, bike route signage, and shared lane markings. Thanks in part to its lobbying, Pittsburgh is transforming into a bike-friendly city. In 2008, it became the first city in Pennsylvania to appoint a full-time bicycle and pedestrian czar. The following year, *Good* magazine called it one of the seven "best burgeoning bike scenes" in North America. The recognition was especially gratifying in light of the fact that two decades earlier, *Bicycling* magazine had named Pittsburgh one of the worst U.S. cities for riders.

The city's bicycling infrastructure is a work in progress. Gaps remain in the 21-mile **Three Rivers Heritage Trail,** begun in 1991. Rather than a continuous route, it's a set of trails along the Allegheny, Monongahela, and Ohio Rivers with names to match the areas they traverse. Print maps are available from **Friends of the Riverfront** (33 Terminal Way, 412/488-0212, www.friendsoftheriverfront.org, 9 A.M.–5 P.M. Mon.–Fri.), which spearheads development of the Heritage Trail. In 2009, the organization launched a digital version featuring more than 200 points of interest. Need wheels? Bring ID and a $10 nonrefundable deposit to the Friends of the Riverfront office, just off East Carson Street in the South Side, to sign up for access to a fleet of fetching cruisers. The bikes are kept in lockers at two sites: along the South Side Trail near 4th Street and along the North Shore Trail just upstream of the 16th Street Bridge. They can only be used on the Heritage Trail. If that's too restrictive for your tastes, choose from a wide array of bikes at **Golden Triangle Bike Rental** (600 1st Ave., 412/600-0675, www.bikepittsburgh.com, open Apr.–Oct., generally 11 A.M.–8 P.M. Tues.–Fri., 10 A.M.–8 P.M. Sat.–Sun., seasonal hours apply). Located along the Eliza Furnace Trail in Downtown, Golden Triangle offers road, mountain, hybrid, touring, recumbent, and tandem bikes. Children's bikes, child trailers, and tag-a-longs that essentially transform an adult bicycle into a tandem are also available. From May through September, Golden Triangle also has a location on the South Side, in front of Cheesecake Factory on South 27th Street. A narrower variety of bikes are available 11 A.M.–8 P.M. Tuesday–Sunday. Steeds at both locations start at $8 per hour or $30 per day.

Pittsburgh's biking community is eagerly anticipating the completion of a trail that will create a vehicle-free corridor from the city to the nation's capital. The **Great Allegheny Passage** (www.atatrail.org) stretches 135 miles from the riverfront city of Duquesne, about 10 miles southeast of downtown Pittsburgh, to Cumberland, Maryland. There it meets the 184.5-mile C&O Canal towpath, which traces the Potomac River to Washington, D.C. When completed, the Great Allegheny Passage will extend all the way to Pittsburgh's Point State

Park, totaling 150 miles. When that day will come—that's anyone's guess.

Bike enthusiasts should mark their calendars for **BikeFest,** Bike Pittsburgh's 10-day celebration of all things cycling. Pittsburgh Trails Advocacy Group (www.ptagtrails.com), an all-volunteer organization that builds and maintains mountain bike trails, hosts the **Mountain Bike Festival,** a series of free organized rides over several summer days. **Pedal Pittsburgh** (412/391-4144, www.pedalpitts burgh.org, May), a fundraiser for the nonprofit Community Design Center of Pittsburgh, showcases inventive architecture. Participants can choose from six courses ranging from six to 60 miles.

HIKING

If a heart-pumping, mind-quieting walk is what you're after, this famously hilly city is happy to oblige. Test your mettle on Canton Avenue in the neighborhood of Beechview, southeast of Downtown. With a grade of 37 percent, it's the steepest street in these parts and, possibly, the world. (*Guinness World Records* tips its hat to New Zealand's Baldwin Street, with a grade of 35 percent.) Of course, hiking isn't quite hiking without soil under your feet. Excellent trails can be found in many city and county parks. A standout: the 35.7-mile **Rachel Carson Trail,** which has its western terminus in North Park and its eastern terminus in Harrison Hills Park. Between the county parks, it visits woods and fields, creeks and steep bluffs, suburbia and farm country. Spurs provide access to the Tudor mansion at Hartwood Acres and the humbler Rachel Carson Homestead, childhood home of the renowned naturalist for whom the trail is named. A hiker's guide is available through the Rachel Carson Trails Conservancy (412/475-8881, www.rachelcarsontrails.org), the volunteer-based organization that maintains the trail. There are no shelters along the trail, which is intended for day hiking. It's not impossible to do the whole trail in one day. In fact, it's encouraged. Scads of brave souls attempt it every summer during the Rachel Carson Trail Challenge, a 34-mile, sunrise-to-sunset endurance hike.

WATER ACTIVITIES

Crisscrossed as it is by three rivers, Pittsburgh offers plenty of opportunities to get off dry land. In fact, the city boasts the second-largest number of registered pleasure boats in the country. About 20 marinas dot Allegheny County's shorelines (see www.fish.state.pa.us/marinas.htm for locations). Boaters can moor at Station Square, the South Side's dining and entertainment complex, for just five bucks an hour or along the North Shore, home to the Steelers and Pirates, for free. Other attractions accessible by boat include Point State Park and Sandcastle water park.

If you're not in possession of a yacht or humbler vessel, you're not out of luck. On game days, you can board a **Pittsburgh Water Limo** (412/221-5466, www.pghwaterlimo.com) and cruise to Heinz Field or PNC Park, chuckling at the fools stuck in traffic and shelling out as much as $25 for parking. Adult fares are $7 for a round-trip to Heinz Field, $6 for a round-trip to PNC Park, or $4 one way. Drinks are a heckuva lot cheaper aboard the heated pontoon boat than inside the stadiums. On Friday and Saturday nights in the summer, Pittsburgh Water Limo ferries party people between the Strip District, Station Square, and the North Shore. The **Gateway Clipper Fleet** (412/355-7980, www.gatewayclipper.com), best known for its year-round cruises, also offers shuttle service from its dock at Station Square to Heinz Field and PNC Park. Tickets are $10 round-trip, $5 one way.

For those who prefer the role of captain to passenger, there's **Kayak Pittsburgh** (www.kayakpittsburgh.org), a project of Venture Outdoors. Its North Shore rental shop is beneath the Roberto Clemente Bridge (also known as the 6th Street Bridge), a stone's throw from PNC Park. Solo kayaks are $15 for the first hour and $8 per additional half hour; tandem kayaks are $20 for the first hour and $10 per additional half hour. Venture Outdoors members pay discounted rates. You don't need experience to set out in the flat-water kayaks, which are more like canoes than sleek whitewater kayaks, but you have to be at least three years old. Kayak Pittsburgh staff offer a short introduction to the sport. The season runs from May to October. Call 412/969-9090 for hours. Kayak Pittsburgh also sets up shop at Lake Elizabeth near the National Aviary. The number there is 412/804-1108.

If you get hooked on river boating, hook up with the **Three Rivers Rowing Association** (412/231-8772, www.threeriversrowing.org). The organization offers rowing, kayaking, and dragon boating programs for all skill levels. It has two boathouses on the Allegheny River, both off Route 28 within four miles of Downtown. One is under the 31st Street Bridge on the island known as Washington's Landing, and the other is in the Millvale Waterfront Park near the 40th Street Bridge. TRRA hosts the **Head of the Ohio Regatta** (www.headofthe ohio.org, fall), which attracts competitive rowers from across North America and thousands of spectators. It's also responsible for the colorful Pittsburgh Dragon Boat Challenge, part of the extravaganza that is the **Three Rivers Regatta** (412/875-4841, www.threerivers regatta.net, July 4th weekend).

Despite having almost 40 miles of river shoreline, Pittsburgh isn't exactly a fishing mecca. Pennsylvania has far more scenic waterways, devoid of post-industrial detritus. But Pittsburghers' zeal for fishing has lured major tournaments to the city. The Forrest Wood Cup, the world's richest bass fishing tournament, was held here in 2009. The Bassmaster Classic came to the Burgh in 2005. Locals who know where to cast can reel in not just bass but also walleyes, saugers, muskies, pike, catfish, and carp. Don't know where or how? Let Venture Outdoors, that tireless promoter of Pittsburgh's natural amenities, hold your hand. Aspiring anglers are invited to join Venture Outdoors' lunchtime fishing posse, the **Downtown TriAnglers** (412/255-0564, www.ventureoutdoors.org). TriAnglers meet at Point State Park or North Shore Riverfront Park 11:30 A.M.–1:30 P.M. Wednesdays from May–September. Rods, bait, and instruction are provided for a $5 season fee. Preregistration isn't required, but a Pennsylvania fishing license is. You can buy one at a sporting goods store or online at www.fish.state.pa.us.

SPECTATOR SPORTS

Founded by Art Rooney in 1933, Pittsburgh's football franchise is the fifth oldest in the National Football League. Originally called the Pittsburgh Pirates in deference to the city's much older ball club, the **Steelers** (100 Art Rooney Ave., 412/323-1200, www.steelers.com) are still property of the Rooney family. Since 2001, they've played at Heinz Field on the North Side. Tickets were terribly hard to come by even before the team captured its sixth Super Bowl title in 2009. There's a waiting list for season seats, and the only official way to purchase tickets to home games is via NFL Ticket Exchange (www .ticketexchangebyticketmaster.com/NFL). The unofficial way: sidling up to scalpers.

Art Rooney's huge clout in the sports world proved invaluable in the mid-1960s, during Pittsburgh's successful bid for a National Hockey League franchise. When it came time to name the expansion team, inspiration came from the Downtown arena that would serve as its home, nicknamed "The Igloo" for reasons apparent to anyone who has seen it. The **Penguins** (Consol Energy Center, 1001 5th Ave., 800/642-PENS, http://penguins.nhl. com) played their first game in the arena in October 1967 and their last in April 2010. The three-time Stanley Cup winners moved to a brand spanking new home across the street— the $321 million Consol Energy Center—in time for the 2010-2011 season. There's a waiting list for season tickets, but individual game tickets can be purchased at the arena box office, at Ticketmaster outlets, online at www.ticket master.com, or by phone at 800/745-3000.

Pittsburgh's Major League Baseball club is its oldest professional sports franchise, dating to the late 1800s. The **Pirates** (115 Federal St., 412/321-2827, http://pittsburgh.pirates.mlb. com) captured two World Series titles while the Steelers were still a twinkle in Art Rooney's eye and three more in the 1960s and '70s. But in recent decades the "Bucs" have faded from the spotlight, which is a polite way of saying they suck. In 2009 they posted their 17th consecutive losing season. In doing so, they made history. No NFL, NHL, NBA, or other MLB team can claim that long of a losing streak. Are season seats at PNC Park available? You betcha. Individual game tickets can be purchased at the ballpark's box office on the corner of Federal and General Robinson Streets, open 8:30 A.M.–6 P.M. Monday–Saturday on non-game days and 8:30 A.M. to the middle of the eighth inning on game days. They're also available on the team's website or by phone at 800/289-2827. Children under 30 inches get in for free.

Pittsburgh doesn't have a professional basketball team. Fortunately for fans of the game, the University of Pittsburgh's men's squad is a perennial winner. In 2009, **Panthers basketball** was ranked number one for the first time in its 101-year history. National Basketball Association teams including the Chicago Bulls and San Antonio Spurs snapped up 2009 graduates. Home games are played at the 12,500-seat Petersen Events Center (3719 Terrace St., 412/648-3054, www.peterseneventscenter.com) at the crest of Pitt's campus in Oakland. Also used by the women's basketball team and for concerts and commencements, the center houses the **McCarl Panthers Hall of Champions**. The tribute to Pitt's athletic overachievers is located in the main lobby, open 9 A.M.–5 P.M. weekdays and during all men's basketball games.

The **Panthers football** program is also impressive. Alumni include NFL legends Mike Ditka, Tony Dorsett, Dan Marino, and Curtis Martin. The team's home base is Heinz Field—same as the Steelers. Tickets to Pitt's athletic events are available online at www.pittsburghpanthers.com, at the ticket office in the lobby of the Petersen Events Center, or by phone at 800/643-7488.

Let's not overlook the ladies. Pittsburgh is home to not one but two women's full-tackle football teams. Formed in 2002, the **Pittsburgh Passion** (724/452-9395, www.pittsburghpassion.com) didn't have an indoor practice facility during its first season. Winter weather didn't stop the players from practicing outside. These days they show their stuff at North Allegheny High School's Newman Stadium (10375 Perry Hwy., Wexford). Season and single-game tickets are available on the Passion website. A former Passion player started the **Pittsburgh Force** (412/583-5774, www.pittsburghforce.net), which played its inaugural season in 2009. Home games take place at Ambridge Area High School's Moe Rubenstein Stadium (909 Duss Ave., Ambridge), and tickets are sold at the gate. The Passion and Force don't face off. The former is a member of the Independent Women's Football League, and the latter, the Women's Football Alliance. Their seasons start in April.

Accommodations

Pittsburgh proper has a pleasant mix of chain hotels and independently owned establishments. And capacity is rarely an issue (though the hospitality industry *was* taxed to the limit when the city hosted a G20 summit in 2009). It lacks budget accommodations, though. It's almost impossible to find a room for less than $100. Pittsburgh's only hostel closed in 2003. A movement to open another, the Pittsburgh Hostel Project (http://pittsburghhostel.org), got off the ground in 2009. But for now, budget travelers have little choice but to bunk down in chain motels on the city's outskirts.

DOWNTOWN
Downtown is home to the city's grandest hotels, and the **◖ Omni William Penn** (530 William Penn Place, 412/281-7100, www.omnihotels.com, $169–399) is the grandest of them all. With 596 guest rooms and suites—beautifully appointed with cherry wood furnishings and windows that actually

open—it's also one of the largest hotels in the Burgh. The list of luminaries who've laid their heads on its pillows (available in foam, feather, or down) includes John F. Kennedy and big band leader Lawrence Welk. You don't have to be a guest to soak up the grandeur. The massive lobby has crystal chandeliers, soaring archways, and plenty of inviting couches and armchairs. Grab a drink from the on-site Starbucks and stay awhile. Also on site is the elegant **Terrace Room** restaurant (6:30 A.M.–2 P.M. and 5–10 P.M. Mon.–Sat., 6:30 A.M.–2 P.M. Sun., $11–32), serving what it calls "new traditional" cuisine. Historic photographs of the hotel, which opened in 1916, decorate its walls.

The old-world charm of the **Renaissance Pittsburgh** (107 6th St., 412/562-1200, www.marriott.com, $199–399) belies its youth. The hotel opened in 2001 in what had been an office building for almost a century. Despite having 300 guest rooms and suites and Marriott as its overlord, the Renaissance pulls off the feel of a boutique lodging. It's smack dab in the heart of the Cultural District, spitting distance from several acclaimed theaters. It's also so close to the Allegheny River that guests on the uppermost floors can take in a Pirates game on the opposite shore without leaving their plush rooms.

The **Doubletree Hotel & Suites** (1 Bigelow Square, 412/281-5800, www.pittsburgh citycenter.doubletree.com, $169–325) is within easy walking distance of the U.S. Steel Tower, the David L. Lawrence Convention Center, and other hives of 9–5 activity. Fittingly enough, it's geared toward business travelers. The business center is open 24 hours, as is the fitness center. High-speed Internet access, remote guest room printing, and shuttle service are all on the house. More than a third of the hotel's 308 accommodations are spacious two-room suites. And while the decor is nothing special, the bedding lives up to its Sweet Dreams trademark. The excellent **Bigelow Grille** (412/281-5013, www.bigelowgrille.com, 6:30 A.M.–10 P.M. daily, $9–39) calls the Doubletree home.

NORTH SIDE

The quickly developing neighborhood that includes PNC Park, Heinz Field, and the Rivers Casino has, surprisingly, just one hotel: Marriott's **SpringHill Suites Pittsburgh North Shore** (223 Federal St., 412/323-9005, www.marriott.com, $169–399). Built in 2005, it's what you'd expect from the brand. The suites are roomy, the breakfast is complimentary, and amenities have the business traveler in mind. Because it's across the street from the ballpark, the 198-room hotel has been home to many young Pirates. (They're wont to stop by SoHo, the in-house restaurant, after a winning game. Don't bother looking for them after a losing one.) A nice perk: complimentary shuttle service within a three-mile area. Not so nice: $18 a day for on-site parking.

There's no shortage of unique, independently owned accommodations within walking distance of the North Side's main attractions. They date to the 19th century, don't charge for parking, and deliver a level of hospitality usually associated with luxury hotels. Perhaps the most original is **◖ The Parador** (939 Western Ave., 412/231-4800, www.theparadorinn.com, $150), a slice of Key West in the heart of Steeler Country. Owner Ed Menzer, whose long career in the hospitality industry included a stint at an oceanfront hotel in Florida, filled the enclosed courtyard of his Caribbean-inspired B&B with tropical plants and something akin to a beach. Inside, geckos, monkeys, and birds stare out from hand-painted murals. Built in the 1870s, the manse boasts three porches, more than 50 stained-and leaded-glass windows, a spectacular formal parlor, and a 2,700-square-foot ballroom with a handcrafted bar that's truly out of the ordinary. Each of its eight guest rooms and suites has a private bathroom and working fireplace. Guests can get their bodies beach-ready at the nearby YMCA for free.

The stone mansion on the corner of West North Avenue and Buena Vista Street was so dilapidated when teachers Karl Kargle and Jeff Stasko snapped it up in 1999 that trees were sprouting from chimneys packed with dirt and pigeon carcasses. It took a few years, but the couple turned the 1880s house into one of the finest B&Bs in the Pittsburgh area, as grand as the day department store baron Russell H. Boggs made it his second home. Mr. Boggs' Room, which boasts views of Allegheny Commons Park and the Downtown skyline, is one of eight guest rooms and suites at **Inn on the Mexican War Streets** (604 W. North Ave., 412/231-6544, www.innonthemexican warstreets.com, $139–189). All have private bathrooms. Most romantic of the bunch is Mrs. Boggs' Room, with its elevated four-poster bed and fainting couch. At $139 for a one-night stay or $119 per night for longer visits, the ornate but windowless Red Room is one of the best values in the Burgh. Guests are more than welcome to tickle the ivories of the baby grand piano in the gorgeous parlor. Better yet, they're welcome to partake in Stasko's famous chocolate chip cookies, which the former teacher of culinary arts has been baking since high school.

Named one of the world's "top 10 hidden gems" by Hotels.com, **The Priory Hotel** (614 Pressley St., 412/231-3338, www.thepriory.com, $125–245) is a 25-room beaut. Built in 1888 as a home for Benedictine priests and brothers who served the church next door (now a magnificent banquet hall), the boutique hotel is anything but austere. It's decorated with antiques and oil paintings, equipped with cable and Wi-Fi, and filled with charm. The rooms are so far from cookie cutter that rates range considerably. A suite that takes up the whole fourth floor boasts a full kitchen and a view of the Pittsburgh skyline. On the other end of the spectrum are two single-person rooms, available for as little as $99 per night. Guests take their breakfast in the same high-ceilinged dining room where the monks took theirs. The doors to the courtyard are swung open on warm days. Complimentary wine is served evenings in the sitting room, where a fire flickers on cold days. On weekday mornings, guests can get a free lift to Downtown or sights on the North Shore.

SOUTH SIDE

Best known for its nightlife, the South Side has precious few lodging options. One, the **Sheraton Station Square Hotel** (300 W. Station Square Dr., 412/261-2000, www.star woodhotels.com, $150–350), has the distinction of being Pittsburgh's only riverfront hotel. A linchpin in the redevelopment of the city's South Shore, once the site of a massive railway complex and now a dining and entertainment destination, the Sheraton is a pricey but sound choice for those who appreciate clean lines and skylines. The nighttime views of Downtown from its six-story lobby and river-facing rooms are nothing short of spectacular. Though separated from the twinkling towers by the Monongahela River, the 399-room hotel is within walking distance of them, thanks to the pedestrian-friendly Smithfield Street Bridge. The Gateway Clipper Fleet of riverboats and the famous Monongahela Incline are also within walking distance. Hotel amenities include an indoor pool, sauna, sundeck, and fitness center. A well-done steakhouse, Pittsburgh Rare, is on site.

Just one block from the South Side's hard-partying main drag, **Morning Glory Inn** (2119 Sarah St., 412/431-1707, www.gloryinn.com, $155–450) is the picture of tranquility. Many a bride's fantasy wedding has come to pass in its brick-paved, gorgeously landscaped Savannah-style courtyard. The B&B also caters to the business traveler with high-speed Internet, meeting rooms, a 50-inch plasma TV that doubles as a touch-screen monitor, and shuttle service to Downtown. Morning Glory offers five cheerful guest rooms and suites in an 1862 brick townhouse and a sprawling suite in what used to be three row houses. It's within walking distance of dozens of restaurants, but you'll want to stick around for breakfast. Innkeeper Nancy Eshelman's repertoire includes cold strawberry soup, heart-shaped waffles, German baked eggs, and homemade biscuits.

OAKLAND AND POINTS EAST

Oakland is a neighborhood dominated by universities and hospitals and, as a consequence, peppered with hotels. The overwhelming majority are chains: Hampton Inn, Quality Inn, Holiday Inn, Residence Inn by Marriott,

PITTSBURGH

Wyndham. For digs with more character, head to Shadyside, the tony neighborhood to Oakland's east.

Pittsburgh's only Select Registry property, (The Inn on Negley (703 Negley Ave., 412/661-0631, www.theinnsonnegley.com, $180–240), is within walking distance of Shadyside's Walnut Street and Ellsworth Avenue, both lined with shops and eateries. It has eight exquisitely decorated guest rooms and ample Victorian charm. Floor-to-ceiling bay windows, a fireplace, a king-sized four-poster bed, and a Jacuzzi make the Cortland Suite particularly romantic. Breakfast is prepared by professional chefs whose curricula vitae include Le Pommier, Café at the Frick, Kaya, and other famed Pittsburgh eateries. A traditional English high tea is served from noon to 4 P.M. by reservation. Chocoholics can opt for piping hot cocoa with freshly baked cookies. Repeat guests may remember the beautifully restored 19th-century house as The Appletree Inn.

The Tea Room at **Sunnyledge Boutique Hotel** (5124 5th Ave., 412/683-5014, www.sunnyledge.com, $189–275, corporate and extended-stay rates starting at $139), another 19th-century stunner, serves tea 3–5 P.M. every day but Monday—and a great deal more. It's an upscale restaurant open to the public for lunch and dinner Tuesdays through Saturdays and brunch on Sundays. The hotel also boasts a cocktail lounge with an exceptional selection of single-malt scotch whiskies, 24-hour concierge service, twice-daily maid service, same-day laundry service, and free shoe shines. Once the home and office of Dr. James McClelland, who founded Shadyside Hospital, Sunnyledge has eight sumptuous guest rooms and suites.

It's nothing but suites at nearby **Shadyside Inn** (5405 5th Ave., 412/682-2300, www.shadysideinn.com, $119–299), a particularly good choice for a longish stay. Monthly rates start at $2,195. You don't need to whip out a calculator to realize we're talking less than $100 a day. (We're talking $73 a day, to be precise about it.) Shadyside Inn also extends deep discounts to guests affiliated with the local universities and hospitals. The hotel is actually a collection of six properties scattered throughout Shadyside—three former apartment buildings and an equal number of converted mansions. The latter are secluded and unmarked, making them ideal for heads of state and Tinseltown types in town for film shoots. Non-mansion suites come in three sizes: studio, one-bedroom, and two-bedroom. All have kitchens, cable, and other home-away-from-home touches. The Wi-Fi is free, as is shuttle service within a three-mile area. Guests who prefer to pedal around the 'hood can hop on one of the hotel's bikes.

Food

Unlike Philadelphia, which is practically synonymous with the cheesesteak, Pittsburgh doesn't have an iconic dish. Pierogies—semicircular dumplings filled with the likes of mashed potatoes and sauerkraut—may be the closest thing, thanks to an influx of Poles during the city's industrial heyday. Pittsburghers reportedly consume more pierogies than the citizenry of any other U.S. city, and Pittsburgh Pirates games feature a race between runners clad in pierogi costumes. French fries also figure prominently in local cuisine. A "Pittsburgh-style" sandwich is stuffed with fries. A "Pittsburgh-style" salad is topped with them. If you haven't figured it out already, this is a meat-and-potatoes kind of town.

If you're not a fan of meat and potatoes, don't despair. While the Burgh has a long way to go before it's considered a dining destination, you'll find everything from Ethiopian fare to vegan hot dogs if you look hard enough (or simply keep reading).

DOWNTOWN AND THE STRIP DISTRICT

American

It's not just God-fearing folk who flock to Downtown's Trinity Cathedral and First Presbyterian Church. The neighboring churches have come to be known as great lunch spots. Trinity Cathedral is home to **Franktuary** (325 Oliver Ave., 412/288-0322, www.franktuary.com, 10 A.M.–3 P.M. Mon.–Fri., under $10), which claims to sell the best New York–style hot dogs in Pennsylvania. Forget what you think about hot dog shops. This place has something for traditionalists, vegans, and foodies alike—plus a sense of humor evident in its motto ("Franks be to God!") and wall art. Standard franks share the menu with a tofu version and the Locavore, made with organic grass-fed beef from a farm some 60 miles north of Downtown. Select from classic toppings like chili and sauerkraut or dress your frank in mango pineapple salsa, fresh mozzarella, artichoke hearts, or other finery. The Pittsburgh frank, topped with a smushed pierogi and coleslaw, is a Franktuary exclusive. The eatery formerly known as Hot Dogma also offers sausages, salads, and fruit shakes.

Our Daily Bread Cafeteria (320 6th Ave., 412/232-0292, www.fpcp.org, 10:30 A.M.–2 P.M. Mon.–Fri., under $10), located on the ground floor of First Presbyterian Church, features house-made soups, sandwiches and wraps, a fruit and salad bar, and daily specials. You guessed it: fish on Fridays.

Every day is fish day at the **Original Oyster House** (20 Market Square, 412/566-7925, www.originaloysterhousepittsburgh.com, 10 A.M.–10 P.M. Mon.–Sat., under $10), which holds the distinction of being Pittsburgh's oldest bar and restaurant. Oysters sold for a penny when it opened in 1870. Today a breaded oyster will set you back a buck seventy, and the size of the fish sandwich will blow your mind. Also popular: the Maryland-style crab cakes, the deep-fried shrimp, and the New England clam chowder, made fresh daily. Quench your thirst with a cold draft or a glass of buttermilk, which sold quite well during Prohibition. If the frozen-in-time joint looks familiar, it's probably because you've seen it in one of 20-plus movies. It's the Marlon Brando of Pittsburgh dining establishments.

Contemporary Cuisine

Pittsburgh's business district has no shortage of restaurants catering to professionals with expense accounts and anyone else willing to spend upwards of $20 an entrée. The **Bigelow Grille** (1 Bigelow Square, 412/281-5013, www.bigelowgrille.com, breakfast from 6:30 A.M. daily, lunch 11 A.M.–2 P.M. Mon.–Sat. and noon–2 P.M. Sun., dinner 5–10 P.M. Mon.–Sat., limited menu 2–5 P.M. Mon.–Sat. and noon–10 P.M. Sun., bar open until 12:30 A.M. Sun.–Thurs. and 2 A.M. Fri.–Sat., lunch $9–17, dinner $21–37) in the Doubletree Hotel & Suites is notable for its reinventions of Steeltown staples, or what it calls "refined presentations of Pittsburgh traditions." Take its haute pierogies, featuring such delicacies as artisan goat cheese and crispy pork belly. At $12, the signature burger is pricey even by fine-dining standards, but consider its consumption an act of eco-consciousness: Bigelow Grille buys the beef and cheddar from family farms in southwestern Pennsylvania. For dinner, try the (house-made) gnocchi tossed with (house-made) sausage and roasted pepper cream.

People are invariably surprised to learn that **Six Penn Kitchen** (146 6th St., 412/566-7366, www.sixpennkitchen.com, 11 A.M.–11 P.M. Mon.–Thurs., 11 A.M.–midnight Fri., 4:30 P.M.–midnight Sat., Sun. brunch 10:30 A.M.–2:30 P.M., lunch/brunch $8–14, dinner $15–34) and the Eat'n Park chain are products of the same parent company. Smack dab in the heart of the Cultural District, Six Penn is the picture of casual sophistication. Eat'n Park restaurants, found throughout Pennsylvania, West Virginia, and Ohio, are best known for smiley cookies. They do share some DNA. Like its plebeian siblings, Six Penn offers a menu of American classics—quintessential comfort foods included—and memorable desserts. But chef Keith Fuller and team bring a worldly sensibility to the table. The results are lobster mac and cheese garnished with salmon roe, country fried quail with fried green tomatoes, seitan "buffalo wings," and such. Pressed-for-time theater-goers can count on attentive service. Six Penn waives its $15 wine corkage on Mondays. On other nights you can bring a bottle without charge if you also buy a bottle from the restaurant.

You'd have to be a finicky drinker indeed to bring your own wine to **Sonoma Grille** (947 Penn Ave., 412/697-1336, www.thesonomagrille.com, lunch 11 A.M.–3 P.M. daily, dinner 5–11 P.M. daily, lunch $8–15,

dinner $16–55), ground-floor tenant of downtown's Courtyard by Marriott. The restaurant boasts a collection of more than 1,000 wines, offering about 100 by the glass. Most are of West Coast provenance, the better to complement the California-inspired cuisine. Belly up to the bar during happy hour—5–7 P.M. weekdays—for $4 glasses of wine and $5 tapas. Or come for dinner on a Monday evening, when prices on many bottles are slashed in half. The menu, which changes monthly, lends itself to sampling a variety of dishes. Finish with a house-made ice cream creation.

THREE SQUARE MEALS, PITTSBURGH STYLE

When celebrity-skewing comedian Kathy Griffin came to Pittsburgh in 2010, she regaled her audience with an account of her meal at homegrown eatery Primanti Bros. Everyone in the sold-out Heinz Hall knew exactly what she was talking about. Primanti's, like steel and the Steelers, is practically synonymous with Pittsburgh.

You can learn a lot about a city from its homegrown eateries. Here are a few that will further your education.

BREAKFAST

On weekend mornings, there's often a line out the door at **Pamela's Diner** (www.pamelasdiner.com, under $10) locations. Fortunately, the line moves quickly. Pamela's is a fast-paced place. Many patrons order without so much as glancing at the menu, and the food comes sooner than you can say "eggs benedict." That's because the restaurant doesn't do eggs benedict – or anything else in the chi-chi category of breakfast foods. Pamela's does scrambled eggs and cheese omelets. It does corned beef hash and home fries. It does what most greasy spoons do. But there's one thing it does differently: pancakes. No light and fluffy flapjacks here. Pamela's pancakes are crepe-like in their thinness, with crispy edges that defy explanation. Then-candidate Barack Obama flipped for them during a 2008 swing through the Keystone State. The following year

he invited co-owners Pamela Cohen and Gail Klingensmith to the White House, where they cooked their famous pancakes for the Obamas and 80 veterans. Head to the **Strip District location** (60 21st St., 412/281-6366, 7 A.M.-3 P.M. Mon.-Sat., 8 A.M.-3 P.M. Sun.) to walk in the president's footsteps. Pamela's also has locations in **Oakland** (3703 Forbes Ave., 412/683-4066, 7:30 A.M.-4 P.M. daily), **Shadyside** (5527 Walnut St., 412/683-1003, 8 A.M.-4 P.M. Mon.-Sat., 9 A.M.-3 P.M. Sun.), **Squirrel Hill** (5813 Forbes Ave., 412/422-9457, 8 A.M.-4 P.M. Mon.-Sat., 9 A.M.-3 P.M. Sun.), **Millvale** (232 North Ave., 412/821-4655, 8 A.M.-4 P.M. Mon.-Fri., 8 A.M.-3 P.M. Sat., 8 A.M.-2 P.M. Sun.), and the South Hills suburb of **Mt. Lebanon** (427 Washington Rd., 412/343-3344, 7:30 A.M.-3 P.M. Mon.-Sat., 8 A.M.-3 P.M. Sun.).

LUNCH

It's not unusual for people to go straight to a **Primanti Bros.** (www.primantibrothers.com, under $10) upon arrival in Pittsburgh. Thanks to TV shows including Travel Channel's *Food Paradise* and *Man v. Food*, Primanti's sandwiches enjoy nationwide fame. Their distinguishing characteristic is the presence of coleslaw and fries. Coleslaw and fries are deli staples, of course. But few delis do what Primanti's does, which is place the traditional sides *inside* the sandwich. For 50 cents, it will throw a fried egg into the mix. Primanti's, which had

Also highly regarded for its wine selection, **❚ Eleven** (1150 Smallman St., 412/201-5656, www.bigburrito.com/eleven, lunch 11:30 A.M.–2 P.M. Mon.–Fri., Sun. brunch 11 A.M.–2 P.M., dinner 5–10 P.M. Mon.–Thurs., 5–11 P.M. Fri.–Sat., 5–9 P.M. Sun., tavern menu 2 P.M.–close Mon.–Fri. and 5 P.M.–close Sat.–Sun., lunch $8–20, dinner $21–55) has been luring foodies to the Strip since 2004, when it opened as the 11th and most ambitious restaurant by Pittsburgh's big Burrito Restaurant Group. Some opening-day dishes, including New York strip steak with pierogies and pan-roasted chicken with risotto, proved so popular that they're still on the menu. Eleven is unique among area restaurants in offering both regular and vegetarian chef's tasting menus ($55 and $45, respectively). A tavern menu ($4–22) available in the first-floor lounge and on the second-floor patio lets budget-minded sophisticates enjoy the modern space. Happy hour—4–6 P.M. weekdays—features $6 martinis and oysters.

Italian

It's often said that if you can make it in New York, you can make it anywhere. TV chef and

17 locations in the Pittsburgh area and three in Florida at last count, dates to the 1930s, when Joe Primanti began selling sandwiches in the Strip District, then crowded with wholesale produce merchants. Many of Joe's customers were truckers on the go; they needed a meal they could eat with one hand. The rest, as they say, is history.

If possible, visit the **original location in the Strip** (46 18th St., 412/263-2142), open 24-7. You'll also find Primanti's in **Downtown** (2 S. Market Square, 412/261-1599, 10 A.M.–midnight daily), **Oakland** (3803 Forbes Ave., 412/621-4444, 10 A.M.–midnight Sun.–Wed., 10 A.M.–3 A.M. Thurs.–Sat.), and the **South Side** (1832 E. Carson St., 412/381-2583, 11 A.M.–2 A.M. Sun.–Thurs., 11 A.M.–3 A.M. Fri.–Sat.).

DINNER

Pamela's and Primanti's are easy on the wallet, if not the arteries. Come dinnertime, consider splurging on a meal on Mount Washington's "Restaurant Row." The eateries along Grandview Avenue aren't necessarily the best in town. Many locals pooh-pooh the pricey lot. But the views they serve up are so incredible that you can forgive an overcooked steak or lackluster dessert. What you'll remember, even years later, is your taste of Pittsburgh's prize-winning skyline.

LeMont (1114 Grandview Ave., 412/431-3100, www.lemontpittsburgh.com, dinner from 5 P.M.

Mon.-Sat. and 4 P.M. Sun., $28-49), which celebrated its 50th anniversary in 2010, bills itself as "the place for special occasions." It's the picture of fancy schmancy, right down to the bow-tied servers. LeMont is known for tableside preparations of chateaubriand, Steak Diane, and more. You can soak up the bling-bling without breaking the bank in the lounge, featuring nightly entertainment. The less ornate **Isabela on Grandview** (1318 Grandview Ave., 412/431-5882, http://www.isabelaongrandview.com, 5-10 P.M. Mon.-Sat., a la carte $26-34, prix fixe $70) is known for its seven-course prix fixe, which is your only option on Saturdays. Seafood lovers favor **Monterey Bay Fish Grotto** (1411 Grandview Ave., 412/481-4414, www.montereybayfishgrotto.com, lunch 11 A.M.-3 P.M. Mon.-Fri., dinner 5-10 P.M. Mon.-Thurs., 5-11 P.M. Fri.-Sat., 5-9 P.M. Sun., lunch $10-23, dinner $23-39), located well above sea level at the top of a luxury apartment building. It offers 15 to 20 varieties of fresh fish on any given day. The **Grandview Saloon** (1212 Grandview Ave., 412/431-1400, www.thegrandviewsaloon.com, 11:30 A.M.-9 P.M. Mon.-Thurs., 11:30 A.M.-10 P.M. Fri.-Sat., 11:30 A.M.-9 P.M. Sun., bar open until 11 P.M. Mon.-Thurs. and 12:30 A.M. Fri.-Sat., $10-35) is notable for its outdoor seating and casual grub, including buffalo chicken fingers and burgers. It's the best choice if you're on a budget.

cookbook author Lidia Bastianich already had two successful restaurants in Manhattan, Felidia and Becco, when she opened **Lidia's** (1400 Smallman St., 412/552-0150, www .lidias-pittsburgh.com, lunch 11:30 A.M.–2 P.M. Mon.–Fri., brunch 11 A.M.–2:30 P.M. Sat.–Sun., dinner 5–9 P.M. Mon.–Thurs., 5–10 P.M. Fri.–Sat., 5–8 P.M. Sun., lunch $9–18, dinner $14–35) in the Strip District, so it stands to reason that Pittsburghers have embraced her brand of Italian cooking. Borrowing a page from Becco's playbook, Lidia's offers unlimited servings of three pasta preparations for a fixed price ($14 at lunchtime and $17 at dinnertime). The lineup, which changes daily, often includes risotto or polenta dishes as well as delectable pastas. But there's more to the restaurant's appeal than all-you-can-eat carbs. The kitchen nails just about every offering, from appetizers like grilled octopus to desserts like tangerine sorbet. Choose from two wine lists: one featuring $28 bottles and another for big spenders. Wines from Bastianich's own vineyards in Italy are available by the glass. The weekend brunch is a popular gut-buster: one entrée and unlimited helpings from the antipasti and sweets tables for $24 per person (children $8).

Seafood

The Strip District's seafood markets are great places to grab lunch—if you don't mind the smells of fresh fish, of course. **Wholey's** (1711 Penn Ave., 412/391-3737, www.wholey.com) and **Benkovitz Seafoods** (2300 Smallman St., 412/263-3016, www.benkovitzseafood.com), which have been around forever, are both fantastic, offering everything from sushi to fish 'n' chips in an old-school setting. But new kid on the block **Penn Avenue Fish Company** (2208 Penn Ave., 412/434-7200, www.pennavefish company.com) is even better. Its chalkboard menu advertises the likes of crab tacos, spicy barbecue shrimp pizza, and mussels in tomato-basil sauce—all under $10. Fish tacos, made with mahi, salmon, and tuna, are marked down on Tuesdays: two for $4.99, three for $6.99, or all you can eat for $8.99. On Wednesdays the market reels in sushi lovers with a $17.99 all-you-can-eat deal.

NORTH SIDE
American

One of the Burgh's most beloved sports figures got into the restaurant game in 2007. **Jerome Bettis' Grille 36** (375 N. Shore Dr., 412/224-6287, www.jeromebettisgrille36.com, opens at 8 A.M. for all Pitt and Steelers home games starting before 2 P.M., $8–50) boasts an astonishing 50 televisions and a patio with views of the Pittsburgh skyline and Heinz Field, where Jerome "The Bus" Bettis wore the number 36 jersey for a decade. Wanna be like The Bus? Start with the cheese-smothered fries, proceed to the Soon to be Famous Deep Fried Cheeseburger, and finish with the one-pound carrot cake, made in-house with fresh carrots and pineapple. The former running back, who retired following the Steelers' 2006 Super Bowl win, also enjoys a Greek chopped salad, if the impressively diverse menu is to be believed. Ask your server about the day's game burger—as in wild game. Bison, boar, ostrich, antelope, and even alligator have made the cut. Take your pick of 36 draft beers, 36 wines, and 36 cocktails. Take three timeouts per half if you're bold enough to take on The 36, a bone-in steak weighing in at—you guessed it—36 ounces.

Asian

A short walk from the National Aviary, (**Nicky's Thai Kitchen** (856 Western Ave., 412/321-8424, www.nickysthaikitchen.com, lunch 11:30 A.M.–3 P.M. Mon.–Sat., dinner 5–9 P.M. Mon.–Thurs., 5–10 P.M. Fri.–Sat., 4–9 P.M. Sun., lunch $7–11, dinner $8–17) offers outstanding takes on familiar dishes like *tom yum* soup and *pad thai,* chef's specials that threaten to ruin you for other Thai eateries, a no-corkage BYOB policy, and a delightful patio. This "may just be the best Thai food we've had in the Western hemisphere," crowed *Pittsburgh City Paper*'s food-critiquing duo after a visit to the restaurant's second location in the Allegheny River town of **Verona** (321

South Ave., 412/828-0339, same hours), about 10 miles northeast of downtown Pittsburgh.

SOUTH SIDE
American

The 500-seat **Grand Concourse** (100 W. Station Square Dr., 412/261-1717, www .muer.com, 11 A.M.–10 P.M. Mon.–Thurs., 11 A.M.–11 P.M. Fri., 11:30 A.M.–11 P.M. Sat., 10 A.M.–9 P.M. Sun. lunch $10–29, dinner $18–39) is the largest restaurant in the city and arguably the most stunning. Set in a former train terminal, it's awash in marble, mahogany, brass, and stained glass. Seafood is its stock-in-trade, but landlubbers can count on a few beef and chicken dishes. The popular Sunday brunch (10 A.M.–2:30 P.M. $24, kids $11) features everything from eggs and bacon to cold smoked fishes and salmon Rockefeller. Its attached sister restaurant, **Gandy Dancer** (11 A.M.–10 P.M. Mon.–Thurs., 11 A.M.–11 P.M. Fri., 4:30–11 P.M. Sat., 10 A.M.–9 P.M. Sun. $8–$18), offers a more casual atmosphere and menu prices to match.

Asian
Nakama Japanese Steakhouse and Sushi Bar (1611 E. Carson St., 412/381-6000, www .eatatnakama.com, 11 A.M.–10 P.M. Mon.–Wed., 11 A.M.–11 P.M. Thurs.–Sat., 1–10 P.M. Sun., bar open until 1 A.M. Mon.–Sat. and midnight Sun., lunch $10–16, dinner $16–70) has racked up so many accolades in so many categories—best trendy scene, best group dining, best ethnic restaurant, among others—that expectations run high round its hibachi tables. It rarely disappoints. House specialties include hibachi chateaubriand, seared scallops, and a seafood combo featuring South African lobster tail. Several surf and turf options take the handwringing out of ordering. Come 4–6 P.M. Monday–Saturday and mention the "early bird special" for 20 percent off a hibachi dinner. Though the sushi bar gets second billing, it's a star in its own right. Cozy up for some of the comeliest maki in all the Burgh—and great people-watching to boot.

Nakama shares the corner of East Carson and 17th Streets with **Cambod-Ican Kitchen** (1701

Grand Concourse

Nakama Japanese Steakhouse and Sushi Bar

E. Carson St., 412/381-6199, www.cambodi cankitchen.com, 4 P.M.–midnight Tues.–Thurs., 4 P.M.–3 A.M. or later Fri.–Sat., Sun. by chance, $8–12). The former is hard to miss, what with the large orange fish suspended over its entrance and the near-constant inflow and outflow of smartly dressed guests. The latter is a different story. Cambod-Ican does so little to announce its presence that South Siders who've passed it countless times couldn't necessarily point you to it. In short, it's a hole-in-the-wall. But Dan and Moeun McSwiggen—he of Pittsburgh, she of Cambodia—have never relied on razzle-dazzle to sell their brand of Cambodian-American fusion. People lined up for their chicken kebabs and fried wantons when the "restaurant" was an aluminum truck. Beloved by barhoppers for its generous portions, low prices, and late hours, the BYOB has also won the hearts of vegetarians with its embrace of tofu. Its fresh-squeezed limeade is a tart treat.

For a steaming curry with a side of sexual innuendo, head to **Thai Me Up** (1925 E. Carson St., 412/488-8893, 11:30 A.M.–2:30 P.M. and 4–10 P.M. Mon.–Fri., noon–10 P.M. Sat., under $10), a teeny BYOB that does a brisk takeout business. The steamed dumplings and lemongrass soup will have you begging for more.

Contemporary Cuisine

You know you're in for a gastronomic surprise when a menu features a glossary of terms. **Yo Rita** (1120 East Carson St., 412/904-3557, www.yoritasouthside.com, à la carte tacos $5–9), which specializes in tacos, is full of surprises. For starters, it's not really a Mexican restaurant. Its glossary includes everything from Idiazabal (a Spanish cheese made from unpasteurized sheep's milk) to kimchi (Korea's national dish) to *tobiko* (flying fish roe, a staple at sushi restaurants). If you think such ingredients have no place on a flour tortilla, you're in for another surprise. Yo Rita's couture tacos are quite simply *fabuloso*. Follow its Twitter feed for the first word on specials like turtle tacos, swordfish ceviche, and prickly pear margaritas.

A date night favorite, **17th Street Café** (75 S. 17th St., 412/381-4566, www.17thstreetcafe .com, 11 A.M.–10 P.M. Mon.–Thurs., 11 A.M.–11 P.M. Fri., 4–11 P.M. Sat., 4–9 P.M. Sun., lunch $7–12, dinner $10–27) offers a menu of mostly Italian-American dishes, along with unsurpassed service. Don't be surprised if owner Pat Joyce drops by your table as you're tucking into wild mushroom raviolis or pecan-crusted tilapia. He came on as executive chef fresh out of culinary school and bought the restaurant more than a decade later. The space is as cozy as they come, which is remarkable considering that it served as a butcher shop and a shot-and-beer joint in its first hundred years. The waitstaff swear they've seen ghosts in the basement, a onetime speakeasy.

Italian

Specializing in Sicilian cuisine, **◖ Dish Osteria and Bar** (128 S. 17th St., 412/390-2012, www.dishosteria.com, 5 P.M.–midnight Mon.–Sat., bar open until 2 A.M., appetizers and salads $4–10, entrées $15–31) is a singular choice for an after-work nibble, a special night out, or a nightcap. After work, self-soothe with house-marinated olives, beef carpaccio served with organic arugula, or mussels steamed with white wine and garlic. Choose from more than a dozen wines served by the glass ($6.50–10). For a special night out, make a reservation. Dish is an intimate space, and it has a following. A tiny kitchen and a keep-it-simple cooking philosophy make for a succinct selection of entrées: a couple of pasta dishes, a couple of steak dishes, and a couple of seafood dishes, plus a handful of reasonably priced specials. Finish with an exquisite dessert, a rich espresso, and a contented sigh. Dish's kitchen doesn't close until midnight, and its bar stays open as late as the law allows—rare for a restaurant of its caliber. The cocktails, like the food, are *perfecto*.

For a New York–style slice—as in very thin and very flavorful—pop into **Pizza Sola** (1417 E. Carson St., 412/481-3888, www.pizzasola .com, 11:30 A.M.–midnight Mon.–Wed., 11:30 A.M.–3 A.M. Thurs.–Sat., 12:30 P.M.–midnight Sun., slice $1.85–5.25, pie $10–22.50), formerly Pizza Vesuvio. It's open until

3 A.M. on the biggest party nights of the week, and that's not the only thing it has going for it. The dough is prepared freshly daily, and the toppings are top of the line, a fact reflected in the prices. A slice of the Carnivore, a red pizza with mozzarella, house-made Italian sausage, pepperoni, and capicola, tops five bucks. Fortunately, one slice is sufficient to sate most appetites. Pizza Sola also offers wings, oven-baked sandwiches, salads, and desserts. Opened in 2002 by two Pittsburgh natives, the South Side pizzeria now has siblings in **Oakland** (114 Atwood St., 412/681-7652, 11 A.M.–midnight Mon.–Thurs., 11 A.M.–3 A.M. Fri., 11:30 A.M.–3 A.M. Sat., 12:30 P.M.–midnight Sun.) and **East Liberty** (6004 Penn Circle S., 412/363-7652, 11:30 A.M.–midnight Mon.–Wed., 11:30 A.M.–1 A.M. Thurs., 11:30 A.M.–3 A.M. Fri.–Sat., 12:30 P.M.–midnight Sun.). Alas, not one delivers.

Vegetarian

No two tables are the same at **The Zenith** (86 S. 26th St., 412/481-4833, www.zenithpgh.com, 11 A.M.–9 P.M. Thurs.–Sat., 11 A.M.–3 P.M. Sun., $10 and under), where your seat could literally be sold out from under you. The vegetarian eatery doubles as an antiques shop, and everything from the glassware to the lamps can be yours for a price. You won't find a better deal than the $10 Sunday brunch. An entirely vegan buffet groans with more than a dozen salads (cross your fingers for crunchy mayo-less slaw and noodles in peanut sauce), breads, pies, and so many Bundt cakes that veganism could easily be confused with hedonism. The cost includes an entrée from the menu, which isn't strictly vegan, and coffee or tea. Thursdays through Saturdays, The Zenith offers a modest variety of salads, sandwiches, and entrées. Have a look-see around the crowded showroom and inside the bathrooms before you leave.

OAKLAND AND POINTS EAST
American

Pittsburgh's university district has no shortage of eateries offering affordable pub grub. Best of the bunch: **Fuel & Fuddle** (212 Oakland Ave., 412/682-3473, www.fuelandfuddle .com, 11 A.M.–2 A.M. daily, $7–14), serving everything from crispy chicken wings to thin-crusted pizzas to alligator stew. Its prominent brick oven proves handy for more than just pizzas. Try the fire-baked brie, which is billed as an appetizer but works well as a dessert. The restaurant boasts a pair of private label beers, Fire Brick Brown Ale and Pumphouse Pale Ale, crafted by Troegs Brewing Company in Harrisburg.

Wings connoisseurs have been in a flutter since a **Quaker Steak & Lube** (3600/3602 Forbes Ave., 412/381-9464, www.quaker steakandlube.com, 11 A.M.–10 P.M. Sun.–Thurs., 11 A.M.–11 P.M. Fri.–Sat., under $10) opened in Oakland. The Pennsylvania-based chain boasts 20-odd wing flavors. You'll have to sign a release form to sample the viciously hot Atomic Wings, known for making grown men cry.

The neon-lit **Original Hot Dog Shop** (3901 Forbes Ave., 412/621-7388, 10 A.M.–3:30 A.M. Mon.–Thurs., 10 A.M.–5 A.M. Fri.–Sat., under $5) is to Oakland what Pink's is to Hollywood: a landmark where hazy memories are made. The O, as it's known, has been feeding the inebriated masses since 1960. It's justly famous for its fries, cooked twice for good measure and doused with cheese if you so choose. So what if your feet stick to the floor?

Hankering for the quintessential American meal? Head to Pittsburgh's Little Italy. **Tessaro's** (4601 Liberty Ave., 412/682-6809, 11 A.M.–11 P.M. Mon.–Sat.) has been serving what many consider to be the city's best burger for more than 20 years. Its flame-grilled patties, made with house-ground meat, weigh in at half a pound. Be prepared to wait. The Bloomfield institution has a legion of regulars.

Shadyside's **Harris Grill** (5747 Ellsworth Ave., 412/362-5273, www.harrisgrill.com, 11:30 A.M.–1 A.M. Mon.–Sat., 10 A.M.–1 A.M. Sun., bar open until 2 A.M. daily, $7–20) inspires similar devotion, which only grew stronger after a 2007 fire shut it down for eight months. A flame logo and a menu replete with puns, pop culture references, and PG-13 cracks sets the tone for the scene. Start with the Goat in a Boat (feta and roasted red pepper dip served with pita wedges) and finish with the Twinkiemissou, a tiramisu of sorts featuring America's favorite snack cake. In between, choose from a vegetarian-friendly selection of salads, sandwiches, and "big things," including a decadent mac and cheese prepared with lobster tail and lump crab meat. Belly up to the bar on a Tuesday night for free bacon. In the warmer months, Harris's outdoor tables are among the most coveted in town, especially 4:30–6:30 weekdays, when drafts and the signature frozen cosmos are half price. Frozen mimosas class up the Sunday brunch buffet (10 A.M.–3 P.M., $15). No reservations. No apologies.

Asian

If backpacking Southeast Asia is on your bucket list, you can all but cross it off after a few trips to **Spice Island Tea House** (253 Atwood St., 412/687-8821, www.spiceisland teahouse.com, 11:30 A.M.–9 P.M. Mon.–Thurs., 11:30 A.M.–10 P.M. Fri.–Sat., $7–14). Deep in the section of Oakland where college students live five or six to a shabby house, the eatery has provided an affordable education in the foods of Indonesia, Malaysia, Burma, Vietnam, Singapore, and their neighbors since 1995. The wealth of options can overwhelm first-timers. Order an appetizer—the Sumatran corn and shrimp fritters are delish—and a pot of tea, and take your time perusing the rest of the menu. For occasions that demand something stronger than Darjeeling or oolong, Spice Island offers a well-edited selection of bottled beers, nearly a dozen wines by the bottle or glass, and champagne cocktails in sugar-rimmed glasses. Dim lighting and thrift-store decor help the imagination travel to distant lands. In the negative column: Parking around here is a pain in the patootie.

Squirrel Hill, a neighborhood known for its large Jewish population, has an inordinate number of Asian restaurants, most of which have a Murray Avenue address. For Chinese, call **Zaw's Asian Food** (2110 Murray Ave.,

412/521-3663, 11 A.M.–9:30 P.M. Tues.–Sat., noon–9 P.M. Sun., under $10) and order takeout. The wee eatery has a counter with a few stools, but you wouldn't want to eat there. To put it mildly, Zaw's is a dump. A thick layer of grime covers the cash register. Dust balls dangle from the air vents. But the grub will keep you coming back. Fast food this is not. Dishes are made with fresh ingredients as they're ordered, which means you'll likely have to wait upwards of 25 minutes for your *chow fun*. Which is why you're going to call ahead, see?

Chaya Japanese Cuisine (2032 Murray Ave., 412/422-2082, www.chayausa.com, 5–9:30 P.M. Mon.–Thurs., 5–9:45 P.M. Fri.–Sat., $12–75) offers some of the best sushi in the Burgh. Devotees were delighted when the first-come, first-served restaurant moved from a tiny storefront with only a handful of tables to a larger space in 2009. Owner and the executive chef Fumio Yasuzawa insists on authenticity in just about every respect. Among his concessions: Americanized portion sizes and the Murray Ave. Roll, featuring salmon and cream cheese, which you'd be hard-pressed to find in his native Japan. Unlike many inland sushi bars, Chaya avoids frozen fish as much as possible, favoring fresh fish flown in from New York or Japan. Its "special combination dinners," which feed two for $45 or less, are an affordable way to sample several traditional dishes. The BYOB charges $2 per wine or beer glass.

If it's Thai you're craving, mosey over to **Bangkok Balcony** (5846 Forbes Ave., 412/521-0728, www.bangkokbalconypgh .com, noon–10 P.M. Sun.–Thurs., noon–11 P.M. Fri.–Sat., $8–18) or its sister restaurant, **Silk Elephant** (1712 Murray Ave., 412/421-8801, www.silkelephant.net, 11:30 A.M.–10 P.M. Sun.–Thurs., 11:30 A.M.–11 P.M. Fri.–Sat., $10–21). In a city blessed with an abundance of Thai restaurants, Bangkok Balcony frequently tops reader polls. Lunch specials, available 11:30 A.M.–3 P.M. weekdays, are a steal at $7.95. While seafood figures prominently in the list of house specialties, most dishes are available with your choice of chicken, beef, pork, shrimp, tofu, or vegetables. Resplendent in red and gold, the second-floor restaurant offers a full bar and Thai dance performances most Thursday and Sunday evenings. After appearing at Bangkok Balcony between 6 and 7, the talent migrates to chef Norraset Nareedokmai's newer Squirrel Hill venture. With its tapas selection ($4–9), well-rounded wine list, and specialty martinis, Silk Elephant is as suited to an after-work stopover as a lazy dinner. Small plates such as salmon rolls, mussels Siam, and Siam Paragon—a marriage of crabmeat and jumbo shrimp consummated in the deep fryer—make it easy to overlook the large plates.

Brewpubs

Some call it sacrilegious. Others call it a shining example of adaptive reuse. The **Church Brew Works** (3525 Liberty Ave., 412/688-8200, www.churchbrewworks.com, full menu 11:30 A.M.–9:30 P.M. Mon.–Thurs., 11:30 A.M.–11 P.M. Fri.–Sat., noon–9 P.M. Sun., pizza served until 11 P.M. Mon.–Thurs.

and midnight Fri.–Sat., lunch $9–16, dinner $11–34, pub menu $8–16), a microbrewery and restaurant in a restored 1902 church building, has been called many things but never "typical." Guaranteed: You've never seen any place like it. With its stained-glass windows, soaring arches, and celestial-hued apse, the Lawrenceville brewpub tends to elicit a "Holy (something or other)!" from first-time visitors. Stainless steel and copper brew vessels occupy the main altar of the former St. John the Baptist Church, which closed its doors in 1993. To the right of the main aisle is the dining section, with seating made from the original pews. The oak planks of the pews were also used to build the long, curving bar to the left of the aisle. You can order from the dining or pub menu on either side, but sit on the left to take advantage of happy hour (4:30–6:30 P.M. Mon.–Fri.) food specials. A courtyard between the church building and onetime rectory provides for outdoor seating in the warmer months. Try a dish as unique as the setting—buffalo and wild mushroom

© SCOTT KEDDY

PITTSBURGH

Admire the stained glass windows of the former St. John the Baptist Church while sipping a brew at Church Brew Works.

meatloaf, for instance, or pierogies filled with the likes of rattlesnake and cactus—or stick to pub staples like chicken wings, onion soup, and oversized sandwiches. You can't go wrong with the pizzas, baked in a wood-fired brick oven. The "Pittsburgh pierogie pizza," topped with potato puree, sautéed onions, and cheddar cheese, is a two-in-one tribute to the city's Italian and Eastern European heritages. The Church Brew Works offers wines and spirits in addition to its signature and seasonal beers. Order the house-made birch beer if you're abstaining. Service can be sluggish, so flag down a waiter before your glass is half empty.

Contemporary Cuisine

It's a darn shame **(C Point Brugge Café** (401 Hastings St., 412/441-3334, www.point brugge.com, 11 A.M.–10 P.M. Tues.–Thurs., 11 A.M.–11 P.M. Fri.–Sat., 11 A.M.–9 P.M. Sun., lunch $8–15, dinner $8–26) doesn't take reservations (except for lunch, and then only for parties of six or more). Waiting for a table as servers whiz by with steamed mussels, steak frites, and hot-out-of-the-oven macaroni gratin is downright torturous. But the torture is worth it. Tucked away in residential Point Breeze, the European-style eatery is the darling of East End foodies. Its name, beer selection, and several signature dishes betray the owners' fondness for Belgium. The Belgian-style frites, served with basil mayo, are simply phenomenal. Golden waffles with notes of caramelized sugar make for particularly long waits during Sunday brunch (11 A.M.–3 P.M., $5–22). Plans for a sister restaurant in the Highland Park neighborhood, Park Bruges Café, were underway in mid-2010.

Ethiopian

Two Ethiopian restaurants have sprouted in the shadow of the magnificent East Liberty Presbyterian Church in recent years, giving Pittsburghers a chance to broaden their palates and an excuse to eat with their hands. Both offer an ample variety of authentic meat and vegetarian dishes and sampler platters for parties unfamiliar with Ethiopian cuisine.

Abay (130 S. Highland Ave., 412/661-9736, www.abayrestaurant.com, lunch 11:30 A.M.–2:30 P.M. Tues.–Sun., dinner 5–10 P.M. Tues.–Sat. and 5–9 P.M. Sun., $12–14) became the city's first Ethiopian restaurant when it opened in 2004. It's a BYOB, so first pay a visit to the wine and spirits store in the nearby Eastside retail complex or overpay for a six-pack of beer at an area bar. Corkage is $2.50 per bottle of wine, $3 per six-pack. Don't be put off by the traditional basket-like tables and backless stools at the front of the restaurant. Abay (pronounced "uh-by") has plenty of regular tables and chairs, including a large round table fit for King Arthur and crew. It accepts reservations for groups of eight or more.

Tana (5929 Baum Blvd., 412/665-2770, www .tanaethiopiancuisine.com, 11 A.M.–2:30 P.M. Tues.–Sun., dinner 5–11 P.M. daily, $11–20) boasts a selection of Ethiopian beers and wines, including a unique honey wine known as *tej*. It makes its own *injera*, the spongy flatbread that doubles as food and eating utensil. (Abay buys *injera* from a bakery that makes nothing else.) Things get lively on Wednesday and Saturday nights, when Tana hosts live music. Jazz is the featured genre on Wednesdays.

French

A stone's throw from East Liberty's "little Ethiopia," **Paris 66** (6018 Centre Ave., 412/404-8166, www.paris66bistro.com, lunch 11 A.M.–2:30 P.M. Tues.–Sat., dinner 5–9:30 P.M. Tues.–Sat., Sun. brunch 10 A.M.–2:30 P.M., $5–17) offers sweet and savory crepes, soups and salads, quiches, puff pastry pizzas, and *plats du jour* amid framed Toulouse-Lautrec prints and a clock showing the time in France. Though inspired by the "city of love," the long, narrow restaurant is too loud to be romantic. Most tables are close enough for making new acquaintances. The savory buckwheat crepes, which French-born owner Frédéric Rongier learned to make from his great-grandfather, are suitable for the gluten-averse. Paris 66, which opened in 2009, is so very un-French in at least one way: It's a BYOB. Corkage is $5 per bottle of wine, $1 per person for beer. Patio dining is available in the warmer months.

For a crepe fix sans table service, try **Crepes Parisiennes,** with locations in Oakland (207 S. Craig St., 412/683-1912, 9 A.M.–5 P.M. Tues.–Fri., 10 A.M.–4 P.M. Sat.–Sun., $10) and Shadyside (732 Filbert St., 412/683-2333, 10 A.M.–5 P.M. Tues.–Sat., 10 A.M.–4 P.M. Sun.).

Italian

Named for a volcanic field not far from Naples, Squirrel Hill's **La Cucina Flegrea** (2114 Murray Ave., 412/521-2082, www.lacucinaflegrea.com, $15–27) serves up regional specialties along with more familiar Italian dishes. Owner Anna Fevola is likely to greet you as you skirt the kitchen en route to one of two small dining rooms. The warm, crusty bread is hard to resist, but save your appetite for the generously portioned entrées. One excellent choice is rigatoni alla vodka, spiked with sun-dried tomatoes and topped with imported Parmigiano-Reggiano cheese. Risotto is available on Wednesdays only. The wine list is heavy on reds from central and southern Italy. Bring your own bottle if you can stomach the $18 corkage.

La Cucina Flegrea isn't the only Italian eatery along Murray Avenue. Three of the Burgh's best pizza joints are found within a two-block stretch. Each offers hoagies and Italian staples such as ravioli and manicotti in addition to pizza by the slice or pie. In business since 1958, **Mineo's Pizza House** (2128 Murray Ave., 412/521-9864, www.mineospizza.com, 11 A.M.–1 A.M. Sun.–Thurs., 11 A.M.–2 A.M. Fri.–Sat., pie $11–29) has enough far-flung devotees that it overnights half-baked frozen pizzas anywhere in the country. Local lore has it that some guy up for some job in California brought two Mineo's pies to his interview after learning that his potential employer hailed from Pittsburgh. He was hired on the spot. Mineo's is the only one of the triumvirate to make Sicilian pizzas in addition to regular-crust red and white pies. **Aiello's Pizza** (2112 Murray Ave., 412/521-9973, www.aiellospizza.com, 11 A.M.–2 A.M. daily, pie $11–31) opened on the same block in 1978.

It's the only one of the three to offer steak as a topping. The youngest of the bunch, **Napoli Pizzeria** (2006 Murray Ave., 412/521-1744, www.napolipizzasqhill.com, 11 A.M.–11 P.M. Sun.–Thurs., 11 A.M.–midnight Fri.–Sat., pie $10–24), has been around for more than 25 years. The 70-ish mother of one of its owners makes the meatballs.

Mediterranean

Casbah (229 S. Highland Ave., 412/661-5656, www.bigburrito.com/casbah, lunch 11:30 A.M.–2:30 P.M. Mon.–Sat., brunch 11 A.M.–2 P.M. Sun., dinner 5–10 P.M. Mon.–Thurs., 5–11 P.M. Fri.–Sat., 5–9 P.M. Sun., lunch $8–16, dinner $19–36) doesn't look like much from the outside. A field hospital (think *M*A*S*H*) comes to mind. Step inside, however, and the truth is revealed: This is one of Pittsburgh's chicest dining destinations. The first door opens into an all-weather patio with the sun-bleached look of a Mediterranean garden. A catwalk of sorts stretches from the entrance to the hostess stand, bringing out your best A-list strut. The dining room, bar, and lounge beyond the next door are so dimly lit in the evening hours that you need a flashlight—or at least a cell phone—to read the ever-changing menu. Ah, the menu: Casbah pays homage to Mediterranean and Northern African cuisines while showcasing the lamb, poultry, and produce of Pennsylvania farmers. Its wine cellar is one of the best in town. Part of the restaurant group behind such highly regarded establishments as Eleven and Soba, Casbah offers roughly 40 wines by the glass and an array of wine flights that allow you to sample three for about the cost of one cocktail. It's also one of the best places in the Burgh to broaden your cheese vocabulary. Try three for $12, five for $16, or seven for $20. The prix fixe Sunday brunch ($22 per person, children 12 and under $12) is a worthy splurge.

Mexican

With offerings like Pennsyltucky Fried Tofu and Thai Curry Burrito, **Mad Mex** (370 Atwood St., 412/681-5656, www.madmex.com,

PITTSBURGH

11 A.M.–1 A.M. daily, $8–12) is a far cry from traditional Mexican. Come November, the already lengthy burrito list includes the Gobblerito—Thanksgiving dinner wrapped in a tortilla. "Vegheads," as the jocular menu calls them, have plenty of options. Just about every burrito and enchilada dish can be made with portobellos or marinated tofu as well as chicken, steak, or shrimp. Vegans can even request soy cheese and tofu sour cream. During happy *hora* (4:30–6:30 P.M. weekdays), the small Oakland restaurant is as crowded with coeds as Cancun during spring break. Drafts and wings are half price, and 22-ounce "Big Azz" margaritas, normally $10, sell for $7. Original, kiwi, strawberry, mango, and raspberry margaritas are always available; be sure to ask about seasonal flavors. Note of warning: Parking in this student-heavy 'hood is a pain in the azz. Mad Mex, a small chain, is part of the big Burrito Restaurant Group family, which also includes Eleven and Casbah.

Middle Eastern

Opened in 1972 by three grad students from Syria, **Ali Baba** (404 S. Craig St., 412/682-2829, www.alibabapittsburgh.com, lunch 11:30 A.M.–2:30 P.M. Mon.–Fri., dinner 4–9:45 P.M. daily, lunch $4–7, dinner $7–15) has never lost touch with the needs of cash-strapped scholars. Most lunch offerings are under $5, dinner specials top out at $15, and even the "premium" beers sell for less than $4.

(If you prefer wine with your lamb kebabs or baked *kibbee,* bring your own.) The $14.95 "maza platter," which has enough hummus, baba ghanouj, tabouli, feta, and olives to serve as dinner for two, is a godsend to the city's vegetarians. Given its low prices and location in the heart of the university district, no one would fault you for envisioning a dive. But the skylighted space is classy enough for visiting lecturers and even ladies who lunch.

Squirrel Hill, to the east of Oakland, boasts two recommendable Middle Eastern restaurants on the same block. Local Lebanese transplants swear by the *mujaddara* at the **Mediterranean Grill** (5824 Forbes Ave., 412/521-5505). The basement-level restaurant is short on ambience, but its food more than compensates for the lack of natural light. **Aladdin's Eatery** (5878 Forbes Ave., 412/421-5100, www.aladdins eatery.com, 11 A.M.–10:30 P.M. Mon.–Thurs., 11 A.M.–11:30 P.M. Fri.–Sat., 11 A.M.–10 P.M. Sun., $6–13), part of a chain with more than two dozen outlets in five states, serves Lebanese-inspired food and arguably the best smoothies in the Steel City. Its wrap-like rolled pitas and pita "pitzas" are good gateways for strangers to Middle Eastern cuisine. The lentil soup is heaven on a wintry day. You'll also find Aladdin's in the Pittsburgh suburbs of **Mt. Lebanon** (630 Washington Rd., 412/344-1111), **Ross Township** (4885 McKnight Rd., 412/369-9600), and **Cranberry Township** (20424 Rte. 19, 724/778-9800).

Information and Services

VisitPittsburgh (800/359-0758, www.visit pittsburgh.com), the official tourism promotion agency for Pittsburgh and the rest of Allegheny County, has several welcome centers stocked with brochures and maps and staffed by knowledgeable folk. If you're flying into Pittsburgh International Airport, look for the welcome center near baggage claim (9 A.M.–4 P.M. Mon., 10 A.M.–5 P.M. Tues.–Fri., 10 A.M.–6 P.M. Sat.,

and 2–6 P.M. Sun.). VisitPittsburgh's Downtown welcome center is located in the Fifth Avenue Palace (120 5th Ave.). Weekday hours are 10 A.M.–6 P.M. Mon.–Fri. and 9 A.M.–5 P.M. April–October. It's open 9 A.M.–4 P.M. Saturday and 10 A.M.–3 P.M. Sunday. The Strip District welcome center inside the Senator John Heinz History Center (1212 Smallman St.) is open 10 A.M.–5 P.M. daily.

The agency's website is also a great place to gather information. Multiple guides are available for the downloading. You can request that a visitors guide be mailed to you, but you may have to wait several weeks for it.

Pittsburgh has two daily newspapers: the *Pittsburgh Post-Gazette* (www.post-gazette.com) and the *Pittsburgh Tribune-Review* (www.pittsburghlive.com), but when it comes to planning their leisure time, most locals reach for the free *Pittsburgh City Paper* (www.pghcitypaper.com), which comes out on Wednesdays. The monthly *Pittsburgh Magazine* (www.wqed.org/mag) also keeps a trained eye on the city's food, arts, and entertainment landscape.

Getting There

Roughly 18 miles from downtown, **Pittsburgh International Airport** (PIT, 412/472-3525, www.flypittsburgh.com) is easily navigable. Thanks to people-moving technologies considered cutting edge when the airport opened in 1992, it's quite possible to traverse hundreds of yards with nary a stride. Moving walkways link the parking lots and a Hyatt Regency hotel with the landside terminal. And trams transport travelers between the landside and airside terminals. PIT is served by about a dozen carriers, including budget airlines JetBlue, AirTran, and Southwest. It's easy to stay occupied while waiting for a plane. Shop in the Airmall, toss back a beer, admire the Alexander Calder mobile above the airside core, or power up your laptop and get some work done. There's free Wi-Fi throughout the four concourses.

At less than $3, the **28X Airport Flyer** (412/442-2000, www.portauthority.org) is the cheapest ride into town (unless, of course, you have a pal in Pittsburgh). It operates seven days a week, including holidays. Service from the airport starts at 5:55 A.M. on weekdays and 6 A.M. on weekends and holidays and ends around midnight. A bus shows up every 20–35 minutes, depending on the time of day. Expect to reach Downtown in about 40 minutes. The bus then makes its way past Duquesne University, Carlow University, and the University of Pittsburgh before reaching the end of its route at Carnegie Mellon University.

SuperShuttle (800/258-3826, www.supershuttle.com) provides shared-van service to Downtown, Shadyside, Oakland, the North Shore, and other neighborhoods. You can book online or by phone or simply stop by the SuperShuttle counter in the airport's ground transportation area. If you're bound for Downtown, you'll pay $18–25. The same trip by cab will set you back $40–45.

It's also possible to arrive in Pittsburgh by rail. **Amtrak** trains (local 412/471-6170, general 800/872-7245, www.amtrak.com) pull into a historic station at 1100 Liberty Avenue in Downtown, just shy of the Strip District. Constructed at the turn of the 20th century, the station building featured a spectacular waiting room that's since been converted into a lobby for well-heeled residential and office tenants. Still, there's something romantic about train travel, especially in a state as scenic as this one. Amtrak's Pennsylvanian, which travels daily between New York City and Pittsburgh, rolls through Amish farmlands and the famous Horseshoe Curve near Altoona. The Capitol Limited route linking Washington, D.C., and Chicago also serves Pittsburgh.

Pittsburgh's **Greyhound** bus terminal (local 412/392-6526, general 800/231-2222, www.greyhound.com) is across from the Amtrak station, at 55 11th Street.

Thanks to **Megabus** (877/462-6342, us.megabus.com), it's possible to get to Pittsburgh from cities including Philadelphia and New York for less than the cost of a cappuccino. Pittsburgh's Megabus stop is under the David L. Lawrence Convention Center, near the intersection of 10th Street and Penn Avenue.

PITTSBURGH

Getting Around

With its rivers, hills, and uncommon street grids, Pittsburgh is notoriously hard to navigate. ("Undoubtedly the cockeyedest city in the United States," marveled newspaper columnist Ernie Pyle in 1937. "It must have been laid out by a mountain goat. It's up and down, and around and around, and in betwixt.") If you're renting a car, spring for a GPS device. Fortunately, a car is not at all necessary—unless you have your heart set on exploring the hinterlands. Neighborhoods including Downtown, the Strip District, the North Shore, the South Side Flats, and Oakland are fairly walkable, and public buses can get you from one to the other. The **Port Authority of Allegheny County** (412/442-2000, www.portauthority .org) operates some 180 bus routes, plus five light-rail routes and the Mount Washington inclines. Its website has a handy "trip planner" feature that spits out suggested itineraries based on your starting point, destination, tolerance for transfers, and willingness to walk. Easier

still, you can call Port Authority and speak to a live trip planner.

The fare structure is zone-based, meaning what you pay depends on the distance you travel. To promote the use of transit, the Port Authority deemed most of Downtown a "free fare zone." There's a bit of fine print: bus rides are free between 4 A.M. and 7 P.M., after which they're $1.50. Trips on the "T," Pittsburgh's light-rail system, are always free within this zone. Standard fares for travel between zones range from $1.50 to $3.25. Transfers are an extra 50 cents. Seniors with ID ride for free, and children 6–11 pay half price. People with disabilities also pay half price except 7–8 A.M. and 4:30–5:30 P.M. weekdays. Check the website for information on weekly, monthly, and annual passes.

If your visit is short, getting acquainted with the public transportation system probably isn't a priority. Cabbing it is always an option. Call **Yellow Cab Co.** at 412/321-8100.

Vicinity of Pittsburgh

Pittsburgh's environs boast quite a few distinctions. Lawrence County is the self-proclaimed Fireworks Capital of America. Indiana County, which lays claim to the title of Christmas Tree Capital of the World, gave us Hollywood legend Jimmy Stewart. Armstrong County was once home to Nellie Bly, the crusading journalist who circled the globe in 72 days in the late 1800s. Indiana County has a town with the unique name of Home; Armstrong County has Parker, the smallest city in the country; and Washington County has 80 buildings constructed almost entirely of poured-in-place concrete—one of Thomas Edison's not-so-bright ideas. But you're interested in destinations, not distinctions, so let me cut to the chase. In the parlance of tourism promoters, these counties are Pittsburgh's "countryside." There

are, indeed, bucolic settings. There are even Amish communities. But there are also highways, drab malls, unsightly industry, and generally depressed areas. That's not to discourage you from leaving the city. By all means, take a daycation. If you know where to go (and you will, if you continue reading), you won't be disappointed.

WASHINGTON AND GREENE COUNTIES

To Pittsburgh's south, Washington County boasts a burgeoning hotel and shopping district centered on a harness race track and casino. It has family-friendly attractions too, including the state's largest and oldest trolley museum. What Greene County lacks in attractions it makes up for in events. Among them:

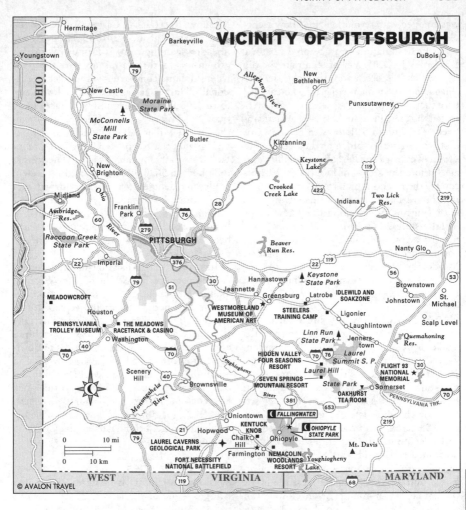

a professional bull riding competition, a festival devoted to a species of swallows, and the **Sheep and Fiber Fest** (724/627-8119, www .sheepandfiber.com, third weekend in May), which celebrates the county's heritage as a wool producer. Between them they have almost 30 covered bridges—cause for an annual festival that's not to be missed.

Meadowcroft

In 1973, University of Pittsburgh archeologists began excavation at a farm in northern Washington County. Over the course of six years, they unearthed evidence that humans have been in the Americas for at least 16,000 years. The site, now known as **Meadowcroft Rockshelter** (401 Meadowcroft Rd., Avella, 724/587-3412, www.heinzhistorycenter.org, noon–5 P.M. Wed.–Sat. and 1–5 P.M. Sun. Memorial Day–Labor Day, open weekends in May and Sept.–Oct., closed Nov.–April, admission $10, seniors $9, children 6–16 $5) was credited with revolutionizing "how archeologists view the peopling of the New World" upon its designation as a National Historic Landmark in 2005. Visitors can tour the dig site, which is protected by an enclosure, and learn about the hunter-gatherers who camped here thousands of years ago. Nearby, two recreated villages illustrate how later Americans lived. The **Indian Village** with its wigwams and "three sisters" garden offers a glimpse of life in Western Pennsylvania some 400 years ago, before the arrival of Europeans. Visitors can try their hand at prehistoric chores: grinding corn with mortar and pestle, cracking nuts with a nutting stone, and such. **Meadowcroft Village** simulates a 19th century rural community, complete with blacksmith shop, covered bridge, and one-room schoolhouse. Meadowcroft is operated by Pittsburgh's Heinz History Center, an affiliate of the Smithsonian Institution.

Pennsylvania Trolley Museum

Home to nearly 50 streetcars, the Pennsylvania Trolley Museum (1 Museum Rd., Washington, 724/228-9256, www.pa-trolley.org, 10 A.M.–4 P.M. Mon.–Fri. and 11 A.M.–5 P.M. Sat.–Sun. Memorial Day–Labor Day, open Fri.–Mon. April–May and Sept.–Dec., closed Jan.–March, admission $9, seniors $8, children 3–15 $5, family $30) transports visitors to an earlier era. The price of admission includes unlimited trolley rides and a guided tour of the car barn, which houses part of the collection. Tours begin at a quarter past the hour; the last begins 45 minutes before closing. On most days, the museum also offers a 1:15 P.M. tour of a 28,000-square-foot building where 30 more trolleys are displayed. It costs an additional $4 for adults, $2 for children. There's a shaded picnic area on the museum grounds, so pack a lunch if you'd like to stay a while. Check the website for special events. In early April, the Easter Bunny comes aboard. Santa makes appearances starting in late November.

The Meadows Racetrack & Casino

Just half an hour from downtown Pittsburgh,

Meadows Racetrack & Casino (210 Racetrack Rd., Washington, 724/503-1200, www .meadowsgaming.com) is Disney World for grown-ups, a thrill-a-minute environment where dreams come true—albeit very occasionally. Harness racing at The Meadows dates to the 1960s. The track hosts live races more than 200 days a year, year-round. It's home to the Delvin Miller Adios, which is to harness racing what the Kentucky Derby or Belmont Stakes are to thoroughbred racing. The winner took home a $620,000 purse in 2009. Delvin Miller, incidentally, was a trainer/driver who won almost 2,500 races and more than $11 million during a racing career that started in his teens and lasted until a mere three months before his death at 83. Adios was his famous bay stallion.

In June 2007, less than nine months after receiving a gaming license, the Meadows opened a temporary casino. A $175 million, 350,000-square-foot permanent casino replaced it in April 2009. Gaming enthusiasts can take their pick of more than 3,500 slot machines and about 60 table games. An on-site bowling center offers 24 lanes, wait service, and a club-like atmosphere on weekends. Dining options range from a food court to the fancy **Bistecca** (4–10 P.M. Sun.–Thurs., 4–11 P.M. Fri.–Sat., $16– 38), a steakhouse and wine bar run by the minds behind Pittsburgh's Cioppino restaurant.

Covered Bridges

Washington County is home to 22 covered bridges—one of the largest concentrations in the country. Seven dot the hills of Greene County. Their jointly hosted **Covered Bridge Festival** (724/228-5520, www.visitwashing toncountypa.com, third weekend in Sept.) tends to be the busiest weekend of the year, a testament to the allure of so-called kissing bridges. Festivities take place at 10 bridges and include live music, horse-drawn wagon rides, crafting demonstrations, and clashing Civil War reenactors. (Incidentally, Canonsburg holds its Pennsylvania Bavarian Oktoberfest the same weekend. The three-day event features two stages of entertainment, a fireworks extravaganza, and, of course, beer. Bottom line: there's a good time around every bend.) Most other times of year, the covered bridges of Washington and Greene Counties are quiet idylls. Visit the website of the Washington County Tourism Promotion Agency, provided above, to request a free driving guide or download a digital version. It's organized into four driving tours and includes descriptions and histories of each bridge. Many are more than a hundred years old.

Bradford and Lemoyne Houses

In the late 18th century, Washington County was a cauldron of political unrest. Its frontier communities, frustrated by the lack of protection from Indian attacks and the high number of absentee landlords, among other things, bridled at a whiskey tax imposed by the newly hatched federal government. Local mobs chased off tax collectors—or worse. The county's deputy attorney general, one David Bradford, was among the leaders of what came to be known as the Whiskey Rebellion. When President George Washington ordered 13,000 troops to the region that bore his name, Bradford fled to present-day Louisiana (Spanish-owned at the time), abandoning his stately stone home in the county seat. The Pennsylvania Historical and Museum Commission assumed control of the **David Bradford House** (175 S. Main St., Washington, 724/222-3604, www .bradfordhouse.org, open May–Oct. 11 A.M.–4 P.M. Wed. and Fri.–Sat., 2–7 P.M. Thurs., other times by appointment, admission $5 or $7 for two) in 1959. Restored to its 18th century design, the house is furnished as it would have been when Bradford and his family lived in it. Visitors can take home a full-sized replica of a Whiskey Rebellion flag for $75, which helps fund operations and repairs to the 1788 house.

History buffs will find more to love around the corner at the **LeMoyne House** (49 E. Maiden St., Washington, 724/225-6740, www .wchspa.org, 11 A.M.–4 P.M. Tues.–Fri., admission $5, students $3). Built in 1812, the house served as a stop on the Underground Railroad. It's named for Francis Julius LeMoyne, the physician who risked his personal freedom by sheltering runaway slaves in defiance of the Fugitive Slave Law of 1850. The National Historic Landmark is now a museum filled with period artifacts and headquarters of the Washington County Historical Society.

Spectator Sports

Baseball fans tired of watching the Pittsburgh Pirates struggle ought head south to Consol Energy Park, just off Interstate 70 in Washington County. The 5,000-seat ballpark is home to a professional team that wins more often than not. The **Washington Wild Things** (724/250-9555, www.washingtonwildthings .com), members of the Frontier League, played their inaugural season in 2002 and reached the playoffs in each of their first six seasons. Single-game tickets start at an affordable $6. Premier box seats go for $12.

Next to Consol Energy Park is the headquarters of **PONY Baseball and Softball** (1951 Pony Place, Washington, 724/225-1060, www.pony.org), an international program for children as young as 4. It houses a museum as well as offices. Mark McGuire, Alex Rodriguez, and Tony Gwynn are among the 800 plus PONY graduates who went on to Major League Baseball careers. You can catch a glimpse of future baseball greats during the **Pony League World Series.** The eight-team, double-elimination tournament for 13- and 14-year-olds takes place in Washington every August.

Shopping

Shopaholics should race to **Tanger Outlets** (Exit 41 off I-79, 724/225-8435, www.tanger outlet.com/washington, 9 A.M.–9 P.M. Mon.–Sat., 10 A.M.–6 P.M. Sun.), a stone's throw from The Meadows Racetrack & Casino. The outlet center, which opened in 2008, boasts Coach, Calvin Klein, Banana Republic, Tommy Hilfiger, Nike, and about 70 other stores. Visit the website before you go for a rundown on current sales and printable coupons.

PITTSBURGH

Accommodations

One look at the **Montgomery Mansion** (1274 National Pike Hwy., Claysville, 724/663-7767, www.montgomerymansion.net, $99–125) and you'll know why locals call it the gingerbread house. The extra ornate Victorian was built in the 1870s and owned, at one point, by the Catholic church next door. Converting it into a B&B with modern-day amenities was a 12-year project. Period furniture and Persian carpets make the inside as fetching as the outside. Problem is, do you choose the Holly room with its solid copper tub and surround shower or the Heather room with its stained glass doors and private sauna? Rooms at **Grammy Rose's Bed & Breakfast** (405 E. Maiden St., Washington, 724/228-1508, www.grammyroses.com, $95–125), another stunning Victorian, are named for the four granddaughters of proprietors Tim and Rose, whose hospitality makes guests feel like family. In-room HBO is a nice touch but hardly necessary with The Meadows Racetrack & Casino, Tanger Outlets, and other attractions just a few miles away.

Built in 1923, **The George Washington** (60 S. Main St., Washington, 724/225-3200, www.thegeorgewashington.com, $99–380) played host to Harry S. Truman, Al Capone, Marilyn Monroe, and John F. Kennedy before falling into disrepair in the latter part of the century. Several years of renovations by current owner Kyrk Pyros culminated in its reopening as a hotel in 2008. Accommodations range from 600-square-foot rooms to 1,800-square-foot suites complete with Jacuzzis. Amenities include meeting and banquet facilities, two restaurants, and a lounge named for David Bradford, the Whiskey Rebellion leader who lived a stone's throw away. The Pioneer Grill, open for dinner, is notable for its massive murals by the late Malcolm Parcell, a Washington native. Painted in the 1930s and valued at millions, they portray the settling of Washington and the anti-tax uprising that put it on the map.

Chores are part of the fun at kid-friendly ◖ **Weatherbury Farm** (1061 Sugar Run Rd., Avella, 724/587-3763, www.weatherburyfarm.com, one night $169–212, longer stay as low as $92 per night), where guests can help "Farmer Dale" pump the water, feed the animals, and gather the eggs. Doing nothing at all is also encouraged. Accommodations on the beef and sheep farm include two-story suites in a one-time livery stable and rooms in what used to be a summer kitchen. All rooms and suites have en suite baths, most of which have clawfoot tubs. A getaway geared toward grown-ups, **So'Journey Farm** (1841 Bristoria Rd., Holbrook, 724/499-5680, www.sojourneyfarm.com, $130) serves up gourmet meals and a generous helping of serenity. The 45-acre farm is home to grass-fed Scottish Highland cattle, pastured chickens, and one rug-hooking ace happy to share her expertise. Catfish are an easy catch in the spring-fed pond and cooked to order.

Overlooking the banks of the Monongahela River, **The Captain's Watch Inn** (106 Water St., Greensboro, 724/943-3131, www.thecaptainswatch.net, $85–175) makes an excellent base camp for hiking and other outdoor recreation. A few hundred yards downstream from the B&B is the eastern terminus of the **Warrior Trail,** a path worn by Native Americans that stretches more than 60 miles to the Ohio River in West Virginia. Guests can take in the Mon from a wicker rocker on the wraparound verandah or paddle across it in one of the Captain's canoes. Friendship Hill National Historic Site, home of early American politician Albert Gallatin, is within walking distance of the opposite shore. Bicycles are also free to guests.

Food

Born in Frank Sarris's basement, **Sarris Candies** (511 Adams Ave., Canonsburg, 724/745-4042, www.sarriscandies.com, 9 A.M.–9 P.M. Mon.–Sat., 11 A.M.–9 P.M. Sun.) has grown into an operation the size of a football field and a favorite of Pittsburgh-area fund-raising campaigns. The factory store is a sweet tooth's fantasyland, complete with 1,500-pound chocolate castle. Slide into a red and brass booth in the connected Ice Cream Parlour, designed to evoke an old-fashioned soda fountain, and devour a sundae made with Sarris's ice cream and toppings.

"Farm to table" takes on new meaning at **❰ The SpringHouse** (1531 Rte. 136, Washington, 724/228-3339, www.spring housemarket.com, 9 A.M.–9 P.M. Mon.–Sat., noon–9 P.M. Sun., winter hours 9 A.M.–7 P.M. Mon.–Thurs., 9 A.M.–8 P.M. Fri.–Sat., 208>Sat., noon–9 P.M. Sun., $7–12), located on a 420-acre family farm. Part creamery, part country store, and part restaurant, the SpringHouse offers lunch and dinner buffets all week and a breakfast buffet on Saturdays. Wash down a from-scratch dessert with a glass of milk courtesy of the Holstein and Jersey cows grazing out back. Got kids? Check the farm's schedule of special events, which include an Easter egg hunt, hayrides, hog roasts, and breakfast with Santa.

Proving that love is blind, locals pack the timeworn **Shorty's Lunch** (34 W. Chestnut St., Washington, 724/228-9919, 8 A.M.–5 P.M. Mon.–Sat., $5), which has been serving chili dogs, gravy fries, and other greasy goodies for more than 70 years. Another favorite of locals, **Old Mexico of Washington** (250 Oak Spring Rd., Washington, 724/250-7899, www.old mexicoofwashington.com, 11 A.M.–2 P.M. and 5–10 P.M. Mon.–Thurs., 11 A.M.–10 P.M. Fri.–Sat., 11 A.M.–9 P.M. Sun., $5–13) specializes in strong margaritas and sizzling fajitas. Servers who *no habla ingles* boost the authenticity quotient.

Fall-off-the-bone ribs flavored with brown sugar and soy sauce have graced the menu of **The Back Porch** (114 Speers St., Belle Vernon, 724/483-4500, www.backporch restaurant.com, 11:30 A.M.–9 P.M. Tues.–Sat., 4–9 P.M. Sun., $10–29, reservations recommended) since it opened on Valentine's Day in 1975. Also known for its beef, duck, lamb, and seafood dishes, the fine dining restaurant near the bank of the Monongahela River occupies an 1806 landmark said to have served as a stop on the Underground Railroad. Original brickwork is still visible in the dining rooms. A bistro menu is available in the bar area, open 4–9 P.M. Tuesday–Sunday.

The even older **Century Inn** (2175 National Rd. East, Scenery Hill, 724/945-6600, www .centuryinn.com, lunch noon–3 P.M. daily, dinner 4:30–8 P.M. Mon.–Thurs., 4:30–9 P.M. Fri.–Sat., 4–7 P.M. Sun., limited hours in winter, $11–26, reservations recommended) has played host to the likes of George Washington, Andrew Jackson, and James Polk. Its menu changes as often as the chef goes shopping, which is to say it changes daily. Cross your fingers for creamy peanut soup the way Thomas Jefferson liked it. Libations include international microbrews, domestic and imported wines, and some 20 types of single malt Scotch whiskey. In operation since 1794, the antique-filled inn closes for a couple of weeks in January, then serves on Fridays and Saturdays only until April.

Information
The **Washington County Tourism Promotion Agency** (724/228-5520, www.visitwashing toncountypa.com) has offices at 273 South Main Street in downtown Washington and in the food court at Tanger Outlets. The former is open 9 A.M.–4:30 P.M. weekdays and the latter 10 A.M.–6 P.M. Monday–Saturday and noon–4 P.M. Sunday. The website of the **Greene County Tourist Promotion Agency** (417 E. Roy Furman Hwy., Waynesburg, 724/627-8687, www.greenecountytourism.org) is also a good source of information and includes a printable calendar of events.

BEAVER, BUTLER, AND LAWRENCE COUNTIES
The counties to the west and north of Pittsburgh are blessed with spectacular state parks. Recreational opportunities run the gamut, from barbequing on a pontoon boat to rappelling down a rock face. The area also affords visitors a glimpse of two uncommon cultures, including one that's now extinct. When you see how the Harmonists lived in the 19th century or how the Amish live now, you might see your own life in a new light.

Harmony Society Sights
Two towns a half hour's drive from downtown Pittsburgh offer a window into the curious way

of life of the Harmonists, a Christian communal society that gained riches and fame but died out anyway. Adherence to celibacy will do that. Their story begins in southern Germany, where in the late 1700s, a peasant-turned-preacher named George Rapp and his followers split from the Lutheran Church. Life wasn't easy for the separatists. They were harassed and imprisoned; their books, confiscated. In 1803, Rapp made the journey to the United States. He bought a tract of land in Butler County and summoned his followers. There, they formally organized themselves as the Harmony Society. Membership required relinquishment of all possessions to Rapp and the Society. The band of pietists swiftly carved a town, Harmony, out of the wilderness. Convinced that the Second Coming of Christ was around the corner, they adopted celibacy to purify themselves. They channeled their energy into agriculture and industry, earning a reputation for excellent textiles and woolens, wines and whiskey.

The Harmonists didn't stay for long, relocating to Indiana after 10 years, but Harmony hasn't forgotten them. In 1974, the area that includes their surviving buildings was designated a National Historic Landmark District. What used to be a Harmonist warehouse is now the main building of the **Harmony Museum** (218 Mercer St., Harmony, 724/452-7341, www.harmonymuseum.org, 1–4 P.M. Tues.–Sun., admission $5, seniors $4, children 6–17 $3), which houses a modest collection of Harmonist furniture and other artifacts. Visitors can descend into a vaulted stone cellar where wines were fermented. The museum isn't devoted solely to the Society. It also tells the story of those who came before, including Native Americans and a young George Washington, and those who followed, including the Mennonites who purchased the Harmonists' holdings. Mennonite stoneworkers were contracted to construct the limestone wall that surrounds the **Harmonist Cemetery** along Route 68 just east of town. A hundred early Harmonists are buried there in unmarked graves; the single gravestone is that of Rapp's

son, who died in an industrial accident. Test your strength at the one-ton revolving stone gate.

Harmony, not nearly as prosperous as in the days of the Harmonists, is about 30 miles north of downtown Pittsburgh. Closer yet is the Society's third and final commune. The Harmonists moved back to Pennsylvania in 1824, this time settling along the Ohio River in Beaver County, less than 20 miles northwest of Pittsburgh. They called their new home Economy. Six acres of their original holdings are now known as **Old Economy Village** (270 16th St., Ambridge, 724/266-4500, www .oldeconomyvillage.org, open March–Dec. 9 A.M.–5 P.M. Tues.–Sat. and noon–5 P.M. Sun., admission $9, seniors $8, children 3–11 $6). The National Historic Landmark comprises 17 buildings filled with thousands of Harmonist artifacts. Among them is Rapp's impressive house, flanked by a formal garden. Some of the buildings can only be visited during guided tours, which cost an additional $1 and depart from the ticket desk four times on weekdays and twice on Sundays. The visitors center features an exhibit and video that trace the history of the Harmonists, whose economic achievements captured the world's attention. Their diverse business ventures included silk manufacturing, railroad construction, and oil production. By the end of the 19th century, however, only a few Harmonists remained. The Society was dissolved in 1905, and Economy was renamed Ambridge by its new industrial heavyweight, the American Bridge Company.

Raccoon Creek State Park

To the west of Pittsburgh International Airport, Raccoon Creek State Park (3000 Rte. 18, 724/899-2200, www.dcnr.state.pa.us/stateParks/parks/raccooncreek.aspx) is a hiker's paradise. It offers a whopping 44 miles of trails, including a 19.5-mile backpacking loop with two places to bed down. Almost six miles of trails wind through the Wildflower Reserve at the eastern end of the park. Home to more than 700 species of plants, the 314-acre reserve attests to Mother Nature's bottomless creativity. The Wildflower Reserve Interpretive Center (724/899-3611) offers guided walks when her canvas is most colorful. The reserve is open 8 A.M. to sunset and closed to all activities other than hiking. Bikers and equestrians will find more than 15 miles of multiuse trails and roads in the 7,600-acre park. Most trails are open to cross-country skiing.

Small but beautiful, Raccoon Lake has a beach open from late May to mid-September and two boat launches. Canoes, kayaks, and rowboats are available for rent. Ice fishing and ice skating are permitted. If you have the cojones to hike in winter, be sure to do the short loop trail that begins and ends across from the park office on Route 18. It meanders past mineral springs prone to impressive ice formations. Above the springs are the remains of an 1800s resort that attracted believers in the springs' healing powers.

Raccoon Creek State Park allows camping year-round. A modern campground with about 170 tent and trailer sites is open from the second Friday in April through the third weekend in October. Rustic sites are available the rest of the year. The park also has 10 modern cabins and a three-bedroom lodge that sleeps as many as 10 people. Reserve online at www.pa.reserveworld.com or by calling 888-PA-PARKS.

Moraine State Park

Butler County's biggest attraction is Moraine State Park (bisected by east-west Route 422 and north-south Route 528, park office 225 Pleasant Valley Rd., Portersville, 724/368-8811, www.dcnr.state.pa.us/stateParks/parks/moraine.aspx, sunrise–sunset daily), a showpiece of environmental engineering. Like Shel Silverstein's Giving Tree, the land relinquished all it had in the 1800s: first its trees, then its limestone and clay, then its coal, and finally its oil and gas. In the 1900s, humans undid the damage, sealing deep mines, backfilling strip mines, plugging hundreds of gas and oil wells, and planting trees, shrubs, and grasses. The result: a win-win for man and nature. Dedicated in 1970, Moraine State Park offers year-round

recreation. Its greatest asset is the sprawling Lake Arthur, the 3,225-acre product of a dam built on Muddy Creek. Here's a recipe for summertime fun: pack a cooler with your favorite cookout foods, rent a pontoon boat and gas grill from **Crescent Bay Marina** (724/368-9955, www.moraineboatrentals.com), and spend the day cruising the lake. Kayaks, canoes, paddleboats, and motorboats are also available for rent. Bring your own fishing gear; the boat concessionaire sells nightcrawlers. Lake Arthur is a warm-water fishery, replete with northern pike, largemouth bass, channel catfish, and other species. You can learn more about the park's wildlife aboard the *Nautical Nature,* a 45-passenger enclosed pontoon boat operated by the Moraine Preservation Fund (724/368-9185, www.morainepreservation fund.com, cruise $8, seniors $7, children $5, dinner cruise $27, brunch cruise $20). The volunteer organization was instrumental in the reintroduction of osprey, once extirpated from Western Pennsylvania. The boat boards at the McDanel's launch on the northwest end of the lake.

Sailing is hugely popular here. If you're interested in the sport but "Grab that shackle!" is Greek to you, hook up with the **Moraine Sailing Club** (412/203-4053, www.moraine sailingclub.org), which offers lessons. The club's Community Sailing Program gives people with sailing experience but no boat of their own access to a fleet. Races and regattas are held throughout the summer. The annual **Regatta at Lake Arthur** (866/856-8444, www.regatta-at-lake-arthur.com, early August) attracts thousands to the park. Events include sailing, canoeing, and kayaking races; a boat parade open to any and all watercraft; a bass fishing tournament; and "dead fish polo," which finds canoeists thwacking a wet sponge with their paddles. Food and craft vendors are on hand during the weekend-long regatta, designed to showcase the great variety of recreational opportunities at the park.

Moraine boasts two beaches, an 18-hole disc golf course, nearly 30 miles of hiking trails, 20 miles of equestrian trails, a seven-mile paved bicycle trail, and a six-mile, not-for-sissies mountain bike trail. There's a bike rental facility (724/368-9011 or 724/658-7054) on North Shore Drive, about a mile and a half north of Route 422. It's open daily from Memorial Day weekend through Labor Day and weekends in off-peak months. Wintertime brings other recreational opportunities: cross-country skiing, snowmobiling, sledding, iceboating, ice fishing, and ice skating.

What Moraine State Park lacks are overnight facilities. There are 11 modern cabins on its 16,725 acres, which can be reserved online at www.pa.reserveworld.com or by calling 888-PA-PARKS. Backpackers can bed down at a shelter off of Link Road, and groups can reserve a primitive camping area, but anyone else with a yen to sleep under the stars should head to a nearby private campground. Best of the bunch: **Bear Run Campground** (184 Badger Hill Rd., Portersville, 724/368-3564, www.bear runcampground.com, mid-April–late Oct., tent sites $25– 45, RV sites $33–50, cabins and rental units $69–169). The "full-service family vacation center" has more than 300 tent and RV sites, a variety of cabins, free wi-fi, a heated swimming pool, a game room, and more.

McConnells Mill State Park

Just a few miles west of Moraine State Park and much smaller, McConnells Mill State Park (2697 McConnells Mill Rd., Portersville, 724/368-8091, www.dcnr.state.pa.us/stateparks/parks/mcconnellsmill.aspx, sunrise–sunset daily) is the adrenaline junkie's first choice. Its central feature is a steep-sided gorge created by the draining of glacial lakes thousands of years ago. Rocky outcrops, huge boulders, and the swift-flowing Slippery Rock Creek make for challenging hiking, climbing, and whitewater boating. The park has nine miles of hiking trails and two climbing and rappelling areas. One climbing spot is across the creek from the 1800s gristmill that gave the park its name. The other, near Breakneck Bridge, is for more advanced climbers. Rafters, canoeists, and kayakers generally start near a Route 422 bridge upstream of the park.

(There's no boat rental facility in the park.) Depending on water level, Slippery Rock Creek can provide a mild to wild ride; helmets are strongly recommended. Don't even think about going for a swim. More than a few people have drowned in the creek. Fishing is fine.

Guided tours of the aforementioned gristmill, which was retired in 1928, are offered Memorial Day through Labor Day. It can still do its water-powered thing. Corn grinding demonstrations are part of the fun at the **McConnells Mill Heritage Festival,** held the last full weekend in September. Festivalgoers can try their hand at old-time games and crafts and enjoy a Civil War encampment. Best of all, they get to see the forested park in its fall splendor.

Lawrence County Amish Country

Say "Pennsylvania Amish" and people think Lancaster County, several hours to the east of here. But Lawrence County has an Amish community of about 3,300, including the third largest Old Order Amish sect in the U.S. The largest concentration lives around the villages of New Wilmington and Volant, connected by Route 208. How do you experience Amish country? You get behind the wheel and drive— well below the speed limit if you happen to find yourself behind a horse-drawn buggy— and keep a lookout for hand-painted signs advertising goods for sale. The Lawrence County Tourist Promotion Agency (229 S. Jefferson St., New Castle, 888/284-7599, www.visitl awrencecounty.com) publishes a map that indicates the location of one-room schoolhouses, a covered bridge, and **Teena's Quilt Shop** (43 Quilt Shop Lane, Volant, 8 A.M.–5 P.M. Mon.– Sat.), an Amish purveyor of furniture and rugs as well as quilts. The shop, a favorite of bus groups, is on a farm about a mile and a half west of Volant on Route 208.

In Volant itself, Route 208 is an old-fashioned Main Street lined with homes converted to darling shops (www.volantshops .com). One specializes in miniatures, another in nostalgic candies and gums, a third in premium teas. **Native and Nature** (808 Main

St., 724/533-5054, www.nativeandnature
.com) sells jewelry and decorative items with a
Native American flavor, while **James Creek
Galleries** (425 Main St., 724/533-2313, www
.jamescreekgalleries.com) offers reasonably
priced reproductions of classic American furniture and décor. Both are open 10 A.M.–5 P.M.
Monday–Saturday and noon–5 P.M. Sunday.
Leave time for a tasting at **Volant Mill Winery**
(1229 Main St., 724/533-2500, www.volant
millwinery.com, 11 A.M.–5 P.M. Mon.–Thurs.,
11 A.M.–6 P.M. Fri.–Sat., noon–5 P.M. Sun.),
which makes some 20 reds, whites, fruit wines,
and a sparkling pink Catawba.

A must-stop while cruising the Amish countryside: the **Apple Castle** (277 Rte. 18, New
Wilmington, 724/652-3221, www.applecastle
.com, 9 A.M.–5:30 P.M. Dec.–July, 9 A.M.–8 P.M.
Aug.–Nov.), a fifth-generation family farm that
grows about 50 varieties of apples. The farm
market sells apples year-round and a variety of
other fruits and vegetables when they ripen. Its
inventory also includes cheese, local eggs, apple
butter, honey, and, often, baked goods made
by Amish neighbors. But the Apple Castle is
most famous for its honey wheat and apple
spice donuts. Wash one down with a glass of
fresh cider. The market is a good landmark if
you're searching for Poverty Point Road, part of
the driving route recommended by the tourism
agency. Pranksters love to steal the street sign.
Poverty Point is the first left after the Apple
Castle if you're driving north on Route 18.

Accommodations
Jacqueline House (3213 Rte. 956, New
Castle, 724/946-8382, www.jacquelinehouse
.com, $100–175) hosts John and Ida Felix
know a thing or two about pampering. The
couple owned a day spa for 11 years. Among
the spa services offered at their B&B: poolside
pedicures. Each of four guestrooms have private baths, queen beds, and cable TV.

Food
Not far from Moraine and McConnells Mill
State Parks, **◖ North Country Brewing Co.**
(141 S. Main St., Slippery Rock, 724/794-

2337, www.northcountrybrewing.com,
11 A.M.–11 P.M. Mon.–Thurs., 11 A.M.–midnight Fri.–Sat., 11 A.M.–10 P.M. Sun., $8–23)
is not what you'd expect from a bar in a college town. No Coors or wine coolers here. The
beers are handcrafted on site, the wines are
made in PA, the live entertainment is frequent,
and the grub ain't boring. The menu—plenty
mindful of herbivores—includes deep-fried
frog legs and elk burger. Owners Bob and Jodi
McCafferty are environmental stewards, or-
ganizing community cleanups and helping
to maintain the North Country Trail, which
stretches across seven states and comes within
a couple of miles of its eponymous brewpub.
They use local grains and fruits in their beers
and local produce and meats in their dishes.
And their operation is powered by renewable
energy. Now that's something to drink to.

The grand, Italianate-style **Harmony Inn**
(230 Mercer St., Harmony, 724/452-5124,
www.historicharmonyinn.com, kitchen
11 A.M.– 9 P.M. Sun.–Thurs. and 11 A.M.–
10 P.M. Fri.–Sat., bar open until midnight
Sun.–Thurs. and 2 A.M. Fri.–Sat., $8–17)
predates the Civil War and is reputedly
haunted—by friendly ghosts, of course. The
barkeeps and regulars are also a chummy lot.
The portions are large; put down your fork
before you're too full for the homemade desserts. Mexican and German specialties share
the menu with American fare. The haunt is a
stone's throw from the Harmony Museum.

Up in Amish country, **Tavern on the
Square** (108 N. Market St., New Wilmington,
724/946-2020, www.thetavernonthesquare
.blogspot.com, 11 A.M.–8 P.M. Mon.–Thurs.,
11 A.M.–9 P.M. Fri.–Sat., noon–5 P.M. Sun.,
$8–15) serves deep-fried green beans, sand-
wiches on fresh-baked croissants, and homemade pierogies, among other things. Once a
stop on the Underground Railroad, the tavern
is now famous for its sticky buns.

Information
You can download the latest visitors guides to
Beaver, Butler, and Lawrence Counties from
the websites of their respective tourism bureaus:

Beaver County Recreation & Tourism Department (Bradys Run Park Recreation Facility, 121 Bradys Run Rd., Beaver Falls, 724/770-2062, www.visitbeavercounty.com); **Butler County Tourism & Convention Bureau** (310 E. Grandview Ave., Zelienople, 724/234-4619, www.visitbutlercounty.com); and **Lawrence County Tourist Promotion Agency** (229 S. Jefferson St., New Castle, 888/284-7599, www.visitlawrencecounty.com).

ARMSTRONG AND INDIANA COUNTIES

Northeast of Pittsburgh and crisscrossed by waterways, Armstrong County beckons boaters and anglers. To its east, Indiana County offers miles and miles of rail-trails, the lovely Yellow Creek State Park with its 720-acre lake, an Amish community, and a museum dedicated to one very beloved screen legend.

Jimmy Stewart Museum

The star of *It's a Wonderful Life* got his start in life in the town of Indiana, about 60 miles from Pittsburgh. Born in 1908 in his parents' home on Philadelphia Street, James Maitland Stewart lent a hand in his family's hardware store long before he landed on the silver screen. He was a decorated Boy Scout before he was a decorated military pilot. Fans can learn about his roots and rise to fame at the Jimmy Stewart Museum (835 Philadelphia St., Indiana, 800/835-4669, www.jimmy.org, 10 A.M.–5 P.M. Mon.–Sat., noon–5 P.M. Sun., admission $7, seniors $6, children 7–17 $5) on the third floor of the public library. Dedicated in 1995 in celebration of Stewart's 87th birthday, the museum has several galleries and a 50-seat theater. Its collection includes something from each of Stewart's 81 films, including a propeller blade autographed by the cast of *Flight of the Phoenix*. A gallery devoted to *It's a Wonderful Life* features photos of cast members, posters, and a note from director Frank Capra. Visitors can watch film clips and career retrospectives in the theater with its velvet drapes and wine-colored seats. Full-length films are shown Saturdays and Sundays at 2 P.M. Stewart's lengthy filmography includes *Mr. Smith Goes to Washington, Vertigo,* and *The Philadelphia Story,* for which he won an Academy Award. He gave the Oscar statuette to his father, who proudly displayed it in his hardware store.

The museum isn't Indiana's only tribute to its favorite son, who died in 1997. The county airport, northeast of town, is named for him. A bronze statue of the screen legend stands on the lawn of the Indiana County Courthouse, next door to the museum. (There's a full-sized fiberglass replica in the museum.) On the other side of Philadelphia Street, a sundial marks the former location of J.M. Stewart & Co. Hardware. One block west on Philadelphia Street, a plaque identifies the doorstep that led to the house in which the actor was born. To see the house he moved to at age 5, head east on Philadelphia Street, make a left onto Jimmy Stewart Boulevard, and proceed to a set of concrete steps. His boyhood home at the top of the steps, 107 N. 7th Street, is still a private residence. Every November, Indiana marks the beginning of the holiday season with the *It's a Wonderful Life* **Festival and Parade** (724/463-6110, www.downtownindiana.org). A large decorated Christmas tree joins Jimmy on the courthouse lawn.

Smicksburg Amish Country

Like Volant and New Wilmington in Lawrence County, Indiana's County's Smicksburg is a place where cars share the roads with horse-drawn buggies. The area is home to more than 280 Old Order Amish families. Where there's a community of Amish, there's usually good shopping, and Smicksburg is no exception. The town has about 20 specialty shops—not counting Amish home-based businesses. With two locations, **The Drying Shed** (118 E. Kittanning St., 814/257-0192, and 23043 Rte. 954, 814/257-8101, www.smicksburgdryingshed.com, 10 A.M.–5 P.M. Mon.–Sat., noon–5 P.M. Sun.) has cornered the market in dried floral arrangements. Owners Patty and Alan Painter grow rows of sunflowers, celosia, lavender, and other plants on their nearby farm to keep pace with demand. They also sell sap buckets, rusty tin stars, jelly cupboards, and other country crafts. For locally crafted furniture, head to **Downtown Smicksburg Amish Country** (21875 Indiana Rd., 814/257-8696, www.smicksburgfurniture.com, 10 A.M.–5 P.M. Mon.–Sat., noon–5 P.M. Sun.). You'll find everything from gun cabinets to cradles, plus a wide variety of specialty foods and Amish-made goods such as baskets and doilies.

Just north of town, **Smicksburg Community Cheese** (24062 Rte. 954, 814/257-8972, www.smicksburgcheese.com, 8 A.M.–5 P.M. Mon.–Sat., noon–5 P.M. Sun.) is a locavore's delight. Amish farmers supply about 80,000 pounds of milk a week to the factory, which makes more than 30 varieties of cheese. Stop in to sample uncommon creations like chocolate cherry cheddar and chicken soup cheese. Locally made cheese deserves a locally made wine. No problem. Smicksburg's **Windgate Vineyards & Winery** (1998 Hemlock Acres Rd., 814/257-8797, www.windgatevineyards .com, noon–5 P.M. daily) has collected more than a hundred awards at regional and national

competitions since opening its doors in 1987. Amish Country White, full-bodied and fruity, and Eye of the Buck, an oak-aged red, are among the recent winners.

Accommodations

John Truett was living in Tampa, Florida, when an eBay real estate listing caught his eye. For sale: a century-old church and the house beside it, formerly a rectory for Episcopal clergy, in a Pennsylvania town he'd never of. Truett clicked "place bid." In October 2009, three and a half years after quitting his job with the Walt Disney Company and moving to the town he'd never heard of, he opened the **❰ The Old Parsonage B&B** (156 Siberian Ave., Leechburg, 724/236-0061, www.oldparson agebandb.com, $100–150) in the onetime rectory. Truett, a nondenominational minister, is quite catholic in his decorating tastes. There's an Egyptian-themed guestroom complete with sarcophagus and a Victorian-themed guestroom. There's also a honeymoon suite, perfect for couples who wed next door. Truett transformed the dilapidated church into the darling

© JOHN TRUETT

The Old Parsonage B&B and Enchanted Abbey Wedding Chapel

PITTSBURGH

Enchanted Abbey Wedding Chapel. The B&B is just a few minutes' walk from Leechburg's riverfront and unique shops such as Books and Beans and Graff Gourmet & Specialty Foods. The River's Edge Canoe & Kayak is less than two miles upstream.

After 30 years as a registered nurse, Marcia Andrews found the courage to pursue a life-long dream. At 51, she enrolled in the Culinary Institute of America, where she met celebrity chef Julia Child. **Chez Nan Bed & Breakfast** (249 S. Walnut St., Blairsville, 724/459-0383, www.chez-nan.com, $99–129) is the culmination of that dream, a retreat constructed with the same care that Child put into beef bourguignon. Thick robes, fluffy towels, and, of course, tasty breakfasts are all part of the recipe. Chez Nan's two suites and one guestroom share a spa-like bathroom.

Just two blocks from the campus of Indiana University of Pennsylvania, **Heritage House** (209 S. 6th St., Indiana, 724/463-3430, www.heritagehousesuites.com, $100–200) was among the grandest homes east of Pittsburgh when it was built in 1870. In the 1940s, the three-story brick house was divided into eight apartments, several of which have now been converted to spacious suites for nightly, weekly, or extended stays. Amenities include private bathrooms, full kitchens, wi-fi, cable TV, and laundry access.

Food

Renowned for its fresh seafood, flown in weekly from Hawaii, ◖ **1844 Restaurant** (690 Rte. 66, Leechburg, 724/845-1844, www.1844restaurant.com, 5–10 P.M. Thurs.–Sat. and daily to private parties, $12–36) is reason alone for Pittsburghers to make the 45-minute trip to southern Armstrong County. 1844 opened in 1974 in a nine-room brick farmhouse built in the 1830s. Bob Gorelli, its proprietor then and now, does the produce and meat shopping. He's handyman, gardener, and bartender too. Son Brandon, who washed dishes in his teens, now presides over the kitchen, serving an ambitious menu that includes both sashimi and linguini. Prime rib is the restaurant's specialty. Its signature sushi roll is a marriage of prime rib, smoked gouda, and wasabi cream sauce. Ask for a table in the Keeping Room when making a reservation. Elegant and rustic with it fieldstone walls and ceiling-high fireplace, it once served as a root cellar.

Black Forest Restaurant und Bier Haus (208 N. River Ave., Parker, 724/399-1100, www.blackforestpa.com, 4–9 P.M. Thurs.–Sat. and daily to private parties, $13–25), a little slice of Germany in the littlest city in the U.S., attracts big appetites with its $24.95 all-you-can-eat buffet on Saturdays. Proprietor Cindy Irwin owes her cooking style to a childhood in the German enclaves of Pittsburgh's North Side. Her menu boasts four types of schnitzel, five types of German sausage, German potato salad, and Bavarian sauerkraut, among other Deutschland dishes. The full bar serves close to 30 German beers along with the likes of Coors Light and Bud Light. Cap your meal with a decadent cocktail or a slice of Black Forest cake or German apple pie.

Speaking of pie, it's absolutely criminal to pass by **Dean's Diner** (2175 Rte. 22 Hwy. W., Blairsville, 724/459-9600, $5–20) without stopping for a slice. The 24-hour diner, which celebrated its 75th anniversary in 2009, offers 15 to 20 varieties daily, including coconut cream with sky-high meringue, banana cream, peanut butter cream, peanut butter and chocolate, peanut butter and chocolate *and* banana, apple, cherry, peach, apricot, and blueberry. For Boston cream, come on a Sunday. The pie baker, who slips in every evening, also makes cake donuts. Way back when, Dean's was located in the heart of Blairsville. In 1953, when the new Route 22 bypassed the town, it moved to its present location along the highway. It was a smart move. Business was so good that a dining room was soon added to the stainless steel diner with its nine booths and long Formica counter. The menu has changed little. Hot roast beef sandwiches, hamburgers, meatloaf, and fried chicken are hot sellers.

For well-executed Italian in a homey setting, try **Pie Cucina Ristorante** (181 E. Brown St., Blairsville, 724/459-7145, www.piecucina.com,

11 A.M.–10:30 P.M. Mon.–Fri., 4–10:30 P.M. Sat.–Sun., $8–22). It's got the usual: pizza, pasta, eggplant Parmesan, steaks, veal, chicken, and seafood. It's also got a great patio.

Information

Request a visitors guide to Pittsburgh's northeast neighbor on the website of the **Armstrong** **County Tourist Bureau** (125 Market St., Kittanning, 724-543/4003, www.armstrong county.com). They'll also send a golf-specific guide if you ask. The website of the **Indiana County Tourist Bureau** (2334 Oakland Ave., Suite 7, Indiana, 724/463-7505, www.visit indianacountypa.org) features a downloadable visitors guide.

Laurel Highlands

The Laurel Highlands are to Pittsburghers what the Hamptons are to New Yorkers: respite from urban bustle. As early as the 1800s, Pittsburghers of certain means fled to this mountainous region southeast of the "Smoky City" to escape industrial pollution and summer heat. Captains of industry built second homes; the less affluent filled boarding houses. Today the region's forests, peaks, and rivers attract not only Pittsburghers but also outdoors enthusiasts from Baltimore, Washington, D.C., and other cities within a half-day's drive. And its most renowned attraction, Fallingwater, draws visitors from around the world. Don't be surprised to hear a medley of languages if you visit the architectural masterpiece, which *Smithsonian* magazine named to its Life List—28 places to see before you die—along with India's Taj Mahal and Peru's Machu Picchu. What few people know is that Fallingwater is just one of *three* Frank Lloyd Wright houses in the Laurel Highlands.

"Laurel Highlands" is a label applied to the adjacent counties of Westmoreland, Fayette, and Somerset. "Laurel" is for the flowering shrubs that typically bloom in June. "Highlands" is for the terrain. The region is home to Mount Davis, the highest peak in Pennsylvania at 3,213 feet above sea level. Not surprisingly, it's home to ski resorts, including the state's largest. It's a region that lends itself to travel budgets big and small. Accommodations range from Falling Rock, where guests enjoy 24-hour butler service and 1,200-thread-count sheets, to trailside shelters that cost a few bucks a night. You can dine at Lautrec, one of only 21 restaurants named to the Forbes Travel Guide five-star list for 2010, or the Big Mac Museum Restaurant, a shrine for fans of the seven-ingredient burger.

SIGHTS
◖ Ohiopyle State Park

The 19,000-acre Ohiopyle State Park (724/329-8591, www.dcnr.state.pa.us/stateParks/parks/ohiopyle.aspx) is an outdoor lover's delight and the region's largest tourist draw. Its star attraction is the curiously spelled Youghiogheny ("yaw-ki-GAY-nee") River, better known as the "Yough." From spring to early fall, thrill-seekers take to its frothy waters in rafts, kayaks, and closed-deck canoes. The Lower Yough, which starts at the heart of the park, is the busiest section of white water east of the Mississippi. Its Class III and IV rapids aren't for the faint of heart. Unless you're an experienced white-water boater, find yourself a guide. You don't have to look far. There's an outfitter around every bend in the tiny village of Ohiopyle, nestled within the park. The Middle Yough begins at the easternmost part of the park and ends near town. Class I and II rapids make the Middle Yough ideal for beginning kayakers, rafters with young children, and anglers.

The park isn't just for paddlers. It's crisscrossed with 79 miles of hiking trails. Several short trails explore the 100-acre Ferncliff Peninsula, a unique botanical habitat. Created by a meander in the northern-flowing river, the National Natural Landmark contains plants sprung from seeds swept up in Maryland and

© LAUREL HIGHLANDS VISITORS BUREAU

Ohiopyle State Park

West Virginia. The 70-mile **Laurel Highlands Hiking Trail,** one of the finest rugged paths in Pennsylvania, has its southern terminus in Ohiopyle. (Contact Laurel Ridge State Park at 724/455-3744 for more information and to reserve overnight shelters, located every 8–10 miles along the trail.) For easy biking, there's the **Great Allegheny Passage** (www.atatrail.org), a rail-trail that stretches from just outside Pittsburgh to Cumberland, Maryland, and traces the Yough through Ohiopyle. After a heavy snowfall, it's a magical cross-country skiing route. The park also has trails for mountain biking, horseback riding, and snowmobiling. Rock climbers have no trouble keeping busy. For old-fashioned fun that requires no gear, park near the Route 381 bridge crossing Meadow Run, just south of the village of Ohiopyle, and follow the path at the back of the parking lot. It leads to two natural water slides.

Ohiopyle's campground is open from the beginning of March to late December. For now, only a few of the 226 campsites have electric hookups. The park also has some platform tents, yurts, and rustic cottages. Reserve online at www.pa.reserveworld.com or by calling 888/727-2757.

The village of Ohiopyle has four major outfitters. All but one offer overnight lodging in the area. **Wilderness Voyageurs** (103 Garrett St., 800/272-4141, www.wilderness-voyageurs .com) is the oldest of the bunch. It offers rafting trips on the Lower Yough as often as three times a day starting in March. Rental equipment is available for experienced rafters who prefer an unguided trip.

Wilderness Voyageurs also offers guided rafting on the class IV-V Upper Yough in Maryland and the class III-IV Cheat Canyon section of the Cheat River in West Virginia. Families with small children and others who prefer ripples to rapids can float down the Middle Yough with a guide or on their own. Bike-rental is available year-round and multi-day bike tours are available from May through October. It also offers fly-fishing, kayaking, and rock climbing instruction.

Laurel Highlands River Tours (4 Sherman St., 800/472-3846, www.laurelhighlands.com) and **Whitewater Adventurers** (6 Negley St., 800/992-7238, www.wwaraft.com) also date to the '60s. Like Wilderness Voyageurs, they facilitate rafting on the Lower Yough, Middle Yough, Upper Yough, and Cheat River. Laurel Highlands River Tours offers canoeing and kayaking instruction, plus guided rock climbing, mountain biking, and hiking tours. Whitewater Adventurers arranges guided fishing trips. You can raft all but the Cheat with **Ohiopyle Trading Post** (4 Negley St., 888/644-6795, www.ohiopyletradingpost .com), which boasts an on-site ice cream shop.

⟨ Fallingwater

What do you get Brad Pitt for his birthday? If you're Angelina Jolie, you spring for a private tour of Fallingwater (1491 Mill Run Rd., Mill Run, 724/329-8501, www.fallingwater.org), Frank Lloyd Wright's architectural masterpiece. ("He's so hard to buy for," Jolie quipped during their 2006 visit.) What Jolie paid is between her and the Western Pennsylvania Conservancy, which owns the house. Regular tours are $18 for adults, $12 for children 6–12, and last about an hour. Children under six aren't permitted. The tours are offered 10 A.M.–4 P.M. daily except Wednesday from mid-March through Thanksgiving weekend. Winter hours are more limited. Weather permitting, tours are offered Fridays, Saturdays, and Sundays in December; daily for about a week after Christmas; and the first two full weekends in March. Fallingwater is closed in January and February. In-depth tours include rooms not seen on the shorter tour and cost $55. They're off-limits to children under nine. All house tours are guided. More than 150,000 tourists snake through the National Historic Landmark each year, making reservations a must. Grounds-only passes, which allow visitors to take in the exterior of the house and the landscape, are available year-round for $8. Check the website for information on other ways to explore Fallingwater, including sunset tours and brunch tours. In 2009 the Conservancy introduced InsightOnsite, a three-day seminar that includes conversations with Fallingwater's director and curators, dinner in the house, and time to meander through it unguided. Participants sleep in simple housing within the natural area that's home to Fallingwater. Priced at $1,500 per person for double occupancy and $2,000 for single occupancy, tickets sell fast.

© ROBERT P. RUSCHAK, COURTESY OF WESTERN PENNSYLVANIA CONSERVANCY

Fallingwater

Wright designed Fallingwater in 1935 for the Kaufmann family of Pittsburgh, owners of eponymous department stores that later became part of the Macy's chain. The Kaufmanns wanted a vacation home with a view of a favorite waterfall. Wright decided to cantilever the house over the 30-foot falls. "I want you to live with the waterfall," he told them. The result is breathtaking—a visual and aural feast. Concrete terraces and a glass-walled living room project over the water, which provides a constant soundtrack. Fallingwater made such a splash when it was featured on the cover of *Time* magazine in 1938 that Wright, who was believed by many to be retired or dead, never wanted for work again. His last major work was Manhattan's Guggenheim Museum, which opened to the public in October 1959, six months after Wright's death at 91. The Kaufmanns used Fallingwater until 1963, when Edgar Kaufmann Jr. entrusted it to the nonprofit conservancy. Their artworks and furnishings, many of which were designed by Wright, still fill the house.

The museum shop carries everything from furniture reproductions to postcards. Fallingwater Café, also located in the visitors center, offers soups, sandwiches, and salads made with locally sourced vegetables and meats and herbs plucked from a garden on the property.

Kentuck Knob

Six miles south of Fallingwater is a less famous but similarly dazzling Frank Lloyd Wright creation. Kentuck Knob (723 Kentuck Rd., Chalk Hill, 724/329-1901, www.kentuckknob.com) sits high above the Youghiogheny River Gorge, wedged into the brow of a hill. Like Fallingwater, it's entwined with the terrain. Wright was 86 when ice cream magnate I.N. Hagan and his artist wife, Bernardine, beseeched him to design a house for their 80-acre mountain property. The Uniontown couple had visited the Kaufmanns at Fallingwater and fallen in love with the architect's work. Wright was overbooked—at work on the Guggenheim in New York, Beth Sholom Synagogue in the suburbs of Philadelphia, and about a dozen residences. "Of course," he told them. "Come on out." Wright never saw the completed home, a symphony of native sandstone,

WRIGHT OVERNIGHT

If Fallingwater and Kentuck Knob whet your appetite for all things Wright, don't leave the Laurel Highlands without visiting – or reserving – the **Duncan House** at **Polymath Park Resort** (1 Usonian Dr., Acme, 877/833-7829, www.polymathpark.com). It's one of only six Frank Lloyd Wright homes in the United States open to the public for lodging.

The Duncan House was built in 1957 in Lisle, Illinois. How it got to this wooded resort five miles from the Donegal exit (#91) of the Pennsylvania Turnpike is a long story. To hear it, book a tour of the resort, which also boasts two houses designed by Wright apprentice Peter Berndtson. Tours are offered on Sundays from March through November. They're $22 for adults, $16 for children 6-12. Children under 6 aren't permitted. For $37 you can tour the houses *and* enjoy a three-stage brunch at the resort's Wright-influenced Tree Tops Restaurant.

By Wright standards, the Duncan House is a modest structure. The architect envisioned mass production of such prefab homes. But even his least expensive design was too expensive to take off. No matter. Rarity magnifies their appeal. The Duncan House has all the Wright stuff: built-in cabinetry, an oversized fireplace, clerestory windows, exposed roof lines. You'll also find stuff that belonged to its original owners, including a pastel-hued hair dryer and bathroom scale. The meat grinder and other original kitchen appliances are just for show; overnight guests are asked to use the microwave and modern gadgets. The house sleeps as many six people. It's $425-575 per night, and a two-night minimum applies. You can also bunk at **Berndtson's Blum House** or **Balter House** – less cachet but more comforts.

© LAUREL HIGHLANDS VISITORS BUREAU

Kentuck Knob in winter

tidewater red cypress, glass, and flagstone. In fact, he set foot on the site only once, when local builders were laying the foundation.

The Hagans lived in the house for 30 years, then sold it in 1986 to Peter Palumbo, a British baron, property developer, and art collector. He and his family vacationed at Kentuck Knob for a decade before opening it to the public. They still entertain there on occasion, and the house is still filled with their furniture, family photos, and artwork. A shuttle ferries guests from the visitors center to the house, about a third of a mile away. Don't pass up the opportunity to walk back. Drink in the view from the crest of the hill before meandering through fields and woods dotted with sculptures.

Regular tours are $16 for adults, $10 for children 6–12, and last about 45 minutes. Children under six aren't permitted. From April through November, they're offered 10 A.M.–4 P.M. daily except Wednesday, when they start at noon. Call or check the website for winter hours. The $55 in-depth tour includes secondary spaces and lasts about 75 minutes. It's open to architecture buffs nine and older.

Sunset tours, Sunday brunch tours, and private tours are also available.

Fort Necessity National Battlefield

Anyone with an interest in world history should visit Fort Necessity National Battlefield (1 Washington Pkwy., Farmington, 724/329-5512, www.nps.gov/fone, 9 A.M.–5 P.M. daily, admission $5, children 15 and under free), where the fuse that ignited the French and Indian War was lit. It was here that a young George Washington fought his first battle—on the side of the British. And it was here that he surrendered for the only time in his military career.

Start in the Interpretive and Education Center, where a film and exhibits tell the story of the July 3, 1754, battle at Fort Necessity. A short paved path leads from the visitors center to a reconstruction of the fort built by Washington's men. The French burned the fort after their victory here, leaving few clues for historians and archaeologists. Debate over its shape raged for decades. Some experts claimed the fort was triangular, while others believed it

PITTSBURGH

© LAUREL HIGHLANDS VISITORS BUREAU

battle reenactment at Fort Necessity National Battlefield

to be diamond-shaped. The diamond camp triumphed in 1932, when the fort was first reconstructed. But both sides ate crow in the 1950s, when archaeologists unearthed evidence of a circular fort. That's what you'll find today.

Five miles of hiking trails meander through the meadow and woods around the fort. Cross-country skiing is permitted in winter. Some of the trails lead to a picnic area and another to **Mount Washington Tavern,** which served as a stagecoach stop in the mid-1800s. It no longer offers food, drink, and lodging to weary travelers; instead it's a museum focusing on life along the National Road, the first federally funded highway. It's open April 15–November 1. Consult the visitors center for hours. The picnic area and tavern can also be reached by car.

Jumonville Glen, the wooded hollow where Washington confronted a band of French soldiers several weeks before the battle at Fort Necessity, is several miles away. From the fort or tavern, follow U.S. 40 (a.k.a. the National Road) west for about four miles, hang a left at Jumonville Road, and continue until you reach the glen. You'll pass by **Braddock's Grave,** a granite monument to the British

commander-in-chief killed in 1755 during a disastrous advance on Fort Duquesne in present-day Pittsburgh. General Edward Braddock was buried under the road his men had built en route to the French fort; the surviving soldiers marched over his grave to prevent enemies from finding and desecrating the body. Jumonville Glen and the parking area at Braddock's Grave are open during summer months only.

Laurel Caverns Geological Park

The road leading from U.S. 40 to Laurel Caverns Geological Park (Skyline Dr., near Chalk Hill, 724/438-2070, www.laurelcaverns .com, 9 A.M.–5 P.M. daily May–Oct., weekends in Apr. and Nov. until Thanksgiving, admission $10, seniors $9, children grades 6–12 $8, grades K–5 $7) is five miles long and isolated. Don't let that deter you. The 435-acre park features Pennsylvania's largest cave. Guided tours depart every 20 minutes and last about an hour. The cave is 52 degrees year-round, so bring a sweater or jacket no matter when you visit. Not far from the natural cave you'll find Kavernputt, a fake cave with an 18-hole miniature golf course. Admission is $5.

Nemacolin Woodlands Resort

Picture the Ritz Paris. Now picture a convincing knockoff of the legendary hotel in an unlikely setting; picture it in rural, working-class Pennsylvania. It's hard to imagine—until you pull into the driveway of the Chateau Lafayette, one of three hotels at the sprawling Nemacolin Woodlands Resort (1001 LaFayette Dr., Farmington, 724/329-8555, www.nemacolin.com). The chateau's guest rooms feature vaulted ceilings, crystal chandeliers, and marble-slathered bathrooms with jetted tubs. And it's not even the fanciest hotel on the property.

Nemacolin is an all-ages playground with a dizzying number of amenities and activities. It has a full-service spa, high-end shops, two golf courses, five swimming pools, and about a dozen restaurants. Its Shooting Academy is one of the country's top sporting clays facilities. WildSide, its family entertainment emporium, features a bowling alley, pool tables, dozens of arcade games, a climbing wall, and—of all things—an exotic bird habitat. What else? You can climb inside a beast of a vehicle at the Off-Road Driving Academy, challenge friends to a paintball battle, try your hand at archery, zip across a 250-foot cable, or fly-fish at nearby streams and lakes. Winter options include cross-country and downhill skiing, snow tubing, snowshoeing, and even dog sledding. You don't have to be an overnight guest to partake in the fun or food. Pittsburghers have been

---

THE WHODUNIT THAT CHANGED HISTORY

The secluded ravine known as **Jumonville Glen** looks much as it did in May 1754, when a party of French soldiers made their camp there. There's no monument to the famous skirmish that took place when George Washington came upon them. A natural rock outcropping marks the site, and discreet signs tell the story. We know how the story ended: The leader of the French detachment, Joseph Coulon de Jumonville, lay dead. But its beginning is shrouded in mystery.

On May 24, four days before the skirmish, Washington and the frontiersmen under his command arrived at Great Meadows, a natural clearing in the woods that struck him as an ideal site for an encampment. Water was plentiful, there was grass for the animals, and the treeless terrain would make it easier to see an enemy coming. "A charming field for an encounter," he called it. Washington was 22, a newly commissioned lieutenant colonel in the Virginia militia, and he'd never come under fire.

When he learned that a group of French soldiers had been spotted several miles away, Washington left Great Meadows with about 40 men. They marched all night. On the morning of May 28, they surrounded the French, who had not posted sentries. A shot was fired, and then hundreds more. "I heard the bullets whistle, and, believe me, there is something charming in the sound," Washington would

write after the clash. When it ended, all of the Frenchmen were dead or captured, save for one who escaped.

Who fired the first shot? We don't know. What were the French doing there? We don't know that either. The French survivors claimed they'd been attacked without cause. They were coming to talk, not attack, they explained. Washington felt certain they were spies rather than diplomats. Upon his return to Great Meadows, he ordered the construction of a small fort. He called it **Fort Necessity.**

The French force that attacked Fort Necessity on the morning of July 3 was 600 strong and assisted by 100 Indians. It was led by the brother of the slain Jumonville. Washington's militiamen and the regular British troops who'd joined them numbered about 400. Hours of sporadic fighting were followed by several hours of negotiations. Near midnight, Washington surrendered, signing a "capitulation" penned in French. With his signature, he unwittingly accepted responsibility for the assassination of Jumonville.

Washington and his remaining troops returned to Virginia. The following year he would retrace his steps, passing through Great Meadows as a volunteer aide to British general Edward Braddock. He would never again refer to war as "charming."

© ANNA DUBROVSKY

Nemacolin Shooting Academy features
35 sporting clay stations.

known to drive 65 miles and back for a meal at world-class Lautrec or Aqueous. Private jets cut the travel time; the resort has its own airfield.

Nemacolin is the brainchild of Joseph Hardy III, founder of 84 Lumber Co., and it strongly reflects his passions and whims. About $45 million in art, rare automobiles, and antique planes are scattered about the property. Free tours of the collection depart from the chateau lobby at 3 P.M. daily. A polo field abuts the Wildlife Academy, shared by potbellied pigs, sheep, and the sled dog team, among other animals. More exotic beasts, including white lions, black bears, and a cougar named Shasta, prowl wildlife habitats scattered throughout the resort.

Nemacolin's wine cellar, the largest private cellar in Pennsylvania, holds an estimated 25,000 bottles. Resident sommeliers host tastings at 4 P.M. Wednesdays, Fridays, and Saturdays. Weekday tastings are $20. Reservations are required for Saturday's "reserve" tasting, which features more exclusive wines and costs $35. Foodies can have their fun too. Nemacolin's award-winning chefs show off their skills Saturdays at 11 A.M. Reservations are required for the $99 cooking

class. Feel free to bring Fido or Fluffy when you visit. Nemacolin Wooflands Pet Resort & Spa (724/329-9663, www.nemacolinwooflands .com) opened in 2009.

Seven Springs Mountain Resort

The state's largest ski resort boasts 13 slopes, 18 trails, and consistently high marks from readers of *Ski* magazine. But snow is seasonal inventory. The average ski season lasts just four months, ending with a whimper near the end of March. That's why Seven Springs (777 Waterwheel Dr., Seven Springs, 800/452-2223, www.7springs.com, all-day lift ticket $50–70, children 6–11 $40–53, seniors 70–79 pay half price, octogenarians and older ski for free, all-day ski rental $29–34, all-day snowboard rental $38–42, snow tubing $15–25 per two-hour session) works hard to position itself as a year-round destination. There's fly-fishing. There's golf. There's paintball and bowling, horseback riding and swimming. There's a downhill bike park, 24-foot climbing wall, and 1,980-foot alpine slide. In fact, Seven Springs hosts more visitors between ski seasons than during the winter months, due in large part to its conference facilities.

The resort also plays host to concerts, festivals, and other special events. Its food and booze festivals, in particular, are among the highlights of the region's social calendar. They include the two-day **Brewski Festival** (spring), the summertime **Wine & Food Festival,** and a daylong tribute to all things cacao, **A Chocolate Affaire** (Sept.). **Autumnfest** weekends feature crafts, live entertainment, and leaf peeping from the unique vantage point of a chairlift.

Robert Nutting, a newspaper mogul and part owner of the Pittsburgh Pirates baseball team, purchased Seven Springs in 2006 from the family that founded it in 1932. A flurry of enhancements ensued. Rooms, restaurants, and lounges were refurbished. A high-speed six-passenger chairlift was added. The resort introduced an Orvis-endorsed fly-fishing program. In 2009 it unveiled the full-service Trillium Spa. A sporting clays complex two years in the making also opened in 2009.

Seven Springs Mountain Resort

The resort's "something for everyone" approach extends to its restaurant portfolio. Visitors can grab a slice of pizza, load up at a buffet, or settle in for a romantic dinner at Helen's, the original home of Seven Springs' founders.

Hidden Valley
Four Seasons Resort
Like rival Seven Springs, Hidden Valley (1 Craighead Dr., Hidden Valley, 814/443-8000, www.hiddenvalleyresort.com, all-day lift ticket $25–54, children 6–17 and seniors 65–69 $25–42, seniors 70 and over $15, all-day ski rental $27, all-day snowboard rental $33, snow tubing $12–14 per two- or three-hour session) is under new-ish ownership. The Buncher Company, a Pittsburgh-based real estate developer, purchased the tired property in 2007 with plans to rejuvenate and expand it. The company lured Seven Springs' CEO and a mountain manager from Vermont, installed a new chairlift and snow-making guns, and replaced the entire ski and snowboard rental fleet. But the biggest changes are still to come. Buncher plans to build a new hotel adjacent to the ski lodge and develop hundreds of pristine acres.

Hidden Valley is considerably smaller and quieter than Seven Springs and rarely the choice of nightlife-loving singles. It attracts some 200,000 people a year; Seven Springs tallies 1.2 million. The skiing is cheaper at Hidden Valley, but Seven Springs has four times as many skiable acres. During the warmer months, Hidden Valley offers golfing on the mountaintop, fishing in Lake George, tennis, horseback riding, and mountain biking. The more adventurous may wish to try mountainboarding, an off-season alternative to snowboarding.

Flight 93 National Memorial
On Sept. 11, 2001, United Airlines Flight 93 crashed into a field near Shanksville, Pennsylvania, at 580 miles per hour. Soon after, a grieving public began journeying to the remote site to pay respects to the 40 passengers and crew who perished while trying to wrest back control of the hijacked plane. They created temporary memorials: homespun collages of flowers, flags, scrawled tributes, and all manner of personal effects—from ball caps to Nerf balls. Legislation calling for a permanent memorial was signed into law in 2002, and a

design was chosen three years later. Acquiring the land necessary for the planned Flight 93 National Memorial (Lambertsville Rd., about 3 miles south of its juncture with US Rte. 30, 814/443-4557, http://www.nps.gov/flni) proved difficult. It wasn't until November 2009 that ground was broken. The first phase of construction is expected to be completed by Sept. 11, 2011, the 10th anniversary of the coordinated terrorist attacks that killed nearly 3,000 people. In the meantime, pilgrims can view the crash site from the so-called Western Overlook, the hilltop that served as a command post in the aftermath of the tragedy. The crash site itself is accessible only to relatives of Flight 93 passengers and crew.

Fort Ligonier

The hilltop Fort Ligonier (200 S. Market St., Ligonier, 724/238-9701, www.fortligonier .org, 10 A.M.–4:30 P.M. Mon.–Sat. and noon– 4:30 P.M. Sun. Apr. 15–Nov. 15, admission $8, children 6–14 $5) went by Post at Loyalhanna when it was constructed in September 1758. General John Forbes renamed it after ousting

the French from the forks of the Ohio River, a site he named Pittsburgh. Loyalhanna was a staging area for his British-American army, the last in a chain of fortifications leading to his target. It was so well situated that it remained in use even after the French and Indian War ended in 1763, serving as a support base for the British when Native American tribes bridled at their policies in "Pontiac's War." Not once was it taken by an enemy.

After it was decommissioned from active service in 1766, the fort fell into disrepair. Over time, surface traces all but disappeared. Lucky for us, a full-scale reconstruction sits on the original site. The 200-square-foot inner fort encloses the barracks, underground magazine, officers' quarters, and other structures. A 1,600-foot-long outer retrenchment surrounds the fort. Sandwiched between the two is General Forbes's hut. A walkthrough can take most of an hour. Don't be surprised if hammering accompanies your history lesson; the complex requires near-constant upkeep.

Even more impressive than the fort is the museum near its entrance. Here, relics vastly

reenactment at Fort Ligonier

outnumber reproductions. They include the mundane—canteens, coins, chamber pots, cannon balls, and gin bottles—as well as show-stoppers such as a pair of pistols that belonged to George Washington. The collection owes much to a creek that passed by the fort. Soldiers, their families, and the merchants and artisans who followed them threw their cast-offs into the creek, where oxygen-free silt made a swell preservative. The collection includes a 250-year-old apple excavated from the streambed, along with 120,000 other artifacts, when the museum was being built in the 1960s.

The Anglo-French conflict in North America was part of the Seven Years' War, and Fort Ligonier Museum houses the only exhibit that tells the story of the global bloodshed with original objects from every theater. One case holds the coat of a British naval officer whose abdomen was pierced by a cannonball off the coast of Spain. Another displays elephant trunk armor from India. It took museum director Martin West seven years to collect the objects in the exhibit, which was completed in 2008.

Be aware that Fort Ligonier is closed for

five months of the year. The best time to visit is mid-October, during **Fort Ligonier Days** (724/238-4200, www.ligonier.com). The three-day festival commemorates the successful defense of Loyalhanna from a French attack on October 12, 1758. Reenactors flood the town of Ligonier, setting up camp on the grounds of the fort. Food and craft booths pop up all over town, church ladies cook up a storm, and the community puts on a parade. Best of all: twice-daily battle reenactments.

Idlewild & SoakZone

The state's oldest amusement park—and the country's third oldest—is three miles west of downtown Ligonier. Drive by Idlewild & SoakZone (U.S. 30 E., Ligonier, 724/238-3666, www.idlewild.com, admission $29.99, seniors $20.99, children 2 and under free, next day pass $15.99) in April, and you may not notice it. Drive by a few weeks later, and you can't miss it. From late May through Labor Day, the amusement park is awash with families.

Idlewild opened in 1878 as a picnic and camping area for Pittsburghers who traveled

Idlewild & SoakZone

to the country by train. The Ligonier Valley Railroad had a station on the property. The railroad was abandoned in the 1950s, but Idlewild was not. By then, America's love affair with the automobile was in full bloom, and Idlewild had grown into a bona fide amusement park, complete with a three-row carousel. Today Idlewild has seven theme areas, including SoakZone Waterpark. Olde Idlewild is home to the antique carousel along with two roller coasters and other major rides. The remaining areas are tamer and geared toward young children. Among them is Mister Rogers' Neighborhood of Make-Believe, where children can meet King Friday XIII, X the Owl, Henrietta Pussycat, and other stars of the children's show. Fred Rogers himself designed the attraction.

On weekends in late September and October, Idlewild dons faux spider webs and reopens for **HallowBoo**, an all-ages Halloween celebration. Admission is $21.99. Come in costume if you like, but steer clear of racy or gory getups. They're an Idlewild no-no, along with masks on adults.

Steelers Training Camp

Want a ticket to watch the Pittsburgh Steelers at Heinz Field? Good luck. Tickets to home games are harder to come by than cauliflower in a candy shop. But you can catch the players in action—for free!—at their summer training camp on the campus of **Saint Vincent College** (300 Fraser Purchase Rd., Latrobe, 724/532-6600, www.stvincent.edu). *Sports Illustrated* Senior Editor Peter King called it "the best training camp in the NFL, the best venue for watching real football in the NFL, and my favorite place to soak in what sports should be." The annual training camp has been held at Saint Vincent since 1968.

The Steelers arrive in mid-July and leave about a month later. Check the team's website, www.steelers.com, for training camp dates and times. Often the schedule isn't confirmed until sometime in June or early July. The Steelers prefer privacy in the mornings, but their late afternoon practices are open to the public. After practice, fans jostle for autographs in designated areas.

Saint Vincent Gristmill

At Saint Vincent Gristmill (Beatty Rd., Latrobe, 724/537-0304, www.saintvincentgristmill.com, 9 A.M.–4 P.M. Mon.–Sat.), just north of Saint Vincent College, Benedictine monks grind grain much as they have for 150 years. The fruits of their labors are available at the Gristmill General Store, which also carries jams, honey, and other products. The Gristmill Coffeehouse (724/537-2858, 8 A.M.–9 P.M. daily) offers free wireless Internet access and occasional live entertainment.

Museums

It comes as a bit of a surprise to discover a first-rate museum in the foothills of southwestern Pennsylvania. The **Westmoreland Museum of American Art** (221 N. Main St., Greensburg, 724/837-1500, www.wmuseumaa.org, 11 A.M.–5 P.M. Wed.–Sun., open until 9 P.M. Thurs., suggested donation $5, children under 12 and students free), 35 miles east of Pittsburgh, counts among its collection works by Winslow Homer, Mary Cassatt, John Singer Sargent, and other nationally recognized names. Even more impressive is its trove of art inspired by southwestern Pennsylvania. Art historian William Gerdts observed that the museum "pioneered regional investigations" in his encyclopedic *Art Across America*. Pastoral landscapes by George Hetzel and other 19th-century artists enamored of the region's mountains, woodlands, and streams contrast sharply with depictions of its 20th-century industrial might. Take in William Coventry Wall's *On the Monongahela*, with its verdant hills, dirt path, and single log cabin. Then take in Otto August Kuhler's *Steel Valley, Pittsburgh,* with its riverside mills, barges, and billows of smoke. Separated by 65 years, the paintings speak volumes about the American experience.

The museum has come to be known as a venue for a made-in-America musical art form. It hosts accomplished jazz artists on the third Thursday of the month from September through June. Performances begin at 7:30 P.M. Tickets are $10 for members of the museum's

"WON'T YOU BE MY NEIGHBOR?"

Before Dora the Explorer, before Teletubbies, and even before Big Bird, there was **Mister Rogers**. *Mister Rogers' Neighborhood* began airing in 1968 and continued to captivate kids even after the death of its creator and host. Fred McFeely Rogers was an unlikely television personality. Born in Latrobe, about 40 miles southeast of Pittsburgh, Rogers was more interested in spirituality than celebrity. Several years before the public television program debuted, he graduated from Pittsburgh Theological Seminary and was ordained a Presbyterian minister. "I went into television because I hated it so," he once told CNN, "and I thought there was some way of using this fabulous instrument to be of nurture to those who would watch and listen."

Rogers taped almost 900 episodes of his eponymous show. They began the same way, with Rogers returning to his television home, slipping into more comfortable clothes, and singing: "Would you be mine, could you be

mine, won't you be my neighbor?" (For many years, his mother knitted the cardigan sweaters that were his signature.) He took viewers on field trips, showing them how things like crayons are made and how things like bulldozers work. And he took them to his Neighborhood of Make-Believe, a kingdom of puppets. Rogers tackled any topic that might weigh on a child, be it war or the first day of school. He even explained, in song, that you can't be pulled down the bathroom drain. He composed all the music for the series. Produced in Pittsburgh, *Mister Rogers' Neighborhood* remained in syndication until September 2008. Some stations still air it.

Rogers died in February 2003 at the age of 74. A few months later, the **Fred Rogers Center** (300 Fraser Purchase Rd., Latrobe, 724/805-2750, www.fredrogerscenter.org) was established at Saint Vincent College in his native Latrobe with the mission of advancing early learning and children's media.

COURTESY OF ROB MATHENY

The "Tribute to Children" Memorial, on Pittsburgh's North Shore, honors Fred Rogers with a sculpture by Robert Berks.

PITTSBURGH

Westmoreland Jazz Society, $15 for nonmembers, and $3 for students.

The **Southern Alleghenies Museum of Art at Ligonier Valley** (1 Boucher Ln. and Rte. 711, Ligonier, 724/238-6015, www.sama-art.org, 10 A.M.–5 P.M. Tues.–Fri., 1–5 P.M. Sat.–Sun., free admission) houses an exceptional paperweight collection. The weights are ingeniously displayed so that visitors can see them from all angles. One of four SAMA branches, the museum hosts an annual juried exhibition that showcases the work of artists from the 19 southwestern counties of Pennsylvania.

The **Compass Inn Museum** (1382 U.S. 30, Laughlintown, 724/238-4983, www.compassinn.com, 11 A.M.–4 P.M. Tues.–Sat. and 1–5 P.M. Sun. May–Oct., 3–7 P.M. Sat.–Sun. Nov.–mid-Dec., admission $9, students through high school $6, children 5 and under free) is a restored stagecoach stop filled with period furnishings. Costumed docents lead 90-minute tours of the inn, built in 1799, and three reconstructed outbuildings, all the while explaining how people lived and traveled in the early 1800s. Tours begin whenever visitors arrive. From November through mid-December the museum is open on weekends only for one-hour candlelight tours.

If you're jonesing for booze—and even if you're not—make your way to **Joe's Bar** (202 W. Main St., Ligonier, 724/238-4877, 11 A.M.–2 A.M. Mon.–Sat., noon–2 A.M. Sun.) in Ligonier. Bring the kids. To the naked eye, Joe's is a smoky beer-and-shot joint. But walk beyond the bar and you'll enter a **taxidermy museum** that's at once ghastly and impressive. If you've never seen a rhinoceros, red lechwe, or blue wildebeest up close, here's your chance. Globetrotting hunter Joe Snyder couldn't keep all his trophies at home, so he displayed them in his bar. They take up four rooms on two floors. A massive elephant head, trunk raised and ears flared, hangs from the ceiling. Three elephant feet repurposed as stools hug a table. A fourth was stolen during Fort Ligonier Days, when thousands squeeze into the dimly lit bar.

Other Sights

Britain's troubles in North America didn't end with its victory over the French in 1763. Within months, the Native American uprising known as Pontiac's Rebellion had begun. A pivotal clash came at **Bushy Run Battlefield** (Rte. 993, near Jeannette, 724/527-5584, www.bushyrunbattlefield.com, park open 9 A.M.–5 P.M. Wed.–Sun. year-round, museum open Apr.–Oct. only, admission $5, seniors $4.50, children 3–11 $3), about 30 miles southeast of Pittsburgh. Here, 400 British soldiers led by Swiss-born Colonel Henry Bouquet defeated a large force of Native Americans bent on seizing Fort Pitt. Guided tours and interpretive programs explain the significance of the British victory, which opened western Pennsylvania to settlement.

Within a decade of Pontiac's Rebellion, settlers were seething at the British. In May 1775, more than a year before the Continental Congress adopted the Declaration of Independence, colonists in Westmoreland County signed a direct challenge to British authority known as the Hanna's Town Resolves. In 1782, near the close of the Revolutionary War, Hanna's Town was attacked and burned by Native Americans and their British allies. You can imagine what it once was at **Historic Hanna's Town** (809 Forbes Trail Rd., Greensburg, 724/836-1800, www.starofthewest.org, 10 A.M.–4 P.M. Wed.–Sat. and 1–4 P.M. Sun. June–Aug., weekends only May and Sept.–Oct., admission $4, seniors $3, children 5–18 $3), which includes a reconstructed tavern/courthouse and three log houses. The wagon shed houses an authentic 18th century wagon.

For another taste of frontier life, make your way south to the **Somerset Historical Center** (10649 Somerset Pike, Somerset, 814/445-6077, www.somersethistoricalcenter.org, 9 A.M.–5 P.M. Tues.–Sat. Apr.–Oct., 9 A.M.–5 P.M. Tues.–Fri. Nov.–Mar., admission $6, seniors $5.50, children 3–11 $3). The focus here is regional agricultural history, "not the history of great men and great battles," says Charles Fox, who administers the Pennsylvania Historical and Museum Commission site. The center celebrates the commonplace, showcasing the tools and other belongings of workaday farmers. Among its artifacts: an electric chicken plucker and a kerosene-powered slide projector. From April through October, visitors can roam the grounds, where farmsteads from the 1770s and 1830s have been recreated. The center is busiest the weekend after Labor Day, when it hosts **Mountain Craft Days.** Craftspeople in traditional costumes demonstrate all things country, from butter churning to barn raising, as part of the festival.

A stone's throw away is the site of a 2002 mine flood that captivated the world. The **Quecreek Mine Monument for Life** (151 Haupt Rd., Somerset, 814/445-4876, www .quecreekrescue.org, dawn to dusk daily) commemorates the successful rescue of nine coal miners trapped 240 feet below ground for almost 80 hours. A seven-foot statue of a coal miner guards the entrance to the monument park, where an arbor garden and granite markers pay tribute to the miners and rescue workers.

ENTERTAINMENT AND EVENTS
Performing Arts
Pennsylvania's oldest professional summer stock theater, the **Mountain Playhouse** (7690 Somerset Pike, Boswell, 814/629-9201, www .mountainplayhouse.org), offers Broadway-quality entertainment in a setting quite the opposite of Broadway. Think shimmering lake and thick woods instead of flashing marquees and thick crowds. The 393-seat theater is housed in an 1805 gristmill that was moved, log by log, from its original site about 20 miles away. The performance season begins in June, ends in October, and includes a mix of genres. Farce is a specialty of the house, which opened in 1939. Theater-goers needn't go far for dinner before the show. The *Wine Spectator* award-winning Green Gables Restaurant is a short walk from the playhouse.

Located across from the Westmoreland County Courthouse in downtown Greensburg, the handsome **Palace Theatre** (21 W. Otterman St., Greensburg, 724/836-8000,

www.thepalacetheatre.org) hosts a wide variety of acts, from local ballet and theater companies to internationally known entertainers like Bill Cosby and Joan Baez. The 1,369-seat theater dates to 1926 and almost had a date with a wrecking ball. Purchased in 1990 by a nonprofit organization now known as Westmoreland Cultural Trust, it has undergone more than $10 million in renovations. Many of its original features remain intact, including a candlelight chandelier in the lobby and a goldfish pond on the mezzanine level.

Festivals and Events
More than 100 locals make up the cast of *The Legend of the Magic Water,* a song-filled account of the discovery of maple syrup. The pageant has been a **Pennsylvania Maple Festival** (Meyersdale, 814/634-0213, www .pamaplefestival.com, Mar.) tradition since 1971. First held in 1948, the folksy celebration of Pennsylvania's sweetest commodity put Meyersdale on the map and gave the town its nickname: Maple City, USA. Highlights include sugaring demonstrations, a parade, auto shows, a Maple Queen contest, and spotza making. What's spotza, you say? It's a taffy-like treat made by pouring boiled maple syrup over crushed ice. (Native Americans, who shared the recipe with settlers, used snow.) Events take place throughout Meyersdale, but the hub of activity is Festival Park. Admission to the park is $4 for adults, $1 for children 6–12.

More than 150,000 people turn out for the **Westmoreland Arts & Heritage Festival** (Twin Lakes Park, Greensburg, 724/834-7474, www.artsandheritage.com, first week of July, free), an arts-infused Fourth of July celebration. Its centerpiece is the Artist Market, featuring the work of 200 plus craftspeople and artisans from across the country. The four-day festival also features a juried exhibition of fine art, dozens of live performances, and ethnic food aplenty.

Kilted bagpipers turn out en force for the **Ligonier Highland Games** (412/851-9900, www.ligoniergames.org, weekend after Labor Day), a celebration of all things Scottish.

Brawny athletes flip giant logs. Highland dancers show off their footwork. Scottish fiddlers face off. And the Guinness flows. The bulk of the festivities take place at Idlewild on the Saturday after Labor Day, a few days after the amusement park mothballs its rides and attractions. Admission is $15 for adults, $12 for seniors, and $5 for children 12 and under.

Squeeze as many as you can into the family van. Admission to **Overly's Country Christmas** (Westmoreland Fairgrounds, Greensburg, 724/423-1400, www.overlys .com, late Nov.–Jan. 1) is $10 per carful. The holiday light display had its beginnings more than 50 years ago, when Harry Overly first decorated his rural home with a few strands of light. Encouraged by his children's delight, he stepped up his game. Year after year, the lights got brighter, and the crowds got bigger. After 35 years, the spectacle outgrew its creator's seven-acre property and, in 1993, found a home at the Westmoreland Fairgrounds. These days it features more than two million lights, a walk-through country-themed Christmas Village, and a life-sized nativity scene complete with live animals. Visitors can roast marshmallows around the bonfire, hop in a horse-drawn wagon or sleigh, and, of course, meet Santa. Proceeds benefit at-risk families.

Some towns put fun on ice in winter. Not Ligonier. Each January it invites artists to create masterpieces from blocks of ice during the two-day **Ligonier Ice Fest** (724/238-4200, www.ligonier.com).

The Seven Springs Mountain Resort (777 Waterwheel Dr., Seven Springs, 800/452-2223, www.7springs.com) plays host to concerts, festivals, and other special events throughout the year. Its food and booze festivals, in particular, are among the highlights of the region's social calendar. The two-day **Brewski Festival,** held in the spring, features specialty beers from dozens of breweries and a buffet groaning with beer-basted chicken, mussels and shrimp broiled in beer, beer bread, chocolate stout cake, and more. The summertime **Wine & Food Festival** is a two-day celebration of fine cuisine and Pennsylvania wines, complete with grape-stomping contests. A daylong tribute to all things cacao, **A Chocolate Affaire,** takes place in September. On its heels: **Autumnfest** weekends, which feature crafts, live entertainment, and, best of all, leaf peeping from the unique vantage point of a chairlift.

SHOPPING
Ligonier Diamond
Historic Ligonier is a diamond of a town, worthy of a stroll any time of year. Its epicenter, known as the Diamond, is surrounded by speciality shops. At **Equine Chic** (100 E. Main St., 724/238-7003, www.equinechic.com, 10 A.M.–5 P.M. Tues.–Sat.), you'll find horse-shaped cookie cutters, pewter napkin rings in the shape of stirrups, and other equestrian home accents.

When life calls for a cashmere sports jacket, head to the **Post & Rail Men's Shop** (104 E. Main St., 724/238-9235, www.ligonier.com/postandrail/, 9:30 A.M.–5 P.M. Mon.–Sat.). It offers classic clothing, personal attention, and expert tailoring, plus leather armchairs for waiting ladies. If you haven't guessed it already, this is horse-and-hound country. For almost 50 years, the famous Mellon family hosted steeplechase races on its property, Rolling Rock Farms, just east of town. Fox hunting remains a Ligonier Valley tradition. It's not unusual to see hunters in breeches and boots grabbing a coffee or meal in town.

The kid in you will appreciate a stop at **The Toy Box** (108 S. Market St., 724/238-6233, www.toyboxligonier.com, 10 A.M.–5 P.M. Mon.–Sat.), a six-room store that puts Toys "R" Us to shame with its selection of playthings. It carries everything from puzzles to plush toys—and horse collectibles, of course.

For refreshments, head to **Abigail's Coffeehouse** (104 W. Main St., 724/238-9373, 7 A.M.–5:30 P.M. Mon.–Fri., 8 A.M.–5:30 P.M. Sat.), which serves ice cream and smoothies as well as coffee.

ACCOMMODATIONS
Under $100
Growing use of the Great Allegheny Passage

has given birth to a number of affordable lodgings in towns along the rail-trail. The Laurel Highlands' only hostel opened in 2009 in Rockwood, 30 trail miles east of Ohiopyle. The **Hostel on Main** (506 Main St., Rockwood, 814/926-4546, www.hostelonmain.com, shared room $15–22 per person, private room $50 for first two people) brings back memories of dorm life with its bunk beds and quiet hours. Bed linens are included in the overnight fee; blankets and towels can be rented for $2 apiece. If rooming with strangers doesn't sit right with you, reserve the hostel's private room, which sleeps up to six. The onetime general store has three private guest bathrooms, a living room stocked with games and books, and a kitchen with a refrigerator, microwave, and coin-operated washer/dryer. Check-in is 5–8:30 P.M. at Rockwood Mill; check-out is 7–9 A.M. The hostel is closed 9 A.M.–5 P.M.

Couples may prefer the **Rockwood Trail House Bed & Breakfast** (131 Rockdale Rd., Rockwood, 888/916-2453, www.rockwood trailhouse.com, $76–96), with its queen-sized beds. The Great Allegheny Passage's Rockwood trailhead is just outside the door of the colonial-style house. It's no wonder that proprietors Lynn and Debra Sanner built a bike shop in 2006. The shop is an authorized Trek dealer. Rental bicycles, child bicycle trailers, and jogging strollers are available. Wi-Fi is available two doors down at **Rockwood Mill Shoppes** (450 W. Main St., Rockwood, www.rockwood millshoppes.com), a former feed and lumber mill now occupied by retailers and eateries.

Meyersdale, 16 trail miles southeast of Rockwood, also has a B&B-cum-bike shop: **Gram Gram's Place** (508 Main St., 814/634-0461, www.gramgramsplace.com, $65–75). The B&B has three comfy en suite guest rooms. The bike shop has a wide selection of parts and accessories, Sun Bicycles, and a rental fleet of adult, child, and trailer bikes.

$100–200

A Select Registry member, the **Inne at Watson's Choice** (234 Balsinger Rd., Uniontown, 724/437-4999, www.watsonschoice.com, $105–145) is a superb choice of country-style lodging. The wonderfully secluded 1800s farmhouse has seven en suite guest rooms. Picture comfy wingback chairs, checkered curtains, and painted country armoires. Across a courtyard from the inn, **Harvest House** ($115–225) offers four more guest rooms and a suite made for romance. The latter features a whirlpool tub and two-person shower. Innkeepers Bill and Nancy Ross serve a country breakfast to guests of both properties in the inn's rustic dining room, complete with heavy stone fireplace.

Collectively known as **Huddleson Court** (7712 Somerset Pike, Boswell, 814/629-9201, www.huddlesoncourt.com, $75–360), the accommodations on the pastoral grounds of Green Gables Restaurant and the Mountain Playhouse range from rooms in a central building to standalone cottages with woodland or lake views. They're charming, every last one of them. The Sugar Maple and Daylily rooms are an exceptional value—no more than $115 during the Mountain Playhouse's performance season and as low as $75 during the off-peak months of November through May. Four one-bedroom suites fetch $85–185 per night. Beaverdam Creek Cabin, with its woodburning fireplace, stone staircase, and cozy loft bedroom, is the stuff of storybooks. Families can feel at home in one of two two-bedroom cottages or the four-bedroom Gristmill House. Guests will find board games, DVDs, maps of area hiking trails, and wireless Internet access—not to mention fine dining—at Green Gables. Call or check the website for information about overnight packages that include dinner at the restaurant and/or a show.

Drenched in pink and delightfully frilly, **Campbell House Bed & Breakfast** (305 E. Main St., Ligonier, 724/238-9812, www .campbellhousebnb.com, $90–159) is a stone's throw from the Ligonier Diamond and historic Fort Ligonier. Patti Campbell calls her eponymous B&B "an adult getaway," recognizing that tots could easily mistake whimsical collectibles and heirlooms for toys. Part innkeeper and part romance facilitator, Campbell offers an elopement package complete with marriage

Campbell House Bed & Breakfast

© GEORGE SUBREBOST

ceremony, wedding cake, and a boutonniere for the groom. Already married or not quite there? Ask about her couples massage package. In addition to the B&B's six rooms and suites, Campbell offers two efficiency motel rooms. They're a bargain at $80 per night or $360 per week, but you'll have to pay extra for her delectable breakfasts.

Lesley's Mountain View Country Inn (327 Mountain View Rd., Donegal, 724/593-6349, www.shol.com/mtview, single occupancy $85–95, double occupancy $150–210) offers antique-furnished and nicely understated rooms in a restored 1850s farmhouse and chestnut barn. Rates include a full breakfast. The barn houses not only several guest rooms but also an upscale restaurant, **Lesley's** (5–10 P.M. Thurs.–Sat., $22–38), with a menu designed around local, seasonal ingredients.

An expansive marble foyer and gold leaf chandeliers greet guests at the **Inn at Georgian Place** (800 Georgian Place Dr., Somerset, 814/443-1043, www.theinnat georgianplace.com, $105–195), a 22-room

Georgian mansion built in 1915 for a local coal and cattle baron. Its 11 guest rooms and suites range from quaint to dignified. Guests are treated to a gourmet breakfast. An on-site restaurant is open for lunch and afternoon tea daily, dinner Tuesday–Sunday, and brunch on Sunday. The bar, D.B.'s Publick Room, serves noon–10 P.M. daily.

If skiing is what brings you to the Laurel Highlands, there's little reason to look beyond **Seven Springs Mountain Resort** (777 Waterwheel Dr., Seven Springs, 866/437-1300, www.7springs.com, winter $159–284, summer $159–229) for lodging. Located at the base of the mountain, the Main Lodge Hotel has a whopping 418 rooms and suites. The decor is nothing remarkable—standard mid-range hotel stuff—but what does that matter? There's too much to do on the 5,500-acre resort to be hanging in your room. The 10-floor hotel is attached to the main lodge, which houses eateries and bars, specialty shops, a heated pool and hot tubs, a game room, and more. Seven Springs' convention center, also

The Inn at Georgian Place is a mansion built in 1915.

attached to the main lodge, boasts a bowling center, exercise room, and racquetball court. Families and small groups may be better off renting a condo or townhouse at the resort. Luxury rentals are available at Southwind, a gated community at the top of the mountain with its own chairlift and trail system. Call for rates.

Over $200

❰ Nemacolin Woodlands Resort (1001 LaFayette Dr., Farmington, reservations 866/344-6957, www.nemacolin.com) offers 335 rooms and a level of luxury unmatched in the Pittsburgh region. The most modest of its three hotels is the Tudor-style **Lodge** (room $319–349, suite $379–439), built in 1968 when the property was a Pittsburgh industrialist's private game reserve and expanded by Nemacolin founder Joseph Hardy III. It houses a good deal of the Hardy family art collection, including Tiffany lamps and Norman Rockwell prints. Room decor evokes an English country inn. **Chateau Lafayette**

(regular room $389–449, regular suite $529–599, club room $589–659, club suite $659–779, presidential $2,999) is Hardy's tribute to the grand hotels of Europe. With its vaulted ceilings, crystal chandeliers, and two-story Palladian windows, the hotel built in 1997 aptly emulates the famed Ritz Paris, a century older. It's home to a cigar bar, a high-end jewelry store, and Lautrec, Nemacolin's most celebrated restaurant. Round-the-clock butler service is available to guests of the fifth-floor club level. White-gloved and professionally trained, butlers do everything from booking dinner reservations to preparing romantic baths, complete with flower petals and flickering candles.

Butler service is available to every guest of **Falling Rock** (room $489–729, suite $659–809), Nemacolin's newest and most exclusive lodging. It's as understated as the chateau is ornate, a reverent nod to architect Frank Lloyd Wright, whose Fallingwater and Kentuck Knob houses are less than 20 minutes away. The hotel sits on the 18th green of the Pete Dye–designed

The Chateau Lafayette was modeled after the famed Ritz Paris in France.

© JEFF GREEN/NEMACOLIN WOODLANDS RESORT

Mystic Rock golf course, a good distance from the hub of activity at Nemacolin. As such, it's closed from mid-November through April except for private buy-out functions. It features 42 guest rooms and suites, a clubhouse that World Golf Hall of Famer Vijay Singh called the finest in America, and an infinity pool reserved for Falling Rock guests. Aqueous, Nemacolin's upscale steakhouse, is on-site. Guests can take their pick of 10 pillow types, including water pillows, buckwheat pillows, and, yes, anti-snore pillows.

Families and groups should inquire about Nemacolin's townhouses, which start at $389 per night, and luxury homes, priced as high as $3,000. The resort's most affordable lodging option is **Maggie Valley** ($135–150), an RV park named for Joseph Hardy's daughter, now president and owner of Nemacolin. Amenities include satellite TV with premium channels, high-speed Internet access—and room service. The 20-space park is open from April through November.

If Nemacolin's high-season rates leave you gasping for air, consider a midweek visit sometime after Thanksgiving and before mid-May, when rates are as low as $229 for a room at the Lodge and $279 for a room at Chateau Lafayette. A two-night minimum stay applies on weekends. If you're planning to visit on a holiday, plan on a three-night minimum stay.

FOOD

You won't find a "dining district" in this mostly rural region, unless you count Nemacolin Woodlands Resort and Seven Springs Mountain Resort with their restaurant collections. (Bear in mind that a good number of Nemacolin's eateries aren't open during the colder months, and several of Seven Springs' aren't open during the warmer ones.) The Laurel Highlands' recommendable restaurants are scattered about. It's well worth your time to search them out, as they offer some of the best dining experiences this side of Philadelphia.

Lautrec

In 2007, Nemacolin Woodlands Resort handed

the reins of its flagship restaurant, ((**Lautrec** (1001 LaFayette Dr., Farmington, 866/344-6957, www.nemacolin.com, 6–9 P.M. Thurs., 6–10 P.M. Fri.–Sat., $98–135, up to $295 with wine pairings), to 28-year-old David Racicot. Three years earlier the self-taught chef had opened Aqueous, Nemacolin's upscale steakhouse, and snagged a AAA Four Diamond rating. The gastronomic glitterati expected great things. Racicot blew their expectations out of the water. Before the year was through, AAA awarded Lautrec its highest honor, making it Pennsylvania's first new Five Diamond restaurant in 13 years. Today it's also on the exclusive Forbes Travel Guide five-star list. Racicot has moved on, but Lautrec's reputation remains impeccable.

Though named for the French artist, Lautrec presents a dining experience best described as modern American. That means Burgundy snails, Maine lobster, mushroom risotto, and yuzu can all find their way onto the menu. Unconventional cooking techniques transform even common ingredients—cauliflower, for example—into artworks. A la carte dining isn't an option here. Guests can choose between a seven-course prix fixe and a nine-course chef's tasting. Needless to say, dinner can take hours. Wine connoisseurs can order a bottle from the state's largest private wine cellar or opt for the sommelier's pairings. The service is really something else. Waitstaff are not only well versed in the food and the placement of forks but are also remarkably friendly. So while men are urged to wear jackets and denim is verboten, the atmosphere in the rounded, richly hued dining room is entirely unstuffy.

More Fine Dining

A Laurel Highlands landmark, **Green Gables Restaurant** (7712 Somerset Pike, Boswell, 814/629-9201, www.mountainplayhouse .org, lunch noon–4 P.M. weekdays, brunch noon–4 P.M. Sat. and 11 A.M.–4 P.M. Sun., dinner 5 P.M.–close Tues.–Sun., $9–32, reservations suggested) started life in 1927 as a roadside sandwich stand. Over the next several decades, owner James Stoughton expanded his

© NEMACOLIN WOODLANDS RESORT

the dining room of Lautrec

eatery room by room, eventually adding terraces and a banquet room with an intricately inlaid dance floor and hand-hewn beams rescued from old barns. Along the way, he established a professional summer stock theater, the Mountain Playhouse, on his property. The meal-and-theater experience is truly special, but Green Gables is a worthwhile destination even when the playhouse is on hiatus. Come for lunch for a meal under $15 and a chance to explore the enchanting grounds in daylight. Come for dinner for artful entrées such as tomatillo-braised bison short ribs and prosciutto-wrapped pork tenderloin.

Seven Springs Mountain Resort's contribution to the fine dining scene is **Helen's** (777 Waterwheel Dr., Seven Springs, 800/452-2223, ext. 7691 during day or 7827 in evening, www.7springs.com, hours vary by season, $16–50), once the sylvan home of the resort's founders. It's particularly romantic when there's snow piled outside and frosting the trees. The Caesar salad is tossed tableside for two. Light eaters can order a half portion of most entrées, including grilled South African lobster tails, braised lamb chops, and pheasant with thyme jus.

The stone Hopwood House, built in 1790 in the village of the same name, played host to Abraham Lincoln and half a dozen other U.S. presidents. In 1994, the French took it over, transforming the onetime tavern into **Chez Gerard** (1186 National Pike/Business U.S. 40, Hopwood, 724/437-9001, www.chezgerard.net, 5 P.M.–close Thurs.–Sun., open for lunch and dinner Mon.–Wed. by reservation for eight or more, $19–65). "Fusion" isn't in chef William Severac's vocabulary. This is food prepared "in the way of the French by the French," says the French native. Severac's delightful wife, Muriel, runs the front end. In the way of the French, she won't present a check until it's asked for. The $50 prix fixe dinner includes your choice of appetizer, main course, and dessert, plus an assortment of cheeses, a salad, and house-made *mignardises*—lavender- and ginger-flavored truffles. Everything on the menu can be ordered individually. Particularly

popular are the sautéed Dover sole, filleted at tableside and $15 extra when ordered as part of the prix fixe, and grilled duck breast. Chez Gerard went BYOB in 2009 for a more affordable dining experience. There's no corkage fee.

Casual Fare

Not long after meeting McDonald's founder Ray Kroc at a Chicago restaurant show, Jim Delligatti bought into the Golden Arches dream and began opening franchises in the Pittsburgh area. In 1967, the entrepreneur added a new hamburger to the menu of his Uniontown McDonald's. Delligatti's invention, the Big Mac, was rolled out nationally the following year, becoming such a fixture on the fast food landscape that Pittsburgh was temporarily renamed Big Mac, USA, on the sandwich's 25th anniversary. Its 40th was celebrated with the opening of the **Big Mac Museum Restaurant** (9051 Rte. 30, North Huntingdon, 724/863-9837, www.bigmacmuseum.com, lobby 5 A.M.–midnight, drive-thru open 24 hours, free admission, food under $5) off the Irwin exit (#67) of the Pennsylvania turnpike. Order *twoallbeefpattiesspecialsaucelettucecheesepicklesonionsonasesameseedbun*, check out the Big Mac memorabilia, and snap a photo in front of the world's largest Big Mac statue.

A stone's throw from the Ohiopyle State Park visitors center, **The Firefly Grill** (25 Sherman St., Ohiopyle, 724/329-7155, www.thefireflygrill.com, 11 A.M.–8 P.M. daily April–Oct., $4–9) has been feeding outdoor adventurers since 2001. Its wraps, sandwiches, and salads are fuel enough for a long bike ride or river trip, but few can pass up the fresh-cut fries. Veggie heads have plenty to choose from, including a gyro loaded with hummus, vegetables, and feta. A 32-ounce hand-squeezed lemonade is just $2.50. Want something harder to quench your thirst? **Ohiopyle House Cafe** (144 Grant St., Ohiopyle, 724/329-1122, www.ohiopylehousecafe.com, open Memorial Day–Labor Day 11 A.M.–9 P.M. Sun.–Thurs., 11 A.M.–10 P.M. Fri.–Sat., $9–26) boasts a full bar, a fantastic deck, and homemade potato chips.

Built for the town's first mayor, the turn-of-the-20th-century Victorian now known as the **Ligonier Tavern** (137 W. Main St., Ligonier, 724/238-4831, www.ligonier tavern.com, 11:30 A.M.–9 P.M. Mon.–Thurs., 11:30 A.M.–10 P.M. Fri.–Sat., noon–8 P.M. Sun., bar open late, $6–23) was the first home in Ligonier with indoor plumbing. Today it's locals' first choice for a casual, high-quality meal. Homemade is the name of the game here. The tavern even has an in-house bakery. Its creamy artichoke dip caught the attention of *Bon Appetit* magazine some years ago. The burgers, pasta dishes, and signature crab cakes are also popular.

Don't be fooled by the name. **Oakhurst Tea Room** (2409 Glades Pike/Rte. 31, Somerset, 814/443-2897, www.oakhursttearoom.com, 11 A.M.–9 P.M. Tues.–Sat., 11 A.M.–8 P.M. Sun., winter hours may vary, $9–29) isn't a finger sandwiches sort of place. Quite the opposite: It's best known for all-you-can-eat buffets. The restaurant, family owned since 1933, acquired its name and teapot collection during Prohibition, when gentlemen gathered there for "tea" (wink, wink). Originally, the Oakhurst offered endless chicken and waffles for 50 cents. Chicken and waffles is still on the menu—though not immune to inflation—along with a whole lot more. Most everything is made from scratch with fresh, not frozen, ingredients. Although à la carte is always an option, the buffet is the way to go. At $8.45 for adults and $3.95 for children under 12, the luncheon buffet is a steal. It's available 11 A.M.–3 P.M. Tuesday–Saturday. At 4 P.M., Oakhurst unveils its "smorgasbord buffet," featuring more than 30 hot items. The feast, also available all day Sunday, is $12.95 for adults, $6.50 for children. Those who prefer to start their Sunday with eggs, pancakes, sausage, and the like can opt for the brunch buffet, priced at $10.95 for adults, $5.50 for children. A buffet loaded with crab legs, clams, mussels, shrimp, and Iceland cod reels in seafood lovers on Friday evenings. Adults pay $28.95 for the seafood and smorgasbord buffets; children pay half that. All buffets have an out-of-this-world dessert bar. The rather nondescript restaurant, capable of seating some 500 people, is six miles west of the Pennsylvania Turnpike's Somerset exit (#110) and 12 miles east of the Donegal exit (#91). It's a 10-minute drive from Hidden Valley Resort.

Tables inside **Out of the Fire Café** (3784 Rte. 31, Donegal, 724/593-4200, www.out ofthefirecafe.com, 4–8 P.M. Tues.–Thurs., 11 A.M.–9 P.M. Fri.–Sat., 11 A.M.–8 P.M. Sun., $6–30) afford a view of the open kitchen, where flames dance for chef/owner Jeff Fryer. Tables on the deck come with breezes and a mountain view. Tough call. Choosing a starter is an easy one. Smoked salmon is the restaurant's raison d'être, and platters of the stuff show up on both the lunch and dinner menus. Fryer, who got his first taste in 1974 and set out to perfect the smoking process, also offers a smoked salmon quesadilla, salads topped with smoked salmon, and smoked salmon wraps and sandwiches. But Out of the Fire Café isn't a one-note operation. Its hand-cut steaks, cooked over a wood-fired grill, and seafood entrées are also fantastic. And don't overlook the $5 sides, which include smoked gouda macaroni and cheese. Bring your favorite beer or wine. Reservations are recommended on weekends.

INFORMATION

Before your visit, visit the website of the **Laurel Highlands Visitors Bureau** (800/333-5661, www.laurelhighlands.org) to download a guide to the region or request that one be mailed to you. The bureau's main visitors center in Ligonier Town Hall (120 E. Main St., Ligonier) is open 8:30 A.M.–4:30 P.M. Monday–Friday. A second visitors center is located in the Somerset County Chamber of Commerce building (601 N. Center Ave., Somerset, 9 A.M.–5 P.M. Mon.–Thurs., 8 A.M.–5 P.M. Fri., and 9 A.M.–1 P.M. most Saturdays). The visitors center at Ohiopyle State Park is off Route 381 in a train station circa 1912. (Today the rail bed is a crushed limestone trail, part of the Great Allegheny Passage.) You can rifle through the brochure racks from dawn to dusk year-round. Information specialists are on hand 10 A.M.–4:30 P.M. daily May–October. On Fridays, Saturdays, and Sundays from Memorial Day to Labor Day, they stick around until 6 P.M.

GETTING THERE AND AROUND

The Laurel Highlands region is a driving destination. Donegal, its approximate center and a gateway to Ohiopyle State Park, is 50 miles southeast of Pittsburgh. The Pennsylvania Turnpike (I-76) traverses the region, with exits at Irwin (#67), New Stanton (#75), Donegal (#91), and Somerset (#110). Other east–west arteries include I-70, the historic National Road (U.S. 40), and the historic Lincoln Highway (U.S. 30). North–south highways U.S. 119 and U.S. 219 also find their way to the Laurel Highlands.

Pittsburgh International Airport (PIT) is the nearest major airport. Latrobe's **Arnold Palmer Regional Airport** (LBE), named for the golf legend who grew up less than a mile from its runway, offers charter flights to Atlantic City, New Jersey, and several Nevada destinations. Commuter service to and from Detroit was discontinued in mid-2009.

If you'd rather leave the driving to someone else, contact one of the tour services listed on the website of the Laurel Highlands Visitors Bureau (www.laurelhighlands.org).

THE ALLEGHENIES

These mountains we call the Alleghenies used to be a real headache. They didn't make it easy on settlers traveling west, where land and opportunity awaited them. Traversing the mountains by wagon took ages and not a little bit of gumption. They stymied canal systems. They baffled railroad builders. In time, of course, engineers tamed this section of the Appalachian range. They threaded a rail line right through the Alleghenies and, later, highways. What made the region so challenging two centuries ago—peaks and valleys, wide rivers and dense woods—is what makes it appealing today. It calls to hikers, cyclists, boaters, anglers, and wildlife watchers. The scenery makes getting from point A to point B so pleasant that the region's image-makers promote motor touring more zealously than they do most destinations.

That's not to say that the destinations are ho-hum. They include towns rich in history, the state's largest inland lake, its highest skiable peak, and a premier mountain biking trail. Towns like Johnstown, Altoona, and Bedford are so diligent about preserving their heritage that visitors can virtually taste life as a steelmaker, railroader, or frontiersman. State College is home to Pennsylvania State University and the mega parties that are Nittany Lions football games. Countless villages offer quaint bed-and-breakfasts and quietude. The region is especially quiet in winter, when amusement parks, show caverns, and even some museums are closed, boats are in storage, and the open road is less welcoming.

HIGHLIGHTS

(Johnstown Inclined Plane: The world's steepest vehicular funicular (try saying that three times) carried people to safety during two deadly floods in the 20th century. Hop on for killer views of "Flood City" (page 425).

(Horseshoe Curve: The 1854 feat of engineering that allowed trains to traverse the Alleghenies is still awe-inspiring after all these years (page 434).

(Berkey Creamery: Best. Ice Cream. Ever. (page 445).

(Seven Points Marina and **Lake Raystown Resort:** Where else in Pennsylvania can you rent a houseboat for a few days of peaceful, easy living? Nowhere (page 462).

(Omni Bedford Springs Resort: The mineral-rich springs at this luxury resort were believed by Native Americans to have curative powers. "Take the waters" and decide for yourself (page 478).

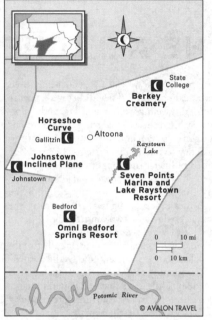

LOOK FOR **(** TO FIND RECOMMENDED SIGHTS, ACTIVITIES, DINING, AND LODGING.

Johnstown Inclined Plane

© JOHNSTOWN CONVENTION & VISITORS BUREAU

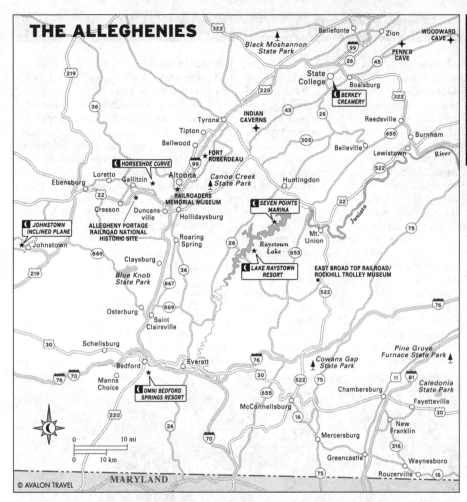

THE ALLEGHENIES

(map showing locations including Black Moshannon State Park, Bellefonte, Zion, Woodward Cave, Penn's Cave, State College, Boalsburg, Berkey Creamery, Tyrone, Indian Caverns, Reedsville, Burnham, Belleville, Lewistown, Tipton, Bellwood, Fort Roberdeau, Horseshoe Curve, Altoona, Canoe Creek State Park, Huntingdon, Loretto, Gallitzin, Railroaders Memorial Museum, Seven Points Marina, Ebensburg, Cresson, Duncansville, Hollidaysburg, Mt. Union, Johnstown Inclined Plane, Allegheny Portage Railroad National Historic Site, Johnstown, Roaring Spring, Raystown Lake, Lake Raystown Resort, East Broad Top Railroad/Rockhill Trolley Museum, Claysburg, Blue Knob State Park, Osterburg, Saint Clairsville, Schellsburg, Bedford, Everett, Cowans Gap State Park, Pine Grove Furnace State Park, Manns Choice, Omni Bedford Springs Resort, Chambersburg, Caledonia State Park, Fayetteville, McConnellsburg, New Franklin, Mercersburg, Greencastle, Waynesboro, Rouzerville, MARYLAND)

© AVALON TRAVEL

0   10 mi
0   10 km

PLANNING YOUR TIME

It's possible to digest Johnstown's heritage sights in a day. Plan on catching the sunset and a nightcap at the top of the famous inclined plane. Altoona is also doable in a day—unless you're a diehard rail fan. If that's the case, book a room at a B&B where you can watch the choo-choos go by and take a few days to explore the various railroad-related sights. Be aware that most of them, including the Railroaders Memorial Museum and Horseshoe Curve National Historic Landmark, are closed during the chilliest months.

If you're visiting State College, chances are you're the parent of a Penn Stater, a prospective student, or a nostalgic alumnus. I wouldn't presume to tell you how long to stay. Raystown Lake and the Bedford area are vacation destinations. The former attracts boaters, mountain bikers, and other outdoorsy types. The latter, with its historic "springs resort," attracts a well-heeled crowd. Suggested stay length: as long as possible.

Johnstown and Vicinity

Johnstown was once an unrivaled steel producer, a magnet for the industry's innovators and working-class immigrants. Its industrial base disintegrated, and its immigrants assimilated, but the city hasn't paved over its past. Johnstown's rivers are still lined with former mills, some of which have found new tenants. Its cityscape is still ornamented with ethnic churches, though many no longer house parishes. In a sense, the city is a museum of its former self, and that serves it well. One of its newer industries is tourism, driven largely by heritage attractions. Steelmaking is only part of its story. The better-known part is the Great Flood of 1889, which razed large swaths of the city and killed about 2,200 people—the largest single-day loss of life in the United States before September 11, 2001. There are two museums dedicated to the disaster: one in the downtown area and another about 10 miles northeast of Johnstown, at the site of the dam that burst on that day. The flood was the biggest news story of the latter 19th century after the assassination of Abraham Lincoln. The riveting tale of rich and poor, rated R violence, and rebirth hasn't lost its power to fascinate.

Flood City, as Johnstown was dubbed after two more deadly floods, has more recently become known as a motorcycle town. Bikers are fond of the scenic routes on all sides of the valley in which Johnstown is cradled. Every June, they descend upon the city in great numbers for a motorcycle rally that may be the largest in the state. Johnstown holds another distinction, one recognized by Guinness World Records. The Johnstown Inclined Plane, which climbs 900 feet from the river valley, is the world's steepest vehicular inclined plane. No visit is complete without a trip to the top.

SIGHTS
Johnstown Flood Museum
The 26-minute documentary shown hourly at the Johnstown Flood Museum (304 Washington St., Johnstown, 814/539-1889, www.jaha.org, 10 A.M.–5 P.M. daily, open until

Johnstown

THE 40-FOOT WAVE

In Hollywood's hands, the story of the Johnstown Flood of 1889 would probably begin like many thrillers: with an idyllic scene. The camera would pan the South Fork Fishing and Hunting Club, a summer retreat for Pittsburgh's wealthiest industrialists and financiers. It would zoom in on the likes of Andrew Carnegie and Henry Clay Frick fishing on the club's private Lake Conemaugh, their wives strolling with parasols, their children sailing. Then the camera would dive beneath the surface to take in the expensive game fish and, finally, the dam holding back the lake. The dam, we'd discover, is in dire need of repair.

A night of torrential rain found the lake swollen on the morning of May 31, 1889. In Johnstown, 14 miles downstream, there was water in the streets. Residents weren't terribly concerned, even as they lugged belongings to the upper stories of their homes and businesses. Johnstown's position in a river valley meant that flooding was a fact of life.

At Lake Conemaugh, club officials rounded up laborers to fortify the dam and relieve pressure from its breast. Despite their furious efforts, the dam crumpled shortly after 3 P.M., unleashing 20 million tons of water. Witnesses would later describe a 40-foot wave of water and debris rushing toward Johnstown. The wave was so powerful that bodies of victims were found as far away as Cincinnati. Some people swept up by the wave were deposited on a massive pile of wreckage that accumulated at the Pennsylvania Railroad Company's stone bridge in Johnstown. About 80 who survived the wild ride perished when the debris caught fire.

In the weeks and months after the disaster, the death toll climbed to 2,209. More than 750 of the victims were never identified, their bodies so badly mangled. Journalists, photographers, doctors, and relief workers, including American Red Cross founder Clara Barton, rushed to Johnstown. Donations of money, food, clothing, medical supplies, furniture, and even lumber for rebuilding arrived from all over the world. The South Fork Fishing and Hunting Club contributed 1,000 blankets.

Suits against the club proved fruitless, the courts ruling that the flood was an act of God. But its elite members were condemned in the court of public opinion. One newspaper cartoon depicted them sipping champagne on the clubhouse porch as the flood leveled Johnstown. In fact, only a handful of members were on premises that deadly day. It was spring yet; most of them were still in their city manses. And they would never return.

Webster & Albee, Publishers, Rochester, N. Y.

Views of Johnstown, Pa.

Johnstown and Conemaugh Va[...]   91. 1889.

7 P.M. Memorial Day–Labor Day, admission $7, seniors $6, children 3–18 $5) is a first-rate primer on the 1889 disaster. *The Johnstown Flood*, produced by filmmaker Charles Guggenheim, won an Academy Award for best documentary, short subject. The museum also features a large relief map that illustrates the flood's path and an original "Oklahoma house," which served as temporary housing for people left homeless by the flood. Its collection of artifacts includes an undershirt worn by a 6-year-old during the flood, the contents of a victim's pocket, and a quilt used to drag people to safety. A morgue book lists details about bodies and body parts recovered from the debris. One particularly fascinating exhibit spotlights the news reports, many of them inaccurate, that turned the world's attention to Johnstown.

The museum occupies the former Cambria Library, which was built to replace a library destroyed by the flood. The structure was paid for by steel magnate Andrew Carnegie, a member of the fishing and hunting club that owned the neglected dam blamed for the devastation. Tickets to the museum include admission to other attractions operated by the Johnstown Area Heritage Association: the Frank & Sylvia Pasquerilla Heritage Discovery Center and the Wagner-Ritter House & Garden. No need to rush through them. Tickets are good for five days.

Frank & Sylvia Pasquerilla Heritage Discovery Center

The Heritage Discovery Center (201 6th Ave., Johnstown, 814/539-1889, www.jaha .org, 10 A.M.–5 P.M. daily, open until 7 P.M. Memorial Day–Labor Day, admission $7, seniors $6, children 3–18 $5) occupies a former brewery in the Cambria City section of Johnstown, where thousands of European immigrants settled in the 19th and early 20th centuries. In 1880, 85 percent of the neighborhood's residents were foreign-born. Appropriately enough, the center's main exhibit is the interactive America: Through Immigrant Eyes. Upon entry, visitors choose

a card with a photo of an immigrant character—a 12-year-old peasant from Poland, for instance—and follow their character's path from the old country to Johnstown's ethnic neighborhoods.

The Discovery Center also houses the **Iron & Steel Gallery** and **Johnstown Children's Museum**. The centerpiece of the Iron & Steel Gallery is a film that tells the story of the Cambria Iron Company, whose rise and fall ushered Johnstown's. *The Mystery of Steel*, which premiered in 2009, includes historic photographs and high-definition footage shot in local mills before they were shuttered in 1992. Infrared heaters in the theater help give

RECOMMENDED READING

If Johnstown's attractions leave you hungry for more information about the cataclysm of 1889, pick up David McCullough's *The Johnstown Flood*. The page-turning account of America's worst inland flood, first published in 1968, was McCullough's first book. The social historian researched the disaster while the last survivors were still alive. Later books earned him two Pulitzer Prizes and two National Book Awards. Here's a nibble:

Johnstown of 1889 was not a pretty place. But the land around it was magnificent. From Main Street, a man standing among the holiday crowds could see green hills, small mountains, really, hunching in close on every side, dwarfing the tops of the houses and smokestacks.

The city was built on a nearly level flood plain at the confluence of two rivers, down at the bottom of an enormous hole in the Alleghenies. A visitor from the Middle West once commented, "Your sun rises at ten and sets at two," and it was not too great an exaggeration.

viewers a sense of the atmosphere in a working steel mill. The Children's Museum on the third floor of the Discovery Center also opened in 2009. Hands-on exhibits geared toward children 3–10 explore regional geology, culture, and industries.

Discovery Center tickets are good for admission to other attractions operated by the Johnstown Area Heritage Association: the Johnstown Flood Museum and the Wagner-Ritter House & Garden. Tickets can be used over a five-day period.

Wagner-Ritter House & Garden

A house museum two blocks from the Heritage Discovery Center tells the story of the German immigrants who once occupied it. Three generations of a working-class family lived in the Wagner-Ritter House (418 Broad St., Johnstown, 814/539-1889, www.jaha.org, 11 A.M.–4 P.M. daily Apr.–Oct., admission $7, seniors $6, children 3–18 $5, includes admission to Heritage Discovery Center and Johnstown Flood Museum) from the time it was built in the 1860s through 1990. The house withstood the 1889 flood, even though water rose so high that family members were able to pull a woman to safety from a second-floor window. The Johnstown Area Heritage Association restored the house to its 19th-century appearance, peeling back 14 layers of wallpaper in some areas and decorating it with original furnishings and family heirlooms. Hops, cabbages, potatoes, and other crops grow in a German-style raised-bed garden behind the house. A permanent exhibit in the adjacent visitors center tells the story of the family and the immigrant community of which it was a part.

◖ Johnstown Inclined Plane

In the aftermath of the Great Flood, communities sprang up in higher elevations. One of those was Westmont, which sits atop Yoder Hill. The hill, with its 70.9 percent grade, was too steep for a road. So an inclined railway was built to carry people, horses, and wagons to the tony neighborhood 900 feet above the river

valley. The Johnstown Inclined Plane (upper station 711 Edgehill Dr., Johnstown, 814/536-1816, www.inclinedplane.com, 7:30 A.M.–10:30 P.M. Mon.–Thurs., 7:30 A.M.–11 P.M. Fri., 9 A.M.–11 P.M. Sat., 9 A.M.–10 P.M. Sun. Apr.–Sept., 11 A.M.–9 P.M. Sun.–Thurs., 11 A.M.–10 P.M. Fri.–Sat. Oct.–Dec., 11 A.M.–7 P.M. Sun.–Thurs., 11 A.M.–10 P.M. Fri.–Sat. Jan.–Mar., fare $4 round-trip, $2.25 one way, children 2–12 $2.50 round-trip, $1.50 one way, seniors free) began operating in June 1891 and hauled about a million passengers a year in its heyday. It was both commuter line and lifeline. During the deadly floods of 1936 and 1977, the world's steepest vehicular inclined plane carried people out of the valley to safety.

The lower station is accessible from downtown by a footbridge that crosses Route 56. If driving east on Route 56, pull onto the ramp that leads to the incline and either park there or continue across a bridge that spans Stonycreek River and drive right onto a cable car. The fare for automobiles is $6 one way. Motorcycles ride for $4 and bicycles for free.

© ANNA DUBROVSKY

Johnstown Inclined Plane

observation deck at the upper station of Johnstown Inclined Plane

There's a visitors center up top, where you can learn more about Johnstown's various floods and pick up information about area attractions. An observation deck affords a bird's-eye view of greater Johnstown and insight into the path of the 1889 floodwaters, which crashed into Yoder Hill. Ice cream and other refreshments are sold on the deck during the warmer months. **City View Bar & Grill,** which shares an entrance with the visitors center, offers a wide selection of eats year-round. If time allows, take a drive or stroll along Westmont's **Luzerne Street,** which boasts the longest stretch of American elms in the country.

Cable cars aren't the only way to climb Yoder Hill. A trail between the foot and top of the incline takes hikers past large steel sculptures made with remnants from local plants. The **James Wolfe Sculpture Trail** is named for the sculptor.

Grandview Cemetery

Many of the 2,209 victims of the 1889 flood are interred at Grandview Cemetery (801 Millcreek Rd., Johnstown, 814/535-2652, gates open at 7:30 A.M. daily, close at dusk May–Oct. and 5 P.M. Nov.–Apr.) on Yoder Hill, a mile south of the inclined plane's upper station. A monument dedicated in 1892 overlooks the Unknown Plot, where 777 unidentified victims are buried.

Thunder in the Valley

For four days in June, Johnstown becomes biker heaven. The streets fill with all manner of motorcycles: pimped-out choppers, dirt bikes, drag-racing machines—you name it. Thunder in the Valley (814/536-7993, www.visitjohns townpa.com) doesn't discriminate. The rally attracted about 3,500 motorcycling enthusiasts in 1998, its first year. Now, more than 200,000 pour into Johnstown and surrounding communities during the fourth weekend in June. The city's hotels burst at the seams; Altoona, Bedford, Ligonier, Indiana, and other towns absorb the overflow.

Thunder isn't a leather-clad bacchanalia. It's

Thunder in the Valley

a family-friendly event that attracts plenty of non-riders. Motorcycle manufacturers show off their latest models. Vendors peddle chaps, helmets, jewelry, and other biker accoutrements. There's live music, a children's play area, charity rides, stunt shows, and a parade.

Johnstown Flood National Memorial

Two grassy abutments are all that remain of the infamous South Fork Dam at the Johnstown Flood National Memorial (733 Lake Rd., South Fork, 814/495-4643, www.nps.gov/jofl, 9 A.M.–5 P.M. daily, admission $4, children 15 and under free), operated by the National Park Service. On each anniversary of the May 31, 1889, flood that killed 2,209 people, candles are lit on the ruins and on the farm of Elias Unger, who was president of the South Fork Fishing and Hunting Club when the dam broke. Exhibits at the visitors center seek to convey the fearsome power unleashed by the failure. In 2006, the Park Service acquired the vast clubhouse where Pittsburgh's elite swilled

brandy and smoked cigars. Rangers lead tours of the clubhouse during the summer months.

Museums and Galleries

The **Southern Alleghenies Museum of Art at Johnstown** (Pasquerilla Performing Arts Center at the University of Pittsburgh at Johnstown, 450 Schoolhouse Rd., 814/269-7234, www.sama-art.org, 9:30 A.M.–4:30 P.M. Mon.–Fri., free admission) exhibits selections from SAMA's permanent collection of American art and hosts an annual juried show of work by local artists.

The first eye-catching artwork at the **Bottle Works Ethnic Arts Center** (411 3rd Ave., Johnstown, 814/536-5399, www.bottleworks.org, 10 A.M.–4 P.M. Tues.–Fri., 11 A.M.–3 P.M. Sat., free admission) is the building itself. It once housed the Tulip Bottling Company, a soda pop manufacturer founded by immigrants. Now it's plastered in colorful murals. The center, which celebrates the region's ethnic heritage, has a gallery, black box theater, and studios.

© JOHNSTOWN CONVENTION & VISITORS BUREAU

The **Community Arts Center of Cambria County** (1217 Menoher Blvd., Johnstown, 814/255-6515, www.caccc.org, 10 A.M.–5 P.M. Mon.–Fri., 10 A.M.–3 P.M. Sat., free admission) is home to a collection of more than 875 dolls, Dorothy and her Oz crew included. Rotating exhibits highlight the work of regional and national artists. The center hosts a summer concert series and several annual events, including the Log House Arts Festival over Labor Day weekend.

Other Sights

Coal mining and railroading take center stage at the **Portage Station Museum** (400 Lee St., Portage, 814/736-9223, www.portagepa.us, noon–5 P.M. Wed.–Sat., free admission) about 20 miles east of Johnstown. The museum and the Portage Area Historical Society, which manages it, occupy a restored 1926 railroad depot building. A 173-square-foot model train display features nearby railroad attractions, including the Horseshoe Curve and the depot itself, which was used by the Pennsylvania Railroad until 1954. On the first Saturday of each month, engines from different time periods pull as many as 40 cars around the miniature tracks. A documentary chronicles the 1940 Sonman Mine explosion, which killed 63 miners near Portage.

For a taste of the coal miner's life, head to the **Seldom Seen Tourist Coal Mine** (Rte. 36, 4 miles north of Patton, 814/247-6305 in season, 814/674-8939 off-season, www.seldomseenmine.com, noon–5 P.M. Sat.–Sun. in June and Thurs.–Sun. July–Aug., admission $9, children 4–12 $6), a family-run mine that operated from 1939 to 1963. Former miners take visitors deep underground, where coal was once dug by hand, loaded on cars, and hauled from the mine by mules.

ENTERTAINMENT AND EVENTS

Bars

Tulune's Southside Saloon (36 Bridge St./ Rte. 403, Johnstown, 814/536-1001, www.southsidesaloon.com, 4 P.M.–2 A.M. Tues.–Sat.,

---

SPORTS, STEEL MILLS, AND THE SILVER SCREEN

The Johnstown Chiefs aren't the city's first minor league ice hockey team. The Johnstown Jets played there from 1950 to 1977, inspiring the 1977 cult hockey film *Slap Shot*. Paul Newman stars as the player-coach of the fictional Charlestown Chiefs, a failing team in a town troubled by mill closings. The movie is based on a screenplay by Nancy Dowd, whose brother played for the Jets, and parts of it were filmed in Johnstown. When the city got a new franchise in 1988, the owners let fans pick the team name. They voted to name their real-life hockey team after the movie version.

The second of two major movies filmed in Johnstown also has a sports theme. *All the Right Moves,* starring Tom Cruise, is the story of a high school football player with dreams of landing a college scholarship and escaping his steel town. The 1983 drama/romance was filmed entirely on location in Johnstown and Pittsburgh during the season of the Western Pennsylvania Interscholastic Athletic League.

---

food $8–10) boasts the area's largest selection of imported and craft beers—large enough to fill an eight-page menu—and a strict "no jerks allowed" policy. Beers run the gamut from a $3 Guatemalan lager to a $65 Belgian brew, vintage 2000. The kitchen, open until 10 P.M. on weeknights and 11 P.M. Friday and Saturday, dishes up burgers, Bavarian pretzels, and other beer-friendly grub.

Performing Arts

The **Pasquerilla Performing Arts Center** at the University of Pittsburgh at Johnstown (450 Schoolhouse Rd., Johnstown, box office 800/846-2787, www.upjarts.com) imports talent from around the world for its annual performance series, which spans multiple genres: Broadway musicals, classic rock tributes, comedy shows, music concerts, dance performances, and even acrobatic theater. The performance hall is home to the **Johnstown Symphony Orchestra** (814/535-6738, www .johnstownsymphony.org), founded in 1929. Not to be missed is the annual Opera Festival, during which world-renowned opera artists perform with the orchestra. Local songbirds organized as the Johnstown Symphony Chorus accompany the orchestra in at least two concerts a year. Homegrown dance and theater groups also take the stage on occasion.

Johnstown's version of Shakespeare in the park takes place at Powell Stackhouse Park in Westmont, just outside the city. The **Band of Brothers Shakespeare Company** (814/539-9500, www.bandofbrothersshakespeare.org) has raised more than $200,000 for the park since its first *Macbeth* in 1991.

Festivals and Events

Johnstown's three-day **PolkaFest** (St. Mary's Byzantine Catholic Church, 411 Power St., Johnstown, 814/536-7993, www.visit johnstownpa.com/polkafest, weekend after Memorial Day, free) attracts several thousand fans of polka music and dance. Nationally renowned Polish and Slovenian polka bands provide the tunes. St. Mary's also hosts **Jazz Along the River** (814/535-4132, fourth Fri. May–Sept., free), a series that pairs ethnic eats with an American-bred musical art form. The band goes on about 6 P.M. Parish members start serving up stuffed cabbage, kielbasa, pierogies, and other Eastern European specialties about an hour earlier. The **AmeriServ Flood City Music Festival** (814/539-1889, www.jaha.org, late Aug., admission by donation) in downtown Johnstown features three stages and acts from across the country. It replaced the Johnstown FolkFest in 2009.

Today's **Cambria County Fair** (814/472-7491, www.cambriacofair.com, opens Labor Day, admission charged) is held on the same grounds just north of Ebensburg as the original fair in 1891. It's a weeklong celebration of the rural life, complete with livestock exhibits, amusement rides, tractor and truck pulls, square dancing, and the crowning of a fair queen. Cambria County is the second largest producer of potatoes in Pennsylvania, which is cause for an annual celebration in Ebensburg, the county seat. Some 200 crafters and artisans peddle their wares in downtown Ebensburg during **PotatoFest** (814/472-8780, www .potatofest.com, late Sept., free). Food vendors serve up potato soup, potato ham pot pie, sweet potato fries, potato pancakes, potato pizza, and even potato candy.

SPORTS AND RECREATION
Prince Gallitzin State Park

Picturesque Prince Gallitzin State Park (966 Marina Rd., Patton, 814/674-1000, www.dcnr .state.pa.us/stateparks/parks/princegallitzin. aspx), about an hour northeast of Johnstown, is popular with boaters and campers. Motors up to 20 horsepower are permitted on the 1,635-acre Glendale Lake, which has nine public boat-launching areas, three mooring facilities, two marinas, and swimming areas. Rental boats and lake tours are available. The lake is a warm-water fishery with bass, pike, muskellunge, and other game fish, plus a decent population of panfish.

A large modern campground is open from the second Friday in April to the last Monday in October. Ten modern cabins that sleep as many as eight people are available year-round. The park has 12 miles of hiking trails, many of which begin at the Point Trailhead near the campground. The 20-mile snowmobile trail network in the northern part of the park is also open to hikers and mountain bikers. Cross-country skiers must stick to seven miles of marked trails.

Rock Run Recreation Area

More than 50 miles of twisting trails make Rock Run Recreation Area (1228 St. Lawrence Rd., Patton, 814/674-6026, www.rockrun recreation.com) a mecca for owners of all-terrain vehicles and dirt bikes. There's terrain for riders of all levels on the property, which belonged to a coal company as recently as 2002. Primitive camping sites are available on a first-come, first-served basis.

Ice-Skating

Ebensburg's **Lake Rowena** is traditionally one of the first in the area to freeze, and ice skaters are invited to practice triple toe loops (or simply staying upright) in a small, roped-off area. For a report on the lake's condition, contact the Ebensburg Borough Office (814/472-8780, www.ebensburgpa.com). **Planet Ice Skating Center** (195 Jari Dr., Johnstown, 814/262-7465, www.planeticeusa.com) offers year-round skating on an NHL-sized ice sheet, plus trippy colored lights and thumping music.

Spectator Sports

Johnstown's minor league ice hockey team, founded in 1988, is the only original ECHL team still in its original city. The **Johnstown Chiefs** (814/539-1799, www.johnstownchiefs.com) play at the Cambria County War Memorial Arena (326 Napoleon St., Johnstown, 814/536-5156, www.warmemorialarena.com), which also hosts everything from professional boxing to trade shows.

The likes of Tiger Woods have teed up at the annual **Sunnehanna Amateur Tournament for Champions** (814/255-4121, www.sunnehanna.com, June). The four-day, 72-hole tournament at Johnstown's Sunnehanna Country Club is free to spectators. Top amateur baseball players also flock to Johnstown yearly. The **All-American Amateur Baseball Association National Tournament** (814/255-6600, early Aug.) is a 16-team double-elimination tournament that takes place over a week. Most games are played at Point Stadium (100 Johns St., Johnstown, 814/533-5511) at the confluence of Johnstown's three rivers.

ACCOMMODATIONS

National chains dominate the lodging scene in downtown Johnstown, but independent establishments can be found in the hills and valleys around it.

Under $100

Once the homestead of Johnstown founder Joseph Schantz, **Schantz Haus** (687 E. Campus Ave., Davidsville, 814/479-2494, www.schantzhaus.com, $50–75) offers three guest rooms, two of which share a bath. It's located on a working dairy farm; guests can try their hand at milking a cow or bottle-feeding a calf. The Swiss-born Schantz, whose surname was anglicized to Johns, is buried on the farm along with several generations of descendants.

The (**Collins Inn Bed and Breakfast** (114 E. High St., Ebensburg, 814/472-4311, www.nooncollins.com, $77–85) is so replete with antique furnishings that it has the feel of a house museum. The grand bed with decorative scrollwork in the Red Room once belonged to railroad builder Philip Collins, who lived in the 1834 Federal-style stone mansion more than a century ago. During World War I, the local draft board occupied the parlor. Pittsburgh native Gene Kelly ran a dance studio on the property in the 1930s. The Green Dining Room, where breakfast is served, housed Ebensburg's public library at one time. Today the historic home has six guest rooms, each with a private bathroom, and modern amenities including air-conditioning, cable TV, and wireless Internet access.

The garden-themed **Dillweed Bed & Breakfast** (7453 Rte. 403 S., Dilltown, 814/446-6465, www.dillweedinc.com, $75–125) has four flower-festooned guest rooms that share two bathrooms, plus a suite with a small kitchen and full private bathroom. It's adjacent to the 36-mile Ghost Town Trail, and its two-floor Trailside Shop offers snacks and beverages for weary hikers along with country gifts such as scented candles and homemade soaps. On the second Saturday in June, the Dillweed hosts the Pick-A-Dilly Herb Faire, where vendors serve up food, crafts, and gardening tips.

$100-150

The owners of the **King's Springs Farm Bed and Breakfast** (3044 Ben Franklin Hwy., Ebensburg, 814/749-9168, www.kingsspringsbb.com, $135) raise hay, organic beef, flowers, herbs, fruits, and vegetables on their hundred-acre property, so you can bet that breakfast is made with fresh, local ingredients. Guests are free to explore the gardens, pastures, orchard, wooded paths, and two ponds. Rooms boast remote-controlled gas fireplaces, but many guests prefer to relax on the farmhouse's wraparound porch.

Come mating season, the bull elk and red deer stags at **Majestic World Lodge and Retreat** (679 Memory Ln., Portage, 814/693-0189, www.majesticworldlodge.com, $95–120) erupt in bugles and roars. Some vacationers come to the getaway at 3,000 feet specifically for the chorus. Majestic offers rustic rooms in its lodge along with a four-bedroom rental house that can sleep more than 15. Guests can arrange for a guided hunt on the property.

FOOD
Johnstown

Johnstown eateries eschew pomp in favor of a laid-back vibe. The city likes its sub sandwiches and hot dogs, and local establishments do a fine job with both. Skip Subway and try a torpedo from **Em's Original Sub Shop** (345 Main St., 814/535-5919, 7 A.M.–8 P.M. Mon.–Fri., 9 A.M.–7 P.M. Sat., $5–10). To look at the menu behind the register is to broadcast your out-of-town-ness. Locals know exactly what they like between their 12 inches of Italian bread. Em's has two other locations in Johnstown and a fourth in Somerset. Coney Island may be in Brooklyn, New York, but **Coney Island Lunch** (127 Clinton St., 814/535-2885, www.coneyislandjohnstownpa.com, 6 A.M.–4 A.M. Mon.–Sat., $2–6) is a Johnstown landmark. It's been around and owned by the same family since 1916. Locals pile into the joint after bars close to ward off hangovers with hot dogs smothered in homemade chili sauce—just $1.50 a pop. A more exotic choice is the "sundowner," a

cheeseburger topped with mustard, chili sauce, chopped onions, and a fried egg. Just two hours after it closes, Coney Island reopens to serve up eggs and hotcakes.

"If it swims we have it," promises **The Fish Boat** (544 Main St., 814/536-7403, www.thefishboat.com, 10 A.M.–5:30 P.M. Mon.–Thurs., 9 A.M.–6:30 P.M. Fri., 10 A.M.–5 P.M. Sat., $4–15), an otherwise humble seafood market and restaurant. The Fisherman's Delight platter offers a bit of everything: haddock, scallops, clams, shrimp, oysters, and a crab cake, plus your choice of sides. Baked fish is the Friday special at **Phoenix Tavern** (200 Broad St., 814/536-3981, kitchen 11 A.M.–midnight Mon.–Fri., noon–midnight Sat., bar open until 2 A.M., $4–10) in Cambria City, a section of Johnstown that's peppered with churches. Sandwiches, salads, and pizzas are available any day of the week. The pierogi pizza—mashed potato, cheese, butter, and onions—is a nod to the neighborhood's ethnic heritage.

The similarly casual **Boulevard Grill** (165 Southmont Blvd., 814/539-5344, www.blvdgrill.com, kitchen 11 A.M.–10 P.M. Mon.–Thurs., 11 A.M.–11 P.M. Fri.–Sat., 3–9 P.M. Sun., bar open until midnight Mon.–Thurs., 2 A.M. Fri.–Sat., 11 P.M. Sun., $4–25) serves everything from hot dogs to filet mignon in a wood-paneled setting. Sports fans take note: The ivy in front of the banquet facility reportedly grew from clippings taken from Chicago's Wrigley Field.

The Holiday Inn in downtown Johnstown is home to the more upscale **Harrigan's Cafe & Wine Deck** (250 Market St., 814/361-2620, www.harriganscafewinedeck.com, restaurant 6 A.M.–10 P.M. weekdays, 7 A.M.–10 P.M. weekends, lounge open until midnight Sun.–Thurs., 2 A.M. Fri.–Sat., $8–33), notable for its Mediterranean cuisine and extensive wine list. On Fridays, Harrigan's serves sushi, ceviche, and seafood carpaccio 5–8 P.M. At **Nyko's Restaurant on Scalp** (935 Scalp Ave., 814/254-4099, www.nykosrestaurant.com, 11 A.M.–11 P.M. Mon.–Sat., $8–29), sushi lovers needn't wait until Friday. Nyko's is known for its selection of nigiri and maki, but there are options aplenty for diners who don't walk on the raw side, including Korean-style barbecued beef, pan-roasted pork chops, and pasta entrées.

"Comfort food" and "health conscious" are an improbable duo of restaurant descriptors. The romantic ☾ **Back Door Café** (402 Chestnut St., 814/539-5084, www.the backdoorcafe.com, 4–9 P.M. Tues.–Thurs., 4–10 P.M. Fri.–Sat., $10–25) proves it's possible with dishes loaded with fresh seasonal ingredients, many of them local. There's a brick oven on premises but no deep fryer. The ever-changing menu always includes a variety of flatbread pizzas with toppings such as sautéed Hungarian hot peppers or wild mushrooms handpicked by chef Tom Chulick.

Ambience reaches new heights at **City View Bar & Grill** (709 Edgehill Dr., 814/534-0190, www.inclinedplane.com/cityview.html, 11 A.M.–10 P.M. Tues.–Thurs., 11 A.M.–midnight Fri.–Sat., 10 A.M.–10 P.M. Sun. May–Oct., closes one hour earlier Tues.–Thurs. and Sun. Nov.–Apr., $8–20) atop the historic inclined plane. The views from the indoor and balcony dining areas upstage entrées like slow-roasted pork ribs and pork medallions with fruit chutney.

Ebensburg

The borough of Ebensburg, about 20 miles northeast of Johnstown, is bursting with Italian restaurants, including the classily cozy **Amici's** (102 S. Center St., 814/471-0366, www.amicisebensburg.com, 3–9 P.M. Mon.–Thurs., 3–10 P.M. Fri.–Sat., $7–25) with its copper bar and stained glass windows. Seafood lovers will appreciate the penne pasta with shrimp and crabmeat in *fra diavolo,* a spicy tomato cream sauce. **Donatello's** (124 W. High St., 814/472-4688, www.dona tellosrestaurant.com, 4–9 P.M. Tues.–Thurs., 4–10 P.M. Fri.–Sat., $12–28) owners Enzo and Nancy Pirrone opened restaurants in Germany and the Midwest before bringing their Italian

cuisine to Ebensburg. A seafood-heavy antipasti menu is prelude to entrées such as *meda-glione:* breaded veal and eggplant layered with ham and Swiss cheese, baked with mozzarella, and topped with pink sauce. Looking for pizza or calzones? You won't find them at Amici's or Donatello's.

INFORMATION AND SERVICES

The **Greater Johnstown/Cambria County Convention and Visitors Bureau** (814/536-7993, www.visitjohnstownpa.com) operates information centers in downtown Johnstown (416 Main St., 8:30 A.M.–4:30 P.M. Mon.–Fri., 11 A.M.–3 P.M. Sat.–Sun.) and at the top of the inclined plane (711 Edgehill Dr., 11 A.M.–5 P.M. Mon.–Fri., 11 A.M.–3 P.M. Sat.–Sun.). Johnstown has a daily newspaper, *The Tribune-Democrat* (www.tribune-democrat.com) and a monthly lifestyle magazine, *Johnstown Magazine* (www.johnstownmag.com).

GETTING THERE AND AROUND

Johnstown is about 70 miles east of Pittsburgh. It's reachable by U.S. 219, U.S. 22, and Routes 56, 403, and 271. Pittsburgh International Airport (PIT) is the nearest major airport, but **John Murtha Johnstown-Cambria County Airport** (JST), five miles east of Johnstown, offers direct service to and from Washington, D.C.

Amtrak (800/872-7245, www.amtrak .com) provides train service to Johnstown via its Pennsylvanian line, which connects New York City and Pittsburgh. **Greyhound** (800/231-2222, www.greyhound.com) offers bus service to the city.

Bus service in and around Johnstown is provided by **CamTran** (814/535-5526, www .camtranbus.com). The base fare is $1.50. One-day passes are available ($4.15 adults, $2.10 students). Passes may be purchased at the transit center (551 Main St.) in downtown Johnstown. Exact fare is required when paying on a bus. Call **Greater Johnstown Yellow Cab** (814/535-4584) if you need a lift.

Altoona and Vicinity

Altoona is a product of the railroad industry, the demise of which hasn't diminished the city's appeal to rail fans. For the first half of the 19th century, what's now Altoona was farmland and wilderness. The tract's location at the eastern foot of the Allegheny Mountains—a formidable obstacle as railroads moved west across America—made it attractive to the Pennsylvania Railroad. The PRR, or "Pennsy," transformed it into a base camp, and thousands of workers arrived to help design, build, test, and repair trains. By 1945, the Altoona Works had become the world's largest rail shop complex. The area was so important to the nation's transportation infrastructure that it was a Nazi target during World War II. (Six saboteurs deposited by submarines off the shores of Florida and Long Island were executed. Two more were returned to Germany after serving prison sentences.)

Peacetime brought a decline in the demand for rail services, and the subsequent construction of a nationwide highway system marked the end of the railroading era. The Altoona Works were largely dismantled. The roundhouse, one of the largest in the country, was torn down in the 1960s. But there are traces of bygone days. A railroad museum occupies the 1882 building that housed the Pennsy's testing labs. Some 50 trains a day still snake around the Horseshoe Curve, the railroad's ingenious answer to the problem posed by the mountain range. Steam engines were retired more than 50 years ago, but the soot they produced still necessitates frequent dusting in the city built for railroaders.

SIGHTS
Railroaders Memorial Museum
A life-sized replica of a steam locomotive dominates the lobby of the impressive Railroaders Memorial Museum (1300 9th Ave., Altoona, 814/946-0834, www.railroadcity.com, 10 A.M.–5 P.M. Mon.–Sat. and 11 A.M.–5 P.M. Sun. May–Oct., open Fri.–Sun. Nov.–Dec., admission $10, seniors $8, children 4–12 $7), located in the former Pennsylvania Railroad master mechanics building in downtown

© ANNA DUBROVSKY

Railroaders Memorial Museum

Altoona. Three floors of interactive exhibits tell the story of the Pennsy, the enormous task of crossing the Allegheny Mountains, and the rail barons and laborers who made it happen. Regularly shown films help visitors make sense of the engineering marvel that is Horseshoe Curve. Museum tickets are good for access to the trackside viewing area at the curve.

Horseshoe Curve

How do you solve a problem like the Allegheny Mountains? The answer came from a young civil engineer named J. Edgar Thompson, who designed a way for trains to ascend gradually—about 90 feet per mile—along the mountain contour. The Horseshoe Curve (look for signs near 40th St. in Altoona, 814/946-0834, www.railroadcity.com, open daily Apr.–Oct. and weekends in Nov., admission $6, combo tickets good for admission to Railroaders Memorial Museum available) opened for rail traffic in 1854, revolutionizing east–west transport of people and the raw materials essential to industry. Today the Curve is owned by the Norfolk Southern

Railway, which hauls everything from ethanol to appliances over the Alleghenies. It's rare for an hour to pass without at least one train making an appearance. Amtrak's Pennsylvanian passenger train can be spotted about 5:20 P.M. on its way from New York City to Pittsburgh. You can ride a funicular or climb roughly 200 steps to reach a trackside viewing area, dotted with benches and picnic tables. Turn your back to the tracks for a striking panorama of the mountain landscape, which has changed hardly at all since the Curve's earliest days.

Allegheny Portage Railroad National Historic Site

Before there was the Horseshoe Curve, there was the Allegheny Portage Railroad. The first railroad to overcome the Allegheny Mountains was completed in 1834. A series of 10 inclined planes operated by stationary steam engines hoisted canal boats over the summit, allowing for continuous barge traffic between Philadelphia and Pittsburgh. The canal and railroad system cut travel time

© PATRICIA GATES, ALLEGHENY MOUNTAINS CONVENTION & VISITORS BUREAU

an aerial view of Horseshoe Curve

between the two cities to 3–5 days—as opposed to three or more weeks by horse and wagon. It remained the fastest way to traverse wild Pennsylvania until 1854, when it was rendered obsolete by the opening of the Horseshoe Curve.

The Allegheny Portage Railroad National Historic Site (110 Federal Park Rd., Gallitzin, 814/886-6150, www.nps.gov/alpo, 9 A.M.–5 P.M. daily, admission $4, free for children under 16), about 12 miles west of Altoona, features a historic tavern and a replica of an engine house. Exhibits and models tell the story of the ingenious—and dangerous—mode of transport that inspired an account by Charles Dickens. Deadly accidents were common because the ropes that pulled barges up from Johnstown on the west side of the Alleghenies or Hollidaysburg on the east side were wont to break. Horses pulled the barges along level sections of the railroad and through the **Staple Bend Tunnel,** the first railroad tunnel in the United States. The 900-foot tunnel was carved through solid rock by Welsh coal miners in the early 1830s and used until 1852, when the Pennsylvania Railroad bypassed it. Today it's an outlying part of the National Historic Site and can be reached via a 2.5-mile hiking and biking trail.

Other Railroading Sights

One mile from the Allegheny Portage site, **Gallitzin Tunnels Park & Museum** (411 Convent St., Gallitzin, 814/886-8871, www.gallitzin.info, park open dawn–dusk daily year-round, museum open 11 A.M.–5 P.M. Tues.–Sun. May–Dec., free admission) boasts a restored 1942 Pennsylvania Railroad N5C caboose and killer views of trains entering and exiting the 3,605-foot Allegheny Tunnel, built in the early 1850s. A bridge overlooking the tracks has camera ports so photographers can get unobstructed shots.

Canal Basin Park (101 Canal St., Hollidaysburg, 814/696-4601, park open dawn–dusk daily, visitors center 11 A.M.–5 P.M. Tues.–Fri., 9 A.M.–3 P.M. Sat., 1–5 P.M. Sun., closed in winter, free admission) gives visitors a window into canal culture. Hollidaysburg, about six miles south of Altoona, once had two large water basins connected by a canal lock. Boats were pulled out of the lower basin and onto the Allegheny Portage Railroad. The park features a replica of the lock mechanisms and other displays about the canal system.

Amusement Parks

The Altoona area has not one but two amusement parks. One of the great things about them is that admission is free. **Lakemont Park & The Island Waterpark** (700 Park Ave., Altoona, 800/434-8006, www.lakemontparkfun.com, regular season May–Sept., closed Tues. and Wed., call or check website for hours, all-day ride-and-slide pass $9.95, evening pass $7.95) boasts the world's oldest roller coaster. Leap-the-Dips was built at the park in 1902 and named a National Historic Landmark in 1996. It costs $2.50 to ride the antique coaster, even if you have an all-day pass. The seen-better-days amusement park has about 30 rides and attractions, including go-kart tracks, an 18-hole mini golf course, paddle boats, and an arcade. The **Altoona First Festival,** which features hundreds of craft vendors, caps the season in September. Lakemont reopens its doors in late November for **Holiday Lights on the Lake** ($8 per car), which runs through early January.

Most amusement parks make a name for themselves with thrilling rides. **DelGrosso's Amusement Park** (Old U.S. 220, Tipton, 814/684-3538, www.delgrossos.com, May–Sept., rides and attractions open 11 A.M. daily, picnic grounds open 8 A.M., all-day fun pass $12.95–15.95, sundowner fun pass $8.95) is famous for its food. When Altoona railroader Fred DelGrosso bought the park in 1946, he set up a special kitchen in its restaurant to experiment with his mother-in-law's pasta sauce recipe. At first his sauce was used only in the park's restaurant. In time it gave birth to DelGrosso Foods Inc., which today produces pizza sauce, meatballs, and other Italian specialty items along with pasta sauces. Park-goers feast on family recipes during

DelGrosso's Amusement Park

Spaghetti Wednesday, celebrated weekly during the summer. The park's potato salad is something of a legend. It's available daily, along with freshly made pizza. An Italian food festival is held in September. The rides, by the way, are also tempting. Three were added in 2009, including the pirate ship ride Pharaoh's Fury. A "fun pass" wristband is required for access to the water attractions.

Both parks sell individual ride tickets for people who prefer a quickie to a full day of thrills. And both charge extra for go-karts and mini golf.

Museums and Galleries

The **Southern Alleghenies Museum of Art at Altoona** (1210 11th Ave., Altoona, 814/946-4464, www.sama-art.org, 10 A.M.–5 P.M. Tues.–Fri., 1–5 P.M. Sat., free admission) boasts a rare collection of albumen photographic prints by William H. Rau, official photographer for the Pennsylvania Railroad at the turn of the 20th century. An annual juried

exhibition, Artists in Our Midst, showcases the work of local and regional artists. The nearby **Servello Gallery of Art** (1302 11th Ave., Altoona, 814/946-8922, 11 A.M.–5 P.M. Tues.–Sat.) celebrates the career of Joe Servello, a painter, sculptor, muralist, and illustrator of more than 50 books. Works by other area artists are also sold at the gallery.

Downtown Hollidaysburg is home to **art4...** (309A Allegheny St., Hollidaysburg, 814/693-2784, www.art4gallery.com, 10 A.M.–5:30 P.M. Tues.–Fri., 10 A.M.–3 P.M. Sat.), which offers original art and artisan crafts from around the United States and Canada. The artist-owned **Brownstone Art Gallery** (7564 Woodbury Pike, Roaring Spring, 814/224-9953, www.brownstoneartgallery .com, 10 A.M.–6:30 P.M. Wed., 10 A.M.–5 P.M. Thurs.), about 15 miles south of Altoona, specializes in contemporary fine arts.

Fort Roberdeau

Reports of lead deposits brought General Daniel Roberdeau, one of Pennsylvania's representatives to the Second Continental Congress, to a rural area known as Sinking Valley in 1778. The American Revolution was underway, and the Continental Army was badly in need of bullets and musket balls. Roberdeau established a lead mining and smelting operation and built a fort to protect it. Fort Roberdeau (about 10 miles northeast of Altoona, 814/946-0048, www .fortroberdeau.org, 11 A.M.–5 P.M. Tues.–Sat. and 1–5 P.M. Sun.–Mon. May–Oct., admission $4, seniors $3, children $2) also gave area settlers a place to flee from the British and their Indian allies. The stockade and half a dozen log cabins were reconstructed in 1976. Costumed guides tell the story of the fort, put on historical skits, and demonstrate crafts and weapons firing. The remote 230-acre site, which offers nature trails and picnic facilities (but no concession stand), can be tricky to find. It's off Kettle Road, accessible from U.S. 220/I-99 or Route 453. Your best bet is to use the mapping function on the fort's website.

Historic Loretto

In the final years of the 18th century, a young priest named Demetrius Gallitzin arrived at a small, isolated settlement in the Allegheny Mountains. Gallitzin, who'd given up a life of luxury as part of Russia's aristocracy, renamed the settlement Loretto in honor of Loreto, Italy, a Catholic pilgrimage site. Under his guidance—and thanks in no small part to his wealth—Loretto became a hub of Catholicism. His parish, St. Michael's, was the first Catholic church between Lancaster, Pennsylvania, and St. Louis, Missouri. By the time of his death in 1840, Loretto required three priests to minister to its thousands of Catholics. Today, the tiny town about 20 miles west of Altoona is home to a university founded by Franciscan friars, a Franciscan monastery, and a Carmelite monastery.

Father Gallitzin's original log church is long gone. In its place is the **Basilica of Saint Michael the Archangel** (321 St. Mary's St., 814/472-8551, www.geocities .com/smsbasilica). The impressive stone structure, shaped like a Latin cross, was financed by Loretto native and steel magnate Charles M. Schwab. It has three bells, four Italian marble altars, and a communion railing of Mexican onyx. Schwab also donated the life-sized bronze statue of Father Gallitzin that was placed over his tomb in 1899. The nearby **Prince Gallitzin Chapel House** (357 St. Mary's St., 814/472-5441, 9 A.M.–4 P.M. Mon.–Fri. year-round, 1–5 P.M. Sun. during summer) was Gallitzin's home for the last few years of his life. A set of vestments, a chalice, glasses, books, and other artifacts once used by the "Apostle of the Alleghenies" are displayed.

The church wasn't Schwab's only investment in his hometown. He also built an opulent summer estate he called Immergrun (German for "evergreen"). Wanton spending and the stock market crash of 1929 cost Schwab his fortune and his thousand-acre retreat. A portion of the estate became a

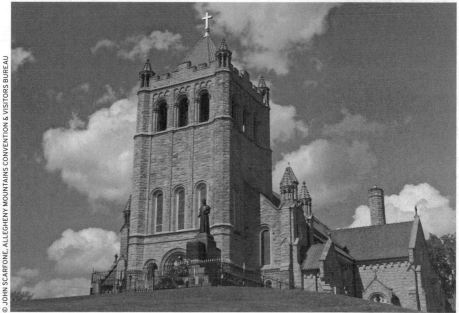

© JOHN SCARFONE, ALLEGHENY MOUNTAINS CONVENTION & VISITORS BUREAU

Basilica of Saint Michael the Archangel

© JOHN SCARFONE, ALLEGHENY MOUNTAINS CONVENTION & VISITORS BUREAU

St. Francis Friary

Franciscan monastery. Schwab's palatial limestone mansion, now the **St. Francis Friary** (141 St. Francis Dr., 814/693-2890), is not open to the public. But its lavish sunken gardens are accessible from sunrise to sunset. Religious and classical sculptures, reflecting pools, and waterfalls operated on Sundays in the summer make the gardens worthy of pilgrimage even for atheists.

Saint Francis University (117 Evergreen Dr., 814/472-3000, www.francis.edu) is home to the main branch of the **Southern Alleghenies Museum of Art** (Saint Francis University Mall, 814/472-3920, www.sama-art .org, 10 A.M.–5 P.M. Tues.–Fri., 1–5 P.M. Sat., free admission), which showcases American art, including Schwab's Tiffany collection. Satellite SAMA facilities can be found in Altoona, Johnstown, and Ligonier.

ENTERTAINMENT AND EVENTS
Performing Arts
The grand **Mishler Theatre** (1212 12th Ave.,

Altoona, 814/944-9434, www.mishlertheatre .org), more than a hundred years old, is home to **Altoona Community Theatre** (814/943-4357, www.altoonacommunitytheatre.com), **Allegheny Ballet Company** (814/941-9944, www.alleghenyballet.com), and the **Blair Concert Chorale** (814/944-7851, www.blair concertchorale.org). The **Altoona Symphony Orchestra** (814/943-2500, www.altoona symphony.org) most often performs at the Mishler but also makes appearances at the Wolf-Kuhn Theatre at Penn State Altoona and at outdoor events. More than 75 professional musicians make up the symphony, founded in 1928. Many performances feature acclaimed guest artists.

The **Cresson Lake Playhouse** (279 Shapiro Rd., Loretto, 814/472-4333, www.cressonlake .com) celebrated its 35th season in 2009. The company performs in a renovated (air-conditioned) pre–Civil War barn in a wooded area about 20 miles west of Altoona.

Festivals and Events
The **Blair County Arts Festival** (814/949-

2787, mid-May) celebrates the area's cultural resources. The weekend event includes a juried fine arts exhibit, a juried crafts market, and a full lineup of performing arts.

The Greater Altoona Economic Development Corp. presents free public jazz concerts by regional artists on select Friday evenings from June through August. **SummerSounds** is held along 11th Avenue in downtown Altoona. The Blair County Historical Society hosts free **Summer Concerts on the Lawn** at Baker Mansion (3419 Oak Ln., Altoona, 814/942-3916, www.blairhistory.org) on Sunday afternoons in July and August.

Stock up on holiday spirit at **Heritage Holidays in the Alleghenies** (Blair County Convention Center, 814/943-4183, www.alleghenymountains.com, Nov.), a craft and gift show with model train displays, live entertainment, and a towering Christmas tree.

SPORTS AND RECREATION
Canoe Creek State Park

The church building near the entrance to Canoe Creek State Park (Turkey Valley Rd.

off U.S. 22, 7 miles east of Hollidaysburg, 814/695-6807, www.dcnr.state.pa.us/stateparks/parks/canoecreek.aspx, park open 8 A.M.–dusk daily, interpretive center open 2–6 P.M. Fri.–Sun. in summer) is a sanctuary, all right—a bat sanctuary. About 14,000 female bats gather in the attic of the onetime house of worship to have their pups each summer. The best time to catch sight of them is after sunset, when they shoot out the attic window to hunt mosquitoes, wasps, beetles, and other prey. If you're an early bird, you can welcome them home just before dawn. There's a small gravel parking lot across the road from the church cemetery. Canoe Creek State Park, which owns the church, boasts one of the largest bat colonies in Pennsylvania. There are additional roosts in a garage near the church and a man-made "bat condo" along Canoe Creek. About 30,000 bats of half a dozen species hibernate in an abandoned limestone mine on park property. Check the park website for a schedule of guided bat programs.

Other summertime activities in the park include swimming and boating. Canoe Lake

© ANNA DUBROVSKY

the bat sanctuary at Canoe Creek State Park

has a sand beach, open 8 A.M. to sunset May–September, with a bathhouse and snack bar. There are boat-launching areas on both sides of the 155-acre lake. A boat rental facility adjacent to the swimming area offers rowboats, paddleboats, kayaks, and canoes. Fishing, including ice fishing, is permitted. The lake is stocked with walleye, muskellunge, bass, trout, and other fish.

Eight miles of hiking trails explore the lakeshore, wetlands, forests, and fields, which provide habitat for more than 200 species of birds and mammals. The park also attracts history lovers; it was the site of several limestone quarries and lime kilns during the heyday of the U.S. steel industry. Six massive cement furnace arches, the remnants of a kiln operated by the Blair Limestone Company, are reachable by road or trail. Biking is limited to a short trail that passes through the historic site. Cross-country skiing is permitted on all hiking trails.

Lower Trail

The 16.5-mile Lower Trail (814/832-2400, www.rttcpa.org) runs alongside the Frankstown Branch of the Juniata River and makes for undemanding hiking, bicycling, horseback riding, and cross-country skiing. In the early 1800s, much of the trail was a towpath for the Pennsylvania Canal. By the 1850s, it was a branch of the Pennsylvania Railroad, which rendered the canals obsolete. The Lower (pronounced like "flower") has six trailheads, all of which are located at or near former railroad stations and can be reached from U.S. 22. The westernmost trailhead, near Canoe Creek State Park, is about a quarter of a mile south of U.S. 22 and reachable by Flowing Springs Road. The eastern terminus is off Main Street in Alfarata. Map boxes can be found at each trailhead.

Spectator Sports

Altoona's minor league baseball team has been the Class AA affiliate of the Pittsburgh Pirates since 1999. The teams renewed their development agreement in 2009, ensuring a relationship through the 2014 season. The **Altoona Curve** (Blair County Ballpark, 1000 Park Ave., Altoona, 814/943-5400, www.altoona curve.com) play in the Eastern League—and play on the region's railroading history. The

© ANNA DUBROVSKY

Blair County Ballpark, home of the Altoona Curve

team's name alludes to nearby Horseshoe Curve as well as the curveball pitch. The facade of the 7,200-seat ballpark evokes a railroad roundhouse. And the stunt-pulling mascots—Steamer and Diesel Dawg—were named for locomotive technologies. The ballpark's open concourse allows fans to keep an eye on the game while eating at a picnic table or mingling on the party deck. House specialties include the "fishdog," a tube-shaped beer-battered fish fillet served on a foot-long hotdog roll. Single-game tickets start at $5. The top-of-the-line "Rail Kings" seats, which feature waiter service, sell for $12.

Outstanding high school football players gather in Altoona every June for the **East West All-Star Game** (800/842-5866, www.east westgame.org), which pits the "beasts of the east" against the "best of the west." Fans can get a sneak peek at future college and National Football League players.

The **International Tour de 'Toona** (814/949-7223, www.tourdetoona.com, summer) was scrapped in 2009 for lack of sponsorship dollars, but organizers promised the bicycle race that started in 1987 would mount a comeback.

ACCOMMODATIONS

Altoona's lodging scene is dominated by chains like the **Courtyard by Marriott** (2 Convention Center Dr., Altoona, 814/312-1800), conveniently connected to the Blair County Convention Center. Bed-and-breakfasts near the city offer an alternative.

Under $100

The brick colonial that is **Elizabeth Rest Bed & Breakfast** (Sabbath Rest Rd., Altoona, 814/940-1842, www.elizabethrest.com, $50–110) was built in 1830. Two guest rooms share a bath. The Chimney Suite has a private bath, living room, and kitchen.

The **Station Inn** (827 Front St., Cresson, 814/886-4757, www.stationinnpa.com, $91–99) "may not meet the expectations of some B&B travelers," its website warns. "The Inn is not air-conditioned; it has no in-room

television, or telephones. No hot tubs or whirlpools. There are no farm animals in the back yard. The Inn has no antiques, no early American furnishings; no homemade bread or jam. We have no tea time. No afternoon wine and cheese." So what's the appeal? Proximity to a busy railroad. (Keep in mind that the rumble of passing trains, while a nuisance to some, is amusement to others.) The front porch and most rooms offer a view of the mainline, and the common room is stocked with rail magazines, books, and memorabilia. Twin beds (extra long for leggy rail fans) give the rooms a dorm-like feel.

$100-150

Rail enthusiasts can also find front-row seats at the **Tunnel Inn** (702 Jackson St., Gallitzin, 814/884-2975, www.thetunnelinn.com, $98–120). Country quilts and Shaker-style furniture complement the inn's railroad motif. Guests can watch passing trains from the roofed deck, outfitted with floodlights for evening viewing, or take a guided spin to other vantage points.

The meticulously appointed **Iron Corbel Inn** (703 Allegheny St., Hollidaysburg, 814/696-0324, www.ironcorbelinn.com, $95–250) in downtown Hollidaysburg is named for architectural features of the Second Empire–style house. Iron columns topped with ladies' faces support the porch, and corbels support the eaves of the mansard roof. Inside the 19th-century manse are marble mantels, crystal chandeliers, and period furnishings. The four elegant guest rooms have private baths. A spacious two-room suite on the third floor boasts a claw-foot tub and separate shower. Luxury linens, terry bathrobes, and other touches make it easy to check out of the world awhile.

FOOD

There's no shortage of national chains in the Altoona area. Thoroughfares are lined with the likes of T.G.I. Friday's and Olive Garden. Locally owned restaurants are a rare breed and most often found in town centers.

Altoona

(**Tom and Joe's Diner** (1201 13th Ave., 814/943-3423, www.tomandjoes.com, 8 A.M.–2 P.M. Mon.–Fri., 7 A.M.–1 P.M. Sat., 7 A.M.–noon Sun., $4–8), across from City Hall in downtown Altoona, was founded in 1933 by brothers named—you guessed it—Tom and Joe. Tom's grandson runs the place today. Like the retro decor (checkered floors, red counter stools, and knotty pine walls), the specials hark back to an era before cholesterol checks. Cap a meal of ham pot pie or liver and onions with a malted shake. Free wireless Internet access adds a touch of modernity.

Authenticity is the hallmark of **Allegro** (3926 Broad Ave., 814/946-5216, www .allegro-restaurant.com, 4–9 P.M. Mon.– Thurs., 4–9:30 P.M. Fri., 4–10 P.M. Sat., lunch 11:30 A.M.–1 P.M. Thurs.–Fri., $14–39), which serves time-honored Italian dishes. The spaghetti is homemade, as are the gnocchi, ravioli, manicotti, and lasagna noodles. The veal menu is extensive, but the specialty of the house is filet Oscar: filet mignon with asparagus, jumbo lump crabmeat, and Mornay sauce. Groups of four or more can order from a family-style menu.

If you're more in the mood for carne asada than pollo piccata, give the Pennsylvania chain **El Campesino** (101 Park Hills Plaza, 814/944-3121, www.elcampesino.net, 11:30 A.M.–10 P.M. Mon.–Thurs., 11:30 A.M.– 10:30 P.M. Fri.–Sat., noon–9 P.M. Sun., $6–20) a chance. The Altoona location is one of six. El Campesino is as good as Mexican gets in these parts and even better after a margarita.

Hollidaysburg

The **U.S. Hotel Restaurant and Tavern** (401 S. Juniata St., 814/695-9924, www .theushotel.com, brunch 10 A.M.–2 P.M. Sun., lunch 11 A.M.–2 P.M. Mon.–Sat., dinner from 4:30 P.M. daily, tavern opens 11 A.M. daily, $7–36) has a rich history dating to 1835, when canals served as expressways and Hollidaysburg was a national transportation center. If you're supping in one of the beautifully restored dining rooms, be sure to check out the barroom,

built in 1905. Its hand-carved mahogany back bar is original, as is the brass foot rail and spittoon trough beneath it. Pub grub and sandwiches are available all day. Steaks and Italian dishes dominate the dinner menu.

Less than two miles west of Hollidaysburg, **Marzoni's Brick Oven & Brewing Co.** (165 Patchway Rd., Duncansville, 814/695-2931, www.marzonis.com, 11 A.M.–11 P.M. daily, $6–23) features exactly what its name suggests: pizza cooked in brick-lined ovens and handcrafted beers. The beers are brewed on premises, and at least eight are on tap every day. Ask for a tour of the brewery if you're curious about the process. There's house-brewed root beer for designated drivers and the underage. In addition to pizza, the restaurant offers sandwiches, pasta dishes, and meat and seafood selections.

INFORMATION AND SERVICES

For brochures, maps, discount cards, and answers to any and all questions about Altoona or the Alleghenies, drop by the **Allegheny Mountains Convention and Visitors Bureau** (1 Convention Center Dr., Altoona, 814/943-4183, www.alleghenymountains.com, 8 A.M.–5 P.M. Mon.–Fri., occasionally open on weekends) in the Blair County Convention Center. The gift shop adjacent to the welcome center has a large selection of made-in-PA keepsakes.

The daily *Altoona Mirror* (www.altoona mirror.com) publishes an entertainment and recreation guide called *Go* on Fridays. The newspaper's annual restaurant guide is available on its website.

GETTING THERE AND AROUND

Altoona is about 95 miles east of Pittsburgh. It's reachable by east–west U.S. 22 or U.S. 220/ I-99, which runs between I-80 to the north of Altoona and the Pennsylvania Turnpike to the south. Pittsburgh International Airport (PIT) is the nearest major airport, but **Altoona-Blair County Airport** (AOO), about 20 miles south of Altoona in Martinsburg, offers direct service to and from Washington, D.C.

Amtrak (800/872-7245, www.amtrak

.com) trains and **Greyhound** (800/231-2222, www.greyhound.com) buses serve the **Altoona Transportation Center** (1231 11th Ave.), which is the primary hub for Altoona's public transit provider, **AMTRAN** (814/944-4074, www.amtran.org). Local taxi services include **Blue & White Taxi** (814/941-2711) and **Yellow Cab Co.** (814/944-6105).

State College and Vicinity

Steelmaking built Johnstown, and railroading built Altoona. Their neighbor State College is the product of a different industry: education. The town is home to Pennsylvania State University, better known as Penn State, which was founded in 1855 as a publicly supported agricultural college. Town and gown have grown in tandem. In 1875, the school had only 64 undergraduates. In 2008, enrollment at its 24 campuses reached 92,613. Almost half of Penn State students are enrolled at the flagship campus, University Park. Their numbers make State College a lively, culturally rich, and commercially robust town. It's also sports obsessed. Penn State's storied football program has made head coach Joe Paterno a household name and "Happy Valley" a much-used nickname for the area. (The valley in which State College is nestled is more properly known as Nittany Valley.)

Penn State long ago expanded its curriculum beyond the agricultural sciences, but farming is still the way of life for many in this region. Farmlands radiate from State College. They're interrupted by mountains and forests and the occasional town, including the particularly quaint Boalsburg and Bellefonte. When Penn State's Nittany Lions play football at home, State College and its neighbors swell with fans. If that's when you visit, you'll see why Penn State was ranked the nation's number one party school. Tranquility awaits you most other times of year.

SIGHTS
Mount Nittany

That tree-covered hump on the horizon? It's probably Mount Nittany, and you should definitely hike it. The mountain is part of a ridge separating two valleys; on a clear day, the crest affords postcard-quality views of both. Its name is derived from the Algonquin "nit-a-nee," which means either "single mountain" or "barrier against the wind," depending on whom you ask. (If you ask, you're liable to get an earful of local folklore about a Native American princess of the same name.) Penn State borrowed the mountain's name for its mascot. In the 1940s, the Lion's Paw Alumni Association bought 525 acres of Mount Nittany to protect it from lumbering and other purposes. The alumni group later formed the Mount Nittany Conservancy (www.mtnittany .org), which has snapped up an additional 300 acres and is shopping for more. The conservancy publishes trail guides, which are available on its website and at area visitors centers.

Finding the trailhead is arguably the trickiest part of the hike. It's at the dead end of Mount Nittany Road, which begins in the quaint village of Lemont. From State College, take South Atherton Street (Business U.S. 322) east to the traffic light at Branch Road. Turn left onto Branch and follow to Mount Nittany Road. Turn right, drive one mile, and—voilà!—there it is. Take your pick of two blazed loop trails: the 4-mile white trail or 5.5-mile blue trail. Both start out rocky and steep. For a view of campus from 1,940 feet, you needn't go farther than the Mike Lynch Overlook, 0.75 mile up the white trail. You can hike Mount Nittany any time of year, but spring and fall are particularly good for wildlife viewing. Winter's leafless trees make for exceptional valley views. Hunting is permitted, so it's wise to wear orange.

If you're short on time or shy of the climb, you can take in Mount Nittany from an observation area between Beaver Stadium and the Bryce Jordan Center on campus. There's no charge to use the high-powered binoculars.

ANATOMY OF A MASCOT

What's a Nittany Lion anyway? The question will brand you an outsider in State College, where the Penn State mascot is revered. Fear not. Here's the lowdown on the region's favorite feline.

Until 1904, Penn State didn't have a mascot. That year, the school's baseball team visited Princeton University, home of the Tigers. When Penn State's Harrison "Joe" Mason was shown a statue of the fearsome mascot, the ballplayer pulled a fast one: He crowed that the Nittany Lion, "fiercest beast of them all," would take down the Tiger. And, indeed, Penn State defeated Princeton that day.

Mason's fabrication had roots in reality. Mountain lions roamed central Pennsylvania when Penn State was founded. A mountain named Nittany was and remains the most prominent natural landmark near campus. Mason put the two together to create a unique symbol of might. A branding whiz couldn't have done it better. Back at Penn State, support for Mason's brainchild was so widespread that the mascot was adopted without so much as a vote.

© CENTRAL PA CVB

Nittany Lions mascot

Beaver Stadium

The best way to experience Beaver Stadium (University Dr. and Park Ave., University Park), den of the Nittany Lions football team, is to go to a home game. Alas, tickets are so prized that even students have to scramble for them. To score a $247 season ticket in 2009, students had to pre-register in May and pray that too many classmates didn't beat them to the punch during a lightning-quick online sale in June. Don't let the lack of a ticket keep you away on game day. Penn State has a tailgating tradition par excellence. Fans with motor homes arrive as early as Thursday to set up camp. On Saturday, the parking lots and fields around Beaver Stadium fill with revelers. There's music. There's food. There's even a good chance you'll find fans (and the occasional scalper) selling extra tickets. "If you haven't been to Happy Valley in the fall, you're missing out on one of the great happenings in all of sports," ESPN's Kirk Herbstreit gushed in 2008.

Beaver Stadium is impressive even when empty. With a seating capacity of 107,282, it's the second largest stadium in the country after Michigan Stadium. It wasn't always a behemoth. Prior to 1960, the home of Penn State football was a 30,000-seat stadium on the west side of campus. That year, it was dismantled and moved in 700 pieces to its current site at the east end, where it was reassembled with 16,000 additional seats. Expansions over the years brought the stadium to its current size. Tours that include the Nittany Lions locker room are offered by the **Penn State All-Sports Museum** (814/865-0044, www.gopsu sports.com/museum, 10 A.M.–4 P.M. Tues.–Sat., noon–4 P.M. Sun., hours vary during game weekends and winter, suggested donation $5, children/students/seniors $3). The 10,000-square-foot museum in the southwest corner of the stadium celebrates the achievements of Penn State athletes and coaches. Visitors can wrap their fingers around a vintage football or compare their shoes to the size 22 sneaks of a Penn State basketball alumnus. The collection also includes the 1973 Heisman Trophy of running back John Cappelletti and the 1952

Olympics gold medal of Penn State graduate and steeplechaser Horace Ashenfelter.

Stroll to the east side of Beaver Stadium for a look at the bronze statue of Joe Paterno, the most famous name in Penn State athletics. The winningest coach in college football is frozen with right arm overhead, index finger raised. Beaver Stadium, by the way, is named not for the dam-building rodent but for James A. Beaver, who served as governor of Pennsylvania and president of the university's board of trustees.

Nittany Lion Shrine

Said to be the most photographed site on campus, the Nittany Lion Shrine resides near the Recreation Building at the west end of Curtin Road. Sculptor Heinz Warneke and stonecutter Joseph Garatti coaxed the crouching lion out of a 13-ton block of Indiana limestone. It was dedicated during homecoming weekend in 1942. In 1966, fans of homecoming rival Syracuse University doused the lion with hard-to-remove paint. Students, faculty, and alumni have guarded (read: partied at) the shrine during homecoming weekend ever since.

◖ Berkey Creamery

This ain't no ordinary ice cream joint. Penn State's Berkey Creamery (corner of Bigler and Curtin Roads, University Park, 814/865-7535, www.creamery.psu.edu, 7 A.M.–10 P.M. Mon.–Thurs., 7 A.M.–11 P.M. Fri., 8 A.M.–11 P.M. Sat., 9 A.M.–10 P.M. Sun.) is a pilgrimage site. People come from near and not so near to indulge in fresh ice cream produced by the country's largest and most sophisticated university creamery. How fresh? How does four days from cow to cone sound? The school's own cowherd can't supply enough milk to meet demand, so the creamery relies on local producers. Don't be deterred by the snaking line to the counter. Most patrons know what they like, and there's no agonizing over one scoop or two. There's only one

the Nittany Lion Shrine

Berkey Creamery

serving size: generous. It's $2.75 whether you take it in a cone or cup. Quarts and half-gallons of the rich stuff are such popular souvenirs that Berkey sells travel bags and dry ice for the road. It also ships ice cream and other products via FedEx. The creamery produces about 100 flavors of ice cream, though only a quarter are available at any given time. Some flavors pay tribute to Penn State personalities and landmarks, e.g. Peachy Paterno and Mint Nittany.

The creamery, which occupies the first floor of the Food Science Building, is a laboratory for students in the College of Agricultural Sciences. They learn the dairy business by working in it, producing milk, cheeses, yogurt, sour cream, frozen yogurt, and sherbet along with the famous ice cream. Want a taste of life in the ice cream trenches? The university's Ice Cream Short Course covers every aspect of production. It's how Ben and Jerry got their start.

Museums and Galleries

Penn State's **Palmer Museum of Art** (Curtin Rd., University Park, 814/865-7672, www.palmermuseum.psu.edu, 10 A.M.–4:30 P.M. Tues.–Sat., free admission) has 11 galleries, a

garden for large-scale contemporary sculpture, and a permanent collection of more than 5,000 works that date from antiquity to present day. Galleries at the student union building, the **HUB-Robeson Center** (814/865-2563, www.sa.psu.edu/usa/galleries), focus on contemporary art.

Local artist Michael Pilato's work is always on display in State College. His 96-by-24-foot wall mural *Inspiration* (Heister St. near E. College Ave., www.pilatomurals.com) depicts more than 300 people from the community.

The village of Lemont, a stone's throw from State College, is home to the nonprofit **Art Alliance of Central Pennsylvania** (814/234-2740, www.artalliancepa.org), which mounts short-term exhibits in its gallery at 818 Pike Street and sells works by area artists in the adjacent **Gallery Shop** (824 Pike St., 814/867-0442, www.gallery-shop.com, 10:30 A.M.–5:30 P.M. Tues.–Fri., 10 A.M.–5 P.M. Sat.).

Historic Boalsburg

On an October day in 1864, three women decorated the graves of fallen Civil War soldiers in a small Boalsburg cemetery. Their respectful gesture would later become an American tradition, giving Boalsburg bragging rights as the birthplace of Memorial Day. Few towns do it up like Boalsburg come the last Monday in May. The village along South Atherton Street (Business U.S. 322), just several minutes east of State College, hosts a daylong festival that culminates in a ceremony at the same cemetery where the three paid their respects. A life-sized statue of the ladies in ground-sweeping skirts stands there today. Boalsburg's reverence for history makes it worth a visit any day of the year. It has three museums, diligently maintained 19th-century homes, and a tavern that opened its doors in 1819. To boot, the quaint village boasts several boutiques worthy of a big city.

Boalsburg was settled in 1808 but called Springfield until 1820, when it was renamed to honor its most distinguished residents, the Boals. The **Boal Mansion Museum** (163 Boal Estate Dr., 814/466-6210, www.boalmuseum .com, 1:30–5 P.M. Tues.–Sun. in spring and fall, 10 A.M.–5 P.M. Tues.–Sat. and noon–5 P.M. Sun. in summer, closed Nov.–Apr., admission $10,

statue of women decorating soldiers' graves in the Boalsburg cemetery

children 7–12 $6) displays the family's many treasures, including original furnishings and military artifacts from the Revolutionary War to World War I. In 1909, a Boal and his French-Spanish wife, a descendant of Christopher Columbus, imported a centuries-old chapel from the Columbus Castle in Spain. It's preserved in a structure of Pennsylvania stone adjacent to the mansion. Artifacts on display in the **Columbus Chapel** include an admiral's desk said to have belonged to the explorer himself and religious statues from the 15th century.

The **Boalsburg Heritage Museum** (304 E. Main St., 814/466-6883, www.boals burgheritagemuseum.org, 2–4 P.M. Tues. and Sat. and by appointment, closed mid-Dec.–Apr., free admission) is an example of a more modest early home, filled with historical and community artifacts.

The site of the **Pennsylvania Military Museum** (S. Atherton St./Business U.S. 322, 814/466-6263, www.pamilmuseum.org, 9 A.M.–5 P.M. Tues.–Sat. and noon–5 P.M. Sun. Apr.–Oct., 10 A.M.–4 P.M. Thurs.–Sat. and noon–4 P.M. Sun. Nov.–Mar., admission $6, seniors $5.50, children 3–11 $4) was once part of the Boal estate. In 1916, with war raging in Europe, Theodore Davis Boal organized a horse-mounted machine gun troop on his property. The men of Camp Boal left for the war in May of 1918. The museum honors them and other Pennsylvania military men and women. It also showcases the tools of war, including the massive gun barrels of a battleship that survived the 1941 Japanese attack on Pearl Harbor. Military service ribbons inspired the cubistic mural on the front facade of the museum.

If you're hungry for more history or just plain hungry, head to **Duffy's Tavern** (113 E. Main St., Boalsburg, 814/466-6241, www .duffystavern.com, kitchen 11:30 A.M.–10 P.M. Mon.–Sat. and 11:30 A.M.–9 P.M. Sun., tavern open until 1 A.M. Mon.–Sat., $7–33), a watering hole since 1819. Boalsburg was a busy stop on a stagecoach route in the early 19th century—busy enough to keep three taverns in business at one point. This one, with its 22-inch stone walls, is believed to have served the gentry.

© ANNA DUBROVSKY

Duffy's Tavern in Boalsburg

Shops suitable for today's gentry include the fragrant **Bella di Vita** (117 E. Main St., 814/466-3404, www.bellasoaps.com, noon–5 P.M. Tues.–Fri., 10 A.M.–5 P.M. Sat., noon–4 P.M. Sun.), a European-inspired trove of kitchenware, house decor, art, stationary, and body products. Owner Linda Esposita makes the soaps herself, using a traditional method from 6th-century France. Cross the street for handcrafted truffles, almond bark, and other confections from the **Boalsburg Chocolate Company** (126 E. Main St., 814/466-6290, www.boalsburgchocolate.com, 11 A.M.–5 P.M. Tues.–Fri., 10 A.M.–5 P.M. Sat.). The flawlessly styled **Riley on Main** (101 E. Main St., 814/466-9200, 10:30 A.M.–5 P.M. Mon.–Sat.) offers vintage and new furniture, jewelry, glassware, and more.

Victorian Bellefonte

The very Victorian town of Bellefonte, 15 miles north of State College, is the seat of Centre County. It owes its (somewhat faded) grandeur to the prosperous and powerful men who called it home in the 19th century: iron and limestone barons, bankers, lawyers, judges, and seven U.S. governors. Much of their real estate is lovingly preserved, which makes Bellefonte attractive to architecture and history buffs, romantics, and the tea-and-scone crowd. It's also popular with anglers. Spring Creek, famous for its large trout, meanders through the storybook town. Bellefonte is never more magical than in winter, when homes, businesses, and county buildings are dressed in holiday finery. The annual **Bellefonte Victorian Christmas** (814/355-2917, www.victorianbellefonte.com, second weekend in Dec.) is a town-wide trip back in time, complete with horse-drawn buggy rides, a gingerbread house contest, tours of historic homes, concerts, and, of course, a Victorian tea party.

Start your visit at pretty **Talleyrand Park** along Spring Creek. Bring breadcrumbs for a closer gander at the waterfowl and trout. On Sunday evenings in the summer, locals gather around the park's gazebo for free concerts sponsored by the Bellefonte Historical and Cultural Association (www.bellefontearts.org). The 1889 train station in Talleyrand is home to the Bellefonte Intervalley Area Chamber of

© ANNA DUBROVSKY

war memorial and courthouse in Victorian Bellefonte

Commerce (320 W. High St., 814/355-2917, www.bellefontechamber.org) and a satellite office of the Central Pennsylvania Convention and Visitors Bureau. You can pick up free maps, information about area attractions, and a Wi-Fi signal.

A former match factory at the edge of Talleyrand Park is now the **American Philatelic Center** (100 Match Factory Place, 814/933-3803, www.stamps.org, 8 A.M.– 4:30 P.M. Mon.–Fri., free admission), headquarters for a society of more than 44,000 stamp collectors. Visitors can learn the ABCs of stamp collecting, browse exhibits of stamp collections and stamp-related memorabilia, and learn about Bellefonte's important role in the early days of airmail. Pilots refueled in the town on their way from New York City to Chicago. A monument honors those who lost their lives en route.

Follow High Street east to the very center of town, where the county courthouse stands. The war memorial in front of the courthouse was designed by the architect responsible for Pennsylvania's Capitol in Harrisburg. A statue at its center depicts Andrew Gregg Curtin, the Bellefonte native who served as governor of Pennsylvania during the Civil War. A later governor, James A. Beaver, lived two blocks north of the courthouse in an 1810 Georgian-style house made of limestone. It's now occupied by the **Bellefonte Museum for Centre County** (133 N. Allegheny St., 814/355-4280, www.bellefontemuseum.org, 1–4 P.M. Thurs.–Sun., by donation), which mounts several thematic exhibitions a year. The nearby **Centre County Library and Historical Museum** (203 N. Allegheny St., 814/355-1516, 10 A.M.–5 P.M. Mon.–Fri., 10 A.M.–4 P.M. Sat., free admission), housed in an 1815 Georgian, has a genealogy research room and displays of artifacts from the Civil War and other periods.

For an ivy-clad Victorian gem, continue to the intersection of North Allegheny and Linn Streets. The **Reynolds Mansion** (101 W. Linn St., 814/353-8407, www.reynoldsmansion.com, $135–245, special events $145–300) is so fetching that it graced the cover of a *Select Registry* guidebook to distinguished inns. Built in 1885 by a wealthy businessman, the B&B is a blend of Gothic, Italianate, and Queen Anne

© ANNA DUBROVSKY

Reynolds Mansion B&B

styles. You don't have to book a room to explore the ornate interior. The Reynolds Mansion is open to the public 11 A.M.–1:30 P.M. daily and until 4 P.M. in December. A self-guided tour of the common areas, including a snuggery where men retired after dinner to sip brandy and smoke cigars, is $3 per adult, $1.50 per child. (These days, women are welcome in the snuggery, but smoking isn't.) For $5 you can also climb the spiral staircase and peek into any available guest rooms. For more Victorian splendor, continue east on **Linn Street.** The three-block stretch of elegant residences between North Allegheny and Armour Streets includes no fewer than four bed-and-breakfasts.

Caverns

An all-water limestone cavern 17 miles northeast of State College wows the Wii generation like it did 19th-century tourists. **Penn's Cave** (222 Penns Cave Rd., Centre Hall, 814/364-1664, www.pennscave.com, open daily Mar.–Nov., weekends only Dec. and Feb., call or check website for hours, cavern tour $14.95, seniors $13.95, children 2–12 $7.95) is a half-

mile wonderland of stalactites and stalagmites, columns and curtains. Tours by motorboat leave on the hour. Joke-cracking guides dole out geology factoids and point out curiously shaped formations (and the occasional beaver). Bring a sweater or jacket even in summer because the temperature inside is a constant 52 degrees. Boats emerge from the tunnel-like cave into the manmade Lake Nitanee, where they linger for wildlife viewing before the return trip. Driving tours of the **Wildlife Park** ($19, seniors $18, children 2–12 $11) are offered April–November. Inhabitants include longhorn cattle, bison, gray wolves, black bears, and bobcats. A cavern and wildlife tour package is available.

When local cave enthusiasts say "the big one," they're talking about **Woodward Cave** (Woodward Cave Dr., Woodward, 814/349-9800, www.woodwardcave.com, open daily mid-May to Labor Day, weekends only to early Oct. and mid-Apr. to mid-May, call or check website for hours, tour $10.50, children 4–12 $5.25). Its spacious rooms include the 200-foot-long Hall of Statues, which features a 14-foot stalagmite known as the Tower of Babel. Woodward Cave is extra chilly—48 degrees

© ANNA DUBROVSKY

Penn's Cave

year-round—so dress accordingly for the 50-minute, five-room tour. It's about an hour's drive from State College, which may make an overnight sensible. The Woodward Cave Campground has hot showers, a snack stand, a game room, and other amenities, plus a packed calendar of events including pig roasts and horseshoe tournaments. Rates start at $18.

ENTERTAINMENT AND EVENTS
Nightlife

Bank on a good time and outstanding brews at **Zeno's Pub** (100 W. College Ave., State College, 814/237-4350, www.zenospub.com, noon–2 A.M. Mon.–Fri., 1 P.M.–2 A.M. Sat.–Sun.), which *BeerAdvocate* called one of the top beer bars on the planet. That's right, the planet. Zeno's shares the Hotel State College complex with **Bill Pickle's Tap Room** (106 S. Allen St., State College, 814/272-1172, www.hotelstatecollege.com/pickles, 11 A.M.–2 A.M. daily), where Guitar Hero–playing patrons provide the entertainment when DJs have the night off, and dance club **Indigo** (112 W. College Ave., State College, 814/234-1031, 10 P.M.–2 A.M. Thurs.–Sun.). On Sundays Indigo hosts "rainbow night" for the LGBTQA (lesbian, gay, bisexual, transgendered, questioning, and allied) crowd. Wednesday evenings in summer, it opens its doors to the underage.

Don't go to **Bar Bleu** (114 S. Garner St., State College, 814/237-0374, www.dantesinc.com/barbleu.htm, 9 P.M.–2 A.M. daily except Tues.) expecting live jazz or blues. That was then. This is now: rock bands and DJs and the obligatory open mic night.

The Saloon (101 Hiester St., State College, 814/234-0845, www.dantesinc.com/saloon.htm, 8 P.M.–2 A.M. daily) fancies itself an English pub, but its famous "Monkey Boy" drink is a State College original. The concoction of clear alcohols emboldens many a student on karaoke Mondays. Bands make the noise most other nights.

Performing Arts

The likes of Cirque du Soleil and Miley Cyrus perform at Penn State's **Bryce Jordan Center** (corner of University Dr. and Curtin Rd., University Park, 814/863-5500, www.bjc.psu.edu), home of Nittany Lions basketball. Word has it that Tim McGraw borrowed a jeep from a Jordan Center employee some years ago to take another performer, Faith Hill, for a spin. Thus began their romance.

Penn State's primary theatrical performance space is the 2,500-seat **Eisenhower Auditorium** (corner of Shortlidge and Eisenhower Roads, University Park, 814/863-0255, www.cpa.psu.edu). Named for a former university president, the modern auditorium hosts some 200 events a year. Wynton Marsalis, David Copperfield, and the Martha Graham and Alvin Ailey dance companies have graced its stage. The **Nittany Valley Symphony** (814/231-8224, www.nvs.org) is a regular user. The full-sized orchestra began as a small band of musicians who came together to perform at the first arts festival in State College in 1967.

The 150-seat **Penn State Downtown Theatre** (146 S. Allen St., State College) is home to the university's professional theater company, **Pennsylvania Centre Stage** (814/863-0493, www.pacentrestage.psu.edu), which can be counted on for high-caliber productions of such works as *Evita, Cabaret,* and *Death of a Salesman.*

State College Community Theatre (814/466-7141, www.scctonline.org) entertains every season but winter at the Boal Barn Playhouse (197 Boal Estate Dr., Boalsburg).

Festivals and Events

More than 125,000 people flood downtown State College and the Penn State campus during the **Central Pennsylvania Festival of the Arts** (814/237-3682, www.arts-festival.com, starts first Wed. after July 4), a tradition since 1967. Artists and craftspeople from around the country exhibit and peddle their work. Musicians, dancers, and puppeteers entertain. All the while, a massive sand sculpture takes shape in Central Parklet. Admission to some performances requires an $8 button.

You don't have to go home when the exhibits

© CENTRAL PA CVB

dinosaur ice sculpture on display during First Night State College

and amusement rides at the **Centre County Grange Fair** (Grange Fairgrounds, Centre Hall, 814/364-9212, www.grangefair.net, starts last Thurs. in Aug., one-day admission $6) close for the night. The weeklong farm-centric fete is one of the largest encampment fairs in the country, with more than 2,000 tent and RV sites. Funnel cake for breakfast, anyone? Penn State hosts the more scholarly **Ag Progress Days** (Russell E. Larson Agricultural Research Center, Rock Springs, 814/865-2081, www.apd.psu.edu, late Aug., free), a showcase of the latest farm machinery, management practices, and research.

First Night State College (814/237-3682, www.firstnightstatecollege.com) is an alcohol-free, arts-focused New Year's Eve celebration known for jaw-dropping ice sculptures. Admission to many performances and crafts workshops requires an $8 button.

SPORTS AND RECREATION

Watching football isn't the only pastime in Nittany Lions country. There are plenty of opportunities to test your own mettle on land, in water, and in the sky. Perhaps the most unique of these is the annual **Penn State Football Fantasy Camp** (817/219-7274, www.pennstatefantasycamp.com, June), where Everyman can live out his football dreams. Penn State coaches and onetime star players put participants through several days of practices, which lead up to a game of flag football at Beaver Stadium. Football fanatics upwards of 70 years old have taken the field.

Black Moshannon State Park

Don't be daunted by the tea-colored waters at Black Moshannon State Park (Rte. 504, 9 miles east of Philipsburg, 814/342-5960, www.dcnr.state.pa.us/stateparks/parks/black moshannon.aspx). They're darkened by plant tannins, not pollution. The bog that hugs Black Moshannon Lake is crowded with sphagnum moss and other wetland plants, including species rarely seen in Pennsylvania. Three carnivorous plants and 17 species of orchids thrive in or near the bog. Thanks to trails and boardwalks that wind through the bog area and surrounding forests, it's possible to get up close to the wildlife. (But don't get too close. The carnivorous plants probably won't catch you, but rangers could.) The 0.3-mile Bog Trail is the easiest of the bunch. If you're more adventurous and not afraid to get your feet wet, try the 7.7-mile Moss-Hanne Trail. Hike it between late July and September if you're fond of blueberries. In winter, the 16-mile trail system is open to cross-country skiers as well as hikers. A couple of the trails connect to much longer trails in the 43,000-acre Moshannon State Forest, which surrounds the park and welcomes mountain bikers and snowmobile riders.

Boating and fishing are permitted on the lake, and rental boats are available during the summer. A sand beach is open from late May to mid-September. When the lake freezes, you can ice skate on a maintained section or ice fish on the rest.

The park's 80-acre campsite is open from the second Friday in April to late December. Rustic cabins with wood-burning stoves and bunk beds provide another seasonal lodging option. Six modern cabins with electric heat are available year-round. Reserve online at www .pa.reserveworld.com or call 888/727-2757.

Fishing and Paddling

The State College area is known for superb angling. In 2009, members of PaFlyFish.com named Bellefonte the best fly-fishing town in the state, citing its proximity to Spring Creek, Penns Creek, Spruce Creek, and other premier fly-fishing waters. Spring Creek, which runs through the town on its way to Bald Eagle Creek, is among the best wild trout streams in the East and even has a section called Fisherman's Paradise.

Riffles and Runs B&B (217 N. Spring St., Bellefonte, 814/353-8109, www.riffles andruns.bellefonte.com, $100–140, special events $140–160) offers fly-fishing instruction and guiding along with two guest rooms with a shared bath.

State College has two specialty stores for fly anglers. More than 30 years old, **Flyfisher's**

Paradise (2603 E. College Ave., State College, 814/234-4189, 10 A.M.–6 P.M. Mon.–Thurs., 10 A.M.–8 P.M. Fri., 10 A.M.–5 P.M. Sat.) employs an FFF-certified casting instructor. Walk in on any given day and you're liable to find a pair of staff members with 80 years of fly-fishing and fly-tying experience between them. New kid on the block **TCO Fly Shop** (2030 E. College Ave., State College, 814/689-3654, www.tcoflyfishing.com, 9 A.M.–6 P.M. Mon.–Sat., 10 A.M.–4 P.M. Sun.) offers a website with loads of information about area waters along with a wide selection of products, instruction, and guide services.

You can explore the waterways that so many fish call home by canoe or kayak. **Tussey Mountain Outfitters** (308 W. Linn St., Bellefonte, 814/355-5690, www.tusseymoun tainoutfitters.com, hours vary by season) rents and sells both. Its paddle pros are happy to provide shuttle and guide services.

Outdoors Gear

Appalachian Outdoors (123 S. Allen St., State College, 814/234-3000, www.appout doors.com, 9:30 A.M.–8:30 P.M. Mon.–Thurs., 9:30 A.M.–9 P.M. Fri., 9 A.M.–8 P.M. Sat., 10 A.M.–6 P.M. Sun.) sells all manner of outdoor clothing and equipment, and its blog offers reviews and tales of adventure.

Flying

If you prefer to live rather than read tales of adventure, head to the **Ridge Soaring Glidersport** (3523 S. Eagle Valley Rd., Julian, 814/355-2483, www.eglider.org), where you can take off in an aircraft without a motor. Seriously.

Sky's The Limit Ballooning (814/234-5986, www.paballoonrides.com, flight $200/person) offers a different way to soar over the State College area. The hot-air balloon lifts off twice a day year-round, barring rain, fog, snow, or strong winds.

Winter Sports

The Alps it's not, but **Tussey Mountain** (341 Bear Meadows Rd., Boalsburg, 814/466-6266, www.tusseymountain.com, early Dec.–late Mar., lift ticket $19–34, complete rental $28, snow tubing 2-hour session $18) attracts Penn Staters in need of a quick skiing fix. It offers several trails for skiing and snowboarding, plus a snow tubing park. Tussey does its best to stay relevant in warmer months with a go-kart track, batting cages, a driving range, a skate park, and the occasional concert.

Spectator Sports

Football may be the crown jewel of Penn State athletics, but the Nittany Lions compete—and frequently trounce—in myriad sports, including baseball, basketball, gymnastics, and wrestling. Ticket information is available on the **Penn State Athletics** website (www .gopsusports.com) and at the ticket office (240 Bryce Jordan Center, University Park, 814/863-1000).

State College is also home to a short-season Class A affiliate of the Pittsburgh Pirates. The **State College Spikes** (814/272-1711, www .statecollegespikes.com) play at Medlar Field at Lubrano Park on the Penn State campus. They share the eco-friendly ballpark with the university's varsity baseball team, which plays

FADE TO WHITE

Penn State athletes weren't always known as the "Blue and White." In 1887, a student committee representing the sophomore, junior, and senior classes convened to weigh options for the school's official colors. Its top picks were presented to the student body and a winner chosen: dark pink and black. Soon, students were sporting blazers and caps in their new school colors. Trouble was, the pink had a habit of fading to white from sun exposure. In 1890, the school traded pink and black for blue and white.

there from March through May. The Spikes' 38-game home schedule begins in June. Single-game tickets cost $6–11. The mascot is a buck with the barest hint of antlers, a.k.a. a spike.

ACCOMMODATIONS

The State College area has a wide array of lodging options, from mom-and-pop motels to exclusive boutiques. Rates can skyrocket for Penn State football games, parents weekend,

© CENTRAL PA CVB

State College Spikes at Medlar Field at Lubrano Park

graduation, the Central Pennsylvania Festival of the Arts, and other busy periods. And they tend to dip when campus is closed.

Under $100

Get your fill of fresh air and baked goods at **Bellefonte/State College KOA** (2481 Jacksonville Rd., Bellefonte, 814/355-7912, www.bellefontekoa.com, campsites start at $33, one-room cabins $68–88, lodges $170–180). The full-amenity campground four miles northeast of Bellefonte has tent and RV sites and a handful of cabins and lodges. It also has a heated swimming pool, a stocked fishing pond, free Wi-Fi, and Amish neighbors who drop by on summer evenings with freshly baked treats.

You don't have to go to the countryside for accommodations in this price range. **The Stevens Motel** (1275 N. Atherton St., State College, 814/238-2438, www.thestevensmotel.com, $42–68, special events $75–180) offers 18 clean rooms, courteous service, and proximity to Penn State. The pet-friendly **Happy Valley Inn** (1245 S. Atherton St., State College, 800/228-4864, www.happyvalleymotorinn.com, $37–49, special events $150–200) has

35 guest rooms and a garden patio for catching rays come summer.

When the **Autoport** (1405 S. Atherton St., State College, 814/237-7666, www.theautoport.com, $75–115, special events $275–300) opened in 1936, it provided travelers with lodging, food, and car repair services. The garage has since been replaced by a coffee shop, but the Autoport still strives to be a full-service stop. There's high-speed Internet service, a heated pool, and a restaurant and bar with almost nightly entertainment.

$100-200

The Penn Stater Conference Center Hotel (215 Innovation Blvd., State College, 800/233-7505, www.pshs.psu.edu/pennstater, $115–225, special events $229–325) is the humbler of two hotels operated by the university's Hospitality Services Department. It looks rather like a dormitory from the outside, but you won't find bunk beds or lava lamps in its 300 guest rooms and suites. The Penn Stater knows well the needs of the PowerPoint crowd. Leisure travelers are also welcome.

Penn State's picture-perfect **(Nittany Lion Inn** (200 W. Park Ave., State College,

© ANNA DUBROVSKY

Nittany Lion Inn

800/233-7505, www.pshs.psu.edu/NittanyLion Inn, $135–285, special events $319–369) is the only hotel on campus. An inviting facade and lobby bespeak a boutique lodging, but in fact the hotel has 223 guest rooms and suites, not to mention meeting facilities and ballrooms. How it manages to feel so intimate may have something to do with the white-glove service.

The eminently elegant **Atherton Hotel** (125 S. Atherton St., State College, 814/231-2100, www.athertonhotel.net, regular rates start at $130, special events up to $315) will shine your shoes while you sleep—for free—but it's doubtful you'll need the service. A complimentary shuttle virtually ensures scuff-free footwear.

Toftrees Golf Resort and Conference Center (1 Country Club Ln., State College, 814/234-8000, www.toftrees.com, regular rates start at $120, special events $299–499) isn't in the pulsing heart of State College, but it's not far. The wooded resort three miles from Penn State's campus offers 102 guest rooms and suites and a variety of golfing/lodging packages. The impeccable **Carnegie House** (100 Cricklewood Dr., State College, 814/234-2424, www.carnegiehouse.com, $165–395)

overlooks the 17th green of the also impeccable Toftrees course. Modeled after Greywalls, the country inn overlooking Muirfield Golf Course in Scotland, the Carnegie House has 22 guest rooms and suites outfitted in antiques and oriental rugs. An in-house restaurant offers contemporary European cuisine amid china, crystal, and silver.

There are B&B options aplenty in this price range. The homey **Great Oak Inn** (104 Farmstead Ln., State College, 814/867-1907, www.greatoakinn.com, $85–200, special events $150–225), just a few minutes from downtown and Beaver Stadium, has three en suite guest rooms. Step back in time (but take Wi-Fi and Wii with you) at Boalsburg's **Springfield House** (126 E. Main St., Boalsburg, 888/782-9672, www.springfieldhousebb.com, $105–135, special events $210–275). Built in the 1800s and completely renovated in 2005, the B&B has five traditionally furnished guest rooms, each with a private bathroom. Chocoholics, take caution: **Boalsburg Chocolate Co.** (814/466-6290, www.boalsburgchocolate.com, 11 A.M.–5 P.M. Tues.–Fri., 10 A.M.–5 P.M. Sat.) is on premises.

Toftrees Golf Resort and Conference Center

© ANNA DUBROVSKY

The Queen B&B on Linn Street in Victorian Bellefonte

Bellefonte is the area's B&B capital. The kingly **Reynolds Mansion** (101 W. Linn St., Bellefonte, 814/353-8407, www.reynoldsmansion.com, $135–245, special events $145–300) has six uniquely decorated guest rooms. Ladies gravitate toward Grace's Garden Room with its turret sitting area and ornate inlaid floor or Louisa's Cherub Room, remarkable for its ceiling mural. Men feel like men in the Colonel's Green Room, which has the only king-sized bed in the house, a working fireplace, and a large black Jacuzzi. Guests can cue up in the billiard room or sip brandy in the snuggery. **The Queen, A Victorian Bed & Breakfast** (176 E. Linn St., Bellefonte, 814/355-7946, www.thequeenbnb.com, $95–245, call for special event rates, weekly and monthly rates available) is preened to perfection. Its tireless owner, Nancy Noll, was named Innkeeper of the Year by the Pennsylvania Tourism & Lodging Association in 2008. Victorian clothes and accessories decorate one room, hunting and fishing collectibles another, and vintage toys a third. The Maid's Quarters, an apartment with

a full kitchen and views of Noll's perennial gardens, sleeps up to four. Noll also rents out a three-bedroom house on an adjoining property for $220–325 per night or $800 per week. Among the other Bellefonte beauties is **Judge Walker's House** (337 E. Linn St., Bellefonte, 814/355-0591, www.judgewalkershouse.com, $95–165, special events $150–175), an artist-owned Queen Anne Victorian with four cozy guest rooms.

FOOD

A town packed with students is by necessity a town packed with eateries. But State College delivers more than typical student grub. There's inventive cuisine among the subs, pizza, and wings. You won't find this volume or variety of restaurants anywhere else in the Alleghenies. College and Beaver Avenues and their cross streets in downtown State College are particularly crowded with dining options. An above-average number of area establishments have large televisions for patrons who want to cheer on the Nittany Lions while chowing down.

American

The Diner (126 W. College Ave., State College, 814/238-5590, www.thedineronline.com, 7 A.M.–4 P.M. Mon.–Thurs., 24 hours Fri.–Sun., $2–7) is almost as legendary as Penn State football, thanks to a sticky bun slathered with butter and cooked until golden brown. "Grilled stickies" have gained so many fans over the decades that the restaurant now ships them anywhere in the country. The 1950s-style **Baby's Burgers & Shakes** (131 S. Garner St., State College, 814/234-4776, www.babysburgers.com, 11 A.M.–9 P.M. Sun.–Thurs., 11 A.M.–11 P.M. Fri.–Sat., $4–7) may not have stickies, but it does have a Wurlitzer jukebox, thick milkshakes, and fries drenched in chili and cheese.

You'll need time to study the thesis-length menu at **The Deli Restaurant** (113 Hiester St., 814/237-5710, www.dantesinc.com/thedeli.htm, 11 A.M.–midnight Sun.–Wed., 11 A.M.–2 A.M. Thurs.–Sat., $7–25). The drinks list alone fills several pages. Management calls

The Deli "eclectic," which may be the only way to describe a restaurant that serves both San Francisco–style cioppino and chimichangas.

The likes of peppered ostrich and pistachio-crusted venison chops grace the menu of the elegantly cozy **American Ale House** (821 Cricklewood Dr., State College, 814/237-9701, www.americanalehouse.net, kitchen 11 A.M.–10 P.M. Sun.–Thurs., 11 A.M.–11 P.M. Fri.–Sat., extended hours in summer, bar open as late as 2 A.M., $9–32). A steam bar makes for sophisticated starters.

Don't get too attached to an entrée at **Harrison's Wine Grill** (1221 E. College Ave., inside Hilton Garden Inn, State College, 814/237-4422, www.harrisonsmenu.com, 11 A.M.–9 P.M. Mon.–Sat., $6–24), because it might not be there next month. Chef Harrison Schailey's specialty is farm-to-table fare. If it's not in season, he's not interested.

Communities around State College offer more fine options. A onetime stagecoach stop, **Duffy's Tavern** (113 E. Main St., Boalsburg, 814/466-6241, www.duffystavern.com, kitchen 11:30 A.M.–10 P.M. Mon.–Sat. and 11:30 A.M.–9 P.M. Sun., tavern open until 1 A.M. Mon.–Sat., $7–33) serves elegant dishes like pork tenderloin with warm fruit in its dining room and more casual fare in the adjacent tavern. You can't miss **Kelly's Steak and Seafood** (316 Boal Ave., Boalsburg, 814/466-6251, 11 A.M.–midnight Mon.–Sat., 2 P.M.–midnight Sun., late-night menu after 9 P.M. Mon.–Thurs. and 10 P.M. Fri.–Sat., $7–45). There's a giant bovine on its roof. The kitschiness belies the kitchen's sophistication. Husband-and-wife chefs Sean and Tien Kelly, who met in Seattle, bring a Pacific Northwest sensibility to dishes such as cedar-plank-roasted salmon. Nowhere else in central Pennsylvania can you find a breakfast sandwich like the "seafood Joe"—scrambled eggs with Dungeness crab, sweet bay shrimp, spinach, onion, mushrooms, and lobster sauce on a toasted English muffin.

For breakfast or lunch in Bellefonte, try **Café on the Park** (325 W. High St., Bellefonte, 814/357-8442, www.cafeonthepark.net, 7 A.M.–3 P.M. Tues.–Sat., 9 A.M.–2 P.M. Sun., $3–8). The diminutive eatery serves omelets, sandwiches, and even ice cream from Penn State's famous creamery.

© ANNA DUBROVSKY

Kelly's Steak and Seafood

© CENTRAL PA CVB

train car at Whistle Stop Restaurant

They won't take your fare at the old train station in Centre Hall. Instead, they'll serve you comfort fare like seafood lasagna and slow-roasted prime rib. Passenger service to Centre Hall ended in the 1950s, and the 1885 station eventually became the **Whistle Stop Restaurant** (104 E. Wilson St., Centre Hall, 814/364-2544, www.whistlestopcentre hall.com, 11 A.M.–8 P.M. Wed.–Thurs., 11 A.M.–9 P.M. Fri.–Sat., 11 A.M.–7 P.M. Sun., $4–22). You'll find the original ticket window inside and a restored passenger car outside.

Two devastating fires in the past few years couldn't keep the **Mount Nittany Inn** (559 N. Pennsylvania Ave., Centre Hall, 814/364-9363, www.mountnittanyinn.com, 11 A.M.–9 P.M. Sun.–Thurs., 11 A.M.–10 P.M. Fri.–Sat., $6–26) down. The restaurant at the summit of Centre Hall Mountain reopened in 2008 to serve up hearty meals and dramatic views of Penn's Valley. A spacious deck allows for alfresco dining.

Asian

Cozy Thai Bistro (454 E. College Ave., State College, 814/237-0139, www.cozythaibistro .com, lunch 11 A.M.–3 P.M. Mon.–Fri. and noon–4 P.M. Sat., dinner 5–9 P.M. Mon.–Thurs., 5–10 P.M. Fri., and 4–10 P.M. Sat., $8–16) pairs fresh herbs with imported seasonings for flavorful renditions of common dishes like *pad thai* and uncommon creations like Cozy Thai canapés—wedges of wheat bread topped with a mixture of deep-fried shrimp and pork.

If you don't like your stir-fry or soup at **Green Bowl** (131 W. Beaver Ave., State College, 814/238-0600, www.thegreenbowl.com, 11 A.M.–9 P.M. Mon.–Thurs., 11 A.M.–9:30 P.M. Fri., noon–9:30 P.M. Sat., noon–9 P.M. Sun., breakfast 8:30–11:30 A.M. Sat.–Sun., $9–12), you've got only yourself to blame. That's because you get to pick the ingredients and sauces that go into your meal. Fortunately, an error in judgment won't leave you hungry. This is an all-you-can-eat establishment. Simply grab another bowl and start over.

Traditional Korean stews swimming with everything from watercress to octopus bring adventurous eaters to **Kimchi Korean Restaurant** (1100 N. Atherton St., State College, 814/237-2096, www.kimchistate college.com, 11:30 A.M.–10 P.M. Mon. and Wed.–Thurs., 11:30 A.M.–10:30 P.M. Fri.–Sat.,

11:30 A.M.–9 P.M. Sun., $7–18). There's chicken teriyaki for the more timid.

Austrian

Don't be surprised if the mom-and-pop **Herwig's Austrian Bistro** (132 W. College Ave., State College, 814/238-0200, www .herwigsaustrianbistro.com, 11:45 A.M.–8 P.M. Mon.–Wed., 11:45 A.M.–9 P.M. Thurs.–Sat., $4–20) closes before its posted hours. Dishes are prepared from scratch daily, and when they run out, the doors shut. Depending on the day, the tongue twisters on the menu board may include *zwiebelrostbraten, erdapfel laberl,* or *geschnetzeltes.* Oh yeah, it's authentic. Customers can bring their own beer or wine after 5 P.M. weekdays and all day Saturday.

Brewpubs

Beer lovers just love **Otto's Pub & Brewery** (2235 N. Atherton St., State College, 814/867-6886, www.ottospubandbrewery.com, kitchen 11 A.M.–10 P.M. Mon.–Sat., 11 A.M.–9 P.M. Sun., bar open as late as 2 A.M., $9–24), which offers about a dozen brews daily and taps a firkin every Friday. The food more than holds its own, thanks to a chef who's partial to fresh ingredients from local producers. Otto's beers even find their way into the entrées.

Elk Creek Café + Aleworks (100 W. Main St., Millheim, 814/349-8850, www.elkcreek cafe.net, 4–10 P.M. Wed.–Thurs., noon–11 P.M. Fri.–Sat., 11 A.M.–6 P.M. Sun., $4–23) is 20-some miles from State College, but its craft beers, from-scratch cuisine, and music hall bring in the crowds. The proprietors strive for a zero-waste operation, so no need to feel guilty about that plateful of Belgian-style fries. The fryer oil powers a diesel Mercedes.

Cajun and Creole

◖ **Spats Cafe & Speakeasy** (142 E. College Ave., State College, 814/238-7010, www .spatscafe.com, noon–9:30 P.M. Mon.–Thurs., noon–10 P.M. Fri.–Sat., $8–35) does New Orleans proud with flawlessly executed Cajun and Creole cuisine. Lazily spinning fans and deep red walls evoke the sensuality of the southern seaport, while dishes like jambalaya, pan-fried gator, and chicken and andouille gumbo make a po' boy out of anyone who passes up this State College gem.

Contemporary

If you give them ample notice, the chef and sommelier at **Zola New World Bistro** (324 W. College Ave., State College, 814/237-8474, www.zolabistro.com, lunch 11:30 A.M.–2 P.M. Mon.–Fri., dinner 5:30–9 P.M. Mon.–Thurs. and 5:30–10 P.M. Fri.–Sat., lighter fare in bar for one hour later, $7–36) can customize a seven- or nine-course tasting menu for you and your party. But the regular menu has much to recommend it, offering the likes of Prince Edward Island mussels in coconut milk and crispy whole red snapper in red chili sauce. Dinner reservations are recommended. If wait you must, you'll do it in style. The bar features leather couches and carefully crafted cocktails.

In 2008, Zola's owners snapped up Bellefonte's most lauded restaurant, the **Gamble Mill** (160 Dunlap St., 814/355-7764, www.gamblemill.com, lunch 11:30 A.M.–2 P.M. Mon.–Sat., dinner 5:30–9 P.M. Mon.–Thurs. and 5:30–10 P.M. Fri.–Sat., $7–36). A former gristmill, the building was condemned and slated for destruction several decades ago. But a local group rallied to its cause, and it became the first building in Bellefonte to be placed on the National Register of Historic Places. Celebrate its preservation with a selection from the 1,600-bottle wine room or a dessert made by the in-house pastry chef. Or both.

Indian

The popular lunch buffet at **India Pavilion** (222 E. Calder Way, State College, 814/237-3400, www.indiapavilion.net, lunch 11:30 A.M.–2:30 P.M., dinner 5–10 P.M. daily except Mon., $7–18) delights vegetarians and omnivores alike. South Indian specialties like *uttapam* and *idli* make an appearance during weekend buffets. *Thalis*—platters laden with a little bit of a lot of dishes—are a good dinner choice for the uninitiated. Bring your own booze if you like. There's no corkage fee.

Italian

Most pizza joints offer an array of toppings. **Hi-Way Pizza** (www.dantesinc.com/hiway.htm, 11 A.M.–9 P.M. Mon.–Thurs., 11 A.M.–10 P.M. Fri.–Sat., noon–9 P.M. Sun., $7–11) does one better, offering a dizzying number of crust options. There's the round Neapolitan and the square Sicilian, the pan pizza and the stuffed pizza, the crispy thin crust (cornmeal or whole wheat) and the flavored crust (roasted garlic, parmesan, or herbed). The standout is the flaky croissant-like crust. The popular "vodka flaky" marries vodka sauce, mozzarella, and prosciutto. Dough and sauces are made in-house. Take your pick of Hi-Way West (428 Westerly Parkway, State College, 814/237-1074) or Hi-Way North (1688 N. Atherton St., State College, 814/237-0375).

The closer-to-campus **Inferno** (340 E. College Ave., State College, 814/237-5718, www.dantes inc.com/inferno.htm, kitchen 11:30 A.M.–9 P.M. Mon.–Thurs., 11:30 A.M.–10 P.M. Fri., noon–10 P.M. Sat., noon 9 P.M. Sun., $6–10) is owned by the same restaurant group but sticks to Neapolitan brick-oven pizzas. Inferno rages on long after the kitchen closes. The full-service bar with its flat-screen TVs stays open as late as the law allows (the wee hour of 2).

Mario & Luigi's (1272 N. Atherton St., State College, 814/234-4273, www.dantesinc.com/marioandluigis.htm, 11:30 A.M.–2 P.M. and 4–9 P.M. Mon.–Thurs., 11:30 A.M.–2 P.M. and 4–10 P.M. Fri., 11:30 A.M.–10 P.M. Sat., noon–9 P.M. Sun., $7–27), yet another *ristorante* in the Dante's Restaurants group, boasts a wood-fired rotisserie where veal, chicken, lamb, or pork can be found roasting on any given night. The owner makes annual trips to Italy to scope out new ideas.

Faccia Luna (1229 S. Atherton St., State College, 814/234-9000, www.faccialuna.com, 11 A.M.–11 P.M. Mon.–Sat., noon–10 P.M. Sun., $6–14) is the brainchild of two Penn State fraternity brothers and now has locations in Virginia and Scranton, as well as State College. The mozzarella sticks are baked, not fried, and the house pizza sauce is an uncommon mixture of crushed tomato and garlic.

INFORMATION AND SERVICES

For brochures, memorabilia, and wireless Internet service, stop by the headquarters of the **Central Pennsylvania Convention and Visitors Bureau** (800 E. Park Ave., State College, 814/231-1400, www.visitpennstate .org, 9 A.M.–6 P.M. daily) across from Beaver Stadium. The CVB has a satellite visitors center in the historic train station at 320 West High Street in Bellefonte.

The *Centre Daily Times* (www.centredaily .com) and Penn State's *Daily Collegian* (www. collegian.psu.edu) provide coverage of local arts and entertainment, as do the monthly *State College Magazine* (www.statecollege magazine.com) and *Town & Gown* (www .townandgown.com).

GETTING THERE AND AROUND

State College is about 45 miles northeast of Altoona. From I-80, take exit 161 (Bellefonte) and follow Route 26 south to U.S. 220 south. The east–west U.S. 322 also leads to the college town. **University Park Airport** (SCE), just a couple of miles from Beaver Stadium, offers daily flights to and from Detroit, Philadelphia, and Washington, D.C. **Greyhound** (800/231-2222, www.greyhound.com) offers intercity bus service to State College. The nearest **Amtrak** (800/872-7245, www.amtrak.com) station is in Lewistown, about 30 miles away.

Local bus service is provided by the Centre Area Transportation Authority, or **CATA** (814/238-2282, www.catabus.com). One-way adult cash fare is $1.25, and transfers are free. Bus drivers don't carry change. Tokens can be purchased at CATA's downtown sales office at 108 East Beaver Avenue and its main office at 2081 West Whitehall Road as well as at several retailers and the information desks at the Nittany Mall and Penn State's HUB-Robeson Center. CATA also provides free transportation within Penn State and between campus and downtown State College. Local taxi services include **AA Taxi Inc.** (814/231-8294, www .statecollegetaxi.com) and **Handy Delivery** (814/355-5555, www.handydelivery.com).

Raystown Lake Region

At 8,300 acres, Raystown Lake is the largest lake entirely within Pennsylvania. Search for it on a map and you won't find a big blue blob. Raystown Lake is a corkscrew of a waterway, 28 miles of zig and zag. That's because it used to be a river. The lake owes its existence to a dam on the Raystown Branch of the Juniata River, built in the early 1970s to provide flood control and recreation opportunities. It succeeded on both levels. Raystown Dam wasn't yet completed when the deadly Hurricane Agnes dumped as much as 19 inches of rain in parts of Pennsylvania. Still, the lake stored so much floodwater that communities along the Juniata and Susquehanna Rivers were spared an estimated $60 million of damage. To boot, the lake has made tourism the second largest industry after agriculture in Huntingdon County. Raystown attracts more than two million visitors a year. The U.S. Army Corps of Engineers places no limits on boat size or horsepower, making the lake a mecca for boating, Jet Skiing, and waterskiing enthusiasts. Thanks to no-wake areas, it's also popular with anglers, bird-watchers, and other connoisseurs of quietude. The island-riddled lake is home to stripers, walleye, musky, crappie, and other game fish. (Bring high-quality tackle. The lake creatures are fighters.) Bald eagles nest in the tree-covered hills that give the lake its snake-like shape.

Under different ownership, a lake of such beauty might be ringed with homes and resorts. But the federal government frowns on development here. Only about 2 percent of the 118-mile shoreline is developed. There are accommodations aplenty in the hills and valleys surrounding the lake, but it isn't impossible to find shorefront digs, especially if your idea of a good time includes a tent. If the shore isn't close enough, you can live *on* the lake. Raystown Lake is the only place in Pennsylvania where you can rent a houseboat—complete with hot tub.

Scenery and recreation aren't the only attractions of the lake region. If you're passionate about railroading history, antique automobiles, or caverns, you'll find your bliss here.

SIGHTS

◖ Seven Points Marina and Lake Raystown Resort

The state's largest marina accommodates about 950 boats, including a rental fleet. Countless carp call the docks home, so bring breadcrumbs or pick up a 50-cent bag of fish food at the marina store. Seven Points Marina (5922 Seven Points Marina Dr., Hesston, 814/658-3074, www.7pointsmarina.com) is also home to the 125-passenger *Princess.* Sightseeing cruises depart at 1:30 P.M. daily July–August. In May, June, September, and October, they're limited to weekends. The 90-minute narrated tours cost $10 for adults, $9 for seniors, and $3 for children 4–12. Bring binoculars for a closer look at the wildlife. Two-hour dinner cruises are offered Saturday evenings from July through Labor Day weekend. The BYOB cruises depart at 6 P.M. Adults pay $33; children 4–12 eat for $12.

If you prefer a boat of your own, you can rent one for a few hours or a few days. Aluminum fishing boats are the smallest and slowest of the rental fleet. The 16-foot, 10-horsepower boats are available for $45 per hour or $100 per day, plus gas and tax. Adrenaline junkies may opt for the 90-horsepower pontoon boats, which come with all the equipment needed for waterskiing or tubing. The eight-person boats cost $125 per hour, $350 per weekday, $400 per day on weekends and holidays. Houseboats aren't available by the hour or day. They can be rented from Monday through Friday or Friday through Monday. They sleep 4–10 (most beds are doubles) and range $900–3,300 June–August. Discounts are available during the preseason (Apr. and May) and postseason (September and October). All of the houseboats have fully equipped galleys and gas grills. A handful boast sliding boards and hot tubs. Dogs are allowed on four.

© HUNTINGDON COUNTY VISITORS BUREAU

Seven Points Marina

You don't have to be a sea dog to rent a boat. The marina, which is privately owned and operates on a lease with the Corps of Engineers, encourages renters to get a boating certificate before they arrive but is authorized to issue temporary certificates. The hardest part of operating a boat is docking it. If you don't have the hang of that, marina staff will do it for you. For those who prefer manpower to horsepower, Huntingdon-based **Rothrock Outfitters** offers rental kayaks and mountain bikes at the marina.

Nearby **Seven Points Beach** is one of two Corps-managed beaches at the lake. Amenities include water trampolines, a snack bar, and showers. The concrete-bottomed beach is generally open from the week before Memorial Day through the week after Labor Day. Swimming is permitted 10 A.M.–8 P.M. within a buoyed area.

Marina and beach are part of the Seven Points Recreation Area, which also includes some 260 campsites, about 500 picnic tables, and an amphitheater that hosts music performances,

movies, and other free programs on Friday and Saturday evenings in the summer.

Lake Raystown Resort, Lodge & Conference Center (3101 Chipmunk Crossing, Entriken, 814/658-3500, www.raystownresort .com) offers a smaller marina than Seven Points but a wider array of lodging options, including campsites with cable hookups, beachfront bungalows, and log cabins perched on cliffs overlooking the lake. The 650-slip marina is home to the ***Proud Mary Showboat,*** used for public cruises from late May through October as well as private events. Ninety-minute sightseeing cruises, offered at 2:15 P.M. daily until Labor Day and weekends thereafter, cost $9.50. Seniors receive a 10 percent discount, and children under six can board for half price. Check the resort website for a schedule of breakfast, happy hour, dinner, and late-night cruises. Prices vary and don't include alcoholic beverages. (Unlike the *Princess* at Seven Points, the *Proud Mary* has a full bar.)

The resort's rental fleet includes fishing boats with 15-horsepower tiller motors, which go for

$30 per hour, $150 per day. Pontoon boats can be rented 8:30 A.M.–5 P.M. or 5:30–7:30 P.M. and range $150–445 per period. A 60-foot-long houseboat with four bedrooms, two full baths, and air-conditioning can be yours Monday–Friday or Friday–Monday for $2,000. Live aboard for a full week for $3,500. Boat rental prices don't include gas or tax. Canoes are available for $10 per hour, $75 per day.

Canoe races and sand art contests are among the organized activities at Buccaneer's Bay Beach, the resort's simulation of a white-sand shore. The property also includes a miniature golf course and a water park with two 380-foot twisting slides, an inner tube ride, and a heated swimming pool.

Heritage Cove Resort

A third boat rental site can be found at the southern end of Raystown Lake. (Interestingly, the Raystown Branch of the Juniata River flows south to north, kinda like the Nile in Egypt.) Heritage Cove Resort (1172 River Rd., Saxton, 814/635-3386, www.heritagecoveresort.com) offers canoes, kayaks, paddleboats, and a pontoon. Resort amenities include a playground, pool, and shuffleboard and volleyball courts.

Historic Huntingdon

The "big town" in Raystown country is the small town of Huntingdon. It's one of the oldest continuously inhabited settlements in Pennsylvania and the seat of Huntingdon County. It's also home to **Juniata College,** a liberal arts school founded in 1876 by members of the Church of the Brethren. Worth visiting is the **Juniata College Museum of Art** (17th and Moore Streets, 814/641-3505, www .juniata.edu/museum, 10 A.M.–4 P.M. Mon.–Fri., noon–4 P.M. Sat., reduced hours during academic breaks, free admission). It occupies Carnegie Hall, which was built in 1907 as the college library and features a grand rotunda and stained glass oculus. The permanent collection includes paintings by key members of the Hudson River School and dozens of portrait miniatures by American and European artists.

In 1988 the college commissioned Maya Lin

DON'T TEMPT THE TEDDY

What do you do if you're boating on Raystown Lake and see a black bear taking a dip? Take a picture, of course. Besides that? Steer clear. Avoid the temptation to speed toward the teddy for a closer look. Bears can grab hold of a boat and come aboard faster than you can say "ahoy," according to Don Brumbaugh, president of the Raystown Striper Club. "Remember," he says, "they're not at all scared of you. In other areas, they'll turn and run." Many of the bears at Raystown Lake were brought there because they did naughty things like pillage trash cans or bird-feeders in residential areas. In other words, they're accustomed to humans hollering at them.

to create an open-air chapel within a nature preserve near campus. The architect responsible for the Vietnam Veterans Memorial in Washington D.C. planted a large circle of rough granite stones on a hilltop and a smooth granite disk on a slightly higher neighboring hill. To reach the *Peace Chapel* from the museum, follow Moore Street north to Cold Springs Road, turn right, continue to Warm Springs Avenue, and take another right. Drive four blocks and turn left onto Peace Chapel Road. The site is open from dawn to dusk. It's not the only example of environmental art in Huntingdon. Look for murals on the corner of Penn and 8th Streets and on the concrete pillars of an abandoned railroad trestle that runs through Portstown Park. Both celebrate the region's history.

History goes 3D during **Mayfest** (814/386-2638, www.mayfestofhuntingdon.com), held on the last Saturday in April. (That's no typo. Huntingdon's Mayfest does indeed take place in April.) Downtown transforms into a patchwork of historical periods—one per block. Costumed performers and vendors help the Renaissance, the tie-dyed days of Woodstock, and other themes come alive. It's the only festival of its kind in the state.

© ANNA DUBROVSKY

the view from Hawn's Overlook

Ridenour and Hawn's Overlooks

For a bird's-eye view of the 225-foot-high dam that created Raystown Lake, head to Ridenour Overlook. It's accessible by winding roads that start at U.S. 22 just south of Huntingdon. Heading east on U.S. 22, watch for a Sheetz gas station on your left. Shortly thereafter, bear right onto Snyders Run Road. Continue to Henderson Hollow/Overlook Road and follow it up the mountain. Bear left at the sign for Ridenour Overlook. A short wooded trail leads from the parking area at Ridenour to a second overlook. The vista from Hawn's Overlook doesn't include the dam but is arguably more breathtaking.

Swigart Automobile Museum

You might recognize one of the mint-condition machines at the Swigart Automobile Museum (12031 William Penn Hwy./U.S. 22, Huntingdon, 814/643-0885, www.swigart museum.com, 10 A.M.–5 P.M. daily Memorial Day–Oct., open until 8 P.M. Fri., admission $6, seniors $5.50, children 6–12 $3). Its 1948

blue Tucker was used in the 1988 film *Tucker: The Man and His Dream,* starring Jeff Bridges. Another celebrity on permanent display: the 1960 Volkswagen named Herbie, a.k.a. "The Love Bug." What started as a private collection in the 1920s now includes about 150 cars, some of which are one of a kind. The museum's 1920 Carroll is believed to be the only surviving automobile built by the Carroll Motor Car Company, and its 1936 Duesenberg "Gentleman's Speedster" is the only 12-cylinder model ever created. Thirty to 35 cars are displayed at any time. The Swigart's "automobilia" includes license plates from every state, radiator emblems that identified a vehicle's manufacturer, and car badges that signified membership in an auto club. Antique bicycles, toys, and automobile artwork round out the collection. The museum's lawn comes alive with candy-colored antiques during the annual auto meet in August.

East Broad Top Railroad

The opportunity to ride a genuine steam

locomotive brings rail fans to rural Rockhill Furnace, home of the East Broad Top Railroad (U.S. 522, Rockhill Furnace, 814/447-3011, www.ebtrr.com, weekends June–Oct., train fares $12–15, children 2–11 $8–15). The narrow-gauge railway was constructed in the 1870s to transport coal from the fields of Broad Top Mountain to Mount Union, where it was transferred to the standard-gauge cars of the Pennsylvania Railroad. After World War II, increased use of oil and gas and competition from roadways took a toll on the East Broad Top. Operations ceased in April 1956, and the railroad was sold to a salvage dealer. But it was never dismantled. A portion of the line was reopened for tourist excursions in 1960, and a National Historic Landmark designation several years later ensured its survival. The EBT is the only original narrow-gauge railroad east of the Rockies. (Its rails are 3 feet apart instead of the standard 4 feet, 8 1/2 inches. Narrow gauge was cheaper and allowed for tighter curves.)

The 33-mile mainline is largely intact, though only a few miles are currently in service. Trains leave the station at 11 A.M., 1 P.M., and 3 P.M. The round-trip through fields and forests lasts about an hour and 15 minutes, with a 10-minute layover at a picnic area called Colgate Grove, where the locomotives turn. You can disembark at the grove, picnic, and catch a later train back—or set up camp on a Saturday and return on a Sunday train. Call the railroad office to reserve a night. Bring your own vittles because none are sold at Colgate Grove. The gift shop at the station sells snacks, and a lunch cart beside the roundhouse offers burgers, hot dogs, fries, and other carnival-style fare.

Tours of the 1882 roundhouse, home to half a dozen steam locomotives built between 1911 and 1920, are available for $8. The EBT's collection of vintage equipment includes two gas-powered motorcars and a variety of track cars used by crews that maintained the railroad. Ride a motorcar for $5 or a track car for $2.

COME WEDNESDAY, GO TO THE BIG VALLEY

You won't find Big Valley on a Pennsylvania map, and that's fine by the Amish and Mennonite communities that call it home. Unlike their brethren in the Lancaster region, the "plain people" of the bucolic Big Valley have managed to stay out of the limelight for more than 200 years. The wide valley nestled between two long ridges is more properly known as Kishacoquillas Valley, in honor of a Shawnee chief who warned settlers of attacks by other tribes, but "Kishacoquillas" doesn't roll off the tongue like "big." The valley floor is a tapestry of more than 1,000 farms. Wednesday is a good day to visit the largest of its five towns and villages: wee little Belleville. From daybreak to midafternoon, Amish and Mennonites mingle with worldlier folk at the **Belleville Sale and Livestock Auction** (717/935-2146), where everything from pies to piglets trades hands. Vendors peddle produce and flowers, new junk and old treasures.

Chickens squawk and children romp. To find the action from Belleville's Main Street (Route 655), simply follow the parade of horse-drawn buggies. White-topped buggies belong to the most conservative of the valley's Amish. Black tops and yellow tops signify membership in more progressive congregations. Big Valley is believed to be the only place where the three coexist.

The drive from either State College or Huntingdon takes about 40 minutes. Since an early arrival ensures the best selection, consider spending Tuesday night at **Brookmere Winery** (5369 Rte. 655, Belleville, 717/935-2195, www.brookmerewine.com, tasting and store hours 10 A.M.–5 P.M. Mon.-Sat., 1–4 P.M. Sun.). That's right, at a winery. In 2008, winemakers Ed and Cheryl Glick transformed an 1866 mansion into a B&B with four guest rooms, all with private baths. Rates at the **Vineyard Inn** range $95–175.

THE ALLEGHENIES

Rail fans, consider bunking across the street from the station at the **Iron Rail Bed & Breakfast** (371 Meadow St., Rockhill Furnace, 814/447-3984, www.ironrailbandb.com, $70–110). Once the home of the railroad's superintendent, the 1885 Victorian was completely renovated in 2007. It has four guest bedrooms and a sitting room with an antique piano. A tree-shaded side porch affords views of the EBT complex.

Rockhill Trolley Museum

Next door to the East Broad Top, the Rockhill Trolley Museum (430 Meadow St., Rockhill Furnace, 814/447-9576, www.rockhilltrolley.org, 11 A.M.–4 P.M. weekends June–Oct., admission $6, children 2–12 $3) is home to about 20 city, suburban, and interurban trolley cars that operated in places near (e.g., Philadelphia) and far (e.g., Portugal). Today, those in working condition operate on what was once a branch of the East Broad Top Railroad. Trolleys depart every half hour.

Among the dozen or so operable cars is a 1924 curved-side car that once plied the streets of York, Pennsylvania. After York Railways ceased streetcar operations in 1939, the car was sold for use as a summer home along Conewago Creek north of the city. In 1972, it was flooded and knocked off its foundation by Hurricane Agnes. Its owners donated the derelict car to the museum, and a worldwide search for missing parts ensued. Volunteer restorers bought wheels and motors from Japan, seats from Chicago, and cane covering for the seats from China.

Rockhill's fleet also includes the only open car operating in Pennsylvania. Assembled in balmy Rio de Janeiro in 1912, it was acquired by the museum in 1965, brought to New York aboard a coffee bean ship, and transported to rural Rockhill Furnace by railroad and highway. In addition to streetcars, the museum owns a handful of cars used to maintain track, remove snow, and move freight cars.

Of course, the Belleville market isn't the only opportunity to witness a way of life that's little changed since the 18th century. Follow any road branching from Route 655 and you're liable to find Amish farms. It shouldn't be long before you see a sign at the bottom of a lane advertising carrots or cabbage or rabbits or pine furniture. Drive down the lane for the goods and a closer gander. Be aware that the Amish don't do business on Sundays. If you spot dozens of buggies outside a home, chances are they're worshiping inside.

The simplicity of life in the valley so impressed Nick and Tara Richtscheit during a visit in the 1990s that the couple decided to make it their home. Now they show visitors around in horse-drawn wagons. **Dayze Gone Bye Carriage Rides** (41 Water St., Allensville, 814/553-5149 or 717/483-0099, www.dayzegonebye.com) are available by appointment.

Nick juggles driving with his duties as police chief of a borough just outside the Big Valley. On Wednesdays you'll find him at the Belleville Sale with ponies and a kid-sized carriage.

Don't leave the valley without a visit to **A.J. Peachey & Sons** (72 Barrville Rd., Belleville, 717/667-2185, www.ajpeachey.com, restaurant 6 A.M.-7 P.M. Mon.-Thurs. and Sat., 6 A.M.-8 P.M. Fri., $6-13, grocery store 7 A.M.-7 P.M. Mon.-Thurs. and Sat., 7 A.M.-8 P.M. Fri., gift shop 9 A.M.-7 P.M. Mon.-Sat.). Part restaurant, part grocery store, and part gift shop, A.J. Peachey is a one-stop for all things Amish, including locally made horseradish, apple butter, and pickled red beets. The restaurant features breakfast, lunch, and dinner buffets, complete with homemade desserts. Quality meats are an A.J. Peachey specialty. Call ahead if you want to cart off a quarter of beef.

© HUNTINGDON COUNTY VISITORS BUREAU

Rockhill Trolley Museum

The museum's season runs through October, but cars are called into service in late November and early December, when the trolley line is flanked with lighted decorations. Check the museum's website for information about Polar Bear Express, Santa's Trolley, and other special events.

Caverns

The Raystown region boasts Pennsylvania's largest concentration of caves. Closest to the lake and three miles west of Huntington is **Lincoln Caverns** (7703 William Penn Hwy./ U.S. 22, Huntingdon, 814/643-0268, www .lincolncaverns.com, open 9 A.M. daily Mar.– Nov., admission $11.95, seniors $10.95, children 4–12 $6.95), discovered in 1930 during the construction of U.S. 22. During the summer months, tours of the limestone cave's winding passageways and otherworldly rooms depart every few minutes; the last leaves at 5 P.M. or 6 P.M. In spring and fall, tours depart about every half hour until 4 P.M. Tours are limited to weekends in December and by appointment

in January and February. Each hour-long tour includes a visit to Whisper Rocks, a second cave discovered in 1941. Check the website for special events such as speleology workshops, February's Batfest, and October's Ghosts and Goblins tours. The temperature in the cave is a constant 52 degrees Fahrenheit, so bring a sweatshirt or jacket even in summer. For a modest fee, you can stay overnight at the primitive Warrior Ridge Campgrounds at Lincoln Caverns. There's no charge to use the picnic pavilions, nature trails, or meditation chapel.

Pennsylvania's largest limestone cave can be found on the banks of Spruce Creek about 18 miles northwest of Huntingdon. **Indian Caverns** (5374 Indian Trail, Spruce Creek, 814/632-7578, www.indiancaverns.com, 10 A.M.–5 P.M. daily June–Aug., weekends only Apr.–May and Sept.–Oct., admission $12, students and seniors $10.50, children 4–12 $6.50) opened to the public in 1929. But humans had been visiting for eons. Arrowheads and other artifacts found in the cave indicate that Native Americans used the

© HUNTINGDON COUNTY VISITORS BUREAU

Lincoln Caverns

cave more than 400 years ago. In the early 19th century, it served as a hideout for the outlaw David "Robber" Lewis and his entourage. Tours leave every hour 11 A.M.–4 P.M. from Memorial Day through Labor Day and cover almost a mile of cavern, including a naturally phosphorescent room. The temperature is a constant 56 degrees. Visitors can fish on a catch-and-release basis or picnic on cave property along Spruce Creek, a renowned trout stream. Fish food and fishing permits are available, but the visitors center doesn't stock rods, reels, or other fishing supplies.

ENTERTAINMENT AND EVENTS
Performing Arts
Juniata College (1700 Moore St., Huntingdon, 814/641-3333) hosts touring musicians, dance companies, and theater groups at its **Halbritter Center.** To boot, Juniata's theater department mounts several productions a year, and its choral and instrumental ensembles offer free concerts.

The **Playhouse at McConnellstown** (11680 Raystown Rd./Rte. 26, McConnellstown, 814/627-0311, www.littletheater.com) has a wee house—just 76 seats—but a wide-ranging repertoire.

Festivals and Events
The Huntingdon County Arts Council (814/643-6220, www.huntingdoncountyarts.org) sponsors weekend-long folk music festivals: **Folk College** (www.folkcollege.com, May, registration fee charged) at Juniata College and the **Greenwood Furnace Folk Gathering** (www.folkgathering.com, Sept., registration fee charged) at Greenwood Furnace State Park. Registrants participate in workshops, jam sessions, and concerts.

Thousands of Christian music fans flock to the Agape Farm near Mount Union for **Creation** (www.creationfest.com, late June, admission charged), a four-day festival on 400 acres. There's music from morning to night, worship services, water baptisms, and a whole lot more. Revelers hike "Jesus Mountain" behind the main stage for heavenly views.

The **Huntingdon County Fair** (10455 Fairgrounds Access Rd., Huntingdon, 814/643-4452, www.huntingdoncountyfair.com, early Aug., admission charged) is an agricultural expo extraordinaire, complete with midway rides, live music, a fair queen contest, and a demolition derby. A museum dedicated to agricultural history, normally open by appointment only, is open throughout the week.

Festivals abound in the fall. Alexandria's annual heritage festival, **Hartslog Day** (Main St., Alexandria, 814/669-4313 or 814/669-4555, second Sat. of Oct., free) features more than 200 craftspeople. The **Maple Harvest Festival** at Shavers Creek Environmental Center (3400 Discovery Rd., Petersburg, 814/863-2000 or 814/667-3424, www.outreach.psu.edu/shaverscreek, late Mar., admission charged) is a celebration of the first harvest of the year. Costumed interpreters demonstrate sugaring techniques used by Native Americans, pioneers, and modern farmers. The pancakes are plentiful and the sausage organic.

SPORTS AND RECREATION

Boating isn't the only draw of Raystown country. The region is chockablock with creeks, parks, forests, hiking trails, and wildlife. It's long been known for world-class fishing. In 2009, with the opening of the Allegrippis Trail System, it became a mecca for mountain bikers.

Allegrippis Trail System

Built by the International Mountain Bicycling Association, the Allegrippis Trail System is more than 30 miles of sustainable single-track trails arranged as stacked loops. Novice bikers can stick to the easiest dips and rollers while those with more experience can hop onto more challenging loops. The trails, which traverse ridges, woods, and the shores of Raystown Lake, also make for excellent hiking, cross-country skiing, and snowshoeing. A detailed map can be purchased at the Raystown Lake Region Visitors Center. Proceeds benefit the nonprofit Friends of Raystown Lake, which maintains the trails. The main trailhead is along Baker's Hollow Road near the Susquehannock Campground entrance. There's also a trailhead with several parking spots along Seven Points Road near the camper check-in building.

Rothrock Outfitters (418 Penn St., Huntingdon, 814/643-7226, www.rothrock-

riding the Allegrippis Trail System

© HUNTINGDON COUNTY VISITORS BUREAU

outfitters.com) offers rental bikes and a whole lot of expertise. Bikes and helmets are available at Seven Points Marina as well as the retail store in downtown Huntingdon. Convenience comes at a price. Renting a bike at Seven Points costs $40 for the first day. Pick it up at the store and pay just $27.

Bird-Watching

At least 19 bald eagles called Raystown Lake home as of January 2009. Birders will find a whole lot more to crow about in the region. In spring, shorebirds are a sure thing at the man-made **Old Crow Wetland** off U.S. 22 near Hoss's Steak and Sea House (9016 William Penn Hwy./U.S. 22, Huntingdon). More than 150 avian species have been inventoried in **Whipple Dam State Park** (20 miles northeast of Huntingdon off Rte. 26, 814/667-1800, www.dcnr.state.pa.us/stateParks/parks/whippledam.aspx).

For guaranteed sightings of golden and bald eagles, owls, and other birds of prey, head to Penn State's **Shavers Creek Environmental Center** (3400 Discovery Rd., Petersburg, 814/863-2000 or 814/667-3424, www.outreach.psu.edu/shaverscreek, 10 A.M.–5 P.M. daily Feb.–mid-Dec., free admission). It's home to injured raptors that can't fend for themselves in the wild. The 79-inch wingspan of the golden eagle got her in trouble; she brushed two power lines at once. Other birds in residence have cars and hunters to blame for their disabilities. They star in the Meet Our Birds of Prey show presented at 2 P.M. every Saturday and Sunday April–November. The environmental center's annual Birding Cup, held the first weekend of May, challenges teams to identify as many species as possible in a 24-hour period. A team called Birding the Midnight Oil holds the record of 160 species. (No, the caged fauna don't count.)

Fishing

Raystown Lake. Juniata River. Spruce Creek. Standing Stone Creek. Aughwick Creek. Shavers Creek. Great Trough Creek. The list of waterways goes on and on, and so does the fishing season. Pros have been casting their lines in this region for decades. Hobbyists unfamiliar with the area may wish to hire a guide.

Lake Raystown is well stocked with boat charter services. Sparky Price is the record-shattering angler behind **Trophy Guide Service** (814/627-5231, www.trophyguide.com). The 53-pound striper he pulled out of the lake is the largest the state has seen. **Striper Guide Service** (814/599-6754, www.striper-guide.com) operates several boats that split up the lake and signal each other when fish are biting. Lake Raystown Resort's **Angry Musky Outfitters** (814/658-3500, www.raystownresort.com) offers customized fishing packages that include lodging and licensing as well as guide service by the hour.

Open since 1986, **Spruce Creek Outfitters** (4910 Spruce Creek Rd., Spruce Creek, 814/632-3071, www.sprucecreekoutfitters.org, open daily Apr.–June, Mon.–Sat. July–Sept., Tues.–Sat. Oct.–Mar., hours vary) specializes in fly-fishing on the Little Juniata River, which is thick with wild brown trout.

Hiking

Several hiking trails wind through the Army Corps of Engineers lands that hug Raystown Lake. The **Hillside Nature Trail** behind the Raystown Lake Region Visitors Center snakes through songbird habitat and serves up a scrumptious view of Seven Points Marina. The **Old Logger's Trail** offers about five miles of hiking between the Seven Points and Susquehannock campgrounds. Exhibits along the trail explain how proper forest management improves food and cover for wildlife. The **Riverside Nature Trail** starts at Branch Camp, a primitive camping area at the northernmost end of the lake. It's but half a mile long but rich with wildlife and plant species. For serious hikers, there's the **Terrace Mountain Trail,** which spans the eastern side of the lake. The 30-mile route has five access points, so hikers can tackle it all at once or in segments. Overnight camping with potable water is available at two access points, and primitive camping is permitted at designated spots along the trail. Some sections are open to mountain bikers and horseback riders. For trail conditions and more information, contact the Army Corps (814/658-3405, http://raystown.nab.usace.army.mil).

Twelve miles of trails traverse **Trough Creek State Park** (Rte. 994, 5 miles east of Rte. 26, 814/658-3847, www.dcnr.state.pa.us/stateparks/parks/troughcreek.aspx), a gorge formed as Great Trough Creek cuts through Terrace Mountain and empties into Raystown Lake. Among the wondrous sights: the large boulder known as Balanced Rock because it clings to the edge of a cliff, beautiful Rainbow Falls, mountain laurel blooms in June, rhododendron blooms in July, and an occasional copperhead.

Greenwood Furnace State Park (Rte. 305, 5 miles east of Rte. 26 at McAlvey's Fort, 814/667-1800, www.dcnr.state.pa.us/stateparks/parks/greenwoodfurnace.aspx) was once a sooty iron-making village. The furnace was retired in the early 1900s, but traces of the company town remain. Trails within the park and the surrounding block of Rothrock State Forest offer glimpses of ruins along with picturesque views. A charcoal hearth and colliers hut can be found along the half-mile **Chestnut Spring Trail.** The park is the northern terminus of the 72-mile **Standing Stone Trail** (www.hike-sst.org), also known as the Link Trail because it connects the even longer Mid State and Tuscarora Trails. It passes through four state game lands and two state forests on its way to Cowans Gap State Park. The **Thousand Steps** are a particularly popular section. Quarry workers built the stone stairs in the 1930s to shorten their commutes to work sites on Jacks Mountain. To trace their steps, look for a parking area along U.S. 22 about two miles west of Mount Union.

Hunting

It's not called Huntingdon County for nothing. The home of Raystown Lake is also home to a plethora of wild game: whitetail deer, rabbit, turkey, grouse, pheasant, fox, duck, goose, and bobcat, to name a few. A Pennsylvania hunting license is required. Hunting is a year-round recreation at Raystown, but a specific season

applies to each game type. Check the website of the Pennsylvania Game Commission (www.pgc.state.pa.us) for hunting seasons and regulations. Hunting and fishing licenses are available at **Big 4 Outdoors** (11559 William Penn Hwy./U.S. 22, Huntingdon, 814/644-6800, www.bigfouroutdoors.com, 9 A.M.–8 P.M. Mon.–Fri., 9 A.M.–5 P.M. Sat., 10 A.M.–3 P.M. Sun., reduced hours Apr.–mid-July). The hunting supply store specializes in archery and has a TechnoHUNT indoor archery range.

Scuba Diving

There's lots to see in Raystown Lake, including remnants of buildings that were consumed when the dam was constructed. Unfortunately, there's no scuba shop in the area, so divers should bring their own gear.

Snowmobiling

Rothrock State Forest offers 191 miles of snowmobile trails, which open after the last day of regular or extended rifle deer season and usually close on April 1. Several state parks and game lands also allow dashing through the snow. The state's Department of Conservation and Natural Resources maintains a listing of snowmobile trails by county: www.dcnr.state.pa.us/recreation/snow/snowcoun.htm.

Spelunking

Huntington County has more than 150 known caves, including Indian Caverns and Lincoln Caverns. If the show caves don't slake your spelunking thirst, contact the Huntingdon County Cave Hunters (cavehunters@yahoo.com), a chapter of the National Speleological Society.

ACCOMMODATIONS

Raystown Lake is the only place in Pennsylvania where you can rent a houseboat. But there's plenty of lodging on dry land, including more than 1,500 campsites, 300 rental homes and cottages, and some charming B&Bs.

Under $50

Bring camping gear for the cheapest digs. **Nancy's Camp,** a year-round tent-only site on the western shore of Raystown Lake, is one of several campgrounds operated by the Army Corps of Engineers (814/658-3405, http://raystown.nab.usace.army.mil). Fifty sites are available on a first-come, first-served basis for $10 apiece. The registration box can be found near the comfort station. **Susquehannock Camp,** another Corps site, occupies a wooded peninsula on the western shore. The primitive campground, open from mid-May through mid-September, has about 60 sites, many of which can accommodate a camper. Sites are $12 per night and can be reserved through the federal recreation portal www.recreation.gov. For electric service and hot showers, head to the Corps-managed campgrounds at **Seven Points Recreation Area,** with some 260 sites organized in six loops. Sixty percent of the sites can be reserved through recreation.gov starting in mid-May; the rest are available on a first-come, first-served basis. The campgrounds at Seven Points open as early as April and close in September or October.

Waterfront campsites are available at **Lake Raystown Resort, Lodge & Conference Center** (3101 Chipmunk Crossing, Entriken, 814/658-3500, www.raystownresort.com, campgrounds open Apr.–Oct., $39–55). The 250-site campgrounds boast water, electric, sewer, and cable hookups, plus wireless Internet service. **Heritage Cove Resort** (1172 River Rd., Saxton, 814/635-3386, www.heritagecoveresort.com, May–Oct., $36–45) has 195 campsites with water, electric, and sewage hookups. The resort also has two- and three-bedroom cottages that can be rented for a full week ($1,350), Thursday–Sunday ($700), or Sunday–Thursday ($865).

$50-100

The Inn at Edgewater Acres (7653 Edgewater Acres Circle, Alexandria, 814/669-4144, www.edgewateracres.net, $99) is a super-sized bed-and-breakfast built around a 1762 farmhouse. Each of its 20 rooms has a private bathroom and either a king bed or two single beds. There's not a bad view in the house; half the rooms face the mountains, and the other half the Juniata River.

$100-200

☾ **The Inn at Solvang** (10611 Standing Stone Rd., Huntingdon, 814/643-3035, www.solvang.com, $100–135) looks like something

© ANNA DUBROVSKY

The Inn at Solvang

out of *Gone with the Wind*. The three-story brick mansion with four massive columns sits at the end of a tree-lined lane off Route 26 about four miles north of Huntingdon. (It's easy to miss the turnoff. Look for an ornate "S" between two white posts.) Gourmet breakfasts are served on fine china, but the atmosphere is far from prim. Guests are welcome to curl up on elegant period furniture with a classic plucked from the bookshelves or fish on the stream that runs through the property. The inn has four guest rooms and a wood-paneled suite that sleeps as many as four.

The rooms and suites in the lodge at **Lake Raystown Resort, Lodge & Conference Center** (3101 Chipmunk Crossing, Entriken, 814/658-3500, www.raystownresort.com, $96–199) have private balconies overlooking the marina. Bring your own towels if you prefer to stay in one of the resort's rustic camping cabins ($111–139 per night), beachfront bungalows ($1,350 per week), or lakeside villas ($800–850 per three- or four-night stay, $1,500–1,600 per week).

Over $200

For a romantic getaway à la Tarzan and Jane, swing over to **Junglewood** (2553 Timberlake Dr., James Creek, 800/673-9211, www.shybeaverlakeviewest.com, $225), perched high above Raystown Lake. The vacation home feels like a treehouse—a treehouse with a large hot tub overlooking the lake.

FOOD

Like many recreation areas, Raystown Lake is blessed with homespun eateries that you can walk into water-soaked or mud-splattered and still be greeted with a smile. Burgers, hoagies, pizza, ice cream, and other foods that don't call for utensils are the norm. But exceptions can be found.

Huntingdon

Start your day at **Standing Stone Coffee** (1229 Mifflin St., 814/643-4545, www.standingstonecoffeecompany.com, 6:30 A.M.–10 P.M. Mon.–Thurs., 6:30 A.M.–midnight Fri., 7:30 A.M.–midnight Sat., noon–7 P.M. Sun.),

which roasts its own java. Pair your drip-brewed or French-pressed coffee with a mini quiche, baked oatmeal, or other breakfast item. Come lunchtime, $4–6 buys you a panino or deli sandwich. Salads and a daily soup are also on offer. Standing Stone has free Wi-Fi and—get this—a self-service laundry. So you can refuel, update your Facebook status, and wash your duds all at the same time.

In 2008, a tea bar, bakery, and gift shop opened in a former bank building. Appropriately enough, the house tea at **Abigail's** (501 Penn St., 814/641-7158, www.abigailsatthehub.com, 10:30 A.M.–3 P.M. Mon., 10:30 A.M.–7 P.M. Tues.–Fri., 8:30 A.M.–3 P.M. Sat., under $10) is called Bankers Blend. Abigail's also serves coffee, espresso drinks, and tea lattes. Scones and muffins are baked fresh each morning, and sandwiches, wraps, and salads are available for larger appetites. The chicken salad—made with pecans, apricots, raisins, and celery—is a best seller.

For dinner, there's ◖ **Mimi's** (312 Penn St., 814/643-7200, www.mimisrestaurant.net, 4:30–10 P.M. Mon.–Sat., bar open as late as 2 A.M., $15–25), a restaurant and martini bar that's hands down the swankiest joint in town. Entrées include pasta dishes, pork tenderloin sautéed with shiitake mushrooms, and New York strip steak. The lengthy cocktail menu takes a while to digest. Signature drinks include Mimi's Martini, made with vodka, Tia Maria, and Irish cream, and Mimi's Mango Freeze, a mixture of mango rum and mango pulp. In the interest of fairness, there's a frozen drink named for Mimi's husband, Jamie. The fashionable, friendly couple can often be found tending bar and mingling with diners.

The husband and wife behind **Boxer's Café** (410 Penn St., 814/643-5013, 11 A.M.–10 P.M. Sun.–Thurs., 11 A.M.–11 P.M. or midnight Fri.–Sat., under $10) refuel their modified vehicles with oil used in the kitchen's fryers. With wings, Cajun fries, and breaded mushrooms on the menu, there's nary a shortage. The eco-conscious restaurateurs favor local and organic foods, eschew Pepsi and Coke for sodas from Pennsylvania-based Catawissa Bottling

Company, and use biodegradable containers for takeout. Named for the dog breed, not the fighting sport, Boxer's is known for its large selection of import beers and microbrews.

Near Huntingdon

Pray that a freight train stops on the tracks behind **Miller's Diner** (11740 William Penn Hwy./U.S. 22, Mill Creek, 814/643-3418, www.millersdiner.com, 6 A.M.–8 P.M. Mon.–Sat., 8 A.M.–2:30 P.M. Sun., $7–11) while you're digging into a plate of home-cookin'. When railroad engineers and conductors pop into the restaurant, everyone gets a token for a free slice of pie. The extensive menu features chicken-fried steak, meatloaf, veal parmigiana, and other comfort foods. For unlimited eats, come for the breakfast buffets on Saturdays and Sundays, the Sunday lunch buffet, or the Friday dinner buffet.

The nearby **Mill Stone Manor** (11979 William Penn Hwy./U.S. 22, Huntingdon, 814/644-0619, www.themillstonemanor.com, fine dining $18–25, casual dining $7–16) is a motel with a restaurant open to the public for dinner. Wear your fancy pants for seating in the fine dining section, where barroom appetizers like calamari and quesadillas introduce ballroom entrées like bacon-wrapped scallops and lobster ravioli. For lower prices, a laxer dress code, and a burger-heavy menu, opt for the casual dining area, sunroom, or bar. Food is served 5–10 P.M. Tuesday–Thursday, 4–10 P.M. Friday and Saturday, and 2–8 P.M. Sunday. Drinks are served until the bar closes, whenever that may be.

About a half mile farther east on U.S. 22, next to the Swigart Automobile Museum, another down-home diner woos travelers with free Wi-Fi and large plates. **Top's Diner** (12151 William Penn Hwy./U.S. 22, Mill Creek, 814/643-4169, www.topsdiner.net, 6 A.M.–8 P.M. Mon.–Thurs., 6 A.M.–9 P.M. Fri.–Sat., 7 A.M.–8 P.M. Sun., $3–15) also boasts an outdoor dining area, so you can have a side of sunshine with your sweet potato hotcakes or meatloaf melt (homemade meatloaf, provolone, and sauce on grilled sourdough). For all-you-can-eat honey-stung fried chicken, arrive on a Wednesday.

Alexandria

The itsy-bitsy borough of Alexandria, about eight miles north of Huntingdon, is home to **The Inn at Edgewater Acres** (7653 Edgewater Acres Circle, 814/669-4144, www.edgewateracres.net, $9–25), a 20-room B&B that opens its dining room to the public for dinner Thursday–Saturday and Sunday brunch. Reservations are recommended as guests get first dibs on tables. The elegant inn snagged a full beverage license in 2009, so you can enjoy a Pinot Noir with your pan-seared duck breast.

No reservations needed for **Main Street Café** (214 Main St., 814/669-4494, $12–25), a sports bar with some 15 televisions. A torch-lit deck offers Juniata River views more captivating than any broadcast. Wings are a big seller here, but the restaurant also caters to the fine-dining crowd with steaks and such. Main Street opens at 11 A.M. daily. The kitchen closes at 11 P.M. on Fridays, Saturdays, and Wednesdays and 10 P.M. on other days. The bar stays open until patrons pile out or 2 A.M., whichever comes first.

INFORMATION AND SERVICES

The hilltop **Raystown Lake Region Visitors Center** (6993 Seven Points Rd., Hesston, 9 A.M.–5 P.M. daily Memorial Day–Labor Day, hours vary in off-season) is a good place to start your "Raycation," as the folks who market the lake like to say. It houses the Huntingdon County Visitors Bureau (814/658-0060, www.raystown.org) and Army Corps rangers (814/658-3405, http://raystown.nab.usace.army.mil). You'll find bushels of free brochures, a gift shop, and exhibits on the region's history, geology, and wildlife. Boat launch permits can be purchased here. A deck affords majestic views of the lake and Seven Points Marina.

GETTING THERE AND AROUND

Huntingdon, the commercial center of the lake region, is about 35 miles east of Altoona near the intersection of U.S. 22 and Route 26. The nearest major airport is in Pittsburgh, about 125 miles away. The closer Altoona-Blair County Airport (AOO) in Martinsburg and University Park Airport (SCE) in State College offer commuter services. **Amtrak** (800/872-7245, www.amtrak.com) provides train service to Johnstown via its Pennsylvanian line, which connects New York City and Pittsburgh.

A car is nearly essential for exploring the region. If you arrive in Huntingdon by train, you can rent one at **Enterprise Rent-A-Car** (100 S. 4th St., 814/643-5778, www.enterprise.com). If you travel light, you could get away with renting a bicycle from **Rothrock Outfitters** (418 Penn St., 814/643-7226, www.rothrock-outfitters.com), less than 500 feet from the train station.

Bedford and Vicinity

As British troops carved a wagon road over the Allegheny Mountains in 1758, they stopped to construct fortifications along the way. One of these, Fort Bedford, sat on a bluff overlooking the Raystown Branch of the Juniata River. The supply fort built to support Britain's campaign against the French had the side effect of transforming a backwoods into a bona fide town. Bedford homesteads became hot property because the fort provided protection from Indian attacks.

Bedford got even hotter in the 1800s, when word spread of mineral-rich springs with curative powers. People traveled great distances to "take the waters." The luxe Bedford Springs Hotel attracted a bevy of politicians and other upper-echelon types during the 19th and early 20th centuries. In 1858, President James Buchanan received the first transatlantic telegram at the resort, which had come to be known as his "summer White House." It closed in the 1980s but reopened in 2007 after a $120 million restoration and expansion. Thanks to its rebirth and relatively low property costs, the

Old Bedford Village

Bedford area is once again gaining popularity as an idyllic retreat for city folk.

SIGHTS
Historic Bedford

Fort Bedford deteriorated in the 1770s, but a museum suggestive of a blockhouse stands near the site. The **Fort Bedford Museum** (110 Fort Bedford Dr./Juliana St., 814/623-8891, www.fortbedfordmuseum.org, 11 A.M.–7 P.M. daily May–second Sat. of Oct., other hours by appointment, admission $5, seniors $4.50, students 6–18 $2) houses a model of the irregularly shaped fort and a variety of military and civilian artifacts. The jewel of its collection is a 1758 flag that hung in the officers' quarters. It was a gift from England's fourth Duke of Bedford, for whom the fort was named.

The **Espy House** (123 East Pitt St.) served as President George Washington's headquarters during the Whisky Rebellion. Snap a few pictures, but don't expect its current occupants to invite you inside. For a warm welcome, try the **Golden Eagle Inn** (131 E. Pitt St., 814/624-0800, www.bedfordgoldeneagle.com, meal $8–36, rooms $150–180). Travelers have been stopping here for a bite to eat and a bed to sleep in since the late 1700s. (Bedford's Pitt Street was once part of the Forbes Trail, the route cut by British troops in 1758 and followed by many a stagecoach driver.) The **Bedford County Arts Council** (137 E. Pitt St., 814/623-1538, 11 A.M.–5 P.M. Tues.–Sat., free admission) occupies the house next door, built in 1814 for Dr. John Anderson. The doctor saw patients in the front and operated Bedford's first bank in the back, where a vault remains. The council hosts rotating exhibits and occasional coffeehouses.

Antique woven bedcovers get an exhibit space of their own in Bedford. The **National Museum of the American Coverlet** (322 S. Juliana St., 814/623-1588, www.coverletmuseum.org, 10 A.M.–5 P.M. Mon.–Sat., noon–4 P.M. Sun., admission $6, seniors $5) occupies a building that was used as a school from 1860 until 1999. The local architect responsible for Dr. Anderson's house built the

---

WASHINGTON SLEPT HERE

Farmers in western Pennsylvania didn't take kindly to a federal excise tax imposed on whiskey producers in 1791. They took out their irritation on tax collectors and other government representatives (think tar and feathers). When their bullying turned to outright insurrection in 1794, President George Washington invoked martial law to summon a force of nearly 13,000. He led the militia army as far west as Bedford. While his men camped in open fields, Washington slept in the home of Colonel David Espy – the nicest digs in town. It was the first and only time a U.S. president would command troops in the field.

By the time troops reached the Pittsburgh area, the epicenter of the so-called Whiskey Rebellion, most of the rebels had fled into the hills. The federal government had proven its might. The whiskey tax remained in force until 1801. In 1984, the Espy House was named a National Historic Landmark.

Bedford County Courthouse (200 S. Juliana St.) in the late 1820s. Two self-supported circular stairways lead to a second-floor courtroom bedecked with portraits of judges.

The **Bedford County Visitors Bureau** (131 S. Juliana St., 800/765-3331, www.bedfordcounty.net, 9 A.M.–5 P.M. Mon.–Fri. year-round and Sat. May–Oct.) offers free guided tours of downtown's historic sites on Fridays June–October. Tours start at 3:30 P.M. and last about 90 minutes. If you have a portable video player, you can download a 75-minute walking tour from the bureau's website any day of the year.

Old Bedford Village

A "living history village" two miles north of downtown leaves nothing to the imagination. When Old Bedford Village (220 Sawblade Rd., Bedford, 814/623-1156, www.oldbedfordvillage.com, 9 A.M.–5 P.M. daily except Wed. Memorial Day–Labor Day, Thurs.–Sun. after Labor Day–Oct., admission $10, students $5) isn't staging reenactments of pre-21st century battles, its costumed artisans are demonstrating coopering, quilting, candle making, and other early American crafts. The village has more than 40 original and reconstructed structures, including a two-story log farmhouse from the 1700s and an octagonal schoolhouse built in 1851.

(Omni Bedford Springs Resort

Bedford doctor John Anderson wasted no time when Native Americans led him to mineral-rich springs on the southern outskirts of town. In 1796 he bought a 2,200-acre swath of countryside that included the springs. Soon, patients were arriving from near and far to bathe in and drink the reputedly curative waters. At first the savvy doctor housed them in tents. In 1806 he built a hotel with stone quarried from a nearby mountain. The resort grew along with its popularity, opening one of America's first golf courses in 1895 and an indoor pool

fed by spring waters a decade later. Musicians serenaded the swimmers from a balcony overlooking the pool. By the time it closed in 1986—timeworn and cash-strapped—the Bedford Springs Hotel had hosted 11 presidents and a long list of captains of industry, celebrities, and other bigwigs.

Reopened in 2007 after a restoration and expansion to the tune of $120 million, the resort offers the luxuries they enjoyed and then some. Now known as the Omni Bedford Springs Resort (2138 Business U.S. 220, Bedford, 814/623-8100, www.omnihotels.com, weekend room rates start at $339 Memorial Day weekend–Oct., $259 Nov.–Dec., $229 Jan.–late Apr., $289 late Apr.–Memorial Day weekend), it boasts a 30,000-square-foot spa that uses water from a spring discovered during the makeover and products inspired by local botanicals like wild honeysuckle and Indian cucumber. The restored golf course was named the top playable classic course in Pennsylvania by *Golfweek* magazine. New Italian marble flooring surrounds the lavish indoor pool, and private cabanas ring the outdoor pool. The

the indoor pool at the Omni Bedford Springs Resort

© OMNI HOTELS

fitness center features the latest cardiovascular and weight-training equipment.

You don't have to be a guest of the resort to enjoy the 18-hole golf course (until 2:50 P.M. $99–119, after 3 P.M. $69–79, special rates for golfers 15 and under) or the **Springs Eternal Spa.** And you don't have to spend an arm and a leg to have a fantastically soothing spa experience. Book any service—from a $20 eyebrow wax to a $245 body treatment—and you can spend all the time you like sipping tea in the coed lounge, strolling in the adjacent garden, or moving between steam room, hot-water pool, and cold-water pool as part of the spa's signature self-guided bathing ritual.

Dining options include the **1796 Room,** an upscale steak and chop house, and the casual **Frontier Tavern,** where you can wash down a burger with a Pennsylvania microbrew. A fire pit outside the bar and lounge beckons s'mores lovers.

Gravity Hill

There's a spot in suburban New Paris, about 15 miles from Bedford, where a car in neutral will roll uphill—or so it's said. To see for yourself, follow U.S. 30 west from Bedford to Schellsburg, turn north onto Route 96, drive about four miles, turn left onto Bethel Hollow Road, drive about two miles to an intersection with a stop sign for oncoming traffic, and bear right. Within a quarter of a mile, you'll see "GH" spray-painted on the road. Continue past the first "GH" and stop at the second "GH." Put your car in neutral. Take your foot off the break pedal. Defy gravity.

Wise men say that Gravity Hill (www .gravityhill.com) is an example of an optical illusion, not of supernatural forces. It's a trip either way. You can pick up a guide to Gravity Hill at the Bedford County Visitors Bureau (131 S. Juliana St., Bedford, 800/765-3331, www.bedfordcounty.net, 9 A.M.–5 P.M. Mon.–Fri. year-round and Sat. May–Oct.) or print directions from the Gravity Hill website.

Covered Bridges

The visitors bureau is also the place to go for information on Bedford County's covered bridges, which number 14. Most were built in

© PATRICIA GATES, ALLEGHENY MOUNTAINS CONVENTION & VISITORS BUREAU

Bedford County covered bridge

the 1800s in the Burr-truss style, named for designer Theodore Burr, and are still drivable. Recommended driving tours range from 30 minutes to three hours.

Coral Caverns

A show cave about 15 minutes west of Bedford boasts the fossilized remains of coral and other sea creatures that lived more than 400 million years ago. Coral Caverns (Cavern St., Manns Choice, 814/623-6882, www.coral caverns.com, 10 A.M.–5 P.M. weekends mid-May–mid-Oct., admission $11, children 11 and under, $5) has plenty of stalagmites and stalactites, too.

ENTERTAINMENT AND EVENTS
Performing Arts

The **Bedford County Players** (814/623-7555, www.bedfordcountyplayers.com) stage musicals and other shows May–December at the Gardner Memorial Theater within Old Bedford Village. A second local theater company, **Four Little Sisters Dinner Theater** (154 N. Richard St., Bedford, 814/624-0010, www.fourlittlesistersdinnertheater.yeeep.com) came onto the scene in 2009.

Pennsylvania Consort (814/733-2920, www.artsinbedfordpa.org) sponsors a six-concert classical music series. Concerts are held in the fall and spring at Bedford United Methodist Church. Tickets are $7 in advance or $8 at the door. The group also sponsors Summer Music on the Square, a series of free Saturday afternoon concerts at the gazebo on the corner of Juliana and Penn Streets in Bedford.

Festivals and Events

The weeklong **Bedford County Fair** (just west of downtown Bedford on Business U.S. 30/W. Pitt St., 814/623-9011, www.bedford-fair .com, late July, admission charged) offers the usual: animal exhibitions, live music, midway rides, and a queen competition. Be sure to check out the unusually large **Coffee Pot** (www.lhhc.org/coffeepot.asp) at the entrance to the fairgrounds. The 1920s structure was once a lunch stand along the Lincoln Highway, America's first coast-to-coast road. It was moved to its present location in 2003.

More than 400 craft booths line Bedford's streets and squares for the annual **Fall Foliage Festival** (800/765-3331, www.bedfordfall festival.com, first two weekends of Oct., free). The celebration features an antique car parade, a quilt show and sale, and plenty of children's activities.

SPORTS AND RECREATION
State Parks

Blue Knob State Park (124 Park Rd., Imler, 814/276-3576, www.dcnr.state.pa.us/ stateparks/parks/blueknob.aspx) in northwestern Bedford County is home to Blue Knob, Pennsylvania's second-highest mountain after Mount Davis. The dome-shaped mountain makes for breathtaking views and challenging hikes. Mountain biking, horseback riding, snowmobiling, cross-country skiing, hunting, and fishing are all permitted in the park. **Blue Knob All Seasons Resort** (Overland Pass, Claysburg, 800/458-3403, www.blueknob .com, lift ticket $23–55, 8-hour downhill skis rental $28, snow tubing 2-hour session $15–18) offers downhill skiing—with a vertical drop of 1,072 feet—on land leased from the park.

Boaters may prefer the smaller **Shawnee State Park** (132 State Park Rd., Schellsburg, 814/733-4218, www.dcnr.state.pa.us/ stateparks/parks/shawnee.aspx) with its 451-acre lake stocked with warm-water game fish. Paddleboats, canoes, and rowboats can be rented during the summer. A swimming beach is open 8 A.M.–sunset from late May to mid-September. Ice skating is permitted near the Colvin boat launch when the lake is frozen.

Both parks offer modern campsites starting the second Friday in April. Blue Knob's 45 tent and trailer sites close in late October. Shawnee has almost 300 sites and a camping season that stretches to late December. Reserve online at www.pa.reserveworld.com or call 888/727-2757.

Biking

Bedford County is home to Cannondale Bicycle Corp.'s U.S. factory, but that's not the only reason it's beloved by cyclists. They also dig its lightly traveled roads, scenic vistas, and an abandoned section of the Pennsylvania Turnpike now known as the **Pike 2 Bike** (www.pike2bike.org) trail. You can print out maps and turn-by-turn directions for more than 20 rides from www.bedfordcounty.net/ bikeloops, including an easy 12.2-mile loop that takes in four covered bridges.

If you don't have a bicycle, head to **Fat Jimmy's Outfitters** (109 Railroad St., Bedford, 814/624-3415, www.fatjimmys.com, 9 A.M.–6 P.M. Mon.–Thurs., 9 A.M.–8 P.M. Fri., 9 A.M.–6 P.M. Sat., 1–7 P.M. Sun.). Rentals start at $20 per day.

Grouseland Tours (467 Robinsonville Rd., Clearville, 814/784-5000, www.grouseland .com), about 25 miles southeast of Bedford, not only rents and sells Cannondales but also leads fully supported road rides and mountain bike tours. A daylong rental ranges from $35 for a bicycle with front suspension to $55 for a tandem. The rental cost is halved for riders taking a Grouseland tour. Tour rates depend on the length of the ride and the number of riders. Grouseland also offers camping at $5 per person.

Boating

Novice paddlers will appreciate the slow-moving Raystown Branch of the Juniata River. Canoe and kayak rentals start at $25 per day at **Fat Jimmy's Outfitters** (109 Railroad St., Bedford, 814/624-3415, www.fatjimmys.com, 9 A.M.–6 P.M. Mon.–Thurs., 9 A.M.–8 P.M. Fri., 9 A.M.–6 P.M. Sat., 1–7 P.M. Sun.). The riverside **Woy Bridge Campground** (190 Campground Rd., Everett, 814/735-2768, www.bedford .net/canoe, May–Oct.), about 15 miles east of Bedford, rents kayaks and canoes along with campsites and a handful of cabins. On-site daily rates are $15 for canoes and $12 for kayaks. There's no shuttle service, but you can take canoes and kayaks off-site for $25 and $20 per day, respectively. Rates drop after the first two days.

Horseback Riding

Greenridge Horse Ranch (130 Horse Ranch Rd., Artemas, 814/784-5223, www.greenridge horseranch.com) promises to have you riding "the cowboy way" in no time. Trail rides start at $40 for a 90-minute three-mile trip. A full-day trip with about five hours in the saddle costs $125. Pony rides are $25 per half hour. The ranch is closed from Thanksgiving through December, when deer hunters roam the woods.

Spectator Sports

Race cars tear up the half-mile dirt track at the Bedford County Fairgrounds on Friday evenings from mid-April through August. The **Bedford County Speedway** (108 Telegraph Rd., Bedford, 814/623-0500, www.bedford speedway.com) also hosts special events like monster truck shows.

ACCOMMODATIONS
Under $100

Clean rooms, low rates, and gracious hosts of Pennsylvania Dutch stock greet guests at **Judy's Motel** (3521 Business U.S. 220, Bedford, 814/623-9118, www.bedfordcounty .net/hotels/judys, $36–44), 1.5 miles south of Pennsylvania Turnpike exit 146.

The full-service **Friendship Village Campground** (348 Friendship Village Rd., Bedford, 814/623-1677, www.friendship villagecampground.com, $22–100) has tent and RV sites, rustic cabins, and cottages complete with air-conditioning and cable TV. Amenities include a convenience store, a bass-stocked lake, and a miniature golf course. On Saturday evenings campers are treated to a "gospel sing" and free popcorn made over a campfire.

$100-200

The impeccable **Chancellor's House Bed and Breakfast** (341 S. Juliana St., Bedford, 814/624-0374, www.thechancellorshouse .com, $110–150) in Bedford's historic district has three guest rooms with private bathrooms and a wide front porch complete with rocking chairs. Antique furnishings and modern amenities await at **Golden Eagle Inn** (131 E. Pitt St., 814/624-0800, www.bedfordgolden eagle.com, $150–180), which has 16 guest rooms and suites.

Nature lovers can explore miles of trails through privately owned wetlands and woods at **Whitetail Wetlands** (967 Dunnings Creek Rd., New Paris, 814/839-2622, www.white tailwetlands.com, $75–200). The lodge has three guest rooms, a kitchenette for self-pre-pared meals, a baby grand piano, and work-ing fireplaces. Primitive camping sites are also available.

An idyllic vacation on a working sheep farm? That's right. Guests aren't asked to lend a hand at **Monsour Sheep Farm** (120 Oppenheimer Rd., Bedford, 814/623-8243, www.monsour vacationhomes.com), which has several vaca-tion homes along with a flock of more than 1,000 ewes and lambs. Accommodations range from a one-room log cabin with a wood-burn-ing stove ($75 per night) to a five-bedroom farmhouse that sleeps as many as 15 ($299 per night for groups up to 10). A two-night minimum stay is required. Come in May for a chance to bottle-feed a newborn lamb.

Over $200

Fronted by columns of solid white pine and rows of balconies, the recently renovated **Omni Bedford Springs Resort** (2138 Business U.S. 220, Bedford, 814/623-8100, www.omnihotels.com, weekend room rates start at $339 Memorial Day weekend–Oct., $259 Nov.–Dec., $229 Jan.–late Apr., $289 late Apr.–Memorial Day weekend) offers 216 luxuriously appointed guest rooms and a hand-ful of suites. They're divided between a historic building and a modern spa wing. The latter is advisable if you plan to spend much time luxu-riating in the fabulous spa, swimming in the indoor or outdoor pools, or exercising in the state-of-the-art fitness center.

More than 200 years old, the resort amid mineral-rich springs oozes with history. Eleven presidents have slept here. A guest ledger signed by President James Buchanan on the eve of the Civil War is displayed in the lobby, as is a copy of the first transatlantic telegram, which Buchanan received at the resort in 1858. Wall after wall in the National Historic Landmark is decorated with black-and-white images of long-ago guests.

Today's guests can pass the time fishing on a private lake or stocked trout stream (kids can have the chef cook their fresh catch), hiking or biking 25 miles of trails (knobby walking sticks provided), or playing a game of golf, tennis, bocce ball, or badminton. Roasting marshmallows around a fire pit is an evening tradition. The executive chef's cooking work-shops are also quite popular.

FOOD

Sink into a plush sofa with an expert espresso drink at **HeBrews Coffee Company** (103 S. Richard St., Bedford, 814/623-8600, www .hebrewscoffeecompany.com, 7 A.M.–3 P.M. or 4 P.M. Mon.–Thurs., 7 A.M.–7 P.M. Fri.–Sat.). For a glass of iced tea and a slice of fresh-baked pie, you can't beat **The Eatery** (100 S. Juliana St., Bedford, 814/623-9120, 10 A.M.–5 P.M. Mon.–Sat., noon–3 P.M. Sun., $6–9). The café tucked inside the mammoth Founders Crossing crafts and antiques co-op also offers soups, salads, and sandwiches.

The Green Harvest Co. (110 E. Pitt St., Bedford, 814/623-3465, www.thegreenharvest co.com, 7 A.M.–5 P.M. Mon.–Sat., under $10) is your best bet for a healthy and satisfying breakfast or lunch. The vegetarian-friendly eat-ery takes the peanut butter and jelly concept to new heights. Try the Apple PB sandwich, made with all-natural peanut butter, apples, bacon, and cheddar, or the PB Starter with its local jam and sliced bananas. Hungry for a hot meal? Order one of the panini or indi-vidual flatbread pizzas. Green Harvest sells its own line of seasonings, condiments, and dip, spread, and salad dressing mixes, plus fine foods from farther reaches.

The historic **Golden Eagle Inn** (131 E. Pitt St., Bedford, 814/624-0800, www.bedford goldeneagle.com, brunch 11 A.M.–1:30 P.M.

Sun., lunch starting at 11:30 A.M. Tues.–Sat., dinner starting at 5 P.M. Thurs.–Sat., $8–36) serves American cuisine "with a Colonial flavor." Its screened-in porch provides a lovely setting for digging into dishes such as spinach quiche, stuffed eggplant, and grilled lamb chops. The **Bedford Tavern** (224 E. Pitt St., Bedford, 814/623-9021, www.bedford-tavern.com, kitchen 5–9 P.M. Tues.–Wed., 5–10 P.M. Thurs.–Sat., 4–9 P.M. Sun., bar open as late as 2 A.M., $4–34) is known for its seafood—frog legs, snow crab legs, and fried oysters included—and "all you care to eat" dinners. It opens at 1 P.M. when the Pittsburgh Steelers are playing.

A few miles west of town is the **C Jean Bonnet Tavern** (6048 Lincoln Hwy., Bedford, 814/623-2250, www.jeanbonnettavern.com, 11 A.M.–10 P.M. daily, $7–34), which serves up the likes of lamb stew, roasted duck with raspberry liqueur sauce, and dry-aged strip loin steak. Its 16-strong selection of draft beers is heavy on Pennsylvania microbrews. If the thick

fieldstone walls of the 1760s landmark could talk, they'd tell of farmers meeting in opposition to a federal whiskey tax and the troops sent to quell their insurrection in 1794. Diners can warm up by old hearth fireplaces in winter or catch a breeze on the outdoor dining porch (a newer amenity) in summer. Tired travelers can stay in one of four guest rooms, priced at $100–120 per night.

Waitstaff in colonial dress serve up country-style meals at the curio-filled **Slick's Ivy Stone Restaurant** (8785 William Penn Rd., Osterburg, 814/276-3131, www.slicks ivystone.com, 11 A.M.–8:30 P.M. Tues.–Fri., 4–8:30 P.M. Sat., 11 A.M.–7 P.M. Sun., closed late Dec.–Mar., $10–22), about 12 miles north of Bedford.

Dining options at the Omni Bedford Springs Resort (2138 Business U.S. 220, Bedford, 814/623-8100, www.omnihotels.com) include the **1796 Room** (5:30–10 P.M. Mon.–Sat., $25–40, reservations requested), an upscale steak and chop house, and the casual **Frontier**

© THE ALLEGHENIES

The beer selection at Jean Bonnet includes several Pennsylvania microbrews.

Tavern (kitchen open 11:30 A.M.–10 P.M. daily, bar closes at midnight Sun.–Thurs. and 2 A.M. Fri.–Sat., $8–16), where you can wash down a $14 burger with a Pennsylvania microbrew.

INFORMATION AND SERVICES

The **Bedford County Visitors Bureau** (131 S. Juliana St., Bedford, 800/765-3331, www .bedfordcounty.net, 9 A.M.–5 P.M. Mon.–Fri. year-round and Sat. May–Oct.) in downtown Bedford has brochures devoted to everything from covered bridges to birding hot spots. Brochure racks can also be found at **HeBrews Coffee Company** (103 S. Richard St., Bedford, 814/623-8600, www.hebrews coffeecompany.com, 7 A.M.–3 P.M. or 4 P.M. Mon.–Thurs., 7 A.M.–7 P.M. Fri.–Sat.) and the 24-hour **Gateway Travel Plaza** (16563 Lincoln Hwy., Breezewood, 814/735-4011, www .gatewaytravelplaza.com), located off exit 161 of the Pennsylvania Turnpike near the intersection of I-76 and I-70.

GETTING THERE AND AROUND

Bedford is about 100 miles east of Pittsburgh and 140 miles northwest of Baltimore and Washington, D.C. The east–west Pennsylvania Turnpike (I-76) and U.S. 30 pass through Bedford County, as does the north–south U.S. 220/I-99. To reach downtown Bedford from the turnpike, take exit 146 and turn right onto Business U.S. 220. The vast majority of visitors arrive and sightsee by car. There are no commercial flights into Bedford County Airport (HMZ).

LAKE REGION

When Pennsylvanians say they're taking a beach vacation, odds are they're going out of state. Maybe they're driving to the Jersey Shore or the Outer Banks of North Carolina. Maybe they're flying to Florida or The Bahamas or even farther. Ask them about the seashore in their backyard, and many will answer with blank stares. *A seashore? In Pennsylvania?*

That's to be expected. People who know their geography think of the United States as having three coastlines: the East Coast, the West Coast, and the Gulf Coast. Pennsylvania borders none of those. But it does border the "Fourth Seacoast," as Congress dubbed the Great Lakes in 1970. The five freshwater lakes on the nation's border with Canada are ocean-like in more ways than one. They offer sandy beaches, sloping dunes, and surfable waves.

And they're vast. At more than 4,500 miles, the U.S. Great Lakes shoreline is longer than the East and Gulf Coasts combined.

The northwest corner of the Commonwealth abuts Lake Erie, shallowest and warmest of the Great Lakes. Pennsylvania's share of the shoreline is small—less than 80 miles—but of note. Presque Isle, a peninsula attached to the mainland just west of the city of Erie, is a natural wonderland. Just seven miles long, it boasts six distinct ecological zones and, consequently, an incredible diversity of plants and animals. *Birder's World* magazine named it one of the best places in the country for bird-watching. It's one of the best—if not *the* best—place in Pennsylvania to watch the sun set. And its beaches are hands down the best in the state.

While Presque Isle is the number one reason

HIGHLIGHTS

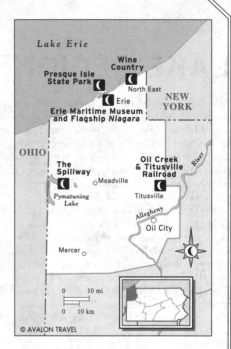

Lake Erie

Wine Country

Presque Isle State Park

North East

NEW YORK

Erie

Erie Maritime Museum and Flagship *Niagara*

OHIO

The Spillway

Meadville

Oil Creek & Titusville Railroad

Pymatuning Lake

Titusville

Allegheny River

Oil City

Mercer

0   10 mi

0   10 km

© AVALON TRAVEL

◖ **Presque Isle State Park:** A National Natural Landmark, this sandy peninsula is sheer bliss for beach lovers and birders (page 489).

◖ **Erie Maritime Museum and Flagship** *Niagara:* The airy museum brings to life the Battle of Lake Erie, a major American victory during the War of 1812. It's doubly interesting when Pennsylvania's official flagship is docked behind it (page 496).

◖ **Wine Country:** Home to more than half a dozen wineries, the town of North East is a first-rate day-trip destination, especially during the harvest months of September and October, when the air is heavy with the scent of grapes (page 499).

◖ **The Spillway:** At this heavily visited spot on man-made Pymatuning Lake, ducks walk on the backs of fish. Seriously (page 511).

◖ **Oil Creek & Titusville Railroad:** Soak up Pennsylvania's oil heritage during a 27-mile round-trip journey through "the valley that changed the world." Better yet, bike in one direction and take the train in the other (page 521).

LOOK FOR ◖ TO FIND RECOMMENDED SIGHTS, ACTIVITIES, DINING, AND LODGING.

to visit the Lake Region, it's certainly not the only one. Erie County is a major grape grower, and you can guess what that means: wineries. Erie, its county seat and largest city, is home port to Pennsylvania's official state ship, a faithful reconstruction of an 1813 brig that sealed one of the most important naval victories in American history. She's a sight to behold, especially when she's sailing, and the opportunity to live on board as part of her crew is truly unique. Another unique opportunity awaits at manmade Pymatuning Lake, within an hour's drive of Erie. There, the simple pleasure of tossing crumbs to chubby carp and ducks is punctuated by the "holy crap!" sight of a duck scrambling over a fish's back.

Nowhere else does the state sanction feeding of wildlife. Like Presque Isle, Pymatuning is a magnet for birders. You can bet money that you'll spot a bald eagle there. Nearby Erie National Wildlife Refuge rounds out the region's bird-watching triple bill. As the birthplace of the modern oil industry, northwest PA also has special appeal to history buffs. Their triple bill: the former boomtowns of Titusville, Oil City, and Franklin.

PLANNING YOUR TIME

There are good times to visit northwest PA, and then there are bad times to visit northwest PA. Winter is a bad time. Why? Three words: lake effect snow. Lake effect snow is

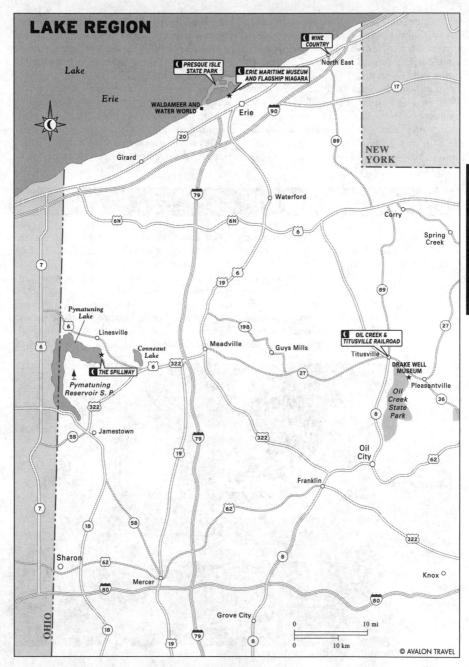

LAKE REGION

Lake

Erie

WINE COUNTRY

North East

PRESQUE ISLE STATE PARK

ERIE MARITIME MUSEUM AND FLAGSHIP NIAGARA

WALDAMEER AND WATER WORLD

Erie

90

17

20

89

NEW YORK

Girard

79

Waterford

6N

6N

6

Corry

7

19

6

Spring Creek

89

27

Pymatuning Lake

6

Linesville

6

Conneaut Lake

322

Meadville

198

Guys Mills

27

OIL CREEK & TITUSVILLE RAILROAD

Titusville

DRAKE WELL MUSEUM

Pleasantville

THE SPILLWAY

Pymatuning Reservoir S. P.

322

36

Oil Creek State Park

8

58

Jamestown

19

79

322

Oil City

62

Franklin

62

58

322

Sharon

62

8

Knox

Mercer

80

18

Grove City

19

79

8

80

OHIO

0   10 mi

0   10 km

© AVALON TRAVEL

what happens "when a mass of sufficiently cold air moves over a body of warmer water, creating an unstable temperature profile in the atmosphere," according to weather.com. To put it in plain terms, the city of Erie and its surrounds get buckets and buckets of snow. With an average annual snowfall of nearly 90 inches, Erie is one of the 15 snowiest cities in the country. That would be great if the attractions in this corner of the state included ski resorts, but when locals want to hit the slopes, they head to New York's Peek'n Peak. Among the very few reasons to visit in winter is to gaze at the otherworldly ice dunes along the shore of Lake Erie. Holing up in a B&B with your honey is another.

If you're going to visit Presque Isle in summer, which, of course, is the most popular time to visit the beach-lined peninsula, plan well ahead. Accommodations fill quickly. Do the same if you're planning on wine-tasting during the harvest months of September and October.

Erie and Vicinity

With a population of roughly 104,000, Erie is Pennsylvania's fourth largest city after Philadelphia, Pittsburgh, and Allentown. Its relative largeness has much to do with its location on Presque Isle Bay, a natural harbor formed and sheltered by the peninsula for which it's named. Erie was a speckle of a town when the United States declared war on Great Britain in 1812. With Canada under British control, the Great Lakes became a theater of war. As one of the few American settlements on Lake Erie and the only one with a good harbor, Erie was a natural staging ground. Virtually overnight, it transformed into a naval shipbuilding center. In August 1813, a fleet of warships left Presque Isle Bay and headed west to meet the enemy. The engagement on September 10 opened with several hours of intense cannon fire and ended

Erie, with a view of the Bicentennial Tower

© HENRYK SADURA/123RF.COM

with a victory for the Americans. The Battle of Lake Erie marked the first time in history that an entire British naval squadron was defeated and captured.

Erie's reputation as a maritime center was sealed, and its harbor quickly became a major stop on the Great Lakes. Completed in 1844, the Erie Extension Canal moved passengers and freight from the port city to the Pittsburgh region. Railroads came to Erie less than a decade later. Its impressive transportation systems made it appealing to industry, and by the end of the 19th century, the city was renowned for its metalworking factories. Its contribution to the World War I effort included more than 1,400 cannons. In the early 1900s Erie was also regarded as the freshwater fishing capital of the world. At one point in the 1920s, a record 144 commercial fish tugs operated out of the city. The bayfront was crowded with fish-processing houses, icehouses, shipbuilders and chandlers, and restaurants, hotels, and boardinghouses serving the men who worked the fishing fleet. Erie's commercial fishing industry eventually fell victim to overfishing and pollution. By the

turn of the 21st century, only one commercial fisherman was still in business. The not-so-crowded bayfront is now home to a museum devoted to Erie's maritime heritage, including its great fishing past. Local waters continue to attract sports and recreational anglers.

Erie remains an industrial city. Locomotive manufacturer GE Transportation has its world headquarters here and tops the list of largest employers. The plastics industry also has a significant presence in Erie. The heyday of lake trade is long past, but Erie's harbor is still in the business of import and export. It's now able to handle the large vessels that carry cargos between the Atlantic Ocean and the Great Lakes via the St. Lawrence Seaway, a system of locks and canals completed in 1959.

◖ PRESQUE ISLE STATE PARK

If Presque Isle (814/833-7424, www.dcnr .state.pa.us/stateparks/Parks/presqueisle.aspx) weren't property of the state, the sandy peninsula would almost certainly be crowded with million-dollar vacation homes. It's that

© ANNA DUBROVSKY

Presque Isle State Park

stunning. Just seven miles long, the spit jutting into Lake Erie boasts more than a dozen beaches, a 19th-century lighthouse, and a remarkable diversity of plant and animal life. The National Natural Landmark is unlike any other place in Pennsylvania. Indeed, it's more like Southern California than the rest of the Commonwealth. (More precisely, in *summer*, it bears some resemblance to SoCal—inline skaters, kite-flyers, and all. In winter, there's nothing California-ish about it. California doesn't have ice dunes, for one thing.)

The claw-shaped peninsula is attached to the mainland four miles west of downtown Erie and widens as it stretches northeastward. It forms and protects Presque Isle Bay, the deep harbor that put Erie on the maritime map. The peninsula refuses to stay put. It's been creeping eastward ever since it formed thousands of years ago. Not being a geologist, this author is ill-equipped to explain the forces of erosion and deposition. Suffice it to say that wind and water are forever pushing sand from the peninsula's neck toward its eastern end, known as Gull Point. That's a problem the U.S. Army Corps of Engineers has been battling since the early 1800s. Today the agency's anti-erosion

arsenal includes 58 breakwaters, which are aligned parallel to the beaches and partially block the waves. The Corps also steps in when storms cause breaches in the neck of Presque Isle—French for "almost an island"—and turn it into a bona fide island. It's happened at least four times since 1819.

Presque Isle is reached via Peninsula Drive (Route 832) or by boat. If you're driving, stop at the **Tom Ridge Environmental Center** (301 Peninsula Dr., Erie, 814/833-7424, www.trecpi.org, 10 A.M.–6 P.M. daily, free admission), or TREC for short, to learn about Presque Isle's history and ecosystems and grab a map of the 3,200-acre park. Named for a former Pennsylvania governor who served as the nation's first secretary of homeland security, the airy and eco-friendly facility houses 7,000 square feet of interactive exhibits, a small orientation theater showing a free 15-minute movie, and the **Big Green Screen Theater** (814/838-4123, 45-minute films shown on the hour 11 A.M.–5 P.M. daily, ticket $7.50, seniors $6, children 2–12 $5.50) with its four-story, 45-foot-wide screen. It also has a café and a lovely shop full of whimsical gifts, including model sailboats, miniature lighthouses, wind chimes,

Presque Isle Bay

© ANNA DUBROVSKY

© ANNA DUBROVSKY

Tom Ridge Environmental Center

and beach glass jewelry. Be sure to climb (or take the elevator) to the top of TREC's 75-foot observation tower for views of Lake Erie. You can spot Canada on a clear day.

Presque Isle is strictly a day-use park, so if you're planning to spend the night, you'll have to do it on the mainland. Book accommodations well in advance if visiting in the summer.

Beaches

Plenty of Pennsylvania's interior lakes advertise sandy beaches (that Mother Nature had *nothing* to do with), but none can deliver surf swimming or a water horizon. Lake Erie is so large that Presque Isle beach-goers see nothing but water and sky when they gaze northward. It's almost like being at the ocean. In at least one way, it's better than being at the ocean: There's no risk of being stung by jellyfish. Presque Isle's beaches are open 10 A.M.–7:30 P.M. daily from Memorial Day weekend to Labor Day unless otherwise posted.

If you're toting a cooler, take your pick of beaches. If not, you may want to choose a beach with a food and beverage concession: Beach 6, Beach 8 (Pettinato Beach), Beach 10 (Budny Beach), or Beach 11. Beach 6 has the added benefit of sand volleyball courts, which attract a lot of teens. Families with small children may prefer Beach 11, a sheltered beach with shallow water, a bathhouse with changing areas, and a playground. Beach 7, also known as Waterworks Beach, is the only other beach with playground equipment. It's notable in that its restrooms and picnic tables and even the water's edge are ADA accessible. If you're looking for a deserted beach, you've come to the wrong place. The Mill Road Beaches, a group of adjacent beaches with shaded picnic areas, are your best bet for a quiet and romantic experience.

Free concerts bring music lovers to Beach 1 on Wednesday evenings in June and July. The **Sprint Sunset Music Series** (814/838-5144, www.discoverpi.com) is presented by the nonprofit Presque Isle Partnership.

Trails

Bicyclists, inline skaters, and joggers circuit the peninsula on the paved **Karl Boyes Multipurpose National Recreation Trail.** Named for a late state legislator, the route is nearly 14 miles long and ADA accessible. Bicycles, tricycles for kids and adults, four-wheeled surreys, and inline skates can be rented from Memorial Day through Labor Day. The concession, **Yellow Bike** (814/835-8900), is about 2.5 miles from the park entrance in what's known as the Waterworks area. In winter, part of the multi-use trail is left snow-covered for cross-country skiers.

Maritime history buffs can retrace the steps of lighthouse keepers on the **Sidewalk Trail.** At the north end of the 1.25-mile trail is the **Presque Isle Lighthouse.** Its brick tower was built in 1873 and raised to 68 feet in the 1890s. Before electric bulbs came into use, keepers climbed to the top every four hours to refill an oil lamp. Today the light is automated, and the attached dwelling, home to nine keepers until 1944, is a residence for park staff. At the south end of the trail is Misery Bay, named such because of the hardships endured by sailors based there during the War of 1812. Lighthouse keepers followed the Sidewalk Trail to their boathouse in the bay when they needed supplies from the mainland. Once a wooden boardwalk, the trail was resurfaced with concrete in 1925.

Hikers can take their pick of about a dozen unpaved trails, none longer than two miles. The 1.5-mile **Gull Point Trail** is particularly popular. It begins at the east end of Beach 10 (Budny Beach) and makes a loop through Gull Point, a resting spot for migrating shorebirds. For the benefit of feathered visitors, the state closes the easternmost section of Gull Point to humans from April through November. There's an observation platform at the edge of the special area.

An old firing range used for training during World War II is visible from the **North Pier Trail.** The 0.7-mile path traces the shoreline from Beach 11 to North Pier, a popular fishing spot and home to the **North Pier Light,** which has been guiding ships into Erie's harbor since 1858. Also notable is the **Dead Pond Trail,** a two-mile journey over former sand dunes and through oak-maple forest, pines, and sand plains.

Boat Tours and Taxi

It would be a shame to leave Pennsylvania's Great Lakes port without logging some boat time. Various watercraft can be rented on Presque Isle and in Erie's Bayfront District, but you also have the option to leave the navigating to pros. **Presque Isle Boat Tours** (814/836-0201, www .piboattours.com, fare $16, children 5–12 $9) offers 90-minute voyages aboard the *Lady Kate* on weekends from mid-May through mid-June, daily from mid-June through Labor Day, and on weekends through the remainder of September. The 110-passenger vessel docks near Presque Isle's Perry Monument, a tribute to the sailors who fought under Commodore Oliver Hazard Perry during the War of 1812. Knowledgeable guides describe points of interest, including historic lighthouses and the nature preserve at the eastern end of the isle, as she cuts through the water. Reservations are recommended.

A water taxi plies the harbor from Memorial Day weekend until the weather takes a nasty turn in September or October, stopping at Presque Isle's Waterworks ferry dock once an hour. Known as the **Presque Isle Aquabus** (814/881-2502, noon–6 P.M. Mon. and 10 A.M.–6 P.M. Tues.–Sun., all-day fare $7 for adults, $4 for children under 12, one-way fare $4 for adults and children), the taxi leaves Dobbins Landing on Erie's waterfront on the hour, heads west to Liberty Park, and then crosses the bay, arriving at Presque Isle on the half hour. From there it returns to Dobbins Landing. On weekends from early July through Labor Day, it sometimes stops at South Pier, near a popular waterfront campground, before returning to Dobbins Landing.

Presque Isle's interior lagoons, home to herons, beavers, turtles, and a host of other critters, also beg to be explored by boat. Free pontoon tours are offered Thursday–Sunday from Memorial Day weekend through June and daily from July until early September. Call or check the website of the Tom Ridge Environmental Center (814/833-7424, www .trecpi.org) for a departure schedule. Be sure to preregister for sunset rides, which fill quickly.

Water Sports

Just about anything you can do at the ocean, you can do here, including waterskiing, windsurfing, kayaking, fishing, and scuba diving. For boaters, Presque Isle offers four launching areas and a marina with almost 500 slips. All of the boat launches are on the bay side of the peninsula. Vista Launch, closest to the park entrance, is only recommended for small boats and Jet Skis. Niagara and Lagoon Launches can accommodate small- and medium-sized watercraft. The four-lane West Pier Launch, located near the marina, is recommended for larger vessels. Open May through October, the marina (814/833-0176) can accommodate boats as long as 42 feet. Slips are highly coveted, so call ahead to determine availability. During the off-season, call the main park office rather than the marina. Beaching of boats along the shoreline is permitted except at the easternmost portion of Gull Point from April through November and within 100 feet of designated swimming areas.

Presque Isle Canoe & Boat Livery (814/838-3938), located on Graveyard Pond across from Misery Bay, rents watercraft by the hour. Open weekends from mid-April through mid-October and daily from Memorial Day through Labor Day, the livery offers canoes, kayaks, rowboats, paddleboats, small motorboats, and pontoon boats. It also rents fish finders and rods and reels.

Bowfishing is permitted, but you'll need your own gear for that. Famous for its walleye fishing, Lake Erie also yields perch, bass, trout, and steelhead. Presque Isle Bay teems with panfish, muskellunge, northern pike, crappie, and smelt. The peninsula's piers, boat landings, and interior lagoons are popular shore-fishing areas.

Snorkeling is prohibited, but certified scuba divers can swim with the fishes. Divers must register at the ranger station on the bay side of the peninsula, about two miles from the park entrance.

Winter Activities

Presque Isle is quite a magical place in the dead of winter. Lake ice, wave surge, and freezing spray conspire to create otherworldly ice dunes. Look for them on the lake side of the peninsula. Wintertime activities include ice skating, ice fishing, iceboating, cross-country skiing, and snowshoeing. A concession in the Waterworks area offers rental skis and snowshoes on weekends from mid-November through March, provided there's snow.

Bird-Watching

Presque Isle is an ecological wonderland, home to a whopping array of plants and animals. Its birds get the most press. More than 320 species have been spotted on the peninsula, named one of the country's top birding spots by *Birder's World* magazine. Part of the reason for the incredible diversity of birdlife is Presque Isle's location along the Atlantic Flyway, a major bird-migration route. The sandspit is to migrating birds what a turnpike service plaza is to

motorists: a place to eat and rest. Shorebirds that migrate from beyond the Arctic Circle to South America and back again "pull over" at Presque Isle in April and September. Waterfowl migration can be observed in March and from late November through December. Come in mid-May or September to commune with warblers.

Shorebirds can be viewed from an observation platform at the edge of the Gull Point Natural Area. The protected area at the east end of the isle is closed to the public from April through November, but the platform can be reached by hiking the Gull Point Trail. For an eyeful of wetland birds, kayak or canoe the interior lagoons. In the hot summer months, morning and early evening are the best times for birding.

The **Presque Isle Audubon Society** (814/860-4091, www.presqueisleaudubon.org), a chapter of the National Audubon Society, offers field trips and workshops throughout the year. It sponsors the local Christmas Bird Count and the annual Festival of the Birds, three days of organized birding activities during the height of spring migration.

OTHER SIGHTS
Waldameer and Water World

Located just short of the entrance to Presque Isle State Park, Waldameer (3100 W. Lake Rd., Erie, 814/838-3591, www.waldameer.com, open weekends in May, daily except Mon. Labor Day weekend through Memorial Day, free admission) is the 10th oldest amusement park in the country. It celebrated its 100th anniversary in 1996 with an ambitious expansion and continues to add new attractions almost yearly. The Ravine Flyer II, a wooden coaster unveiled in 2008, garnered the Best New Ride award from *Amusement Today,* a trade newspaper. It's one of four coasters at the family-owned amusement park. Two, including a 1951 coaster, are tame enough for little kids. Waldameer has 30-some rides in all, including a 140-foot drop tower and a Ferris wheel that affords fantastic views of Presque Isle and Lake Erie. Water World, a water park added in 1986, features a variety of tube and body slides, a lazy river attraction, a massive hot tub, and kiddie pools.

There's no charge for parking, admission to Waldameer, the thrice-daily song-and-dance performances in its Showtime Theater, or use of its unreserved picnic tables and grills. Use of the rides requires purchase of a wristband or rechargeable Wally Card, which works like a debit card. Wristbands, good for unlimited riding, are $20.95 for adults, $13.45 for children under 48 inches tall. After 6 P.M., prices drop to $16 for adults, $11 for children. Wally Card "points" are $1 apiece and can be used for midway games, gift items, and food as well as rides, which require 1.5, 3, or 4.5 points. Admission to Water World requires a wristband. Water World wristbands are $15.75 for adults, $11.25 for children under 48 inches tall. Combo wristbands good for unlimited use of both parks are $23.45 for adults, $16.95 for children. Two-day combo passes are also available.

Bayfront District

Once crowded with shipyards and crisscrossed by railroad tracks, Erie's Bayfront District is slowly transforming into a recreational destination. It's home to the fantastic Erie Maritime Museum, which opened in 1998. Local and intercity buses deliver passengers to a sprawling transportation center, built a few years later, just east of the museum. West of the museum is a $44 million convention center that opened in 2007 after seven years in the making. It's connected by a water-spanning pedestrian bridge to an eight-story Sheraton, which became the city's first bayfront hotel when it opened in 2008. Recreational marinas, boat launches, and an outdoor amphitheater also dot the evolving waterfront.

First stop for many visitors is the **Bicentennial Tower** (814/455-6055, 9:30 A.M.–10 P.M. daily Memorial Day–Labor Day, 10 A.M.–5 P.M. or 6 P.M. daily for remainder of Sept., noon–4 P.M. Sat.–Sun. Oct.–Mar., 10 A.M.–5 P.M. or 6 P.M. daily in Apr., 10 A.M.–8 P.M. daily May 1–Memorial Day, admission $3, children 7–12 $2, free admission first Sun. of each month), which sits on a pier at the foot of State Street, Erie's main drag. Built for the 1995 celebration of the city's 200th birthday, the tower measures 187

feet to the top of its flagpole. Its two observation decks, both reachable by stairs or elevator, afford views of Presque Isle, the natural harbor it forms, and downtown. Souvenirs and snacks are available in the lobby. For a sit-down meal and a taste of Key West, drop anchor in the nautically inspired **Smugglers Wharf** (3 State St., Erie, 814/459-4273, www.smugglers wharfinc.com, opens at 11:30 A.M. daily Mother's Day–Oct. 15 and Wed.–Sun. rest of year, closes between 7 P.M. and 11 P.M., $9–20). Other eateries within spitting distance of the tower include the Sheraton's Bayfront Grille and the uber-casual Rum Runners. Boats can dock right beside the latter.

The *Victorian Princess,* a pretty paddlewheeler that plies the bay from May through October, docks beside the Bicentennial Tower. **Victorian Princess Cruise Lines** (814/459-9696, www.victorianprincess.com, sightseeing cruise $12, happy hour cruise $14.95, meal cruises $17.95–32.95) offers a lunch cruise on Tuesdays and Thursdays; a happy hour cruise on Wednesdays; a dinner cruise on Tuesdays, Thursdays, and Fridays; and brunch and early

Victorian Princess

dinner cruises on Sundays. Call or check the website for a schedule of shorter sightseeing cruises. The 112-foot-long ship has two enclosed, air-conditioned decks and an open-air deck. It also has a cash bar. (Cruise prices don't include alcoholic beverages.) Reservations and advance payment are required.

Other bayfront attractions include **Harbor View Miniature Golf** (36 State St., Erie, 814/874-3536, www.harborviewminigolf.com, open May–Sept., game $6, seniors $4.50, children 3–12 $4) and **Liberty Park,** a popular spot for picnicking or catching the sunset. The waterfront park is about a quarter-mile west of the Bicentennial Tower and adjacent to Bay Harbor Marina. It features a large children's play area and an outdoor amphitheater that's host to a free summer concert series, **8 Great Tuesdays** (814/455-7557, www.porterie.org). You could walk from the Bicentennial Tower to Liberty Park, but it's more fun to take a taxi—a water taxi, that is. **Presque Isle Aquabus** (814/881-2502, noon–6 P.M. Mon. and 10 A.M.–6 P.M. Tues.–Sun., all-day fare $7 for adults, $4 for children under 12, one-way fare $4 for adults and children) operates from Memorial Day weekend until the weather takes a nasty turn in September or October. It leaves from the pier at the foot of State Street, a.k.a. Dobbins Landing, on the hour and arrives at Liberty Park about a quarter past. Five minutes later it departs for Presque Isle. Typically the water taxi returns to Dobbins Landing after visiting the peninsula, but on weekends from early July through Labor Day, it first stops at South Pier, near Lampe Marina and its popular campground.

A passion for **boating** is what brings many people to the Bayfront District. If you have your own boat, peruse the website of the Erie-Western Pennsylvania Port Authority (814/455-7557, www.porterie.org) for information on marinas and boat launches on Presque Isle Bay and adjacent waters. The port authority operates the popular **Lampe Marina,** located just outside the harbor entrance. Lampe has 252 slips that accommodate boats as long as 30 feet, public launch ramps, and 24-hour security. **Perry's Landing Marina** (W. Bayfront Parkway, 814/455-1313, www.perryslanding marina.com), just west of Liberty Park, is also commendable. It has a clubhouse with a heated swimming pool and two-tiered sundeck.

If you don't have your own boat, you're not out of luck. **Port Erie Sports** (Chestnut Street Boathouse, 402 W. Bayfront Parkway, Erie, 814/452-2628, www.porteriesports.com, 6 A.M.–9 P.M. daily weather permitting) rents runabouts, Jet Skis, offshore fishing and bay fishing boats, kayaks, and canoes. Water-skis, tubes, and fishing equipment and bait are available. The staff is happy to acquaint first-time boat drivers with the various watercraft. Port Erie Sports also carries a selection of rental bicycles, including beach cruisers and kids' bikes.

Anglers unfamiliar with Erie's waters are best off letting someone else do the driving. The *Edward John* (814/881-7611, www.edward johnperchfishing.com), a 52-foot perch-pursuing party boat, departs at 7 A.M. and 4 P.M. daily from its slip near the Bicentennial Tower. Captain John Nekoloff is a 20-year veteran of the U.S. Coast Guard. Each trip is several hours long and costs $32 for adults, $27 for seniors, and $22 for children under 16. It's also possible to reserve the whole boat, which can accommodate as many as 40 passengers. Private trips range from $785 to $985 depending on the day. Prices include bait; rods and reels can be rented on board for $3 a set.

Scuba divers and sailing enthusiasts can also find a friend in the Bayfront District. **Lakeshore Towing** (814/453-6387, www .lakeshoretowing.com) offers diving charters from Wolverine Park Marina, a transient facility at the corner of State Street and the Bayfront Parkway. Lake Erie is strewn with shipwrecks at various depths. Lakeshore Towing charges $65–85 for wreck dives depending on the depth. Night dives and custom training dives are also available. Also operating out of Wolverine Park Marina, **Lake Effect Sailing** (814/434-0600, www.lakeeffectsailing .com, $50 per hour for group of up to 6, 2-hour minimum) offers private charters on a 32-foot cutter named *Namaste*.

◖ Erie Maritime Museum and Flagship *Niagara*

America's attempts to seize Canada from the British during the oft-forgotten War of 1812 didn't go so well. The initial three-pronged offensive was a full-out failure, with Detroit falling to the British in August of 1812. An elaborate attempt to attack Montreal the following year was also unsuccessful. But 1813 wasn't without a bright spot for the United States. On September 10, nine U.S. ships under Commodore Oliver Hazard Perry defeated a British squadron of six vessels on Lake Erie. "We have met the enemy and they are ours," Perry famously wrote in a post-battle dispatch. The victory forced the British to retreat from Detroit and lifted the nation's morale, at least temporarily. (A year later the British would march into Washington, D.C., and torch public buildings, doing serious damage to morale.) The Erie Maritime Museum (150 E. Front St., Erie, 814/452-2744, www.eriemaritime museum.org, 9 A.M.–5 P.M. Mon.–Sat. and noon–5 P.M. Sun. Apr.–Oct., 9 A.M.–5 P.M. Thurs.–Sat. Nov.–Mar., admission $8, seniors $7, children 3–11 $5) brings to life the dramatic events of the Battle of Lake Erie. One exhibit features a replica of the battered hull of the *Lawrence,* Perry's original flagship. The replica was fired upon with cannons to approximate the damage done to the real deal. After the 20-gun brig was disabled and most of its crew wounded or killed, Perry transferred to her undamaged sister ship (the *Niagara*), hoisted his battle flag, and sailed to victory.

The Battle of Lake Erie didn't unfold near Erie's shores. It was fought near Put-in-Bay, Ohio. But Erie is rightfully proud of its role in the American victory. Six of the nine U.S. ships that sailed into battle, including the *Niagara,* were built in Erie. If that sounds unremarkable, consider that Erie had roughly 500 residents at the outbreak of the war. It had oak trees but not a single sawmill. Turning the remote town into a warship-building center required the recruitment of shipwrights, blacksmiths, and laborers from other parts. Pittsburgh sent rigging and anchors. Philadelphia contributed canvas for the sails. Cannons arrived from the nation's capital. The fleet was completed in a matter of months.

The museum on Erie's waterfront is home port to the Flagship *Niagara,* a reconstruction of Perry's relief flagship. When the square-

Erie Maritime Museum

© ANNA DUBROVSKY

© ANNA DUBROVSKY

Flagship *Niagara* at Erie Maritime Museum

generating plant, isn't solely devoted to the Battle of Lake Erie. Visitors can learn about Erie's lighthouses, its once-booming fishing industry, and its rich shipbuilding heritage. An exhibit on square-rigged ships features a working mast with sails. One section of the museum tells the story of the USS *Michigan,* the Navy's first iron-hulled warship. Launched in Erie in 1843, she operated on the Great Lakes for just short of 80 years. Many Erie residents have ancestors who crewed on the iron steamer, which was renamed *Wolverine* in 1905. Her prow, saved from the scrapper's torch, is on display.

Erie Land Lighthouse

Scuba divers love Lake Erie for its abundance of shipwrecks. The number of sunken ships would undoubtedly be much higher were it not for Presque Isle Bay's historic lighthouses. One, the Erie Land Lighthouse, sits high on a bluff at the foot of Lighthouse Street, overlooking the harbor entrance. Built in 1867, it's the third lighthouse at this site. The first, erected in 1818 about 200 feet west of the present tower, was one of the first lighthouses on the Great Lakes. It was demolished after it began to sink. A second lighthouse was built in 1857 but also proved unstable, lasting just 10 years. The 49-foot conical tower that stands today is no longer operational and closed to the public but is still a magnet for lighthouse fans.

Erie County Historical Society Museums

The Erie County Historical Society (419 State St., Erie, 814/454-1813, www.eriecounty history.org) operates several museums in and around the city. Most impressive is the **Watson-Curtze Mansion** (356 W. 6th St., Erie, 814/871-5790, 11 A.M.–4 P.M. Wed.– Sat., 1–4 P.M. Sun., admission $4, seniors $3, children 5–12 $2, family $10), a house museum that provides a glimpse into life during Erie's industrial heyday—life as the upper crust knew it. The 24-room mansion, built in the Richardsonian Romanesque tradition in 1891, is named for Harrison F. Watson, its first owner, who manufactured heavy-duty

rigged wooden vessel is in port, museum visitors are treated to guided tours. She sails during the warmer months, visiting other Great Lakes ports. If you're 16 or older, in good health, and crave a taste of the seafarer's life, you can apply to be a live-aboard trainee for a minimum of two weeks. An appetite for spartan conditions is required. Though the present *Niagara,* completed in 1990, has auxiliary propulsion engines and modern navigation equipment, she emulates the original in just about every other way. That means no showers, no hot water, and no privacy. Trainees live out of duffel bags, sleep in hammocks, and bathe out of buckets. (Soaping up and going for a swim also does the trick.) To preserve the back-in-time vibe, use of cell phones and laptops is not permitted. Sailing excursions of just a few hours are offered when the ship isn't en route to another port. A day sail from the Erie Maritime Museum is $60 for Pennsylvania residents, $70 for out-of-state visitors. Visit the museum website for a training program application or schedule of day sails.

The museum, housed in a former electricity

paper used in construction, and Frederick Felix Curtze, its second owner, who presided over an iron works. It's one of the few manses on the section of West 6th Street known as "Millionaire's Row" that have retained their original integrity. Open for self-guided tours, the three-story museum is filled with decorative woodwork, hand-painted friezes, stained glass windows, elaborate fireplaces—12 in all—and 19th-century furnishings.

In 1959 the mansion's carriage house was transformed into the **Erie Planetarium** (814/871-5790, admission $4, seniors $3, children 5–12 $2, family $10). Primarily used by Boy Scout troops and other organized groups, the small planetarium offers public shows on Saturday afternoons throughout the year and Thursday afternoons in the summer. Call the planetarium or check the Erie County Historical Society website for a schedule.

The historical society's headquarters on State Street, just half a mile from the Watson-Curtze Mansion and planetarium, houses the **Museum of Erie County History** (11 A.M.–4 P.M. Tues.–Sat., admission $4, seniors $3, children 5–12 $2, family $10). Its main exhibit gallery presents a timeline of events from pre-settlement to recent times. Next door at 417 State Street is the 1839 **Cashier's House** (11 A.M.–4 P.M. Tues.–Sat., included in admission to Museum of Erie County History), so called because it was built for the chief executive officer of Erie's branch of the Bank of the United States. The interior of the three-story townhouse is CEO-worthy with its marble flooring, coffered ceilings, keyhole-shaped doorways, and egg-and-dart molding.

The historical society operates two more house museums in the town of Girard, about 16 miles southwest of downtown Erie. The **Battles Museums of Rural Life** (436 Walnut St., Girard, 814/454-1813, ext. 32, tours by appointment, admission $4, seniors $3, children 5–12 $2, family $10), located on 130 acres of farmlands and woods, are Civil War–era houses. Exhibits interpret two centuries of agricultural life in Erie County.

Special admission rates are available for history buffs who care to see two or more museums in one day.

Erie Art Museum

It's easy to mistake the Erie Art Museum (411 State St., Erie, 814/459-5477, www.erieartmuseum.org, 11 A.M.–5 P.M. Tues.–Sat., 1–5 P.M. Sun., admission $4, seniors and students $3, children under 12 $2, free admission every Wed.) for a bank or government building. The stately Greek Revival–style structure, completed in 1839, has served as both during its lifetime. As northwest Pennsylvania's only art museum, it provides a showcase for local artists and an opportunity for local residents to experience art from around the world. The museum's 6,000-object permanent collection includes religious paintings from Tibet, photographs from 19th-century Japan, and European prints. Its pride and joy is a collection of about 100 bronze and stone sculptures from ancient India. Admission is free on Wednesdays. Also free: the two-day **Erie Art Museum Blues & Jazz Festival** (Frontier Park, first full weekend of Aug.), featuring local, regional, and national acts.

Erie Zoo

Erie Zoo (423 W. 38th St., Erie, 814/864-4091, www.eriezoo.org, 10 A.M.–5 P.M. daily Mar.–Nov., Mar. admission $7, seniors $6, children 2–12 $4, Apr.–Nov. admission $8, seniors $6, children 2–12 $5) is home to some 500 animals representing 100 species, including the warthog, the red panda, the white-cheeked gibbon, the black-footed penguin, and the gray kangaroo. It's as much botanical garden as it is menagerie, boasting more than 600 species of plants. **ZooBoo,** a nightly event during the second half of October, is a rare opportunity to explore the grounds after dark. Compact enough to see in two or three hours, the zoo is next door to Glenwood Park, one of Erie's largest municipal parks. Allow extra time for a picnic in the park or a little orangutan action on its playground.

Presque Isle Downs & Casino

Presque Isle Downs & Casino (8199 Perry Hwy.,

Erie, 814/860-8999, www.presqueisledowns
.com, casino open 24 hours) isn't on Presque
Isle or even nestled on Lake Erie. But that didn't
stop the "racino," which opened in 2007, from
adopting the name of Erie's main attraction.
Located at exit 27 of I-90, the casino and thoroughbred racing track are major attractions in
their own right. The atmosphere is particularly
electric when the thunder of hooves competes
with the ding-ding-ding of slot machines. Live
racing begins in early May and continues until
late September. Post time is 5:30 P.M. Horse-
racing fans descend on Presque Isle Downs even
when there's no action on its mile-long oval
track to watch broadcasts of races in other parts
of North America. **The Downs Clubhouse &
Lounge** (814/866-8775, 11 A.M.–11 P.M. Wed.–
Thurs., 11 A.M.–2 P.M. Fri.–Sat., 11 A.M.–11 P.M.
Sun., $9–17), a three-tiered casual dining res-
taurant, is a popular gathering spot for both live
racing and simulcast racing because it overlooks
the track and has a plethora of plasma TVs. It
serves up live entertainment on Friday and
Saturday nights. The racino's eateries also include the upscale, adults-only **La Bonne Vie
Steakhouse** (814/866-8359, opens at 5 P.M.
Wed.–Sat., $27–49) and a buffet restaurant
open for breakfast, lunch, and dinner daily. If
you love crab legs, hit the buffet on a Friday or
Saturday evening.

◖ Wine Country

The massive ice sheet that covered part of the
northern United States tens of thousands of
years ago left lovely gifts on its way out, among
them the Great Lakes. On the southern shores
of Lake Erie, it left ridges of soil and gravel
that proved splendid for grape growing. How
splendid? The Lake Erie grape belt is North
America's largest grape-growing region outside of California. And it's the largest Concord
grape–growing region in the world.

Concord grapes aren't the only variety cultivated in this prolific region. Recent decades
have seen a profusion of small wineries, and
a good deal of land has been replanted with
premium wine grapes. Today some 20 wineries make up the 40-mile **Chautauqua-Lake**

Erie Wine Trail (www.chautauquawinetrail
.org), so named because the bulk of it is in
Chautauqua County, New York. The town of
North East, so named because of its location
in Erie County, is the wine trail's *southwest* terminus. Go figure. Located 15 miles northeast
of downtown Erie near the New York border,
North East is home to more than half a dozen
wineries. The town milks its viticulture heritage, which dates to the mid-1800s, for all it's
worth. Grapes festoon the website of its chamber of commerce, its high school athletes are
known as the Grapepickers (their fans are filled
with "Picker Pride"), and its charming lodgings
include the Grape Arbor B&B and Vineyard
B&B. The social highlight of the year is the
three-day **Wine Country Harvest Festival**
(Gravel Pit Park and Gibson Park, 814/725-
4262, www.nechamber.org, last full weekend
of Sept., admission charged at Gravel Pit).
WineFest traditions include a cruise-in, an arts
and crafts show, a champagne breakfast featuring local bubbly, and, of course, grape stomping. Wine samples are a buck an ounce.

You certainly don't have to wait until
WineFest to see what North East's wineries
are up to. **Mazza Vineyards** (11815 E. Lake
Rd./Rte. 5, North East, 814/725-8695, www
.mazzawines.com, 9 A.M.–8 P.M. Mon.–Sat.
and 11 A.M.–4:30 P.M. Sun. July–Aug., 9 A.M.–
5:30 P.M. Mon.–Sat. and noon–4:30 P.M. Sun.
Sept.–June), a popular stop on the wine trail,
offers tastings and tours year-round. Established
in 1972 by Italian-born brothers, the winery
has a distinctly Mediterranean look. But don't
expect to sample Chianti and Montepulciano
d'Abruzzo inside. The Mazza brothers thought
the land better suited for Germanic varieties and
became known for Riesling in the early years.
Mazza Vineyards still offers Riesling, but today
it's better known for sweet, fruity wines made
from Niagara, Concord, and Catawba grapes—
varieties born in the USA. It's also known as a
pioneer of Pennsylvania ice wines. Producing an
ice wine can be tricky business. At Mazza, Vidal
Blanc grapes are left on the vine for two or three
months after they ripen, getting ever sweeter
but losing their looks. When the temperature

© ANNA DUBROVSKY

Mazza Vineyards

dips below 15 degrees and the shriveled buggers freeze, they're picked by hand (sometimes in two or three feet of snow) and pressed immediately. The result is a honey-like dessert wine that sells for upwards of $40 a bottle. Mazza also produces a couple of faux ice wines, made by harvesting grapes and then freezing them artificially. They sell for about $25 apiece. Just about everything else on the menu is under $15, including oak-aged dry reds such as Cabernet Sauvignon and Chambourcin.

Mazza Vineyards has a sister winery about half an hour away in New York, Mazza Chautauqua Cellars, and another just five minutes away, **South Shore Wine Company** (1120 Freeport Rd./Rte. 89, North East, 814/725-1585, www.ss.mazzawines.com, 10 A.M.–5:30 P.M. Mon.–Sat. and noon–4:30 P.M. Sun. May–Oct. with extended hours Mon.–Sat. in July and Aug., noon–5:30 P.M. Mon.–Fri., 10 A.M.–5:30 P.M. Sat., and noon–4:30 P.M. Sun. Nov.–April). The latter is rich in history. Its tasting room occupies a stone cellar built in the 1860s as part of Erie County's first winery. Prohibition closed the original South Shore

Wine Company in the 1920s. The Mazza family restored the historic wine cellar and revived the name in 2007. The wine selection is different from Mazza Vineyards' and more limited. If you're visiting in the warmer months, buy a bottle and enjoy it with a cheese plate, sandwich, or salad in the patio café.

You can't order food on the open-air patio at **Penn Shore Winery** (10225 E. Lake Rd./Rte. 5, North East, 814/725-8688, www.pennshore.com, 9 A.M.–5:30 P.M. Mon.–Thurs., 9 A.M.–8 P.M. Fri.–Sat., and 11 A.M.–4:30 P.M. Sun. July–Aug., 9 A.M.–5:30 P.M. Mon.–Sat. and 11 A.M.–4:30 P.M. Sun. Sept.–June), but you can feast on the view of row upon row of grapevines. Penn Shore snagged one of the first two "limited winery" licenses issued after passage of the Pennsylvania Limited Winery Act of 1968, which allowed grape farms to break into the wine biz, and opened its doors in 1970. Tours of the wine cellars are offered daily from June through August; large parties can take a look-see any time of year.

Arrowhead Wine Cellars (12073 E. Main Rd./Rte. 20, North East, 814/725-5509, www

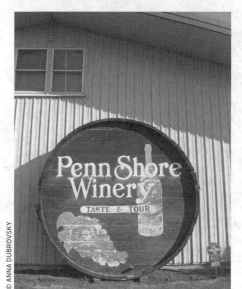

© ANNA DUBROVSKY

Take a tour of the Penn Shore Winery wine cellar.

.arrowheadwine.com, 10 A.M.–6 P.M. Mon.–Sat. and noon–5 P.M. in summer and fall, winter and spring hours vary) is a relative newcomer. Nick and Kathy Mobilia opened the winery on their 250-acre fruit farm in 1998. But their wines are perennial medalists at the Pennsylvania Farm Show and other competitions. Their peaches, sweet and sour cherries, frozen pitted sour cherries, and freshly pressed grape juice for home winemaking are also held in high esteem and sold seasonally at the farm stand adjacent to the winery. Amateur winemakers will also want to visit **Presque Isle Wine Cellars** (9440 W. Main Rd./Rte. 20, North East, 814/725-1314, www.piwine.com, 8 A.M.–6 P.M. Mon.–Sat. and 8 A.M.–2:30 P.M. Sun. during grape harvest season late Sept.–mid-Oct., 9 A.M.–5 P.M. Mon.–Sat. rest of year), which sells all manner of equipment and raw materials.

ENTERTAINMENT AND EVENTS
Concert Venues
Tullio Arena (809 French St., Erie, 814/452-4857, www.erieevents.com) in downtown Erie

is a concert venue as well as home to the city's professional basketball, ice hockey, and indoor football teams. The likes of Elton John, Rod Stewart, Cher, Kiss, Barry Manilow, and Alan Jackson have rocked the arena, named for Erie's first Italian-American mayor. Disney on Ice, World Wrestling Entertainment, and Ringling Bros. and Barnum & Bailey have also entertained audiences there.

Boats drop anchor within listening distance when bands perform at the **Liberty Park amphitheater** (W. Bayfront Parkway, 814/455-7557, www.porterie.org) on Erie's waterfront. Bring a blanket or chair to listen from dry land; the open-air venue adjacent to Bay Harbor Marina doesn't have seating. It's host to a free summer concert series, **8 Great Tuesdays** (814/455-7557, www.porterie.org), that has welcomed Arlo Guthrie and Big Bad Voodoo Daddy in recent years.

Performing Arts
Erie's lavish **Warner Theater** (811 State St., Erie, 814/452-4857, www.erieevents.com) was built, surprisingly enough, during the Great Depression. Within months of opening its doors in 1931, the movie palace initiated a vaudeville season, and Bob Hope made an appearance soon thereafter. Today the theater hosts the **Erie Broadway series** (814/452-4857, www.eriebroadwayseries.com) and concerts by touring musicians. It's also home to the **Erie Philharmonic** (814/455-1375, www.eriephil.org), which predates the Warner, and the younger **Lake Erie Ballet** (814/871-4356, www.lakeerieballet.org).

Founded in 1916, the **Erie Playhouse** (13 W. 10th St., Erie, 814/454-2852, www.erieplayhouse.org) is one of the oldest community theaters in the country. Homeless at times in its history, the theater is now ensconced in a 1940s movie house that seats about 440. More than 20 plays, musicals, youth theater shows, and special events are offered yearly. **The Station Dinner Theatre** (4940 Peach St., Erie, 814/864-2022, www.canterburyfeast.com) is best known for "A Canterbury Feast," a long-running musical comedy set in medieval times.

LAKE REGION

Performers do double duty, serving the victuals while staying in character. The dinner theater also cooks up farces and musical tributes.

Festivals and Events

Dozens of juried artists and crafters showcase their work during the **Erie Summer Festival of the Arts** (Liberty Park, 814/838-0971, www.eriesummerfestivalofthearts.org, last full weekend of June, free). The three-day event on the city's waterfront features loads of live entertainment. A few weeks later, thousands of motorcyclists roll into town for **Roar on the Shore** (814/833-3200, www.roarontheshore .com, mid-July, free). The bike rally kicks off with the Bringin' in the Roar Bike Parade, led by a celebrity grand marshal. Rock frontman and reality TV star Bret Michaels and professional daredevil Robbie Knievel have done the honors. Bikers ride en masse through Presque Isle State Park and to places including Erie County's grape-growing region during the three-day event, a fund-raiser for area charities. Rock and roll plays a big role in the festivities.

Another major event in July is **Discover Presque Isle** (Presque Isle State Park, 814/838-5138, www.discoverpi.com, last weekend of July, free), a celebration of the superb state park and a fundraiser for the nonprofit organization devoted to making it even better. It has all the fixings of an arts festival—art and craft vendors, musical entertainment, and plenty of food—plus an emphasis on sporty fun. Festival-goers can try their hand at rock climbing, archery, and kayaking, compete in beach volleyball and sand sculpting, and explore the peninsula alongside professional naturalists. A challenging duathlon kicks off the final day.

Downtown Erie gets its turn in the spotlight during **Celebrate Erie** (State St., 814/870-1200, www.celebrateerie.com, mid- or late Aug., free). The four-day extravaganza highlights the city's culinary and cultural offerings. Fireworks over the bayfront serve as grand finale. Head to the **Erie Heritage Festival** (Liberty Park, 814/454-1813, www

.erieheritagefest.com, Sat. after Labor Day, free) for the granddaddy of grand finales. The Erie Philharmonic and the Flagship *Niagara* team up to perform Tchaikovsky's 1812 Overture, with the latter providing cannon fire. Church bells and fireworks amp up the show. Tchaikovsky had the Napoleonic Wars in mind, but the triumphant orchestral work is a fitting end to the one-day celebration of Erie's maritime heritage, which has its roots in the War of 1812. The festival also features a living history exhibition and an ethnic marketplace.

Stars of such films as the original *Texas Chain Saw Massacre* and *Dawn of the Dead* turn out for the cleverly named **Eerie Horror Fest** (Warner Theatre, Erie, 814/873-2483, www.eeriehorrorfilmfestival.com, Oct., admission charged, free for children 12 and under). Started in 2004, the four-day event is part indie film festival and part fan convention. Horror, science fiction, and suspense films culled from hundreds of submissions are shown on the big screen. Fans can have a bloody good time among celebs, film company reps, and merchandise vendors at the Carnival of Carnage Expo. Bring cash if you're keen on getting autographs.

SPORTS AND RECREATION
Splash Lagoon

Long after Erie's harbor freezes over and ice dunes form on the lakeshore, the city remains a destination for splish-splashing fun. Lake-effect snowstorms have no affect on Splash Lagoon (8091 Peach St., Erie, 814/217-1111, www.splashlagoon.com, call or check website for hours). It's always a balmy 84 degrees at the indoor water park, located south of downtown at exit 24 of I-90. Splash Lagoon's attractions range from toddler-friendly play areas to slides dope enough for teenage adrenaline junkies. The "Hurricane Hole," dopest of them all, involves shooting through a tube at 40 miles per hour and circling a funnel before plunging into 6 feet of water. Milder attractions include "Adventure Bay," a four-foot-deep pool complete with foam alligators and oversized lily pads, and a lazy river lined with larger-than-life fish statues decorated by local artists. Splash Lagoon also has several whirlpools, including one exclusively for adults. In 2010 construction began on a 250,000-gallon wave pool.

Admission to Splash Lagoon is only guaranteed with purchase of a package that includes an overnight stay at an affiliated hotel. Walkways connect the water park to three hotels: Comfort Inn (8051 Peach St.), Residence Inn by Marriott (8061 Peach St.), and Holiday Inn Express (8101 Peach St.). Several nearby hotels are also affiliates. Packages can be reserved through Splash Lagoon's website or by calling 866/377-5274. A limited number of day passes are available to nonguests when the water park isn't at capacity. Day pass rates are $34.95 for guests over 48 inches tall and $24.95 for the shorter set. After 4 P.M., rates drop to $26.95 and $19.95. A $9.95 spectator pass is available for visitors who don't plan to get wet. Splash Lagoon's dry attractions include an arcade with more than 110 games and a crafts room. Adults can pass the time sipping piña coladas out of carved coconuts in the full-service bar adjacent to the arcade. Access to **Lazer Tag at Splash Lagoon** (814/864-9463), a large laser tag arena next door to the water park, does not require an overnight package or day pass. A half-hour session is $10 per person. Reservations are recommended.

Family First Sports Park

A stone's throw from Splash Lagoon is a sprawling sports and recreation complex. Family First (8155 Oliver Rd., Erie, 814/866-5425, www.familyfirstsportspark.com, call or check website for hours) runs leagues and clinics in sports including basketball, volleyball, soccer, and football. In winter it's a haven for golfers, who can fine-tune their game at the 38-station indoor driving range, take a lesson from a PGA-certified pro, or play a round of virtual golf. Family First's golf dome also features a miniature golf course. With spring comes a broader range of diversions. Outdoor amenities include a 34-foot rock wall, a go-kart track, bumper boats armed with cannons, batting cages, and not one but two mini golf courses. An all-day

pass good for unlimited access to go-karts, bumper boats, the climbing wall, and more is $20 from Memorial Day weekend through Labor Day. Earlier in spring and later in fall, the pass costs $16.

Spectator Sports

Erie is home to several professional sports teams. Oldest of the bunch is its minor league baseball team, founded in 1995. The **Erie SeaWolves** (Jerry Uht Park, 110 E. 10th St., Erie, 814/456-1300, www.seawolves.com), which play in the Eastern League, are the AA affiliate of Major League Baseball's Detroit Tigers. Their 6,000-seat ballpark, affectionately referred to as the Uht, features a two-level picnic area down the right field line and a short porch in left field. ("Short porch" is baseball jargon for an outfield wall that's uncommonly close to home plate. It makes for plenty of homers.) It's not unusual for home run balls to careen off the wall of the adjacent Tullio Arena, home to Erie's basketball, ice hockey, and indoor football teams.

Minor league basketball came to Erie in 2008 with the expansion of the NBA Development League. The **Erie BayHawks** (814/790-5600, www.eriebayhawks.com) are affiliated with the National Basketball Association's Cleveland Cavaliers and Toronto Raptors. The **Erie Otters** (814/452-4857, www.ottershockey.com) are one of only three U.S.-based teams in the Ontario Hockey League. More than 20 Otters have been selected at the National Hockey League Entry Draft since the franchise relocated to Erie from Ontario in 1996. Erie's American Indoor Football Association franchise got a new name in 2010: the **Erie Storm** (814/452-4857, www.stormerie.com). Previously known as the RiverRats, the team traded its rodent logo for one featuring the city's Bicentennial Tower. An events calendar that includes SeaWolves, BayHawks, Otters, and Storm games is available on the website of the Erie County Convention Center Authority (www.erieevents.com), which operates the ballpark and Tullio Arena (809 French St.).

Auto-racing fans can get their fix at **Lake**

Erie Speedway (10700 Delmas Dr., North East, 814/725-3303, www.lakeeriespeedway .com), a NASCAR-sanctioned short track about 15 miles east of downtown Erie. Half a dozen types of cars take to the 3/8-mile asphalt oval on Saturday evenings from May through early September. A fireworks show caps the night. The 8,000-seat speedway also hosts special events such as monster truck competitions and Crash-A-Rama, a chance for regular folks with old beaters (and good helmets) to have a smashing good time.

ACCOMMODATIONS
Waterfront

Not surprisingly, many people who come to Erie when it's best to come to Erie—in summer—want to be near the water. Surprisingly, waterfront accommodations are scarce in this waterfront city. There's no lodging on Presque Isle and just one hotel on Erie's bayfront. A seashore-style vacation requires advance planning—or a good deal of luck. At **Sara's Campground** (50 Peninsula Dr., Erie, 814/833-4560, www.sarascampground.com, $23–32 per night, $138–192 per week), a stone's throw from the entrance to Presque Isle State Park, you can pitch a tent on a private beach. But Sara's doesn't accept reservations. Its 100-some campsites are doled out on a first-come, first-served basis, ostensibly because they're worth the gamble.

Lampe Marina Campground (foot of Port Access Rd., Erie, 814/454-5830 May–Oct., 814/455-7557 Nov.–Apr., www.porterie.org, $25 Sun.–Thurs., $30 weekends and holidays), open May through October, accepts reservations up to six months in advance. Operated by the Erie-Western Pennsylvania Port Authority, the campground near the entrance to Erie's natural harbor has 42 campsites with water and electric hookups, a dump station, and fantastic views. All sites have picnic tables; some also have fire rings. On one side of the campground is the popular Lampe Marina with its free public boat launch. (Boat slips are an additional $20 per day when available.) On the other is a pier popular with anglers and anyone who likes

to watch boats go by. Erie's water taxi makes stops at the pier on weekends during peak tourist season, whisking campers to the Bayfront District and Presque Isle State Park.

The water taxi also docks near the ◖ **Sheraton Erie Bayfront Hotel** (55 W. Bay Dr., Erie, 814/454-2005, www.sheraton .com/erie, $109–209), which opened in 2008 near the Bicentennial Tower. It's connected to the Bayfront Convention Center by a water-spanning walking bridge and has all the amenities you'd expect from a hotel that caters to conference-goers, including a fitness facility and business center open round-the-clock. All 200 guest rooms are nonsmoking. Many feature bay or marina views to match the nautical color scheme. Bring a swimsuit for the indoor pool and sunscreen for the adjacent deck. And bring your pooch if you like; the hotel provides dog beds. There's one restaurant on-site, the classy but casual Bayfront Grille, and several more within spitting distance.

About 15 minutes east of downtown Erie is an altogether different waterfront option: the family-owned **LakeView on the Lake** (8696 E. Lake Rd./Rte. 5, Erie, 814/899-6948, www.lakeview erie.com, $99–225). This is the sort of place to bring that stack of books you've been meaning to work your way through. Adirondack chairs dot the mini-resort, which sits atop a 120-foot bluff overlooking Lake Erie. Guests can reach the water via a wooden staircase. Many return year after year for the spectacular sunsets and laid-back vibe. LakeView has several types of accommodations: a six-room motel, six simple cottages of various size, and "Annie's Retreat," a one-bedroom home away from home with a living room, dining room, full kitchen, two bathrooms, and private deck. Amenities include a heated outdoor pool and lawn enough for bocce, badminton, and horseshoes.

Inland Erie

That's it for waterfront accommodations, but there are plenty of places to bed down within a few minutes of Presque Isle State Park and its sandy beaches. They're a shabby bunch, with a few exceptions. The **Glass House Inn** (3202

© ANNA DUBROVSKY

LAKE REGION

The Boothby Inn was built in 1888.

W. 26th St., Erie, 814/833-7751, www.glass houseinn.com, summer rates $86–140, off-season rates $59–85) is a very pleasant motel owned by a very pleasant couple. Its 30 rooms are equipped with refrigerators, microwaves, coffeemakers, and wireless Internet. The small outdoor pool is open for hours after Presque Isle's beaches close for the day. Another good option is the 131-room **Bel-Aire Clarion Hotel and Conference Center** (2800 W. 8th St., Erie, 814/833-1116, www.belaireclarion.com, $70–170), offering complimentary airport transportation, an exercise room, an indoor pool and hot tub, and a restaurant and bar. Breakfast is a bargain at $4 per person. The hotel woos families with in-room Nintendo game systems and business travelers with free weekday newspapers and meeting facilities.

If romance is on the agenda, consider a bed-and-breakfast in downtown Erie or wine country to its east. The impeccably decorated ☾ **Boothby Inn** (311 W. 6th St., Erie, 814/456-1888, www.theboothbyinn.com, $130–175, $20 discount Sun.–Thurs. except

June–Aug.) is Erie's only Select Registry property. It's an 1888 manse on "Millionaire's Row," a section of West 6th Street once home to manufacturing and shipping magnates and now home to a good deal of college students. Owners Wally and Gloria Knox spent the better part of a year restoring and updating the house, adding five bathrooms, before opening it as a B&B in 2001. They're walking encyclopedias on local history, not to mention gracious hosts. A guest galley on the second floor is always stocked with complimentary wine, beer, soda, and snacks. Its coffee machine clicks into action an hour before a full breakfast is served in the formal dining room or delightful garden patio. Each of four guest rooms—Africa, Japan, France, and Scotland—reflects the Knox's own travels. The 1872 **George Carroll House** (401 Peach St., Erie, 814/459-2021, www.georgecarrollhouse.com, $75–90), another renovated mansion in downtown Erie, offers seven guest rooms, a plainer aesthetic, and a lower price point. Breakfast is a continental affair.

North East

Wine lovers should make a base camp in North East, a town known for vineyards and Victorian architecture. The **Grape Arbor Bed & Breakfast** (51 E. Main St., North East, 814/725-0048, www.grapearborbandb.com, $95–175) consists of two side-by-side mansions in the center of town. Built as private homes in the 1830s, they housed a stagecoach tavern, professional offices, and a primary school before their rebirth as a B&B. Grape Arbor's eight guest rooms and suites are traditionally furnished, outfitted with wireless Internet, and named for varieties of grapes grown in the region. The Cabernet Suite boasts a private entrance through a side porch, a built-in gas fireplace, and a two-person Jacuzzi. Also grape-themed, **Vineyard Bed & Breakfast** (10757 Sidehill Rd., North East, 888/725-8998, www.vineyardbb.com, $70–95) offers cheaper, country-style accommodations. Innkeepers Clyde and Judy Burnham have lived in the turn-of-the-20th-century farmhouse since 1953. Breakfast includes their homemade grape juice.

AND FOR DESSERT . . .

Listen up, chocolate lovers: Pass on dessert when dining in Erie. Pay the bill, get in the car, and drive straight to **Romolo Chocolates** (1525 W. 8th St., Erie, 814/452-1933, www.romolochocolates.com, 8 A.M.–8 P.M. Mon.–Fri., 9 A.M.–8 P.M. Sat., 10 A.M.–5 P.M. Sun., open until 10 P.M. daily June–Aug.), showplace of master chocolatier Tony Stefanelli. At one end of the building, modeled on an Italian villa, is an airy café. Sink into a couch with a cup of the signature cocoa, made with dark chocolate, cream, and milk. If it's warm outside, order the iced version and have a seat on the patio. The strawberry cocoa – imagine chocolate-covered strawberries in liquid form – is especially delightful. Romolo's Cocoa Café also serves coffees and teas, espresso drinks, and ice cream and baked goods made on site. At the other end of the building is a theater-style chocolate shop, where you can observe the last stages of the candy-making process as you browse shelves lined with truffles, caramels, nougats, and other confections. Between them is Mercato, a gift shop geared toward sweet tooths.

© ANNA DUBROVSKY

FOOD
Bayfront District

Erie's Bayfront District is not yet a bona fide dining and entertainment hub, but it's edging toward that goal. There's now a small cluster of restaurants at the foot of State Street, near the Bicentennial Tower. They have just the recipe for a hot summer day: outdoor tables and cold drinks. The most casual of the bunch is ◖ **Rum Runners** (133 E. Dobbins Landing, Erie, 814/455-4292, 11 A.M.–2 A.M. daily Apr.–Oct., kitchen closes between 10 P.M. and

midnight, $3–13), named for the bootleggers who braved the unpredictable waters of Lake Erie to bring Canadian booze into Prohibition-era America. Boats can dock right beside its large waterfront patio, which hosts live bands on Fridays and Saturdays throughout the summer. Rum Runners isn't much to look at (think Dairy Queen), and its fare is nothing fancy (think seafood baskets and burgers), but the bay view, jolly vibe, and potent signature drink—a frozen blend of rum, liqueurs, and fruit punch—make the seasonal eatery a favorite among locals and

---

The sweets emporium is named for Stefanelli's Italian-born grandfather, who immigrated to New York City around the turn of the 20th century and learned the candy-making trade there. The Great Depression brought sugar rationing and drove many candy makers out of the city. Romolo Stefanelli settled in his wife's hometown of Erie, where he began making candy in the basement of his father-in-law's house. By the mid-1950s the operation had outgrown the basement and the backyard. He opened a store on West 8th Street and shortly after passed the reins to his two sons. The business thrived. Today there are four **Stefanelli's Candies** (www.stefanelliscandies.com) stores in Erie, including the original (2054 W. 8th St., Erie, 814/866-8200, 10 A.M.–6 P.M. Mon.-Sat., 11 A.M.–4 P.M. Sun.), but there hasn't been a Stefanelli at the helm since the early 1990s. Tony Stefanelli, who studied the art of candy making under his grandfather, father, and uncle, opened Romolo Chocolates in 1994, shortly after Stefanelli's was sold out of the family. His two 30-something sons are Romolo chocolatiers, his wife runs the café, and his brother helps in the back.

Erie has not two, but three homegrown chocolatiers. Established in 1903, **Pulakos 926 Chocolates** (www.pulakoschocolates.com) has three locations. Its flagship store (2530 Parade St., Erie, 814/452-4026, 9:30 A.M.–5 P.M. Mon.-Sat.) is at Parade and East 26th Streets in downtown, but in summer many locals

favor the West 26th and Elmwood Avenue location (1301 W. 26th St., Erie, 814/456-3815, 9:30 A.M.–7 P.M. Mon.-Sat., noon–5 P.M. Sun.), which serves freshly made ice cream, milkshakes, and old-fashioned sodas.

Ask a group of locals if they prefer Romolo, Stefanelli's, or Pulakos, and you'll likely get a heated debate. Pulakos has long been known for its chocolate-covered strawberries (far-flung fans pay upwards of $80 to have them overnighted) and Stefanelli's for its "sponge candy," a melt-in-your-mouth confection with an airy, crispy center and a coat of chocolate. But Romolo does a brisk business in both, and the youngest brand on the block may well be the most traditional. "We do things like my grandfather wanted us to," says Tony Stefanelli, whose grandfather introduced sponge candy to Erie. "We use older style machines. We don't use any kind of enzyme or thinner when we're working with our chocolate. We don't use preservatives." That doesn't mean there's no room for new ideas. "When my father was alive, he would let my kids coat anything they wanted to coat with chocolate," he recalls. "My daughter was a grape freak, so we coated some red seedless grapes when I opened Romolo, she was in her early 20s, but that was the first thing she asked for." He made a batch and put some on a tray for customers. The rest, as they say, is history. Today the shop sells upwards of 10 pounds of chocolate-covered grapes a day.

tourists. In 2008 its owner opened an all-seasons restaurant a stone's throw away. The Caribbean-inspired **Rum Runners Cove** (2 State St., Erie, 814/454-7160, www.rumrunnerscove.com, 11 A.M.–2 A.M. Mon.–Sat. and 11 A.M.–10 P.M. Sun. in summer, kitchen closes at 10 P.M. Mon.–Thurs., 11 P.M. Fri.–Sat., and 9 P.M. Sun., hours vary in off-season, $7–19) features a seafood-heavy menu and a thatch-roofed outdoor bar. Food options are limited to starters, soups, salads, and sandwiches until 4 P.M., when they expand to include entrées such as coconut-crusted Hawaiian sunfish, filet mignon stuffed with crabmeat, and the ever-popular seafood fettuccine. The Cove carries the tropical theme to its logical conclusion: key lime pie.

Right across from it is another port of call for seafood lovers, **Smugglers Wharf** (3 State St., Erie, 814/459-4273, www.smugglerswharfinc.com, opens at 11:30 A.M. daily Mother's Day–Oct. 15 and Wed.–Sun. rest of year, closes between 7 P.M. and 11 P.M., $9–20). It's been around since the 1970s—long enough for grapevines to claim nearly every inch of its covered porch. The effect is casually romantic and not quite in sync with the "Welcome, matey!" atmosphere of the nautically accented interior. Try the lobster roll, the Great Lakes walleye, or the coconut shrimp. Those who prefer turf to surf swear by the slow-roasted prime rib. Spiked coffee drinks are a specialty of the bar and especially satisfying when there's a chill in the air.

The **Bayfront Grille** (55 W. Bay Dr., Erie, 814/454-2005, www.sheraton.com/erie, 6:30 A.M.–10 P.M. Mon.–Sat., 6:30 A.M.–9 P.M. Sun., $8–27) is the most upscale option in the area but hardly hoity-toity. Part of the Sheraton Erie Bayfront Hotel, it offers something none of the others do: breakfast. It's also notable for its spicy clam chowder, griddle cakes of crabmeat and roasted corn, seafood ravioli, and salad of baby arugula, plantains, and goat cheese. Choosing a side is no easy task with options like seasoned fries and risotto with sun-dried tomatoes and crab.

Downtown

State Street, Erie's main drag, boasts a good

© NATALIE KAZMIERCZAK, MOLLY BRANNIGANS

Be sure to try the fish and chips at Molly Brannigans.

number of restaurants and bars. But judging an establishment by the size of the crowd inside could lead you astray. That's because the city has a couple of colleges, and students generally gravitate toward cheap grub and suds. Colm McWilliams came to Erie from Ireland to attend one of those colleges and stayed to open **Molly Brannigans** (506 State St., Erie, 814/453-7800, www.mollybrannigans.com, 11 A.M.–midnight Sun.–Thurs., 11 A.M.–2 A.M. Fri.–Sat., $8–15), one of the State Street standouts. The Irish pub, which also has locations in Pittsburgh and Harrisburg, is furnished from floor to ceiling with items imported from the Emerald Isle, including a bar salvaged from a hotel. A large fireplace lends a cozy feel to the high-ceilinged space. The menu includes burgers, wraps, and other standard American fare, but the big movers here are shepherd's pie and the fish and chips platter, featuring a half-pound of deep-fried haddock. Wash it all down with a Guinness combo—a pint consisting of the quintessentially Irish stout and another draft beer. The "half & half" (Guinness and Harp), "dirty ole Englishman" (Guinness and Boddingtons), and "dark side of the moon" (Guinness and Blue Moon) combos are particularly popular.

With its flat-screen TVs, jukebox, and stage, **Nelson's** (1033 State St., Erie, 814/454-4500, 4 P.M.–2 A.M. Mon.–Sat., 3 P.M.–2 A.M. Sun., $8–16) looks like the sort of place more concerned with good times than good food. But the two go hand in hand at the live music venue, which opened just in time to ring in 2009. You'll be singing a happy tune when you tuck into an order of Prince Edward Island mussels, a po' boy stuffed with organic rock shrimp, or a burger made from locally raised grass-fed beef.

Foodies with more disposable income congregate at **1201 Kitchen** (1201 State St., Erie, 814/464-8989, www.1201restaurant.com, 5–10 P.M. Mon.–Sat., $14–36), which serves "Latin/Asian inspired food," including the best sushi in town. Named for its address, the chic chef-owned restaurant changes its menu every few weeks, giving understated names like "fried chicken" and "land & sea" to entrées as original as the artwork on its walls. Kobe beef and scallops almost always make the cut. Reservations are strongly recommended and a must if you'd like to experience the chef's table—a five-course meal with wine pairings for $60 per person.

Not every recommendable restaurant in downtown Erie has a State Street address. One block west of the thoroughfare is the **Brewerie at Union Station** (123 W. 14th St., Erie, 814/454-2200, www.brewerie.com, 11:30 A.M.–10 P.M. Mon.–Thurs., 11:30 A.M.–1 A.M. Fri.–Sat., $7–19), which isn't too proud to offer bottles from other Pennsylvania breweries along with drafts of its own creations. The menu is heavy on comfort foods: beer-battered pickles, pulled-pork nachos, fried bologna and grilled cheese sandwiches, and even a burger topped with bacon, chorizo, and a fried egg. Housed in Erie's passenger train station, the brewpub hosts the **Erie Micro Brew Festival** (www.eriebeerfest.com) in April and live music most Friday and Saturday nights. There was a time when dozens of passenger trains lumbered through the 1927 station daily. Today it's a stop on just one Amtrak route.

An early-20th-century firehouse provides the atmospheric setting for another off-State eatery, **The Pufferbelly** (414 French St., Erie, 814/454-1557, www.thepufferbelly.com, 11:30 A.M.–9 P.M. Mon.–Thurs., 11:30 A.M.–11 P.M. Fri.–Sat., 11 A.M.–8 P.M. Sun., $7–23). It's best known for its all-you-can-eat Sunday brunch (11 A.M.–3 P.M., $16.99), featuring made-to-order omelets and cut-to-order roast beef, among other things.

For an authentic Italian dinner, head to **Colao's Ristorante** (2826 Plum St., Erie, 814/866-9621, www.italianrestauranterie.com, 5–9:30 P.M. Mon.–Thurs., 5–10:30 P.M. Fri.–Sat., $11–23).

Presque Isle

Presque Isle's dining scene consists of a few concession stands, but one of the region's most adored eateries is just outside its entrance. You can't miss **Sara's** (25 Peninsula Dr., Erie, 814/833-1957, www.sarasandsallys.com, open Apr.–Sept., 10:30 A.M.–9 P.M. Apr.–Memorial Day and Labor Day–Sept., 10:30 A.M.–10 P.M.

Sara's, near the entrance to Presque Isle State Park

© ANNA DUBROVSKY

LAKE REGION

Memorial Day–Labor Day, $2–7) with its red-and-white striped awning, bustling picnic tables, and six-foot hot dog statue. Its menu, like its decor, pays tribute to 1950s malt shops. Even its prices are on the retro side. Five bucks gets you a foot-long hot dog smothered with homemade chili and a Coke in an old-fashioned glass bottle. A bacon cheeseburger with a basket of homemade onion rings will set you back $7. Save room for soft-serve ice cream; Sara's is famous for its Creamsicle-like "orange vanilla twist." From Memorial Day through Labor Day its owner opens a 1957 stainless steel diner parked nearby for customers who want to eat in air-conditioned comfort.

Another place to grab a bite near Presque Isle is **Waldameer** (3100 W. Lake Rd., Erie, 814/838-3591, www.waldameer.com, open weekends in May, daily except Mon. Labor Day weekend through Memorial Day). The amusement park doesn't charge for parking or admission, and it's dotted with concession stands offering the likes of fresh-cut fries and funnel cake.

INFORMATION

If you're driving to Erie from New York via I-90 west, look for the Pennsylvania welcome center near the state line. It's stocked with brochures about attractions in the region and throughout the state. Personalized travel counseling is available 7 A.M.–7 P.M. daily; the restrooms are always open. If you're driving from Ohio via I-90 east, you can load up on brochures at a rest stop about a mile past the state line. **VisitErie** (208 E. Bayfront Parkway Ste. 103, Erie, 814/454-1000, www.visiterie.com, 8:30 A.M.–5 P.M. Mon.–Fri.), Erie County's tourism promotion agency, staffs an information desk inside the rest stop from late May through September. Once in Erie, head to VisitErie headquarter inside the Intermodal Transportation Center or the **Tom Ridge Environmental Center** (301 Peninsula Dr., Erie, 814/833-7424, www.trecpi.org, 10 A.M.–6 P.M. daily) for answers to any questions about where to go and how to get there. Before you hit the road, request a free copy of the *Erie All Seasons Visitors Guide*

via VisitErie's website. A downloadable version is available.

GETTING THERE AND AROUND

Erie is in Pennsylvania's northwest corner, about 130 miles north of Pittsburgh and 100 miles from Cleveland, Ohio, and Buffalo, New York. If you're coming from Pittsburgh or other points south, you'll arrive via I-79. I-90 is the major east–west thoroughfare, but if you value scenery over speed, follow the coastal Route 5 into town.

Erie International Airport, Tom Ridge Field (814/833-4258, www.erieairport.org), with a booking code of ERI, is served by three major airlines offering service between Erie and Cleveland, Detroit, and Philadelphia. **Amtrak** (800/872-7245, www.amtrak.com) provides train service to the city via its Lake Shore Limited line. **Greyhound** (800/231-2222, www.greyhound.com) buses pull into the Intermodal Transportation Center (208 E. Bayfront Parkway, Erie) in the Bayfront District.

Local bus service is provided by the **Erie Metropolitan Transportation Authority** (814/452-3515, www.emtaerie.com), or EMTA. A good way to get the lay of the land is to hop on an EMTA Route 20 Bay Liner Trolley—a bus in the guise of an old-timey trolley that runs between the bayfront and downtown's 14th Street via State Street every day but Sunday. Bay Liner service from the Intermodal Transportation Center begins at 6:16 A.M. on weekdays and 10 A.M. on Saturdays. You'll find taxis at the airport and the Intermodal Center. Call **Erie Yellow Cab** (814/461-8294, www.erieyellowcab.com) if you need a lift from elsewhere in the area.

A water taxi plies Presque Isle Bay from Memorial Day weekend until the weather takes a nasty turn in September or October. Known as the **Presque Isle Aquabus** (814/881-2502, noon–6 P.M. Mon. and 10 A.M.–6 P.M. Tues.–Sun., all-day fare $7 for adults, $4 for children under 12, one-way fare $4 for adults and children), it leaves from the foot of State Street on the hour, heads west to Liberty Park, and then crosses the bay, arriving at Presque Isle on the half hour.

Pymatuning and Vicinity

Lake Erie isn't the only body of water luring boaters, anglers, and bird-watchers to Pennsylvania's northwest corner. Less than an hour south of the Great Lake's shoreline is a great lake named Pymatuning. Unlike Lake Erie, a thousands-year-old product of geologic forces, Pymatuning is relatively young and the product of a man-made dam. It's Pennsylvania's largest lake and the centerpiece of its largest state park. (Lake Erie is much larger, of course, but it's no more Pennsylvania's than the Pacific Ocean is America's.) Man-made though it is, Pymatuning has long been a destination for ardent observers of the natural world. The state's first migratory waterfowl refuge was established there in 1935, shortly after the dam was constructed. A few years later Pymatuning became the site of the state's first wildlife education center. From 1968 to 1980, only three pairs of bald eagles were known to nest in Pennsylvania, and all of them were in the Pymatuning area. The raptors can now be found in many areas of the state, but the frequency of sightings at Pymatuning brings birders back again and again. There's something else that brings people back again and again—something delightfully freakish. At Pymatuning, ducks walk on the backs of fish. That's right, *on their backs.* Read on.

Just a few miles east of the state's largest lake is its largest natural lake. Conneaut Lake is popular with the speedboating set and home to the *Kaylee Belle,* the only authentic paddlewheel boat on Pennsylvania waters. East of Conneaut is the city of Meadville, home to a very old market house and the very unusual Johnson-Shaw Stereoscopic Museum. And east of Meadville is the Erie National Wildlife Refuge, a federally managed haven for waterfowl and, like Pymatuning, a paradise for birdwatching enthusiasts.

PYMATUNING LAKE

At roughly 17,000 acres, Pymatuning is Pennsylvania's largest lake by a wide margin. (Boosters of the 8,300-acre Raystown Lake

in the Alleghenies region are quick to point out that Pymatuning spills into Ohio, making Raystown the largest lake *entirely within* the Commonwealth. The fact of it is that Pennsylvania has the lion's share of Pymatuning and its 70-mile shoreline.) The lake is the product of a dam on the Shenango River near the small town of Jamestown, about an hour south of Erie. Constructed in the 1930s, the dam transformed a vast swamp into one of Pennsylvania's most visited destinations.

The U.S. 6 town of Linesville, widely regarded as the gateway to Pymatuning, bills itself as the place "Where the Ducks Walk on the Fish." The phenomenon occurs at a reservoir spillway just south of town. You'll pass a large fish hatchery and then Ford Island, a renowned bird-watching site, on the way.

Pymatuning Lake is the centerpiece of identically named parks in Pennsylvania and Ohio. Pennsylvania's **Pymatuning State Park** (724/932-3141, www.dcnr.state.pa.us/stateparks/Parks/pymatuning.aspx) is the largest park in the state system and has the most campsites—roughly 650. It also has three marinas, five beaches, and seven miles of hiking trails. The park's northernmost campground, marina, and beach are minutes from Linesville and can be reached from U.S. 6. Campgrounds, marinas, and beaches are also found off Route 285 near the town of Espyville and off U.S. 322 near Jamestown. For information on facilities in Ohio's Pymatuning State Park, call 440/293-6030 or visit www.dnr.state.oh.us/parks/pymatuning/tabid/781/Default.aspx.

(The Spillway

Want to see a monkey atop an elephant? Buy a ticket to a circus. Want to see a duck atop a fish? Buy a loaf of bread and head to the spillway (Hartstown Rd., 2 miles south of U.S. 6 at Linesville) on Pymatuning Lake. Each year, hundreds of thousands of people visit the spillway to hurl breadcrumbs (or whole loaves) at the fish and waterfowl that congregate there. The fish—big, mean-looking carp—are so thick that they form a writhing carpet on the water's surface. A carp with its sights set on a saltine or slice of Wonder bread will sometimes leap out of the water and somersault over its brethren. To say that ducks walk the carp carpet is a bit of an overstatement. Once in a while, a duck in hot pursuit of baked goods will scramble over a fish or two. It's a magical moment that keeps many families coming back year after year.

In 2008 state conservation officials tried to put a stop to the decades-old bread-tossing tradition, arguing that the carp were eating too many carbs (or something like that). Visitors could still feed the fish special pellets sold at a state-run concession stand, they said. The "let them eat pellets" proclamation incited a public outcry, attracting the attention of state legislators. Attacked like a hamburger bun in the heart of the spillway, the Department of Conservation and Natural Resources backed down.

The bread hurling begins with the spring thaw and continues through late fall. Refreshments, souvenirs, and fish food are available at the spillway concession stand, which is generally open weekends mid-April to Memorial Day, daily through Labor Day, and weekends only for the remainder of September.

Linesville Fish Hatchery

Anglers and anyone who's owned an aquarium will enjoy a visit to the state-run fish hatchery (13300 Hartstown Rd., Linesville, 814/683-4451, www.fish.state.pa.us/images/fisheries/fcs/linesville/fcs.htm, 8 A.M.–3:30 P.M. daily, free admission) about a mile north of the spillway. Built in 1939, the hatchery raises millions of gilled swimmers each year: about a dozen warm-water species as well as trout destined for Lake Erie's tributaries. Its visitors center features a two-story aquarium filled with walleye, crappie, perch, catfish, bass, and other warm-water fish; a collection of vintage fishing equipment and boat motors; and plenty of mounted trophy fish, including the state

record muskellunge—a 54-pounder pulled from nearby Conneaut Lake in 1924. Kids get a kick out of an interactive exhibit that tests their fish identification skills.

A platform overlooking the hatch house gives visitors a chance to observe workers bringing in adult fish, stripping the eggs out, fertilizing them, and otherwise going about their day. Though fish rearing is a year-round business at Linesville, there's less to see during the coldest months. Sometime in October or early November, hatchery workers drain the 10,000-gallon aquarium, releasing the fish into Pymatuning. Production ponds are also drained. They remain empty until the ice comes off the lake in March or early April.

The hatchery grounds are popular with birdwatchers. Bring binoculars or a spotting scope to scan the skies and trees for bald eagles. Bring a picnic basket if you plan to stay awhile; there are tables and benches on the property but no concession stand.

Pymatuning Wildlife Learning Center

More than 300 mounted specimens of native birds and mammals can be seen at the Wildlife Learning Center (12590 Hartstown Rd., Linesville, 814/683-5545, www.pgc.state.pa.us, 8:30 A.M.–4 P.M. Thurs.–Sun. Apr.–Sept., free admission) on Ford Island, about midway between the spillway and the hatchery. Operated by the Pennsylvania Game Commission, the center is something of a natural history museum. Many of the animals are displayed in habitat dioramas, including a mountain stream scene, a bobcat cavern, and a bald eagle nest. Two hulking bucks lock antlers in a battle for dominance. (The pair died in combat and were found in their strange embrace.) Unlike most natural history museums, the center is more or less in the middle of nowhere, which means it's quite possible to see living versions of some mounted creatures just outside its doors. Bald eagles are spotted almost every day. Come in April or May, before the trees leaf out, for the best views of their nests. Bluebird boxes, a bat condominium, and other wildlife houses and feeders around the center virtually guarantee animal sightings. A quarter-mile nature trail beginning at the center and ending at the parking lot also provides wildlife-watching opportunities.

Ford Island overlooks a section of Pymatuning Lake overseen by the Game Commission, the state agency charged with managing wildlife and regulating hunting. For decades, the Game Commission has gone out of its way to make the area inviting to Canada geese and other migratory waterfowl. It's been extremely successful. Opportunities to hunt in the waterfowl refuge are limited and highly coveted. Visit the Game Commission's website or call the regional office at 814/432-3187 for more information.

Boating and Fishing

Pymatuning Lake isn't a destination for adrenaline junkies. A 20-horsepower limit rules out Jet-Skiing, waterskiing, wakeboarding, and the like. (Head to nearby Conneaut Lake if that's what floats your boat.) If you enjoy peace and quiet and pretty scenery, you'll enjoy Pymatuning. Ditto if you enjoy sailing or canoeing. The lake's Pennsylvania shores are dotted with boat ramps and three public marinas: the 170-slip Linesville Marina (814/683-4339) on the north shore, the 184-slip Espyville Marina (724/927-2003) on the east shore, and the 203-slip Jamestown Marina (724/932-3267) on the south shore. Generally open from late March or early April through October, the marinas rent a variety of watercraft, including motorboats, pontoons, and canoes. Fishing tackle, bait, and snacks are available.

Common species in the warm-water fishery include walleye, muskellunge, crappie, bluegill, and largemouth and smallmouth bass. Anglers can cast anywhere on the lake with a fishing license from either Pennsylvania or Ohio, but shore fishing requires a license from the appropriate state. Popular shore fishing spots include an 850-foot breakwater at Espyville Marina and piers adjacent to Linesville Marina and on the Shenango River just below the dam.

Outdoorspeople can be found on Pymatuning even in the dead of winter. Iceboating is permitted everywhere on the lake. Anglers pull walleye, perch, and crappie out of the frigid waters.

Campgrounds and Beaches

Pennsylvania's Pymatuning State Park has three campgrounds, one near each of the marinas. They usually open in mid-April and close in late October. Beaches are within easy reach of the marinas and campgrounds and are open from the weekend before Memorial Day through Labor Day, weather permitting. Campgrounds have modern facilities, including showers and flush toilets, and a mix of electric and non-electric sites. Not a camper? Reserve one of the modern cabins near Linesville Campground and Jamestown Campground. The two- and three-bedroom cabins have a furnished living area, kitchen/dining area, and bathroom. Bring your own linens, towels, cookware, and tableware. The 20 cabins at the southern/Jamestown end of the state park are rentable year-round. The northern/Linesville end has five cabins, all wheelchair accessible and rentable from mid-April to late October. Reserve campsites and cabins online at www.pa.reserveworld.com or by calling 888/727-2757.

OTHER SIGHTS
Pymatuning Deer Park

Known for its bald eagles and other native wildlife, the Pymatuning area is also home to some not-so-native animals: African lions, Siberian tigers, camels, and various primates. You'll find them at Pymatuning Deer Park (804 E. Jamestown Rd., Jamestown, 724/932-3200, www.pymatuningdeerpark.com, 10 A.M.–6 P.M. Mon.–Fri. and 10 A.M.–7 P.M. Sat.–Sun. mid-May–Labor Day, 10 A.M.–6 P.M. Sat.–Sun. for remainder of Sept., admission $6.50, seniors and children 2–15 $5.50), a family-owned attraction near the southern end of Pymatuning Lake. Established in 1953, the menagerie has grown to more than 250 animals and birds, both domestic and exotic. Its petting zoo, miniature train ($2), and pony rides ($2) are hugely popular with pint-sized visitors. The animal park encourages feeding of many animals, including bears, primates, emus, and deer. Don't bring yesterday's left-overs; only park-sold animal food ($1 per package) is permitted.

Conneaut Lake

Less than 10 minutes from Pymatuning's shores, Conneaut Lake is the largest natural lake in Pennsylvania. Let's get this clear: It's not very large. At 934 acres, it's a puddle relative to the 17,000-acre Pymatuning. But the glacial lake near the town that shares its name has a certain appeal, as evidenced by the vacation homes along its shores. Pymatuning is no deeper than 35 feet, and the state imposes a 20-horsepower limit on the man-made lake. Conneaut is almost 70 feet deep, and there's no horsepower limit. So speedboating, water-skiing, Jet-Skiing, and the like—prohibited on Pymatuning—are kosher on Conneaut. You'll need your own watercraft, however. Rentals are hard to come by.

The boatless can experience Conneaut Lake from the decks of a paddlewheeler. The *The Barbara J.* (11934 Conneaut Lake Rd., Conneaut Lake, 814/382-7433, www.silver shores.net, Sunday brunch cruise $15) offers Sunday brunch cruises from June through Labor Day. She departs from her dock at Silver Shores Restaurant promptly at 11 A.M. and returns 90 minutes later. Tickets are sold at the waterfront eatery.

Built for the Columbus Zoo in 1969, the *Kaylee Belle* (814/439-0066, www.conneaut lakepark.com/kayleebelle.html, 1-hour narrated cruise $10, children under 12 free) now docks at **Conneaut Lake Park** (12382 Center St., Conneaut Lake, 814/382-5115, www.conneaut lakepark.com), an amusement park that has seen better days. Opened in 1892 as a picnic area, the park is best known for its classic Blue Streak coaster, installed in 1938. In recent years it's become known for financial woes and some lousy luck. Its rides stood idle in 2007 due to lack of funds. In early 2008 an arson fire destroyed its century-old Dreamland Ballroom, where Perry Como and Doris Day once sang. Just two months later its old bowling alley

Conneaut Lake Park

collapsed. Most of the rides—but not the Blue Streak—opened for the 2009 season, and the trustees that run the debt-laden park promised improvements in years to come. Anyway, about the *Kaylee Belle:* She plies Conneaut Lake every day the park is open and on weekends for about a month after Labor Day, departing on the hour 10 A.M.–6 P.M. Passengers are welcome to bring food and beverages on board. A great place to get those beverages is the **Conneaut Cellars Winery** (12005 Conneaut Lake Rd., Conneaut Lake, 814/382-3999, www.ccw-wine.com, 10 A.M.–6 P.M. daily). Established in 1982, the winery produces about 20 varieties of white, red, rose, and sparkling wines. Tastings and guided tours of the 6,400-square-foot winery are free. Tours are offered at 11 A.M. and on the hour 1–5 P.M. There's no vineyard here; Conneaut Cellars buys its grapes from Lake Erie growers.

Meadville

About 15 minutes from Conneaut Lake and 25 from Pymatuning, the city of Meadville offers quaint B&Bs and cultural attractions. It's a college town—about 2,100 of its roughly 13,000 residents are students of Allegheny College, a liberal arts institution founded in 1815—and the county seat of Crawford County. (It's also the birthplace of actress Sharon Stone. Years before famously uncrossing her legs in *Basic Instinct,* she enjoyed local fame as Miss Crawford County.) The **Meadville Market House** (910 Market St., Meadville, 814/336-2056, 9 A.M.–5 P.M. Mon.–Fri., 9 A.M.–6 P.M. Wed.–Thurs., 8 A.M.–4 P.M. Sat.), a community gathering spot since 1870, is a good place to start the day. It's home to a greasy spoon known for its breakfasts. It's also a destination for locally made crafts and specialty foods, including baked goods and homemade pasta. During the growing season, farmers sell their produce outside. The **Meadville Council on the Arts** (814/336-5051, www.meadville councilonthearts.com) occupies the second floor of the Market House and showcases the work of area artisans in a gallery open noon–4 P.M. Wednesdays and Fridays and 10 A.M.–2 P.M. Saturdays. It also operates a small theater and spacious dance studio.

The **Baldwin-Reynolds House Museum** (639 Terrace St., Meadville, 814/333-9882, www.baldwinreynolds.org, tours on the hour noon–3 P.M. Wed.–Sun. mid-May–Aug., admission $5, children 6–18 $3) is another of Meadville's cultural attractions. The Greek Revival mansion was built in the 1840s for U.S. Supreme Court Justice Henry Baldwin. He died within a year of moving in, and for a few years his dream home served as a finishing school for girls. In 1847 his widow deeded the property to her nephew, William Reynolds, a young Pittsburgh attorney and graduate of Allegheny College. Reynolds moved his family to Meadville, became one of its most influential businessmen, and served as its first mayor. The house stayed in the Reynolds family until 1963, when it was purchased by the Crawford County Historical Society. Visitors are led through more than 20 rooms, including Justice Baldwin's study with his original sofa and secretary desk. Reynolds family furnishings and other 19th-century antiques are displayed throughout the three-story manse. Tours last 60–90 minutes and include a peek inside an 1883 doctor's office that was transported to the museum grounds.

Meadville also has a museum devoted to stereoscopy, a parlor pastime in the days before television and Nintendo. The **Johnson-Shaw Stereoscopic Museum** (423 Chestnut St., Meadville, 814/333-4326, www.johnsonshaw museum.org, 10 A.M.–4 P.M. Wed.–Fri. and 10 A.M.–5 P.M. second Sat. of the month Apr.–Sat., other times by appointment, admission $5, seniors and students $3) houses a collection of stereoviews—photographs that appear three-dimensional when viewed through a binocular-like device—made by the Keystone View Company. Founded in Meadville in 1892, the company was the nation's leading manufacturer of stereoviews by the early 20th century. Another unusual attraction is the **Greendale Cemetery** (700 Randolph St., Meadville, 814/336-3545, www.greendale cemetery.org). More than 150 years old, Greendale has so many stories to tell that there's an iPhone app, iGreendale, to guide visitors to points of interest. The park-like cemetery is absolutely enchanting in springtime, when more than 1,500 rhododendrons bloom.

ENTERTAINMENT AND EVENTS
Performing Arts

Opened in 1885, the **Academy Theatre** (275 Chestnut St., Meadville, 814/337-8000, www.theacademytheatre.org) welcomed more than its fair share of traveling troupes thanks to Meadville's location along railroad lines between New York City and Chicago. These days the performers who take its stage are mostly local (and there's no passenger train service to Meadville). The theater began showing films in the early 1900s and still does. They're mostly of the artsy or foreign persuasion. The **Riverside Inn** (1 Fountain Ave., Cambridge Springs, 814/398-4645, www.theriversideinn.com), which also dates to 1885, is a hotel-cum-dinner theater open from April through December. It squeezes about a dozen shows—lighthearted productions like *Love, Sex, and the IRS; Drinking Habits;* and *Hot Flashes*—into its season.

Festivals and Events

More than two dozen hot air balloons take flight over Meadville every Father's Day weekend. The **Thurston Classic Hot Air Balloon Event** (Allegheny College, Meadville, 814/336-4000, www.thurstonclassic.com, late June, free) pays tribute to Samuel Sylvester Thurston, a Meadville hotel operator who took up ballooning in 1860, and the son who followed in his footsteps. The younger Thurston launched his balloon from the roof of the still-standing Meadville Market House on at least one occasion.

The likes of Abraham Lincoln and Daniel Boone—or men who look a lot like them—turn out for the **Pymatuning Pioneer & Arts Festival** (Pymatuning State Park, 724/927-9473, www.pymatuningpioneerdays.com, last full weekend of July, admission $1), featuring a Civil War encampment and an Indian encampment. Festival-goers can count on demonstrations of old-school skills like butter churning

Thurston Classic Hot Air Balloon Event

© CRAWFORD COUNTY CONVENTION & VISITORS BUREAU

and cow milking, a pie-eating contest, and live entertainment. "Big name" and local bands take turns entertaining crowds at the **Crawford County Fair** (Rte. 77, Meadville, 814/333-7400, www.crawfordcountyfair.net, Aug., admission charged), billed as the largest agricultural fair in Pennsylvania. It's got all the hallmarks of an ag fair: lots of livestock, lots of food, amusement rides, truck and tractor pulls, and a pageant. Actress Sharon Stone won the coveted Miss Crawford County crown in 1975.

SHOPPING

Bill Campbell's pottery is sold in some 600 galleries in the United States and Virgin Islands, but opening his own store a few miles from his production facility was a gamble. The big question: Would people come out to the country for his elegant, richly colored porcelain? They did. The **Campbell Pottery Store** (25579 Plank Rd., Cambridge Springs, 814/734-8800, www.campbellpotterystore.com, 10 A.M.–5 P.M. daily Mar.–Dec.), about 20 minutes north of Meadville and half an hour south of Erie, is well worth a detour. Heck, it's a destination in its own right. It took Bill and his wife, Jane, a decade to transform a large barn built in the mid-1800s into a showplace for his pottery and fine crafts from across the country. There are three floors to explore. The basement level, once a dirt-floored milking area, is now a gallery used for group or solo shows, demos, workshops, and other special events. The barn's painstakingly restored fieldstone foundation gives the Stonewall Gallery it name. Exquisite creations in a variety of mediums and price ranges fill the ground level and loft area, where massive hand-hewn beams and other original architectural features compete for the eye's attention. In addition to the largest selection of Campbell Pottery in the world, including experimental pieces available nowhere else, you'll find handcrafted soaps, baby goods, decorative items for home and garden, and sophisticated jewelry. The store offers complimentary coffee and tea, shipping anywhere in the continental United States, and a bridal registry. Come in July to be greeted with acres of daylilies.

SPORTS AND RECREATION
Erie National Wildlife Refuge
About 30 miles east of Pymatuning Lake is another **bird-watching** mecca. Established in 1959 as a haven for migratory birds, Erie National Wildlife Refuge (11296 Wood Duck Ln., Guys Mills, 814/789-3585, www.fws.gov/ northeast/erie, headquarters 8 A.M.–4:30 P.M. Mon.–Fri., outdoor facilities open daily from 30 minutes before sunrise to sunset, unless otherwise posted) consists of two expanses of federal land. It attracts some 240 species of birds, including waterfowl, bald eagles and other raptors, shorebirds, and marsh birds. A detailed bird brochure is available at the refuge headquarters, located on the larger and more intensely managed tract. The 5,206-acre Sugar Lake Division, as it's called, lies in a narrow valley on the outskirts of Guys Mills, about 10 miles from Meadville. A two-loop trail near the headquarters offers a 1.2- or 1.6-mile jaunt through wetlands, meadows of upland grasses, and mixed forests. In winter it's popular with

cross-country skiers and snowshoers. It's possible to spot a variety of birds without stepping foot outside the headquarters. An indoor bird observation area with seating, binoculars, and bird identification materials overlooks feeding stations installed outside. Thanks to microphones placed under the stations, visitors can even listen to the banter of the feasting birds. The 3,594-acre Seneca Division is about 10 miles north of Sugar Lake Division, or four miles southeast of the town of Cambridge Springs.

Beaver ponds, swamps, wet meadows, and other wetlands cover almost a third of the refuge, attracting large numbers of migrating waterfowl in March and early April and again from September to November. Small flocks of shorebirds such as sandpipers and yellowlegs appear in the summer and feed on the mudflats. More than 100 bird species nest on Erie Refuge, including wood ducks, Canada geese, mallards, bald eagles, red-tailed hawks, American kestrels, and great blue herons. Several dozen varieties of mammals also make their home here. White-tailed deer, beavers, muskrats, and woodchucks are the most commonly seen.

Meadville Area Recreation Complex
The 47-acre recreation complex known as the MARC (800 Thurston Rd., Meadville, 814/724-6006, www.marc4fun.com) is owned and operated by the Meadville Area Recreational Authority, but you don't have to be a local resident to make use of its pools, ice arena, skateboard park, tennis courts, and other facilities.

Whispering Pines Golf Course and AvalancheXpress
Just minutes from Conneaut Lake, Whispering Pines Golf Course (15630 Middle Rd., Meadville, 814/333-2827, www.golfwhispering pines.com) offers 18 holes of golf amid rolling hills and eastern white pines. You'd expect the place to be dead once snow blankets those hills. You'd be wrong. In winter the public golf course transforms into AvalancheXpress (open Fri.–Sun. and holidays in winter, $10–18 per

person), a snow-tubing park with a 900-foot-long hill. Snowmaking machines keep the hill white, and a lighting system keeps thrill-seekers there long after the sun sets.

ACCOMMODATIONS

If you're a camper, you won't have trouble finding a place to lay your head near Pymatuning Lake. Pymatuning State Park has hundreds of campsites—more than any other state park in Pennsylvania, in fact—and 25 cabins. Should you encounter a No Vacancy sign, take your business to **Pineview Camplands** (15075 Shermanville Rd., Linesville, 814/683-5561, www.pineview camplands.com, open Apr. 15–Oct. 15, primitive site $15–20, site with hookups $20–30). It's extremely well situated: Pymatuning is a few minutes away in one direction, and Conneaut Lake is a few minutes away in another.

There are no hotels on Pymatuning's shores. Conneaut Lake had quite a few during its heyday as a resort area in the late 19th and early 20th centuries. **Hotel Conneaut** (12382 Center St., Conneaut Lake, 814/213-0120, www.clphotelconneaut.com, $55–250) is the lone survivor. Room rates were $1 per day when it opened on the grounds of Conneaut Lake Park, the amusement park on the western shore, in 1903. Its longevity is rather remarkable for a wooden structure. In 1943 it was struck by lightning, and the resulting blaze destroyed more than half of its roof. Rebuilding while the nation was engaged in a war effort was infeasible, so the charred portion was demolished and the number of guest rooms cut in half to 150. Little has changed since then. The hotel is still seasonal, operating only during the summer months. Most rooms don't have air-conditioning; ceiling fans and lakefront breezes usually do the trick. Televisions are also a rarity. Guests can get their TV fix in a common room on the first floor or ward off withdrawal symptoms with a board game or a cruise on the *Kaylee Belle,* an authentic paddlewheeler that docks in front of the hotel. Rooms range in size from singles to two-bedroom suites. Because it intends to see its 200th anniversary, smoking and burning candles are strictly forbidden.

Like Hotel Conneaut, the ⟨ **Riverside Inn** (1 Fountain Ave., Cambridge Springs, 814/398-4645, www.theriversideinn.com, rooms and 1-bedroom suites $75–140, 2- and 3-bedroom suites $220–355) is the lone survivor of a once-booming resort industry. In the late 1900s, the rural village of Cambridgeboro, about 25 miles northeast of Conneaut Lake, gained renown for its mineral springs. Dozens of hotels and rooming houses sprang up to accommodate believers in the water's healing powers, and by the end of the century, Cambridgeboro had been renamed Cambridge Springs. The mineral water craze didn't last long. While other grand hotels closed, the 1885 Riverside Inn adapted. Instead of therapeutic baths and electrical treatments, it now offers golf packages, artist workshops, a dinner theater, fine dining, and a taste of a bygone era. The Victorian beauty on the banks of French Creek is open from April through December.

Year-round accommodations can be found in Meadville. The college town has a mix of budget hotels and B&Bs. With 63 spacious rooms and a solicitous staff, **Americas Best Value Inn** (11237 Shaw Ave., Meadville, 814/724-6366, www.americasbestvalueinn .com, $70–80) is a winner in the former category. It's just off I-79 on the southern outskirts of town. **Mayor Lord's House** (654 Park Ave., Meadville, 814/720-8907, www .mayorlords.com, $89–129), best of the B&Bs, is in the heart of Meadville, just two blocks from Allegheny College. The beautifully restored house was built in the 1920s for a former mayor of Meadville. Both Americas Best and Mayor Lord's House offer Internet access, cable TV, and a complimentary continental breakfast. **Bethaven Inn** (386 Hamilton Ave., Meadville, 814/336-4223, www.bethaveninn .com, $65–75), another close-to-campus B&B, is a homelier and cheaper alternative.

FOOD

If you work up an appetite feeding the fish and fowl at the spillway, head to **Rebecca's Family Restaurant** (144 W. Erie St., Linesville, 814/683-3484, www.goodfoodlinesville.com,

6 A.M.–2:30 P.M. Sun.–Tues., 6 A.M.–9:30 P.M. Wed.–Sat., $5–20). Delightfully cozy with its hand-hewn log furniture, river rock fireplace, and an expansive brick wall uncovered during a gut renovation in 2007, the casual eatery in the heart of Linesville is known for phenomenal pies and its "cinnamon roll sundae." Cleaning your plate before dessert? A pleasure. Named for the owners' daughter, Rebecca's does everything from eggs to meatloaf sandwiches to steak dinners just right. It offers a breakfast buffet on Saturdays and Sundays. Come 4–6 P.M. for a hearty dinner at a price that matches your arrival time.

As the largest town in the area, Meadville has the widest selection of recommendable restaurants. For a quick bite, **The Pampered Palate** (748 N. Main St., Meadville, 814/337-2100, www.pamperedpalate.net, 6 A.M.–6 P.M. Mon.–Fri., 7 A.M.–5 P.M. Sat., $6) can't be beat. Start with a crock of French onion soup topped with three bubbling cheeses or save your appetite for an oversized sandwich on your choice of breads. The pressed sandwiches are especially satisfying and include a vegetarian version stuffed with portobello mushrooms and roasted peppers and tomatoes. Beverage options abound, ranging from a simple cup of coffee to flavored hot chocolate drinks and "frozen explosions" in varieties such as white chocolate turtle and cookie dough. **Julian's Bar & Grille** (299 Chestnut St., Meadville, 814/337-8513, 11 A.M.–9 P.M. Mon.–Sat., $6–19) is another good choice in the center of town. The jazz-themed joint offers creatively prepared sandwiches, burgers, pasta dishes, steaks, and occasionally live music.

On the southern outskirts of town, **Chovy's!** (18228 Conneaut Lake Rd., Meadville, 814/724-1286, www.chovysitaliancasual .com, 11 A.M.–11 P.M. Mon.–Thurs., 11 A.M.– midnight Fri.–Sat., 11 A.M.–10 P.M. Sun., kitchen closes 1 hour before closing time, $8–27) serves up southern Italian cuisine and a warm, lively atmosphere. The pastas are imported from Italy, the soups and sauces made from scratch, and the crisp Italian bread baked hourly. The menu takes the guesswork out of

food and wine pairing, suggesting a wine for everything from its thin-crusted white pizza and black Angus burger to its bone-in rib-eye and seafood linguini. More than 25 bottles are priced at $25 or less. Meat lovers can't help but love the nearby **Montana's Rib & Chop House** (11142 Highline Dr., Meadville, 814/333-2000, www.meadvilleribandchophouse.com, 11 A.M.–11 P.M. daily, $6–23), a brand seen only in Montana and Wyoming before the opening of the Meadville location in late 2009. It's best known for its pork ribs, which are marinated for 24 hours, slow cooked, and then finished on the grill. Buffalo rib-eye steak and pot roast are also customer favorites.

Ten miles north of Meadville and very definitely worth the drive is (**Sprague Farm & Brew Works** (22113 U.S. 6/U.S. 19, Venango, 814/398-2885, www.sleepingchainsaw.com, hours vary seasonally, generally open Thurs.– Sat., $3–13), a brewpub in a refurbished dairy barn. Brian and Minnie Sprague, its husband and wife owners, like to point out that producing beer isn't all that different from

Sprague Farm & Brew Works is a brewpub in an old dairy farm.

LAKE REGION

producing milk. "It used to be grain in, milk out. Now it's grain in, beer out," she quips. They serve their suds in glass milk jugs. The Spragues opened their out-of-the-way brewery in 2006, took top honors at the Erie Micro Brew Festival in 2009, and added a pub later that year. Fresh beer and joviality are the main attractions, but they also offer a selection of Pennsylvania wines and a menu that includes soft pretzels, made-in-Erie Smith's hot dogs, sandwiches and wraps, and mini kebabs. Don't have a designated driver? Book a stay at the Sprague's Sleeping Leaf Lodge ($150 per night for first 2 people, $5 per additional person, $825 per week), a five-bedroom farmhouse within stumbling distance of the pub.

INFORMATION AND SERVICES

The folks at the **Crawford County Convention and Visitors Bureau** (16709 Conneaut Lake Rd., Meadville, 814/333-1258, www.visit crawford.org, 8:30 A.M.–4:30 P.M. Mon.–Fri.)

are happy to answer questions about their region. Their office is usually closed on weekends, but you'll find brochures outside its doors. If you're traveling with a laptop, you'll also find a Wi-Fi signal, handy for perusing the CVB's website.

GETTING THERE AND AROUND

Pymatuning Lake, about an hour's drive from Erie, is accessible from the east and west by U.S. 6 and U.S. 322 and from the north and south by Route 18. **Greyhound** (800/231-2222, www.greyhound.com) provides bus service to Meadville. Private jets can land at Port Meadville Airport (GKJ), but passenger aircraft can't get any closer than **Erie International Airport, Tom Ridge Field** (814/833-4258, www.erieairport.org), with a booking code of ERI. It's served by three major airlines offering service between Erie and Cleveland, Detroit, and Philadelphia.

Oil Country

In 1857, a New York native named Edwin Drake arrived in the northwest Pennsylvania town of Titusville with a mission: bore a hole in the planet and bring up petroleum. Most people thought he was off his rocker. To be sure, there was crude oil in this corner of the world. It oozed from the banks and bed of the creek flowing through Titusville, giving the Allegheny River tributary a rainbow sheen and its name, Oil Creek. Hundreds of years before Drake's arrival, Native Americans had dug pits along the creek, waited for oil to rise to the surface of the water that collected in them, and then skimmed off the oil, which they prized for medicinal purposes. White settlers had also gotten the hang of gathering oil from natural seeps.

But Drake wasn't interested in a gallon here, a gallon there, and it was his method that struck locals as ludicrous. No one in Titusville had ever attempted to drill for oil. Drake's mission

was ridiculed as "Drake's folly." Boy, were the locals wrong. By the end of 1860, there were more than 70 producing wells in and around Oil Creek. U.S. oil production that year totaled 509,000 barrels, up from about 2,000 barrels in 1859. "Drake's folly" had given birth to the modern oil industry.

The local oil rush didn't last long, but it certainly hasn't been forgotten. It's the basis for the region's tourism industry. A full-scale replica of Drake's engine house and derrick stands on the site of the original. An excursion train chugs through the state park in summer and fall, its passengers taken back in time by guides whose forbears witnessed oil fever. Titusville, which bills itself as the "Birthplace of the Oil Industry," and Oil City, located 16 miles to its south where Oil Creek flows into the Allegheny River, celebrate their oil heritage with yearly festivals. The latter has a daily newspaper named *The Derrick*. Graceful

they're thick with trees, which is why OC & T tickets are in hot demand in October. Be sure to make a reservation during leaf-peeping season. From June through September, it's unusual for the sightseeing excursions to sell out, so you should be able to buy tickets on arrival. A special rate of $50 for two adults and up to three children ages 3–12 is available during those months. It doesn't apply to murder mystery train rides ($59 per person, including buffet dinner) and other special excursions.

Sitting on tracks next to the home station is the **Caboose Motel** (800/827-0690, www .octrr.org/caboosemotel.htm, open May–late Oct., $90). Each of its 21 caboose cars has a king-sized bed or two double beds, a heat and air-conditioning unit, and a television. Overnight packages with reduced train fares are available.

Drake Well Museum

In 1876 the engine house and derrick over Edwin Drake's history-making oil well were dismantled and sent to Philadelphia, where they were reassembled and displayed at the Centennial Exhibition, the first major World's Fair held in the United States. Millions of people got a look at the simple drilling tools that launched a giant industry. The tools found their way back to Titusville and now are part of the collection at the Drake Well Museum (202 Museum Ln., Titusville, 814/827-2797, www.drakewell.org, call or consult website for hours, admission $6, seniors $5, children 3–11 $3), whose doors are spitting distance from the hole Drake drilled in 1859. The boards, however, were never returned. Fortunately for museum-goers, a board-for-board copy of the well house was constructed in 1945 using 1860s photographs. Working reproductions of Drake's steam engine and boiler were installed in 1986. It's best to visit May through October, when the steam engine and other oil field machinery on the museum grounds are running. The sight of oil flowing from a pipe in the original hole is enough to give a history buff goosebumps.

The museum, whose main building closed

© ANNA DUBROVSKY

Oil pours from a pipe in Edwin Drake's history-making hole in the ground.

Victorian buildings throughout the region bear testimony to the great wealth born of oil. The most vibrant city in oil country, Franklin, has such an abundance of them that it's been dubbed the "Victorian City."

SIGHTS
⟨ Oil Creek & Titusville Railroad

There's no better way to experience the Oil Creek Valley—"the valley that changed the world," as local boosters call it—than aboard a vintage train. The OC & T (home station 409 S. Perry St., Titusville, 814/676-1733, www .octrr.org, runs weekends June–Oct. and select weekdays July–Aug. and Oct., ticket $17, seniors $15, children 3–12 $11) snakes along Oil Creek from Titusville to Rynd Farm Station at the southern tip of Oil Creek State Park, crossing multiple bridges on its 27-mile round-trip journey. Guides regale riders with colorful stories of the oil boom days, when the banks of the creek were thick with derricks. Today

© ANNA DUBROVSKY

Drake Well Museum

in late 2009 for a major renovation and was expected to reopen in mid-2011, does more than tell the tale of Drake's innovation and the ensuing oil mania. Operated by the Pennsylvania Historical and Museum Commission, it illustrates how oil has seeped into the very fabric of our lives. Native Americans used the petroleum that literally bubbled out of the ground to treat animal skins and their own cuts and burns. In the years since Drake coaxed it out of the earth, its uses have multiplied manifold. Petroleum distillates power cars, planes, and ships—you knew that. But did you know they're found in hundreds of products, from lipstick and golf balls to syringes and artificial hearts? Not to mention that polyester shirt you pull out for 1970s theme parties.

Oil Creek State Park

The creek banks that attracted so many fortune seekers after Edwin Drake struck oil in 1859 now attract bicyclists, hikers, history buffs, and fly-fishing enthusiasts. Stretching from the site of Drake's well in the north to just outside Rouseville in the south, Oil Creek State

Park (main entrance off Rte. 8, 1 mile north of Rouseville, park office 1080 Petroleum Centre Rd., Oil City, 814/676-5915, www.dcnr .state.pa.us/stateparks/Parks/oilcreek.aspx) is threaded with more than 50 miles of trails. The most popular is a 9.7-mile paved trail along Oil Creek. Custom-made for leisurely bike rides, it's dotted with historical markers, picnic tables, benches, and restrooms. Rental bicycles (8 A.M.–4 P.M. weekdays and 10 A.M.–6 P.M. weekends Memorial Day–Labor Day, some weekdays earlier in May and later in Sept., $5 per hour, $10 per day, $25 family special) are available at the park office, located near the southern trailhead. The northern trailhead is near Drake Well Museum. The park also boasts a backpacking trail. Thirty-seven miles long and named for the volunteer who created it in the 1980s, the Gerard Trail winds through the whole park, passing scenic vistas, waterfalls, and historic sites. Yellow blazes identify the main trail. Connecting loops blazed in white allow for shorter day hikes.

Vestiges of the oil rush are so few that a full-scale tableau was erected at the southern

a heron at Oil Creek State Park

end of the park, on the site of a farm that was overrun by oil opportunists in the mid-1860s. The farmer, a certain Mr. Benninghoff, pocketed some $6,000 a day during the madness. The Benninghoff Farm tableau features six 35-foot oil derricks and an oil barge. At the northern end of the park is the Hunt Farm tableau, reflective of mom-and-pop oil operations of the mid-1900s. Like movie sets, the tableaus are all form and no function. The buildings are empty, and the machinery doesn't work.

Oil Creek, which joins the Allegheny River in Oil City, is known for its bass and trout. Boughton Run, Toy Run, and Jones Run, which empty into the creek at the northern end of the park, provide brook trout fishing. The creek also lures canoeists. Because water levels can change on a dime, canoeists should call the park office for conditions. March, April, and May are usually the best months for paddling.

Camping isn't permitted in the park except in two hike-in areas along the Gerard Trail. Both have tent sites and Adirondack-style shelters with fireplaces. Reservations are required.

Tyred Wheels Museum

If you like antique automobiles, you'll like Gene Burt. His collection grew so large that he opened a museum. In addition to 25 antique cars and planes, Tyred Wheels (1164 Russell Corners Rd., Pleasantville, 814/676-0756, 1–5 P.M. Sat.–Mon. Memorial Day weekend– Labor Day, admission $3.50, children 8–16 $2) displays more than 5,000 miniature vehicles. Burt's collecting interests extend to old radios, dollhouses, tin toys, bicycles, pedal cars, and even spark plugs. When the weather's nice, he's easily coaxed into taking museum visitors for a spin in one of his antique cars. Tyred Wheels is off Route 227 between Pleasantville and Plumer, about 20 minutes from either Titusville or Oil City.

DeBence Antique Music World

Prepare for an aural feast at DeBence (1261 Liberty St., Franklin, 814/432-8350, www .debencemusicworld.com, 11 A.M.–4 P.M. Tues.–Sat. and 12:30–4 P.M. Sun. Apr.–Oct., by appointment Nov.–Mar., admission $8, seniors $7, high school and college students

© OIL REGION ALLIANCE

Tyred Wheels Museum

$5, children 3–14 $3), home to more than 100 player pianos, nickelodeons, calliopes, and other old-time automatic musical instruments. The tinkling of music boxes, the tunes of Irving Berlin and John Philip Sousa, and the nostalgia-inducing strains of merry-go-round organs punctuate tours of the incredible collection, which was started in the 1940s by Jake and Elizabeth DeBence. In 1965 the couple retired to a farm in the Franklin area, filling a barn with these iPods of yesteryear. After Jake's death, area residents formed a nonprofit and raised more than $1 million to purchase the collection and a place to display it. It now resides in a former five-and-dime in downtown Franklin.

The mechanical marvels date from the mid-1800s to the 1940s. Many are very rare. The museum's Berry-Wood A.O.W. orchestrion, which was designed for use in moving picture houses and does the work of a 10-piece orchestra, is the last of its kind. Also notable is a massive disc-playing music box made by the Regina Music Box Company of Rahway, New Jersey, in the 1890s. It came into the DeBence collection when its owner, an elderly woman, had to move into a nursing home. She came back year after year to listen to the exquisite instrument. Loudest of them all is a circa 1920 Wurlitzer Military Band Organ, which the manufacturer guaranteed would "produce lively, enjoyable music of such great volume" that crowds would gather.

ENTERTAINMENT AND EVENTS
Performing Arts

Fans of whodunits have a killer time aboard the **Oil Creek & Titusville Railroad's Mystery Train** (409 S. Perry St., Titusville, 814/676-1733, www.octrr.org, ticket $59). The evening begins with a buffet dinner at the Perry Street Station and, naturally, a murder. Dessert is served—and the crime is solved—after a train ride along Oil Creek. The OC & T offers half a dozen murder mystery train rides during its June–October operating season.

The **Barrow-Civic Theatre** (1223 Liberty St., Franklin, 814/437-3440, www.barrow theatre.com) in downtown Franklin boasts a year-round season. Dedicated in 1993, the venue sometimes attracts touring performers but primarily showcases local talent. Shows by its Old Time Radio Troupe, dedicated to the art of the audio play, are a particular treat.

Festivals and Events

The region's oil heritage is celebrated not once but twice a year. Both the **Oil Heritage Festival** (814/676-8521, www.oilheritage festival.com, late July, free) in Oil City and the **Oil Festival** (814/827-2941, www.titusville chamber.com, second weekend of Aug., free) in Titusville feature an arts and crafts show, a parade, concerts, and fireworks. But the region's biggest fete isn't about oil. It's about a fruit. Franklin's **Applefest** (814/432-5823, www.franklinapplefest.com, first weekend of Oct., free) started as a pie-baking contest in 1983 and has grown into a three-day affair that attracts more than 100,000 people. The apple dumplings, apple cider, and other festival fare are big draws. So is the enormous antique and classic car cruise. The abundance of apple trees in the Franklin area is owed in part to the fabled Johnny Appleseed, who lived there in the opening years of the 19th century.

Classic cars are an Applefest staple.

The Oil City Arts Council (814/676-1509, www.ocartscouncil.com) presents a variety of cultural events throughout the year, including **First Night Oil City** (Dec. 31, admission charged), an alcohol-free New Year's Eve celebration, and the **Oil Country Bluegrass Festival** (Feb., by donation). Its **Arts in the Park** (Justus Park, Fri. evenings July–Aug., nominal fee) and **Arts in the Transit** (National Transit Building, 206 Seneca St., Oil City, second Fri. of each month Sept.–May, admission charged) concert series serve up jazz, folk, and other genres.

ACCOMMODATIONS
Titusville

There isn't *that* much to do in the mostly rural oil region, so there's a lot to be said for amenity-rich lodging. 【 **Oil Creek Family Campground** (340 Shreve Rd., Titusville, 814/827-1023 or 800/395-2045, www.oilcreek campground.com, campsite $22–26 per night and 7th night free, cabin $30–50 per night or $190–280 per week, camper $70–75 per night or $430 per week) fits the bill. It has a heated swimming pool, an 18-hole disc golf course, a fishing pond stocked with smallmouth bass and bluegill, a playground, a miniature train, a softball field, basketball and volleyball courts, and horseshoe pits. And that's not all. This place has a llama petting pen. The long-necked critters enjoy apples, pears, and grapes, so shop accordingly. Situated within walking distance of Oil Creek State Park, the campground has a variety of campsites, from secluded tent sites to full hook-up sites. A handful of cabins and 30-foot campers are available for rent.

What **Bromley's Hillhurst Bed & Breakfast** (701 N. Perry St., Titusville, 814/827-1101, www.bromleys-hillhurst.com, $95) lacks in llamas it makes up for in on-site massages. The turn-of-the-last-century manse boasts a grand staircase, fireplaces galore, and a great room with a player piano. It's packed with antiques and old-fashioned dolls, and guests who love that sort of thing will love its gift shop. The guest suites are spacious and the breakfasts sumptuous.

© OIL REGION ALLIANCE

Caboose Motel

Titusville's other notable accommodations are the **Caboose Motel** (409 S. Perry St., Titusville, 800/827-0690, www.octrr.org/caboosemotel.htm, open May–late Oct., $90) and the **Knapp Farm** (43776 Thompson Run Rd., Titusville, 814/827-1092, www.theknappfarm.com, $70). Geared toward rail fans, the former sits on train tracks next to the home station of the Oil Creek & Titusville Railroad and consists of 21 caboose cars furnished with beds, heat and air-conditioning units, and televisions. Geared toward horse lovers and hunters, the latter offers B&B accommodations, guided trail rides, and hunts for pheasant, partridge, quail, wild turkey, and deer.

Oil City and Franklin Area

Oil City's lodging options are few, which is good for business at **Americas Best Value Inn & Suites** (1 Seneca St., Oil City, 814/677-1221, www.oilcityhotel.com, $69–99). Formerly known as The Arlington Hotel, it's centrally located near the confluence of Oil Creek and the Allegheny River, walking distance from the Venango Museum and National Transit Building. Amenities include a restaurant and lounge, an outdoor pool overlooking the Allegheny, and a guest laundry. Wireless Internet, continental breakfasts, and access to a nearby YMCA are complimentary.

Turtle Bay Lodge (472 President Village Rd., Tionesta, 814/677-8785, www.turtlebaylodge.com, $100–150) is anything but centrally located, and that's part of its appeal. It's on the banks of the Allegheny in a village named President, about 10 miles east of downtown Oil City. Owners Ray and Jan Beichner named four guest rooms after U.S. presidents and the fifth and frilliest after their granddaughter. Each has a king-sized bed, television, and private bathroom. Ideal for a do-little getaway with friends or extended family, the entire lodge can be rented for $500 per night. Rates include continental breakfast.

Franklin's heart-of-it-all hotel is the **Quality Inn & Conference Center** (1411 Liberty St., Franklin, 814/437-3031, www.qualityinn.com, $89–99), offering rooms with refrigerators and microwaves, whirlpool suites, free Wi-Fi and breakfast, an exercise facility, and privileges at the local YMCA to boot. The very Victorian town also has a couple of recommendable B&Bs: **The Lamberton House** (1331 Otter St., Franklin, 814/432-7908, www.lamberton house.com, $60–135), complete with an outdoor hot tub, and **Hager's Peach Basket** (1501 Liberty St., Franklin, 814/437-7699, www.hagerspeachbasket.com, $95).

FOOD

The oil region has precious few notable restaurants, and with the exception of Titusville's **Blue Canoe Brewery** (113 S. Franklin St., Titusville, 814/827-7181, www.thebluecanoe brewery.com, 3 P.M.–midnight Tues.–Sat., 12:30–10 P.M. Sun., $9–20), they're concentrated in Franklin. If you're new to the airy Blue Canoe, start with a sampler paddle of seven beers. The food doesn't play second fiddle to the house-brewed suds, which find their way into the peel-and-eat shrimp, the bratwurst platter, and the chargrilled steaks, among other menu items. Vegetarians needn't despair. The brewpub offers a smoked tofu sloppy joe and a couple of hand-tossed pizzas with nary a pepperoni slice.

The lousy thing about the **AmaZing Foods Café** (1327 Elk St., Franklin, 714/437-3663, www.amazingfoodscatering.com, 8 A.M.–2 P.M. Mon.–Fri., $4–9), the public face of a catering operation in downtown Franklin, is that it's not open on weekends. Boo to that. Yay to its delectable pancakes, piping hot oatmeal, and other morning starters. There's a Mediterranean tinge to the lunch menu of sandwiches and sides. AmaZing is all about fresh, sustainable ingredients, so it changes its menus often but is always true to its name.

The **French Creek Café** (1242 Liberty St., Franklin, 814/437-6860, 11 A.M.–3 P.M. Mon., 7:30 A.M.–3 P.M. Tues.–Sat., $5–8) is also an excellent choice for a casual breakfast or lunch. Regulars swear by the veggie scrambler (two eggs, rosemary potatoes, roasted red peppers, caramelized onions, asiago, and more), but the apple pancakes with cinnamon butter and caramel sauce are hard to resist. Come lunchtime, the eatery offers a variety of panini sandwiches, all served with hummus and pita chips made fresh daily.

◖ Bella Cucina (1234 Liberty St., Franklin, 814/432-4955, www.bellacucina pa.com, lunch 11 A.M.–2 P.M. Mon.–Sat., dinner 5–9:30 P.M. Tues.–Sat., lunch $7–12, dinner $14–33) promises a "divine dining" experience and delivers. Its Italian name belies the eclecticism of its cuisine. Dishes range from traditional meatballs over linguini to ginger-crusted pork medallions painted with a Thai-style sauce. Seafood lovers are particularly well served, though choosing between the signature crab cakes, scallops topped with sweet and sour sauce, and Norwegian salmon is no picnic. Speaking of picnics, there's a sizable oak tree inside the otherwise traditionally decorated establishment.

The grand, columned building known as **The Commons at Franklin** (1340 Liberty St., Franklin, www.thecommonsatfranklin .com) houses two very dissimilar restaurants: an Irish pub and the candlelit, anniversary-worthy Terrace. **McGinnis' Irish Pub & Grill** (814/437-7736, 11:30 A.M.–10 P.M. Tues.–Thurs., 11:30 A.M.–11 P.M. Fri.–Sat., 10:30 A.M.–2:30 P.M. Sun., $7–15) offers old-world specialties, plenty of American grub, and hybrids like its signature burger, which is topped with boxty, 'kraut, Swiss and Gruyère cheeses, and spicy thousand island dressing. Portions are more than generous, but you'd be doing yourself a disservice if you didn't start with the creamy redskin potato soup and finish with the bread pudding soaked with warm whiskey sauce. The bar, which remains open as late as 2 A.M., always has Guinness on tap and prides itself on its specialty martinis. Reservations are recommended for McGinnis' Sunday brunch ($13.99 for adults, $6.99 for children 3–10), an all-you-can-eat affair. Upstairs, **The Terrace** (814/437-7771, 5–9 P.M. Thurs. and Fri., $22–30) serves the likes of slow-roasted duck confit and house-made truffled pappardelle. Its opening in 2010 bolstered Franklin's culinary cred.

LAKE REGION

INFORMATION

The **Oil Region Alliance** (217 Elm St., Oil City, 814/677-3152, www.oilregion.org, 8 A.M.–5 P.M. Mon.–Fri.) promotes tourism in Titusville, Oil City, Franklin, and other municipalities within a 708-square-mile area known as the Oil Heritage Region. Its website is a good source of information about the region, which was designated a Pennsylvania Heritage Area in 1994 and a National Heritage Area a decade later. If you're in the area, stop by its office in downtown Oil City or the home station of the **Oil Creek & Titusville Railroad** (409 S. Perry St., Titusville, 9:30 A.M.–5 P.M. Sat.–Sun. in June and Sept., Wed.–Sun. in July, Aug., and Oct.) to load up on brochures.

GETTING THERE AND AROUND

The cities of Franklin, Oil City, and Titusville lie along Route 8, a north–south route stretching from Erie to Pittsburgh. Continental Connection flies daily between Cleveland and Franklin's **Venango Regional Airport** (814/432-5333, www.flyfranklin.org). The larger **Erie International Airport, Tom Ridge Field** (814/833-4258, www.erieairport.org) is 50 miles north of Titusville, the northernmost of the cities. The airports' booking codes are FKL and ERI, respectively.

PENNSYLVANIA WILDS

May as well leave your cell phone at home when you visit the Pennsylvania Wilds. It won't work in many parts of the vast and lightly populated region. To say that north-central Pennsylvania has more trees than people is a colossal understatement. More than 80 percent of the Wilds—a brand the state cooked up—is forestland. Perhaps that's why one county in the region advertises itself as "God's Country." Philadelphia has more than twice as many residents as the 12 counties that make up the Wilds. Given these facts, you can probably guess the region's primary commodities: solitude, scenery, and recreational opportunities galore.

Almost a third of the Wilds—about two million acres—is public land, open to anyone with an itch to explore. There's room for just about every form of outdoor recreation, from hunting to hang-gliding. Anglers and boaters will find thousands of miles of streams and waterways, including more than 2,000 wild trout streams. Hikers will find trails at every turn. The region isn't just for rugged types. It's for berry pickers, leaf peepers, and stargazers. It's for anyone with a yen for nature. Pennsylvania's only national forest, the river gorge known as the "Grand Canyon of Pennsylvania," and the largest free-roaming elk herd in the northeastern U.S. can all be seen without so much as leaving your car.

The wealth of natural resources that makes the region so attractive to outdoorspeople made it irresistible to 19th-century oil and lumber barons. The industries created boomtowns like Bradford ("High-Grade Oil Metropolis of the

HIGHLIGHTS

◖ Allegheny Reservoir: The 24-mile-long lake born of a 1960s anti-flooding project is a stunner whether you're gazing at it from a perch in Pennsylvania's only national forest or gliding across it in a kayak (page 532).

◖ Zippo/Case Museum: Dedicated to the handsome lighter that has appeared in more movies than John Wayne (who himself carried a Zippo), this museum speaks volumes about American culture (page 535).

◖ Colton Point and Leonard Harrison State Parks: Both afford breathtaking views of the gorge known as "Pennsylvania's Grand Canyon" (page 546).

◖ Pine Creek Rail Trail: Get high on nature and some low-impact exercise on the 60-mile trail that winds through wondrous Pine Creek Gorge, open to hikers, bikers, snowshoers, skiers, and even covered wagons (page 547).

◖ Dark Sky Park: Good-bye, light pollution. Helloooo, heavenly bodies! Cherry Springs State Park offers some of the best stargazing on the eastern seaboard (page 550).

◖ Benezette: This itty-bitty town is ground zero for communing with the largest herd of free-roaming elk east of the Rockies (page 575).

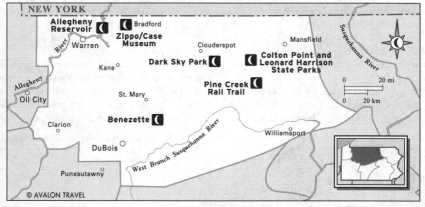

LOOK FOR ◖ TO FIND RECOMMENDED SIGHTS, ACTIVITIES, DINING, AND LODGING.

World") and Williamsport ("Lumber Capital of the World") and scarred the landscape. A century ago, the breathtaking Pine Creek Gorge was a smoldering wasteland of tree stumps, sawdust, and ash. Pennsylvania elk were unheard of. But the earth healed, thanks in part to government conservation efforts. As for the towns, they faded from the limelight. Their populations dwindled. Their mansions fell into disrepair. Today many Pennsylvanians from other parts would be hard-pressed to name a town in the Wilds (though Punxsutawney, made famous by a groundhog and a Bill Murray movie, might come to mind eventually). That may change if the region continues to attract nature lovers and families grateful for low-cost recreation. In recent years it has attracted another demographic: natural gas explorers. If their bullish predictions prove accurate, the Wilds may very well snag a new "capital" crown.

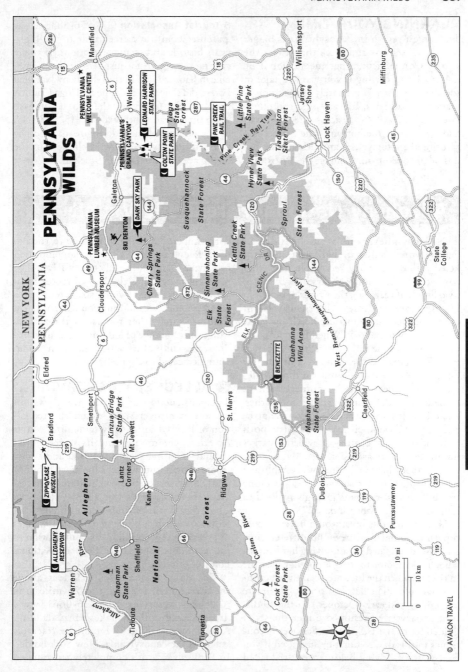

© AVALON TRAVEL

PLANNING YOUR TIME

The largest region in Pennsylvania is bigger than some states—and more than twice the size of Connecticut. That means you'll be doing a lot of driving if you want to take in the major sights. Fortunately, the region is made for road trips. Its east–west thoroughfares are U.S. 6 (Route 6) across the upper half and I-80 across the bottom. The former is a favorite of motorcyclists and other aficionados of the open road. Contact the **PA Route 6 Tourist Association** (877-276-8836, www .paroute6.com) for a free guide to the highway's historic and scenic attractions. If you're visiting the region for just two or three days, take in Kinzua Dam in the Allegheny National Forest and Pine Creek Gorge in Tioga County, traveling U.S. 6 between the two. If you have more time, head south via U.S. 15, U.S. 219, or any number of meandering roads, and pay a visit to Pennsylvania's wild elk herd or the birthplace of Little League Baseball.

Allegheny National Forest and Vicinity

The river valleys and steep hillsides of Pennsylvania's only national forest are blanketed with black cherry, red maple, and other hardwoods. They didn't always look like this. Two hundred years ago, the woods of northern Pennsylvania were thick with shade-tolerant eastern hemlock and American beech and laced with white pine and oak. When European settlers arrived in the early 1800s, they cut trees to make cabins and barns and to clear land for farming. As the nation grew, so did the demand for timber. Sawmills, tanneries reliant on hemlock bark for turning hides into leather, and railroads sprouted across the state's northern tier. The wood chemical industry, born near the end of the century, provided a market for virtually every accessible tree. By the time the Allegheny National Forest was established in 1923, the land was so barren and so prone to wildfires that residents jokingly referred to it as the "Allegheny brush patch."

Worries that the forest would never recover proved unfounded. A new and different forest arose, dominated by sun-loving hardwoods. They make motor touring a popular pastime in the fall, when the hills are ablaze with crimson and gold. (The best leaf peeping is in late September and early October.) In the 1940s, timber harvesting resumed under the strict guidelines of the U.S. Forest Service. It continues to this day, so don't be surprised if you find yourself driving behind a trailer loaded with timber. The biggest change to the national forest came in 1965, with the completion of Kinzua Dam on the Allegheny River. The resultant reservoir is the hub of recreational activity in the forest, which spans more than half a million acres in four counties. Warren, Bradford, and other towns on the forest's fringes offer a range of lodging and dining options, plus cultural attractions including a museum dedicated to Zippo lighters.

◖ ALLEGHENY RESERVOIR

The construction of Kinzua Dam was not without controversy. It forced the relocation of Pennsylvania's only remaining Native American community and its sacred burial ground, inspiring a federal lawsuit and a song recorded by country legend Johnny Cash. But the U.S. government saw the dam as necessary armament in its war against flooding. The Army Corps of Engineers estimates that Kinzua Dam has prevented flood damages in excess of $360 million. Its contribution to the recreational appeal of Allegheny National Forest is priceless.

The dam, which rises 179 feet above the streambed, created the 24-mile-long Allegheny Reservoir (814/726-0661, www .lrp.usace.army.mil/rec/lakes/kinzuala.htm). Also known as Kinzua Lake, the reservoir straddles the Pennsylvania–New York border. In Pennsylvania, it's completely surrounded

Allegheny Reservoir

by Allegheny National Forest. In New York, it's bordered by Allegany State Park and the Allegany Indian Reservation of the Seneca Nation. (Yep, the spelling varies.) The reservoir's shoreline is dotted with campgrounds, picnic areas, and boat launches.

Kinzua (pronounced "KIN-zoo") Dam itself is in Warren County, nine miles east of the city of Warren. From Warren, head east on U.S. 6 for about two miles and turn left (east) on Route 59, which leads to a parking lot at the top of the dam. Check out the giant carp that congregate on one side of the dam and the hydroelectric facilities on the other. Displays at the Army Corps' **Big Bend Visitor Center** (Rte. 59, 814/726-0678, 10 A.M.–3:45 P.M. daily Memorial Day weekend–Labor Day, weekends Sept.–Oct.), just downstream of the dam, illustrate the hydroelectric process. The outflow area is a popular fishing spot.

Two nearby overlooks offer bird's-eye views of the river valley (and attract rock climbers). Leaving the dam, drive east on Route 59 for about three miles. Just before reaching a bridge that crosses the reservoir, turn right onto Longhouse Scenic Drive (Forest Road 262). Make the first right off Longhouse to reach **Jakes Rock Overlook.** The access road to **Rimrock Overlook,** Forest Road 454, is about three miles farther east on Route 59. Follow the forest road until it ends at a parking lot. A short hike leads to the viewing area atop a large rock face. There are picnic areas at both overlooks.

Between the overlooks is the 200-boat **Kinzua-Wolf Run Marina** (Rte. 59, 13 miles east of Warren, 814/726-1650, www.kinzua marina.com, 10 A.M.–6 P.M. Mon.–Fri. and 8 A.M.–8 P.M. Sat.–Sun. Memorial Day–Labor Day, by appointment in May and Sept.), which rents pontoon boats, motorboats, canoes, and kayaks as well as boat slips. The nautical-themed **Docksiders Café** (814/726-9645, www.kinzua marina.com/cafe.htm, 11 A.M.–11 P.M. May–Labor Day, kitchen closes at 10 P.M., $6–15) overlooks the marina. Docksiders serves burgers and sandwiches all day and fish entrées for dinner, beefing up its menu on Tuesday, Friday, and Saturday evenings with three styles of prime rib. If you're starved for cell phone service, look for the bell hanging from the ceiling to the left of the bar. Stand directly beneath it, cross your fingers, and you'll probably get a signal. The entrance to **Kinzua Beach** is across Route 59 from the marina.

Recreation Areas

You can pitch a tent just about anywhere in the Allegheny National Forest (see www.fs.fed.us/r9/forests/allegheny for restrictions), but amenities like bathrooms and boat launches are concentrated in designated recreation areas. Several of these are located along the Allegheny Reservoir. The largest recreation area along the reservoir is **Willow Bay.** It's on the eastern shore of the reservoir along Route 346, about 16 miles west of Bradford. Willow Bay has 101 campsites and six rustic cabins with electricity—the only cabins in the forest system. Facilities include a concrete boat launch and a large picnic area overlooking the reservoir. Pontoon boats, canoes, and other means of flotation are available for rent.

Two other modern campgrounds, **Dewdrop** and **Kiasutha,** are located along Longhouse Scenic Drive (Forest Road 262) on the western shore of Kinzua Bay, a southern branch of the reservoir. Both have concrete boat launches. The latter also has a picnic area, a grassy swimming beach, and a handful of rental canoes. **Red Bridge,** located along Route 321 on the eastern shore of Kinzua Bay, has campsites with full hookups (electric, water, and sewage), but it doesn't have a boat launch, picnic area, or beach.

Willow Bay is open year-round. Dewdrop and Kiasutha are open from Memorial Day weekend through Labor Day. Red Bridge is open from the first weekend in April through the second weekend in December. For periods from Memorial Day through Labor Day, some campsites can be reserved through the federal recreation portal www.recreation.gov or by calling 877/444-6777. To reserve a site during fringe seasons, contact concessionaire Allegheny Site Management (814/368-4158, www.alleghenysite.com). Campsite fees are

$18–30; the four-person cabins at Willow Bay rent for $45 per night.

The Forest Service also operates five primitive campgrounds along the reservoir that can only be reached by foot or boat. Handsome Lake, Hooks Brook, Hopewell, Morrison, and Pine Grove are open year-round and have vault toilets and water pumps. Campsites are available on a first-come, first-served basis for $10 per night. Camping on the reservoir's shores is prohibited except in these designated areas.

Fishing

The Allegheny Reservoir has produced record-setting walleye, northern pike, and channel catfish. That shouldn't come as a surprise; "Kinzua," after all, is Seneca for "place of many big fishes." Keep in mind that a Pennsylvania fishing license doesn't fly in New York's share of the reservoir, where jurisdiction is divided between the state and the Seneca Nation. Be sure to have a license from the appropriate agency for the portion of lake you're fishing. When he's not competing in professional walleye tournaments, Charlie Brant of **Allegheny Guide Service** (www.alleghenyguideservice .com) can help you pull in a trophy fish. He can be reached at 814/757-9514 or 814/688-7556.

OTHER SIGHTS
Historic Warren

The city of Warren boasts a 28-block National Historic District, thanks to house-proud lumber and oil barons of the 19th and 20th centuries. Ask for a self-guided walking tour brochure at the **Warren County Historical Society** (210 4th Ave., 814/723-1795, www .warrenhistory.org, 8:30 A.M.–4:30 P.M. Mon.–Fri. year-round and 9 A.M.–noon Sat. in summer). The society's headquarters is itself a historic property, an 1870s Second Empire–style house that's especially enchanting come Christmastime. The tour ends at the **Warren County Court House** (204 4th Ave., 8:30 A.M.–4:30 P.M. Mon.–Fri.), site of a 1954 courtroom shooting that left a judge dead and captured the nation's attention. You can still find bullet holes in the woodwork.

Near Warren

The hodgepodge of artifacts at the **Wilder Museum** (51 Erie Ave., Irvine, 814/563-7773, www.warrenhistory.org/wilder_museum .htm, 5–8 P.M. Thurs., 1–4 P.M. Fri., and 11 A.M.–2 P.M. Sat. Apr.–Oct. and 9 A.M.–3 P.M. Tues. in summer, by donation) includes a one-handed clock invented in Warren and a two-person vacuum. With 14 exhibit rooms, the museum operated by the Warren County Historical Society even has space for a 1963 Mercedes-Benz. Tiny Irvine is about eight miles west of Warren along U.S. 6.

Call ahead to make sure someone is in at the **Simpler Times Museum** (Rte. 62, 5 miles north of Tidioute, 814/484-3483, open by chance or appointment), an oversized private collection of equipment related to the oil and farming industries. Oil scouts poured into Tidioute and other nearby towns in the latter half of the 19th century, drilling well after well. By the early 1900s there were 13 refineries within a six-mile radius of Warren. (The United Refining Company, founded in 1902, is still standing.) Bruce Ziegler and his wife began collecting vestiges of the oil boom and farming equipment in the mid-1990s. In 15 years they amassed more than 90 gasoline pumps, hundreds of gasoline signs and globes, 100 tractors, and more than a dozen antique cars, among other things. The Simpler Times collection is housed in five buildings on their property.

Penn-Brad Oil Museum

The city of Bradford, east of the Allegheny Reservoir on U.S. 219, was once a small lumber town named Littleton. Its population exploded in the late 1800s with the discovery of a prolific oil field. In 1881, at the height of production, the field produced three-fourths of the world's oil output, and Bradford reigned as the "High-Grade Oil Metropolis of the World." The first billion-dollar field is still in business, though on a much smaller scale. Bradford's Minard Run Oil Company, owned by the same family since its establishment in 1875, is still prospecting. American Refining Group's Bradford refinery, established in 1881, is the world's oldest

the Penn-Brad Oil Museum

© ALLEGHENY NATIONAL FOREST VACATION BUREAU

continuously operating crude oil refinery. The McDonald's in downtown Bradford has the usual—Big Macs, McNuggets, fries—and a working oil well in its parking lot. Drilled in the 1870s, the well still produces about a barrel a day. (What it lacks in quantity, Pennsylvania oil makes up for in quality. Its high paraffin content makes it a prized lubricant.) The Penn-Brad Oil Museum (U.S. 219, Custer City, 3 miles south of Bradford, 814/362-1955, 10 A.M.–4 P.M. Tues.–Sat. and 1–4 P.M. Sun. Memorial Day–Labor Day, admission $5, seniors $4.50, children under 12 free) takes visitors back to oil boom times. Its large collection of oil field artifacts boasts a 72-foot-tall drilling rig.

◖ Zippo/Case Museum

The most visited museum in the region isn't dedicated to art or history but a little bit of both: the Zippo lighter. The Zippo was born in the early 1930s, after Bradford native George G. Blaisdell noticed a friend fumbling with an Austrian-made lighter. Blaisdell decided to make a lighter that was easier to use and handsome to boot. The first lighter he produced is one of hundreds of models and prototypes displayed at the museum within the Zippo/Case Visitors Center (1932 Zippo Dr., Bradford, 814/368-1932, www.zippo.com, 9 A.M.–5 P.M. Mon.–Sat., 11 A.M.–4 P.M. Sun., open until 7 P.M. Thurs., free). The museum tells the uncommonly compelling story of how a lighter became a cultural icon with more than 1,000 movie, TV, and stage credits under its belt. Its collection includes contemporary artworks created with Zippos and examples of "trench art"—lighters decorated by servicemen during wartime. "If I had a farm in Vietnam and a home in hell I'd sell my farm and go home," one soldier carved on his Zippo. Knives made by W.R. Case & Sons Cutlery, a subsidiary of Zippo Manufacturing Company since 1993, are also exhibited.

Visitors can watch technicians at work in the Zippo Repair Clinic. The company fixes or replaces any broken Zippo, no matter how mangled, free of charge. (Tours of the factory, elsewhere in Bradford, are not available.) The store adjacent to the museum sells the complete line of Zippo and Case products, including collectors' items not found anywhere else.

Eldred World War II Museum

Even before the United States entered World War II, the town of Eldred was contributing to the Allied effort. A munitions plant serving British armed forces began operating in the Eldred area in mid-1941. Production for American troops began after the Japanese attack on Pearl Harbor in December of that year. The National Munitions Company employed 1,500 people—mostly women—and produced eight million bombs, mortar shells, and fuses in less than four years. The plant has since been dismantled, but Eldred hasn't forgotten its role in the global conflict. The Eldred World War II Museum (201 Main St., Eldred, 814/225-2220, www.eldredwwiimuseum.net, 10 A.M.–4 P.M. Tues.–Sat., 1–4 P.M. Sun., admission $5, children free) tells the story of the home front and the war abroad through artifacts, automated dioramas, and videos. An extensive library

Eldred World War II Museum

boasts rare and out-of-print books. Eldred is about 17 miles east of Bradford at the junction of Routes 346 and 446.

Kinzua Sky Walk

When the Kinzua Bridge was built in 1882, it was the highest and longest railroad bridge in the world. Measuring 301 feet tall and 2,053 feet long, the bridge spanning Kinzua Creek was heralded as a work of engineering genius. Originally built of iron, it was reconstructed of steel less than 20 years later to handle heavier trains loaded with coal, timber, and oil. Long after it was outranked by other bridges and discarded by the Erie Railroad in 1959, sightseers packed excursion trains to cross it. A *New York Times* writer described soaring over the Kinzua gorge as "more akin to ballooning than railroading." But after more than a century of service, the man-made marvel was no match for Mother Nature. In July 2003, in the midst of an extensive restoration, a tornado ripped 11 of the bridge's 20 towers from their concrete bases, strewing them on the valley floor.

The bridge was not rebuilt. But the state

"AS LONG AS THE GRASS SHALL GROW"

Kinzua Dam flooded lands that had been promised to the Seneca Nation by President George Washington. Native American folksinger Peter La Farge wrote a song about the plight of the Senecas, which Johnny Cash recorded in 1964. "As Long as the Grass Shall Grow" is the first song on Cash's *Bitter Tears* album.

> *. . . On the Seneca reservation there is much sadness now*
> *Washington's treaty has been broken, and there is no hope no how*
> *All across the Allegheny River, they're throwing up a dam*
> *It will flood the Indian country, a proud day for Uncle Sam . . .*
> *As long as the moon shall rise*
> *As long as the rivers flow*
> *As long as the sun will shine*
> *As long as the grass shall grow*

is transforming six surviving towers into the Kinzua Sky Walk, a walkway ending at an overlook with a glass floor. Located in **Kinzua Bridge State Park** (Rte. 3011/Lindholm Rd., 4 miles north of Rte. 6 at Mount Jewett, 814/965-2646, www.dcnr.state.pa.us/stateparks/parks/kinzuabridge.aspx), the Sky Walk is arguably the best place in Pennsylvania to revel in the colors of fall.

Mount Jewett Heritage Mural

The region's natural and cultural assets are on full display in the U.S. 6 town of Mount Jewett—on the wall of a building. The Mount Jewett Heritage Mural (Main St., www.kongho.com) is a 3,600-square-foot celebration of the national forest, the Allegheny River, and the area's diverse wildlife. The Viking ship at its center never sailed the Allegheny; it pays homage to the Swedish immigrants who settled in Mount Jewett in the 19th century. The four-story mural also depicts the octagonal Nebo Chapel, the still-standing Lutheran church they built on a hilltop west of town. Muralist Kong Ho, a Chinese immigrant and professor of art at the University of Pittsburgh at Bradford, turned the wall into a work of art in 2004.

Smethport Mansion District

Fifteen miles east of Mount Jewett, U.S. 6

merges with Main Street in the borough of Smethport, governmental seat of McKean County. As lumber and oil riches poured into Smethport in the latter half of the 19th century, mansions mushroomed along its tree-lined streets. Begin your tour of the Mansion District at the **McKean County Courthouse** on Main Street/U.S. 6 between Church and

Smethport Mansion District

PENNSYLVANIA WILDS

State Streets. You'll find walking tour brochures at a kiosk on the lawn of the courthouse. Don't miss the McKean County Historical Society's **Old Jail Museum** (502 W. King St., 814/887-5142, 1–4 P.M. Tues.–Thurs. Apr.–May, Mon.–Fri. June–Aug., Tues.–Thurs. Sept.–Oct., admission $4, seniors and children 6–12 $2) housed in—you got it—Smethport's old jail. The local history museum boasts the largest collection of artifacts related to the Civil War's Bucktail Regiment, which was organized in Smethport.

Across the Border

Warren and McKean Counties abut New York, and a drive across the border opens new avenues of entertainment and recreation. The **Seneca Allegany Casino & Hotel** and the **Seneca-Iroquois National Museum,** off I-86 in Salamanca, New York, are less than 20 miles from Bradford and within 50 of Warren. **Holiday Valley,** a ski and golf resort in Ellicottville, New York, is 26 miles north of Bradford on U.S. 219. Other New York attractions within a short drive of the border include the **Lucy-Desi Museum** in Lucille Ball's hometown of Jamestown and the gigantic boulders of **Rock City Park** near the city of Olean.

ENTERTAINMENT AND EVENTS
Performing Arts

The **Struthers Library Theatre** (302 W. 3rd Ave., Warren, 814/723-7231, www.struthers librarytheatre.com) in the heart of Warren's Historic District was built in 1883. It's home to the **Warren Players** (www.warrenplayers.com), an amateur theater company organized in 1930, and an annual film series. The **Warren Concert Association** (814/723-2348, www.warrencon certassociation.com) brings everything from bluegrass to baroque to the Struthers.

The **Bradford Creative & Performing Arts Center** (814/362-2522, www.bcpac.com) presents music, theater, and dance by talented Bradfordians as well as professional artists and troupes from around the country. Performances are held in the Bradford Area High School auditorium or the 500-seat Bromeley Family Theater on the campus of the University of Pittsburgh at Bradford.

The hexagon-shaped **Verna Leith Sawmill Theatre** at the Cook Forest Sawmill Center for the Arts (140-170 Theatre Ln., Cooksburg, 814/927-6655, www.sawmill.org) hosts performances by area theater groups and Clarion University from late May through mid-September. The lights go down at 8 P.M. Come early to shop at the **Sawmill Center Craft Market,** where more than 200 artisans sell their work.

Festivals and Events

For two summer days, Kane's Evergreen Park is the site of a fledgling fine arts show, **Art in the Wilds** (814/837-7167, www.artinthewilds .org, late June, free), that offers up works in a wide array of mediums. Wood is the favored medium at the **Johnny Appleseed Festival** (814/968-3906, www.johnnyappleseedfest.net, early Oct., free) in the forest town of Sheffield. In addition to chainsaw carving, the three-day event features contests between professional lumberjacks from as far away as New Zealand.

Perfectly sane people plunge into insanely cold water during Warren County's **Winterfest** (814/726-1222, www.wcvb.net, Jan., free) at Chapman State Park. In addition to the "polar bear plunge," the weekend festival includes ice fishing and snow-sculpting contests, sled dog races, and sleigh rides.

SPORTS AND RECREATION
Hearts Content National Scenic Area

In the mid-1800s, a lumber company spared a 20-acre parcel of virgin timber about 15 miles southwest of Warren. It was donated to the Forest Service in 1922, and in 1934, the remnant tree stand and 102 surrounding acres were designated the Hearts Content National Scenic Area. A mile-long interpretive trail winds through the stand of mostly white pine and eastern hemlock, some of which are

Warren County's Winterfest

300–400 years old. To reach the area, take the Mohawk exit of U.S. 6 and follow Pleasant Drive south for 11 miles. At the hard curve, turn left onto a gravel road and continue south for four miles. The scenic area is on the left side of the road. A campground built by the Civilian Conservation Corps in 1936 is on the right. Its 26 campsites are available on a first-come, first-served basis.

State Parks

The 805-acre **Chapman State Park** (4790 Chapman Dam Rd., off U.S. 6, Clarendon, 814/723-0250, www.dcnr.state.pa.us/stateparks/parks/chapman.aspx) is sandwiched between national forest and state game lands about nine miles south of Warren and serves as a trailhead for hundreds of miles of hiking, biking, cross-country skiing, and snowmobiling trails. Adventurers loath to leave their vehicles on public roadways can park at Chapman for free. The 68-acre Chapman Lake has a boat launch, mooring spaces, fishing piers, and a sand beach open from late May

to mid-September. Rental canoes, kayaks, paddleboats, and bicycles are available. In winter, there's a skating area on the lake and a seven-acre groomed slope for sledding and tobogganing. Visitors can defrost by the wood-burning stove in the park's warming hut.

The towering, wide-girthed white pines and hemlocks of the "Forest Cathedral," a National Natural Landmark at **Cook Forest State Park** (Rte. 36, Cooksburg, 814/744-8407, www.dcnr.state.pa.us/stateparks/parks/cookforest.aspx), have been around since the days of Pennsylvania's founding. It's one of four old-growth timber areas in the 8,500-acre park south of Allegheny National Forest. Word is that some of the trees are 450 years old, having survived a large forest fire in 1644. The park has an environmental learning center and offers interpretive programs year-round. The Clarion River, which flows along the eastern border of the park, is popular with paddlers and anglers.

Campsites, cabins, and picnic pavilions in both state parks can be reserved online at www.pa.reserveworld.com or by calling 888/727-2757.

ATV Riding

The national forest has more than 100 miles of trails for all-terrain vehicles and motorbikes. The easiest is the 39-mile **Timberline** trail system, which includes many old roads and railroad grades. It ties into the more challenging **Marienville** trails, which total 37 miles. **Willow Creek** is a 10-mile loop trail rated "more difficult." The northern loop of the 22-mile **Rocky Gap** trail is reserved for expert riders.

The trails are open to ATVs and motorbikes from the Friday before Memorial Day through the last Sunday in September. All but Willow Creek and a portion of Marienville are also open from late December through March. Trails are marked with yellow diamond-shaped blazes. Riding on unmarked routes is a major no-no, as is riding without a $35 annual permit. Directions to trailheads, trail condition reports, and a permit application can be found on the Allegheny National Forest website (www .fs.fed.us/r9/forests/allegheny).

Allegheny Recreation Rentals (217 W. Washington St., Bradford, 814/817-1283, www.rentrecreation.com) offers ATVs as well as scooters, bicycles, camping equipment—just about anything an adventurer might need.

Bicycling

The national forest's ATV and snowmobile trails are open to mountain bikers, as are its gated roads. Bikes are also permitted on some hiking trails. Road cyclists can pedal through the forest on U.S. 6. The state-endorsed BicyclePA Route Y generally follows U.S. 6 from one end of the state to the other.

Boating and Paddling

There's no horsepower limit on the deep waters of the **Allegheny Reservoir** or on **Tionesta Lake** (Rte. 36, just south of Tionesta, 814/755-3512, www.lrp.usace.army.mil/rec/lakes/tionesta.htm), an Army Corps project at the southwest corner of the national forest. On

summer weekends, nonmotorized watercraft are better off on less trafficked waterways.

The **Allegheny River** below Kinzua Dam sees a good number of professional canoe and kayak races, but it's gentle enough for novices. Contact the Pennsylvania Fish & Boat Commission (814/337-0444, www.fish.state .pa.us) for a free guide, *Middle Allegheny River Water Trail,* to the 107-mile, island-peppered section from Kinzua Dam to Emlenton. Better yet, drop $30 for the spiral-bound and water-resistant *Allegheny River Paddling Guide,* chock-full of practical information like where to camp or buy a cup of coffee. It's published by the amiable owners of **Allegheny Outfitters** (2101 Pennsylvania Ave. E., Warren, 814/723-1203, www.alleghenyoutfitters.com), which facilitates canoe and kayak trips on the 15-miles stretch between Kinzua Dam and the national forest's Buckaloons recreation area. The livery is open daily from Memorial Day weekend through Labor Day, shuttling paddlers to the dam every hour from 10 A.M.–2 P.M. on weekdays and 9 A.M.–5 P.M. on weekends. Its sister livery, **Indian Waters** (10074 Rte. 62, 5 miles north of Tidioute, 814/484-3252, www .alleghenyindianwaters.com), offers day trips of 5–15 miles and overnight journeys as far as Emlenton. It's open Thursday through Monday from Memorial Day weekend through Labor Day. Shuttles leave every hour 10 A.M.–2 P.M. on weekdays and 8 A.M.–5 P.M. on weekends. (Don't say who told you, but owners Piper and Josh Lindell can be cajoled into earlier trips.) Both liveries offer river trips by reservation before Labor Day weekend and after Memorial Day.

Tionesta-based **Outback Adventures** (Rte. 62, next to Tionesta Bridge, 814/755-3658, www.escape.to/outback) specializes in trips on **Tionesta Creek** as well as the Allegheny River. The creek makes for a magical float in early spring; by June, water levels are generally too low for canoeing. Outback Adventures also operates a riverfront campground.

The **Clarion River,** one of the major tributaries of the Allegheny, was once believed to be the most polluted river in Pennsylvania (think acid mine drainage). You wouldn't know it from the recovered section that snakes along the southern border of the national forest and continues past Cook Forest State Park. **Cook Forest Canoe Rental** (Rte. 36 at Clarion River Bridge, Cooksburg, 814/744-8094, www.cookforest canoe.com, daily June–Aug., weekends Apr.–May and Sept.–Oct.) offers canoes, kayaks, tubes, and transportation to launch points. The nearby **Pale Whale Canoe Fleet** (6 River Rd., 0.25 mile from Rte. 36, Cooksburg, 814/744-8300, www.canoecookforest.com, Apr.–Oct.) even rents floating coolers.

Fishing

The national forest's reservoirs and hundreds of miles of streams are home to dozens of species of fish. Like the Allegheny Reservoir, the Allegheny River below Kinzua Dam is known for trophies. The river town of Tidioute is the longtime host of the **Pennsylvania State Championship Fishing Tournament** (814/484-3585), held the last weekend in September. The section between the dam and the city of Warren rarely freezes, allowing for open water fishing even in winter. **Allegheny Guide Service** (www.alleghenyguideservice.com) founder Red Childress specializes in river fishing. He can be reached at 814/723-5912 or 814/688-2309. U.S. Coast Guard Master Captain Josh Jekielek is the trout-centric angler behind **Northcountry Outfitters** (814/726-1570, www.alleghenytroutfishing.com). He offers walk-and-wade trips throughout the national forest region as well as drift boat trips on the Allegheny River.

Hiking

Hundreds of miles of hiking trails snake through the Allegheny National Forest and public and private lands on its borders. The **North Country National Scenic Trail,** which stretches from New York to North Dakota, traverses the length of the national forest. Printed guides are available through the North Country Trail Association (616/897-5987, www.north countrytrail.org).

Trails near the Allegheny Reservoir include the **Morrison Trail,** an 11.4-mile loop that can be broken into two shorter loops. The trailhead parking lot is off Route 59, seven miles east of Kinzua Dam. The trail leads to the primitive Morrison campground on the shores of the reservoir. The 34-mile **Tracy Ridge Trail** system includes a reservoir-skirting portion of the North Country Trail. The system of interconnecting loops starts at the Tracy Ridge recreation area, located along Route 321 about 3.5 miles south of the juncture with Route 346.

Trails in the southern part of the forest include the 9.6-mile **Buzzard Swamp** system, near the town of Marienville. Buzzard Swamp—a string of 15 man-made ponds—offers some of the best wildlife viewing in the forest, especially during the spring waterfowl migration. From Marienville, follow Lamonaville Road 2.5 miles east to reach the northern trailhead. Buzzard Swamp Road, a.k.a. Forest Road 157, is about a mile south of Marienville and leads to the southern trailhead.

Guides to these and other trails are available on the Allegheny National Forest website (www.fs.fed.us/r9/forests/allegheny) and at Forest Service and tourism promotion offices.

Horseback Riding

Riding is permitted in most parts of the Allegheny National Forest. A number of ranches on its borders supply well-mannered horses. The 600-acre **Flying W Ranch** (Rte. 666, Kelletville, ranch 814/463-7663, restaurant 814/463-5001, www.theflyingwranch.com) offers trail rides and overnight pack trips, along with accommodations ranging from primitive campgrounds to a five-bedroom farmhouse. Flying W hosts the **Allegheny Mountain Championship Rodeo** in July, which features steer wrestling, bronco riding, and other man-versus-wild spectacles.

Sixty dollars buys a two-hour trail ride and a steak dinner at **Hickory Creek Wilderness Ranch** (Economite Rd., Tidioute, 814/484-7520, www.hickorycreekranch.com). Trail rides of up to six hours leave from the ranch's campground, where humans and their horses can share a site. The ranch welcomes professional bull riders for July's **Battle on Bull Mountain.**

Skydiving

The **Freefall OZ Skydiving Center** (off New York Rte. 417, Ceres Township, PA, 814/697-7218, www.freefallozskydiving.com, 9 A.M.–sunset daily spring–fall) offers tandem jumps and freefall instruction—and killer breakfasts. Owners Ash and Celeine Easdon-Smith turned a century-old barn on their property into a rustic-chic B&B, **Oz's Homestay** (www.ozhomestay-huntinglodge.com, $119–139). Ash, who hails from Australia, crafted much of the furniture from trees from the 122-acre property. Pilots can land on the couple's private airstrip.

Winter Sports

The national forest has more than 300 miles of snowmobiling trails and about 50 miles of cross-country skiing trails. The only groomed skiing trail is **Laurel Mill,** located three miles west of the town of Ridgway on Spring Creek Road. Visit the Allegheny National Forest website (www.fs.fed.us/r9/forests/allegheny) for trail maps and snow conditions.

ACCOMMODATIONS

Campgrounds and cabins abound in the national forest region, but it also offers unique lodging options like the Lodge at Glendorn, a member of the uber-exclusive Relais & Chateaux group.

Under $100

Kane Manor (230 Clay St., Kane, 814/837-6522, www.kanemanor.com, $49–69) was built in the final years of the 19th century for Elizabeth Kane, widow of Thomas L. Kane, the abolitionist and Civil War general for whom the town of Kane is named. Today it's a B&B with 10 guest rooms, period furnishings, Kane family mementos, and an impressive portico overlooking the lush grounds.

Hand-crocheted afghans and homemade baked goods await at **The Inn on Maple Street Bed & Breakfast** (115 E. Maple St., Port Allegany, 814/642-5171, www.theinnonmaplestreet.com, $75–165), one block off U.S. 6 in picturesque Port Allegany. (Don't go looking for a port in town. Its name honors its history as a launching point for canoe journeys down the Allegheny River.) Innkeeper Jay D. Roush will deliver a breakfast basket to your room if you can't bear to change out of the fluffy bathrobes.

$100-200

The **Horton House Bed & Breakfast** (504 Market St., Warren, 814/723-7472, www.hortonhousebb.com, $178–238) is named for Isaac Horton, the lumber magnate who built the 7,500-square-foot house (of wood, naturally) in the late 1800s. Its seven rooms are so lovingly decorated that it's hard to tell which were the servants' quarters. Guests can soak in the outdoor hot tub year-round.

Built in 1934 at the "gateway" to Cook Forest State Park, **(Gateway Lodge** (14870 Rte. 36, Cooksburg, 814/744-8017, www.gatewaylodge.com, rooms $95–125, suites $199–250, cabins $129–215, weekly rates available for cabins) has morphed into the picture of rustic elegance in the hands of Deb Adams, its owner since 2006. It boasts fireside Jacuzzis, private balconies, and great food and wines. The restaurant, which serves breakfast ($10) and dinner ($8–45), is open to the public. So is the onsite spa, which offers a menu of massages, facials, and hand and foot treatments.

Over $200

Pull up to the **(Lodge at Glendorn** (1000 Glendorn Dr., Bradford, 814/362-6511, www.glendorn.com, rooms from $199, suites and cabins from $449) and a staff member or two will be waiting outside to greet you. Sink into a velvety couch in the all-redwood main lodge and another will offer you a drink. Come dinnertime, a seasoned server will produce a menu written just for you. Prefer to have the executive chef cook for you in the privacy of a hilltop cabin? Just ask. The effect is rare and

the Lodge at Glendorn

priceless: You'll feel like you own the place. Indeed, for almost 70 years, Glendorn was a private estate, an idyllic retreat for the oil-rich Dorn family. They opened it to the public in 1995, and it quickly earned a reputation as one of the nation's premier hideaways. The fenced 1,280-acre property, which abuts the Allegheny National Forest, is so secluded that many area residents don't know what or where it is—all the better for guests like Denzel Washington, who stayed there during filming of 2009's runaway-train thriller *Unstoppable*. One of only two Orvis-endorsed fly-fishing lodges in Pennsylvania (the other is Nemacolin Woodlands in the Laurel Highlands region), Glendorn offers the fly fisher nearly three miles of privately managed trout angling. Other amenities include three trout-filled ponds, a 60-foot pool, tennis courts, a trap and skeet shooting range, and a vast trail system. Most activities, including horseback riding, snowmobiling, cross-country skiing, snowshoeing, and curling, are free to guests. You don't have to be a guest to experience fine dining at Glendorn (breakfast $15, lunch $29, dinner $75–105).

FOOD
Bradford
The 【 **Option House** (41 Main St., 814/368-4780, www.theoptionhouserestaurant.com, dinner 5–10 P.M. Thurs.–Sat., lounge 4:30–11 P.M. Thurs.–Sat., $9–25) is so named because of its 19th century clientele: men who traded options at the Bradford Oil Exchange next door. The exchange is long gone, but the name is still fitting. Today's clientele can choose between the pub-like Trading Room Lounge with its long oak bar or the formal Peacock Parlors dining room. The original dumb waiter has been completely restored—along with the rest of the elegant restaurant—and carries drinks between the first- and second-floor bars. Food options range from cheese-smothered fries to lobster tail.

Kane
You can swirl, sniff, sip, and go—or stay a while—at **Flickerwood Wine Cellars** (309 Flickerwood Rd., 814/837-7566, www.flickerwood.com, 11 A.M.–6 P.M. Mon.–Thurs., 10 A.M.–9 P.M. Fri.–Sat., noon–6 P.M. Sun.). The award-winning winery added a lounge in 2007 where guests can savor a glass of wine while noshing on cheese and pepperoni, chicken skewers, mini quiches, and other hors d'oeuvres. Flickerwood's reds, whites, and blushes are the creations of Ron Zampogna, who served the red, white, and blue as a Forest Service employee for 36 years. The winery is located off Route 6 just east of Kane.

Warren
The 【 **Plaza Restaurant** (328 Pennsylvania Ave. W., 814/723-5660, 7 A.M.–8 P.M. Mon.–Sat., $6–9) is "still doing things the hard way," according to its owner, whose Greek-born father opened the diner in 1959. In other words, it still makes just about everything from scratch—from mashed potatoes to heavenly pies. Skip the standard diner grub and order a Greek specialty like souvlaki or spinach pie.

PENNSYLVANIA WILDS

And don't you dare pass up dessert. The graham cracker pie is especially delightful. **Legends** (809 Jackson Ave. Ext., 814/723-9170, www.legends.dinerz.com, 5–9 P.M. Tues.–Sat., $8–18) is known as much for its decor as its steaks, seafood, and massive sandwiches. A 1953 Santa Fe caboose serves as one of its dining rooms, an ice-filled clawfoot tub serves as the salad bar, and desserts are laid out in the open trunk of a 1949 pink Cadillac. Crank telephones, vintage gas pumps, pump organs, and other antiques decorate every corner.

Kitsch-free and chic, **The Cafe** (211 Liberty St., 814/726-3082, www.thelibertystreetcafe.com, 5–9 P.M. Tues.–Sat., reservations recommended, $18–34) offers a frequently changing menu of world cuisine. Nowhere else in the Wilds can you find Vietnamese pork pho, Thai red curry chicken, and Italian osso bucco on the same menu.

Westline

The town of Westline is a speckle on forest maps. Find it and you'll be rewarded with fine French cuisine. **The Westline Inn** (Westline Rd., 814/778-5103, www.westlineinn.com, opens at 3 P.M. Sun.–Thurs., noon Fri.–Sat., dinner 5:30–9 P.M. Mon.–Thurs., 5:30–10 P.M. Fri.–Sat., 3–7 P.M. Sun., bar closing time varies, reservations recommended, $9–30) offers escargot bourguignonne, crepes stuffed with seafood, bouillabaisse, and the like. Chef Jon Pomeroy cooks in the French provincial style, meaning steaks are cooked in a broiler, not on an open grill. Prefer an American-style burger? Ask for the pub menu. First, though, you have to find the place. From the intersection of U.S. 6 and U.S. 219, head north on 219 for five miles to a sign pointing left to Westline. Follow the narrow road for three miles.

INFORMATION AND SERVICES

The headquarters of the **Allegheny National Forest** (4 Farm Colony Dr., Warren, 814/723-5150, www.fs.fed.us/r9/forests/allegheny, 8 A.M.–4:30 P.M. Mon.–Fri.) are about five miles north of downtown Warren on Route 62. You'll find free brochures on recreation in the forest as well as T-shirts, topographical maps, books on plants and birds, and other merchandise. Two ranger districts also offer a wealth of informational materials. The **Bradford Ranger District** (29 Forest Service Dr., Bradford, 814/362-4613) can be found near the junction of Routes 59 and 321, 11 miles east of the dam. The lower part of the forest is overseen by the **Marienville Ranger District** (131 Smokey Ln., Marienville, 814/927-6628, 8 A.M.–4:30 P.M. Mon.–Fri., 7 A.M.–4:30 P.M. Sat., 7 A.M.–1 P.M. Sun.).

The Army Corps of Engineers operates the seasonal **Big Bend Visitor Center** (Rte. 59, nine miles east of Warren, 814/726-0678, 10 A.M.–3:45 P.M. daily Memorial Day weekend–Labor Day, weekends Sept.–Oct.), just downstream of Kinzua Dam. For a daily summary of water conditions, call 814/726-0164.

The national forest stretches across four counties represented by three tourism promotion agencies, each of which can supply a plethora of information about the region. The **Warren County Visitors Bureau** (22045 U.S. 6, Warren, 814/726-1222, www.wcvb.net, 9 A.M.–4:30 P.M. Mon.–Fri., 11 A.M.–4 P.M. Sat.) is about six miles west of downtown Warren. The **Allegheny National Forest Vacation Bureau** (800/473-9370, www.visit anf.com), which represents McKean County, has its headquarters in downtown Bradford (80 E. Corydon St., 9 A.M.–5 P.M. Mon.–Fri.). In cooperation with the Forest Service, the vacation bureau operates a seasonal visitors center at the Foote Rest Campground (3183 U.S. 219, Lantz Corners) near the intersection of U.S. 6 and U.S. 219. It's open 8 A.M.–9 P.M. on weekends and 9 A.M.–5 P.M. on weekdays in the summer. The lower part of the forest lies in Forest and Elk Counties, which are represented by the **Great Outdoors Visitors Bureau** (175 Main St., Brookville, 800/348-9393, 8:30 A.M.–4:30 P.M. Mon.–Fri.).

GETTING THERE AND AROUND

The forest region, like the rest of the Wilds, is driving country. The national forest is roughly framed by Route 62 on the west and U.S. 219 on the east. U.S. 6 wriggles through it. Another east–west road, Route 59, passes by Kinzua Dam and over the Allegheny Reservoir, the recreational heart of the forest.

Bradford Regional Airport (BFD) and **DuBois Regional Airport** (DUJ) offer direct service to and from Cleveland, as does New York's **Chautauqua County Airport-Jamestown** (JHW), about 25 miles north of Warren. The larger **Erie International Airport** (ERI) and **Buffalo Niagara International Airport** (BUF) are within a two-hour drive of the forest.

Pine Creek Gorge and Vicinity

Pine Creek Gorge is Pennsylvania's take on the Grand Canyon. The glacially carved canyon starts near the U.S. 6 village of Ansonia and continues south for 47 miles. Most visitors take in its majesty from state parks on opposite rims near its northern end, where the gorge is about 800 feet deep. At Waterville, near its southern end, Pine Creek Gorge is a whopping 1,450 feet deep and almost a mile wide. Whopping, of course, is a relative term. The real Grand Canyon, in Arizona, is as deep as 6,000 feet and 10 miles wide on average.

Still, Pennsylvania's version is "one of the finest examples of a deep gorge in the eastern United States," according to the National Park Service, which has seen them all.

The heavily treed gorge, like Allegheny National Forest to its west, was logged nearly bare during the 1800s. Pine Creek, the largest tributary of the West Branch of the Susquehanna River, served as a major thoroughfare for the lumber industry. It carried countless logs toward the city of Williamsport, the world's lumber capital during the latter half of the 19th century.

PENNSYLVANIA WILDS

© TIOGA COUNTY VISITORS BUREAU

Pine Creek Gorge, Pennsylvania's Grand Canyon

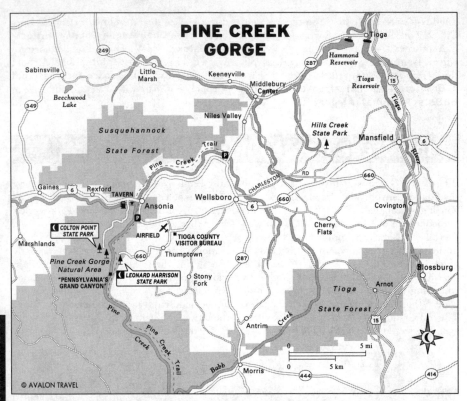

In 1883, a railroad was threaded through the canyon. It transported timber to mills, hemlock bark to tanneries, coal, and people. The last freight train passed through the gorge in October 1988. The conversion of the railway to a multi-use recreation trail began several years later. By 2008, the Pine Creek Rail Trail had grown to 60 miles. It's shared by hikers, bikers, horseback riders, cross-country skiers, and snowshoers. The swift waters of Pine Creek, which has been carving its namesake gorge for thousands of years, beckon anglers and paddlers.

COLTON POINT AND LEONARD HARRISON STATE PARKS

On the west rim of the gorge, there's Colton Point State Park. On the east, there's Leonard Harrison. The former is accessible from U.S. 6 at Ansonia, though the road leading to it is easily missed. You'll find Colton Road between a small gas station and the Burnin' Barrel Bar. Follow it for five miles to Colton Point and its series of scenic overlooks.

The better-groomed Leonard Harrison offers superior views of the canyon (and bathrooms with plumbing). From the town of Wellsboro, follow Route 660 west for 10 miles to the park. You can stop at the **Tioga County Visitors Center** (2053 Rte. 660, Wellsboro, 570/724-0635, www.visittiogapa.com, 8 A.M.–4:30 P.M. Mon.–Fri. year-round, 9 A.M.–1 P.M. Sat. May–Oct., 9 A.M.–1 P.M. Sun. Oct.) along the way. The state park office at the entrance to Leonard Harrison (4797 Rte. 660, Wellsboro, 570/724-3061, www.dcnr.state.pa.us/stateparks/parks/

leonardharrison.aspx, 8 A.M.–4 P.M. Mon.–Fri. spring–fall or as staffing allows) handles queries about both parks. The main overlook and an environmental interpretive center are a quarter of a mile up the road.

Both parks have picnic tables and pavilions, several miles of hiking trails, and campgrounds open from the second Friday in April until the third Sunday in October. Colton Point's campground with its rustic toilets is a product of the Civilian Conservation Corps era of the 1930s. Campsites are available on a first-come, first-served basis. The Leonard Harrison campground has modern facilities, including hot showers. Several campsites have electricity. They can be reserved online at www.pa.reserveworld.com or by calling 888/727-2757.

◖ PINE CREEK RAIL TRAIL

Humans have traveled through the gorge for hundreds of years. Native Americans followed footpaths along Pine Creek when its waters weren't navigable by canoe. Later, trains carrying people and the building blocks of a new nation chugged alongside the creek. It's a beaten path, all right. But to traverse the 60-mile Pine Creek Rail Trail is to experience unspoiled wilderness. Dramatic outcrops, gushing waterfalls, and diverse flora greet today's visitor.

HOW LOW CAN YOU GO?

You don't have to take on the whole of the Pine Creek Rail Trail. There are more than a dozen access areas, separated by sections of various lengths.

Section	Distance (miles)
Wellsboro Junction to Ansonia	7.6
Ansonia to Darling Run	1
Darling Run to Tiadaghton	7.7
Tiadaghton to Blackwell	8.4
Blackwell to Rattlesnake Rock	1.8
Rattlesnake Rock to Cedar Run Bridge	2.7
Cedar Run Bridge to Hilborn Fields	3.4
Hilborn Fields to Slate Run	2.5
Slate Run to Black Walnut Bottom	1.8
Black Walnut Bottom to Ross Run	2.6
Ross Run to Cammal	2.5
Cammal to Dry Run	5.3
Dry Run to Waterville	1.1
Waterville to Bonnell Flats	4.5
Bonnell Flats to Torbert Bridge	3.1
Torbert Bridge to Torbert	1.7
Torbert to Jersey Shore	2.3
Total	**60**

PENNSYLVANIA WILDS

© ANNA DUBROVSKY

on the Pine Creek Rail Trail

Then there's the wildlife. The woods are home to coyote, deer, wild turkeys, and black bears, among other creatures. River otters were reintroduced to the canyon in the 1980s and fishers in the 1990s. Even bald eagles have returned to the gorge.

The gently graded gravel path starts at Wellsboro Junction, an erstwhile railway junction at U.S. 6 and 287, about three miles north of downtown Wellsboro. It follows wriggly Marsh Creek to its confluence with Pine Creek and accompanies the latter to the town of Jersey Shore, just shy of the West Branch of the Susquehanna River. Darling Run, about nine trail miles from Wellsboro Junction, is a popular point of entry for hikers and bikers. It's located along Route 362, a mile and a half south of U.S. 6 at Ansonia and about seven miles west of Wellsboro. The horseback trailhead is along Marsh Creek Road near the junction of U.S. 6 and Route 362 at Ansonia. Horses are restricted to the dirt access road that runs alongside the trail for nine miles. Even

covered wagon tour of Pine Creek Gorge

© ANNA DUBROVSKY

non-equestrians can have a giddy-up experience of the gorge. **Mountain Trail Horse Center** (877/376-5561, www.mountaintrailhorse.com, 2-hour wagon ride $20–30, children 4–12 $10–15) offers covered wagon rides most days from late May through October. Its hand-crafted wagons, pulled by teams of Percheron draft horses, are larger and cushier than the Conestogas of yore. (Pioneers didn't have the pleasure of padded seats and shock absorbers.) Call or check the website for departure times. Walk-ins are welcome, but be sure to make a reservation from late September through mid-October, when the gorge is awash with autumn colors and demand is highest. Wagons leave from a barn on U.S. 6 in Ansonia. Mountain Trail also offers horseback trail rides and multi-day trips year-round.

Maps of the trail are available at state park, forestry, and tourism promotion offices. The trail traverses two state forests, Tioga and Tiadaghton. There are camping areas on public forestlands and private property along the trail.

DOWNTOWN WELLSBORO

The gateway to the Grand Canyon of Pennsylvania is the exceedingly charming town of Wellsboro, where gaslights burn 24/7. It's small enough to see in one day, and that's exactly why some visitors stay a few. Wellsboro's manicured town square, tree-lined streets, and general absence of hustle and bustle are almost as soothing as a spa getaway. Almost.

Let the calming begin at the town square, better known as "the green," across from the county courthouse on Main Street. The fountain statue at its center, *Wynken, Blynken, and Nod,* was inspired by an 1889 lullaby of the same name and depicts three children sailing across the sky in a wooden shoe. The bronze sculpture is a replica of the marble original in Denver. Wellsboro has another Denver connection. Its **Gmeiner Art and Cultural Center** (134 Main St., 570/724-1917, www.gmeinerarts.com, 2–5 P.M. daily, by donation) was a gift of the late Arthur Gmeiner, a Denver entrepreneur and philanthropist who was born not far from Wellsboro. Exhibits change frequently. So does the inventory at the

Wellsboro's *Wynken, Blynken, and Nod* fountain statue

© TIOGA COUNTY VISITORS BUREAU

Artisan's Shoppe (17 1/2 Crafton St., 570/724-5166, www.artisansshoppe.com, 10 A.M.–5 P.M. Mon.–Sat.), where dozens of local artists display and sell their work. Buying a piece buys you some peace of mind; profits benefit a local animal rescue group.

Information about local events, attractions, and businesses is available at the **Wellsboro Area Chamber of Commerce** (114 Main St., 570/724-1926, www.wellsboropa.com, 8:30 A.M.–4:30 P.M. Mon.–Fri.). You'll find brochures on the porch even when the chamber is closed. Pause in the front yard to meet Wellsboro's oldest resident: a massive elm tree that's been growing since the 1700s.

OTHER SIGHTS
Tioga Central Railroad

The passenger trains that once served this region are long gone, but it's still possible to ride the rails. The Tioga Central Railroad (Rte. 287, 3 miles north of downtown Wellsboro, 570/724-0990, www.tiogacentral.com, Sunset Limited $24, children 4–12 $12, Sunset

© ANNA DUBROVSKY

Tioga Central Railroad

Limited dining car $44, children 4–12 $22, children under 4 $10) operates an excursion and charter train on a 34-mile railroad extending from Wellsboro Junction to just south of Corning, New York. Dinner, brunch, and sightseeing trips are available from Memorial Day weekend through October. Santa climbs aboard for special excursions in late November and early December.

The train first passes by the Marsh Creek Wetlands, a bird-watching hot spot better known as "The Muck." It crosses over creeks and through fields where deer graze. Ask the conductor about any eagle nests along the way. Most excursions end at Hammond Lake, where it's not unusual to spot ospreys and other raptors. The train has two locomotives, one for the northbound trip and another for the return. Meals are prepared in the kitchen car under the supervision of a chef who favors local growers, which means the corn on your plate could have been in the field two hours earlier.

Pennsylvania Lumber Museum

It's hard to imagine what north-central Pennsylvania looked like when work, not play, attracted people to its woods. The Pennsylvania Lumber Museum (U.S. 6 between Galeton and Coudersport, 814/435-2652, www.lumber museum.org, 9 A.M.–5 P.M. Wed.–Sun., winter hours may vary, admission $6, seniors $5, children 3–11 $3) makes it a little easier. Thousands of artifacts, including a 1912 logging locomotive, tell the story of the state's forest industries. Visitors can tour an operational steam-powered sawmill and a recreated logging camp complete with blacksmith shop, horse barn, and mess hall. A cabin constructed in 1936 by the Civilian Conservation Corps, President Franklin D. Roosevelt's army of forest re-builders, stands near the parking lot. Modern-day "woodhicks" demonstrate axe throwing, bark peeling, cross-cut sawing, and other skills during the museum's annual **Bark Peelers' Convention,** held the weekend nearest July 4.

◖ Dark Sky Park

To feast your eyes on heavenly bodies, head to **Cherry Springs State Park** (Rte. 44, 15 miles southeast of Coudersport, 814/435-

5010, www.dcnr.state.pa.us/stateparks/parks/cherrysprings.aspx). Thanks to its exceptionally dark night sky, the tiny park is one of the best places in the eastern seaboard for stargazing. In 2008, Cherry Springs was designated as the second International Dark Sky Park by the International Dark-Sky Association, an Arizona-based nonprofit that agitates against light pollution. (Pennsylvania had already patted itself on the back, declaring Cherry Springs its first Dark Sky Park in 2000.) The fact that Cherry Springs sits atop a mountain, shielded by forest, has much to do with its spectacular night sky. It doesn't hurt that the airspace above it sees little traffic.

The park's stargazing field offers a 360-degree view of the sky. If you plan to stay for just a few hours, park at the defunct Cherry Springs Airport and walk to the field. You can drive onto the field if you're staying overnight. It's best to set up camp and equipment before nightfall. If you arrive after dark, you have to enter the field sans headlights. On a dark-moon weekend, some 200 amateur astronomers and their equipment could be scattered across the field. Four small observatories can be reserved online at www.pa.reserveworld.com or by calling 888/727-2757.

The park's location affords an excellent view of the nucleus of the Milky Way. If you can't tell Sagittarius from Scorpius, check the park's schedule of free public stargazing programs. Cherry Springs also hosts two yearly "star parties" attended by hundreds of amateur astronomers, lecturers, and equipment vendors. For a personal sky tour, contact local star guru Stash Nawrocki of **Crystal Spheres: Adventures in Stargazing** (814/848-5037, crystalspheres@gmail.com).

ENTERTAINMENT AND EVENTS
Performing Arts
The Art Deco **Arcadia Theatre** (50 Main St., Wellsboro, 570/724-4957, www.arcadiawellsboro.com) in downtown Wellsboro was built in 1921 for silent pictures. These days it shows the fruits of Hollywood's labors and art house films on four screens. Since 2002, the Arcadia has also presented live theater productions, including *Aida, Godspell,* and Stephen Sondheim's *Assassins.*

Festivals and Events
The blooming of Pennsylvania's state flower is cause for much merrymaking in Wellsboro. The **Pennsylvania State Laurel Festival** (570/724-1926, http://laurelfestival.tripod.com) starts the second weekend in June and continues through the third. Events include a road cycling race, a 10K foot race, a crafts fair, and not one but two parades—one featuring local pets and the other a more traditional showcase of musical units, floats, and contenders for the Laurel Queen crown. The

A DIMLY LIT TUSSLE

The world's first night football game was played on September 28, 1892, on a field in Mansfield, Pennsylvania. Electric lights and the game of football were both novelties, so organizers weren't surprised that a crowd of thousands gathered to watch it. The players wore little padding and no helmets, and the lighting was so minimal that it was hard to tell which team had the ball (a larger, rounder forebear of today's versions). Before either squad could score, the referee deemed it too dangerous to continue.

A reenactment of the anticlimactic but historic game is the highlight of Mansfield's **Fabulous 1890's Weekend** (570/662-3442, http://1890sweekend.com, last weekend in Sept.). Mansfield University students and area residents play by the rules of 1892 in uniforms created 100 years later for a commercial for General Electric, which supplied the lights for the first night game. The game is followed by fireworks, just as it was in 1892. The Fabulous 1890's parade also strives for historical accuracy, which means no motors and a whole lot of horses.

latter parade is always on the third Saturday in June.

The parade of renowned musicians who perform at the **Endless Mountain Music Festival** (570/662-5030, box office 570/787-7800, www.endlessmountain.net, summer, admission charged) makes it one of Pennsylvania's premier classical music events. The international festival was born in 2006, after a vacation in Wellsboro convinced acclaimed conductor Stephen Gunzenhauser that mountain scenery and world-class music would be a potent combination. By 2009, it had grown to 16 concerts over 17 days. The festival features solo recitals, chamber music concerts, and an orchestra of musicians from around the world—conducted, of course, by the maestro who fell in love with the mountains.

The hills are alive with the buzz of chainsaws during the **Woodsmen's Show** (814/435-6855, www.woodsmenshow.com, early Aug., admission charged) at Cherry Springs State Park. ESPN watchers may recognize the pro lumberjacks who face off in events like two-man logrolling, ax throwing, and tree felling. Amateurs can also test their skills. Chainsaw artists create masterpieces on-site over the course of the weekend. The three-day **Hickory Fest** (570/439-4079, www.hickoryfest.com, mid-Aug., admission charged) brings the finest in bluegrass and acoustic music to canyon country.

True nostalgics should visit Wellsboro the first full weekend in December, when Main Street is transformed into an early Victorian marketplace for the **Dickens of a Christmas** celebration. Costumed food and craft vendors, carolers, and street-corner thespians help turn back the clock.

SHOPPING
Wellsboro
The bulk of Wellsboro's shops line Main Street. No national chains here. Wellsboro's answer to Barnes & Noble is **From My Shelf Books** (87 Main St., 570/724-5793, www.wellsboro bookstore.com, 9 A.M.–6 P.M. Mon.–Sat., 11 A.M.–3 P.M. Sun.). The ever-changing stock of new and gently used books includes out-of-print treasures. The nearby **Shabby Rue** (69 Main St., 570/723-8809, www.shabbyrue.com, 10 A.M.–5 P.M. Mon.–Thurs., 10 A.M.–7 P.M. Fri.–Sat., 11 A.M.–3 P.M. Sun.) deals in treasures for the home. **Dunham's** (45 Main St., 570/724-1905, www.dunhamswellsboro.com, 10 A.M.–5:30 P.M. Mon.–Sat., noon–4 P.M. Sun.), one of the oldest family-owned department stores in the country, has called Wellsboro home since 1905. During the Great Depression, when rural folk had no way of getting to town, Dunham's turned a truck into a "rolling store" stocked with dry goods, hardware, and candy.

Adventurers can stock up on gear and apparel by the likes of Marmot, Kelty, and SIGG at **Wild Asaph Outfitters** (71 Main St., 570/724-5155, www.wildasaphoutfitters.com, 10 A.M.–8 P.M. Mon., 10 A.M.–5:30 P.M. Tues.–Thurs., 10 A.M.–6 P.M. Fri., 10 A.M.–5 P.M. Sat., by chance Sun.). The store, opened by a pair of women not long after they finished a thru-hike of the Appalachian Trail, is a good source of information about area trails and rock-climbing spots. **Country Ski & Sports** (81 Main St., 570/724-3858, www.countryski andsports.net, 9:30 A.M.–6 P.M. Mon., Tues., and Thurs., 9:30 A.M.–5 P.M. Wed. and Sat., 9:30 A.M.–8 P.M. Fri., hours vary in Dec.) offers kayaks in the warmer months, skiing and snowboarding equipment in the colder ones, and bikes all year-round.

SPORTS AND RECREATION
Biking
Bikers who want a bumpier ride than the Pine Creek Rail Trail provides can find any number of backcountry routes in and around the gorge. The Asaph section of the Tioga State Forest, site of the **Laurel Classic Mountain Bike Challenge** (www.twistedspokes.org, Sept.), boasts a course with quad-busting climbs and creek and log crossings. Longtime biker Bill Yacovissi recommends more than a dozen loops, mostly on unpaved state forest roads, on his Pine Creek Canyon Bike Rides website (www.pinecreekbikerides.com). **High**

Mountain Adventures (570/787-3099, www .highmountainadventures.net) offers customized mountain bike expeditions as well as off-road jeep tours.

Paddling and Fishing

Paddlers can sightsee and fish for hours or days on Pine Creek. Sadly, the window of opportunity is small. With no dams, Pine Creek relies on snowmelt and rainfall for its flow-jo. As spring turns to summer, water levels begin to drop. Paddlers must find other waters—or pray for thunderstorms heavy enough to swell the creek again.

Maps of the Pine Creek Rail Trail indicate creek access areas. The 54-mile state-designated Pine Creek Water Trail begins at the Big Meadows access area at Ansonia. The road leading to it is on the south side of U.S. 6, opposite a church. Don't put in at Big Meadows if you're looking for a quickie float. The first advisable take-out is 17 miles downstream, at the village of Blackwell. It takes about six hours to get there, though vigorous paddlers can do it much faster and an

kayaking on Pine Creek

unhurried angler can take much longer. A few sections approach Class III (difficult) water, so novice paddlers would be wise to hire a guide. **Pine Creek Outfitters** (U.S. 6 at Ansonia, 570/724-3003, www.pinecrk.com, 9 A.M.–6 P.M. daily, closed late Dec.–Jan.) offers daily raft tours from March to late May. Guided trips may continue into June if water levels allow. The outfitter also rents rafts, canoes, kayaks, and wetsuits, along with bikes for cycling the Pine Creek Rail Trail. Shuttle service and sage advice are available for anyone paddling the creek, biking the rail-trail, or hiking the West Rim Trail.

The upper stretches of Pine Creek and its many tributaries offer some of the finest trout fishing in the Northeast. The lower part of the creek (downstream of Waterville) is better known for warm-water species. Vehicles can access the western riverbank from Ansonia by turning onto Colton Road and then left onto Owasee Road, which traces the creek for about four miles. There are ample pull-offs along Route 414, which hugs the creek from Blackwell to just north of Waterville. **Slate Run Tackle Shop** (Rte. 414, Slate Run, 570/753-8551, www.slaterun.com, 8 A.M.–6 P.M. Sun.–Thurs., 8 A.M.–8 P.M. Fri.–Sat., reduced hours in winter) is a full-line Orvis dealer with an impressive inventory (thousand-dollar fly rods included) and an equally impressive acquaintance with local waters. Staff gladly dispense directions to sections of stream and can tag along to provide on-stream instruction.

Hiking

While short, the steep rim-to-creek trails at Colton Point and Leonard Harrison State Parks can challenge even experienced hikers. The highlight of **Colton Point's Turkey Path,** a three-mile down-and-back trail, is a 70-foot cascading waterfall less than half a mile from the trailhead. No one will call you a turkey if you end your descent there. **Leonard Harrison's Turkey Path** is two miles down and back, leading to a vista and waterfall before reaching the canyon floor. There's no bridge across Pine Creek, so hikers can't waddle down one Turkey Path and up the other.

Longer treks through canyon country can be had on state forestlands. As its name suggests, the 30-mile **West Rim Trail** traverses the western rim of Pine Creek Gorge, affording spectacular views of the valley. Its northern terminus is on Colton Road one mile south of U.S. 6 at Ansonia. The southern terminus is on Route 414 at the Rattlesnake Rock access area, two miles south of the village of Blackwell. Contact Tioga State Forest (570/724-2868, fd16@state.pa.us, www.dcnr.state.pa.us/forestry/stateforests/tioga.aspx, 8 A.M.–4 P.M. Mon.–Fri.) for more information about the trail. It connects with Pennsylvania's longest backpacking trail, the **Mid State Trail** (http://hike-mst.org), at Blackwell.

As if that weren't enough, backpackers can reach the 42-mile **Black Forest Trail** from the southern end of the West Rim Trail by following the Pine Creek Rail Trail to Slate Run. The Black Forest trailhead on Slate Run Road can also be reached via Route 414. The very difficult loop trail darts into and out of the gorge several times. Contact Tiadaghton State Forest (570/327-3450, fd12@state.pa.us, www.dcnr.state.pa.us/forestry/stateforests/tiadaghton.aspx, 8 A.M.–4 P.M. Mon.–Fri.) for information.

Skiing

The rail-trail and state forestlands offer hundreds of miles of cross-country skiing. Downhill skiers and snowboarders will find Pennsylvania's steepest slopes and plenty of natural snow at **Ski Denton** (5661 U.S. 6, Coudersport, 814/435-2115, www.skidenton.com, lift ticket $15–42, all-day ski rental $24–27, snow tubing 2-hour session $10), 34 miles west of Wellsboro between Galeton and Coudersport. Its trails are open to mountain bikers in the warmer months. **Ski Sawmill** (383 Oregon Hill Rd., Morris, 570/353-7521, www.skisawmill.com, lift ticket $17–35, all-day ski rental $20–25), 18 miles south of Wellsboro, has 12 slopes, a terrain park, and a tubing area with four runs. Both ski areas offer limited and rather spartan accommodations.

Snowmobiling

There are hundreds of miles of snowmobile trails on public lands surrounding Pine Creek Gorge. The **PA Grand Canyon Snowmobile Club** (4814 U.S. 6, 12 miles west of Wellsboro, 570/724-2888, www.pagrandcanyonsnowmobileclub.com) is a good source of information about trails at the northern end of the gorge. Trails from the clubhouse lead everywhere from the west rim of the canyon to local watering holes.

Guided Tours

Nature Quest (570/723-1643, www.naturequestadventures.com) arranges eco-journeys of every stripe, including birding excursions by foot or bike, overnight fly-fishing trips, and multi-day adventures that combine horseback riding and rafting.

ACCOMMODATIONS
Under $50

It doesn't cost a cent to camp on state forestlands within the spectacular Pine Creek Gorge, but it does require a permit. Contact **Tioga State Forest** (570/724-2868, fd16@state.pa.us, 8 A.M.–4 P.M. Mon.–Fri.) about camping in the Tioga County portion of the gorge and **Tiadaghton State Forest** (570/327-3450, fd12@state.pa.us, 8 A.M.–4 P.M. Mon.–Fri.) about the lower portion in Lycoming County. The county line is between the villages of Blackwell and Cedar Run, about 20 miles from the northern mouth of the gorge. Some state forest camping areas have amenities like potable water and vault-style bathrooms. For those who prefer a touch more luxury, there are modern campgrounds and other accommodations on private property in the gorge. You'll find them at Blackwell and points farther south.

One such campground is **Pettecote Junction** (400 Beach Rd., Cedar Run, 570/353-7183, www.pettecotejunction.com, campsite $20–30, cabin $100). The proprietors aren't exaggerating when they advertise "direct access." The campground is wedged between Pine Creek and the rail-trail. Not surprisingly, it offers rental canoes, tubes, and bikes. In addition to tent and RV sites, Pettecote Junction has several cabins that sleep 4–8 people.

Canyon Country Campground (130 Wilson Rd., Wellsboro, 570/724-3818, www.camp inpa.com, Apr. 15–Oct., campsite $21–29, cabin $47–68) isn't in the gorge but has an enviable location near its eastern rim. A walking trail leads from the campground to Leonard Harrison State Park and its acclaimed overlooks. Campground amenities include a game room, playgrounds, and a laundry room that doubles as a lending library (and Wi-Fi hot spot).

$50-100

It's not hard to imagine former guest Groucho Marx striding through the **Penn Wells Hotel** (62 Main St., Wellsboro, 570/724-2111, www .pennwells.com, $75–140, winter $50–100). Built in 1869 on the site of Wellsboro's first inn, the hotel pulses with history. Soak in the vibe of bygone days in the lobby or adjacent bar, but stay in one of the more recently renovated rooms if you can. The hotel's restaurant is open to the public and particularly hopping during Friday night fish fry and Sunday brunch. The hotel's younger sister, the **Penn Wells Lodge** (4 Main St., Wellsboro, 570/724-3463, www.pennwells.com, $80–95, winter $60–70), offers larger rooms, an indoor pool, and a Jacuzzi. It's vintage in its own way, having opened in 1960.

Pine Creek is just outside the backdoor of the **Cedar Run Inn** (281 Beulah Land Rd., Cedar Run, 570/353-6241, www.pavisnet .com/cedarruninn, room $40–45 per person, room and meals $70–75 per person), which is reason enough to book one of its 13 guest rooms. Even more reason: The country inn is home to one of the finest restaurants (dinner only, reservations recommended, $17–25) in the region.

The streamside **Hotel Manor** (392 Slate Run Rd., Slate Run, 570/753-8414, www.hotel-manor.com, $90) was rebuilt in the summer of 2004 after a fire destroyed the logging-era original. The speed at which it was rebuilt—five

© ANNA DUBROVSKY

Penn Wells Hotel

PENNSYLVANIA WILDS

months—speaks to its popularity with anglers and others. The hotel has 10 guest rooms, each with its own bathroom and a queen bed, and a restaurant (noon–9 P.M. Mon.–Thurs., noon–11 P.M. Fri., 11 A.M.–11 P.M. Sat., 8 A.M.–9 P.M. Sun., hours vary in winter, $9–25) featuring meaty fare and an expansive deck.

Guests of the **Cammal Bed & Breakfast** (7697 Rte. 414, Cammal, 570/753-8020, www.cammal.net, $65–75) don't have to go far to find groceries, hand-dipped ice cream, or hunting and fishing supplies. They have to go downstairs. The four guest rooms are atop a general store 50 yards from the Pine Creek Rail Trail. Alas, the bathroom is shared. The B&B also offers a two-bedroom apartment with a full kitchen and bathroom.

$100-200

A B&B-cum-sheep farm, **Arvgården** (5159 Arnot Rd., Wellsboro, 570/724-4337, www.arvgarden.com, $105) offers solitude in a rural setting within easy reach of Wellsboro. Guests of the Swedish-style B&B can visit with the New Zealand–style sheep, check out the looms used to turn their wool into woven items, or explore the farm's bird habitats. Owners Keith and Hilma Cooper share the bounty of their garden during breakfast.

Stay in Paris, or stay in Provence. No matter which room you choose at the lovely **La Belle Auberge** (129 Main St., Wellsboro, 570/724-3288, www.nellesinns.com, $119–219, winter $99–179), you'll be staying in the lap of luxury. The B&B is a richly decorated slice of France whose proprietor also owns the Wellsboro Diner, better known for its slices of pie. Chocolates, handmade soaps, robes, and slippers await guests in four rooms, two of which have private Jacuzzis. On-premise massage services take the pampering over the top.

The three rooms at **Wellsboro Inn on the Green** (3 Charles St., Wellsboro, 800/661-3581, www.wellsboroinnonthegreen.com, $115–185, winter $99) take their names from the *Wynken, Blynken, and Nod* statue in the town square, which the B&B overlooks. Nod, a garage-turned-guesthouse, is a page out of a Pottery Barn catalog, while Wynken and Blynken take a more flouncy approach to elegance. Music by the

La Belle Auberge B&B

© ANNA DUBROVSKY

breakfast at Wellsboro Inn on the Green

PENNSYLVANIA WILDS

likes of Dean Martin accompanies divine breakfasts served at private tables. Innkeepers Cindy and Rob Fitzgerald also own the aptly named **Crossroads Bed & Breakfast** (131 S. Main St., Mansfield, 800/661-3581, www.crossroadsbb.com, $115–165, winter $99–125) at the corner of U.S. 6 and U.S. 15 in nearby Mansfield.

It's easy to reach the Pine Creek Rail Trail from **Bear Mountain Lodge** (8010 U.S. 6, Wellsboro, 570/724-2428, www.bearmountainbb.com, $109–249). Just walk or bike half a mile down a country road. What's hard is leaving the den of creature comforts. Two of the four guest rooms have private decks complete with hot tubs, and the other two have whirlpool baths. All have natural-gas fireplaces, flat-screen TVs, and queen beds of hickory, white cedar, or black cherry—crafted locally. You can hardly blame guests for hibernating when they could be hiking.

FOOD
Wellsboro

Ask for the Grand Canyon at **The Native**

Bagel (1 Central Ave., 570/724-0900, http://nativebagel.tripod.com, 7 A.M.–7 P.M. Mon.–Fri., 7 A.M.–3 P.M. Sat., 7 A.M.–2 P.M. Sun., $3–7) and you won't get directions to the Pine Creek Gorge. You'll get a triple-decker sandwich with ham, turkey, bacon, and barbecue sauce. Sandwiches are named for local attractions and made with breads that couldn't be more local. Loaves, bagels, and pastries are made on-site.

A local institution, the **Wellsboro Diner** (19 Main St., 570/724-3992, 6 A.M.–8 P.M. Mon.–Sat., 7 A.M.–8 P.M. Sun., $5–15), serves up meatloaf, mashed potatoes, and the like in a deliciously authentic setting. The 1938 Sterling diner car was placed at the corner of Main Street and East Avenue in 1939 and hasn't budged since.

True to its name, **Timeless Destination** (77 Main St., 570/724-8499, www.timeless destination.com, 11 A.M.–9 P.M. Mon.–Thurs., 11 A.M.–10 P.M. Fri.–Sat., noon–9 P.M. Sun., closes 9 P.M. Fri.–Sat. in winter, $7–26) serves Italian-inspired cuisine that never goes out of

© TIOGA COUNTY VISITORS BUREAU

Wellsboro Diner

style. Pair a hand-tossed pizza with a local wine or tuck into a plate of linguini with clams.

The thick cuts of filet mignon at the dinner-only **Steak House** (29 Main St., 570/724-9092, www.thesteakhouse.com, 5–9 P.M. Mon.–Sat., $8–38) are tasty as is, but ask for the bourbon-flavored butter anyway. Save room for an after-dinner drink. Perhaps because of their surname, third-generation owners Chris and Geoff Coffee offer a world of spiked coffee options: Irish coffee, Italian coffee, Mexican coffee, and more.

With 16 draft beers behind its 150-year-old bar, the ◖ **Wellsboro House** (34 Charleston St., 570/723-4687, www.wellsborohouse.com, kitchen 5–9 P.M. Mon.–Wed., noon–9 P.M. Thurs.–Sat., bar closing time varies, $8–25) could draw a crowd if it served little more than hot wings. But convivial owners Chris and Laura Kozuhowski wouldn't hear of that. Their take on hot wings is a buffalo chicken sandwich dressed with crumbly bleu cheese and diced celery. The Wellsboro House is generally closed on Sunday, but not during football season. Look no further than the menu's South Philly cheesesteak to guess which team the Kozuhowskis root for.

West of Wellsboro

There are several options for a satisfying meal on the stretch of U.S. 6 between Galeton and Wellsboro. Among them is the **Burnin' Barrel Bar** (5440 U.S. 6, 570/724-1333, 11 A.M.–close Tues.–Sat., noon–close Sun., winter hours vary, $6–16), which couldn't be more convenient to the west rim of Pennsylvania's Grand Canyon. It's 11 miles west of Wellsboro via U.S. 6, just shy of the turnoff to Colton Point State Park. The Burnin' Barrel serves steak sandwiches, burgers, hoagies, and triple-decker clubs in a setting that's kid-friendly by day. Weekends bring dinner specials like snow crab legs and spare ribs, plus live music. Leave your mark by leaving a signed dollar bill. Hundreds of them share wall space with mounted animals, license plates, and neon beer signs.

It shouldn't surprise you to find big game mounts at the **Antlers Inn** (3591 U.S. 6,

814/435-6300, www.antlersinnpa.com, 4:30–9 P.M. Mon.–Wed., 11 A.M.–11 P.M. Thurs.–Sat., 11:30 A.M.–9 P.M. Sun., $11–23). It might surprise you that the Antlers is as elegant as it is rustic, wholly suitable for a first date or anniversary. The restaurant and attached sports bar seat 180, but decorating touches like a four-sided indoor waterfall create intimate spaces for indulging in the likes of ham steak, bacon-wrapped meatloaf, and seafood rigatoni. Deep-fried cheesecake makes frequent appearances on the dessert menu.

Used to be you could catch a trout in the pond behind the **Log Cabin Inn** (3501 U.S. 6, 814/435-8808, opens at 4:30 P.M. Tues.–Sat. and noon Sun., $11–31) and have the restaurant prepare it for your dinner. Its current proprietors did away with that, but the cozy inn founded in 1932 is still highly regarded for its fish dishes. Try the whole trout—de-boned, breaded, and pan-fried—or the haddock with crabmeat stuffing. Exercise restraint at the impressive soup and salad bar so you don't fill up before the main course arrives.

South of Wellsboro

Cedar Run Inn (281 Beulah Land Rd., Cedar Run, 570/353-6241, www.pavisnet.com/cedarruninn, dinner only, reservations recommended, $17–25) is home to one of the finest restaurants in the region. Anglers and hunters can wash up at an old marble sink beneath a mounted buck before digging into the house pâté, a medley of clams and herbs baked with parmesan cheese. Be sure to call ahead for restaurant hours; they vary throughout the year. Dinner is served most Fridays and Saturdays. The restaurant is also open Wednesdays and Thursdays from mid-April through October and Sundays in October.

Mansfield

In the U.S. 6 town of Mansfield, 13 miles east of Wellsboro, mornings find locals lined up at **Gramma's Kitchen** (1080 S. Main St., 570/662-2350, 7 A.M.–3 P.M. Mon.–Sat., $2–6) for freshly baked bread. The pies and cookies at the friendly-as-grandma's breakfast and lunch

spot are also homemade. You can order breakfast right up to closing time.

The chef-owned 🍷 **Wren's Nest** (102 W. Wellsboro St., 570/662-1093, www.wrensnestpa.com, lunch 11:30 A.M.–2 P.M. Tues.–Fri., dinner 5–9 P.M. Mon.–Sat., $7–29) offers fine dining in an 1856 cottage and the occasional live jazz night. Chef James Fry has an enviably short commute (he lives at the Wren's Nest with his family), reserving his energy for creations like blackened ahi tuna steak topped with guacamole.

INFORMATION

If you're arriving via U.S. 15 south, look for the state-run welcome center seven miles south of the Pennsylvania–New York line. Personalized travel counseling is available 7 A.M.–7 P.M. daily; the restrooms are always open.

The **Tioga County Visitors Center** (2053 Rte. 660, Wellsboro, 570/724-0635, www.visittiogapa.com, 8 A.M.–4:30 P.M. Mon.–Fri. year-round, 9 A.M.–1 P.M. Sat. May–Oct., 9 A.M.–1 P.M. Sun. Oct.) is conveniently located just a few miles east of the entrance to Leonard Harrison State Park and its glorious views of Pennsylvania's Grand Canyon. The visitors center has loads of information about the gorge and other area attractions. The county seat, Wellsboro, also has an advocate in the **Wellsboro Area Chamber of Commerce** (114 Main St., 570/724-1926, www.wellsboropa.com, 8:30 A.M.–4:30 P.M. Mon.–Fri.).

The **Potter County Visitors Association** (118 N. Main St., Coudersport, 814/274-3365, www.pottercountypa.org, open by chance) can be counted on for information about westerly attractions like the Pennsylvania Lumber Museum and Cherry Springs State Park. If no one is in, brochures can be found across the street at the Hotel Crittenden (133 N. Main St., Coudersport).

South of Blackwell, Pine Creek and its eponymous rail-trail cross from Tioga County into Lycoming County, represented by the **Lycoming County Visitors Bureau** (210 William St., Williamsport, 800/358-9900, www.vacationpa.com, 8:30 A.M.–5 P.M.

Mon.–Fri., 8 A.M.–3 P.M. Sat., 11 A.M.–3 P.M. Sun.).

GETTING THERE AND AROUND

The east–west U.S. 6 passes through both Wellsboro and the village of Ansonia, gateway to Colton Point State Park on the gorge's west rim. The east–west Route 660 runs between U.S. 15 and the entrance to Leonard Harrison State Park on the gorge's east rim, passing through Wellsboro on the way. The north–south Route 287 also passes through Wellsboro.

Private aircraft can fly into **Grand Canyon Airport,** just a few miles from the rim of the canyon. Commercial planes can't get any closer than New York's **Elmira Corning Regional Airport** (ELM), 55 miles northeast of Wellsboro.

Williamsport and Vicinity

The largest city in the Wilds region is the not-so-large city of Williamsport, population roughly 30,000. It's situated on the West Branch of the Susquehanna River. In the latter half of the 19th century, so many logs were floated down tributary streams and captured by a log boom at Williamsport that the city became known as the "Lumber Capital of the World." Its riverfront was crowded with sawmills—more than 30 at the peak of logging activity in Pennsylvania. Its West Fourth Street was crowded with the opulent residences of lumber barons. They moved to (literally) greener pastures as the lumbering era waned, but their showplaces still stand on the street known as Millionaires Row. The local high school's sports teams go by Williamsport Millionaires.

The city that once claimed to have more millionaires per capita than any place in the world now prides itself on a different distinction: birthplace of Little League Baseball. Every August, 16 teams of preteen ballplayers and tens of thousands of fans converge on the Williamsport area for the Little League Baseball World Series. A museum dedicated to Little League serves as a year-round pilgrimage site for little kids with big dreams.

LITTLE LEAGUE SIGHTS

In 1938, an oil company clerk named Carl Stotz decided to start a baseball program for boys in his hometown of Williamsport. He rounded up neighborhood children and began experimenting with different equipment and field dimensions. By the summer of 1939, Stotz had found sponsors for three teams of 10 and a name for his program: Little League. The first game on June 6, 1939, pitted Lundy Lumber against Lycoming Dairy. The uniforms, stats sheets, and other artifacts of Little League's first season are displayed at the **Peter J. McGovern Little League Museum** (525 U.S. 15, S. Williamsport, 570/326-3607, www.littleleague.org/museum, 10 A.M.–5 P.M. Mon., Thurs., and Fri.–Sat. and noon–5 P.M. Sun. Memorial Day–June, 10 A.M.–5 P.M. Mon.–Sat. and noon–5 P.M. Sun. July–Labor Day, 10 A.M.–5 P.M. Fri.–Sat. Labor Day–Memorial Day, admission $5, seniors $3, children 5–13 $1.50), named for the first president of Little League Baseball. Visitors can learn how Williamsport's three-team league grew into the world's largest organized youth sports program with more than 2.5 million players. The museum's collection includes balls signed by U.S. presidents and professional players, photographs of major leaguers with their Little League teams, and the uniform Williamsport native and baseball great Mike "Moose" Mussina wore when he represented local restaurant Johnny Z's as a Little Leaguer.

The museum is part of Little League International's 66-acre complex in the borough of South Williamsport, across the Susquehanna River from Williamsport. It overlooks two

© LYCOMING COUNTY VISITORS BUREAU

Learn how a three-team league became the largest organized youth sports program.

stadiums used during the annual **Little League Baseball World Series** (571/326-1921, www.littleleague.org, Aug.). Admission to all 32 games of the series is free, but tickets are required for seats in the Howard J. Lamade Stadium for the championship game. Tickets are distributed via a lottery system. To request as many as four tickets, send a letter to World Series Tickets, Little League International, 539 U.S. 15, P.O. Box 3485, Williamsport, PA 17701. Lamade Stadium has seating for about 7,500. The terraced hills beyond the outfield fence can accommodate another 35,000. The **Grand Slam Parade** (800/358-9900, www.vacationpa.com) through downtown Williamsport kicks off the series.

The World Series, first held in 1947, wasn't always played in South Williamsport. Before 1959, the action unfolded on a field across the street from Williamsport's minor league ballpark, Bowman Field. The original field, now named the **Carl E. Stotz Field** (1741 W. 4th St., Williamsport, 570/323-1308, www.league lineup.com/originalleagueinc), is still in active

use. It's operated by Original League Inc., a youth baseball organization born of a rift between Stotz and Little League International in the 1950s. Surviving members of the three teams that faced off in 1939 gather at the field during World Series week and give tours of its memorabilia-filled clubhouse.

MILLIONAIRES ROW HISTORIC DISTRICT

A drive down the one-way West 4th Street belies the wealth that once flowed into Williamsport in the form of tens of millions of logs. The moneyed have moved elsewhere. Their erstwhile homes show their age. More than a few house students from the nearby Pennsylvania College of Technology. But a stop here and there reveals Williamsport's rich history.

First stop is the Lycoming County Historical Society's **Thomas T. Taber Museum** (858 W. 4th St., 570/326-3326, www.tabermuseum.org, 9:30 A.M.–4 P.M. Tues.–Fri., 11 A.M.–4 P.M. Sat., 1–4 P.M. Sun., closed Sun. Nov.–Apr., admission $5, seniors $4, children $2.50), a modern building amidst the Victorian-style structures of West 4th, a.k.a. Millionaires Row. The museum skillfully chronicles the history of the region, which didn't start with the arrival of loggers. Visitors can explore a gallery devoted to Native Americans as well as a string of period rooms that illustrate the lifestyles of subsequent inhabitants. The Taber is also home to more than 300 toy trains, one of the finest collections in the country. A dozen of the models are one of a kind.

A real train car sits outside the **Peter Herdic Transportation Museum** (810 Nichols Place, 570/601-3455, www.phtm.org, 10 A.M.–3 P.M. Tues.–Sat., admission $5, seniors $4, children under 12 $3), a stone's throw from the Taber. Named for Williamsport's most prominent lumber baron and the inventor of a horse-drawn taxi called the "herdic," the museum celebrates transportation achievements as wide-ranging as the birch bark canoe and the public bus. As the hub of the 19th-century lumber industry and the home of so many millionaires, Williamsport was at the head of the line for transportation innovations. Herdic himself oversaw the construction of a streetcar railway that went into service in 1865. Early trolleys were pulled by horses and had small stoves to keep passengers warm in winter. Williamsport went electric in 1891, a year before Philadelphia. And while buses muscled the city's trolleys out of operation in 1933, visitors with vivid imaginations can almost hear the clatter of trolley wheels on steel rails during a **Williamsport Trolley Tour** (570/326-2500, http://ridervt.com/trolley.htm, May–Oct., fare $5, seniors $4, children under 12 $3). Motorized trolleys depart from the transportation museum at 10:45 A.M., 12:15 P.M., and 1:45 P.M. Tuesday–Friday and 10:45 A.M. and 12:15 P.M. Saturday. The trolleys and transportation museum are operated by River Valley Transit, Williamsport's public transit provider, and tickets are interchangeable. Trolleys make stops at the riverfront Susquehanna State Park, where the Hiawatha Paddlewheel Riverboat docks, and River Valley's 3rd Street parking garage. Riders can hop on or off at any of the three stops.

No stop along Millionaires Row elucidates the Williamsport of yore better than the **Rowley House Museum** (707 W. 4th St., 570/322-3460, www.preservationwilliamsport.org). The Queen Anne Victorian with its stained-glass windows and elaborate woodwork was built in 1888 for Edwin A. Rowley, one of the wealthiest men in Pennsylvania, who spared no expense. Its restoration is an ongoing project of Preservation Williamsport, which opens the magnificent house for tours by appointment. The volunteer-run organization also masterminds Williamsport's annual **Victorian Christmas** celebration. Quite a few mansions along West 4th Street and in other neighborhoods are open to the public during the November event.

OTHER SIGHTS
Hiawatha Paddlewheel Riverboat
The gaily painted *Hiawatha* Paddlewheel Riverboat (1 Hiawatha Blvd., 570/326-2500, www.ridehiawatha.com, May–Oct., public cruise $7.50, seniors $7, children 3–12 $3.50) is not the same *Hiawatha* that ferried Sunday picnickers from Williamsport to a park on the opposite side of the Susquehanna River a century ago. That Hiawatha was caught in ice in the winter of 1914 and crushed during the breakup of the ice that spring. This one is her spitting image. River Valley Transit, which operates the excursion boat, offers hour-long public cruises up and down the Susquehanna every day except Monday from June 1 through Labor Day. In May, September, and October, public cruises are limited to Saturday and Sunday. The season is peppered with longer cruises, including meal cruises, karaoke cruises, concert cruises, and wing night cruises complete with $5 pitchers. The *Hiawatha* docks in Susquehanna State Park, accessible via the Reach Road exit of U.S. 220. The park has picnic areas with grills, restrooms, swings, and a public boat launch.

Inspiration, Lycoming County
For a mega dose of *Inspiration,* pull into the parking lot across from Williamsport's

Community Arts Center in the 200 block of West 4th Street. Muralist Michael Pilato's *Inspiration, Lycoming County* (www.pilato murals.com) spans the three-story walls that frame the lot. The wraparound mural, which has a three-dimensional quality that's a hallmark of Pilato's work, is a visual history of the Williamsport area. It was a work in progress as of 2010. When it's complete, the mural will feature a foldout stage and sound system for live music.

Woolrich Company Store

In the early 1800s, a young British immigrant named John Rich traveled from one Pennsylvania logging camp to another selling woolen fabrics, socks, coverlets, and yarn from the back of a mule cart. The company he founded in 1830 is still ticking, and its flagship store warrants a trip to the woodsy village that shares its name. You don't have to be a lumberjack to appreciate the inventory at the original Woolrich Company Store (39 Boardman Dr., Woolrich, 570/769-7401, www

.woolrich.com, 9 A.M.–6 P.M. Mon.–Thurs. and Sat., 9 A.M.–9 P.M. Fri., noon–5 P.M. Sun.). Woolrich's longevity has much to do with an ever-expanding product line. The company that made army blankets during the Civil War and woolen bathing suits in the 1920s now hawks everything from hosiery to home furnishings. Customers can even snag a dog coat inspired by Woolrich's classic Buffalo Check Shirt, worn by generations of outdoorsmen (and scores of mussy-haired dorm dwellers). The 31,000-square-foot store in the stoplight-free village of Woolrich, about 20 miles west of Williamsport, would be at home on New York's Madison Avenue. Natural light bathes a natural-like indoor fountain. An adjoining café serves breakfast and lunch. Shoppers will find photos of the building and village in earlier times amid current-season Woolrich styles offered at 20 percent below suggested retail prices and deeply discounted discontinued items. The store also carries merchandise by comfort-peddling brands like Life Is Good, Clarks, and Crocs.

PENNSYLVANIA WILDS

Woolrich made army blankets during the Civil War.

In the late 1980s, Woolrich had 10 plants in the United States and another near Montreal. Today, the company outsources most of its production and licenses other manufacturers to produce goods under its venerable brand. But it still operates a woolen mill—America's oldest—within walking distance of the flagship store. The village of Woolrich takes a no-nonsense approach to street names. You'll find the cemetery on Cemetery Street, the park on Park Avenue, and the mill—you guessed it—on Mill Street. The towering evergreens that line the road into town were planted in 1930 in memory of M. B. Rich, who incorporated the family business founded by his grandfather.

Piper Aviation Museum

In 1937, a fire destroyed the Bradford, Pennsylvania, factory of aircraft manufacturer William T. Piper. The man who would come to be known as the "Henry Ford of Aviation" relocated to an abandoned silk mill in Lock Haven, a river city about 25 miles west of Williamsport.

It was there that his company, Piper Aircraft, produced the legendary J-3 Cub, the low-cost, easy-to-fly airplane that "taught the world to fly." An estimated four out of five pilots who flew in World War II received their training in a Piper Cub, and a military version of the two-seat, single-engine plane won the war's last dogfight. Lock Haven is no longer home to Piper Aviation (new owners consolidated manufacturing in Florida in the 1980s), but it is home to the Piper Aviation Museum (1 Piper Way, Lock Haven, 570/748-8283, www.pipermuseum .com, 9 A.M.–4 P.M. Mon.–Fri., 10 A.M.–4 P.M. Sat., noon–4 P.M. Sun., closed Sun. Dec.–Mar., admission $6, seniors $5, children 7–15 $3, family rate $12). The museum, which occupies a former Piper engineering building, preserves all things Piper, from vintage aircraft to flight journals. Every June, Piper devotees from around the country take a **Sentimental Journey** (570/893-4200, www.sentimentaljourneyfly-in .com) to the William T. Piper Memorial Airport, adjacent to the museum.

Piper planes descend on Lock Haven during the annual Sentimental Journey.

ENTERTAINMENT AND EVENTS

Bars

Located a beer pong toss from the Pennsylvania College of Technology campus, **Kimball's** (972 2nd St., Williamsport, 570/322-1115, www.kimballspub.com, 11 A.M.–2 A.M. Mon.–Fri., 5 P.M.–2 A.M. Sat.–Sun., kitchen closes at 10 P.M., food $5–9) is steadfast in its support of craft brewers, including Pennsylvania's own Sly Fox, Troegs, Victory, and Weyerbacher. The bar hosts an open mic night, Quizzo (team trivia) games, and, occasionally, a band. Beer connoisseurs should also pay a visit to **Bavarian Barbarian Brewing Co.** (429 W. 3rd St., Williamsport, 570/322-5050, www.bavarianbarbarian.com). The production brewery, which opened its doors in 2007, offers samples, growlers, cases, and kegs of its creations 2–6 P.M. Tuesday–Thursday, 2–8 P.M. Fri., and 9 A.M.–8 P.M. Saturday.

More of a rum-swiller? The Caribbean-themed **Rumrunners Pub & Eatery** (241 Market St., Williamsport, 570/322-0303, www.rumrunnerspub.com, 4–11 P.M.

Mon.–Thurs., 4 P.M.–1 A.M. Fri., 5 P.M.–1 A.M. Sat., 5–11 P.M. Sun., food $7–22) stocks more than a hundred varieties. Yah, mon. The kitchen sends out island-style and Italian dishes and hybrids like a pizza topped with pineapple, sweet red peppers, and jerk chicken. Bands crank up the beach vibe on Saturday nights.

Performing Arts

Williamsport's cultural hub is the **Community Arts Center** (220 W. 4th St., Williamsport, 570/326-2424, www.caclive.com), a 1920s vaudeville theater turned modern performance venue. The acoustically exemplary theater seats just over 2,100 people for concerts, dance performances, plays, comedy acts, and movies. The likes of Jerry Seinfeld, Ray Charles, Barry Manilow, and B. B. King have brought down the house. Local performing arts organizations, including the **Williamsport Symphony Orchestra** (570/322-0227, www.williamsportsymphony.com), also take the stage.

All about local talent, the **Community**

DRIVE-INS A SHORT DRIVE AWAY

The drive-in movie theater is slowly fading to black in many parts of America. Not in these parts. The Williamsport area has not one but two drive-in theaters. Both show double features for less than the price of a single movie at many indoor theaters. They're open rain or shine during the warmer months. The **Harvest Moon Drive-In** (U.S. 220, Linden, 570/398-1018, www.moondrivein.com, Fri.-Sun., admission $6, children 4-12 $2), midway between Williamsport and Jersey Shore to its west, has been in business for more than 50 years. Come dusk, two mammoth screens come alive with recently released films. The scratchy speakers of yesteryear are gone; today the sound is transmitted through car radios. But the snack bar menu harks back to a time when cholesterol wasn't a dirty word. The Moon Carfeteria serves up hot dogs and cheeseburgers

drenched in homemade chili, beer-battered haddock sandwiches, homemade pizzas, pierogies, and deep-fried anything (deep-fried clam strips, deep-fried cheese ravioli, deep-fried pickles, and deep-fried Snickers candy bars, to name a few).

The pet-friendly **Pike Drive-In** (5798 U.S. 15, Montgomery, 570/547-7232, www.pikedi.com, Fri.-Sun., admission $7, seniors and college students $5, children 7-12 $3), just three miles south of the Little League Museum in South Williamsport, boasts three screens. Its fryer isn't as busy as Harvest Moon's, but movie-goers can still sock it to their arteries with "The Joe," a hamburger topped with a hot dog. Dinner at the independently owned drive-ins can be had for less than the cost of popcorn at a movie house. (Jumps for dead car batteries are free.)

Theatre League (100 W. 3rd St., Williamsport, 570/327-1777, www.ctlnet.org) produces about 10 plays a year and hosts concerts that run the gamut from bluegrass to barbershop. Its intimate theater-in-the-round can be found in the McDade Trade and Transit Centre, Williamsport's bus hub.

Professional summer stock theater can be found in a barn that once housed registered Holstein cattle. The tireless **Millbrook Playhouse** (258 Country Club Ln., Mill Hall, 570/748-8083, www.millbrookplayhouse.com, tickets $18, students $10, children under 12 $8) generally squeezes four main stage productions, an equal number of cabaret performances, and a couple of children's musicals into a two-month season. Alumni of the theater founded in 1963 include *Twin Peaks* star Kyle MacLachlan and Michael Tucker of *L.A. Law* fame. Come fall, Millbrook raises funds with Brews in the Barn, a beer-tasting extravaganza complete with live entertainment and a picnic-style dinner. The borough of Mill Hall is about 30 miles east of Williamsport, near Lock Haven.

Founded in 1831, Williamsport's **Repasz Band** (www.lycoming.org/repaszband) is one of the oldest community bands in the country. It played at Appomattox Court House in Virginia when General Robert E. Lee surrendered to General Ulysses S. Grant. It played during the inaugurations of Presidents Theodore Roosevelt and William Howard Taft. Its eponymous *Repasz Band March* played on an episode of *M*A*S*H*. Today the band plays pieces from its lengthy repertoire at free indoor and outdoor concerts throughout the area.

Festivals and Events

Live music, meet-the-artist events, and extended store hours enliven downtown Williamsport on the **First Friday** (570/326-1971, www.williamsport.org) of every month. The Williamsport Symphony Orchestra produces the annual **Pops in the Park** (570/322-0227, www.williamsportsymphony.com, free) series, which brings regional talent to the bandshell at Brandon Park (Packer Street, Williamsport) on select Sunday evenings in the summer.

Free outdoor concerts are all the rage in Lock Haven. The city (570/893-5900, www

free concert at Lock Haven's J. Doyle Corman Amphitheater

.lockhavencity.org) sponsors concerts not once but twice a week from June through August, dishing out classic rock, country, swing, polka, and other musical genres. On Friday evenings, bands perform at Triangle Park at Bellefonte Avenue and West Main Street. The Sunday evening venue is the uniquely charming **J. Doyle Corman Amphitheater** at Jay and Water Streets. The amphitheater is built into the levee that guards Lock Haven from flooding by the West Branch of the Susquehanna River, and the stage floats on the water. Boats drop anchor around the stage for "front-row seats." On rainy days, the concerts move to a Lock Haven University auditorium at West Church and 3rd Streets.

Bluegrass fans flock to the little borough of Loganton, 17 miles south of Lock Haven, for three days each June. Regional and national acts perform at the **Smoked Country Jam Bluegrass Festival** (570/753-8878, www .smokedcountryjam.com, admission charged), which benefits the Lupus Foundation of Pennsylvania. The one-day **Billtown Blues Festival** (570/584-4480, www.billtownblues .org, June, admission charged) brings more than a dozen names in blues to the Lycoming County Fairgrounds (300 E. Lycoming St., Hughesville). The festival celebrated its 20th year in 2009 with performances by the likes of guitarist Bob Margolin, who played with blues legend Muddy Waters in the 1970s.

Downtown Williamsport heats up in mid-February, when thousands take to the streets for **Mardi Gras** (570/326-4700). The two-day celebration features fireworks and a parade complete with bead-tossing float riders.

SPORTS AND RECREATION
Pine Creek Rail Trail
The southern trailhead of the 60-mile Pine Creek Rail Trail is in the town of Jersey Shore, a 20-minute drive from Williamsport. The trail shortly meets Pine Creek and follows it into the deepest section of what's known as Pennsylvania's Grand Canyon. It's beloved by hikers, bikers, cross-country skiers, and snowshoers.

State Parks
Nestled in Tiadaghton State Forest, **Little Pine State Park** (4205 Little Pine Creek Rd., Waterville, 570/753-6000, www.dcnr.state .pa.us/stateParks/parks/littlepine.aspx) offers big fun for hikers and anglers. The 2,158-acre park has 14 miles of trails, and the Mid State Trail (http://hike-mst.org), Pennsylvania's longest and wildest trek, passes through it. A 94-acre lake and 4.2 miles of stream provide good fly, bank, and boat fishing. Rental paddleboats, canoes, kayaks, and rowboats are available from Memorial Day weekend to Labor Day. Come snowfall, two acres of slopes are set aside for sledding and tobogganing. Snowmobilers can access more than 100 miles of groomed trails in the surrounding state forest.

The park's modern campground, open from the first weekend in April through mid-December, has 99 sites, most of which have electricity. The campsites, three cottages, and two yurts can be reserved online at www .pa.reserveworld.com or by calling 888/727-2757. To reach the park from Williamsport, take U.S. 220 south to the Pine Creek Exit near Jersey Shore. Follow Route 44 north 11 miles to Waterville, and turn right onto Little Pine Creek Road/Route 4001. Continue four miles to the park.

Farther from Williamsport but worth the trip is **Hyner View State Park** (Hyner View Road, Hyner, 570/923-6000, www.dcnr.state.pa.us/stateparks/parks/hynerview.aspx), which boasts one of the finest lookouts in the state. Sprinting off the lookout is a popular pastime (for those strapped into a hang glider). From Waterville, continue on Route 44 for about 12 miles. Turn left onto Hyner Mountain Road, left at Ritchie Road, and right at Hyner View Road. From the famed lookout, you can see miles of the West Branch of the Susquehanna River. To see hang gliders and paragliders launch from the state's highest active site, visit the six-acre park around Easter, Memorial Day, Fourth of July, Labor Day, or the **Pennsylvania State Flaming Foliage Festival,** celebrated in the nearby town of Renovo during the second full weekend of October. That's when the **Hyner**

Hang Gliding Club (www.hynerclub.com) hosts "fly-in" events of 3–5 days. The landing zone is a grassy stretch near the river that once served as an airport. Come nightfall, it's aglow with the campfires of gliders and their groupies.

Boating and Paddling

A boat launch at **Susquehanna State Park** (Reach Rd. and Arch St., Williamsport, 570/988-5557, www.dcnr.state.pa.us/stateparks/parks/susquehanna.aspx), home of the Hiawatha Paddlewheel Riverboat, provides access to the West Branch of the Susquehanna River and the Hepburn Street Dam, which is deep enough for waterskiing. There's no horsepower limit.

Other boat access areas are scattered along the banks of the West Branch. Downriver from Williamsport, **Country Ski & Sports** (836 Broad St., Montoursville, 570/368-1718, countryskiandsports.net, 10 A.M.–8 P.M. Mon. and Fri., 10 A.M.–6 P.M. Tues. and Thurs., 10 A.M.–5 P.M. Wed. and Sat.) sells and rents canoes and kayaks and offers paddling

clinics to boot. Upriver, **Rock River & Trail Outfitters** (57 Bellefonte Ave., Lock Haven, 570/748-1818, www.rockriverandtrail.com, 10 A.M.–5 P.M. Mon.–Thurs., 10 A.M.–6 P.M. Fri., 9 A.M.–3 P.M. Sat., other hours by appointment) offers guided kayaking trips and shuttle service. The four-season, fully insured outfitter rents kayaks, comfort bikes, and snowshoes.

Fishing

Pine Creek and Loyalsock Creek, tributaries of the West Branch of the Susquehanna ("Suskie" to in-the-know anglers), are among the more popular fishing streams in the Williamsport area. The former empties into the West Branch near Jersey Shore, about 15 miles west of Williamsport, and the latter at Montoursville, about eight miles east of the city.

Fly fishers will find a selection of more than 350 hand-tied flies at **McConnell's Country Store & Fly Shop** (10853 Rte. 44 N., Waterville, 570/753-8241, www.mcconnellscountrystore.com, 7 A.M.–7 P.M.

paddling the West Branch of the Susquehanna River

Sun.–Thurs., 7 A.M.–9 P.M. Fri.–Sat., winter hours 7 A.M.–5:30 P.M. Sun.–Thurs., 7 A.M.–9 P.M. Fri., 7 A.M.–7 P.M. Sat.), 12 miles north of Jersey Shore in the village of Waterville, where Little Pine Creek meets the "Big Pine." McConnell's offers guides as well as gear.

Hiking

The 59-mile **Loyalsock Trail** runs roughly parallel to Loyalsock Creek, which empties into the West Branch of the Susquehanna River at Montoursville, just east of Williamsport. It's a strenuous trail that rewards hikers with spectacular vistas. The western terminus is on Route 87, about nine miles north of I-180/U.S. 220 at Montoursville. The Alpine Club of Williamsport (570/322-5878, www.lycoming.org/alpine), which maintains the trail, sells a detailed guide with full-color maps. The trail also appears on the free public-use map for Loyalsock State Forest (570/946-4049, fd20@state.pa.us, www.dcnr.state.pa.us/forestry/stateforests/loyalsock.aspx). For gear, backpackers need look no further than **Lyon Camping & Supply** (361 Broad St., Montoursville, 877/368-5966, www.lyoncamping.com, 10 A.M.–6 P.M. Mon., Tues., and Thurs., 10 A.M.–3 P.M. Wed. and Sat., 10 A.M.–7 P.M. Fri.).

The 90-mile **Donut Hole Trail,** one of the state's most challenging, parallels the West Branch of the Susquehanna River through Sproul State Forest (570/923-6011, fd10@state.pa.us, www.dcnr.state.pa.us/forestry/stateforests/sproul.aspx). Its eastern terminus is in Farrandsville, 30 miles west of Williamsport. **Rock River & Trail Outfitters** (57 Bellefonte Ave., Lock Haven, 570/748-1818, www.rockriverandtrail.com, 10 A.M.–5 P.M. Mon.–Thurs., 10 A.M.–6 P.M. Fri., 9 A.M.–3 P.M. Sat., other hours by appointment) offers shuttle service.

In Ralston, about 25 miles north of Williamsport along Route 14, **Wilderness Treks** (570/995-5544, www.wildernesstreks inc.com) takes hikers on guided tours of lush forest and a once-thriving coal town turned ghost town. Hikes start at $27.50 and end with lunch at the Ralston General Store on Thompson Street.

Scuba Diving

For the lowdown on local dive sites and gear galore, hunt for **Sunken Treasure Scuba Center** (664 Geiler Hollow Rd., Jersey Shore, 570/398-1458, summer hours noon–9 P.M. Mon. and Fri., 10 A.M.–5 P.M. Tues. and Thurs., 9:30 A.M.–1 P.M. Sat., hours vary Sept.–May). From U.S. 220, take Route 287 north for 0.7 mile and turn left. Continue for 0.8 mile to Sunken Treasure on the right.

Spectator Sports

Famous for its small-fry ballplayers, Williamsport is also home to a team of grownups. The **Williamsport Crosscutters** (1700 W. 4th St., Williamsport, 570/326-3389, www.crosscutters.com), a short-season Class A affiliate of the Philadelphia Phillies, play home games at historic Bowman Field. Built in 1926, it's the second oldest minor league park in the country. The Crosscutters share it with the Wildcats of the Pennsylvania College of Technology.

ACCOMMODATIONS
Under $100

The house Pennsylvania governor John Andrew Schulze built after his 1823–1829 term didn't stay in his family. It was seized and sold to pay a legal debt. In 2007, it opened as the **Governor Schulze House Bed and Breakfast** (748 Broad St., Montoursville, 570/368-8966, www.govshulzehouse.com, $80–120), a tastefully decorated retreat that caters to business travelers and honeymooners alike. The latter are best off in the Eck Suite with its corner Jacuzzi and curtained four-poster bed.

Breakfast is served by candlelight at the historic **Bodine House** (307 S. Main St., Muncy, 570/546-8949, www.bodinehouse.com, $85–140), and a fire greets guests on cold mornings. That's not for lack of modern conveniences. Built in 1805 and listed on the National Register of Historic Places, the antique-filled house has en suite bathrooms wireless Internet access, and air conditioners in each of three guest rooms. A two-story carriage house, built circa 1900, accommodates as many as six guests. The center of heritage-rich Muncy is within walking distance.

$100-200

The **Ⅽ Genetti Hotel** (200 W. 4th St., Williamsport, 570/326-6600, www.genetti hotel.com, $90–295) has welcomed the likes of Gene Kelly, Rita Hayworth, and Robert Kennedy since opening in 1922. Thanks to a major renovation in 2006, the landmark offers the comforts and amenities of a modern hotel along with a heaping of historic charm. The pet-friendly Genetti has an outdoor pool and an American restaurant. Barring a special event, guests get a complimentary continental breakfast. At 10 floors, the hotel is Williamsport's tallest building. It's as centrally located as it gets, next door to the Community Arts Center.

The Peter Herdic House, Williamsport's finest restaurant, doesn't serve breakfast.

Its tireless proprietors are busy at their inn next door. Breakfast is served on weekends at the **Peter Herdic Inn** (411 W. 4th St., Williamsport, 570/326-0411, www.herdic house.com, $95–200), a Millionaires Row mansion with original silver and brass chandeliers. The painstakingly decorated inn has six guest accommodations, including a scarlet-hued suite with a private balcony and Jacuzzi.

It's hard to believe that river water once lapped the walls of the resplendent Queen Anne Victorian that opened in 2008 as the **Aurora Leigh Bed & Breakfast** (302 W. Church St., Lock Haven, 570/748-6530, www.aurora leighbandb.com, $95–155). The 19th-century mansion two blocks from the Susquehanna is chockablock with original features, including parquet floors and hand-carved wainscoting. (Not everything is original. Innkeepers Tracy Brundage and Peter Bellis added three bathrooms during a yearlong renovation.) The sumptuous, uniquely decorated guest rooms—Pemberley, Mandalay, Kingsbere, and Saint Ive's—are named for locales real and fictional

Peter Herdic Inn

© LYCOMING COUNTY VISITORS BUREAU

that figure in classic literature. Guests are welcome to browse the collection of more than 500 books in the Red Room Library, named in tribute to Charlotte Bronte's *Jane Eyre*.

As remote and tranquil as its name suggests, the **Serene View Farm Bed & Breakfast** (80 Engle Mill Ln., Williamsport, 570/478-2477, www.sereneviewfarm.com, $100–140) sits on 128 acres of critter-filled woodlands and meadows about 20 miles northeast of Williamsport. The 1890s farmhouse has a wraparound porch complete with rocking chairs, a family room with an original, working cook stove, and three homey guest rooms. Need a stronger dose of serenity? Innkeepers Maggie and Larry Emery can arrange for an on-site massage.

Nature lovers have another fine option in the **Creekview Country Cottage Bed and Breakfast** (552 Tescier Rd., Muncy, 570/546-7715, www.creekviewcountrycottagebnb .com, $110–150), a half-mile from pavement on a country road named for the innkeeper's grandparents. The sylvan homestead overlooking Little Muncy Creek has two private cottages and a main house with two guest rooms. The lovely Treehouse Cottage boasts seven skylights and French doors that open to views of the creek.

FOOD
Williamsport
Mr. Sticky's (1948 E. 3rd St., 570/567-1166, www.mrsticky.biz, 6 A.M.–7 P.M. Mon.–Tues., 6 A.M.–9 P.M. Wed.–Sat., 7 A.M.–6 P.M. Sun., $2–8) raisons d'être are freshly baked and unapologetically addictive sticky buns. Phil Poorman and his family opened the restaurant in 2003 after several years of peddling their buns from concession trailers. Now they serve soups, salads, and sandwiches on homemade rolls along with four varieties of gooey buns: original sticky, walnut sticky, cinnamon bun with cream cheese icing, and cinnamon bun with peanut butter icing and milk chocolate shavings.

Award-winning microbrews and frequent live entertainment are reason enough to hop to the **Bullfrog Brewery** (229 W. 4th St., 570/326-4700, www.bullfrogbrewery.com, opens 11 A.M. Mon.–Sat., 9 A.M. Sun., $5–23), but the food is also something to croak about. The Bullfrog buys its baked goods from local bakeries and its beef from a free-range co-op (great news for anyone biting into the "mammoth" burger, which weighs in at one pound). Beers are brewed on-site and include the Williamsporter, a dark ale with a chocolaty finish, and the slightly floral Billtown Blonde, built to evoke the city's earliest breweries. On Sundays, the Bullfrog opens early for brunch and serves up free jazz starting at noon. Call or check the online calendar for information about performances throughout the week, some of which have a cover charge. The kitchen is open until 11 P.M. Monday–Wednesday, midnight Thursday–Saturday, and 10 P.M. Sunday. The Bullfrog is always open until midnight and closes as late as 2 A.M. if business is, um, hopping.

The Valley Inn (204 Valley St., Duboistown, 570/326-3383, www.thevalley-inn.com, 11 A.M.–11 P.M. daily, bar closes at 2 A.M., $6–20) dipped its toes into the froth in 2005, adding a brewing operation called Abbey Wright Brewing Co. The restaurant just across the river from Williamsport serves beers from around the world along with its own, plus wine and booze. Famous for its wings—served with your choice of 13 homemade sauces—the kitchen also turns out sandwiches, burgers, pizzas, and entrées like braised pork shank and beef stroganoff.

The au courant **Barrel 135 Wine Bar & Bistro** (135 W. 3rd St., 570/322-7131, lunch 11 A.M.–2 P.M. Mon.–Fri., dinner 5–10 P.M. Tues.–Sat., bar open as late as 2 A.M. Tues.–Sat., $6–23) offers sushi and small plates, salads and sandwiches, and a handful of meat and seafood entrées, plus live music on Friday nights. Chef-owned **33 East** (33 E. 3rd St., 570/322-1900, www.33east.com, 5–10 P.M. Mon.–Sat., $15–29), yet another contemporary restaurant that takes its name from its address, makes just about everything in-house, including its complimentary sourdough bread. Hot sellers include the penne pasta with lobster and filet of beef with garlic mashed potatoes. Its cocktail lounge, which stays open until about midnight, offers nibbles in the $7–12 range.

Founded in 1984 as a maker of fine pastas and sauces, **DiSalvo's** (341 E. 4th St., 570/327-1200, www.disalvopasta.com, lunch 11:30 A.M.–2 P.M. Wed.–Fri., dinner 5–9:30 P.M. Mon.–Thurs. and 5–10 P.M. Fri.–Sat., lunch $9–14, dinner $16–28) now enjoys a reputation as Williamsport's finest Italian restaurant. Offerings range from simple wood-fired pizzas to a $50 aged steak. The house gnocchi is creamy heaven.

Don't let memories of school cafeterias keep you from **Le Jeune Chef** (1098 Hagan Way, 570/320-2433, www.pct.edu/lejeunechef, lunch 11:30 A.M.–1:30 P.M. Mon.–Fri., dinner 5:30–8 P.M. Wed.–Sat., reservations recommended, lunch $7–13, dinner $8–30) on the Pennsylvania College of Technology campus. The restaurant offers real-world training for students in the college's School of Hospitality and a fine-dining experience for patrons. Call or check the website to see if Le Jeune Chef— French for "the young chef"—is offering an à la carte menu or multi-course meal.

Epicurean delights await at the onetime home of Williamsport's most extravagant lumber baron. Built in 1854, the ☚ **Peter Herdic House** (407 W. 4th St., 570/322-0165, www.herdichouse.com, 5–9 P.M. Tues.–Sat., lunch during Dec., reservations recommended, $10–30) opened as a restaurant 130 years later. Appetizers include such delicacies as escargot, chicken and duck livers sautéed with onion and bacon, and locally smoked shad. Owners and sisters Marcia and Gloria Miele are so fond of local producers that they name names on the menu. The roasted hen? It's from an herbicide-free farm less than 50 miles away. Other priorities prevail when it comes to the 75-bottle wine list. The Mieles have traveled to Burgundy and Tuscany to sample vinos. Be sure to explore the ornate

Old Corner is known for its burgers.

property before or after your meal. There's a wisteria-covered patio for outdoor dining and a lounge with its own menu (think free-range chicken wings). Swear to tell the truth and nothing but the truth at the bar, which served as a witness stand in a courtroom since demolished.

Lock Haven

It's not much to look at, but the **Old Corner** (205 N. Grove St., 570/748-4124, www.the oldcorner.com, 11 A.M.–midnight daily, bar closes at 2 A.M., $3–8) is revered for its burgers cooked to order at budget prices. Its sandwiches, flatbread pizzas, and salads (mixed greens!) are also commendable. The neighborhood hang has but a handful of tables; don't be shy to cozy up to the bar.

Dutch Haven Restaurant (201 E. Bald Eagle St., 570/748-4779, www.dutchhaven restaurant.com, 11 A.M.–8:30 P.M. Wed.–Thurs., 11 A.M.–9 P.M. Fri., 5–9 P.M. Sat., 10 A.M.–2 P.M. Sun., $6–18) is a happy marriage

© CLINTON COUNTY ECONOMIC PARTNERSHIP

Dutch Haven Restaurant will satisfy your craving for German food.

PENNSYLVANIA WILDS

of German and American cuisines. Whether your tastes run toward schnitzel and spatzle or steak and fries, you'll almost surely leave stuffed. Come Sunday, Dutch Haven puts on a buffet of eggs, pancakes, ham, turkey, homemade sticky buns, and a whole lot more.

INFORMATION

You can download a visitors guide to Williamsport and other Lycoming County communities from the website of the **Lycoming County Visitors Bureau** (210 William St., Williamsport, 800/358-9900, www.vacationpa.com, 8:30 A.M.–5 P.M. Mon.–Fri., 8 A.M.–3 P.M. Sat., 11 A.M.–3 P.M. Sun.), or pop by its headquarters in downtown Williamsport for brochures. **Williamsport. com** (http://williamsport.com), an online city guide, offers a calendar of events, a directory of businesses, and even a list of gas prices at area pumps.

For information about the Piper Aviation

Museum, the original Woolrich Company Store, and other attractions in Clinton County, Lycoming's neighbor to the west, contact the **Clinton County Economic Partnership** (212 N. Jay St., Lock Haven, 570/748-5782, www.clintoncountyinfo.com, 8 A.M.–5 P.M. Mon.–Fri.).

GETTING THERE AND AROUND

U.S. 15, U.S. 220, and I-180, a spur of I-80, meet in Williamsport. **Williamsport Regional Airport** (IPT), offers direct service to and from Philadelphia. **Susquehanna Trailways** (800/692-6314, www.susquehannabus.com) makes stops in Williamsport, Muncy to its east, and Lock Haven to its west. Bus transportation between Williamsport and other points in Lycoming County is provided by **River Valley Transit** (570/326-2500, www .ridervt.com). For a cab, call **Billtown Cab Co.** (570/322-2222).

Elk Region and Vicinity

Majestic elk once roamed throughout Pennsylvania. But as the human population increased in the mid-1800s, the elk population dwindled. By the end of the century, every last elk had fallen victim to unregulated hunting and habitat loss. Which is why it's no small matter that north-central Pennsylvania is today home to the largest herd of free-roaming elk east of the Rockies. In 2009, roughly 800 elk prospered in an 835-square-mile range stretching across Elk, Cameron, and Clearfield Counties. The heart of the elk region is the remote village of Benezette, so tiny that elk-viewing visitors outnumber residents at times.

The eastern elk that populated Pennsylvania in the days before white settlers are long extinct. The animals we see today are descendants of 177 Rocky Mountain elk from Yellowstone National Park and other parts that were released in Pennsylvania between 1913 and 1926. For a while there, the future of the big beasts looked not so bright. Only a few dozen elk remained in Pennsylvania in the mid-1970s. But the population rebounded. By 2001, the herd had grown large—and unruly—enough that the state approved the first elk season in 70 years. More than 50,000 hunters paid $10 apiece to participate in a lottery for 30 licenses. The elk hunt has continued every year since then, with 60 licenses awarded in 2009. (If the notion of hunting these handsome creatures offends, consider that hunters are very much to thank for the flourishing herd. License fees and donations from sportsmen's groups have been used to turn acres upon of acres of abandoned strip mines and other forest openings into elk-friendly habitat.)

The best time to visit is during elk mating season, a.k.a. the rut. It starts in September and winds down in October. During the rut, Elk County reverberates with the bugling of mature bulls. The piercing call is an invitation

elk viewing

to cows and a challenge to rival bulls. Bulls battle for control of cow harems, locking antlers until the weaker of the two retreats. Much of the action takes place in the open, where it's easier for harem masters to stand guard. Bring binoculars and a camera with ample zoom capabilities; stay well clear of the frays.

In winter, snow and ice make the country roads riskier and some areas inaccessible. The upside: If you find elk, you'll probably find a large number. The animals congregate in lower elevations, where they're more likely to find food. A good bet is to travel Route 555, which connects the villages of Weedville and Driftwood and passes through Benezette. The 26-mile road hugs the Bennett Branch of Sinnemahoning Creek, and elk can oft be seen along the water.

Elk continue to feed near streams in the spring, gradually moving out of the valleys as higher elevations green up. (If you have a mantel just begging for a pair of elk antlers, this is the time to go scavenger hunting. Bulls drop their antlers in late winter or early spring—finders keepers.) Come summer, when food is plentiful throughout the range, it's unusual to see large groups of elk. The hottest months are the worst for elk viewing because the beasts skulk in the relative coolness of dense forest. No matter when you visit, the best times to view elk are the first hour or two of daylight and just before dusk. That's when they're most likely to be grazing on legumes, grasses, and forbs in open fields.

(BENEZETTE

The capital of elk country is the Route 555 village of Benezette. Elk can often be found near town (and occasionally in town) in large part because the state and conservationists roll out the green carpet. Area forest openings are planted with alfalfa, clovers, and other food crops irresistible to elk. By attracting elk and other animals to clearings on public land, these buffets also serve human visitors hungry for wildlife sightings.

The **Elk Country Visitor Center** (134 Homestead Dr., Benezette, 814/787-5167,

© ANNA DUBROVSKY

Hicks Run viewing blind

ELK FAQS

What exactly are elk?
The elk is the second largest member of the deer family in North America. The moose is larger. Good luck finding one of those in Pennsylvania.

How do I distinguish elk from white-tailed deer?
For one thing, white-tailed deer are common throughout the Commonwealth. Free-roaming elk can be found only in a handful of counties in the Wilds region. Elk are much larger than white-tailed deer. A mature male elk, a.k.a. a bull, weighs 600–1,000 pounds. His female counterpart, a.k.a. a cow, is a relative featherweight at 500–600 pounds. Elk have the barest hint of a tail; white-tailed deer have longer tails with white undersides. Elk have darkish necks; white-tailed deer have a white throat patch. The antlers of bulls sweep backwards; those of bucks (male deer) curve forward.

Why can't bulls just get along?
Normally they do. For the bulk of the year, bulls roam on their own or in small "bachelor groups." It's not until mating season that they butt heads – literally. Their battles over the ladies rarely end in serious injury.

Can I feed the elk?
Absolutely not. In fact, Pennsylvania law prohibits it. Elk that are habituated to humans generally have shorter life spans than elk that steer clear of them. Think poachers. Think car-elk collisions.

How close can I come to the elk?
Elk will let you know how close is too close. When they sense danger, they raise their heads, cock their ears forward, and move stiffly. They sometimes bark to warn their comrades. Or they simply flee. Try not to make the elk flee. It ruins things for other viewers, and it stresses the elk. They're particularly vulnerable in wintertime, when they need every ounce of energy just to survive.

If elk are so precious, why are elk burgers on the menu?
The elk on the menu wasn't part of Pennsylvania's free-roaming herd. It was raised on a farm.

a bull elk

© PA GREAT OUTDOORS VISITORS BUREAU

www.elkcountryvisitorcenter.com, hours vary by season), located just north of town off Winslow Hill Road, is a good place to start an elk-spotting adventure. Opened in 2010, it features exhibits about elk and wildlife conservation, a "4D" theater (admission $3, children under 5 free) presenting a 22-minute show every half hour, and panoramic windows that look out at elk feeding areas. A series of trails and wildlife viewing areas are accessible from the center.

If you continue along Winslow Hill, heading away from Benezette, you'll soon arrive at another popular elk viewing area, **Dent's Run** (Winslow Hill Rd., 3.5 miles from Route 555 in Benezette). The vantage point overlooks fields where many a bull have locked antlers to win the affections of cows. The fields are also visited by white-tailed deer, wild turkeys, foxes, and even bobcats and black bears. Scan the skies for hawks and other birds of prey.

Another premier viewing area, **Hicks Run**, is 8.5 miles east of Benezette on the north side of Route 555. There was a village here in the early 1900s, which is why you'll pass a small cemetery on your way to a covered viewing blind. The blind affords a front-row view of elk and other animals in a wide clearing planted with succulent snacks.

Driving in circles is rather effective as elk spotting goes. Try the following loop. From Benezette, follow Winslow Hill Road for 2.2 miles, turn right to stay on Winslow Hill Road, continue for 0.7 miles, and bear right at Summerson Road. Continue on Summerson to Route 555, and turn right to return to Benezette. Repeat as necessary.

If you spot elk while driving, don't stop in the middle of the road. Find a place to pull off, being careful to avoid shoulders near sharp bends and private driveways. (If you see cars parked along a road, it's safe to assume that elk are nearby.) Keep in mind that people who live in places like Benezette value peace and quiet; they don't necessarily appreciate the growing wave of ecotourism. Don't go traipsing through private lands without permission. Certainly don't honk if you find yourself in traffic.

ELK SCENIC DRIVE

Elk Scenic Drive is a 127-mile route peppered with 23 sites of interest to nature lovers, including the viewing areas near Benezette. It winds through three state forests and three state game lands, starting and ending at points on I-80. From the west, leave I-80 at Penfield exit 111 at Route 153. From the east, take Snow Shoe exit 147 at Route 144. Look for distinctive signage.

All but a few of the sites require diverging from the main route. The journey can take a few hours or a few days, depending on your level of interest in sites such as Kettle Creek State Park, with its 167-acre stocked trout lake, a 26-mile equestrian trail, and a wetland teeming with gray catbirds, swamp sparrows, and other wildlife. It's not unusual for animals to amble across roads, so drive carefully. Be especially alert when you see an "elk crossing" sign. A mature bull with headgear bigger than a Vegas showgirl's can weigh as much as a car.

GUIDED ELK VIEWING

Spotting elk is never a sure thing, but you can stack the odds by hiring an experienced guide. Few know elk habits better than the husband-and-wife team behind **Hicks Run Outfitters** (814/787-4287, hicksrunoutfitters@yahoo.com). Jeff and Janet Coldwell, along with Janet's daughter, Cody, happily lead photographers, hunters, and anyone else seeking a close encounter of the elk kind off the beaten track. Call **PA Elk Range Adventures** (814/486-0305, http://paelkrangeadventures.tripod.com) to explore the range alongside nature photographer and writer and self-described hunting "addict" Phil Burkhouse. **Nature Quest** (570/723-1643, www.naturequestadventures.com) offers day and multi-day elk treks by various means of travel: foot, mountain bike, canoe, horse, or some combination thereof.

BEYOND ELK
St. Marys

Elk aren't the only attraction in these parts. The city of St. Marys, a 20-mile drive from Benezette, is not only Pennsylvania's second largest city by land area after Philadelphia but also the home of **Straub Brewery** (303 Sorg St., St. Marys, 814/834-2875, www .straubbeer.com). The award-winning brewery, family owned since 1872, has a fiercely loyal following in places where its beers can be found. Alas, distribution is limited to parts of Pennsylvania and Ohio. The beer is free of sugar, salt, and preservatives and just plain free to brewery visitors age 21 and older. Come between 9 A.M. and 4:30 P.M. on a weekday or before 1 P.M. on a Saturday to drink from the keg known as the "eternal tap." Tours are also free and open to anyone 12 or older. They're conducted 9 A.M.–noon weekdays. Call in advance if you want to make sure you visit when bottles are rolling off the line. For safety's sake, be sure to wear closed-toe footwear. The brewery's drive-up store is open 8:30 A.M.–8 P.M. Monday–Thursday and 8:30 A.M.–9 P.M. Friday and Saturday.

An early Straub coaster is part of the collection of the **Historical Society of St. Marys & Benzinger Twp.** (99 Erie Ave., St. Marys,

FACE TIME WITH PHIL

The resurrection of Pennsylvania's elk herd is a good story, but it's a different animal that grabs headlines year after year. That would be Punxsutawney Phil, the world's most famous weather forecaster (apologies to Al Roker). His hometown of Punxsutawney is a bit southwest of the elk range and more than a bit enamored of its renowned resident. Six-foot fiberglass effigies of the furry seer are scattered throughout town.

Unless you've been in a burrow for the last couple of decades, you probably know that Phil comes out of his hole every February 2, a.k.a. Groundhog Day, to predict if spring weather is around the bend or still weeks away. You may have seen him portrayed in *Groundhog Day,* the 1993 comedy starring Bill Murray. Maybe you caught him on *Oprah.* But the groundhog who inspired a Beanie Baby isn't so famous that you can't see him in person. Most days of the year, you'll find Phil and his groundhog entourage at their pad in downtown Punxsy, the **Groundhog Zoo** at Punxsutawney Memorial Library (301 E. Mahoning St., 814/938-5020, www.punxsutawneyboro.com/library). The critters are visible from inside or outside.

The best time to visit, of course, is **Groundhog Day** (www.groundhog.org). In the dark of night, thousands of people gather at **Gobbler's Knob** (1548 Woodland Ave. Ext.), a clearing just south of town, to await Phil's prognostication. He delivers it at daybreak. (Sadly, Phil himself does not address the crowd. That's left to men in top hats and bow ties who call themselves the Inner Circle.) The annual prediction is occasion for several days of festivities, including magic acts, musical performances, hayrides, and a sleepover at the community center. Lovebirds can marry at "Phil's Wedding Chapel" with Punxsutawney's mayor as officiant and an Inner Circle member as witness. The community also honors its favorite citizen in the summer. The weeklong **Punxsutawney Groundhog Festival** (814/938-2947, www.groundhogfestival.com, week of July 4) features free concerts, a craft show, and fireworks.

Book lodging well in advance if you're planning a Groundhog Day visit. Bill Murray bedded down at the **Pantall Hotel** (135 E. Mahoning St., 800/872-6825, www.pantallhotel. com, normally $64-139, inquire about special event rates), built in 1888. (*Groundhog Day* the movie was not, in fact, filmed in Punxsutawney. The actor visited of his own accord.) Being the only hotel in town hasn't made it lazy. The Pantall has undergone extensive renovations without shedding its turn-of-the-20th-century classiness. Its restaurant, the **Coach Room,** (7 A.M.-9 P.M. Tues.-Sat., 7 A.M.-3 P.M. Sun., $6-16) is best known for a bountiful Sunday brunch but a wise choice anytime.

The **Punxsutawney Area Chamber of Commerce** (102 W. Mahoning St., 800/752-7445, www.punxsutawney.com, 9 A.M.-5 P.M. Mon.-Fri., souvenir shop also open 10 A.M.-4 P.M. Sat.), a stone's throw from the Pantall, hawks

814/834-6525, www.smhistoricalsociety.com, 10 A.M.–4 P.M. Tues., 1–4 P.M. and 6–8 P.M. Thurs., other times by arrangement). The museum is crammed with artifacts dating to the founding of Sanct Marien Stadt—St. Marys, as we know it—by German Catholic immigrants in 1842. The nation's first Benedictine convent was established here in 1852. You can pray with the Benedictine Sisters of Elk County at **St. Joseph Monastery** (303 Church St., St. Marys, 814/834-2267, www.benedictine sistersofelkcounty.org) any day of the week.

Ridgway

The seat of Elk County was founded as a lumbering town in the 1820s. Lest you forget Ridgway's long association with wood, streets and parks are decorated with chainsaw carvings 5–6 feet high. Pop by the **Ridgway-Elk County Chamber of Commerce** (300 Main St., Ridgway, 814/776-1424, www.ridgway chamber.com, 10–4 Mon.–Fri., brochures always accessible) for a guide to these so-called Enchanted Woodlins. While you're there, grab a walking tour map of the "Lily of the Valley"

all things groundhog, from a fuzzy groundhog golf club cover to the official Groundhog Day Habanero Hot Sauce. You can also grab a free guide to the 32 fiberglass Phils, each decorated by a different artist.

Are Phil's predictive abilities good enough to merit all the fuss? Members of the Inner Circle will tell you he's never wrong. They'll also tell you there's been only one Phil since the Knob

tradition began in 1887. You can explore the science and lore of weather forecasting at the kid-centric **Punxsutawney Weather Discovery Center** (201 N. Findley St., 814/938-1000, www.weatherdiscovery.org, 10 A.M.-4 P.M. Mon.-Tues. and Thurs.-Sat., closed Wed. and Sun., admission $4, children under 2 free). As for their second claim, you'll have to make up your own mind.

© EDDIE-S

Gobbler's Knob, the home of Punxsutawney Phil

National Register Historic District. More than 700 buildings reflect Ridgway's century of significance in the lumber industry.

There's a real buzz in town in late February, during the **Ridgway Chainsaw Carvers Rendezvous** (814/772-0400, www.chain sawrendezvous.org). The noncompetitive showcase of ear-splitting sculpting attracts hundreds of wood and ice carvers from around the world, thousands of spectators, and television cameras. Feel inspired to take chainsaw to wood? Learn how at **Appalachian Arts Studio** (17245 Boot Jack Hill, Ridgway, 814/772-0400, www.appalachian-arts.com), owned by the couple responsible for the Rendezvous. Classes in pottery, painting, photography, and other arts are also available. Those who prefer collecting to creating can find works by local and regional artists at the gallery of the **Elk County Council on the Arts** (237 Main St., Ridgway, 814/772-7051, www.eccota.com, 10 A.M.–5 P.M. Tues.–Fri., 10 A.M.–2 P.M. Sat.).

One of the loveliest things to do in Ridgway is to leave it by way of the **Clarion/Little Toby Trail** (www.pavisnet.com/tcrtt). The rail-trail extends 18 miles to Brockway, following first the Clarion River and then Little Toby Creek. It offers hikers, bikers, and cross-country skiers pretty vistas and a pretty good workout. The Ridgway trailhead is on Water Street, one block off Main Street. Nearby **Love's Canoe** (3 Main St., Ridgway, 814/776-6285, 9 A.M.–5 P.M. Mon.–Fri., 7 A.M.–6 P.M. Sat.–Sun.) rents and sells bicycles and skis, along with canoes for those who'd rather paddle out of Ridgway.

ENTERTAINMENT AND EVENTS
Performing Arts

The **Paul G. Reitz Theater** (36 E. Scribner Ave., DuBois, 814/375-4274, www.reitzthe ater.com), home of the Reitz Theater Players, was a house of God for more than a century. The church-turned-theater presents everything from Appalachian clogging to Slovenian-style polka to one-act plays by local playwrights.

Festivals and Events

The **Elk County Summer Concert Series** (814/772-7051, www.eccota.com, free) brings live music to various venues on Friday evenings. The picnic pavilion at **Laurel Mountain Winery** (1754 Old Grade Rd., Falls Creek, 814/371-7022, www.laurelwines.com, 10 A.M.–6 P.M. Wed.–Sun.) transforms into a live music venue on select summer evenings. A logo wine glass is free with paid admission. Call or check the website for "sunset at the winery" dates. A homemade wine contest is among the highlights of **Tasting in the Wilds** (Ridgway, www.ridgwayheritagecouncil.org, late July, admission charged), a daylong celebration of wine, beer, food, and fine arts.

SPORTS AND RECREATION
State Parks

Don't sleep in if you're camping in **Sinnemahoning State Park** (8288 1st Fork Rd., Austin, 814/647-8401, www.dcnr.state .pa.us/stateparks/parks/sinnemahoning.aspx). Early morning is prime time for observing elk, white-tailed deer, and other animals in the fields along the First Fork Sinnemahoning Creek. A wildlife-viewing area is at the north end of the park along Route 872, 14 miles north of its junction with Route 120 and the village of Sinnemahoning. There's also much stirring at sunset, particularly during the summer months, when the large elevated house next to the viewing kiosk is home to dozens of bats. The winged things head out on errands just before dark.

Wildlife viewing isn't the only pastime at the park nestled in Elk State Forest. About 1,400 of the park's 1,910 acres are open to hunting and trapping. A dam built on the creek in the 1950s created a 142-acre reservoir renowned for panfish, especially bass. Nearby creeks and runs also provide good fishing. Boating is permitted on the reservoir. Park naturalists offer educational pontoon boat rides from Memorial Day to Labor Day and guided elk watches ($15 per person, $30 per family with one-week advance notice) in the fall. The park's 35-site modern campground is open from the second weekend in April to late December. Snowmobilers can make use of a 25-mile trail system in the park and adjacent state forest after deer season ends in December.

Named for the popular trout stream that flows through it, **Kettle Creek State Park** (97 Kettle Creek Park Ln., Renovo, 570/923-6004, www.dcnr.state.pa.us/stateParks/parks/kettlecreek.aspx) attracts not only anglers but also hunters, boaters, sunbathers, picnickers, hikers, horseback riders, mountain bikers, snowmobilers, and cross-country skiers—not to mention numerous species of wildlife. The centerpiece of the park is the 167-acre Kettle Creek Reservoir. A boat launch and sandy beach can be found at the northern end of the reservoir, about 10 miles northwest of Route 120 and the village of Westport via Kettle Creek Road. Sailing and windsurfing are permitted. The park provides access to the middle section of the 90-mile Donut Hole Trail and many miles of equestrian, biking, and snowmobiling trails in sprawling Sproul State Forest. Hunting and trapping are permitted in most of the 1,793-acre park and in the adjacent forest. The park has two campgrounds with a total of about 70 sites, open from early April through deer season in December. The lower campground has sites right along Kettle Creek.

Campsites in both parks, as well as a four-bedroom house at Sinnemahoning State Park, can be reserved online at www.pa.reserveworld.com or by calling 888/727-2757.

Hiking

Elk country offers several backpacking trails in addition to many short ones. The **Quehanna Trail** passes through the Quehanna Wild Area, the largest state-designated wild area at nearly 50,000 acres. The strenuous loop of 70-plus miles can be accessed at Parker Dam State Park (Mud Run Rd., near Penfield, 814/765-0630, www.dcnr.state.pa.us/stateparks/parks/parkerdam.aspx), among other places. Connector trails allow for shorter treks. Contact Moshannon State Forest (814/765-0821, fd09@state.pa.us, www.dcnr.state.pa.us/Forestry/stateforests/moshannon.aspx) for a trail map

© CLINTON COUNTY ECONOMIC PARTNERSHIP

PENNSYLVANIA WILDS

hiking in Sproul State Forest

and camping guidelines. Cross-country skiers should also get their hands on the free map; there are more than 50 miles of marked skiing trails in the Quehanna Wild Area.

The 34-mile **Bucktail Path** takes its name from a storied Civil War regiment of Pennsylvania woodsmen and requires a good deal of soldiering on. It calls for steep climbs, stream crossings, and a comfort level with isolation. The southern trailhead is on Grove Street in the Route 120 village of Sinnemahoning. From there, hikers ascend to a ridge top before entering the Johnson Run Natural Area of Elk State Forest. The Bucktail is the only trail into the natural area, a blast from Pennsylvania's pre-settler past. The northern terminus is at Sizerville State Park (199 E. Cowley Run Rd., Emporium, 814/486-5605, www.dcnr.state.pa.us/stateParks/parks/sizerville.aspx). Contact Elk State Forest (814/486-3353, fd13@state.pa.us, www.dcnr.state.pa.us/forestry/stateforests/elk.aspx) for more information about the trail.

The western terminus of the 90-mile **Donut Hole Trail** can be found in the village of Jericho, less than a mile east of Sinnemahoning on Route 120. Contact Sproul State Forest (570/923-6011, fd10@state.pa.us, www.dcnr.state.pa.us/forestry/stateforests/sproul.aspx) for information.

ACCOMMODATIONS
Under $100

A stay at the **Bennett House Bed and Breakfast** (14019 Rte. 555, Benezette, 814/787-4842, www.bennetthousepa.com, $80) is rather like visiting Grandma. Innkeeper Ginger McCoy is liable to greet you with a hug and send you on your way with Christian literature. The three guest rooms are small and plain and the bathrooms shared, but the location is hard to beat. Hicks Run, one of the most prolific elk-viewing areas, is just two miles from the homestead that once belonged to Ginger's great-great-grandfather. Eggs served for breakfast are courtesy of her hens.

Rooms at the **Old Charm Bed and Breakfast** (444 Brusselles St., St. Marys, 814/834-9429,

www.visitoldcharm.com, $72–82) are, indeed, charming. But don't take "old" the wrong way; the B&B is blessed with contemporary amenities including en suite bathrooms and wireless Internet access. The Old Charm Gift Shoppe (Tues. by chance, noon–5 P.M. Wed.–Sat.) carries chocolates and candles and prettily packaged baskets of locally produced goods.

The third-floor suite at the elegant **Victorian Loft Bed and Breakfast** (216 S. Front St., Clearfield, 814/765-4805, www.victorianloft.com, $75–130), big enough for two couples or a family, boasts a whirlpool tub overlooking the West Branch of the Susquehanna River. Antique silver and china place settings greet breakfasters in the formal Victorian dining room. Innkeepers Tim and Peggy Durant also offer a one-bedroom traditionally decorated pad in downtown Clearfield ($75–125) and a divinely secluded three-bedroom cabin in Moshannon State Forest ($110–150). Ask about biweekly and monthly rates if you're staying awhile.

$100-200

A stone's throw from the Elk Country Visitor Center, the three-bedroom **Elk Mountain Homestead** (401 Homestead Dr., Benezette, 814/787-7530, www.experienceelkcountry.com, $115–230, weekly $860–1,100, rates good for up to 6 people, $30 per night for each additional person) offers sweeping views of fields, woods, and the critters that inhabit them. Proceeds from the rental of the state-owned farmhouse benefit conservation efforts. The house, which sleeps as many as 10 people, has a fully equipped kitchen, two showers, and a covered viewing platform. Light sleepers should consider shutting their windows during the fall, when bulls bugle all night long.

The six modern cabins at **Wapiti Woods** (Rte. 555, 4 miles west of Benezette, 814/787-7525, www.wapitiwoods.com, $160, weekly $995) boast indoor wood burners, creek-facing porch entryways, and off-the-charts coziness. Two of the knotty pine masterpieces also have whirlpool tubs. (Suds bunnies should ask for the "romance" cabins.) The 34-acre retreat along the Bennett Branch of Sinnemahoning Creek has its very own wildlife-wooing feed plot.

Built in 1998, **The Inn at Narrows Creek** (44 Narrows Creek Ln., DuBois, 814/371-9394, www.narrowscreek.com, $85–125) plausibly portrays a 19th-century New England inn. Each of six guest rooms and suites has a private bathroom and distinctive theme, e.g. angels, sunflowers, and Americana. Be the first to claim the hammock in the grove of hickory trees out back. Bring home a bit of the coziness by shopping at the on-site folk art store, open 10 A.M.–5 P.M. Wednesday–Saturday.

The cheery Jerome Powell Suite at the **(Towers Victorian Inn** (330 South St., Ridgway, 814/772-7657, www.towersinn.com, $110–149 May–Oct., $80–125 Nov.–April) pays tribute to the lumber baron who built the Italianate mansion in 1865. But the most stately of guest accommodations is named for town founder Jacob Ridgway. The inn has a two-bedroom carriage house that sleeps as many as seven in addition to six rooms and suites in the main house. Hikers, bikers, and boaters can arrange for drop-off and pick-up service.

Over $200
Hot tubs and satellite TV await at **Elk Terrace Lodge** and **Winslow Meadow Lodge** (Elk Terrace Dr., Benezette, 814/772-6850, www.elkterracelodge.com and www.winslowmeadowlodge.com, $225 for 2 adults), sibling rental properties just minutes from Benezette. If such comforts just make it hard to leave the grounds, that's okay. Elk have a habit of visiting the three- and four-bedroom lodges.

Your majesty may enjoy a stay at **MacDarvey Castle** (near Benezette, 814/546-2043, http://macdarvey.tripod.com, 1–5 bedrooms $225–400 per night, 2-night minimum), undoubtedly the most unusual lodging in elk country. The boxy hilltop castle is the work of a certain Marcy and Dave (its name is an anagram of theirs), whose tastes tend toward turrets and gold filigree. Guests can gaze upon grazing elk from 67 windows, shoot pool in the "dungeon," or feast in the dining room. You'll be king or queen of the castle whether you rent one bedchamber or all five; it's rented to just one group at a time. Dragon not included.

FOOD
When it comes to high-quality grazing, elk have it somewhat better than humans in these parts. Restaurants are few and far between and tend toward pub grub. But the pub grub is rather good in some cases and downright colossal in one.

Benezette
The **Benezette Hotel** (95 Winslow Hill Rd., 814/787-4240, www.benezettehotel.com, 11 A.M.–2 A.M. Mon.–Fri., 7 A.M.–2 A.M. Sat.–Sun., dinner until 9 P.M., late-night menu until midnight, $4–18) is so centrally located that it's frequently referenced in directions to elk viewing areas. It serves everything from wings to "wedgies" (grilled steak or ham, cheese, and vegetables enfolded in a 12-inch pizza shell), along with beer and other beverages. Wrangle a table on the patio and you may spot a live one as you bite into an elk burger.

St. Marys
Gunners (33 S. St. Marys St., 814/834-2161, www.gunners.biz, kitchen 11 A.M.–10 P.M. Mon.–Sat., bar open until midnight Mon.–Thurs. and 2 A.M. Fri.–Sat., $4–24) hits the mark with a jovial atmosphere and just-right steaks. Call or check the website for the entertainment lineup. A player piano does the job most evenings.

Clearfield
With 72 hours notice, **(Denny's Beer Barrel Pub** (1452 Woodland Rd., 814/765-7190, www.dennysbeerbarrelpub.com, 10 A.M.–midnight Mon.–Sat., 11 A.M.–11 P.M. Sun., $4–22) can cook up a burger that weighs in at more than 100 pounds. Two or three pounds of beef is more than enough for most guests. Finish a two-pounder in an hour and you get a free T-shirt, half off the $15.95 price, and a plac[e] in the restaurant's Hall of Fame. The $21.[ ] three-pound burger is free if you finish it in

minutes. Give the restaurant a day's notice if you get it in your head to try the six-pound "Ye Olde 96er" ($35.95) or the 15-pound "Belly Buster" ($49.95). Hamburger challenges have made the restaurant famous—Food Network famous—but the real challenge may be deciding on a dish from the 16-page menu. In addition to 30-some burgers, Denny's Beer Barrel Pub offers wings in dozens of flavors, pizzas, steak and seafood dishes, Irish fare, Mexican *comida,* and more.

The family-run **Moena** (215 E. Market St., Clearfield, 814/765-1564, www.moenas.com, lunch 11 A.M.–1:30 P.M. Tues.–Fri., dinner 5–8:30 P.M. Tues.–Thurs., 5–9 P.M. Fri.–Sat., $5–22) is named for the Italian village from whence the family originated. The restaurant's rendition of filet scaloppini, veal Caprese, chicken Napoli, and the like would make the ancestors proud.

INFORMATION
The **PA Great Outdoors Visitors Bureau** (75 Main St., Brookville, 800/348-9393, www .visitpago.com, 8:30 A.M.–4:30 P.M. Mon.–Fri.) is a fount of elk-viewing tips and other information. It speaks for Cameron, Clarion, Elk, Forest, and Jefferson Counties.

GETTING THERE AND AROUND
The main corridor through elk country is the east–west I-80. Benezette, its unofficial capital, is about 140 miles northeast of Pittsburgh and a 70-mile drive from State College.

DuBois Regional Airport (DUJ) offers direct service to and from Cleveland. State College's **University Park Airport** (SCE) offers direct service to and from Detroit, Philadelphia, and Washington, D.C.

BACKGROUND

The Land

If you look at a map of the original 13 American colonies you will see that Pennsylvania is located right in the middle. The "Keystone State" was so-named since Pennsylvania is geographically in the center of the arch formed by the other colonies, similar to the keystone that stonemasons put in the middle of an arch to hold the rest of the stones together. Today Pennsylvania is surrounded by the states of New York, New Jersey, Delaware, Maryland, West Virginia, and Ohio. It has a land area of 44,820 square miles, ranking 33rd in area among the 50 states, and has 1,239 square miles of water surface. The elevation in the state ranges from its highest peak of Mount Davis in Somerset County (3,213 feet above sea level) to its lowest point at sea level, on the banks of the Delaware River outside Philadelphia.

It was for good reason that King Charles II of England in 1681 coined the name Pennsylvania, translated from Latin to mean "Penn's Woods." When early Europeans first explored the eastern shores of North America they were awed by the vastness and density of the forest as trees covered more than 90 percent of Pennsylvania's territory. Its moderate climate, abundant rainfall, and rich soils gave rise to dense forests with plants and animals

© ANNA DUBROVSKY

unknown to European settlers. A famed natural scientist named John Bartram was traveling up the Susquehanna River in 1743 and found forests so thick that "it seems almost as if the sun had never shown on the ground since the creation." Today, more than 17 million acres, almost 60 percent of the state, are covered by a quality hardwood forest, and Pennsylvania is the nation's largest producer of hardwood lumber (over 1 billion board feet per year). The State Forest system, comprising 2.1 million acres, is one of the largest public forest ownerships in the eastern United States.

GEOGRAPHY

The variety of natural landscapes in Pennsylvania is the result of millions of years of continents shifting and crashing into one another, creating the state's mountains and valleys. The Appalachian mountain range, which bisects present-day Pennsylvania, was formed some 480 million years ago and marks the first of several mountain-building plate collisions that culminated in the construction of the supercontinent Pangea, with the Appalachians near the center. Compared to the modern-day Himalayas in Asia, the Appalachians once stood as tall and were covered under large glaciations and vast oceans. Weathering and erosion prevailed as Pangea broke apart and the mountains began to wear away. By the end of the Mesozoic era (65 million years ago), the Appalachian Mountains had been eroded to an almost flat plain. It was not until the region was uplifted during the most recent geologic era that the distinctive present topography formed. Broad-topped mountains, called plateaus, include the Allegheny and Pocono ranges of the Appalachian Mountains.

From the Appalachian Mountains, the landscape slopes downward to the east and west forming rolling hills and lowlands that make up the five major land regions. The largest of these land regions is the Appalachian Plateau, which covers most of western and northern Pennsylvania. This region, which includes the regions south and north of Pittsburgh, holds a big share of the state's natural resources; it

was the location of the world's first successful oil well and a source of rich veins of coal. East of the Appalachian Plateau is the Appalachian Ridge and Valley, a region of narrow and steep mountain peaks and numerous valleys that resemble parallel arcs if viewed from space. Grouping the valleys of Cumberland, Lebanon, and Lehigh together made up the Great Appalachian Valley, an area that stretches from the south-central border with Maryland to the eastern border with New Jersey. Farther southeast is the region called the Piedmont Plateau, an area of low hills, ridges, and valleys that has some of the richest farmland in the state and, some say, of the country. Due to the soil conservation techniques practiced by the Amish since the early colonial days the area has remained agriculturally productive even through the industrial pillaging of the 19th and 20th century. The remaining two regions are close to water and the smallest regions of the five—the Atlantic Coastal Plain and the Erie Lowland or Erie Plain. The Atlantic Coastal Plain covers the extreme southeastern corner of the state while the Erie Plain covers the extreme northwestern corner of Pennsylvania.

The River Valleys

Three major river systems in Pennsylvania drain more than 90 percent of the state's land: the Delaware, Susquehanna, and the combined Allegheny, Ohio, and Monongahela Rivers. These river systems were important in the development of the state's transportation systems and industries such as steel and lumber. The Delaware River is the main river of the eastern part of the state and actually defines the jagged eastern border of the state. The river separates Pennsylvania from New York and New Jersey as it serpentines through narrow rapids and wide regions from New York to the Delaware Bay. This is the same river of the famous "Delaware Crossing," which involved an improvised boat crossing undertaken by George Washington's army during the American Revolution on Christmas Day 1776.

Due to its access to the Atlantic Ocean, the Delaware is a major shipping lane that is second only to the Mississippi River in the amount of commerce it carries each year. The Upper Delaware offers some of the finest recreational opportunities in the northeastern United States. In particular, sightseeing, boating, camping, hunting, fishing, hiking, and bird-watching are popular activities in the river area.

Running north to south through the central part of the state is the Susquehanna (sus-ka-HAN-na) River, renowned for its fantastic fishing and recreation. Anglers can fish for muskies, walleye, smallmouth bass, panfish, catfish, and carp. The river meanders 444 miles from its origin near Cooperstown, New York, until it empties into the Chesapeake Bay at Havre de Grace, Maryland. In a similar north-to-south manner, the Allegheny River flows down the western portion of the state. This river begins as a spring in a farmer's field off of Route 49, a couple of miles east of the little town of Colesburg and nine miles from Coudersport in the upper Appalachian Mountains of northern Pennsylvania. The Allegheny River joins the Monongahela (mo-non-ga-HAY-la) River in Pittsburgh to form the westward-pointing Ohio River, which eventually flows into the Mississippi. The Ohio provides 35 percent of all of the water that empties out into the Gulf of Mexico.

CLIMATE

In spite of its proximity to the ocean, Pennsylvania has a humid continental climate that is due to the prevailing winds from the west. These prevailing westerly winds carry most of the weather disturbances from the interior of the continent into the state, so that the Atlantic Ocean has only a limited influence upon the climate. Pennsylvania is also situated in the conflict zone between polar air masses from the north and tropical air masses from the south. These air masses create large annual, daily, and day-to-day temperature ranges that Pennsylvanians experience in four distinct seasons. In addition, local elevation and geological features can drastically vary the climate.

Winters usually bring snow to most of the state (more to the mountainous areas), with temperatures ranging from below zero Fahrenheit to the high 30s Fahrenheit. The coldest time of the year is usually January, with northern latitudes recording colder temperatures and southeastern locations with milder temperatures. In summer the temperature rarely breaks 100 degrees, yet the humidity is often high, especially in the months of August and September. Evenings during the summer months cool down from their daytime highs, which average in the 80s in July. Spring and autumn are the best times to travel to Pennsylvania as the temperatures are moderate and the state is covered in greenery in the spring and is blanketed in brilliant colors in the autumn. The spring months of March through May see the temperatures slowly ramping up from an average of 40s to 70s, while the autumn months of September through November see the reverse.

The state averages 41 inches of precipitation each year, which helps trees and other plants grow abundantly. The greatest amount of precipitation usually occurs in spring and summer months, while February is the driest month, having about two inches less than the wettest months. Thunderstorms, which average between 30 and 35 occurrences per year, are concentrated in the warm months and are responsible for most of the summertime rainfall. Sometimes tropical systems from the south (or their remnants) affect the state by causing flooding rains, especially in the eastern portion of the state. Tornadoes can and do occur but they usually cause minor damage. Yet in May 31, 1985 a total of 21 tornadoes killed 65 people, injured 707, destroyed over 1,000 homes, and caused $380 million (1985 figure) in damage. A rare F-5, the strongest tornado, nearly leveled the town of Wheatland in Mercer County.

Among the major population centers, Philadelphia and Pittsburgh have similar temperatures with annual mean temperatures of 54°F and 50°F, respectively, and similar precipitation amounts of 42 inches and 37.8 inches, respectively. However, Pittsburgh usually has more snow (44 inches) as compared with 21 inches for Philadelphia. The greatest weather extremes usually occur in the northeastern and north-central part of the state. The average number of cloudy days increases from the southeast corner of the state near Philadelphia (average of 160 cloudy days) to the northwest corner of the state near Erie (average of 205 cloudy days).

ENVIRONMENTAL ISSUES

When the first Europeans settled in Pennsylvania, the horizon-to-horizon forest had many 400-year-old trees. Trees that densely covered the state were cut down by early settlers who viewed them as obstacles to agriculture and timber for cabins and barns. Since 1682, the advancing human population has conquered the vast forests that covered the state. The last bison was shot in 1801, and the last native elk in 1867.

As the Industrial Revolution progressed in the 19th century, Pennsylvanians cut, mined, quarried, hunted, harvested, and in other ways extracted nature's bounty with unrelenting enthusiasm and voraciousness. By 1900, Pennsylvania had lost more than 60 percent of its forests. Its polluted waterways, denuded landscapes, impoverished soils, extinct and disappearing plant and animal life and foul air motivated many to embrace new conservation and preservation ethics. Fears of a "timber famine" gave birth to a national conservation movement for the protection and rejuvenation of forests for future use. In the early 20th century, Pennsylvania passed a broad network of laws to restrict the pollution of its waters and air, protect wildlife, and regulate extraction of natural resources. It established fish, game and forest commissions to conserve and manage these resources. In addition, the state acquired more than four million acres of land and established 20 state forests for timber conservation, plant and wildlife preservation, and recreation. Unfortunately, most of the damage was done and is irreversible: Pennsylvania has lost as many as 156 species of native vascular plants and vertebrates in the past 300 years. An additional 351 species have become endangered or threatened. Moreover, 56 percent of Pennsylvania's wetlands have been lost since 1780.

Yet old challenges endured and new threats emerged during the 20th century. Leaded gasoline, acid rain, DDT, PCBs, and other carcinogens polluted the water and the air, wreaking havoc on the flora and fauna of the state (the Fish and Boat Commission issues an annual advisory on which areas and fish to avoid). By 1999, Pennsylvania led the nation in toxic discharges into its surface water, had the worst acid rain problem in the nation, and was the nation's largest importer of municipal waste. The state was second in the number of Superfund toxic waste sites, rate of suburban sprawl, and toxic air emissions from coal mining and processing; third in toxic air emissions from coal, oil, and electrical utilities; and fourth in the release of toxic chemicals from manufacturing. Pennsylvania has the distinction of being the home to the town of Centralia, where an exposed seam of coal caught fire in 1961, forcing the entire community to flee the area as the underground fire continues to this day and is expected to burn for decades more. No single event drove home the potential costs of industry more than the accident at Three Mile Island, which in 1979 ended the American romance with nuclear energy. Yet the greatest danger to Pennsylvania's remaining wildlife is the risk of habitat destruction by sprawl: the building of parking lots, shopping malls, and houses.

The introduction of nonnative insects, plants, and diseases has caused millions of dollars in damage and altered the forest ecosystem. Certain parts of the state have been overrun by Norway maple, Japanese knotwood, autumn olive, and other plants imported from abroad. A popular plant with home gardeners called the purple loosestrife escaped into the wild and rapidly displaced native plants, choked wetlands, and caused millions of dollars of economic damage. The Asian long-horned beetle, which entered the country in wooden pallets from China, threatens to cause billions of dollars in damage by attacking a wide range of American trees. Multi-agency surveys are in place to detect threats before they become established in the state.

One native threat to the state, unbeknownst to the average tourist, has been the white-tailed deer. All but gone from Penn's woods at the beginning of the 20th century, deer now exist in unprecedented numbers, averaging 60 deer per square mile. They overgraze the native plants of the forest while leaving the nonnative plants untouched, contribute to the spread of Lyme disease, and cause thousands of motor vehicle accidents each year. By eating and killing off the seedlings and saplings that regenerate woodlands they have radically altered the state's forests.

Conservation efforts by the state and private organizations have made great strides in turning back the clock to the pre-European settlement days. By the 20th century, the state passed stricter wildlife-protection laws and enforced those that were already on the books. Over the last 100 years the state's Fish and Game Commission has reintroduced beaver from Canada, elk from Wyoming, white-tailed deer from Michigan, cottontail rabbits from Kansas and Missouri, and quail from Mexico. Using the fees paid each year by hunters and fishers, they set up hatcheries and nurseries to restock the state's streams and forests with shad, trout, ruffled grouse, pheasant, and other species. River otters, once ubiquitous across Pennsylvania before over-trapping and poor water quality, are thriving after being reintroduced throughout the state starting in the mid-1990s. Likewise, several bird species, such as the osprey, the peregrine falcon, and bald eagle, are slowly increasing in population. In 1983 the state contained three bald eagle nests (easily counted because of their great size); by 2009 that number was up to 155 nest sites.

Flora and Fauna

FLORA

Pennsylvania is situated in the middle of the transitional zone between the great northern and southern forests of eastern North America. The mixed hardwoods of the southern forests—the broadleaf oak, hickory, chestnut, and walnut—merged into mixed softwood and hardwood forests of the north—the great white pine, hemlock, sugar maple, beech, and birch. The forest that you see today is largely the result of two things: the exploitation of timber at the turn of the 20th century, which devastated the old-growth variety of trees, and 87 years of Mother Nature's forces and management by the Forest Service. Various disturbances such as wind, fire, insects, disease, deer, and human intervention worked together to create the unique conditions for hardwood trees to become established and flourish (over 108 species of native trees and many others introduced from Europe and Asia). Pennsylvania's forests contain more hardwood growing stock than those of any other state, providing raw material for a forest-products industry that earns $5 billion per year while employing nearly 100,000 people.

Located primarily in the north-central part of Pennsylvania are 20 sites that are designated "old-growth" or virgin forests. These forests contain trees that have attained great age (usually 300 to 400 years old) and exhibit characteristic features such as large trunk diameters. Most of the sites are within what is known as the Lumber Heritage Region, the 15 counties from which most of the timber resources were extracted in the 19th and early 20th centuries. Although industrialization removed the majority of these trees, those that are left from that era are usually in areas that were inaccessible, such as steep slopes, or accidents of boundary overlaps. Within Cook Forest State Park, nine different old-growth forest areas—covering over 2,200 acres—can be found within boundaries of the park.

Within 45 minutes of Cook Forest are three of Pennsylvania's other premier old-growth sites: Heart's Content Scenic Area, Anders Run Natural Area, and the 4,000-acre Tionesta Scenic and Research Natural Area, which contains hemlocks more than 500 years old. Every Fall, the deciduous trees in the state put on an unrivaled blaze of glory along its highways, country roads, and coastline with rich and vibrant hues of red, orange, yellow, and brown.

Spring in Pennsylvania brings abundant rainfall and glorious blooms of native wildflowers and flowering shrubs. Throughout spring, yellow forsythia, azaleas, rhododendrons, trilliums, elderberries, honeysuckles, and mountain laurels bring splashes of color to the state's forests, fields, and roadsides. This colorful display brings thousands of tourists from the Commonwealth and surrounding states each spring. Mountain laurels, the state flower of Pennsylvania, normally begin to bloom late in May and their pink and white blossoms are in evidence well into June. They are particularly abundant in the mountainous sections of the state, particularly the Laurel Highlands in the south and the Allegheny Mountains in the northeast. The distinctive plant, with its three- to five-inch lustrous, dark green leaves, is used extensively as ornamental shrubbery. Pennsylvania's climate also ensures wild berries such as cranberries, blackberries, thimbleberries, strawberries, and elderberries throughout the early spring and into the fall season. Wild strawberries, noticeable by their smaller size compared to their cultivated cousins, can be seen in early May through June throughout the state. High-bush cranberries grow in northern Pennsylvania and can be recognized by their three-lobed leaves and large seeds.

FAUNA

he white-tailed deer, the icon for the state mal, is undoubtedly one of the most in-ntial species of wildlife in Pennsylvania. provide the greatest wildlife value to the s of this state as watchable wildlife, a huntable resource, and venison for countless families. Much of Pennsylvania's rural cultural heritage is closely linked to this species. Around 1900, the Game Commission estimated that only about 500 white-tailed deer remained in the state. The commission began bringing deer from Michigan and Kentucky in 1906 and continued through the 1920s. Seeing a deer in the forest (or in the headlights) is no longer a rare event in much of Pennsylvania. Since development has dramatically reduced their habitat they are frequently sighted, therefore keep a lookout along roads. Along with deer, the garden variety of forest critters are commonly seen in Pennsylvania, including: wild rabbits, black and gray squirrels, raccoons, foxes, minks, opossums, skunks, and woodchucks. Beavers, nearly extinct due to over-trapping (prime pelts netted $65 each in colonial times), are now abundant in each state county. Less common, but still found around campsites and cabins, are black bears, which are mostly found in the north-central and northeastern counties of the state. Black bear attacks in the eastern United States are rare, yet bears dependent on eating human food can become slightly aggressive when people get between them and food. Rarer still are wildcats, which live in northern mountain habitats.

Between 1913 and 1926, the Pennsylvania Game Commission attempted to restore an elk herd by releasing 177 western elk from Wyoming. A recent survey indicated the herd size to be more than 600 animals, typically found in southwestern Cameron and southeastern Elk Counties. Elk are much larger than white-tailed deer, weighing between 700 and 1,000 pounds with a height of about five feet. Males are usually sporting a set of backward curving antlers that can have as many as 16 points, while females are somewhat smaller and antlerless. The elks' coat can vary from dark brown to reddish, depending on the season, yet a large buff-colored patch covering the rump is characteristic signature. Elk are best observed at dawn and dusk, in September and October during the mating season, and from a safe distance. They can be very dangerous, especially bulls during the mating season.

Snakes

Hikers and campers should be aware that most snakes in Pennsylvania are harmless, although there are three native poisonous snake species that inhabit the state (northern copperheads, timber rattlesnakes, and the eastern massasauga rattlesnake). All these venomous snakes possess an indentation or pit on each side of the head between the eye and nostril, a vertically elliptical eye pupil resembling that of a cat, and a single row of scales on the underside of the tail. Reports of venomous snakebites in the state are rare, with bites usually occurring while a person is trying to catch or carelessly handle one of these snakes. All of these species are usually non-aggressive and prefer to avoid confrontation, usually moving away from an approaching human or remaining completely still as a threat passes by.

Birds

Bird-watching, or birding, has become a popular activity in Pennsylvania thanks to the 373 species of birds. The largest number and species of birds may be found during May when migration for most long-distance migrants is well under way. In some locations more than 150 species have been recorded in 24 hours; these include flycatchers, wrens, thrushes, and orioles. Bird song all but ends in August as the nesting season is usually over for most species. The ruffed grouse, known as the state game bird and sometimes called the partridge or pheasant, is easily recognized by their territorial drumming and the roar of their wings when they take flight. Distinguishable characteristics include a plump body, feathered legs, and mottled reddish-brown color. Great horned owls, the largest and most widely distributed resident owl in Pennsylvania, are powerful birds of prey that feed on a wide variety of mammals and birds. They are most often detected when vocalizing during the mating and breeding season in fall through winter. A nesting female may sit on eggs through the

worst of weather and sometimes is seen covered with snow.

In the Water

With 83,184 miles of stream and rivers and over 4,000 inland lakes and ponds, Pennsylvania has notoriety for its popular game fish, including trout, bass, muskie, walleye, steelhead, and panfish. The Allegheny, Monongahela, and Ohio Rivers around Pittsburgh are clean enough these days to support 40 species of fish. Clean enough that they attracted the Bassmaster Classic in 2005 and the Forrest Wood Cup in 2009, which are professional bass fishing competitions. The Susquehanna River and its tributaries, Roaring Creek and Hemlock Creek, feature wild and stocked trout and smallmouth bass. Potter County boasts a huge collection of Class A wild trout streams, while Oil Creek State Park offers excellent fly-fishing for walleye and smallmouth bass. Many streams are stocked to ensure good fishing and regulated with minimum size and daily limits by the Fish and Boat Commission. Lake Erie is sometimes called the freshwater fishing capital of the world thanks to trout, perch, walleye, smallmouth bass, northern pike, and muskie. In recent years, more attention has been given to the threat of nonnative species and the impact these species have on native wildlife within the Lake. Nonnative fish (e.g., round goby) and invertebrates such as the zebra mussel or rusty crayfish are currently occurring in high densities in Lake Erie drainage and may be seriously impacting native fauna by eliminating them from their former ranges.

One positive trend in wetland wildlife is the increase in river otters, which had drastically declined in the state because of fur trapping and destruction of river water quality. Through a state reintroduction program that started in 1982, more than 110 river otters have been released in Pennsylvanian rivers and streams. Otters were reintroduced in several watersheds across northern Pennsylvania and as far south as the lower Susquahanna River and Youghiogheny River. You might notice a river otter due to its playful antics, particularly its practice of repeatedly sliding down stream banks into the water. Amphibians such as frogs, salamanders, and turtles can also be seen throughout the state. One turtle in particular, the bog turtle, is a 3- to 4.5-inch-long turtle species usually found in southeastern and eastern Pennsylvania. Development and selfish collectors who find them irresistibly cute have decimated their population, and as a result they have received federal threatened status. Eastern hellbenders, large and wondrously ugly amphibians, are usually found in the western part of the state and can live to be 30 to 50 years old. They are a superb indicator of the health of the environment and can provide an early warning of when an ecosystem is in trouble since they prefer clean and clear-flowing rivers and streams.

History

ANCIENT CIVILIZATION

The first people to live in Pennsylvania were part of the earliest waves of human migration that came during the end of the last Ice Age (about 30,000 to 10,000 years ago), when lower ocean levels exposed the Bering Land Bridge between Siberia and Alaska. These Paleo-Indians, as archaeologists call them, were a nomadic hunter-gatherer tribe that fashioned tools from stone, bone, and wood in order to hunt mammoths, elk, and moose but did not plant crops or build permanent dwellings. A Paleo-Indian archaeological site in Pennsylvania, the Meadowcroft Rockshelter, which is 30 miles southwest of Pittsburgh, shows evidence of human occupation possibly as early as 16,000 years ago, meaning it may be the earliest documented site of human occupation in North America. About 13,000 years ago ice glaciers located in the northeastern and northwestern parts of the state began to recede. During the Archaic Period (8000–1000 B.C.), as the climate slowly got warmer, Indian hunter-gatherers continued to seek shelter at Meadowcroft, but their technology diversified and they began to hunt deer, elk, bear, and turkey in deciduous forests with a rich understory of berries and other plant foods.

The Fishbasket Old Town archaeological site in Clarion County, Indian Jasper Quarries in the Lehigh Valley, and Indian Paint Hill in Warren County have yielded arrowheads, stone axes, sinkers for fishing nets, and other Archaic Period artifacts. By the Late Woodland Period (A.D. 1000–1500), there were two major Indian tribe population centers that congregated along the major river systems of the Delaware and the Susquehanna. The northern and southern parts of the Delaware Valley were inhabited by the Lenapes or Delawares. To the west, close to modern-day Lancaster County, the northern Susquehanna Valley was home to Iroquoian-speaking peoples called the Susquehannocks. Numerous tribes, which can't be identified with certainty, inhabited western Pennsylvania before the Europeans arrived but were eliminated by wars and diseases in the 17th century. The Iroquois Nation, a confederacy of numerous tribes joined together, lived mostly in present-day New York yet traveled to present-day northern Pennsylvania to hunt.

EUROPEAN EXPLORATION AND SETTLEMENT

The age of discovery in Europe brought a desire for territorial gains beyond the seas, first by Spain and Portugal and later by England, France, the Netherlands, and Sweden. Captain John Smith, famous for later establishing the Jamestown settlement, journeyed from Virginia up the Susquehanna River in 1608, visiting the Susquehannock people. Later in 1609 Henry Hudson, an Englishman in the Dutch service, sailed the *Half Moon* into Delaware Bay and made contact with the Lenape, thus giving the Dutch a claim to the area. Not until 1640, however, did the Dutch establish their first trading post at Fort Nassau (near present-day New Jersey), which soon developed a fairly prosperous exchange of Dutch items for Indian beaver pelts. Surprisingly, the Swedes were the first to establish a settlement in the Delaware Bay area, called New Sweden, beginning with the expedition of 1637–1638, which established a small colony of Swedes near the current site of Wilmington, Delaware. Governor Johann Printz of New Sweden relocated the capital to Tinicum Island in 1643, which was 20 miles south of present-day Philadelphia. There he directed a rough band of conscripts, army deserters, and debtors to build new blockhouses and log cabins as well as a new fort that aimed four cannons at a Dutch trading station. In the 1640s, Holland and Sweden were at peace yet competition in the fur trade created on-going tensions between Printz and his Dutch counterpart, Peter Stuyvesant, governor of New Netherlands. After some skirmishes between the two groups, the settlers lived and worked together peaceably and established an effective legal system that punished crimes based on fines rather than imprisonment.

In 1664 King Charles II of England decided to give all the land between Connecticut and Maryland to his brother, James, Duke of York. As a result of this declaration, the Dutch decided to seize the Hudson and Delaware Valleys, in spite of English claims to these regions. During the war that followed, the British captured New Amsterdam, whose name they changed to New York, and English laws and civil government were introduced to the region in 1676. By 1680, Pennsylvania included Swedes (the largest nationality in the region) along with lesser numbers of Dutch, Finnish, German, French, Welsh, and English settlers.

WILLIAM PENN AND THE QUAKERS

During the late 17th century, England was undergoing religious upheaval as Protestants persecuted Catholics, Catholics persecuted Protestants, and both persecuted other religious beliefs. A new Protestant sect called the Religious Society of Friends came in the spotlight due to its rejection of rituals and oaths, its

opposition to war, and its simplicity of speech and dress. Outsiders tended to call the followers of this sect Quakers because they were said to quake and tremble when they rose to speak during their religious services. George Fox, the radical preacher credited with founding the Quakers, was decried a heretic and his followers were widely persecuted and imprisoned. William Penn, a charismatic young aristocrat who frequented the king's court and was trusted by the Duke of York (later known as King James II), embraced Fox's teachings. Despite high social rank and an excellent education, Penn shocked his upper-class associates by his conversion to Quaker beliefs that insisted that God valued each individual equally–a drastic change to the British class system. King Charles II of England owed a large sum of money to Penn's father, a deceased admiral in the British Navy. Seeking a haven in the New World for persecuted Quakers, Penn asked the king to grant him land in the territory between Lord Baltimore's province of Maryland and the Duke of York's province of New York. With the duke's support, Penn's petition was granted. By giving Penn a colony, the king managed to pay off an outstanding debt and at the same time get rid of people that constantly challenged English laws and the legitimacy of the Anglican Church, the nation's established church. On March 4, 1681, King Charles II of England granted 45,000 square miles of land, an area almost as large as England itself. King Charles named the new colony "Penn's woods" (in Latin, Pennsylvania) in honor of the admiral.

The old manorial system in Europe was breaking down, creating a large class of landless people ready to seek new homes. In addition, wars in southern Germany caused many Germans to migrate eventually to Pennsylvania. The Reformation led to religious ferment and division, not only with Quakers, Puritans, and Catholics from England, but with Pietists, Mennonites, and Lutherans from the Rhineland, Scotch Calvinists via Ireland Amish from Switzerland, and Huguenots from France. Penn guaranteed the settlers of h new "Holy Experiment" freedom of religious worship, yet Pennsylvania's charter restricted the right to vote and to hold political office only to Protestants. In addition, Penn's Holy Experiment did not extend the protections of his charter to enslaved Africans and African Americans.

CITY OF BROTHERLY LOVE

Penn's first visit to Pennsylvania in 1682 brought 100 prospective colonists, one-third of whom would die after smallpox broke out during the voyage. His ship, the *Welcome,* was the first of a fleet of 23 ships that carried more than 2,000 men, women, and children to Pennsylvania in the next year. Penn's agents recommended that the capital be established on a sparsely settled peninsula at the confluence of the Schuylkill and Delaware Rivers, far from the Dutch and Swedish settlements that were previously established. Named Philadelphia, or "City of Brotherly Love," the peninsula was also one of Penn's original three counties, along with Bucks and Chester. Rather than simply occupy the land without consent of the Lenape people, Penn wrote letters and met with Lenape chiefs, asking permission to "enjoy the land with your love and consent."

The capital city of Philadelphia laid claim to most of Penn's attention during his first months. He appointed a surveyor general and immediately directed him to lay out "a greene country town where every house be placed in the middle of the plot, so that there may be ground on each side, for gardens, or orchards or fields and so that it will never be burnt, and always be wholesome." Penn also called for the creation of parks by directeing that "four squares be set aside for physical recreation" and that a "ten-acre Center square be reserved for a House of Public Affairs." In addition, he mandated that land for "Publick Houses" be set aside on every block as community gathering places. A city grid pattern was developed that set precedent for future American towns; streets running east–west were to be amed after trees, and those running north–uth were to be numbered. During his second visit in 1699–1701, Penn lived at a country estate he had built north of Philadelphia on the Delaware River that was known as Pennsbury Manor. Forced to return to England in 1700 to protect his control of the colony from the government and forced to remain there because of poor health, Penn spent only five years in Pennsylvania over his two visits. Penn's colony paved the path for the future of the young American republic by providing a democratic form of government and a legacy of toleration, which can still be seen in the First Amendment's protection of religious liberty. Thanks to its central position in the colonies and its wealth, Philadelphia became the largest and most important city in the colonies by the time of the American Revolution.

EXPANSION AND THE COLONIAL WARS

As immigrants arrived in waves to North America, many were drawn to Pennsylvania by its reputation as "the best poor man's country," since the land was cheap and plentiful, taxes were low, and no state church hounded religious dissenters. The vast majority of these immigrants stepped ashore in the Delaware River ports of Philadelphia or New Castle, yet they did not stay there for long. The quickest way to acquire property and independent livelihood was to move west, into the frontier region of the lower Susquehanna Valley. This westward expansion intruded on Native Americans who had only recently settled in the area, already displaced by expanding colonial populations elsewhere. In diplomatic councils with colonial leaders, these Indians often reminded their counterparts of William Penn's pledge to always deal peacefully and fairly with them; unfortunately, Penn's successors were not so principled. In the Walking Purchase of 1737, the Lenape agree to give away the amount of land a person could walk in a one day. The shrewd colonists cheated by hiring athletes to run in relays, covering much more land than the Lenape thought they were giving away.

In the years 1753 and 1754, the French sent troops south from their Canadian territory to occupy and claim the Ohio Valley. For the French, the Allegheny-Ohio watershed was part of a highway that linked their imperial dominions in Canada and Louisiana, and securing it would make the continent's interior their own. George Washington of Virginia failed to persuade the French to leave, and in 1754 they defeated his militia company at Fort Necessity, about 10 miles southeast of present-day Uniontown. Washington's humiliating defeat touched off an international crisis that became the French and Indian War in North America, which pitted the British versus French and Indian forces. The decade of warfare involved European armies that cut roads through the wilderness to build forts on strategic waterways, Native Americans who conducted raids against colonial homesteads for scalps and captives, and colonial militias and vigilantes who attacked and in some cases murdered Indians regardless of their political sympathies. While this war had many theaters around the globe, much of its blood and treasure were spilled in western Pennsylvania along French forts at Erie (Fort Presque Isle), Waterford (Fort LeBoeuf), Pittsburgh (Fort Duquesne), and Franklin (Fort Machault). In 1755, General Edward Braddock led a British army into the Pennsylvania wilderness to take Fort Duquesne, only to be decimated by French and Indian forces. British might returned in force in 1758 when General John Forbes cut his own route across southern Pennsylvania from Carlisle to the Forks of the Ohio, forcing the French to abandon Fort Duquesne and making possible the construction of Fort Pitt, a fortress designed to cement British supremacy in the region. After the war, the Native Americans were disillusioned with the British, and Ottawa war chief Pontiac sparked a widespread native resistance movement known as Pontiac's Rebellion. Pennsylvania, a state celebrated by colonists and Native Americans alike for its peaceful intercultural relations, had become a killing ground in which each side became convinced that its future rested on extirpating the other. Two military campaigns in 1763 and 1764 by Colonel Henry Bouquet

brought the hostilities to an end at the Battle of Bushy Run and a subsequent punitive expedition against the Delawares and Shawnee in the Ohio Country. As the 1760s gave way to the Revolutionary Era, the British would find that governing an American empire was more difficult than conquering one.

THE REVOLUTIONARY WAR

On the eve of the American Revolution, Pennsylvania was a multi-ethnic colony of about 250,000 inhabitants, with an ethnic mixture of mainly English, Germans, and Scots-Irish. Pennsylvania's role as a supplier of raw materials for British manufacturers as well as consumers of their products was in stark contrast to colonies like Massachusetts and Virginia, where resistance to imperial measures was common, especially after 1765 when the British Parliament began to impose a series of revenue-raising taxes. The First Continental Congress met in Philadelphia in 1774 with delegates from each of the colonies except Georgia to protest the commerce restrictions and taxes. By the time the Second Continental Congress convened in May 1775, the opening salvo of the War for American Independence had already been fired in the Massachusetts, and Pennsylvania joined the 12 other colonies in a war for national liberation against Great Britain. During the American Revolution, the Pennsylvania State House—today known as Philadelphia's Independence Hall—became the center for the wartime business of the new United States government, except when the British threat caused the capital to be moved successively. While Congress was sitting in York, Pennsylvania (October 1777 to June 1778), it approved the Articles of Confederation, the first step toward a national government. The final military victory at Yorktown, Virginia, in 1781 assured political independence, greater social equality, and more economic freedom. But at the end of the war, Pennsylvanians, like the rest of American people, still had to determine how to govern themselves and how to adapt to the new, more egalitarian society that was taking shape in the new nation.

By the end of the war, Pennsylvania had won control of the disputed areas in the northeast and received title to most of the disputed lands in western Pennsylvania, extinguishing all Indian claims to their lands within the state. Pennsylvania became the first state to begin the gradual abolition of slavery; by 1800, all but 55 of Philadelphia's more than 6,400 blacks were free. Philadelphia grew in importance as the nation's financial and cultural center and well as its capital from 1783–1789 and 1790–1800. The city boasted the nation's first museum (1786), first stock exchange (1791), first paved road and turnpike (1792), the largest public building (the State House), and largest market.

INDUSTRIALIZATION AND THE CIVIL WAR

Into the 1790s large areas of the northern and western parts of the state were undistributed or undeveloped. The state adopted generous land policies and distributed free "Donation Lands" to Revolutionary veterans. The immigrant tide into the state increased as Irish fled the potato famine of the late 1840s and Germans fled the political turbulence of their homeland. In 1820 more than 90 percent of the working population was involved in agriculture, by 1840 more than 77 percent of the 4.8 million employed persons in Pennsylvania were in agriculture. As agriculture began to decline into the 1860s, there was increased industrialization as Pennsylvania became the leading iron manufacturer in nation. The state was blessed with iron ore deposits, vast forests that provided charcoal, abundant coal beds that also supplied fuel, limestone used as flux, and streams for water power. By 1861, the factory system became the foundation of the state's industrial greatness as noted by the shift to machinery in the textile industry. Leather-making, lumbering, shipbuilding, publishing, and tobacco and paper manufacture all prospered throughout the 1800s.

The expression "underground railroad" may have originated in Pennsylvania, where numerous citizens, especially Quakers, aided the escape of slaves to freedom in Canada. During the Civil War, Pennsylvania played an important role in preserving the Union as Confederate forces invaded Pennsylvania three times by way of the Cumberland Valley, a natural highway from Virginia to the North. Pennsylvania's multifaceted resources with its railroad system, iron and steel industry, and agricultural wealth were essential factors in the economic strength of Union cause. In June 1863, General Robert E. Lee turned his 75,000 men northward on a major invasion across the Mason-Dixon line into Pennsylvania. Confederate forces captured Carlisle, Pennsylvania, and advanced to within three miles of Harrisburg. In a bitterly fought engagement in Gettysburg, the Union army threw back the Confederate forces in the war's bloodiest battle, with 51,000 casualties, marking the major turning point in the struggle to save the Union.

With the end of the war came an era of industrialization led by entrepreneurs who built the mills, mines, and factories of the late 19th century. Businessmen like Henry Clay Frick, Andrew Carnegie, Joseph Wharton, and William Scranton saw fortunes to be made as the coming of mass-produced steel in the 1870s created a modern industrial society in Pennsylvania. These new mills, mines, and factories created a labor shortage. While most of the state's pre-1861 population was composed of ethnic groups from northern Europe, the later period brought increased numbers of Slavic, Italian, Scandinavian, and Jewish immigrants. Between 1900 and 1910, during the height of this "new immigration," Pennsylvania witnessed the largest population increase of any decade in its history. Several important labor struggles took place in the state, such as the Homestead Steel Strike of 1892, igniting the birth of the modern labor union movement.

THE WORLD WARS

As an industrial state, Pennsylvania followed a predictable course that involved devastating economic slumps and financially invigorating wars throughout the 20th century. Although the state continued to be an industrial powerhouse, its national prominence began to subside as economic development became more widespread into the western and the southern parts of the country. Pennsylvania's resources and manpower were of great value in World War I as shipyards in Philadelphia and Chester were decisive in maintaining maritime transport. African American migration from the South intensified after 1917, when World War I restricted European immigration, and again during World War II.

The effects of the Great Depression were drastic, as 24 percent of the state's work force was unemployed in 1931, and later in 1933 unemployment reached 37 percent. Only the war-related production demands of World War II, which began in Europe in 1939, restored vitality to the state's economy. Tagged as the "Arsenal of America," factories poured out planes, tanks, armored cars, fuel, and guns. A steady stream of war goods flowed over its railroads and highways. Pennsylvania was second only to New York in the number who served, and it can be said that one out of every seven members of the armed forces in World War II was a Pennsylvanian. In 1940 the Commonwealth was the second largest state in the nation with a population two-thirds that of New York.

Pennsylvania played a key role in the development of major technologies from the late 19th century into the 20th century. George Westinghouse, an American entrepreneur and engineer based in Pittsburgh, invented the railway air brake and was a pioneer in the electrical industry. Westinghouse's electrical distribution system, which used alternating current based on the extensive research by Nikola Tesla, made it possible to provide electricity to the nation's homes and factories. The state became a center for electronics during World War II, when the first computer, ENIAC, was constructed at the University of Pennsylvania in Philadelphia. The first all-motion-picture theater in the world was opened on Smithfield Street in Pittsburgh on June 19, 1905, where the term "nickelodeon" was coined. The first commercial radio broadcast station in the world was KDKA in Pittsburgh, which started daily schedule broadcasting on November 2, 1920.

CONTEMPORARY TIMES

After World War II the coal, steel, and railroad industries declined considerably in Pennsylvania. Oil and natural gas were by then regarded as so much more convenient to use than coal for heating buildings, while the railroads were losing ground to the growing trucking industry. The state's steel production began to contract in 1963, although the nation's output, stimulated by the Vietnam War, rose to its all-time maximum in 1969 of 141 million tons. The decline in manufacturing jobs has been followed with an increase in education and health services as well as high-tech industry jobs.

Although the state continues to be one of the largest coal-producing states in the nation, a natural gas boom with the Marcellus Shale that covers two-thirds of the state will create new economic opportunities. Both Philadelphia and Pittsburgh, along with numerous other Pennsylvanian cities, are undergoing revitalization efforts to reclaim abandoned or underused industrial and commercial facilities and are trying to reverse the "brain drain" of talented people moving out of the state. Newly constructed sports stadiums, convention centers, and art centers have attracted new businesses, which in turn have brought hotels, restaurants, and housing to previously blighted sections. This transformation is also seen in the landscape as once-polluted rivers become viable for fishing and recreation and unused railways are converted to trails. In fact, recognition to the state has come from *Forbes* magazine in its 2010 "America's Most Livable Cities" listings: The Pittsburgh metropolitan area received the number one ranking and the Harrisburg-Carlisle metropolitan area received the number five ranking.

Government and Economy

GOVERNMENT

Pennsylvania uses the designation of "Commonwealth" instead of "State," just like Virginia, Kentucky, and Massachusetts. The designation is a remnant from the founding days of William Penn, when to be a commonwealth meant power was derived from equally free and independent people rather than a hierarchical and/or feudal system under a king. When the United States separated from Great Britain and its monarchy and became part of a democratically governed nation, the term commonwealth lost its meaning. The State Seal does not use the term, but it is a traditional, official designation used in referring to the state, and legal processes are in the name of the Commonwealth. In 1776, the state's first constitution referred to Pennsylvania as both "State" and "Commonwealth" (either term can be used correctly today). In Pennsylvania, all legal processes are carried out in the name of the Commonwealth. The Capitol and center of the state government has been located in Harrisburg since 1812, by authority of an act of February 21, 1810. Philadelphia and then Lancaster were earlier capital cities. The present Capitol building was dedicated in 1906, after an earlier building was destroyed by fire in 1897.

At the federal level, Pennsylvania is represented by two members of the United States Senate and 19 members of the United States House of Representatives. Like the United States, Pennsylvania's state government is defined by a constitution, which was originally drafted in the State Constitutional Convention of 1776 with amended constitutions in 1790, 1838, 1874, and 1968. And, like that of the United States, Pennsylvania's government comprises three equal and independent branches: the executive, legislative, and judicial. The legislative branch makes commonwealth laws, a responsibility carried out by the General Assembly. The General Assembly is made up of 253 members—a Senate with 50 members and a House of Representatives with 203 members.

The executive branch administers commonwealth laws and is overseen by the governor. The governor serves a term of four years and, if reelected, may serve a maximum of two terms in succession. And the judicial branch preserves the rule of law and guarantees citizens' rights by resolving disputes through the courts. The judicial branch consists of the Supreme Court, the Superior Court, the Commonwealth Court, courts of common pleas, community courts, and municipal/traffic courts in Philadelphia. Justices and judges are elected statewide and their regular term is 10 years, with those in the magisterial district judges and municipal/traffic courts in Philadelphia serving a term of six years.

At the local level there are four general types of municipalities in Pennsylvania (counties, cities, boroughs, and townships) along with active authorities and school districts. With 67 counties, 56 cities, and over 4,000 boroughs, townships, and active authorities, Pennsylvania local government is quite the mosaic. All operate under the laws of the Commonwealth yet each is distinct and independent of other local units and may operate under its own code of laws, although they may overlap geographically and may act together to serve the public.

The state has swung from being a Republican-leaning state during much of the 20th century to a more Democratic-leaning state in the 21st century, as it has backed the Democratic presidential candidate in every election since 1992. Both Philadelphia and Pittsburgh are Democratic strongholds in the state, often delivering huge margins for Democrats in statewide elections, while rural areas tend to be more conservative and support Republicans. City suburbs tend to be the swing areas that can change political views based on a candidate's social and fiscal positions. Overall, the state tends to support officials that have a more pro-life and gun-supporting stance. On the state government level, the senate and representative seats are usually evenly divided between both major parties. The governorship has been frequently held by

Republicans since 1861 with Democratic governors recently gaining a foothold in the office.

ECONOMY

At different times in history Pennsylvania was the worldwide leader in the production of leather, lumber, steel, zinc, pig iron, coal, coke, glass, cement, and aluminum. Ironically, Pennsylvania's earlier domination in industrial development created a major liability within factories and mills. The enormous capital investment, past and present, left a complex now less efficient than newer industrial centers elsewhere. In steel, Pennsylvania's integrated mills have been less efficient than the South's mini-mills and the new steel complexes abroad in Japan and China. Yet Pennsylvania is still a national leader in specialty steel products.

Agriculture is concentrated in the fertile counties of the southeast, and prized farmlands lie in the Great Appalachian Valley, where the best agricultural soil can be found. In 2008 there were 63,200 farms, which take up 27 percent of the state's land area. The top agricultural commodities produced in terms of receipts are dairy products followed by cattle, agaricus mushrooms, and greenhouse products. Other principal agricultural products include eggs, corn, wheat, oats, and poultry. The tourism industry is also an economic booster to the state as Pennsylvania is the fourth-most visited state in the country, according to state industry tourism representatives. Tourism generates more than $10 billion in wages and benefits each year and benefits 400,000 Pennsylvanians.

Heavy industry has declined in general, but the state still manufactures metal products, transportation equipment, foodstuffs, machinery, chemicals, and a wide variety of products. Manufacturing, which provided 960,000 jobs in the 1990s, has about 560,000 jobs as of May 2010. Education and health services, in contrast, recorded about as much growth as manufacturing lost, going from 750,000 jobs in 1990 to 1.1 million jobs in 2010.

The tremendous consumer power of Pennsylvania is reflected in ranking sixth in total retail sales receipts, fifth in the number of retail establishments, and seventh in the number of wholesale establishments in 2003 and 2004. An important statistical measure of a state's economic vitality is the gross state product (GSP), the equivalent, for the 50 states and the District of Columbia, of the nation's gross domestic product (GDP). In 2008 Pennsylvania was ranked sixth in the country with a GSP of $553 billion, behind Texas, Illinois, Florida, New York, and California.

The recession of 2008, which is slowly turning around, has caused a loss of 242,000 private sector jobs in Pennsylvania. Enactment of the Recovery Act in 2009 infused $27 billion into the state, with the majority of the funds going to residents and businesses in the form of tax credits, yet a large amount is going to job training and unemployment services. Another promising sign is that the Marcellus Shale Formation, located in the western two-thirds of the state, is providing an economic natural gas boom.

People and Culture

DEMOGRAPHY

An estimate of Pennsylvania's population by the U.S. Census Bureau in 2009 is 12,604,767, which is a 6.0 percent increase since the 1990 census. Pennsylvania had long been the second most populous state in the nation, behind New York, but in 1950 it fell to third due to California. In 1980 Texas also exceeded our population, as did Florida in 1987 and Illinois in 1990, leaving Pennsylvania in its current sixth rank in population. Eighty percent of Pennsylvania's population growth comes from international immigration, and 20 percent from the excess of births over deaths within the population already residing. The numbe of residents leaving Pennsylvania each year larger than the number of other states' residents migrating into Pennsylvania each year, so entrants from other states are not a positive factor in the state's present overall population growth. A U.S. Census Bureau population projection for 1995 to 2025 shows the state to rank second to last in projected population growth.

Even though most of Pennsylvania is rural, nearly 70 percent of the population lives in urban areas.

The trends across the state show that in western Pennsylvania only Butler County experiences robust growth; only six other western counties have escaped net population decline since 2000. Estimates to July 1, 2006, show all the southeastern counties except Philadelphia have continued to grow, as did Monroe, Pike, and Wayne. All the other northern tier counties and most of the contiguous counties immediately to the south of them had net population losses except Forest. Pennsylvania's population has continued to get older as the median age has increased from 38 years in 2000 to estimates showing it will be 40 years in 2010. In 2000, Pennsylvania had the second oldest state population, behind Florida, as measured by percentage of people over 65.

RACE AND ETHNICITY

Based on 2008 county and state population estimates, the racial composition of the state is 81.4 percent Caucasian (non-Hispanic), 10.8 percent African American, 2.4 percent Asian, 4.8 percent Hispanic, and 0.2 percent American Indian. Compared to the national average, the African American percentage is slightly less than the national average of 12.8 percent while the Hispanic percentage is considerably less than the national average of 15.4 percent. The largest concentrations for these two groups are found in Philadelphia County (45 percent of the county residents are African American while 13 percent are Hispanic).

The census figures from 2000 show that the majority of residents have ancestry of Germanic origin. This is followed by residents with Irish, Italian, English, and African American origins.

The late 19th and early 20th centuries brought increased numbers of Slavic, Scandinavian, and Jewish immigrants from the eastern Mediterranean and Balkan regions. Many of the new immigrants settled in the east-central and Ohio Valley regions where the anthracite and bituminous coal-mining jobs were located. You will still find self-contained ethnic enclaves that have increased interest in preserving distinctive ethnic traditions. The 2000 census figures listed 508,291 Pennsylvania residents, or 4.1 percent of the total state population, as foreign born. Although this number is up from 1990 (3.1 percent of total state population), it is considerably lower than the national average of 11.1 percent. The immigrant population has primarily been from former Soviet Union republics, India, and China. The Latino population in the state is mostly composed of Puerto Ricans, with smaller numbers of Cubans and Central Americans.

RELIGION

Religion played the major role that lead to the founding of Penn's colony. In a Declaration of Rights issued in 1682 by William Penn, the idea that individuals have a natural right to worship according to the dictates of their own conscience was a radical, even subversive notion. At the time, no nation in Europe embraced it. Pennsylvania's religious composition at the beginning of the 21st century can be judged by statistics compiled by the Association of Religion Data Archives. A total of 8,448,193 individual religious adherents are believed to presently exist, amounting to 68.8 percent of Pennsylvania's population according to the Association of Religion Data Archives; 1,331,835 (or 15.8 percent) of that total figure is estimated because numerous congregations are known to exist but have no record of their total adherents. These unaccounted faiths include the Church of Christ, Scientist and various African American denominations. The archives identified 115 different faiths in Pennsylvania with the breakdown showing Catholics as the largest religious group, followed by Methodists,

Lutherans, Presbyterians, and Jewish denominations. Other smaller faiths include Baha'i, Buddhism, Church of Jesus Christ of Latter-day Saints, Hindu, Jain, Jewish, Muslim, Tao, Unitarian Universalism, and Zoroastrian. Although Quakers (Society of Friends) were part of the majority religious denomination in Pennsylvania's early years, the number of adherents to the faith is only 11,800.

Pennsylvania Germans belonged largely to the Lutheran and Reformed churches, but there were also several smaller sects, such as German Baptist Brethren or "Dunkers," Schwenkfelders, and Moravians, the largest groups of which are the Amish and Mennonites, who number 99,500 followers. Pennsylvania has the second largest Amish settlement in the country, which is located in the Lancaster County area (Holmes County in Ohio is first). Other Amish settlements can be found in Mifflin, Indiana, and New Wilmington Counties.

LANGUAGE

As in other states in the United States, English is the dominant language in Pennsylvania. The 2000 census figure shows that 10,583,054 Pennsylvanians—91.6 percent of the population five years old or older—speak only English at home. Two distinctive dialects are noticeable when listening to native Pennsylvanians. One of these is the Midland dialect, which is significant as foundation for speech across the Midwest and Western United States. In the northern counties of the state you hear predominantly the Northern dialect, which has its origins in upstate New York State. In much of south-central Pennsylvania, descendants of the colonial Palatinate German population retain their speech as Deutsch, often misnamed Pennsylvania Dutch. Travels around the state will show that names of numerous rivers and towns have Native American origins, such as Punxsutawney, Aliquippa, Pocono, Towanda, Susquehanna, and Shamokin.

ESSENTIALS

Getting There and Around

BY AIR

Pennsylvania's two major airports are in Pittsburgh and Philadelphia. Pittsburgh's airport, frequently listed as one of the world's best airports by various travel publications, does not have hub status with any of the major airlines, yet US Airways handles the majority of flights. On the opposite end of the state, Philadelphia International Airport was the 11th busiest airport in the world in terms of aircraft activity in 2008. As of 2010, the airport is the primary international hub for US Airways with approximately 20 other airlines also providing flights. Smaller airports that deal with local and regional flights, including flights to and from certain Canadian cities, are located in Allentown, Erie, Harrisburg, Johnstown, Latrobe, State College, Wilkes-Barre/Scranton, and Williamsport.

BY CAR

Between 1903 and 1911 Pennsylvania took the lead in creating the road system you see today throughout the state. The 120,623 miles of rural and urban highways rank the state ninth among the 50 states. When the Pennsylvania Turnpike opened in 1940, it was the first high-speed, multi-lane highway in the country and

© HUNTINGDON COUNTY VISITORS BUREAU

set the pattern for modern super-highways throughout the nation. The Turnpike is a toll road with prices varying depending on the distance traveled. Exits on the turnpike occur every 10 miles or so with 24-hour service plazas providing fast-food dining options, fuel, public telephones, restrooms and other amenities. Along with the Turnpike (I-76), the other major east–west highway is I-80, which does not serve any major cities in Pennsylvania and serves mainly as a cross-state route to and from New York City. The western part of the state has I-79 as the main north–south highway from near Morgantown, West Virginia, up to Erie. I-81 serves the same purpose in the east, going from the New York–Pennsylvania border area near Binghamton and crossing the state until it splits near Scranton, where I-476 heads to Philadelphia. For road trip ideas, visit the state-sponsored website visitPA.com, which has 20 ready-to-ride trip ideas.

The consequence of being the first to develop highway and road systems is that it can't meet current conditions, either from increased use or temperature and weather changes. Many highway on-ramps and off-ramps were constructed during the early automobile era when vehicles were only able to reach a 45-mph top speed; therefore, they tend to be short considering today's faster speeds. The latest 2010 survey from *Overdrive* magazine ranks Pennsylvania as again having the worst roads in the nation; this has occurred 13 out of the 19 years of the survey. In 2010 the American Society of Civil Engineers rated Pennsylvania's roads a D minus, down from grade of D when graded in 2006. The quality of the roads is very apparent when coming from Ohio or West Virginia, which has received significant infrastructure federal funding. Unfortunately, simply keeping the road system from degrading, let alone improving it, requires more than is currently available in the budget. As an old saying goes, driving conditions in Pennsylvania revolve around two seasons: winter and construction. In the rural majority of the state, large snowfalls render most secondary roads impassable, but major thoroughfares like interstates are well plowed and salted. Still, car travel anywhere should be done with extreme care in the winter, especially on steep roads and by those unfamiliar with driving on snow or ice. The beginning of spring and into summer is the season when PennDOT (the state transportation department) begins paving, line painting, or road-widening projects with travel lanes typically reduced.

The highway speed limit in Pennsylvania is usually 55 mph in urban areas and 65 mph in rural areas. The Turnpike maintains the 65 mph limit regardless of urban or rural designation except through tunnels or snaking sections. Seatbelt use is mandatory for those seated in the front seats, yet it has a secondary enforcement standard (a fine will be issued to those who are pulled over for other citations). Pennsylvania has not yet enacted a ban on hand-held cell phone or text messaging usage while driving, although the cities of Philadelphia, Allentown, Erie, and Harrisburg have enacted bans. Wild animals can be a major problem when driving on rural interstates and roads, especially deer, which can cause severe car damage and injury if hit.

BY BUS

Numerous bus companies service Pennsylvania, most notably **Greyhound** (800/231-2222, www.greyhound.com). Major bus terminals are located in Erie, Pittsburgh, Altoona, State College, Harrisburg, Scranton, Allentown, and Philadelphia. The majority of Greyhound routes run across the state following the major east–west interstates. Travel times can vary depending on the number of stops and transfers in a particular route. Based on July 2010 prices, a Pittsburgh to Philadelphia bus ride with Greyhound is approximately $55 when purchased online and takes about seven hours with three stops in between.

BY RAIL

Pennsylvania used to be served by dozens of passenger railroads back in the era of railroad travel, but now only **Amtrak** provides passenger service (800/872-7245, www.amtrak.com

Philadelphia is home to one of Amtrak's busiest stations, at 30th Street, which is served by the Acela Express service linking Washington, D.C., with New York City and Boston. Journey time to Philadelphia from Washington, D.C., is 95 minutes; from New York City it's 1 hour; and from Boston it's 5 hours. Free transfers to the urban transportation system, run by SEPTA, are available to Amtrak passengers (request upon ticket purchase). Pittsburgh has daily Amtrak services to Chicago, New York City, Philadelphia, and Washington, D.C.

BY BOAT

Ferry services that cross from Wiggins Park in Camden, New Jersey, to Penn's Landing in Philadelphia are operated by RiverLink Ferry System (215/925-5465, http://riverlink-ferry.org). The ferry season runs Saturday and Sunday only in May and September with daily service between Memorial Day and Labor Day. Regular hours for the 2010 season were 9:30 A.M.–6P.M. with departures from Philadelphia every hour on the hour beginning at 10 A.M. Departures from Camden are every hour on the half hour beginning at 9:30 A.M. Tickets are available at the Penn's Landing

ferry terminal (Philadelphia) or Wiggins Park ferry terminal (Camden). On the other side of the state there are no ferry services from any of the lakeside towns of Lake Erie, either to Canada or neighboring states. Pennsylvania has three of the country's busiest ports with Philadelphia, Erie, and Pittsburgh, providing access to the extensive 900-mile U.S. inland waterway system.

INTERCITY MASS TRANSIT

If you are flying into a major city, it is very likely that there is some sort of mass transit to and from the airport as well as within the city boundaries. In Philadelphia, the Southeastern Pennsylvania Transportation Authority (SEPTA, 215/580-7800, www.septa.org) has interconnecting buses, trolleys (streetcars), subways, and elevated railways. Pittsburgh's Port Authority of Allegheny County (PAT) has an efficient network of buses serving the various districts and a light-rail system that currently serves the downtown and South Hills area only. Harrisburg is served by Capital Area Transit (CAT), which provides public bus, paratransit, and commuter rail service throughout the greater metropolitan area.

Tips for Travelers

CONDUCT AND CUSTOMS
The Amish

Just as the Amish do not carry personal photographs or display them in homes, they do not want others to take photographs of them. Many visitors to Lancaster County find it difficult not to take photographs. Yet, if there is one thing that appears to frustrate the Amish, it is tourists attempting to take their picture, especially ones in which faces are recognizable and considered to be a "graven image" or sign of vanity. Amish families typically use a horse and buggy as their primary mode of transportation, therefore please be aware of them on Pennsylvania's many two-lane roads. Buggies e difficult to miss as they have a red reflector

triangle on their backside. When driving by them on roads the etiquette calls for drivers to slow down as they approach and wait until a clear path is available for passing. Even though horses are accustomed to cars, it's wise to pass with enough room and a slow speed.

Liquor Laws

Pennsylvania has some of the nation's most restrictive and bizarre liquor laws, which have existed since Prohibition ended in 1933. Unlike in most states, the convenience of buying alcohol while at the supermarket or convenience store is not available. Wine and liquor are only available at state-owned stores monitored by the Pennsylvania Liquor Control Board or wineries.

These state-owned stores (many of them labeled as "Wine & Spirits Shoppes") usually have a limited selection, tend to be expensive, and are closed or have limited hours on Sunday.

Pennsylvania laws require bars and taverns to close by 2 A.M. If you would like to purchase beer to go (especially a local beer) it is recommended that you buy it at a beer distributor. Although these beer distributors only sell beer in 24-packs and larger as required by a law, it is much cheaper than buying beer to go from a restaurant or bar. Bars are only allowed to sell up to 12 beers to go to any individual (though if you step out the door, you can step back in and buy two more 6-packs). Many restaurants do not have alcohol on their menus due to the huge expense of obtaining a liquor license from the state. Not surprisingly, Pennsylvanians try to purchase much of their liquor in neighboring states like West Virginia or Maryland, where a half gallon of whisky sells for about one-third less. Yet to control their monopoly, the Liquor Control Board has made this cross-border alcohol transport illegal. Don't worry—there aren't any border checks, although undercover state troopers have been known to monitor vehicles with Pennsylvania licenses at border liquor stores.

SENIORS AND TRAVELERS WITH DISABILITIES

Thankfully the state has a large elderly population (second in the nation) that has instilled the need for senior-friendly facilities and services. In fact, Pittsburgh hosted the 2005 Summer National Senior Games when 10,000 senior athletes converged to the city. Many attractions and events offer senior discounts, so remember to inquire. AARP has a state-by-state guide to transportation assistance, which provides links to transportation services, including dial-a-ride, bus tokens and/or transit passes for fixed-route scheduled services, and taxi vouchers. In addition, each county has Aging and Disability Resource Centers that list transportation options for seniors and people with disabilities. Major metropolitan areas such as Pittsburgh, Harrisburg, and Philadelphia have numerous transportation options, such as wheelchair-accessible bus lifts, yet this is unlikely in smaller Pennsylvania towns. While the vast majority of attractions and accommodations make every effort to comply with federal law, the historic nature of the state along with cash-strapped municipalities means that some structures are not disability friendly. In 2009 lawsuits prompted the Pennsylvania Department of Transportation to budget millions over the next decade to replace 117,000 handicapped curb ramps along state roads and add curb cuts to sidewalks. Unfortunately, with the limited budget for highways and roads, sidewalks are typically not maintained sufficiently for wheelchair access, especially in certain municipalities not covered by the state.

GAY AND LESBIAN TRAVELERS

Although the state would probably not be classified gay-friendly, Philadelphia was the site of some of the nation's first gay rights protests in 1965, is home to one of the nation's oldest and most respected gay newspapers, and was the first to pass domestic partners law that provided a tax break for gay and lesbian couples. Pittsburgh and Philadelphia, both cities that lean toward the liberal end of the political spectrum, are quite accepting of gay and lesbian travelers. The areas around and between the two cities tend to have a religious conservative philosophy that is less friendly to gays and lesbians. In small towns throughout the state, the best approach is to simply avoid standing out. This means keeping public displays of affection and politics discussions to a minimum. For additional information about the gay and lesbian locale contact the Gay and Lesbian Community Center of Pittsburgh (www.glccpgh.org/, 412/422-0114) or the William Way Community Center in Philadelphia (www.waygay.org/, 215/732-2220).

HEALTH AND SAFETY

As in most states, tourists visiting Pennsylvania shouldn't be concerned about any immediate and grave risks to health or safety while traveling through the state. Travelers with medical or health issues are encouraged to bring extra supplies of medications and copies of prescriptions in case of an emergency. Larger cities, such as Philadelphia, Pittsburgh, Erie, Williamsport, York, Allentown, and Scranton, all have quality hospitals, urgent-care clinics, and pharmacies that are close to the metropolitan population center. Due to the expense of medical coverage in the United States, it is wise for international travelers to carry international health insurance. Likewise, domestic travelers should check whether they are in-network or out-of-network coverage with Pennsylvania hospitals. Emergency rooms are required to take true emergency cases regardless if a patient can pay for services.

Crime rates for Pennsylvania show the state as a whole to be low in rankings. Philadelphia and Reading used to be in the top 20 in crime statistics, yet new policing strategies have resulted in significant crime drops over the last couple of years. Violent crimes are rare, with the most common being thefts. As usual when traveling, use common sense—blend in with other people, don't leave valuables visible inside your car, etc. Crime in smaller cities and towns is virtually unknown.

The Elements

Summer months can be especially humid and hot in Pennsylvania, with temperatures reaching in the 90s and humidity ranging from 50 percent to 75 percent. Extreme heat and humidity can pose serious problems for the elderly, infants and children up to the age of four, the overweight, people who work or exercise outdoors, and people with heart or respiratory problems. Heat exhaustion is the body's response to an excessive loss of water and salt contained in sweat. Warning signs include heavy sweating, paleness, muscle cramps, fatigue, dizziness, headache, nausea or vomiting, and fainting. Stay hydrated and in the shade. Seek medical attention immediately if the symptoms are severe or if the person has heart problems or high blood pressure.

Winter months in Pennsylvania are not especially cold, yet travelers should bring adequate winter gear (thick coat, gloves, and hat) if traveling during that season. Winter is also the most difficult driving season to deal with due to the snow and ice along with the fewer hours of daylight. Make sure your vehicle is in good condition, especially by ensuring your vehicle has snow or all-season tires. Remember to clear the ice and snow from your vehicle before driving. In Pennsylvania, drivers are required by law to remove snow and ice from their vehicles before traveling. Failure to do so can lead to a $200–1,000 fine. Be sure the windshield washer reservoir is adequately filled with a freeze-resistant cleaning solution. Drive slowly. Even if your vehicle has good traction in ice and snow, other drivers will be traveling cautiously.

Ticks and Lyme Disease

Lyme disease is the most common tick-borne illness in North America and Europe. According to the Centers for Disease Control, Pennsylvania has more Lyme disease cases than any other of the states. The disease is caused by the bacterium that is harbored and spread by deer ticks, which feed on the blood of animals and humans. To contract Lyme disease, you must be bitten by an infected deer tick. Before bacteria can be transmitted, a deer tick must take a blood meal, which can take more than 48 hours of feeding. If you know you've been bitten and experience signs and symptoms of Lyme disease—rash, flu-like symptoms, joint pain, numbness—particularly if you live in an area where Lyme disease is prevalent, go to the nearest medical facility as soon as possible. The rash often resembles a bull's-eye, with a red ring surrounding a clear area and a red center, yet many victims don't show a rash. You're more likely to get Lyme disease if you spend time in grassy and heavily wooded areas where ticks carrying the disease thrive. As a precaution, wear long pants when hiking and tuck the bottoms into your socks or use tape to prevent access to attachment sites. Permanone, a tick repellent containing permethrin, may be applied to clothing only (avoid skin contact). This product may provide protection for a day or longer.

Information and Services

MONEY

Commercial establishments in the United States accept only the national currency, the U.S. dollar. Most of these establishments will accept cash, debit cards, credit cards, travelers checks, and personal checks from U.S. banks. It's likely that rural areas in the state will only accept cash and don't have access to automated teller machines (ATM), so carry a reasonable amount of cash when visiting those areas. U.S. paper currency is all the same size and color, with the number in the corner indicating the dollar amount. Coins come in these denominations: penny ($0.01), nickel ($0.05), dime ($0.10), quarter ($0.25), and half-dollar ($0.50).

CELL PHONES AND WI-FI HOT SPOTS

Cell phone signals are usually strong in the metropolitan areas across Pennsylvania yet are weak in the rural and mountainous areas, especially the north-central part of the state. There are numerous dead zones when driving through the state along the Turnpike or I-80, especially on highways that are far from civilization. Wi-Fi hot spots are numerous, yet the majority are restricted to paying customers at a retail establishment or require payment for a limited time subscription. Philadelphia has a municipal Wi-Fi network that is free to use that covers certain public spaces such as parks and other recreational areas. Both Pittsburgh International Airport and Philadelphia International Airport offer free Wi-Fi access to travelers. Amtrak is working on adding free Wi-Fi access to all of its trains, which would certainly make traveling by rail in the United States a lot more pleasant.

MAPS AND TOURIST INFORMATION

Each region in the state has a convention and visitors bureau that has an online website with itineraries, planning tools, and up-to-date information. Along with information provided in this book, these websites have extensive listings of hotels, activities, events, festivals, transportation, sports, restaurants, cultural attractions, and shops. In addition, many of the 67 counties have their own tourism website promoting tourism to that specific county. The PA Tourism & Lodging Association has an online gateway to Pennsylvania bed-and-breakfasts, inns, farm vacations, boutique hotels, and other unique accommodations. A leisure travel organization, such as the American Automobile Association (AAA) or a travel agency, can provide maps of the entire state and select cities.

RESOURCES

Suggested Reading

HISTORY

Ellis, Joseph J. *Founding Brothers: The Revolutionary Generation.* Winner of the 2001 Pulitzer Prize for History, this book explores the oft-contentious relationships between America's founding fathers. Read it en route to Philadelphia, where so many of their squabbles played out.

Kraybill, Donald B. *The Amish of Lancaster County.* Donald Kraybill, a professor at Lancaster County's Elizabethtown College and a nationally recognized authority on Anabaptist groups, has authored or edited more than 20 books. His latest is an easily digestible explanation of the lifestyle of the Lancaster County Amish, complete with full-color photographs.

McCullough, David. *The Johnstown Flood.* First published in 1968, this riveting account of the 1889 flood that killed more than 2,000 people in a Pennsylvania steel town was David McCullough's first book. The Pittsburgh-born historian has since won two Pulitzer Prizes and the Presidential Medal of Freedom.

McIlnay, Dennis P. *The Horseshoe Curve: Sabotage and Subversion in the Railroad City.* This is the gripping story of the Nazi plot to destroy the Pennsylvania Railroad's Horseshoe Curve during World War II. Published in 2007, the book includes eyewitness accounts of the execution of six saboteurs

convicted of the failed plot. Author Dennis McIlnay, who lives within a few miles of the targeted section of rail track, delves into the history of the Pennsylvania Railroad and the construction of the Curve while he's at it.

FICTION

Chabon, Michael. *The Mysteries of Pittsburgh* and *Wonder Boys.* Michael Chabon's first two novels are set in Pittsburgh, where the Pulitzer Prize–winning author went to college. The main character in *Wonder Boys* was inspired by one of his professors at the University of Pittsburgh. Both books were adapted into films.

Dillard, Annie. *An American Childhood.* Annie Dillard's enchanting memoir paints a vivid picture of Pittsburgh in the 1950s.

Shaara, Michael. *The Killer Angels.* Winner of the 1975 Pulitzer Prize for Fiction, this superbly crafted historical novel tells the story of the Battle of Gettysburg. The page-turner was adapted into the 1993 film *Gettysburg,* another excellent treatment of the Civil War's bloodiest battle.

OUTDOORS

Carson, Rachel. *Silent Spring.* Pennsylvania-born biologist and nature writer Rachel Carson has been called the mother of the modern environmental movement—largely because of this 1962 book on the harmful effects of pesticides.

Egan, Timothy. *The Big Burn: Teddy Roosevelt and the Fire that Saved America.* This is the story of a devastating blaze that killed more than 100 firefighters. It's also the story of Gifford Pinchot, America's first forester and one of Pennsylvania's favorite sons.

MAGAZINES

Pennsylvania Heritage. Historians, curators, and archivists contribute to this liberally illustrated magazine, copublished by the Pennsylvania Historical and Museum Commission and the Pennsylvania Heritage Society. To receive the quarterly magazine, become a member of the Heritage Society at www.pa-bookstore.com or by calling 717/787-9123.

Pennsylvania Magazine. Showcasing the state's places, people, and events since 1981, *Pennsylvania Magazine* is published six times a year. Request a free issue or subscribe at www.pa-mag.com or by calling 800/537-2624.

Pennsylvania Pursuits. Published by the Pennsylvania Tourism Office, this seasonal magazine is "dedicated to life, liberty, and the pursuit of happiness in Pennsylvania travel." Articles on everything from major attractions to under-the-radar restaurants to ice fishing find their way into the free mag. Subscribe at www.visitpa.com/pursuits or by calling 800/847-4872.

Internet Resources

TRAVEL
Pennsylvania Tourism Office
http://visitPA.com
Pennsylvania's official tourism website provides information on just about every attraction in the Commonwealth, plus trip ideas for those not sure where to start. Visiting from Spain, France, Russia, or China? You'll find travel information in your native tongue.

HISTORY
Pennsylvania Historical & Museum Commission
www.phmc.state.pa.us
The website of Pennsylvania's official history agency is a good starting point for information on the people and events that shaped the Commonwealth.

http://explorepahistory.com
WITF, Harrisburg's PBS and NPR affiliate, organizes this website in conjunction with the Pennsylvania Historical and Museum Commission. You could spend days engrossed in the stories behind the 2,000-odd historical markers that dot the state.

CULTURE
Amish Studies
www2.etown.edu/amishstudies
This site, maintained by the Young Center for Anabaptist & Pietist Studies at Lancaster County's Elizabethtown College, answers frequently asked questions about the Amish.

OUTDOORS
Pennsylvania Bureau of State Parks
www.dcnr.state.pa.us/stateparks
This site provides detailed descriptions of Pennsylvania's state parks, which numbered 117 at last count. The companion reservation site, www.pa.reserveworld.com, allows you to search for parks by region and amenities such as white-water boating and beach swimming.

National Parks in Pennsylvania
www.nps.gov
About 30 of Pennsylvania's historic sites, scenic trails, and river corridors are part of the National Park System. Visit this site for a comprehensive listing.

Pennsylvania Trails
www.explorepatrails.com

Launched by the state Department of Conservation and Natural Resources in late 2009, ExplorePAtrails.com allows outdoorsy types to find and share information on thousands of miles of land and water trails.

Pennsylvania Fish & Boat Commission
www.fish.state.pa.us

Purchase a fishing license, register a boat, read up on regulations, or submit a request for the state agency's free publications. The site boasts a number of interactive maps designed for anglers and boaters.

Pennsylvania Game Commission
www.pgc.state.pa.us

Hunters can find information on seasons, bag limits, and everything else they need to know on the website of Pennsylvania's wildlife management agency.

LODGING

Pennsylvania Campground Owners Association
www.pacamping.com

This trade association represents more than 200 individually owned and operated campgrounds. Search its online directory or request a free copy of the printed version.

PA Tourism & Lodging Association
www.painns.com

This is a handy directory of bed-and-breakfasts, inns, boutique hotels, and other unique accommodations represented by the PA Tourism & Lodging Association.

Index

YZ

List of Maps

Acknowledgments

This book is dedicated to my grandmother, who passed away three months shy of its publication. In the last year of her life, "Is the book finished?" was invariably the first question she asked me. I would have loved to see her hold it in her hands, this baby of mine, but at least I had the chance to say, "I'm done, babushka, *finally*."

So many people helped me get there that I could fill several pages with shout-outs. But this book is already much too thick. For that, I offer a heartfelt apology to my editor, Shari Husain, who suffered my long-windedness and occasional whininess with remarkable grace. Patience and good-naturedness seem to run in the Avalon Travel family. I'm grateful to acquisitions director Grace Fujimoto, who made my year when she gave me this gig; production coordinator Elizabeth Jang, who sifted through the 800-plus photos I collected; and cartography editor Brice Ticen, who's responsible for the snazzy maps in these pages. Thanks also to *Moon Philadelphia* author Karrie Gavin, who generously shared her knowledge of the state's largest city.

I owe a lot to Pennsylvania's dedicated tourism promoters, who answered my incessant questions and made it possible for me to see a great deal in a limited time. I'm especially grateful to Cara O'Donnell, Julie Donovan, Kristin Mitchell, Eric Ash, Sean Waddle, Lisa Rager, Christie Black, Ed Stoddard, Christine Pennsy, Carla Wehler, Linda Devlin, Lori Copp, Peter Lopes, Donna Schorr, Nina Kelly, Alicia Quinn, Joel Cliff, Carl Whitehill, and Rick Dunlap.

As I traveled around this unique state, I picked the brains of everyone from barflies to museum curators. They shared juicy tidbits that no amount of googling could have yielded (though Google also deserves a thanks here). A special thank you to Jeff and Janet Coldwell for teaching me most of what I know about elk, Noelle Owens for letting me blow the train whistle, and the Ranck family for showing me how to make popcorn on the cob. I thank everyone who gave me food to eat and a place to lay my head. For giving me a taste of life with a butler at my beck and call: Damn you, Nemacolin Woodlands!

Thank you to the fellow travel writers I met along the way for sharing their knowledge, their wit, and their booze. I'm thrilled to be part of a club that's dedicated to mixing work and pleasure. To Dan Bard, who lent me his laptop when mine was MIA and left us too soon: You are missed.

My greatest gratitude goes to my family and friends: for pointing me to their favorite PA spots, for forgiving my absences and absentmindedness, for whisking me away when I needed it, and for their unwavering confidence in me. I thank Amy for her feedback on my book proposal. I thank Shannon for sizing up northeast PA's restaurants and resorts. I thank Amanda for her *mi-casa-es-su-casa* hospitality and masterful pep talks. I thank Ioana for being the Bernstein to my Woodward in Philly, for mobilizing a team of research assistants at the 11th hour, and for reminding me that this is exactly what I wished for.

And then there's George, who saw me at my most unkempt, at my most unglued, and never ran screaming. The most reasonable explanation is that he expects this book to sell at the rate of *Twilight* and make us filthy rich. It's also possible that this wonderful man, who possesses a most unlikely combination of handiness and braininess, loves me as much as I love him. I'm going to make it up to him for all those unkempt, unglued moments—even if it takes a lifetime.